MENTAL HEALTH LAW

POLICY AND PRACTICE

Third Edition

PETER BARTLETT

AND

RALPH SANDLAND

OXFORD
UNIVERSITY PRESS

OXFORD
UNIVERSITY PRESS

Great Clarendon Street, Oxford OX2 6DP

Oxford University Press is a department of the University of Oxford.
It furthers the University's objective of excellence in research, scholarship,
and education by publishing worldwide in

Oxford New York

Auckland Cape Town Dar es Salaam Hong Kong Karachi
Kuala Lumpur Madrid Melbourne Mexico City Nairobi
New Delhi Shanghai Taipei Toronto

With offices in

Argentina Austria Brazil Chile Czech Republic France Greece
Guatemala Hungary Italy Japan Poland Portugal Singapore
South Korea Switzerland Thailand Turkey Ukraine Vietnam

Oxford is a registered trade mark of Oxford University Press
in the UK and in certain other countries

Published in the United States
by Oxford University Press Inc., New York

First Published 2000
Second Edition 2003
Third Edition 2007

British Library Cataloguing in Publication Data
Data available

Library of Congress Cataloging in Publication Data
Data available

Typeset by Newgen Imaging Systems (P) Ltd., Chennai, India
Printed in Great Britain
on acid-free paper by
Ashford Colour Press Ltd, Gosport, Hampshire

ISBN 978–0–19–927827–5

3 5 7 9 10 8 6 4 2

Outline Contents

Detailed Contents vii

Preface xi

Table of Cases xix

Table of Statutes xxxiii

Table of Secondary Legislation xlv

1 **Conceptualising Mental Health Law** 1

2 **Problems of Definition** 33

3 **An Overview of the Contemporary Mental Health System** 59

4 **Admission to Hospital** 111

5 **The Process of Civil Confinement** 155

6 **Mental Disorder and Criminal Justice** 199

7 **Treatment in Hospital** 275

8 **Leaving Hospital** 353

9 **Control, Care and Community** 435

10 **Mental Capacity: Broad Issues and Basic Concepts** 497

11 **The Mental Capacity Act 2005** 545

12 **Legal Responses and Advocacy for Clients** 579

Bibliography 609

Index 647

Detailed Contents

Preface   xi

Table of Cases   xix

Table of Statutes   xxxiii

Table of Secondary Legislation   xlv

1 **Conceptualising Mental Health Law**   1

   1.1 Introduction   1

   1.2 Who are the insane?   2

   1.3 Other interests: mental health care   11

   1.4 Sources of law   17

   1.5 Concluding comments   31

2 **Problems of Definition**   33

   2.1 Introduction   33

   2.2 The statutory structure   34

   2.3 Mental illness   46

   2.4 Schizophrenia: a case study   50

   2.5 Cautionary tales?   54

3 **An Overview of the Contemporary Mental Health System**   59

   3.1 Introduction   59

   3.2 The rise and fall of asylum-based provision   71

   3.3 Community care   82

   3.4 Inside the institutions   95

   3.5 Concluding comments   108

4 **Admission to Hospital**   111

   4.1 Introduction   111

   4.2 Informal admission   112

   4.3 Civil confinement: standards and justifications   120

4.4 Detention for assessment or treatment: substantive issues   126

4.5 Other mechanisms of confinement: substantive issues   133

4.6 The criteria in action   138

4.7 Other options?   145

4.8 Concluding comments   153

5 **The Process of Civil Confinement**   155

5.1 Introduction   155

5.2 The context of admission under Part II   156

5.3 Nearest relatives and approved social workers   159

5.4 The mechanics and dynamics of admission   173

5.5 Challenging the legality of admission under Part II   185

5.6 Concluding comments   197

6 **Mental Disorder and Criminal Justice**   199

6.1 Introduction   199

6.2 Diversion from prosecution   203

6.3 Court-based diversion before the sentencing stage   214

6.4 The special verdict   239

6.5 Sentencing as diversion   242

6.6 Transfer from prison to hospital   263

6.7 Concluding comments   272

7 **Treatment in Hospital**   275

7.1 Introduction   275

7.2 Medical treatment for mental disorder   277

7.3 Medical treatment in hospital: law and practice   288

7.4 Emergency measures: treatment or control?   333

7.5 Concluding comments: back to the critique of the medical
     model of treatment for mental disorder   345

8 **Leaving Hospital**   353

8.1 Introduction   353

8.2 Leave and recall   354

8.3	Discharge from hospital: the law	362
8.4	Mental health review tribunals: preliminaries and process	373
8.5	Substantive powers of discharge	397
8.6	Tribunal and decisions	419
8.7	Challenging MHRT decisions	424
8.8	Absence without leave	429
8.9	Concluding comments	433

9 Control, Care and Community   435

9.1	Introduction	435
9.2	Services for mentally disordered persons in the community	437
9.3	Assessing entitlement, and the nature and scope of the duties owed	450
9.4	A 'seamless' service?	470
9.5	Control in the community	485
9.6	Concluding comments	495

10 Mental Capacity: Broad Issues and Basic Concepts   497

10.1	Introduction	497
10.2	Legal structures of capacity	498
10.3	Tests of capacity	505
10.4	Capacity in context	518
10.5	How should decisions be made for those lacking capacity?	526
10.6	Who should make decisions for those lacking capacity?	538
10.7	Concluding comments	542

11 The Mental Capacity Act 2005   545

11.1	Context and overview of the Act	545
11.2	The principles of the Act and the meaning of incapacity	549
11.3	Best interests	552
11.4	Decisions by substitutes	557
11.5	Advance decisions regarding treatment	569
11.6	Rough edges	571

12 **Legal Responses and Advocacy for Clients**   579

    12.1 Introduction   579

    12.2 Mental health review tribunals and judicial review   580

    12.3 Controlling the starting gate: s. 139   583

    12.4 Criminal prosecutions   590

    12.5 Civil actions for damages   593

    12.6 Applications under the Human Rights Act   600

    12.7 Complaint processes   602

    12.8 Advocacy   604

Bibliography   609

Index   647

Preface

The job of keeping abreast of developments in mental health law remains as difficult as ever. As with the previous two editions of this book, this third edition has been written against the backdrop of possible impending reform of mental health law. Nonetheless, we decided to proceed with this new edition on the grounds that the 2nd edition was already substantially out of date, whether or not there was to be substantive reform to the current Mental Health Act 1983. We were fortified in this view by the knowledge that, had we waited for the reform process to be complete before publishing the first or second editions, those editions would be yet to appear! Most significant of those changes to the law which have taken place since the publication of the second edition is the passage of the Mental Capacity Act 2005. The Act is set to come into operation in 2007, some eighteen years after the House of Lords (in *F v West Berkshire Health Authority* [1989] 2 All ER 545) forcibly underlined the need for Parliamentary intervention to reform the law of capacity. It is discussed in detail in chapter 11, but read on: there are already significant proposals to reform the 2005 Act.

Outside Parliament, the senior judiciary have also been active. This has generally, although not always, altered the law in the direction desired by the government, with the consequence that a number of the intended statutory reforms have in fact already occurred through the mechanism of judicial interpretation of the 1983 Act. The Human Rights Act 1998 has proven to be a trigger of litigation intended to change both procedural and substantive law, and the response of the judiciary in the domestic courts and the European Court of Human Rights has often been controversial. There have also been a variety of new policy initiatives in this period. Acute outpatient services have been prioritised, for example, sometimes to the detriment of other services, and the shift of some mental health services from the public to the private sector has largely been completed. These changes, and many more discussed in the main text of this book, raise or re-pose questions of quality of service, accountability and transparency.

And yet, wholesale statutory reform has so far been elusive. This is not for the want of trying on the part of the government. The process of reform of the 1983 Act began in earnest in the late 1990s. The resulting draft Mental Health Bill of 2002 (Department of Health, 2002d) promised wholesale change to the law. That Bill was subsequently abandoned, as was the later, modified, version which appeared in 2004 (Department of Health, 2004a). Both were beset with controversy and engendered significant and widespread opposition, much of it challenging the fundamental policy assumptions about the purpose of mental health law that were built into those draft Bills. The essential charge was that the reform proposals paid too much attention to questions of risk and control and too little to the interests of service users and the professionals who operate the system.

On 16 November 2006, the government began its third attempt to reform the law, when it introduced its latest Mental Health Bill into the House of Lords (HL Bill 1,

2006–7; Department of Health, 2006p). This Bill was anticipated during the drafting of the following text, and the general intention of the government had been signalled by a variety of briefing papers (Department of Health, 2006a), which are referred to in the body of this volume. Nonetheless, on questions of detail, the reader should consult the Bill itself. As anticipated, the Bill constitutes a set of amendments to the Mental Health Act 1983 and Mental Capacity Act 2005, and the government has also compiled a version of these Acts as they would appear if the Bill passed unamended. There is little chance of that – see further below – so helpful though these consolidations are, they must be approached with some caution. They are available on the Department of Health website. No doubt if the Bill is successful, revised versions of these consolidations will similarly be made available there.

The overall changes proposed by the Bill include the following.

Throughout the Act, the Bill would slightly alter the definitions of the roles of key players. 'Responsible medical officers' would become 'responsible clinicians' – and would no longer need to be medical doctors. This takes forward the earlier proposal to that effect, discussed at p. 297 of this book, although the government has rethought the job title, having previously proposed 'approved clinicians'. Nothing seems to turn on this change of preferred nomenclature. The key point is that, in appropriate circumstances, the key professional in charge of an individual's care might be a clinical psychologist, for example. In addition, as discussed at p. 87, 'approved social workers' (ASWs) would become 'approved mental health professionals', and would no longer need social work qualifications to perform the role, although a training regime is provided for by cl. 18 of the Bill.

The Bill alters the presumptive list of nearest relatives only marginally, by the express inclusion of civil partners in the same category as husbands and wives. The criteria for the replacement of a nearest relative (NR) are expanded, however, to include a broad criteria that 'the nearest relative of the patient is otherwise not a suitable person to act as such' (cl. 29(3)(e)). The Bill would further for the first time allow the patient to apply for the replacement of his or her nearest relative: cl. 29(2)(za). How much difference this will in fact make for patients is doubtful. If patient and ASW agree that someone else ought to be appointed, then under the existing Act, the ASW may already launch an application for the NR to be replaced. If the patient and his or her professional carers disagree as to the appropriateness of the NR, it may well be because the patient wants a NR who will be more proactive in challenging professional decisions. Notwithstanding that the current Act seems to suggest a role for the NR that is independent of the professionals, the current case law is exceptionally generous to professionals who wish to remove NRs who exercise that role: see pp. 165–173 below. It is thus extremely doubtful that applications by patients to replace nearest relatives on the basis of a failure to adequately challenge professionals will meet with any success. Effectively, patients are likely to find that they may have whoever they want as their NR, so long as that person agrees with the professionals. As discussed below at p. 172, it is not obvious that this meets the concerns of Article 8 of the ECHR and the settlement in the case of *JT* v *United Kingdom* [2000] 1 FLR 909.

As anticipated (see, e.g., pp. 43, 132), the four-fold division of mental disability is to be done away with. The different standards of efficacy of treatment that apply under s. 3 of the existing Act depending on the type of disability are also to be abolished: the test will instead be consistent for all people with mental disabilities, and it will be that 'appropriate treatment' is available. This is in turn reflected in the provisions in part IV regarding treatment, where SOADs in sections 57 and 58 would approve treatment if it is 'appropriate', rather than the current standard which refers to the 'likelihood of the treatment alleviating or preventing a deterioration of the patient's condition'. When the new test is combined with the definition of 'treatment' found in recent case law (see pp. 297–299), which covers everything from 'cure to containment', it is apparent that the it would license detention in circumstances in which the patient is not 'treatable' by reference to any conventional understanding of that term.

The definition of mental disability will still be circumscribed in ways that raise some of the issues addressed under the existing Act. The restrictions to the definition as it relates to people with learning disability (clauses 1(2A) and 1(4) of the Bill) raise many of the same issues as currently arise regarding the mental impairments (see p. 38, below), although the difference between serious and non-serious mental impairment would be abolished (p. 37). 'Dependence on alcohol or drugs' is expressly precluded from inclusion as a mental disorder: cl. 1(3). A current difficulty exists that because of similar wording under the 1983 Act, it is difficult to find services for people with these difficulties who also have other mental disorders, and there has been considerable debate as to how far addiction to alcohol (as distinct from drunkenness) for example comes under the Act: see pp. 42–6. Given this context, it is not obvious that the proposed clause makes the situation clearer.

Again as anticipated, the Bill proposes the introduction of community treatment orders – CTOs (clause 25 of the Bill proposes new sections 17A to 17G of the 1983 Act) – and the corresponding abolition of aftercare under supervision (currently found in sections 25A to 25J of the 1983 Act), as discussed at pp. 491–495 in this volume.

How significant the inclusion of CTOs would be is an open question. As discussed at pp. 354–357 below, the courts have effectively introduced them by exceptionally generous readings of the leave of absence provisions contained in s. 17 of the existing Act. Quite how the new provisions will interface with s. 17 leave is not clear, as the Bill does nothing to restrict the provisions of such leave, and the existing jurisprudence therefore arguably remains in effect. Prior to granting s.17 leave for a period beyond seven days, responsible clinicians would be required to 'consider' whether the patient should instead be placed under a CTO, but it is not clear what factors they should take into account. CTOs would have a much more ornate statutory structure than s. 17 leave; it seems likely that s. 17 leave will remain preferable by clinicians when it can be justified.

The provisions regarding CTOs will no doubt be subject to considerable debate as the Bill progresses. The substantive criteria for their imposition are notably weak. The individual would have to be detained pursuant to s. 3 (admission for treatment) immediately prior to the granting of the CTO. In addition, the following criteria would have to be met (cl. 17A (5)):

(a) the patient is suffering from mental disorder of a nature or degree which makes it appropriate for him to receive medical treatment;

(b) it is necessary for his health or safety or for the protection of other persons that he should receive such treatment;

(c) subject to his being liable to be recalled as mentioned in paragraph (d) below, such treatment can be provided without his continuing to be detained in hospital;

(d) it is necessary for his health or safety or for the protection of other persons that he should be liable to be recalled to hospital for medical treatment; and

(e) appropriate medical treatment is available for him

As discussed regarding other criteria for compulsion below (pp. 126–133), these lack substantive rigour. Health, safety, and protection of others are disjunctive. The minimum threshold would thus appear to be that someone has a disorder that makes it appropriate for him or her to receive medical treatment in the interests of his or her health, that it can be provided in the community, and that it would be necessary for his or her health that the individual be liable to be recalled to hospital. This is not very strong. It is further open to some question what clause (d) means. It may be necessary for someone's health or safety that they be recalled to hospital; but in what sense can the threat of such recall – being 'liable' to be recalled – be necessary for those ends?

The CTO could prescribe where the individual would live, lay down a variety of conditions regarding medical treatment, or require 'that the patient abstain from particular conduct' (cl.17B). It is not obvious how broadly those criteria would be read; on their face, the last in particular is very broad indeed.

The proposed power of recall to hospital of a 'community patient' (i.e., one under a CTO) is also very broad. Such recall may be based on the belief of the responsible clinician that medical treatment in hospital is required, and there is a risk (the degree of which is not defined) to the health or safety of the patient or to the protection of others if such recall were not made (cl. 17E(1)). This does not require a failure by the patient to comply with the CTO. Failure to attend for examination when required by the CTO is itself a separate ground for recall to hospital (cl.17E(2)), even if the risks contained in cl. 17E(1) are not present.

A community patient would be able to apply to the Review Tribunal both when the CTO was made, and in the event that he or she was recalled to hospital. The first CTO would be for a maximum period of six months; thereafter, renewals could be for up to one year (cl. 20A(3)).

Treatment of community patients is dealt with in clauses cl. 28 of the Bill, which would add new sections 64A to 64K to the 1983 Act. Those sections are convoluted, but in essence require both a valid consent and approval of a SOAD if the treatment would have required such certification if the individual had remained detained rather than placed on a CTO. The consent may come from the patient, if competent, or from an

LPOA or deputy under the MCA, if any. Absent such consent, the treatment may nonetheless be given to an incompetent adult patient if the responsible clinician has no reason to believe that the patient objects to being given the treatment, or 'he does have reason to believe that the patient so objects, but it is not necessary to use force against the patient in order to give the treatment' (cl. 64D(4)(b)). It is unclear the intended scope of this provision: would it be justifiable, for example, to place drugs covertly in the patient's soup to avoid having to force the patient to take the medication? In any event, the treatment must not conflict with an advance decision to refuse treatment under the MCA, or the decision of an LPOA or deputy under that Act.

Children who are community patients are to be subject to a somewhat different set of statutory provisions, laid out in cl. 28 of the Bill and intended to take effect as ss. 64E and F of the 1983 Act.

The Mental Health Bill also amends the Mental Capacity Act 2005, to take account of the decision in *HL v United Kingdom* Application No. 45508/99, (2005) 40 EHRR 32 (see pp. 114–20 below). The Bill generally corresponds to the briefing paper discussed in the chapters that follow, although it is appropriate to express some disappointment regarding the drafting of the amendments: schedule A1 to the Act, which contains many (but not all) of the amendments flowing from *HL*, runs to approximately forty pages, almost the entire length of the MCA 2005 as originally enacted. The statute had in general been a model of legislative drafting. Regrettably, and unlike the situation under the existing Act, if the Bill is passed, it is not obvious that a reasonably competent practitioner or carer will be able to understand the Act.

The similarity of the Bill to the briefing paper means that the problems identified below remain. As expected, it is the people who deprive persons lacking capacity of their liberty who will instigate the process of providing rights for those people.

A draft Code of Practice was published to accompany the *HL* amendments to the MCA 2005, and is available on the Department of Health website.

These notes are written at the beginning of February 2007, as this volume is in the final stages of production. At this time, the Bill has received second reading in the House of Lords (published as HL Bill 34, 2006–07). There is no certainty that it will reach the statute books, and if it does, it is not obvious that it will resemble the version of November 2006. Already, the House of Lords has made important amendments.

Most significantly, they have included a requirement under sections 2 and 3 of the MHA 1983 that the individual's disorder must result in 'impaired decision making' if these civil sectioning powers of the Act are to be used. The government has in the past objected vehemently to such a provision; it seems unlikely that they will choose to allow it to pass now. And as we write there are rumours of further significant changes as the Bill goes to third reading in the Lords, including perhaps an attempt to introduce an enhanced treatability standard as a condition of confinement. How accurate these rumours prove to be is anyone's guess as we write. The government's decision to introduce the Bill in the Lords means that they cannot force it through using the Parliament Acts. The fight therefore may well be a long way from over.

The 2006 Bill is not the only point where the government's agenda has shifted. Just prior to Christmas 2006, the government altered the timetable for the implementation of the Mental Capacity Act 2005. Previously, the Act was to come into effect in its entirety on 1 April 2007, and that expectation is reflected in the body of this volume: see, eg., pp. 23, 118, 549, 563 below. Implementation is now to be done in two stages. The Independent Mental Capacity Advocates will be introduced on 1 April 2007, as will the new offence of ill-treating a person lacking capacity; the Court of Protection and provisions regarding Lasting Powers of Attorney will take effect from October 2007. The ministerial statement of 18 December 2006 is not entirely clear on which of these dates the remaining provisions of the Act are to come into force. The new definitions of incapacity and best interests must presumably come into effect on the earlier date, as they are integral to the role of the IMCAs. Similarly, the authority to make decisions related to personal care and treatment – the statutory version of the current necessity defence – must come into effect on 1 April, as the role of the IMCA is defined in terms of the exercise of this authority. It is not yet clear on which of the dates the new, statutory provisions regarding advance refusals of treatment will take effect. This is potentially significant, as the statutory regime will tighten the formalities requirements for some advance decisions. It is further unclear when the new provisions regarding research will take effect.

Pending the introduction of the new Court of Protection, issues relating to the interpretation of the Act or its application in specific circumstances should presumably be raised in the High Court.

As can be seen, the law relating to mental disorder is in a state of considerable change. It is our view that this makes the approach of this textbook all the more pertinent. In the preface to the first edition, we said that in our view it was almost immoral to divorce the study of mental health law from the social situation of the people most directly involved. We continue to subscribe to that view. Our approach, accordingly, remains unabashedly to consider not merely the content of the formal law, but also as far as possible the socio-legal, historical, sociological, and cultural issues surrounding that law. Mental health law, be it the law as it has developed to date or the law as it is to be reformed in the future, is about power: it involves at its heart the forcible confinement and medication of people, many of whom are amongst the most vulnerable in society. These powers do not fall evenly on everyone. Psychiatric powers are applied differently by gender and race, and disproportionately on the poor. While cheap Marxist platitudes are unhelpful, the realities of psychiatric power in society equally cannot be ignored. Although these issues certainly apply at the micro level, in the way individuals are administered under the existing law, they are perhaps particularly important in times of reform. In chapter 1.3, we identify a variety of interest groups. These groups have not all been able to punch with the same weight in the reform debates, and it is appropriate to have real concern that the people identified as having psychiatric disorders may be marginalised in the face of high power and better funded actors. We would argue that an approach that acknowledges their concerns is more important than ever before.

At the same time, we remain fixed in our view that the purpose of a textbook is to challenge its readers to further inquiry, not to provide snappy answers to snappy questions. Indeed, implicit in our placement of academic study of mental health law in the context of social and professional practice, it is our view that such simple answers to questions of social regulation do not exist. We will have succeeded in our enterprise not if our readers think they have found solutions, but instead if we have inspired them to greater consideration of the problems.

As usual, we have received sterling support from our colleagues at Oxford University Press, including Helen Tyas, Ness Plaister, and Melanie Jackson. Peter wishes to record his thanks to his domestic partner Rick, for yet again demonstrating considerable patience over the grind which the creation of this book has inevitably involved. Once again, we also thank the students who have subscribed to our mental health module since its inception in 1995, and in particular those of them that have shared their experiences of the mental health system, either as patients or staff, with us and with their colleagues. They have not merely provided invaluable insights into the law in practice; they have also served as a reminder that the dividing line between 'them' and 'us' is largely illusory.

Peter Bartlett
Ralph Sandland
February 2007

Table of Cases

A (A Mental Patient) v Scottish Ministers and Advocate-General (Scotland) [2002] SC (PC) 63, [2002] HRLR 6[right] ... 29, 602

A, D and R v Scottish Ministers [2001] UKPC D5, [2002] UKHRR 1[right] ... 254, 351, 401, 404, 434

A (Male Sterilisation), Re [2000] 1 FLR 549[right] ... 505, 534–5, 537

A Metropolitan Borough Council v DB [1997] 1 FLR 767[right] ... 521, 522

A v A Health Authority and Another, In Re J (A Child), R (S) v Secretary of State for the Home Department [2002] EWHC 18[right] ... 505

A v Secretary of State for theHome Department [2004] UKHL 56, [2005] 2 AC 68, [2005] 2 WLR 87, [2005] 3 All ER 169[right] ... 195

AD v East Kent Community NHS Trust [2002] EWCA Civ 1872[right] ... 103

Aerts v Belgium (2000) 29 EHRR 50[right] ... 63, 247, 264, 267, 370

Airedale NHS Trust v Bland [1993] 2 WLR 316[right] ... 335, 536, 537, 559

AK (Medical Treatment: Consent), Re [2001] 1 FLR 129[right] ... 528

Alexander Machinery (Dudley Ltd) v Crabtree Ltd [1974] ICR 120[right] ... 420

Ann R (By her Litigation Friend Joan T) v Bronglais Hospital Pembrokeshire and Derwen NHS Trust [2001] EWHC Admin 792[right] ... 175

Anufrijeva v Southwark London Borough Council [2003] EWCA Civ 1406, [2004] 2 WLR 603[right] ... 469

Ashingdane v UK (1984) 6 EHRR 69; (1985) 7 EHRR 528[right] ... 63, 342, 417, 589

Associated Provincial Picture Houses Ltd v Wednesday Corporation [1948] 1 KB 223[right] ... 101, 102, 193, 194, 195, 296, 311

Attorney-General v Guardian Newspapers (No. 2) [1990] 1 AC 109[right] ... 554

Attorney-General v O'Driscoll (No. 2) [2003] JRC 117[right] ... 225

Attorney-General v Prior (2001)[right] ... 241

Attorney-General's Reference (No. 3 of 1998) [1999] 3 All ER 40 (CA)[right] ... 234

Avon County Council v Hooper and Another [1997] 1 All ER 532 (CA)[right] ... 472

B (Consent to treatment: Capacity), sub. nom B (Adult: Refusal of Medical Treatment), Re B V NHS Hospital Trust [2002] EWHC 429, [2002] 2 All ER 449, [2002] 1 FLR 1090[right] ... 309, 511

B v Croydon District Health Authority [1995] 1 All ER 689; (1994) 22 BMLR 13 (HC)[right] ... 6, 7, 303, 304, 305, 306, 307, 308, 309, 320, 348

B v Mental Health and Review Tribunal and Secretary of State for the Home Department [2002, QB Admin][right] ... 29

B(A) v B(L) (Mental Health Patient) [1980] 1 WLR 116 (CA)[right] ... 170

Baldwyn v Smith [1900] 1 Ch 588[right] ... 500

Banks v Goodfellow (1870) 5 QB 549[right] ... 502, 532, 543

Barclay-Maguire v UK Application No. 91/7/80 (December 1981)[right] ... 389

Barker v Barking Havering and Brentwood Community Healthcare NHS Trust [1999] 1 FLR 106[right] ... 92, 189, 192, 355, 356, 357, 581

Bartram v Southend Magistrates Court [2004] EWHC 269[right] ... 238–9

Battan Singh v Amirchand [1948] AC 162 (JCPC)[right] ... 498, 510

Beaney (Deceased), Re [1978] 2 All ER 595[right] ... 500, 502, 517, 552

Benjamin and Wilson v UK (2003) 36 EHRR 1[right] ... 415, 416, 417

Bennett v Bennett [1969] 1 WLR 431[right] ... 502

Bevan, In re [1912] 1 Ch 196[right] ... 569

Bezicheri v Italy (1989) 12 EHRR 210[right] ... 344, 390

Birkin v Wing (1890) 63 LT 80[right] ... 498

Bolam v Friern Hospital Management Committee [1957] 2 All ER 118 (HC)[right] ... 290, 291, 294, 312, 538, 594

Bolitho v City and Hackney HA [1997] 4 All ER 771, [1997] 3 WLR 1151, [1998] AC 252[right] ... 291, 294, 594

Bollan v UK Application No. 42117/98 [right] ... 343

Bone v Mental Health and Review Tribunal [1985] 3 All ER 330 (DC)[right] ... 419–20, 425

Brand v The Netherlands [2001] Hudoc reference REF00006531, Application No. 49902/99[right] ... 247, 464

Briscoe, Re [1998] COD 402 (HC)[right] ... 164, 169, 188

Broadmoor Hospital Authority v Robinson (1998) *The Times*, 15 October (HC)[right] ... 102, 103

Brown v Stott [2001] 2 WLR 817[right] ... 229

Buckley v UK [1997] EHRLR 435[right] ... 338

Buxton v Jayne [1960] 1 WLR 783[right] ... 595

C (A Patient), Re [1991] 3 All ER 866[right] ... 532

C (Adult: Refusal of Medical Treatment), Re [1994] 1 All ER 819, [1994] 1 WLR 290 (HC)[right] ... 23, 289, 304, 305, 307, 308, 319, 325, 497, 522, 525, 528

C (Mental Patient: Habeas Corpus), Re [2002] EWHC 243 (Admin)[right] ... 189

Campbell v Secretary of State for the Home Department *see* R v Oxford Regional Mental Health and Review Tribunal, ex p Secretary of State for the Home Department [1988] 1 AC 120, [1987] 3 All ER 8 (HL)

Caparo Industries plc v Dickman [1990] 2 AC 605[right] ... 596

Carter v Metropolitan Police Commissioner [1975] 1 WLR 507[right] ... 137, 587

Cassidy v Ministry of Health [1951] 1 All ER 574[right] ... 600

CH and MH v Merton Primary Care Trust [2004] EWHC 2984[right] ... 462

Chester v Afshar [2004] UKHL 41, 2004 WL 2289136 (HL), [2005] 1 AC 134, [2004] 4 All ER 587, [2004] 3 WLR 927[right] ... 595

Child, ex p (1854) 15 CB 238[right] ... 112

Christie v Leachinsky [1947] AC 573[right] ... 101

Christine Goodwin v UK (2002) 35 EHRR 18, (2002) 2 FLR 487[right] ... 351, 468

CL, In re [1969] 1 Ch 587[right] ... 535

Clunis v Camden and Islington Health Authority [1998] 2 WLR 902[right] ... 366, 468, 469, 595

Clunis v UK, 11 September 2001[right] ... 366–7

Cocks v Thanet District Council [1983] AC 286[right] ... 469

Cotterham v UK [1999] 1 MHLR 97[right] ... 389

Council of Civil Service Unions v Minister for the Civil Service [1984] 3 All ER 935 (HL)[right] ... 191, 193

Cozens v Brutus [1973] AC 854[right] ... 47

Crookdale v Drury [2003] EWHC 1938[right] ... 450

D (Mental Patient: Habeas Corpus), Re [2000] 2 FLR 848[right] ... 168

Davey, In re [1981] 1 WLR 165[right] ... 502–3

De Sousa v Portugal [2006] EWHC 455[right] ... 190

Dent v Bennett (1839) 4 My & Cr 268[right] ... 533

Derbyshire County Council v Akril [2005] EWCA Civ 308[right] ... 443

Devi v West Midlands AHA [1980] 7 CL 44 (HC)[right] ... 334, 335

D(J) (Court of Protection), In Re [1982] 1 Ch 237[right] ... 529–30, 532, 533

Dlodlo v Mental Health Review Tribunal for the South Thames Region (1996) 36 BMLR 145[right] ... 221, 372

DN v Switzerland Application No. 27154/95 [2001] ECHR[right] ... 385

Director of Public Prosecutions v Blake [1989] WLR 432 (CA)[right] ... 208, 212

Director of Public Prosecutions v Cornish (1997) *The Times*, 27 January (CA)[right] ... 212

Drew v Nunn (1879) 4 QB 661[right] ... 561, 565, 566

Drew v UK (2006) 43 EHRR SE2[right] ... 243 *see also* R v Drew [2003] UKHL 25, [2003] 1 WLR 1213, [2003] 4 All ER 557

D'Souza v DPP [1992] 4 All ER 545 [right] ... 432

Dulles' Settlement, In re [1950] 2 All ER 1013[right] ... 126

Durham v Durham (1885) 10 P 80[right] ... 502, 542

E v Norway (1990) 17 EHRR 30[right] ... 389–90

Edwards v UK (2002) 35 EHRR 19[right] ... 216, 217

Egglestone and Mousseau and Advisory Review Board, Re (1983) 42 OR (2d) 268[right] ... 581

Engel v The Netherlands (No. 1) [1976] 1 EHRR 647[right] ... 228, 401

Evans v Knight and Moore (1822) 1 Add 229[right] ... 511

Everett v Griffiths [1921] 1 AC 631 (HL)[right] ... 595

F (Mental Health Act: Guardianship), Re [2000]
  1 FLR 192[right] ... 38, 490, 503, 536

F v West Berkshire Health Authority [1989] 2 All
  ER 545, [1990] 2 AC 1[right] ... xi, 116, 305,
  306, 504, 550, 555, 559

Fell, Re (1845) 3 Dowl & L 373, 15 LJ (NS) MC 25
  QB[right] ... 121

Fletcher v Fletcher (1859) 1 Fl & Fl
  420[right] ... 339

Freeman v Home Office [1984] QB 524
  (HC)[right] ... 292, 293

Furber v Kratter (1988) unreported
  (HC)[right] ... 589

Gillick v West Norfolk and Wisbech Area Health
  Authority [1985] 3 All ER 402[right] ... 522

Glaser v UK (2001) 33 EHRR 1[right] ... 367

Goserelin case (R v Mental Health Act
  Commission, ex p X (1988) 9 BMLR 77
  (DC))[right] ... 308, 325, 328, 348, 407,
  515, 525

Grant v Mental Health and Review Tribunal
  (1986) 26 April 1986 (DC)[right] ... 405

H&M v DPP [1998] Crim LR 653
  (CA)[right] ... 208, 212–13

Hadfield's Case (1800) 27 Howell's St Tr
  1281[right] ... 18

Hall and Carter v Wandsworth London Borough
  Council [2004] EWCA Civ 1740[right] ... 479

Harnett v Fisher [1927] AC 573[right] ... 595

Harwood v Baker (1840) 3 Moore
  282[right] ... 510

HE v A Hospital NHS Trust [2003] EWHC 1017,
  [2003] 2 FLR 408[right] ... 528

Herczegfalfy v Austria (1992) 15 EHRR
  437[right] ... 294, 310, 312, 313, 316, 317, 339

Hill v Chief Constable of West Yorkshire [1989]
  AC 53[right] ... 367

HL v UK Application No. 45508/99 (2005) 40
  EHRR 32 (Bournewood case)[right] ... 26,
  113, 115, 116, 117, 118, 119–20, 150, 190, 276,
  294, 362, 497, 504, 549, 559, 571, 572, 573,
  574, 576

HM v Switzerland (2002) 26
  February[right] ... 410

Holgate v Lancashire Mental Hospitals Board
  [1937] 4 All ER 294[right] ... 366

Hutchinson Reid v UK (2003) 37 EHRR
  211[right] ... 29, 63, 189, 351, 402

Imperial Chemical Industries Ltd v Shatwell
  [1965] AC 656 (HL)[right] ... 589

Imperial Loan Company v Stone [1892] 1 QB
  599[right] ... 500, 552

IRC v National Federation of Self-Employed and
  Small Businesses Ltd 2 All ER 93 (HL), [1982]
  AC 617, [1981] 2 WLR 722 (HL)[right] ... 192

Islington London Borough Council v University
  College London Hospital NHS Trust [2005]
  EWCA Civ 596[right] ... 472

J, Re [1992] 4 All ER 614[right] ... 525, 560

Jenkins v Morris (1880) 14 Ch 674[right] ... 501,
  512

John (Julie), Re [1998] COD 306
  (DC)[right] ... 188

Johnson v UK (1999) 27 EHRR 296[right] ... 29,
  361, 363, 371, 407, 412, 413

Jones v Commission for Social Care Inspection
  [2004] Civ 1713[right] ... 444

JT (Adult: Refusal of Medical Treatment),
  Re [1998] 1 FLR 48[right] ... 307

JT v UK [2000] 1 FLR 909 (ECHR)[right] ... 165,
  354, 554

K, Re and F, Re [1988] 1 All ER 358[right] ... 565,
  566

K v UK (1998) 40 BMLR 20[right] ... 358, 371

Keenan v UK [1998] 26 EHRR
  CD64[right] ... 314

Kinsey, Re (1999) 21 June, unreported
  (HC)[right] ... 364

Knight v Home Office [1990] 3 All ER
  237[right] ... 61

Kolanis v UK (2006) 42 EHRR 12[right] ... 30,
  413–14, 468

Koniarska v UK Application No. 33670/96
  (2000) 12 October (unreported)
  [right] ... 401, 402

Kudla v Poland (2002) 35 EHRR 11
  K[right] ... 216, 217, 265

Kynaston v Secretary of State for Home Affairs
  (1981) 73 Cr App R 281 (CA)[right] ... 192,
  368

Leigh v Gladstone (1909) 26 TLR
  139[right] ... 307

Litwa v Poland (2001) 22 EHRR 53[right] ... 401

M, Petitioner 2003 SLT 219 (Outer
  House)[right] ... 321

McClelland v Simon S [2000] 1 MHLR
  6[right] ... 171

M'Adam v Walker (1813) 1 Dow
  148[right] ... 499

Makin (s. 3, Mental Health Act 1983), Re (QBD, 4 May 2000)[right] ... 178

Manches v Trimborn (1946) 174 LT 344[right] ... 501–2

Manchester City Council v MI, [1999] 1 MHLR 132[right] ... 171

Masterman-Lister v Brutton and Co, Jewell and Home Counties Dairies [2002] EWCA Civ 1889[right] ... 497, 561, 574, 604, 605

MB (Medical Treatment), Re [1997] 2 FLR 426[right] ... 508, 521, 535

Mental Health and Review Tribunal v Hempstock [1997] COD 443 (HC)[right] ... 398, 411

MH v SSDH [2005] UKHL 60, [2005] 1 WLR 1209, [2004] EWCA Civ 1609[right] ... 376

Miller v The Queen (1985) 24 DLR (4th) 9[right] ... 343

Mitchell v Homfray (1881) 8 QBD 587[right] ... 533

M'Naghten's Case (1843) 10 C & F 200[right] ... 239, 240, 241

Moore v Care Standards Tribunal [2005] EWCA Civ 627, [2005] 1 WLR 2979[right] ... 445

MP v Nottinghamshire Healthcare NHS Trust, Secretary of State for the Home Department, SSH [2003] EWHC 1782[right] ... 425

MP v Nottinghamshire Healthcare NHS Trust, SSHD, SSH [2003] EWHC 1782[right] ... 409

Narey v Customs and Excise Commissioners [2005] EWHC 784[right] ... 232

Nevmerzhitsky v Ukraine Application No. 54825/00 (unreported) 5 April 2005[right] ... 316, 317

Newham London Borough Council v S and Another (Adult: Court's Jurisdiction) [2003] EWHC 1909 (Fam), [2003] All ER (D) 550; [2003] EWHC 2278[right] ... 505, 534, 573

NHS Trust A v M, NHS Trust B v H [2001] Fam 348[right] ... 314

Norfolk and Norwich Healthcare (NHS) v W [1996] 2 FLR 613[right] ... 521

North Devon Homes Ltd v B 2003 WL 1202659[right] ... 480

Norton v Canadian Pacific Steamships [1961] 1 WLR 1057[right] ... 589

Nottidge v Ripley (1849) The Times, London, 27 June[right] ... 121

O'Connor v Donaldson, 422 US 563 (USSC, 1975)[right] ... 146

O'Neill v Morrison (1994) unreported (CA)[right] ... 595

O'Reilly v Mackman [1982] 3 All ER 1124[right] ... 192

Osman v UK (2000) 29 EHRR 245[right] ... 367

Palmer v Tees HA (2000) 2 LGLR 69 (CA)[right] ... 367

Park, In the Estate of [1954] P 89[right] ... 502

Pauline Lines v UK [1997] EHRLR 297[right] ... 389

Pearce v United Bristol Healthcare NHS Trust [1999] PIQR 53 (CA)[right] ... 291, 595

Pembrey v General Medical Council [2003] UKPC 60[right] ... 572

Perkins v Bath District Health Authority (1989) 4 BMLR 145 (CA)[right] ... 397

Pfizer v Ministry of Health [1965] 1 All ER 152[right] ... 593

Pickering v Liverpool Daily Post and Echo Newspapers plc [1991] 1 All ER 622[right] ... 394

Poplar Housing and Regeneration Community Association Ltd v Donoghue [2001] 3 WLR 183[right] ... 192

Porter v Magill [2001] UKHL 67, [2002] 2 AC 357, [2002] 2 WLR 37, [2002] 1 All ER 465[right] ... 375

Pountney v Griffiths [1976] AC 314 (HL)[right] ... 100, 299, 338, 584

Poyser and Mills Arbitration, Re [1963] 1 All ER 612 (HC)[right] ... 420

Pretty v UK (2002) 35 EHRR 1[right] ... 602

PS v Germany Application No. 33900/96 (2002)[right] ... 230

R (A Minor) (Wardship: Consent to Medical Treatment), Re [1991] 4 All ER 177[right] ... 115, 551

R, on the application of Mohammed Latif 2002 WL 31422140[right] ... 233

R (Burke) v General Medical Council [2005] EWCA 1003[right] ... 570

R (E) v Bristol City Council [2005] EWHC 74[right] ... 166, 171, 172

R (Enduring Power of Attorney), Re [1990] 1 Ch 647[right] ... 563, 564

R (Home Secretary) v Mental Health and Review Tribunal [2004] EWHC 1029 (Admin)[right] ... 130–1

R (IH) v Home Secretary, Health Secretary [2003] UKHL 59[right] ... 29

R (MH) v Secretary of State for Health [2005] UKHL 60, reversing [2004] EWCA Civ 1609[right] ... 573

R (MH) v Secretary of State for Health, ex p W [2004] All ER Digest 188; R v Mental Health and Review Tribunal, ex p W [2004] EWHC 3266 (Admin)[right] . . . 402

R (N) v Dr M and Others (2002) WL 31676213[right] . . . 582

R (On the application of M) v Secretary of State for Health [2003] EWHC 1094[right] . . . 166, 171, 172, 554

R (P) v Mental Health and Review Tribunal for East Midlands and Northeast Region [2002] EWCA Civ 697[right] . . . 40–1

R v Alfred B [2001] EWCA Crim 1104 (CA)[right] . . . 248

R v Anglia and Oxfordshire Mental Health and Review Tribunal, ex p Hagan [2000] Lloyd's Rep Med 119[right] . . . 399

R v Antoine [1999] 2 Cr App R 225 (CA), [2001] 1 AC 340[right] . . . 223, 227, 234, 235, 236

R v Ashworth Hospital Authority, ex p H [2002] EWCA Civ 923, [2003] 1 WLR 127 (H)[right] . . . 420, 424–5, 429, 434

R v Ashworth Hospital, ex p B [2003] EWCA Civ 547, [2005] UKHL 20, [2005] 2 AC 278, [2005] All ER 289, [2005] 2 WLR 695[right] . . . 300, 316, 372, 398, 399

R v Ashworth Hospital, ex p E 2001 WL 1479868 E[right] . . . 101

R v Ashworth Hospital, ex p H [2001] EWHC Admin 872, [2002] 1 FCR 206, [2002] EWCA Civ 923, [2003] 1 WLR 127[right] . . . 102, 385, 387, 411

R v Ashworth Hospital (now Mersey Care NHS Trust), ex p Munjaz, R v Airedale NHS Trust (Appeal) ex p S [2005] UKHL 58, [2005] 3 WLR 793, [2005] HRLR 42[right] . . . 22, 30, 264–5, 299, 340, 341, 344, 345

R v Ashworth Special Hospital, ex p M (2000) 2000 WL 1480059 (QB)[right] . . . 341

R v Ashworth Special Hospital and Secretary of State for Health, ex p N [2001] EWHC Admin 339[right] . . . 30, 100

R v Aspinall [1999] 2 Cr App R 115, (1999) 49 BMLR 82[right] . . . 206–7, 208, 210, 212

R v Avon County Council, ex p M [1994] 2 FCR 259 (HC) M[right] . . . 452, 453

R v Avon and Wiltshire Mental Health Partnership NHS Trust, ex p KW [2003] EWHC 919, 2003 WL 1823101[right] . . . 385

R v Ayan M 2000 WL 544040[right] . . . 252

R v Barking and Dagenham London Borough Council, ex p L [2002] 1 FLR 763 (CA)[right] . . . 461, 469

R v Barnet, London Borough Council, ex p G [2003] UKHL 57[right] . . . 460

R v Berkshire County Council, ex P [1997] 95 LGR 449 (HC)[right] . . . 451, 481

R v Bexley NHS Care Trust, ex p Grogan [2006] EWHC 44[right] . . . 475

R v Birch (1989) 11 Cr App R(S) 202 (CA)[right] . . . 244, 247, 248, 249, 250, 251, 256, 257, 259, 264

R v Blackburn [2005] EWCA Crim 1349[right] . . . 212

R v Blackwood (1974) 59 Cr App R (S) (CA)[right] . . . 250

R v Borkan [2004] EWCA Crim 1642[right] . . . 223

R v Bournewood Community and Mental Health NHS Trust, ex p L [1998] 2 WLR 765; [1998] 3 WLR 107 (HL); [1999] 1 AC 481[right] . . . 26, 113, 115, 116, 117, 118, 119–20, 150, 190, 276, 294, 362, 497, 504, 549, 559, 571, 572, 573, 574, 576

R v Bradford Crown Court, ex p South West Yorkshire Mental Health NHS Trust [2003] EWCA (Civ) 1857[right] . . . 229

R v Brent London Borough Council, ex p Mawcan (1994) 26 HLR 528 (HC)[right] . . . 480

R v Bristol City Council, ex p Penfold [1998] COD 210 (QB)[right] . . . 451, 460, 482

R v Broadmoor Special Hospital Authority, ex p S and Others (1998) *The Times*, 17 February[right] . . . 99–100, 299, 372

R v Buckland [2000] 1 WLR 1262, [2000] 1 All ER 907, CA[right] . . . 243

R v Budgen [2001] EWCA Crim 1708[right] . . . 248

R v Camden and Islington Health Authority, ex p K [2001] 3 WLR 553, [2001] MHLR 24[right] . . . 30, 448, 464, 465, 466

R v Camden London Borough Council, ex p B [2005] EWHC 1366[right] . . . 450, 465

R v Camden London Borough Council, ex p P [2004] EWHC 55[right] . . . 439–40

R v Camden London Borough Council, ex p Pereira [1998] 31 HLR 317[right] . . . 479

R v Canons Park Mental Health Review Tribunal, ex p A [1994] 2 All ER 659 (CA)[right] . . . 130, 403, 404

R v Cardiff Local Health Board, ex p Keating [2005] EWCA Civ 847, [2006] 1 WLR 158[right] . . . 64

R v Central Criminal Court, ex p Young [2002] EWHC 548 QBD[right] . . . 236

R v Central London County Court and Another, ex p London [1999] 3 WLR 1 (CA)[right] . . . 173

R v Chippenham Magistrates' Court, ex p
   Thompson (1995) *The Times*, 6 December
   (DC)[right] ... 222, 238

R v Clare T [2003] EWCA Crim 17, 2003 WL
   1202680 (CA)[right] ... 244

R v Clarke (1762) 3 Burr 1362[right] ... 112

R v Clayton 2000 WL 664424[right] ... 208

R v Cleveland County Council, ex p Cleveland
   Care Homes Association and Others (1993)
   158 Local Government Reports 641
   (HC)[right] ... 444

R v Coate (1772) Lofft 73[right] ... 112

R v Codere (1916) 12 Cr App
   R 21[right] ... 543

R v Collins and Ashworth Hospital, ex p Brady
   (2001) 58 BMLR 173 (QB)[right] ... 307, 309,
   311, 313, 320, 348

R v Commissioner of Police of the Metropolis,
   ex p Blackburn [1968] 1 All ER 763; (No. 2)
   [1968] 2 All ER 319; (No. 3) [1973] 1 All ER
   324 (CA)[right] ... 464

R v Constantini [2005] EWCA Civ
   821[right] ... 239

R v Cowan [2004] EWCA Crim
   3081[right] ... 250

R v Cox [1991] Crim LR 276 (CA)[right] ... 208,
   212

R v Cox [2004] EWCA Crim 123[right] ... 248

R v Cox (Maurice) [1968] 1 WLR
   308[right] ... 236

R v Criminal Injuries Compensation Board, ex p
   Lawton [1972] 3 All ER 582[right] ... 430

R v Czarnota [2002] EWCA Crim
   785[right] ... 250

R v Daniel F George R 2000 WL
   1544620[right] ... 252

R v Daniel O 2001 WL 1476329[right] ... 252

R v Department of Health, ex p Source
   Informatics Ltd [1999] 4 All ER
   185[right] ... 21

R v Deputy Governor of Parkhurst Prison, ex p
   Hague [1992] 1 AC 58 (HL)[right] ... 264

R v Doncaster Metropolitan Borough Council, ex
   p W [2003] EWHC 192, [2004] EWCA Civ
   378, [2004] 1 MHLR 201[right] ... 412, 413,
   465, 466, 467, 601

R v Dorset County Council, ex p Beeson [2002]
   Civ 1812, [2001] EWHC Admin
   986[right] ... 442, 443

R v DPP, ex p Ferris [2004] EWHC
   1221[right] ... 227, 229

R v Dr F and DE, ex p Wirral Health Authority
   and Wirral Borough Council [2001] MHLR
   66[right] ... 364

R v Dr H, South West London and St George's
   Mental Health NHS Trust and Dr B, ex p K
   [2003] EWHC 357 (Admin), 2003 WL
   933333[right] ... 284

R v Dr M and Others, ex p N [2003] 1 WLR
   562 [2002] EWCA Civ 1789 (CA)[right]
   ... 312

R v Dr SS and Dr AC, ex p PB [2005] EWHC
   86[right] ... 315, 319

R v Drew [2003] UKHL 25, [2003] 1 WLR 1213,
   [2003] 4 All ER 557[right] ... 243, 249, 260,
   261, 265 *see also* Drew v UK (2006) 43
   EHRR SE2

R v Ealing District Health Authority, ex p Fox
   [1993] 1 WLR 373; 3 All ER 170
   (HC)[right] ... 464, 466, 560

R v East London and City Mental Health NHS
   Trust and Snazell, ex p Count Franz von
   Brandenburg [2001] EWCA Civ 239; [2002]
   QB 235; [2001] 3 WLR 588, [2001] 1 MHLR
   36; [2004] 2 AC 280, [2003] UKHL 58, [2004]
   1 All ER 400; [2003] 3 WLR 1265; [2003]
   EWHL 58[right] ... 30, 372, 427, 429, 468

R v East Sussex County Council, ex p Dudley
   [2003] EWHC 1093[right] ... 461, 462

R v Egan [1997] Crim LR 225 (CA)[right] ... 234,
   235

R v Fairhurst (1996) 1 Cr App R (S)
   242[right] ... 248, 249

R v Feggetter and MHAC, ex p John W [2002]
   WL 498885, CA, [2002] EWCA
   554[right] ... 30, 322, 324, 332, 582

R v Finnegan and DE, ex p Wirral Health
   Authority [2001] EWCA Civ
   1901[right] ... 424, 429

R v Fleming (1993) 14 Cr App R (S) 151
   (CA)[right] ... 248

R v Friend [1997] 2 Cr App R 231,
   CA[right] ... 224

R v Galfetti [2002] EWCA Crim
   1916[right] ... 246, 262

R v Gardiner (1967) 51 Cr App R
   187[right] ... 251, 256

R v Gardiner, ex p L [1986] 2 All ER 306
   (DC)[right] ... 355

R v Gill [2004] EWCA Crim 3245 2004 WL
   3089232[right] ... 212

R v Gloucestershire County Council and Another,
   ex p Barry (1995) 30 BMLR 20[right] ... 360,
   449, 454, 455, 456, 457, 496

R v Gloucestershire County Council, ex p
   Mahfood and Others (1996) 8 Admin LR
   180[right] ... 449

R v Goode [2002] EWCA Crim
   1698[right] ... 251, 252

R v Gordon (1981) 3 Cr App R(S) 352 (HC)[right] . . . 246

R v Governor of Broadmoor, ex p Argles (1974), unreported[right] . . . 188

R v Grant [2002] 1 Cr App R 38 (CA)[right] . . . 231, 236

R v Griffiths [2002] WL 1311144[right] . . . 271, 272

R v H and Secretary of State for the Home Department [2003] UKHL 1[right] . . . 223, 228

R v Haddock [2005] EWJC 921 (Admin)[right] . . . 317

R v Hall (1988) 86 Cr App R 159[right] . . . 36–7, 38

R v Hallstrom and Another, ex p W (No. 1) [1985] 3 All ER 775 (CA)[right] . . . 185, 192, 193, 197, 355, 357, 424, 582, 583

R v Hallstrom, ex p W (No. 2) [1986] 2 All ER 306[right] . . . 114–15, 132, 489

R v Harding (1983) The Times, 15 June (CA)[right] . . . 246

R v Haringey London Borough Council, ex p O [2004] EWCA Civ 535[right] . . . 484

R v Hasani [2005] EWHC 3016 (Admin), [2006] 1 All ER 817[right] . . . 227

R v Havering London Borough Council, ex p Johnson [2006] EWHC 1714[right] . . . 191, 461–2

R v Hayes (1981) 3 Cr App R (S) 330[right] . . . 256

R v Hennessey [1989] 2 All ER 9[right] . . . 240

R v Holmes [1979] Crim LR 52[right] . . . 592

R v Home Secretary, ex p K [1990] 3 All ER 562[right] . . . 407, 408

R v Home Secretary, ex p Leach [1994] QB 198 (CA)[right] . . . 299

R v Horseferry Road Magistrates' Court, ex p K [1996] 3 All ER 733 (CA)[right] . . . 239

R v Hospital Managers of Royal Park Hospital, ex p FTT [2003] EWCA Civ 330[right] . . . 189, 363

R v Hothi [2005] EWCA Crim 1803[right] . . . 248

R v Howell (1985) 7 Cr App R (S) 360[right] . . . 248, 249

R v Huntercombe Maidenhead Hospital, ex p SR [2005] EWHC 2361, [2006] ACD 17, 2005 WL 2273357[right] . . . 365

R v Hussein [2005] EWCA Crim 3556[right] . . . 225

R v Hutchinson (1997) 2 Cr App R (S) 60 (CA)[right] . . . 248

R v IA [2005] EWCA Crim 2077, [2006] 1 Cr App R (S) 91[right] . . . 248, 260

R v Islington London Borough Council, ex p Batantu (2001) 33 HLR 76 (QB)[right] . . . 451, 456, 460, 482, 484

R v Islington London Borough Council, ex p HP [2004] EWHC 7[right] . . . 451

R v Islington London Borough Council, ex p Jones [2005] EWHC 662 (QBD)[right] . . . 231

R v J [2003] EWCA Crim 3309, 2003 WL 22769342[right] . . . 205, 212

R v Jefferson, Skerritt, Readman and Keogh [1994] 99 Crim App R 130 (CA)[right] . . . 207, 208, 212

R v Jones 2000 WL 976077[right] . . . 252

R v Kamara [2002] EWCA Crim 1559[right] . . . 250

R v Kenny [1994] Crim LR 284[right] . . . 213

R v Kensington and Chelsea London Borough Council, ex p Kujtim [1999] 4 All ER 161[right] . . . 451, 460

R v Khan (1987) 9 Cr App (S) 455[right] . . . 250

R v Kirklees Metropolitan Borough Council, ex p C [1993] 2 FLR 187 (CA)[right] . . . 112, 113, 115, 126, 584

R v KM [2003] EWCA Crim 357[right] . . . 230, 236–7

R v Lambert 2001, WL 720273, [2001] UKHL 37, [2002] 2 AC 545, [2001] 3 WLR 206, [2001] 3 All ER 577[right] . . . 101

R v Lang and Others [2005] EWCA Crim 2864[right] . . . 243, 244

R v Law-Thompson [1997] Crim LR 674[right] . . . 212

R v Leicester County Council, ex p S [2004] EWHC 533 (Admin)[right] . . . 452

R v Leonard Cheshire Foundation (LCF), ex p Heather [2002] 2 All ER 936, [2002] HRLR 30, [2002] EWCA Civ 366[right] . . . 191, 192, 462

R v Lewis (Martin) [1996] Crim LR 260 (CA)[right] . . . 206

R v Lewis-Joseph [2004] EWCA Civ 1212[right] . . . 223

R v Lincoln (Kesteven) Justices, ex p O'Connor [1983] 1 WLR 335 (DC)[right] . . . 221, 238

R v Lincolnshire Health Authority, ex p Collins [2001] EWHC Admin 665[right] . . . 462

R v London South and West Region Mental Health and Review Tribunal, ex p M [2000] Lloyds Rep Med 143 (QB)[right] . . . 400

R v M (John) [2003] EWCA Crim 3452[right] . . . 224, 225

R v M, K and H [2001] EWCA Crim 2024, [2002]
1 WLR 824 (CA)[right] ... 227–8, 229, 230,
235

R v Macrow [2004] EWCA Crim
1159[right] ... 250

R v Maloney and Doherty [1988] Crim LR
523[right] ... 212

R v Manchester City Council, ex p Stennett
[2002] UKHL 34, [2001] QB 370
[right] ... 448

R v Maria TK [2001] EWCA Crim
400[right] ... 252

R v Martin 2000 WL 877792[right] ... 252

R v Mbatha (1985) 7 Cr App R (S)
373[right] ... 248, 249

R v Mental Health Act Commission, ex p Smith
(1998) The Times, 15 May (HC)[right] ... 100

R v Mental Health Act Commission, ex p X
(1988) 9 BMLR 77 (DC) (Goserelin
case)[right] ... 308, 325, 328, 348, 407, 515, 525

R v Mental Health and Review Tribunal; Ian
Stuart Brady and Secretary of State for the
Home Department, ex p Mersey Care NHS
Trust [2004] EWHC 1749[right] ... 393, 394

R v Mental Health and Review Tribunal, ex p B
[2002] EWHC Admin 1553[right]
... 386, 391

R v Mental Health and Review Tribunal, ex p B
[2003] EWHC Admin 815
(Admin)[right] ... 397

R v Mental Health and Review Tribunal, ex p
Booth [1998] COD 203 (HC)[right] ... 411

R v Mental Health and Review Tribunal, ex p C
[2005] EWHC 17[right] ... 408

R v Mental Health and Review Tribunal, ex p
Central and North West London Mental
Health NHS Trust [2005] EWHC
337[right] ... 378

R v Mental Health Review Tribunal, ex p
Clatworthy [1985] 3 All ER 699
(HC)[right] ... 44, 45, 385, 420, 434

R v Mental Health and Review Tribunal,
ex p Cooper [1990] COD 275
(HC)[right] ... 407, 408

R v Mental Health and Review Tribunal,
ex p East London and the City Mental
Health NHS Trust (QBD (Admin))
[2005] EWHC 2329, 2005 WL
2996870[right] ... 386, 421

R v Mental Health and Review Tribunal, ex p G
[2004] EWHC 2193[right] ... 410

R v Mental Health and Review Tribunal, ex p KB
and Seven Others [2002] EWHC Admin
639[right] ... 390, 391

R v Mental Health and Review Tribunal, ex p
Kelly (1997) 22 April, unreported
(HC)[right] ... 396, 424, 434

R v Mental Health and Review Tribunal,
ex p Li [2004] EWHC 51
(Admin)[right] ... 421

R v Mental Health and Review Tribunal, ex p M
[2005] EWHC 2791[right] ... 375

R v Mental Health and Review Tribunal, ex p
Mersey Care NHS Trust [2003] EWHC
1182[right] ... 419

R v Mental Health and Review Tribunal, ex p N
[2001] EWHC Admin 1133[right] ... 399

R v Mental Health and Review Tribunal, ex p
Pickering [1986] 1 All ER 99[right] ... 420

R v Mental Health Review Tribunal, ex p Pierce
(1997, unreported) (HC)[right] ... 399

R v Mental Health and Review Tribunal, ex p S
[2002] EWHC 2522 (QBD)[right] ... 385

R v Mental Health and Review Tribunal, ex p
Secretary of State [2001] EWHC Admin
849[right] ... 419

R v Mental Health and Review Tribunal, ex p
Secretary of State [2004] EWHC
2194[right] ... 410

R v Mental Health and Review Tribunal, ex P
Secretary of State for the Home Department
(1987) The Times, 25 March
(HC)[right] ... 387

R v Mental Health and Review Tribunal, ex p
Secretary of State for the Home Department
[2003] EWHC 2864[right] ... 420

R v Mental Health and Review Tribunal, ex p
Secretary of State for the Home Department
(2005) EWHA Civ 616[right] ... 407

R v Mental Health and Review Tribunal, ex p
Secretary of State for the Home Department
(2005) EWHC 2468 (Admin)[right] ... 407

R v Mental Health and Review Tribunal, ex p
Secretary of State for the Home Department,
PH [2002] EWCA Civ 1868, PH[right] ... 409,
435–6, 493

R v Mental Health and Review Tribunal, ex p SR
[2005] EWHC 2923 (Admin)[right] ... 377

R v Mental Health and Review Tribunal, ex p SS
[2004] EWHC 650, 2004 WL
960902[right] ... 396

R v Mental Health and Review Tribunal, ex p T
[2002] EWHC Admin 247[right] ... 394

R v Mental Health and Review Tribunal, ex p W
[2004] EWHC 3266 (Admin)[right] ... 402

R v Mental Health and Review Tribunal, ex
Secretary of State [2001] EWHC Admin
849[right] ... 408

R v Mental Health and Review Tribunal, ex
Secretary of State for the Home Department
[2001] ACD 62[right] ... 387

R v Mental Health and Review Tribunal London
North and East Region, ex p PW [2001] 1
MHLR 146 (HC)[right] ... 424

R v Mental Health and Review Tribunal London
South and West Region, ex p C [2001] MHLR
110[right] ... 344, 363, 389, 390

R v Mental Health and Review Tribunal and
Managers of Homerton Hospital (East
London & City Mental Health NHS Trust),
ex p CS [2004] EWHC 2958
(Admin)[right] ... 356

R v Mental Health and Review Tribunal North
and East London Region, ex p H [2000] CO
2120/2000, [2001] 3 WLR 512, [2002] QBD
1[right] ... 29, 385, 400, 403, 580

R v Mental Health and Review Tribunal
(Northern Region), ex p N; R v Mental Health
and Review Tribunal, ex p DJ [2006] QB 468,
[2006] 2 WLR 850, [2005] EWCA Civ
1605[right] ... 393

R v Mental Health Review Tribunal and Others,
ex p Hall [1999] 1 WLR 1323
(CA)[right] ... 409, 464

R v Mental Health and Review Tribunal and
Secretary of State for the Home Department,
ex p LH [2001] 1 MHLR 130
(HC)[right] ... 370, 398, 417

R v Mental Health Review Tribunal for the South
Thames Region, ex p Smith (1998) *The Times*,
9 December (HC); [1999] COD 148[right] ...
127, 402, 421

R v Mental Health and Review Tribunal, Torfaen
County Borough Council and Gwent Area
Health Authority, ex p Hall [1999] 3 All ER 132
(HC)[right] ... 447

R v Mental Health and Review Tribunal and W, ex
p Epsom and St Helier NHS Trust [2001]
EWHC Admin 101[right] ... 356, 405, 419, 425

R v Mental Health and Review Tribunal for the
West Midlands and North West Regions, ex p
Ashworth Hospital [2001] EWHC Admin
901[right] ... 392

R v Mental Health Tribunal for the North Wales
Region, ex p P (20 May 1990), unreported
(DC)[right] ... 405

R v Mersey Health Care NHS Trust, ex p DR
[2002] EWHC 1810, 2002 WL
1654941[right] ... 356

R v Merseyside Mental Health Review Tribunal,
ex p K [1990] 1 All ER 694[right] ... 370–1,
406, 407

R v Midlands and North West Mental Health and
Review Tribunal, ex PD [2004] EWCA Civ 311,
2004 WL 412965[right] ... 357, 375

R v Ministry of Defence, ex p Smith [1996] QB
517 (CA)[right] ... 193, 194

R v Mitchell (1997) 1 Cr App R (S) 90
(CA)[right] ... 248

R v Morse [1991] Crim LR 195[right] ... 207, 208

R v Nafei [2004] EWCA Crim 3238, [2005] 1 Cr
App R (S) 24[right] ... 249

R v National Asylum and Support Service, ex p
Westminster City Council [2002] UKHL
38[right] ... 460

R v Newcastle-upon-Tyne City Council, ex p
Dixon (1993) 158 Local Government Reports
441 (HC)[right] ... 444

R v Newham London Borough Council, ex p
P 2000 WL 1741487[right] ... 451

R v Newham London Borough County Council,
ex p Bibi 2000 WL 1544686[right] ... 462

R v Newington (1990) Cr App R 247
(CA)[right] ... 591, 592, 593

R v Newman [2000] 2 Cr App R (S)
227[right] ... 243

R v North and East Devon Health Authority,
ex p Coughlan [2001] QB 213, [2000] WLR
622 [2000] All ER 850[right] ... 456, 461,
462, 472, 475

R v North East London Regional Mental Health
and Review Tribunal, ex p T [2000] CLY 4173
(HC)[right] ... 420

R v North West London Mental Health NHS
Trust and Others, ex p Stewart [1997] 4 All ER
871, [1998] 2 WLR 189[right] ... 221, 360

R v North Yorkshire County Council, ex p
Hargreaves (No. 1) (1994) Medical Law
Reports 121 (HC)[right] ... 68

R v North Yorkshire County Council, ex p
Hargreaves (No. 2) (1997) *The Times*, 12 June
(HC)[right] ... 449

R v Nottingham Healthcare NHS Trust,
ex P M [2002] EWCA Civ 1728, [2002]
EWHC Admin 1400 (HC)[right] ... 270,
416

R v Nottingham Mental Health and Review
Tribunal, ex p Secretary of State for the Home
Department (1988) *The Times*, 12 October
(HC)[right] ... 387

R v Nwohla [1995] Crim LR 668[right] ... 256

R v Offen [2001] 2 Cr App R (S) 10,
CA[right] ... 243

R v Officer (1976) *The Times*, 20
February[right] ... 246

R v Oldham Metropolitan Borough Council, ex p Garlick; R v Tower Hamlets London Borough Council, ex p Ferdous Begum [1993] 2 All ER 65 (HL)[right] ... 479, 480, 484

R v Omara [2004] EWCA Crim 431[right] ... 227

R v O'Neill (1990) 16 October, unreported (Crown Court)[right] ... 208, 212

R v Oxford Regional Mental Health and Review Tribunal, ex p Secretary of State for the Home Department [1988] 1 AC 120, [1987] 3 All ER 8 (HL)[right] ... 379–80, 392, 396, 409, 411, 413

R v Oxfordshire Mental Healthcare NHS Trust, ex p F [2001] EWHC Admin 535[right] ... 299

R v Oxfordshire Mental Healthcare NHS Trust, ex p H [2002] EWHC 465[right] ... 427

R v Oxfordshire Mental Healthcare NHS Trust and Oxfordshire Health Authority [2001] 1 MHLR 140 (HC)[right] ... 370

R v Page and R v Secretary of State for the Home Department, ex p Hurlock [2001] EWHC Admin 380[right] ... 359

R v Palmer (1991) Legal Action, 21 September (Crown Court)[right] ... 208, 212

R v Parole Board, ex p Bradley [1990] 3 All ER 828[right] ... 368

R v Partnerships in Care Ltd, ex p A [2002] 1 WLR 2610[right] ... 192

R v Pathfinder NHS Trust, ex p W [1999] 1 MHLR 142 (HC)[right] ... 398, 427

R v Paul Lee S [2001] EWCA Crim 743[right] ... 246

R v Pemberton (1996) 24 June, unreported (CA)[right] ... 250, 252

R v Pinder, in re Greenwood (1855) 24 LJ (NS) QB 148[right] ... 121

R v Plymouth City Council, ex p Cowl [2001] EWCA Civ 1935 [2002] 1 WLR 803, [2002], 1 All ER 633 [2002] 1 WLR 810[right] ... 461

R v Podola [1960] 1 QB 325 (DC)[right] ... 224, 225

R v Powys County Council, ex p Hambridge (No. 1) (1998) 1 FLR 643 (HC), [1998] LGR 627[right] ... 449, 450, 457

R v Powys County Council, ex p Hambridge (No. 2) (2000) BMLR 133 (CA)[right] ... 446

R v Preston, ex p DPP [2003] EWHC 729[right] ... 206

R v Pritchard (1836) 7 C & P 303[right] ... 224, 231, 232, 238, 240

R v Rampton Hospital Authority, ex p W [2001] EWHC Admin 134[right] ... 269

R v Ramsgate Justices, ex p Kazmarek (1985) 80 Cr App R 366 (DC)[right] ... 238

R v Redbridge LB, Camden LB, ex p N [2003] EWHC 3419 (Admin)[right] ... 441

R v Reid [2005] EWCA Crim 392[right] ... 249

R v Reynolds [1999] 2 Cr App R (S) 5[right] ... 251

R v Ristic [2002] EWCA Crim 165[right] ... 251

R v Riverside Mental Health Trust, ex p Huzzey (1998) 43 BMLR 167 (HC)[right] ... 364, 365

R v RMO, ex p PS [2003] EWHC 2335[right] ... 314

R v RMO and SOAD, ex p JB [2006] EWCA Civ 961[right] ... 312, 313, 317

R v RMO and SOAD, ex p T [2005] EWHC 1688[right] ... 315

R v Robbins [1988] Crim LR 744[right] ... 37

R v Robertson (1968) 52 Cr App R 690, [1968] 1 WLR 1767[right] ... 223–4

R v Roden [2006] EWCA Civ 1211[right] ... 248

R v Runighian [1977] Crim LR 361[right] ... 339, 584

R v S and Others, ex p B [2006] EWCA Civ 28[right] ... 319, 321

R v St Helens Borough Council, ex p Haggerty [2003] EWHC 803, [2003] HLR 69[right] ... 462

R v St Leonce [2004] EWCA Crim 1154[right] ... 252

R v Secretary of State for the Environment, Transport and the Regions, ex p Alconbury [2001] 2 WLR 1389 (HL)[right] ... 195

R v Secretary of State for Health, ex p Borough Council Hammersmith and Fulham (and Others) (1997) The Independent, 15 July (HC)[right] ... 479

R v Secretary of State for Health, ex p L [2000] 1 MHLR 191[right] ... 100

R v Secretary of State for the Home Department, ex p A [2002] EWHC Admin 1618, [2003] 1 WLR 330[right] ... 359, 360–1

R v Secretary of State for the Home Department, ex p Abdul Miah [2004] EWHC 2569 (Admin)[right] ... 270

R v Secretary of State for the Home Department, ex p Brind [1990] 1 All ER 649[right] ... 407

R v Secretary of State for the Home Department, ex p C [2002] EWCA Civ 647[right] ... 379

R v Secretary of State for the Home Department, ex p Carroll, Al-Hasan, and Greenfield [2001] EWCA Civ 1224, [2002] 1 WLR 545, [2001] HRLR 58, 2001 WL 753465[right] ... 100

R v Secretary of State for the Home Department, ex p D [2002] EWHC 2805[right] ... 417

R v Secretary of State for the Home Department, ex p Daly [2001] 2 AC 532 (HL)[right] ... 102, 103, 193, 194, 195, 196, 311, 424, 455–6

R v Secretary of State for the Home Department, ex p DB [2006] EWHC 659 (Admin)[right] ... 98, 102

R v Secretary of State for the Home Department, ex p Didlick [1993] COD 412 (DC)[right] ... 372

R v Secretary of State for the Home Department, ex p H & Others [1994] 3 WLR 1110[right] ... 268

R v Secretary of State for the Home Department, ex p Harry [1998] 3 All ER 360 (HC)[right] ... 97, 369, 398, 434

R v Secretary of State for the Home Department, ex p K [1990] 1 All ER 703 (DC)[right] ... 264, 371, 372

R v Secretary of State for the Home Department, ex p L [2005] EWCA Civ 2, [2006] 1 WLR 88[right] ... 371–2

R v Secretary of State for the Home Department, ex p OS [2006] EWHC 1903 (Admin)[right] ... 359

R v Secretary of State for the Home Department, ex p P [2003] EWHC 2953[right] ... 414

R v Secretary of State for the Home Department, ex p Pickering (1990, unreported) (CA)[right] ... 369

R v Secretary of State for the Home Department, ex p Powell (1978, unreported)[right] ... 368–9

R v Secretary of State for the Home Department, ex p S [2003] EWCA Civ 426[right] ... 430

R v Secretary of State for the Home Department, ex p Samoo [2001] UKHRR 1150[right] ... 195

R v Secretary of State for the Home Department, ex p Stroud (1993) COD 75[right] ... 418

R v Secretary of State for the Home Department, ex p T [1994] 1 All ER 794 (DC)[right] ... 266

R v Secretary of State for the Home Department, ex p T [2003] EWHC 538[right] ... 265, 372

R v Secretary of State for the Home Department and National Assembly of Wales, ex p D [2004] ex p D [2004] EWHC 2857 (Admin)[right] ... 265, 267, 268

R v Secretary of State for the Home Department and Secretary of State for Health, ex p IH [2002] EWCA Civ 646, [2001] 1 MHLR 100[right] ... 380, 386, 400, 410, 411, 412, 413, 414, 465, 466, 467, 468

R v Secretary of State for the Home Office, ex p Gilkes [1999] 1 MHLR 6 (HC)[right] ... 267

R v Secretary of State for Social Services, ex p Association of Metropolitan Authorities [1986] 1 All ER 164[right] ... 164

R v Sefton Metropolitan Borough Council, ex p Help the Aged and Others [1997] 4 All ER 532[right] ... 458, 460

R v Shetty, ex p IR [2003] EWHC 3022[right] ... 270

R v Slater (1996) 7 October, unreported[right] ... 252

R v Slough BC, ex p M [2004] EWHC 1109, [2006] EWCA Civ 655[right] ... 439

R v Snaresbrook Crown Court, ex p K 2001 WL 1422891[right] ... 271, 272

R v South Western Hospital Managers and Another, ex p M [1994] 1 All ER 161 (HC)[right] ... 30, 169, 184, 188, 372, 426, 427

R v Southend Borough Council, ex p J [2005] EWHC 3457[right] ... 450

R v Southwark Borough Council, ex p K [2001] EWCA Civ 999, [2001] HLR 31 , (2000 WL 1791525) (CA)[right] ... 451–2, 453, 483

R v Southwark London Borough Council, ex p Mooney [2006] EWHC 1912[right] ... 484

R v Staines [2006] EWCA Crim 15[right] ... 260, 261

R v Stockton on Tees Borough Council, ex p Stephenson [2005] EWCA Civ 960[right] ... 68, 440

R v Stone, R v Dobinson [1977] 1 All ER 341[right] ... 593

R v Sullivan [1984] AC 156 (HL)[right] ... 240

R v SW Staffs Primary Care Trust [2005] EWHC 1894[right] ... 453

R v SW Thames Mental Health and Review Tribunal, ex p M [1998] COD 38 (HC)[right] ... 377

R v Swindon Borough Council, ex p Stoddard (1998) 2 July, unreported (DC)[right] ... 273, 451

R v Tower Hamlets London Borough Council, ex p Abdul W [2002] EWCA Civ 287[right] ... 302, 441, 456, 460, 482, 484

R v Trent Mental Health and Review Tribunal, ex p Ryan (1991) unreported CA[right] ... 40

R v W and Another [1994] Crim LR 130 (CA)[right] ... 208

R v Walch [2003] EWCA Crim 1603[right] ... 249

R v Walsall Metropolitan Borough Council, ex p P and R (2001) 26 April, unreported[right] ... 462

R v Walton [2003] EWCA Crim 2254[right] ... 248

R v Wandsworth London Borough Council, ex p
G [2003] EWHC 2941, [2004] EWCA Civ
1170[right] ... 451, 463

R v Wandsworth London Borough Council,
ex p Spink [2005] EWCA Civ 302, [2005] 1
WLR 2884, [2005] 2 All ER 954[right] ...
455, 496

R v West Allerdale Magistrates Court, ex p Bitcon
[2003] EWHC 2460[right] ... 221

R v West London Mental Health NHS Trust, ex p
K [2005] EWHC 1454 (Admin), [2006] EWCA
Civ 118 [2006] 1 WLR 1865[right] ... 360

R v West London Youth Court, ex p J [2000] 1
WLR 2368, [2000] 1 All ER 823[right] ... 208

R v Westminster City Council, ex p M, P, A and X
(1997) 1 CCLR 85[right] ... 481–2

R v Wigan Metropolitan Borough Council, ex p
Tammadge [1998] 1 CCLR 581[right] ... 482,
484

R v Wirrall Metropolitan Borough Council, ex p
B (1994) The Times, 3 May (HC)[right] ... 480

R (Wheldon) v Rampton Hospital Authority
[2001] EWHC Admin 134[right] ... 131

R (Wilkinson) v RMO Broadmoor Hospital and
MHA Second Opinion Approved Doctor
[2001] EWCA Civ 1545; [2002] 1 WLR 419
(CA)[right] ... 29, 30, 188, 190, 195, 309, 310,
311, 312, 313, 314, 315, 316, 317, 320, 321, 323,
332, 424, 463, 582, 590, 601, 602

Raninen v Finland [1997] 26 EHRR
563[right] ... 316

Reeves v Commissioner of Police [1999] 3 WLR
363[right] ... 309

Reid v Secretary of State for Scotland [1999] 2 AC
512, [1999] 2 WLR 28, [1999] 1 All ER
481[right] ... 129, 298–9, 404, 405, 434

Rhodes v Bate (1866) 1 Ch 252[right] ... 533

Richardson v London County Council [1957] 1
WLR 751[right] ... 579, 586

Roberts, Re (Deceased) [1978] 1 WLR
653[right] ... 502

Robertson v Fife Council [2002] SLT
951[right] ... 442

Rouse v Cameron, 373 F 2d 451
(1966)[right] ... 146

Roux v UK [1997] EHRL 102, [1997] EHRLR
102[right] ... 388, 389

Ruddle v Secretary of State for Scotland (1999)
GWD 29-1395[right] ... 404

RW v Sheffield County Council [2005] EWHC
720 (Admin)[right] ... 481

S (a Minor) (Consent to Medical Treatment), Re
[1994] 2 FLR 1065[right] ... 522

S (Adult: Refusal of Medical Treatment), Re
[1992] 4 All ER 671[right] ... 521, 522

S (Adult Patient: Sterilisation: Patients' Best
Interests), Re [2000] 3 WLR 1288
(CA)[right] ... 294

S (Adult Patient) (Inherent Jurisdiction: Family
Life), Re [2002] EWHC 2278, [2003] 1 FLR
292[right] ... 505, 534, 573

S (Hospital Patient: Court's Jurisdiction), Re
[1995] 3 All ER 290 (CA)[right] ... 497, 504,
541

S (Hospital Patient: Foreign Curator), Re [1996]
Fam 23[right] ... 541

S (Medical Treatment: Adult Sterilisation), Re
[1998] 1 FLR 944[right] ... 537

S v Airedale NHS Trust[right] ... 344

S-C (Mental Patient: Habeas Corpus), Re [1996]
1 All ER 532 (CA)[right] ... 184, 187, 188, 189,
191

St George's Healthcare NHS Trust v S [1998] 2
FLR 728, 3 All ER 673 (CA)[right] ... 177, 185,
187, 308, 309, 521, 522

SC v UK (2005) 40 EHRR 10[right] ... 229

Seal v Chief Constable of South Wales Police
[2005] EWCA Civ 586, [2005] 1 MHLR
137[right] ... 583

Secretary of State for the Home Department v
Mental Health and Review Tribunal for Wales;
Secretary of State for the Home Department v
Mental Health and Review Tribunal for
Merseyside RHA [1986] 3 All ER 233
(HC)[right] ... 409, 410

Secretary of State for the Home Department v
Robb [1995] 1 All ER 677 (HC)[right] ... 306,
307, 308, 309

Shah v Barnet London Borough Council [1983] 1
All ER 226 (HL)[right] ... 168, 169

Sheffield City Council v E [2004] EWHC
2808[right] ... 502, 543

Shoesmith, In re [1938] 2 KB 637[right] ... 585

Sidaway v Board of Governors of the Bethlam
Royal Hospital and the Maudsley Hospital
[1985] 1 AC 870[right] ... 290, 291, 595

Smee v Smee (1879) 5 P 84[right] ... 532

Smirek v Williams [2000] 1 MHLR
38[right] ... 170

Smith and Grady v UK (1999) 20 EHRR
493[right] ... 194, 195

Snook v Watts (1848) 11 Beav 105[right] ...
498

South West London and St George's Mental
Health NHS Trust v W [2002] EWHC
1770[right] ... 264, 270, 299, 364

Spier, In the Estate of (Deceased), Re [1947] WN 46[right] ... 517

Stead v Thornton 3 B & Ad 357[right] ... 566

T (Adult: Refusal of Treatment), Re [1992] 3 WLR 782 (CA)[right] ... 289, 293, 309, 335, 508, 521, 522

T v Chase Farm Hospital 2000 WL 1479976 (HC), T[right] ... 189

T v T [1988] 1 All ER 613 (HC)[right] ... 489

T v UK and V v UK [2000] Crim LR 187[right] ... 229

T and V v UK (1999) 7 BHRC 659[right] ... 310

Tameside and Glossop Acute Services Trust v CH [1996] 1 FLR 762 (FD)[right] ... 303, 304, 305, 306, 307, 308, 339, 348, 521, 523–5

Tarbuck v Bispham 2 M & W 2[right] ... 566

TB, Re [1967] Ch 247[right] ... 535

TF (An Adult: Residence), Re [2000] 1 MHLR 120[right] ... 504, 505, 573

Tinsley v Sarkar [2005] EWHC 192[right] ... 464

Twine v Bean's Express Ltd [1946] 1 All ER 202[right] ... 589

Van der Leer v The Netherlands (1990) 12 EHRR 567[right] ... 389

Varbanov v Bulgaria Application no. 31365/96 (2000)[right] ... 267

VE (Mental Health Patient), Re [1973] 1 QB 452[right] ... 185–6

W (A Minor) (Medical Treatment: Court's Jurisdiction), Re [1992] 3 WLR 758[right] ... 115, 551

W (Adult: Refusal of Treatment), Re [2002] C8002041[right] ... 289, 309

W (EEM), Re [1971] 1 Ch. 123[right] ... 535, 536

W, Re [1970] 2 All ER 502[right] ... 561

W v Edgell and Ors [1990] 1 All ER 835 (CA)[right] ... 384

W v L [1974] QB 711[right] ... 47, 170, 171

Walker, Re [1905] 1 Ch 160[right] ... 500, 552

Ward v Commissioner of Police for the Metropolis [2005] UKHL 32[right] ... 136, 179

WC v South London and Maudsley NHS Trust and David Orekeye [2001] EWHC Admin 1025[right] ... 168

Wednesbury case *see* Associated Provincial Picture Houses Ltd v Wednesday Corporation [1948] 1 KB ... 223

Whitbread (Mental Patient: Habeas Corpus), Re [1997] 39 BMLR 94[right] ... 164

Whitbread v Kingston and District NHS Trust (1997) *The Times*, 14 July, (1998) 39 BMLR 94[right] ... 155, 169, 174, 188

Winch v Jones [1985] 3 All ER 97 (CA)[right] ... 587, 588, 595

Winterwerp v The Netherlands (1979–80) 2 EHRR 387[right] ... 28–9, 189, 196, 231, 351, 358, 363, 368, 371, 376, 393, 400, 401, 403, 407, 412, 413, 574

Wyatt v Stickney, 325 F.Supp 781 (MD Ala. 1971)[right] ... 146

X (Minors) v Bedfordshire County Council [1995] 3 All ER 353[right] ... 595

X v A, B and C and the MHAC (1991) 9 BMLR 91[right] ... 588

X v Bedfordshire County Council [1995] 3 All ER 353[right] ... 469, 596, 597, 598

X v UK (1982) 4 EHRR 118[right] ... 190, 361, 374, 380, 401, 404, 416, 427, 492

Yonge v Toybee [1910] 1 KB 215[right] ... 605

Youngberg v Romeo 457 US 307 (USSC, 1982)[right] ... 146

Z v UK [2001] 2 FLR 612; (2002) 34 EHRR 3[right] ... 598

Zinnerman v Burch, 494 US 113 (USSC, 1990)[right] ... 150

Table of Statutes

This table contains current UK legislation, followed by proposed legislation, foreign legislation, European legislation and international legislation

Access to Medical Reports Act 1988
  s. 7(1) ... 322
Armed Forces Act 1996
  Sch. 7
    Part III
      para. 1 ... 263

Bail Act 1976 ... 218
  s. 3(6) ... 215
  s. 3(6)A ... 215
  s. 4(1) ... 215
  s. 4(4) ... 215
  Sch. 1
    Part I ... 217
      para. 2 ... 215
      para. 2A ... 215, 217
      para. 3 ... 217
      para. 5 ... 217
      para. 7 ... 215, 217
      para. 8(1) ... 215
      para. 8(2) ... 215
      para. 9 ... 219

Care Standards Act 2000 ... 95, 118, 446, 469, 556
  Part I ... 444
  Part II ... 91, 444
  s. 2(2) ... 91
  s. 2(3)(b) ... 444
  s. 2(6) ... 445
  s. 3 ... 445
  s. 3(1) ... 66
  s. 3(2) ... 444
  s. 3(2)(b) ... 91
  s. 3(3) ... 444
  s. 5 ... 444
  s. 6 ... 444
  s. 6(2) ... 444
  s. 11 ... 444
  s. 20(1)(B) ... 444
  s. 21 ... 444
Carers (Recognition and Services) Act 1995 ... 13, 68
Children Act 1989 ... 167, 439
  Part III ... 455
  s. 4 ... 167
  s. 85 ... 115

Chronically Sick and Disabled Persons Act (CSDPA) 1970 ... 446, 454
  s. 2 ... 449, 450, 457, 458
  s. 2(1) ... 449, 454, 455, 456, 459, 463, 464
Civil Partnership Act 2004 ... 167
Community Care (Delayed Discharge) Act 2003 ... 476
  s. 11(3) ... 476
Community Care (Direct Payments) Act 1996 ... 479
Community Care and Health (Scotland) Act 2002 ... 475
Community Care (Residential Accommodation) Act 1998 ... 441
Contempt of Court Act 1981
  s. 2 ... 394–5
County Asylums Act 1808 ... 18, 19, 75
  s. 17 ... 112
  s. 23 ... 112
County Asylums Act 1845 ... 18, 19, 72, 75, 76
Crime and Punishment (Scotland) Act 1997
  s. 6 ... 260
Crime (Sentences) Act 1997 ... 243, 260, 262, 263, 417
  s. 2 ... 257
  s. 6 ... 257
  s. 28 ... 414
  s. 47(1) ... 254
  s. 49(1) ... 262
Criminal Appeals Act 1968
  s. 16A ... 223
  s. 16B ... 223
Criminal Appeals Act 1995
  s. 9 ... 212
Criminal Justice Act 2001
  s. 39 ... 273
Criminal Justice Act 2003 ... 244, 417
  s. 142 ... 242
  s. 142(2)(d) ... 242
  s. 143 ... 242
  s. 148(1) ... 242
  s. 153 ... 242
  s. 154 ... 245
  s. 155(2) ... 242
  s. 157(1) ... 242
  s. 157(3) ... 242

s. 166 ... 242
s. 166(2) ... 242
s. 177 ... 244
s. 207 ... 244
s. 224(2) ... 242
s. 225 ... 243
ss. 225–8 ... 243
s. 225(2) ... 242
s. 225(3) ... 243
s. 225(4) ... 243
s. 226 ... 243
s. 227 ... 242, 243
s. 227(1)(b) ... 242
s. 227(2)(a) ... 242
s. 227(2)(b) ... 242
s. 227(3) ... 242
s. 227(4) ... 242
s. 227(5) ... 242
s. 228 ... 243
Sch. 15
    Part 1 ... 242
    Part 2 ... 242
Criminal Justice and Public Order Act 1994
s. 25 ... 219
s. 34 ... 207
s. 36 ... 207
s. 37 ... 207
Criminal Law Act 1967
s. 3(1) ... 339
Criminal Lunatics Act 1800 ... 223
Criminal Lunatics Act 1860 ... 18
Criminal Procedure (Insanity) Act 1964 ... 224,
    228, 229, 232, 237, 238, 239, 300, 383
s. 4 ... 223, 227, 229
s. 4(1) ... 223
s. 4(2) ... 226
s. 4(3) ... 226
s. 4(4) ... 226
s. 4(5) ... 225
s. 4(6) ... 227, 231
s. 4A ... 226, 227, 228, 229, 236
s. 4A(1) ... 226
s. 4A(2) ... 226, 227, 230, 233, 234, 238
s. 4A(2)(a) ... 227
s. 4A(2)(b) ... 227
s. 5 ... 227, 231, 232, 239
s. 5(1)(a) ... 372
s. 5(2) ... 227, 235
s. 5(2)(a) ... 231, 232
s. 5(2)(b) ... 232
s. 5(2)(c) ... 232
s. 5(3) ... 235, 239
s. 5(3)(b) ... 232
s. 5(4) ... 231, 232
s. 5A ... 231
s. 5A(1)(c) ... 231
s. 5A(2) ... 233

s. 5A(3) ... 232
s. 5A(4) ... 232
s. 5A(6) ... 232
Sch. 1
    para. 1(2) ... 232
    para. 1(3) ... 232
    para. 1(4) ... 232
Sch. 1A ... 233
    para. 1(1) ... 233
    para. 1(2) ... 233
    para. 2(1) ... 233
    para. 3(1) ... 233
    para. 4 ... 233
    para. 4(3) ... 233
    para. 5 ... 233
    para. 5(3) ... 233
    para. 8 ... 233
Criminal Procedure (Insanity and Unfitness to
    Plead) Act 1991 ... 224, 226, 227, 228, 229, 230,
    231, 232, 233, 238, 239, 241
Part II ... 96
Part III ... 96
s. 2 ... 223, 226
s. 3 ... 231
s. 4A(4) ... 234
s. 5 ... 224
Sch. 1
    para. (1) ... 232
    para. (2) ... 232
Sch. 2
    para. 6 ... 238
    para. 8(2) ... 238
    Part III ... 238
Criminal Procedure (Scotland) Act 1975
s. 59A ... 260
s. 174ZA ... 237

Disability Discrimination Act (DDA) 1995 ... 27,
    446
s. 22 ... 480
Disabled Persons (Services, Consultation and
    Representation) Act 1986 ... 457, 496
s. 4 ... 457
Domestic Violence, Crime and Victims Act
    (DVCVA) 2004 ... 226, 239
Part III
    Ch. 2 ... 383, 396
s. 22 ... 225
s. 24 ... 231

Enduring Powers of Attorney Act (EPAA)
    1985 ... 528, 546, 547, 548, 561, 563
s. 8(2)(b)(i) ... 563

Financial Services Act 1986
s. 7(1) ... 236

Health Act 1999 ... 88
  s. 26 ... 474
  s. 30 ... 474
  s. 31 ... 474
  s. 31(1) ... 474
Health Service Commissioner Act 1993 ... 603
Health Service Commissioner (Amendment)
  Act 1996
  s. 6 ... 603
Health Services and Public Health Act (HSPHA)
  1968 ... 446–7
  s. 45 ... 438, 439, 446, 463
  s. 45(4)(b) ... 446
Health and Social Care Act 2001 ... 88
  Ch. 2
    Parts 3 and 4 ... 87
  s. 2 ... 88
  s. 45 ... 474
  s. 46 ... 474
  s. 49 ... 475
Health and Social Services and Social Security
  Adjudications Act 1983
  s. 17 ... 446, 447, 472
Homicide Act 1957 ... 235
Housing Act 1996 ... 481
  s. 167(2) ... 482
  s. 189(1) ... 479
  s. 189(1)(c) ... 479
  s. 191 ... 480
  s. 193(2) ... 479
  s. 197 ... 481
  s. 198 ... 481
  s. 198(1) ... 481
  s. 199 ... 481
Human Fertilisation and Embryology Act
  1990 ... 558
Human Rights Act (HRA) 1998 ... xi, 23, 26,
  27–8, 29, 30, 59, 99, 165–6, 167, 171, 187, 189,
  194, 277, 296, 309, 323, 361, 367, 389, 403, 426,
  434, 580, 582, 590, 600–2
  s. 3 ... 323, 601
  s. 6 ... 191, 196, 323
  s. 6(1) ... 196–7, 311, 380, 393, 462, 463, 468
  s. 6(2) ... 393, 467
  s. 6(3) ... 380, 468
  s. 6(3)(a) ... 311, 392–3
  s. 6(3)(b) ... 462
  s. 7(1) ... 196
  s. 8 ... 196
  s. 8(1) ... 601
  s. 9 ... 391

Idiots Act 1886 ... 19
Immigration Act 1971 ... 266
Incapacity (Scotland) Act 2000
  s. 47(2) ... 285

Inebriates Act 1898
  s. 1 ... 43
  s. 2 ... 43
Insolvency Act 1986
  s. 423 ... 443

Limitations Act 1980
  s. 28 ... 606
Local Authority Social Services Act 1970 ... 438
  s. 7 ... 438, 446
  s. 7A ... 438
  s. 7D ... 469
  s. 7E ... 438
Local Government Act 1888
  s. 3(vi) ... 18
  s. 86 ... 18
  s. 111 ... 18
Lunacy Act 1890 ... 18–19, 121, 159, 596
  s. 139 ... 339

Madhouses Act 1774 ... 17
Madhouses Act 1828 ... 17
  s. 29 ... 112
Magistrates' Courts Act 1980
  s. 142 ... 246
Mental Capacity Act (MCA) 2005 ... xi, 21, 23,
  26, 27, 39, 114, 118–19, 120, 160, 186, 276, 283,
  294, 335, 498, 499, 505, 516, 522, 534, 545–78,
  579
  Part V ... 545
  s. 1 ... 546–7
  s. 1(1) ... 549
  s. 1(2) ... 497, 549, 550
  s. 1(3) ... 550
  s. 1(4) ... 517, 550
  s. 1(5) ... 548, 550, 562
  s. 1(6) ... 550
  s. 2 ... 225, 319, 325, 551, 569
  ss 2–3 ... 547
  s. 2(1) ... 551
  s. 2(2) ... 551
  s. 2(3) ... 551
  s. 3 ... 225, 551, 569
  s. 3(1) ... 225, 551
  s. 3(1)(b) ... 225
  s. 3(1)(c) ... 225
  s. 3(2) ... 551
  s. 3(3) ... 225, 551
  s. 3(4) ... 516, 551
  s. 4 ... 536, 547, 552, 553, 555, 556, 558, 562
  s. 4(1) ... 553
  ss. 4(1)–(7)D ... 555
  s. 4(2) ... 553
  s. 4(3) ... 553
  s. 4(4) ... 553
  s. 4(5) ... 553, 572

s. 4(6) ... 552
s. 4(7) ... 554, 556
s. 4(9) ... 555, 556
s. 5 ... 550, 567, 568
s. 6(4) ... 558
s. 6(5) ... 118, 558
s. 7 ... 567, 568, 569
s. 7(2) ... 569
s. 8 ... 569
s. 8(2) ... 569
s. 8(2)(b) ... 563
s. 9(4) ... 562
s. 11(2) ... 552
s. 11(5) ... 558
s. 11(6) ... 118, 558
s. 11(7)(a) ... 558
s. 11(8) ... 561
s. 15 ... 559
s. 16(4)(b) ... 560
s. 16(5) ... 560
s. 17 ... 559
s. 18 ... 559
s. 19 ... 560
s. 19(9)(b) ... 572
s. 20(1) ... 500, 552, 558
s. 20(2) ... 558
s. 20(4) ... 560
s. 20(12) ... 558
s. 20(13) ... 118, 558
s. 22(3) ... 559
s. 22(4) ... 564
s. 23 ... 559
s. 23(1) ... 563
ss. 24–26 ... 547
s. 25 ... 570
s. 25(2) ... 570
s. 25(3) ... 570
s. 25(4) ... 570
s. 25(4)(c) ... 570
s. 25(5) ... 571
s. 26(1) ... 569
s. 26(2) ... 571
s. 26(3) ... 571
s. 26(5) ... 571
s. 27 ... 558, 559
s. 28 ... 558, 576
s. 28(1) ... 575
s. 28(2) ... 575
s. 29 ... 558, 573
ss. 35–41 ... 556
s. 36 ... 556
s. 44 ... 548
s. 62 ... 546
s. 64(1) ... 567, 570
Sch. 1 ... 563, 572
Mental Deficiency Act 1913 ... 19, 43, 82, 488,
    503, 546
s. 2(b)(vi) ... 43

Mental Deficiency Act 1926 ... 82, 503, 546
Mental Deficiency Act 1939 ... 82, 503, 546
Mental Health Act (MHA) 1959 ... 19–20, 43, 44,
    47, 60, 79, 82, 116, 138, 256, 266, 268, 294, 299,
    301, 302, 332, 345, 347, 373, 374, 395, 421, 488,
    499, 503, 539, 546, 587
s. 4(5) ... 44
s. 5 ... 584
s. 25(2)(a) ... 295
s. 34 ... 488
s. 128 ... 593

Mental Health Act (MHA) 1983 ... xi, 9, 17, 18,
    20, 23, 24, 26, 27, 33, 36, 37, 39, 40, 42, 46, 57,
    60, 66, 82, 86, 91, 97, 100, 107, 108, 115, 116,
    117, 118, 119, 121, 129–30, 137, 145–6, 148,
    154, 155, 156, 159, 161, 166, 172, 181, 186, 191,
    199, 200, 231, 239–40, 272, 308, 324, 332, 339,
    340, 347, 349, 439, 444, 445, 447, 487, 575, 579
Part II ... 21, 81, 91, 135, 136, 137, 141, 155,
    156–8, 162, 184, 185, 197, 222, 245, 294, 330,
    354, 362, 363, 372, 377–8, 379, 399, 431, 488,
    489, 490, 576, 590
Part III ... 21, 91, 202, 256, 264, 367–73, 557
Part IV ... 220, 221, 275, 276, 281–2, 289, 292,
    296, 297, 299, 300, 302, 303, 306, 308, 315,
    318, 320, 327, 334, 335, 347, 348, 357, 558,
    575, 576
Part VI ... 21
Part VII ... 16, 21, 499, 500, 534, 539, 542, 546,
    547, 548, 552, 559, 560, 561, 583
Part IX ... 590, 592
s. 1 ... 112, 124, 232, 245, 251, 489
s. 1(2) ... 34, 35, 39, 126, 129, 205, 258, 355,
    503, 576
s. 1(3) ... 35, 42–6, 202, 215
s. 1(4) ... 255
s. 1(5) ... 255
s. 2 ... 25, 35, 111, 122, 123, 124, 125, 126–8,
    129, 133, 134, 135, 138, 139, 140, 146, 158,
    163, 164, 169, 173, 174, 178, 179, 184, 187,
    188, 221, 268, 296, 300, 302, 376, 377–8, 387,
    388, 390, 391, 399, 402, 423, 426, 431, 464,
    557, 573, 596, 600
s. 2(2) ... 126, 134
s. 2(2)(a) ... 127
s. 2(2)(b) ... 122, 127, 128, 134, 400
s. 2(3) ... 174
s. 2(4) ... 363
s. 3 ... 25, 35, 37, 47, 111, 122, 123, 124,
    128–33, 134, 135, 138, 139, 146, 163, 164,
    165, 169, 173, 174, 176, 177, 178, 179, 184,
    187, 188, 192, 193, 220, 221, 245, 246, 264,
    268, 269, 293, 298, 299, 300, 302, 303, 324,
    330, 355, 356, 364, 365, 372, 377–8, 379, 381,
    387, 388, 389, 390, 402, 403, 405, 420, 426,
    427, 428–9, 430, 464, 489, 494, 557, 576, 582,
    596, 600
s. 3(2) ... 128–9, 134

s. 3(2)(a) . . . 132, 404
s. 3(2)(b) . . . 36, 37, 38, 129, 134, 355, 403, 489
s. 3(2)(c) . . . 122, 132
s. 3(3) . . . 174
s. 3(3)(b) . . . 129
s. 4 . . . 123, 124, 134–5, 138, 140, 174, 176, 177,
    297, 431, 432, 464
s. 4(1) . . . 134
s. 4(2) . . . 134
s. 4(2)(c) . . . 557
s. 4(3) . . . 177
s. 4(4) . . . 363
s. 5 . . . 35, 123, 124, 133, 138, 233, 362,
    376, 464
s. 5(2) . . . 134, 138, 139, 188, 297, 431
s. 5(3) . . . 134
s. 5(4) . . . 134, 138, 139, 297, 431
s. 5(4)(a) . . . 122, 134
s. 5(7) . . . 134
s. 6 . . . 35
s. 6(1) . . . 179, 184–5
s. 6(1)(a) . . . 179
s. 6(3) . . . 183, 185, 186, 187–8
s. 6(6) . . . 577
s. 6(12) . . . 180
s. 7 . . . 38, 114, 268, 489, 576, 590, 591, 600
s. 7(2)(a) . . . 489
s. 7(2)(b) . . . 489, 577
s. 7(5) . . . 490
s. 8 . . . 35, 489, 490, 503, 504, 557
s. 8(1) . . . 114, 488, 577
s. 8(2) . . . 490
s. 9 . . . 490
s. 11 . . . 123, 164, 168, 354, 489
s. 11(1) . . . 163, 489
s. 11(2) . . . 163, 173
s. 11(3) . . . 123, 163, 164
s. 11(4) . . . 164, 169, 188
s. 11(5) . . . 177, 188, 268
s. 11(6) . . . 36, 175, 184
s. 11(7) . . . 174
s. 12 . . . 123, 176, 220, 221, 242, 250, 490
s. 12(1) . . . 174
s. 12(2) . . . 137, 175, 176
s. 12(3) . . . 176
s. 12(4)(a) . . . 176
s. 12(4)(b) . . . 176
s. 12(4)(c) . . . 176
s. 12(5) . . . 174
s. 13 . . . 123, 174, 428, 489
s. 13(1) . . . 163, 164, 174, 179, 182
s. 13(2) . . . 177
s. 13(4) . . . 174
s. 14 . . . 123, 163
s. 15(1) . . . 183, 184
s. 15(2) . . . 184
s. 15(3) . . . 184
s. 16 . . . 377, 378, 398
s. 16(1) . . . 300

s. 16(2) . . . 403
s. 17 . . . 97, 297, 354, 355, 356, 358, 359, 361,
    362, 585
s. 17(1) . . . 357
s. 17(2) . . . 355
s. 17(3) . . . 357, 358
s. 17(4) . . . 358, 360
s. 17(5) . . . 355
s. 18 . . . 432
s. 18(1) . . . 432
s. 18(1)(a) . . . 430
s. 18(1)(b) . . . 430
s. 18(1)(c) . . . 430
s. 18(2) . . . 432
s. 18(3) . . . 489
s. 18(4) . . . 431, 489
s. 18(4)(a) . . . 431
s. 18(4)(b) . . . 431
s. 18(5) . . . 431
s. 18(6) . . . 429, 430
s. 19 . . . 97, 123, 358, 359, 439
s. 20 . . . 132, 320, 355, 356, 364, 398, 492
s. 20(1) . . . 363
s. 20(2) . . . 123
s. 20(2)(a) . . . 377
s. 20(2)(b) . . . 377
s. 20(4) . . . 122, 131, 132, 355, 364
s. 20(4)(a) . . . 355
s. 20(4)(b) . . . 131, 355
s. 20(4)(c) . . . 355, 403
s. 20(6) . . . 489
s. 21 . . . 431
s. 23 . . . 125, 163, 169, 173, 297, 364, 365, 367,
    368, 375, 378, 397, 402
s. 23(1) . . . 169, 363, 367
s. 23(2) . . . 21
s. 23(2)(a) . . . 165, 363
s. 23(3) . . . 363
s. 23(4) . . . 363
s. 24 . . . 365
s. 25 . . . 22, 146, 169, 364–5, 378, 397, 402
s. 25(1) . . . 364, 365
s. 25(1)(b) . . . 364
s. 25A . . . 377, 584–5
s. 25A-J . . . 21, 492
s. 25B . . . 377
s. 25C . . . 377
s. 25D . . . 492, 584
s. 25D(4) . . . 492
s. 25G(1) . . . 492
s. 26 . . . 167, 169
s. 26(2) . . . 167
s. 26(2)(b) . . . 167
s. 26(3) . . . 167
s. 26(4) . . . 168
s. 26(5) . . . 167, 169
s. 26(6) . . . 163, 167
s. 26(7) . . . 163, 167
s. 29 . . . 168, 169, 171, 173, 198, 377

s. 29(3) ... 169
s. 29(4) ... 173
s. 34(1) ... 91, 297
s. 35 ... 35, 219, 220–3, 233, 246, 250, 297, 376
s. 35(2) ... 220
s. 35(2)(a) ... 220
s. 35(2)(b) ... 220, 221, 222
s. 35(3) ... 219
s. 35(4) ... 219
s. 35(5) ... 219
s. 35(6) ... 219
s. 35(7) ... 219
s. 35(10) ... 432
s. 36 ... 219, 220, 221, 233, 246, 250, 376
s. 36(1) ... 220
s. 36(3) ... 219
s. 36(4) ... 219
s. 36(5) ... 219
s. 36(6) ... 219
s. 36(8) ... 432
s. 37 ... 35, 221, 222, 231, 239, 243, 244, 245,
    246, 247, 248, 250, 251, 252, 255, 257–8, 259,
    260, 261, 262, 264, 265, 266, 271, 299, 359,
    367, 368, 372, 379, 388, 399, 408, 431, 464
s. 37(1) ... 244, 245, 489
s. 37(1A) ... 243
s. 37(2)(a) ... 231, 246, 247
s. 37(2)(a)(i) ... 246
s. 37(2)(b) ... 247
s. 37(3) ... 221, 224, 238, 239
s. 37(4) ... 231, 246, 297
s. 37(5) ... 246
s. 37(7) ... 246
s. 38 ... 233, 256–7, 262–3, 376
s. 38(1)(a) ... 262
s. 38(1)(b) ... 262
s. 38(2) ... 262, 557
s. 38(3) ... 262
s. 38(4) ... 262
s. 38(5) ... 262
s. 38(7) ... 432
s. 39 ... 246
s. 39(2) ... 430
s. 39(3) ... 557
s. 40 ... 246
s. 40(4) ... 378
s. 41 ... 247, 248, 249–63, 265, 359, 360, 367,
    379, 408
s. 41(1) ... 250, 256
s. 41(2) ... 250, 258
s. 41(3) ... 254, 359
s. 41(3)(a) ... 254
s. 41(3)(aa) ... 353
s. 41(3)(b) ... 254
s. 41(3)(c) ... 255, 360, 398
s. 41(3)(c)(i) ... 359
s. 41(3)(d) ... 255, 360
s. 41(5) ... 368, 378
s. 41(6) ... 255, 320, 368

s. 42 ... 361, 367–8, 409, 418
s. 42(1) ... 368, 378
s. 42(2) ... 270, 368, 371, 398, 417
s. 42(3) ... 371, 372, 389, 396, 409, 413
s. 42(5) ... 418
s. 43 ... 250
s. 43(1)(c)(i) ... 361
s. 44 ... 250, 263
s. 45A ... 257, 258, 260, 261, 415, 464
s. 45A(1) ... 257
s. 45A(2)(a) ... 258
s. 45A(2)(b) ... 257, 258
s. 45A(2)(c) ... 258
s. 45A(3)(a) ... 257
s. 45A(4) ... 258
s. 45A(10) ... 260
s. 45B ... 257
s. 45B(2) ... 258
s. 45B(2)(a) ... 415
s. 45B(2)(b) ... 415
s. 46 ... 263, 300
s. 46(3) ... 466
s. 47 ... 35, 255, 263–4, 265, 266, 267, 269, 415,
    419, 464
ss. 47–9 ... 263–4
s. 47(1) ... 264, 266
s. 47(2) ... 266, 267, 268
s. 47(3) ... 265, 266
s. 47(4) ... 264
s. 48 ... 220, 266, 267, 414, 415, 464
s. 48(2) ... 266
s. 49 ... 265, 266, 270, 415
s. 49(1) ... 265, 266
s. 49(2) ... 265, 414
s. 49(3) ... 320
s. 50 ... 379, 416, 418, 419
s. 50(1) ... 258, 270, 416
s. 50(1)(a) ... 270
s. 50(1)(b) ... 270, 417, 418
s. 50(2) ... 265, 268
s. 50(3) ... 265, 268, 270
s. 51(2) ... 271
s. 51(3) ... 271
s. 51(4) ... 271
s. 51(5) ... 271
s. 51(5)(a) ... 271
s. 51(5)(b) ... 271
s. 51(6) ... 271
s. 54(1) ... 220, 221, 246
s. 55(1) ... 246
s. 56 ... 334
s. 56(1) ... 220, 318, 357
s. 56(1)(a) ... 297
s. 56(1)(b) ... 221, 297
s. 56(1)(c) ... 297
s. 56(2) ... 318
s. 57 ... 285, 298, 318, 319, 320, 324, 326, 327,
    328, 333–4, 497, 525, 576, 584
s. 57(1)(a) ... 318

s. 57(1)(b) ... 318, 328
s. 57(2) ... 318, 328
s. 57(2)(a) ... 318, 325, 515, 526
s. 57(2)(b) ... 318
s. 57(3) ... 318
s. 58 ... 125, 298, 318, 319, 320, 322, 323, 324, 325, 326, 327, 328, 333, 497, 547, 570, 575, 576
s. 58(1)(a) ... 318, 325
s. 58(1)(b) ... 318, 320, 506
s. 58(2) ... 319
s. 58(3)(a) ... 319, 325, 326
s. 58(3)(b) ... 315, 319, 320, 322, 327, 328, 334
s. 58(4) ... 319
s. 59 ... 319
s. 60 ... 320
s. 61 ... 320, 325, 327
s. 61(2) ... 328
s. 62 ... 298, 327, 334, 335
s. 62(1) ... 333
s. 62(2) ... 320
s. 62(3) ... 334
s. 63 ... 7, 125, 289, 299–317, 318, 320, 328, 333, 335, 339, 399, 404, 506, 524, 547, 570, 575, 582
s. 64 ... 401
s. 64(1) ... 297
s. 64(2) ... 327
s. 65 ... 374
s. 65(1A) ... 374
s. 65(1B) ... 374
s. 65(4) ... 374
s. 66 ... 377, 378, 401
s. 66(1) ... 377
s. 66(1)(a) ... 125, 377
s. 66(1)(b) ... 125, 377
s. 66(1)(c) ... 490
s. 66(1)(d) ... 377, 378
s. 66(1)(e) ... 377
s. 66(1)(f) ... 125, 377, 378
s. 66(1)(g) ... 377
s. 66(1)(h) ... 377
s. 66(1)(i) ... 377
s. 66(1)(ii) ... 377
s. 66(2) ... 469
s. 66(2)(a) ... 125, 377
s. 66(2)(b) ... 125, 377
s. 66(2)(d) ... 377
s. 66(2)(e) ... 377
s. 66(2)(f) ... 125, 377
s. 66(2)(g) ... 377
s. 67 ... 379, 490
s. 67(1) ... 379
s. 68 ... 401
s. 68(1) ... 379
s. 68(2) ... 379
s. 68(5) ... 379
s. 69 ... 377
s. 69(1)(a) ... 378

s. 69(2) ... 378
s. 69(2)(a) ... 378
s. 70 ... 377, 378, 379
s. 70(a) ... 378
s. 70(b) ... 378
s. 71 ... 380
s. 71(1) ... 379
s. 71(2) ... 380
s. 71(4) ... 379
s. 72 ... 186, 397, 403, 405, 421, 422, 580
ss. 72–5 ... 397
s. 72(1) ... 185, 377, 399, 400, 403, 405, 406, 407, 419, 420
s. 72(1)(a) ... 399, 406
s. 72(1)(a)(ii) ... 400, 410
s. 72(1)(b) ... 399, 406, 408, 409, 420
s. 72(1)(b)(i) ... 402, 403, 404, 405
s. 72(1)(b)(ii) ... 402
s. 72(1)(b)(iii) ... 378, 402
s. 72(2) ... 403, 405
s. 72(3) ... 397, 406, 580
s. 72(3A) ... 398, 580
s. 72(4A) ... 378
s. 72(5) ... 300, 398, 399
s. 72(7) ... 405, 406
s. 72(b)(ii) ... 410
s. 73 ... 406, 407, 408, 414, 415, 421, 422
s. 73(1) ... 400, 406, 408, 419
s. 73(1)(a) ... 406
s. 73(1)(b) ... 406, 407–8
s. 73(2) ... 407, 408, 412
s. 73(3) ... 408, 415
s. 73(4)(a) ... 409, 413
s. 73(4)(b) ... 409
s. 73(5) ... 409
s. 73(7) ... 380, 397, 411, 412
s. 74 ... 401, 406, 408, 414, 416, 418
s. 74(1)(a) ... 414
s. 74(1)(b) ... 415–16, 417, 418
s. 74(2) ... 415
s. 74(3) ... 415, 418, 419
s. 74(4) ... 414–15
s. 74(5) ... 415
s. 74(5A) ... 415, 417
s. 74(6) ... 415
s. 75 ... 382, 408
s. 75(1) ... 396
s. 75(1)(a) ... 380
s. 75(1)(b) ... 379
s. 75(2) ... 379, 406, 418
s. 75(3) ... 408
s. 76 ... 384
s. 77(1) ... 377
s. 77(2) ... 377, 381
s. 77(2)(f) ... 381
s. 78 ... 374
s. 78(2)(h) ... 383
s. 78(6) ... 382
s. 78(8) ... 189, 425–6

s. 79 ... 378
s. 79(1) ... 378
s. 94 ... 35
s. 94(2) ... 499
s. 96 ... 559
s. 97 ... 559
s. 99 ... 499
s. 114 ... 87
s. 114(1) ... 160
s. 114(2) ... 87, 160
s. 114(3) ... 160, 161
s. 115 ... 178
s. 117 ... 21, 125, 357–8, 411, 438, 439, 447–9,
    464, 465, 466, 467, 468, 469, 470, 492, 496,
    556, 584, 598, 599
s. 117(2) ... 447, 464
s. 117(2A) ... 447
s. 118 ... 22, 341
s. 118(2) ... 318
s. 120(1) ... 603
s. 121(2)(a) ... 318
s. 124 ... 468
s. 126 ... 590
s. 126(3) ... 590
s. 127 ... 585, 590, 591, 592, 593
s. 127(1) ... 590, 591
s. 127(2) ... 591
s. 127(2A) ... 591
s. 127(4) ... 592
s. 128 ... 590
s. 128(1) ... 430
s. 128(3) ... 430
s. 129 ... 590, 593
s. 129(1)(a) ... 178
s. 129(b) ... 178
s. 129(d) ... 178
s. 130 ... 592, 593
s. 131 ... 35, 111, 112, 115, 123, 158, 275,
    439, 584
s. 132 ... 112, 324, 606
s. 132(1) ... 222
s. 132(1)(b) ... 375
s. 132(2) ... 375
s. 132(3) ... 376
s. 134 ... 103
s. 134(1)(b) ... 102
s. 134(2) ... 102
s. 134(4) ... 103
s. 135 ... 35, 123, 135–6, 137, 138, 177, 179,
    180, 297, 376, 432
s. 135(1) ... 124, 126, 135, 174
s. 135(2) ... 179
s. 135(2)(a) ... 179
s. 135(2)(b) ... 179
s. 135(4) ... 135
s. 135(5) ... 180
s. 136 ... 35, 111, 123, 124, 126, 136–8, 139–40,
    142, 144, 179, 203, 204, 297, 362, 376, 464
s. 136(2) ... 137

s. 137 ... 590
s. 137(1) ... 179
s. 137(2) ... 179
s. 139 ... 192, 339, 583–90, 592–3, 596, 601, 602
s. 139(1) ... 192, 583, 584, 586, 588, 590, 601,
    602
s. 139(2) ... 192, 424, 587, 588, 592
s. 139(3) ... 583, 585, 592
s. 139(4) ... 583
s. 145 ... 126, 132, 406, 407, 584
s. 145(1) ... 91, 104, 297, 298, 299, 345, 404,
    407
Sch. 1
    para. 3(a) ... 359
    para. 3(b) ... 360
    para. 3(c) ... 360
    Part I
        para. 1 ... 359, 379
        para. 2 ... 378
        para. 8 ... 367, 378
        para. 9 ... 378
    Part II
        para. 2 ... 97
        para 2 ... 431
        para 3 ... 97, 359
        para 4 ... 431
        para 5 ... 97
        para. 7 ... 367
Sch. 2 ... 374
    para. 1 ... 374
    para. 3 ... 374
    para. 4 ... 374, 382
    para. 6 ... 374

Mental Health (Amendment) Act 1975 ... 186
Mental Health (Amendment) Act 1982 ... 161
Mental Health Bill (MHB) 2002 ... xi
Mental Health (Care and Treatment) (Scotland)
    Act 2003 ... 45–6
asp. 13
    s. 328(1) ... 41
Mental Health (Patients in the Community) Act
    1995 ... 92, 431, 433, 492, 495
    s. 2(1) ... 431, 591
    s. 3 ... 433, 493
    s. 10(a) ... 433
    s. 16(5)(b) ... 433
    s. 17 ... 493, 494, 495
    s. 20 ... 433
    s. 20(2) ... 433, 439
    s. 20(4) ... 433
    s. 21 ... 433
    s. 21A ... 433
    s. 21B ... 433
    s. 21B(2) ... 433
    s. 21B(2)(b) ... 433
    s. 21B(3) ... 433
    s. 21B(4) ... 433
    s. 21B(6) ... 433

s. 21B(10) ... 433
s. 25A ... 493
s. 25A(1)(a) ... 492
s. 25A(4)(a) ... 493
s. 25A(4)(b) ... 493
s. 25A(4)(c) ... 493
s. 25B ... 493
s. 25E ... 493
s. 66(1)(f) ... 433
s. 66(2)(f) ... 433
Sch. 1
   para. 18 ... 591
Mental Health (Public Safety and Appeals)
   (Scotland) Act 1999 ... 401, 404
ASP 1
   s. 3 ... 41
s. 328(2) ... 46
Mental Health (Scotland) Act 1984 ... 401, 606
s.17(1) ... 41
Mental Treatment Act 1930 ... 19, 79
s. 1 ... 112
Misuse of Drugs Act 1971 ... 99

National Assistance Act (NAA) 1948 ... 86, 481
   Part III ... 438, 439–46, 449, 463
   s. 21 ... 191, 439, 440, 441, 442, 448, 458, 459,
      460, 472, 479, 481, 482, 483, 484, 556
   ss. 21–28 ... 439
   s. 21(1) ... 460, 483, 484
   s. 21(1)(a) ... 439, 440, 441, 482, 483
   s. 21(2A) ... 441
   s. 21(4) ... 441
   s. 21(5) ... 473
   s. 21(6) ... 441
   s. 21(8) ... 482, 483
   s. 22 ... 441, 448, 458, 459
   s. 22(5) ... 441
   s. 24 ... 441
   s. 24(1) ... 441
   s. 26 ... 191
   s. 26(1) ... 443
   s. 26(1A) ... 443–4
   s. 29 ... 439, 446, 447, 449, 450, 454, 459, 556
   s. 29(1) ... 445
   s. 29(5) ... 446
   s. 45 ... 447
National Health Service Act 1946 ... 86
National Health Service Act (NHSA) 1977 ... 91,
   444, 446, 464
   s. 1(1) ... 64, 360
   s. 1(2) ... 472
   s. 3(1) ... 64, 360
   s. 3(1)(e) ... 64
   s. 4 ... 65–6
   s. 21 ... 438, 439, 447, 463
   s. 21(1)(b) ... 447
   s. 22 ... 438

s. 47(1) ... 470
s. 47(3) ... 470
Sch. 8 ... 438, 439, 447, 463
   para. 2(1) ... 447, 463
National Health Service and Community Care
   Act (NHSCCA) 1990 ... 86, 88, 90, 439,
   450–69, 479, 481
   Part III ... 437
   s. 4 ... 88
   s. 21 ... 452
   s. 22 ... 470
   s. 46 ... 66, 470, 471
   s. 46(1) ... 87, 437, 449
   s. 46(2) ... 87, 437
   s. 46(3) ... 67, 438, 449, 450, 454, 458, 463
   s. 47 ... 174, 450, 451, 454, 456, 458, 460,
      465, 471
   s. 47(1) ... 454, 455, 457, 460, 478, 481, 482
   s. 47(1)(a) ... 450, 455, 457, 460
   s. 47(1)(b) ... 450, 455, 460
   s. 47(2) ... 457
   s. 47(2)(a) ... 457
   s. 47(3) ... 478
   ss. 48–50 ... 437
   s. 50 ... 469
   s. 66(1) ... 583
   Sch. 9
      para 24(7) ... 583
   Sch 10 ... 469
National Health Service Reform and Health Care
   Professionals Act 2002 ... 88
   s. 23 ... 62
Nationality, Immigration and Asylum Act 2002
   s. 62 ... 266

Police and Criminal Evidence Act (PACE)
   1984 ... 136, 140
   Code C ... 204, 205, 209, 211, 212
      para. 1.4 ... 209
      para. 1.7(b) ... 207
      para. 3.15 ... 206, 209
      para. 3.16 ... 210
      para. 3.19 ... 207
      para. 3.5(c)(ii) ... 209
      para. 9.5 ... 210
      para. 10.12 ... 206
      para. 11.1 ... 206
      para. 11.15 ... 206
      para. 11.16 ... 212
      para. 11.17 ... 206, 212
      para. 11.19 ... 206
      para. 11.20 ... 206
      para. 12.3 ... 211
   s. 15 ... 136, 179, 180
   s. 15(4) ... 180
   s. 15(5) ... 179
   s. 15(6) ... 180
   s. 16 ... 136, 179, 180

s. 16(3) ... 180
s. 16(4) ... 180
s. 17(1)(d) ... 432
s. 17(1)(e) ... 136
ss. 76–8 ... 205, 212
s. 76(2)(a) ... 205
s. 76(2)(b) ... 205, 208
s. 77 ... 208, 214
s. 77(1) ... 204–5
s. 78(1) ... 205
s. 117 ... 432

Powers of Criminal Courts (Sentencing) Act
2000 ... 417
s. 12(1) ... 228, 232
s. 80(2)(b) ... 260
s. 81 ... 214
s. 82 ... 214, 259
s. 82A ... 242
s. 109 ... 243, 244, 257
s. 110 ... 243–4
s. 111 ... 243–4
s. 115 ... 246

Regulation of Commissions in Lunacy Act 1853
s. 2 ... 499
s. 47 ... 499

Sale of Goods Act 1979 ... 569
Sex Offenders Act 1997 ... 92
Sexual Offences Act 1956 ... 593
s. 7 ... 37, 593
s. 8 ... 506
s. 9 ... 593
Sexual Offences Act 1967
s. 1(3) ... 37, 506
s. A ... 37
Sexual Offences Act 2003 ... 506, 593
Social Services and Social Security Adjudications
Act 1983
s. 17 ... 450
Supreme Court Act 1981 ... 559
s. 18 ... 229
s. 31(3) ... 192
s. 31(4) ... 190
s. 31(6) ... 191

Trial of Lunatics Act 1883
s. 2 ... 239

Vagrancy Act 1714 ... 74

Proposed legislation

Mental Health Bill 2002 (draft) ... 62, 222, 283,
285, 296, 373, 386, 494

cl. 2(6) ... 39
cl. 115 ... 285
cl. 118 ... 283
Part 5 ... 276
Mental Health Bill 2004 (draft) ... 222, 285–6,
296, 373, 386, 494
cl. 46(6)(b) ... 63
cl. 194 ... 286

Canadian (Ontario) legislation

Consent to Treatment Act
SO 1992
c. 31, s. 17(1) ... 539
Mental Health Act, c.M.7
s. 13 ... 115
Substitute Decisions Act 1992
SO 1992
c. 30 ... 529

European legislation

Charter of Fundamental Rights of the European
Union 2000 ... 27
European Convention on Human Rights and
Fundamental Freedoms (ECHR) 1950 ... 23,
27–8, 558
Art. 2 ... 28, 102, 196, 197, 216–17, 317, 367,
394, 462, 582
Art. 3 ... 28, 102, 195, 196, 197, 216, 243, 247,
265, 284, 292, 294, 310, 311, 313, 314, 315,
316, 317, 321, 339, 342, 343, 344, 462, 582,
598
Art. 4 ... 28, 196, 197
Art. 5 ... 28, 113, 116, 117, 118, 148, 189, 190,
196, 197, 247, 264–5, 342, 343, 344, 356, 370,
384, 400, 401, 409, 412, 417, 464, 548, 571,
598, 602
Art. 5(1) ... 361, 368, 371, 400, 406, 410, 434,
493
Art. 5(1)(e) ... 28, 29, 63, 117, 189, 231, 233,
241, 264, 267, 351, 355, 356, 358, 370, 400,
401, 405, 410, 412, 413, 414, 467
Art. 5(3) ... 216, 376
Art. 5(4) ... 189, 190, 344, 355, 361, 372, 374,
376, 380, 385, 389, 390, 391, 400, 406, 412,
413, 414, 416, 417, 428, 429, 434, 467, 469,
573, 574
Art. 5(5) ... 601, 602
Art. 6 ... 28, 196, 197, 223, 225, 227, 228, 229,
230, 247, 271, 317, 320, 321, 323, 384, 408,
443, 574, 605
Art. 6(1) ... 216, 228, 321
Art. 6(2) ... 228
Art. 6(3) ... 228, 230

Art. 7 ... 28, 196, 197, 316
Art. 8 ... 28, 100, 101, 102, 172, 191, 195, 196,
    230, 247, 265, 267, 271, 284, 292, 294, 311,
    313, 315, 316, 317, 321, 323, 324, 339, 342,
    343, 344, 354, 355, 367, 382, 384, 394, 408,
    417, 453, 456, 462, 480, 484, 582
Art. 8(1) ... 100, 284, 310, 319, 342, 343, 394,
    416, 456
Art. 8(2) ... 100, 102, 197, 284, 310, 319, 342,
    343, 456, 463
Art. 9 ... 28, 196
Art. 9(2) ... 197
Art. 10 ... 28, 196

Art. 11 ... 28
Art. 12 ... 28
Art. 13 ... 194, 598
Art. 14 ... 147–8, 315, 317, 484, 602
Treaty of Amsterdam 1997 ... 27

International legislation

United Nations Declaration on the
    Rights of Mentally Retarded Persons
    1971 ... 34

Table of Secondary Legislation

Adults with Incapacity (Specified Medical
Treatments) (Scotland) Amendment
Regulations 2002 (SSI 2002/302) ... 285

Ashworth, Broadmoor and Rampton
Amendment (No. 2) Directions 2002 ... 99

Care Homes Regulations 2001 (SI I
2000/6539) ... 444

Care Trusts (Applications and Consultation)
Regulations 2001 (SI 2001/3788) ... 474

Civil Procedure Rules (CPR) 1998 ... 574
Part 54.20 ... 191
r. 6.6 ... 605
r. 21.1 ... 604
r. 21.2 ... 604
r. 21.3 ... 605
r. 21.3(4) ... 605
r. 21.4 ... 605
r. 21.4(3) ... 605
r. 21.6 ... 605
r. 21.7 ... 605
r. 24.2 ... 586
r. 54 ... 190, 191
Sch. 1 ... 425, 426

Data Protection (Subject Access Modifications)
(Health) Order 2000
Art. 5(1) ... 322

Domestic Violence, Crime and Victims Act 2004,
Commencement Order No 1, SI 2005/579
para. 3 ... 226

Incapacity (Specified Medical Treatments)
(Scotland) Regulations 2002
SSI 2002/275 ... 285

Legal Services Commission (Community Legal
Services (Financial) Regulations 2000, SI
2000/516 ... 382

Mental Capacity Act 2005 (Independent Mental
Capacity Advocates) (General) Regulations
2006, SI 2006/1832
reg. 4(2) ... 557

Mental Health Act 1983 (Remedial) Order 2001
(SI 2001/3712) ... 399, 403

Mental Health (Hospital, Guardianship and
Consent to Treatment) Regulations 1983 (SI
1983, No 893) ... 126, 128, 134, 135, 327
Part III, reg. 13 ... 490

reg. 4 ... 173
reg. 14 ... 169
reg. 14(1) ... 169
reg. 14(2) ... 169
reg. 16 ... 318, 325
Sch. 1 ... 327

Mental Health (Nurses) Order 1998
(SI 1998/2625) ... 134

Mental Health Review Tribunal Rules
1960 ... 395
r. 24(1) ... 395

Mental Health Review Tribunal Rules 1983 (the
1983 Rules), SI 1983/942 (amended by SI
1996/314 and SI 1998/1189) ... 395, 604
r. 2(1)(a) ... 382
r. 3(1) ... 381
r. 3(2) ... 381
r. 3(2)(e) ... 381, 382
r. 4(1) ... 382
r. 4(1)(a) ... 382
r. 5 ... 384
r. 6 ... 390
rr. 6–8 ... 382
r. 6(1)(a) ... 382, 389
r. 6(1)(b) ... 382, 389
r. 6(2) ... 382
r. 6(3)(a) ... 383
r. 6(3)(b) ... 383
r. 6(4) ... 383, 384
r. 6(5) ... 383
r. 7 ... 382
r. 8(1) ... 374
r. 8(2) ... 375
r. 8(3) ... 375
r. 10 ... 580
r. 10(2) ... 382
r. 10(3) ... 382
r. 10(4) ... 382, 383
r. 10(6) ... 393
r. 11 ... 384, 581
r. 12 ... 382, 581
r. 12(2) ... 383, 384
r. 12(3) ... 384, 393, 581
r. 13 ... 382, 386
r. 14(1) ... 382
r. 14(2) ... 393
r. 15 ... 382
r. 16 ... 386
r. 16(1) ... 384
r. 17 ... 382
r. 18(1) ... 381
r. 18(2) ... 381

r. 19 ... 382
r. 19(1) ... 381
r. 19(2) ... 381, 384
r. 20 ... 382, 580
r. 21(1) ... 394, 395
r. 21(3) ... 393
r. 21(4) ... 393
r. 21(5) ... 393, 394
r. 22(1) ... 392, 394
r. 22(2) ... 396
r. 22(5) ... 392, 394
r. 23 ... 581
r. 23(1) ... 419
r. 23(2) ... 419
r. 24(1) ... 419
r. 24(2) ... 419
r. 24(4) ... 398
r. 26 ... 382
r. 28 ... 382
r. 29(cc) ... 388
r. 30 ... 387
r. 31 ... 387, 390, 391
r. 32 ... 387
r. 32(2) ... 387
Sch.
    Part A ... 382
    Part B, para. 1 ... 382, 389
    Part C ... 382
    Part D ... 383
National Assistance Act 1948 (Choice of
    Accommodation) Directions 1992
    para. 2 ... 452
    para. 3 ... 452
National Assistance (Assessment of Resources)
    Regulations 1992 (SI 1991/2977)
    reg. 25 ... 442
    para. 20 ... 458, 459
National Assistance (Residential
    Accommodation) (Additional Payments and

Assessment of Resources) (Amendment)
    (England) Regulations 2001 (SI
    2001/3441) ... 441–2
National Assistance (Residential
    Accommodation) (Disregarding of Resources)
    (England) Regulations (SI 2001/3067) ... 441,
    460
National Assistance (Sums for Personal
    Requirements and Assessment of Resources)
    (Amendment) (England) Regulations 2006 (SI
    2006/674) ... 441
NHS Bodies and Local Authorities Partnership
    Arrangements Regulations 2000 (SI
    2000/617) ... 474
Northern Ireland Order, SI 1986/595 (NI 4);
    Reed, 1996: 5 ... 41

Police and Criminal Evidence Act 1984 (Code of
    Practice C and Code of Practice H) Order 2006
    (SI 2006/1938) ... 204

Rules of the Supreme Court (RSC) Ord. 94
    r. 11 ... 425
    r. 11(6) ... 425, 426

Safety and Security in Ashworth, Broadmoor and
    Rampton Hospitals Directions, The,
    1999 ... 99
Safety and Security in Ashworth, Broadmoor
    and Rampton Hospitals Directions,
    The, 2000
    para. 2 ... 100
    para. 6 ... 99
    para. 8 ... 99
    para. 10 ... 99
    para. 11 ... 99
    para. 29(3) ... 100

1

Conceptualising Mental Health Law

In the serene world of mental illness, modern man no longer communicates with the madman: on one hand, the man of reason delegates the physician to madness, thereby authorizing a relation only through the abstract universality of disease; on the other, the man of madness communicates with society only by the intermediary of an equally abstract reason which is order, physical and moral constraint, the anonymous pressure of the group, the requirements of conformity. As for a common language, there is no such thing; or rather, there is no such thing any longer; the constitution of madness as a mental illness, at the end of the eighteenth century, affords the evidence of a broken dialogue, posits the separation as already effected, and thrusts into oblivion all those stammered, imperfect words without fixed syntax in which the exchange between madness and reason was made. The language of psychiatry, which is a monologue of reason *about* madness, has been established only on the basis of such a silence.

Foucault, 1965: x–xi

1.1 Introduction

In his usual rather dense style, Foucault encapsulates many of the paradoxes at the root of the study of mental health and illness, and sets the stage for many of the themes that will be of significance in this volume. The centrality of a medical model of insanity is asserted, imposing a scientific order onto the profoundly unordered world of the mad. While madness is displayed in the form of a disease, sanity is a constraint, both physical and moral, into which the insane person is confined through pressure of the group, the sane. All of this is a construction of the reasoned, and reflects the world of the reasoned; to the insane person, it is an alien landscape.

The situation is yet more complex than Foucault posits here, however, because mental health law, like psychiatry, is also a language 'of reason about madness'. The two languages, law and psychiatry, sometimes speak symbiotically and sometimes in uneasy juxtaposition in the pages that follow. Each are paradigms of rationality in their way, and thus each is faced with the same problem: how to impose order onto madness, a realm that would seem *ex hypothesi* to be lacking order, to be irrational.

This may sound hopelessly abstract, but a few examples will clarify. How exactly, if at all, can mental health (or perhaps more importantly, mental illness) be defined, and are the existing legal and medical definitions clear, consistent, and appropriate? How can we impose reason, rationality, onto the irrational? Does the process of definition not imply a logical structure in madness, a structure that cannot be assumed to exist in madness by its very nature? At what point do mad people acquire rights and corresponding responsibilities and authority over what happens to them? Are we content that these languages of mental health and illness remain exclusive of the voices of their client groups, and if not, how are those voices to be included in an understanding of law and policy in the mental health area? And if mental health law and psychiatry are both discourses of reason about madness, what do those discourses tell us about the reasoned people who create them? If, as Foucault claims, the languages of mental health law and psychiatry develop in the silence of those they affect, what do our views of how the insane are understood and when we should intervene in their care tell us about us, the people who construct the languages about the insane?

These are some of the big issues at the heart of this book. There is no pretence that they will be solved; indeed, it is a fundamental belief of the authors that the purpose of a text such as this is not to present solutions, but instead to articulate problems for discussion and investigation. The first three chapters concern broad issues of interest, such as the general structure of mental health services, including (in Chapter 2) the definitions of mental illness and mental disorder. Chapters 4 and 5 concern civil confinement, and Chapter 6, criminal confinement. Chapter 7 concerns treatment for mental disorder, Chapter 8, the law and procedure surrounding mental health review tribunals, and Chapter 9, community care. Chapters 10 and 11 concern the law of civil capacity, and Chapter 12 contains an overall discussion of the efficacy of legal remedies for those with psychiatric difficulties, and an introduction to advocacy for this particular client group.

1.2 Who are the insane?

Issues of psychiatric and legal definition will be reserved for Chapter 2, but it is appropriate at the outset at least to start the discussion of who the insane are. The newspapers would leave us in little doubt. In their eyes, the insane are a threat, a lurking menace in society, a hidden and violent element, which may erupt without notice. The Glasgow Media Group analysed news items about the mentally ill for the month of April 1993, mainly in the tabloid press and on television. It found 323 stories relating to dangerous or violent behaviour by people with mental illness – roughly twice as many as concerned their other categories (stories about harm to self, prescriptive or advice columns related to treatment or care, and stories critical of accepted definitions) combined (Glasgow Media Group, 1996: 47–81; see also Thornicroft, 2006: ch. 6). These may no doubt be in part a function of the economics of publishing – scaremongering sells newspapers – but the Glasgow Group further makes a persuasive case that these representations have an effect on public perceptions. The image is profoundly misleading. The vast bulk of those with psychiatric difficulties are simply not dangerous (Bowden, 1996: 17–22; Thornicroft, 2006: ch. 7). Not only that, but the numbers of persons killed by people with psychiatric problems have been steadily falling since the 1970s: Taylor and Gunn, 1999.

The images do not stop with violence, however. The mentally ill are perceived as homeless and poor: the deserted of society. There may well be some truth in these allegations in many cases, although much depends on how mental illness is defined, and in particular regarding homelessness, whether substance addiction is considered a mental illness. Certainly, many of those who have been involved with the psychiatric system are poor, although it is a fair question to ask the degree to which this is due to a prejudice of employers against hiring people who have been institutionalised (see Thornicroft, 2006: ch. 3). The image is nonetheless of people who have fallen through the net, tragic figures, lonely, to be pitied rather than valued.

These images cannot tell the whole story. There are countervailing images. When we think of the mentally ill, we might alternatively think of Virginia Woolf, Robert Schumann, Sylvia Plath, or Vincent Van Gogh. The image of the mad artistic genius is, in its way, a part of Western cultural imagination. The connection between madness and genius excited considerable academic debate in the nineteenth century, and more recently, the US psychologist Kay Redfield Jamison has argued for a correlation between manic depression and artistic genius (Jamison, 1993). The image of the insane person as genius, warranting respect rather than pity or fear, is a refreshing counterweight to the images of the insane person as dangerous lunatic, or homeless vagrant. It becomes possible to ask whether madness is something to be valued rather than disparaged. Rather than silencing the mad, should we encourage them to speak?

In the end, all of these images must be approached with considerable caution, since the mad artistic genius, like the mad killer, focuses on the statistically rare exception. The reality, in the overwhelming number of cases, is likely to be characterised by banality rather than extremes. Current estimates are that mental illness will affect roughly one in six adults in Britain per year, although psychotic illnesses are much less common, at closer to one per cent of the population. Depression alone will affect roughly half of women and a quarter of men before the age of 70 (Department of Health, 1998a: 10). This would suggest that it is not appropriate to think in terms condescendingly of 'them', but rather, somewhat more humbly, of 'us'. The frequency suggested by the statistic would suggest that any generalisation may well mislead as much as it informs.

That is perhaps particularly important in so far as it challenges the popular sense that everyone with mental difficulties must somehow be the same. Different difficulties affect people differently. It is simply wrong, for example, to expect that people with mental illness will also have intellectual limitations. The fact that an individual is profoundly depressed or hearing voices, for example, does not mean they are unable to understand complicated information, and process it at a reasonably sophisticated level. Certainly, some people with mental illness are not intellectually high achievers, but others are very bright indeed, and most are somewhere in the middle. The experience of people affected would suggest that the stereotype associating mental illness with lack of mental ability remains widespread, a depressing comment on how far society has yet to come in understanding both mental illness and developmental disabilities.

A similar warning ought to be made regarding developmental disabilities. Frequently, one hears the phrase 'mental age' used regarding people in this group. It is, at best, a caricature. People develop in different ways and at different rates, and the person 'with a mental age of six' may well have little in common with a six-year-old child. To refer to a 25-year-old woman in this way is unhelpful: in a very real sense, she is still a 25-year-old woman. Rather than to identify her with the child she manifestly is not, it is far more sensible to consider her actual situation, understanding and abilities, and proceed accordingly.

Romanticisation of mental illness, whatever image is adopted, is unlikely to be helpful. That said, it is surely appropriate to provide some sort of starting point to understanding what it feels like to be mentally ill. The writings of those who have experienced mental illness first hand provide invaluable reading to the student beginner in the area. A selection is provided in the bibliography (Mays, 1995; Hart, 1995; Dunn *et al.*, 1996; Jamison, 1996; Lewis, 2002; Pegler, 2002; Read and Reynolds, 1996; Styron, 1990). These readings drive home the point that mental illness, particularly in its more extreme forms, can be a profoundly unsettling and unpleasant experience. Consider U.A. Fanthorpe's description (1996: 52–4) of the experience of depression:

Again I find myself waking miserably early, even before the summer birds; again I find music unspeakably painful; again my speech becomes slow, and my arms seem grotesquely long; again I'm afraid to go out, because people will see at a glance that there's something wrong, and shun me; I can't face the garden because, although in one part of my brain I know the blackbirds are just making their usual evening calls, I'm convinced that the cats are after them and that it's my fault; above all, my vocabulary shrinks to such an extent that the only word I'm really at home with is 'sorry'.

When I'm badly depressed I long above all things to be a prisoner. I imagine this as a life where you don't make choices, where the pattern of life is plain and involuntary. Life in depression is like this anyway, but it retains the illusion of choice. If you had to do the sad things you are doing because someone had ordered that you should, indeed because you'd deserved it, the despair might (you think) go.

Linda Hart (1995: 19) described the sensations accompanying her schizophrenia as follows:

The top half of my head feels quite light but the thread that runs down from my head to my stomach is soaked in a deep despair. Maggots in my belly multiply. Rotting flesh. Want to drink bleach to cleanse them or a sharp knife to cut them out. They told me I needed a psychiatrist and not a medical surgeon back in September. They said Graham [the psychiatrist] would get rid of the maggots but he hasn't.

These are not pretty images, and one would be inhuman not to feel considerable sympathy for the individuals affected by these experiences. Yet sympathy is a double-edged sword, because it can easily lead to a paternalist impulse to intervene whether the individual likes it or not, 'for their own good'. The result is a risk of marginalising the person we intend to help, and the re-enforcement of the gulf of silence of which Foucault speaks.

This is not merely a civil rights point, nor an abstract issue of discourse construction. It is, in part, a practical point: if intervention is to be successful in the long term, its subject must, in the end, be supportive of the intervention. In the environment of intrusive surveillance in a psychiatric facility, it is possible to force a patient to take drugs they do not wish to take. It is much more difficult outside that environment, and if the patient is not convinced at that time of the continuing benefits of medication, it seems unlikely that he or she will continue taking it.

This marginalisation further presupposes a gap between the individual and his or her disorder, or a 'real' person who has been subverted by the disorder into someone else of an unknown character. Such an articulation is contained in the following passage, in which an author describes his first interview with Leslie, the mother of a mentally ill man (Karp, 2001: 3–4):

Near the beginning of our first conversation she said that 'so much has happened in three years that I don't even know where to begin... It's overwhelming'. There was, though, one thing that she absolutely wanted to bring up right away and have me understand... She went on to explain that 'Mike has the potential for violence. And... because I know this is being recorded, it's really important to me for you to know that he is innately a very, very sweet and kind person. But [because of] the disease he gets very paranoid. His disease has made him a danger to others...I mean, he wouldn't even step on a bug, you know? But this illness is so [awful] and he has attacked his brother and attacked his sister'. Throughout our nearly ten hours of talk, Leslie repeatedly sought assurance that I would not confuse Mike with his disease.

Such a clear division is presupposed in much of the popular and professional understanding of mental disorder, and articulates the experiences of many people affected by mental disorders. It is further implied in a medical model of mental illness, where imagery in pharmaceutical advertisements, for example, will frequently refer to the drug as allowing for the return of a person, previously 'lost'. At the same time, other accounts call into question whether the disorder is readily distinguishable from the person with the disorder. This ambiguity is apparent in Marie Cardinal's description (1996: 108):

But for my children, I might let myself go completely, stop fighting, perhaps, for the struggle against the Thing was exhausting. More and more, I was tempted by the medication that delivered me to a nothingness which was dull and sweet.

In this articulation, it is the medication, the alternative to the disorder, which is a void, a nullity. The disorder itself is in Cardinal's reality. This image of mental illness as constructive of self is similarly evident in Sheila MacLeod's description (1996: 81) of her anorexia:

Two facts emerge immediately from this résumé. The first is that I felt my battle to be with authority, whether in the form of teachers, matrons, parents, or even nature itself. The second is that, up until this point, I was winning. It seems to me that anorexia nervosa acts as a metaphor for all the problems of adolescence. But instead of meeting each problem separately and assessing it for what it is, the anorexic thinks she has a master plan, designed to solve them all at one stroke. She is convinced that it works; it can't fail. It is like a dream come true. It is euphoria.

When I first came across Szasz's dictum, 'Mental illness is a self-enhancing deception, self-promoting strategy', I considered it to be a harsh judgement on a fellow creature. But when I substituted 'anorexia nervosa' for 'mental illness' I could see the truth in what Szasz was saying, and realize at the same time that his judgement was not so harsh. After all, if the self is felt to be nothing, any strategy adopted to enhance or promote it, desperate though it may be, is a step towards what most of us would consider to be health, and an action necessary for survival. The anorexic's skinny body proclaims, 'I have won; I am someone now'.

In this view, the disorder is intrinsic to the self and constitutive of who the individual is. As such, it need not necessarily be viewed in simplistically negative or undesirable terms. Lewis notes (2002: xv):

If you can cope with the internal nuclear winter of depression and come through it without committing suicide – the disease's most serious side effect – then, in my experience, depression can be a great friend. It says: the way you've been living is unbearable, it's not for you. And it teaches you slowly how to live in a way that suits you infinitely better. If you don't listen, of course, it comes back and knocks you out even harder the next time, until you get the point.

Over twenty years I've discovered that my depression isn't a random chemical event but has an emotional logic which makes it a very accurate guide for me.

A similarly complex vision regarding schizophrenia is discussed by Chadwick (1997). This is not to suggest that either Chadwick or Lewis rejoiced in their disorders. It is instead to suggest that a simplistically dismissive view of the values associated with the disorder may deny an important aspect of the experience of the individual patient.

This view of mental illness as intrinsic to self receives judicial acknowledgement in the case of *B v Croydon District Health Authority* (1994) 22 BMLR 13 (HC). That case involved a patient suffering from a personality disorder, not anorexia, which nonetheless manifested itself in the refusal of food to the point of near self-starvation. The primary issue before the trial court was whether the patient had the capacity to consent to treatment, in this case feeding. Thorpe J (as he then was) cites (at p. 19) an expert witness, a forensic psychiatrist, as identifying the relation between the individual and the personality disorder as a factor for the court's consideration:

The third feature is the patient's necessity to control her own internal world and her relationship with others. In a pathological way, she uses maladapted methods to control distress in herself and to control others around her. Her need to use abnormal coping mechanisms stems from her abnormal development. In relation to this feature, Dr Eastman poses the question: Have we the right to remove the only mechanism that remains to her without the prospect of being able to help her to cope in other ways?

The court gives considerable credence to this concern (at p. 22):

Here the patient has developed in adolescence an individual personality which can be medically classified as disordered. But the disorder is the person and we must question the justification of depriving such a person of all that is available without the prospect of being able to help her to cope in other ways.

In this formulation, intervention will affect the core of who the individual is. This raises an obvious ethical problem: should the state apparatus be used to enforce this kind of personal alteration?

Various points may be made about this approach. First, the comments occur in an appraisal of capacity. While a similar logic may ethically apply to other branches of mental health law, capacity is a field with its own idiosyncrasies: see Chapters 10 and 11. Second, the decision of Thorpe J on capacity was expressly doubted by the Court of Appeal, albeit in comments that are summary and *obiter*: see [1995] 1 All ER 689.

Finally, while the relation between the individual and the disorder was clearly a matter considered by Thorpe J, and a factor in his decision that B had the capacity to consent to treatment, it did not in the end preclude him from ordering the provision of tube-feeding as treatment, pursuant to s. 63 of the Mental Health Act (MHA) 1983. The intricacies of this part of the decision will be discussed in Chapter 7. The instant point is instead that the centrality of the disorder to the individual is a factor that raises ethical issues regarding intervention; it does not necessarily determine whether intervention is ethically justified. A number of positions may be potentially adopted here. At one extreme, it might be claimed that intervention, and particularly intervention over the patient's objection, is rarely, if ever, justified on the basis that it constitutes extraordinarily intrusive meddling with an individual's personality and psyche. At the other, it might be argued that intervention is frequently justified, on the basis that, after the intervention, many people are grateful. This 'thank you theory' will be examined in more detail in Chapter 4, in the context of civil confinement. Intermediate positions are also possible. Presumably, the wishes of the affected individual may be a significant factor; it would seem positively cruel not to support an individual who wishes to be free of the trait. Thorpe J distinguishes between alterations to an individual's normal personality, and a situation where the disorder is intrinsic to the personality. In *B v Croydon*, there was 'no overlay of illness upon the patient's norm' (p. 22). This might be distinguished from a situation where a medically defined variation appears in an already existing personality, where intervention might be justified to restore the pre-existing personality. The difficulty with this approach, of course, is to determine how long the disorder must exist before it becomes integral to personality. In addition, it does not solve the question of what to do when the cure will remove more than the disorder. Marie Cardinal's reference to a 'nothingness which was dull and sweet' suggests a cure removing not only the disorder, but also other parts of her nature as well.

Students of mental health law are often quick to adopt a medicalised model of mental illness, that it is appropriately the realm of a specialised, medical practitioner. Certainly, medicine will often have a role to play, and this is acknowledged by most, but not all, people affected by mental disorder. Those in the subject group, however, will often understand their experience in a multifaceted way. William Styron, for example, writes (1996: 57):

I shall never learn what 'caused' my depression, as no one will ever learn about their own. To be able to do so will likely for ever prove to be an impossibility, so complex are the intermingled factors of abnormal chemistry, behaviour and genetics. Plainly, multiple components are involved – perhaps three or four, most probably more, in fathomless permutations.

Certainly, those with mental health problems often receive medical attention. Usually this is voluntary on their part, but at the same time, there may be an element of ambivalence to it, even when the treatments work relatively according to plan, and thus alleviate the condition. U.A. Fanthorpe describes this ambivalence (1996: 52) as follows:

When depression hits me, the last thing I want to do is see the doctor, because it seems hard to define anything 'wrong'. When I have finally made myself go, and the doctor has slotted me back into a medical definition again, the reactions are odd: relief at knowing where I am again and what I have to do, but at the same time resentment that this has happened again, the same symptoms, prescriptions, general fears, and dreariness.

John Bentley Mays (1995: xiv, xv) describes the medicalisation of his condition, in his own eyes as much as those of the doctors, more expressly in terms of alienation, reflecting the Foucaultean vision with which this chapter commenced:

Yet the forensic language I invoke springs from nothing in my own heart or mind, is no more original than my routine complaining. Rather, it slides down on the page out of clinical case histories and medical records, a portrait of the *nobody*, nameless, extinguished, who is the topic of the technical literature on depression.

I have read the literature now that provides me with terms of order, pretending to study the technical language of depression – but really studying the way of looking, of writing, embodied in such texts. It is a poetry of the scalpel's quick slash, the spurt and stanching of blood, clamping back successive layers of skin, fat, muscle, the probe with a point of gleaming metal of the nothingness at the centre. Writing myself up as a *case*, I experience myself, pleasurably, obscenely, as object. The former exacerbation of subjectivity is gone, now that the cyst known as *soul* is lanced, and all that remains is flesh, killed by the invasion of medical power, stiffening, cooling.

A similar ambivalence can be seen in attitudes to medication itself. Gwyneth Lewis describes her experience of antidepressant medication (2002: 72–3) as follows:

After three weeks the anti-depressants began to kick in. These affected the quality of my depression but without changing its nature. What they gave me was some psychic space, a small but crucial distance between me and the horrors. Like a line of crustacean riot police, they pushed back the nightmares clamouring for my attention. This gave me a narrow cordon sanitaire in which to move, some room to breathe. The mental crowds were still there, of course, but they had less power over me, as if the anarchists had turned into paparazzi. The lightning of intrusive cameras was blinding, but at least I was free to move out of their way and into the foyer.

Fanthorpe, Mays and Lewis describe continuing and successful relations with their respective medical advisers, and acknowledge the benefits they have received from medication: there is no element of sour grapes here. At the same time, they display a real sense of ambivalence to a medical model of their experience, and a resistance to any simplistic association between drugs and cure.

This is significant not merely as an insight into the way those in the affected group perceive their condition; it is also significant because of the way the world, or at least social policy, reacts to this uncertain relationship with the medical model. The silence between the insane and the rational is becoming further enforced, as the failure to follow medical advice is increasingly perceived as an unacceptable act of deviance. The response can take several forms. While mental capacity – the practical ability to make decisions – is not lost simply because an individual has a mental illness or developmental disability, it has long been a matter of concern that disagreement with a doctor may trigger a finding that the psychiatric patient lacks capacity to make treatment decisions. This generally has the effect of removing from the patient the legal right to refuse treatment (see Chapter 11). Further, government discussion surrounding proposals to reform the Mental Health Act 1983 would suggest that non-compliance with medical advice is not to be tolerated. Thus, at the press conference establishing the expert panel to consider reform, the then Minister of State for Health, Paul Boateng, spoke of the 'responsibility' of patients to comply with the care they were offered: 'Non compliance can no longer be an option when appropriate care in appropriate settings is in place. I have made it clear to the field that this is not negotiable.' (Department of Health, 1999a: AC, para. 11). In the White Paper published two years later, the point was only slightly softened: 'Care and treatment should involve the least degree of compulsion that is consistent with ensuring that the objectives of the [care] plan are met.' (Department of Health, 2000c: para. 2.11) Patients are to be as free as is possible, it would seem, as long as they do what they are told.

This position is problematic. Is it reasonable or appropriate to expect unswerving adherence to treatment in a professional context perceived by the patient as alienating? Will this breakdown not be exacerbated if the doctor/patient relationship is not as successful as it appears to have been in the cases of Mays and Fanthorpe? Can the enforcement into treatment be justifiable, when all the indications are that psychiatry is not an exact science. Should the law really be used to enforce compliance with treatment when such levels of uncertainty exist? Many patients embrace the treatments that medicine has to offer, but others are content to live with their disability, even when a treatment exists. The Hearing Voices Network, for example, assists people who hear voices to live with their voices and to get on with their lives (see James, 2001). Many do so, quite successfully. Whether their refusal to take medication is the result of the adverse effects of the medication, a view that the 'cure' affects their self-perception, or because they view their disorder as an integral part of who they are, is it obvious that their views should be subordinated to a medical vision of their condition?

A broader view of the nature of mental disorder is consistent with public perceptions of insanity. The British studies uniformly indicate that the public perceives behaviour typical of mental disorders as caused by a wide range of factors. Social and environmental factors are identified as causes more frequently than physiological or moral factors (see analysis contained in Glasgow Media Group, 1996: 5–8). Nor is this multifaceted view the preserve of the laity. While medical professionals hotly dispute the relative significance of various factors, few would now question the relevance of social and environmental factors to the occurrence of mental disorder. There is a risk that this view may fuel a different stereotype, that the mentally ill individual is really a malingerer, who should simply buck up and get on with their life. It is difficult to see this view accurately describing many of the people affected with mental illness. At the same time, the public perception of mental illness as more than just medical gives additional credence to the broader views of those affected. In short, everyone else agrees: mental disorder is not just a medical matter, suggesting that this view, when held by people directly affected, should not be dismissed lightly.

Students new to mental health law sometimes perceive mental illness as something that can be cured permanently, rather like measles, where with appropriate treatment the patient is free of the malady forever. This is often a misleading view, particularly in the case of serious mental illness. The better image is of a chronic condition, at best controllable, which may affect the individual for much of their life. This, again, has social policy implications: if intervention is to be enforced on the individual, is it to be enforced in perpetuity? This seems extremely intrusive to the life of the individual affected, and must therefore be approached with considerable hesitancy.

Viewed in this light, mental health law and policy might be seen as dispiriting subjects. Those affected by mental illness often face a selection of possible courses of action, none of which on balance is particularly appealing. Continuation with the experience of disorder may not be an attractive option, and medicine may either provide an incomplete answer, or entail adverse effects perceived by the individual to be as unpleasant as the disorder. Alteration of the social, cultural and environmental factors that may contribute to the malady is extremely difficult to achieve in practice. Forced intervention, be it through confinement in hospital, enforced medication or control of the individual in the community, seems both intrusive and not obviously effective except perhaps in the very short term. One of the difficult things for new students in this area to understand fully is that here, as with many areas of law, there will often be no good solution possible for a client. Instead, there will be a selection of problematic or downright bad possibilities from which a choice must be made.

At the same time, it would be wrong to assume that all persons with mental health difficulties live miserable lives. Again, generalisations are likely to be unhelpful here, but like most of the rest of us, it is reasonable to understand this client group as happy with some parts of their lives, unhappy with others, having some good times and some bad times. While it is inappropriate for the student of mental health law to ignore the realities of the life imposed by the reality of the mental condition, it would be equally inappropriate to romanticise the mental disorder in a way that obliterates the remainder of the life of the individual.

1.3 **Other interests: mental health care**

People with mental disabilities or disorders are, of course, the client group who are the objects of the psychiatric system, and thus of mental health law, but they are not the only people with interests in the delivery of mental health care. Mental health care is delivered in a system, in part based in the National Health Service, in part elsewhere in the state social services network, and in part in the private sector. A detailed survey of the range of interests operating in this system, and the sociology of how those interests interact, is beyond the scope of this chapter, but a brief survey of some of the players will provide an indication of the complexity of the influences on mental health policymaking.

The prime medical personnel involved in the care of the mentally ill are, of course, nurses and doctors, primarily general practitioners and psychiatrists. These people work in conjunction with social workers, psychologists, community mental health nurses, health visitors, social service agencies and, particularly in recent years, health administrators in the administration of the mental health system.

It is abundantly clear that the vast bulk of these people have a real and honest concern about the people in their care. The power-hungry doctor who has no interest in his patients but merely a desire to control may make good television drama, but it has little to do with the reality of the individuals involved in the mental health system. That said, the individuals listed above are all professionals, operating in an administrative system. Vast sociological literatures exist on the way people operate in such bureaucracies, and strive to enhance professional status. The tensions may be within individual professions: psychiatrists, for example, have tended historically to feel undervalued among medical specialisms. Tensions may run between groups: nurses have long been working to see their own profession recognised in the broader medical hierarchy, and social workers have similarly struggled for professional recognition. Such professional issues will be noted further in Chapters 5 and 7.

Such projects of status enhancement are clearly a part of the sociological and historical fabric of the administration of mental health. They are not generally crass attempts at power-grabbing, but manifest themselves instead primarily in articulation and formation of the values and expertise of the group in question. The group will no doubt sincerely believe, often entirely appropriately, in the value of the expertise it has to bring to a specific set of issues; the result is nonetheless the privileging of a set of assumptions, or of a specific way of looking at things. It is this process that may result in the person with the mental health difficulty being unable to recognise himself or herself in clinical descriptions. Other ways of looking at things, whether those of the individual with the difficulty or of the other professions, are implicitly challenged or marginalised in the process. Perhaps unintentionally, the knowledge or expertise of the profession becomes the exercise of power, in potential conflict with other professions or ways of looking at things.

On a more mundane note, the professionals noted above are also all human, with understandable concerns about job satisfaction and job conditions. The image of the doctor, willing to abandon all family or personal life and devote himself or herself entirely to the care of patients, has a romantic appeal, but does not represent reality in most cases. The professionals, entirely reasonably and like the rest of us, must balance priorities.

These day-to-day pragmatic issues have become increasingly important in recent years. The policy drive in the last twenty years has been towards economic efficiency in services provided by the state. The result has been a service stretched beyond reasonable limits. Deahl and Turner describe general psychiatric wards, particularly in London, where bed occupancy rates are routinely in excess of 120 per cent capacity, where virtually all admissions are emergencies (1997: 6). Government moves to introduce supervised discharge and supervision registers in the mid-1990s for those released from psychiatric facilities (see Chapters 3 and 9) are a further pressure to hold hospital and other medical personnel responsible when things go wrong following discharge, with no extra resources. The results were perhaps predictable: there was a crisis of morale in much of the mental health services. Deahl and Turner claimed that the burnout period for a psychiatric nurse on an adult general psychiatric ward is seven months, and cite a study that 88 per cent of consultant psychiatrists wished to leave the profession (1997: 6). The picture is of a set of professionals, overworked and disillusioned, unable to provide the sort of service that they think it appropriate to give, and which would match their professional ideals and ideology.

How are we to approach this in a social policy or a legal context? Should we abandon our vision of a health service able to provide the continuing framework of care required by those suffering from chronic conditions, such as many mental illnesses? Should we design policy on the basis that service will be minimalist, able to intervene only in crisis situations, targeting care at those in most need while leaving those with less pressing problems to their own devices? How should law approach these situations? In the law of negligence, for example, should doctors be given an increased margin of appreciation for their errors, on the basis of working conditions that are far from ideal? Or should the courts continue to insist on standards of professional practice that the public may feel it has a right to expect, but which professionals themselves feel they are no longer able to provide?

Not all of those with an interest in the care and treatment of the mentally ill are contained within the public sector. Overflows of patients from NHS psychiatric wards may be moved to private facilities, simply to alleviate space pressures. Further, many of the facilities, such as group homes, through which community care is offered are provided by the private sector. Sometimes, these private-sector providers are non-profit organisations, established through charities such as MIND; in other cases, they are standard businesses, run with a profit motive. Either way, the shift to the private sector means that maintenance of standards and control of staffing are out of direct government control. Regulation is theoretically possible, but complicated by the fact that, if unattractive standards are set, the private operator can fold up shop, a possibility the government can little afford given the inability of the NHS to service the demand. This is not a desirable option from the private operator's viewpoint either, since considerable investment will have been made. In this balance, policy must be made.

Care is not, of course, the exclusive preserve of the professionals. Families and friends also provide care, and there is considerable US evidence to suggest that the role of families is pivotal to relapse (Dixon *et al.*, 1995; 2000). The specific role of these informal carers will depend on the circumstances. Sometimes, they provide housing, with or without a day centre providing a formalised programme during the day. Sometimes, the person with mental illness will reside elsewhere, whether in hospital, at a group home, or alone in the community. Here, the role of family and friends may be to provide a sense of community and support, or it may also be to provide some sort of overview, to ensure that the appropriate services are being provided.

These services and the people who provide them have traditionally been largely taken for granted in the administrative structure of mental health. This is difficult to justify, because such carers provide important services, in conditions that may be very difficult. Some public support is available for these activities (see Carers (Recognition and Services) Act 1995) and there have been some recent moves to increase public funding to assist or relieve carers, for example, by allowing them to take the occasional weekend break from their caring duties. Such programmes seem appropriate acknowledgements of services performed that, at their best, provide the person with the mental disorder an optimal home environment, at minimal cost to the state.

The family role can also be perceived as much more problematic. Particularly at the onset of an illness, the family may have little understanding of mental disability, and may react with stereotyped views (Thornicroft, 2006: ch. 1). Further, perhaps even more than with the professional actors, the interests of the service provider and those of the mentally ill person are difficult to disentangle, suggesting difficulties with formal control of these individuals over the decisions that are made about mentally ill family members. Like other service providers, but perhaps more than other service providers, the family and friends of the individual will have an emotional and practical interest in the fate of the individual. The effect of the condition on relations within the family and, if the affected person is a breadwinner forced to cease employment, on the economic life of the family, can be profound. More poignantly, it can be profoundly painful to witness the onset of mental illness in a loved one. Karp comments, regarding his attendance at a support group for friends and family of persons with mental disorder (2001: 22):

On any given evening I might hear about the unimaginable pain surrounding the decision to have a child removed from one's home by the police, the powerlessness of visiting a spouse or child in a hospital who is so muddled by powerful medications that he or she can barely speak, the shame that accompanies hating someone you love because of what their illness has done to you and your family, the guilt that lingers from the belief that you might somehow be responsible for another person's descent into mental illness, the confusion associated with navigating the Byzantine complexities of the mental health system, the fear associated with waiting for the next phone call announcing yet another suicide attempt by someone close to you, the disappointment that a talented son or daughter may never realize even a fraction of their potential, the exhaustion that accompanies full-time caregiving, or the frustration of being unable to take even a brief vacation. Pain, powerlessness, shame, guilt, confusion, fear, disappointment, exhaustion, frustration: these emotions are the currency of conversion among the Family and Friends group members.

It is difficult to see how family members can be expected to divorce these feelings from their views of the person with the disorder, and what ought to happen to that person. Unsurprisingly, Karp's study finds family carers building practical and emotional walls, setting up 'boundaries of obligation', to use his term, in their care relationships. The result is a paradox: it is the family's intimate knowledge and relationship with the affected person that creates the appeal of their greater involvement; at the same time, this same factor creates the risk that decisions will be made on criteria other than the best interest of the affected person.

The private interests in the mental health field extend well beyond carers. Pharmaceutical manufacturers are a particularly clear example of these other interests. Pharmaceuticals are big business: roughly one quarter of the prescriptions dispensed by the NHS are to affect the central nervous system, to alter moods, states of mind or behaviour (Lacey, 1996: xiii). Clearly, medication for mental illness has brought considerable benefits in many cases. At the same time, the adverse effects of medication can be profoundly unpleasant. The precise nature of these adverse effects will, of course, depend on the patient and medication in question, but they can be significant enough to dissuade patients from continuing the treatment. Ron Lacey (1996: 118) makes the point this way, regarding depot antipsychotic medications, long-lasting medications injected into patients at intervals of weeks or months.

Whilst they can relieve the torment of the symptoms of serious mental illness for many people, they can also reduce an individual to an unprotesting zombie-like state. For some patients the use of depot antipsychotics is little more than an exchange of one form of human misery for another. Drowsiness, lethargy, loss of motivation, impotence, stiffened muscles, shaking hands, physical restlessness, severe anxiety and persistent constipation may be more distressing to some people than a fixed belief that their thoughts are being controlled by the international brotherhood of Freemasons. For others these side effects are a small price to pay for the relief that the drugs give them from a much more distressing and terrifying psychotic inner reality.

The varieties of psychiatric medication and their adverse effects will be discussed in greater detail in Chapter 7; suffice it here to say that, while their benefits should not be ignored or underestimated, they are not problem-free, miracle drugs.

Pharmaceutical manufacturers spend a considerable amount of money advertising their products, particularly in specialist medical, nursing and health care journals related to mental illness and disability. Unsurprisingly, the advertisements emphasise the potential benefits of the medications, and place the adverse effects in very small print, either at the bottom of the page or off to the side. More interesting are the images used to sell the drugs, often reflecting themes discussed elsewhere in this chapter, although usually with a particularly sugary gloss. Thus, images of a patient's return to true self-hood as a result of the drug, or scenes of restored domestic bliss, are common. Perhaps more worrying are advertisements that, often very subtly, suggest the use of medications as an efficient control of patients. These are presumably directed to the harassed doctor, presenting a fast and efficient way to restore order onto their ward or into the local psychogeriatric nursing home. Are the advertisements effective? The continued use of large advertising budgets by these firms would suggest that they think so. A field trip to the medical library for a critical viewing of these advertisements is instructive to the student who is new to mental health law.

All these groups – patients, the varieties of medical personnel, social workers, hospitals and NHS health trusts, private caregivers, families, and pharmaceutical companies – make use of lobbyists and pressure groups to press their views. Sometimes, these roles are performed by professional organisations, such as the Royal College of Psychiatrists, the College of Physicians, or the British Medical Association; sometimes, they are performed by charities, such as MIND, Mencap, or the National Carers' Association. Sometimes, large organisations such as pharmaceutical companies will hire lobbyists directly. Once again, there is a considerable sociological literature on how these bodies work. If the group represents a variety of different persons or providers, decisions about what position is to be lobbied for may become complex. This may be particularly complex in some of the groups in the charitable sector, for example, which do not 'represent groups' per se, but exist instead primarily to focus attention on sets of issues. While MIND, for example, endeavours to give particular consideration to the views of users, its mandate and membership is considerably broader than this.

Lobby or pressure groups may further have independent interests involving their reputations or financial integrity that may influence them in addition to, or, occasionally, at odds with, the interests of the groups they represent. If a private firm of lobbyists is hired, for example, the firm will have a profit motivation. Even in the charitable sector, the financial integrity of the organisation must remain a factor in its priorities. Amendments to the way in which services are provided has complicated this, since in the last two decades, government has increasingly provided funding in the charitable sector. Nationally, the government provided £175m of £3,000m in charitable revenues in 1976, or roughly six per cent; by 1984, this had grown to £1bn of charitable revenue of £10bn, or 10 per cent (Prochaska, 1988: 4). By 1999, somewhere between 35 and 40 per cent of charitable income was thought to come from government sources (Whelan, 1999: 3). While these figures reflect the entire charitable sector, mental health charities have garnered at least their share of this new money. Indeed, as the charities have found an increasing role for themselves in the provision of community mental health services, their financial relations with government have intensified. The effect on these organisations is ambiguous. On the one hand, government relies on these organisations more than ever before to fulfil government objectives; at the same time, the organisations rely increasingly on government, to provide the funding for their activities. It is difficult to see that this uneasy relationship would not have its effect on the role of these charitable organisations to comment upon and to influence government policy.

Lying across all these interests is, of course, the government. It would be an error to think of the government as a monolith: like the remainder of the system, it is composed of parts, which may be characterised as much by competition as cooperation. The clearest of these possibly divergent interests arises between central and local government. The tradition in this country has long been for local government to have a particularly central role in service provision. Thus, the actual purchase, and some of the provision, of community care rests at the local authority level, where policymaking rests primarily with central government. The same is true of healthcare provision, which will be administered at the local level, in the context of central regulation. In each case, much of the core funding will originate with the central government. This suggests that local and central interests may well disagree on a wide variety of issues, from priorities in service provision, to, most pivotally, the appropriate level of funding for service provision.

Even central government must be understood as a complex entity. Mental health care will span a variety of offices and departments. Disability benefits for those living in the community are a social security issue. The Court of Protection, which handles the property and affairs of those found incapable of so doing themselves under Part VII of the MHA 1983, is a part of the Lord Chancellor's Department. Psychiatric treatment in hospital is, of course, a matter for the Department of Health. Within government, status is measured largely in terms of staff allocations and budget. The way in which programmes are divided between departments is thus profoundly relevant to the status of the departments concerned, with corresponding impact on government policy. The interests of a variety of departments in mental health services re-enforces that mental health policy may be as much a function of competitive negotiation between government departments as it is of cooperation.

Throughout the system, lawyers can be expected to be active. They will be hired, either to lobby for specific interests or to represent clients in specific situations, by all of the parties noted above. Here again, while the lawyer should, of course, defend the interests of those clients with all ferocity, limited only by professional standards such as the duty to uphold the dignity of the court, other factors can creep into the picture. Practising lawyers quickly learn that their individual reputations are profoundly significant to the attainment of their career aspirations and, sometimes, to the success of their causes. In practice, this may affect how the lawyer presents a case, and occasionally, what arguments will be made. Similarly, the realities of private legal practice require a cash flow. The lawyer representing clients in mental health as much as any other cannot, in the end, ignore that reality. This is seen with clarity in some of the debates surrounding legal aid. Certainly, availability of legal aid is likely to be vital to many poor psychiatric patients if their rights are to be protected. At the same time, the reason it is vital is because, without an appropriate legal aid structure, lawyers simply cannot afford to accept many cases: the issue here is about the economics of running a law office as much as it is about abstract notions of rights.

The resulting picture is of a complex system of actors and interests in the provision of mental health care. It would be unduly cynical to take the view that the people with the mental health problems, the people whom the system ought most to support and assist, are ignored. It would be fair to say that the users of mental health services have not traditionally been as successful as the professional groups in having their voices heard directly. This problem is complicated by the fact that the users of mental health services do not speak with one voice. They range from enthusiastic proponents of medication to people denying entirely the relevance of a medical model to insanity. User views instead tend to be filtered through a professionalised view of best interests. While it would be inappropriate to deny the good faith of much of this professional concern, the other factors noted above may distort or influence the message. If it is inappropriate to say that the person with mental health difficulties is absent from policy formation, it is certainly inappropriate to deny the other factors that influence policy formation.

1.4 Sources of law

1.4.1 The roots of the Mental Health Act

Mental health law is as old as law itself. The earliest codified reference in the English statute book is contained in a 1324 statute defining the Royal Prerogative, giving the king jurisdiction over the persons and property of 'idiots' and those who 'happen to fail of [their] Wit': *De Prerogativa Regis*, c. ix, x. Nonetheless, much of the care of the insane in medieval and early modern England occurred outside the realm of statute, and it was not until the eighteenth and, particularly, nineteenth centuries that the insane became, increasingly, subject to statutory jurisdiction. These statutes may have been the precursors of the MHA 1983, but they were markedly different in form. Specifically, for much of the nineteenth century, mental health law was not contained in a single Act, but instead in a variety of streams of statutes, each quite distinct from the others. Four nineteenth-century streams, and one additional one from the early twentieth century, warrant particular note, because they combine in somewhat amended form to comprise the MHA 1983.

One set of legislation governed private madhouses. The Madhouses Act of 1774 required private madhouses to be licensed by the College of Physicians if in London, or otherwise by the local magistracy. In 1828, this legislation was replaced by a new Madhouses Act. While amended repeatedly over the course of the century, this Act set the structure for these establishments for much of the nineteenth century. The College of Physicians lost its formal role. Up to 1845, madhouses outside London were inspected and licensed by the Justices of the Peace. In London, these inspection and licensing functions were conducted by a new body, the Metropolitan Commissioners in Lunacy. With an amending statute of 1845, the Metropolitan Commissioners were renamed the Commissioners in Lunacy, with jurisdiction to inspect madhouses throughout the country, although their licensing authority remained restricted to London. Admission to private madhouses was upon the application of a family member, supported by two certificates of insanity signed by medical practitioners not directly associated with the madhouse.

The Madhouse Acts covered only private madhouses and charitable hospitals. While these may occasionally have been quite extensive in size, they were not the vast public asylums of popular memory, which were instead governed by a series of County Asylum Acts. The first of these was passed in 1808. This Act allowed asylums for the relief of the insane poor to be built on the county rates. The facilities were overseen by a committee of Justices of the Peace until 1888, when they were passed to local authority control: Local Government Act 1888, ss. 3(vi), 86, 111. Throughout the nineteenth century, these facilities were generally restricted to paupers, although in practice a somewhat wide definition of that term might sometimes be employed. Admission was by order of a Justice of the Peace, upon the application of a poor law relieving officer, supported by one medical certificate, almost invariably signed by the poor law medical officer. The frequent rewritings of, and amendments to, the County Asylum Acts in the nineteenth century did little to change this structure, although legislation in 1845 made county asylum provision mandatory for the first time.

The nineteenth century also saw a string of statutes relating to clarifying, modernising, and rationalising the procedures relating to the Royal Prerogative powers. These powers allowed control over the person or property and affairs of an individual to be taken over, once incapacity to make relevant decisions had been shown (see Chapters 10 and 11). This power thus related to decision-making authority, not institutional confinement. Technically, the Royal Prerogative vested authority over lunatics and idiots in the monarch, who by tradition granted the power to make determinations of lunacy and idiocy to the Lord Chancellor at the beginning of each reign. By the beginning of the century, the Lord Chancellor in turn delegated the inquisition into the lunacy of an individual to three Commissioners. This panel of three was reduced to a panel of one in 1833. Where originally the Commissioners had been judges, they became, in 1842, barristers of at least ten years' standing. In 1862, the Commissioners lost the authority to try lunacy and idiocy matters where a jury was requested. That was removed to the common law courts, where the Commissioners continued to try lunacy or idiocy when no jury was requested. This gives a flavour of the nineteenth-century statutes relating to Chancery jurisdiction.

Finally, the nineteenth century saw a stream of statutes devoted to the detention of criminal lunatics. The initial statute was forced by *Hadfield's Case* (1800) 27 Howell's St Tr 1281, where it was held (at p. 1354) that notwithstanding a successful plea of insanity in defence of an attempted murder, the prisoner 'for his own sake, and for the sake of society at large, must not be discharged'. Legislative authority was provided for such detentions later that year. For the next half-century, criminal lunatics were included in county asylum legislation, but the construction of Broadmoor Asylum, opened in 1863, was reflected legislatively by a new stream of statutes devoted to criminal lunacy specifically, commencing with the Criminal Lunatics Act 1860.

The Lunacy Act 1890, is sometimes perceived as a watershed statute. In a sense it is, in that, for the first time, it combines the four legislative streams relating to the laws of insanity into one statute. Further, it was in effect for much of the twentieth century, not being formally repealed until 1959, and the MHA 1983 still resembles it in general structure. In its historical context, however, the 1890 Act is something of an anticlimax, although it did make some changes. For the first time, for example, privately paying patients could not be admitted to psychiatric facilities without the order of a Justice of the Peace. If the 1890 Act consolidated the various strands into one statute, however, it did not consolidate the strands themselves: for example, the paupers who had been under the jurisdiction of the County Asylum Acts continued to be subject to a set of rules quite different from private patients.

The first half of the twentieth century offered two significant developments. The first was to add yet another strand of legislation, the Mental Deficiency Acts, commencing in 1913. These seem to have been given short shrift by legislative historians of insanity, which is unfortunate: not only did they provide the basis of the current guardianship provisions of the MHA; they also provided the legislative framework for some early care in the community, before the Second World War (Thomson, 1998; Walmsley *et al.*, 1999). This provision was not negligible: by 1939, almost 90,000 people were controlled by these Acts in England and Wales, nearly half of which were living in the community (Walmsley *et al.*, 1999: 186). Further, they provided a legislative framework for an increasingly ornate social discourse relating to developmental disabilities. While 'idiocy' was expressly covered under the nineteenth-century legislation, for much of that period little distinction was made between this and 'lunacy'. The Idiots Act of 1886 began to acknowledge the distinctness of problems relating to developmental disability; the differential nature of the issues, and a different set of social responses, was given clearer articulation by the Mental Deficiency Act 1913.

The second development was that the Mental Treatment Act 1930 introduced informal admissions for the first time. In law, this is extremely significant. Up to this time, there was no distinction between admission to, and confinement in, a psychiatric facility. From 1930, it became possible for an individual to be admitted to a psychiatric facility without a formal and binding order of admission. For the first time, the patient might also be free to leave. While this admission route took some time to gain widespread popularity, it now accounts for around 90 per cent of psychiatric admissions.

It is in this legislative context that we must understand the Mental Health Act 1959. The creation of the National Health Service in 1948 had largely removed the distinction between public and private facilities, with the incorporation of charitable hospitals into the public sector. The old legislative distinctions appeared to make less and less sense. Where the 1890 Act had left the distinctions largely untouched, but included all legislative strands in one statute, the 1959 Act actually tried to consolidate the divergent strands into one. The solution of the 1959 Act was largely to ram the different processes together. For example, where compulsory admission before that time had been in the hands of poor law or social service officials if the patient was poor and the family if the patient was able to afford private care, under the new system both admission mechanisms were combined for all patients, so that all compulsory admissions required both family and social services involvement.

The 1959 Act did make a few significant changes. First, admissions were now removed from Justices of the Peace. The process allowed admission instead upon the agreement of a mental welfare officer and the nearest relative of the patient, accompanied by certification of mental disorder by two doctors. This may have reflected existing practice in any event, for there is evidence that, in some areas at least, Justices of the Peace were signing multiple copies of blank orders of admission, in anticipation of applications from poor law relieving officers and medical officers (Forsythe *et al.*, 1999: 83). Nonetheless, albeit perhaps unintentionally, the 1959 Act is said to have had the effect of moving power from hospital administration and judicial officers directly to treating physicians (Fennell, 1996: 168–9). Secondly, the Act introduced mental health review tribunals. For the first time, a dedicated mechanism was created by which patients could challenge their confinement. Finally, the 1959 Act moved the *parens patriae* power to an entirely statutory footing. Where the previous legislation of this power had functioned as amendments of the common law, the 1959 Act subjected guardianship and conservatorship to a purely statutory régime.

The MHA 1959 once again placed mental disorder and developmental disorder in the same statute, an approach continued under the MHA 1983, currently in force. The result has been a mixed blessing. On the one hand, legislation combining the responses to be available in appropriate circumstances, irrespective of whether an individual suffers from mental illness or developmental disability, increases the flexibility of responses in a way that must be to the benefit of both groups. At the same time, the combined statute means that the legislative space to consider problems specific to each of these groups has disappeared. This would seem to have worked to the disadvantage of those with developmental disabilities, which, in discussions related to the current Act, are overshadowed by issues of mental health and illness. This is reflected in the title of the Act: why should people with developmental disabilities be subject to a 'mental health' Act, when they are not, per se, mentally ill? Indeed, this book can be justly criticised for this bias. While purporting to discuss the ambit of the MHA 1983 as a whole, much of the discussion does show an inappropriate assumption that the prime users of the legislation are mentally ill, not developmentally disabled.

The MHA 1983, still currently in force, albeit as amended, kept the basic provisions of the 1959 Act. The new Act was passed in a climate where patient rights were treated more seriously than ever before. There were some changes in nomenclature: 'mental welfare officers' became 'approved social workers', and 'mental subnormality' and 'severe mental subnormality' became 'mental impairment' and 'severe mental impairment' respectively, for example. Some more substantive changes were also made at this time, however. Treatment while in a psychiatric facility was, for the first time, brought into the legislative realm, albeit only for those confined in the facility. That inclusion nonetheless made it equally clear, for the first time, that those not covered by the provisions – that is, those informally admitted – had the same rights regarding treatment as the common law provides to people outside the facility. In addition, the powers of personal guardians were significantly reduced. The guardian could now only determine where the person might reside (but not require him or her to be returned there, if, for example, he or she were wandering), and where they might attend for treatment (but not to consent on the person's behalf). While they can also ensure access to the individual by social services or medical personnel, they have authority to make no other decisions for the individual. This triggered a process of law reform, eventually resulting in the passage of the Mental Capacity Act 2005 (MCA 2005): see Chapter 11. In the interim, the courts expanded common law on an ad hoc basis to fill the apparent gap.

Most of the changes since 1983 have occurred in the realm of a forest of policies, guidance, and directives from the Department of Health. These have been legion, introducing best practice policies for a wide variety of matters relating to psychiatric care. While these have been enforced through administrative audit and similar mechanics of government – woe betide a provider who fails to develop the administratively appropriate care plans for patients – they have no formal legal effect. The courts may look to them, of course, but will not be bound by them when they do not reflect statute or common law: see, for example, *R v Department of Health, ex p Source Informatics Ltd* [1999] 4 All ER 185. The trend towards this form of extralegal regulation is typical across government, and is certainly prevalent in health matters generally. The move raises questions of accountability: while some of the guidances have considerable effect, they will not have been scrutinised by Parliament.

In the 1995, in response to two *causes célèbre*, significant amendments were made to the Act regarding control of patients released into the community. The 1983 Act already made the provision of aftercare in the community mandatory for people who were released from civil confinement in psychiatric facilities (s. 117). The 1995 amendments allowed service providers in the community to be appointed, who would ensure that the patient live in a specific place, attend a specific place for treatment (although there is no power to require that the person consent to the treatment), and could require access to the individual by other service providers (s. 25A–25J; see further, Chapter 9). The particular relevance of these provisions in an historical context is the blurring of control between the institution and the community and, perhaps more significantly, the debate surrounding the introduction of these provisions turned from a language of rights, the predominant discourse in the 1983 debates, to a language of risks. That latter language has proven central to the government's thinking regarding mental health reform in the last few years.

What are we to make of this long and somewhat tortuous history? Perhaps what is striking is less how much things have changed, as how much they have remained the same. While the distinctions between public and private admissions have disappeared under the current Act, the structure is otherwise reminiscent of the strands of nineteenth-century law identified above: Parts II and VI on admission to facilities, including removal of patients to the various parts of the UK; Part III on criminal confinement; Part VII on management of property and affairs. On a more minute level, the continuities are similarly notable. The current role of the approved social worker (ASW) looks remarkably similar to that of the poor law relieving officer, 150 years ago.

At the same time, the context of the Act has changed markedly, making interpretation complex. When the Act contains the old nineteenth-century clauses, as it often does, their relevance or applicability is no longer clear. Take, for example, the provisions defining the right of the nearest relative to insist on the release of a patient, contained in s. 23(2). This originates in the nineteenth-century statutes. If the confinement was in the private sector, the relative was responsible for paying the patient's upkeep, and therefore was perceived to have the right to demand the release of the patient, to limit their own financial exposure. If instead the patient was confined in a county asylum, the right to order release was conditional on an undertaking by the person ordering the release that the individual would no longer be chargeable on the poor law. The right to release was thus a way to enforce public economy in care provision, and to limit the shame of the family at receiving poor relief. Neither of these justifications continues to exist; yet the section remains in relatively unamended form. Justifications may continue to exist for the inclusion of the role, but they are *ex post facto*.

These nineteenth-century rights to order the release of the patient were circumscribed if the patient were 'dangerous to other persons or to himself', a restriction remaining in s. 25 of the Act; yet how are we to read that section, given the standard of confinement introduced in 1959 and still in force, that the civil confinement is 'necessary for the health or safety of the patient or for the protection of other persons'? If it is the same standard, the right of the nearest relative is removed in all cases where the patient is rightly confined, rendering the power a nullity. If the standards are different, how are they different? The answer would have to be to introduce a relatively low standard for 'health' in the 1983 provision, since it is difficult to see how 'safety' of the patient or 'protection of other persons' provides the necessary flexibility to provide a standard different from 'dangerous'; is this really consistent with the meaning of the 1959 standard as a whole? Does the phrase 'the health or safety of the patient or for the protection of other persons', when read as a whole, not instead imply a relatively high standard of risk to health? And should the determination of modern standards of confinement be based on arcane arguments about nineteenth-century legal history?

The MHA 1983 is full of this sort of difficulty. Its construction and interpretation can be fiendishly difficult. A Code of Practice, most recently revised in 1999, has been issued to assist those charged with the Act's administration (Department of Health and Welsh Office, 1999). In a sense, this only complicates matters further, because the Code contains material supplementary to the legal standards of the Act. While the Code is not legally binding on practitioners, it is identified as something the Secretary of State is obliged to produce by s. 118 of the Act. As such, while service providers may depart from it, they are required to give the Code 'great weight' and to depart from it only when they have 'cogent reasons' for doing so (*R (Munjaz)* v *Ashworth* [2005] UKHL 58, para. 21). The result can appear to establish ambiguities in the standards to be applied: one is reminded of the Japanese proverb that a person with a clock knows the time; a person with two clocks is never sure. Even without reference to issues of social policy in interpretation, the MHA therefore provides a veritable panoply of difficulties, testing the lawyer's skills in statutory interpretation to their limit.

1.4.2 Potential reform

Reform of mental health law and mental capacity law has long been in the air. The project to reform the mental capacity legislation started with a project of the Law Commission in the late 1980s (see Law Commission, 1995). The eventual result was the

MCA 2005, currently expected to take effect in April 2007, almost two decades after the reform process commenced (re revised timetable, see preface to this volume). This statutory reform affects people lacking capacity, that is, people who are unable by reason of mental disability to make decisions (see Chapters 10 and 11). As such, it affects some, but not all, people with psychiatric problems: there is nothing legally inconsistent between having a mental illness or developmental disability and being able to make decisions. Indeed, people with mental illness, like other adults, are presumed able to make decisions unless the contrary is shown: *Re C (Adult: Refusal of Medical Treatment)* [1994] 1 All ER 819. The 2005 Act is not intended to affect the compulsion powers under mental health legislation, although it will be relevant for people without decision-making capacity in the psychiatric system but outside the formal powers of compulsion (see Chapter 11).

From 1998, reform of the MHA 1983 has also been on the legislative agenda. This has not yet borne fruit, although the latest bill has been expected imminently for some time. The purpose of the current discussion is not to chronicle the detail of the proposed reforms; their detailed content will be discussed as it arises elsewhere in this book. Instead, the purpose here is to provide a general guide to their development, range and general content: an overview so that the references to the various reform packages will be comprehensible as they arise in the rest of the book.

Reform of the Mental Health Act grew from two unrelated directions. On one side, the 1997 Labour Party election manifesto had contained a pledge to include Community Treatment Orders. Some legislative reform was therefore going to be necessary, and in part because of the impending implementation of the Human Rights Act 1998, which allowed the provisions of the European Convention on Human Rights to be raised in domestic courts, the government decided a full review of mental health law was appropriate. An expert committee was established, chaired by Professor Genevra Richardson, in October 1998. Over the course of the following year, that committee consulted broadly, before submitting its report to the Department of Health in the summer of 1999 (Department of Health, 1999a).

The Richardson Committee proposed fundamental amendments to the administration of mental health law, based on a set of general principles that would be incorporated into the Act. These were generally the broadly accepted principles of mental health law of the last decades: the desirability of patient autonomy; a preference of informal care over compulsory measures; a preference for the least restrictive manner and environment for treatment; a preference for care reflecting the preferences of the user; the participation of users in all aspects of their treatment and care, in so far as their capacity allows; reciprocity (i.e., that mandatory orders create a corresponding duty to provide a high standard of service); no discrimination, but context-sensitive services based on background, age, gender, sexual orientation, ethnic group, and social, cultural or religious background; respect for carers; the importance of communication and the provision of information to users.

The Committee proposed increased flexibility in the mandatory orders that could be made, including increased powers of coercion in the community. While these powers stopped short of enforced treatment in the community, they would, if the order so specified, allow the confinement of the individual in hospital in the event of non-compliance with treatment. Due process safeguards were included, however: the process would begin with a mandatory assessment period of up to seven days; in that period, with narrow exceptions, only emergency treatment could be administered involuntarily. An application to a tribunal would be necessary within the seven days, for a mandatory order to issue that would allow involuntary treatment. This initial mandatory order would last for up to 28 days; further orders, for which tribunal sanction would be mandatory, would last up to six months.

The Richardson Committee also proposed changing the substantive criteria for the imposition of mandatory powers, according a considerably increased role for the capacity of the patient. The Committee stopped short of saying that people with capacity could never have their decisions overridden, as is the case in other branches of health law, but the views of the competent patient were accorded considerably more emphasis.

The Committee's report, along with a Ministry of Health Green Paper on mental health reform (Department of Health, 1999c), was published in November 1999.

The second influence on the Mental Health Act reforms flowed from the Fallon Committee, appointed in 1998 following concerns about mismanagement and abuse at Ashworth Special Hospital. Its report to the Department of Health and the Home Office, published in 1999 (Department of Health, 1999b), was not restricted to that institution, but included a broader discussion of the law relating to criminals with personality disorder. As will be discussed further in Chapter 2, persons with personality disorders are controversial in legal regulation of mental health, because they are often untreatable. Such untreatable 'psychopaths' (to use the language of the existing legislation) cannot be confined under the 1983 Act. The Committee was concerned that appropriate services ought to be available to members of this group who were treatable, but it was also concerned to ensure that criminals with personality disorders who might still pose considerable danger to the community would not be released at the end of a fixed sentence. The committee proposed that a reviewable sentence be introduced for individuals who remained dangerous.

The Department of Health and the Home Office largely accepted the Fallon Committee's recommendations, and, in the summer of 1999, published a Green Paper exploring the possibility of either strengthening the existing criminal law to make greater use of discretionary life sentences, or creating a new legal framework to allow the confinement of dangerous persons with personality disorders indefinitely, whether or not they were treatable, and whether or not they had come into contact previously with the criminal justice system. Effectively, this would create a parallel system to the Mental Health Act for those with dangerous and serious personality disorder. Unsurprisingly, these proposals were highly controversial. Civil libertarians objected to the unlimited detention of those who had not committed any offence; mental health professionals objected to the detention of those whom they could not treat.

It is at this point that the two streams of mental health law reform were combined: the Department of Health issued one White Paper on mental health reform in December 2000, flowing from its two Green Papers the previous year, and a draft bill in June 2002 (Department of Health, 2000c; 2002d). Perhaps unsurprisingly, given the concern of the Fallon Committee regarding criminals with personality disorder, much of the due-process protections and concerns about general principles, non-discrimination, respect and capacity had disappeared. Instead, much of the language of dangerousness contained in the post-Fallon discussion had entered the picture, along with requirements that persons thought to pose a threat to the public should be treatable, which would be met if their symptoms could be managed.

The White Paper and draft bill were not well received. Service users and their advocates complained about the disappearance of many of the rights-based protections, and the notion that users were to be treated with dignity. Doctors objected that they would be required to warehouse people for whom there was no treatment. Civil rights advocates complained at the demise of due process safeguards, particularly the initial tribunal review at the seven-day period proposed by Richardson. The overall direction of change can be illustrated by reference to the guiding principles contained in the bill. As noted above, the Richardson Committee proposed an array of progressive principles, supportive of patient dignity, liberty and rights. The draft bill contained three general principles, securing: that patients be involved in the making of decisions; that decisions be made openly and fairly; that 'the interference to patients in providing medical treatment to them and the restrictions imposed in respect of them during that treatment are kept to the minimum necessary to protect their health or safety of other persons' (cl. 1(3)). Unlike the Richardson principles, these simply did not reflect the direction and complexity of discussion and debate in the mental health arena in recent decades. As if this were not enough, a subsequent subclause went on to say that the Code of Practice could specify circumstances or decisions or people to which even these minimal principles would not apply (cl. 1(4)). It is unsurprising that the proposals did not receive broad support among users, service providers and carers.

That said, some of the objections are not entirely convincing. Certainly, the language of risk in the debate was prominent; it was, indeed, contained in the guiding principles quoted. At the same time, it was already justifiable to confine an individual whose mental disorder makes this necessary 'for the protection of others' (MHA 1983, ss. 2, 3). Certainly, the requirement that persons with personality disorders and mental impairment be treatable if they are to be confined was to disappear, but there was no meaningful requirement under the existing legislation that persons with other forms of mental illness should have an effective cure. Why should personality disorder be treated differently from schizophrenia? Certainly, the move to a dangerousness standard risks the over-representation of black people in our psychiatric facilities, but the current system stands equally accused of this problem: see Chapter 4.

A subsequent draft bill introduced in 2004 (Department of Health, 2004a) was not well received for similar reasons. This bill was subjected to a highly critical report by a Joint Scrutiny Committee of the House of Commons and House of Lords (House of

Commons and House of Lords, 2005). The government initially defended its focus on safety to the public and to users themselves, stating that it was only users, and medical and social care professionals who seemed concerned by this focus (Department of Health, 2005a: 4). Nonetheless, faced with the opposition of the key players, it decided the following year not to proceed with the bill, and instead to introduce amendments to the MHA 1983.

As a bill has not yet been forthcoming, although a variety of policy statements have articulated the government's general direction, the changes will be modest. Some amendments will be made to the definition of 'mental disorder'. The different standards of 'treatability' required for compulsory admission will be made consistent. Supervised community treatment will be given statutory form. Additional flexibility will be introduced regarding appointment and replacement of 'nearest relatives'. Application for compulsory admission will no longer be managed exclusively by social workers, but by a broader category of 'approved mental health professionals', and in appropriate circumstances, the person in charge of a patient's care will be able to be someone other than a doctor. Some changes are to be made to processes before Mental Health Review Tribunals, to make them proceed more expeditiously. As required by the European Court of Human Rights, some additional protections will be offered for people who are admitted to hospital informally, but who lack the capacity to consent to that admission ('*Bournewood*' patients).

This is a disappointing outcome to a process of reform lasting eight years so far. It is difficult to see that such limited reform will provide long-term legislative stability. Mental health issues have been arising with increasing frequency before the European Court of Human Rights (see Bartlett *et al.*, 2006). As will be seen in the pages that follow, mental health issues are showing up routinely in Human Rights Act litigation. Success in this litigation has been mixed, but it is difficult to see that these challenges will go away, particularly when the 1983 Act is not designed with these human rights issues in mind. Human rights is also a moving target: as human rights develop in domestic and international discourse, evidenced, for example, by new international conventions, the standard of scrutiny under the ECHR is likely to rise. The 1983 Act was passed prior to the significant movements in disability rights of recent years, and already looks antiquated. It is likely to appear increasingly out of step with human rights standards as time passes. It seems inevitable, therefore, that the proposed government amendments will not be the last word.

1.4.3 Other law and mental disorder

The MHA 1983 may provide the core of the law for this text, but it will be clear from the preceding discussion that it cannot stand on its own. The MCA 2005 will also be relevant, and in the silence of the statutes, common law will continue to apply. In addition, other legal subject areas may come into play in understanding the rights of those with mental health problems. The modern law curriculum, frequently modular, is appropriately criticised for treating legal subjects as self-contained packages, with little to do with each other. The study of mental health law allows the law student an ideal opportunity to think across legal subjects, analysing which approach will yield a desirable result. Mental health law spans almost all legal disciplines. The student of mental health law should see this as an opportunity, not a threat, because it allows a reassessment of those disciplines from a new and different angle to that usually forming the base of law school curricula. A brief survey will show how some of these related areas intersect with mental health law.

The MHA 1983 itself involves subjects such as confinement and enforced treatment, performed on statutory justification. These matters tend to be controlled by judicial review, and students should be aware of the relevance of their study of public law to mental health law.

The MHA 1983 is not a complete code, and in the silence of the statutes, the common law will apply. The treatment of people with decision-making capacity who are informally admitted to psychiatric facilities is governed by common law, with the standard rules of consent and medical negligence applicable. When people lack capacity, the MCA 2005 will apply in these situations, creating mechanisms governing decision-making on behalf of people lacking capacity. In this sense, it is really a guardianship statute.

Capacity is, of course, not merely about guardianship; it is a threshold whenever people enter into legal relations. The MCA 2005 creates prospective mechanisms to allow individuals to make decisions on the incapable person's behalf, but it does not alter the pre-existing legal rules applicable when the incapable person has nonetheless entered into relations with others. Here, capacity law, generally based in common law, reaches into virtually the entire law school curriculum. As an illustrative list, there are rules regarding capacity to marry, to engage in sexual relations, to file for divorce, to sign contracts, to commit crimes and to enter a plea when charged with an offence, to serve as trustee or corporate director, to execute a will, and of course to consent to medical treatment. Some of these will be discussed below, requiring some consideration of the broader laws in these areas.

Even regarding mental disorder as distinct from incapacity, the Mental Health Act does not, of course, affect all of the individual's life. A variety of other statutory regimes may also be significant. People with mental disorders face with embarrassing frequency the problems of maintaining jobs and finding places to live (Thornicroft, 2006: ch. 3 and *passim*). The first of these will be subject to employment laws, which articulate the degree to which mental illness can be used to justify dismissal; similarly, both employment and housing are covered by the Disability Discrimination Act 1995 and subsequent amendments to that statute. This may be particularly helpful, because it can require the employer or landlord to make reasonable accommodation to take account of the needs of the disabled person. Disability rights are also noted in the Treaty of Amsterdam 1997, and the Charter of Fundamental Rights of the European Union, signed in Nice in 2000 (2000/C 364/01), suggesting that a European dimension may become increasingly relevant as that treaty is implemented. Particularly if employment fails, the individual may be in need of social services, where a range of disability benefits may be available under social security legislation.

The Human Rights Act 1998 came into effect in October 2000. It allows the provisions of the European Convention on Human Rights to be pleaded in the domestic courts of the UK for the first time. The convention provides an array of classically liberal rights:

- right to life (Article 2);
- prohibition of torture and inhuman or degrading treatment or punishment (3);
- prohibition of slavery and forced labour (4);
- right to liberty and security of person (5);
- right to a fair trial regarding civil rights or criminal charges (6);
- no conviction or punishment for a criminal offence without prior law prohibition (7);
- right to respect for private and family life (8);
- freedom of thought, conscience and religion (9);
- freedom of expression (10);
- freedom of assembly and association (11);
- right to marry (12).

Its introduction in 2000 was an oddity in historical terms, because the Convention itself was drafted in the late 1940s, eventually coming into effect in 1953. It therefore contains the presuppositions about rights current at that time, when the rights of persons with disabilities were not on the political agenda. This different attitude is easily illustrated by reference to the wording of Article 5, the Article protecting citizens from wrongful confinement and deprivation of liberty:

5.1 Everyone has the right to liberty and security of the person. No one shall be deprived of his liberty save in the following cases and in accordance with a procedure prescribed by law:

* * *

e. the lawful detention of persons for the prevention of the spreading of infectious diseases, of persons of unsound mind, alcoholics or drug addicts, or vagrants

The teaming of 'persons of unsound mind', itself a term from a previous age, with alcoholics, drug addicts, and vagrants bespeaks a very different rights culture than that prevailing at the beginning of the new millennium. There can be little doubt that the rights of people with mental disabilities were not in the minds of those ratifying the original text, more than half a century ago, and the early, formative jurisprudence of the Convention was formulated without reference to the needs of people with mental health problems. One might reasonably ask how far we can really look to the introduction of this antiquated language into English law as a way forward for mental health law.

The view from Europe is mixed (see Bartlett *et al.*, 2006). Over the last quarter-century, consistent with the shift in attention towards a rights-based model for those with mental disabilities, the European Court of Human Rights has become involved in reinterpreting and developing its jurisprudence to take account of cases relating to those with mental health problems. This began, in 1979, with the case of *Winterwerp v The Netherlands* (1979–80) 2 EHRR 387, which laid down core standards that Member States must apply, if they are to rely on Article 5.1(e). This case has proven extremely important in establishing fundamental standards in the mental health area. The experience since that time has been mixed. The Court has been strong on ensuring appropriate due process protections, but weak on substantive issues. As perhaps an extreme example, in *Johnson v UK* (1999) 27 EHRR 296, the court held that while an individual who had been, but was no longer, mentally ill had a variety of process rights to challenge their confinement, the fact that they were no longer mentally ill did not mean that they had a right to an immediate and unconditional release from their psychiatric facility. This does seem to be an extraordinarily conservative reading of the phrase 'person of unsound mind' in Article 5.1(e). At the same time, the court has been strong on ensuring appropriate procedural safeguards for those in facilities. Thus the court has held that detention will only be justified on the basis of objective medical evidence. It has provided general statements as to the substantive standards of that evidence, but little guidance specific enough to be useful to policymakers in determining what substantive threshold that evidence must meet (see Bartlett *et al.*, 2006: 42–9). Similarly, the court has established requirements regarding access to a judicial-style procedure to challenge detention, and the availability of hearings before such tribunals at reasonable intervals. It is thus clear that the aspiring mental health lawyer will need to have a good grasp of ECtHR jurisprudence in the future.

Movement on the substantive side of mental health issues has been much more the province of the Committee for the Prevention of Torture and Inhuman or Degrading Treatment or Punishment. The Committee has taken the view that people who are institutionalised are particularly vulnerable to abuse, and therefore form a particularly important part of its mandate. It routinely visits not only prisons, but also psychiatric hospitals, social care homes, and similar institutions, to ensure that appropriate standards are met. Its reports are not as influential in domestic English courts as the decisions of the ECtHR, but they may nonetheless be given some consideration: see, for example *R (Wilkinson) v RMO Broadmoor Hospital and MHA Second Opinion Approved Doctor* [2002] 1 WLR 419 (CA) at paragraph 28 per Simon Brown LJ, regarding the rights of persons with capacity to make treatment decisions.

The experience so far in the British courts is mixed. Thus far there have been a number of procedural successes. The burden of proof before review tribunals is now clearly on the doctor justifying confinement, rather than on the patient applying for release: *R v MHRT North and East London Region, ex p H* [2001] 3 WLR 512, [2002] QBD 1. Scheduling of review tribunal hearings must now be done more promptly: *B v MHRT and Secretary of State for the Home Department* [2002, QB Admin]; *R (IH) v Home Secretary, Health Secretary* [2003] UKHL 59. New procedures are available for courts to determine whether rights have been violated: *R (Wilkinson) v Broadmoor Hospital*. Substantive issues have fared less well. Thus the House of Lords has held that the Human Rights Act imposes no requirement that a person's illness be treatable for that person to be confined: *A (A Mental Patient) v Scottish Ministers* 2002 SC (PC) 63, [2002]

HRLR 6, affirmed *Hutchison Reid* v *the UK* (2003) 37 EHRR 9. Where specific aftercare is a condition of a tribunal's release order for a patient, the Human Rights Act creates no obligation on a health authority to provide the treatment, beyond making reasonable efforts: *R* v *Camden and Islington HA, ex p K* [2001] 3 WLR 553, affirmed *Kolanis* v *UK* (2006) 42 EHRR 12. Challenges to surveillance practices of forensic psychiatric facilities have been generally unsuccessful: *R* v *Ashworth Special Hospital and Secretary of State for Health, ex p N* [2001] EWHC Admin 339; *R* v *Ashworth Hospital, ex p Munjaz* [2005] UKHL 58.

The more interesting question is perhaps whether the Human Rights Act is effecting a cultural change on the judiciary: are they now perceiving issues relating to those with mental health difficulties as human rights questions, rather than mere questions of administrative law? This is a difficult question, because judges do not act with one mindset. There are some indications, however, that judges are approaching matters differently. *R (Wilkinson)* v *Broadmoor and MHA Second Opinion Approved Doctor* [2002] 1 WLR 419 (CA), for example, held that where fundamental rights under the Convention, including legality of psychiatric treatment, were in doubt, the court should not base its decision on the reasonableness of the defendant doctor's view, but should instead decide between expert opinions, making findings of fact as required. Witnesses should be called and cross-examined as necessary. That is a marked departure from standard judicial review procedure, which is generally conducted on the basis of written evidence only.

Also indicative is the re-litigation of the question of whether a patient can be immediately re-sectioned, following release by a review tribunal. Recent litigation under the Human Rights Act has applied increasingly clear rules as to when this can happen: see *R* v *East London and City MH NHS Trust and Snazell, ex p Count Franz von Brandenburg* [2003] EWHL 58. This case is effectively a rehearing of the issue in *R* v *South Western Hospital Managers and Another, ex p M* [1994] 1 All ER 161, yet the court in the more recent case markedly restricted the grounds on which re-application should be made. It is not obvious that there is a direct influence of the Human Rights Act – the recent cases could equally have been decided on the grounds of abuse of process, as the earlier one had been. The question is whether the culture of perceiving the issues had changed, from one of deference to medical professionalism to one acknowledging to a greater degree the rights of the patient in question. Similarly, the case of *R* v *Feggetter and MHAC, ex p John* [2002] EWCA 554 concerned the duty of doctors providing second opinions prior to compulsory treatment of patients to provide reasons. The decision was based on traditional common law principles, but the language of the reasons harkened instead to the human rights discourse contained in *Wilkinson*, above.

How far this cultural shift will move remains to be seen. It is, as yet, early days in the Human Rights Act jurisprudence. There is a final wild card in the equation: under the Human Rights Act, our judges must take into account the ECtHR jurisprudence, but they are not formally bound by it. This may mean a retreat from some of its principles, but it may also mean development in new ways. A variety of other commonwealth jurisdictions have established traditions and jurisprudence of human rights, which may apply more or less forcefully to the English situation, and which may or may not convince English judges. It remains to be seen whether or how these other influences will influence our jurisprudence.

1.5 Concluding comments

This book views mental health law both as a subject in its own right and as a case study. In the former context, it provides an opportunity for law students to exercise their skills in statutory interpretation and case analysis, but it requires more. Mental health law and policy is, by its very definition, an interdisciplinary study. It is not an area where law should be considered independently, divorced from the realities of clinical practice or life for the client in the community. It requires the student to consider how various actors work together, and which interests take precedence over others. Thus, empirical research and sociological approaches will often be as enlightening as pure legal analysis.

Mental health law as case study requires the student to consider the nature of law. As we have seen, mental health law spans the curriculum. In this, it is typical of other types of law – a secret often kept from students, who seem determined to view law in discrete and unrelated subject packages – and the skills acquired by the student in thinking across these legal areas should be expected to assist him or her in any sort of law they eventually practise. If critical theory and sociology may be required to make sense of what mental health law is about, so mental health law provides a way for the undergraduate student to approach these subjects, and once again, these approaches will prove valuable in other contexts. No law operates divorced from the real needs of clients and the pressures of social policy. Mental health law creates a suitable study of how these interact, and an understanding of this can certainly be applied by students to other areas of law.

In closing, this chapter returns to its beginning: silence. It will be clear that in our view, the silence must be broken. This is, in a sense, a lawyer's conceit, because law glorifies the representation of the individual client: in our professional ideology, based in rights theory and liberalism, the model of the lawyer defending the interests and acting on the instructions of the individual client is pivotal. Yet this is not merely conceit. The more offensive conceit would be to treat mental health law as a set of academic constructs, and ignore the people contained within the system. These are real people with real problems. This is true of everyone in the system, but is perhaps most true of the people with mental health difficulties or developmental disabilities: it is their voices that remain largely outside the hearing of policymakers.

If this book argues for the necessity to break down the silence described by Foucault, it should also challenge the reader to question the discourse that has resulted from that silence. If policy has developed through silencing the mad, if it is, as Foucault claims, a discourse of reason about unreason, it then tells us as much, or more, about the reasonable as the mad. For reason to articulate insanity, it must do it with reference to sanity, because this is the only way the border can be understood. In this way, mental health law and policy can be seen as a mirror, in which we see our own values reflected. For Foucault, this language of reason bears no particularly enhanced status. It is instead 'that other form of madness, by which men, in an act of sovereign reason, confine their neighbors, and communicate and recognize each other through the merciless language of non-madness' (Foucault, 1965: ix). If reason is madness, it is nonetheless our madness, and thus something we should strive to acknowledge and understand.

In the first chapter of *Madness and Civilization*, Foucault uses the imagery of the ship of fools, the *stultifara navis*, as the paradigm of a Renaissance view of madness. Foucault seems to have believed that these ships actually existed, a view that has attracted criticisms from historians (e.g. Midelfort, 1980). Foucault also draws a symbolic meaning from this image (1965: 9): 'It is possible that these ships of fools, which haunted the imagination of the entire early Renaissance, were pilgrimage boats, highly symbolic cargoes of madmen in search of their reason.' This is, in a sense, an appropriate metaphor for Foucault's view of the result of the enlightenment: the journey of 'that other form of madness' in search of its reason.

It is also the project of this book.

2

Problems of Definition

When I assert that mental illness is a myth, I am not saying that personal unhappiness and socially deviant behavior do not exist; what I am saying is that we categorize them as diseases at our own peril.

The expression 'mental illness' is a metaphor that we have come to mistake for a fact. We call people physically ill when their body-functioning violates certain anatomical and physiological norms; similarly, we call people mentally ill when their personal conduct violates certain ethical, political, and social norms. This explains why many historical figures, from Jesus to Castro, and from Job to Hitler, have been diagnosed as suffering from this or that psychiatric malady.

Szasz, 1970: 23

Szsaz's arguments are not only wrongheaded, they are also inhumane, since they deny the possibility of help for a condition [schizophrenia] which claims the life of one in ten sufferers.

Leff, 1993: 78

2.1 Introduction

The problem posed by Szasz is real enough. A finding of mental disorder in law can have profound effects on an individual. It serves as a dividing line between the acknowledgement that individuals are responsible for their actions and have authority to make decisions as to what happens to them, and possible intervention depriving the individual of basic rights of citizenship. The MHA 1983 contains extreme powers. People may be confined against their will, or lose control of their property and affairs. They may be treated against their will with powerful chemicals or electricity. Some of these have adverse effects, which may significantly curtail the individual's quality of life, or sense of well-being. Such powerful violations of civil rights require powerful justifications.

At the same time, as the quote from Leff illustrates, there is a sense in society that it is somehow wrong to leave without protection those who are vulnerable to abuse and unable to cope with day-to-day decisions. This too is occasionally expressed in terms of rights. Thus, the United Nations Declaration on the Rights of Mentally Retarded Persons contains a specific right to a guardian able to protect the rights and interests of an incapacitated person: 1971 UN General Assembly, 26th sess., resolution 2856, para. 5. The failure to intervene in an appropriate situation here can leave the individual open to physical, mental or financial abuse, results that are remarkably similar to the risk of over-intervention identified by Szasz.

Whichever way the argument is phrased, whether as the liberal right to be free from intervention, or as the more paternalist question of who should or should not be protected, the issue involves the deployment of power over individuals. This is most easily seen in the overtly legal context: civil confinement under the MHA is obviously the deployment of power. The development of social policy is also the deployment of power, however, for it involves the structuring of society and the creation of social programmes into which the participants will be expected to fit. Even naming individuals as mentally disordered is an exercise of power, because it changes their perceptions of themselves, and the way they are perceived by other people.

If power is to be exercised, it is appropriate to insist that it be exercised properly, for cogent justifications, according to reasonably clear and defensible criteria. The gateway to the powers under the MHA is the concept of 'mental disorder', and four of its sub-categories. This chapter will challenge the stability and clarity of these concepts and the justifications for their use. The result is a quandary that is at the base of mental health law and policy: if we are to take Leff's view seriously, we are obliged to exercise power in aid of those who are most vulnerable; yet it is profoundly problematic to determine who those vulnerable people are, leaving open the possibility of significant civil rights abuses and criticisms.

2.2 **The statutory structure**

The conditions to which the MHA 1983 is to apply are defined in s. 1(2) of that Act:

'mental disorder' means mental illness, arrested or incomplete development of mind, psychopathic disorder, and any other disorder or disability of mind and 'mentally disordered' shall be construed accordingly;

'severe mental impairment' means a state of arrested or incomplete development of mind which includes severe impairment of intelligence and social functioning and is associated with abnormally aggressive or seriously irresponsible conduct on the part of the person concerned and 'severely mentally impaired' shall be construed accordingly;

'mental impairment' means a state of arrested or incomplete development of mind (not amounting to severe mental impairment) which includes significant impairment of intelligence and social functioning and is associated with abnormally aggressive or seriously irresponsible conduct on the part of the person concerned and 'mentally impaired' shall be construed accordingly;

'psychopathic disorder' means a persistent disorder or disability of mind (whether or not including significant impairment of intelligence) which results in abnormally aggressive or seriously irresponsible conduct on the part of the person concerned.

All of these are subject to s. 1(3) of the 1983 Act:

Nothing in subsection (2) above shall be construed as implying that a person may be dealt with under this Act as suffering from mental disorder, or from any mental disorder described in this section, by reason only of promiscuity or other immoral conduct, sexual deviancy or dependence on alcohol or drugs.

2.2.1 'Mental disorder'

Section 1(2) defines 'mental disorder' broadly. While mental illness, severe mental impairment, mental impairment and psychopathic disorder will become significant in their own right for some purposes, it would be incorrect to view mental disorder as simply the sum of these categories, because the definition also includes 'any other disability or disorder of mind'. Thus any arrested or incomplete development of mind will suffice to render an individual 'mentally disordered', even if there is no resulting aggressive or irresponsible conduct that would bring the individual into the scope of one of the defined mental impairment categories. Similarly, the Court of Protection, which is in charge of assuming control and management of property and affairs of those lacking capacity, is able to take the view that persons with difficulties of short-term memory, spatial or temporal orientation, or reasoning difficulties may be placed under its remit in appropriate circumstances. While medical evidence is required prior to the court assuming jurisdiction, a specifically psychiatric diagnosis is not necessary, as long as a disorder or disability of mind is present.

'Mental disorder' is the gateway definition for a number of provisions of the Act. It is the term used, for example, in s. 2, which allows an individual to be confined for up to 28 days; in s. 5, it allows the formal detention of an individual already in hospital for up to six hours; in s. 6, it allows an individual to be confined for 72 hours on a more summary procedure than that in s. 2; in s. 94, it defines the jurisdiction of the Court of Protection; in s. 131, it allows an individual to be admitted on a voluntary or informal basis to a psychiatric hospital; in s. 135, it allows Justices of the Peace to issue warrants to search for and remove individuals believed to be ill-treated; in s. 136, it allows detention by a police officer for up to 72 hours. Mental disorder is, of course, not the only requirement for the use of these powers, but it is the disorder required for the use of the sections.

Other sections of the Act do not require 'mental disorder', but instead a more specific mental condition. Longer term admissions under s. 3, guardianship under s. 8, criminal confinements under ss. 35 and 37, and transfers from prisons to mental hospitals under s. 47, for example, all require that the individual be suffering from one of four specific types of mental disorder: mental illness; severe mental impairment; mental impairment; psychopathy. Where two doctors are required to certify the disability in these sections, they must identify the same category of disorder: see s. 11(6).

Mental illness is not defined under the Act. Discussion of its nature and possible definition will be discussed in detail below. To understand the discussion of the other categories that follows, however, it is appropriate to say that the courts have held that the words of the statute are not specialist terms. Instead, there is some authority that they are terms of ordinary English usage, to be understood as the reasonable person would understand them.

2.2.2 The mental impairments

'Mental impairment' and 'severe mental impairment' are defined in the statute. The distinction between them is significant primarily because of slightly different requirements for civil confinement beyond the first 28 days. For the former, such longer confinement may only occur if a treatment is available that 'is likely to alleviate or prevent a deterioration of his condition' (s. 3(2)(b)); no comparable requirement is contained in the Act for severe mental impairment.

Both definitions require a 'state of arrested or incomplete development of mind'. The causation of these conditions seems irrelevant: they can be a function of genetic, constitutional, or environmental factors, or be caused by disease of the brain (Hoggett, 1996: 39). That said, the definitions would not be broad enough to include degeneration of or injury to a mind 'occurring after that point usually accepted as complete development' (Department of Health and Welsh Office, 1999: para. 30.5).

The definitions do not cover all such cases, however, but only those where the deficit entails 'impairment of intelligence and social functioning', and is also 'associated with abnormally aggressive or seriously irresponsible conduct' on the part of the individual. It is with these criteria that we begin to see the express use of behaviour to determine whether the Act should apply. Here, the use of these factors seems relatively benign from a civil rights perspective. The behaviour here does not define the impairment; it rather serves to restrict the cases of impaired intelligence where the Act may be invoked. Nonetheless, it does start to raise the question of what the priorities of the Act are, and to hint at its social control functions.

The statutory definitions of mental impairment and severe mental impairment are remarkably similar. The difference appears to be a matter of degree. In the former, the arrested or incomplete development of mind is specifically identified as 'not amounting to severe mental impairment'. The former must include 'significant', and the latter 'severe' impairment of intelligence and social functioning. Clearly, this suggests a difference of degree, but it is not obvious that these adjectives actually add very much to the understanding of or differentiation between the two categories.

The phrases 'impairment of intelligence and social functioning', and 'associated with abnormally aggressive or seriously irresponsible conduct' are distinct, and raise somewhat different sets of issues. The case of *R v Hall* (1988) 86 Cr App R 159 discusses the former phrase in a context slightly removed from the MHA 1983. The case involved a charge of intercourse with a 'defective' (to use the term of the statute), pursuant to s. 7 of the Sexual Offences Act 1956. The defendant, Hall, had been the principal of a special school, where Alison Hames had been a student for two years, between the ages of 16 and 18 years. At the age of 18, Ms. Hames moved to a different institution for those with developmental disabilities. Some 18 months later, Hall went to the new institution, collected Ms. Hames, and brought her to a hotel. There, he encouraged her and assisted her to masturbate. He admitted that they had engaged in similar conduct while she had been under his care, at the special school. The issue was whether Ms. Hames was capable of consenting to this behaviour.

The Sexual Offences Act 1956 held that consent could not be given by a 'defective', defined as 'a person suffering from a state of arrested or incomplete development of mind which includes severe impairment of intelligence and social functioning'. This wording is identical to that contained in the test for severe mental impairment. At issue was the meaning of the word 'severe'. Was severity to be gauged in comparison with the population as a whole, or instead with the population of people with impaired intelligence and social functioning? The court favoured the former (at p. 162):

The words of the phrase 'severe impairment of intelligence and social functioning' are ordinary English words. They are not terms of art. The phrase appears in a section which deprives two classes of person of the capacity to consent, girls under 16 and women who are defectives. It is clearly designed to protect girls under 16 because, albeit normally developed mentally, they are clearly regarded by Parliament as not sufficiently mature to consent to what, consent apart, would be indecent assaults. It is also designed to protect women over 16, if defectives, from exploitation. We can see no reason to suppose that Parliament intended to protect only those who were severely impaired compared with other mentally defective persons, but not those who were severely impaired as compared with normally developed persons. The sections do not say so and, on a natural reading of the words, it is in our view clear that severe impairment is to be measured against the standard of normal persons.

While medical evidence would be admissible to determine an individual's level of intelligence, it had no weight on the question of whether the individual was 'severely' impaired; that was an issue for the jury (p. 162). Indeed, in *R v Robbins* [1988] Crim LR 744, which dealt with a similar issue, a finding of 'severe mental handicap' under s. 1(3), (3A) of the Sexual Offences Act 1967 was made without expert evidence being led at all.

Some commentators take the *Hall* case as a guide to the reading of the MHA 1983 definitions (see, for example, Jones, 2006: 17). The similarity of wording is striking, but the respective contexts should equally be noted. While the purpose of the MHA 1983 is certainly to ensure the protection of people with mental impairments, it also provides them with civil rights, and in determination of those rights, the distinction between mental impairment and severe mental impairment can be significant. For example, those with non-serious mental impairment can only be civilly confined under s. 3 of the Act if treatment is available that 'is likely to alleviate or prevent a deterioration of his condition' (s. 3(2)(b)). This provision does not apply to people with severe mental impairment. The broad reading of 'severe mental impairment' that would follow from an uncritical application of the *Hall* decision would correspondingly limit membership in the class of 'mental impairment', limiting the application of s. 3(2)(b). It may be open for the court in *Hall* to find that Parliament intended to protect all mentally impaired people from indecent assaults; it is difficult to make the parallel argument for the MHA 1983 classes, where Parliament has itself drawn distinctions in the Act. The criminal statutes do not contain a distinction between 'severe' and non-severe classes; the MHA 1983 does, and that perhaps makes a difference. It may still be open to argument that, in the context of the Mental Health Act 1983, the severity of mental impairment should be assessed in comparison with other people with mental disabilities, not with the public at large.

It is appropriate to note in passing the difference between *Hall* and the Code of Practice regarding the issue of medical expertise. *Hall* emphasises the lay determination of the 'severity' of mental impairment; the Code of Practice emphasises the professional role in determinations through multidisciplinary assessments, and direct observation of behaviour (Department of Health and Welsh Office, 1999: paras. 30.4, 30.5). Neither reading can be considered a definitive approach for the interpretation of the MHA 1983: not *Hall* because it is about a criminal law defence, and neither the Code, because it is only issued for guidance on good practice. Nonetheless, it is another example of the ambiguities and uncertainties relating to the role of medical professionals in the interpretation and administration of the Act.

This ambiguity of professional role appears as well in the case of *Re F (Mental Health Act: Guardianship)* [2000] 1 FLR 192, which concerned the second branch of the test for the impairments, abnormally aggressive or seriously irresponsible conduct. That case involved a young woman nearing her 18th birthday. She had lived all of her life, along with seven younger siblings, with her parents in a home where she had allegedly been exposed to chronic neglect, including uncleanliness in the home, sexual abuse by visitors to the home, and that generally flowing from the failure of her parents to provide appropriate standards of parenting. All of the children, including F, were removed from the home under a family law emergency protection order.

The remainder of the children were dealt with through family court wardship proceedings, but because of her age, the local social services decided to apply for a guardianship order for F, under s. 7 of the MHA 1983, an application that would require proof that F was mentally impaired. There was no doubt that she had arrested, or incomplete, development of mind; the question was whether this resulted in aggressive or seriously irresponsible conduct. Social services took the view that F's desire to return home was sufficient to meet this standard.

It is not difficult to see why they took this view. To them, a desire to return to what they clearly perceived as an inadequate home, a home in which abuse was alleged to have taken place, must indeed have appeared irresponsible. The Court of Appeal did not see it that way. The legislative history of the section suggested that the drafters perceived guardianship as a restriction on civil liberties, and this suggested a restrictive reading of the conduct criterion. On this point, the court was not guided by the professionals' view. Instead, it was swayed by F's account of her actions, as reported by the trial judge (p. 196):

What she said to me was that she wanted to go home. Her father is getting old, he is ill and he is dying soon. She has lived with him for 17 years and wants to be with him. She was happy at home, had plenty to do, went to the park. Her mother took her. She had always been with her mother and father and brothers and sisters and wanted to get back.

In the views of both the trial court and the Court of Appeal, this was not irresponsible. There was no question that the social services authorities had acted in good faith and with the best of motives, but their reading of the facts was markedly different from that of F – a reminder of the division between professional and client to which Foucault refers.

The government has indicated its intention to do away with the four-fold categories of mental disorder in favour of a single, all-embracing definition. It will probably closely resemble the definition contained in the 2002 draft bill (cl. 2(6)), which likewise would have abolished the separate categories (Department of Health, 2002d):

"Mental Disorder" means any disability or disorder of mind or brain which results in an impairment of disturbance of mental functioning; and "mentally disordered" is to be read accordingly.

The government has also stated that it will be maintaining the restrictions relating to abnormally aggressive or seriously irresponsible conduct, as they apply to the mental impairments (to be renamed 'learning disability') (Department of Health, 2006a: A1, 2). It is not clear how this will be accomplished. It seems likely that some form of definition of learning disability will have to be included in the new Act. This would suggest that the issues discussed above might not quite be consigned to history. That said, persons lacking capacity might alternatively be dealt with under the terms of the MCA 2005. While not all people with learning disabilities lack capacity, a significant number of people will fall under the jurisdiction of both statutes. No safeguard comparable to those regarding aggressive or irresponsible conduct exists in the MCA 2005. For people lacking capacity, it is therefore not clear how far the conduct criteria will be relevant, because compulsion will be available through the MCA 2005. It is further not clear why the conduct criteria are relevant for learning disability, and not for other disorders that do not fall within that category. This might, for example, mean that a person with mild senility associated with old age would be potentially subject to the MHA 1983, where a similar old person with learning disability would not be. It is not obvious that such a distinction makes sense.

2.2.3 'Psychopathic disorder'

The mental impairments are perhaps the easiest starting points in the discussion of s. 1(2), MHA 1983, because at least everyone agrees that arrested or incomplete development of mind exists in an intellectually coherent fashion. The same cannot be said to be true about the other defined term in the subsection, i.e. psychopathic disorder.

The difficulty with this disorder is that its criteria of definition are not distinct from its behavioural ramifications: abnormally aggressive or seriously irresponsible conduct do not merely characterise the malady; they are indistinguishable from it, at least in current medical understanding. Indeed, the term itself is viewed as outdated by the medical profession, which prefers instead to speak of antisocial or dissocial personality disorder.

In the defining of psychopathy, the image of mental health law as a mechanism of social control is perhaps at its strongest. Some aspects of behaviour or personality are defined as illness, without any obvious mechanism to distinguish them from similar, non-ill traits. Do these individuals fail to conform to fundamental behavioural norms because they are unable, or unwilling, to comply? Mental abnormality is inferred from antisocial behaviour, and antisocial behaviour is explained by mental abnormality, in an apparently sealed loop. An examination of the core criteria defining the condition does little to ease concern about this. Classic characteristics include egoism, immaturity, aggressiveness, low frustration tolerance, and the inability to learn from experience. More recently, Prins lists additional indicators: a 'lacuna of super-ego'; the greater-than-usual need for excitement; a capacity for the creation of chaos among family, friends and carers; thrill-seeking; pathological glibness; antisocial pursuit of power; absence of guilt (1995: 311). The result is hesitation even within the psychiatric community. Prins refers to it (1995: 309) as the 'Achilles heel' of psychiatry, citing Peter Tyrer:

[T]he diagnosis of personality disorder is similar to an income tax form; it is unpleasant and unwanted, but cannot be avoided in psychiatric practice.

As noted above, psychopathy as defined in the 1983 Act requires a mental disorder that results in 'abnormally aggressive or seriously irresponsible conduct'. Consistent with, or perhaps compounding, the ambiguities in the categorisation, the courts are content to view a finding of psychopathy as a hybrid between medical professionals and lay opinion. In *R v Trent MHRT, ex p Ryan* (1991) unreported CA, Nolan LJ said:

No doubt whether the conduct is the result of the disorder is again a medical question. Whether it amounts to seriously irresponsible or abnormally aggressive behaviour seems to me, as Dr Shubsachs himself said in his report, to raise questions other than of a purely clinical nature . . . The fact that medical evidence is involved in the definition is of course in itself no reason why it should not be decided by members of the tribunal in the light of their own expertise and examination of the patient.

At the very least, the approach of the court is expressly normative. As with the distinction between mental impairment and severe mental impairment, the pivotal issue is not a matter of medical expertise.

As noted, the definition of psychopathy requires that the disability 'results in abnormally aggressive or seriously irresponsible conduct' on the part of the person concerned. In *R (P) v MHRT for East Midlands and Northeast Region* [2002] EWCA Civ 697, the appellant continued to show some signs of psychopathy, such as a failure to trust, interpersonal relationship difficulties, impulsivity and a tendency to blame others, but he had not shown the conduct specified in the statutory conditions for several years. The Court of Appeal nonetheless upheld the decision of the Review Tribunal that he continued to be within the definition. Chadwick LJ held (at paras. 43–4):

I accept, of course, that the Tribunal must address the question whether the patient suffers from a persistent disorder or disability of mind which is current at the time when the matter is before them. But I do not accept that the disorder of mind cannot fall within the statutory definition of psychopathic disorder unless that disorder causes him, at that time, to engage in abnormally aggressive or seriously irresponsible conduct.

It is enough, in my view, that the disorder of mind has done so in the past and that there is a real risk that, if treatment in hospital is discontinued, it will do so in the future.

See also Pill LJ at para. 23–7, concurring.

This is a very weak reading of the safeguard contained in the Act, and points up the difficulty of psychopathy as a category without diagnostic criteria distinct from behaviour. If a doctor takes the view that a patient may meet the required threshold of aggression or irresponsibility at some time in the future, what evidence can the patient call in rebuttal?

Psychopathy is handled differently in the different mental health legislation in the UK. It does not exist as a separate category either in Northern Ireland or Scotland. The Northern Ireland Order appears to exclude it entirely, and the best view appears to be that those with the disorder cannot, for example, be civilly confined under that ordinance (see Northern Ireland Order, SI 1986/595 (NI 4); Reed, 1996: 5). Until recently, the Scottish legislation, by comparison, included it by implication in the broader category of mental illness. Section 17(1) of the Mental Health (Scotland) Act 1984 referred specifically to individuals suffering from a mental disorder that 'is a persistent one manifested only by abnormally aggressive or seriously irresponsible conduct'. The implied status is now express. The first statute passed by the new Scottish parliament altered the 1984 definition so that it now explicitly includes personality disorder: Mental Health (Public Safety and Appeals) (Scotland) Act 1999, ASP 1, s. 3. This approach is now reflected in s. 328(1) of the Mental Health (Care and Treatment) (Scotland) Act 2003, asp. 13.

The earlier Scottish approach appears to be favoured by the government in its proposed reforms: personality disorders would be included within the rather general definition of mental disorder, cited in the discussion of the mental impairments above, and subject to the same rules regarding the imposition of compulsory powers as are other mental disorders. This would include a less stringent treatability requirement: compulsory admission to be permitted only when treatment is available that is 'appropriate to the patient's mental disorder and all other circumstances of [his or her] case' (Department of Health, 2006a: A2, 2) (see also 2006 Bill discussed in the preface to this volume).

This is a compromise position. Earlier government proposals to remove the treatability requirement for psychopathy had proven extremely controversial. Clinicians feared that they would become jailers, and since dangerousness is so hard to predict, jailers frequently of those who would commit no crime. Civil libertarians similarly objected that such a change would mandate police powers prior to the commission of an offence. These are serious criticisms, but one must wonder why they should apply to some, but not all, mental disorders. Mental illness, other than personality disorder, contains no treatability test in the MHA 1983, and there has been no objection in principle to the use of compulsory powers over other mentally ill people without treatability being demonstrated, or prior to the commission of a criminal offence. If personality disorder is appropriately understood as a psychiatric disorder, why should it not be subject to the same rules as other forms of mental illness? Is the debate thus really about whether personality disorder and psychopathy is, in fact, a mental illness?

Prior to the reform process, there would appear to have been no consensus, even within the psychiatric community, as to how these cases ought to be dealt with, and what reform, if any, would be appropriate to the English legislation. A survey by Rosemarie Cope of psychiatrists working in regional secure units and special hospitals showed a near-even split as to whether psychopathy should remain within the MHA 1983: 53 per cent in favour and 47 per cent against. Of those proposing removal from the Act, roughly 60 per cent favoured the Scottish system, where psychopathic disorder would be contained within the broader concept of mental illness (Cope, 1993: 217). Nonetheless, roughly 10 per cent of Cope's sample appear to have favoured removal of psychopaths from the Act entirely, presumably resulting in something analogous to the Northern Irish model (1993: 226).

Cope's survey was restricted to forensic psychiatrists, however, and may therefore have been more supportive of a continued use of the concept in the Act. Unlike the pattern in forensic services, diagnoses of personality disorders in general psychiatric settings have been falling off considerably in recent years (Pilgrim and Rogers, 1999: 169). This may be a complex statistic to read, however, because the civil confinement of psychopaths requires the disorder to be treatable, the fall in numbers does not necessarily mean a challenge to a medical paradigm of psychopathy or personality disorder; it may instead reflect a scepticism as to whether people with these disorders are amenable to treatment. This would appear to be a serious question: while some of these people do, apparently, respond to different treatments, there does not seem to be any mechanism to determine what treatment, if any, will be effective on a specific individual (Reed, 1996: 6–7).

2.2.4 Section 1(3): promiscuity, immoral conduct, sexual deviancy and drug dependency

Section 1(3) provides that no person may be dealt with as mentally disordered under the 1983 Act, 'by reason only of promiscuity or other immoral conduct, sexual deviancy or dependence on alcohol or drugs'. This restriction applies both to 'mental disorder' and also to the four specifically enumerated types of mental disorder. The word 'only' is significant: the subsection does not preclude the operation of the Act in cases where the impugned conduct is but one manifestation of a more complex disorder.

This section, as so much of the MHA 1983, must be understood in its historical context. Victorian and Edwardian social policy had, to a considerable degree, been intended to enforce morality, particularly onto the poor and marginal. The public, county lunatic asylums were but one mechanism to this end. In addition, the Inebriates Act 1898, ss. 1 and 2 allowed the detention for up to three years in reformatories of habitual drunkards and those committing serious crimes while drunk. While originally conceptualised in terms of moral control, the first decade of implementation saw the role of inebriate regulation increasingly in psychiatric terms (Zedner, 1991: 259–63). A similar ambiguity between socially inappropriate behaviour and institutional control may be seen in the subsequent Mental Deficiency Act 1913, where 'feeble-mindedness' was not clearly distinguished from immoral behaviour. Feeble-minded, unmarried woman giving birth while on poor relief, for example, were to be subjected to confinement in an asylum (Mental Deficiency Act 1913, s. 2(b)(vi)) and there are indications that some local authorities required little further proof of mental status, once the fact of the birth on poor relief was discovered (Zedner, 1991: 275).

The MHA 1959 can be seen as introducing a sea change in this regard, by introducing an earlier version of the current s. 1(3). In part, this can be understood as the continuation of a reconceptualisation of the role of regulation and institutions for the insane, away from overt control and towards a more medicalised vision of treatment. The fact that the impugned behaviour is not of itself sufficient evidence of mental disorder does not make the behaviour acceptable. If the behaviour in question constitutes a crime, as much of the behaviour in the scope of s. 1(3) may, it will instead be categorised as criminal. The express addition in 1983 of drug dependency to the conduct that does not, of itself, indicate mental disorder provides a good example of this new ambiguity. The express removal of drug dependency from the definition of mental disorder does not normalise the behaviour in question, because people are still convicted of drug-related crimes in considerable numbers. In understanding the effect of the section, and the scope of the definitions in s. 1 as a whole, the issue may well not be simply the distinction between mentally disordered as opposed to non-disordered behaviour; it may be the choice of category of deviance, the choice between mad or bad.

The government intends to remove the exclusions in so far as they refer to promiscuity and other immoral conduct, on the basis that these are not mental disorders. In its view, their inclusion is obsolete. The exclusion based on sexual deviancy will also be removed, apparently because it is misunderstood: people are being refused treatment because their underlying disorder manifests itself as sexual deviance (Department of Health, 2006a: A1, 3). The government is quick to deny that homosexuality will be included as a mental disorder as a result of this change. Sexual deviance based on personality disorder may prove more problematic, because, as we have seen, personality disorder is not readily distinguishable from the conduct it entails. It is not obvious, for example, whether paedophilia will be perceived as a manifestation of personality disorder, or simply as bad conduct. The exclusion based on dependence on alcohol or drugs is to remain, since the government takes the view that misuse of such substances is not a mental disorder. This exclusion is to be reworded to make it clear that people who are dependent on such substances are not precluded from treatment for other mental disorders, even if those disorders are related to their substance abuse.

The leading case on the current subsection is *R v MHRT, ex p Clatworthy* [1985] 3 All ER 699. That case involved a man convicted in 1967 of two counts of indecent assault involving inappropriate touching of young girls. On the basis of this conduct, which represented part of a pattern of similar behaviour, he was diagnosed as having a psychopathic disorder. He remained in a secure hospital for 18 years, whereupon his doctors concluded that he could no longer be detained, on the basis that the sole justification for his confinement was his sexually deviant behaviour towards young girls. As it was a confinement under the criminal jurisdiction of the mental health legislation, however, they could only recommend his release, and the review tribunal with the actual decision-making authority did not follow their advice, providing only the barest of reasons for its decision. Clatworthy sought judicial review.

The facts of the case provide a hint of some of the other dynamics of decision-making in this sort of situation. Clatworthy had been confined under the MHA 1959, which contained a provision substantively similar to s. 1(3) of the 1983 Act (MHA 1959, s. 4(5)). While that section refered only to 'promiscuity or other immoral conduct', rather than sexual deviance specifically, it is nonetheless difficult to see that the 1959 phrase is not wide enough to encompass the inappropriate touching. If the doctors in 1985 were serious in their view that this conduct had been the only justification for confinement, it is open to be asked why this objection had not occurred to them 18 years previously.

The issues before the court were not limited to the scope of s. 1(3), but also included an issue as to the adequacy of reasons provided by the tribunal: see Chapter 8. On this latter point, Clatworthy was successful and the case was remitted to the tribunal. Perhaps for this reason, the court is somewhat coy in its treatment of the former point, suggesting, but not expressly making, a finding based on a rather fine distinction (pp. 701–2):

It may at once be observed that the effect of sub-s. (3) is apparently to prevent there being a condition of psychopathic disorder when the abnormally aggressive or seriously irresponsible conduct consequent on the persistent disorder or disability of mind is conduct which is a manifestion of sexual deviancy. It may also be observed that it can be contended that sexual deviancy does not mean tendency to deviation but means indulgence in deviation. That contention would achieve support from its context, the context being promiscuity or other immoral conduct and dependence on alcohol or drugs.

The suggestion would seem to be that the tendency, a sexual attraction to children, may be outside the scope of s. 1(3), but that the conduct, the inappropriate touching of little girls, is covered by the section. The suggestion seems to be that one may treat the sinner, but not the sin.

If tendency is theoretically distinct from behaviour and s. 1(3) were to apply only to the latter, however, it would presumably be the case that an individual could be brought within the scope of the Act if they were to have the tendency to behave in one of the ways enumerated by s. 1(3), even if they were never, in fact, to have acted on that tendency. Thus, to have paedophiliac desires would justify the invocation of the Act, even if the desires had never been acted upon. Can it really have been the intent of the legislature that a desire to drink alcohol to excess could be taken into account in understanding an individual as mentally disordered, even if the individual were, in fact, teetotal? Or that a desire to behave promiscuously might be taken into account even if the individual were to remain chaste?

Such a reading would seem to fly in the face of the historical context of the provision, discussed above. There was no distinction in the framing or implementation of the earlier legislation between the behaviour and the tendency, and confinement in the facilities in question was to curb the tendency as much as the behaviour. Thus Zedner notes that nineteenth-century advocates justified detention of inebriates for up to three years in reformatories 'in order to keep them away from drink long enough to fortify their will to abstain' (1991: 232). The objective was to create moral character, to remodel the individual, not merely to control behaviour (1991: 237, 241–5). It was this sort of violation of liberty that s. 1(3) was to address; if the distinction between tendency and behaviour is adopted, however, it would seem instead to have paved the way for a more expansive violation of the individual's freedom. The earlier legislation at least required the individual actually to have engaged in the specified activity, i.e. to be a habitual drunkard or to engage in immoral sex, for example.

The distinction between tendency and behaviour is in any event problematic, because mental disorders do not comfortably divide from the behaviours that characterise them. Psychopathy is perhaps the paradigmatic example: the condition is defined by the behaviour. This difficulty is acknowledged by the court in *Clatworthy*, in its criticism of the reasons provided by the tribunal (at p. 703):

The grounds for the reasons invite immediately the question: what are the features of psychopathic disorder as defined by the 1983 Act apart from sexual deviancy? The evidence as I read it is that there is no other feature and sexual deviancy is to be discounted under the Act.

In so far as this is the case, the distinction between behaviour and tendency ceases to be meaningful, and in such cases, s. 1(3) should be read as precluding the application of the Act.

Is the distinction between tendency and behaviour defensible based on the statutory wording itself? Does the subsection really refer to behaviour as distinct from tendency? The wording as it relates to promiscuity, other immoral conduct, or sexual deviancy may be at least arguably consistent with the comment of the court, but the phrase 'dependence on alcohol or drugs' is more problematic. The conduct that attaches to this phrase is presumably drunkenness and the actual ingestion of drugs. 'Dependence' on such substances would appear instead to refer not merely to the conduct, but also to the tendency to engage in the conduct in question. This distinction is made expressly in the Mental Health (Care and Treatment) (Scotland) Act 2003, which refers to 'dependence on, or use of' alcohol or drugs (s. 328(2)). If this is a meaningful distinction, it would have to be asked whether it was really the intention of the legislature to refer only to conduct in some of the subsection and to conduct plus tendency elsewhere, without express indication of what is, in the end, a very fine distinction.

It may, nonetheless, be inappropriate to dismiss the distinction too quickly, because it is, in a different sense, consistent with a continuing reconceptualisation of the realm of mental health law away from simple control of behaviour, towards the cure of the individual. The problems to be faced no longer centre on physical control, but instead on remedying a condition. Institutions are to be about treatment, not about simple detention; psychiatrists are to be understood as doctors, not as jailers. It would be consistent with this approach to distinguish between tendency and conduct in the definition section of the Act.

The control of the tendency requires, of course, very different mechanisms from the control of conduct. The tradition has been to view this as a benevolent shift, with physical control associated with a particularly miserable existence for the insane person, and medicalisation with humanitarianism and liberation. Certainly, the intrusiveness of physical confinement ought not to be underappreciated. At the same time, the intrusiveness of the newer techniques has its critics. For Michel Foucault, for example, the move to new forms of control of madness is problematic. For Foucault, this theme of intrusive control of the mind of the individual is consistent from the beginning of nineteenth-century psychiatry. Traditional medical history had accorded the Tukes of York with accolades as great liberators of the insane, for their pioneering work in removing physical restraint from patients at the beginning of the nineteenth century. Foucault's view of this move is much more circumspect (1965: 247):

In fact Tuke created an asylum where he substituted for the free terror of madness the stifling anguish of responsibility; fear no longer reigned on the other side of the prison gates, it now raged under the seals of conscience. Tuke now transferred the age-old terrors in which the insane had been trapped to the very heart of madness. The asylum no longer punished the madman's guilt, it is true; but it did more, it organized that guilt; it organized it for the madman as a consciousness of himself, and as a non-reciprocal relation to the keeper; it organized it for the man of reason as an awareness of the Other, a therapeutic intervention in the madman's existence.

In this vision, where the old ways controlled physically, the new control through imposing self-restraint on the individual, alters the way the insane perceive themselves. Where the old ways left the thoughts and feelings of the individual essentially private, the new used his or her altered self-perception as a method of control.

2.3 'Mental illness'

As we have seen, the MHA 1983 sometimes requires one of the four specific categories of mental disorder, i.e. mental illness, severe mental impairment, mental impairment or psychopathy, to be specified. Mental illness has a particular importance among the four, simply because of the frequency of its use. In 2001–2, roughly 98 per cent of the people detained for treatment under s. 3 of the Act were categorised as mentally ill (Department of Health, 2002c: 6).

The term is not further defined by the Act. Once again, the case law and official information are ambiguous and inconsistent regarding how the term is to be read, and the degree of professional involvement in its interpretation. A memorandum provided by the Department of Health states that the term's 'operational definition and usage is a matter for clinical judgment in each case' (Department of Health and Welsh Office, 1998: para. 10). This would suggest that it is a medical matter, to be interpreted by doctors in a medical framework.

This is difficult to reconcile with the case law, such as it is. The leading case, W v L [1974] QB 711, involved a man who engaged in sadistic behaviour towards animals. There was clear evidence that the man suffered from a psychopathic disorder, but at that time the MHA 1959, in effect, allowed only relatively young psychopaths to be confined. The man was over the relevant age, and was therefore unable to be confined on that basis. One of the issues, therefore, was whether he could also be understood to suffer from 'mental illness'. The majority of the Court of Appeal found that evidence of unusual performance on an electroencephalogram (EEG) indicated that he was also suffering from mental illness. It is however the minority judgment of Lawton LJ that has attracted the bulk of the attention. His Lordship interpreted the words 'mental illness' as plain English (at p. 719):

The words are ordinary words of the English language. They have no particular medical significance. They have no particular legal significance. How should the court construe them? The answer in my judgment is to be found in the advice which Lord Reid recently gave in Cozens v Brutus [1973] AC 854, 861, namely, that ordinary words of the English language should be construed in the way that ordinary sensible people would construe them. That being, in my judgment, the right test, then I ask myself, what would the ordinary sensible person have said about the patient's condition in this case if he had been informed of his behaviour to the dogs, the cat and his wife? In my judgment such a person would have said: 'Well, the fellow is obviously mentally ill.' If that be right, then, although the case may fall within the definition of 'psychopathic disorder' . . . it also falls within the classification of 'mental illness'; and there is the added medical fact that when the E.E.G. was taken there were indications of a clinical character showing some abnormality of the brain. It is that application of the sensible person's assessment of the condition, plus the medical indication, which in my judgment brought the case within the classification of mental illness and justified the finding of the county court judge.

This passage has been read as emphasising a lay interpretation of mental illness. Brenda Hale, for example, rather pointedly refers to it as the 'man-must-be-mad' test (Hoggett, 1996: 32). Michael Cavadino (1991: 299–300) has criticised the test on the basis that it assumes a known and consistent view among lay people as to what mental illness is. He argues that it, in fact, has a medical usage, drawing into question Lawton LJ's statement that it has 'no particular medical significance', and that it is based on an assessment of behaviour rather than on mental condition. He also stresses that Lawton LJ was in the minority, and therefore the legal status of the test is suspect.

Some criticisms of the test are undoubtedly justified. Would the reasonable person on the street view an individual engaged in abnormally aggressive or seriously irresponsible conduct as mentally ill? If so, and the point seems at least arguable, psychopathy becomes its own subcategory of mental illness: all people with 'psychopathic disorder' are also 'mentally ill'. This does not seem far-fetched, because it represents the situation under the Scottish legislation, as we have seen. But it cannot be the legislative intent in England, however, because the statute sometimes provides different conditions for the application of the Act to the two classes; the relevance of these different provisions to psychopaths would be nullified if they might simply and alternatively be categorised as mentally ill.

At the same time, the test is not entirely inconsistent with the approach of the courts to psychopathy and the mental impairments, discussed above. As in those cases, medical expertise is acknowledged, but the decision regarding whether the medical facts are sufficient to satisfy the standard in the Act is a matter that is not restricted to clinical judgment. Such a hybrid approach admittedly fits more easily into the express definitions of those other disorders, where the issues of degree to which the lay view attaches are expressly spelled out in the statute, but a move from such a hybrid view for mental illness begs the question of why medical views should be definitive for that category, but not for the other categories, of mental disorder. Consistency might alternatively be achieved if lay views were removed from the determination of all four subcategories of mental disorder; in that event, the question arises as to whether we are content to place extraordinary powers over individual rights in the hands of one profession, no matter how well intentioned.

The use of a purely medical approach to the administration of the disorder definitions in the Act is problematic for a variety of reasons. The first question is *which* medical approach? There are two primary medical nosologies of mental illness. The one in use primarily in North America is the Diagnostic and Statistical Manual of Disorders, currently in its fourth edition (DSM-IV-TR), published by the American Psychiatric Association. Most of the rest of the world relies primarily on the World Health Organisation standard, the International Classification of Diseases and Related Health Problems, currently in its tenth edition (ICD-10), which contains a classification of mental disorders in Chapter 5.

While converging in format, ICD-10 and DSM-IV are not yet identical, and their content is determined both by cultural specificities and by administrative momentum of the respective formulating organisations (Kendell, 1991). The content reflects political issues and approaches within these organisations: the framers of DSM-IV were criticised by some feminists, from within and outside of the medical professions, for advocating the inclusion of self-defeating personality disorder and premenstrual dysphoric disorder in the nosology, because the classifications were perceived to pathologise women. A rather pointed account of the internal political wrangles of the American Psychiatric Association in the formulation of DSM-IV, and in particular regarding the continued inclusion of these two categories, can be found in Caplan

(1995). The internal administrative tensions she documents serve as a salient reminder that, as discussed in the previous chapter, mental health law is never far from a collection of other complex interests.

Even viewed in its most sympathetic light, the use of these purely medical criteria in a legal context is problematic. Classification systems such as DSM-IV and ICD-10 can be seen as having a variety of objectives: they promote a unified nomenclature for professionals active in research or diagnosis, to ensure consistency in medical professional discourses and practice; they define the direction of those professional discourses, by determining the disorders to be studied (see Boyle, 1990: 4). Neither was designed as a mechanism to determine appropriateness of legal intervention.

Doctors and other medical professionals develop the medical model of mental illness with the objective of providing cures, or, at the very least, alleviating undesirable effects of conditions. Severity of disorder, for example, is not necessarily a factor in development of that approach. Just as we would expect a doctor to treat minor, as well as major, physical ailments, so psychiatry is appropriately concerned with conditions of varying degrees of severity. This search for causes and cures is quite a different project from that of the Act, which may concern appropriateness of intervention, sanctioned by the state and over the objection of the subject. Certainly, the Act requires other legal requirements to be met before these powers can be invoked, but the question remains: is there any obvious reason to use a system developed to promote cure, in the rather different context of rights determination? Are these not simply two separate projects?

A variety of theoretical problems also lie at the root of the medical model of mental illness, which at least arguably suggests that we should embrace it in a legal context only with considerable hesitation. The medical paradigm comes wrapped in a scientific cloak, suggesting objectivity, reliability, and a confirmed basis in physical reality. There is an irony to this public perception, because few pure scientists would characterise their work in such pristine terms (see, e.g., Bird, 1998). For them, science is more likely to be understood as a collection of hypotheses, which explain phenomena to a greater or lesser degree. This may well fit the medical model of mental illness, but its more modest claims equally serve to undermine the desirability of the model in a legal context: should we really be removing rights on the basis of hypotheses?

While a medical model of mental illness would generally suggest a physical cause of a disorder, such causes are generally at best disputed, and often entirely unknown in practice. Often, there will be no test of a mental disorder, in the way in which an X-ray may reveal a broken bone. Instead, diagnosis will initially be through patient symptoms, that is, the history as reported by the individual. These will be supplemented by signs, indications actually witnessed by the doctor. In neither case is this likely to involve identifiable physical abnormalities, but instead behaviours or phenomena. For major disorders, these may involve things such as hallucinations, the patient's belief in things that are profoundly unlikely, such as that the individual is being controlled telepathically, or that the individual is abnormally frightened or depressed without cause. The individual may be behaving or threatening to behave in a way that self-damages, as in the case of a person with a personality disorder who wishes to self-mutilate, or an anorectic patient refusing food. The use of phenomena in this way is both theoretically and practically problematic. Why are these phenomena associated with a disease model at all, when the physical disorder that is central to that paradigm is often unknown?

The absence of objective tests further risks rendering the diagnoses self-fulfilling: individuals believed to have a specific form of disorder will have their behaviour used to confirm that diagnosis. Thus, the hallucinations and delusions that are at the base of psychotic disorders such as schizophrenia may alternatively be caused by known physical factors such as toxic reactions. While good doctors may consider this possibility, the risk is that the doctor working in a psychiatric facility, and therefore expecting to see psychiatric disorders, may diagnose schizophrenia and further inquiry will not be conducted, because, for schizophrenia, there is no further test.

Indeed, once an expectation of psychiatric disorder is raised, all sorts of behaviour may be viewed through a pathological lens to justify that conclusion further. In Rosenhan's study (1973), a variety of sane people gained admission to psychiatric facilities. Rosenhan's paper discusses the fate of these 'pseudo-patients'. To gain admission, they attended at the facility and complained (disingenuously) of hearing unfamiliar voices; the message of the voices was often unclear, but as far as could be understood, they said 'empty', 'hollow', and 'thud'. No further falsifications to the patient's personal history were made. Gaining admission was apparently not a problem, perhaps unsurprisingly because they were describing psychotic delusions, and in almost all cases, a diagnosis of schizophrenia was reached. The falsity of the presenting symptoms was not open to be discovered, of course, because there was no additional, objective test for schizophrenia: symptoms, as described by the patient, are all the doctor has to go on.

What is perhaps more unnerving in the present context is the pathologisation of behaviour on the ward, and of the patient's history. Relationships with parents were reinterpreted and, in Rosenhan's view, distorted to match the existing psychodynamic theories. Aggression was understood as a sign of the continuance of the disorder, never as flowing from heavy-handed or marginalising behaviour by an attendant, nurse or doctor. Even arriving at the cafeteria early for lunch was reformulated by a psychiatrist in one case as indicating the 'oral-acquisitive nature' of the disorder (Rosenhan, 1973: 253). Such reinterpretation to justify existing conclusions is well-known in the sociological literature, both in medical contexts and beyond (see, for example, Garfinkel and Bittner, 1967; Smith, 1990). The fact that this makes diagnoses difficult to falsify ought to give cause for pause, however, when legal controls and compulsions result.

2.4 Schizophrenia: a case study

Schizophrenia provides a case study to examine these problems, although much of what will be discussed in this context will apply, by analogy, to other psychiatric disorders. It is selected here because its nature and the applicability of a medical model to its understanding are matters of current debate, discussed in a variety of sources readily accessible to students (for example, Thomas, 1997; Boyle, 1990; Wing, 1988; Bentall *et al.*, 1988; 1988a). Its significance should not be understated: it is one of the most frequent diagnoses under the Act, and serves as a paradigm in many people's minds for what mental illness is.

Contrary to popular usage, schizophrenia does not, in the overwhelming number of cases, have to do with a so-called 'split personality'. It is instead a psychotic disorder: fundamental to its nature is a fractured relationship to reality. This is typically manifest in hallucinations, particularly hearing voices. An interference in the thinking process is common (i.e. 'delusions'), where the individual believes that others are controlling their thoughts, or know what they are thinking. Similarly, a loss of autonomy may be experienced, where strange physical sensations may be felt, or movements occur, without the patient's will. A lack of emotional engagement with surroundings, poverty of or minimal speech, lack of drive, lack of pleasure, and poor attention may also appear, generally gradually over a longer period than the earlier symptoms.

Schizophrenia is thus diagnosed solely according to symptoms as reported by the patient and observed behaviours. Two separate concepts should be identified in moving from these indicators to a diagnosis. The first is 'reliability': is the medical definition of the disorder clear enough that individuals will be categorised accurately, no matter who is doing the assessment? The second is 'validity', whether the definition actually relates to anything in reality. The difference can be illustrated by using David Pilgrim's example of Santa Claus (1995). We all know the characteristics of Santa Claus: delivers goodies on Christmas Eve from a sleigh drawn by reindeer; white beard; red coat; black boots; unrepentant pipe smoker, etc. We would all know him if we saw him; the definition is reliable. But it does not mean Santa Claus exists; the definition is not in that sense valid.

The reliability of schizophrenia diagnosis has been problematic in the past (Bentall *et al.*, 1988: 305–6). Practice may be improving in this regard. Both the ICD and DSM criteria have become more specific in determining when a diagnosis of schizophrenia can be made. With the development of ICD-10 and DSM-IV, diagnostic criteria are converging, although there are still some differences (see Gelder *et al.*, 1996: 257–9). Increased reliability does not, however, settle the issue of whether the definition actually refers to anything or whether, like Santa Claus, it is a definition devoid of validity.

The causal theories relating to schizophrenia are various, and span genetic, biochemical and social factors. The genetic studies are summarised by Thomas (1997: 31–6). If genetics were the cause of schizophrenia, one would expect the identical twin of a schizophrenic also to have the disorder, because identical twins have the same genetic code. Studies do indicate a much higher probability of this occurring. Thomas cites a study by McGue *et al.*, showing first cousins of people diagnosed as schizophrenic as having a 1.6 per cent chance of developing the disorder, where identical twins of schizophrenics have a 44.3 per cent chance (Thomas, 1997: 33, citing McGue *et al.*, 1985). The difference is indeed suggestive, but hardly conclusive. Certainly, the probabilities of schizophrenia in the identical twin of a schizophrenic are impressively high, but as Thomas points out, one could equally argue the inverse: notwithstanding identical genetic codes, less than half of identical twins of schizophrenics go on to develop the disorder. While there would consequently appear to be a genetic susceptibility, it is not clear whether the triggers in development of the actual disorder are genetic or environmental (Gelder *et al.*, 1996: 268–9). Further, the mode of inheritance is unknown (1996: 280). It is thus obvious that genetics are not the whole story.

Biochemical factors are similarly problematic. The most popular theory is that schizophrenia results from an oversupply of a chemical called dopamine in the brain. This view is not without support. Certainly, neuroleptic medication can assist in the control of symptoms in at least some patients, and this medication would appear to affect dopamine levels. The fact that chemical treatments can control the manifestations of a disorder does not, however, necessarily mean that the disorder itself is biochemically caused. During the press attention and legal proceedings following the disclosure of her relationship with US President, Bill Clinton, Monica Lewinsky admitted to feeling depressed and taking medication to control that depression. The medication may well have helped her; it is not a reason to adopt a biochemical model to understand the causes of her depression.

The first neuroleptics pre-date the dopamine theory: they were discovered to work before the dopamine theory was developed. At least arguably, the theory can be seen to account for the efficacy of the drug, rather than the drug being developed to match a separate theory (Thomas, 1997: 125). Drug efficacy is an awkward measure to use in any event. Not everyone receives the beneficial effects (see Pilgrim and Rogers, 1999). Further, the beneficial effects are not limited to schizophrenia, but also occur in mania. This suggests a more complex picture than simple causation based on dopamine imbalance.

Beyond the issue of drug efficacy, the theory has, at best, mixed empirical and experimental support (Thomas, 1997: 38). While post-mortem studies of the brains of people who had schizophrenia show an increase in dopamine, this may be the result of antipsychotic medication (Gelder *et al.*, 1996: 274). Thus Gelder *et al.* state that, while 'the evidence that dopamine is central to the action of antipsychotic drugs is strong, evidence for the corollary – that dopamine neurotransmission is abnormal in schizophrenia – is weak' (1996: 274).

Neurodevelopment models of schizophrenia also exist (Thomas, 1997: 39–44). Here, the idea is that for any of a variety of reasons, whether maternal illness, birth injury, genetics or other factor, an abnormality in the brain occurs, and schizophrenia is the result. This, like the genetic factors discussed above, seems to apply for a subgroup of the schizophrenic population.

The remaining models are medical theories. Even those relatively devoted to a medical model of schizophrenia acknowledge that the cause is unknown (e.g. Frith, 1994). Validity cannot be shown. While that may give cause for pause, a lack of evidence does not necessarily bespeak a negative: the inability to demonstrate validity does not necessarily mean that the definition is invalid. Should we continue to rely on it, notwithstanding its questionable validity?

The continued utility of the concept in a research context has been disputed. Mary Boyle, for example, applies the work of Imre Lakatos on the philosophy of science to claim that schizophrenia has outlived its usefulness (Boyle, 1994). Her argument is considerably more sophisticated than a claim that a theory needs to explain all evidence. It is instead acknowledged that theories require adjustment in the face of new or inconsistent evidence. The theory is still helpful in a research context if these adjustments are 'content increasing'; if not, the theory itself is open to question. In other words, if adjusting the theory to cope with anomalies actually provides new information or insights, the theory remains useful; if it is merely making excuses for its anomalies, it is no longer helpful.

Boyle suggests that, on such criteria, the concept of schizophrenia ought to be abandoned. In her view, the current research into the disorder is not producing new and helpful knowledge, but rather getting mired in its own contradictions. While she acknowledges increasing definitional rigour has increased reliability of diagnosis, she argues that this does nothing to address whether the disorder, as defined, will be valid. She is critical of the research attempting to move towards validation, again on the basis that it is failing to produce new insights. Thus she criticises the theory that schizophrenia is a result of brain dysfunction on the basis that research has not been able to identify which part of the brain is at issue, and on the basis of the lack of evidence that any schizophrenic people suffered from brain dysfunction prior to treatment. The finding by proponents of schizophrenia that it may have multiple causes is criticised on the basis that these causes have not been identified, notwithstanding considerable empirical investigation. Boyle similarly sees the suggestion that schizophrenia is actually a collection of many subtypes as problematic: they have, in her view, never been convincingly identified (Boyle, 1994: 402).

Needless to say, such views are extremely controversial. They are nonetheless important for the student to consider, lest there be an unjustified sense that the medical conceptualisation of mental illness is somehow accepted or uncontroversial among the experts. Indeed, it is perhaps appropriate to note that some of the most radical critiques of concepts of mental illness have come from practitioners, or at least those with practice experience, themselves. Obvious examples include Thomas Szasz, R.D. Laing, and Michel Foucault.

The search for validation of the concept of schizophrenia can be understood in professional terms: geneticists, neurologists, and medical biochemists each attempting to find an explanation for the condition, based on the training they have received and the intellectual structures of their subdisciplines. Social scientists have made similar enquiries, based on social science methodologies. Reflecting the history of social science research generally, social causes, social reactions, and social constructions of schizophrenia have all been identified. For reviews of the literature, see Thomas (1997: 51–6), Pilgrim and Rogers (1999: 11–20).

Regarding social causes, sociologists have identified class, poverty, and social disintegration as correlatives of schizophrenia. Because schizophrenia is geographically centred in inner cities, sociological debate developed around the question of whether it is caused by increased stress in such environments. The alternative explanation, of course, is that the onset of schizophrenia precipitated a fall in socio-economic status, resulting in a disproportionate move by people with the disorder to the inner cities.

Similarly, sociologists have looked at the ways in which people react to behaviour, labelling it as deviant. The issue here is how people become defined or understood as 'deviant': again, a subject considered by sociologists regarding psychiatric patients at about the same time it was considered for prisoners and other 'deviant' classes. The study here was of patient 'careers', beginning with the way an individual became identified as insane. The argument was that this occurred when professionals identified these individuals as failing to conform appropriately to their appropriate social roles. Once they became so identified, the individuals then moved on to conform to the new role, the 'person with mental illness' role, to which the professional had now assigned them, adopting behaviours and attitudes that were expected of them in this new situation. The work of Erving Goffman (1961), which will be considered more thoroughly in the next chapter, provides a particularly good example of such an approach, carried from the stage of diagnosis or identification into the adoption of the role by the individual. The Rosenhan study (1973), discussed above, is a further example of this: 'illness' was created in the interaction with the professionals. For a view that challenges Rosenhan on some of his conclusions, see Spitzer (1976).

2.5 Cautionary tales?

What are we to make of all this, for purposes of legal regulation? Scholars challenging schizophrenia as a concept do not necessarily argue that people diagnosed with schizophrenia are 'really' just like everyone else. As Boyle points out, challenging an existing paradigm is not to deny the existence of the phenomena that it is intended to explain (Boyle, 1990: 193):

It is not claimed that some people do not behave in strange and disturbing ways or have disturbing experiences. Nor is it claimed that these behaviours and experiences may not cause considerable distress, that they may not be preceded by changes in brain chemistry or that they may not be altered by certain drugs. What is challenged is the current interpretation of these phenomena; the usefulness of 'schizophrenia' or any of its sub-types as an inference from them.

This is all well and good, but it does not provide much assistance in a legal context.

Boyle goes on to provide interesting suggestions on how research might be conducted in the future, but does not purport to analyse how legal intervention and regulation should proceed. In her view, the use of the concept as a basis for legal regulation is problematic, not only because of the claimed unscientific nature of schizophrenia, but also because science cannot be expected to perform what are essentially moral tasks relating to decisions about when intervention is appropriate. She does argue that '[a]cceptance of its [schizophrenia's] non-scientific status, however, might at least help to make clear the need to articulate and radically rethink the assumptions and practices surrounding the law as it relates to bizarre behaviour' (Boyle, 1990: 194).

It would, indeed, be a radical rethink, because law prides itself on its rationality, and its objectivity. The attachment of law to a medical approach can be seen in this light: with the use of a 'scientific' paradigm, the law can use standards that at least appear neutral. If intrusive intervention such as physical confinement and the removal of other civil rights is to be justified, it must be done according to clear and objective criteria. Scientific or medical frameworks are one, but not necessarily the only, approach that yields such apparent objectivity. Thus the insanity defence, for example, will often, in practice, include expert medical testimony, but the test remains (in simple terms) whether the accused understood that the actions in question were wrong, a matter that is not essentially medical (see Chapter 6). Intervention in anticipation of future events is more difficult to structure without reference to some scientific characterisation of the individual. Thus we acknowledge suicide as within the rights of an individual, but would tend to hesitate before allowing a person with a mental illness to commit suicide, if the suicide were thought to be a manifestation of the disorder. Without some form of scientific base, how are we to distinguish these two cases?

At the same time, the problems remain. The apparent neutrality of the medical model may mask inequalities. As we shall see in Chapter 4, people of Afro-Caribbean origin are markedly statistically over-represented in mental health admissions. There is hot dispute about whether this represents a real, higher incidence of a medical disorder, or whether instead the apparent neutrality of the medical paradigm is masking discriminatory implementation. Black people are also over-represented throughout the criminal and policing system; does the supposed neutrality of the medical model protect such over-representation in the psychiatric system from appropriate scrutiny? Similarly, different diagnoses are reflected in differing proportions in people of different genders. Thus women are considerably more likely to be diagnosed with depressive disorders, senile and presenile dementia, and neurotic disorders than are men; men are somewhat more likely to attract diagnoses of schizophrenia, and alcoholism or alcohol psychosis (Pilgrim and Rogers, 1999: 42). Such statistics are not necessarily inconsistent with true neutrality of the model. The increased incidence of senile and presenile dementia may, in part, be explained by the statistically shorter life span of men, which is likely to affect the incidence of a disorder that tends to occur late in life. At the same time, fierce debate continues to exist about how women are characterised by the mental health system.

The difficulty remains as to how a medical model can formulate what is, in the end, a social choice both of what constitutes an illness or disorder, and when intervention or differential treatment is warranted. Homosexuality provides an instructive illustration. It is an interesting example, because this is a case where the psychiatric profession, along with society as a whole, simply decided that something that had been understood as an illness in the past would no longer be considered in pathological terms.

In many ways, theories of homosexuality have mirrored, and continue to mirror, theories of mental illness. In both cases, there have been genetic, physical, and environmental explanations of behaviour that is statistically abnormal. Like mental disorders, homosexuality was for years treated with drugs, psychotherapy, or electrical aversion therapy in psychiatric environments, with ambiguous claims to success. Notwithstanding its disease-like status in scientific terms and this history of treatment, it was decided that an illness model was no longer appropriate. A certain type of behaviour that had previously indicated a mental illness would no longer do so, emphasising the social nature of the whole project of mental illness. In the USA, the matter was decided by vote of the American Psychiatric Association, in 1974. It was not until the introduction of ICD-10 in 1993, 19 years later, that it disappeared from the WHO classification.

It may well be that many psychiatrists in this country had not considered homosexuality a mental illness for years before that time. While that may be relevant for the day-to-day human rights and dignity of gay and lesbian people, it raises a different set of problems for mental health law, policy and regulation, because it suggests that professionals use criteria other than the medical standards to determine who is or is not mentally ill. If professionals are making such individualistic decisions, in what sense is the scientific or medical paradigm being relied on? Are we not left with doctors making individual choices as to what qualifies as an illness, and when intervention is appropriate? If they are expanding beyond the criteria provided in their professional taxonomies, is there any reason that their views should be given particular credence?

Homosexuality also provides an important example of how old ideas die hard. The topic is still frequently raised in chapters relating to sexual disorders in psychiatric texts (see, e.g., Cohen and Hart, 1995: 364–5; Goldberg *et al.*, 1994: 273–4). In the first text, Cohen and Hart expressly recognise that homosexuality is not a disorder under ICD-10. While Goldberg *et al.*, in a text directed to general practitioners, make no reference to treatment or cure, they equally do not specifically note that the condition is not a disorder, and its discussion is placed between transsexualism and sexual disorders of adult life, both conditions that may call for medical intervention or assistance. In their discussion of the causes of homosexuality, Goldberg *et al.* do not merely cite genetic, biochemical and parental role models; in addition, they indicate that 'effeminate' boys are likely to become homosexual, and suggest that boys lacking confidence about their masculinity may be unattractive to the opposite sex, 'so that the adolescent enters the rather less competititive homosexual world' (Goldberg *et al.*, 1994: 274). It is difficult to see that this description matches the experiences of gay men. Instead, it would appear to reinforce historical images of gay men as morally weak and social failures – hardly the imagery of equality and respect that is reflected by the modern political agenda.

The older, pathological conceptions of homosexuality continue to influence current practice. Gay and lesbian psychiatric patients speak not merely of overt discriminatory behaviour in the mental health services, but also of how their sexuality is likely to be used to explain their mental health difficulties. In a survey by MIND in 1997, half of gay and lesbian users of mental health services surveyed were told they would have fewer problems if they tried to alter their sexuality. The continued view of sexuality as a mental health problem is perhaps unsurprising, because homosexual experiences may attract particular attention in textbook instructions on good practice in taking patient histories. Thus, while Cohen and Hart specifically disclaim homosexuality per se as a disorder under ICD-10 (1995: 364), they also specifically urge that information about 'any homosexual activity or other deviations' be specifically requested and noted in compiling the sexual history of a patient (1995: 23).

The example of homosexuality can be seen, in part, as a cautionary tale: for years, intrusive and often unpleasant treatments were used in an attempt to alter a condition that is no longer viewed as pathological. One wonders if there are other disorders that, in time, will benefit from similar changes in social attitudes. In this context, it is an example of the normative side of diagnosis and mental health regulation, and raises the question of whether mental illness or disorder, as defined by the medical profession, is an appropriate gateway to the MHA 1983, or whether a standard reflecting broader social interests should be introduced.

The example of homosexuality further emphasises the difficulties of moving between administrative contexts in the use of medical categories. To be realistic, people concerned about their sexual orientation will, at least sometimes, consult doctors. Unless they are to abandon those people, doctors must develop some form of under-standing of homosexuality, and the role of the medical profession in this context must be articulated. That does not necessarily mean a 'cure' for homosexuality; it may well mean appropriate psychotherapy or peer counselling to come to terms with the indi-vidual's concerns. Nonetheless, it is not obvious that homosexuality can simply be removed from the medical universe. This raises, from another angle, the question of how medical nosology and models relate to legal regulation. Is the threshold of humane medical intervention necessarily the same as for legal or policy regulation? Certainly, other requirements will be necessary to invoke the powers of the MHA, but is the same standard or definition of mental disorder appropriate for the individual who seeks medical involvement as that used for the imposition of state power, through civil confinement? Is the use of a system designed by doctors to provide a structure for care and cure really the appropriate one by which to determine administrative or legal interventions?

The problems of definition discussed in this chapter lie at the heart of mental health law and policy. If a coherent understanding and articulation of the fundamental definitions of mental disorder, which serve as the gateway to the 1983 Act is not attained, it is fair to ask how the Act is to be justified within a civil rights framework. Why is one set of behaviours treated one way, and another differently, if there is no coherent meaning to the terms that define the prerequisite conditions of the Act's appli-cation? Medical frameworks are problematic in this regard, and it is not obvious what other criteria might reasonably be used. On this basis, the justification for the Act is, arguably, dubious.

At the same time, reread some of the personal accounts of mental disorder cited in the last chapter. Is it really justifiable that society does not develop social and legal support for these individuals? Can we really pass by? Is enforced intervention never appropriate? Why?

3

An Overview of the Contemporary Mental Health System

3.1 Introduction

The study of any area of law will be deficient unless the legal rules and procedures in question are studied in their operational context. This truism is, if anything, especially applicable to mental health law, the study of which can never pretend to be an end in itself. This is because law functions here, in the arena of mental health, not as an abstract discourse to be evaluated solely in terms of its internal coherence (although this is obviously an important question), but variously: as the most formal and the most coercive expression of the policy of the state towards persons with mental disorder; as permission and limitation; as the authorisation of a hierarchy that licenses some to invade or significantly curtail the freedom of others, possibly indefinitely. Mental health law is at once a mere tool, a function of policy in the same way that a decision to build a new hospital or fund an outreach programme is a function of policy, and an expression of values, or of compromise between competing values or considerations, which can themselves be unpacked to reveal an untidy conglomeration of political, economic, moral, professional, and systemic, as well as legal and other, forces.

Law must also be seen as a source of the mental health system in its own right (Fennell, 1986). Law, in terms of discourse, ideas, structures, and so on, has had a constructive influence on the contemporary system, a point that has been underscored with the coming into force of the Human Rights Act 1998, and the various changes in practice that litigation under that Act has brought. Thus it can be said that a psychiatric facility is both a physical structure and a legal entity; there is little point in studying the operation of one without reference to the operation of the other. The same, it must follow, is true of those who enter the system. The patient, or client, is in some sense a product of the legal regime, just as he or she is a product of social and medical policy and practice. The tradition in some of the literature has been to see these approaches as conflicting. This is not necessarily appropriate. As Roger Smith (1981) has shown, legal and medical discourses have shown considerable similarity in the past. The mutual reliance of these discourses in both the past and present will be a theme of this chapter, and indeed a recurring theme in this text.

Crucial to understanding the contemporary system is an awareness of its history. The intimacy of the relationship between past, present and future in the delivery of mental health services cannot be overestimated. Mental health policy over the last two and a half centuries has tended to be reactive, and as a consequence has had continually to live with its ghosts, in terms of physical plant, professional discourse, vested interest and, to a greater or lesser extent, public perceptions. To provide an example (although the picture has become more complex in recent years), it has been the policy of successive governments since at least 1960 that the preferred mode of delivery of mental health services, all things being equal, should be in the form of 'care in the community'. Yet throughout the entirety of that period, mental health law, in the form of the Mental Health Acts of 1959 and the current Act of 1983, has been predicated on the view that that 'confinement' is the norm; a view that is an inheritance from earlier legislation that gave expression to such policies. In consequence, the 5–10 per cent or so of patients who are detained in hospital are administered under a relatively developed (albeit controversial) legal regime; but for the majority of hospital inpatients, and the many more who are treated in the community, the relevant law is sketchy and must be pieced together from any number of sources, many of which give expression to a different order of policy imperatives – concerned, for example, with the housing, benefits and general healthcare systems – in addition to a hotchpotch of overlapping legislation, case law and other forms of guidance dealing specifically with community care for mental disorder. The result is both that the policy on care in the community is incoherent and that law and policy are often out of kilter.

Although the current movement towards new mental health law was initially announced as 'a root and branch reform of the law' (Department of Health, 1998h), and although it is clear that the removal of the 'bright line' between the legal status of a patient being treated in hospital and that of one being treated in the community remains a key plank of the much more modest reform proposals published in 2006 (see Department of Health, 2006a, 2006p), there is little evidence that the Mental Health Act will be better integrated with, for example, housing or benefits law and policy, or indeed, with the current web of legislation pertinent to the delivery of community care services, when (or if) the terms of the 2006 Bill become law. Legislation is, of course, not the only mechanism by which to introduce changes in policy; the Care Service Improvement Partnership and the National Institute for Mental Health in England (2006a) has recently published *10 High Impact Changes for Mental Health Services*. These do underline the reality of the shift from inpatient to outpatient service provision as the norm (Change 1) and the importance attached to better coordination of service delivery across health and social services (Change 2), but still there is little to indicate that the state's understanding of the system is consistent with those of its users.

3.1.1 A sketch of the contemporary mental health system

Part of the explanation for such discrepancies is that, immediately upon attempting to define the contemporary mental health system, problems of delimitation present themselves. For example, from the perspective of one 'client group', namely patients judged dangerous enough by a court or the Secretary of State to require the making of a 'restriction order', what counts as 'the system' may be limited to the 'special hospitals' (characterised by their high level of security) and prisons, with transfer into medium and low-security hospital facilities being little more than a postscript to many years spent in 'deep end' provision. A considerable number never leave the 'deep end' of the system. Many of those who have been transferred to a special hospital from prison will be returned to prison, rather than be transferred into hospital conditions of lesser security, if treatment in hospital either proves successful or is shown to be fruitless.

Should prisons be considered as part of the mental health system? The argument that they should is increasingly strong. As discussed in Chapter 6, only a small number of mentally disordered offenders are sentenced to hospital by a court, and the population of our prisons includes a high number of mentally disordered persons. There has long been provision to transfer those in need of treatment for mental disorder to hospital, but even though such transfers increased in the 1990s (see Chapter 6) it remains the case that around 90 per cent of prison inmates have some form of mental disorder (including substance abuse), rising to 95 per cent for juvenile detainees (HM Prison Service, Department of Health and National Assembly for Wales, 2001: 3; see also Rickford, 2003; Rickford and Edgar, 2005; Butler and Kousoulou, 2006: 35), and a significant number have more than one form of disorder: 12–15 per cent of women inmates were found in one study to have at least four out of: neurosis, psychosis, personality disorder, alcohol abuse and drug dependency (Owen *et al.*, 2004). Traditionally, the Prison Service has usually provided health care to prisoners who are not ill enough to warrant transfer to hospital, or for whom no hospital place is available, and so the health care of prisoners has largely been outside of the bounds of the NHS. Such care has also been of lower quality than NHS provision (Reed and Lyne, 2000; Reed, 2002). The High Court in *Knight* v *Home Office* [1990] 3 All ER 237 held that prisoners could expect no better.

Concerted efforts have since been made to change this situation. The *National Service Framework for Mental Health*, which was published in 1999, made it clear that prisoners should be able to expect the same quality of care as others in need (Department of Health, 1999: 9). Also in 1999, the Prison Service and the NHS unveiled plans for a formal partnership (HM Prison Service and NHS Executive, 1999). This was followed in December 2001 by the jointly published *Changing the Outlook: A Strategy for Developing and Modernising Mental Health Services in Prisons* (HM Prison Service, Department of Health and National Assembly for Wales, 2001). This document was blunt about the problem (2001: 5): 'There are too many prisoners in too many prisons who, despite the best efforts of committed prison health care and NHS staff, receive no treatment, or inappropriate treatment for their mental illness, from staff with the wrong mix of skills and in the wrong kind of setting.' *Changing the Outlook* proposed a package of measures to use available resources better, including the provision of treatment in terms of community care to prisoners in their cells rather than routinely moving the mentally ill to separate hospital wings, improved staff training, and improved collaboration between prisons and the NHS.

In addition, funding for an extra 300 medical staff to implement 'In-reach' programmes was promised. By 2006, there were 360 new staff across 102 prisons. An expert group, chaired by the National Director of Mental Health, oversees the whole project. Policy is put into operation through a structure of prison health regional task force teams and the jointly operated Prison Health Policy Unit and a Prison Health Task Force, which began to operate in 2000 and was amalgamated into one unit in December 2002, shortly after the launch of the the Prison Mental Health In-reach Collaborative in November 2002 (HM Prison Service and Department of Health, 2002). The aim of the Collaborative is, essentially, to ensure that the same systems, practices and mechanisms for quality control that exist in the general run of the NHS also function in prisons. Section 23 of the National Health Service Reform and Health Care Professions Act 2002 placed a duty on NHS bodies to cooperate with the prison service, and the Director of Prison Health has also instituted clinical governance in prisons (HM Prison Service, 2003), the development of which will be monitored over forthcoming years. A most significant policy development is that from April 2003 responsibility for funding prison health care (£176m in 2005–6, of which £20m was spent on mental health: Rosie Winterton, Minister's statement, HC Hansard 20 January 2006, Col. 168W; although it was reported in 2001 that half of all expenditure goes on mental health treatment: HM Prison Service and Department of Health and the National Assembly for Wales, 2001: 8) has been gradually been transferred from the Prison Service to the Department of Health, a process that was fully complete by April 2006. At local level, it is now primary care trusts (PCTs) that control such budgets and purchase secondary care, where appropriate, from NHS trusts and independent sector providers.

In so far as these developments promise to improve the historically low quality of treatment for mental illness in prisons, they are to be welcomed. What has been less welcome is the possibility that part of the package would involve treatment under compulsion in prison. One of the most controversial elements in the now abandoned draft Mental Health Bill 2002 was the proposal that, in the divide between hospital-based and community-based treatment under compulsion, prison establishments are to be counted as being in the community, and this would allow treatment to be given under compulsion in prison under civil law powers 'if [the patient] would otherwise have been eligible for a treatment order in the community': Home Office and Department of Health, 2002: para. 3.35. The 2002 draft bill, and the later version published in 2004 and now also withdrawn, was opposed by a broad and diverse coalition for a number of reasons, but this proposal drew particular criticism. The Law Society, in calling for a halt to the progress of the 2002 draft bill on grounds that its central provisions were 'legally, morally and ethically undesirable' described the proposal for compulsory treatment in prison as 'poor practice' (Law Society, 2002: paras. only 1, 122). The General Synod of the Church of England was prompted by the draft bill, which it declared 'unworkable and regressive' and 'preoccupied with issues of public safety', into its first discussion of mental health for eight years. The proposal for the compulsory treatment of patients in prisons was its 'greatest concern' (*The Independent*, 2 March 2003: 7).

It can also be argued that such a proposal offends against the dicta of the European Court in *Ashingdane* v *UK* (1985) 7 EHRR 528 at para. 44, repeated more recently in *Hutchinson Reid* v *UK* (2003) 37 EHRR 211, that: 'In principle, the "detention" of a person as a mental patient will only be "lawful" for the purposes of [Art. 5(1)(e) of the Convention] if effected in a hospital, clinic or other appropriate institution authorised for that purpose.' A technically correct answer to this point is, first, that in the circumstances envisaged by the government, a prisoner's detention would be by reason of having been sent to prison by a court following a conviction for a criminal offence and not by reason of his or her mental disorder. But this is not a very good answer because the net effect is clearly outside the spirit of *Ashingdane*. The view of the Law Society (2002: para. 122) is that any proposal for compulsion in prison also falls foul of the decision of the European Court in *Aerts* v *Belgium* (2000) 29 EHRR 50, in which it was held to be a breach of Art. 5(1)(e) to detain a mentally ill person in unsuitable conditions in prison for seven months until a hospital bed could be located for him. Human rights law, however, deals with questions of fact rather than with sweeping propositions, and a breach of Convention rights will only be found if the particular circumstances warrant it: it is not the case that the detention and treatment of a mentally disordered person in prison is per se in breach of the Convention (the difference between a 'prison' and a 'hospital' is, in any case, very blurred at the margins). But as far as it is possible to tell at the moment, it seems that the proposal for the use of compulsion outside hospital has been abandoned. The bill published in 2004 provided that a patient being treated in the community, who refuses to take necessary medication, should be hospitalised in order for the treatment to be given (see cl. 46(6)(b)), as is also the case with the proposals for supervised community treatment published in 2006 (Department of Health, 2006l; 2006p). But this does not detract from the general point being made here, which is that it is no longer tenable to regard the prison estate as a system separate from the mental health system.

Meanwhile, at the other 'end' of the system, there is a blurring between hospital and community care provision (much of which is in the form of residential accommodation) in terms of physical plant: while in terms of user experience, a patient whose condition involves episodic acute periods may well experience 'the system' as comprising a combination of inpatient and outpatient services, and might also want to include other departments of state – local authority housing departments or benefits agencies, for example – as component parts of the same system. A majority of individuals with mental health problems, such as depression, or with a learning disability never or rarely enter a hospital for the treatment for their mental disorder. One survey has shown that, even for patients with severe and enduring mental health problems, a considerable number (between 10.5 and 13.5 per cent) are dealt with solely by the primary care sector (Callanan *et al.*, 1997). For these patients, 'the system' is to all intents and purposes nothing more or less than their local GP, and the services provided by primary care trusts (PCTs), such as counselling, and/or their local pharmacy. There are clearly significant quantitative and qualitative differences in how, from the point of view of those on the receiving end of the provision of mental health services, 'the system' is experienced.

From a more philosophical point of view, how one understands the concept of 'system' is far from clear. If one conceives of a system in terms of specific physical locations within society – hospitals, prisons, and so on – it can be described fairly easily. But, of course, the premise of community care is that, wherever possible, services should be delivered to persons in their own homes: are the homes of service users to be understood as part of the system? If so, a definition that moves beyond a description of physical plant is required. If the mental health system is seen instead in discursive terms – that is, as a set of doctrines and corresponding practices – the limitation of a 'physical' definition of the system seems to have been overcome. But where, then, is the line to be drawn?

One might attempt to define the system in terms of the professionals who administer it, but this too is problematic. Considerable numbers of people with conditions that the Mental Health Act would identify as 'mental disorders' are cared for primarily informally, by their families or by private facilities. People with developmental disabilities and vulnerable senior citizens are perhaps the obvious examples. The existence of family care for these people may mean that the state has little involvement other than the provision of a GP, or specialised teaching for a child with learning disabilities, or the inspection and licensing of a residential facility for a senior citizen. This sort of private care provision is a part of state policy, but are these people in 'the system'? The answer to this question may depend on the reason the question is being asked. Thus, if the issue is state encroachment on individual care, the answer may be doubtful, since control of care is largely private, although even here, the existence of some supervision over the nursing home, although not over the specific care of the individual, shows how grey the boundaries of the system can be. If the issue is instead the imposition of power relations onto people who may be vulnerable, these people must be considered a part of the subject class of this book, since such private arrangements for care can be as oppressive as the public, and more visible, psychiatric facilities. A part of the legal tradition involves assuming some responsibility for the protection of such persons; in that context, even purely private care cannot be perceived as outside the system.

Inevitably, there is a degree of intractability inherent in such questions. It can be said, however, that the contemporary mental health system is conceptualised by the state as a system of service provision, which is not limited, in theory at least, to specific physical locations. That said, institutional provision remains the dominant mechanism for service delivery. It is the duty of the Secretary of State for Health to promote a comprehensive health service: s. 1(1) of the National Health Service Act, 1977. Section 3(1) of the Act lists a number of forms in which that duty may be performed, comprising various inpatient and outpatient facilities and services. It has been held that the scope of s. 3(1) should be construed widely, to include, as a 'facility' for the purposes of s. 3(1)(e), a scheme providing advice on welfare and other state benefits to mentally disordered persons: *R v Cardiff Local Health Board, ex p Keating* [2005] EWCA Civ 847, [2006] 1 WLR 158, albeit that this was not a health service but a service ancillary to that.

The duty to provide services is delegated to primary care trusts (PCTs), which provide primary (community-based) care and contract for secondary (hospital-based) care from National Health Service (NHS) trusts and independent sector providers.

Much of, but not all, secondary mental health services are provided by specialist NHS mental health trusts. A NHS trust might have exclusive occupation of a hospital site or a number of separate NHS trusts might provide accommodation and services on the same site. Alternatively, a NHS trust might manage accommodation across a range of sites, perhaps in the form of a psychiatric inpatient facility and a 'satellite' hostel for patients who require some form of assisted accommodation before returning to the community, or perhaps in the form of a number of specialist units. The trend is towards larger trusts operating a number of sites. The Mersey Care National Health Service Trust, for example, operates 33 inpatient facilities of various types. By mid-2006, there were, following some amalgamations, 76 specialist mental health trusts in existence. The National Health System in 2004–5 provided a total of 181,784 beds, of which 31,667 were for mental illness and 4,899 for learning disabilities (Department of Health, 2006i). The trend is down: in 2002, 34,000 beds were available for mental illness and 6,000 for learning disability; in 1995, the figures were 39,000 and 15,000 respectively; in 1990–1 they were 55,000 and 23,000 (Government Statistical Service, 2002: Table B16). All NHS long-term accommodation for learning disability is due to have closed by the end of 2006. Much of the slack has, however, been taken up by expansion in the independent sector, and it has been estimated that there were, in fact, only 5 per cent fewer beds in 2001 than in 1994–95, although the fall in NHS beds was 20 per cent during that period (Mental Health Act Commission, 2005: para. 2.51). It is open to debate whether the increased use of the independent sector is beneficial. Independent provision can be more expensive than NHS beds and some PCTs have been reluctant to purchase it. More worrying, perhaps, a significant number of transfers of patients from NHS to independent sector providers – 48,900 at 31 March 2005, representing 18 per cent of the total council supported residents in England (HC Hansard 3 July 2006, Col. 817W) – have been 'out of area', and there is concern that this 'may in effect be re-creating long-stay institutions' (2005: para. 2.22).

According to the government's published data (Department of Health, 2006i), occupancy rates in 2005 averaged 87.9 per cent for mental illness beds and 84.4 per cent for learning disability beds, which is reasonably close to the Royal College of Psychiatrists optimum occupancy rate of 85 per cent (Royal College of Psychiatrists, 1998a). Understaffing must be factored in, however, and Garcia et al. (2005: Figure 12), found a national vacancy rate of 13 per cent, rising to 22 per cent in London for nursing staff. The government's figures are, in any case, disputed. Garcia et al. found average bed occupancy rates of 100 per cent across acute mental health inpatient services in England. The Mental Health Act Commission (2005: para. 2.4) also found occupancy rates in excess of 100 per cent in over half of the 1,591 wards visited between October 2004 and July 2005, and 81 wards had rates in excess of 120 per cent (para. 2.6). Whatever the true figures, it is apparent that the system is, to say the least, stretched; the bed shortages that characterise the NHS generally are particularly acute in some sectors of the mental health estate.

The Secretary of State has a specific duty, currently to be found in s. 4 of the NHS Act 1977, to provide so-called 'special hospitals', defined as those for patients who 'in his opinion require treatment under conditions of high security on account of their dangerous, violent or criminal propensities'. There are three special hospitals that provide such services for England and Wales: Broadmoor hospital in Berkshire, Rampton in Nottinghamshire, and Ashworth in Merseyside. These institutions opened in 1863, 1912 and 1989 respectively, although Ashworth hospital is the combination (in 1989) of two earlier institutions, Moss Side Hospital, which opened in 1933, and Park Lane Hospital, the newest special hospital accommodation, built in the 1970s. The average population of each of these hospitals is around 250–350 patients, and all three accept patients with all types of mental disorder, although the vast majority of patients are either mentally ill or suffer from a psychopathic disorder. Other facilities offer a range of accommodation in terms of security. Regional secure units (RSUs) are operated within the psychiatric NHS trust sector, and offer an interim level of security, whilst medium secure units (MSUs), provide an intermediary level of security between that offered in general psychiatric facilities and that offered by RSUs. The regional and medium secure sector grew markedly in the late 1990s, and by 2000–1, secure units provided 1,950 beds for mental illness, almost a doubling from the 1,080 beds available in 1994–5, and 430 beds, up from 330 in 1994–5, for learning disability (Government Statistical Service, 2002: Tables B22, B23), and there was a further expansion in the early years of the new century to accommodate the programme to relocate patients inappropriately held in the high-security hospitals, through the Accelerated Discharge Programme (ADP), which ran from 2002 to 2004. By 2004–5 there were 2,696 secure beds for patients with mental illness and 503 for patients with a learning disability (HC Hansard 20 July 2006, Col. 665W). Although it is not clear from the data, it seems that this number does not include secure beds for patients with a personality disorder (distinct from mental illness under the terms of the 1983 Act), which would add a sizeable number to this total. Many of these places would previously have been provided by the large asylums, which began to close in significant numbers in the mid-1990s (see later in this chapter). The initiative for the development of secure accommodation has come from within the health service and the Department of Health. Neither RSUs nor MSUs are statutory concepts.

The duty to secure the provision of services (other than health services) to patients in the community lies primarily with local authorities (s. 46, National Health Service and Community Care Act 1990; Local Authority Circular (93)4), although services will also be provided by NHS bodies, housing authorities, and service providers in the charitable, voluntary and independent sectors. The 1990 Act is a coordinating piece of legislation and marks the point of entry into a web of services, legislation, delegated legislation and guidance. (The legal framework for the provision of community care services will be considered in detail in Chapter 9.) A significant proportion of the community care budget is consumed in the provision of residential accommodation of one sort or another. The two main types of unit are homes providing accommodation and personal care, and those providing accommodation and nursing care. Previously known as residential care homes and nursing care homes respectively, all such accommodation is now defined as 'care homes': s. 3(1), Care Standards Act 2000. As at

March 2005, there were 10,217 mental illness beds for adults aged 18–64 in 967 care homes, down from 11, 309 across 1,068 homes in March 2003, and 32,339 beds for adults with learning disabilities in 4,568 locations, down from 35,278 beds in 4,901 locations two years previously (Commission for Social Care Inspection, 2005: Table 7.1).

An ever-increasing amount of this provision is in the private, charitable and voluntary sectors (together the 'independent sector'). By 2001, the independent sector provided 92 per cent of all homes and 85 per cent of places in residential homes (Department of Health, 2001: Table R1). By 2003–4, less than 5 per cent of residential provision for persons with mental illness remained in the public sector (Commission for Social Care Inspection, 2005: 49). Accommodation provided for mentally disordered persons in the form of residential care in the community is only a small part of the broader community care system. In March 2006, there were 440,223 care home beds provided by 18,752 establishments, down from 441, 376 places in 19,762 establishments in March 2005 (Commission for Social Care Inspection, 2006: 20). Of the 267,240 people whose residential or nursing care was funded by local authorities in 2005, only 12,320 had mental health problems and 35,125, a learning disability. The vast majority of such funded places (205, 210 in 2005), are occupied by the elderly (Department of Health, 2005c: Table S1). Thus, although mental health services comprise a significant percentage of hospital provision, such services only occupy a moderate corner of the provision of care in the community.

It has been policy since 1990 (Department of Health, 1990b) that care should be provided to people in their own homes wherever possible, rather than in residential accommodation. Accordingly, the community care system also comprises primary care provision, preventative care and aftercare. For most mentally disordered persons, their GP is the first point of contact with the mental health system. In addition, s. 46(3) of the NSHCCA 1990 requires local authorities to provide (with more or less room for discretion) a wide range of services, which are to be found in any equally diverse number of statutes, to, inter alia, mentally disordered persons in their own homes. These services are delivered by social workers, in tandem with community psychiatric nurses (CPNs), increasingly working out of community mental health centres (CHMCs) or in the form of community mental health teams (CMHTs). They may also be delivered in the form of general social services, for example, domiciliary and other services geared to support independent living. CMHCs and CMHTs will also be amongst the forms in which day care provision is made, and will also refer patients to secondary care services and have been influential in this respect. As Rogers and Pilgrim (2001: 147) explain:

Traditional primary and secondary arrangements between specialist and generalist medical practitioners were disrupted by the introduction of CMHTs. These increasingly became the main referral point through which GPs and other primary care sources gained access to the secondary sector.

This arrangement replaced that of GPs referring to psychiatrists. Research by Barnes *et al.* (1990) found that, in areas where there are CMHCs, there was a reduction in admissions to hospital. In 2001–2, CPNs had 559,000 'first contacts' with patients, followed in 322,000 instances with an 'initial contact' with a treatment provider following referral by a CPN (Department of Health, 2002a: Tables 1, 2 and 3). The number of first contacts increased throughout the 1990s, reaching a peak of 603,000 in 1998–9, after which time the number has fallen (*ibid.*). The average duration of a 'CPN episode', that is, the time from first contact to final contact, was nine months in 2001–2, double the duration (4.5 months) in 1991–2 (*ibid.*). Thus, although the picture is complicated, and there are regional variations, the recent trend is broadly to treat fewer people but for longer periods (of course, these statistics tell us little about absolute levels of mental disorder in the community). The role of social workers and community psychiatric nurses in the mandatory provision of treatment and other services, and in exercising powers of surveillance and control over mentally disordered persons in the community, has increased markedly over the last decade, as successive governments have sought to respond to public concerns about the 'failure' of community care in this regard.

Completing the picture is the relatively 'invisible' but crucially important, component, in the form of caring provided by the family and friends of learning disabled or mentally ill persons. Such provision is recognised in the Carers (Recognition and Services) Act 1995, which gives informal carers the right, in certain circumstances, to require that assistance be provided by a local authority. Conversely, local authorities may properly consider care that is being provided informally when assessing a person's need for services, and decide that it can, in a given case, play a residual role, offering respite care to both clients and their carers: *R v North Yorkshire County Council, ex p Hargreaves* (1994) *Medical Law Reports* 121 (HC); they might also expect that normally a relative will not charge for the care provided: *R v Stockton on Tees BC, ex p Stephenson* [2005] EWCA Civ 960. This 'invisible' element in the system obviously distorts the pattern of community care expenditure. Even so, and despite evidence that spending on care for clients in their own homes increased more quickly from 2002 to 2004 than did spending on residential accommodation (Commission for Social Care Inspection, 2005: 53), local authorities continue to spend greater amounts on residential care than on provision to persons in their own homes. In 2003–4, local authority social service departments spent £332,127m on care home places for persons with mental health problems (£271,970m on residential home care and £60,157m on nursing care) and £1,578,649m (£1,499,301m on residential places and £79,348m on nursing care) for persons with learning disabilities, plus £41,976m and £240,558m respectively on the cost of supported accommodation. This contrasts with total expenditure on home care and day care of £152,949m for mentally ill clients and £899,375 for clients with learning disabilities (Commission for Social Care Inspection, 2005: Table A3). There has also been a significant increase in total spending in recent years. In 1998, for example, £185m was spent on residential care for persons with mental illness (Government Statistical Service, 1998: Table E5).

There are ongoing attempts to pull all of this provision together into a more coherent and uniform, policy and evidence-driven, system. In 1999, the *National Service*

Framework for Mental Health (NSFMH) was published (Department of Health, 1999), listing seven national standards, with a ten-year timescale for implementation:

- the promotion of mental health for all, social inclusion and the combating of discrimination on grounds of mental health;
- people suffering from a common mental health problem should be able to access necessary assessment and treatments;
- services should provide round-the-clock coverage;
- all service users with a care plan should receive optimum care, including preventative care, a written care plan and 24-hour access to services;
- there should be timely access to inpatient care in the least restrictive environment possible;
- those who provide regular care to a person on the Care Programme Approach (CPA, see Chapter 9) are entitled to have their own needs as carers assessed at least once annually;
- by a combination of the above factors, service providers should work to reduce suicides.

The NSFMH proceeds to provide in some detail the evidential base for these standards and to elaborate on their implications for practice. As for their implementation, and that of mental health policy more broadly, a National Director of Mental Health, Professor Louis Appleby, took up post in summer 2000, just as the NHS Plan was published. The National Director chairs the Mental Health Task Force (Department of Health, 2002b), set up at the same time. Its collective task is to push policy forward in various areas, including the NSFMH and, as seen above, the development of prison policy and capacity for dealing with mental health issues. The National Institute for Mental Health for England (NIMHE) was also established in 2001, again under the leadership of Professor Appleby (Department of Health, 2001a), with a brief to coordinate research and disseminate information, to facilitate training, and to develop services. In addition, various recently established bodies, such as the National Institute for Clinical Excellence (NICE), have specific responsibilities; in the case of NICE it is to provide national guidance on the use of treatments.

In September 2004, the pressure and campaigning group MIND issued its report on the first five years of the NSFMH, finding that (2004: 1):

The picture is mixed. Whilst there is no doubt that increased focus has been placed on specialised community based services, which is welcome, this has in many cases been at the expense of attention on other areas such as mental health promotion and inpatient care. After five years, we would expect more comprehensive improvements to have been achieved. Making high profile improvements in some areas whilst allowing others to be left behind is not acceptable.

In December of that year, the Department of Health published its own report on the first five years of the NSF, authored by Professor Appleby (Department of Health, 2004e). Professor Appleby reported that significant improvements had taken place following the implementation of the NSF, together with the NHS Plan and the establishment of the NIMHE, and that 'Most of what has been achieved has been in specialist mental health services. We should be unapologetic about that – it is also where the greatest problems were, as well as the people with the greatest needs' (Department of Health, 2004: 68). 'There are also aspects of specialist mental health services that have not yet been adequately addressed and now need urgent attention. These are inpatient wards, dual diagnosis, support for carers, and information technology', he suggested (Department of Health, 2004: 68). Other areas in need of attention include issues of equality, stigma, discrimination and exclusion, the quality of primary care and the interface between primary and secondary care (Department of Health, 2004: 71–2).

No reform programme, however, can be successful unless funds are adequate and used appropriately. Professor Appleby reported that spending on mental health services had increased by between 20 and 25 per cent in the four years following the introduction of the NSF, but that 'some of the money that has reached front-line services has been spent on the wrong things. It has been used to shore up the old services that the NSF and NHS Plan were intended to change'. In addition, not all trusts have received new money for investment, and there is a noticeable and growing north–south divide. Ultimately, Appleby argues, the problem lies with PCTs, strategic health authorities (established in 2002) and the Department of Health, 'not because they lack concern for mental health care but because when money is tight – and it always seems to be tight, even when (as now) investment is expanding – it is accepted that improving access and reducing waiting times are even more important'. PCTs 'have continued the historical under-funding of mental health that created the problems that we are now grappling with'. Finally, Appleby notes that overall spending on the NHS increased to £63.4bn in 2003–4 and is predicted to reach £92bn by 2007–8; it is important, therefore, that mental health services get not merely a greater amount but also a larger percentage of the total spending, because 'it will be hard for some people to accept that our priority status has been fulfilled if spending on mental health does not at least keep pace with spending on the NHS as a whole'.

By 2006, despite the acknowledged overall increase in NHS funding, stories concerning staff redundancies and other cutbacks were being reported in the media, and the NHS in England recorded a £512m deficit for 2005–6. In April 2006, Health Minister Rosie Winterton, in answer to a Parliamentary Question, stated that 11 of the 84 NHS trusts at that time providing mental health services had announced cuts in spending, totalling £16.5m, which 'amounted to less than 0.3 per cent of the total investment of more than £6bn' (HC Hansard, 18 April 2006, Vol. No. 445, Part No. 136). This was challenged soon after in two reports (Rethink, 2006; The Sainsbury Centre for Mental Health, 2006), the first alleging that cuts of £30m had been planned; the second that finding that over half of trusts had diverted money earmarked for mental health services to compensate for overspending elsewhere, on primary care and acute hospitals, that 75 per cent of trusts had to take special measures to break even, such as freezing vacant posts, and that for 2006–7, many must make reductions of around 3 per cent on their planned budgets. Perhaps most damningly, the Sainsbury Centre report found that, although spending on mental health services had increased by 7.1 per cent, in 2005, the increase for the NHS as a whole was 9.1 per cent, so that, despite concerted efforts being made in some quarters to make the NSFMH a reality, the situation to date is that mental health services are not keeping pace with spending on the NHS as a whole.

Evidently, our mental health system, described here in bare outline, exists in a highly politicised climate. But we should not forget to allocate time to the broader and more fundamental questions: is this the system that we want? How, when and why did it come into being? What is its function or functions (intended or unintended)? To what extent has the 'shape' of the system changed, and with what implications? How well does the system actually work? More pertinently, what is the relevance of such questions for the student of mental health law? Although this book, as a whole, might begin to answer at least some of these questions, it is the questions themselves that will be particularly to the fore in this chapter.

3.2 The rise and fall of asylum-based provision

To say that the interpretation of the historical genesis and development of the contemporary mental health system is a matter of controversy is a substantial understatement. The more one learns of the history of madness and its responses, the better the reasons for this controversy are appreciated. It is both the most fascinating and the most frustrating aspect of this history that, in its detail, one finds the negation of easy generalisation, on more or less any aspect of it. Let us begin with what is not controversial: from its beginnings in a relatively small number of relatively small asylums active at the end of the eighteenth century, specialised institutional provision for the insane grew, over the course of the nineteenth and twentieth centuries, until about the end of the Second World War. From that point, asylum provision has been in a fairly precipitous decline, as public policy has increasingly focused on community care as the primary mode of care provision for people with mental disabilities. The change in provision can be seen clearly in a few statistical indicators. In 1847, there were 21 county asylums in existence; by 1914, there were 97. The size of the average asylum also grew markedly after 1850: the average population was 1,000 by 1900, with a number of institutions at double that rate (Prior, 1996: 67). This growth is matched by the total number of people confined in these asylums. In 1850, total inpatients in county asylums numbered 7,140 (4.03 per 10,000 population). By 1930, they contained 119,659 people (30.14 per 10,000 population), and by 1954, 148,000 people (33.45 per 10,000 population). At this point, however, the decarceration movement was beginning to take effect, and the total inpatient population fell more rapidly than it rose: by 1981, the rate of confinement had more than halved, to 15.5 per 10,000 population. This downward trend continued throughout the 1980s and 1990s. Between 1980 and 1990, there was a further 25 per cent reduction in the number of hospital beds available. Bed numbers fell below 100,000 by 1990, and by 1997–8 the total stock of available psychiatric hospital beds stood at 45,878. By 1997–8, there would remain only two hospitals with more than 1,000 beds

(Government Statistical Service, 1998: Table B17). By the end of the century, both of these hospitals had closed.

There are a variety of explanations for these trends. Regarding the growth of asylums, Jones (1972) emphasises the nineteenth-century social reform movements, and the great men who were their tireless advocates, Sir George Onesiphorus Paul, Charles Wynn, and, perhaps most significantly, Anthony Ashley Cooper, the seventh Earl of Shaftesbury, as promoting an increasingly civilised and humane response to the social problem of madness. The object of these figures was to bring decent and rational provision to some of the most pitiable people of society. Through tireless lobbying, they brought about the expansion of the county asylum movement to the point where it became a symbol of nineteenth-century philanthropy, and the provision of standards, both in those asylums and in private facilities, through the introduction of legislative standards and an effective system of inspection.

This broadly progressive image of nineteenth-century social policy on asylums cannot entirely be dismissed. Certainly, there was an interest in the legislation of lunacy in the nineteenth century, such as had not occurred before; the 1845 County Asylums Act, which made county asylum provision mandatory for pauper lunatics, was undoubtedly a significant boost to asylum construction. But the progressive nature of the reforms is perhaps open to question. The nineteenth-century commentators were fond of citing the horrific care provided in environments where reform had not penetrated. A report from as late as 1845 tells of insane persons outside asylums kept by their families in that place 'commonly devoted to the reception of coals', this being a 'confined, dark and damp corner' between the stairs and the ground floor in which 'may be found at this very time no small number of our fellow-beings, huddled, crouching and gibbering, with less apparent intelligence and under worse treatment than the lower domestic animals' (Jones, 1972: 12). Was previous provision really so bad? And did it really become so much better upon admission to asylums?

Certainly, some of the accounts are extremely unpleasant, but modern scholars are looking to these accounts with an increasingly critical eye. Patricia Allderidge (1985), for example, has challenged much of the disparaging imagery of Bethlem hospital in the eighteenth and early nineteenth centuries, and Roy Porter (1987a) and Rab Houston (1999) have both painted broadly positive pictures of the care of the insane in the private sector in the eighteenth century. For the poor, provision of care was surely more frugal; research by Akihito Suzuki (1991; 1992) would suggest that it would be wrong to perceive even the poor insane as simply ignored by the system. Instead, they appear to have been treated within the poor law system, much as other paupers were.

The question, therefore, becomes not so much a matter of improvement in treatment on an objective scale, but rather of how the Victorians understood the reforms as progressive. Certainly the perception of improved standards was a part of the concern; equally important was the idea that society could be regulated, and individuals controlled, on a large scale. By 1845, the reforms in their legal form matched a fairly classic Benthamite paradigm. Central legislation was put in place, designed to ensure that poor 'lunatics and idiots' would come to the attention of Justices of the Peace, and would be confined in a new system of county asylums. Both these, and the private madhouses catering to the more monied classes, would be inspected regularly, by a specialised board of inspectors, the Commissioners in Lunacy. And consistent with such a Benthamite model, the asylum itself – both its architecture and the regime it would create – would be pivotal to the conception of the reform of the insane person. Surveillance both of the insane in the asylum and at least of the poorer classes of society became pivotal to the ideology of the statute.

The approach that became symbolic of nineteenth-century asylum care was moral treatment. This form of therapy had diverse origins. In England, it originated in a private facility run by Quakers, the York Retreat, in the years following its opening in 1796 (see Digby, 1985; 1985a). In France, it is attributed to Philippe Pinel, at roughly the same time. In contrast to the intrusive physical treatments of his day, Pinel claimed that 'experience affords ample and daily proofs of the happier effects of a mild, conciliating treatment', and 'giving my most decided suffrage in favour of the moral qualities of maniacs' who would exhibit 'indescribable tenderness' and 'estimable virtue' if treated 'morally'. Although not the first to use such techniques 'Pinel, however, explicitly completed the circle: that which is psychologically caused is most effectively psychologically treated' (Bynum, 1981: 42). A similar philosophy was to be found at the York Retreat, in that 'moral treatment as practised at the Retreat, and elsewhere, meant a concentration on the rational and emotional rather than the organic causes of insanity' (Digby, 1985: 53). This entailed a regime that, although varying from exponent to exponent, essentially comprised the provision of a protective, peaceful, civilised and contemplative environment in which 'to help the patient gain enough self-discipline to master his illness' (*ibid.*). As the nineteenth century progressed, and scandalous conditions were revealed to exist at asylums, hospitals and madhouses up and down the country, the York Retreat became a watchword for the humane treatment, and cure, of the insane. By shortly after mid-century, a somewhat mutated form of the Retreat's approach was broadly adopted throughout the country, under the name 'non-restraint'.

The system never worked in the way its framers had intended. The notion of a coordinated, centrally directed network of county asylums, and of surveillance throughout the country, whereby the poor insane would be routinely identified and removed to asylums, came up against well-established local interests, and management of and admission to asylums remained in local hands. Similarly, while it is certainly true that even in the largest of county asylums few people were subjected to physical restraint, moral treatment was not relied upon to the exclusion of chemical intervention, particularly later in the century when the use of opiates became relatively common. While pragmatic issues will be more relevant below, it is also appropriate to note significance of the image of this paradigm of nineteenth-century regulation and care.

As noted, the issues of surveillance, regulation, and control are central to the aspects of the system: surveillance of the community, to ensure the routine diversion of the insane to asylums; surveillance of the insane in the asylum, through appropriate architecture and staffing, to ensure that the insane are properly cared for and appropriately employed; surveillance of the asylum, to ensure that the officers and staff are doing their job properly; surveillance of the insane by themselves, as a method of treatment. Certainly, this can be portrayed as progress. For the insane exposed to the worst of eighteenth-century conditions, there can be little doubt that the nineteenth-century asylum offered an improvement in standard of care: basic comforts, including adequate food, were provided; work was offered to those who were able to do it – generally farm work for men and laundry and needlework for women – but only six hours per day. Perhaps unsurprisingly, there is evidence that some (although not all) individuals wanted admission to this environment (Bartlett, 1999; 1999a.). At the same time, there is a sense in which the systemic approach glorified in the nineteenth century implied its own set of particularly intrusive controls and confinements. In theory, the poor were always under surveillance by local officials; there was to be no escape. Asylums were similarly open to the prying eyes of inspectors.

Similarly, the treatment at the centre of the new ideology has not always been portrayed in positive terms. For Castel (1985: 256), moral treatment is 'this authoritarian pedagogy'. For Foucault, moral treatment differed from what had gone before, the lunatic in chains, not so much because of its greater humanity but rather because of its greater, more penetrative, control of the recipient. Now, the mad would police themselves. The moral treatment practised at York was important not so much for its religious element, but rather its more general strategy (Foucault, 1986: 145, 146):

...to place the insane individual within a moral element where he will be in debate with himself and his surroundings: to constitute for him a milieu where, far from being protected, he will be kept in a perpetual anxiety, ceaselessly threatened by Law and Transgression...the madman...must feel morally responsible for everything within him that may disturb morality and society, and must hold no one but himself responsible for the punishment he receives.

This may sound harsh, but such apparent harshness in part emphasises the success of the project upon which the new asylums were engaged, a project now completely assimilated into our modern understanding: cure, in the asylum, is to be understood as a journey to normalcy. Where previous approaches to mental illness, based on somatic theories, may have implied such a base line in their diagnostic criteria, moral treatment places a concept of normality at the core of treatment: where previously, it might have been how the insane person was identified, now, it becomes that which the insane person must want. This remains pivotal to our understanding of mental health: success is measured in terms of reintegration into society, and invisibility of the individual when returned to that society.

The nineteenth-century reforms further serve as a marker of a new attitude to people with mental health difficulties: they were a class to be treated differently. This is, in fact, merely a stage on a considerably longer progression, commencing with the 1714 Vagrancy Act, which allowed the confinement of the 'furiously mad' poor. A 1744 Vagrancy Act continued this trend, allowing such lunatics to be excused from corporal punishment for failing to work. In this context, the nineteenth-century statutes constitute a continuation of this strategy of classification and differential treatment. This does represent a change from previous legal understanding, however, when the insane poor were dealt with as just another category of deviant. In the eighteenth and nine-teenth centuries, they became a unique class, warranting special treatment or attention. It is a theme that permeates our modern view of the appropriate social approach to insanity. It is what makes it somehow socially acceptable to argue for the protective detention of the insane, or for their increased control in the community, in contexts that would be unthinkable in other elements of the population – again, a profoundly important epistemological shift at the root of our understanding of the insane.

While the social reform theory explains much of the theoretical context of asylum provision, both in the nineteenth century and today, it is problematic in that the legis-lation was not implemented in the way in which it would appear from the statute to have been intended. And the emphasis on the Benthamite model obscures some funda-mentally non-Benthamite influences on the shape of the legislation. The control of the new county asylums remained almost entirely outside the scope of the specialist inspect-orate, the Commissioners in Lunacy. They were instead managed by the local Justices of the Peace until 1888, when they were transferred to local authorities. Similarly, as discussed in Chapter 1, Justices of the Peace controlled admission and discharge processes throughout the nineteenth century. The Commissioners in Lunacy could inspect the facilities. They might squawk, and squawk they occasionally did in their annual reports, but they had minimal actual power to enforce change. Thus, the City of London did not build a county asylum for its pauper lunatics until 1866, more than twenty years after such provision became mandatory, notwithstanding a continuing series of complaints from the Commissioners. Effectively, if local administrations did not wish to comply with the legislation, there was little to force them. The situation relating to the Commissioners was similar in relation to private madhouses outside London, although inside the metropolis they did have licensing power for such private institutions. As a percentage of asylum provision, however, such private establishments were of minimal significance: the large growth in asylum provision in the nineteenth century was in the county asylum sector, over which the Commissioners had no direct influence.

To understand the actual structure and growth of the nineteenth century asylum system, therefore, it is necessary to understand the dynamic of the individuals who were actually doing the administration. Here, the presumptions of the previous discussion become almost universally problematic. Certainly, the nineteenth-century statutes appear to create the insane as a separate class of deviant, and in a sense they were; in the county asylum system, they remained a separate class specifically of deviant poor, and pauper status was required in order for admission. Arguably, the county asylum acts of the nineteenth century are appropriately considered to be a branch of the poor law itself (Bartlett, 1999).

This makes sense chronologically. The County Asylums Act 1808 was of limited effect. The 1845 Act was of considerably greater effect, based not only on the numbers of asylums built, but also on the numbers of people confined. Arguably, the significant change occurring between the two Acts is the replacement of the largely voluntary parish officers of the old poor law, with the professional workforce of the new. While the

1808 Act had given poor law officials the duty to enforce the Acts at the local level, it was only with the post-1834 staffing that the admission processes could be run on the scale the Acts intended. If this approach is correct, the question arises as to when the provision of asylum and other services to people with mental disorders really separates from the provision of poor law, or social services, as we would now call it. The question is perhaps whether they have ever become separate. A reasonable case can be made for the separation for asylum provision when the NHS was created, because it was at that time that the final vestiges of the poor law were laid to rest. For community care, however, the argument looks as strong as ever. Thus as will be seen below, it is only when community care services became claimable on social services budgets rather than health budgets that significant provision began to be made for care in the community.

The poor law connection is significant not merely for its administrative relationship to the asylum, but also because it was reformed at roughly the same time as the asylum law, and it too, at least on paper, introduced an institutional solution through the nineteenth-century workhouse. Prisons also grew apace in this period. Institutional solutions were popular throughout social policy at this time. Can these parallels be considered as flowing from the same causes? Can both reforms be related to the economic changes prompted by the industrial revolution? Again, arguments are not straightforward. Certainly, population growth was rapid and unyielding, and there was a shift from rural to urban living for a significant proportion of the population. Traditional communities and social ties were broken. The result was the beginnings of the creation of a great swathe of urban poverty. As Scull has pointed out, however, the asylum had already been adopted as policy when the majority of the population still lived outside new cities, and before the Acts of 1845, the decision, at county level, to construct an asylum bore little relation to the extent of urbanisation and industrialisation. Scull offers instead an analysis that echoes that offered by Foucault in relation to the previous century. He suggests that explanation should focus on 'the effects of the ever more thoroughgoing commercialization of existence' (1979: 29), resulting in 'the abandonment of long-established techniques for coping with the poor and the troublesome' (1979: 30) without recourse to institutionalisation. For Scull, the new logic of commodification undermined informal methods of responding to insanity based on feudal relations of patronage, essentially converting them from social to economic relations based on waged labour. Madness in the era of capitalism is defined in terms of the requirements of that system, which is to say in terms of the ability to work. Incarceration of the insane freed former carers to work outside the home in the new factories, and in addition 'seemed ideally suited to the means of establishing "proper" work habits among those elements of the workforce who were apparently more resistant to the monotony, routine, and regularity of industrialised labour' (1979: 35).

Proof of such a theory is problematic. It would be naive to ignore the social change that occurred in this period, and the consequent changes to the possibilities of domestic care of the insane. Certainly, the values cited by Scull were significant in the ideology of the new asylums. As we have seen, work was to be provided in the asylum for those able to pursue it. Similarly, an inability to work was one of the factors that might be considered in determining the appropriateness of an asylum admission. It was not, of course, the only one, but Scull's theory is not so crass. It acknowledges that confinement of an insane person may be necessary because of the absence of other care possibilities. It also acknowledges the possibility that those with insane relations might increasingly expect the state to provide care. While certainly an arguable view, such motives are difficult to substantiate. It does not inspire confidence, however, that patterns of institutionalisation of the insane during the period bear no obvious correlation to patterns of economic growth or recession and unemployment in the period, as one might expect if the growth of asylums is to be understood in economic terms.

In all of this discussion of the nineteenth century, doctors, in general, and specialists in mental disorders, in particular, have been conspicuous by their absence. They have long been involved in the treatment of the insane, of course; at some point in the last 250 years, they became particularly central to the administration of insanity. Precisely how and when that colonisation occurred is controversial. Certainly, by the middle of the eighteenth century, the process had begun. Jones (1972: 35) argues that the madness of George III, cured by Dr Willis, gave the image of the mad doctor a considerable boost. That seems undisputed, although the rudiments of professional formation were falling into place before that time, with the opening of a variety of hospitals for the insane in the second half of the eighteenth century. First of these was St Luke's in London, opened in 1751. St Luke's was to be a teaching hospital and centre for medical research, and admitted medical students from the start. Other hospitals or asylums, funded, like St Luke's, by way of public subscription, opened in quick succession: Manchester Lunatic Hospital in 1766; others in Newcastle, Liverpool, York and elsewhere soon followed. Certainly, the doctors running these establishments, and particularly those involved in private madhouses, would complain of low professional status, but, in time, madhouse-keeping became an object of pride rather than shame, 'helping, not hindering, a medical career' (Porter, 1987a: 167). Porter points out that William Battie, the driving force behind St Luke's, was to become President of the Royal College of Physicians.

The movement of medical specialists into the treatment of insanity continued with the development of the county asylums. Andrew Scull (1993) has devoted considerable talent and insight to a claim that the nineteenth century was the period when specialist doctors consolidated their professional status over the insane. Much of his work is extremely perceptive in this regard, examining how the new specialist class of mad-doctors form a profession, complete with professional journals and a professional organisation, the Association of Medical Officers of Asylums and Hospitals for the Insane. It is indisputable that significant medical theory developed in the nineteenth century. That said, for key developments, the medical profession can be seen as followers rather than leaders. Thus, notwithstanding the myth that the policy of non-restraint was introduced by John Conolly at the Hanwell Asylum in London, it would seem instead that it was introduced by the Justices of the Peace in charge of the asylum: see Suzuki (1995). This is significant of a considerably wider phenomenon: while specialist doctors were appointed as medical superintendents of county asylums for much of the nineteenth century, they had remarkably little power. Specifically, they did not control who came into the asylum; that was the role of Justices of the Peace, poor law relieving officers, and poor law medical officers. They similarly did not control who left the asylum: that, once again, was in the hands of the managing committee of Justices.

In the private sector, things were different, because often the facility would be owned by a doctor. If it was not, however, the relations between the owner and the medical officer might presumably be complex. For both the private and county facilities, medical certificates were, of course, required for admission (two for the former, one for the latter); individuals with an interest in the facility to which admission was sought were specifically precluded from signing the forms. As a result, they would frequently be signed not by specialists, but by general doctors. All of this did not, of course, stop the specialist doctors from developing a professional expertise in the treatment of insanity, but it is difficult to see that this specialist group enjoyed particularly administrative or political influence in the nineteenth century. That would arise instead in the twentieth century.

So why did asylums grow? The centralised theory of Jones is problematic, in that the growth required the acquiescence, if not the outright enthusiasm, of the local officials, and the central authorities had no way of enforcing that. Bartlett's theory may account for that more effectively, but it does not explain why private provision also increased markedly in the nineteenth century (although not as greatly as county asylum provision). The fact that such provision increased outside of the administrative framework Bartlett describes suggests that internal administrative dynamics of the poor law cannot solely account for the growth of the asylum system: this must, at least in part, reflect a broader paradigm shift. The increased promise of cure is similarly problematic as an explanation. The use of data sets by modern historians would suggest that the asylums did have a curative role: roughly two thirds of people admitted were released cured within two years of admission (Wright, 1997). Nineteenth-century observers seemed to be unaware of this fact, however, and their reports tended to read from the earliest times as justifications for the failures of cure (see Scull, 1993). Certainly, the nineteenth century favoured institutional solutions more broadly, but it is difficult to see how that broad principle related to specific causal factors. It would seem that we are left with a selection of partial and not entirely convincing explanations; the issues will no doubt be debated by historians for a long time to come.

Accounts of the retreat from the asylum are no less problematic. Contemporary accounts tended to link the fall-off in hospital inpatient numbers with the emergence of a new generation of major tranquillising drugs in the 1950s. The first and most well known of these was chlorpromazine, which was first produced in France in 1950. The drug was first used in the UK in 1954 (where it is known as Largactil), and in the USA in 1955 (under the name Thorazine). There is no doubt that there was a 'drug revolution' in psychiatric practice at this time. As Scull (1977: 80) points out, in the USA, in late 1953, Thorazine was only used (in trials) on 104 patients; by 1955, an estimated two million prescriptions were written. Smith Kline French aggressively marketed the drug, and the company's turnover increased from $53m in 1953 to $347m by 1970.

This explanation seems to have a logical ring to it. If drug therapies can, at the very least, hold symptoms in abeyance, and possibly even 'cure' mental illness, the rationale for a general policy of inpatient treatment is undermined. Of course, huge benefits accrued to the status of the psychiatric profession within the medical, and broader, establishment with the advent of the new drug therapies. Here was confirmation of the organic, somatic model of mental illness, which allowed psychiatry to conform more explicitly to a medical model. The drug revolution also precipitated a change in government policy. The Mental Health Act 1959 recast the relation between 'legalism' and 'medicalism' in favour of the latter (although the process had already begun with the introduction of 'informal' admissions by the Mental Treatment Act 1930: see Chapter 1), and also redrew the map of service provision. From now on, there was to be a greater emphasis, at least at the level of policy, on outpatient and community-based service provision. 'Community care', which had in fact been a constant feature of the social response to mental disorder throughout the age of the asylum, now became government policy. In 1960, Enoch Powell, then Minister of Health, announced that the old Victorian asylums were 'doomed institutions'. According to his Hospital Plan of 1962, inpatient services were to be relocated to the greatest extent possible within general hospitals (and departments of psychiatry were indeed a feature of many general hospitals from the early 1960s) and, so the theory ran, investment was now to be channelled into community care schemes of one sort or another rather than into the maintenance of the Victorian asylum system (see later in this chapter). Moreover, this was seen to be politically feasible, because there was, by this time, a more tolerant attitude on the part of society in general towards mentally disordered persons.

There is, however, good reason to think that this explanation is altogether too neat. For a start, inpatient numbers in some hospitals began to fall *before* the emergence of chlorpromazine. Mapperly hospital in Nottingham, for example, had started to reduce inpatient numbers from 1948 (1948, 1,310; 1956, 1,060), and this pattern continued 'at an unchanged pace even after drugs arrived on the scene'. This was a pattern that can also be seen in hospitals in the USA (Scull, 1977: 82). In some European countries, asylum numbers continued to rise after the introduction of the new drug treatments (Rogers and Pilgrim, 2001: 62). In the UK, there was little correlation between diagnosis, treatment and decarceration: so that, although the new treatments were not appropriate for the majority of hospital inpatients this did not prevent their deinstitutionalisation (Butler, 1993: 37). In short, the preponderance of academic opinion today is to the effect that the link between decarceration and the drug revolution is little more than a modern myth (see, e.g., Butler, 1993: 36; Rogers and Pilgrim, 2005: 177; Scull, 1977: 82).

So what does explain the undeniable fact of decarceration? Scull's argument, which is well known, is that asylums did not cure people, but merely institutionalised them; those working in the system did not need radical sociologists to tell them this. Maudsley, for example, was making the point in the late nineteenth century. But the nineteenth-century campaign for a policy of care in the community failed, or rather it lay dormant until its time came, that is, when its interests coincided with wider ideological and political agendas. Scull's second factor is the development of the welfare state after the Second World War. Scull locates the emergence of decarceration policies in the 1950s in the context of 'the internal dynamics of the development of capitalist societies' (1977: 134). As seen above, Scull has offered a similarly economically oriented explanation of the rise of the asylum a century earlier. In respect of decarceration, he argues that, with the emergence of the welfare state and an accompanying rise in state expenditure on the provision of welfare services, the asylum became too expensive to justify when 'outrelief' was as a general rule easier on the state's pocket. Scull points out that expenditure on social services as a percentage of GDP increased from 10.9 per cent in 1937 to 24.9 per cent in 1973, which has led to 'acute budgetary strains' (1977: 138). For Scull, the impact of the drug revolution should be seen as a subset of these broader economic considerations. The virtue of the new drug treatments, as such, is not so much that they 'work' but that they give credence to a strategy of service provision outside the asylum that is geared by considerations of cost rather than therapy.

Scull's analysis cannot easily be dismissed. It has been pointed out, however, that it is an analysis that is easier to apply to the 1960s, when financial problems, the 'sterling crisis' in particular, were a matter of acute concern for the government of the time. The 1950s, by contrast, were not a time of economic crisis, but rather of rapid economic growth (Rogers and Pilgrim, 2005: 178). Rogers and Pilgrim emphasise 'changes in ideological factors not economic factors' (2001: 63), in particular, the link between Nazi concentration camps and other forms of incarceration that had been made, amongst others, by Deutsch (1973). Scull, in turn, has argued that such comparisons represent little more than 'the hyperbole of muck-raking journalism' (1996: 385). Another undoubtedly important development was the spread of 'open door' policies from the mid-1950s, as psychiatric professionals developed a sensitivity to critical accounts of asylum life, and attempts were made to identify psychiatric facilities more closely with hospitals. The 'open door' policy was itself a function of a broader changes within psychiatric practice. Prior (1993) has shown how the objects of psychiatric discourse have changed throughout the twentieth century, as research in the early decades of the century (Rosanoff, 1917; Lewis, 1929; cited in Prior, 1993) revealed that both that psychiatric disorder was much more prevalent than had previously been appreciated and that many psychiatric disorders had to be evaluated – and treated – in terms of their social context. As Prior explains, 'the discovery of the reservoir of mental illness in the community suggested that the presence of the asylum wall no longer acted as a natural boundary between the sane and the insane' (1993: 110). Many of the mental health problems identified tended to be minor in nature, and inappropriate for hospitalisation.

Although it may not be immediately apparent how the discovery of greater amounts of mental illness (and learning disability) in the community at large is linked to the policy of decarceration, the point is that there has been a shift in the focus of hospital-based services, from dealing with both acute and chronic cases, to a marked focus on acute. This is especially evident over the last few years. The total number of short stay hospital beds for elderly patients suffering from mental illness has risen slightly, from 6,390 in 1994–5 to 7,620 in 2000–1. For other patients, there were 14,380 beds available in 2001, down from 15,210 in 1994–5, although a rise over the previous year's figure of 14,120. In the same period, long-stay beds for elderly patients fell from 10,760 (having stood at 13,660 in 1992–3) to 5,540 and for other patients from 7,830 (having stood at 11,000 in 1992–3) to 4,200 (Government Statistical Service, 2002: Table B23). By the end of 2006, all long-stay beds for the elderly had been transferred to the independent sector. Busfield (1986) has suggested that this shift in orientation from chronic to acute patients can explain the apparent paradox in patterns of hospitalisation in the 1960s, when falling total inpatient numbers coexisted with significant increases in admission rates, from 78,500 in 1955 to 170,000 in 1968 (Scull, 1977: 67). Bott (1976) has argued that the beginnings of this trend are discernible in the 1930s, when first admissions, and numbers discharged, began to rise. It is likely that, as well as reflecting changes in the orientation of psychiatry, these features are a function of the availability, after 1930, of admission to, and discharge from, hospital on an informal basis. Scull is more cynical, arguing that the increase in admissions in this period should be seen in terms of a rearguard action on the part of asylum staff and managers to demonstrate that the asylum was not unable to cure people. A high turnover implies a high cure rate, although in reality, this meant that patients were discharged whether 'cured' or not, and, in the case of long-stay patients, whether 'deinstitutionalised' or not. According to Bean and Mounser (1993: 12) 'everyone gets out, and some, it appears, whether they are ready or not'.

The pattern of ever-increasing admissions continued to be a feature of the system, certainly as far as compulsory admissions under civil law are concerned, throughout the 1990s. There were 16,021 such admissions under Part II of the Mental Health Act 1983 in 1990–1 (excluding the admission of those already in hospital), rising year on year (save for 1995–6) reaching 26,909 in 1998–9 (Department of Health, 2003c: Table 1). Since that time, numbers have stayed fairly constant, with 26,632 admissions in 2000–1, 26,403 in 2002–3 and 26,752 in 2004–5, the last year for which figures are available (Department of Health, 2006c: Table 1). Yet on 31 March 2005, 14,681 persons (including those admitted when already in hospital, who constitute a good chunk of the whole: see Chapter 4) were detained under Part II (2006c: Table 2). This would seem to indicate that duration of stay is relatively short. Ramon (1992: xii) found that 60 per cent of hospital admissions spend less than a month as an inpatient, and more recently, Thompson et al. (2004) found that only 3.2 per cent of patients stayed in hospital longer than 90 days, and only 1 per cent were still in hospital a year after initial admission. Paradoxically, shorter periods of detention can lengthen the overall time that a patient is, episodically, in receipt of inpatient care. The Mental Health Act Commission (2005: para. 2.14) has reported on research conducted in Wales, which found that although 'first admissions were considerably shorter in 1996 than 1896...today's patients will spend longer periods of their lives in hospital than their counterparts a century ago'. This seems to suggest that decarcaration may be, to some extent at least, an ideology that is imposed on the system and individual patients, sometimes inappropriately.

Can the change, at least in part, be attributed to a broader policy shift away from institutional solutions? The beginning of decarceration at the end of the 1940s corresponds to the final end of the poor law and its workhouses, and a move in poor relief generally towards financial assistance to live in the community. If the rise of the asylum can be understood in terms of the favouring of institutional solutions in nineteenth-century social policy, can the twentieth-century move away from the asylum similarly be perceived as just another manifestation of a broader social policy? In this context, it should be emphasised that, notwithstanding the policy focus on asylums in the nineteenth and early twentieth centuries, care in other settings by no means ceased to exist. In part, this emphasises that local practice did not necessarily match official policy discourses. Thus, a steady 25 per cent of those found to be insane in the nineteenth century were cared for in workhouses, and contrary to popular myth, these workhouse wards were not necessarily substandard in accommodation (Bartlett, 1999): many, in fact, became NHS hospitals after 1948. In addition, care outside institutions continued throughout the so-called heyday of the asylum. Systems of boarding out-patients existed in both Scotland and Wales throughout the nineteenth century, whereby insane persons would be housed with family, friends, or paid carers in the community, or lodged on farms (Hirst and Michael, 1999; Sturdy and Parry-Jones, 1999). In England, arrangements tended to be less formal, but outdoor poor relief (doles) to people identified as insane continued throughout the nineteenth century, albeit on a diminishing scale. In the years between the two world wars, there was increasing experimentation relating to care in the community, particularly of those identified as mentally defective (Thomson, 1996). Indeed, by the Second World War, almost 44,000 people in England were living outside the traditional asylum system under statutory guardianship under the Mental Deficiency Acts 1926 and 1939 (Walmsley *et al.*, 1999: 186). On this basis, a move to increased community care can perhaps be seen as a policy reorientation waiting to happen.

3.3 Community care

3.3.1 The development of community care and its impact on hospital-based services

The term 'community care' was first coined by the Royal Commission on Mental Illness and Mental Deficiency (the 'Percy Commission'), which sat from 1954 to 1957. The 1959 Act lifted the concept of guardianship from the Mental Deficiency Act 1913, giving a 'guardian' the powers 'of a parent over his or her 14-year-old child' over a person subject to an order, the criteria for which were, and remain under the 1983 Act, broadly similar to those for confinement. Although nobody was quite sure what such powers entailed (and their detail was amended in 1983), the intention behind guardianship was to provide a community-based alternative to compulsory institutionalisation. Enoch Powell followed up, a year after his Hospital Plan of 1962, with *Health and Welfare: The Development of Community Care* (Ministry of Health, 1963). All of this seems to fit neatly with the view that the policy of decarceration did not exist in isolation, but rather was the mechanism through which a fundamental change was to be effected in the structure of the mental health system: a relocation of the client base of mental health services from institutions to 'the community'. As with decarceration, however, the actuality is somewhat more complex, even paradoxical. No more than a brief outline of some of the relevant factors at play will be considered here. The current legal framework for community care service provision, and prospects for reform, will be considered in Chapter 9.

The first paradox is concerned with the very existence of community care. On the one hand, the policy document published in 1963 was to be the first of many such government documents with similar sounding names. Amongst the most important of these are: *Better Services for the Mentally Handicapped*, a White Paper published in 1971 (Department of Health and Social Security, 1971); its companion document *Better Services for the Mentally Ill*, published in 1975 (Department of Health and Social Security, 1975); the Audit Commission report *Making a Reality of Community Care* published in 1986 (Audit Commission, 1986); the Griffiths Report, *Community Care: Agenda for Action* (Griffiths, 1988). Each of these documents spoke to the failure to translate community care policy into community care practice. As Murphy (1991: 60) pointed out, by 1974 there were 60,000 fewer hospital inpatients than in 1954 'but very few services existed in the community... in most cases these people simply "disappeared" from the official statistics since no one followed up their progress or knew anything about their fate'. In the cash-strapped 1960s, the attraction of care in the community as a cheaper option than institutionalisation, buttressed by permissive legislation regarding the provision of services, ensured that the policy was chronically underfunded. The White Paper of 1975 pointed out that, in the year 1973–4, £300m was spent on hospital services and only £15m on community care provision, and by March 1974, 31 local authorities had no residential accommodation for the mentally ill and a greater number – 63 – did not even have day provision (Busfield, 1986: 348). Although the number of inpatients continued to fall, mental hospitals remained the key locus for the delivery of services. In the early 1980s, all of the hospitals marked for closure by the Hospital Plan of two decades earlier remained open. In part, this is a 'chicken and egg' situation: decarceration policies were delimited by the lack of residential provision 'in the community', but whilst funds remained tied up in hospital services, and hospitals remained willing to admit patients – indeed, as seen above, in ever greater numbers, and usually informally – and the public at large continued to construct the mentally ill as 'other', fuelled by a number of notorious cases, such as that of Graham Young (see Chapter 8), there was a lack of political will, both centrally and locally to make community care a 'reality'. In a very real sense, community care simply did not happen.

On the other hand, recent re-evaluations of the age of the asylum have shown that care in the community has been a constant feature of the social response to mental illness and learning disability: there have always been elements within psychiatry and its (particularly middle-class) client base, which have pursued and sought care outside the asylum (Bartlett and Wright, 1999). In a sense, therefore, 'community care' is nothing new but rather is an approach that existed both before and during the period of the 'great confinement'.

The key to understanding this paradox, which throws much light on the more recent developments, lies in unpacking the concept of 'community'. At a minimum, 'community' is a geographical location, but more importantly, it is also a malleable discursive construct, and is capable of being put to use in a variety of different ways. Bartlett and Wright, for example, use the term as shorthand for care 'outside the asylum', and, in particular, in and by the family. The policy of community care after 1960 was also predicated to a large extent on the assumption that much care that had hitherto been provided in the form of inpatient treatment could be provided – at a fraction of the cost – by and in the family (Lewis, 1989). As women, in fact, provide the vast bulk of 'informal' care (although men may recently have come to play a greater role in this regard, see Arber *et al.*, 1988), whether in a family setting or by way of voluntary work for charitable organisations, the concept of 'community' used here, therefore, implicitly draws on an underpinning set of assumptions about the link between the concepts of care and femininity (Finch, 1984).

Post-1960 community care policy, however, also drew on the notion of 'social reintegration'. 'Community' here is used in a broader sense, to connote not simply the family of the person in need of 'care' but also the community at large. This much is evident from the social work theories that have developed around the concept. Normalisation theory, which emphasises the need for the community to value more highly the contribution that people with mental disorder problems, and learning disabilities in particular, make to society (Brown and Smith, 1992), can be seen as 'treatment' not so much for the client as for the community. The Independent Living Movement argues that community care policy should be geared towards ensuring that persons, who might otherwise be hospitalised, are provided with the means to live independent, participatory lives as members of the broader community (Morris, 1993). Others (see Hume and Pullen, 1994) advocate the 'rehabilitation model', the key elements of which involve helping individuals to (re)learn socially necessary skills, and which, like the Independent Living Movement, emphasises such things as the recognition of the rights of clients, their empowerment in decision-making, and the promotion of normal patterns of life.

At the end of the 1990s the Labour government stated brusquely that 'community care has failed' (Department of Health, 1998a; 1998b). One significant reason for this, although not the reason emphasised by the government, that the 1950s view – that the broader community was prepared for the reintegration of mentally disordered members – was mistaken. And this, in turn, is in significant measure explicable in terms of a failure to understand adequately the multifaceted nature of the concept of 'community' (and its ever-present companion, the 'other', that which is not 'community') before attempting to build a policy on that basis. As early as 1957, research suggested that 'on the whole...people...do not wish to have very much contact with mental illness either on the personal or social level' (Cumming and Cumming, 1957, cited in Prior, 1993: 124).

To say that community care has failed should not, however, be taken to imply that nothing changed. By 1977, one third of admissions into psychiatric hospitals were to wards in general hospitals rather than in mental hospitals (Barham, 1992: 20). Psychiatry became more fully medicalised, and from the start of the 1980s, the old large-scale asylums finally began to close. Initially, this was a painfully slow, ward-by-ward, process, but in the 1990s, the rate of closure speeded up, and was complete by the end of that decade. Accordingly, the 'shape' of the mental hospital system has changed, although the process is by no means complete. As seen earlier in the chapter, the current number of hospital beds available for patients with mental illness or who have learning disabilities (together the 'mentally disordered', as per s. 1(2) of the MHA 1983) – around 35,500 in England in 2005 – represents a decrease over previous years, and it is long-stay beds that are being shed by the NHS. Available beds in nursing and residential care homes, by contrast, rose throughout the 1990s. Residential care beds for persons with a mental illness reached 22,180 in 1994–5 and 37,780 in 2000–1, and in nursing care homes, rose from 24,190 to 28,780 over the same period (Government Statistical Service, 2002: Table B23). Local authorities had long been reluctant to accept fully their responsibilities for the long-term mentally ill and (although to a lesser extent) learning disabled. Various policy initiatives attempted to galvanise local government into action, but it was not until the decision was taken (in 1980) that the cost of residential accommodation could be claimed by way of social security benefits that the residential community care sector finally began to expand, as '[s]uddenly patients could be transferred into the community without burdening the budgets of health and local authorities' (Muijen, 1996: 145). Guaranteed payment by way of bene-fits provided the incentive required for the rapid development of privately run residen-tial homes (see Commission for Social Care Inspection, 2005: Table 7.1, discussed earlier in this chapter). These institutions vary in size from a few hundred to a handful of beds. The latter type of accommodation often takes the form of a so-called 'group home', in which residents live in a semi-communal, family-like arrangement. Perring (1992) identifies four types of group home:

- independent flats for patients immediately leaving hospital;
- homes with 24-hour staffing;
- group homes with daytime staffing;
- hostels on hospital sites.

In addition, social service departments and CPNs, combined into CMHCs and CMHTs (see earlier in the chapter) deliver outreach and other community-based services. The first CMHC opened in 1977, with numbers rising to 54 in 1987, and around 75 ten years later. Today, as the most tangible effect so far of the implementation of the NSFMH, we are approaching national coverage, although this is patchy, and out-of-hours services in particular are currently unsatisfactory (Healthcare Commission and the Commission for Social Care Inspection, 2006).

There has, then, been a sizeable increase in the provision of mental health services in the form of 'community care', although recent statistics indicate that the exponential growth of residential places that was a feature of the 1990s has now peaked (see earlier).

The proposed reform of the Mental Health Act, with the provision of increased powers of treatment in the community and the removal of the rigid legal distinction between hospital-based and community-based treatment regimes, can be expected to prompt further developments. Hence, as far as the future is concerned, although there are forces at work that, for some mentally disordered persons as defined by the MHA 1983 (chiefly the 'psychopathically disordered' and others thought to warrant secure detention on the grounds of the protection of the public), look likely to result in a renewed emphasis on compulsory hospitalisation, the overall trend towards the provision of care outside of hospital looks set to continue for a while yet.

3.3.2 Community care: divergence, convergence and colonisation

In order to understand the general social significance of the contemporary mental health system, it is not sufficient simply to attempt to measure the degree to which there has been a shift from hospital-based to community-based sites of service delivery. An assessment of the degree to which there has been *qualitative* and/or *functional* change in the 'shape' of the system must also be made: and this requires that concepts like 'hospital' and 'community-based' must again be unpacked. It also requires that the provision of community care for those suffering from mental disorder be located in the wider context of the provision of welfare services in the era of decarceration. As noted earlier, social work theories have their place in the provision of care in the community. The services that are the particular concern of this book must be set in the broader context of the development of the welfare state in the period after the Second World War. The establishment of the National Health Service by the National Health Service Act 1946 drew on consensus-based theories of community and 'cradle to grave' protection for all citizens. Other key legislation, notably the National Assistance Act 1948, which finally abolished the workhouse and ushered in the modern social security benefits system, marks the end of incarceration as the policy response to poverty. Community care for mental disorder must be set against this broader context, not simply in terms of a renewed policy preference for 'outrelief', but also in terms of the material development of the welfare state, in particular, in the form of local authority social services departments.

The assumption built into the Powell scheme of the early 1960s was that, in general terms, the responsibility for the provision of social services in the community was to lie with local authorities, but that the provision of services for the mentally ill was the province of health authorities. The consequence was inertia, because hospital-based spending dominated health budgets and local authorities tended to prioritise poverty and disability rather than mental health. The 1975 White Paper redrew the map to an extent, underlining the point that the appropriate response to chronic mental disorder was small-scale residential units in the community, funded by local authorities, but it was not until the National Health Service and Community Care Act 1990 (NHSCCA) that the relationship between local and health authorities in the provision of community care services was drawn with anything approaching precision. This Act removed from the NHS the primary responsibility for the provision of non-hospital services for those requiring long-term care. Now, the responsibility for overall planning of service provision was to lie primarily at the door of local authorities, in consultation with health authorities, independent sector providers and voluntary agencies: s. 46(1), (2), NHSCCA 1990 (see now also Health and Social Care Act 2001, Ch. 2, Parts 3 and 4). Although, from one point of view, this might be seen as something of a poisoned chalice, such an arrangement also has the potential to mark a qualitative shift in the shape of the mental health system to the extent that now mental disorder in 'the community' was as much a social work issue as it was a medical one.

This was certainly the intention of the social work profession, and well before 1990. The involvement of social workers in the delivery of mental health policy was slight in the early years of community care. The first psychiatric social worker had only been appointed in London in 1936, although social workers had a presence in American service delivery as early as 1905 (Prior, 1993: 88). But by the 1970s, social work had become a recognised profession requiring training, and its knowledge base began to build up. The British Association of Social Workers (BASW) campaigned for specialist mental health training for social workers to be built into the law by the reforms that took place in 1983, and s. 114, MHA 1983 now provides that 'approved social workers', who have various statutory functions in relation to detained patients, not least being the responsibility to apply to a hospital for a person to be detained in it under the 1983 Act, must be persons of 'appropriate competence in dealing with persons who are suffering from mental disorder': s. 114(2), MHA 1983. It is not only hospital-related matters that social workers are concerned with. As discussed earlier, there are now various well-developed social work theories of community care. The post-1990 regime devolved power for the provision of services at ground level to social workers as 'care mangers' in social services and 'key workers' in mental health services, and the role of social workers was given sharper definition by legislation in 1995 concerning the 'supervised discharge' of patients from hospital and their continued monitoring thereafter (see Chapter 9). Social workers may also take the role of advocate in respect of the entitlement to services of their clients.

Yet to date, in so far as the social work profession has had aspirations to usurp the role of medical professionals in the delivery of community care services, the project must be counted as unsuccessful. The psychiatric profession still dominates, and indeed the exclusive jurisdiction of social work professionals over hospital-related matters is under challenge, because under current government proposals 'the role will be opened up to a wider group of appropriately trained and qualified mental health professionals such as nurses and occupational therapists' (Department of Health, 2006d: 2) and the title of the role will accordingly change to 'Approved Mental Health Professional'. Further discussion of this point in relation to the admissions process into hospital can be found in Chapter 5. As far as community-based services are concerned, it is clear here too that psychiatry remains the dominant profession (Prior, 1992). There was to be no central funding of specialist mental health training for social workers, and the numbers of such specialists has remained problematically low in the years after 1983 (see Chapter 5). This dominance by the psychiatric profession of services for mentally disordered persons outside of hospital will require further discussion shortly. Staying for the moment, though, with the NHSCCA 1990, it has to be said that this Act is more often discussed in terms of a definitive moment in the emergence of 'managerialism' rather than that of medicalism in the delivery of healthcare services.

In the years following 1979, welfarism was recast, as the concept of 'community' was given a new inflection, emphasising the responsibility of service users and service providers to the broader community in terms of economic efficiency. State services have been increasingly infused with market principles and practices, and the mental health system is no exception. The 1990 Act was intended not only to systematise the provision of community care, but also to revolutionise the structure of the NHS. The immediate precursors of the 1990 Act were the White Papers of 1989: *Caring for People* (Department of Health, 1989a) was concerned with community care; *Working for Patients* (Department of Health, 1989b) with the National Health Service. The immediate concern of each was the same: the cost of community care and the health service, respectively. For instance, in the case of the former, the availability of supplementary benefits (from an uncapped central government fund) for funding residential accommodation had played a large part in causing a rise in expenditure on supplementary benefit from £80m in 1978 to £1.5bn in 1989 (Muijen, 1996: 145). The Audit Commission Report of 1986 (Audit Commission, 1986) pointed out that not only was this a very expensive way of funding community care, but it also built in a tendency for preference to be given to residential accommodation, funded by supplementary benefit, rather than the provision of services to clients in their own homes, the bill for which had to be met from local authority funds.

The 1990 Act abolished this use of supplementary benefit and set in place a system under which the financing of 'residential care' was to be the responsibility of local authorities, while 'nursing care' was that of health authorities. This was only a small part of the picture. The fundamental change ushered in by the 1990 Act was the division of both hospital and community care systems along market lines, with players defined as either 'providers' or 'acquirers' (purchasers) of care: s. 4, NHSCCA 1990. Local social service authorities and health authorities (along with fundholding general practitioners and private clients) were to be 'purchasers' of services. Hospitals and local authority social services departments were to be 'providers' of services, now in competition with private sector suppliers. The Labour administration of the late 1990s abolished the single market in health (by way, inter alia, of the Health Act 1999, the Health and Social Care Act 2001, and the National Health Service Reform and Health Care Professions Act 2002); but the devolution of decision-making power and budgetary control to units of provision, and the distinction between primary and secondary care – with the new primary care trusts (replacing GP fundholding) contracting for the provision of most secondary care (PCTs can provide some such care themselves) from NHS trusts – remains. The government also adopted a policy of funding trusts according to past performance (s. 2, Health and Social Care Act 2001), and of formalising its policy of public–private partnerships.

In previous editions of this book, we suggested that it was the advent of managerialism that posed the real challenge to the dominance of the clinical psychiatrist, and although, subsequently, clinical governance has come more to the fore, this does not so much represent a renaissance for medical criteria as the further infusion of medical criteria with market-type ideas of efficiency and value for money. Key early documents included the White Paper *The New NHS: Modern, Dependable* (Department of Health, 1997a), the NHS Executive's Consultation Document (1998) *A First Class Service – Quality in the new NHS* and its subsequent (1999) *Clinical Governance: Quality in the new NHS*, the *NHS Plan* (Department of Health, 2000a), and *Building a Safer NHS for Patients* (Department of Health, 2001b). More recent reforms, introduced and implemented through a number of further key documents – including *Reforming NHS Financial Flows: Introducing Payment By Results* (Department of Health, 2003d), *The NHS Improvement Plan: Putting People at the Heart of Public Services* (Department of Health, 2004c), *Choose and Book: Patient's Choice of Hospital and Booked Appointment* (Department of Health, 2004d), *Commissioning a Patient-led NHS* (Department of Health, 2005), *Creating a Patient-led NHS: Delivering the NHS Improvement Plan* (Department of Health, 2005a), *Health Reform in England: Update and Next Steps* (Department of Health, 2005b), *Health Reform in England: Update and Commissioning Framework* (Department of Health, 2006e), *Our Health, Our Care, Our Say: A New Direction for Community Services* (Department of Health, 2006f), and *The NHS in England: The Operating Framework for 2006/7* (Department of Health, 2006g) – are designed to give greater say to patients, over time and place of treatment, and to relax, to some extent, the budgetary controls that hospitals managers have hitherto been able to exert over clinical staff.

Indeed, according to the Department of Health, it is already the case that 'Recent health reforms have changed the way that healthcare is commissioned. Under reforms such as payment by results and patient choice, clinical decisions are now direct drivers of financial resources' (2006h: 3). This is technically true, as it is that the system of 'Payment by Results' (PbR) provides PCTs with a financial incentive to increase productivity because there is a direct link between (increased) productivity and revenue. But the new arrangements also provide dilemmas for PCTs when making commissioning choices. PCTs are constrained by national tariffs for services provided and cannot negotiate cheaper prices, and must also factor in the degree to which patients exercise their new 'choose and book' rights to be given treatment at a time and place that best suits them rather than the healthcare body. Moreover, PCTs remain, to some extent, at the mercy of individual GPs and consultants, who determine whether a given patient should be admitted to hospital, or receive some form of outpatient treatment, or not, and so cannot fully control the 'activity', and expenses, that their patients generate (Mannion and Street, 2006). Tight control over budgets will remain the norm, and to this extent, at this early stage in the operation of the reformed system, the jury remains out on the question of the extent to which it is the healthcare professionals or their managers, and their strategic health authorities (which oversee the performance of PCTs), that have the upper hand in determining which services will be delivered.

The third element of this shift, along with this shift from hospital-based to community-based service provision, and from demand-led to supply-led service provision and managerialism, has been a shift from public to private sector provision. Although the cost of residential care, following the coming into force of the 1990 Act, had to be met by local authorities rather than the social security budget, the shift was sweetened by the availability of grant aid to be spent on acquiring services for persons in need by reason of mental illness (see HC(90)24). The availability of grant aid, which was time-limited to three years, depended on the abilities of local authorities to raise 30 per cent of the revenue, which in practice limited its availability to some local authorities, and could not be spent on capital projects (Butler, 1992: 88–9). Moreover, it was stipulated that 85 per cent of grant provision must be spent on the acquisition of independent sector care. This not only limited the potential of local authorities to work in tandem with health authorities (Muijen, 1996: 147) but gave further momentum to the trend of the 'privatisation' of welfare services throughout the 1990s, and as seen earlier, it is now the case that the vast majority of accommodation is to be found in the independent sector.

On one view, which tends to be voiced by those who associate with the 'old' communitarian values of the post-war welfare state (Butler, 1993; Cowen, 1999), this process of reform of the mental health system is seen in terms of a betrayal of that ethos. From a different perspective, one that draws on the Foucauldian themes of service provision as 'discipline' and social control, there is an altogether more sinister aspect to these developments. Cohen has provided the most influential and wide-ranging version of this thesis, in his book *Visions of Social Control* (1985). For Cohen, the development of community-based alternatives to institutionalisation in various contexts – poverty, criminality and mental disorder – should be read as the 'dispersal' of disciplinary strategies, from specialist institutions into society as a whole, involving: a widening of the net of social control; a 'thinning of its mesh', which brings a greater percentage of the population under supervision; a 'blurring' of the distinction between formal and informal methods of control; a greater 'penetration' of the state penal-therapeutic complex into the fabric of society. In its broadest version, this thesis has distinctly Orwellian connotations, of society at large continually under the disciplinary gaze of the state's organs of social control (Mathiesen, 1983). More nuanced versions, however, concede that the target population is limited to society's 'deviant' populations, including persons suffering from mental disorders, but nevertheless argue that the move out of the institution should be seen in terms of the greater 'psychiatrisation' of social problems. Applied to the context of mental health service provision, this is an attractive thesis. As detailed above, the early decades of the twentieth century saw an increase in the scope of psychiatry as new 'illnesses' were discovered in ever-wider sections of the general population (see earlier in this chapter). Rose (1986: 83, in Rogers and Pilgrim, 2001: 73) explicitly couples this with the process of decarceration:

Rather than seeking to explain a process of de-institutionalisation we need to account for the proliferation of sites for the practice of psychiatry. There has not been an extension of social control but rather the psychiatrisation of new problems.

In terms of the present discussion, perhaps the most important point here is that to conceive of community care in terms of new sites for old practices raises the question of the qualitative differences between hospital and community care. It can be argued that, given the rapid growth of residential community-based accommodation, 'decarceration' to date has meant little more than patients being relocated from one institution to another.

Perring (1992) found that, amongst former hospital inpatients discharged into group homes, although there was a preference for the latter, there were distinctly mixed views. It was widely remarked by residents that the new homes were too much like hospitals. Residents remained under supervision, visits by relatives were not encouraged, and there was a tendency amongst staff to 'infantise' residents: classic traits of hospital life (see further below). It was an increasingly notable feature of the 1990s that patients made subject to compulsory detention in a hospital under both civil and criminal powers of confinement, were being admitted into privately run nursing homes. In 1987–8, there were 281 such admissions (Department of Health, 1998d: Table 9). This rose to 463 in 1991–2, 898 in 1996–7 (Department of Health, 2003c: Table 3), 1,413 in 1999–2000, and reached 1,629 by 2004–5 (Government Statistical Service, 2006: Table 1). In 2004–5, 405 patients were sent to an independent hospital by a criminal court or from a prison under Part III of the 1983 Act (Government Statistical Service, 2006: Table 9), compared to only 22 in 1987–8 (Department of Health, 1998d: Table 9). Although such admissions constitute only a tiny proportion of the whole (see Chapters 4 and 6), they nevertheless raise crucial questions about the qualitative difference between hospital accommodation and community care accommodation. For the purposes of the MHA 1983, 'hospital' is defined broadly in s. 145(1) to include, as well as hospitals as defined by the National Health Service Act 1977, any accommodation provided by a local authority for use as a hospital, and s. 34(1) explicitly provides that a mental nursing home that is registered to accept detained patients (under the regime found in Part II, Care Standards Act 2000) is to be defined as an 'independent hospital' for the purposes of Part II of the 1983 Act (s. 2(2) Care Standards Act 2000). Other nursing homes or registered homes are not hospitals for these purposes, but to be registered as a nursing home the establishment in question must offer nursing and personal care to, inter alia, people who have or have had a mental disorder (s. 3(2)(b) Care Standards Act 2000), and are de facto hospitals. As Eldergill (1997: 137) has pointed out, whether a 'detained' patient is 'discharged' into 'the community' can depend solely on whether local provision of hostel accommodation and the like has been made, or purchased, by the health authority or the local authority: if it is the former, it may be defined as a hospital, but not if it is the latter. It can be suggested, therefore, that what constitutes a 'hospital' is essentially an arbitrary question that, ironically, at least in the context of the compulsory admission of patients into 'hospital', is determined more by the custodial rather than therapeutic qualities of the institution in question. Moreover, the vast majority of residential community-based accommodation is outside the provisions of the MHA 1983, which apply only to 'sectioned' patients, and as such, is a space of virtually unfettered medical discretion.

This thesis also garners plausibility from the proliferation of mechanisms for the control and monitoring of mentally disordered persons in their own homes. In the 1990s, 'supervision registers' were introduced, along with systems designed to provide continual monitoring in the form of the 'care plan approach' and 'aftercare under supervision', to sit alongside the already existent powers of guardianship (see Chapter 9). These powers do not extend to the forcible administration of treatment in the community, but the government intends to introduce a new order for supervised community treatment (SCT) in the near future (see preface). Like its forerunner, the medical treatment order, which figured prominently in the now aborted bills of 2002 and 2004, SCT comes very close to, but stops short of, introducing powers to give treatment without consent, although it will be possible to hospitalise a refusing patient within 24 hours, in order for treatment to be given (see Chapter 9). In practice, the threat of compulsion can often have the desired effect, and it is, in any case, possible to treat without consent in a community setting, if that setting is in the form of accommodation provided by a health authority, because it will count as a 'hospital' for these purposes. The recent loosening of the judicial embargo on the use of leave of absence from hospital (see *Re Barker*, discussed in Chapter 8) has, in addition, fashioned a de facto community treatment mechanism of more general application.

The strengthening of measures to control the behaviour of, in particular, mentally ill persons in their own homes has been carried forward on a wave of public concern about the threat to society that such persons constitute and has, in addition to the developments mentioned above, spawned such measures as the Sex Offenders Act 1997. In addition, there have been problems in attempting to provide group home accommodation because of opposition both from local residents and local authority planning authorities. In an illuminating but disheartening piece of research, Jodelet (1991) found that the social stigma of insanity had not left mental disorder, but rather continued to prefigure the interactions of persons so labelled with their 'normal' counterparts, for whom mental disorder continues to function as a motif for 'otherness'. In short, there is plenty of evidence to suggest both that, although patients can be taken out of the asylum, it is not so easy to take the asylum (as the symbol for 'otherness') out of the patients, and that in a very real sense, the move to community care should therefore be seen as a spreading out of the hospital system into a broader and more diverse range of sites, rather than constituting an alternative to hospitalisation. The provision of mental health services to persons in their own homes can, in the same way, be seen as the ever-greater diffusion of that (medicalised) disciplinary strategy.

There is no doubt that the 'dispersal of discipline' thesis accurately captures one important element of mental health policy over the last few decades, particularly in respect of the development of control-oriented powers over the last decade. But it also misses some important truths about both policy and, in particular, practice. As will be discussed in greater detail in Chapter 9, below, the powers of control in the community, as framed by the Mental Health (Patients in the Community) Act 1995, represent a compromise between the interests of control and the civil liberties of the individuals concerned, and bear the influence of a consideration of the provisions of the European

Convention of Human Rights. Any new law will have to give due weight to the Convention rights of patients, various of which will be pertinent, according to the fact situation. In other words, it is the case that, if what is meant by 'control' is the medicalisation of those pockets within the wider community that are inhabited by mentally disordered persons, then, to date at least, 'control' has been hemmed in by the presence of a legalistic discursive input at the level of policy formation. On the other hand, there is little doubt that the control imperative is to the fore at the moment, and the case law suggests that, where treatment can be shown to be medically necessary, it will not, in principle, breach any provision of the Convention (see Chapter 7). In short, there remains plenty of scope for the further tightening of the control of community care patients.

At the level of practice, there has long been an obvious difficulty with theories of social control: the failure of community care has been seen, most often, as a failure of control. Perhaps the dominant theme in public and political discourse concerning mental health over the last decade has concerned homicides and (but to a much lesser extent) suicides committed by mentally disordered persons. In part, this has been because of the failure of service providers to coordinate services effectively. A new blueprint for inter-agency working was published by the Department of Health in 1995 – *Building Bridges: A Guide to Arrangements for Inter-agency Working for the Care and Protection of Severely Mentally Ill People* (1995a) – and this has been followed by a further range of documents, and legislation, that have launched the policy of the Labour government (discussed in Chapter 9). Whether these developments will change the political realities, of a public that perceives the mentally ill as a risk, and inter-agency cooperation that has steadfastly remained at best patchy (Healthcare Commission, 2005; Sainsbury Centre and Mental Health Act Commission, 2005) in the face of many attempts to impose cooperative practices, is yet to be seen.

These policy developments reflect the political reality that the failure of community care as control has dominated the agenda. In the 1990s, there was a constant stream of independent inquiries into homicides and suicides that published reports, such as those following the killing of Jonathon Zito by Christopher Clunis in December 1992. It is true that these cases have been picked up and amplified by the media, and that the public and political reaction has often been out of all proportion to the scale of the problem: there is not an epidemic of murderous mental patients roaming at will throughout society, as some seem to believe (see Chapter 9). Nevertheless, read together, the independent reports paint a depressing picture of overstretched, under-resourced and understaffed community mental health teams, unable to maintain contact with patients who have little wish to cooperate with their 'care plan'. As it was put in the White Paper of 1998 (Department of Health, 1998a), 'while [community care] improved the treatment of many people who were mentally ill, it left far too many walking the streets, often at risk to themselves and a nuisance to others'. *Safety First*, the five-year report of the National Confidential Inquiry into Suicide and Homicide by People with a Mental Illness (Department of Health, 2001j) called for 'a major overhaul of the operation of the Care Plan Approach' (recommendation 9) amongst many others.

It is often not a matter of chance as to who 'falls through the net'. CMCHs have been criticised (e.g. Bean and Mounser, 1993) on the grounds that they tend to concentrate on acute patients at the expense of chronic patients. According to Scull, in the USA, where the same centres can be found, 'very few members of the chronic patient population find themselves being treated [by CMHCs]'.

In part, this is because such centres verge on bankruptcy 'but more importantly, from the very outset, those running these facilities made it clear that the very last people they wished to treat were the psychotic' (Scull, 1996: 388). Smyth and Hoult (2000), on the other hand, suggested that the provision of treatment to acute patients at home has been underdeveloped because of an orthodoxy that holds that acute patients must be in hospital, and although there is evidence that in some parts of the country treatment is increasingly being used (Owen *et al.*, 2000), it remains too often the case that those in need of treatment fall through the net. Howlett (1998: 3) found that there was 'no ownership of the chaotic and dangerous patients', and a key element in explaining this was that, very often, such patients were diagnosed as suffering from an untreatable 'personality disorder' (a 'severe and dangerous personality disorder' or 'SDPD'). The debate over the non-treatment of Michael Stone, who was found guilty in 1998 (he was retried, and again found guilty, in 2001 and appealed unsuccessfully in 2005) of the murder of a mother and daughter in Kent, typifies the situation. Stone had not been offered treatment because his condition was deemed untreatable. Jack Straw, then the Home Secretary, lambasted mental health professionals for their 'refusal' to 'treat' Stone, seeing it as an abdication of responsibility, but the response of professionals was that it was not appropriate to detain and/or treat a person deemed untreatable. The Home Secretary responded by announcing plans in June 1999 for the introduction of preventative custody for such persons (Home Office and Department of Health, 1999; Department of Health and Home Office, 2000a: ch 2), and although those legislative proposals were subsequently abandoned, £70m was made available to provide accommodation for SDPD within the prison estate and £56m for places within the hospital system and in hostels. A significant number of these places are already in operation.

The point here is that this is evidence, not of the spread of 'medicine as control' into the community, but of a general reluctance on the part of both psychiatric and social work professionals to undertake the control of such individuals. It may be that this has changed to an extent in recent years, as increasing amounts of resources have been channelled into community mental health teams, but there is evidence that in some areas community mental health teams are draining staff resources from inpatient care (Mental Health Act Commission, 2005: para. 2.10). Certainly, there has, as of yet, been no significant reduction in hospital admissions: indeed, they have continued to rise, in part, it seems, as a consequence of the actions of community teams (Sainsbury Centre for Mental Health, 2005: 63–4). As far as the spread of residential accommodation is concerned, it is hard to see this as 'social control' in any conspiratorial sense, given that it tends to be those who are least in need of control and most in need of treatment that are provided with accommodation. This is not to dispute that civil liberties issues are absolutely pertinent to the treatment of those who occupy residential or nursing home beds. For Scull, the new system resonates with its history, comprising little more than neo-feudal styles of control (Scull, 1996). And although there is a system of registration and inspection in place (under the Care Standards Act 2000), scandals, such as that concerning the physical abuse and neglect of residents over a period of many years in registered homes licensed and inspected in the Lothians region (*Edinburgh Evening News*, 10 March 2006) and in Cornwall (*The Guardian*, 5 July 2006), give rise to grave doubts about the ability of the system to detect and prevent this sort of abuse. This raises the issue of the experience of life as a hospital inpatient or client of community care residential accommodation. Before leaving our discussion of the mental health system, it is necessary to give this topic separate consideration.

3.4 Inside the institutions

Within the sociology of medicine, the Weberian model of modernist institutions as bureaucratic organisations characterised by the complexity of their social interaction is a popular way of conceptualising the functioning of hospitals. Such models, although useful, can marginalise the experience of the client population. In this latter respect, one author whose work has provided the template for many people's understanding of life in a mental hospital is Erving Goffman. His highly influential *Asylums* was first published in 1961. The book is the product of fieldwork carried out at St Elizabeth's, a large asylum in Washington DC, in the mid-1950s, although it also draws widely on secondary material to support its general thesis. Goffman argued that mental asylums have less in common with general hospitals and more in common with other 'total institutions', such as monasteries or convents. Total institutions are those that erect 'a barrier to social intercourse with the outside and to departure that is often built into the physical plant such as locked doors, high walls, barbed wire, cliffs, water, forests, or moors' (1991: 15–16). These institutions are problematic for Goffman because '[a] basic social arrangement in modern society is that the individual tends to sleep, play, and work in different places, with different co-participants, under different authorities, and without an overall rational plan'. Hence the 'central feature of total institutions can be described as a breakdown of the barriers ordinarily separating these three spheres of life' (1991: 17).

   For Goffman, then, the inmates of total institutions have had their lives spatially collapsed and rationalised, and must adhere precisely to a timetable conceived by somebody else, and to a rational plan, to the details of which they may not be privy. They must do this within a confined space and 'in the company of a large batch of others, all of whom are treated alike and required to do the same thing' (*ibid.*). Moreover, society within the institutions is split artficially into two groups: the inmates and the staff; '[e]ach grouping tends to conceive of the others in terms of narrow hostile stereotypes' (1991: 18). There is no public/private split here. The most personal or private aspects, not merely of inmates' lives, but of their minds, are public domain: a legitimate target for psychiatric intervention. This constitutes what Goffman describes as 'a violation of one's informational preserve regarding self' (1991: 32). The most profound or obvious effect of this is 'disculturation' or 'institutionalisation': the inability of inmates to cope with the demands and strains of life outside, i.e. the fostering in inmates of absolute dependency on the system not only to satisfy but also to define their needs. The 'self is systematically, if often unintentionally, mortified' (1991: 24). Institutionalisation signifies a radical departure in the moral career of inmates. The sense of 'self' developed on the outside, in the context of family and other relationships, is left at the gates, along with the inmate's physical possessions and human dignities. Inmates are, quite literally, 'mortified'.

There is an obvious irony here that Goffman is keen to bring out. If the purpose of mental hospitals to cure or rehabilitate inmates for 'life outside', it seems a peculiar way of going about things to suspend 'life outside' as part of this process. This suspension of 'real life', however, is not 'simply' total, but instead plays on the very fact of that suspension (1991: 23–4):

total institutions do not really look for cultural victory. They create and sustain a particular kind of tension between the home world and the institutional world and use this persistent tension as strategic leverage in the management of men.

Total institutions are coercive. Goffman talks, for example, about the 'obedience test' that new inmates have to go through (1991: 26–7). This, he argues, consists of the inmate accepting the total authority of the staff. The lesson to be leant here, however, is not merely obedience but unquestioning obedience. There can be no visible sign that the inmate questions or disagrees with, or feels injustice at, a staff decision. Inmates learn how to keep their facial expressions to themselves, to remain inscrutable, because attitude is as much a target for intervention as is action. The inmate must learn subordination as much as obedience. This is really the key distinction between institutions in general and total institutions: in the latter, the new inmate must make a number of 'primary adjustments' to the self in order to 'fit' appropriately within the institutional world. There are, however, degrees of totality, and this is because inmates also develop 'secondary adjustments': ways to 'buck the system', including, for example, the development of an inmate culture in opposition to that of the institution, the smuggling of contraband of various descriptions, the development of an economic system based on barter, the 'colonising' of vacant space within the institution, and so on. This is done partly to make life more bearable, but partly for the sense of defiance that comes from 'breaking the rules' per se (1991, pts. 2 and 3).

Goffman does not deny that patients do get out of mental institutions, but his point is that, on release, much of what the inmate has learnt inside dissipates (1991: 70) and, from his point of view, this is not surprising, because institutionalisation prepares inmates only for institutionalisation. What dischargees do take with them back into the community is the stigma of their incarceration and an anxiety about being able to cope with the freedoms and responsibilities of life on the outside. Goffman says that, in his experience, it is these factors, rather than those relating to the patient's medical/mental condition, that occupy the thoughts of staff charged with the responsibility of deciding who gets out. The problems, in other words, that face dischargees and decision-makers, are caused by the fact of institutionalisation and not by the reasons for institutionalisation in the first place (1991: 70–1)

This, then, is the general thesis of *Asylums*. The rest of the book adds the detail, but we have already seen enough to realise that Goffman paints a dismal picture of the asylum, as a place where the logic of control has a far greater influence than medical discourse. There is certainly evidence to substantiate the claims that Goffman makes. For example, inquiries at the special hospitals (in 1980 at Rampton (Home Office, 1980); 1988 at Broadmoor (NHS Advisory Services/Department of Health and Social Security Social Services Inspectorate, 1988); and 1992 at Ashworth (Home Office, 1992)) found conditions not too dissimilar from those of the 'total institutions' described by Goffman: 'insular, closed institutions whose predominantly custodial and therapeutically pessimistic culture had isolated them from the mainstream of forensic psychiatry' (Department of Health, 1999: para. 1.19.7), unable to attract and retain medical staff, with the Prison Officers' Association the dominant professional body. Such institutions cater mainly, although not exclusively, for persons sent to hospital by a criminal court, who can expect to spend a considerable period under detention.

Although for the majority of special hospital patients there is a reasonable prospect of eventual transfer into conditions of increasingly lighter security followed by discharge into the community, the process is held up by the well known problem of delay in securing transfer. Thornicroft (2004) found that there were 280 patients in the high-security hospitals who did not need to be there in the view of their RMOs. One historical reason for this is the reluctance of those (psychiatrists) who control access to medium-security accommodation to accept a special hospital patient (Dolan and Shetty, 1995). If a criminal court has ordered that a defendant be detained in a hospital, and has also made a 'restriction order' or a 'restriction direction' in respect of that defendant (see Chapter 6), significant powers are given to the Secretary of State for the Home Department by the 1983 Act, including the power of veto over any proposal that may be made by a Mental Health Review Tribunal or the patient's doctor, for the transfer of a 'restricted' patient out of a special hospital: s. 19, Sch. I, Part II, paras. 2, 5. A patient may be given leave of absence under s. 17 by way of a 'trial transfer'. This too can only be done with the consent of the Secretary of State (Sch. 1, Part II, paras. 2, 3), who may properly consult others including the Home Secretary's Advisory Board on Restricted Patients (see Chapter 8), before making any decision, and may take into account questions of public safety: *R* v *Secretary of State for the Home Department, ex p Harry* [1998] 3 ALL ER 360 (HC).

Not surprisingly, the Home Office adopts a cautious approach to the giving of consent to transfer proposals from a special hospital doctor or a tribunal. By a combination of these factors, the consequence is that a significant number of patients remain inappropriately in special hospital accommodation (Gostin, 1986a; Hamilton, 1990; Department of Health, 2000). Of course, all of this tends to increase the likelihood that such institutions will fit the 'total institution' model. There was a concerted attempt, following the Tilt Report (Department of Health, 2000, discussed further below) to increase the numbers transferred out of the special hospitals, via the Accelerated Discharge Programme (ADP), which ran from 2002–4, and with some success. For example, Broadmoor discharged 145 patients into conditions of lesser security in 2003–4 (West London Mental Health NHS Trust, 2004). The success of the ADP 'has created its own problem in that it is now more difficult than ever to transfer a patient into the medium secure services as beds are at a premium' (Mersey Care NHS Trust, 2005: 5). At that time (early 2005), Ashworth hospital had '12 patients who are classified as delayed discharges because of the lack of medium secure capacity, despite the intensive efforts of high secure commissioners and ourselves'. The hospital 'hoped the independent sector will provide the solution for these men'. The Secretary of State has powers, given by s. 123, to transfer patients out of a special hospital, whether to another special hospital or to conditions of lesser security, but in R v SSHD, ex p DB [2006] EWHC 659 (Admin) it was said by a representative of the Mental Health Unit at the Home Office, which in practice exercises the powers of the Secretary of State, that s. 123 will only be used in 'the most exceptional circumstances', without the consent of the receiving institution.

The circumstances surrounding the reports mentioned above were similar to those that were at play over the last century, with government action prompted by scandal, concern, and the lobbying activities of a concerned few. This was also the pattern of events preceding subsequent inquiries, at Broadmoor in 1997 and Ashworth in 1997–9, but the nature of the complaint had changed: now the special hospitals were not too austere, but instead too open. Both inquiries were prompted by concerns that security was lax, and that drugs and pornography were widely available. The inquiry at Broadmoor was brief and showed that, on the whole, the regime had improved since the report of a decade earlier, although there were still significant concerns about security. In contrast, the *Report of the Committee of Inquiry into the Personality Disorder Unit, Ashworth Special Hospital* (Department of Health, 1999b) (the Fallon Report) presented to Parliament by the Secretary of State for Health in January 1999, showed that most of the allegations that had prompted the setting up of a Committee of Inquiry in 1997 were, indeed, true. The allegations in question had been made by a former patient of the personality disorder unit (PDU). The most serious concerned the availability of pornography, including child pornography, and the presence in the PDU of the child of a former patient, brought in by him, so the inquiry team found, as part of a plan to have her 'groomed for paedophile purposes'. There were many other lapses or plain absences of security and of management: patients ran businesses from the hospital and there was very little in the way of the barriers to communication with the outside world that were described by Goffman: Internet access, for example, was freely available. At the same time, the institutions remained isolated in terms of their relation to the rest of the hospital system. The Fallon Inquiry concluded that the custodial, security-inclined regimes that had been detailed in the reports of the 1980s and early 1990s no longer existed, but now 'the pendulum may have swung too far away in the other direction', making a mockery of the notion of a 'high security' hospital. *The Independent* newspaper put the point more bluntly in the headline to its coverage of the publication of the Fallon Report: 'Ashworth run by inmates not staff' (*The Independent*, 6 January 1999: 6).

In Goffman's terms, the Fallon Report details the extent to which 'secondary adjustments' can fashion an entirely different regime if 'policy' becomes a vacuum. Following Fallon – indeed, before the report was published – policy moved sharply back in the direction of increased security and control. Fallon recommended that security at Ashworth should be subject to independent and regularly repeated review. The response of the Department of Health was to commission a wider review of security at all three special hospitals by a team led by Sir Richard Tilt (Department of Health, 2000), and this led to 86 detailed recommendations. The Department of Health produced *The Safety and Security in Ashworth, Broadmoor and Rampton Hospitals Directions* in 1999 (Department of Health, 1999f), which have since been revised on a number of occasions (most recently in 2003). The Directions now require routine and random searches of patient's rooms and persons (para 6, 2000 Directions), as well as regular searches of communal areas (para. 8). There are also stringent requirements for staff and visitors to be searched (paras. 10, 11). The Directions had to be amended in 2002 (*The Ashworth, Broadmoor and Rampton Amendment (No. 2) Directions 2002*) to exclude mental health review tribunal members from being searched when entering or leaving hospital premises. This gives some indication of how heavy-handed the Directions in their initial form were and to a large extent remain (Mental Health Act Commission, 2001: 5.23–5.43).

Other Directions require random testing for the use by patients of 'illicit substances', defined as controlled drugs under the Misuse of Drugs Act 1971 and alcohol (2000 Directions, para. 14), an absolute ban on Internet access and on access to other computerised equipment, such as games consoles (2000 Directions, para. 20) and mobile phones (para. 26), as well as Directions concerning the opening and inspection of incoming and outgoing patient mail (paras. 22, 24) and, when a patient is judged to be 'high risk' following a risk assessment, required by para. 30, various other intrusive actions are possible, such as the routine monitoring of patients' telephone calls (paras. 27–9). For other patients, such monitoring may be done on a random and routine basis. In short, the object of the Directions is to plug all gaps in security identified by the Fallon and Tilt reports.

There is no doubt that the Directions impinge significantly on the rights and liberties of special hospital inmates and move the regimes markedly back in the direction of the 'total institution' model. The security of perimeters, the increase in the use of CCTV, and the strengthening of internal security all also followed in the wake of the Tilt Report, even though Tilt found that abscensions from the special hospitals are rare (23 from 1990–9, and none after 1996: Department of Health, 2000: 8). It might be suggested that we are currently in the midst of a not-altogether-unexpected moral panic about the security of the special hospitals. Legal challenges by patients to the reintroduction of these more draconian policies, that were heard before the coming into force of the Human Rights Act 1998, scored little success. In *R v Broadmoor SHA, ex p S and*

Ors (1998) *The Times*, 17 February, three patients at Broadmoor sought judicial review of the decision of the hospital authority to introduce a policy of random and routine searching, replacing the 'for cause' policy that had hitherto been applied. Not surprisingly, the application was rejected in the High Court and that decision was upheld in the Court of Appeal. It was held that the power to detain for treatment implied a power to do that which was necessary for the success of that treatment, which included the right to search, as long as that was not exercised unreasonably in the circumstances.

A similarly expansive reading of the 1983 Act was provided in *R v Mental Health Act Commission, ex p Smith* (1998) *The Times*, 15 May (HC), which relied on the above decision, and that in *Pountey v Griffiths* [1976] AC 314, to hold that the powers of admission, detention and treatment necessarily implied broader powers of management and control. After the coming into force of the 1998 Act, the High Court in *R v Ashworth Special Hospital Authority and Anor, ex p N* [2001] EWHC Admin 339 heard an application from a patient that the policy of randomly recording and listening to 10 per cent of patients' outgoing telephone calls, that had been introduced by para. 29(3) of the 2000 Directions, was in breach of the right to privacy protected by Art. 8 of the Convention. The court laid out the Directions and the evidence from Fallon and Tilt that showed that unimpeded access to telephones constituted a security risk, before concluding that, although the policy did breach Art. 8(1) it was justifiable as proportionate, because, although the patient in question had not been judged to be 'high risk', he was nevertheless a member of a class of dangerous individuals (i.e. special hospital patients) and so the infringement of his privacy was justified by reference 'to the extent of the threat, the established degree of manipulation which can occur and the possible serious consequences to patients, staff and members of the public' (at para. 20). This was so even though N had been conditionally recommended for transfer and so evidently was not dangerous enough to require the conditions of security that pertain in the special hospitals.

A robust approach was also taken in *R v Secretary of State for Health, ex p L* [2000] 1 MHLR 191. In this case, a patient detained following conviction for murder, who, following the tightening of security at Rampton had been denied visits from his nephews and nieces, challenged para. 2 of the 2000 Directions. This forbids visits, to special hospital patients detained by reason of sex offending or homicide, from children outside a parent–child relationship unless authorised following a risk assessment. In L's case, he had waited two years for an assessment, as a consequence of which he argued that the link with his family had been broken, in breach of Art. 8(1) ECHR. The High Court refused to accept argument that, as the Directions treat those convicted of homicide as prima facie sex offenders, they are irrational. It further held that the ban on unauthorised visits by children complied with Art. 8(2) as a proportionate measure aimed to protect children.

The tenor of these judgments strongly suggest that only rarely will any special hospital patient be able successfully to challenge the substance of the Directions. In *R v Secretary of State for the Home Department, ex p Carroll, Al-Hasan, and Greenfield* [2001] EWCA Civ 1224, [2002] 1 WLR 545, [2001] HRLR 58, 2001 WL 753465, the

Court of Appeal upheld the first instance decision, that as long as there is good reason, so-called 'squat searches' (which require the person being searched to strip and squat so that the genital area and anus can be examined for concealed contraband of one type or another) are, in principle, lawful. In that case, the good reason was that sniffer dogs had detected the possible presence of explosives in an area of the prison to which only a limited class, including the two applicants, had access. A search of that area had been carried out and nothing found, after which the decision was taken to search the living quarters of those prisoners, and to carry out squat searches. No particular prisoner was under suspicion, and prisoners were not, out of concerns for security, informed of the reason for the search. C and A-H, two of the prisoners, refused to consent and were subsequently disciplined for failing to obey a lawful order. The Court of Appeal distinguished earlier case law, which is to the effect that reasons must usually be given for a personal search (*Christie* v *Leachinsky* [1947] AC 573), holding that 'loss of liberty, security and control are essential parts of the disciplinary process of a prison. Searches, even strip searches, are routine and, for a routine search, reasons need not be given' (at para. 68). The only protection the court was prepared to allow was that the decision to carry out a personal search should be taken by an officer of governor grade and that there should be contemporaneous recording of the reasons necessitating the search. It is clear that all of this reasoning is equally applicable to the special hospitals. The court did not consider the application of human rights law to this question because the incidents occurred before the coming into force of the HRA 1998, and it was decided by the House of Lords in *R* v *Lambert*, 2001 WL 720273, [2001] UKHL 37, [2002] 2 AC 545, [2001] 3 WLR 206, [2001] 3 All ER 577 that the HRA did not have retrospective application. Nevertheless, it seems clear from the case law discussed above that the Human Rights Act has so far had limited impact on the freedom of regimes to implement the security measures deemed necessary.

Patients have also been unsuccessful in challenging other decisions pertaining to their management. In *R* v *Ashworth Hospital Authority, ex p E* 2001 WL 1479868 E, a male patient wished to be allowed to dress as a woman in the hospital, but his freedom to do so had been restricted to the extent that he was only allowed to keep and wear a small number of female undergarments, and then only in the privacy of his own room. The reason given for this by E's doctor, Dr S, was that, in his opinion, E was a fetishistic transvestite who was sexually aroused by cross-dressing and the more so in public, and who also had a history of inappropriate sexual behaviour towards women, to the extent that to allow him to wear female clothing in public spaces in the hospital 'would be likely to be associated with unwise behaviour' (para. 8). It was also Dr S's view that wearing female attire might undermine E's treatment plan, inhibit his possible transfer, and increase the risk of an escape attempt, E having previously attempted to abscond whilst dressed as a woman. Although there was evidence from another doctor that to refuse to allow E to wear female clothing subjected him to unnecessary stress, the High Court preferred the evidence of Dr S, to hold that the restrictions of E were *Wednesbury* reasonable (para. 36); and that there was no breach of Art. 8, because although the powers to control such things as mode of dress are not apparent on the face of the 1983

Act (see Chapter 7), they are nevertheless 'in accordance with the law' as required by Art. 8(2) as being both available and forseeable in their effect (once the earlier case law discussed above is taken into account) (para. 42). On the question of necessity, Richards J cited from the speech of Lord Steyn in *R v SSHD, ex p Daly* [2001] 2 AC 532 (HL) (discussed further in Chapter 5), and charged himself to conduct an 'appropriately intensive scrutiny' of the decision of Dr S and his colleagues as to whether there was indeed a pressing social need for the infringement of Mr E's rights and whether such action as was taken was proportionate. He reminded himself that 'it must be borne in mind that the hospital authority is the decision maker in this case . . . it is not for the court to engage in a full merits review so as to reach its own independent decision on the matter' (para. 45). His conclusion was that the hospital had made out its case and the restriction was justified.

That decision was applied in *R v SSHD, ex p DB* [2006] EWHC 659 (Admin), a case involving a male-to-female transsexual transferred from prison to Ashworth hospital, which only accepts male patients. Ashworth permitted DB to wear female dress in her room, but demanded that she wear gender-neutral clothes in public areas. DB argued that her rights under Arts. 3 and 8 ECHR had been breached, and pointed inter alia to the fact that the hospital authorities felt that her transfer and continuing detention at Ashworth were inappropriate, both because DB did not require high-security conditions and because, given her transsexualism, the placement was inappropriate. The High Court found that Ashworth had been sufficiently sensitive to DB's situation and there was no breach of either Article, and, indeed, Davies J recorded his disquiet (para. 51) that the claim should have been thought appropriate to have been brought at all.

In *R v Ashworth Hospital, ex p H* [2001] EWHC Admin 872, [2002] 1 FCR 206, H, a carrier of the Hepatitis C virus and claiming to be sexually active within the hospital, challenged the decision of the hospital to refuse to supply him with condoms as in breach of Arts. 2 and 8 ECHR. This decision was made in line with the hospital's 'no sex' policy, and on the basis that the hospital doubted H's claim to be sexually active. The High Court found in favour of the hospital on both counts, holding that sexual activity between patients was unlikely to occur, and so there was no 'real and immediate threat to life' and hence no breach of either Article, and that the policy was justified on grounds of security (condoms might, in its view, be used as currency or for smuggling purposes). The 'no sex' policy was also justifiable on security grounds. The court also dismissed arguments based on more traditional judicial criteria. Thus, the blanket ban on the issuance of condoms was neither '*Wednesbury* unreasonable' nor 'irrational' (see Chapter 5).

It is not easy to find examples of successful challenges by patients to aspects of the regimes operated in the special hospitals. There is one example, *Broadmoor Hospital Authority v Robinson* (1998) *The Times*, 15 October (HC), in which a more restrictive approach to the interpretation of the 1983 Act was taken. Special hospital managers have powers under s. 134(1)(b) of the 1983 Act to withhold outgoing mail from a special hospital patient to avoid 'likely' distress or danger to other persons, and under s. 134(2) in respect of incoming mail, which may be withheld in the interests of the safety of the patient or for the protection of others. Managers have corresponding powers to open and inspect any mail: s. 134(4). *Robinson* involved a patient who had written an account of his time in Broadmoor, which had been submitted to a publisher. An injunction had been obtained by the hospital managers on the grounds that the publication of the patient's memoirs would distress other patients and expose the defendant to risk of assault. The court held that s.134 could have no effect when an item of post sent by a patient had reached its destination, and that the injunction should be discharged because it had the practical effect of undermining the limitations of managers' powers found in that section.

This is likely to be an isolated example, however, given the change in climate since the 1990s, and that the Security Directions now place stricter requirements to monitor mail on the special hospitals; it is clear from *R v Secretary of State for the Home Department, ex p Daly* [2001] 2 AC 532 (HL) that there can be no blanket policy of searching detainees' legal correspondence in the absence of the detainee, although it is equally clear that even legal privilege may be overridden for cause. The government and the courts at present talk with one voice, and the message is that, all things being equal, security considerations outweigh the rights of individuals. Even so, it is not clear that special hospital patients necessarily feel secure themselves: bullying, particularly in personality disorder wards seems to be a very common but underacknowledged problem (Ireland and Snowden, 2002), with 20 per cent of both patients and staff reporting having seen someone been bullied in the preceding week in one survey (Ireland, 2004; see also Ireland, 2006; Ireland and Bescoby, 2004), and there are significant differences between the experiences of women and men, in Ashworth at least, Ireland (2004a: para. 1.3.2.) finding that 3 per cent of men, but 30 per cent of women, reported being bullied in the previous week. Bullying can take the form of sexual harassment, which, MIND (2002) has reported, remains a major problem (see also *AD v East Kent Community NHS Trust* [2002] EWCA Civ 1872). Scandalous stories about the rape and sexual abuse of female patients by male patients in Broadmoor broke in March 2003, prompting the Department of Health to pledge the relocation of all female patients out of the hospital within three years (Dillon, 2003), although there were still 42 women amongst the total of 273 patients held in the hospital in January 2006 (West London Mental Health NHS Trust, n.d.).

It may, of course, be argued that special hospitals are atypical institutions. Indeed they are: yet there is evidence to support a Goffman-influenced understanding of the modern experience of hospitalisation from all sections of the hospital system. The Rosenham research, discussed in the previous chapter, provides one example. Research by Bott (1976: 133) discussed by Barham (1992: 8) found that the barrier between staff and inmates was rigidly enforced, because '[t]alking to patients is dangerous because it threatens to puncture the barrier that keeps sanity and madness in their proper places', while Christine Perring (1992: 134) found that clinical staff take a fatherly role, nursing staff, a motherly role, and that inmates are correspondingly infantised, irrespective of the actual gender of the participants. The ninth biennial report of the Mental Health Act Commission (MHAC, the latterday version of the Lunacy Commissioners, 2001) discloses one example of bad practice in which a ward office contained a 'patient information whiteboard' in clear view of patients, which contained both confidential medical information and more informal 'unflattering assessments' of patients (MHAC, 2001: para. 2.31). Although the MHAC insisted that the practice be discontinued, it does provide an example of the way in which medical staff can lack respect for the autonomy of patients in their charge. The strategic deployment of 'family' is a well-documented feature of the regime in women's prisons, particularly the New Holloway, which, after opening in 1976 used 'family' as a structuring dynamic within the regime (which was overtly therapeutic), for example, by dividing inmates into 'family units'. The enforcement of discipline and subordination through regulation of contact with family is also a well-documented research finding.

Many more examples of institutions and regimes that exhibit this or that feature of Goffman's model might be drawn from the literature. There is also much autobiographical work that supports Goffman's contention that hospital inpatients must adhere to the regime or suffer the consequences, which places therapy of the mildest kind in a continuum with the use of shock treatment or drugs and, ultimately, when all else fails, straightforward violence and torture-like techniques based on deprivation or segregation, and which sees them as a function of the 'mortification' rather than 'treatment' of patients (Perrucci, 1974). The boredom of institutional life is well documented (see, for example, Anon., 1996). In short, there is little doubt that the characteristics and techniques described by Goffman have been widely deployed in both time and space, and although the view of many ex-inpatients who have been transferred into community-based residential accommodation is that the latter is less 'total' accommodation than that provided by mental hospitals, it is also well documented that many of the conditions of total institutions pertain in such accommodation (see Perring, 1992; Barham, 1992: 21–8). Within the general hospital sector, 'restraint' and 'seclusion' are still practised: moral treatment and medical treatment have still not totally ousted their historical predecessors, but have rather colonised their techniques. As will be discussed later (see Chapter 7), these practices today come under the definition, in s. 145(1) MHA, 1983, of 'treatment'.

As the continued, even increased (Mental Health Act Commission, 1999: para 10.2), use of such practices indicates, mental hospitals continue to be institutions characterised by high levels of violence (Shah, 1993). It is difficult to give precise details of the incidence of patient attacks on staff, because abuse is significantly under-reported by staff (Thackrey and Bobbit, 1990), and much of the research tends to be retrospective, based on analysis of reported incidents (Cheung et al., 1997). The attitude of staff to reporting abuse often depends on whether the patient is viewed as morally responsible for his or her behaviour (Crichton and Calgie, 2002). In a prospective study, involving 220 patients and 279 staff in an 11-ward facility comprising both locked and unlocked accommodation and housing both short and long-stay patients, Cheung et al. (1997) recorded 477 assaults. Of these, 296, or 62.1 per cent, were verbal, 181, or 37.9 per cent, physical, with or without accompanying verbal abuse. Although around a third of all assaults had no obvious precursor, the majority stemmed from interactions with staff, with the staff member either denying some request or 'assisting with patient's activities of daily living' (Cheung *et al.*, 1997: 48) (whatever that means) or requesting the patient to take medication. Use of weapons was rare and physical injuries usually minor. Only two incidents required the attention of a doctor, with a further seven requiring some sort of first aid. Around a third of those assaulted did, however, feel 'substantially shaken' by the incident.

Of the 220 patients covered by the research, around half committed an assault (whether verbal or physical), although men were markedly more aggressive than women. In general, patients on locked wards were involved in a greater mean number of incidents than other patients, and assaults on such wards tended to be less likely to arise out of interactions with staff and therefore less predictable. Patients with schizophrenia and schizo-affective disorders accounted for 80 per cent of physical assaults, and only six patients were responsible for nearly two thirds of all violent incidents. The authors found 'all of them to be suffering from treatment resistant schizophrenia' (Cheung *et al.*, 1997: 51). This research also confirmed the patterns of inmate violence against staff that have emerged from a large number of research projects. The findings that a high number of violent incidents are attributable to a few patients, and that men are more likely to be aggressive than women, are typical. Violence against staff is not the only reason for some form of active intervention. The prevention of patient-on-patient violence, and self-harm, are also pressing concerns (Crichton, 1995).

The Department of Health established its 'zero tolerance' campaign in 1999, and the National Task Force on Violence Against Social Care Staff was created in the same year. The Task Force reported in 2000 (National Task Force on Violence Against Social Care Staff, 2000) and a National Action Plan was launched in January 2001 (Department of Health, 2001) with a £2m budget, and an aim to reduce patient violence by 25 per cent by March 2005 compared to March 2002 (National Task Force on Violence Against Social Care Staff, 2001: para. 8.2). No mechanism was set up to monitor changes in the levels of violence, however, and in 2006, the Health Minister, Rosie Winterton, conceded, in answer to a question in Parliament, that the government did not know and had no way of knowing whether the target reduction had been met (HC Hansard, 29 June 2006, Col. 623W). There is, however, evidence that levels of patient violence have fallen, but remain high. In its Annual Report for 2005, the Healthcare Commission (2006: 3) surveyed 209,000 hospital staff, of which 12 per cent had suffered physical violence at the hands of patients or their visitors in the previous year and 26 per cent had experienced harassment, verbal abuse or bullying, down from 14 per cent and 27 per cent respectively in 2004. This supplemented data on the quantum of violence published by the Healthcare Commission in 2005 (Healthcare Commission, 2005). Covering 265 units of provision, the research generated 6,500 questionnaires completed by staff, patients and visitors. Although there were significant differences between different types of unit of provision (see further Davis, 1991), in global terms, 78 per cent of nursing staff had experienced violence or threats of violence or had otherwise felt unsafe, and 89 per cent had witnessed violence or threats. For clinical staff, the figures were 41 per cent and 62 per cent respectively, and for non-clinical staff, they were 32 per cent and 57 per cent respectively. More than a third – 36 per cent – of service users had experienced, and 47 per cent had witnessed, violence or threats, as had 18 per cent and 33 per cent respectively of visitors (Healthcare Commission, 2005: 27). Best practice is now detailed in NICE guidelines (National Institute for Health and Clinical Excellence, 2005).

Turning to self-harm, and in particular to suicide, there are more than 5,906 deaths recorded as suicide in 2004 (Office for National Statistics, 2006). An unknown further number attempt suicide. Around a quarter of those who commit suicide will have had contact with the mental health system in the year before their death (Department of Health, 1998a: para. 1.7, 1.8). Suicide in hospital and prison facilities is a matter of special concern (Brahams 2004). Around four in every thousand persons admitted to a mental hospital will commit suicide (Ganesvran and Shah, 1997), although the greatest risk is in the days immediately after discharge (Johnson *et al.*, 1993). Suicides are statistically more probable for all categories of mental disorder (Ruschena *et al.*, 1998), although those suffering from schizophrenia seem to be more at risk than others (Rossau and Mortensen, 1997). Patients at most risk tend to be young, male and with antisocial personality traits (Johnson *et al.*, 1993), and there is evidence to suggest, although for reasons that are not clear, that, controlling for other variables, secure hospital accommodation carries a higher risk of suicide than either prison or general hospital facilities (Haycock, 1993).

There is also evidence from Australia that suicide rates in hospitals can be affected by legal changes requiring staff to be more sensitive to the risk (Ganesvran and Shah, 1997). In Goffman's terms, suicide is the ultimate 'secondary adjustment', but the starkness of the statistics on suicide, and the complexity of the situation, makes one think long and hard about the role of theory. It must not be to offer glib or easy explanations for such problematic issues. As seen earlier in the chapter, the prevention of suicide is the seventh of the seven national standards introduced by the NFSMH. The *Report of the Confidential Inquiry into Suicide and Homicide by People with Mental Illness* (Department of Health, 2001d) confirmed the above research findings, and further found that those most at risk of suicide are often without close personal ties and unemployed, and that around 20 per cent of suicides are potentially preventable, if closer supervision and monitored compliance with treatment were more readily available. The NSFMH set this as a target, which equates to 7.3 deaths by suicide per 100,000 population, for the reduction in the number of suicides by 2010. The most recently available data (Care Service Improvement Partnership and National Institute for Mental Health, 2006) indicates some success in meeting this target. In 2004, there were 8.56 deaths per 100,000 population, down from 9.2 per cent in the mid-1990s.

Goffman's thesis, as might be expected, has not gone unchallenged, on philosophical, methodological and empirical grounds. Sedgwick (1982), for example, has argued that Goffman's theory is too sweeping and so both underplays the extent to which mental hospitals resemble other hospitals, even from the point of view of the patient, most of whom are not detained, and is insensitive to the historical contingencies that must be taken into account when applying a theoretical model. For instance, Goffman draws, in quick succession, on TE Lawrence's description of barracks life in the airforce, practices in a nunnery, and the practice of flogging on nineteenth century warships, to illustrate his thesis, all in the space of a few pages (Goffman, 1991: 37–9), and gives the reader the impression that all are mere examples of a general phenomenon with no particularities or variation to speak of. There is no well-defined qualitative element in Goffman's understanding of a total institution.

There is, for example, as much autobiographical work that contradicts Goffman's views as supports them. Many patients do experience their treatment as beneficial, even if their first impulse had been to resist. Moreover, a central tenet of Goffman's thesis has been undermined by the shift in focus of hospital services to acute care (Cavadino, 1989: ch. 5). In the years of the great confinement, a considerable number of patients spent years, if not decades, inside asylums. The average length of stay in the 1950s had fallen to approximately ten years, compared to twenty to forty years before the Second World War. As already mentioned, these days 60 per cent of hospital admissions spend less than a month as an inpatient. Rather than being 'total' institutions, contemporary mental hospitals are better characterised in terms of managed chaos. The biennial reports of the Mental Health Act Commission leave the reader in no doubt: the 2001 Report (MHAC, 2001: para. 3.5) states that the Commission 'continues to be concerned that the pressures on inpatient beds reported in our last four Biennial Reports continues to hamper achievement', the consequences being delays in admission, patients moved during admission, inappropriate use of leave in order to free beds, inefficient use of staff time spent locating available beds (*ibid.*). Bed occupancy rates are 'well over 100 per cent' in many hospitals (*ibid.*), and patients, who were in theory 'detained' under the MHA 1983, had to be sent home on leave to attend hospital on a daycare basis. The problem is particularly acute in London (MHAC, 1997: para. 4.1), and this goes some way towards explaining the greater involvement of London police with mentally disordered persons in public places, many of whom will be homeless (Abdul-Hamid and Cooney, 1997).

The policy of bed closure has left the remaining system under-resourced for the numbers with which it is required to deal. Hence, although some wards are 'bright, cheerful and clean', others are of low quality, providing 'bleak conditions for patients' (MHAC, 2001: para. 3.17). These observations 'remained valid' by the time of the 2003 Report (MHAC, 2003: para. 8.81), and although plans to modernise inpatient care, with £30m funding, were announced in 2004 (Appleby, Department of Health, 2004: 73), the 2005 MHAC Report (2005: para. 2.1) described inpatient care as employing a 'fire-fighting' approach, under which 'the delivery of a therapeutic service can be impossible', and emphasised that 'some direct intervention to ameliorate overcrowding and related problems must be taken' (2005: para. 2.28), continuing to list a catalogue of problems familiar to readers of earlier Reports (2005: para. 2.40), with the safety of female patients being a particular cause for concern (2005: para. 2.44). The extent to which such a picture corresponds to Goffman's model is open to question. There is limited interaction between patients and nursing staff, for example, although this seems to be more because of the pressure caused by staff shortages, which is particularly acute in RSUs (MHAC, 2001: para. 3.14; 1997: para. 4.4.2.), than because of an 'us and them' philosophy. This, in turn, affects the standards of care and the ability of institutions to provide individualised attention. Staff morale is often low, and some hospitals have been forced to close beds (*ibid.*). At care homes, which must be visited by the MHAC if accommodating 'detained' patients under the MHA 1983, concerns were with failure in record-keeping and adherence to procedures rather than with ward conditions. But, as discussed above, the residential home sector is periodically rocked by scandal, which tends to encourage a certain degree of scepticism about the abilities of third-party inspection always to detect even significant problems. Of course there are some parts of the system, the newly built MSUs for example, that are said to provide high quality accommodation (MHAC, 1997: para. 4.4.1.), but these too are now subject to the same pressures to be found elsewhere in the system (MHAC, 2001: para. 5.69).

3.5 Concluding comments

It is not easy to digest of all this information, and it may be that this is because it sends out conflicting messages. In a very real sense, it is misleading to think of the state provision of mental health services as a singular system. Notwithstanding the move toward statutory integration of administrative structures and standards, the various 'streams' identified in Chapter 1 continue to coexist. The special hospitals, albeit now integrated into their local NHS trusts, should be thought of as a separate system, in which the emphasis is very much more on containment than cure. In 1999, the Fallon Report recommended, in straightforward terms, that the special hospitals should be closed, and provision made for its patients in a range of smaller units. The Secretary of State for Health rejected this plan on the very day that the report was published. The matter had already been raised a year earlier in a confidential report made by the High Security Psychiatric Commissioning Board to the Secretary of State, which was leaked to the media (*The Independent*, 23 March 1998: 2). Resource limitations simply do not allow the abandonment of the three special hospitals, whatever their limitations. But the civil liberties implications are significant. The confidential report also expressed the view that between 850 and 1,000 of the 1,520 persons detained in special hospitals do not need to be held in conditions of high security, but cannot be transferred for want of alternative accommodation, and this view was reiterated strongly by the Tilt Report (Department of Health, 2000, see Chapter 8). There has since been significant progress in transferring suitable persons into conditions of lesser security, but more remains to be done. Black people are significantly over-represented in special hospitals, and this, in itself, is a real cause for concern (Boast and Chesterman, 1995; Commission for Healthcare Audit and Inspection, MHAC, CSIP and NIMHE, 2005). But it seems highly likely that the special hospitals will continue to function in the forseeable future as the nearest approximation to an ideal-type 'total insitution' that is to be found in our mental health system.

General psychiatric hospital provision, by contrast, has moved significantly into the mainstream of healthcare provision and such facilities are very much more part of that general hospital system. As such, they share the problems of that system – limited funds, staff shortages, an emphasis on 'throughput' and the dominance of managerial rather than clinical (or social-control-oriented) imperatives. If the problem for patients in the special hospitals is getting out, for those in need of acute care services, the problem can be getting in – and staying in long enough. In some respects, these facilities, when adequately funded, can conform most closely to the ideal of the asylum as 'refuge' or 'retreat' from the rigours of society that inspired the pioneers of moral treatment (Wallcraft, 1996). If a Goffman-type thesis can be made out in respect of this sector, it can only be through a detailed consideration of the treatments that it provides. This will be undertaken in Chapter 7.

Even so, generalisation remains a problem: for example, different wards in the same facility negotiate the balance between treatment and control differently. Wards ostensibly in 'the community' may, in fact, be more secure than those in hospitals; detained patients may be held in conditions of lesser security than 'informal' patients. The recently begun process of unearthing the hidden history of care in the community (Bartlett and Wright, 1999) is a reminder that much of what has passed as 'the' history of the treatment of mental disorder is only a part of that history, and that the role of institutionalisation has been routinely overemphasised by 'traditionalists' and 'revisionists' alike. But are we now at risk of making the opposite mistake: spinning a tale of the shift from institutional to community-based provision, when, in fact, much of that provision in the community is in residential form? The old asylums, as visible icons, may have gone (although many remain and have been converted to other uses), but are they truly 'abolished', or merely rendered more diffuse and opaque, now spread over very many sites, not infrequently 'out of area'; harder to see, maybe, but no less real? Some (Priebe and Turner, 2003) are now arguing that, despite plans for greater powers of compulsion in the community (see Chapter 9), for assertive outreach and home treatment, we are entering a period of 'reinstitutionalisation', as evidenced by the rise in forensic (secure unit) beds (which diverts funds that would otherwise be spent on community care), the widening of the criteria for admission proposed by the government, and, we might add, the building programme to provide accommodation to house severely personality-disordered patients. Priebe and Turner conclude that 'supported housing [residential accommodation] seems to be taking the place that used to be held by the old style asylums' (2003: 175).

It may be improvident to make any too-firm predictions, given the state of flux and uncertainty that characterises contemporary mental health law, policy, and practice, and the mental health system. Nevertheless, it can be cautiously suggested that one feature of the system that will remain fundamentally unchanged is that our response to mental disorder will continue to be framed within the two polar points of the history considered in this chapter. Our response to mental disorder is prompted both by concern about the plight of fellow human beings and by a desire to control behaviour judged to be dangerous or antisocial. Managerialism and the influence of market principles are vital questions when investigating how the system works. But in terms of function, the overarching perspectives of benevolence and control, medicalism and custodialism *are* accurate: they reflect our motives, and their inherent ambiguity. In large part, the degree to which one or the other is emphasised is a matter of perspective, judgment and interpretation. But to understand the mental health system fully, in terms of its broader social function and in its microscopic interactions with service users, it is perhaps necessary to learn to live with the paradox that it is both at once – and often the failure of both. Caught in the middle of this juxtaposition of the mundane, the bizarre and the poignant, as the intended beneficiaries of political and professional initiatives, and of social work and sociological theories, are the users of the service. Although the voices of service users risk being drowned out by those of the others, this must be resisted, if we are not to lose sight of the special contribution to our understanding of our mental health system that its users can make. We shall leave the final words in this chapter to the voice of one user:

> Joe's making a stool
> I'm weaving a basket
> someone's making coffee
> Dee says I can sing
> and she does.
> Jane won't make an ashtray
> Arthur's sulking because the priest wouldn't rechristen him *Jesus*.
> Jane still won't make an ashtray. instead she becomes a dog
> grr Woof!
> Dogs don't make ashtrays.
> Dee's singing the national anthem
> Arthur blesses me.
> Sydney hasn't spoken all morning, or yesterday or the day before, gggrrrr Woof!
> *Shit* said Joe
> *I'm going to discharge myself from this place it's driving me mad*
>
> realising what he had said, he starts to laugh
> i also start to laugh
> the man on my left (who didn't hear Joe) starts to laugh as well. we all laugh.
>   except Sid
> who wants to die (and means it)
> then we had coffee

(Lewis, 1996)

4

Admission to Hospital

I came out of my dream and back to stark reality when I opened my eyes that October morning. I looked around me: four grey walls reached to a high ceiling...There was a dirty blood-stained blue door with a small port-hole of reinforced glass in it but it was covered over the outside by a curtain: the door, too, was locked from the outside. There was no furniture in my tiny cell, nothing save a mattress, a pillow and a blanket. I had not even got my clothes, and there was no chamber pot. I huddled under my blanket for warmth.

(Zaki, 1995: 3)

4.1 Introduction

Roughly 250,000 persons per year are admitted to psychiatric facilities in England and Wales. While it is unwise to generalise about their views of admission, the above quotation serves as a reminder that many do not perceive it as a happy experience. They arrive through a variety of legal mechanisms. The overwhelming majority – about 90 per cent – are admitted 'informally' under s. 131, Mental Health Act 1983. People admitted under this section are not confined in any legal sense. While we will argue below that the practical situation of these people often makes it misleading to think of them as entering and remaining in the facility voluntarily, nonetheless, in law, they are free to leave at will. The preponderance of these admissions must be emphasised, because the litigation and the literature are rather misleadingly skewed towards persons civilly or criminally confined. In fact, persons subject to detention are a relatively small minority of the hospital population. Of those formally confined ('sectioned'), most are admitted for assessment under s. 2. About two thirds as many (3 per cent of admissions) are admitted for treatment under s. 3. In addition, a much smaller number are admitted pursuant to the police powers contained in s. 136, or findings of mental disorder at various stages in the criminal process (see Chapter 6).

The mechanism of entry is important not merely because of the right to leave. Persons admitted informally keep the same rights to consent to treatment as anyone else in society. Persons confined have very different rights regarding treatment (see Chapter 7). The different categories of confinement further have some variations in length of confinement permitted and discharge procedure (see further below, and

Chapters 5 and 8), so even between classes of confinement, the mechanism of admission is of considerable importance.

While the distinctions between the formal categories are thus definitive of legal rights, patients are often sufficiently uninvolved in the mechanics of the admission that they do not know what category they are under. This is further complicated by the movement of numerous patients between categories at various times in their hospital stay. Studies suggest that, notwithstanding the duty in s. 132 that detained patients be informed of their status and of avenues of redress, 40 to 50 per cent of civilly confined patients did not know they had been confined (Toews *et al.*, 1984; Bradford *et al.*, 1986; Monahan *et al.*, 1995; Goldbeck, 1997). This emphasises the divergence of textbook law and law in practice: large numbers of patients appear to lack basic information relevant to their situation.

4.2 Informal admission

Section 131 of the MHA 1983 allows the admission of anyone who 'requires treatment for mental disorder'. 'Mental disorder' refers to the definition in s. 1 of the Act, discussed in Chapter 2. The court in *R v Kirklees Metropolitan Borough Council, ex p C* [1993] 2 FLR 187 (CA) held that s. 131 applied to treatment only, not to assessment of a patient, creating a potential lacuna in the Act. The court dealt with the problem by holding that 'there has never been any doubt that an adult patient may be lawfully admitted to hospital for assessment, provided he or she consents, just as he or she may be admitted to hospital for an operation' (p. 191, per Lloyd LJ). The court thus established a second and independent basis for informal admission, founded in the common law.

As a matter of law, the existence of such an authority for informal admission outside the statute is not self-evident, because informal admission appears to be a concept unknown to the common law. In the eighteenth century, in law if not in practice, cases such as *R v Clarke* (1762) 3 Burr 1362 and *R v Coate* (1772) Lofft 73 would suggest that legal authority had to be sought to house a lunatic in a psychiatric facility. Certainly, the care of the insane in this period was not understood on the model of an informal patient. This was clarified by nineteenth-century statutes, which expressly precluded informal admission. This was built into the initial legislation establishing county asylums in 1808, where all admissions were by order of Justices of the Peace, and no inmate was permitted to be at large without order of the Justices: see ss. 17, 23, County Asylum Act 1808. For private sector institutions, the restrictions date from s. 29 of the Madhouse Act 1828. It is only with the statutory intervention of s. 1, Mental Treatment Act 1930, that informal admissions were generally permitted (see Chapter 1). Prior to that, consent of the patient to admission does not appear to have been relevant to legal substance. It was instead relevant only to the question of procedure: throughout the period, strangers acting without apparent encouragement of the patient were denied standing to press for a remedy (see *R v Clarke*, and *Ex p Child* (1854) 15 CB 238).

If the finding in *Kirklees* is surprising in law, it is less so given modern attitudes sympathetic to voluntary admission, particularly in comparison with civil confinement. On the surface at least, the problems of coercion, of concern to the civil libertarian, disappear. In addition, the patient is likely to be more involved in the treatment programme, to be less alienated and dissatisfied with the experience of hospitalisation, and therefore more amenable to seeking assistance in hospital in the event that he or she encounters problems in the future. The balance of power between patient and psychiatrist is, at least partly, redressed, creating a closer approximation of a regular doctor–patient relationship. The increased trust between doctor and patient may improve treatment compliance after release, and create a better medical result. The image is of therapeutic alliance, rather than the imposition of care and treatment by force.

These are laudable arguments indeed. The difficulty is that often, these admissions are not 'voluntary' in any conventional sense. Since the pioneering study by Gilboy and Schmidt in 1971, it has been recognised that coercion often operates in voluntary admissions. Studies abroad find that something like a half of informally admitted patients feel coerced during their admission (Monahan *et al.*, 1995; Poulsen, 2002). Pressure may be effected in a variety of ways. At its simplest, it may be purely situational. Psychogeriatric patients, for example, may be unable, due to physical weaknesses, to exercise their right to leave. At a slightly more complex level, an individual living with a caring family may have no option but to follow the family's decision to admit the individual, because they may have nowhere else to live and, often, few means of finding alternative accommodation and living support. As 'relief of carers' was the prime major reason for admissions to acute wards of the London hospitals studied by Flannigan *et al.* (1994a), this sort of coercion might be expected to be not uncommon.

Carers and others may not rely simply on the situational vulnerability of the client, but may use other tactics, from gentle encouragement or reasoning, through to threats or physical violence, to encourage the individual to enter the facility. The motives are legion. A lawyer representing a client on a minor criminal charge may see 'willingness' to undergo psychiatric treatment as a useful bargaining chip in a sentencing hearing. Police officers or medical staff may wish to avoid the increased bureaucracy that flows from civil confinement. Medical staff may believe the therapeutic justifications for voluntary admissions noted above, and encourage patients to adopt that route rather than confinement for that reason. The medical staff also have an additional power, however: they can threaten confinement unless the patient consents to voluntary admission, and perpetuate that threat each time the patient expresses a wish to leave the facility (see Rogers, 1993). When such a direct manipulation is used, it is difficult to see the confinement as voluntary in any meaningful sense. It is now clear that under certain circumstances, informal admissions may nonetheless violate an individual's right to liberty under Art. 5 of the ECHR: see *HL* v *UK* Application No. 45508/99, (2005) 40 EHRR 32, discussed below.

While the statistics would suggest that most people admitted to hospital find their stay beneficial overall (Monahan *et al.*, 1995, and studies cited therein; Nicholson *et al.*, 1996), there are obvious drawbacks to even informal hospital admission. Institutional rules limit freedom, and the individual is removed from society for a period. Hospitalisation is also expensive both to the taxpayer and, if private care is received, to the patient or the insurer. The practical situation of these informal patients currently is arguably worse than that of confined patients. As will be discussed in Chapter 8, at least a confined patient can challenge his or her committal. If the patient is competent to consent to medical treatment, his or her position is stronger as an informal patient, because he or she can refuse medication (although problems of coercion similar to those we have been discussing will arise in the case of such 'voluntary' treatment as well, and competent patients refusing treatment may find themselves sectioned in short order so that their refusal can be circumvented). If the patient lacks that capacity, however, he or she has been in a considerably weaker position than a confined patient, because the Act provides safeguards relating to second opinions prior to treatment and tribunal hearings to challenge confinement only for confined patients. An informal patient lacking capacity, by comparison, has been able to be treated by the doctor without any procedural safeguards, on the basis of the doctor's view of the patient's best interests. The MCA 2005, when it takes effect in the spring of 2007, will provide an enhanced legal framework over these treatment decisions (see further Chapters 7, 10 and 11). Further, proposed amendments to that Act are be introduced shortly, in the same package as the mental health amendments, to provide enhanced safeguards against admission of people lacking capacity.

Informal admission does not affect all groups equally. Statistically, women, and particularly white women, are admitted at a considerably higher rate than their proportion of the population as a whole (Pilgrim and Rogers, 1999: 42; Bebbington *et al.*, 1994: 746; Ineichen *et al.*, 1984: 601). The indications are that this imbalance is particularly prevalent in the informal category, with women admitted informally at roughly one and a half times the rate of men. If the system is working properly, this preponderance of informal admissions is a good thing, suggesting a relationship of trust between women and the psychiatric establishment; it seems equally fair to question whether the statistics instead represent the disempowerment of women in current society. In this latter scenario, women's informal admission would result from acquiescence to the non-legal forms of authority discussed above, rather than an active choice of hospitalisation as the best available option.

4.2.1 Parents, guardians, and *Bournewood*

The law has dealt with these non-voluntary informal admissions in a variety of ways. The first concerns the power of a guardian appointed under s. 7 of the 1983 Act. The details of these appointments will be discussed in Chapter 9, but here, suffice it to say that the Act allows guardians to be appointed for persons with mental disorders, where warranted by their welfare or the protection of others. The powers of these guardians are restricted by the Act, but s. 8(1) allows the guardian to require the patient to reside in a specific place. According to *R v Hallstrom (No. 2)* [1986] 2 All ER 306, p. 312, there is nothing in the Act to prevent this power being used to admit the patient into a hospital. The patient would not be detained under the confinement powers of the MHA 1983, and would therefore be an informal patient. Paragraph 13.10.a of the Code of Practice argues against the use of this power in this way for anything other than a short stay, but it is difficult to see statutory support for that limitation. In *Kirklees*, the Court of Appeal held that violation of the Code would not create a wrong that could be subjected to judicial scrutiny if the statute was complied with, even, as in that case, where the guardian was a public authority. The Code's prohibition may thus discourage guardians from admitting patients, but cannot prevent it should it occur. The result would be an informal patient without the legal authority to leave, and no obvious forum to require some form of assessment of his or her predicament. He or she could, of course, challenge the guardianship order before a review tribunal, but that would involve a set of criteria quite different from a challenge to a specific decision of a guardian to place the patient in the psychiatric hospital. Other jurisdictions expressly allow review tribunal applications in such situations: see, e.g., Ontario Mental Health Act, CSO, c. M.7, s. 13 regarding children over the age of 12. The 1983 Act contains no such provision.

A similar difficulty concerns the admission of children as informal patients, on the authority of a parent. It is clear from *Kirklees* that a parent (or, more correctly, a person or body, such as a local authority with 'parental responsiblility') has the right to admit a child to a psychiatric hospital. Section 131 of the 1983 Act specifically allows children over the age of 16 years, capable of expressing wishes, to be admitted informally on their own authority. If the child wishes not to be admitted, however, his or her competence seems not to be an issue here, because at common law, the wishes of a competent child under the age of 18 years can be overriden by his or her parent: *Re R (A Minor) (Wardship: Consent to Treatment)* [1991] 4 All ER 177; *In Re W (A Minor) (Medical Treatment: Court's Jurisdiction)* [1992] 3 WLR 758. At the end of three months, the Health Authority is under a duty to notify the local authority of the residency, and the local authority must investigate to ensure that the welfare of the child does not require its intervention (s. 85, Children Act 1989), but such *post facto* investigation is not a substitute for admission standards (see Sandland, 1994).

Both of these situations concern the patient who has a guardian. What happens in the case of an adult patient without a legal guardian, and without the capacity to consent to admission? This was the situation in *HL v UK* Application No. 45508/99 (2005) 40 EHRR 32 (also called '*Bournewood*', based on the title of proceedings in the domestic litigation). In that case, L, an adult with profound developmental disabilities, lived with a family who cared for him, but who were not legally his guardians. L had a history of becoming agitated, coupled with mild self-harm, which the family had been able to control in the three years that L had lived with them. While at a day centre, he became agitated and was admitted as an informal patient to a psychiatric facility. While agitated in the admission ward, he was generally compliant, and did not attempt to leave the acute ward following the admission. Had he made such a move, formal confinement proceedings would have been commenced, and L would not have been allowed off the premises; but such formal proceedings had not been necessary. Notwithstanding repeated requests by the family for L's return, the hospital refused to discharge him into their care.

At issue in the domestic litigation was whether individuals such as L, who acquiesce rather than assent to their admission and who lack the capacity to make a decision as to where they will reside in any event, can be admitted informally and remain in hospital under these circumstances or whether they must be sectioned under the formal confinement powers of the MHA. Before the European Court of Human Rights, the issue was whether these conditions engaged the right to liberty under Art. 5 of the ECHR.

The questions are of considerable practical relevance. During the domestic litigation, the Mental Health Act Commission estimated that requiring the use of such formal confinement powers would increase the use of those powers by 48,000, from 26,000 to 74,000 persons per year, an increase of 184 per cent. The persons subject to formal confinement powers on a given day would increase by 22,000, from 13,000 to 35,000, a rise of 169 per cent: *R* v *Bournewood Community and Mental Health NHS Trust, ex p L* [1999] 1 AC 481. Shortly after that case, during the reform process of the Mental Health Act, the Department of Health estimated that the specialist mental health services dealt with 44,000 acquiescing incapacitated people at any given time (Department of Health, 2000c: para. 6.1.)

The House of Lords held that the MHA 1983 envisaged the informal admission of acquiescing incapable patients. Lord Goff reached this view by citing paragraph 291 of the Percy Commission report, the report that led to the 1959 Mental Health Act (Royal Commission on the Law Relating to Mental Illness and Mental Deficiency 1954–1957, 1957). Certainly, it does seem that the Percy Commission did advocate informal admission, not merely for assenting patients, but for 'all who need [treatment] and are not unwilling to receive it' (1957: para. 291). As a general principle, this interpretation of the Percy Commission is beyond reproach.

The House of Lords then approached the case in the context of wrongful confinement. In that context, Lord Goff held that any question of detention of L would have arisen only had he attempted to leave the hospital, which he did not. Further, any confinement that would have occurred would, in this case, have been justified by the principles of best interests and necessity, derived from *F* v *West Berkshire Health Authority* [1989] 2 All ER 545. It is much less obvious that the House of Lords was correct in these aspects of L's case (see Bartlett, 2003). The Percy Commission expressly addressed the situation of a family member asking for the release of an incompetent, acquiescing patient. In the event that the family member was the nearest relative, the Commission stated that 'there can be no question of a barring certificate, even on grounds of danger to the patient or to others, in relation to patients admitted informally, whom the hospital has no authority to detain' (para. 305(ii)). If the person requesting were not the nearest relative, it would seem that the patient should nonetheless be released if the relative had made reasonable plans to care of the patient (para. 305(iv)). The House of Lords was apparently not referred by counsel to this paragraph of the Percy Report, and it is not referred to in its judgment. In any event, these aspects of the House of Lords' judgment are largely superseded by the decision of the European Court of Human Rights.

The European Court of Human Rights took the view that L's right to liberty under Art. 5 of the ECHR was engaged. Article 5 rights were specifically not dependent on whether the individual manifested a wish to leave the facility (*HL* v *UK* Application No. 45508/99 (2005) 40 EHRR 32, para. 90). Instead, the key factor was that the staff of the hospital exercised 'complete and effective control over his care and movements' (para. 91). Had he attempted to leave, he would have been prevented from so doing, and visits from his carers were restricted by the hospital staff. The Court continued (para. 91):

Accordingly, the concrete situation was that the applicant was under continuous supervision and control and was not free to leave. Any suggestion to the contrary was, in the Court's view, fairly described by Lord Steyn as 'stretching credulity to breaking point' and as a 'fairy tale'.

The evidence was conflicting as to whether the ward on which L was kept was actually locked. The Court held that this was not determinative of the question of detention (para. 92).

Article 5(1)(e) does allow the deprivation of 'persons of unsound mind', a category into which L fell, but subject to conditions. The confinement must be according to a procedure proscribed by law. Substantively, the law must be sufficiently clear to allow an individual to foresee the reasonable consequences of actions. The Court declined to decide whether the doctrine of necessity met the latter, substantive, threshold, but it held that it did not meet the former, procedural criterion (para. 120):

In this latter respect, the Court finds striking the lack of any fixed procedural rules by which the admission and detention of compliant incapacitated persons is conducted. The contrast between this dearth of regulation and the extensive network of safeguards applicable to psychiatric committals covered by the 1983 Act (paragraphs 36 and 54 above) is, in the Court's view, significant.

In particular and most obviously, the Court notes the lack of any formalised admission procedures which indicate who can propose admission, for what reasons and on the basis of what kind of medical and other assessments and conclusions. There is no requirement to fix the exact purpose of admission (for example, for assessment or for treatment) and, consistently, no limits in terms of time, treatment or care attach to that admission. Nor is there any specific provision requiring a continuing clinical assessment of the persistence of a disorder warranting detention. The nomination of a representative of a patient who could make certain objections and applications on his or her behalf is a procedural protection accorded to those committed involuntarily under the 1983 Act and which would be of equal importance for patients who are legally incapacitated and have, as in the present case, extremely limited communication abilities.

On this basis, the Court found a violation of Art. 5.

The House of Lords and European Court of Human Rights decisions are overlapping, but not precisely contradictory. As things stood after both decisions, it was lawful for incapable, acquiescing patients to be admitted informally, as long as the conditions of the admission did not amount to a deprivation of liberty under Art. 5. Quite how many people were therefore affected is unclear: deprivation of liberty is determined by the facts of individual situations, and it cannot be assumed that all incapable acquiescing individuals were deprived of their liberty. Nonetheless, it became clear that legal reform would be necessary.

The MCA 2005, in the form it was passed in 2005, offered little help to the *Bournewood* problem. The MCA 2005 will, when it comes into effect (probably in April 2007), introduce a statutory best interests test for persons lacking capacity, and formalise processes for substitute decision-making for those individuals (see Chapter 11). While these individuals might 'restrain' an individual in certain circumstances, the MCA 2005 is clear that any deprivation of liberty under Art. 5 is outside the authority of these individuals (MCA 2005, ss. 6(5), 11(6), 20(13)). While the new Court of Protection might, presumably, order admission in *Bournewood* situations, it seems unlikely that this will prove practical as the sole process for doing so, given the numbers of admissions likely to be involved (re revised timetable and 2006 Bill regarding *HL*, see preface).

The government published its intentions regarding a legislative response to *Bournewood* in June 2006, with the intent, it would seem, that it will be introduced in the same package of measures as the amendments to the MHA 1983 (Department of Health, 2006b). The amendments will affect people in hospitals and care homes registered under the Care Standards Act 2000. The staff of these institutions will be required to identify persons who lack capacity and are being (or risk being) deprived of their liberty. The facility then applies to a 'supervising body' – the primary care trust (PCT) for hospitals in England, the local authority for care homes in England, and the National Assembly in Wales – for authorisation of the deprivation of liberty. The supervising authority will then obtain assessments on the following matters:

- whether the individual is over the age of 18 (age assessment);
- whether the individual suffers from a disorder or disability of the mind (mental health assessment);
- whether the individual lacks capacity to decide whether he or she should be a resident in the facility (mental capacity assessment);
- whether there is already a control in place under the MHA 1983 (such as a guardianship) that conflicts with the proposed authorisation (eligibility assessment);
- whether the authorisation is in the best interests of the person, consistent with the overall definition in the MCA 2005, including that it is necessary for the person to be a patient in the facility to prevent harm to the patient, and that the authorisation is a proportionate response to the likelihood and seriousness of that harm (best interests assessment).

The duration of the authorisation is to be dependent on the circumstances of the case, subject to a maximum of one year. Reapplications at the end of an authorisation will be permitted if appropriate.

The MCA 2005 allows an individual, when competent, to sign a 'lasting power of attorney', appointing a substitute decision-maker in the event the individual loses capacity. It also allows the court to appoint a 'deputy' to make such decisions. While it would seem that the authorisation process will need to be followed, even when such a substitute or deputy agrees with the admission to the facility, the grant of an authorisation cannot be in conflict with the decision of such a person.

If the authorisation is granted, a 'representative' will be appointed to keep in touch with and support the person lacking capacity. The representative's powers will include the right to apply for a review or appeal of the authorisation. Consistent with the approach of the MCA 2005 generally, regarding admissions to care homes and hospitals, this person will normally be a friend or family member, but in the absence of such a person, a professional advocate will be provided.

The authorisation does not restrict other legal justifications for these admissions: the powers of parents and of guardians under the MHA1983 will remain in place. Further, in the event that an authorisation is not granted, detention under the MHA 1983 will continue to be available, assuming the criteria in that Act are satisfied. For example, the 'harm' requirement in the proposals will allow authorisation only in the event that the harm was to the patient himself or herself; if failure to admit the individual would result in harm not to that individual but to someone else, it will apparently be necessary to resort to the MHA 1983.

The proposals will further require the use of the MHA 1983 detention procedures in the event that the individual objects to the admission, or 'would object if they were in a position to do so' (Department of Health, 2006b: 2). It is not obvious how this hypothetical requirement is to be implemented. It may well be the case that whether the person would or would not have objected if able to do so is purely speculative. (Re 2006 Bill on this point, see preface.)

The proposals represent a clear improvement on the current situation. There remain some difficulties, however. The people who are to be subject to the legal safeguards are to be identified, at first instance, by the staff of the hospital or care home, based on the subjective criteria that they lack capacity and are deprived of liberty. This raises a practical question: will adequate training and support be provided to the staff members (in both the public and the private sector) to ensure that these decisions can be appropriately and systematically made? Quite what 'capacity' means in the context of a decision to be admitted to a facility is not unproblematic (see later in this chapter); its assessment may be similarly difficult. It also raises a theoretical difficulty: the decision as to whether legal safeguards will apply will rest at first instance with the person depriving the individual of liberty. This raises an issue of conflicting interests: while most of the administration will fall to the supervisory body, an application to that body will still mean an increased workload for the staff making the application, with a corresponding pressure not to invoke the safeguards. It is not clear how or whether there will be an external audit of their decisions in this regard. In other contexts, it will be reasonable to expect the person whose liberty is in question to have a role in challenging any failure to provide legal safeguards, but such an expectation cannot be assumed for people lacking capacity.

Bournewood patients will be primarily contained in hospitals or registered care homes, and thus within the scope of the proposed legal reforms. Some *Bournewood* patients will not be in these facilities, however. For such people, whose liberty is curtailed in family homes and similar environments, the government proposes that an application to the new Court of Protection under the MCA 2005 should be necessary (Department of Health, 2006b: 6). Once again, the question is how this requirement will be enforced. It seems unlikely that families will have sufficient knowledge of the law to know that such an application is made, and it is obvious that not all families will be able to afford such an application. There is no systematic enforcement mechanism to ensure compliance with the MCA 2005 as a whole; it is not obvious how this provision will be enforced.

4.3 Civil confinement: standards and justifications

In theory (but as we have seen, not necessarily in practice), informal admission does not involve intervention by the state to confine the individual in the psychiatric hospital. With civil confinement ('sectioning'), this is not the case. The sectioning of an individual is clearly an instance of the state's coercive power intruding on the freedom of the individual. While the objective of civil confinement is not punitive, the intrusiveness of the violation must be understood as requiring clear justification.

Traditionally, the justifications have concerned the need to protect the individual or others in society (the 'dangerousness' criterion), or the more paternalist justification of acting for the benefit of the individual, with 'benefit' usually understood in medical terms. There has been an implication in some of the discourse regarding these criteria that the former is a creature of US constitutional law, while the latter is consistent with the English way of doing things. This is misleading on both counts. While the US Bill of Rights has certainly resulted in a more interventionist jurisprudence than has existed in England, it has always stopped short of finding dangerousness as an express requirement for confinement, and indeed, when alternative options are considered at the end of this chapter, a system of therapeutic criteria designed to meet the rights standards of the US Constitution will be discussed.

Similarly, the dangerousness criterion is not an American invention. Prior to the statutory development of asylum law in the nineteenth century, the legal issue was a defence to an action for wrongful confinement. Confinement of a lunatic would be allowed 'to prevent apparent mischief, which might ensue: as, to restrain the plaintiff, non sane, from killing himself, or others, burning a house, or other mischief' (Comyn, 1822: vol. 6, p. 544, pl. 3.M.22.) While thus well established by the beginning of the nineteenth century, the roots of the criterion are much older. Brook's abridgement from the sixteenth century contains another similar statement referring specifically, as in Comyn, to restraining the lunatic from killing, or doing mischief such as setting fire to a house (Brook, 1573: 'Faux Imprisonment', pl. 28, vol 1, p. 330).

In the nineteenth century, confinement criteria were codified by a series of statutes. With minor variations over the century, the standard required that a lunatic, idiot or person of unsound mind was 'a proper person to be taken charge of and detained under care and treatment': see Lunacy Act 1890, form 8. Notwithstanding this broad wording, out of a concern for civil rights of the insane, the courts imported the dangerousness language from the wrongful confinement context. The legislation was held to be justified by public order. Thus in *Re Fell* (1845 3 Dowl & L 373, 15 LJ (NS) MC 25 QB, Patteson J commented (at p. 29) that: 'These statutes were passed for the protection of the public...' That, in turn, led to a standard of dangerousness. In *Nottidge* v *Ripley* (*The Times* London, 27 June 1849, p. 7), for example, Sir Frederick Pollock CB stated in his charge to the jury, 'it is my opinion that you ought to liberate every person who is not dangerous to himself or others...and I desire to impress that opinion with as much force as I can'. See also *R* v *Pinder, in re Greenwood* (1855) 24 LJ (NS) QB 148 at 151, per Coleridge J).

Far from being a foreign interloper, therefore, the dangerousness standard forms a part of English legal culture. In so far as it reflects an attempt to preserve public peace and safety, it represents an obviously legitimate public interest. The desire to protect individuals from harming themselves is less evidently a public interest, but if paternalist, it is at the less interventionist side of that spectrum. As a guiding justification for civil confinement, it also has the disadvantage that a person, even if not susceptible to treatment, might remain confined in perpetuity, due to mental illness and the mere risk of behaving in a fashion dangerous to self or others. This is particularly problematic because, as we shall see, dangerousness is notoriously difficult to predict. It also reinforces imagery of the asylum as a place of confinement and, by implication, not of treatment. Neither governments, nor the medical professionals working in the facilities, nor the public, find that imagery attractive.

Even in the nineteenth century, the dangerousness criterion was contested. In an open letter to the Lord Chancellor, responding to *Nottidge*, the Commissioners in Lunacy expressly denied a requirement of dangerousness prior to confinement, claiming instead that '[t]he object of these Acts is not, as your Lordship is aware, so much to confine lunatics, as to restore to a healthy state of mind such of them as are curable, and to afford comfort and protection to the rest' (Parliamentary Papers, 1849 (620) xlvi 381 at 4.) The twin justifications of the desirability of treatment and need for protective custody are essentially paternalist. The two strands are worth distinguishing, however. The former is an essentially medical paternalism, which continues to resonate in the mental health discourse and the MHA 1983. Its attractiveness lies in its promise, accurate or not, that things will be made better for the individual.

The attractiveness is nonetheless problematic in terms of legal logic. As several commentators have pointed out (Hoggett, 1996; Price 1994) it is a non sequitur to hold that because a patient's condition can be said to warrant hospitalisation, the patient should be *forced* to enter hospital. As a matter of law, what is the public interest that justifies such extreme intervention as the confinement of an individual to effect his or her treatment or cure? There may be an economic benefit, in that the individual may, if sufficiently improved in mental state, be much more employable, but if the claim is an economic one, the benefits presumably need to be balanced against probable costs of treatment, an exercise for which few would argue. The more appealing claim has to do with doing something good for somebody, a justification based on charity. This too is problematic, however. Intervention is justified only if there is likely to be real benefit to the proposed patient – but how likely and how much benefit? And on what basis is it justifiable to enforce such good will onto people with mental disorders, when we do not do so onto people with physical disorders, where the same arguments may apply when a person refuses hospitalisation?

A claim that intervention is permissible on behalf of those unable to help themselves is not justified, because the standard is based on treatability, not incapacity in decision-making. These two classes are considerably different in membership. It remains a distinct problem to locate a state interest in imposing confinement for purposes of cure or assistance on people who do not lack mental capacity, and do not want the help.

These difficulties are even clearer regarding the second justification of the Commissioners. The argument for protective custody is a different sort of paternalism, a claim that, even if the patient's condition will not be improved, it is an act of kindness to confine the individual. This attitude exists expressly for people with mental illness or severe mental impairment who are already detained under s. 3. Renewal of such detention can be justified in part when 'the patient, if discharged, is unlikely to be able to care for himself, to obtain the care which he needs or to guard himself from serious exploitation' (s. 20(4)). The notion of protective custody is much diminished in the professional discourses. It does still exist in the popular discourse regarding people on the streets rightly or wrongly understood to have psychiatric difficulties, particularly when those people are begging or sleeping rough. Arguments for confinement of this class must be approached with some care. Options, perhaps including hospitalisation, should be offered to these people, but it is difficult to see the state interest in using a coercive power to confine them.

The current English legislation is a conjunction of a variety of approaches. For example, a prerequisite for most confinements refers to 'the health or safety of the patient or for the protection of other persons' (MHA 1983, s. 3(2)(c); see also ss. 2(2)(b), 5(4)(a)). Criteria relating to dangerousness and therapeutic benevolence are expressly included, even in the space of a single paragraph of the statute. Defenders of the 1983 Act would claim a triumph of English pragmatism and compromise. The rationales of the approaches are markedly different, however, and they do not necessarily sit easily together. Detractors would call the statute incoherent (Price, 1994). The tensions between the various approaches will be apparent throughout the discussion that follows.

The 1983 Act is somewhat complex, and an overview in advance may be of assistance in understanding the more detailed discussion that follows. The civil confinement structure is summarised graphically in Figure 4.1. Essentially, civil admissions may be for assessment (s. 2) or for treatment (s. 3). An admission for treatment allows the detention of the individual for up to six months for initial admission and first renewal, and for up to a year for subsequent renewals. An admission for assessment allows detention of the individual for 28 days. It is not renewable. At the end of that time, the individual must either be released, continued as an informal patient, or admitted for treatment under the usual procedures for a s. 3 admission.

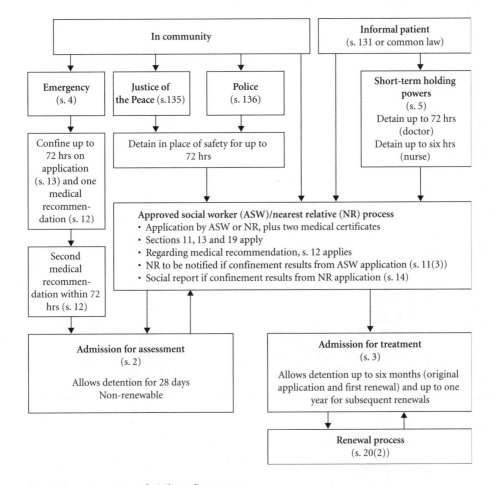

Fig. 4.1 An overview of civil confinement

• Patients transferring between facilities maintain their status (s. 19)

• Upon lapse of authority to detain, patients in hospital revert to informal status (s.131)

For admission under either s. 2 or s. 3, an application must be made by the nearest relative of the individual or, in practice much more frequently, by an approved social worker (ASW) (see Chapter 5). The application must, in general, be accompanied by certificates from two medical practitioners. There are several ways in which short-term intervention may be instituted, to allow for the assessments of the medical practitioners or social worker to be completed. First, in an emergency (s. 4), one medical certificate will suffice for an admission for assessment, as long as the second is furnished within 72 hours. Secondly, an informal patient may be detained for up to 72 hours by a doctor, or, when immediacy is necessary, up to six hours by a nurse (s. 5). A Justice of the Peace, upon application by an approved social worker, may require detention in a place of safety, for up to 72 hours, of mentally disordered individuals who are being ill-treated, neglected, or not kept under proper control, or who are living alone and unable

	For assessment	For treatment	Emergency	Urgent inpatient	Justices of the Peace	Police
Section	2	3	4	5	135(1)	136
Mental disorder criteria	Any mental disorder that warrants patient's detention in hospital for assessment for at least a limited period	Must suffer from one of the specific categories of disorder defined in s. 1, to a nature or degree that makes it appropriate to receive medical treatment in a hospital. If psychopathic disorder or mental impairment, treatment must be likely to alleviate or prevent deterioration of condition	As s. 2 admission	If application by doctor, no criteria If application by nurse, as for s. 2 admission	Any mental disorder	Any mental disorder
Substantive thresholds	Ought to be so detained in the interests of his or her own health or safety or with a view to the protection of other persons	Necessary for patient's health or safety, or for protection of other persons, that such treatment be provided, and it cannot be provided unless detained under this section	Compliance with s. 2 would involve undesirable delay	If application by doctor, merely that application 'ought' to be made regarding inpatient If by nurse, inpatient receiving treatment for mental disorder, and not practical to refer to doctor	Has been, or is being, ill-treated, neglected or kept otherwise than under proper control; or living alone and unable to care for him/herself	In public place and in need of immediate care and control, and necessary in the interests of the person or for the protection of other persons

Maximum detention authorised	28 days, non-renewable	Six months (original certificate and first renewal); one year (subsequent renewal)	Absent second medical certificate, 72 hours. If second certificate, becomes s. 2 admission	By nurse, six hours. By doctor, 72 hours	72 hours in place of safety	72 hours in place of safety
Treatment rights	Treatment provisions of ss. 58 and 63 apply	Treatment provisions of ss. 58 and 63 apply	Treatment provisions of ss. 58 and 63 do not apply	Treatment provisions of ss. 58 and 63 do not apply	Treatment provisions of ss. 58 and 63 do not apply	Treatment provisions of ss. 58, 63 do not apply
Other notes	Discharge under ss. 23 et seq. Review of detention available under ss. 66(1)(a) and 66(2)(a) within first 14 days of confinement	Discharge under ss. 23 et seq. Review of detention available under ss. 66(1)(b) and (f) and 66(2)(b) and (f), once prior to first renewal and once per renewal thereafter Duty exists to provide aftercare under s. 117	Discharge under ss. 23 et seq.	Designed to allow assessments by ASW and doctor(s) Discharge under ss. 23 et seq.	Designed to allow assessment by ASW and doctor(s) No statutory provision re. discharge	Designed to allow assessment by ASW and doctor(s) No statutory provision re. discharge

Table. 4.1 Confinement criteria

to care for themselves (s. 135(1)). Finally, mentally disordered individuals found by police officers in public places may also be removed to a place of safety for up to 72 hours (s. 136). Prescribed forms for most of these purposes are contained in the Mental Health (Hospital, Guardianship and Consent to Treatment) Regulations 1983 (SI 1983, No. 893).

The substantive criteria differ for each of these interventions. A brief outline of these criteria, along with the basic effects of confinement under the various categories, is in Table 4.1. There is a curious failure of the literature to analyse in detail the meaning of these criteria. As we will see, the courts have sometimes given relatively broad interpretations to the substantive criteria. Given the intrusion into the civil liberties of those confined, however, we would respectfully argue that the statutes ought instead to be strictly construed (see *In re Dulles' Settlement* [1950] 2 All ER 1013). Careful consideration of the standards is therefore appropriate.

4.4 Detention for assessment or treatment: substantive issues

4.4.1 Admission for assessment under s. 2

The substantive criteria for admission for assessment are contained in s. 2(2) of the 1983 Act:

> 2(2) An application for admission for assessment may be made in respect of a patient on the grounds that—
>
> (a) he is suffering from mental disorder of a nature or degree which warrants the detention of the patient in a hospital for assessment (or for assessment followed by medical treatment) for at least a limited period; and
>
> (b) he ought to be so detained in the interests of his own health or safety or with a view to the protection of other persons.

To begin with, the patient must be suffering from 'mental disorder', in the sense of the generic definition in s. 1(2): see Chapter 2. It is not necessary to specify the patient's condition with any greater clarity at this stage: this, after all, is the purpose of the intended assessment. The test is phrased in the present continuous ('is suffering') so that a person who has been but is no longer suffering from mental disorder is outside the scope of this section.

The section implies that this determination ought to be made prior to the confinement. This interpretation is given further credence by Forms 3 and 4 of the regulations (SI 1983/893), the medical recommendations upon which the confinement is based, which require the signing doctors to be of the opinion that the criteria of s. 2(2) are satisfied, including the existence of the mental disorder. This is at variance with the *obiter* view of Lloyd LJ in *R v Kirklees Metropolitan BC* (1993) (see earlier) that because the definition of 'patient' in s. 145 includes a person who *appears to be* suffering from a mental disorder, admission under s. 2 would be lawful if the assessment subsequently revealed that the patient is not mentally disordered (p. 190). His Lordship held that: 'Any other construction would unnecessarily emasculate the beneficial power under s. 2 and confine assessment to choice of treatment.' This is not necessarily correct, because the purpose of assessment is also, and as a prior requisite for the administration of treatment, to attain with greater precision the nature of the particular patient's mental disorder or explore avenues of treatment (Code of Practice, para. 5.2; Department of Health and Welsh Office, 1999). Many patients are, in fact, rediagnosed shortly after admission (Bean, 1980).

The mental disorder must be of 'a nature or degree that warrants the detention of the patient in a hospital for assessment (or for assessment followed by treatment) for at least a limited period'. 'Nature' and 'degree' do not have the same meaning. It was held in *R v MHRT for South Thames Region, ex p Smith* [1999] COD 148 that the former refers to the particular disorder itself, including the features of the underlying condition and its prognosis, while the latter referred to the current manifestations of the disorder. In the view of the court, these were intentionally listed as alternative requirements in the statute. While the expert evidence was that the degree of Smith's disorder did not warrant confinement, its nature did, and therefore he could be legally confined on the basis that the condition might cease to be static. The *Smith* case itself concerned a patient whose disorder was controlled by medication, but who had a history of ceasing medication and becoming ill. The decision held that patients with such a history could be confined, even when taking their medication. This has led to criticism that patients who cease their medication with ill effects at some time following a previous release may remain liable to unjustly prolonged detention in subsequent admissions, because of that history (Armstrong, 1999).

If the distinction between nature and degree is taken to its logical end, the situation might, in fact, be more serious, because 'nature' would appear to refer in the section to the disorder itself, not to the patient's intentions regarding treatment compliance. If that is the case, even patients with no history of ceasing treatment might have disorders of a nature but not degree warranting confinement. In that event, s. 2(2)(b) might still preclude the confinement, but the safeguards contained in s. 2(2)(a) nonetheless appear remarkably weak after *Smith*.

The clear implication is that some types of mental disorder are *not* of a nature or degree that requires hospitalisation. Typically, however, the Act does not specify with any precision the limits of the powers given to those charged with its operation (Bean, 1986: 39). Nonetheless, the remainder of the section provides some guidance as to how this might be understood. Clearly, the provisions reflect a concern to safeguard the rights of mentally disordered persons from unwarranted compulsory hospitalisation. By the same token, they mean that the decision whether a patient should be admitted under s. 2 is not simply a clinical, medical one. It should also incorporate an assessment of the prospects for the patient if *not* hospitalised. Issues relevant to this assessment include the individual's home environment and the accessibility of other support networks, whether the formal provision of 'care in the community' or networks of friends and family. This is further reflected in the requirement that the ASWs certify that 'detention in hospital is in all the circumstances of the case the most appropriate way of providing the care and medical treatment of which the patient stands in need' (Form 2, SI 1983/893). Even if hospitalisation is required, an assessment must be made as to whether 'detention' is justified. Thus, the doctors providing medical certificates in support of the application are required to provide reasons as to why informal admission is not appropriate in the circumstances (Forms 3 and 4, SI 1983/893).

Under s. 2(2)(b), an individual can only be admitted if he or she 'ought to be so detained in the interests of his own health or safety or with a view to the protection of other persons'. The interpretation of this section is problematic. On the one hand, the structure of the paragraph as one continuous phrase suggests an intent that it should be read as a coherent whole. On the other, as we have seen, it is a simple disjunction of two separate justifications of confinement, beneficence and dangerousness, making such a coherent reading problematic. The difficulty becomes apparent in assessing how broadly the term 'health' is to be read. The gloss in the Code of Practice divides the health, safety and protection into three paragraphs, and italicises the 'or' between them, creating an impression that a very wide view of the health grounds would justify confinement (para. 2.6). The section itself does not do that, however. While it would be incorrect to read a dangerousness requirement as pervading all terms in the paragraph, it remains appropriate to follow the standard rule of statutory construction that items in a list modify each other to some degree. In that event, a reasonably serious risk to health would be required to justify confinement. That seems appropriate: confinement is an extreme mechanism, and ought only to be used for serious threats to the health of an individual.

The importance of this approach can be seen in considering the glosses placed on the criteria. The view of the Mental Health Act Commission, the Law Society Mental Health and Disability Committee, and the Department of Health are all that the section is broad enough to include a risk to mental health of the individual (Jones, 2006: 29). In the event of real and serious risk to the mental health of an individual, this may be a defensible position; the risk is that it will be overused. It would, for example, be a serious violation of an individual's right to make treatment decisions, if failure to take psychiatric medication routinely triggered these criteria.

4.4.2 Admission for treatment under s. 3

The criteria for admission for treatment are contained in s. 3(2):

3(2) An application for admission for treatment may be made in respect of a patient on the grounds that—

(a) he is suffering from mental illness, severe mental impairment, psychopathic disorder or mental impairment and his mental disorder is of a nature or degree which makes it appropriate to receive medical treatment in a hospital; and

(b) in the case of psychopathic disorder or mental impairment, such treatment is likely to alleviate or prevent a deterioration of his condition; and

(c) it is necessary for the health or safety of the patient or for the protection of other persons that he should receive such treatment and it cannot be provided unless he is detained under this section.

The structural similarities to s. 2 will be immediately apparent. As under s. 2, the patient must at the time of the application actually be suffering from the mental disability; here, unlike in s. 2, not any mental disability will do. Section 3 instead requires that the patient be suffering from one of the four specific sorts of mental disorder identified by s. 1(2) and, pursuant to s. 3(3)(b), each medical certificate must identify the same s. 1(2) category. It is not possible to admit a person under s. 3 on the grounds that he or she is suffering from 'any other disorder or disability of mind', as is possible under s. 2. The mental disorder must be of a nature and degree that makes it appropriate for them to receive treatment in a hospital. Analogous to the discussion of the criteria in s. 2, this would suggest that some disorders are inappropriate for hospital treatment; as with s. 2, the assessment must be made on the basis of both clinical and social factors. It must be 'necessary' (perhaps a slightly higher threshold than 'ought' in s. 2?) for the health or safety of the patient or for the protection of other persons that the treatment be given, with the attendant difficulties on how these substantive criteria are to be read.

Unlike s. 2, s. 3 requires that the treatment in question cannot be provided without detention under the section, and the medical certificates require reasons to be given why this is the case (Form 11, SI 1983/893). This requirement is the cornerstone of the policy in the Act to tie compulsion to mandatory admission. In recent years, this requirement has been subject to ongoing erosion, in an effort to make the mandatory treatment provisions that flow from s. 3 available to enforce treatment on people who for all intents and purposes live in the community. This jurisprudence is discussed in Chapter 8.

To what degree must the treatment be effective? For those with psychopathic disorders or (non-severe) mental impairment, s. 3(2)(b) of the statute prescribes that the treatment be likely to alleviate or prevent a deterioration of the patient's condition. This has come to be known as the 'treatability test'. It is not clear, however, that many psychopathic or mentally impaired individuals can be 'treated' in any conventional sense. How can treatment be expected to affect an 'arrested or incomplete development of mind', as required for a finding of mental impairment?

A similar issue arises regarding psychopaths where, as noted in Chapter 2, there is considerable dispute among doctors as to whether the condition is treatable. This divergence of opinion was noted by Lord Hope in *Reid* v *Secretary of State for Scotland* [1999] 1 All ER 481 at p. 493, a case decided under Scottish law, but on principles held by the House of Lords also to be applicable to England:

Medical opinion which says that this condition is not susceptible of treatment in a hospital may be capable of being reconciled with the statute in a practical way, because those who hold to this opinion will refrain from recommending that a hospital order should be made in cases of this kind.

This is no doubt correct, but it is, at best, a sorry attempt to justify the statute, because it suggests that the decision as to whether an individual will be confined under the

MHA 1983, or released (often to face criminal sanctions), is a function, not of the characteristics of the individual or the disorder, but instead of the doctor's belief about the treatability of psychopathy. As the patient has no right to choose a doctor upon assessment, but is instead assigned the doctor on duty, this turns basic decisions about the individual's civil rights into a lottery. It is difficult to see this as a justifiable situation.

The clearest exposition of the treatability test may be found in *R v Canons Park Mental Health Review Tribunal, ex p A* [1994] 2 All ER 659 (CA). That case revolved around a person with psychopathic disorder, where the proposed treatment was group therapy. This, of course, requires the cooperation of those participating in order to be effective, and A refused to participate. Roch LJ, dissenting on other grounds, provided the following principles as a guide to treatability (at pp. 679–80):

First, if a tribunal were to be satisfied that the patient's detention in hospital was simply an attempt to coerce the patient into participating in group therapy, then the tribunal would be under a duty to direct discharge. Second, 'treatment in hospital' will satisfy the 'treatability test' although it is unlikely to alleviate the patient's condition, provided that it is likely to prevent a deterioration. Third, 'treatment in hospital' will satisfy the 'treatability test' although it will not immediately alleviate or prevent deterioration in the patient's condition, provided that alleviation or stabilisation is likely in due course. Fourth, the 'treatability test' can still be met although initially there may be some deterioration in the patient's condition, due for example to the patient's initial anger at being detained. Fifth, it must be remembered that medical treatment in hospital covers 'nursing and also includes care, habilitation and rehabilitation under medical supervision'. Sixth, the 'treatability test' is satisfied if nursing care etc. are likely to lead to an alleviation of the patient's condition in that the patient is likely to gain an insight into his problem or cease to be uncooperative in his attitude towards treatment which would potentially have a lasting benefit.

In *Canons Park* itself, Roch LJ held that the treatability test had been satisfied.

While the principles enunciated by Roch LJ appear innocuous enough at first glance, they are problematic. The first principle holds that detention should not be used in order to coerce consent to treatment; yet the fourth principle acknowledges that there may be an initial reluctance to consent based, for example, on anger at admission, and the sixth principle holds that rendering the patient cooperative in attitude toward treatment is a therapeutic objective. It is, on a practical level, difficult to see how confining a patient through the period of their initial anger with the hope of rendering them cooperative is different from the coercion prohibited by the first principle.

The breadth of 'treatment' under the 1983 Act will be discussed further in Chapter 7, but the court in *Canons Park* is not alone in adopting an expansive meaning to justify confinement. In *Reid*, the sheriff (the judicial officer hearing the case initially) held that in the structured and supervised setting of the state hospital, Reid's 'anger management' improved, and he became less aggressive. This allowed Lord Hutton to conclude that the treatability test was satisfied, on the basis that 'treatment which alleviates the symptoms and manifestations of the underlying medical disorder of a psychopath is "treatment" within the meaning of [the Act] even if the treatment does not cure the disorder itself' (p. 514). Similarly, *R (Home Secretary) v MHRT* [2004] EWHC 1029

(Admin) concerned a patient alleged to have a psychopathic disorder. In the view of his medical team and the court, he was clearly dangerous; the question was whether he was treatable. He was deriving no benefit from treatment programmes, but could seem to cope in the structured environment of the hospital. The court held that this was enough (para. 16):

The Tribunal accepted that the hospital could prevent deterioration by his continuing in custody. Having accepted that factual proposition, it seems to me it was bound to conclude that the condition was susceptible to treatment in that it would prevent deterioration of the symptoms of the mental disorder were he suffering from a mental disorder.

Detention itself, it would seem, can be 'treatment'.

While this escapes the difficulty of how such a constitutional condition can be 'treated', it does so at some cost, because by focusing on symptoms and manifestations rather than the disorder itself, it emphasises the social control and policing functions of the statute. This is consistent with the courts' overall approach to the test. In *R (Wheldon)* v *Rampton Hospital Authority* [2001] EWHC Admin 134, Elias J took the view that the treatability test was 'far from satisfactory', because of course it means that the court may be required, in effect, to direct the release of somebody who is a real danger to the public' (para. 16). In that case, he was content to hold that the test was satisfied, on the slimmest evidence that benefit would actually result to the patient (para. 35):

I recognise that it may be said that those treatments have been proposed in hope rather than out of experience, and that it is possible that the various medical officers and social workers recommending such treatment do not necessarily believe that it is likely to achieve any benefits for Mr Wheldon. But there are passages in the documents before me which make it plain that there is a belief that they will bring about an improvement: I refer, for example, to a letter which Dr Page wrote to the Medical Director of Broadmoor Hospital, in which she states: 'The view of the clinical team is that Mr Wheldon would benefit from an alternative placement.'

Given these cases, it is difficult to see the treatability test as much of a safeguard to patient rights.

For those diagnosed with mental illness or severe mental impairment, there is no express treatability test in s. 3. This is not an oversight. The Percy Commission had recommended that the treatability requirement apply across the board, but this suggestion was rejected on the basis that hospitalisation might offer asylum in times of crisis to some mentally ill or severely mentally impaired people, notwithstanding the untreatability of their condition (Royal Commission on the Law Relating to Mental Illness and Mental Deficiency 1954–1957, 1957: para. 240). This is consistent with the conditions for renewal of s. 3 detentions, as they approach their expiry at the end of six months, where something analogous to a treatability test is included. The conditions for such renewals are contained in s. 20(4). While broadly similar to those in s. 3, they do not restrict the treatability test to mental incapacity and psychopathy: s. 20(4)(b). For cases of mental illness or severe mental incapacity, however, an alternative is available to the requirement that treatment 'alleviate or prevent a deterioration' of the patient's condition (s. 20(4)):

... in the case of mental illness or severe mental impairment, it shall be an alternative to the condition specified in paragraph (b) above that the patient, if discharged, is unlikely to be able to care for himself, to obtain the care which he needs or to guard himself against serious exploitation.

On this reading, it would be possible to detain an individual who is not actually treatable. Particularly if an expansive definition of 'health' is adopted under s. 3(2)(c), as discussed above, these individuals will not necessarily be dangerous to self or others. While asylum may be an important option to leave open for individuals in this situation, it is less obvious that it should be imposed, using coercive powers.

There has, perhaps, been some retreat from that extreme position. In *R v Hallstrom, ex p W (No. 2)* [1986] 2 All ER 306, the court held (at p. 315) that there must be some treatment to be given to the patient while confined in the facility:

'Admission for treatment' under s. 3 is intended for those whose condition is believed to require a period of treatment as an inpatient. It may be that such patients will also be thought to require a period of outpatient treatment thereafter, but the concept of 'admission for treatment' has no applicability to those whom it is intended to admit and detain for a purely nominal period, during which no necessary treatment will be given.

The phrase 'and his mental disorder ... makes it appropriate for him to receive treatment in a hospital' in section 3(2)(a) also leads to the conclusion that the section is concerned with those whose mental condition requires in-patient treatment.

Some hesitation may be appropriate in interpreting this case here, because the facts in that case are quite different from the current discussion. The case involved an individual detained under s. 3, on long-term leave of absence in the community. Renewal of the detention was sought to allow the mandatory treatment provisions of the 1983 Act to remain in effect in the community when the patient was, immediately, given a leave of absence. That is quite a different situation from admission to a facility where treatment is not available.

The argument based on *Hallstrom* may well be moot, because the expansive definition of treatment under s. 145 of the 1983 Act is open to be invoked: see Chapter 7. If mere nursing constitutes treatment for purposes of ss. 3 and 20 (as it clearly does under that definition), confinement of the mentally ill or severely mentally impaired would be justified if it were appropriate that they receive some nursing care, and, if the detention is to continue beyond six months, that they were believed to be unable to care for themselves, or open to exploitation.

In its package of reforms to the MHA 1983, the government proposes to abolish the four separate categories of mental disorder. Consistent with this, it proposes to do away with the differing treatability standards. Instead, compulsory admission will be available only if 'medical treatment which is appropriate to the patient's mental disorder and all other circumstances of their case is available' (Department of Health, 2006a: A2, p. 2). Appropriateness of treatment is not merely to be determined with reference to medical factors. While the briefing sheet cites cultural factors and the distance the patient must travel to access services as other indicators of appropriateness, it will be interesting to see how the range of factors is defined legislatively. In particular, one might well imagine the government arguing that public protection constituted a factor relevant to 'appropriateness' of treatment to the individual's case, allowing social control factors a central place in the new criteria.

The briefing document does state that compulsion will only be permitted if the treatments proposed are actually available. Again, the precise wording of the statute may be of importance here. While the provision may provide detained patients with a right to 'appropriate' treatment, it is not obvious that this will be a right to the most desirable treatment for their case. Even if the eventual statutory text appears to provide substantive rights here, courts have an intense dislike of statutory provisions that purport to provide rights to standards of health or social services. There is, therefore, little more than optimism to suggest that this provision will provide any more than the most minimal right to standards of care.

4.5 Other mechanisms of confinement: substantive issues

Sections 2 and 3 are the fundamental mechanisms of civil confinement under the MHA 1983. Supporting them are a variety of other provisions to facilitate admissions under ss. 2 or 3 in difficult situations. These allow control to be taken of the individual, typically for up to 72 hours, to allow the processes leading to a s. 2 or s. 3 admission to take place.

4.5.1 Admission of patients already in hospital

Section 5 allows an application under ss. 2 or 3 to be made in respect of an informal patient already in that hospital. In most cases, this will be used regarding an informal patient in a psychiatric ward, but the section is not formally restricted in that fashion, and it may be used to confine a patient in a different ward of the hospital, being treated for a reason other than mental disorder. The section is restricted to inpatients, however, and persons resident outside the facility but receiving treatment at outpatient clinics are beyond its scope.

The trigger of an application under s. 5 may well be the intent or attempt of an informal patient to leave the hospital. In these circumstances, there may well be insufficient time to follow the regular application processes before the patient leaves. To account for this problem, a 'holding power' is provided for doctors and nurses, giving authority to detain an inpatient who is not yet technically compulsorily admitted.

The provision relating to doctors is notably lax in its requirements. It is available only to the doctor in charge of the patient's treatment, usually a consultant psychiatrist, or in their absence, their named delegate, usually a junior doctor (s. 5(3); Hall *et al.*, 1995). There is no separate substantive standard in the Act for the exercise of this holding power, except that the doctor thinks that an application under ss. 2 or 3 of the Act 'ought' to be made. Consistent with that, the doctor does have to provide reasons why informal status is no longer suitable: SI 1983/893, Form 12. The result is that the patient may be confined for 72 hours (s. 5(2)).

Nurses of the 'prescribed class' (s. 5(4),(7); see the Mental Health (Nurses) Order 1998 (SI 1998/2625)), also have a holding power, of six hours' duration (s. 5(4)). Here, there are substantive criteria stated in the section. Unlike the remainder of the section, individuals subjected to this detention must actually be receiving treatment for mental disorder. In addition, it must appear to the nurse:

(a) that the patient is suffering from mental disorder to such a degree that it is necessary for his health or safety or for the protection of others for him to be immediately restrained from leaving the hospital; and

(b) that it is not practicable to secure the immediate attendance of a practitioner for the purposes of furnishing a report under subsection (2) above [the doctor's holding power].

Notwithstanding the similarity in wording between s. 5(4)(a) and ss. 2(2)(b) and 3(2)(b), there are significant differences. Section 5(4)(a) requires the necessity of immediate restraint, for the health or safety of the patient or the protection of others. The necessity of immediate restraint is, on its face, a stricter test than 'ought' to be detained for assessment (s. 2(2)), and perhaps even than the necessity of treatment (s. 3(2)). It is certainly not a test that will be met simply because a mentally disordered patient wishes to leave the psychiatric ward at a time when no doctor is at hand. The nurse is placed in a position where he or she must make a decision on the criteria. How far this is reflected in practical realities is doubtful. Given the realities of hierarchy in the staffing of psychiatric wards, it is difficult to believe that the criteria prescribed by the 1983 Act will be the only matters on the nurse's mind.

4.5.2 Emergency admission (s. 4)

Section 4(1) of the Act provides a reordering of the s. 2 process in cases of 'urgent necessity'. The application of the ASW or nearest relative requires medical certification from only one doctor, rather than two. This allows the individual to be detained in a psychiatric hospital for up to 72 hours. If a second medical certificate is provided in this period, the admission becomes a s. 2 admission.

The criteria for admission are as in s. 2, but in addition, the statement of the nearest relative or ASW must attest that the case is one of urgent necessity, and that resort to the processes of s. 2 would involve 'undesirable delay': s. 4(2). While the statute appears to place the responsibility for this matter in the hands of the applicant, the forms place it squarely on the doctor providing the medical certificate. Where the applicant's nearest relative or ASW must merely certify the urgent necessity, and the undesirable delay, the doctor must estimate the delay that would result from following the procedure in s. 2, and explain the harm that would result to the patient, those caring for the patient, or other persons (Form 7, SI 1983/893).

The Code of Practice makes it clear that the provision is to be used for cases of 'genuine emergency' only, not those of 'administrative convenience' (para. 6.2). Interestingly, 'emergency' is understood by the Code as a function of carers to cope (para. 6.3). Evidence of an emergency includes the existence of significant risk of mental or physical harm to the patient or to others, the danger of serious harm to property, and the need for physical restraint of the patient. The Code actively discourages the use of this provision for convenience of doctors to examine the patient inside rather than outside hospitals, and ASWs unsatisfied with the unavailability of second doctors in these contexts are told to take the matter up with the relevant health authority (paras. 6.4 and 6.6).

4.5.3 Powers of Justices of the Peace in s. 135

Section 4 will be effective in cases of urgency, when an approved social worker or nearest relative feels it necessary to act quickly. It will not be successful if an ASW lacks the information required for an application under ss. 2 or 3, nor if doctors are not given access to the patient, so as to provide the required medical certificates. In such situations, reference should be had to s. 135(1).

The substantive provisions of the subsection allow an ASW to make an application to a Justice, if:

there is reasonable cause to suspect that a person believed to be suffering from mental disorder—

(a) has been, or is being, ill-treated, neglected or kept otherwise than under proper control, in any place within the jurisdiction of the justice, or

(b) being unable to care for himself, is living alone in any such place.

On these grounds, the Justice may issue a warrant for a constable, accompanied by an approved social worker and, if desired, a medical practitioner (s. 135(4)), to enter specified premises by force if necessary and, if thought fit, to remove the subject of the order to a place of safety for up to 72 hours, with a view to an application under Part II of the Act.

The 'reasonable cause' standard in the subsection harkens back to standards of criminal law for search warrants. The social worker's belief need only be that the individual is suffering from 'mental disorder', not one of the specific types required for a s. 3 admission. It is clear from the subsection that the justification for the intervention must be protection of the subject from ill-treatment or neglect by others or by himself or herself, but the statute offers no further express guidance as to the degree of harm required to justify the order.

It is clear that removal to a place of safety will only be justified with a view to commencing proceedings under Part II of the Act. Should that standard inform the degree of harm or neglect that ought to be required by the Justice of the Peace, prior to granting the order? The argument against such a standard would be that social workers ought to have access to people at risk of harm or neglect, even if the risk is insufficient to warrant confinement under Part II, in order to inform those people of options other than involuntary hospitalisation, including home support services such as Meals on Wheels, or community care. Early intervention through this mechanism might allow the implementation of such programmes with the patient's consent, and minimise the risk of hospitalisation in the future. The argument against is that, as we have seen, coercion operates in many ways, and a forced entry to the individual's home, for example, such as might be justified by this sort of order, is bound to create an effect on the individual. There is no doubt a risk that, intentionally or otherwise, an individual may feel pressured into adopting a programme that they would prefer, without the coercion, to avoid. In the event that this results in an informal hospital admission, the result would be a coerced hospitalisation without the criteria of Part II being met, and a resulting circumvention of the safeguards of the 1983 Act.

It would appear that ss. 15 and 16 of the Police and Criminal Evidence Act 1984 (PACE) probably apply to warrants under this section (*Ward* v *Commissioner of Police for the Metropolis* [2005] UKHL 32, para. 27; see also Jones, 2006: 500). Indeed, the police powers of entry under s. 17(1)(e) of PACE 1984 provide an alternative although similar mechanism. Under this subsection, a constable may lawfully effect entry for the purposes 'of saving life or limb or to prevent serious damage to property'. Although it is clear that warrants are rarely issued under this section, it is not known how often the police are called in to use these alternative powers of entry.

4.5.4 Police powers under s. 136

As we have seen, the emergency provisions of the 1983 Act allow an expedited process on application by the nearest relative or an approved social worker. Section 135 allows access to people at risk in private places, in the event that there is no carer, or where the carer or nearest relative is being uncooperative. Section 136, by comparison, provides for situations in which intervention may be required concerning people found in public places:

If a constable finds in a place to which the public have access a person who appears to him to be suffering from mental disorder and to be in immediate need of care or control, the constable may, if he thinks it necessary to do so in the interests of that person or for the protection of other persons, remove that person to a place of safety within the meaning of section 135 above.

Due to the immediacy of the need to act in some situations, but unlike the other situations considered so far, there is no application process prior to intervention. Instead the constable makes an on-the-spot assessment.

There are, nonetheless, standards that must be satisfied. Any mental disorder will suffice, but the individual must also be 'in immediate need of care or control', and arrest (and therefore subject to PACE 1984: Jones, 1999: 398) must be 'necessary . . . in the interests of that person or for the protection of other persons'. Once again, these sections are a peculiar combination of dangerousness and beneficence themes. The requirement of immediacy of need suggests the impracticability of using one of the other admission mechanisms in the 1983 Act; it may or may not import to the standard a sense of gravitas. The requirement that arrest be 'necessary', rather than merely potentially beneficial, reflects the intrusiveness of the intervention. The clause regarding 'protection of others' (although presumably not protection of their property) resonates in a dangerousness framework, where the clause referring merely to the 'interests of the person' suggests a very wide beneficence theme, not obviously consistent with the seriousness suggested by the earlier language.

The result of intervention does little to clarify the situation. The result is detention, for up to 72 hours, 'for the purpose of enabling him to be examined by a registered medical practitioner and to be interviewed by an approved social worker, and of making any necessary arrangements for his treatment or care' (s. 136(2)). Unlike the s. 135 intervention, there is no express expectation that an application under Part II will be pursued.

The powers of intervention are given specifically to constables, and the ability of the police to make these decisions, and specifically to diagnose mental disorder, has been subject to strong criticism (Thomas, 1986; Gostin, 1986a). The concerns regarding diagnostics appear not to have been well founded. Despite the fact that individual officers have very little training for, or experience of, s. 136 (Rogers, 1990), and typically have to make judgments about mental disorder on the spot with 'no advance warning' and 'little organisational back-up' (Rogers, 1990: 229), the evidence shows that 'the vast majority of police referrals are mentally ill and in need of treatment' (Fahy, 1989: 320). For example, Rogers found a 95 per cent correlation rate between assessments by the police and later professional assessments (1990: 232), whilst Bean (1980) found in his research that only one patient detained by the police was *not* compulsorily admitted into hospital. While these findings suggest considerable congruence between police practice and psychiatric practice, they do little to advance discussion on the appropriateness or legality of police actions with reference to the non-diagnostic criteria of the section.

Police intervention under this section is restricted to any 'place to which the public have access'. This has been given a relatively wide reading by the courts. Thus it includes the communal areas in a tenement block (*Carter v Commissioner of Police for the Metropolis* [1975] 1 WLR 507 (CA)). With this criterion, there is evidence that the use of the Act may be being extended. Rogers (1990) for example, found that 19 per cent of 'removals' made under s. 136 were not from public places.

The 72-hour detention period is a *maximum* and the detention should cease as soon as possible after the examination (which should preferably be carried out by an 'approved' doctor under s. 12(2): see Code of Practice, para. 10.12), interview and necessary arrangements have occurred. The appropriate maximum for detention under this section was the subject of considerable controversy before the passage of the 1983 Act, with some (Gostin, 1975) arguing for a much shorter maximum period of detention. That it was decided to retain the 72-hour period that had pertained under the 1959 Act means that the fallibilities of the system were accommodated by the legislation, at the expense of a concern for the rights of persons so detained. The present law gives rise to the fear that the need for prompt medical examination once detained is capable of being undermined, so that it is possible to be held for a considerable period of time in a police cell on the basis of a constable's 'diagnosis' of mental disorder.

Removal is, in theory to a 'place of safety' as defined by s. 135, above. As Bean has pointed out, this 'For all practical purposes... means a police station, for very few hospitals will accept patients on the recommendation of a police constable, and there are few "other places where the occupier is willing to temporarily receive the patient"' (Bean, 1986: 56; Rassaby and Rogers, 1987; Mokhtar and Hogbin, 1993).

4.6 The criteria in action

For most of the lifespan of the MHA 1959, the emergency admission section was the most frequently used compulsory power of admission. Its usage began to decrease in the 1970s (from 60 per cent of all compulsory admissions in 1972 to 29 per cent in 1984), mainly as a result of implementing policies at local level to ensure the involvement of a psychiatrist in the admission procedure (Beebe *et al.*, 1973), and this decrease was given extra impetus by the passage of the 1983 Act, as the architects of that Act had intended (Barnes *et al.*, 1990: 61). In 2003–4, s. 4 was used in 7 per cent of compulsory civil detentions in England (Department of Health, 2004b). It is now s. 2 that is most frequently invoked (53 per cent of civil detentions in 2003–4), with 38 per cent being admissions for treatment. The statistics for the use of s. 3 are significant, having risen from 2,012 admissions in 1986, to 5,500 in 1991–2 to 9,070 in 2001–2 (Department of Health, 1998a; 2002c).

These bare statistics hide a number of factors as Barnes, Bowl and Fisher's nationwide survey (1990) demonstrated. The most significant finding was widespread regional variation in the use of the various sections (1990: 75–91). Further, Barnes *et al.* found that the statistics for *outpatient admissions* understated the level of compulsion by around 50 per cent, as for every two outpatient admissions, one person already in hospital is either sectioned or 'promoted' from s. 2 to s. 3 status under s. 5 (1990: 61). This proportion has since increased: 19,483 of the 45,718 detentions in 2003–4 (43 per cent) were of people already in hospital. Indeed, such admissions now account for 61 per cent of the uses of s. 3 under the MHA 1983 (Department of Health, 2004b). To add to the confusion, Bean (1980) and Cavadino (1989) found that those operating the system (principally, psychiatrists and social workers) develop their own idiosyncrasies and preferences for the uses of a particular section, which can have little relationship to the formal criteria. Hence, any generalisation must be treated with caution.

Detention pursuant to s. 5(2) of patients informally in hospital was used on 8,894 occasions in 2003–4, and the nurse's holding power in s. 5(4) on 1,779 occasions (Department of Health, 2004b). In a variety of studies in different hospitals, s. 5(2) accounted for between 3 and 7 per cent of all compulsory admissions (see Brown, 1991; Pourgourides *et al.*, 1992; Hall *et al.*, 1995). It is not so much the incidence per se, as the manner in which s. 5(2) is used that is controversial. Bean (1980: 147) found evidence that patients would be admitted informally and then quickly placed on a 'section 30' (now s. 5(2)). More recent research indicates that this practice continues fairly unabated, despite the clear advice of the Code of Practice, para. 8, and especially para. 8.9. In Hall *et al.*'s year-long study of 61 consecutive admissions under s. 5(2) at one hospital, on 23 occasions (38 per cent of the total) the holding powers were invoked within 24 hours of the patient's informal admission (1995: 233). Similar findings were made by Joyce *et al.* (1991) (38 per cent within 24 hours) and Brown (1991) (33 per cent within 24 hours). Of those held under s. 5, 43 per cent revert to informal status at the end of the 72-hour period, and the remainder divide roughly evenly between s. 2 and s. 3 admissions (Department of Health, 1998d: Table 7).

These figures are, of course, open to interpretation. Hall *et al.* (1995) argue that the high incidence of the use of these powers following the admission of informal patients 'may indicate, for example, that there is a genuine clinical need for a short period of detention at times of particular crisis in some conditions' (1995: 235). Concern has been registered elsewhere, however, that the doctor's confinement power under s. 5 is a 'trial period' of compulsory detention (Bean and Mounser, 1993). That would clearly be an abuse, because the subsection is expressly intended to provide a window to allow an application elsewhere under the 1983 Act.

The incidence of coercion in informal confinement has been discussed. Even for those persons who remain in hospital on an informal basis at the expiry of the 72 hours, it is reasonable to speculate that the use of the s. 5(2) or s. 5(4) power might well be perceived by the patient as a coercive act, severely restricting the reality of their option to leave the facility. Much research has shown that around 50 per cent of inpatients are unaware of their legal status (see Monahan *et al.*, 1995, for a review), and thus the voluntary nature of the informal status of many of these patients is rendered suspect.

Although numbers are now declining, about 10 per cent of compulsory confinements result from the police powers in s. 136 (Department of Health, 1995d). These official statistics must be treated with caution for at least three reasons.

First, because there is considerable variation between jurisdictions and practitioners regarding ss. 2 and 3, there is similarly vast regional variation in the use of s. 136. In particular, recourse to s. 136 in Greater London is markedly greater than elsewhere. The Thames Regional Health Authorities were responsible for 90 per cent of s. 136 assessments in 1984 (Spence and McPhillips, 1995: 48). Bean (1986: 58) says that if one goes by official statistics, 'the use of section 136 is almost confined to the Metropolitan District in London'. As long ago as 1965, Rollins claimed that London was 'the sump into which the chronic psychotics from all over the UK, and indeed, farther afield, [were] drained' (cited in Spence and McPhillips, 1995: 48). By the same token, in many police areas, s. 136 powers seem to be virtually obsolete.

Second, the official statistics may obscure the fact that some police forces act in the manner contemplated by s. 136 without actually invoking the section or making a record of its use (Fahy, 1989). It is not known how many persons arrested by the police are subsequently released without being admitted to hospital under Part II or s. 131 of the Act (Bean, 1986: 58). The relationship between the police, social services and psychiatric professionals seems to be negotiated locally. Bean recounts how, in Nottingham in the 1980s, the practice was that the police, on arresting a person suspected to be suffering from mental disorder, would first contact a psychiatrist. Whether an ASW was contacted depended on the psychiatrist's diagnosis. If the psychiatrist decided against compulsory detention, the patient was either charged (usually with a minor offence) or released. As Bean says (1986: 56): 'Section 136 was being used – but not in the manner prescribed by legislation. No patient was officially recorded as being detained yet, in all other respects, section 136 was used in the manner legally prescribed.'

Given the potential for wide regional variation (further examples are documented in Bean, 1986: ch. 5), it is virtually impossible to decide with any certainty how the police do, in fact, deal with mentally disordered persons 'found' in public places. From the fact that there is widespread regional variation, however, coupled with research that shows it is common police practice to carry out stop and search procedures that are not 'officially' recorded as required by PACE Guidelines (McKenzie *et al.*, 1990), it *can* be stated with a fair degree of certainty that the official picture will be under-representative of the actual use of these powers. This, in turn, problematises *any* finding derived from the recorded use of s. 136: things may be worse (or better) than they appear to be.

Third, the use of s. 136 is, in any event, somewhat arbitrary, in the sense that its invocation does not depend solely on the officer's assessment of the mental health of the person in question, but rather that this consideration is weighed against the behaviour of the person in question. In general terms, if a criminal offence has been committed, the officer is less likely to invoke the section, and the more serious the offence, the less likely is it that s. 136 will be used (Bean, 1980). Other factors, such as the relationship between the police and the other relevant agencies at the local level, and the alternatives to use of s. 136, both formal and informal (availability of family members to take care of their relative and so on), also affect the decision about whether to take the person into custody. Rogers (1990: 231) found that police stations in neighbouring areas responded to the attitude of their local magistrates' court, so that in an area in which magistrates disapproved of the bringing before a court of an obviously mentally disordered person, s. 136 was much more frequently used (1990: 231).

Many comparable factors apply, of course, to other compulsory admission powers, and specific extraneous factors seem to have an effect in determining the method of admission. Mokhtar and Hogbin (1993: 192), for example, found that if family members were involved, admission was by s. 4 or s. 2; in no s. 136 arrest situation was a relative present.

4.6.1 Race and psychiatric detention

The detention criteria and their application have different impacts on different segments of the population. Black people from the Caribbean, and particularly men of this group, are statistically over-represented in the detention statistics, and the disparity increases with the level of coercion. The largest recent study appears to be that of Audini and Lelliott (2002). They considered data from 26 areas of England and Wales, comprising 9.2 million people, or 18 per cent of the English and Welsh population. In these areas, they found that Afro-Caribbean black people were more than six times more likely than white people to be sectioned, and detentions of black men, eight times more frequent than those of white men (2002: 223). This prevalence is reflected in secure forensic settings as well, where it would seem that Afro-Caribbean black men were roughly 5.6 times as likely to be admitted as white men (Coid *et al.*, 2000).

Smaller studies confirm these overall trends, but indicate geographic variation in prevalence. Flannigan *et al.*'s (1994) study of inner London in the early 1990s, found that black Caribbean people comprised 23 per cent of the hospital psychiatric population in South Southwark, and 16 per cent in Hammersmith and Fulham, being respectively 2.1 and 2.9 times their prevalence in the population of those districts as a whole. Both white people, and persons of other ethnic backgrounds, were confined in smaller percentages than their prevalence in the population. Where white people were admitted informally in 80 per cent of cases, black people from the Caribbean were admitted informally only 55 per cent of the time. Instead, they were compulsorily detained under ss. 2 or 3 twice as frequently as whites (35 per cent as compared with 17 per cent for whites), and under the emergency power of s. 4 three times as frequently (10 per cent rather than 3 per cent for whites: Bebbington *et al.*, 1994; see also Pilgrim and Rogers, 1999: ch. 4).

These findings are consistent with other research. Bean *et al.* (1991) found that people of Afro-Caribbean origin were two and a half times as likely to be the subject of a s. 136 arrest as others living in the same area, and that this likelihood was increased for young males. In Rogers's research (1990), Afro-Caribbean people were twice as likely to be referred under this section as others, and again the discrepancy was greater still for young males (1990: 233). These findings are further consistent with research carried out into the use by the police of their stop and search powers under PACE and other legislation (Jefferson, 1988; Norris *et al.*, 1992), and taken at face value would seem to be good evidence of discriminatory police practice. There is further evidence that the disparity is increasing. Lelliott and Audini (2003) studied the use of Part II of the MHA 1983 from 1991 to 1997, and found a 31 per cent increase in confinements of white people, and a 38 per cent increase in the confinement of black people. In the seven local authorities that served as the basis of their study, 67 white people per 100,000 population were confined in 1997. For black people, this figure was 397 per 100,000 (Lelliott and Audini, 2003: 69).

The research findings regarding the statistical over-representation of black people in the psychiatric system are overwhelming. No comparable consensus exists regarding ethnically Asian people, however. Audini and Lelliott's (2002) study indicates that they are over-represented by 65 per cent relative to white people (2002: 223). Other studies find this ethnic group under-represented in psychiatric populations: see, e.g. Coid *et al.*, 2000; Bhui *et al.*, 2003: 114.

Predictably, the disproportion of black people in the psychiatric system has generated considerable controversy. It has been alleged by some that the police use s. 136 as a 'mental health sus law' (Black Health Workers and Patients' Group, 1983), that it is used in a discriminatory fashion, and that, although the section repeats the *parens patriae* police powers pattern of the Part II admission sections, its purpose is social control rather than assistance for persons with mental health problems. Similar arguments are made, although generally with somewhat less vehemence, about admissions under the other detention sections of the 1983 Act.

Certainly, express or implied racial bias in the mental health and law enforcement systems is one possible explanation for the over-representation and negative experiences of black people (see Sashidharan, 2001), but there are others. If one adopts a medical model, specific types of mental illness may be particularly prevalent in black communities, as are certain types of physical illness, such as sickle-cell anaemia. Even if one does not adopt a medical model, other factors such as pressures related to minority status might well be expected to increase mental disorder. Alternatively, cultural factors that minimise healthcare facilities for black people, or trust in healthcare professionals by black people, might be expected to result in a move away from informal admission toward confinement, and confinement through police intervention rather than GP or other medical route. Predictably, these bases are hotly disputed (see Littlewood and Lipsedge, 1997 for a summary of the literature).

There is certainly evidence that race can be a factor in how doctors perceive patients. Using standardised case-vignettes with the race of the subject varied, a study by Loring and Powell (1998) in America showed a marked increase in willingness of American psychiatrists to diagnose schizophrenia, predict dangerousness and advocate confinement in the cases of black people than of white people in otherwise similar scenarios. While the rate of diagnosis of schizophrenia per 100,000 population for black people is almost double the rate for white people, (Bebbington *et al.*, 1994: 743), some English studies would suggest that this is not a function of race, but of other factors (Littlewood and Lipsedge, 1997; Lewis *et al.*, 1990) Other aspects of the American study have been replicated here, however. Lewis *et al.* used a similar methodology to the Loring study, concluding that the race of the patient influenced clinical predictions and attitudes of British psychiatrists, to the degree that a stereotype could be extracted (1990: 413):

This stereotype consists of an illness of short duration, more likely to lead to violence, in which criminal proceedings are slightly more appropriate, and in which neuroleptic medication is less likely to be necessary. It most easily fits the rubric of brief/acute reactive psychosis and may be especially strong in a male patient.

Such a finding is perhaps unsurprising. Similar stereotypes unfortunately exist more broadly in society; there is no obvious reason to suspect that psychiatrists will be mystically immune to such influences.

These broader biases may be significant in the apparent overuse of s. 136. In Rogers's survey, police initiated contact in only 8 per cent of the cases where the individual was subsequently arrested. Instead, the process was instigated in 42 per cent of instances by passers-by, in 15 per cent by neighbours and 13 per cent by members of the referee's family (1990: 228). The police, in other words, are cast in a *reactive* role, and so cannot be held responsible for the characteristics of those detained. Consistent with broader social prejudice, Rogers (1990: 233) also found that Afro-Caribbeans were more often referred by strangers and passers-by, and less often referred by friends or relatives, than other groups. Rogers concludes that 'this entails the police acting as a "conveyor belt" for community prejudices due to public perceptions of black people's deviant behaviour constituting a threat to public law and order'.

Similar complicating factors exist for other civil confinements. The study of Soothill *et al.* of compulsory admissions in Birmingham and Lancaster show well over half as originating in the home (1990a: 183). While this study is not restricted to black patients, it does serve as a reminder that doctors are not the only actors in the system.

There are other indications that simple medical bias does not, or does not entirely, explain the disproportion of involuntary admissions of black people. The Bebbington study of inner London did not support that ethnicity per se was a factor in confinement, instead finding that 'the two major factors independently associated with compulsory admission are diagnosis of schizophrenia and challenging behaviour' (Bebbington, 1994: 748). This study, like the ones cited above, does not support a claim of misdiagnosis based on racial factors.

The reasons for the high diagnosis rate for schizophrenia have been the subject of considerable discussion. Some of these explanations place the social understanding of race as a factor both in the definition and prevalence of the diagnosis. Others do not: Eagles (1991) provides an array of medical alternatives to psychosocial models. Of particular interest for current purposes, the over-representation of cases is, according to some research, based in a specific subcategory. The study by Thomas *et al.* shows that Afro-Caribbeans born abroad were, in fact, less likely than whites to be confined. The disproportion was in black people born in this country (1993: 94). This is significant not only for epidemiological reasons, but also because of the implications for theories centred on racist practice: it is difficult to believe that racially discriminatory attitudes on the part of doctors, social workers, and the police would distinguish between individuals of the same race born in the UK and those born abroad.

In this context, the difference in admission mechanisms and the apparent overuse of s. 136 might be seen to relate not to behaviour of doctors, but cultural factors among black people, and particularly black men. It does seem clear that black people have more complex pathways into psychiatric care: see Bhui *et al.*, 2003; Bhui and Bhugra, 2002. A hesitation to approach existing medical services, for example, might reasonably be expected to create a shift away from physician-led admission to police-led processes. Only 41 per cent of those in Spence and McPhillips's study were registered with a GP, for example (1995: 49). In Mokhtar and Hogbin's (1993) study, s. 136 admissions were less likely than s. 4 admissions to have previously used social and community mental health services. The introduction of a physician at the relatively late stage of hospitalisation may limit the possibilities of negotiation and extralegal coercion that, as we have seen, can result in informal admission. Consistent with this model of black people avoiding the system, Mokhtar and Hogbin defend s. 136 as 'a valuable "back up" for those who would otherwise fall through the net and fail to benefit from the Mental Health Act'. They call for an expansion of its use on the grounds that there is a 'hidden group' who are not using mental health community services and who are not being picked up by the police (1993: 195). The solution may well not be so simple, however, because decay of trust, whether by reputation in the community or by flowing from experience in the system, is not necessarily easily remedied. It is thus a cause of concern that Afro-Caribbean black patients, particularly those born in the UK, are apparently significantly less satisfied with the treatment they receive in the psychiatric service than white people: Parkman *et al.*, 1997.

The over-representation of black people is thus problematic. Certainly, on therapeutic bases, it does appear that the typical 'customer' is in need of some help, and that, as a group, such people are typically reluctant to seek help at an early stage. At the same time, the failure of black people to make contact voluntarily with existing medical and community mental health services seems to suggest that society has not yet found a selection of services that this community considers appropriate. That suggests a failure in healthcare policy, and it would seem deeply offensive to use the rather crude power of civil confinement rather than to address that systemic problem.

The typical profile of the person detained in psychiatric facilities straddles a number of 'problem populations' who have historically been the target of social control strategies. The probability of detention is heightened by being young, male, unemployed, single and homeless (see, e.g., Rogers and Faulkner, 1987; Spence and McPhillips, 1995; Thomas *et al.*, 1993). There is a real sense in which the problems discussed here raise questions of housing and social policy (see further the discussion of community care provision in Chapter 9) as much as of mental health policy. They also raise questions of policing policy. As Coid *et al.* note, the prevalence of black people in high-secure psychiatric facilities is roughly equivalent to their prevalence in prisons (2000: 245). To advocate increased use of the police as the appropriate response is therefore deeply problematic.

In recent years, the government has published a variety of policy documents and 'action plans' relating to race and mental health. A significant one flows from an inquiry into the death of David 'Rocky' Bennett, who died in 1998 in a medium-secure psychiatric facility, during a period of restraint by staff. The action plan and response address the safety and training issues inside facilities that were directly relevant to that death, but extends to consider issues relating to race and psychiatric confinement more generally (Department of Health, 2005d). Equally important, the National Institute for Mental Health in England, an organ of the NHS, published a strategy document for improvement of mental health services for black and minority communities in 2003 (NIMHE, 2003b). Both of these documents press all of the right political buttons. They speak intelligently of the need to provide services of relevance to ethnic communities, to involve members of those communities in the planning of those services, and to ensure staff are appropriately trained so that they can deal effectively and appropriately with members of those communities. Fine words – but the problems of race in mental health are not merely within the health service: they are also reflections of broader cultural factors. It remains to be seen how the action plans will translate into service provision, and whether they can alter these long-standing patterns.

4.7 Other options?

The English Act has its problems. As we have seen, the criteria reflect divergent and conflicting theoretical bases. There is no overriding theoretical justification provided for confinement, but instead a collection of two centuries of statutory tinkering. Its apologists would argue that it works, at least most of the time; its detractors would point to its lack of clarity: that it is difficult to tell whether it works, because it is difficult to tell what it is intended to do.

The recent reform process collapsed for much the same reason: there was no consensus as to what mental health law, and in particular, the use of compulsion, ought to do. In this sense, mental health law is at a crossroads. On the one hand, social policy is said to have become markedly more risk-averse in recent years. Policy is also becoming increasingly intrusive into the lives both of the public and of professionals. The perception is now that people in the community 'fall through the cracks' in legislative provision, rather than legislation being appropriately limited by civil rights concerns. These factors militate towards an intrusive policy of coercion in mental health. At the same time, the rise of anti-discrimination law and practice means that previous justifications for intervention can no longer be accepted uncritically: why coerce people with mental disabilities when we would not coerce others in the population? Unless we come up with new and coherent answers to the overarching question of what mental health law is supposed to do, it is difficult to see how reforms can be successfully accomplished.

There have traditionally been three justifications for coercion of people with mental disabilities: dangerousness, incapacity, and therapeutic benefit. These will be discussed in turn in the remainder of this chapter. As will be clear, they are all problematic in policy terms.

4.7.1 Dangerousness

A number of commentators have criticised the draft bill for its focus on the dangerousness of people with mental health problems. Some real concern here is appropriate, because, as we have seen, people with mental health problems have only a marginally elevated incidence of dangerous behaviour relative to the population as a whole, and a risk is that a statute paying undue attention to this issue will perpetuate a damaging stereotype.

At the same time, dangerousness is one of the usual standards for psychiatric coercion in North America (see Monahan, 2006), and as we have seen, it is not a foreign concept in English mental health law. Indeed, it is contained in the 1983 Act, which allows confinement on the basis of 'the protection of other persons' (s. 2 and 3) and restricts discharge by the nearest relative if the patient is 'dangerous to other persons' (s. 25). For contagious diseases, doctors can, with appropriate safeguards, quarantine people for the public safety, whether or not treatment is available; this is merely part of the police powers of the state to protect its citizens from harm. Is there an obvious reason that governance of mental health should be different?

There are a variety of difficulties with this approach. One of particular concern to doctors is that confinement without appropriate treatment turns them into jailers. While there was a run of cases discussing the right to treatment in the USA, it would appear that many of these cases flow from inadequate funding of psychiatric facilities, rather than from disorders not being amenable to treatment: see, for example, *O'Connor* v *Donaldson*, 422 US 563 (USSC, 1975); *Rouse* v *Cameron*, 373 F 2d 451 (1966); *Wyatt* v *Stickney*, 325 F.Supp 781 (MD Ala. 1971); *Youngberg* v *Romeo* 457 US 307 (USSC, 1982). The current objection is instead based on the idea that psychiatric facilities should be institutions of health, and not of social control. Anselm Eldergill makes the point as follows (2002: 343):

The evidence suggests that present medical interventions have, like liberal prison regimes, the reformation of the individual as their aim. This is unacceptable because the proper function of medical science and practice is to treat individual suffering attributable to disease or injury, not to alleviate the suffering of society; and, in the field of mental health, to treat those diseases or injuries which interfere with the development or expression of an individual's personality, not to reform her or his personality by reference to some social or political norm.

The line between these two concepts is however, as discussed in Chapter 1, not nearly as clear as Eldergill suggests. People are brought into coercive psychiatric structures when their behaviour becomes sufficiently antisocial to be perceived to warrant intervention. Whether that is defined in terms of illness or in terms of dangerousness, the result is still social control.

More problematic are the practical problems of dangerousness. With the physical illnesses for which quarantine may be imposed, there are generally clear diagnostic tests to ensure that only those people who, in fact, have the dangerous condition are confined. The same is not true of dangerousness predictions. The most extensive trial has been recently completed in the USA, by the MacArthur project (Monahan *et al.*, 2001). Their strongest statistics involved 939 people, at several sites. Of these, 176 were, in fact, violent over the course of the study. Using a variety of statistical methods, they were able to arrive at five risk bands, summarised in Table 4.2.

The level of prediction attained by the MacArthur team is extremely impressive relative to previous risk studies; it will be clear that even this result is far from perfect. Even in the most dangerous risk category, 5, roughly one quarter of the class did not turn out to be violent in the following year, and would therefore be wrongly confined if subsequent violence were the justification for the imposition of compulsion. If we restricted our confinement criteria so that only those in that most dangerous category 5 were subject to compulsion, we would only have included just over a quarter of the

Table 4.2

Risk class	Number of cases in class	Percentage of class violent	Number of people violent	Percentage of total violent people contained in this class	Number of people not violent in class
1	343	1.2	4	2	341
2	248	7.7	19	11	237
3	183	26.2	48	27	135
4	102	55.9	57	32	45
5	63	76.2	48	27	15

Source: Adapted from Monahan *et al.*, 2001: Table 6.7

people who would be violent during the following year. To catch half of the violent people, we would have to extend our criteria so that people in classes 4 and 5 would be subject to compulsion. That would, in fact, catch 59 per cent of the people who would be violent in the following year – 105 in number – but an additional 60 people, or 37 per cent of those within the criteria, would not in fact have been violent. Even with the MacArthur figures, therefore, a dangerousness standard will result in the imposition of compulsion on a significant number of people who would not, in the end, be violent. We would have severe reservations about a criminal system where 37 per cent of those convicted were not in fact guilty; is there any reason we should lower our standards for mental health compulsion? (See, generally, Dershowitz, 1970; Crawford, 1984).

It should be emphasised that the MacArthur study is the best available. As its authors acknowledge, its criteria are too complex to be used unaided in a clinical environment (Monahan *et al.*, 2001: 127), although a computer programme has now been developed to assist practitioners (Monahan *et al.*, forthcoming). Any other prediction mechanism used in practice will provide *less* accurate results than those above, compounding the problem of 'false positives' subjected to compulsion. Studies generally find that between a half and three quarters of those identified as dangerous by psychiatric professionals do not, in the end, turn out to be violent (studies are surveyed in Bowden, 1996; Monahan, 1988; Monahan, 1981).

Systems of dangerousness prediction also frequently use criteria considerably removed from the mental disorder in question as part of their assessment. West, for example, concludes that actuarial evidence based on factors such as sex, age, marital status, and criminal record are 'generally more efficient than clinical judgments of attitude, personality or mental state' at predicting future crimes involving sexual molestation (1996: 55). Yet the premise of mental health legislation is that confinement prior to criminal act is justified by issues of mental disability, not by demographic characteristic. There are further obvious HRA issues. Article 14 of the ECHR prohibits discrimination on the basis, among other things, of sex, race, social origin, birth or other status. West's criteria are thus subject to challenge, in so far as factors such as age and sex are used to determine detention within the meaning of Art. 5. Even the MacArthur criteria, which are better on the most obviously discriminatory criteria than most systems, contain potential problems. Whether the patient was abused as a child, whether their father had been involved in crime, whether the patient was employed, and age all figured in some of their statistical calculations to reach the above results (Monahan *et al.*, 2001: Figure 5.2). Monahan himself argues that the only criterion currently precluded under American law for these purposes is race (2006: 429). This may well be an accurate statement of American law, but for current purposes, it misses the point: is it ethical to subject people to intrusive mandatory powers on these bases?

The expansion of factors further highlights the question of whether prediction of dangerousness is an appropriate medical function. This has always been an issue: when exercising their clinical judgment, it seems clear that doctors are no better at predicting dangerousness than other people, nor do they restrict themselves in this regard to medical criteria (see, e.g., Montandon and Harding, 1984, and studies cited therein). The use of doctors to administer the confinement processes in North America is thus suspect. The issue is not simply one of expertise, but also conflict of interest. Doctors are trained to work in a therapeutic frame of reference. It is difficult to see that such a framework could fail to influence their decisions regarding confinement, undercutting the implementation of the dangerousness standard. While symbolically significant in distinguishing mental health law from other state police functions, the use of doctors to administer the confinement process may thus serve to undercut the dangerousness standard, which serves as the justification of confinement.

Some of this difficulty may be countered by clear statutory directions to doctors as to how dangerousness is to be assessed. As we have seen, the MHA 1983 provides no guidance whatsoever in this regard. This may be compared to the legislation in Ontario, where the relevant criteria read as follows (CSO, c. M7):

15(1) Where a physician examines a person and has reasonable cause to believe that the person,

(a) has threatened or attempted or is threatening or attempting to cause bodily harm to himself or herself;

(b) has behaved or is behaving violently towards another person or has caused or is causing another person to fear bodily harm from him or her; or

(c) has shown or is showing a lack of competence to care for himself or herself, and if in addition the physician is of the opinion that the person is apparently suffering from mental disorder of a nature or quality that likely will result in,

(d) serious bodily harm to the person;

(e) serious bodily harm to another person; or

(f) serious physical impairment of the person,

the physician may make application in the prescribed form for a psychiatric assessment of the person.

Here is a dangerousness standard where the doctor is provided with clear and legally enforceable standards as to what must be shown prior to confinement. It is now a quarter of a century old, and progress in determination of dangerousness may warrant reconsideration of its content; as a guide to the level of clarity that should be expected, however, it serves as a helpful model.

Nonetheless, the problems of confinement of those who would not, in the end cause harm to themselves or others remains: prediction of dangerousness is not an exact science. And some of the problems identified elsewhere in this chapter relating to the existing English system, apply equally in the USA, under dangerousness systems. In so far as the over-representation of black people in the civil confinement structure is understood as a civil rights issue, for example, it is equally an issue in US jurisdictions (see, for example, Lawson *et al.*, 1994 and studies cited therein) This is unsurprising, given the findings, discussed above, that psychiatrists are more likely to perceive black people as dangerous; it does mean that the civil rights problem does not disappear due to a change in the criteria.

At the same time, if dangerousness is not the solution, what other options are available?

4.7.2 Admission and capacity

In the face of the government proposals, a number of commentators have raised the possibility for a markedly increased role for capacity in the criteria for compulsion: see Buchanan, 2002; Gunn and Holland, 2002; Szmukler and Holloway, 2000; cf. Bartlett, 2003a. The idea is intellectually appealing, because it most closely mirrors the situation for patients with physical illnesses. If we are serious that people with mental health problems ought to be treated without discrimination, how better to accomplish this result than in making capacity the cornerstone of psychiatric compulsion? Indeed, the Richardson Committee itself envisaged a markedly enlarged role for capacity in the thresholds of compulsion, although they stopped short of proposing that it would be the sole criterion as it would be for compulsion related to physical illnesses (Department of Health, 1999a: para. 5.95).

For treatment, this seems to be an entirely workable solution. In 1986, the Province of Ontario, Canada, introduced a system where treatment could not be enforced on a competent patient without consent. This rule applied equally to psychiatric and non-psychiatric treatment, and in a psychiatric context, to voluntary and involuntarily admitted patients. It has proven workable in practice, and there is no obvious reason it could not be introduced in England (for discussion, see Bartlett, 2001). As noted above, however, Ontario continues to use a dangerousness standard for psychiatric confinement. The question for current purposes is whether a capacity model might also be imposed onto confinement in a psychiatric facility.

Capacity and its role in mental health law generally will be discussed at some length in Chapters 10 and 11, and some of the detail of that discussion will apply to consideration of capacity to consent to psychiatric admission. For present purposes, however, capacity may be taken to mean an ability to understand, remember, and evaluate the information necessary to make a specific decision. It is not a global concept: an individual may have capacity to consent to admission to a psychiatric hospital, but not have capacity to make a will, for example. At issue is the information required for the specific decision to be made. In the event that the individual lacks capacity, he or she loses the authority to make the decision in question, which would be made by a substitute, such as the potential clinical supervisor, in the case of admission to a psychiatric facility.

This raises the question of what information someone would need to understand, in order to decide whether or not to be admitted to a psychiatric facility. Questions of circumstances in which one needs to have capacity have been litigated in highly visible cases in both England and America: *Bournewood*, above, and *Zinnerman v Burch*, 494 US 113 (USSC, 1990). The litigation has not been helpful at proscribing the definition of capacity required for these situations, however.

Obviously, the individual would have to understand that they were being admitted to a psychiatric facility. Presumably, the reason for the admission will usually be treatment. Should the individual be competent to consent to the treatment, in order to be competent to consent to the admission? Neither result seems desirable here. If it were considered that the patient did need treatment capacity, then a patient who was otherwise competent to consent to the admission could still be forced into the facility, even if their failure to agree to the admission was not based on a factor related to the treatment in question. If, instead, the individual did not need to be competent to consent to the treatment in order to have capacity to consent to the admission, a refusal to go into hospital would mean that a treatment only available in hospital would be denied him or her, notwithstanding that *ex hypothesi* the patient is not competent to make decisions about that treatment.

To have capacity to decide asylum admission, does the individual need to understand the ramifications of failing to enter the asylum? Is asylum admission to be understood as an isolated decision, or as part of a more complex decision as to where the individual lives, among which may be several choices? Should the question also involve questions of capacity to decide to remain in the community? Assume for the moment that asylum admission and some form of community care arrangement can be considered alternative decisions, with no obvious third option. In that event, a decision regarding one is effectively a decision regarding the other, yet the capacity criteria for these decisions may be markedly different. For example, capacity to remain in the community may include capacity to seek out and enter into care relationships such as with meals providers and home help, and capacity to manage one's accommodation. For the individual to have capacity to decide to live in the community, how far should we insist that he or she be able to make decisions about the intricacies of these matters? Should understanding be required, or is it enough that they are in a situation where social services will provide? If daily needs are catered for, does the individual need to understand how that occurs? This suggests, at the very least, that incapacity on its own should not be enough to justify an enforced admission to a psychiatric or other facility, because it serves as a reminder that the admission takes the individual out of their former home, a move that can perhaps be traumatic and must be justified. It is for this reason that the Law Commission, in their report on mental incapacity, introduced in addition to incapacity a standard of 'vulnerability', defined as an inability to care for the self or to protect the self from serious exploitation, to be required prior to public law interventions: Law Commission, 1995: para. 9.5–9.6. It is further quite appropriate that the government's proposals regarding *Bournewood* patients, discussed earlier, would similarly require a higher threshold prior to intervention than mere incapacity.

Perhaps most difficult is the question of how far individuals would need to understand their own psychiatric condition, and in particular, their dangerousness to themselves or others, in order to have capacity to make decisions about asylum admission. If such understandings are required, much of the practical advantage of the capacity standard over that of dangerousness disappears, because all of the difficulties of assessment return, and the social control ramifications continue, merely under the guise of a neutral capacity test. If dangerousness is to be a factor in any event, it may perhaps be to the advantage of both patient and clinician to have a clear dangerousness standard placed in the statute, whatever the apparent social control imagery, rather than for the matter to be determined in the murkier twilight of a capacity determination.

These questions do not appear to have been considered at any length by the proponents of a capacity test. If such a test is to be adopted, they do require consideration.

4.7.3 The Stone system

North American psychiatrists are not unaware of the contradictory roles they are expected to perform when dangerousness is the criterion for admission (see, e.g., Roth, 1979). Their concern tends to be less with the integrity of the dangerousness criteria, than with their own role as therapeutic professionals. They dislike being recast in a police function, arguing that this undermines both professional dignity and the therapeutic relationship with their patients. Rather than arguing for their removal as administrators of the confinement process, however, these psychiatrists tend to argue for a different standard, based on therapeutic criteria.

Therapeutic justifications for confinement import quite a different theoretical framework, with different corollaries. Unlike a structure based on incapacity or dangerousness, confinement on therapeutic criteria is generally seen to go along with forced treatment during confinement, because it seems bizarre to confine on the basis of treatability, and then not to treat.

The challenge in this context is to develop criteria that, while therapeutic, are justifiable violations of the rights of the person confined. We do not impose treatment on people for physical disease or disorders; without reference to the police power of the state, why should we impose psychiatric treatment?

One justification is found in the attitudes of the patients after the fact. A significant proportion of civilly confined patients, even if objecting to confinement when it occurred, reported finding the confinement broadly beneficial following discharge. In a study by Edelsohn and Hiday (1990), 55 per cent of civilly committed patients objected at the time of admission, but after the fact, only 31 per cent felt the confinement unjustified. In a study by Kane (1983), roughly two thirds of the civilly confined people who objected to confinement at the time, reported at discharge that their commitment was fortunate. (For further discussion of these and similar studies, see Monahan *et al.*, 1995; Hiday, 1992.) If intervention were able to be restricted to these individuals who subsequently agreed with its appropriateness after the fact, surely that would not violate civil rights?

In the mid-1970s, Alan Stone, a US psychiatrist, attempted to develop a therapeutically based, but rights-aware, set of admission criteria. Under Stone's criteria, confinement would be justified only if all of the following criteria were met:

(a) a reliable diagnosis of severe mental disorder must be made;

(b) the immediate prognosis must be one of major distress;

(c) an effective treatment must exist;

(d) the patient must offer incompetent refusal of treatment;

(e) the proposed treatment must be reasonable (i.e., the reasonable patient would consent).

The criteria are designed to mix the gravitas that is appropriately a prerequisite for state intervention ('severe mental disorder', immediate major distress), with selection of individuals who can actually be assisted by the mental health system ('effective treatment must exist'). The treatment refusals of mentally competent patients are to be respected and will serve as a bar to confinement; there is a reality check to treatment desirability in the objective 'reasonable patient' test.

Stone's criteria, like the dangerousness test and the incapacity standard, are problematic in practice. Psychiatry is not an exact science, and reliability of diagnosis occurs only in a minority of cases (Crawford, 1984: 143, and studies cited therein). Equally problematic in practice are the value judgments contained in the conditions. 'Severe' disorders, 'major' distress, and 'effective' treatment are all highly subjective, and thus militate against patient challenge and correspondingly against patient rights. 'Incompetent' refusal and 'reasonable' consent as concepts have large legal and medical literatures of their own. They are thus more readily assumed into a patient rights framework, but they are also highly problematic in application.

Many of these problems are more appropriately discussed elsewhere in this text; suffice it here to say that, for the apparent protections to patient rights to be real, the administration of the system might become unwieldy. Enforcement of the criteria cannot depend on patient intervention, because the patient is expected to lack treatment capacity. It therefore cannot be assumed that the patient is in a position to press for his or her rights. Protections must be built in, to ensure the criteria are met as a matter of routine. Truly independent medical diagnoses would be necessary to ensure the reliability of the diagnosis. The doctor(s) recommending treatment would, presumably, not do so unless they thought a reasonable patient would consent to it. Consistent with this, in Hoge *et al.*'s study (1989: 172) of implementation of Stone, in a sample of 483 treatments, not a single doctor recommending treatment thought a reasonable patient would refuse it. Independent involvement would also be necessary at this stage, if the criterion is to provide meaningful protection. As will be seen below, a similar argument can be made regarding determination of treatment competence. The result is likely to be a highly complex administrative structure. That may be appropriate: civil confinement is a serious intervention, after all. It is not, however, likely to meet with political success in times of economic restraint; nor is it likely to meet with the approval of doctors, who tend to prefer the practice of medicine to administration.

Interestingly, the studies would suggest that it would result in a decrease, rather than an increase, in confinements, relative to the dangerousness test. Hoge *et al.* (1989: 173) found that barely more than half of the people who would be likely to be confined under Massachusetts' current dangerousness standard would be confined under Stone. Their study did not include the procedural protections of various administrators assessing for the different criteria above, suggesting that, with appropriate safeguards, the numbers might be even lower. Again, this is not necessarily a problem, because there is no reason to believe that the success of a model is directly proportional to the number of people confined under it; it does suggest that one cannot assume that therapeutic criteria, when civil rights protections are included, will result in high committal rates.

More problematic is that no study seems to have assessed whether the persons who would be confined under the Stone system are the patients who would go on to believe that their confinement had been beneficial. The structure of the criteria seem designed to select out these individuals, making this a reasonable speculation, but hard evidence is currently lacking.

4.8 Concluding comments

The discussion of the issues raised in this chapter reveals the complexity of the issues involved. Various points, however, do emerge. First, there is no rigid distinction between the informally and the compulsorily detained patient. Whether one is admitted under a 'section' or 'informally' is dependent on a whole host of variables, to do with issues of time and resources, social status, age, gender and race, the power dynamics of the relationship between the patient, psychiatrist, second opinion doctor, ASW and the patient's relatives (we examine further some of these relationships in the next chapter). Informal admission does not necessarily imply the patient's consent, nor does compulsory admission necessarily imply the patient's refusal to consent (although this is more often the case). Bean found that 'Most of the compulsory patients gave passive resistance, and most of the voluntary patients actively or passively surrendered' (1980: 120). The majority of patients who are compulsorily admitted (certainly under ss. 2 and 4) stay in hospital after the expiry of the section, although compulsory powers will often come back into play if the patient attempts to leave hospital. The legal status of the patient is, in practice, unhelpful in determining whether compulsion is present in the admission.

The foundation of this edifice of ambiguities is similarly uncertain. The legal standards of confinement offer no clear interpretive framework, and the courts in this century have adopted a remarkably laissez-faire attitude to interpretation. Standards have, in practice, moved out of the legal arena into the professional realm, raising considerable questions about the rule of law in this area. These questions are particularly important, given the civil rights implications of confinement.

It is to professional practice that we must turn to understand the application of the 1983 Act, yet it is very hard to generalise about this area of law. Widespread regional variation in application and idiosyncrasies of the actors involved defy any attempt to theorise in a predictive sense. The very notion of '*a system*' does not capture sufficiently the federal nature of mental health provision. Each location in which services are provided or in which the 1983 Act operates is, itself, a fairly autonomous system in numerous ways (in the power given to consultant psychiatrists and the discretion given to ASWs, for example), even if these micro-systems are subject to 'interference' from each other and to restraint from outside in the form of central policy and resourcing, or its absence.

It is to these relationships, both as prescribed in the 1983 Act and in so far as possible as they operate in practice, that we turn in the next chapter.

5

The Process of Civil Confinement

5.1 Introduction

The compulsory admission of a person into a psychiatric facility is not only a question of diagnosis or of moral justification for the confinement of the dangerous. It is also a matter of compliance with a detailed legal process. On its face, the MHA 1983 sets up a relatively straightforward scheme. An application for admission to hospital must be addressed to the managers of the hospital in question, and can only be made by an approved social worker (ASW) or the nearest relative (NR) of the person to be confined. Such applications must be 'founded on' two medical recommendations, although one will suffice in an emergency. Completion of the necessary paperwork gives legal authority to the applicant to convey the person to be admitted to the hospital in question, and provided that the receiving officer of the hospital is satisfied that the relevant paperwork appears to be in order, the managers of the hospital are then legally empowered to detain the subject of the application in the hospital.

The practice is not quite so straightforward. The Court of Appeal has held that, as long as the various requirements of the admissions process have been complied with, an admission will not be unlawful if compliance was not in the chronological sequence implied in the statute. Hence, although an application must be 'founded on' the necessary medical recommendations, the application documents can be completed before the medical recommendations have been given: *Whitbread* v *Kingston and District NHS Trust* (1997) *The Times*, 14 July. This is a problematic reading of the MHA 1983, because 'founded on' does seem to imply that the application should follow the necessary medical recommendations. It also raises due process considerations, because it allows the possibility that an applicant for admission can certify that the *medical* criteria for admission are met without first having that opinion corroborated by doctors. Yet it also reflects the fact that the social processes that lead to the compulsory confinement of a person in a psychiatric hospital are dynamic rather than linear, and the various actors involved may interrelate in a variety of ways. Moreover, there are more potential actors involved in the admissions process than indicated on the face of the MHA 1983. An admission to hospital under Part II will involve some combination of: the patient; his or her relatives, carers, friends and neighbours; ASWs or other social workers; community psychiatric nurses (CPNs); psychiatrists and other doctors, particularly GPs; police officers. The MHA 1983, the accompanying Code of Practice (Department of Health and Welsh Office, 1999) and the Memorandum on the Act (Department of Health and Welsh Office, 1998), contemplate that it will be possible for those involved to work together effectively, yet there is reason to think that this is not always easily possible. The various professionals involved will each, to some extent at least, be a product of their professional training and this will be reflected in the perspective through which the admissions process is viewed. The attitude of relatives, friends and other non-professionals will also vary according to numerous factors. Some nearest relatives, for example, may actively seek hospitalisation while others may oppose it. Some may act in what objectively appear to be the best interests of the patient; others may not. Those to be admitted will also vary in their attitude to that prospect. Of course, the consent of the patient is not required for an admission under Part II, and from a civil libertarian perspective, there is a risk that the voice of the patient will be drowned out by those of the others involved. Given all of the permutations that this dynamic process allows, and add the fact that such tensions are set within a broader framework in which control of both personal freedom and professional territory and status are at stake, it is apparent that there is as much likelihood of discord as there is of harmony.

In seeking to work through these issues, this chapter will open with a brief consideration of the background against which the formal admissions process must function. It will then turn to the role given by law to approved social workers and nearest relatives, before considering how the admissions process is intended to work, how it does, in fact, work, and how it is limited in its effectiveness by its multidisciplinary nature. Finally, some space is given over to the question of how a legally flawed admission may be challenged by, or on behalf of, the patient.

5.2 The context of admission under Part II

5.2.1 How do its patients come to the attention of the mental health system?

Soothill *et al.* concluded, from their international survey into the source of referral for mentally disordered patients in six countries, that 'a picture emerges of individuals troubled by mental illness over a considerable period, in whom a crisis or breaking point is reached in their own homes, and who are admitted to hospital for several weeks' (1981: 343). In a later replication study analysing data from two hospitals in a seventh country (England), this conclusion was fortified (Soothill *et al.*, 1990a). Of 103 compulsory new admissions analysed in the English study, around 55 per cent of referrals in both hospitals (which covered very different catchment areas in socio-economic terms) were from the patient's home. This was lower than the international survey (69 per cent), but was still easily the most frequent source of admissions. Of the remainder, just under 20 per cent were referred from another hospital; just over 20 per cent were referred from the police and courts (although this was more marked in one hospital, at 22 per cent, than the other, at 13 per cent). One person in each hospital was referred from a public place (1990a: 183). These findings are broadly in line with those of a number of other studies (Huxley, 1985: ch. 1).

Of those patients referred from their own homes, a number initiate the admission process themselves by self-referral to their GPs, even if this is not always with a formal psychiatric complaint (Huxley, 1985: 9). It is a common research finding that GPs vary in their knowledge of psychiatry and ability to detect mental health problems (see Bean, 1980). In Goldberg and Huxley's research (discussed in Huxley, 1985: 9), GPs' non-detection of mental disorder, and decision, even when a disorder was suspected, not to refer the patient to a psychiatrist, constituted the largest filter of potential compulsory admission, with 230 consulters being reduced down to only 17 referrals. Equally worrying is an apparent lack of understanding of mental health law by GPs: Peay et al., 2001. If, following a GP's referral, a psychiatrist takes the view that the patient should be compulsorily detained, then an ASW will become involved and the formal process of application for admission will begin.

Other sources of first referral are the family and relatives of the patient, and, less frequently, neighbours and friends. These, put together with self-referrals, either via a GP and psychiatrist or, less often, directly to a local authority social services department (SSD), tend to account for 40 to 50 per cent of patients brought to the attention of an ASW; in some studies, self-referral is more common than referral by relatives, while in others the reverse is true. There are examples in the research of fairly low referral rates from these 'informal' sources, according to variables such as whether the person referred lived alone or not, and whether the process was initiated as a result of violence on behalf of the person to be admitted (Gondolf et al., 1991), with a correspondingly higher referral rate through the primary and secondary healthcare systems, or from the police. The rate of self-referral would seem, as Soothill et al. (1990b) argue, to render problematic the claim that compulsory detention is 'about' social control. For such persons, the picture here accords much more closely with the medical model, of persons recognising themselves as 'ill' and seeking treatment from the 'health' services. Indeed, it is no easy matter to be detained. Barnes et al. (1990: 13) found that 'for every seven people detained, three are referred for the use of compulsion but not so detained'. In Bean's study, there were 125 non-admissions out of 325 cases considered for admission (1980: 174). Although in one study, self-referral accounted for 33 per cent of the total, however, the more usual figure is around 12 to 18 per cent (see Appelbaum, 1985). This means that around 80 per cent of compulsorily admitted patients are admitted as a result of some other person taking the initiative in seeking 'help'.

5.2.2 **Who is admitted?**

Not surprisingly, it is those who show obvious signs of severe disorder who are most likely to be 'diagnosed' as mentally disordered by laypersons (including GPs), to be referred by a GP, to be recommended for compulsory admission by a psychiatrist, and to be admitted under s. 2 (Huxley, 1985). Soothill *et al.* (1990b) found, in their study of 53 consecutive compulsory admissions into a hospital in Birmingham, that 27 of those admitted (51 per cent of the total) posed no significant danger to themselves or other persons, a similar finding to that made by Bean in his larger study (1980). On this basis, they argue that 'the 1983 Act allows the professional judgment of the clinician to remain paramount. The essential focus remains as a psychiatric question with the dangerousness issue as of only residual concern . . . quite simply, dangerousness is not the primary issue of concern in terms of compulsory admission' (1990b: 24). As we saw in the last chapter, this is controversial in that diagnostic techniques are a long way from scientific.

Research has found that a variety of other factors are also relevant. A key indicator, not surprisingly, is previous admission. Being 'socially isolated', single, divorced or separated and female, or unemployed also render a person more likely to consult. The middle-aged, and separated, divorced or widowed persons were more likely to be diagnosed by a GP as mentally disordered, although young, single men were more likely to be referred by GPs, along with separated, divorced and widowed females. Those more likely to thought by the psychiatrist to be in need of hospitalisation were single, male and of social class V (Huxley, 1985: 10). These findings echo across a range of other studies. For example, as far as social class was concerned, Bean (1980) found that, out of 200 patients admitted under Part II *and* s. 131, none were of social class I and few (5 per cent) were of social class II, whereas 61 per cent were from social classes IV and V (1980: 111). Only in social class V was the likelihood of being admitted under Part II equal to that of being admitted informally, and this perhaps goes some, but not all, of the way towards explaining the high incidence per capita of the population of persons from ethnic minorities amongst those compulsorily admitted (see Chapter 4, and Moodley and Thornicroft, 1988).

Summarising this information, it can be said that, although the admissions process is very often prompted by therapeutic considerations, it is focused on socially rather than medically problematic individuals. The above research also shows that often, although others involved are important filters, it will be a psychiatrist who is the main instigator of the admissions process. Yet, as far as the law is concerned, only an ASW or an NR may be the applicant. Thus it can be seen that the way in which potential inpatients come under consideration for confinement contains the potential to undermine the legal conceptualisation of that process and who should drive it forward. This is, of course, all the more true when, as in 19,483 of the 45,718 uses of Part II in 2003–4 (Department of Health, 2004b: Table 2), the patient is already in hospital.

5.3 Nearest relatives and approved social workers

Under the Victorian procedure, admission of paying patients to psychiatric facilities was on the application of a relative, and admission of pauper patients was on the application of poor law officials, with the proviso that the nearest relative of such paupers could generally obtain their discharge, on the undertaking that the individual would no longer be a drain on public funds. Medical certificates in a form noticeably similar to those under the current Act (one for paupers, two for private patients) were also required. Pauper patients, who constituted the vast majority of patients in Victorian asylums, always had their admission subject to the scrutiny of a Justice of the Peace, and this safeguard was extended to private patients under the Lunacy Act 1890.

The routine involvement of Justices of the Peace was removed for all confinements in 1959. Otherwise, the remnants of the Victorian processes can still be seen in modern admissions, although, with the fusion of private and pauper status following the introduction of the National Health Service in 1948, statutory change has resulted, at least in theory, in involvement of both nearest relatives (now more closely defined than in Victorian times) and social workers (the modern inheritors of traditional poor law roles) in all confinements. Under the law since 1959, now the MHA 1983, the patient's nearest relatives, and ASWs have coexistent powers to make an application for compulsory admission. It was hoped by the Percy Commission (Royal Commission on the Law Relating to Mental Illness and Mental Deficiency 1954–1957, 1957: para. 403) that the majority of applications would be made by nearest relatives, with help from an ASW only if necessary, although, as the Commission suspected, this is not how the system has subsequently proven to operate. At least in theory, the choice between the two applicants is not necessarily important anyway, because, unlike Victorian law, the modern Act requires, whoever is the applicant, that the other of these figures be consulted in the process.

The existing process is thus very much the vestige of its nineteenth-century predecessors. The role and power of the family throughout the admission flows from middle class Victorian ideologies of public and private life; the role of doctors reflects both the gradual occupation of medicine as expert in the field of madness in the eighteenth and nineteenth centuries, and the reality of doctors being the only reliably educated professionals in the poor law administrative system; the social workers represent the municipal need to regulate relations between society and the asylum. The political justifications for the continued roles of these actors have changed over time. Thus modern arguments for the involvement of nearest relatives are likely to focus on the knowledge of that individual of the specifics of the patient's life. The new justifications do not necessarily correspond to the roles prescribed in the 1983 Act, however, which were framed based on earlier justifications. The tensions between the roles of the various actors are amongst the key themes in this chapter, and that the historical justifications for these roles is at odds with the contemporary reality is at least part of the explanation of those present tensions.

With the abolition of the hearing before the Justice of the Peace, an expressly legal voice was removed from the admission structure. The late Victorian introduction of this safeguard had been based, in part, on concerns regarding civil rights and wrongful confinement. The removal of this voice thus raises the question of where, if at all, in the current system, these issues will be raised. In addition, a traditional focus of legal hearings had been to serve as clearing house for divergent discourses. The efficacy of these legal hearings in this regard is dubious; certainly, the Percy Commission saw them as a mere formality. The problem of mediation between the divergent discourses is real, however, as will be discussed later in the chapter. The abolition of these hearings, while simplifying the system and perhaps rendering it less intrusive on patients, removed the chance to use them as a way of mediating between the divergent discourses.

5.3.1 Approved social workers

In practice, the vast majority of applications for admission are made by ASWs, and even when an nearest relative is nominally the applicant, it is usual for the ASW to play a significant role. Cavadino (1989), for example, found that only three out of 47 applications for compulsory admission were made by the patient's NR, and an ASW was involved in all three (see also Bean, 1980; Barnes *et al.*, 1990). It is to be expected that ASWs will predominate in the application process. It will be a rare NR who has the legal and procedural knowledge to make an application without help.

The ASW, by comparison, is trained in these matters. The Act requires that they have 'appropriate competence in dealing with persons who are suffering from mental disorder': s. 114(2). Local SSDs 'shall appoint a sufficient number of approved social workers for the purpose of discharging the functions conferred on them [i.e. ASWs] by this Act' (s. 114(1)), and in so doing authorities 'shall have regard to such matters as the Secretary of State may direct' (s. 114(3)), by way of training and qualifications. As such, ASWs are constructed by the 1983 Act as specialists with autonomous decision-making capabilities. This, however, has not been without controversy. For the equivalent post under the 1959 Act (the mental welfare officer or MWO), there was no requirement for the possession of any special skills or training over and above that required to undertake social work, and appointment policy was a local matter. Bean's research (1980) found numerous examples of inefficiency, lack of expert knowledge, and actions of dubious legality by MWOs, and constituted a strong argument for the introduction of specialist training. Such factors dovetailed with the views of MIND, who saw a specialist social worker as a potentially powerful advocate for patients vis-à-vis the psychiatric profession (Gostin, 1986a), and of the British Association of Social Workers (BASW), which was keen to reconstruct mental health within a discourse founded on a welfarist rather than medical foundation and so enhance its claim to professionalisation, in juxtaposition to the medical profession in general and psychiatry in particular. As Prior (1992: 111, giving examples) notes, '[p]rofessional aggrandisement, using mental health legislation as the lever, was clearly evident in the social work press during the period 1981 to 1983'. The case for 'welfarisation' was also strengthened by the attacks on psychiatry coming from the antipsychiatry movement, which itself was bolstered by empirical research casting doubt on the claims to expertise of psychiatrists (e.g. Cocozza and Steadman, 1978), and the scandalous conditions revealed to exist in some hospitals (Barnes *et al.*, 1990: 19–23).

There was, however, much opposition to the specialisation of mental health social work from within the social work profession, from local authorities and from psychiatrists. For psychiatry, the problem was one of professional control of territory, both in terms of geography (because the emergence of welfarism as an alternative discourse was part of the wider shift out of the asylum: see Chapter 3) and in terms of client base, coupled with a general low regard for the capabilities of social workers and a concern that the power given to ASWs is such that, on occasion, acute patients may be denied the treatment they need (Bluglass, 1987). For local authorities the problem was that the government expected the training for approved social workers to be implemented without an increase in central funding (Prior, 1992: 111). Finally, although the BASW was in favour of professionalisation, NALGO, the social workers union, objected to specialisation in principle, and to the fact that the ASW requirements placed new conditions of service on social workers if they were to continue to carry out the work they had been doing since 1959. Alternatively, if ASW status entailed new responsibilities, then a salary increase should be forthcoming to reflect this fact. NALGO also argued that social workers who had been carrying out the functions of the new ASW prior to the implementation of the 1983 Act should not be required to undergo training. The government eventually accepted this argument, so that those who had been in post as an MWO immediately prior to the Mental Health (Amendment) Act 1982 (that is, 27 October 1982) or had 'gained substantial experience' as a MWO in the period 1975–82 need not hold the Certificate of Qualification in Social Work (CQSW) or Central Council for Education and Training in Social Worker (CCETSW) equivalent; that is, they need not be qualified social workers (Department of Health, 1986: cl. 7(a)).

But in the long run, it was the pro-training/specialisation viewpoint that, as we have seen, now represents the letter of the 1983 Act. The CCETSW set up an examination for qualified social workers. In directions made pursuant to s. 114(3) (Department of Health, 1986), it is provided in cl. 7(a) that, in order to be eligible for approval by a local authority, a person should: (a) be a qualified social worker (unless exempt under the deal worked out with NALGO); *and* (b) have received appropriate training for mental health work *and* have appropriate professional experience and have demonstrated 'an appropriate level of professional competence'. Approval should be for a period not exceeding five years: cl. 7(b)(iii). In order to deal with the problems of funding specialised mental health training, and to cope with the fact that NALGO boycotted the examination for post-qualification mental health training, cl. 7(c) provided that, until 27 October 1988, local authorities could make 'transitional approvals' of social workers of at least two years who had carried out the duties of an MWO or had acted under the supervision of an ASW in the execution of duties under the 1983 Act. This latter provision reflected the fact that, although the new enhanced role for social workers appeared on the face of the new legislation, the politics of the Act's implementation meant that the putting into practice of the new scheme had effectively floundered. Four thousand social workers were approved under cl. 7(c), which was approximately 80 per cent of those operating in the mid 1980s (Prior, 1992). In practice, therefore, the professionalisation and specialisation of mental health social work took off only very slowly.

For much of the life of the 1983 Act, many ASWs made few assessments and applications for involuntary admission. This is, in part, because of the specifics of their employment. In 1992, a majority of ASWs were employed outside specialist mental health teams. Only 26 per cent were employed in specialist mental health social work teams in the community (Huxley et al., 2005: 509). Substantial numbers of ASWs were therefore largely inactive in mental health matters. In 1990, almost a third of ASWs were performing only one assessment a year, and must be considered substantially inactive for purposes of Part II assessments (Huxley et al., 2005: 510).

The professional requirements were tightened in the early 1990s. To attain ASW status, a social worker was required undergo around 12 weeks of training, and attend refresher courses at regular intervals (Central Council for Education and Training in Social Work, 1993). The numbers of ASWs performing only one assessment a year dropped, from 30 per cent in 1990, to 23 per cent in 1992. By 2002, a study of ASWs showed that 88 per cent of ASWs were active, and the minimum number of compulsory admissions by any ASW was 12 (Huxley et al., 2005: 510). The number of assessments performed can be assumed to be significantly greater, as on average only half of the assessment performed resulted in an involuntary admission (2005: 509). ASWs may thus now be taken to have a case load sufficient to give them meaningful experience and potential expertise in these assessments.

Consistent with this, more recent research seems to indicate that ASWs are sometimes able to make a better judgment about the need for hospitalisation than are psychiatrists, and it is claimed that this is because of the training in issues such as discrimination and disadvantage that ASWs receive (Hatfield et al., 1997). Further, research by Peay et al. suggests that ASWs do have a reasonable understanding of mental health law (2001: 52) and are more hesitant than psychiatrists in recommending involuntary admission of individuals (Peay, 2003: ch. 1).

At the same time, the numbers of ASWs seems increasingly inadequate to the task established by the MHA. By 1998, 60 per cent of social services departments reported an insufficient number of ASWs (Huxley et al., 2005: 509). In 2002, Huxley's study found 21 per cent of jobs vacant, with 68 per cent of social service departments reporting recruitment problems and 30 per cent retention problems (Huxley et al., 2005: 511). Huxley's team identified better pay and conditions in other forms of social work to be a factor in these recruitment difficulties, as well as the stressful nature of statutory responsibilities under the Act (Huxley et al., 2005: 511; see also Evans et al., 2005).

The government's current intent is to remove the specific role of social workers in the admission of patients, instead allowing an 'approved mental health professional' to examine the individual, along with the doctors (Department of Health, 2006a: A4, p. 2). This class might include nurses and occupational therapists, but specific training, based on the current ASW training, will be required. This is a controversial change. It was argued before the Richardson Committee that ASWs retained an independent and non-medical perspective to the compulsion process, that they were able to deal with the social and domestic aspects of the individual's admission, and that they were specifically trained for this role (Department of Health, 1999a: para. 5.11). The last of these cannot be convincing on its own: there is no reason other professionals might not be trained for the role; the second reason appears much more convincing. The Richardson Committee was sceptical about the degree to which ASWs would behave more independently of doctors than would other mental health professionals, but this does nonetheless seem to be a coherent objection to the proposals. Research by Peay suggests that ASWs are more hesitant to confine people than psychiatrists, and that their views do have some sway in confinement decisions (2003: ch. 1). The bulk of nursing training, by comparison, occurs within a medical frame of reference, and in so far as the decision to impose mandatory measures on an individual is not simply a medical decision, it is not obviously desirable to move toward further medical involvement in the making of the decisions.

It seems odd, given the protracted and complicated battle over the nature of ASW status, that a nearest relative, who need have no professional training whatever, is equally able to make an application for admission of the patient (s. 11(1), MHA 1983). The reason, as we have seen, flows from Victorian processes, and Victorian ideologies of the family and local government. Now, both are to be involved in all compulsory admissions. An ASW must, prior to making the application, consult with the nearest relative, who may block an application for admission under s. 3. Upon admission following an application by an NR, the receiving hospital must contact the patient's local SSD, which must then detail a social worker (although not necessarily an ASW) to interview the patient and provide a report on the patient's circumstance to the hospital: s. 14.

In respect of admission under s. 2, this consultation process is governed by s. 11(3) of the Act:

> Before or within a reasonable time after an application for the admission of a patient for assessment is made by an approved social worker, that social worker shall take such steps as are practicable to inform the person (if any) appearing to be the nearest relative of the patient.

Under s. 13(1) the ASW must do so 'having regard to any wishes expressed by relatives of the patient'. This does not give the NR a power of veto (although he or she must also be informed, under s. 11(2), of their powers of discharge in s. 23: see Chapter 8), nor does it give the relatives an express right to be consulted. It does, however, require the ASW to take into account the views of the NR other relatives of the patient, as defined by s. 26(6) and (7) (see below), in the event that the ASW is aware of those views.

The 1983 Act gives NRs rather more power in respect of an application by an ASW for admission for treatment. Section 11(4) states that an application for admission under s. 3:

> shall not be made by an approved social worker if the nearest relative of the patient has notified that social worker, or the local social services authority by whom that social worker is appointed, that he objects to the application being made and, without prejudice to the foregoing provision, no such application shall be made by such a social worker except after consultation with the person (if any) appearing to be the nearest relative of the patient unless it appears to that social worker that in the circumstances such consultation is not reasonably practicable or would involve unreasonable delay.

If admission for treatment under s. 3 is contemplated, therefore, the ASW *must* consult with the person appearing to be the NR prior to making the application, unless this is not reasonably practicable or would involve unreasonable delay. As a s. 3 admission is, by definition, not an emergency, practicability and unreasonableness should be interpreted so as to allow consultation if at all possible.

There is limited case law on the required extent of the consultation process. Perhaps due to the context of the case, Phillips LJ, in *Re Whitbread (Mental Patient: Habeas Corpus)* [1997] 39 BMLR 94, focuses on the relationship between the consultation and the NR's right to object to the application:

No express provision is made as to when consultation should take place. Counsel for the respondents conceded that a nexus must exist between the consultation and the application subsequently made. The consultation must relate to the application. It must place the nearest relative in a position, if so minded, to object to that application ... Provided that the social worker explains to the nearest relative that he or she is considering making an application and why, the nearest relative will be afforded the opportunity for objecting to the application that the Act requires.

In this articulation, the NR is not asked for involvement, nor need they be expressly told of their legal right to veto the admission. It is difficult to see that such a limited consultation would encourage the active involvement of the NR in the admission process, as seems to be implied by the statutory scheme.

A broader reading, more consistent with the statutory scheme but by a lower court, is contained in *Re Briscoe* [1998] COD 402. In that case, Tucker J held that merely informing the NR of a pending application would not suffice. Instead, he cited *R v Secretary of State of Social Services, ex p Association of Metropolitan Authorities* [1986] 1 All ER 164 to the effect that the essence of consultation was 'communication of a genuine invitation to give advice and a genuine consideration of that advice'. This must surely be the better interpretation, because the duty to take the views of relatives into account contained in s. 13(1) applies to s. 3 admissions, as well as those under s. 2. It seems unduly legalistic to separate that general duty from the duty to consult under s. 11. There is further no obvious reason why the legislature would require, in s. 11(3), that for s. 2 admissions, the NR be told of their power to order the discharge of the patient under s. 23(2)(a), but not include a similar requirement for s, 3 admissions, unless it was anticipated that the consultation would be a full exchange of views, with the NR being made aware of their right to veto the admission.

5.3.2 Nearest relative

The role of the nearest relative in mental health law has been controversial for many years. At the root of the dispute lie a variety of tensions on the nature of mental health law and social policy. The most obvious of these is the tension between lay and professional views. If we understand mental health law and practice as a domain of professionals, it is not obvious in theory what the family member will have to bring to the process. Such arguments quickly become less simple, however. As society moves increasingly away from hospitalisation and the total institution towards community care, the role of familial carers becomes pivotal: ongoing family support may be a key determinant of whether an individual's community placements are successful. That does not, of course, make the question of professional power go away. Indeed, it may complicate it into a question of further colonisation, because the professional may view the road to success as requiring not only the patient, but also the relevant carers, to subscribe to the authority and the views of the professional. Such family carers are not generally subject to express legal controls, however, so working relationships must be established by less direct means. Often, this will not be a problem. Whether because of a genuine agreement with professional views, an intersection of interests, or deference to authority, family members like patients themselves frequently agree with the professionals. These tend to be the relationships invisible to law: when there is no dispute, law tends not to notice. It is when there is disagreement, as in the cases involving replacement of NRs below, that matters are drawn to legal attention.

The justifications for the involvement of the family are similarly problematic. In part, it is because the family is thought to be a locus of care, when the individual is not in hospital; it is also, as we have seen, the vestige of Victorian family values concerning public and private. Each of these is problematic in its own terms. The realities will not necessarily measure up to the ideologies: not every family is a caring family. *JT v UK* [2000] 1 FLR 909 (ECHR) involved a patient whose stepfather was said to have sexually abused her. Unsurprisingly, Ms T did not wish her NR, her mother who was still living with the stepfather, to be involved in the decisions about her care, nor indeed for the mother to have any knowledge of her whereabouts. The case was settled before the European Court of Human Rights on the basis that the government would amend the Act to allow the patient to appoint the NR. To date, that amendment has not been made, although the government has indicated an intention to amend the law regarding nearest relatives in the forthcoming legislative reforms (Department of Health, 2006a: A5) (for provisions of the 2006 Bill, see preface). In 2003, relying on *JT*, a declaration of incompatibility with the Human Rights Act was made regarding the existing provision in the MHA 1983: *R (M)* v *Secretary of State for Health* [2003] EWHC 1094. The subsequent case of *R (E)* v *Bristol City Council* [2005] EWHC 74 declined a declaration of incompatibility, instead construing the statute so that inappropriate nearest relatives could not be 'practicably' consulted: see further below.

Even when the reality does measure up to the image, problems may result. In strong nuclear families, care may continue to be understood as a private family function, not a public one, creating direct conflicts with the public and professional nature of the MHA and its administration. And the realities faced by caring families create manifold conflicts of interest, because the realities of care must be balanced against the remainder of family life and responsibilities: see, for example, Karp, 2001.

This, of course, risks conflict with the civil rights of the patient. A civil libertarian is unlikely to see how it is justifiable that a patient be admitted for 'relief of carers', notwithstanding that this was the most frequent major reason cited for acute admissions to hospital in an Inner London study (Flannigan *et al.*, 1994a: 752), and the Code of Practice does include 'the needs of the patient's family and others with whom he or she lives' as a relevant factor to be taken into account by an applicant in assessing whether an application for admission should be made (Department of Health and Welsh Office, 1999: para. 2.6). Equally of concern here is the revival in the last twenty years of the ideology of the family, a belief in family involvement as a cornerstone of social policy, whether or not the family implied by the ideology bears any relation to the relations of people in individual cases. In a system based increasingly on community care, support structures in the community are increasingly important; those structures will often be based in the family. To marginalise involvement of the family in the hospitalisation process arguably puts the continued set of relations between the medical professionals, the family, and the patient at risk, thus threatening the community support that the patient will need upon discharge.

This last factor suggests we may not have moved as far as we might have thought from the original Victorian issues regarding family involvement. Under the current regime the role of the NR is not simply that of alternative applicant for admission.

These tensions are reflected in policy and its implementation. According to Cavadino's research (1989), ASWs tend towards the view that it is inappropriate for the patient's relatives to make the application because this may harm relationships within the family. This view is echoed in the Code of Practice (para. 2.35), and it was once the policy of MIND and the BASW that the role of NR should be abolished completely (Cavadino, 1989: 117). This would also enhance the position of social workers in the system, who may need to protect their area of expertise and professional power from encroachment by laypersons, and to assert their role in the admission process vis-à-vis the medical professionals. It is nonetheless not obvious that the role of the NR should be removed completely. There may well be cases where the relative is aware of realities of the patient's life relevant to admission, and of wishes of the patient that may warrant respect. It is not obvious that professionals have access to this sort of information, and without such consultations being legally mandatory, they may not occur in a system facing continual cutbacks and where administrators are under increasing stress.

The legal definition of a NR is found in s. 26 of the MHA 1983. The NR of a patient will normally be the person nearest to the beginning of the following list:

(a) husband or wife;

(b) son or daughter;

(c) father or mother;

(d) brother or sister;

(e) grandparent;

(f) grandchild;

(g) uncle or aunt;

(h) nephew or niece.

Other persons with whom the patient had been residing for at least five years at the time of admission to hospital are added as a final class on this list by s. 26(7). Those entitled include relatives of both 'the whole blood' and half blood: s. 26(2). If there is more than one person of the relevant class, the elder will be the NR, and relatives of the whole blood are preferred over those of half blood: s. 26(3). Relatives living abroad, separated spouses, and relatives under the age of 18 other than parents or spouses, are discounted (s. 26(5)), but cohabiting partners of at least six months' standing are included, as long as the patient is separated from anyone to whom the patient is married: s. 26 (6). Since the introduction of the Human Rights Act 1998, the Secretary of State has taken the view that gay and lesbian partners are also to be accepted as cohabiting partners under s. 26(6): see Cho, 2002. The government has further indicated that the statutory definition will be amended to include gay civil partners in the definition of nearest relative when the MHA 1983 is next amended (Department of Health, 2006a: A5, 2). The government briefing sheet is silent on what status these people will be given. It will be consistent with the intent of the Civil Partnership Act 2004 that they will be considered equivalent to a heterosexual married spouse, although an amendment to this effect was apparently rejected by the government during the passage of the 2004 Act (Jones, 2006: 191). It may therefore be that they will be considered cohabiting partners, in which case cohabitation for six months would be required for them to be considered as 'husband or wife' under s. 26 (see s. 26(6)).

Even with the clarifications, the provisions are problematic if the objective is to select what would commonly be understood as the 'nearest' relative. For example, 'father' includes an unmarried father only if he has parental responsibility acquired in accordance with the requirements of s. 4, Children Act 1989, and members of the father's family similarly can only be the patient's nearest relative if the father has parental responsibility: s. 26(2)(b). Statutory responsibility acquired under the Children Act 1989 terminates on the child's 18th birthday, and so it would seem that all paternal 'relatives' of the adult offspring of unmarried parents are debarred from NR status, even if, for example, the unmarried parents do not cohabit and the adult patient is (and may perhaps have been since childhood) cared for by the father or his family.

Notwithstanding the general rule that persons higher up the list take precedence over those lower on the list, where the patient 'ordinarily resides with or is cared for by' one of his relatives listed as (a) to (h) above, or was so before admission to hospital, that relative is the NR of the patient: s. 26(4). The leading case on care in this context is *Re D (Mental Patient: Habeas Corpus)* [2000] 2 FLR 848, but it provides limited assistance. Lord Justice Otton allowed that relevant factors would include duration, continuity and quality of care provided by the relative (para. 14), but otherwise did not expand on the language of the statute. He did hold that the word 'ordinarily' qualified 'resides' only, and not also the care requirement. On the facts of the case, care that was more than minimal, but well short of long-term and ongoing support, was sufficient to invoke the provision (para. 15).

The provision regarding ordinary residence is similarly difficult to apply in practice. The test contained in *Shah* v *Barnet London Borough Council* [1983] 1 All ER 226 (HL) at 235 has been used: ' "ordinarily resident" refers to a man's abode in a particular place or country which he has adopted voluntarily and for settled purposes as part of the regular order of his life for the time being, whether short or long duration'. This was applied in *WC* v *South London and Maudsley NHS Trust and David Orekeye* [2001] EWHC Admin 1025. The difficulty is that individual lives do not fit into such neat boxes. Thus, in *WC* itself, the patient had resided with his wife when his relationship with her was proceeding successfully, and with his mother when it was not. At the time of his admission, he was residing with his mother. As regarding patients already in hospital, the statute refers to the last ordinary residence, suggesting a preference for the mother as the carer; but the court found otherwise on the facts. It does not appear that the statute provides a place for the patient's choice in these situations (re proposal in 2006 Bill allowing patient to apply for replacement of NR, see preface).

The NR of the patient, as defined by statute, is thus not necessarily the nearest relative as understood either by the patient, or by the colloquial use of that phrase. References to age and legitimacy may have been justifiable under the Victorian family ideology; they are not obviously appropriate if the concern is to identify the person best placed to know and act upon the patient's wishes and best interests. It is possible for a NR to delegate his or her functions, and there can be an application to a county court to remove and replace an NR (under s. 29, see below), but the former depends on the agreement of the existing NR and the latter is only used when there is concern about the abilities of the existing NR to perform his or her duties satisfactorily. Neither option is likely to afford much assistance to a de facto but not *de jure* NR.

Determination of who is the NR can thus be a complicated affair. For purposes of the consultations required by s. 11 at the time of admission, it is sufficient that the person contacted by the ASW *appears* to be the NR. The courts have steadfastly refused to impose any duty of reasonable enquiry on the ASW in this regard. The test is the honesty of the ASW's belief, not its reasonableness: *Whitbread* v *Kingston and District NHS*

Trust (1998), 39 BMLR 94; *D* v *Barnet Healthcare Trust* (above). That said, the ASW does appear to be required to apply the statute properly to the facts of which he or she is aware. In *R* v *South Western Hospital Managers and Anor, ex p M* [1994] 1 All ER 161 (HC), a patient, M, had been admitted under s. 3. The ASW involved in the case had consulted as NR the patient's mother, a resident of Eire, and had also discussed the situation with the patient's uncle, resident in the UK, who was not opposed to the admission. Laws J held that there had been a failure to comply with s. 11(4) because M's mother was disbarred from acting as NR by operation of s. 26(5)(a) (see above), and this was so notwithstanding that s. 11(4) requires the ASW to consult the person 'appearing to be the nearest relative'. He held that a person could not appear to be the patient's NR 'where, on the facts known to the social worker, the person in question is legally incapable of being the statutory nearest relative'. To consult that person defined as the NR but only in the capacity of a 'mere' relative, as happened here, will not suffice: of particular importance is the need to explain the powers to object to the patient's admission and those of discharge available to the NR under s. 23 (*In the Matter of Briscoe* [1998] COD 402 (HC)).

As we have seen, the MHA 1983 provides a variety of roles for the NR upon the admission of the patient. As will be discussed in more detail in Chapter 8, the NR also has a continuing power to order the release of the patient at any time in a s. 2 or s. 3 detention, subject to an overriding authority of the hospital to detain the patient if 'dangerous': ss. 23(1), 25. The authority of the NR over the confinement therefore remains throughout its full duration. The MHA 1983, then, gives the patient's NR a good deal of power. The person who is the patient's NR by operation of s. 26 may not, however, always be in the best position to act. This possibility is anticipated by various provisions. A NR can delegate the power to act to any other person, other than one prohibited from so acting under s. 26(5), or under reg. 14, Mental Health (Hospital, Guardianship and Consent to Treatment) Regulations 1983, SI 1983/893. This must be done in writing (reg.14(1)) and communicated to the local SSD, or hospital if the patient has already been admitted: reg.14(2). It is the responsibility of ASWs to suggest that a delegation be made in appropriate circumstances (Department of Health and Welsh Office, 1999: para. 2.17).

It is also possible for a county court, on the application of any relative, an ASW, or a person with whom the patient was residing prior to hospitalisation, to substitute an individual to act in place of the nearest relative defined by statute: s. 29. While the court has near infinite discretion as to whom to appoint, the grounds for the application are limited: they are contained in s. 29(3). Either there must be no NR under s. 26, or the prescribed NR must be incapable of acting due to mental illness or other disability, or the prescribed NR 'unreasonably objects' to an application for treatment or assessment, or the NR has exercised 'without regard to the welfare of the patient or the interests of the public', his or her power to order the discharge of the patient from hospital or guardianship. The powers accorded to the NR require his or her continuing involvement in the detention and treatment of the patient, and it is obviously important in that regard to ensure that the most appropriate person is exercising that authority on behalf of the patient.

The difficult cases under this section are those where the relative allegedly 'unreasonably objects' to the application for treatment. In these cases, the exercise of professional power over the NR can be seen with particular clarity, whether or not one agrees with the result. That appearance is noted by Lady Justice Hale in *Smirek v Williams* [2000] 1 MHLR 38 at paras. 14–15:

I am bound to say that this case illustrates several aspects of the mental health law which give rise to the greatest possible sense of injustice on the part of patients and from time to time their families.

. . . it illustrates the overriding of the views of the nearest relative, and in practice how difficult it is for the nearest relative to avoid being found unreasonable if his views differ from those of the hospital. In this particular case, even more will there be a sense of injustice as his views are the same as those of a Mental Health Review Tribunal. Relatives must in those circumstances wonder why they have any role at all.

The problems inherent in these applications exemplify a variety of the complexities of involvement of the NR in the sectioning process.

To found an application, the court must be given evidence that the proposed application for admission is necessary: *B(A) v B(L) (Mental Health Patient)* [1980] 1 WLR 116 (CA). The test of the unreasonableness of the objection was established by *W v L*, [1974] QB 711. That case involved the objection of a wife to the confinement of her husband, and the test was established by Lord Denning, at 717–8:

This brings me to the final question: is the wife unreasonable in objecting to the making of an application for the husband's detention? This is a difficult question. One can see that she is pulled both ways: on the one hand, she is devoted to her husband and wants him to be with her; on the other hand, she is devoted to her baby and wants the baby to be with her too. No doubt she feels that she can cope. She says she knows her husband better than anyone else does; she will see that he takes his tablets; she is quite satisfied that neither she nor the baby will be in danger. So if you look at it from her own point of view, she may not be unreasonable. But I do not think it correct to look at it from her own point of view. The proper test is to ask what a reasonable woman in her place would do in all the circumstances of the case . . .

So we come to this: looking at it objectively, what would a reasonable woman in her place do when faced with this problem? It seems to me that a reasonable woman would say: my husband ought to go in for treatment and he ought to be detained until he is cured. It is too great a risk to have him home whilst the baby is so small. Her objection is therefore unreasonable.

Should such an objective test be used? Is the question what the 'reasonable' NR would do? This raises the question, not discussed in the case, as to why the NR should be included in the decision process at all. If it is merely to ensure the provision of relevant information to the doctor, an objective test is defensible; although it is not obvious why a veto to admission would be available in that case. If it is instead to provide an acknowledgement that the NR, as an individual family member, might have something distinctive to bring to the determination, the case for an objective test is more difficult to make out, because such individuality is removed by the objective test. When such individuality is removed, any disagreement with the social worker and doctors is bound to look unreasonable.

Indeed, the facts of *W* v *L* can be read in that way. Lord Denning presents the case as the wife driven to unreasonableness in the conflicting desires to be near her baby and her husband. Lawton LJ goes so far as to say that the case comes 'to the right conclusion in deciding to safeguard this little baby from the possibility of harm' (719–20). In fact, the baby had been placed in care voluntarily by the wife, so was apparently in no danger whatsoever, at least in the short term. The husband was, in fact, taking his medication. The husband and wife had been living together for some weeks without dangerous or violent incident. The use of an objective test allowed the court not to consider the balance that the wife had chosen to strike. Objectively, it would seem, in the view of the court, the reasonable woman ought to have her baby with her, and she ought to follow the advice of the medical experts about her husband.

The application of this objective test effectively undercuts the independent role of the NR, because it allows findings of fact adverse to the NR effectively to determine the matter. In *Manchester City Council* v *MI*, [1999] 1 MHLR 132, for example, the issue was whether allegedly aggressive behaviour by the patient flowed from mental disorder or from epilepsy. The NR, herself a nurse, had medical evidence from the patient's GP and from an independent expert neurologist attesting to the fact that MI did indeed have epilepsy. The court also had evidence from a senior social worker and two consultant psychiatrists that MI had chronic schizophrenia and Tourette's syndrome. The court preferred the latter evidence, and therefore held that the objection to MI's admission was unreasonable. With respect, this asks the wrong question, because it presupposes that the reasonable NR must reach the same view of conflicting medical evidence as the court. If the NR is to have a meaningful role in these circumstances, the question must instead be whether the NR is unreasonable in believing one set of expert medical opinion over another, or was deciding unreasonably given that view of the evidence.

While the courts occasionally deny it, it is difficult to see that s. 29 applications do not, in the end, collapse into a question of the court's view of the best interests of the patient, and the courts are loathe to take a view divergent from the patient's medical officers. Indeed, in *McClelland* v *Simon S* [2000] 1 MHLR 6, the trial judge went so far as to find that the NR's 'attack on [the psychiatrist's] opinion is but one indication of the unreasonableness of Mr S's objection to his mother's continued detention in hospital' (p. 6). While Lady Hale, in the Court of Appeal, expressly disagreed with that finding, it does suggest an approach of extreme sympathy to medical opinion at trial.

The obvious person who is precluded from applying under s. 29 is the patient him or herself. As noted above, this has led to a declaration of incompatibility under the Human Rights Act: *R (M)* v *Secretary of State for Health* [2003] EWHC 1094. Subsequently, the issue was revisited in *R (E)* v *Bristol City Council* [2005] EWHC 74. In that case, the nearest relative would have been the patient's sister, who apparently had no interest in fulfilling the role. The patient, E, expressed a competent view that she did not want the sister fulfilling the role, and E's medical advisers and, indeed, the respondent council agreed that it would be not in E's best interests for the sister to continue in this role. Like the court in *R (M)*, Bennett J held that for her to continue to do so would be in violation of E's rights under Art. 8 of the ECHR, but unlike the court in *R (M)*, he did not issue a declaration of incompatibility. Instead, the court held that consultation with the sister in these circumstances would not be 'practicable', and therefore need not occur.

Whatever the merits of this decision in the specific case, it is not an ideal solution. It stretches language a considerable degree. There was no indication that it would be practically difficult to contact the sister; merely that it was inappropriate under the circumstances. If that were the result Parliament had wanted, it could surely have been clearer on the point. *R (E)* is also a particularly clear case on the merits. E had capacity, and did not want the sister involved. She clearly trusted the social services personnel, and indeed attempted to execute a power of attorney appointing them as her nearest relative. It is much less clear how or why a nearest relative should be excluded under other circumstances. The risk is, of course, that this will occur when convenient for professional carers. The result was also not the appointment of a nearest relative more agreeable to E. It was instead an exclusion of the existing nearest relative, the sister: E was left with no nearest relative. Nearest relatives have, however, an important role in the statutory system of the MHA 1983. If such a role is justified, it is unfortunate that there was no mechanism for E to appoint some independent person to fulfil that role.

In this context, the intent of the government to alter the MHA 1983 to allow patients to apply to court for the replacement of their nearest relatives is a good thing. The government's proposal is considerably wider, however: it intends that not only the patient, but also the approved mental health professional, any relative of the patient, or anyone living with the patient will be able to apply to replace the statutory nearest relative, 'where it reasonable that the person should not be able to act as the NR' (Department of Health, 2006a: A5, 2). This is a broader criterion than that contained in the current s. 29. As noted above, it is certainly arguable that the courts already give insufficient credence to the views of the nearest relative. If the purpose of the nearest relative is to provide a counterweight to the professional, it is obvious that it is not desirable to give these professionals yet further scope to displace the nearest relative, only on the basis that his or her continuation in the role is not 'reasonable'.

It is further obvious that the approach does not address the problem that the original litigation in this area was intended to solve. It is the patient's Art. 8 right to privacy that is being violated, according to *R (E)* (para. 16–17). That right is violated whenever an individual not of the patient's choosing is made privy to private information about the patient, and can therefore be violated whether or not the nearest relative is acting 'reasonably'. If the Art. 8 right is to be taken seriously, people must be able to appoint their own nearest relatives (or, presumably, decline to have a nearest relative) without a legal threshold relating to how well the statutory nearest relative is doing his or her job. Indeed, one of the reasons the patient may wish the statutory nearest relative replaced is that the patient views the current nearest relative as too 'reasonable', in the sense of being too compliant to the wishes of the approved mental health professional or the medical team.

Under the government's plans, it is further not clear how the new nearest relative will be chosen. Conspicuously absent from the government's briefing sheet is any suggestion that the competent patient will be able to choose the person to fulfil this role. Will the individual have to pass the scrutiny of the court, or of the approved mental health professional? If so, the indications in the existing jurisprudence regarding s. 29 would suggest that the nominee's compliance to the approved mental health professional and the treatment team may figure large in the appointment process. If, however, there is an argument for the involvement of a nearest relative or similar figure, it must surely be that they serve as a counterpoint to these professional views. It is difficult to see this as a likely outcome of a controlled appointment process.

If an NR objects to the admission for treatment under s. 3 of a patient already detained for assessment under s. 2, the 28-day period of detention under s. 2 may be extended until the application under s. 29 is heard, and for a further seven days if that application is successful (s. 29(4)), to allow the formalities of a s. 3 admission to be complied with. It has also been held that an interim order can be made under s. 29, and that a patient may be admitted under s. 3 during the currency of such an order if there are cogent reasons to admit the patient before the s. 29 application can be finally determined: *R v Central London County Court and Anor, ex p London* [1999] 3 WLR 1 (CA). Particularly offensive was that this order was made *ex parte*, that is, without proper notice to the NR: p. 5. Quite why that failure occurred is not obvious, because it would seem that the hospital was in touch with the NR. The Court of Appeal rejected the submission that if, on the subsequent full hearing of the application under s. 29, the interim order were to be discharged and no other order made, the patient would have been disadvantaged unfairly by the making of an interim order. But in such a case, the patient will have been lawfully admitted under s. 3 over the objections of the (now reinstated) lawful NR, and although the NR will then have a power to discharge the patient under s. 23, that power can be vetoed by the RMO if the patient is thought to be dangerous (see Chapter 8). In any case, a power to discharge is a poor replacement for a power to prevent admission.

5.4 The mechanics and dynamics of admission

5.4.1 Prerequisites for the making of an application for an admission

Whoever the applicant is, the application must be made to the hospital managers of the receiving hospital (s. 11(2)), and must be made on the correct form (SI 1983 No. 893, reg. 4 and Forms 1, 2, 4, 5, 8, and 9). It is the responsibility of the applicant to ensure, if compulsory admission is warranted, that all the requirements for a valid application are satisfied. Although, in general, the decision whether or not to make an application is in the discretion of the potential applicant (whether ASW or NR), s. 13(1) places a duty to make an application on an ASW 'in any case where he is satisfied that such an application ought to be made and is of the opinion... that it is necessary or proper for the application to be made by him'. In making this decision, an ASW must also consider the options for treatment or assistance without hospitalisation, and an assessment pursuant to s. 13, MHA 1983 may double as an assessment for entitlement to community care services under s. 47, National Health Service and Community Care Act 1990 (see Chapter 9). An NR can initiate the assessment process under s. 13(4), MHA 1983, which gives an NR the right to request an SSD to 'direct an approved social worker as soon as practicable to take the patient's case into consideration under [s. 13(1)] with a view to making an application for his admission'. A request under s. 13(4) places the SSD under a duty of care towards the patient. The ASW may well also owe a duty of care to the patient in these circumstances: see s. 12.5, below. If the ASW after consideration decides that an application is not required, his or her reasons must be supplied to the NR in writing: s. 13(4).

5.4.1.1 The medical recommendations

An application for admission under Part II must be 'founded on' the necessary medical recommendations: ss. 2, 3, 4. Under the terms of the statute the medical recommendations 'shall be signed *on or before the date of the application*' (s. 12(1)), but, following the decision in *Whitbread* (1997) *The Times*, 14 July, this does not mean that the medical recommendations must precede the making of the application. The Code of Practice states that medical and social work assessments should be carried out jointly unless there are good reasons for separate assessments (Department of Health and Welsh Office, 1999: para. 2.3). If it is not possible to gain access to the patient in order to carry out an assessment, recourse should be had to s. 135(1) (see Chapter 4) or to any powers of forced entry that the police may lawfully use (Department of Health and Welsh Office, 1999: para. 2.24).

For ss. 2 and 3, there must be two medical recommendations: ss. 2(3), 3(3). The two doctors may examine the patient together or separately (s. 11(7)), but where separate examinations take place, they must not be more than five days apart: s. 12(1). The practice of requiring the agreement of two doctors is a function of a Victorian fear that doctors are easily corruptible, the idea being that each would police the actions of the other (Bean, 1986: 43). The 1983 Act, like its Victorian antecedents, also includes additional safeguards against potential collusion or improper use of medical recommendations. Section 12(5) disbars the following persons from acting as the second opinion doctor: the applicant for admission (some ASWs or NRs may be doctors); the professional partner or assistant of the first recommending doctor; any practitioner who has a financial interest in the hospital to which the patient is to be admitted; close relatives of the patient.

Today, since doctors are normally salaried and have little financial motive for the confinement of patients, the argument about corruption seems unpersuasive. The requirement is instead better understood as a civil rights protection, ensuring a reasonable degree of medical certainty and consistency before confinement may occur. Reflecting that, while each recommendation may contain diagnoses of more than one of the specified forms of mental disorder, there must be agreement on at least one form of mental disorder if any subsequent application is to be effective: s. 11(6). As we have seen, however, a joint examination is possible, and even if examinations are performed separately, the Code of Practice requires the two doctors involved to discuss the patient with each other (para. 2.25). This, on its face, would undercut the civil rights protection, which would be strengthened if each doctor were required to reach an independent judgment. In the view of the Code of Practice, good practice also dictates that the recommending doctors discuss the situation with the applicant (para. 2.26), although there is no legal duty in the MHA 1983 to do so.

Of the two medical recommendations, one 'shall be given by a practitioner approved for the purposes of this section by the Secretary of State as having special experience in the diagnosis or treatment of mental disorder': s. 12(2). This person will usually be a professional psychiatrist, although the Code of Practice now encourages SSDs to take steps to encourage other doctors including GPs to apply for approval (para. 2.41). The power to approve practitioners under s. 12(2) has been delegated to health authorities (SI 1996/708).

The second recommending doctor must be a registered medical practitioner who has previous acquaintance with the mentally disordered person, unless the approved doctor already has such previous acquaintance (s. 12(2)), or unless this is not practicable. This typically means that the second doctor will be the patient's GP. Such limited case law as exists on the point would suggest that the acquaintance can be very limited indeed. In *Ann R (By her Litigation Friend Joan T) v Bronglais Hospital Pembrokeshire and Derwen NHS Trust* [2001] EWHC Admin 792, the GP in question had only just accepted R as a patient. His first real connection with her was at a meeting of the local social services department, concerning her potential confinement. Thereafter, he visited her for five minutes, and scanned, but did not read, her medical record when he eventually received it from the Family Health Authority. This constituted his prior acquaintance, prior to a second visit at which he conducted the assessment. Scott Baker J held that the section specifically did not require prior 'personal' acquaintance. While para. 2.29 of the Code of Practice did refer to such personal knowledge, this was guidance only, and not binding. The GP had gained sufficient knowledge in the case conference with social services that he was not coming at the matter cold, but with some knowledge of her background. In the court's view, this was all that was required.

The balance contemplated by the 1983 Act, then, is a mix of substantive expertise, and experience with the particular patient. There are a number of reasons, however, why the system has a tendency to break down in practice. First, not everyone will have a GP (Spence and McPhillips, 1995), or have a GP that knows them well. That said, a high number of those admitted compulsorily have been admitted before (*ibid.*), so there may well be someone available who has previous acquaintance with the patient. If the patient has no GP, or if the GP cannot practicably be contacted, the Code of Practice takes the view that the second recommending doctor should also be 'approved' (para. 2.29). Second, when GPs are involved in the admission process, it tends to be very much in a subordinate role to the appointed psychiatrist. Bean (1980:162, 163) found that 'GPs, generally speaking, knew little of the [Mental Health] Act, and knew little of psychiatry'. Consequently, and also because of the hierarchy within the medical profession between generalists and specialists, the GPs did what the psychiatrists told them to do (Bean, 1986: 44). The hopes for balance and mutual restraint, then, have not been realised. Not more than one of the medical recommendations may be given by a practitioner on the staff of the receiving hospital (s. 12(3)), unless to delay on these grounds would involve 'serious risk to the health or safety of the patient' (s. 12(4)(a)), *and* one of the practitioners works 'for less than half the time which he is bound by contract to devote to work in the health service' in the receiving hospital (s. 12(4)(b)), *and*, where one of the recommending doctors is a consultant, the other does not work in a grade under that consultant's directions: s. 12(4)(c).

Bean's view of the limited knowledge of general practitioners is given support by Peay *et al.* (2001). Peay attempted to compare the legal knowledge of those involved in the psychiatric process, using a postal questionnaire. The encouraging finding from this survey is that s. 12(2) approved psychiatrists and ASWs scored reasonably well in the questionnaire. The authors comment that 'put at its simplest, a patient is relatively unlikely to encounter an ASW or s. 12(2) psychiatrist with poor legal knowledge' (2001: 53). As a patient is required to be examined by both an ASW and a s. 12(2)-approved doctor, normally, but not necessarily, a psychiatrist, the odds are presumably correspondingly increased that at least one person examining the individual will be aware of the legal standards of confinement.

The findings regarding GPs, whether s. 12(2) approved or not, is not nearly so encouraging. While all but 22 of the 573 GPs responding to the survey had participated in a mental health assessment, their knowledge was considerably less than that of the psychiatrists or ASWs. While the overall findings are comparative between the professional groups rather than purporting to establish absolute scales, answers to specific questions reported by Peay are striking. Only two thirds of the s. 12-approved GPs, and half of the remaining GPs, knew that criteria for a s. 3 admission included that the person needed detention in the interests of their health. Only 59 per cent of the former group and 67 per cent of the latter realised that the admission criteria do not require the individual to lack capacity to consent to treatment (2001: 47).

For admission under s. 4, the situation is different. Here, there need be only *one* medical recommendation, which need not be made by a psychiatrist, but which should be made by a doctor with previous acquaintance with the patient if practicable: s. 4(3). Section 4 should only be used in cases of 'urgent necessity', and the Code of Practice (para. 6.2) states that s. 4 should never be used for administrative convenience. In particular, patients 'should not be admitted under section 4 rather than section 2 because it is more convenient for the second doctor to examine the patient in, rather than outside, hospital' (para. 6.4). If, as this implies, medical convenience does not render the situation one of urgent necessity, the use of s. 4 for this reason would render the confinement illegal. This argument has yet to be tested in the courts.

5.4.1.2 The approved social worker interview

The applicant, whether ASW or NR, must have personally seen the patient no more than 14 days prior to the date of the application for admission: s. 11(5). If the intending applicant is an ASW, he or she 'shall interview the patient in a suitable manner and satisfy himself that detention in a hospital is, in all the circumstances of the case, the most appropriate way of providing the care and medical treatment of which the patient stands in need': s. 13(2). The patient should be given the option of this interview being conducted in private (unless the ASW has reason to fear physical harm) or in the presence of some other person such as a friend: (Department of Health and Welsh Office, 1999: para. 2.13). An interpreter trained to act in a psychiatric context should be present if the patient and ASW do not speak the same language (1999: para. 2.14); a relative, friend or neighbour of the patient should only be used as a last resort. The Code of Practice advises that 'it is not desirable for a patient to be interviewed through a closed door or window except where there is serious risk to other people' (para. 2.12.a). Instead the powers of intervention accorded to the Justice of the Peace under s. 135 (see Chapter 4) should be used.

One function of this interview should be to ensure that the legal grounds of confinement, as discussed in the previous chapter, are satisfied before an application is made. It was said, in *St George's Healthcare NHS Trust v S* [1998] 2 FLR 728, 3 All ER 673 (CA), that for an admission for assessment, an ASW is not required to be certain that the patient definitely is mentally disordered. Indeed, it 'cannot be a final diagnosis. [An ASW] is entitled to be wrong: so are the medical practitioners on whose medical recommendations her application is based' (per Judge LJ at p. 690). But his lordship made clear that an ASW is required to 'believe' that the person to be admitted for assessment is mentally disordered. This is logical: more precise diagnosis may constitute the need for assessment in hospital. The same reasoning does not apply to admissions under s. 3, however, which would seem to imply that an ASW or the recommending doctors are *not* entitled to be wrong for such admissions. In practice the question is largely irrelevant, however, because a person who is found not to be mentally disordered after admission should be discharged, and if not is entitled to apply for habeas corpus (see later in this chapter) in either case.

Section 13(2) is not concerned solely with medical questions, however, but rather with the broader question of the 'appropriateness' of confinement. The BASW has taken the view that, in addition, the following constitute the role of the social worker in the admission process (BASW, 1980, quoted in Jones, 2006: 94):

(a) to investigate the client's social situation and how it has developed; and to estimate, in consultation with others involved, the extent to which the social and environmental pressures have contributed to the client's observed behaviour;

(b) to apply professional skill to help modify any contributory personal relationship or environmental factors;

(c) to mobilise the resources of the health service, the community service and acknowledge and use the community as a therapeutic resource;

(d) to ensure that any intervention is the least restrictive necessary in the circumstances;

(e) to ensure strict compliance with the law.

The emphasis of these criteria would ensure that confinement is the least restrictive option. While that is unquestionably desirable, training and expertise in the application of these criteria may, as we have seen, remain problematic. Equally problematic is the reduction of the legal standards of admission to only one of a list of social work responsibilities in the area. The risk is that the provisions of ss. 2 and 3 will be seen only as factors in admission policy, rather than legal standards that are *sine qua non* of confinement.

The high professional standard implied in these criteria are nonetheless laudable. A somewhat different image is presented by the comments of Burton J in *Re Makin (s. 3, Mental Health Act 1983)* (QBD, 4 May 2000), that 'certainly, given the experience of professionals, it is not suggested that 20 minutes or 15 minutes or even 10 minutes, would be too short for an interview'. The image presented here seems well removed from the lofty professional ideals of the BASW cited above.

This mandatory requirement to interview the patient will often be straightforward, in the sense of the patient not actively resisting the process of hospitalisation, but not infrequently there is resistance. A prospective inpatient may refuse to speak to the ASW or to allow the ASW access to the patient's home, or may be verbally or physically violent towards the ASW or others involved in the admission process such as psychiatrists (Dean and Webster, 1991). The medical model approach for compulsory admission is backed up by a system of graduated coercion to ensure that hospitalisation is not thwarted by the patient's lack of cooperation. An ASW has powers of entry and inspection under s. 115, MHA 1983, which are exercisable 'at all reasonable times' in respect of premises (other than hospitals) 'in which a mentally disordered patient is living, if he has reasonable cause to believe that the patient is not under proper care'. Section 115 does not, however, permit forced entry, and so is of little use if consent to enter the premises in question is not forthcoming. Under the 1983 Act, it is an offence for a person 'without reasonable cause' to refuse to allow an inspection of any premises (s. 129(1)(a)), as it is to 'refuse to allow the visiting, interviewing or examination of person by a person authorised in that behalf by or under this Act' (s. 129(b)) and to 'otherwise obstruct any such person in the exercise of his functions': s. 129(d). But, whilst an ASW who is refused entry to premises may use the fact that an offence or offences has or have thereby been committed as a bargaining chip, this is unlikely to be the appropriate course of action on many occasions. In particular, this does not address the question immediately at hand, of the need to interview the patient.

As we have seen (see Chapter 4), powers of intervention are also given to Justices of the Peace and police, under ss. 135 and 136. These allow the person to be kept in a place of safety for up to 72 hours. This is not necessarily a guarantee that an interview will take place, if an interview is defined to mean a conversation to which both, or all, participants contribute: the patient may refuse to speak. If this occurs, the ASW's assessment 'will have to be based on whatever information the ASW can obtain from all reliable sources'. If all else fails, therefore, the patient can seemingly be admitted into hospital in the absence of an ASW interview. The use of 'reliable sources' (whatever that means) is not an alternative to interviewing, however, because an ASW is required to make such enquiries in any case under s. 13(1).

5.4.1.3 The execution of an application

Execution of the application is pursuant to s. 6(1):

> An application for the admission of a patient to hospital under this Part of the Act, duly completed in accordance with the provision of this Part of this Act, shall be sufficient authority for the applicant, or any person authorised by the applicant, to take the patient and convey him to the hospital.

This authority subsists for 14 days from the date of the last medical recommendation in the case of s. 2 and s. 3 admissions (s. 6(1)(a)), and for 24 hours in the case of s. 4 admissions (s. 6(1)(b)), after which time it will lapse.

Once the application is executed in this fashion, the patient is deemed to be in legal custody: s. 137(1). By s. 137(2), the person responsible for conveying the patient to hospital 'shall . . . have all the powers, authorities, protection and privileges which a constable has within the area for which he acts as constable'. This includes the right to use reasonable force, to sedate the patient (in which case, a nurse, doctor or specialist ambulance person should accompany the patient to hospital – Code of Practice: para. 11.14)), and the power to arrest any person obstructing the execution of the application.

If access to the patient is denied, s. 135(2) allows a Justice of the Peace, at the instigation of the applicant for committal or a constable, to issue a warrant authorising a constable to enter the premises. The Justice must be satisfied that the patient is to be found on the premises in question (s. 135(2)(a)), and 'that admission to the premises has been refused or that a refusal of such admission is apprehended': s. 135(2)(b). It has been argued that the general requirements in relation to the execution of warrants for entry and search by police constables, contained in ss. 15 and 16 of PACE 1984, also apply here (see Jones, 2006: 500–1), and Baroness Hale, in *obiter*, has given tentative support to this view: see *Ward v Commissioner of Police for the Metropolis* [2005] UKHL 32. The most important of these requirements for present purposes are that the warrant authorises entry on one occasion only (s. 15(5)), and that the warrant has a life of one month from the date on which it is made (s. 16(3)), and must be executed at a reasonable time, unless there is reason to believe that the search would thereby be frustrated: s. 16(4). As Jones notes, however, s. 15(4), PACE states that the '*constable* [making the application for the warrant] shall answer any questions that the Justice of the Peace hearing the application . . . puts to him', which seems to imply that ss. 15 and 16 are relevant only when the applicant for the warrant is a constable. Further evidence that the drafters of ss. 15, 16, PACE did not have s. 135, MHA 1983, in mind is that, by s. 15(6), PACE, the identity of the person sought should, so far as is practicable, be specified on the warrant, whereas s. 135(5), MHA 1983 provides that the name of the patient need not be given either in the information laid before the Justice on the warrant. If this is correct, it would mean that only warrants applied for under s. 135 by police constables are covered by these provisions, with warrants applied for by an ASW not being covered.

5.4.1.4 Taking the patient to hospital

The applicant remains personally responsible for the proper conveyance to hospital of the patient, but may delegate the power to convey the patient to another person: s. 6(12). Conveyance is to be by the 'most humane and least threatening' method, consistent with the safety of the patient and others, taking into account the patient's preferences, the views of friends and relatives involved with the patient, the views of the professionals involved in the application, any potential violence on the part of the patient, and the impact of particular modes of conveyance on the patient's relationship with the community to which he or she will return (Department of Health and Welsh Office, 1999: para. 11.3). The police should usually be asked to help if the patient is likely to be violent or dangerous (1997: para. 11.7). Dean and Webster (1991: 190) found that 15 per cent of compulsory admissions involved the use of 'restraint' by the police, and 55 per cent involved either verbal or violent resistance to the conveyance and admission. In such circumstances, the preferred mode of transport remains by ambulance, although, if this is not possible, a suitable police vehicle may be used (Department of Health and Welsh Office, 1999: para. 11.7). A violent or dangerous patient should never be conveyed by car (1999: para. 11.6).

5.4.2 Is multidisciplinary teamwork possible?

The assumption behind the compulsory admission procedure is that the various persons involved can act effectively in tandem. The Code of Practice contemplates an approach based on teamwork and a 'framework of cooperation and mutual support' (Department of Health and Welsh Office, 1999: para. 2.3). The reality can be somewhat different. As already discussed, for example, GPs tend to accept that, in matters of psychiatric expertise, they are outranked by specialist psychiatrists, and the contemplated partnership between the specialist and the person with knowledge of the particular patient often fails to materialise. It is not unreasonable to conclude that the 'safeguard' of requiring two medical recommendations, apparent on the face of the 1983 Act, frequently does not exist in practice. This discrepancy between theory and practice can be seen in other aspects of the operation of the MHA 1983, such as the high number of s. 136 arrests that are not made in 'a place to which the public has access' (Rogers, 1990) or unlawful admissions that occur as a result of breaches of the letter of the 1983 Act by ASWs (Bean, 1980). These examples are, however, of improper uses of the 1983 Act *within* agencies or professions. Whilst here it is sufficient to say that the agency or profession does not always do what in law it should, a simple theory/practice opposition is not a sufficiently rigorous analytical model to understand compulsory admission as a dynamic process involving inter-agency cooperation.

A potential inpatient may be seen differently by each of those involved in the admission, as at once a legal actor with legal rights, a 'medical case', a 'social work problem', an actual or potential threat to public order, and a family member. It is worth pointing out that all of these perspectives are applied to the patient, and offer solutions defined by their understanding of the patient's problem and into which the patient is expected to fit himself or herself. The patient's own understanding of his or her problems is at risk of disappearing in the clash of the professional titans. These discourses may well offer competing rather than complementary interpretations of the situation at hand, each grounded in its own particular context and subject to its own imperatives and agendas, as well as the need to maintain, enhance, or acquire professional standing. To illustrate this argument, we shall look at the relationship between ASWs and psychiatrists, although similar sorts of argument may apply between any of the actors, both in informal and involuntary admissions. The relative importance of the discourses, and the nature of the tensions that result, will be a function of the individual case.

5.4.2.1 The interaction of doctors and social workers

The Percy Commission framework, intended to engender harmonious cooperation between ASWs and doctors, seems instead to have put into legislative form a relationship based on friction. In part this can be put down to the low esteem in which the two professions seem to hold each other (Cavadino, 1989: 114); in part, it is also a question of territory and power. For those who are medically qualified, the decision to admit is primarily a medical one, but the law usurps their clinical autonomy by giving ASWs a power of veto over the admission process. Moreover, under the terms of reference of the admission process, the recommending doctors are required to stray into the professional territory of the ASW, whilst the applicant is also required to state that the patient is suffering from mental disorder, notwithstanding that the applicant will not be trained in psychiatry. In addition, there do appear to be significant differences between ASWs and psychiatrists that are likely to exacerbate tensions. Bean (1980: 157), for example, found that social workers tend, on the whole, to rate patients lower in terms of dangerousness to others than do psychiatrists. For the psychiatrist, this displays either a lack of skill at diagnosis or a lack of realism in the social worker's assessment; for the ASW, it is more likely to be seen as the manifestation of civil liberties-based concerns, coupled with scepticism about the professional abilities of psychiatry to 'cure' patients.

It is important to realise, however, that such differences are more than of view; they are of perspective. ASWs bring to bear a social-work standpoint that may well be more influenced by concerns about autonomy and coercion, and even theses such as those of Szasz, Goffman and Foucault (Cavadino, 1989: 116). The hope of the Department of Health that a multi-agency approach to admission would work effectively fails to appreciate the non-transferability of knowledge or information across discursive contexts. There is a real sense in which doctors and ASWs, in their professional roles, do not talk the same language. Research shows that the two professions do, indeed, bring different 'models' of mental disorder to their task (Bean, 1980: 167) and this brings with it the risk of what Bean calls 'unstable interaction' (1980: 168), making the rule enforcement procedures unpredictable; this instability, Bean found, was lessened to the extent that the approved doctor took control of the situation, interviewing the patient with the GP and social worker, and supervising the transfer to hospital (*ibid.*). The role of the ASW was reduced to no more than a rubber stamp. Psychiatrists do, indeed, view themselves as the senior professionals involved, with ASWs occupying a subordinate role. Here is the dilemma for ASWs: either accept a subordinate role, which is a dereliction of the duty imposed under s. 13(1), and which in autopoietic terms reduces the ASW to the role of 'social worker-within-psychiatry' (King, 1991), but which may well mean that the admission process works relatively smoothly (if not always lawfully), or assert the independent nature of the social work role, and risk an unhappy working relationship with the psychiatrist and accept the resulting tensions and doctrinal inconsistencies in the admission process.

Peay's research examines the dynamics of decisions made jointly by ASWs and psychiatrists in detail. Her methodology involved forty pairs of ASWs and psychiatrists making decisions regarding admission of the same fictional patient, based on a mock clinical record-and-video interview. In analysing these decision-making processes, she does not find an ideal world where ASWs and psychiatrists respect and benefit from each other's expertise, but instead concludes that 'such good decision-making practices were not the common pattern' (Peay, 2003: 17). She describes a complex set of dynamics, leading to decisions of varying quality. Consistent with the view of professional discourses noted above, express reference to legal criteria was almost entirely absent (2003: 29). The outcome of these decisions was apparently based on broad ethical notions and interpersonal dynamics of the decision-makers, some related to professional values, some not. Unsurprisingly, therefore, the views of professionals within each profession differed markedly, and the decisions reached by the pairs were also notably inconsistent – a problem when an individual's civil rights are at stake.

Some in social work argue that a greater commitment by all involved parties to the concept of teamwork is the only way to rescue social workers from their secondary status in the compulsory admission process (Huxley, 1985), whilst others think that social work should strive to attain a position of professional status equal to that of psychiatrists by adopting an attitude of greater assertiveness in dealings with other professionals (Rabin and Zelner, 1992). We would argue that both strategies will be thwarted, not so much because the psychiatrist is on 'home turf' and in the dominant position (although this is, of course, important, as Rogers (1993) found in her research into the relationship between police officers and psychiatrists), but because the ultimate goal – of an effective working relationship – is simply not possible to achieve. If, however, this would seem to be the case in any particular instance (and the empirical literature throws up no examples), then we would suggest that, in the terminology of autopoiesis, it is the 'psychic' rather than 'social' actors who are communicating effectively, which means that the professionals involved must abandon their occupational discourses and interrelate instead as citizens. This would also seem to indicate that common ground is only found when professional perspectives and roles are abandoned in favour of a shared 'common sense' perspective, a 'common sense' language in which communication is possible. There are consequent theoretical problems, however: why would we involve professionals, only to require them to discard their professional roles? And if they discard these roles, will decisions really be made on a transparent and consistent basis?

5.4.3 Scrutiny and rectification of documents on arrival at hospital

A hospital may accept a patient if the application 'appears to be duly made and to be founded on the necessary medical recommendations' (s. 6(3), MHA 1983), and this will involve the formal receipt of the various documents connected with the admission. Again following Victorian precedent, admission documents are to be routinely scrutinised, with rectification of some defects possible in some circumstances. The Victorian justification for this process was to ensure both the civil rights of those unjustifiably confined, but also to avoid the release of those appropriately confined, but by documents with technical defects. Without these provisions, such technical improprieties might, in Victorian times, have allowed parishes or poor law unions to escape payment of maintenance fees to the county asylum. In modern times, the process serves to protect the hospital from litigation flowing from the confinement, a function also served in Victorian private sector care.

Rectification of documents is considered at length in Keywood (1996). The receipt, scrutiny and rectification of admission documents should be conducted by staff specifically delegated for the purpose and knowledgeable about the relevant law (Department of Health and Welsh Office, 1999: para. 12.1). Because 24-hour cover is required for this function, it may, in appropriate circumstances, be delegated to senior nursing staff. The function of the receiving officer is specifically phrased in juxtaposition to rectification (1999: para. 12.3(b)): 'to detect errors which cannot be corrected at a later stage in the procedure.' Accuracy is to be checked with the applicant, if an ASW. The Act allows a 14-day window for this purpose at the beginning of the confinement (s. 15(1)), but the Code of Practice makes it clear that it should occur either immediately upon admission, or on the next working day, if admission occurs at night, on weekends or public holidays when appropriate staff are unavailable (1999: para. 12.4(a)) The medical certificates are to be scrutinised medically, to ensure that they show adequate grounds for confinement (1999: para. 12.4(b)).

The powers to 'rectify' a document authorising the admission and detention of a person under Part II are contained in s. 15(1), and seem broad. An application form, or any documentation relating to the medical recommendations upon which the application in question is founded, which 'is found to be in any respect incorrect or defective' may, with the consent of the hospital managers, be amended by the person who signed it. In addition, if a medical certificate is found wanting in either form or substance, it may be replaced with a fresh and proper one (s. 15(2)), with the exception that s. 15(2) may not be used when medical certificates identify different mental disorders in violation of s. 11(6), in documentation in support of a s. 3 admission for treatment: s. 15(3).

The powers in s. 15(1) have, however, been interpreted fairly restrictively by the courts. In *R* v *South Western Hospital Managers, ex p M* [1994] 1 All ER 161 (HC) it was said (at p. 177) that the rectification process is limited to errors or omissions on the face of the various documents. This means, for example, that s. 15(1) cannot be used if the social worker or doctor does not have legal status to sign the certificate. In the case of the doctor, of course, a new certificate might be sought from a different doctor under s. 15(2); this option will not be available if the social worker is not 'approved', as defined by the Act. Jones (2006: 105) suggests that an unsigned admission document cannot be rectified, and this is also the view of the Department of Health (Department of Health and Welsh Office, 1998: para. 46) because an unsigned document 'cannot be regarded as an application or medical recommendation'. By extension, rectification cannot cure a failure to include one of the required forms, so that, for example, a purported admission for treatment supported by only one medical opinion cannot be saved because it requires two such opinions. Finally, rectification is unable to cure a defect that has arisen because a necessary event in the procedural chain has simply not taken place: *ex p M* (see earlier). Thus, in that case, consultation with the wrong person as the NR could not be rectified. A similar reading of rectification was reached in *Re S-C (Mental Patient: Habeas Corpus)* [1996] 1 All ER 532 (CA) by Bingham MR, who held (at p. 537) that the rectification procedure cannot be used to correct 'a fundamentally defective application'. This would seem to limit rectification to cases of inaccurate record-taking, and not to papering over procedural improprieties. The Memorandum gives examples of the sorts of defects that can be rectified. These are: the leaving of blank spaces or the failure to delete inapplicable alternatives (relating, for example, to the particular ground in ss. 2 or 3 upon which the admission is based); inaccuracies in recording the name of the patient (Department of Health and Welsh Office, 1998: para. 48).

The receiving examination may be successful at identifying this type of defect, but it is difficult to see that it will be successful at identifying defects not apparent on the face of the documents. It would not, for example, have identified the deficiency in consultation with the NR, which was the issue in *ex p M* (for facts, see earlier in this chapter). The result places admission staff in a difficult position. It is perhaps for this reason that, in *ex p M*, Laws J held that, although the conveyance to hospital in that case was not lawful because there had been a failure to consult the patient's NR, and the test in s. 6(1), being objective, such that, for a conveyance to be lawful, the application must be 'duly completed', this did not affect the legality of the patient's subsequent detention, which requires only that the application 'appears to be duly made': s. 6(3). The Court of Appeal in Re SC held that Laws J had been wrong to hold that, if s. 6(3) is complied with, the patient's detention is lawful, notwithstanding a failure to comply with s. 6(1), because this involved a non sequitur (the assumption that, because there was a power to detain, an unlawful admission was rendered lawful). Laws J's analysis was in all other respects explicitly approved by Bingham MR (at p. 156), and by a unanimous Court of Appeal in St George's Healthcare NHS Trust (see earlier in this chapter). Thus, there is nothing in any of these cases to contradict the view expressed in the Memorandum (Department of Health and Welsh Office, 1998: para. 46) that 'the officer scrutinising the form may take statements at face value', and as long as this is done, the hospital will be protected from any liability if it is subsequently shown that the admission was flawed in some way. This raises the question of how a patient is able to challenge detention on grounds that it is in some, less than obvious, way unlawful.

5.5 Challenging the legality of admission under Part II

5.5.1 Challenging the legality of admission by way of an application to a mental health review tribunal

The main mechanism in the MHA 1983 by which patients may challenge the legality of their detention in hospital is the Mental Health Review Tribunal (MHRT) (for detailed discussion of the tribunal system, see Chapter 8). Tribunals must order the immediate discharge of any patients detained under Part II of the Act if the criteria for admission cannot be made out to the satisfaction of the tribunal. There is also a general discretion to order the discharge of a Part II patient 'in any case': s. 72(1). The established wisdom is, however, that MHRTs do not have jurisdiction to hear applications relating to the admission of a person into a hospital, but are instead limited to considering whether grounds for continued detention exist. This is because s. 72(1) limits the consideration of a MHRT in the exercise of its duty to discharge to the situation 'then' pertaining. This reading of the power of MHRTs is based on dicta of Ackner LJ in R v Hallstrom and Anor, ex p W [1985] 3 ALL ER 775 (CA), at 784–5. Ackner LJ based his view on two distinct elements: as well as the relevance of the use of 'then' in s. 72(1), it was also the case that a MHRT, because it must hear applications from persons 'liable to be detained', is not competent to hear an application from a person whose detention is defective.

As Eldergill (1997: 575) has pointed out, however, Neill and Glidewell LJJ expressly declined to express an opinion on the point in that case, which was in any case only of obiter status, and in the earlier case of Re VE (Mental Health Patient) [1973] 1 QB 452, the Court of Appeal held that a MHRT should discharge a patient if the initial admission had been flawed. It must be conceded that Re V is not on all fours with the situation under discussion here. That case was decided under the 1959 Act, which provided that no application for admission for treatment for psychopathy could be made in respect of patients over the age of 21. V, a 40-year-old patient, had been admitted for treatment diagnosed as suffering from mental illness. On her application to a MHRT for discharge, the tribunal declined to make the order sought, but came to the opinion that she had been wrongly diagnosed and the correct diagnosis was psychopathy. The question arose whether, given that if V had been so diagnosed initially, she would not have been liable to be detained, the tribunal should have ordered discharge consequent upon reclassifying her mental disorder. The Court of Appeal decided that, in such a situation, the patient must be discharged. There is no scope under the 1983 Act for holding that a patient in such a situation 'must' be discharged, because the criteria for mandatory discharge are closely defined by that Act (and the Mental Health (Amendment) Act 1975 was enacted to overrule *Re V* to the extent that it placed an *obligation* on MHRTs to discharge in similar circumstances). But to put the case at its lowest, *Re V* arguably supports the view that such issues may be considered by a MHRT, including whether to exercise its discretion to discharge. On the other hand, as Eldergill concedes, a narrow reading of *Re V* would find it consistent with the conventional view, that discharge may be ordered when a patient's detention is no longer justified, as opposed to it being authority to examine the initial admission, which is thought to be confined to the High Court in the exercise of its powers of judicial review and habeas corpus (see below).

There is nothing in the MHA 1983, however, that limits the discretion of MHRTs to discharge; to concede that only the High Court may quash an admission does not mean that a MHRT may not order discharge, because this is not the same thing at all. That a patient may not in law be 'liable to be detained' because of some flaw in the admission process does not mean that a person *in fact* detained is not *liable* to be detained by the hospital managers at that point, on the basis of s. 6(3) (see earlier in this chapter). Eldergill (1997: 591) concludes, on the basis of these and other less substantial points, that there is no reason why a tribunal should not be able to consider the legality of an admission to hospital in the context of its discretionary powers of discharge, but that the views of Ackner LJ are now so well established that, if 'unconsidered', the best practical advice is that this view prevails, so that 'the tribunal must confine its attention to those matters expressly referred to in section 72' (1997: 591). This is an unfortunate conclusion: to limit the discretion of a tribunal is also to limit the chances for release of detained patients. Elsewhere in the Act – in the powers of hospital managers and doctors to make an order for discharge, for example (see Chapter 8) – discretionary power to release is not fettered in this way. Moreover, as a technical legal matter, where, as here, there seems to be some ambiguity about the scope of a statutory provision, it should be resolved in favour of the liberty of the subject. Technical arguments should not be employed to defeat this principle, even if they can 'technically' be made.

Nevertheless, such an argument has not yet been accepted by a court, and until such time as it is, the only option open to a patient to challenge the legality of his or her admission, short of absconding (see Chapter 8) has been to look to the High Court, and request that it exercise its (discretionary) powers of judicial review or issue a writ of habeas corpus. The traditional explanation of the difference between the two is that, although there is an area of potential overlap, judicial review is the appropriate avenue by which to challenge a decision that its maker was lawfully empowered to make but which has been made unlawfully, for example, by taking into account some irrelevant factor, whereas habeas corpus should be used when the claim is that there was no juris-diction for a decision to hold a person in custody. The traditional similarity between them is that neither is an appeal against the merits of a decision but each rather consti-tutes an examination of the procedures that must be gone through in decision-making, or of the accuracy of facts upon which an admission is based. In essence, this explan-ation remains correct, but the impact of the Human Rights Act 1998 now requires that the traditional explanation be qualified somewhat.

5.5.2 The writ of habeas corpus

'Habeas corpus' approximates to 'you must have the body', and is an ancient prerogative writ, which can be found in Magna Carta, designed to protect persons from illegal detention, whether in prison, hospital or some other place. It requires the person having custody of the applicant to present the body of that person before a court and show legal cause for the detention. An admission to hospital will be unlawful if some condition precedent is not satisfied. An example is provided by *St George's Healthcare NHS Trust* (see earlier in this chapter). S had been admitted under s. 2 after presenting at a primary healthcare centre to register with a GP. S was 36 weeks pregnant. Pre-eclampsia was diagnosed and S was advised that there was a risk to herself and to her baby, and that a caesarean section operation was necessary; S refused to give her consent to this procedure. She was seen by an ASW and two doctors and quickly admitted to a mental hospital, then transferred to another hospital, at which the operation was per-formed and a child delivered. A week later, having returned to the mental hospital, S's detention under s. 2 was terminated and she immediately discharged herself. The Court of Appeal held that S's admission to hospital had been unlawful because it had been prompted by concerns about her pregnancy and not by the question of whether or not she warranted hospitalisation for any mental disorder. The ASW and recommending doctors had not turned their minds to that question. Therefore, it could not be shown that S was suffering from mental disorder. This was a precedent fact that had not been established and, had S not already been discharged, she would have been entitled to apply for a writ of habeas corpus 'which would have led to her immediate release' (753).

The applicability and scope of an action for habeas corpus was discussed by the Court of Appeal in *Re S-C* (see earlier in this chapter). S-C had been admitted to hospital under s. 3, pursuant to an application for admission made by an ASW who had consulted S-C's mother as NR, knowing that, in law, her NR was actually her father, and that he objected to her admission. Sir Thomas Bingham MR held that, in such a case, a writ of habeas corpus could be made. Although hospital managers are entitled to rely on an application for admission that 'appears to be duly made' by virtue of s. 6(3), and are therefore protected from a claim of false imprisonment, the initial admission remained unlawful. As mentioned earlier in the chapter, the contrary view of Laws J in *ex p M* was explicitly overruled on this point as, presumably by implication, were other cases inconsistent with this ruling, such as *R v Governor of Broadmoor, ex p Argles* (1974), unreported (see Gunn, 1986: 295). The Master of the Rolls held that, were it otherwise, the 'horrifying' result would be that, as long as an application for admission *appeared to be* lawful, it would be so, whatever failures or omissions lay behind the face of the document. Even so, a writ was not issued in *Re S-C*, because the hospital managers were not before the court and the case was adjourned for a week to allow them to appear and show cause for S-C's continued detention (in the event, S-C was discharged in the interim and the court made no order).

Thus, although on one level *Re S-C* amounted to a reassertion of the applicability of habeas corpus to unlawful detention in a hospital, it also demonstrates that, even on a successful application, it does not necessarily follow that the patient's immediate release will be forthcoming. Later cases have followed this pattern. In *Re John (Julie)* [1998] COD 306 (DC) a patient, J, had been detained under s. 3 although her NR had not been consulted. When J's solicitor questioned the legality of her detention, the s. 3 detention was discharged, and she was held under s. 5(2) before being 'readmitted' under s. 2. It seemed clear that the reason for the admission under s. 2 was that J's NR was known not to be prepared to consent to her admission, and so the use of ss. 5(2) and 2 was in the manner of a holding operation until J's NR could be replaced. It was held that her detention under s. 2 was prima facie lawful and, because those who had engineered it were not available to be cross-examined as to their motives, J's application for habeas corpus had to be dismissed. The judgment carries the danger of implying that, as long as those who play fast and loose with the statutory scheme stay away from court, there will be no effective (that is, immediate) sanction (although this decision probably does not survive that of the Court of Appeal in *Wilkinson*, see below). In *Re Briscoe* [1998] COD 402 (HC), in which an application was, in theory at least, successful, the court followed *Re S-C* in allowing the hospital managers in question two days to show why the writ should not be made, because the court was concerned that immediate release would be anti-therapeutic. Thus, habeas corpus, even when successfully pleaded, cannot be relied upon as a mechanism to secure immediate release, even if it is clear that a precedent fact, such as the duty to consult with the patient's NR prior to making the application, has not been satisfied.

This is unfortunate. Without an order for immediate release, the writ loses its potency. Moreover, the courts have also been keen to emphasise the limits of the scope of the habeas corpus. In *Whitbread v Kingston and District NHS Trust* (1997), *The Times*, 14 July (CA), a patient sought a writ on the grounds the consultation that an ASW must have with the patient's NR before making an admission for treatment (s.11(4)) must, as had not happened in this case, follow the interview with the patient required by s.11(5). The Court of Appeal held that there was no necessary chrono-logical sequence that the various requirements of a compulsory admission must adhere to: it is enough that they are all complied with. The court emphasised that it is only when there has been some non-compliance (or fraud) that a writ for habeas corpus will go. In *Barker* v *Barking Havering and Brentwood Community Healthcare NHS Trust* [1999] 1 FLR 106, the Court of Appeal played down the advantages of habeas corpus and emphasised the wider range of remedies available by way of judicial review (see below), and withdrew somewhat from the position that had been taken in *Re S-C*, in which the ground that was 'appropriately' covered by habeas corpus had been drawn fairly widely. Lord Woolf MR expressed a strong preference that, wherever possible, actions should be commenced by way of an application for judicial review, unless it is clear that an action for habeas corpus was the only appropriate action. Such situations will be rare: habeas corpus has always been a remedy of last resort, to be used only when all avenues have been exhausted. Thus, in *T* v *Chase Farm Hospital* 2000 WL 1479976 (HC), T, who had been granted conditional discharge from a hospital but had not been released, sought a writ of habeas corpus on the basis that her health had improved to the extent that, at her next tribunal hearing, she should be entitled to absolute discharge. The court held that habeas corpus could not be used as a mechanism to pre-empt the decision of the tribunal, and would not allow the application to proceed.

Unlike with judicial review (see below), the effects of the Human Rights Act 1998 in terms of developing the writ of habeas corpus in this context have, to date, been minimal. Indeed, the 1998 Act may mark the virtual extinction of habeas corpus applications, at least in the context of detention by reason of mental disorder, because the requirements of Art. 5 ECHR, brought into domestic law by the Act, cover much the same ground. Under Art. 5(1)(e), the detention of a person of 'unsound mind' must be 'lawful', and the European Court has recently reiterated that 'the Convention here refers essentially to national law and lays down the obligation to conform to the substantive and procedural rules of national law': *Hutchinson Reid* v *UK* (2003) 37 EHRR 21 at para. 46. Article 5(1)(e) also requires that it be 'convincingly shown' by reference to objective evidence that the detained person is suffering from 'unsound mind': *Winterwerp* v *The Netherlands* (1979) 2 EHRR 387. Article 5(4) requires that: 'Everyone who is deprived of his liberty by arrest or detention shall be entitled to take proceedings by which the lawfulness of his detention shall be decided speedily by a court and his release ordered if the detention is not lawful.' Damages are also payable for breach of a Convention right, but not on a successful habeas corpus application. Between them, these requirements obviate the need for the writ of habeas corpus.

Certainly, there has only been a trickle of cases following the coming into force of the 1998 Act. In *Re C (Mental Patient: Habeas Corpus)* [2002] EWHC 243 Admin, C sought a writ of habeas corpus on the basis that a tribunal had not properly considered medical evidence indicating that he should be released from hospital. The court, following *T* v *Chase Farm Hospital*, held that such matters were for the tribunal (from the decision of which there is the possibility of both review and, under s. 78(8) of the 1983 Act, appeal: see Chapter 8) and dismissed the application. In *R* v *Hospital Managers of Royal Park Hospital, ex p FTT* [2003] EWCA Civ 330, the Court of Appeal upheld the decision of the High Court, that there was no action for habeas corpus when two of three members of a committee appointed by a hospital to review a patient's detention were of the view that a patient should be discharged, but their view was vetoed by the third member. The main significance of this case here is that, although it involved an application for habeas corpus, there is no discussion of this power in the judgment, whereas the court does consider the situation under Art. 5.

Moreover, it is not just that Art. 5 is increasingly being used when previously an application for habeas corpus would have been made. It is also the case that the scope of habeas corpus has been held to fail to comply with the requirements of the Article. In *HL v UK* (2005) 40 EHRR 32, para. 137, the European Court held that habeas corpus was in breach of Art. 5(4) 'as not being wide enough to bear on those conditions which were essential for the "lawful" detention of a person on the basis of unsoundness of mind since it did not allow a determination of the merits of the question as to whether the mental disorder persisted', applying its own earlier judgment in *X v UK* (1982) 4 EHRR 118, which is to the same effect. Decisions such as this, and in the domestic courts in cases such as *Wilkinson* (see below) may push a habeas corpus hearing more in the direction of a full merits review than would otherwise have been the case, but it seems more likely that, given its 'last resort' status, habeas corpus will continue its slide into relative obscurity in this area, even if it remains alive and well as a useful mechanism for other constituencies, such as prisoners and, in particular, persons seeking to challenge extradition orders (see, for example, *De Sousa v Portugal* [2006] EWHC 455).

5.5.3 Judicial review

5.5.3.1 The remedies available and access to them

The basis of the High Court's contemporary powers of judicial review is also to be found in the ancient prerogative powers of the Crown. In essence, 'judicial review' refers to the High Court's powers to examine decisions taken on behalf of the state (including central and local government and the various state agencies, such as the National Health Service), in order to determine whether such decisions have been properly made. These powers give litigants access, if successful, to an impressive array of remedies. These are:

- *certiorari* – the power to quash (nullify) a decision;
- *mandamus* – the power to compel a public authority to perform a public duty, to consider a matter that does fall within its remit, or to reconsider a matter in which it has been judged to have acted unlawfully;
- *prohibition* is a lesser used, but sometimes extremely useful, power to prevent an unlawful action by way of an injunction.

The court may also make an award for damages, by virtue of s. 31(4), Supreme Court Act 1981 and r. 54, Civil Procedure Rules 1998. The provision of an appropriate remedy on a successful application for judicial review is technically discretionary, but there is a 'very limited ambit [to] that discretion in practice when the liberty of the subject is at stake' (per Sir Thomas Bingham MR in *Re S-C* at 153), and the High Court must now give reasons for refusing to grant relief on a successful application: s. 31(6), Supreme Court Act 1981 and r. 54, CPR 1998. Access to these remedies has, however, tradition-ally been limited by technical requirements, and by the courts' view of their role.

As far as technical requirements are concerned, there are three. The first is that judi-cial review, as a public law mechanism, applies only to the policies and actions of those operating using public law powers or performing a public law function. As Gunn (1986a) notes, that decisions relating to the compulsory admission of a person into a mental hospital are amenable to judicial review seems simply been assumed by the courts. But that assumption is not contentious, because decisions taken under the authority of the MHA 1983 are, as is normally required, administrative decisions grounded in statutory power (*Council of Civil Service Unions* per Lord Diplock at 949). What is more contentious is the application of judicial review to the private sector, which, as seen as Chapter 3, has grown markedly over recent years as much residential provision has been contracted out by local authorities. In *R v Leonard Cheshire Foundation (LCF), ex p Heather* [2002] 2 ALL ER 936, [2002] HRLR 30, the Court of Appeal held that judicial review is the appropriate mechanism by which to determine whether a particular body, in this case, a charity providing residential accommodation in the community, can be said to be performing a public function (Woolf CJ at para. 38). But the court held that LCF, in accommodating residents that would otherwise have been accommodated by the local authority pursuant to its duty in s. 21, National Assistance Act 1948 (see further Chapter 9), which provision the authority had con-tracted out to the Foundation under the powers to do so in s. 26 of the same Act, was not performing a public function. Nor was it a 'public authority' under s. 6, Human Rights Act 1998, and as such, did not have to comply with Convention rights (in this case, the right to family life in Art. 8, said by the applicants to have been breached by LFC's decision to close their accommodation). The local authority clearly is a public authority for these purposes, but had not breached Art. 8 in its decision to contract out the provision of accommodation to LCF (see also *R v Havering LBC, ex p Johnson* [2006] EWHC 1714, discussed in Chapter 9).

On the scope of 'public authority' under s. 6 of the 1998 Act, and also, by implication, the scope of 'public function' for judicial review purposes, Woolf CJ held all that had been contracted out was the mechanism for service delivery, not the duty to provide the service (para. 33) and for a private body to provide services to, or on behalf of, a public body did not make that private body a public one. His consolation prize to the appli-cants, that once the High Court has determined that judicial review is not available it may use the powers in Part 54.20, CPR 1998 to transfer proceedings elsewhere for their private law rights to be ascertained, is little comfort, because it is not clear, in the absence of a clear promise not to close the home (see Chapter 9), that any of the private law rights of the applicants have been infringed.

This is a significant decision that denies both judicial review and Convention rights to the many thousands of persons living in independent sector care homes (see Chapter 3 and Markus, 2003), notwithstanding that they would otherwise, as was the case until the last few years, most frequently be housed in local authority accommodation. Consideration must, however, be given to the precise fact situation. The Court of Appeal in *LCF* distinguished its earlier decision in *Poplar Housing and Regeneration Community Association Ltd* v *Donoghue* [2001] 3 WLR 183, in which it had been held that, as a local authority housing department and a private housing association had become so closely intertwined that they effectively operated as one unit, actions taken by the housing association were amenable to judicial review. Shortly after the Court of Appeal gave its judgment in *LCF* , Keith J held in the High Court, in *R* v *Partnerships in Care Ltd, ex p A* [2002] 1 WLR 2610 that a patient, in a privately run care home in which she was detained under s. 3 of the MHA 1983, could challenge a decision to change the focus of the care provided in the home by way of judicial review.

LCF was considered at first instance by Keith J (who, as a High Court judge is not bound by the decision of other High Court judges at first instance), but the appeal was not mentioned. Arguably therefore *ex p A* is *per incuriam*, particularly as the House of Lords [2002] 2 ALL ER 936 subsequently refused permission to appeal. On the other hand, it may be that, as that case involved detained patients and Keith J found a public interest in the care of such patients, *LCF* is distinguishable in any case. But it is not a point of distinction that we would support. From the point of view of service users – some of whom will have been placed in residential accommodation by local authorities or NHS bodies, and some of whom will fund their own placements, and who may be housed by local authorities, NHS bodies or independent sector providers – the precise mechanism by which their accommodation is provided is a mere technical matter. However it is achieved, there should be equity of respect for the human and moral rights of service users.

The second technical requirement is that the leave of the High Court must be sought under s. 31(3) Supreme Court Act 1981 and the CPR 1998 before an application for judicial review can be brought. As leave is not required for an application for a writ of habeas corpus, the decision in *Barker* (above), that proceeding by way of judicial review is to be preferred, can be seen as a mechanism to monitor applications before they reach a substantive hearing. The purpose of the requirement of seeking leave is to screen out 'groundless, unmeritorious or tardy harassment' (*O'Reilly* v *MackMan* [1982] 3 ALL ER 1124, per Lord Diplock at 1133) of those charged with exercising statutory responsibilities. Leave will be granted if the patient can show that his or her complaint is worthy of fuller investigation: see *IRC* v *National Federation of Self-Employed and Small Businesses Ltd* 2 ALL ER 93 (HL).

The third requirement comprises the hurdle potentially presented by s. 139(2), MHA 1983. This provides that no civil proceedings may be brought without the leave of the High Court, and, by s. 139(1), that if leave is given liability can only be established if bad faith or lack of reasonable care can be shown (see Chapter 12). In *R* v *Hallstrom and Anor, ex p W (No.1)* [1985] 3 ALL ER 775 (CA), however, it was held that judicial review did not constitute 'civil proceedings' and therefore s. 139 did not apply. Hence, a patient will only need to seek leave once and will not need to show bad faith or negligence (as would be the case under s. 139(2): *Kynaston* v *Secretary of State for Home Affairs* [1981] 73 Cr App R 281, per Lawton LJ at 285) to succeed on the substantive application. An example of a successful challenge to the legality of an admission under s. 3 is provided by *Hallstrom*, in which a patient's detention was renewed only in order that immediate leave of absence be given, as a device to get around the embargo on treatment without consent in the community (see Chapter 8). Gunn (1986: 293) gives the example of an application for admission made by a NR, the main purpose of which was to get the patient out of their house for the NR's benefit as another situation in which an order for *certiorari* might properly be made.

5.5.3.2 Substantive powers of review

Judicial review has traditionally proceeded in line with the constitutional orthodoxy, that Parliament is sovereign, and has a political mandate to make law and to delegate that power, and to give decision-making powers to various state agencies and their officials. In the light of this, the appropriate task of a court of judicial review is not, in general terms, to consider the substantive content of any law, policy or decision, but merely to review the manner and process of its making. In *Council of Civil Service Unions* v *Minister for the Civil Service* [1984] 3 ALL ER 935 (HL), Lord Diplock said (at 950) that the main three heads of judicial review, which are neither discrete nor necessarily exhaustive, are:

- *illegality* – the decision-maker does not have the legal authority to make the decision, for example, by reason of lack of required qualifications, or has failed to exercise a discretionary power;

- *irrationality* – a decision-maker cannot use a power, given for one purpose, for another purpose, and cannot consider irrelevant, or fail to consider relevant, information, or make a decision which is so unreasonable that no other decision maker in a similar situation could make it (this test is known as '*Wednesbury* unreasonableness', after the case, *Associated Provincial Picture Houses Ltd* v *Wednesbury Corpn* [1948] 1 KB 223);

- *procedural impropriety* – if the statute giving the power or duty in question prescribes procedures, a decision will be reviewable if those procedures are not followed; decisions must accord with the principles of natural justice, such as the right to a hearing, the right to impartiality and freedom from bias in decision-making, and a (circumscribed and far from general) right to know reasons for a decision.

In practice, it is the *Wednesbury* test that has been the most important element of the substantive powers of judicial review, because it has been taken to mean, in the words of Lord Cooke of Thornton in *R* v *Secretary of State for the Home Department, ex p Daly* [2001] 2 AC 532 (HL), at para. 32, that 'there are degrees of unreasonableness and that only a very extreme degree can bring an administrative decision within the legitimate scope of judicial invalidation'. It is true that the test was developed to some extent by the decision in *R* v *Ministry of Defence, ex p Smith* [1996] QB 517 (CA), in which it was held that, in cases involving human rights, the courts should carry out a 'heightened scrutiny' of the policy or decision in question, which came to be known as the 'Super-

Wednesbury test'. The policy in question in that case was that which provided that homosexuality in the armed forces undermines morale and threatens security and so homosexuality constitutes grounds for dismissal from the forces. The House of Lords carried out an 'anxious scrutiny' of the policy but found it to be lawful.

It is now possible, however, to talk of 'the death of *Wednesbury*' (O'Doherty, 2003), and the reason for this is the impact of the Human Rights Act 1998 on the nature and scope of judicial review proceedings. A year or so before the 1998 Act came into force (October 2000), the European Court of Human Rights found, in the case of *Smith and Grady* v *UK* (1999) 20 EHRR 493, that the system of judicial review in England and Wales, as applied in *ex p Smith*, was in breach of Art. 13 of the ECHR, which guarantees that national courts will provide a remedy for breach of substantive Convention rights. This was because the '*Wednesbury* reasonableness' or 'irrationality' test did not allow the courts to consider whether the human rights of the applicant had been breached and, if so, whether for good cause and in an appropriate manner.

After the passage of the Human Rights Act, the House of Lords was given the opportunity to clarify the approach to be taken in *R* v *Secretary of State for the Home Department, ex p Daly* [2001] 2 AC 532 (HL). The House confirmed that courts hearing judicial review cases must now 'themselves form a judgment whether a Convention right has been breached (conducting such enquiry as is necessary to form that judgment) and, so far as permissible under the [Human Rights] Act, grant an effective remedy' (Lord Bingham at 546). This means that courts must now consider (i) if an applicant's human rights have been breached, and if so, (ii) whether the reason for this is permitted by the Convention, and if so, (iii) whether the infringement of the applicant's right is proportionate to the harm that it thereby seeks to avoid. The English courts have long resisted the continental principle of proportionality, but now it is part of domestic law. In *Daly*, Lord Steyn (at 547) considered the implications of this for judicial review. He said:

there is an overlap between the traditional grounds of review and the approach of proportionality. Most cases would be decided in the same way whichever approach is adopted. But the intensity of review is somewhat greater under the proportionality approach. Making due allowance for important structural differences between various convention rights, which I do not propose to discuss, a few generalisations are perhaps permissible. I would mention three concrete differences without suggesting that my statement is exhaustive. First, the doctrine of proportionality may require the reviewing court to assess the balance which the decision maker has struck, not merely whether it is within the range of rational or reasonable decisions. Secondly, the proportionality test may go further than the traditional grounds of review inasmuch as it may require attention to be directed to the relative weight accorded to interests and considerations. Thirdly, even the heightened scrutiny test developed in *R* v *Ministry of Defence, ex p Smith* [1996] QB 517, is not necessarily appropriate to the protection of human rights.

As such, although 'This does not mean that there has been a shift to merits review' (548), nevertheless 'the intensity of the review . . . is guaranteed by the twin requirements that the limitation of the right was necessary in a democratic society, in the sense of meeting a pressing social need, and the question whether the interference was really proportionate to the legitimate aim being pursued' (at 548). Moreover, the intensity of the review is dependent on the subject matter (548): 'In law, context is everything.'

The situation has clearly changed following this decision, although as Starmer (2003: 21) notes, the ramifications of *Daly* are not yet clear. One issue that needs to be unpacked is the concept of proportionality, particularly as it differs from a full merits review. In *Smith and Grady*, the European Court, in the name of proportionality and review, had analysed and rejected a report by the Ministry of Defence's Homosexuality Policy Assessment Team, which purported to demonstrate support for the reasons justifying the policy of excluding homosexuals from the armed forces, thus concluding that a breach of the applicants' Art. 8 rights to respect for privacy had not been justified by the UK government. If this is a review, rather than an assessment of the UK's policy on the merits, then, as Leigh (2002: 271) puts it, 'Nevertheless, the narrowness of the margin conceded by the court [between review and appeal on the merits] collapses the distinction practically to vanishing point'. The same point can be illustrated by reference to the post-*Daly* decision of the Court of Appeal in *R v RMO, Broadmoor Hospital and Ors, ex p Wilkinson* [2001] EWCA CIV 1545 (discussed in detail in Chapter 7). In that case, the Court of Appeal, purportedly following *Daly*, held that, at least when a detained mental patient's Art. 3 rights to freedom from inhuman or degrading treatment are jeopardised, in the words of Hale LJ (at para. 83), 'Super-*Wednesbury* is not enough. The appellant is entitled to a proper hearing, on the merits, of whether the statutory grounds for imposing this treatment upon him against his will are made out'. How is this to be understood?

One mechanism, employed by Lord Nolan in *R v Secretary of State for the Environment, Transport and the Regions, ex p Alconbury* [2001] 2 WLR 1389 (HL) at para. 61, is to make a distinction between a hearing 'on the merits', which is really an appeal on the substance of the policy or decision in question – impermissible according to *Daly* – and a review 'of the merits'; this does not really answer Leigh's point. A better answer is that proportionality of review, when 'context is everything', means that, at one end of the scale, there may be little distinction between the proportionality approach and the traditional *Wednesbury* approach, while at the other end, there is little difference between review of the merits and review on the merits. As a rule of thumb, for example, a specific claimed breach of human rights should be subject to a more intensive scrutiny than more general matters of policy. The battle between conservative, moderate and more radical elements of the judiciary is ongoing, however (see *R v Secretary of State for the Home Department, ex p Samoo* [2001] UKHRR 1150, in which the import of *Daly* was minimised by Dyson LJ in the Court of Appeal; see also Leigh, 2002: 276–7). It is, as yet, too early to predict with certainty just where the dust will settle, particularly as the senior judiciary are still uncertain of the extent to which constitutional questions require them to adopt an attitude of deference to their various political masters in Westminster and elsewhere in Europe (Thompson, 2005), although, as Lord Bingham stated in *A v SSHD* [2004] UKHL 56, [2005] 2 AC 68, [2005] 2 WLR 87, [2005] 3 All ER 169 at para. 29, when a decision is more legal than political (as will usually be the case in the context of mental health law), deference must not stop the courts from performing their constitutional responsibility to clarify the law and protect the rights of citizens.

The second question that is posed, rather than answered, by *Daly* relates to Lord Steyn's mention that his discussion of proportionality bracketed 'important structural differences between various convention rights, which I do not propose to discuss'. This seems to be a reference to the fact that the principle of proportionality only figures in the reasoning of the European Court in cases in which it is mandated by the Convention. Articles 2, 3, 4 and 7 may not be breached on grounds of proportionality, and it would be 'wholly inappropriate' (Leigh, 2002: 277) if the national courts were to begin to allow 'proportionate' breaches of these rights to stand. This seems to mean that for these Convention rights at least, on the merits, review or appeal is required, which as we have seen, chimes with the decision of the Court of Appeal in *Wilkinson*. On the other hand, case law subsequent to *Wilkinson* has rather reduced the impact of that decision, by limiting the circumstances in which a substantive hearing will be ordered, and by lowering the threshold necessary to satisfy the Convention requirement (imposed in *Winterwerp*) to 'convincingly show' the court that the breach in question is necessary (see Chapter 7). This, arguably, is to reintroduce proportionality through the back door, so that where there is a prima facie justification for a breach, the case is unlikely to get to court and unlikely to be successful if it does.

The applicant in *Wilkinson* sought to have his case heard by the European Court of Human Rights, essentially arguing that the law as enunciated by the Court of Appeal did not sufficiently protect his human rights under Arts. 3, 6, and 8 of the Convention. However, in 2006 the Court declared his various claims inadmissible (*Wilkinson v UK*, application no 14659/02). In summary, then, it can be said that, despite the changes in approach that have already taken place, the precise effects of the 1998 Act on the operation of judical review remain uncertain.

5.5.4 Section 6(1) of the Human Rights Act 1998

In addition to requiring changes to the way in which judicial review functions, the Human Rights Act 1998 also introduced, in s. 6(1), a requirement that public authorities must not act in a way incompatible with a Convention right, and s. 7(1) allows a 'victim' of a breach of a Convention right by a public authority to bring an action against it, and if a breach of s. 6(1) is found, damages or some other suitable remedy is available under s. 8 of the 1998 Act. Section 6(1), in itself, can be seen as adding a new head of redress to judicial review when it is the use of a discretionary power that is at issue. But it also provides a directly enforceable remedy for breach of human rights by a public authority in and of itself. Although what counts as a 'public authority' has been narrowly defined (see earlier in the chapter), those various government agencies that provide services for the mentally disordered are clearly covered by the term. It is true that s. 6 in these circumstances provides no better protection of Arts. 5, 6, 8, 9, and 10 than does judicial review, because, in any case, the terms of the Convention allow breaches if proportionate, and if 'necessary in a democratic society in the interests of national security, public safety or the economic well-being of the country, for the prevention of disorder or crime, for the protection of health or morals, or for the protection of the rights and freedoms of others' (see Arts. 8(2) and 9(2). In fact, for Arts. 5 and 6, more precise criteria apply).

But for Arts. 2, 3, 4 and 7, in respect of which the Convention allows no breach, there is a very strong case, given the plain wording of s. 6(1), that nothing less than full merits review of the substance of the decision in question is permissible under the terms of the 1998 Act, whatever the approach taken on judicial review. It remains to be seen how these powers develop in future. There are advocates of both fusion and separate development of the common law and Convention rights amongst the judiciary. It can be said that we are witnessing something of a 'Europeanization' of judicial review in the UK (Hilson, 2003), but where the process will eventually lead can only, at present, be a matter of conjecture. It can be said, however, that the likelihood of the High Court coming to the aid of aggrieved patients is markedly higher than was the case before the coming into force of the 1998 Act.

5.6 Concluding comments

As the discussion in this chapter shows, at its worst, the process of admission under Part II can be little more than 'legalism' in its entirely negative sense: a set of tiresome bureaucratic requirements that are a source of irritation for, but do not actually impede, those who control admissions 'on the ground'. Even when the courts have found that an admission to hospital is unlawful, therapeutic considerations are, as in the habeas corpus cases, frequently allowed greater weight than a civil libertarian might wish to see. It does seem innocuous that the courts espouse a rhetoric of individual freedom, find that it has been infringed in the case before them, and then decline to grant the order sought. In other cases (those of H and Hallstrom provide examples), law has proved able to allow patients and their relatives a means by which to challenge successfully the exercise of power by professionals.

But successful challenges are conspicuous by their rarity. It is important to remember that many, although by no means all, admissions under Part II proceed with the consent and agreement of all those involved, with the exception of the patient, because, by definition, the compulsory powers of confinement should not be used if the patient consents to hospitalisation, and the paperwork involved provides a positive incentive to avoid the use of the compulsory powers. Yet consent may not, of course, always be genuine, and this is true of those involved in the admissions procedure as it is of patients. The evidence suggests that the admissions procedure is driven principally by psychiatrists. Although ASWs are in the role of applicant, an application must be accepted by the hospital and so there is, in practice, a power of veto reserved to psychiatrists over the decision-making abilities of ASWs. Of course, there will be cases, perhaps the majority, in which there is little scope to disagree that hospitalisation is required, whatever perspective one brings to that question. But on occasion, differences in perspective will matter. It will be a strong-minded ASW who resists making an application when requested to do so by a psychiatrist. Conversely, without the requisite medical recommendations, an ASW cannot make an application. GPs are similarly likely to endorse the views of the specialist. In practice, there are various ways around an impasse: find another doctor, find another ASW, remove a recalcitrant NR under s. 29, and so on. But it remains the case that, despite the strict legal situation, admission to hospital is under the control of the psychiatric profession, and that control is inhibited more by questions of resources than by legal restraints. Against the broader background of the 'medicalisation of mental disorder', however, such a conclusion is perhaps not surprising.

6

Mental Disorder and Criminal Justice

6.1 Introduction

In the first edition of this book, we noted that government policy – broadly, that mentally disordered offenders should be 'diverted' from the criminal justice system into the mental health system – was at variance with popular and media understandings of mental disorder and criminality, which tended to conflate, rather than separate, mental disorder and criminality, seeing them as 'natural' bedfellows (Health Education Authority, 1997). This is no longer so clearly the case (Peay, 2002: 747). It is not entirely accurate to say that the policy of diversion has been abandoned: all of the various circulars, policy documents, legislation and case law that form the doctrinal basis of that policy still apply; the various agencies continue to implement diversionary practices at various stages of the criminal justice process; the government has no plans to remove the powers of the courts to send mentally disordered offenders to hospital rather than to prison. But there has clearly been a sea change in the attitude of the government. There has been shift towards the greater use of a criminalised, rather than a medicalised, model of mental disorder, with a marked increase of emphasis on risk management and control over care or treatment (see Gray *et al.*, 2002). This, coupled with the government's project to increase the quality of treatment for mental disorder in prisons, perhaps indicates the abandonment of the policy – always more honoured in the breach – to ensure that mentally disordered persons are not housed in prisons.

Yet it is problematic to talk about policy shifts in such easy and polarised terms. Within this general trend towards a risk paradigm, a distinction is made between those judged a significant risk to public safety (in some shape or form) and those who are judged to pose little or no risk. For the former group (which includes some, but not all, mentally disordered offenders and also includes some patients detained under Part II of the 1983 Act), the second half of the 1990s saw significant expansion, with a doubling of secure unit accommodation. For the latter group, inpatient provision was markedly reduced, and shifted into the private sector (see Chapter 3). There is thus something of a bifurcation in policy, deriving from an economy of risk management, with a tightening of control for the former group and the scaling down of provision for the latter. We should not be surprised if one consequence of this policy is that a greater number of mentally disordered persons, in the absence of appropriate support in the community, come into contact with the criminal justice system. At the same time, however, central government policy is only one factor that impacts on practice; professional discourse and ethics, as well as legal rights, are all also vital factors. Local initiatives – to improve the detection of mental illness in police stations and courthouses, and to fashion a practical therapeutic alternative to the criminal process, for example – are relatively independent of government policy. There are also the limitations on any policy imposed by the finite nature of resources.

At a more conceptual level, the problem inherent in attempting to evaluate either the functioning of a policy of diversion, or any claimed shift away from that policy, is that, even in the civil law provisions of the Mental Health Act, there is a dense and complex weave of medical and criminological ideas. The criteria for civil confinement, as seen in Chapter 4, treats 'abnormally aggressive or seriously irresponsible conduct', neither of which is a medical concept, as integral to the definitions of mental impairment, severe mental impairment and psychotic disorder (see Chapter 2). Responsible medical officers (RMOs) are given powers to veto an application for discharge made by a nearest relative of the patient on the grounds of the 'dangerousness' of the patient (see Chapter 8), and so on. The degree of overlap between the two concepts of madness and criminality, in both the popular and the political imagination, and reflected in the law, is such that such interconnectedness can seem inevitable, even natural.

Yet there is much reason to think that the extent of the linkage of mental disorder with criminality is a projection, dictated more by the way in which each is constructed and responded to, both by the state and the public at large, than by any innate qualities of the concepts themselves. As Peay (1997: 687) has pointed out, 'the overwhelming correlates of violence are male gender, youth, low socio-economic class, and the use/abuse of alcohol or drugs, and not the diagnosis of major mental disorder'. Yet there is no policy in contemplation to detain men, or the poor (or reckless drivers, or any number of other potentially dangerous and identifiable groups) on preventative grounds of public protection. It is important always to bear in mind the politicised and partial nature of the constructions of mental disorder that underpin much governmental discourse. For example, the White Paper of 2000 (Home Office and Department of Health, 2000a: para. 1.5) estimated that there are between 2,100 and 2,400 men in the population with DSPD and who pose a threat to the public at large. These figures were based on analysis of the prison population, those detained in secure hospitals, and 'community estimates'. But it was not until July 2002, in answer to a Parliamentary Question, that the government disclosed its information, that only 124 of those individuals were actually in the community, and that the vast bulk are already detained in prison or in a secure hospital (Hansard [HL] Col. 5088, 23 July 2002). Needless to say, this disclosure did not receive the fanfare that accompanied the publication of the White Paper in 2000. We do not advocate indifference to those 124 individuals and the risks they may pose to self or others, but the point is that the media, and the public, are allowed and encouraged to develop a wholly inaccurate idea of the extent of the risk actually posed, and of the extent of the link between mental disorder and violence.

Nevertheless, the political reality is that the two concepts are always already conflated. We should not forget that it is only, and precisely, the construction of the mentally disordered as 'other' that allows the imposition of legal controls that do not apply to other sections of the community, and the mentally disordered as such are similarly situated alongside the 'criminal other' by any world view that divides society into the normal and the deviant. If the policy of the present government is to place greater emphasis on risk management and dangerousness, and less on the medicalisation of mental disorder, then perhaps it should be understood as a shift in emphasis in the way that the relation between the two concepts is structured, rather than any broader shift from one to the other model. This is not to deny, however, that the way in which the tension between treatment and control is negotiated in policy and legislative terms impacts significantly on the practical reality of the mental health system as it is experienced, by patients and professionals alike.

Long and Midgely (1992) trace the linkages made in professional and popular understandings of the concepts of criminality and madness in the nineteenth century. The causes of each were understood in much the same way, which meant that the 'two could be viewed together, two sides of a common problem' (1992: 64–5). At the same time, the problem of 'criminal lunatics' was very much in the public eye (see Chapter 1). When professional disenchantment with the potential to cure either the insane or the criminal set in, towards the end of the century, the view of the 'incurable criminal lunatic' as the archetype of both mental illness and criminality, gained ground accordingly, in popular as well as professional discourses (Foucault, 1988). In part, this mythology (for mythology it largely is) has been maintained to the present day, through a series of folk devils with a roll call that begins with Jack the Ripper, and includes Crippen, Hindley and Brady, Sutcliffe, Nielson, and which in recent years has taken on a broader complexion with homicides and other crimes committed by persons released from hospitals into care in the community (see Chapter 9). The 'criminal lunatic', and the conflation of the two concepts that such a person is set up to represent, is part of our cultural furniture, a staple in drama, from Hammer Horror to *Fatal Attraction*. In part also, though, it can be argued that this linkage is a professional tactic or technology of professional dominance. Szasz (1970), for example, has famously argued that the emergent profession of psychiatry campaigned successfully for a strategic linkage of the concepts of criminality and madness in the nineteenth century, in order to stake out a professional stamping ground for themselves within the asylum and the prison, and since then has protected that linkage from attempts to separate it. It is certainly the case that the modern prison has been a continuous home for psychiatry. As Long and Midgely point out, right from the start of its life in 1842, Pentonville prison's inmate population featured an over-representation of 'lunatics' by almost ten times more than would have been expected; a feature of imprisonment that, as will be seen, has changed little today.

Despite this, since at least 1800, the 'official' state response to crime and mental disorder has been structured around the supposition that there should be a separation, rather than a conflation, of criminality and madness. The healthcare system and the criminal justice system are, in theory at least, distinct systems pursuing different goals.

Mentally disordered offenders, however, render that distinction problematic, and when a person who is, or is suspected to be, mentally disordered comes into contact with the criminal justice system, the appropriate state response is far from clear. Each such individual represents, in microcosm, the dilemma of policy: treatment or punishment? Despite the activities of the current government (and, indeed, its Conservative predecessors) it remains the case, according to a government circular still in force (Home Office, 1990: para. 2), that 'it is government policy that, wherever possible, mentally disordered persons should receive care and treatment from the health and social services'. The circular proceeds to outline, and encourage the use by the various agencies of the criminal justice system of, the various legal mechanisms that are available to 'divert' mentally disordered offenders and suspects into the mental health system.

This has never been a blanket policy. Part III of the MHA 1983 functions more as a *threshold* than as a simple gateway between the two systems. Not all of those who can be *clinically* classified as mentally disordered will meet the criteria for diversion out of the criminal justice system under the terms of the 1983 Act. For example, the exclusion from the mental health regime by s. 1(3) of the 1983 Act (see Chapter 2) of those whose disorder only manifests in the form of the misuse of drugs or alcohol explains a sizeable proportion of the mentally disordered, sentenced prison population as measured by clinicians (see Brooke *et al.*, 1996, and below). There are other varieties of diversion, for example a decision by the police or the Crown Prosecution Service not to proceed with a prosecution, that are not governed by such strictly defined criteria, but it is nevertheless the case that the 1983 Act does not attempt, nor should the Home Office Circular of 1990 be thought to advocate, a policy of diverting *all* people who could be said to be mentally disordered in some way. Even when it can be shown that an individual does satisfy the criteria for diversion required by the 1983 Act, there is usually a discretion whether to act on that evidence. This is because the well-being of the offender is not the only concern, which must be balanced against the need to protect the public and to punish the culpable. And within the framework of the criminal justice system, there may well be other options open, such as opting for a non-custodial criminal disposal, which can amount to a de facto diversionary measure.

The preference for a policy of diversion depends on the view taken of mental disorder and criminality. Szasz, for example, holds that there should be no diversion, that hospitals should not be places of compulsory confinement; this follows from his understanding of mental disorder as a construction of the psychiatric professions. If, on the other hand, one concedes that, on occasion at least, the presence of mental disorder negates *mens rea*, then there can be no guilt and therefore no punishment. Rarely, if ever, is the situation so straightforward in practice. Even if a person can be shown to be mentally disordered, to show that there is a relationship between his or her disorder and offending is quite another question. By and large, the current regime avoids these difficulties altogether, and makes diversion dependent solely on the presence of mental disorder (in fact, specific forms of mental disorder are usually required) without attempting to link that disorder with the offending behaviour, preferring rather to balance the two factors when deciding on disposal. We do not seek in this chapter to challenge that approach as such. Nor do we wish to challenge what, until recently, has been the established orthodoxy that diversion is a 'good thing': we think that it is. Instead, the aim is to evaluate diversion on its own terms: does the law, policy and practice of diversion actually work?

6.2 Diversion from prosecution

6.2.1 Early diversion from the criminal process

Police officers are empowered by s. 136 MHA 1983 to remove to a place of safety a person found in a place to which the public have access and who appears to be mentally disordered and in need of care or control (see Chapter 4). This, in itself, may function as a diversionary measure, because the s. 136 powers may be used even when the person in question has, or may have, committed an offence. There is research evidence to suggest that, in deciding whether to proceed, factors such as the practicalities of pressing charges and the perceived seriousness of an individual's mental state are taken into account (Rogers, 1990). A decision not to proceed with criminal charges will often involve officers in negotiation with hospitals or social service departments. As was discussed in Chapter 4, around one in ten of hospital admissions are consequent upon the use of s. 136 powers, but in practice early diversion is something of a lottery, because much will depend on the availability of local alternatives that satisfy the officer in question that a decision not to proceed can be taken (Greenberg *et al.*, 2002). Rowlands *et al.* (1996) found that the most common form of diversion used by the police is to grant bail to a suspect after having arranged for an outpatient psychiatric assessment, although there was a high rate of failure to attend for such an assessment, particularly amongst substance abusers. Psychiatric services were able, however, to maintain contact with a sizeable number of persons, although most were not formally diverted until the stage of court disposal, when probation orders and discharges were reasonably common.

All of this depends on the abilities of police officers to detect the presence of mental disorder. This issue will be discussed in further detail below, but it is worth pointing out here that schemes in magistrates' court to identify, and if appropriate divert, those with mental disorders (see further below) have, for a considerable time now, also functioned in police stations (Laing, 1995); the process gathered momentum following the proposal to that effect made by the Royal Commission on Criminal Justice (1993, para. 92). An early and seemingly successful diversion scheme has been running in Birmingham since 1992. The scheme involves a community psychiatric nurse (CPN) being present at police stations to screen for mental disorder problems and arrange for care to be given where necessary. In the first six months of this scheme, only one individual identified as requiring psychiatric intervention by the CPN eventually went to court to face the criminal charges in question (Laing, 1995: 372; see also Riordan *et al.*, 2000).

James (2000) discusses the outcome of a diversion scheme developed to be run across three busy central London police stations by community psychiatric nurses (CPNs), who screened police station arrivals and took referrals from custody sergeants or police doctors (known as forensic medical examiners or 'FMEs', see further below), and who liased between these actors, the detainees' legal and other representatives (see further below), and detainees. The CPNs were also proactive in finding diversionary options for suitable cases, whether in the form of admission to a hospital or referral to community-based services (the CPNs running the scheme were attached to a CMHT, thus facilitating communication between the police station and the CMHT). James' conclusion is that 'The CPNs managed to find a role in the custody suite which gained the confidence of custody sergeant, FME, and local community health service . . . the CPNs succeeded in acting as a catalyst for the effective usage of resources already extant' (2000: 549, 553). Even where diversion schemes are active, however, a proportion of those held in police stations who are mentally disordered are not noticed by those running the scheme (7 per cent on average, according to Vaughan *et al.*, 2001).

The preponderance of research shows that s. 136 or informal diversion is 'unlikely to be used when evidence of a notifiable crime is present' (Robertson *et al.*, 1996: 176). The police, most often, prefer to leave the decision about diversion to the court. There is, of course, the intermediary stage, at which a case put forward by police will be reviewed by an officer of the Crown Prosecution Service (CPS). The task of the CPS is to establish both that there is sufficient evidence for a case to proceed, and that it is in the public interest that a prosecution should be brought. One factor that should incline against proceeding is 'significant' mental illness, although this has to be balanced against the likelihood of repetition of the alleged offence. For some, it is not obvious that diversion on grounds of mental illness is to be encouraged, because it can amount to a denial of an accused person's right to test the evidence against him or her in a court, and so be seen to treat mentally ill persons as second-class citizens (Carson, 1989b). There is little evidence on how these tasks are discharged by the CPS, but such evidence as there is (Cooke, 1991) suggests that, like the police, the CPS prefers to let evidentially strong cases proceed, and leave the diversion decision to the courts.

6.2.2 Diversion within the criminal process

Most mentally disordered persons who enter police custody are not immediately diverted out of the criminal process, but are instead funnelled into a second variant of diversion, which is found in Code of Guidance C, Police and Criminal Evidence Act 1984 (PACE), a revised version of which came into force on 25 July 2006 (The Police and Criminal Evidence Act 1984 (Code of Practice C and Code of Practice H) Order 2006, SI 2006/1938. This is concerned with the diversion of mentally disordered criminal suspects, along with other 'vulnerable' detainees, such as juveniles, into an investigative regime with greater safeguards than are ordinarily implemented. Code C was initially introduced in response to a highly publicised litany of miscarriages of justice involving persons with learning disabilities (the 1984 Act uses, and defines in s. 77(1), the term 'mental handicap') or mentally ill persons based on confession evidence given in police interviews. The Royal Commission on Criminal Procedure was set up in 1978 following the case in which an 18-year-old man with learning disabilities was, with two others, convicted of the murder of Maxwell Confait on the basis of confession evidence later shown not to have been true. Other notable appeals based on pre-PACE practice include those of Stefan Kiszko and Judith Ward. PACE extended the existing system of safeguards to cover mentally ill, as well as learning disabled, criminal suspects. The introduction of Code C has not, however, ameliorated concerns about miscarriages: in 1994, the pressure group, Justice, reported 89 suspected miscarriages by reason of disputed confession evidence (Justice, 1994); for a recent example, involving on a post-PACE case, see *R v J* [2003] EWCA Crim 3309, 2003 WL 22769342.

Continued concerns about the treatment of mentally disordered persons in police custody are partly explicable in terms of uncertainties and gaps in the regime laid out by the Code, as will be discussed below. But part of the explanation lies in the fact that Code C is targeted at police officers and has, as its primary aim, to ensure that evidence gathered in police interviews can survive challenge under ss. 76–8 of PACE. Section 76(2)(a) requires a court to exclude evidence obtained by oppression, and s. 76(2)(b) requires that evidence obtained in circumstances likely to render any confession unreliable be excluded, unless the prosecution can prove beyond reasonable doubt that it was not, in fact, so obtained. Section 78(1) gives the discretion to exclude evidence that would adversely affect the fairness of the proceedings if admitted. Section 77(1) places a duty on a trial judge to warn a jury of the dangers of relying solely on the uncorroborated confession evidence of a mentally handicapped (but not mentally ill) person obtained in the absence of an independent third party. Code C, therefore, is, in a sense, only incidentally concerned to protect the rights of mentally disordered suspects and it is not concerned to divert offenders away from prosecution on grounds of mental disorder. This is a good example of the point that, at the general level, the policy is not diversion per se. Section 77(1) contemplates that a prosecution of a mentally disordered offender should go ahead, as long as the safeguards therein are adhered to, even if there has been a breach of the Code, and not that there should be no prosecution. In effect, the diversion question is then passed to the court.

6.2.2.1 The operation of the 'appropriate adult' scheme

6.2.2.1.1 The role of the 'appropriate adult'

Code C prescribes a particular regime to apply when a vulnerable suspect is detained in a police station. A vulnerable suspect is one who is a juvenile or who is 'mentally vulnerable or mentally disordered', and the Code, in note of guidance 1G, defines 'mental disorder' by reference to s. 1(2) MHA 1983, and 'mentally vulnerable' as 'any detainee who, because of their mental state or capacity, may not understand the significance of what is said, of questions or of their replies'. Thus, the Code seems to cover a wider constituency of adults than does the Mental Health Act 1983. Code C requires that when such a person is detained or interviewed by police officers in connection with an alleged offence, their interests and rights are protected by the presence of an independent third party known as the 'appropriate adult' (AA). In general terms, the function of an AA is 'to befriend, advise and assist' the detainee (Royal Commission on Criminal Justice, 1993: para. 4.103). More precise guidance is found at para. 11.17 of Code C:

> If an appropriate adult is present at an interview, they shall be informed:
>
> - they are not expected to act simply as an observer; and
> - the purpose of their presence is to:
>   - advise the person being interviewed;
>   - observe whether the interview is being conducted properly and
>   - facilitate communication with the person being interviewed.

The presence of an AA does not depend on whether or not a mentally disordered suspect is to be interviewed. An AA should be asked by the custody officer to attend at the police station in any case (Code C: para. 3.15). If the detainee is cautioned in the absence of an AA, that caution must be given again when the AA arrives (Code C: para. 10.12). If the detainee is not to be interviewed, that may well be the extent of the AA's involvement. Most persons – around 70 per cent (Robertson *et al.*, 1996: 299) – detained at a police station are not, in fact, interviewed. When interviews do occur, they tend to be of short duration, with half being conducted within twenty minutes and 75 per cent within half an hour (Robertson *et al.*, 1996; McConville and Hodgson, 1993).

If there is to be an interview, para. 11.15 of Code C provides that a 'mentally disordered or otherwise vulnerable person must not be interviewed regarding their involvement or suspected involvement in a criminal offence or offences, or asked to provide or sign a written statement under caution or record of interview, in the absence of the appropriate adult', unless an officer of superintendent rank or above considers that delay will be likely to lead to interference with evidence, physical harm to other people or serious damage to property, or might alert other suspects who have not yet been arrested (para. 11.1). If an interview is held in the absence of an AA on the basis of para. 11.1, it must last only as long as is necessary to avert the risk there referred to (paras. 11.1, 11.19), and a record of the grounds for the decision must be made (para. 11.20). Case law has established that it is not necessary to await the arrival of the AA before taking bodily samples: *R v Preston, ex p DPP* [2003] EWHC 729. The detained person should be told that he or she may consult privately with the AA at any time (para. 3.18). At the commencement of any interview, the AA should explain his or her role to the detainee while the tape is running. In this way, the role of AA is parallel to that of the attending solicitor, and in *R v Lewis (Martin)* [1996] Crim LR 260 (CA), it was said that the functions of each were essentially similar. Lawyers do not necessarily have training in mental health matters, however, and legal advice at police stations can be of low quality (Hodgson, 1997: 787, 794). Surely, the reason that a suspect should have the services of an AA in addition, if wanted, to those of a solicitor, is that it is intended that the AA will bring special knowledge of the particular suspect or expertise in dealing with persons who are mentally ill or have learning difficulties that, by implication, a solicitor is not expected to have. Moreover, it is not obviously the responsibility of a solicitor to 'facilitate communication' with the suspect. In *R v Aspinall* [1999] 2 Cr App R 115,

(1999) 49 BMLR 82, this sort of argument was accepted, and the court emphasised that the role of the AA, in safeguarding the interests of the interviewee, is broader than, and distinct from, that of an attending solicitor.

The detail of the role remains unclear (Williams, 2000), however. For example, a solicitor might advise a 'no comment' interview: should an AA still attempt to 'facilitate communication'? As Fennell (1994: 67) has said, the 'danger is that the role of facilitating communication may be over-emphasised to the extent that the [AA] becomes an agent of the interrogating officers'. The situation in *R v Jefferson, Skerritt, Readman and Keogh* [1994] 99 Crim App R 130 (CA) came very close to realising this concern. In this case, the Court of Appeal upheld a decision not to exclude confession evidence obtained by interview of a juvenile suspect in the presence of his father as AA, on the grounds that the father had, on occasion, robustly joined in the questioning of his son, because this, it was held, had not impeded the father's ability to perform a protective role. Given what is known about the suggestibility, or the urge to confess or to please others, that some vulnerable persons exhibit (Royal Commission on Criminal Justice, 1993: 57), this in itself is a questionable decision. It also points to the broader uncertainties about the function of the AA and the interrelationship of that role with that of legal representative: the AA is charged to ensure that an interview is 'fair', but what does this mean? (See Nemetz and Bean, 2001: 601.) Should an AA take an 'interventionist' or a 'passive' role? If it is the former, how should the demarcation of the role of AA from that of legal adviser be expressed (White, 2002)? What if there is no legal representative? AAs have an independent right to request the presence at the police station of a solicitor (Code C: para. 3.19), although this fact does not seem to be well known and, as in *R v Morse* [1991] Crim LR 195 (see later in the chapter), an AA may decline legal advice. How does this affect the role of the AA? What are the implications of the truncation of the 'right to silence' by ss. 34, 36 and 37 of the Criminal Justice and Public Order Act 1994 (see Fennell, 1994a: 58–60, Gray *et al.*, 2001) for AAs? A key distinction between the situation of a solicitor and that of an AA is that there is no privilege in any statements made by the detainee to the AA (Home Office, 2003a: 2). This can create a dilemma for an AA charged on the one hand to protect the rights of the detainee, and, on the other, having no legal right to withhold information from the police, even if the detainee assumed that any information disclosed to the AA would remain confidential. Is it possible to 'befriend' a detainee and pass on his or her confidences to the investigating officers? In summary, although it is possible to give an account in broad terms of the appropriate role of an AA, the more the detail is examined, the less clear the appropriate role becomes; the more clear it becomes that to act as an AA is potentially extremely difficult.

6.2.2.1.2 Who should act as AA?
Despite the apparent complexities of the role of the AA, there is no requirement that an AA be given suitable training. For mentally disordered suspects, Code C provides that the AA should be a relative or guardian of the suspect, or a person with experience of dealing with mentally disordered or mentally vulnerable people, or failing that, some other responsible person (para. 1.7(b)). A police employee may not act as an AA, nor

may a lawyer attending the police station in a professional capacity, nor a probation officer (unless specifically requested by the detainee): *R v O'Neill* (1990) 16 October, unreported (Crown Court). An AA must be an adult (*R v Palmer* (1991) *Legal Action*, 21 September (Crown Court)), who is able effectively to communicate in English (*H&M v DPP* [1998] Crim LR 653 (CA)), and who is able in fact to empathise with the suspect: *DPP v Blake* [1989] WLR 432 (CA). If an interpreter is used, that person cannot also function as AA, because an interpreter must be impartial and an AA may not be: *R v West London Youth Court, ex p J* [2000] 1 WLR 2368, [2000] 1 All ER 823. An AA should take an active role in events and so needs the mental capacity to fulfil the role. In *R v Morse* [1991] Crim LR 195, the father of a juvenile suspect acted as the AA during a police interview, but a psychologist later gave evidence that the father was of low IQ and was probably unable to appreciate the gravity of the situation and what was expected of him as an AA. The confession evidence obtained in the interview was excluded by a Crown Court under s. 76(2)(b), PACE, holding that the prosecution had failed to discharge its burden, of proving that the unsuitability of the father to act as the AA had not raised doubts about the reliability of the evidence.

There are cases going the other way. In *R v W and Anor* [1994] Crim LR 130 (CA), the Court of Appeal emphasised that it is concern about the manner in which evidence was obtained, and not about the truth of the evidence, that triggered consideration of s. 76 (see also *R v Cox* [1991] Crim LR 276 (CA)). The court nevertheless upheld a decision to admit evidence obtained by way of police interview of a juvenile suspect in the presence of her mother acting as an AA, even though the mother herself was a person who, if detained, would require the presence of an AA, being 'mentally handicapped' as defined in s. 77 PACE and suffering from psychosis. This was on the basis that the mother's psychotic thoughts were apparently concerned exclusively with her neighbours, and she was, in fact, capable of acting rationally in connection with the events in question. This is, perhaps, an unfortunate decision. It seems wrong, in policy terms, that a person whom the AA regime is intended to protect can herself act as an AA for a third party. Other worrying decisions include *Jefferson, Skerritt, Readman and Keogh* (discussed earlier), on the facts of which it is doubtful that the detainee would have felt befriended by his AA. These cases show the Court of Appeal being prepared to sanction an AA in situations that seem to depart from the spirit of protection behind the scheme, and that the courts have been satisfied with a bare minimum in terms of what is required of an AA. It may be that the trend has been bucked by *Aspinall* (see earlier, and Kerrigan, 2000), in so far as the court emphasised the importance attached by the statutory scheme, not only to the attendance of an AA, but to that person's active involvement and active pursuance of his or her responsibilities towards the detainee. In the later Court of Appeal decision in *R v Clayton* 2000 WL 664424, however, the court rejected the appeal against conviction of a defendant sentenced to six months' imprisonment for indecent assault. The appellant claimed that, because of poor legal advice at the time of his arrest, he had not been interviewed in the presence of an AA when his state of mental health at that time required it, and so his confession should have been excluded. The Court of Appeal held that the trial judge had dealt properly with the matter by advising the jury that the confession evidence should be treated with caution.

Although parents most commonly act as AAs in respect of juvenile detainees, there is, in fact, a preference amongst police officers for social workers to be used for adult detainees (Brown *et al.*, 1993), although Bean and Nemetz (n.d.) found that, in one Midlands area, victim support volunteers were preferred, and there is more recent evidence that volunteers function better than either social workers or parents of juvenile detainees (Pierpoint, 2001). Code C, in Note of Guidance 1D, advises that a trained AA is to be preferred to a relative of the suspect, unless the suspect wishes, as might be commonly the case, that a relative act as AA, which preference 'should be respected, if practicable'. An untrained AA may do more harm than good, however, by giving the appearance, but not the reality, of third-party protection (White, 2002), yet to secure the services of an AA who is not a member of the detainee's family is not to guarantee that that person has suitable training. For example, some local authorities, unable through pressure of resources to spare full-time staff for this work, use social work volunteers who may well have no specialist training. Not all schemes are run by local authorities; others are in the charitable or voluntary sector, and here it is more likely that non-professionals will operate the scheme. In a recent review of the national situation, Pritchard (2006: 5, 7) found that 49 per cent of all schemes operate solely through the use of volunteer AAs, with training of between 0 and 60 hours, the average being 16.5 hours. Suitable AAs can be hard to find, as Robertson and his colleagues discovered when researching the use of AAs in London: the researchers were coopted to act as AAs during their fieldwork 'to avoid lengthy delays for police and detainee' (1996: 309). Bean and Nemetz, (1997; Nemetz and Bean, 2001) reported the establishment of schemes run by teams of volunteers that, although patchy in terms of national coverage, could in their view provide 'a model for the future' (2001: 603), and by 2004, things had moved on to the extent that the National Appropriate Adult Network (NAAN) was established, and in 2005, promulgated National Standards for recruitment, support, training and standards of service delivery (NAAN, 2005; 2005a; 2005b). It is not clear, however, for the reasons discussed above, whether even having dedicated and trained AAs will resolve the more intractable problems inherent in the role.

6.2.2.1.3 Detecting the need for an 'appropriate adult'

As with diversion out of the criminal justice system altogether, the efficacy of this scheme depends on the ability of police officers to detect the presence of mental disorder. Key to this is the role of the custody officer, usually a sergeant, who has a general responsibility for the welfare of detained persons and to ensure that no person is detained longer than is necessary. It is the duty of the custody officer to activate the particular requirements of Code C in respect of any person about whom he or she 'has any suspicion, or is told in good faith ... may be mentally disordered or otherwise mentally vulnerable, in the absence of clear evidence to dispel that suspicion' (para. 1.4). He or she 'must' inform an AA if he or she 'has any doubt' that a person may be mentally vulnerable or mentally disordered (Code C, note 1G: paras. 3.5(c)(ii) and 3.15), and to arrange for a

FME to examine the detainee if it appears to the custody officer that the detainee is suffering from mental disorder (Code C: paras. 3.16, 9.5). It is apparent from the case law, confirmed by research carried out for the Royal Commission on Criminal Justice (the Runcimann Commission) (Gudjonsson *et al.*, 1993), that very often custody officers miss the presence of disorder, with AAs being present at 4 per cent of all interviews of adult suspects, yet being required in around 15 per cent. Other research reports even lower AA attendance rates. Bean and Nemetz (1994), in a retrospective analysis of 21,000 police custody records, found that an AA was arranged in only 38 cases, a rate of 0.016 per cent. The expected rate is between 10 and 100 times that. This situation is perhaps not surprising. Police custody suites can be very busy places, and individuals with no history of mental disorder can react in a bizarre manner to the fact of arrest and detention (Gudjonsson, 1992). The influence of alcohol or drugs can be confused with the presence of mental disorder (Palmer, 1996: 634–5), and there is evidence to suggest that persons with learning difficulties or who are otherwise vulnerable, for instance by reason of illiteracy, may try to disguise their difficulties (Hodgson 1997: 787). There is also evidence to suggest that custody officers in London are more adept at detecting the need for an AA than their colleagues elsewhere (Roberston *et al.*, 1996).

Palmer's (1996) study of police practices in Yorkshire confirmed the findings of earlier research that, although major disorders may be detected, minor disorders frequently are not. Palmer's research also highlighted the frequently made point that the lack of assistance given to police officers by way of a definition of mental disorder results in officers applying their own definitions. As one interviewee said, '[t]here is no test really as far as I can work out' (cited in Palmer, 1996: 634) and so some officers interpret the need for an 'adult' to indicate that it is detainees who exhibit 'childlike' behaviour who are to be defined as mentally disordered. In *Aspinall* (see earlier), the detainee, who was in receipt of medication for schizophrenia, was adjudged by all concerned not to need the presence of an AA, because his illness was not then acute. He was also convicted in the Crown Court and it took the Court of Appeal to affirm that an AA should have been called to attend, even if the detainee appeared to be lucid. This appears to be a fairly common situation. Bean and Nemetz (1994) found, in their sample of 21,000 cases, 50 examples of detentions in which mental disorder was recognised, but in which an AA was nevertheless not called. It is not surprising, then, that the constant refrain of commentators is to emphasise the need for more and better training of police officers, and custody officers in particular, in matters of learning disability, mental health and illness (e.g. Glover-Thomas, 2002: 182). But good training can only follow well thought-out policy. As Nemetz and Bean (2001: 600) have recently pointed out, it may not be readily apparent that a person suffering from psychopathic disorder and hence covered by the AA scheme, 'who may be highly intelligent, well aware of what is going on, and well able to understand the significance of the questions put to him', is in need of an AA. The police are less likely to be enthusiastic about a system that, from a police perspective, can be seen as offering unnecessary protection and leverage to at least some detainees. More generally, the point is that the AA scheme is poorly thought-out, confusing or opaque to those who have to operate it at ground level.

6.2.2.1.4 The role of the forensic medical examiner and the question of 'fitness for interview'

Code C of PACE 1984 requires that, before a mentally disordered person can be interviewed, he or she must be examined by an FME, and 'The custody officer shall not allow a detainee to be interviewed if the custody officer considers it would cause significant harm to the detainee's physical or mental state' (para. 12.3). FMEs are often GPs who work on a part-time basis for the police, attending to the injuries that police officers sustain in the course of their duties, as well as carrying out physical and mental health checks on detainees when required. There have long been concerns about the suitability of GPs (Royal Commission on Criminal Justice, 1993: para. 90), and although some forces, including the Metropolitan police force, do require FMEs to undertake relevant training, in other areas of the country, FMEs will not necessarily have any specialist training in recognising mental disorder. A further cause for concern is that it is apparently the practice in some police forces not to call an AA until a suspicion of mental disorder has been confirmed by an FME examination (Palmer, 1996: 638). Yet it is clear, from Code C of PACE, that an AA should be contacted at the same time as the FME, and the task of the FME is to report on fitness for interview and not on the need for an AA. That is a decision solely in the province of the custody officer.

There are three possible conclusions that an FME may reach on examining a detainee: that he or she is not fit for interview; that he or she is fit if there is an AA present; that he or she is fit without the presence of an AA. What is not clear is *how* any conclusion should be arrived at. Before 1994, the decision was left totally to the FME concerned, but in that year the British Medical Association and Association of Police Surgeons issued guidance on the meaning of 'fitness for interview' (British Medical Association and Association of Police Surgeons, 1994). This guidance advised that fitness for interview should be assessed by reference to: an assessment of the detainee's competence to understand the situation and questions to be put to him or her; whether there was a need for an AA to be present; the expected length and conditions of the intended interview. It also recommended that the detainee be reassessed after interview. This guidance is less helpful than it might be, however, because it does not discuss yardsticks, nor how to discern into which of the three categories any given individual fits (Norfolk, 1997). It is clear that, on occasion, there is a failure to identify the presence of mental disorder, an infamous example being that of Travis Clarke (Laing, 1995: 374), who took his own life only hours after having been judged at no risk of suicide by an FME. Gudjonsson (1995) has suggested an approach that asks whether any statement made by the interviewee would be 'necessarily reliable', and if the answer to that question is 'no', then the detainee is not fit to be interviewed. Norfolk similarly advocates a functionalist approach, such that a person should be regarded as unfit if there is a 'substantial risk' that any statement made is likely to be unreliable, and where there is a 'significant risk' any interview should only proceed in the presence of an AA (Norfolk, 1997: 231). Although there will be problems with any chosen form of words, it is surely correct to emphasise that fitness for interview is concerned with the reliability of any information gathered, rather than the abilities of the interviewee to 'cope with' the experience of being interviewed. It seems that, in practice, custody officers are on occasion more cautious than FMEs and, no doubt with at least one eye on the requirements of ss. 76 to 78 PACE, will bail a suspect to return to the police station at a later date if the officer feels that he or she is not at that time fit for interview, or will contact an AA to be present during interview, even if the FME states that the suspect is fit to be interviewed (Robertson *et al.*, 1996). As *Aspinall* shows, however, this will not always be the case.

6.2.2.1.5 Should 'appropriate adults' be retained?

There are examples to be found – *O'Neill* (see earlier) is one – of police officers actively impeding a person attempting to assume the role of AA. But it is by far more common to find that persons called on to act in that capacity, in fact, do very little other than observe the proceedings (Littlechild, 1995: 541; Palmer, 1996: 641; Hodgson, 1997: 790). This is perhaps not surprising, given the difficulties of trying to determine exactly what is expected of an AA, and the fact that the AA has trespassed into the heartland of police territory, described by Simon Holdaway as 'an "inner sanctuary" of police stations where police are in total control, and social workers (and others) are potential challengers' (Holdaway, 1983, cited in Littlechild, 1995: 542). The police station, and in particular the interview room, can be a daunting and disempowering environment for those not accustomed to it.

And yet the presence of an AA is constructed in the current scheme of things as a vital mechanism by which the interests of the detainee are protected. There are many reported cases in which evidence obtained at interview has been held inadmissible by a court for want of the presence of an AA (see, for example, *R* v *Maloney and Doherty* [1988] Crim LR 523; *R* v *J* [2003] EWCA Crim 3309, 2003 WL 22769342, *R* v *Blackburn* [2005] EWCA Crim 1349 – being appeals referred by the Criminal Cases Review Commission under s.9 Criminal Appeal Act 1995 – and *Palmer, Blake, O'Neill* and *Aspinall* discussed above). But the courts have also consistently held that the absence of an AA at the interview of a mentally handicapped suspect is not sufficient per se to render the suspect's confession inadmissible. Instead, the court should look to the circumstances of the interview and form a view of the effect of the absence of an AA on it: *DPP* v *Cornish* (1997) *The Times*, 27 January (CA). Quite how a court is to ask this hypothetical question of itself is far from clear – does it imply a 'reasonable AA' for example, or should the court consider what the effect of the absence of a *particular* AA may have been? Nevertheless, in *R* v *Law-Thompson* [1997] Crim LR 674, in *Aspinall*, and again in *R* v *Gill* [2004] EWCA Crim 3245 2004 WL 3089232, the Court of Appeal reiterated the stance in *Cornish*.

By the same token, in cases such as *Cox* and *Jefferson*, when there is an AA present, the courts have been reluctant to exclude evidence, even if the AA seemed, in fact, to do very little or even 'sided with' the investigating officers, or where there has been a breach of Code C of PACE. In the *H&M* case, for example, the Court of Appeal decided that although there had been a breach of para. 11.16 (now para. 11.17) of Code C, because an AA had not been identified formally and the person who acted as de facto AA was unaware of the responsibilities attendant on the role, there had been no substantive injustice as a result and the interests of the vulnerable persons (in that case, juveniles) had, in fact, been protected and there was no reason therefore to exclude evidence obtained in interview.

The message from the Court of Appeal in these cases is twofold. First, when there is an independent third party present, he or she will only be judged not to be an AA if the standard of assistance to the detained person is very poor indeed. Second, even when there is no AA, evidence will only be excluded if, in the opinion of the trial court, there is good reason to think that the evidence is *in fact* unreliable. This marks a shift away from the approach taken by the Court of Appeal in cases like *R v Kenny* [1994] Crim LR 284, where it was emphasised that the issue for the court was whether the breach of the Code made it *likely* that evidence obtained was unreliable. Both elements of the message give cause for concern, because the Court of Appeal is seemingly prepared to endorse the provision of a low, or at least variable, quality service to mentally disordered detainees, the long history of miscarriages involving such persons notwithstanding.

Whether the AA system should continue in its present form is open to question. Gudjonsson *et al.* (2000: 85) found that whilst 58 per cent of police officers thought that the presence of an AA offered significant protection to a detainee, only one in three lawyers shared that view. It is difficult to know how to read such findings. Fennell has suggested that the way forward is to abolish the role of AA, and instead put in place a scheme that ensures that mentally disordered suspects are automatically attended at the police station by 'fully qualified solicitors with special training in advising mentally disordered clients' (1994a: 67). This has the merit of avoiding the existing overlap in terms of personnel, but it does not necessarily mean that the fundamental tension between the protective and facilitative elements of the role of legal adviser and AA will be any better reconciled. There seems to be a consensus that the key is effective training, but not all think that it is members of the legal profession who should be trained. Hodgson (1997), for example, has pointed out that the term 'vulnerable' covers a wide range of conditions, even excluding consideration of juvenile suspects, and so there should be a variety of professionals – social workers, community psychiatric nurses – who would be recognised, on completion of both a generic and specialist training programme, as 'authorised' AAs, available to the police in need of the particular type of specialist help. Certainly, the CPNs who operated the scheme described by James (2000) (see earlier in this chapter) acted as AAs in addition to their other functions. At present, most AAs are volunteers, although various schemes also utilise a variety of social work and healthcare professionals (Pritchard, 2006), and training, in either case, is patchy nationally.

But trained personnel would not answer all the problems of the current system. There is, as Palmer (1996: 643) notes, a lack of strategic planning on the part of government, and if the commitment is towards developing a nationwide, 24-hour responsive scheme, then some sort of national framework is required to deliver it. Bean is clear in his view that 'we have to believe that the Appropriate Adult is the best system there is, and its failings are as much political as jurisprudential' (2001: 109). This is the intention of the National Appropriate Adult Network, but it is early days, and there are considerable resources implications attached to any set of proposals for change that would, in effect, professionalise what has hitherto been a largely voluntary, shoestring operation. Parents and relatives may attend at police stations free of charge, but the quality of service that such persons can realistically be expected to provide by way of safeguarding the position of the detainee is low. Pritchard (2006) found that, amongst providers, there is most support for the idea that statutory responsibility for organising AA schemes should be given to local authorities, although this does not preclude the contracting out of service provision to the voluntary and charitable sectors. At the moment, there is no single body in charge of the provision of AAs nationally, and there is no secure source of funding: sometimes funds come from local authorities or police forces; sometimes from charitable donations. Pritchard also found that underfunding is a fact of life for the vast majority of providers. Other substantive changes are required – for instance, the limitation of s. 77, PACE to mentally handicapped persons is anomalous. The protection offered by the section should be extended to all vulnerable interviewees. And if there are to be trained specialist AAs, then it behoves the courts to recognise their worth and to exclude vigilantly evidence obtained in the absence of the detainee's AA: at present, the courts have done little to give shape or definition to the role of AA (Pierpoint, 2006). Even with all this done, it would still be necessary to clarify the nature of the role of advocate, which means not only providing internal coherence but also some guidance on its relationship to that of attending solicitor. Perhaps the real virtue of Fennell's suggestion is that it offers a solution that simply avoids this latter problem.

6.3 Court-based diversion before the sentencing stage

Virtually all criminal prosecutions open in a magistrates' court. Much of the throughput of magistrates' courts is in terms of one-off court appearances at which the case against the defendant is proven, or, more commonly, there is a guilty plea, and the defendant is convicted and sentenced immediately. Such cases are typically trivial in nature and most are dealt with by way of a fine. In such a case, it is very rare that the defendant will have any further contact with officers either of the criminal justice system or the mental health services after conviction. In a significant minority of cases, however, progress through the system is less rapid. More serious offences, known as 'indictable offences', can only be heard by the Crown Court and require that the defendant is remanded, on bail or in custody, for considerable periods of time awaiting a court date. For middle order ('either way') offences, either the defendant or the bench may elect for Crown Court trial. In some cases, magistrates will convict but then pass the case to the Crown Court for sentencing. In others, for example, if a court is considering passing a prison sentence in certain circumstances or is dealing with a member of a class of offenders, reports of various types, including psychiatric reports, must be called for (ss. 81, 82 Powers of Criminal Courts (Sentencing) Act 2000), and cases adjourned for that purpose. This means that the engagement with the trial process can, for some, be a protracted experience.

There are a number of legal mechanisms for the diversion of mentally disordered suspects from the judicial process before conviction and sentencing, although these are, in the main, intended to facilitate either the trial – for example, by providing the accused person with treatment to allow the trial to proceed – or the sentencing process – by gathering information relevant to that process – rather than to divert the accused person out of that process. Nevertheless, on occasion, a defendant may never become fit to be tried, or reports may lead to a more informally engineered diversionary disposal. It is also possible, in certain circumstances, for a court to make a long-term diversionary order for the hospitalisation of an accused person by way of final disposal of the case, without convicting the defendant.

6.3.1 Bail or remand? Questions of policy, practice and resources

In strict theory, remand in custody is the exception not the rule. Virtually all accused persons have the same entitlement to bail. Section 4(1) of the Bail Act 1976 introduced a statutory presumption in favour of granting bail to accused persons, including persons whose case is adjourned after conviction to enable reports to be made: s. 4(4). The presumption can be rebutted for various reasons, to do with the likelihood of reoffending, absconding, interfering with witnesses, or having committed offences whilst on bail (Sch. 1, Part I, paras. 2, 2A, Bail Act 1976). It is possible to attach conditions to a bail order, relating, for example, to attendance for medical report or treatment, place of abode and so on: s. 3(6), (6)A, Bail Act 1976. Home Office guidance (1990) urges magistrates to work in cooperation with the health service, and para. 8(1) requires magistrates to give consideration to alternatives to remand in hospital, such as the attachment as a condition to an order granting bail that the defendant stay in a hospital or attend as an outpatient. Moreover, according to para. 7, 'a mentally disordered person should never be remanded to prison simply to receive medical treatment or assessment', and the power to remand instead to hospital rather than to prison 'should be used wherever possible to obtain a medical report on an accused person's condition': para. 8(2).

The remand prison population has, however, continually been found to contain a high number of mentally disordered persons (Taylor and Gunn, 1984; Williams *et al.*, 2005). A more recent survey, which sampled 9.4 per cent of the male unconvicted prison population of England and Wales (Brooke *et al.*, 1996), found that 63 per cent had some form of psychiatric disorder. The largest diagnostic group was 'harmful drug or alcohol misuse', which is defined as a form of mental disorder by the psychiatric profession but is excluded from the ambit of the 1983 Act by virtue of s. 1(3). Parsons *et al.* (2001) found 59 per cent of female remand receptions with at least one mental disorder, excluding substance abuse. Research carried out by Birmingham *et al.* (1996) at Durham prison, which did exclude substance abuse, found that 26 per cent of remand receptions had a form of serious mental disorder. Brooke *et al.* (1996) are quick to point out that, although 55 per cent of their sample was in immediate need of medical treatment '[m]ost ... could be provided by health services in prison'. Yet in the view of the researchers, 9 per cent of the sample (64 individuals) should have been in hospital

(1996: 1526), which, extrapolating to the remand prison population as a whole (13,463 in July 2006, comprising 8,462 untried and 5,001 convicted but unsentenced prisoners, amounting to around one in six of the total prison population of 79,319 – Home Office 2006: 2) suggests that, on any one day, there are several hundred persons remanded into custody who need to be in hospital. Singleton *et al.* (1998), in a sample of 3,000 prisoners, found 10 per cent of remand prisoners (and 7 per cent of sentenced prisoners) to be suffering from a psychotic disorder. This research also found that only 10 per cent of prisoners did *not* have at least one of personality disorder, drug or alcohol dependency, neurosis, or psychosis, and 78 per cent of remanded males prisoners were diagnosed as having a personality disorder, most commonly an antisocial personality disorder (Coid *et al.*, 2002: 248). In 2005, the Department of Health and the National Institute for Mental Health in England (2005) produced templates for best practice at every stage of a prisoner's 'pathway' through prison, from initial reception and first night, through to release and aftercare. The effect of this advice remains to be seen.

In *Kudla* v *Poland* (2002) 35 EHRR 11 K, a remand prisoner suffered from a personality disorder and depression. He also had suicidal tendencies, which were found by the prison's medical officers to constitute a grave risk to his life. K was, nevertheless, held on remand for well over three years, during which time he made numerous suicide attempts. For nearly all of that time, he had been housed in a remand centre with no psychiatric ward. The European Court found that K had been provided with necessary medical care and supervision whilst remanded. After one suicide attempt, he had been placed in hospital. His condition was continually monitored, and although the Polish government conceded that more attention might have been given to K's psychiatric state, a majority of the court concluded that K's treatment had not reached the levels of severity required to trigger Art. 3 (para. 99). The court further held (at para. 93) that Art. 3 cannot be interpreted as 'laying down a general obligation to release a detainee on health grounds or to place him in a civilian hospital to enable him to obtain a particular kind of medical treatment'. Each case will turn on its facts, although the court emphasised that Art. 3 is not easily invoked. It did, however, find a breach of the requirement of Art. 5(3), which requires that a person arrested or detained is prima facie entitled to a speedy trial or release pending trial. The time spent on remand could not be explained by the Polish government to the satisfaction of the court, which emphasised that 'only very compelling reasons' (para. 114) would persuade the court that a remand of such length could be justified. (K's conviction and sentence were subsequently successfully appealed against for irregularities found by the European Court to breach Art. 6(1).)

In *Edwards* v *UK* (2002) 35 EHRR 19, the European Court found the UK to be in breach of its positive obligation to protect the right to life, imposed by Art. 2 of the Convention. E, a remand prisoner, who at the time of his arrest had acted violently and shown indications of developing schizophrenia, was housed in a prison cell with another remand prisoner, L. L was also schizophrenic, and with a known history of violence and who had, in fact, been violent immediately before being placed in the cell with E. A few hours later, L violently assaulted and killed E. The Court found a further breach of Art. 2 on the grounds that the subsequent inquiry into the incident had been carried out in private and without satisfactory procedures with respect to powers to compel witnesses. Although this case reveals deficiencies in the ability of criminal justice personnel to recognise significant mental illness, or to act when mental illness is recognised at various points of the process from arrest to prison reception, the court found specific fault with the system for screening receptions (at para. 62: 'The defects in the information provided to the prison admissions staff were combined in this case with the brief and cursory nature of the examination carried out by a screening health worker who was found by the Inquiry to be inadequately trained and acting in the absence of a doctor to whom recourse could be made in the case of difficulty or doubt.' It also cited the findings of the inquiry into the incident, which had concluded that there had been 'a systemic collapse of the protective mechanisms that ought to have operated to protect this vulnerable prisoner' (at para. 33).

This judgment is concerned with only one prison, Chelmsford; the picture that is painted is a familiar one in the literature. Birmingham *et al.* (2000) have argued that the 'one size fits all' system of screening of prison receptions that currently operates should be abandoned in favour of a more tailored and focused approach that provides a fuller assessment of those most likely, based on past psychiatric history, to be mentally disordered on reception to prison, and the Department of Health has recently attempted to initiate more nuanced system (Department of Health and National Institute for Mental Health in England, 2005). Of course, all of this occurs against the backdrop of the continuing rise in the prison population and the ongoing 'crisis' in our prison system (Cavadino and Dignan, 2002: ch. 6), and as elsewhere, the ability of any scheme to improve the provision of mental health care depends on the degree to which it is funded, and its ability to compete with the other priorities for time and money. Between them, the decisions in *Kudla* and *Edwards* demonstrate that, although such considerations may be taken into account and mentally disordered persons may be remanded in prison in less than ideal conditions, this course of action does place some minimum requirements on prison authorities to improve the systems that, as *Edwards* and the academic research demonstrate, are frequently lacking at present.

Reasons for refusing bail are to be found in Sch. 1, Part I, Bail Act 1976. An accused person may be remanded to prison if the court is satisfied that this is required for his or her 'protection', which is capable of wide definition (para. 3), if it has not been practicable to carry out reports so as to enable a decision about bail to be made: para. 5; or if it appears to the court that it would otherwise be impracticable to complete any necessary inquiry or report: para. 7. Paragraph 2A now provides in addition that bail may not be granted unless the court is satisfied that there is no significant risk of offending whilst on bail. Dell *et al.* (1991) found that remand in custody for psychiatric reports was common. Of course, the courts do not remand defendants, mentally disordered or not, in custody simply because they can. A key problem is the lack of access to information that would enable a diversionary measure to be adopted *before* a defendant is remanded in custody. A number of 'bail information schemes' have been set up since the mid-1980s, but detecting persons suffering from mental disorder, out of the constant stream of people who pass through the court system, can be like looking for a needle in a haystack

(Brabbins and Travers, 1994). Accordingly, the spread of court-based diversionary schemes specifically aimed at mentally disordered defendants has also been a noticeable development in recent years. In the mid-1980s, such schemes were relatively unknown; by the turn of the decade, 48 schemes were in existence (Blumenthal and Wessely, 1992), increasing to more than a hundred by 1995 (Department of Health, 1995c, cited in Peay, 1997) and 136 by 2005 (Centre for Public Innovation, 2005: 16). Even by 2005, however, 'The national picture is far from ideal. Many areas have no provision at all. Many others rely on one lone worker, most often a community psychiatric nurse' (National Association for the Care and Rehabilitation of Offenders, 2005: 14). Of schemes surveyed by NACRO in England and Wales in 2004, one third operated with only one CPN, and although 42 per cent had three or more staff members, 50 per cent had no input from a psychiatrist or psychologist (2005: 5). Over two thirds (69 per cent) of schemes are 'reactive', only assessing those referred to them (2005: 9).

As to such schemes as do exist, NACRO found that 'each of the schemes visited differed in set up, composition and working practices; there was no "norm" in place. The schemes had developed over varying lengths of time and had evolved in relation to service provision from local mental health and criminal justice agencies' (Centre for Public Innovation, 2005: 33). A relatively well-resourced and well-staffed scheme is described by James *et al.* (1997). This scheme operates across several central London boroughs and five magistrates' courts. Accused persons suspected to be in need of psychiatric attention are cross-remanded to one of the courts, at which a team comprising two consultant psychiatrists, an ASW, a senior nurse, a research worker and an administrator have office and interview accommodation. Assessments are requested by the defence and by the court, and assessment takes place in the court building, reports to the court are immediately available, and team members have access to inpatient hospital beds, including those in a secure unit. There are many variations on schemes such as this (see, for example, the scheme that operates in Leeds, described in Greenhalgh *et al.* (1996) or that in Hampshire, explained by Austin *et al.*, 2003). Although there are divergent findings about the impact of such schemes, and numbers diverted are typically modest (see Cooke, 1991; Evans and Tomison, 1997; Exworthy and Parrott, 1997; James *et al.*, 1997), there is more agreement that the availability of a court-based diversion scheme can impact considerably both on the time taken for reports to be compiled and made available to sentencers and on the interval between initial arrest and arrival in hospital: in one study this latter figure was reduced from an average of fifty to eight days (James and Hamilton, 1991), although there have been claims more recently that the system is in crisis (Rickford and Edgar, 2005).

Even when a defendant has been identified as a potential candidate for bail or some other form of diversion by a court-based scheme or otherwise, the Bail Act nevertheless requires the balancing of the needs of the individual concerned for treatment with the considerations in the Act. The experience of James *et al.* (1997: 39) was that '[t]he most serious cases of violence would in any case be remanded into custody for reasons of public safety'. It is not possible to grant bail where a defendant, having a similar conviction or one for culpable homicide, is charged with murder, attempted murder, manslaughter, rape or attempted rape (s. 25, Criminal Justice and Public Order Act 1994), nor is it possible to remand a person convicted of murder to hospital for assessment (s. 35(3) MHA 1983) or a person accused of murder for treatment (s. 36(2)). In cases where the decision as to bail is one for the court, the factors to be considered include the nature of the offence, the strength of the evidence, and the strength of the accused person's community ties (Sch. 1, Part I, para. 9, Bail Act 1976), and it is easy for these factors to conspire in the direction of remand to prison for mentally disordered suspects. The net effect of this is that diversion schemes tend to operate around an axis governed by the seriousness of the alleged offending behaviour, focusing on the less serious offences, which, it can be suggested, is not sufficiently sensitive to the need for treatment.

Perhaps the main limitation of court-based diversion at present is the lack of resources, both in the courts and in terms of medical facilities. The ability of an advocate to suggest remand to hospital rather than prison is constrained by the fact that it is not always easy to find a hospital place, particularly if secure hospital accommodation is required, as Greenhalgh *et al.* (1997) and NACRO (2005: 5), amongst others, have discovered. Partly, this is because there is a general shortage of beds, but in addition, there is a certain degree of resistance within the mental health system towards accepting offender patients, partly because such patients tend to be more 'difficult' than others (Coid, 1988), and partly because of the pressure that criminal justice admissions place on already oversubscribed local hospital accommodation (James *et al.*, 1998). At present, the efficacy of court-based diversion depends on local initiatives and must be funded out of local budgets. Although there is national guidance, there is little in the way of national strategy and structure. As a consequence, many in need of treatment slip through the net, and must take their chances at the next stage of the process.

6.3.2 Remand to hospital: the law

Section 35 of the MHA 1983 provides a general power to remand a defendant in a magistrates' court or the Crown Court to hospital 'for a report on his mental condition'. Section 36 confers a power, exercisable only by the Crown Court, to remand to hospital for treatment. In many ways, the two sections are similar: in either case, a court shall not remand an accused person to hospital unless satisfied, on the written or oral evidence of a doctor or manager at that hospital, that a bed will be available within seven days and that the accused can be detained in a place of safety in the meantime: ss. 35(4), 36(3). A period of remand may not last more than 28 days (ss. 35(7), 36(6)), but may be renewed if evidence is provided of the need to remand further to complete the process of assessment (s. 35(5)), or treatment (s. 36(4)); the accused person need not be brought back before the court on such occasions provided that he or she is legally represented: ss. 35(6), 36(5). No person can be remanded for longer than 12 weeks in total: ss. 35(7), 36(6). There are also significant differences between the two sections, although the import of these has been lessened by decisions of the Court of Appeal.

6.3.2.1 Remand of an accused person to hospital for treatment under section 36

Section 36 is only applicable to an accused person in respect of whom the Crown Court is satisfied, on the written or oral evidence of two doctors, at least one of whom must be 'approved' under s. 12 (s. 54(1)), that the accused 'is suffering from mental illness or severe mental impairment of a nature or degree which makes it appropriate for him to be detained in a hospital for treatment': s. 36(1). The wording of this test is identical to that to be found in relation to civil detention for treatment under s. 3. A person in need of treatment by reason of mental impairment or psychopathic disorder cannot be remanded under s. 36, apparently because of the view that persons suffering from these conditions would be of problematic treatability. As one might expect, given that this is remand for treatment, a patient detained under s. 36 is subject to the powers of compulsory treatment without consent contained in Part IV of the 1983 Act: s. 56(1). Section 36 is used rarely: it was used on 12 occasions in England in 2004–5 and 12 during the previous year, down from 25 in 2001 (Government Statistical Service, 2006: Table 1). This compares with 33 uses in 1996–7, and 48 in 1990–1 (Department of Health, 2003c: Table 1). Although the falling use of s. 36 is in line with the pattern in respect of other diversionary measures, which show a general decline over recent years, the infrequency of use of s. 36 is also partly explained by the increased use of the Secretary of State's powers in s. 48 to transfer unsentenced prisoners from prison to hospital, used with greater frequency from the mid-1990s (see later in this chapter), and the tendency of court-based diversions schemes to come into play somewhat earlier in the process in magistrates' courts (Blumenthal and Wessely, 1992), when it is s. 35 that is the relevant provision. But when the numbers remanded under both sections are compared to the thousands of mentally disordered people remanded to prison for medical assessments, the underuse of the powers to remand to hospital is truly shocking.

6.3.2.2 Remand under section 35

Section 35 is indeed used more frequently than s. 36, although the number of orders made in 2004–5, at 118 (Government Statistical Service, 2006: Table 1), was lower than any previous year in the decade, and remarkably down on the 419 such orders made in 1990–1 (Department of Health, 2003c: Table 1). The powers contained in s. 35 are exercisable in respect of an 'accused person', defined in s. 35(2). In respect of the Crown Court, an accused person is one who is awaiting trial or has been arraigned for trial for 'an offence punishable by imprisonment' (s. 35(2)(a)), with the exception of the offence of murder. So far as magistrates' courts are concerned, an accused person is defined in s. 35(2)(b) to include:

> any person who has been convicted by the court of an offence punishable on summary conviction with imprisonment and any person charged with such an offence if the court is satisfied that he did that act or made the omission charged or has consented to the exercise by the court of the powers conferred by this section.

Thus, a person may be remanded to hospital by magistrates without the bench being satisfied that he or she did the act alleged, if that accused person consents to the remand. But if that person has not been convicted, he or she cannot be remanded under this provision without consent unless the bench is satisfied that the defendant did the act or omission charged. If the defendant refuses to or lacks capacity to consent, a magistrates' court may, when there is a firm diagnosis by two s. 12 'approved' doctors that the defendant is suffering from mental illness or severe mental impairment, make a hospital order (see later in this chapter) under s. 37 instead of remanding the defendant to hospital under s. 35. This may be done without convicting the offender if the court 'is satisfied that the accused did the act or made the omission charged' (s. 37(3)), and does not require the consent of the offender: *R v Lincoln (Kesteven) Justices, ex p O'Connor* [1983] 1 WLR 335 (DC). This mechanism can achieve the same effect as an order made under s. 35, which provides an identical test (s. 35(2)(b)), with the important differences that a s. 37 order will not be time-limited and a patient detained under s. 37 is subject to the powers of treatment without consent contained in Part IV of the 1983 Act. All of this, these days, is subject to financial considerations. In *R v West Allerdale Magistrates Court, ex p Bitcon* [2003] EWHC 2460 a magistrates' court made an order under s. 35, for B to be remanded to a private nursing home. B's local PCT refused to fund his placement, however, basing its decision on the view of a psychiatrist, that only remand in prison would be appropriate. The court then revoked its order. When B sought judicial review of that decision, the High Court held that the magistrates' court had no choice but to act as it had.

Notwithstanding that the medical criteria for remand under s. 35 are similar to those for civil commitment for treatment under s. 3, and that the court must be satisfied, on the basis of the evidence of one doctor (who must be 'approved': s. 54(1)), that there is reason to suspect that the defendant is suffering from one of the four specified types of mental disorder required for admission under that section, remand under s. 35 does not allow the treatment without consent of the remandee under the provisions of Part IV of the 1983 Act, because this is expressly excluded by s. 56(1)(b). It has long been the practice that, where necessary to treat such persons without their consent, then they would, during the duration of the remand, also be sectioned under ss. 2 or 3 of the Act, despite long-standing doubts about the legality of such 'double detention' (Fennell, 1991b). In *Dlodlo v Mental Health Review Tribunal for the South Thames Region* (1996) 36 BMLR 145 and *R v North West London Mental Health NHS Trust and Ors, ex p Stewart* [1997] 4 ALL ER 871, [1998] 2 WLR 189, however, the Court of Appeal decided that there is no embargo on the application of the provisions of one part of the 1983 Act to a person already detained under another part. Jones (2006, 218–19; see also Fennell, 1991b) has laid out a number of strong arguments against the holding in *Stewart*, which include:

- this defeats the clear intention of Parliament that there should be no compulsory treatment of persons remanded for reports, as evidenced by s. 56(1)(b);
- why is there a separate provision – s. 36 – that provides for remand for treatment to a more limited category of patient (only the mentally ill and severely mentally impaired)?

- a person detained under Part II could be 'discharged' by a tribunal (see 8.4) but would still be liable to be detained under s. 35;

- the powers of RMOs, for example, to grant leave of absence, in respect of patients detained under Part II would not, in fact, be exercisable;

- the duty of hospital managers under s. 132(1) to ensure that the patient understands the legal basis for detention and the avenues open by way of challenge to continued detention could only be carried out with difficulty.

In short, the argument is that the 1983 Act is clearly not set up to contemplate all the myriad complications relating to the legal status of a patient subject to 'dual detention'. Nevertheless, the Court of Appeal has ruled in favour and there is little objection from within psychiatry (Gunn and Joseph, 1993). The Mental Health Bills of 2002 and 2004 would have given explicit powers to treat those held on remand, but the 2006 proposals, of more limited scope, make no mention of this situation. It is our view, however, that this is a necessary reform. There is little reason to object in principle, particularly as the alternative is remand in prison. Other proposals seem to have fallen with the fall of the 2002 and 2004 Bills. For example, a person remanded in hospital cannot be given leave of absence by his or her RMO. A common complaint of RMOs is that the constraints of a remand order impact negatively on the ability to construct a satisfactory care plan, if leave of absence is seen as an important part of that plan. The proposal, now apparently abandoned, to relax the time limits on remand might have encouraged the greater use of remand in hospital, as one reason for the current underuse of these powers is that the time limits imposed by ss. 35 and 35 of the 1983 Act are thought by some medical professionals to be too short to allow satisfactory treatment to be given (although, as *Kudla* shows, remand cannot be for any longer duration than is reasonable in the circumstances).

In addition, it seems that there will be no reworking of the potentially problematic wording of s. 35(2)(b) of the 1983 Act, the general thrust of which is to allow magistrates to remand to hospital both convicted, and in the circumstances detailed, unconvicted defendants. In one important respect, it seems that the wording of the provision frustrates that intention. The problem is with the reference to 'an offence punishable on *summary* conviction' because this comprises only summary offences (triable only in a magistrates' court) and offences that are 'triable either way' (which may be dealt with in either a magistrates' court or the Crown Court), which comprise petty and moderately serious offences. The most serious of offences are triable *only* 'on indictment', that is, only in the Crown Court. Such offences, as a matter of law, simply *cannot* result in a 'summary conviction', which means that a person charged with such an offence cannot be remanded to hospital by magistrates. This was the view of the law taken in *R v Chippenham Magistrates' Court, ex p Thompson* (1995) *The Times*, 6 December (DC), in which it was held that a 'hospital order' in s. 37, which uses the same phraseology as s. 35, could not be made by magistrates in relation to an indictable offence. There would seem to be no good reason for the narrow scope of this provision as a matter of policy and it may well be explicable as clumsy drafting. If this is so, then the opportunity should be taken to put it right. The law on remand in hospital will, however, feel the effects of the proposed reformulation of the definition of mental disorder and abolition of the current 'treatability' test, which, if enacted, would widen the ambit of the powers to remand for treatment, specifically to include those with personality disorders.

As this discussion shows, the area of remand, whether, as is usual, in custody or, relatively rarely, in hospital is beset with difficulties both in terms of resources and frameworks. As this chapter so far has also shown, the main problems with the current system are to do with the ability to recognise mental disorder, and the chronic underuse of the option of remand to hospital rather than to prison by the courts. This is partly about lack of funding, but it also an indication that the courts have not been convinced by the merits of the policy of diversion. In the light of this, there is a pressing need to improve the quality of medical care for mental disorder in prisons and the system for transfer from prison to hospital. As seen elsewhere in this text (Chapter 3), steps have recently being taken in this regard. But the need to encourage the more systematic use of the power to remand to hospital rather than prison is, if anything, more vital, if the remand to hospital system is not to become de facto obsolete. New law can help, but attitudinal change, both on the part of the courts and psychiatrists too often unwilling to accept remanded patients, is the real key.

6.3.2.3 Fitness to stand trial

Remand to hospital is not the only pre-trial diversionary mechanism available for consideration: an alternative is to find that the accused person is not fit to be tried. The conviction of a person who was unfit to plead at the time of trial will be unsafe and will be set aside (*R v Lewis-Joseph* [2004] EWCA Civ 1212). This is because it has long been the accepted wisdom of common law, and now of Art. 6 of the Convention, that there should be no trial of a person who is unable to understand the proceedings, and so cannot respond to the charge against him or her 'with that advice and caution that he ought' (Blackstone, 1793, in Mackay, 1995: 216). At the same time, though, society needs to be protected from those who 'present a continuing danger' to it (per Lord Bingham CJ in *R v Antoine* [1999] 2 Cr App R 225 (CA) at 227; see also the speech of Lord Bingham in *R v H and SSHD* [2003] UKHL 1 at para. 2). Section 2 of the Criminal Lunatics Act 1800, which put this view on a statutory basis, provided that a person found to be insane, by a jury empanelled for that purpose, should not be tried but instead 'kept in strict custody'. This was more or less the position until recently, with the caveat that the triggering concept was subsequently widened and is now that of 'disability' rather than 'insanity': s. 4, Criminal Procedure (Insanity) Act 1964 ('the 1964 Act') as substituted by s. 2, Criminal Procedure (Insanity and Unfitness to Plead) Act 1991 ('the 1991 Act'). There is a right of appeal against any order made under these Acts: s. 16A,B Criminal Appeals Act 1968.

The possibility that a defendant is under such disability as prevents him or her being tried may be raised by the defence 'or otherwise' (s. 4(1), 1964 Act), in any case, before a Crown Court. There must, however, be at least some medical evidence that supports a finding of unfitness: Kennedy LJ in *R v Borkan* [2004] EWCA Crim 1642. In *R v Robertson*

(1968) 52 Cr App R 690, [1968] 1 WLR 1767, it was held that, if the issue is raised by the defence, the burden of proof is on it to establish on a balance of probabilities that the defendant is unfit, but in *R v Podola* [1960] 1 QB 325 (DC), it was held that the criminal law burden of proof – beyond reasonable doubt – applies when the issue is raised by the prosecution. Recourse to the Acts of 1964 and 1991 is not possible in a magistrates' court (s. 5, 1991 Act), although, as discussed earlier, magistrates may use their powers in s. 37(3) MHA 1983 to achieve much the same ends.

There is no statutory definition of the concept of 'disability' or 'unfitness to plead' as it is commonly, but misleadingly, described. The leading case remains *R v Pritchard* (1836) 7 C & P 303, in which it was held, per Baron Alderson, that a defendant is unfit for trial if unable to plead to the indictment, or if not 'of sufficient intellect to comprehend the course of the proceedings in the trial so as to make a proper defence, to challenge a juror to whom he might wish to object and to comprehend the details of the evidence' (see also *R v Friend* [1997] 2 Cr App R 231, CA). That this 'cognitive' test is capable of allowing departures from its spirit is evident from *Podola*, in which a person suffering from amnesia about the events relevant to the charge was held not to be unfit. It may well be that such a person can understand the proceedings, and so on, but without a memory of the relevant events, it is not clear how he or she could decide on a plea, instruct a lawyer effectively, provide evidence or testimony to contradict that of the prosecution and its witnesses, or make any number of other decisions that are required of a defendant in a criminal trial. In *R v M (John)* [2003] EWCA Crim 3452, the Court of Appeal did not disagree with a judge's direction given to a jury, which comprised the following six factors (at para. 20). To be fit to plead, the defendant must be capable of: '(1) understanding the charges; (2) deciding whether to plead guilty or not; (3) exercising his right to challenge jurors; (4) instructing solicitors and counsel; (5) following the course of the proceedings; (6) giving evidence in his own defence.' This test seems to move closer to the 'decisional competence' approach advocated by some commentators (Duff, 1986; Grubin, 1993; Mackay, 1995), who seek a broader test of unfitness, which would include some assessment of the defendant's ability not merely to understand but to make relevant decisions before and during the process of trial.

The trial judge in *R v M* elaborated on various aspects of the test. He explained, for example, that the sixth point required that, to be found fit, 'the defendant must be able (a) to understand the questions he is asked in the witness box, (b) to apply his mind to answering them, and (c) to convey intelligibly to the jury the answers which he wishes to give' (para. 24), which does seem to require something more than simply cognition. But it is possible that a defendant might 'go through the motions' without being decisionally competent. It seems that an ability simply to answer questions from counsel, even if the answers reveal little understanding of the those questions, will be acceptable as evidence of fitness to stand trial. The judge in *R v M* went on to explain that: 'It is not necessary that [the defendant's] answers should be plausible or believable or reliable.' For Mackay (2002: 733), decisional competence constrasts with 'competence to assist counsel', or 'a rudimentary understanding of the trial process'. He (2002: 732) cites research (Polythress *et al.*, 2002) to show that, in order to take a truly proactive part in proceedings, it is decisional competence that is required.

In *R* v *M* , as in *Podola*, the substantive outcome was that a defendant with significant short term memory problems was found fit for trial. If the defendant proved unable to remember events referred to in cross-examination, 'He is entitled to say that he has no recollection of those events, or indeed of anything that happened during the relevant period]' (para. 24). It is not clear that this is necessarily the best course for a defendant in this position to take, and raises prior questions, for example, about whether to give evidence in one's own defence or not, which would be required by a full-blown 'decisional competence' approach but which are not relevant under the current approach (Gray *et al.*, 2001). In the last edition of this text, we argued that it would be preferable for the concept of unfitness or disability to be grounded in the test for capacity proposed by the Law Commission, which has since taken statutory form as ss. 2 and 3 of the Mental Capacity Act 2005. Section 3(1) of the 2005 Act provides that 'a person is unable to make decisions for himself if he is unable (a) to understand the information relevant to the decision, (b) to retain that information, (c) to use or weigh that information as part of the process of making the decision, or (d) to communicate his decision (whether by talking, using sign language or any other means)'. In Jersey, in *Attorney General* v *O'Driscoll* (No. 2) [2003] JRC 117, the Royal Court of Jersey decided not to follow *Pritchard* and instead adopted essentially this test (see further Mackay, 2004). Although s. 3(3) of the 2005 Act does provide that 'The fact that a person is able to retain the information relevant to a decision for a short period only does not prevent him from being regarded as able to make the decision', it would seem at least arguable that a defendant such as that in *R* v *M* would have been classified as unfit under this test, on the particular grounds of not satisfying the requirements of s. 3(1)(b) and therefore also s. 3(1)(c). As we shall discuss presently, the law on unfitness and the insanity defence was reformed in 2004, but it seems clear that still further changes are required. As the test in the Mental Capacity Act is rolled out across most areas of law and policy, it seems increasingly innocuous that in this area there is continued reliance on a test formulated in, and against the state of knowledge of, the early nineteenth century. There is an argument to be made, that Art. 6 requires that a more defensible test of disability be engineered than that which currently exists.

Historically, it has been for a jury to determine whether a defendant is unfit, but s. 22 of the Domestic Violence, Crime and Victims Act 2004 altered this, and it is now provided that the question of unfitness is to be decided 'by the court without a jury': s. 4(5), 1964 Act. Although there was some disquiet expressed in Parliament as the 2004 Act went through the law-making process, that the removal of the jury from elements of the criminal justice system is an attack on democracy (see HC Hansard, 27 October 2004, Cols. 1524–35), there is always the one-size-fits-all criticism of juries – that they can produce perverse yet unchallengeable decisions – to put against such arguments; there are cases that support the point (see, for example, *R* v *Hussein* [2005] EWCA Crim 3556, in which a jury found a defendant fit to plead, although the defence and prosecution were in agreement that he was not). The issue is usually raised early in the trial process, at arraignment. If unfitness is raised at any later stage, such as in the course of trial, it 'shall be determined as soon as it arises' (s. 4(4)), but this is subject to a discretion in the court to delay consideration of the issue until the opening of the defence case: s. 4(2). This may be a suitable option if there is reason to believe that the prosecution case is weak, such that the court may direct, or the defence submit, that there is no case to answer. In such circumstances, the defendant must be acquitted and the question of unfitness 'shall not be determined': s. 4(3).

Until the reforms introduced by the 1991 Act, the consequences of a determination of the question of unfitness were straightforward. If fit for trial, the defendant was tried in the normal way; if not, the court was required to make an order committing the defendant to hospital (a 'hospital order'), without limit of time, coupled with a 'restriction order' (see later in the chapter), which effectively gives to the Home Secretary power to determine when, if at all, the defendant is released from hospital, or remitted to prison to stand trial. These orders had to be made following a finding of unfitness to plead by a jury. Hence, under the pre-1991 system, there was the possibility that a defendant would be made subject to a hospital order, even though the court may not have considered whether the grounds for the making of such an order in the Mental Health Act had been made out; indeed, it may not even have heard medical evidence. There is evidence that this possibility was, in fact, realised in a number of cases (Mackay, 1990: 251). The prospect of indefinite detention meant that the question of unfitness was rarely raised, and increasingly so through the 1980s until by 1989 there were only 11 such cases nationally (Mackay 1995: 222). This meant, in practice, the failure of this mechanism as a diversionary measure and, by implication, also that the rules of natural justice were often not observed. Moreover, because it was usual for a finding of unfitness to be made before the defence case had been put, there was the possibility that an offender found unfit to plead may have been acquitted had that case been heard, which, according to Grubin (1991: 543) was indeed the situation in seven of the 295 cases of persons found unfit between 1976 and 1988.

The 1991 Act introduced three main innovations to address these concerns, regarding the procedure following a finding of unfitness, the lack of a place for medical evidence in that procedure, and the disposal options open to the court. These reforms did not solve all of the problems identified with the operation of the 1964 Act, however, and further changes were introduced by the Domestic Violence, Crime and Victims Act 2004, the provisions of which relating to unfitness to plead (and the insanity defence; see below) came into force on 31 March 2005 (The Domestic Violence, Crime and Victims Act 2004 Commencement Order No 1, SI 2005/579, para. 3). The discussion below will focus on the law that has been in force since that date.

The first substantive change introduced by the 1991 Act was, by s. 2, to insert a new provision, s. 4A, into the 1964 Act. This provides that, if the court has determined that the defendant is under such disability that he or she is unfit for trial, the trial process will halt. Then, a jury shall determine whether or not it is satisfied that the defendant did the act or made the omission with which he or she is charged: s. 4A(1),(2). This is to be done either on the evidence that has already been heard, or on the prosecution evidence and that given by a person appointed by the court to act for the defence: s. 4A(2)(a),(b). This is described in the long title to the 1991 Act as a 'trial of the facts'. Its purpose is to divert from the consequences of a finding of unfitness defendants who would not have been found guilty of the offence charged. A jury that is not satisfied – and the test seems to be that which is usually applied in criminal courts, of 'beyond reasonable doubt' (Home Office, 1991: para. 9; see also the speech of Lord Hutton in *Antoine* in the House of Lords [2001] 1 AC 340 at 376) – that the defendant did the act or made the omission in question must acquit: s. A(4).

The courts have been posed some problems by the apparently mandatory nature of ss. 4(6) and 4A(2), coupled with s. 5(2) (discussed further below), under the terms of which the court 'shall' determine the question of fitness as soon as it arises, the jury 'shall' then determine whether the accused did the act or omission in question, and the court 'shall' then make one of the orders available to it. If the accused is found, and remains, unfit, there is no problem, but in cases where the mental state of the accused fluctuates, things have not been so straightforward. In *R v Omara* [2004] EWCA Crim 431, the Court of Appeal held that, once a finding of unfitness has been made, a trial of the facts must follow, even if, as in that case, the defendant had in the meantime become well. In *R v DPP, ex p Ferris* [2004] EWHC 1221, Maurice Kay LJ, sitting in the Divisional Court, held that the wording of s. 4A(2) is mandatory, in a case in which a trial had recommenced after an earlier finding of unfitness and a trial of the facts which found that D did the act charged, and had then stopped a second time, again on grounds of unfitness. The court held that the statute required that there must be a second trial of the facts, and the jury charged to determine whether D did the act in question must not be informed of the earlier finding. In both of these cases, the court expressed a dissatisfaction with the statute as it is presently worded, and the policy argument, that there is nothing to be gained by finding for a second or subsequent time that the defendant did the act or made the omission in question. The policy reasons did seem to prevail, however, in *R v Hasani* [2005] EWHC 3016 (Admin), [2006] 1 ALL ER 817. The Divisional Court held that 'the ss. 4A and 5 procedures are inapplicable if, following a further s. 4. hearing, the court has found the accused person fit to plead' (para. 14), noting that it would be 'a quite absurd waste of time and money' for a trial of the facts to take place when it is known that the accused is fit to stand trial, as it would if the court had to make an order for absolute discharge because of an earlier, and now out-of-date, finding that the accused was unfit. The court accepted that it had departed from the literal rule of statutory interpretation in reaching this conclusion, instead following the rule that statutory provisions must where possible be given a sensible meaning (para. 14). It is submitted that the approach in *Hasani* is to be preferred, notwithstanding that judicial rewriting of the statute is entailed. As the Court of Appeal noted in *Omara*, the statute, as it is currently constructed, risks breach of the Art. 6 rights of the defendant.

The general compatibility of the trial of the facts procedure with Art. 6 ECHR was litigated in *R v M, K and H* [2001] EWCA Crim 2024, [2002] 1 WLR 824 (CA), a conjoined appeal involving three defendants accused of serious sexual offences. It was argued before the court that a trial of the facts was no fairer to a defendant found to be unfit than was a full trial. In a trial of the facts, just as in a full trial, the defendant would be unable to participate in the proceedings rendering a trial of the facts 'unfair' within the meaning of Art. 6(1). It was further argued that a trial of the facts is to be conceptualised as a criminal trial, thus bringing Art. 6(2) into play, and allowing the argument that the presumption of innocence guaranteed by Art. 6(2) was not adhered to, and that the defendant in such a hearing would not have 'adequate time and facilities for the preparation of his defence', or be able to defend him or herself, or examine witnesses, or cause that to be done by counsel of his or her own choosing, as required by Art. 6(3). The Court of Appeal rejected these submissions, holding, on an application of *Engel* v *The Netherlands* (No. 1) [1976] 1 EHRR 647, that, as a trial of the facts is not a criminal trial, the 'criminal charge provisions of Article 6 do not apply' (at para. 19).

One of the appellants appealed further to the House of Lords (*R* v *H and Secretary of State for the Home Department* [2003] UKHL 1). The sole question on the appeal was whether the trial of the facts procedure breaches the protection provided by Art. 6 of the Convention to those involved in criminal proceedings. Lord Bingham, giving the opinion of the House, held that it does not. His reasoning was essentially similar to that of the Court of Appeal. He applied the three-part test developed by the European Court in *Engel*. This provides that, in order to determine the status of proceedings, it is necessary to consider (1) if the proceedings in question are categorised as criminal under domestic law, (2) the nature of the offence, and (3) the severity of any penalty. Lord Bingham noted that the proceedings are not categorised as criminal by the Acts of 1964 and 1991, which provide, as seen above, that a trial of the facts occurs only when a criminal trial has been halted. On the second and third points, Lord Bingham said (at para. 18) that: 'Whether one views the matter through domestic or European spectacles, the answer is the same; the purpose and function of the section 4A procedure is not to decide whether the accused person has committed a criminal offence. The procedure can result in a final acquittal, but it cannot result in a conviction and it cannot result in punishment.' As such, although 'the procedure under section 4A must always, of course, be conducted with scrupulous regard for the interests of the accused person . . . if properly conducted [it] is fair' (at para. 20).

Therefore, the procedure did not of itself in any way breach any provision of Art. 6. This is perhaps unfortunate. In support of his conclusion that there is no punitive disposal available following a trial of the facts, Lord Bingham emphasised that an absolute discharge (as had been ordered at first instance in this case and in the case of K) is not a punishment, but an alternative to punishment according to the definition in s. 12(1) Powers of Criminal Courts (Sentencing) Act 2000. But, as will be discussed further below, a court may now also, since 1991, require that a person, found on a trial of the facts to have committed the act or made the omission charged, be made subject to a 'supervision order', which in substance is remarkably similar to a psychiatric probation order; probation has, since 1991, been defined as a punishment (before that date it was conceptualised as an alternative to punishment). Thus, it can be argued, the distinction between what is or is not, at an abstract or principled level, 'punitive' under the 1964/1991 Acts regime is perhaps more problematic than Lord Bingham, sticking closely to technical definitions that may have scant relationship to how any particular disposal is experienced by the person subject to it and the facts of the case before him, suggests. And, although it is true that a trial of the facts does not 'determine any criminal charge' against the defendant (see further below) as required to bring Art. 6(1) into operation, it is only because a defendant has been charged with a criminal offence that the trial of the facts procedure will have been activated. The court does, in most circumstances, make a final disposal following such a trial, and so there is in truth a 'determination', just as in truth the punitiveness of any disposal is in the eye of the beholder. The slippery quality of this question is underlined by the fact that subsequently, in *R v Bradford Crown Court, ex p South West Yorkshire Mental Health NHS Trust* [2003] EWCA (Civ) 1857, the Court of Appeal held that the s. 4A procedure could be classified as involving 'a criminal cause of matter' for the purposes of determining the applicability of the right to appeal under s. 18 of the Supreme Court Act 1981. In *R v DPP, ex p Ferris* [2004] EWHC 1221, Maurice Kay LJ, at para. 17, provided a rather bemusing explanation:

when classification is necessary proceedings under Section 4A may be civil for some purposes, as was found in the case of *H*, and essentially criminal for other purposes, as was found in the *Bradford Crown Court* case. On any basis, the proceedings . . . bear some of the hallmarks of both civil and criminal proceedings: civil to the extent that they do not and cannot involve conviction or punishment in the penal sense; criminal in the sense that the rules of criminal evidence, including those relating to the burden and standard of proof, apply, and the result may be loss of liberty.

The implication of this seems to be, in essence, that a court may chose to emphasise either the criminal or the civil aspects of the s. 4A procedure as it wishes, and the implication of that is that it was open to the appellate courts in *H* to have bestowed a greater degree of protection on those subject to that procedure than was the case.

Rose LJ in the Court of Appeal gave further consideration to the question of 'fairness'. The court noted that although the right to a fair trial in Art. 6 is 'an absolute right, the content of that right varies'. The ability of defendants to pursue their defence actively varies, and for some, age or unfitness will constitute a disadvantage. The court 'should do its best to minimise that disadvantage, but it may be unable to remove it totally'. In *T v UK* and *V v UK* [2000] Crim LR 187 (see also *SC v UK* (2005) 40 EHRR 10), the European Court required national law and process 'to reduce as far as possible' the disadvantages of the defendants, also recognising, in the words of Lord Bingham in *Brown v Stott* [2001] 2 WLR 817 at 836, cited by Rose LJ in *K, M and H*, 'the need for a fair balance between the general interest of the community and the personal rights of the individual'. The court concluded that 'If Article 6 applies, it has not been infringed in any of the cases before us'. This means that only if there is some departure from or abuse of the ss. 4 and 4A procedures, which pushes the disadvantage to a particular defendant beyond that which is reasonable in the circumstances, will the Convention rights of the defendant be at issue. An example is provided by the decision of the Court of Appeal in

R v KM [2003] EWCA Crim 357. KM had been found, on a trial of the facts, to have committed the act of murder. This finding was based on a witness statement, to the effect that KM had been part of a group who had stabbed a young boy to death, had wiped the knife in question clean after the attack, and had verbally admitted to his involvement in the attack. The statement was made by another member of the group, and had been read to the jury, with no opportunity for those representing KM to challenge its veracity. On appeal, the Court of Appeal held that there was a breach of Art. 6(3). Citing the decision of the European Court in *PS v Germany* Application No. 33900/96 (2002), that Art. 6(3) requires that evidence be available for cross-examination, and the right to challenge evidence against oneself can only be limited where strictly necessary (for example, to protect the Art. 8 rights of witnesses who have been subject to intimidation), the Court of Appeal held (at para. 61) that to admit the witness statement in question in evidence unduly disadvantaged KM. The decisive factor in this case was that the witness in question had a vested interest 'in pinning the murder on the defendant' (para. 61).

In all three of the cases initially under appeal in *K, M and H*, an application had been made before the trial judge for a stay of proceedings to be ordered so that the Art. 6 question could be determined, or on grounds that to proceed against the accused was an abuse of process. In all three cases, that request had been denied and, in at least one case, the trial judge was of the view that he had no power to order a stay once a finding of unfitness had been made. This was because of the wording of s. 4A(2), which provides that once a finding of unfitness has been made 'it *shall* be determined by a jury [emphasis added]' whether or not the defendant committed the act or made the omission charged against him. The Court of Appeal held that these words are procedural rather than mandatory, and do not limit the inherent powers of the courts to stay proceedings, at any stage of the process: 'An abuse application, whenever made, must be founded on matters independent of the defendant's disability, such as oppressive behaviour of the Crown or agencies of the State, or circumstances or conduct which would deprive the defendant of a fair trial e.g. destruction of vital records . . .'. The court specifically disapproved the approach taken in the *K* case at first instance, in which the judge, considering the application for a stay, balanced the rights of the individual against the general good in determining whether the defendant had committed the act in question. Such questions, said the court, were for the CPS, in deciding whether a prosecution should be brought. Once the case had come to court, they were immaterial, and 'The public interest in having serious allegations investigated is a factor behind the general principle that the power to order a stay should be exercised sparingly, even when there are proper, i.e. non-disability related grounds'. In summary, then, the House of Lords and Court of Appeal in *K, M and H* found the procedures relating to a finding of unfitness and to a subsequent trial of the facts to be neither in breach of the human rights of disabled defendants nor to be an abuse of the court process.

The second innovation introduced by the 1991 Act, and amended in 2004, addressed the possibility that a hospital order might be made, although there was no mechanism to ensure that medical evidence be heard before its making. It is now provided that a court may not find a defendant unfit to plead except on the written or oral evidence of two or more doctors, at least one of whom must be 'approved': s. 4(6), 1964 Act. Nonetheless, after 1991, there remained a considerable degree of incongruence between the 1964/1991 Acts regime and the MHA, because under the former, the jury (now the court) considers the *Pritchard* test, and this test only asks if the defendant is or is not fit for trial, and not whether he or she suffers from a mental disorder that would justify his or her detention under the MHA. The medical evidence required by s. 4(6) need only to relate to the question of fitness, leaving open the possibility that a person who, on an application of the *Pritchard* test, is found unfit, might be placed on a hospital order, only to be discharged by the RMO, hospital managers or a tribunal (see Chapter 8), because the criteria for continued detention under the 1983 Act – which are narrower than the *Pritchard* test – are not met, as happened in the case of Glenn Pearson in 1986 (Emmins, 1986).

Not only is such a situation potentially self-defeating, it is also arguably in breach of Art. 5(1)(e) ECHR's requirement that no person shall be deprived of his or her liberty, save, inter alia, for 'the lawful detention . . . of persons of unsound mind', and as is well known, the European Court of Human Rights in *Winterwerp* v *The Netherlands* (1979) 2 EHRR 387 held that, for detention to be lawful, there must be objective medical evidence that the person to be detained is mentally disordered such as to justify detention. In *R* v *Grant* [2002] 1 Cr App R 38 (CA), the court left open the possibility that a breach of Art. 5(1)(e) would be found in a case in which objective medical evidence that the defendant is mentally disordered was absent. To remedy this, a replacement s. 5 and a new s. 5A were inserted into the 1964 Act by s. 24 of the 2004 Act, and it is now provided that a 'hospital order' made under the 1964 Act has the meaning given by s. 37 of the 1983 Act: s. 5(4) 1964 Act. Now, therefore, 'To make a hospital order, the court must have the evidence required by the 1983 Act: that the defendant is mentally disordered and requires specialist medical treatment. This means that there must be medical evidence that justifies his detention on grounds of his mental state' (Department of Health, 2004: para. 90), which requirement is imposed by s. 37(2)(a) (see later in the chapter).

The third main reform, introduced in 1991, concerned choice of disposal following a finding of unfitness and that the defendant did the act in question. Until this Act, there was no choice: a person found unfit had to be sent to hospital indefinitely and placed under restrictions. Section 3 of the 1991 Act changed this situation by introducing a range of disposals, as s. 5 of the 1964 Act, a redrawn version of which was inserted by s. 24, DVCVA 2004. A court may still make a hospital order, but now with or without restrictions: s. 5(2)(a), 1964 Act. A restriction order, designed to protect the public (see below) can be attached at the discretion of the court, even if medical evidence does not support that option, as long as it can be said that the decision of the court is a reasonable one given the totality of the circumstances: *R* v *Isleworth Crown Court, ex p Jones* [2005] EWHC 662 (QBD). The making, by a Crown Court, of an order for admission to hospital requires the managers of the hospital specified in the order to admit that person: s. 37(4), MHA 1983; s. 5A(1)(c), 1964 Act. Before the 2004 Act, the making of a hospital order was not the end of the process. It was for the Secretary of State to decide whether or not to issue a warrant for the admission of the defendant into hospital within the 'relevant period', which was two months: Sch. 1, paras. 1(2), (3), (4), now repealed. In the new system, there is no longer a role for the Secretary of State. The effect of the making of a hospital order is automatic, and not subject to his or her discretion.

There are no criteria governing the making of a restriction order (see later) in addition to a hospital order on the face of the Acts of 1964 and 1991. In *Narey* v *Customs and Excise Commissioners* [2005] EWHC 784, Laws LJ, sitting in the Divisional Court with David Steel J to hear an appeal by way of case stated, held that the criteria in s. 41 of the MHA 1983 do not apply to s. 5 of the 1964 Act (para. 13), but then went on to hold that 'the only possible justification for restriction without limit of time must be that the [defendant] poses a risk of serious harm to the public' (para. 17), which is the wording employed in s. 1. This case was decided before the 2004 reforms came into force, and would seem to be rendered otiose by them, because s. 5(4) of the 1964 Act now provides that reference to a restriction order in s. 5(2)(a) carries the meaning given by s. 41, so that the same criteria, and requirements as to medical evidence (discussed in detail later in the chapter), do now apply under both routes into a restriction order.

Whether or not a restriction order is made is crucial to the defendant, not simply because such defendants will be subject to a more restrictive hospital regime and to greater restrictions on release, but also because, when a court makes a restriction order in addition to a hospital order, the defendant can be remitted directly to court, or to a prison or remand centre, for trial, if, following treatment, he or she is well enough to stand trial: s. 5A(4), 1964 Act. Before 2004, it was explicitly provided that any other disposal made by the court was to be treated as final: Sch. 1, paras. (1), (2), 1991 Act, now repealed. Presumably, it was felt that it was no longer necessary to be explicit, because the clear implication of s. 5A(4) is that, without both a hospital and a restriction order, there is no power to remit and the disposal is, therefore, in practice final. The power to remit is vested solely in the Secretary of State, and may only be exercised if, after consultation with the defendant's RMO, he or she 'is satisfied that that person can properly be tried', which, presumably, should involve a reapplication of the *Pritchard* test.

If the offence that the defendant is found, on a trial of the facts, to have committed is murder, there is no option but to make a hospital order and a restriction order without limit of time (s. 5(3), 1964 Act), but *only* – and this is another significant change introduced in 2004 – if the criteria for a hospital order are made out: s. 5(3)(b), 1964 Act. If they are not, 'the court's options are limited to a supervision order or absolute discharge' (Home Office Circular, 2005: para. 12). For offences other than murder, the court may, instead of making a hospital order, with or without restrictions, make a 'supervision order' (s. 5(2)(b), 1964 Act) or discharge the defendant absolutely: s. 5(2)(c). If an order for absolute discharge is made, s. 12(1) of the Powers of Criminal Courts (Sentencing) Act 2000, which provides the jurisdictional basis to make such an order, applies, but is modified by s. 5A(6) of the 1964 Act, to the effect that the sentencing court must be of the opinion that it is inexpedient to inflict punishment, and that an absolute discharge 'would be most suitable in all the circumstances of the case'. There is no guidance about when a community-based disposal is to be preferred over the making of a hospital order.

In some instances, it will be appropriate for courts to use the new powers in s. 5A(2) to remand an accused to hospital under ss. 35 and 36 of the 1983 Act, or to make an interim hospital order under s. 38. These powers are available if an accused has been found unfit and a trial of the facts has concluded that he or she did the act in question, but a disposal under s. 5 has not yet been made. It is, however, not possible to make a hospital order unless there is medical evidence in support of that option, and so, provided that the decision to make a hospital order rather than a supervision order or an order for absolute discharge is bona fide, the law as it now stands is in compliance with the requirements of Art. 5(1)(e) of the Convention. If a hospital order is made instead of a community-based option for inappropriate reasons, such as a lack of resources to fund a particular defendant's care in the community, the situation may be different: *R, on the application of Mohammed Latif* 2002 WL 31422140, para. 12.

Supervision orders are only available under the 1964 Act. The details of the scheme are found in Sch. 1A to the Act. Supervision orders are similar to guardianship orders (see Chapter 9) in some respects, but provide for considerably more nuanced control over the subject of the order. A supervision order (which can only be made if the court is satisfied that it is the most suitable means of dealing with the accused or appellant: para. 2(1)), is an order requiring the person in respect of whom it is made to be under the supervision of a social worker or probation officer, from within a specified social service or local justice area (para. 3(1)) for up to two years: para. 1(1). An order can include a treatment component for all or some of its duration, if there is medical evidence from at least two doctors, at least one of whom is 'approved', that the subject of the order is in need of treatment but his or her condition is not such as to warrant hospitalisation: paras. 1(2), 4, 5. Treatment may only be given on an outpatient basis (paras. (3), 5(3)) in a specified hospital or other place, and under the direction of a specified doctor (para. 4(3)), but there is also provision for an order to include a requirement as to residence (para. 8), and so the subject of a supervision order may be de facto hospitalised by the terms of an order. There is, however, no sanction for any breach of the terms of an order, and this is because the supervision order, new in 2004 (although replacing the similar 'supervision and treatment order'), 'is designed to enable support and treatment to be given to the defendant to prevent recurrence of the problem which led to the offending' (HM Stationery Office, 2004: para. 96). The usefulness of the new order, which aims only to 'provide a framework for treatment' (*ibid.*) remains to be demonstrated.

Despite these reforms, the area of unfitness to plead remains controversial. One particular issue is the precise meaning, on a trial of the facts, of the phrase 'did the act or made the omission charged against him as the offence' in s. 4A(2) of the 1964 Act. The view of the government, at the time the 1991 Act was passed, was that a trial of the facts should be limited to an inquiry into whether the defendant had committed the *actus reus* of the offence in question, because otherwise there would be little to distinguish a trial of the facts from a full trial, for which the defendant is not meant to be fit

(Mackay and Kearns, 1997: 650). As White (1992) pointed out, however, the *actus reus* of some offences – he gave the example of theft – embrace notions of intention. This very point arose in *R v Egan* [1997] Crim LR 225 (CA). The court held that 'did the act or made the omission' meant *all* the ingredients of the offence, so that on a trial of the facts on a charge of theft, a defendant is entitled to be acquitted unless the prosecution can show both that he or she took the property in question, and that this was done dishonestly and with an intention permanently to deprive. Although, on this view, a trial of the facts is in fact barely distinguishable from a full trial, and so raises the conceptual problems referred to above, it was the view of the court in *Egan* that to hold that 'act' should be defined narrowly risks subverting the underlying intention behind s. 4A(4) of the 1991 Act, because it would leave open the possibility of injustice, namely that a defendant, who would have been acquitted had the case gone to trial, would not be acquitted on a trial of the facts. *Egan* was not an authority of any longevity, however. In *Attorney-General's Reference (No. 3 of 1998)* [1999] 3 ALL ER 40 (CA), a differently constituted Court of Appeal held that *Egan* 'appears to have been decided per incuriam' (per Judge LJ at 48). This view was, strictly, *obiter*, because the court in *Attorney-General's Reference* was concerned with the question of the 'special verdict' of insanity rather than with the issue of fitness to plead. As Judge LJ pointed out, however, in both contexts a 'trial of the facts' is required, which is identical and the product of the same legislative history, and hence 'whether the case is proceeding on the ground of insanity or unfitness to plead . . . the issue is identical, that is, whether or not the defendant did the act or made the omission alleged, but nothing in the legislation suggests that if the jury has concluded that the defendant's mental state was such that . . . his mental responsibility for his crime was negatived, it should simultaneously consider whether the necessary *mens rea* has also been proved' (at 47).

In *R v Antoine* [2001] 1 AC 340, in which the appellant had been found on a trial of the facts to have committed the act of murder, the House of Lords approved *Attorney-General's Reference* and disapproved *Egan* (at 372). The reasoning of Lord Hutton, giving the leading opinion, is deceptively simple. Section 4A(2) of the 1964 Act requires the jury to consider whether the accused 'did the act or made the omission charged against him as the offence'. 'Act' is accordingly counterposed to 'offence', the difference between them being the presence of *mens rea*. Hence a trial of the facts is concerned only with the questions of whether the accused committed the *actus reus* of the offence. To this, he added a policy consideration (at 373): 'The risk would be that if a defendant who killed another person and was charged with murder was insane at the time of the killing and was unfit to plead at the time of his trial by reason by that insanity, then *mens rea* could not be proved because of the insanity existing at the time of the alleged offence, and the jury would have to acquit the defendant and he would be released to the danger of the public.' The policy consideration is valid, but the distinction between *actus reus* and *mens rea* that underpins Lord Hutton's analysis of the statutory provisions is, with respect, problematic. The point is that the two elements of a crime – *actus reus* and *mens rea* – derive their legal significance from each other. An act is only a constituent part of a crime if accompanied by the necessary mental element. It is not a crime for

A to kill B. It is only a crime if A kills B unlawfully, that is with intention, recklessly or negligently. As Smith (2000: 622) notes, the decision in *Antoine* 'seems to be a novel departure. No other occasion when the actus reus, standing alone, has been held to have any legal consequences comes to mind'. Moreover, there is a certain logic to the argument that when a defendant has been found not guilty by reason of insanity, as required by the special verdict, it is perverse to investigate his or her *mens rea* at the time of the offence. But the argument is less persuasive in the context of unfitness to plead. This is because such a finding carries no implications about the defendant's state of mind at the time of the offence, but only at the time of trial. And, of course, the possibility of injustice noted by the Court of Appeal in *Egan* has been resurrected by these decisions.

This is unfortunate whatever the offence charged, but the most serious consequences are felt when the approach in *Antoine* is combined with the requirement of s. 5(3), 1964 Act, which, as mentioned above, require the imposition of a hospital order and unlimited restriction order if the offence charged is murder, and if the grounds for a hospital order are present. The key issue remains the accessibility of defences that would have been available had the case gone to trial. In *Antoine*, Lord Hutton did say that 'If there is objective evidence which raises the issue of mistake or accident or self-defence, then the jury should not find that the defendant did the "act" unless it is satisfied beyond reasonable doubt on all the evidence that the prosecution has negatived that defence' (at 376). These defences cannot be raised 'in the absence of a witness whose evidence raises the defence' (377). In other words, they cannot be raised by reference to the state of mind of the accused. 'Objective evidence', accordingly, means the evidence of person other than the accused.

These defences, if successful, lead to acquittal, and therefore partly answer the objection made above, but it remains the case that it is possible that a defendant, who would have been able to plead self-defence, mistake or accident on the basis of his own evidence had the case gone to trial, can be found to have done the act on a trial of the facts. Moreover, the defences of diminished responsibility and provocation introduced by the Homicide Act 1957 cannot be accessed on a trial of the facts. These defences, which apply only when a defendant is charged with murder, can, if successfully pleaded, reduce a conviction from murder to manslaughter; a finding on a trial of the facts, that the act of manslaughter is proven, frees the court to chose the most suitable disposal as per s. 5(2) of the 1964 Act. But these defences go the question of *mens rea* rather than *actus reus*, and it is clear from the authorities that these defences cannot be accessed on a trial of the facts.

In *Antoine*, the argument of the defendant was that he should be able to put the defence of diminished responsibility to the jury. Lord Hutton, in rejecting that argument, pointed out (at 365) that, following a finding of unfitness the defendant is no longer liable to be convicted of murder – as decided in *K, M and H*, a trial of the facts is not a criminal trial and does not seek to establish whether or not a criminal offence has been committed. And it is only when all the ingredients of the offence of murder have been made out that the defence of diminished responsibility can be triggered, thus reducing the conviction for what would otherwise be murder to manslaughter. Because the s. 4A procedure does not require all the ingredients of the offence to be made out, the process never reaches the point at which diminished responsibility becomes a relevant consideration. The court also pointed out that, if a person found to have done the act of manslaughter on a trial of the facts subsequently became fit for trial, he or she could not be tried at that stage for murder because the finding of manslaughter at the trial of the facts would also have entailed an acquittal on the charge of murder (at 367).

In *Antoine*, Lord Hutton left open the question of the category into which the defence of provocation fell (376). Was it an 'objectively' verifiable defence, or did it go to the forbidden territory of *mens rea*? In *R v Grant* [2002] 1 Cr App R 38, the Court of Appeal decided that it was the latter. G killed her partner. She was subsequently found unfit to plead. Before a trial of the facts took place, defence counsel submitted that he should be allowed to place a defence of provocation before the jury. The judge rejected that request, and G was subsequently found to have committed the *actus reus* of murder and a hospital order and a restriction order were duly made. G appealed on the basis that the judge was wrong to refuse to allow the defence of provocation to be put to the jury. The Court of Appeal applied *Antoine*, holding that although 'the distinction applied in *Antoine* between *actus reus* and *mens rea* is not clear-cut... in our judgment provocation falls clearly on the *mens rea* side of the dividing line' (at para. 45), and that the considerations relevant in that case were equally relevant to the defence of provocation (at para. 46).

There is thus, on the law as it stands at present, no way for a defendant charged with murder and subsequently found to be unfit to plead to access the defences of diminished responsibility or provocation. There is currently no *charge* known to law of 'diminished responsibility manslaughter' or 'manslaughter by reason of provocation'. Given the harsh consequences of a finding that the defendant committed the *actus reus* of murder following a finding of unfitness to plead, it is to be hoped that prosecutors keep the possibility of injustice in mind when laying charges, and that a charge of manslaughter rather than murder is brought in appropriate cases (see *R v Cox (Maurice)* [1968] 1 WLR 308). This would allow the courts access to a broader range of disposals.

It is arguable whether the distinction between objective and subjective, and the distinction between *actus reus* and *mens rea*, is sustainable. The defences of accident, mistake and self-defence can be understood as subsets of the general defence of 'no *mens rea*' and so it can be suggested that, by allowing these defences, the House of Lords in *Antoine*, maintaining the distinction between an act and its meaning on the one hand, deconstructs or undermines that distinction on the other. Shortly afterwards, the Divisional Court was forced to concede that, if a mental element is part of the *actus reus* (in that case, the *actus reus* of the offence, under s. 7(1) Financial Services Act 1986, was 'concealing' material facts, and to conceal, rather than, say mislay or overlook, requires intention), then the state of mind of the defendant can be inquired into to that extent (see *R v Central Criminal Court, ex p Young* [2002] EWHC 548 QBD). Clearly, to say the least, the core distinction between 'act' and 'offence', is one beset with difficulties. This was further made apparent in *R v KM* [2003] EWCA Crim 357, in which the Court of Appeal upheld the trial judge's view that the accused 'did the act' if he or she took part in a criminal enterprise either as a principal or a secondary party. The upshot of this decision was that KM should be found to have committed the act of murder if he had inflicted one of the two fatal knife wounds during a group attack on a young boy, or if he had inflicted one of the other non-fatal wounds or, most controversially, if 'he was a person who took part in what he knew at the time was a knife attack' (per Potter LJ at para. 47), that is, had been a member of the group even if he had not actually used a knife against their collective victim.

Our humanistic concern with this decision is that it allows, as in this case, a young man unfit for trial on the grounds of having the 'intellectual capacity of a young child' and who 'was so suggestible and lacking in understanding that he could not follow the court processes' and 'would have been unable to give intelligent or coherent evidence' (Potter LJ at para. 3) to be stigmatised as having committed the act of murder, when it is *possible* that his actual involvement and his understanding was minimal. Our legalistic concern is that *KM* provides a further example of the problematic policy of attempting to determine whether a criminal act has been committed without recourse to questions of *mens rea*. The requirement that 'he knew at the time it was a knife attack' entails consideration of the state of mind of the accused. This was, according to Potter LJ at para. 42 'a matter of inference from the independent evidence of witnesses and not from the evidence of the defendant', but this only dissimulates the fact that the defendant's *mens rea* is absolutely pertinent to this determination, and the evidence of any third party is in reality evidence, once-removed, of what the defendant him or herself understood to be the situation.

Mackay and Kearns (1997: 650–1) suggest that the approach taken in Scotland has the potential to provide both conceptual clarity and substantive justice. Section 174ZA, Criminal Procedure (Scotland) Act 1975, which came into force on 1 April 1996, requires that, as part of a trial of the facts, the court must be satisfied that there are, on a balance of probabilities, no grounds for acquitting the defendant: *mens rea* must therefore be considered, but the court need not be satisfied beyond reasonable doubt that there are no grounds for acquitting the defendant, so less than a full trial will be required. It can be argued that this is splitting hairs – either a trial court does consider the state of mind of the defendant or it does not – or alternatively, if *mens rea* is to be an issue it should not be in this watered-down version, which can still lead to a finding against the defendant in circumstances that, on a full trial, would have led to acquittal. One option would be to remove the mandatory requirements that follow a finding that the defendant committed the act of murder. But even this would not be totally satisfactory, because the defendant would still carry the stigma of a murderer. This seems to lead to the conclusion that, where justice requires, the defendant should have available, on a trial of the facts, all of the defences that would otherwise be available on a full trial. It seems as if there is no way to reconcile completely the requirements of conceptual clarity and those of substantive justice to the defendant, in which case the latter should prevail.

These reforms do seem to have encouraged the increased use of the 1964 Act, particularly in recent years. As mentioned above, in 1989, there were only 11 cases of unfitness to plead. Initially, the enactment of the 1991 Act seemed to make little difference, but there were 31 cases in 1994, 35 cases in 1995 and 33 in 1996 (Mackay and Kearns, 2000: 534). The most common diagnosis was schizophrenia, and it is overwhelmingly males who are found to be unfit (2000: 535). This research also showed that unfitness is usually uncontested by the prosecution. More recent statistics on all cases of unfitness have yet to be published, but in 2001, 46 restriction orders were made following a finding of disability (a doubling over 2000 numbers), rising to 51 in 2004 (Home Office Research, Development and Statistics Directorate, 2005: Table 3). This is a good indicator of patterns in the total number of cases, because around 45 per cent of all cases of disability are disposed of by means of a hospital order and restriction order (Mackay and Kearns, 2000: 545). The leap from 2000 to 2001 may be more to do with the wish to avoid mandatory minimum sentences than a direct consequence of the 1991 reforms. Nevertheless, although the data is ambiguous, and the numbers involved are small, the greater use of a plea of unfitness is to be welcomed.

6.3.2.4 Magistrates' courts and unfitness to plead

Although the Acts of 1964 and 1991 are not generally applicable in magistrates' courts, it is only a magistrates' court that can revoke or amend a supervision and treatment order: Sch. 2, Part III, 1991 Act. An application for an order to be revoked can be made by a supervising officer or a supervisee, and may be revoked if 'having regard to the circumstances which have arisen since the order was made, it would be in the interests of the health or welfare of the supervised person that the order should be revoked': Sch. 2, para. 6, 1991 Act. It is difficult to know what a magistrates' court would make of this provision, because there are so few cases, but it is likely that, in practice, the opinion of the supervisor would be determinative, whether the application was for a revocation or an amendment. An order cannot be 'amended' to extend its duration beyond two years from the date on which it was made: Sch. 2, para. 8(2).

Magistrates can, in fact, achieve much the same effect as an order made under the Acts of 1964 and 1991. This is because magistrates may make a hospital order under s. 37(3) of the 1983 Act without convicting the defendant if, on a trial of the facts identical to that contained in s. A(2) of the 1964 Act, the bench is satisfied that the defendant did the act or made the omission that constitutes the *actus reus* of an offence punishable on summary conviction with imprisonment, which includes offences triable 'either way' even if the defendant wishes to elect for Crown Court trial (*R v Ramsgate Justices, ex p Kazmarek* (1985) 80 Cr App R 366 (DC)), but not offences that are triable only on indictment, since such offences are not punishable on *summary* conviction: *R v Chippenham Magistrates' Court, ex p Thompson* (1995) *The Times*, 6 December (DC). It has been said that magistrates will only very rarely have need to use this power: *R v Lincoln (Kesteven) Justices, ex p O'Connor* [1983] 1 WLR 335 (DC). When it is used, it must be used in accordance with the diagnostic criteria employed by the MHA 1983 rather than the *Pritchard* test. A guardianship order was usefully made in *Bartram v Southend Magistrates Court [2004]* EWHC 269. B, suffering from paranoid schizophrenia and having failed to take prescribed medication, stabbed and killed his dog, believing it to be possessed by an evil spirit. He was charged with causing unnecessary suffering to an animal. It was clear to all that B was unfit to plead and the court, being satisfied that B did the act of killing the dog, made an order under s. 37(3). B's condition responded well to treatment in hospital and his mental state became stable and cooperative. The magistrates' court took this to mean that B was no longer mentally ill and held that there was therefore no scope for the further use of s. 37, and it proposed to try his case. B sought judicial review of that decision, which was successful, the Divisional Court holding that, although B was stable and not now in need of hospitalisation, psychiatric reports indicated that he remained liable to further acute attacks and that the continued use of s. 37, now to make a guardianship order, was not merely legally possible, it was also the best way to dispose of the case.

6.4 The special verdict

The 'special verdict' offers an alternative to conviction. The legal basis of the special verdict remains s. 2 of the Trial of Lunatics Act 1883, which now provides that a person who was 'insane' at the time the alleged offence was committed may be found 'not guilty by reason of insanity'. Like the law relating to disability to stand trial, the special verdict is subject to the regimes laid down by the Acts of 1964, 1991 and 2004 discussed above; as with unfitness, before the 1991 Act, the only disposal available was indefinite detention in a hospital. The situation now is that the range of disposals discussed earlier in the context of unfitness are also available if a special verdict is returned (s. 5 1964 Act), again with the exception that an order committing the defendant to hospital with restrictions must be made if the offence in question is murder and the grounds for a hospital order can be made out: s. 5(3), 1964 Act. As with unfitness, the issue of insanity may be raised by defence, prosecution or the court, and must be demonstrated by the defence on the balance of probabilities (*R v Constantini* [2005] EWCA Civ 821). It is established that the defence is available both in the Crown Court and on summary trial in magistrates' courts: *R v Horseferry Road Magistrates' Court, ex p K* [1996] 3 All ER 733 (CA).

Neither the 1991 Act nor the 2004 Act, however, did anything to change the definition of insanity, and the leading authority remains the infamous *M'Naghten's Case* (1843) 10 C & F 200, in which Tindal CJ (at 210) laid out the '*M'Naghten* rules'. That is, to establish the defence of insanity:

it must be clearly proved that, at the time of the committing of the act, the party accused was labouring under such a defect of reason, from disease of the mind, as not to know the nature and quality of the act he was doing; or if he did know it, that he did not know that what he was doing was wrong.

These words, which have since set as firm as any statutory provision, set up a similar mismatch with the criteria for admission and detention under the MHA 1983 as that discussed earlier in the context of disability; in so far as this test is also inconsistent with that in *Pritchard*, there is, in fact, a three-way mismatch between the relevant legal regimes (Howard, 2003).

The possibility that a person found insane on an application of the *M'Naghten* test can be sent to hospital without the court having to consider whether there is objective medical evidence of a mental disorder warranting hospitalisation was removed in 2004. But it can be argued that the latest round of reforms did not go far enough. If the function of the *M'Naghten* test is to differentiate the dangerous (in need of detention in a hospital) from those who are not (and so are able to access the alternative of non-insane automatism, which provides a complete defence), or the morally blameworthy from those who are not, there is general agreement that it fails (Baker, 1994; Kerrigan, 2002). From a psychiatric point of view, the problem is that the *M'Naghten* test focuses on cognition (understanding) rather than conation (motivation or volition, reasoning), and would, for example, label children as insane rather than as, on a conational model, merely immature. In addition, at present, in England and Wales (Scotland does not apply the *M'Naghten* rules) the definition of insanity is premised on an internal/external causes model: if the cause of the actions in question is 'internal', insanity is the issue. This distinction has produced manifest injustices, such as that in *R v Sullivan* [1984] AC 156 (HL), in which it was held that psychomotor epilepsy came within the *M'Naghten* definition of insanity, or in *R v Hennessey* [1989] 2 ALL ER 9, in which it was held that hyperglycaemia was also caught by the concept of a 'disease of the mind'. Bizarrely, the courts have always insisted that the definition of insanity to be used in criminal trials is a matter of law, yet, of course, in reality *M'Naghten* constitutes the legal 'freezing' of a particular phase in the development of psychiatric knowledge and theory, and in consequence, the legal definition of insanity is not coterminous with modern medical knowledge.

Situations like those in *Sullivan* or *Hennessey* will not generally be problematic in practice under the current law: the broader range of disposals and the need for medical evidence in support of hospitalisation means that, in such cases, a hospital order need not, or cannot, be made. Additionally, despite their rigidity as a matter of legal doctrine, the research evidence is that, although the rules are usually (but not always) referred to by psychiatrists reporting to the court, 'wrong' is more often than not (68 out of 100 cases: Mackay *et al.*, 2006: 405–6) interpreted to mean, given the defendant's (often confused or deluded) understanding of the events in question, 'morally wrong', rather than the, stricter, 'legally wrong'. As Mackay *et al.* (2006: 407) state, 'psychiatrists may in many respects be adopting a pragmatic approach by augmenting the strict scope of the *M'Naghten* rules and the courts by accepting this interpretation are in reality continuing to accept a wider interpretation of the rules', which does embrace notions of conation. Yet there is still an argument to be made that any test that catches such cases is in need of reform. In 2002, the government stated its intention to redraw the test as part of the reform of mental health law (Department of Health and Home Office, 2002: para. 4.3), but, as seen, the test itself was not, in fact, altered in the reforms of 2004. The suggestion of the Butler Committee was that the definitions of insanity (and unfitness) be abolished and replaced with the criteria used for detention for treatment under s. 3,

MHA 1983 (Home Office and Department of Health and Social Security, 1975: para. 18.37). It was felt, however, that this would be to widen the criminal law definition to an unacceptable extent, allowing an escape route for many who are in fact culpable; demeaning to the dignity of persons with mental disorders by denying them the right to a trial, depending on the perspective taken (Carson, 1989b). In Jersey, in *Attorney General v Prior* (2001) (see Mackay and Gearty, 2001), the argument that the *M'Naghten* rules breach Art. 5(1)(e) has been accepted (although on the equivalent of the pre-2004 Act law). The Royal Court of Jersey instead adopted the definition of insanity offered to the court by Professor Mackay, namely that a person is insane for the purposes of the insanity defence if at the time of the offence 'his unsoundness of mind affected his criminal behaviour to such a degree that the jury consider that he ought not to be found criminally responsible'. A jury (or judge, as is now the case) might only reach such a conclusion if there is medical evidence to support that view. Given that the *M'Naghten* test is 'offensive, and no longer meaningful in either a clinical or a common language context' (Mental Health Act Commission, 2005: para. 5.21), it is difficult, in our view, to dispute the preferability of this test over the *M'Naghten* approach.

It is too early to tell what effect the 2004 reforms will have on the use of the insanity defence. Before the 1991 Act reforms, the insanity defence was used no more than two or three times annually, if that. The inflexibility of defence, the harshness of the consequences of its use, and the availability of a preferable alternative of the defence of diminished responsibility, introduced in 1957, and the abolition of the death sentence for murder in 1965, together meant that it was no longer clear that indefinite detention in a psychiatric hospital was preferable to a criminal disposal from the point of view of the accused. Although the 1991 Act did encourage greater use of defence, the evidence was slow to emerge. The defence was used seven times in 1991 but only six times in 1992 (the year the 1991 Act came into force), five in 1993, and eight in 1994. It was used 12 times in 1995, however, and has never since been below double figures, being used 17 times in 1999 (the highest total for a single year) and 15 in 2001 (Mackay *et al.*, 2006: Table 1). Mackay *et al.* (2006: 2) point out that there were more cases (72) in the second five years of the operation of the 1991 Act (1997–2200) than there had been in the whole of the period 1975–91 (69). The most recently available Home Office data shows that in 2004, eight people found to be insane were disposed of by way of hospital and restriction orders (Home Office Research, Development and Statistics Directorate, 2005: Table 3). In their research, Mackay *et al.* found that, in 1997–2001 there were such orders were made in 27 cases, comprising 37.5 per cent of the total (2006: Table 8), which would suggest that there were approximately twenty uses of the defence in that year, with over half of them involving a community-based disposal. The defence is used for a broad number of disorders, but 50 per cent of all cases involved a primary diagnosis of schizophrenia, and it is most often used in cases of homicide or serious offences against the person, overwhelmingly involving male defendants aged 20 to 40 (2006: Tables 2, 3 and 5). The numbers involved are so small that it is difficult to talk of trends, and it is clear that the use of the special verdict is a rare event, but such increase in its use as there is is to be welcomed.

6.5 Sentencing as diversion

The relevance of mental disorder to the substantive criminal law is beyond the scope of this text, as is detailed discussion of the sentencing options open to a court on convicting an offender. Nevertheless, it is appropriate to point out that, prima facie, at least the principles of punishment, crime reduction, public protection, reform, rehabilitation and reparation that are to be found in s. 142 of the Criminal Justice Act 2003 apply to all offenders, mentally disordered or not (although these considerations do not apply if a court makes a hospital order: s. 142(2)(d)). That Act contains a graded system of sentencing, which attempts to engender proportionality in sentencing practice. A prison sentence, and a community sentence, must not be passed unless the court is satisfied that the offence committed is serious enough (defined in s. 143) to warrant it, and the sentence passed must be the shortest that is commensurate with the seriousness of the offence: ss. 155(2), 148(1), 153, 2003 Act. A person who is, or appears to be, mentally disordered cannot be imprisoned unless the court has first obtained a medical report from a s. 12 MHA approved doctor (s. 157(1)), and has also considered any information about that person's mental condition (whether given in a medical report, a pre-sentence report or otherwise), and the likely effect of such a sentence on that condition and on any treatment which may be available for it: s. 157(3). A court may decide, on the basis of such evidence, that a defendant's mental disorder amounts to mitigation, in which case it may pass a lesser sentence than it otherwise would have done (s. 166) and may, in particular, make a community-based disposal even if the seriousness of the offence in question would normally result in a custodial sentence: s. 166(2).

There are exceptions to these general rules, however, and in particular s. 227 provides that an extended prison sentence may be passed on conviction of a specified violent or sexual offence. A 'specified offence' is one of the 153 listed in either Parts 1 (violent offences) or 2 (sexual offences) of Sch. 15 to the Act. To pass such a sentence, the court must be of the opinion that there is otherwise a significant risk of serious harm to members of the public (s. 227(1)(b)). An extended sentence comprises the term that would have been given for the offence, or 12 months if the term that would have been imposed is less than that (ss. 227(2)(a), (3)), and a further period, the 'extension period', which must not exceed five years for a specified violent offence or eight years for a specified sexual offence (ss. 227(2)(b), (4)), nor must the total sentence exceed the maximum permissible for the offence: s. 227(5).

If the offence is 'serious', defined in s. 224(2) as being a specified offence for which the maximum available sentence is life or at least ten years' imprisonment, the court must, if the offender would otherwise be liable to imprisonment for life, impose a life sentence, if it considers that such a sentence can be justified, either taken on its own or together with one more other offences associated with it (s. 225(2)), and must also state a minimum term to be served before release can be considered (s. 82A of the Powers of Criminal Courts (Sentencing) Act 2000). If the offence in question is not covered by s. 225(2), either because it is not an offence for which the defendant would otherwise have been liable to life imprisonment or because, in the view of the court, such a sentence, although available, is not justified, the court must pass a 'sentence of imprisonment for public protection' (s. 225(3)), which is a indeterminate prison sentence: s. 225(4) (see further Thomas, 2004). These new sentencing powers have been given a restrictive interpretation by the Court of Appeal in *R v Lang and Ors* [2005] EWCA Crim 2864, emphasising, for example, that it must be shown that there is a significant risk both of the defendant committing further specified offences and of serious harm being thereby caused.

Concern has, in the past, been voiced that longer than normal sentences are being passed disproportionately in cases involving mentally disordered offenders. Solomka (1996: 241) found that 65 per cent of all cases heard by the Court of Appeal over a five-month period involved a psychiatric report. Not surprisingly, in around 40 per cent of those cases where a report was called for, a personality abnormality or disorder ('psychopathic disorder' in legal terms) was identified. The treatability of psychopathically disordered offenders has long been a matter of concern, which means that hospitalisation is often not an option. Once consigned to passing a prison sentence for an offence of sex or violence, the provisions of the 2003 Act apply and Crown Court judges are obliged to push offenders 'up tariff'.

The current situation is markedly less severe than was the case before the reforms initiated in the 2003 Act. This is because, first, the 2003 Act abolished the 'penal aberration' (Thomas, 2004: 702) that was s. 109 of the Powers of Criminal Courts (Sentencing) Act 2000, (previously to be found in the Crime (Sentences) Act 1997), which required that a life sentence be passed for a second serious violent or sexual offence absent 'exceptional circumstances', which were not intended to include mental disorder (Laing, 1997: 507). That this was the effect of s. 109 was confirmed, with 'regret' by the Court of Appeal in *R v Newman* [2000] 2 Cr App R (S) 227, and by the House of Lords in *R v Drew* [2003] UKHL 25, [2003] 1 WLR 1213, [2003] 4 All ER 557. The House of Lords held that s. 109 of the 2000 Act (and s. 37 of the MHA 1983, the scope of which was ousted by s. 109) did not per se breach Art. 3 of the Convention. This was on the basis that (i) it had been established that s. 109 carried a rebuttable presumption that the reason for a life sentence was that the defendant in question was dangerous, and did not apply if the defendant was able to demonstrate otherwise (*R v Offen* [2001] 2 Cr App R (S) 10, CA; for an example, see *R v Buckland* [2000] 1 WLR 1262, [2000] 1 All ER 907, CA), and (ii) Parliament was entitled to decide to send a person in need of medical treatment for mental disorder to prison rather than hospital, noting that, where necessary, there are powers to transfer a mentally disordered prisoner to hospital (see below). This view was subsequently upheld in the European Court, holding that D's application for a substantive hearing before the Court was inadmissible (*Drew v UK* (2006) 43 EHRR SE2).

The second reason why the post-2003 situation is an improvement on its predecessor is that the 2003 Act also amended s. 37(1A) of the MHA 1983, so that the availability of a hospital order to a sentencing court is not affected by the passage of ss. 225–8 of the 2003 Act (ss. 226 and 228 apply the provisions of ss. 225 and 227, with slight modifications, to juvenile offenders), as was and remains the case in respect of ss. 110 and 111 of the

Powers of Criminal Courts (Sentencing) Act 2000 Act, which prescribe mandatory minima for third-time drug trafficking and domestic burglary offences. This effectively restores the pre-1997 position, so that sentencing courts will always, unless the defendant has been convicted of murder, have the option of making a hospital order instead of sending a convicted person to prison, if the conditions for the making of such an order (on which, see below) can be made out. But – and this is the reason that the old law is laid out in some detail above – the relevant provisions of the 2003 Act only apply after their commencement, which was 4 April 2005. For offences committed before that time, but after 1 December 1997, when what became s. 109, 2000 Act first came into force, s. 109 continues to apply. Given that it is not at all unusual, for sexual offences in particular, that offences do not come to light for a considerable period, the old law (and indeed, the pre-1997 law, in which there were no mandatory minima) is likely to be relevant for some, if not many, years to come (Thomas, 2004: 707). The advice of the Court of Appeal is that where possible defendants should only be sentenced on the basis of the most recent offences, although this may not be possible if the earlier offences are more serious than those committed after 4 April 2005: *R v Lang and Ors* [2005] EWCA Crim 2864 per Rose LJ at para. 3.

In addition to the standard sentencing options, including the making of a 'community order' (formerly a probation order) with a requirement to accept treatment for mental disorder attached (ss. 177, 207, Criminal Justice Act 2003), the courts can send a mentally disordered person to hospital instead of prison by making a 'hospital order', which can be given additional bite by the addition of a 'restriction order', or to prison with immediate reception into a hospital, in the form of a 'hospital direction' coupled with a 'limitation direction'. In absolute terms, these orders are rarely used: less than half of one per cent of all disposals between 1992 and 1996 were hospital orders, and of these only a quarter had restrictions attached (Street, 1998: 101).

6.5.1 Hospital orders

The power to make a 'hospital order' is contained in s. 37 of the 1983 Act. The order is an alternative to imprisonment. The court has the discretion to make a guardianship order rather than a hospital order: s. 37(1). This is only rarely done, however, and in a case in which a community-based disposal is deemed preferable to detention, a community order is likely to be preferred over guardianship, because conditions relating to the acceptance of treatment can be attached: *R v Clare T* [2003] EWCA Crim 17, 2003 WL 1202680 (CA) (although the order requires the consent of its subject). Whenever a s. 37 order is made, the defendant passes out of the criminal justice system altogether, and cannot be brought back into that system. In the leading case on the use of hospital and restriction orders, *R v Birch* (1989) 11 Cr App R(S) 202 (CA), Mustill LJ explained (at 210) that the option for sentencers of being able to sentence an offender to hospital:

is intended to be humane by comparison with a prison sentence. A hospital order is not a punishment. Questions of retribution and deterrence . . . are immaterial. The offender who has become a patient is not kept on any kind of leash by the court.

Nor does the Home Office monitor the subsequent history of patients sentenced to hospital under s. 37 if restrictions are not also imposed under s. 41 (Home Office Research, Development and Statistics Directorate, 2005: 26). The criteria for making an order under s. 37 are substantially the same as for civil confinement under s. 3, and psychiatrists and review tribunals have similar powers to discharge hospital order patients as apply to patients detained under Part II of the 1983 Act (see Chapter 8).

Unrestricted hospital orders were made on 657 occasions in 2004, up from 559 in 2003 (Home Office Research, Development and Statistics Directorate, 2005: Table 18). This compares with 749 in 1999, 717 in 1996 and 649 in 1995, this being the fewest number of orders made in a year in the 1990s, the highest number being 789 in 1990. By contrast, 288 hospital orders coupled with restriction orders were made in 2004 (2005: Table 3). Of those persons in respect of whom a court made a hospital order without restrictions in 2004, 215 had been convicted of a violent offence, including 19 convictions for homicide other than murder (2005: Table 18). It is not possible to make an unrestricted hospital order in respect of a conviction of murder: s. 37(1). Of the rest, 124 had been convicted of criminal damage including arson. A further 37 had been convicted of a sexual offence. A similar number had been convicted of burglary (40), robbery (44) or for theft or handling (40), 62 had been convicted of other indictable offences, and 94 of summary offences (*ibid.*).

It is very difficult to talk about trends, given the very small numbers involved, but there are generally fewer hospital orders made than a decade ago in a considerable number of categories. The one offence category that clearly bucks this trend is homicide other than murder (four orders made in 1994, five in 1995, but 22 in 2003 and 19 in 2004), which indicates that the increase in claims of unfitness to plead is not at the expense of hospital orders made following homicide. And it does seem that the making of hospital orders on summary conviction is in a long-term decline – there were 159 such orders in 1990 and 145 in 1991, compared to 84 in 1993 and 94 in 2004. The import of this is, however, unclear. It may be that magistrates' courts are failing to use hospital orders in appropriate cases, but on the other hand, the use of hospital orders following summary conviction is a potential cause for concern, because it is likely that many of this group will spend more than 12 months – the maximum prison sentence that may be given in a magistrates' court on conviction for a summary offence (s. 154 Criminal Justice Act 2003) – in hospital. Although information on the average period spent by hospital-order patients in hospital is hard to come by, it is unlikely that all are discharged within the first six months following the making of the order by the court. There is much else we do not know about the making of hospital orders: for example, which courts made the orders in question, or whether there are significant regional variations in orders made as a percentage of total convictions.

The statistics do, nevertheless, indicate that, although, as might be expected, a good number of persons in respect of whom hospital orders are made have been convicted of an offence with an element of actual or potential dangerousness to others, the range of offences in respect of which hospital orders are made is relatively broad. This suggests that the courts do see the order as a therapeutic response, and its use is not linked to the offence but the need for hospital treatment. In *R v Paul Lee S* [2001] EWCA Crim 743, the Court of Appeal held that the making of a hospital order does not depend on any link between the offending behaviour and the disorder.

Before making a hospital order, the court must be satisfied, on the written or oral evidence of two doctors, one of whom must be approved (s. 54(1)), that the defendant is suffering from one or more of mental illness, psychopathic disorder, severe mental impairment or mental impairment of a nature or degree that makes it appropriate for him or her to be detained in a hospital for treatment: s. 37(2)(a). It is not necessary that both doctors agree that one of these disorders is all that the defendant is suffering from, although they must both diagnose the presence of the same disorder: s. 37(7). As with admission under s. 3, there is a treatability requirement in respect of psychopathic disorder and mental impairment: s. 37(2)(a)(i). There have long been concerns about the treatability of persons diagnosed as suffering from psychopathic disorder, with the result that many such persons have received a prison sentence rather than a hospital order. It is this perceived problem with the operation of s. 37 that provided the initial impetus to introduce in 1997 what are now known as 'hospital and limitation directions', and, later, the current proposals for reform, discussed further below.

As with orders made under ss. 35 or 36, an order under s. 37 'shall not be made' unless the court is provided with evidence (which may be written or oral) from the doctor who will be in charge of the patient's treatment (the 'responsible medical officer' or RMO), or from the managers of the intended recipient hospital, that arrangements are in train for the admission of the defendant within 28 days of the making of the order: s. 37(4). Section 39 gives the court powers to request from the relevant primary care trust or health authority, information as to the availability of hospital accommodation, and s. 40 gives authority for the defendant to be conveyed to and detained in the hospital named in the order. If the admission cannot occur immediately, the defendant may be conveyed to and detained in a 'place of safety' (defined in s. 55(1) to include a police station, prison, remand centre or other hospital). A practical problem may arise if, after an order has been made and the assurance of a hospital place has been given, that place is then withdrawn. In such a situation, the Secretary of State may direct that the patient be admitted to another specified hospital (s. 37(5)), or the sentencing court may substitute a sentence under s. 115 of the Powers of Criminal Courts Act 2000 or s. 142 of the Magistrates' Courts Act 1980.

There has been an acknowledged problem, since at least the mid-1970s, of hospitals refusing to take some hospital-order patients (see *R v Officer* (1976) *The Times*, 20 February; *R v Gordon* (1981) 3 Cr App R(S) 352 (HC); *R v Harding* (1983) *The Times*, 15 June (CA)), which does not appear to have abated, because despite the expansion in medium-secure provision over the last decade and a half or so, the pressure on beds both in medium-security and high-security accommodation remains at crisis point (see Chapter 3). In *R v Galfetti* [2002] EWCA Crim 1916, the defendant had been convicted and the court wished to make a hospital order, but it took nine months before a bed could be found, at which time the hospital order was eventually made. The Court of Appeal, although finding this to be an 'excessive delay' (at para. 43), held that there was no breach of any of Arts. 3, 5, 6 or 8 of the Convention in the delay itself, because the court is able to monitor the delay and take action if required, thus satisfying the 'reasonable time' requirement of Art. 6 (para. 48). Nor was there any breach of a Convention right in activating the order so long after it had originally been made, because there was evidence before the court when the order was finally made that justified its making, and the defendant had been transferred to hospital where he had received appropriate treatment in the meantime (para. 49). But the court did say that, if a hospital bed cannot be located within an appropriate time, the sentencing court may have to consider the use of another disposal (per May LJ at para. 48). The court bemoaned the lack of powers available to it to secure a hospital bed with promptitude, and did draw attention to the fact there there is no mechanism to enable a person in Galfetti's position to appeal against an order adjourning his sentence indefinitely. In *Brand v The Netherlands* [2001] Hudoc reference REF00006531, the Court declared inadmissible the argument based on Art. 3, of a person held in prison awaiting the availability of a hospital bed, because he had, on the facts, not suffered adversely or been denied treatment whilst in prison, and thus could not be said to have suffered inhumane or degrading treatment. The Court distinguished the decision in *Aerts v Belgium* (2000) 29 EHRR 50, in which it had unanimously found breaches of Art. 5(1)(e) when a defendant sentenced to hospital had waited for seven months in *unsuitable* surroundings in prison for a hospital bed to become available.

In addition to the requirements of s. 37(2)(a) being met, s. 37(2)(b) provides that before a court may make a hospital order it must be 'of the opinion, having regard to all the circumstances including the nature of the offence and the character and antecedents of the offender and to the other available methods of dealing with him' that a hospital order is the most suitable disposal. In *Birch*, the Court of Appeal suggested the following order of deliberations. First, a sentencing court should decide, on normal sentencing principles, whether the defendant should be compulsorily detained or whether some form of community-based sanction such as probation with treatment-related conditions would be more appropriate. This is known as the 'custody threshold'. If it is decided that detention is required, the second question is whether the conditions contained in s. 37 are satisfied and, if so, whether the making of such an order is preferable to the imposition of a prison sentence.

According to the court in *Birch*, there are only two reasons for sending a mentally disordered person in respect of whom the conditions in s. 37 are satisfied to prison: (1) 'the offender is dangerous and no suitable secure accommodation is available' (Mustill LJ at 215) and; (2) where 'notwithstanding the offender's mental disorder there was an element of culpability in the offence which merits punishment' (*ibid.*). In short, the court must decide whether the offender perpetuated a crime primarily 'of illness' or 'of wickedness' (*ibid.*). The thrust of the court's approach, though, was in favour of diversion from prison, Mustill LJ holding that 'even where there is culpability, the right way to deal with a dangerous and disordered person is to make an order under section 37 and 41' (s. 41 is considered below), and that it is inappropriate to pass a prison sentence out of a concern that the defendant will be released earlier from hospital than would be the case if sent to prison. In this, the Court of Appeal in *Birch* was following its own earlier authorities, *R v Howell* (1985) 7 Cr App R (S) 360 and *R v Mbatha* (1985) 7 Cr App R (S) 373, which are to the same effect. *Birch* has subsequently been followed on many occasions, the Court of Appeal consistently taking an approach that holds, in essence, that if the conditions for a hospital order are made out, and there is a bed available, then that is the course that the court should ordinarily take (see, for example, *R v Fairhurst* (1996) 1 Cr App R (S) 242, *R v Mitchell* (1997) 1 Cr App R (S) 90 (CA), *R v Hutchinson* (1997) 2 Cr App R (S) 60 (CA), *R v Alfred B* [2001] EWCA Crim 1104 (CA), *R v Walton* [2003] EWCA Crim 2254, *R v IA* [2005] EWCA Crim 2077, [2006] 1 Cr App R (S) 91, and *R v Roden* [2006] EWCA Civ 1211). In all of these cases, the Court of Appeal substituted orders under ss. 37 and 41 for a prison sentence. The court has also shown itself prepared to replace a prison sentence with an unrestricted hospital order when satisfied that the appellant poses no risk to the public: see, for example, *R v Budgen* [2001] EWCA Crim 1708, *R v Cox* [2004] EWCA Crim 123, *R v Hothi* [2005] EWCA Crim 1803.

One long-standing exception to the consistency of this line of cases is *R v Fleming* (1993) 14 Cr App R (S) 151 (CA), in which it was held acceptable to pass a sentence of life imprisonment rather than to make a hospital order on the basis that, in that case, the ultimate decision about the release of the defendant would be one for the Home Secretary, rather than, if a hospital order was imposed, for a tribunal. Clearly, the court felt that, in some situations, tribunals could not be trusted not to release dangerous offenders prematurely. In *Mitchell*, however, Otton LJ pointed out that this was wrong in law – it is the discretionary lifer panel of the parole board that decides whether discretionary lifers should be released, not the Home Secretary – and held that *Fleming* 'is better disregarded' (at 93), a view endorsed by Rose LJ in *Hutchinson* (at 63). Nevertheless, the approach in *Fleming* finds support in *Birch*, in which Mustill LJ (at 214) held (seemingly inconsistently with the general tenor of his judgment in that case) that the sentencing court could properly consider 'the practical effect of all the orders'. This, as Baker (1992: 48) argued, might be seen as 'an invitation to disposing courts to impose prison sentences on offenders whom they believe to pose a risk, no matter how badly in need of treatment they are and, presumably, to rely on the Home Secretary's discretion to transfer them to hospital afterwards if necessary', which is precisely what had been done, for example, in *Fairhurst* at first instance.

A patient transferred to hospital from prison can be returned to prison, if treatment given in hospital is successful or of no beneficial effect. A patient discharged by a tribunal may be released straight into the community, and it is not surprising that some trial courts are uneasy about the latter prospect. The criteria that a tribunal must apply – which, inter alia, require that discharge be ordered if the applicant is no longer sufficiently mentally disordered – are narrower than those considered by the parole board, where the main concern is risk, and there is also less scope for the recall of a patient discharged by a tribunal compared to a prisoner, particularly a discretionary lifer, released from prison on licence. Concerns about the laxity of the tribunal system are, however, largely without foundation. It can be no easy feat to leave hospital for those sent there

MENTAL DISORDER AND CRIMINAL JUSTICE 249

by a court, particularly if, as is usual in cases in which the defendant is perceived to constitute a risk to the public, a restriction order is appended to the hospital order (see Chapter 8). Nevertheless, in *R v Drew* [2003] UKHL 25, Lord Bingham, expressing the unanimous view of the House of Lords, held that 'we would accept that these differing conditions [i.e. as to the consequences of a court choosing one course rather than the other] are a matter to which sentencing judges and appellate courts should try to give appropriate weight'.

But it is clear that the orthodoxy established in *Birch* – that prison should only be preferred over hospital in exceptional cases – remains intact, at least for now. In *Drew*, where the point was not argued directly, Lord Bingham continued: 'The difficulties caused to prison managements by the presence and behaviour of those who are subject to serious mental disorder are, however, notorious, and we would need to be persuaded that any significant change in the prevailing practice was desirable.' This does not mean, of course, that mentally disordered offenders are never sent to prison: far from it, and there are plenty of examples of the Court of Appeal upholding a prison sentence, even when the grounds for a hospital order are made out, recent instances including *R v Walch* [2003] EWCA Crim 1603, *R v Nafei* [2004] EWCA Crim 3238, [2005] 1 Cr App R (S) 24, and *R v Reid* [2005] EWCA Crim 392. In *Nafei*, in which N had been sentenced to 12 years' imprisonment for his part in the importation of cocaine with a street value calculated at £1.8m, the court emphasised the lack of a causal connection between N's schizophrenia and his offence (distinguishing *Birch*, *Howell*, *Mbatha*, and *Fairhurst* on this basis), holding that it was within the discretion of the sentencing judge to take such a view.

6.5.2 Restriction orders: s. 41

The profile of offending of those given a hospital order with restrictions leans more noticeably towards the more serious offences than that of those given hospital orders without restrictions. In *Birch*, Mustill LJ explained (at 211) the effect of a 'restriction order' being added to a hospital order:

No longer is the offender regarded simply as a patient whose interests are paramount... Instead, the interests of public safety are regarded by transferring the responsibility for discharge from the responsible medical officer and the hospital... to the Secretary of State and the Mental Health Review Tribunal. A patient who has been subject to a restriction order is likely to be detained in hospital for much longer than one who is not, and will have fewer opportunities for leave of absence.

Even when a restriction order patient leaves hospital, it is overwhelmingly likely that that discharge will be conditional in the first instance, and a conditionally discharged restriction order patient remains liable to recall to hospital (see Chapter 8). A hospital order made under s. 37 order, coupled with a restriction order made under s. 41, can therefore be understood as the conceptual intersection between treatment and punishment or protective custody. This option is designed to accommodate those who are both mad and 'bad', or dangerous.

An order under s. 41 cannot be made by a magistrates' court (s. 41(1)), although that court may commit to the Crown Court if of the view that a hospital order, coupled with a restriction order, is required: ss. 43, 44. A s. 41 order is not freestanding, but must be attached to a s. 37 order. The requirements of s. 37 must therefore be met as a prerequisite to the making of a s. 41 order. In addition, a s. 41 order can only be made where the court is of the view, given the nature of the offence, the history and antecedents of the offender, and the risk of reoffending, that 'it is necessary for the protection of the public from serious harm': s. 41(1). This question must be addressed explicitly by the sentencing court (*R* v *Czarnota* [2002] EWCA Crim 785). The meaning of 'serious harm' was considered in *Birch*. Mustill LJ held that 'harm' here is 'not limited to personal injury. Nor need it relate to the public in general' (213). The condition may be met where there is a risk of serious harm to 'a category of persons, or even a single person... Nevertheless, the potential harm must be serious, and a high possibility of a recurrence of minor offences will no(t)...suffice' (213). The court overruled earlier cases where orders had been made on this basis, but did approve the case of *R* v *Khan* (1987) 9 Cr App R (S) 455, in which, although the offences in question were fairly minor (reckless driving), the risk that was thereby posed to the public was serious. In *R* v *Cowan* [2004] EWCA Crim 3081, hospital and restriction orders had been made following C's conviction for common assault. Although the harm caused in that case was fairly minor, hence the offence charged, it was in the view of the sentencing judge merely good fortune that C's victims had not sustained greater injuries. The Court of Appeal upheld the first instance decision, accepting that, although the case was marginal, it was 'on the side of the margin calling for a restriction order' (Douglas Brown J at para. 10). In *R* v *Pemberton* (1996) 24 June, unreported (CA) an appeal was allowed against the making of a s. 41 order because the trial judge had considered there to be a 'serious risk' of harm. The Court of Appeal, citing *Birch*, pointed out that it is the potential harm and not the risk of its occurrence that must be serious. It is clear that harm includes psychological harm: *R* v *Macrow* [2004] EWCA Crim 1159. A court may conclude that there is such a risk even if the defendant has no history of violence, if the medical evidence supports that conclusion (*R* v *Kamara* [2002] EWCA Crim 1559). Nevertheless, as Street (1998: 14) found, in his analysis of all restriction orders made in 1992 and 1993, there do appear to be cases, which are not appealed, in which a s. 41 order has been made although 'the risk of serious future harm was not readily apparent'.

In arriving at its decision, s. 41(2) requires that the court hear oral evidence from at least one of the doctors who have already given evidence about the suitability of a s. 37 order, and although this need not as a matter of law be a s. 12 approved doctor it should, as a matter of good practice, be a doctor on the staff of the hospital at which the defendant will be detained if the order is made: *R* v *Blackwood* (1974) 59 Cr App R (S) (CA). As Akinkunmi and Murray (1997: 55) note, however, this is not always easily possible. For example, staff at the Bentham Unit (a specialised unit designed to accept persons remanded to hospital by a court under ss. 35 and 36) have found that a problem has arisen on sentencing subsequent to a period of remand, because only they have the expert medical knowledge of the patient that the court needs to decide whether or not a hospital order should be made but they do not intend to accept a patient on a long-term basis under a hospital order.

It is the responsibility of this doctor or doctors (it is unusual in practice for a sentencing court to hear only the evidence of one doctor) to advise the court on the question of risk. Although risk assessment is a technical matter, Street found that 'psychiatrists largely took the straightforward view that those offenders who committed the most serious offences were the most likely to pose a risk to others in the future' (1998: 24). Recommendations to the court come in various shades, from a firm recommendation that a restriction order is required, through a recommendation that a hospital order be made with no opinion expressed about a restriction order, although it is rare for psychiatrists who recommend a hospital order to oppose positively the making of a restriction order. In a number of cases, there will be no express recommendation, because some psychiatrists feel that it is not the role of the doctor to become too closely associated with the sentencing process. But in the majority – 70 per cent – of cases in which a restriction order is made, there had been a preponderance of medical evidence to the effect that the defendant did pose a risk of significant harm to others, even if there was not always a positive recommendation that a s. 1 order be made (Street, 1998: 28).

This still means, however, that 30 per cent of restriction orders are made even though there is no consensus amongst medical witnesses that the defendant poses a significant risk. As the facts of *Birch* demonstrate, medical evidence does not need to be followed by the sentencing judge. In that case, three approved doctors gave evidence that the defendant who, acting under diminished responsibility as a result of her mental disorder, had killed her husband, did not present a danger of significant harm to the public or any individual. Nevertheless, the trial judge made a restriction order and his decision was upheld by the Court of Appeal, where it was pointed out that, under the terms of s. 41, unlike those of s. 37, the trial judge need not follow any medical recommendations that are made. The decision, ultimately, is one for the court. The Court of Appeal, in the later case of *R v Reynolds* [1999] 2 CR App R (S) 5, made comments that might be seen to contradict this: 'On hearing the evidence there must be at least some basis upon which the doctor is able to say, and persuade the court, that a restriction order is appropriate.' We share the view expressed by Jones (2006: 257) that in so far as these comments are at odds with *Birch*, they should be seen as *per incuriam*; and the views expressed in *Birch* were reiterated by the Court of Appeal in *R v Ristic* [2002] EWCA Crim 165 and *R v Goode* [2002] EWCA Crim 1698. In *Birch*, the Court of Appeal approved, as good law under the 1983 Act, the dicta of Parker CJ in *R v Gardiner* (1967) 51 Cr App R 187 that, for crimes of violence, particularly where there is a prior history of such offending, or of mental disorder manifesting as violence, 'there must be compelling reasons to explain why a restriction order should not be made'.

Each case, however, must be decided on its own circumstances, including the seriousness of the offence, the medical evidence and prognosis, and any other relevant factors. It would seem to follow that, because there is a general discretion to ignore medical advice in the interests of public safety, a decision to add a restriction order will be harder to appeal than the making (or not making) of a s. 37 order in the first place, and indeed this is generally the case. If there is a medical recommendation in favour of s. 41, an order can be made even though some, or even the preponderance, of medical opinion is against it (see, for example, *R* v *IS* [2004] EWCA Crim 957, *R* v *Jones* 2000 WL 976077 and *R* v *Daniel O* 2001 WL 1476329). Even when there are no medical recommendations in favour of s. 41, the court may, if it is reasonable to do so, make an order. For example, in *R* v *Goode* [2002] EWCA Crim 1698, four doctors were unanimous in their view that a s. 37 order alone was required, and that there was no risk of reoffending. The judge nevertheless made a s. 41 order, and that decision was upheld by the Court of Appeal, because there was evidence from which it was reasonable for the court to conclude that there was a low risk of serious reoffending. In an unusual case, *R* v *Martin* 2000 WL 877792, the defendant, already detained in hospital under s. 37, was sentenced to s. 37/41, having been convicted of criminal damage for setting fire to a mattress in the hospital. He appealed against the sentence because he wished to leave the hospital and preferred the option of prison. As the first instance judge had followed medical advice as to the desirability of a s. 41 order, the appeal was held to be without substance.

The Court of Appeal has, however, made plain that it will allow an appeal and rescind a s. 41 order if the trial court falls into error on the law (*Pemberton*), if the judge bases the decision on his or her own views in contradiction of the medical evidence (*R* v *Daniel F George R* 2000 WL 1544620, in which the judges' views about the effects of long-term cannabis use were found to have coloured his judgment) or, as in *R* v *Slater* (1996) 7 October, unreported, and *R* v *St Leonce* [2004] EWCA Crim 1154, where the Court of Appeal is satisfied that there had not, in fact, been a serious risk of harm if the order had not been made. The court has also been prepared to allow an appeal when, on the evidence then available, a s. 41 order was properly made at first instance but has subsequently been shown to have been unwarranted in reports ordered by the appeal court (*R* v *Maria TK* [2001] EWCA Crim 400) or because the restrictions that attend s. 41 impact negatively on the treatment plan for the defendant whilst in hospital (*R* v *Ayan M* 2000 WL 544040, a case in which the RMO wished to use leave of absence as part of the defendant's care plan, which intention would have been hindered if a restriction order had been made, because of the powers given to the Secretary of State to veto leave of absence if a restriction order is made: see Chapter 8).

As already mentioned, 288 restriction orders were made by a court in 2004. This is up drastically from the 198 made in 2003, although 2003 was a low point, there having been 216 such orders in 2002, 237 in 2001, 212 in 2000 and 259 in 1999 (Home Office Research, Development and Statistics Directorate, 2005: Table 3). The longer trend is upwards: only 156 restriction orders were made by a court in 1991 (Home Office Research, Development and Statistics Directorate, 2002: Table 3). The vast majority – 231 – of defendants who were made subject to a restriction order in 2004 were diagnosed as suffering from mental illness, and a further 21 had a mental illness coupled with another disorder. Numbers for psychopathic disorder, mental impairment, and severe mental impairment were 20, 12 and 0 respectively, and three defendants had a dual diagnosis of mental impairment and psychopathic disorder (Home Office Research,

Development and Statistics Directorate, 2005: Table 4). As with hospital orders, both property offences and offences of violence feature in the statistics, although the latter are more prominently represented here, with 35 offences of manslaughter and 93 of 'other violence' amongst the 288. There were 19 restriction orders made following conviction of a sexual offence and 43 following conviction for arson. There were 39 restriction orders following property offences of various kinds, and 59 orders were made following a conviction for other offences, which would no doubt include some of a minor nature (2005: table 5).

Street (1998) found that, apart from restriction order patients being more likely to have committed a dangerous offence and more likely to have, or likely to have more, previous convictions than hospital order patients, there was very little to distinguish the two groups in terms of age, sex or age at first conviction. The majority of all patients are in the 21–39 years age range (Home Office Research, Development and Statistics Directorate, 2005: Table 11), and 90 per cent were male, being first convicted at around twenty years of age (Street, 1998: 31). *Within* the group of restriction-order patients, however, there were significant variables. Men were much more likely to be sentenced to a restriction order than women, but women were twice as likely as men to have a main diagnosis of psychopathic disorder, and less likely to be diagnosed as mentally ill (which echoes the finding of Milne *et al.*, 1995). Black defendants were nearly all (96 per cent) diagnosed as mentally ill, compared with 69 per cent of white defendants (Street 1998: 10). Other research has found a wide discrepancy in the frequency with which black defendants have a diagnosis of schizophrenia (see Chapter 4). In general terms, Street found a significant over-representation of black African or Caribbean people (21 per cent of those given a restriction order) compared with the population as a whole (at around 2 per cent). The reasons for this are complex and disputed, and the arguments have been rehearsed at various points throughout this text. Street did find that white defendants made subject to a restriction order were less likely than black defendants to have committed a crime of violence, at 75 per cent compared with 85 per cent, although this hardly explains the width of the discrepancies that exist; other studies, such as that carried out by Shubsachs *et al.* (1995) at Rampton found no significant differences on a number of indicators, including offence. In a helpful review of the literature and issues, Boast and Chesterman (1995) conclude that the high incidence of black people at the deep end of mental health services represents the outcome of social disadvantage, and both direct and indirect discrimination at various decision-making points 'lower down' the system, from the diagnosis of disorder to the perception of the police and the courts of the (perceived) relation between ethnicity, dangerousness and risk. Equally depressing statistics, however, cut across barriers of race. Street (1998: 12) found that the typical recipient of a restriction order is long-term unemployed (90 per cent of all orders made in 1992 and 1993), long-term single (68 per cent) and, with the exception of mentally impaired persons, a high percentage (41 per cent) lived alone. Around 20 per cent, rising to almost 40 per cent of mentally impaired defendants, lived in hostels, bed and breakfast establishments or were homeless. Restriction orders, in short, are overwhelmingly made in respect of some of the most economically and socially disadvantaged in society.

The government has repeatedly emphasised that, even where there is no obvious link between the presence of mental disorder and offending behaviour, treatment for the mental disorder in question is likely, at the general level, to reduce recidivism (Department of Health, 1999a: ch. 8.3). At the same time, however, the view expressed in the White Paper of 2000 was that, although hospital and restriction orders should bestow 'direct therapeutic benefit' to the person subject to the order in most cases, 'this will not be a requirement for a compulsory order to be imposed' (Department of Health, 2000: para. 4.2), which is to be achieved by the removal of the legal relevance of the various subcategories of mental disorder and also of the current treatability test, which is the preferred strategy for bringing those with a diagnosis of severe and dangerous personality disorder (SDPD) within the criteria for these orders. It seems that, in the government's plans, the need for treatment is to be linked not to therapeutic concerns, but instead to the offence, and the degree of risk thereby implied.

The case of *A, D and R v Scottish Ministers* [2001] UKPC D5, [2002] UKHRR 1 (see further Chapter 8) was concerned with the release of restricted patients who had initially, but wrongly, been thought treatable. The Privy Council held that such patients could, on the grounds of public safety, continue to be detained, even if not treatable. The relevance of that decision here is that, if the expanded concept of mental disorder and the removal of the treatability requirement were to be implemented, this decision would resonate also at the point of admission. Under the various propoals introduced over the last few years, including those currently being taken forward, it will be lawful to make a hospital order and a restriction order even when it is known that the defendant is not susceptible to treatment, on the grounds of public protection. As discussed in Chapter 8, there is currently little assistance in the case law of the European Court for those who would wish to dispute this view (see also Gostin, 2000).

6.5.2.1 The nature of the restrictions and the restricted patient regime

There are few restrictions on the way in which a restricted patient is treated (in the broad sense of this term) when in the hospital system (Baxter, 1991). Until recently, for example, there was no legal requirement that a s. 41 patient be held in secure accommodation such as a special hospital, although the situation now is that the court may specify not only the hospital but also the unit within the hospital in which the subject of the order is to be detained: s. 47(1), Crime (Sentences) Act 1997. In a sense, therefore, a restriction order is not aimed so much at the restricted patient as at the medical professionals responsible for his or her care (Baker, 1992: 32). It is the clinical freedom of the RMO that is curtailed by a restriction order. As such the restriction order is one of the best examples of the legal institutionalisation of a hierarchy of concerns that places control above treatment. The restrictions are set out in s. 41(3), and s. 41(3)(a) provides that 'none of the provisions of Part II of this Act relating to the duration, renewal and expiration of authority for the detention of patients shall apply'. There can be no application to a tribunal except in circumstances specified: s. 41(3)(b) (see Chapter 8). The patient cannot be given leave of absence, or be transferred or discharged, by the RMO without the consent of the Secretary of State: s. 41(3)(c). If leave of absence is granted the patient can be recalled to hospital at any time by the Secretary of State: s. 41(3)(d) (see Chapter 8). Whilst a restriction order is still in effect, any hospital order will also continue (s. 41(4)), although the bringing to an end of a restriction order (by the Secretary of State or a tribunal) does not mean that a patient is no longer liable to be detained. Instead, such a patient is treated as though on a s. 37 order from the date of the cessation of the restriction order: s. 41(5), known as a 'notional s.37', a term which also applied to a prisoner transferred from prison to hospital under s. 47 of the 1983 Act without restrictions (see later; and Mental Health Act Commission, 2005: paras. 5.66–5.70 for further discussion).

It is perhaps misleading, however, to explain the effect of a restriction order simply in terms of a list of restrictions. Restricted patients do tend to begin their time in hospital at the deep end of the hospital system, although not necessarily in a special hospital (2005: para. 5.113), and are, for the most part, keenly aware of their status. Restricted patients are subject to ongoing monitoring by the mental health unit (MHU) of the Home Office, by way of mandatory annual reports that must be made to the MHU by each patient's RMO (s. 41(6)), and the MHU and the Home Secretary tend towards caution in their attitude to the release of restriction-order patients. A restricted patient will feel the state breathing down his or her neck much more keenly than other detained patients. Moreover, the effects of a restriction order continue after release from hospital, because virtually all restricted patients are, in the first instance, discharged condition-ally, and unless and until discharge is made absolute, are liable to recall to hospital (see Chapter 8).

The restricted patient regime does not only apply to those sentenced to a restriction order by a court, but also includes most patients transferred to hospital from prison, those hospitalised after having been found unfit to be tried, and those found not guilty by reason of insanity. Many can expect to spend long periods in hospital before being considered for release. Of the 3,282 restricted patients detained in hospital in England and Wales on 31 December 2004 (up from 2,694 in 1997, 3,002 in 2001: Home Office Research, Development and Statistics Directorate, 2002: Table 15), 83 had been in hos-pital for more than 30 years, 200 for between 20 and 30 years, 593 for between 10 and 20 years, 643 between five and ten years, 639 between two and five years and 927 (including 192 patients on remand) less than two years (Home Office Research, Development and Statistics Directorate, 2005: Table 15). Of those detained for long periods, a numerically small, but statistically significant, number of patients with psychopathic disorder – 33 out of a total of 412 – had been detained for more than 30 years. By way of comparison, 30 mentally ill patients had been detained as long, but this was out of a total of 1970 (2005: Table 15). Another 125 psychopathically disordered patients had been detained for between 10 and 20 years, and 48 for between 20 and 30 years. Yet what is more remarkable is that many patients in all disorder categories spend a considerable number of years in hospital. It is clear that a restriction order is by no means a 'soft option' compared with imprisonment, at least in terms of time served.

6.5.2.2 Restriction orders of limited duration

An order under s. 41 may be made 'either without limit of time or during such period as may be specified in the order': s. 41(1). In the early years of the regime inaugurated by the passage of the MHA 1959, almost half of restriction orders made were of limited duration, but the Court of Appeal turned its face against limited duration orders in *Gardiner* (see earlier), given that prognosis is usually uncertain at the time of sentencing. From 1968 onwards such orders became much more rare (Robertson, 1989), as remains the case. Limited duration orders now account for around 5 per cent of all restriction orders: 72 out of 1448 s. 41 orders made in the decade 1983–93 (Romilly *et al.*, 1997: 564). It seems likely that this pattern will not change in the foreseeable future. The Court of Appeal reiterated the view taken in *Gardiner* in both *Birch* and *R* v *Nwohla* [1995] Crim LR 668.

An analysis of the use of limited duration restriction orders in the ten years following the passage of the MHA 1983 (Romilly *et al.*,1997) found, perhaps not unexpectedly, that the profile of offenders for which such orders are made was less serious than that of those sentenced without limit of time. Of more interest, when a limited duration order was made, it was often on the initiative of the trial judge acting against (11/72) or without (30/72) medical opinion as to the suitability of such an order. Firm medical recommendations leading to an order being of limited duration were relatively rare (26/72); it was rarer still that the reason for the medical recommendation for a limited duration order was a firm prognosis for effective treatment within the specified time period, which forms the basis of the stance taken by the Court of Appeal. Often, such a recommendation was made in an attempt to dissuade the judge from making an order that, in the opinion of the doctor in question, would have been even more undesirable – whether an unlimited s. 1 order or a prison sentence. Romilly *et al.* conclude that, as far as generalisation is possible, when a limited-duration s. 41 order is made, it reflects a judicial desire to pass a sentence that, in terms of time in confinement, is commensurate to the tariff. The guidance of the Court of Appeal in *R* v *Hayes* (1981) 3 Cr App R (S) 330, that this practice is inappropriate, seems to have gone unheeded by the lower courts.

The Butler Committee recommended the abolition of limited duration restriction orders when the law was reformed in 1983, but that view was rejected on the grounds that the order was useful when a firm prognosis was possible at the time of trial. The evidence is strong, though, that the order is used in this way only rarely, and is used more often as a covert way to introduce a punitive element into a treatment order in a way that departs from the spirit of the general policy of diversion. The argument for abolition, therefore, is now that much stronger than it was in the early 1980s. The Government intends to abolish the time-limited order (see Department of Health, 2002: para. 2.13 and Department of Health, 2006p). The fate of this particular proposal remains to be seen: it does not feature amongst those made by the government in 2006.

6.5.3 Hospital and limitation directions

Under the regime contained in Part III of the 1983 Act, as initially enacted, a patient sentenced to hospital could not be transferred to prison at a later date. Although s. 38

provides for interim hospital orders (see below), this provision, as the Court of Appeal noted in *Birch*, has not been popular with sentencers. There were calls for a number of years for greater flexibility to be crafted into the system. In addition, there has long been concern about the particular problem of psychopathically disordered offenders, given the dubious treatability of this condition, making it unclear that a hospital order under s. 37 (usually coupled with an order under s. 41) was always appropriate. In such cases, the accused person would, on conviction, receive a prison sentence, and although there is the possibility of transfer to hospital from prison, this is not a realistic prospect for the majority of offenders; transfer may happen late into the sentence of imprisonment, with the consequence that the offender continues to be detained in a hospital after the expiry of the sentence given, which raises its own set of ethical and legal problems (see below). Conversely, in some cases, ss. 37/41 orders have been made, only for those charged with treating the subject of the order to discover that he or she is not, in fact, treatable, with the consequence that the function of hospitalisation, in practice, is purely custodial.

Sentencing courts have also sometimes displayed concern that a defendant sentenced to hospital may be released inappropriately early. Hospital orders are made rarely in cases involving psychopathic disorder – only 20 patients diagnosed as psychopathic were admitted to a hospital under ss. 37 and 41 in 2004, compared with 231 mentally ill offenders (Home Office Research, Development and Statistics Directorate, 2005: Table 4). Psychopathically disordered offenders are also more likely to be recalled after discharge than are other categories of mentally disordered offenders. In practice, most psycho-pathically disordered offenders are given a punitive disposal that frequently means that there is little further involvement by the mental health services, during or after custody, until, in those few cases where it does, disaster strikes.

The White Paper, *Protecting the Public* (Home Office, 1996) and an ensuing consult-ation document (Department of Health and Home Office, 1996) signalled governmen-tal acceptance of, at least some version of, these arguments, and s. 6 of the Crime (Sentences) Act 1997 inserted new sections – ss. 45A and 45B – into the 1983 Act, which now provide for 'hospital and limitation directions' to be made by a sentencing court. Now, a court is not faced with a stark choice between sending a defendant either to prison or to hospital, but may instead direct that the disposal is initially to a hospital, but with the reassurance that, if hospitalisation proves unsuccessful, the prison sen-tence passed can be activated. A 'hospital direction' is defined in s. 45A(3)(a) as 'a direc-tion that, instead of being removed to and detained in a prison, the offender may be removed to and detained in such hospital as may be specified in the direction'. A hos-pital direction can only be made following the conviction of the defendant in a Crown Court (s. 45A(1)), and in circumstances in which the court has considered making a hospital order under s. 37 but has decided that a sentence of imprisonment would be more appropriate (s. 45A(2)(b)) because a hospital order will not be sufficient to protect the public from harm, or because of the operation of s. 2 of the 1997 Act (now s. 109 of the 2000 Act) under which a mandatory life sentence must be passed (Home Office Mental Health Unit, 1997), if applicable: see 6.5.

Confusingly, however, the conditions that must be met before a hospital direction can be made are the same as those relevant to the making of a hospital order under s. 37.

As under that section, a court contemplating making a hospital direction must be satisfied on the written or oral evidence of two doctors (who need neither be 'approved' nor even psychiatrists) that the mental disorder from which the defendant is suffering is of a nature or degree that makes it appropriate for him to be detained in a hospital for medical treatment (s. 45A(2)(b)) and that 'such treatment is likely to alleviate or prevent a deterioration of his condition': s. 45A(2)(c). Section 45A also introduced the 'limitation direction', which is 'a direction that the offender be subject to the special restrictions contained in s. 41'. There is no scope to make a hospital direction without also making a limitation direction. The court must hear oral evidence from at least one of the two doctors who gave evidence under subsection (2) before making the two directions, but as the wording of s. 45A(4) is similar to that of s. 41(2) (see 6.5.2), it would seem clear that, as under that section, the final decision is for the court.

It may well be asked what difference there is between directions made under s. 45A and orders made under ss. 37 and 41. It is certainly the case that this sentencing option ended up being closer to that already available to a sentencing court than was originally envisaged. There are, however, two significant differences. First, a hospital direction can only be made if 'the offender is suffering from psychopathic disorder': s. 45A(2)(a). As mentioned above, the new powers were born out of a perceived need for flexibility in the sentencing of psychopathic offenders in respect of whom there was uncertainty about the efficacy of treatment (Reed, 1994), and resurrected an earlier proposal along the same lines (Peay, 1988). The 1996 consultation document retained this rationale, explaining that a hospital direction and limitation direction would be appropriate where the outcome of treatment was uncertain, but as seen above, in the new powers as actually enacted, there is a treatability requirement identical to that imposed under s. 3. At some point in the transition to the statute book, the initial justification for hospital and limitation directions has been lost.

The consultation document also explained the need for the new directions in cases where it was not clear that the making of a hospital order, with or without restrictions, would 'sufficiently address the risk to the public posed by the defendant' (Department of Health and Home Office, 1996: para. 1.4). This is because, on discharge from hospital, a patient detained on a s. 37 order, even one with restrictions attached, has to be discharged into the community; even though such discharge can be conditional in the case of restricted patients, and even though there is a certain logic in the discharge of patients from hospital who have apparently responded successfully to treatment or are found not to be treatable, the concern about the presence of known dangerous psychopathically disordered persons in the community was, and is, such that, in political terms, something had to be done. Accordingly, the second main difference between the powers added in 1997 and the existing orders is that, by s. 45B(2), a hospital direction is to have effect as a transfer direction and a limitation direction as a restriction direction, which means that, on discharge, a s. 45A patient may be transferred to prison to serve out his or her sentence: s. 50(1). Laing (1996: 138) has argued that this may undermine the doctor/patient relationship for s. 45A patients, either by offering patients who do not wish to confront their problems an escape route from hospital (Mental Health Act

Commission, 1995: 72) or by providing a disincentive to respond as well as might otherwise have been the case for patients who do not wish to return to prison. But within the frame of reference in which the new directions were concocted – the need to convince sentencers that detention in a hospital would not increase the chances of early release back into the community – this problem seems to be unavoidable. Simply, without the backstop of prison, there would be no meaningful distinction between these powers and the established orders, and so no encouragement for sentencers, who have been reluctant to make hospital orders in cases involving psychopathically disordered offenders, to make hospital directions.

The final justification for the new directions that is made in the consultation document is that hospital and limitation directions would be appropriate in cases where 'a punitive element in the disposal is required to reflect the offender's whole or partial responsibility' (para. 1.4). Subsequently, however, the reference to 'responsibility' was conspicuous by its absence from the Home Office Circular that accompanied the 1997 Act (Home Office Mental Health Unit, 1997). This may be because the possibility that hybrid orders should be used to denote the offender's responsibility was heavily criticised (Eastman, 1996; Laing, 1996), as it had been in earlier forms (Peay, 1988; Committee on Mentally Abnormal Offenders, 1975: para. 19.5) and in other contexts (Dell, 1982), on the grounds that it seeks to draw psychiatrists into the sentencing process, notwithstanding that 'psychiatrists are likely to resist such direct involvement in sentencing decisions, both on ethical grounds and because there is no scientific basis upon which such advice could be given to a court' (Eastman, 1996: 488), which is to say that criminal responsibility is not a medical concept.

Yet, in truth, culpability is a key element in the decision-making process. In order to get to the point at which it is proper to consider making a hospital direction, the sentencing court must first go through the process laid down by the Court of Appeal in *Birch*. As discussed earlier, this requires the judge to consider: first, the making of a non-custodial disposal; second, if detention in some form is required, whether a hospital order can and should be made. And the only reasons to decide against making a hospital order when the criteria are satisfied are to protect the public when there is no secure hospital accommodation available, or to recognise the culpability of the offender when punishment is warranted. Thus, considerations of culpability will be firmly to the fore when the judge is at this stage of the reasoning process. Hospital directions, therefore, which should not be considered until this point as an alternative to imprisonment after it has been decided that for the reasons outlined above a hospital order – even coupled with a restriction order – is not appropriate, are reserved for dealing with those (psychopathically disordered) offenders who, by definition, are either particularly dangerous or particularly culpable (as discussed earlier; in *Birch*, Mustill LJ held that orders under ss. 37 and 41 are 'even where there is culpability, the right way to deal with dangerous and disordered persons . . . '). Moreover, having rejected a non-custodial disposal, or as part of that decision, the court is required to obtain and consider a report on a mentally disordered offender under s. 82 of the Powers of Criminal Courts (Sentencing) Act 2000 and, having rejected the option of a hospital order, the court must go on to consider, either before, or as part of, the deliberations concerning whether to make a hospital direction, the appropriate sentence length.

This means that the psychiatric profession will be drawn into the sentencing process by the new directions. Eastman and Peay see this as 'a fundamental shift in thinking which will have a radical impact on the relationship between courts and psychiatrists' (1998: 105), in that involvement in the sentencing process is being foisted on psychiatric professionals against their wishes. From a more theoretical perspective, the reasoning process attendant on making hospital and limitation directions attests to a particularly graphic example of the complexity of the fusion of psychiatric and jurisprudential discourses that constitutes a new density to the 'micropractices' of power/knowledge. There are other reasons to be concerned about hospital and limitation directions. For instance, how is it possible to justify the applicability of the new directions solely to psychopathic offenders who, although likely to be culpable to a greater or lesser extent for the crimes that they commit, are not necessarily more likely to be culpable than other mentally disordered offenders? Part of the answer is, no doubt, that, in *political* terms, psychopathic offenders are perceived to be a particularly problematic group, about whom 'something must be done', but this is akin to saying that the 1997 Act provisions can be read as the latest instalment in the historical project of demonising the criminal psychopath as the epicentre of both badness and madness.

Less esoterically, perhaps, the limited target group of the 1997 reforms constitutes a missed opportunity to keep some significantly mentally disordered offenders out of prison. The equivalent Scottish legislation (s. 59A, Criminal Procedure (Scotland) Act 1995, as inserted by s. 6, Crime and Punishment (Scotland) Act 1997) has, from the outset, been available for all forms of mental disorder, and there is provision in s. 45A(10) of the 1983 Act for the English and Welsh legislation to be similarly extended by order of the Secretary of State. Indeed, it seems that it was only financial and resources reasons that explain the current limitation to psychopathic disorder (Eastman and Peay, 1998: 98). In *Drew*, Lord Bingham expressed the 'hope that further thought may be given to exercise of the power conferred by section 45A(10)' (para. 21), and the Court of Appeal added its voice in *R v IA* [2006] Cr App R (S) 91 and *R v Staines* [2006] EWCA Crim 15. This is perhaps a twin-edged sword. On the one hand, a defendant given a prison sentence on the basis that, despite being mentally disordered, his or her culpability is such that a hospital order, even coupled with a restriction order, is inappropriate might otherwise be hospitalised if the reach of s. 45A were to be extended beyond psychopathic disorder. This was almost certainly the situation in *Drew* (see Lord Bingham at para. 21). On the other hand, at present, the combination of s. 80(2)(b) of the Powers of Criminal Courts (Sentencing) Act 2000 and the availability of hospital directions risks pushing psychopathically disordered offenders 'up tariff' by attaching the hospital direction to a 'longer than normal' sentence. If an order under s. 45A was available in respect of offenders exhibiting any form of mental disorder, it might be that sentencing courts would prefer such orders over those contained in ss. 37 and 41 because of the 'safety net' of return to prison as a backstop, which would, in this broader statutory sentencing context, constitute an important shift in diversion policy at the general level, because the balance between treatment and punishment would move significantly towards the latter. Such concerns are, to date, largely academic. Hospital and limitation directions have barely been used in England and Wales – three occasions in 2000 and 2001 (Home Office Research, Development and Statistics Directorate, 2002: Table 4), only twice in 2004 (Home Office Research, Development and Statistics Directorate, 2005: Table 4). and not at all in 2004–5 (Government Statistical Service, 2006: para. 5.13). Nor is there any greater enthusiasm in Scotland, where the directions are not limited to psychopathically disordered offenders. Only two hospital and limitation directions were made between 1 July 1998 and 31 May 2000, and neither involved a psychopathically disordered offender (Scottish Executive Central Research Unit, 2001).

It is not surprising, in view of the rarity of use of s. 45A, that little case law has been generated. The only significant appellate decision to date, *R v Staines* [2006] EWCA Crim 15, does perhaps demonstrate the potential usefulness of the section for its current, limited, target group. S, 18 years of age and whose life had been an 'unmitigated and profound tragedy' (Tomlinson J at para. 2), killed a man who had befriended her. She told police officers and social workers that she had heard voices that had told her to carry out the attack. S was convicted in December 2000 of manslaughter by reason of diminished responsibility and given a discretionary life sentence. The judge also made an order under s. 45A, partly because of doubts about her diagnosis and treatability, partly because of concerns for public protection, and partly to mark her culpability for the offence. This was a case, then, in which all three of the justifications for making an order under s. 45A were, in the view of the sentencing judge, present.

Three and a half years later, S successfully applied for leave to appeal against her sentence. Her argument was that orders under ss. 37 and 41 of the 1983 Act should have been made in her case. Her grounds were (i) that she had responded to treatment following her arrival in hospital (S was, in fact, already in Broadmoor at the time of her trial, having been transferred from prison whilst on remand in prison) and therefore there was no need for the possibility of her transfer to prison, which possibility also had a deleterious effect on her treatment; (ii) that she had been wrongly diagnosed as suffering solely from a personality disorder, because she also suffered from a mental illness that had been present at the time of the offence and therefore reduced her culpability to a greater extent than appreciated by the sentencing court; and (iii) the fact that S was technically a prisoner meant that her release was a matter for the parole board rather than, as would be the case if she had been merely a patient, a mental health review tribunal, with the consequence that there was less scope to fine-tune the supervision and treatment of S if, and when, released into the community.

The Court of Appeal rejected all three arguments. It was not satisfied that the option of return to prison had, in fact, proven any significant impediment to S's treatment in Broadmoor (para. 27). It was not satisfied, although there was conflicting evidence, that the diagnosis of psychopathic disorder, accepted by the sentencing court, was incorrect (para. 23). Nor, therefore, would it accept that S's culpability was less than that judged by the sentencing court and, following *Drew*, a prison sentence was appropriately given to mark S's culpability. Finally, the court held that the parole board was able to impose conditions, relating to medical treatment, similar to those that could be imposed by a tribunal, and that the fact that S was a prisoner whose release would be considered by the parole board 'affords to the public a significantly enhanced and desirable degree of protection from the risk of danger from the appellant' (para. 30). There was, as such, no reason to interrupt the sentencing decisions made at first instance. There is little doubt that the availability of the hybrid order kept S out of prison. At first instance, it was found that, despite her disorder, S bore 'a considerable degree of responsibility for this savage killing'. She had a long history of being abused and abusing others, and had been convicted of a previous, serious, attack on the same victim. She had been subject to a 'very urgent transfer' to hospital whilst on remand in prison because of fears for her own safety and that of others in the prison, and had responded to treatment whilst in hospital. At the same time, the safety of the public had been assured. There can be little surprise that her appeal was unsuccessful, or that it appeared to the appeal court that the availability of the hybrid order had allowed a win–win outcome in this case.

In lieu of the failure of the 1997 Act to provide for the originally intended target population of patients of uncertain treatability, sentencers should be encouraged to make greater use of their powers, contained in s. 38 MHA 1983, to make an interim hospital order. An order under s. 38 can be made provided that an offender is suffering from one of the four specified forms of mental disorder (s. 38(1)(a)), and that two doctors, one of whom is employed at the hospital to be specified in the order (s. 38(3)), have given evidence to the court's satisfaction that there is 'reason to suppose that the mental disorder from which the offender is suffering is such that it may be appropriate for a hospital order to be made in his case': s. 38(1)(b). An order under s. 38 can only be made by a court on convicting a defendant of an offence punishable with imprisonment. As with an order under s. 37, it must be certified that the arrangements have been made for the reception of the defendant into hospital within 28 days of the making of the order and that there is a place of safety available if necessary: s. 38(4).

The idea of the interim order is to give adequate time to assess the treatability of the defendant's disorder, which may not be available under the remand powers. An interim order should not, however, be used as a holding device until a suitable long-term hospital placement can be made, if it is clear at the outset that the preferable order is one under s. 37: *R v Galfetti* [2002] EWCA Crim 1916, per May LJ at para. 7. If, following the making of a s. 38 order, the defendant is judged suitable for hospitalisation, a full hospital order may be made without the defendant being brought back before the court, provided that his or her legal representative has the opportunity to be heard: s. 38(2). If not, the defendant may be sentenced to a term of imprisonment. Until 1997, the maximum duration of an interim hospital order was six months (s. 38(5)), but this was extended to 12 months by s. 49(1) of the Crime (Sentences) Act 1997 – the same legislation that introduced the hospital and limitation directions. An order under s. 38, as amended, should be able to deal satisfactorily with the initial justification for the introduction of hospital and limitation directions, which view is bolstered by the fact that, according to government statistics, 69 persons were admitted to hospital in 2004–5 by virtue of either s. 38 or ss. 44 or 46 (Government Statistical Service, 2006: Table 1). This data does not disclose how those 169 admissions were divided between those sections, although it is likely that most were under s. 38. Section 44 deals with persons committed to Crown Court by a magistrates' court, with a view to a restriction order being passed, and is unlikely to be used much, and s. 46, which dealt with members of the armed forces, was, in fact, repealed by the Armed Forces Act 1996, Sch. 7, Part III, para. 1. It is tempting to conclude on this basis that hospital and limitation directions as currently structured have little practical value over and above the other available orders, and should be seen to reflect (confused) political imperatives. In retrospect, the main significance of the introduction of hospital and limitation directions may be as a sign of the increasing political emphasis on control over treatment.

6.6 Transfer from prison to hospital

If the measure of the success of the policy of diversion is the number of mentally disordered persons who end up in prison, then there is a good argument to say that the policy has failed. As Peay (1997: 668) succinctly states '[m]any, if not most, "disordered" offenders do not receive the therapeutic "hospital order" disposal, even though their culpability may be mitigated, if not absolved, by their mental state'. Despite the policy of, and mechanisms to secure the practice of, diversion of offenders suffering from mental disorder from the penal to the hospital system, the numbers of such persons amongst sentenced prison populations has been consistently well documented (see earlier). In some instances, this will be because an offender's mental health is negatively affected by prison conditions, but there is little doubt that some of those in prison suffering from mental disorder were suffering at the time of conviction. Research has shown that prison screening programmes can fail to detect mental disorder (Birmingham et al., 1996), although it has more recently been suggested that screening programmes have a reasonable detection rate (Hardie et al., 1998). Gunn et al. (1991) found that 3 per cent of prisoners required transfer to hospital, which amounts to several hundred individuals. Mechanisms for the transfer of such persons from prison to hospital have long been a feature of mental health legislation. Although it is possible to transfer such persons back to prison from hospital, there is no mechanism to transfer a person initially sentenced to hospital to a prison; as we have seen above, persons sentenced to hospital pass out of the criminal justice system once and for all. It was this gap that the reforms introduced by the Crime (Sentences) Act 1997 attempted to plug.

The current law, with respect to the transfer of a person from prison to hospital, is to be found in ss. 47–9 of the 1983 Act. Section 47 provides for the transfer of sentenced prisoners. The medical criteria to be satisfied are identical to those contained in ss. 3 and 37. Two doctors, at least one of whom must be 'approved', must examine the patient and agree that he or she is suffering from one of the four specified forms of mental disorder (s. 47(4), although it is not necessary that they agree that this is all that the patient is suffering from), to a nature or degree that makes it appropriate for him or her to be detained in a hospital for treatment. There is also a treatability test in respect of psychopathic disorder and mental impairment: s. 47(1). In *South West London and St George's Mental Health NHS Trust* v *W* [2002] EWHC 1770, a prisoner diagnosed as suffering from psychopathic disorder was transferred under s. 47 to a hospital near the end of his prison sentence under a care plan that proposed staged introduction of leave and eventual further transfer to a hostel, and eventually, release into the community. The court held that this plan amounted to 'treatment', even though there would be no more than 'psychological supervision' of W whilst in hospital, because graduated release would be more likely to prevent a deterioration, or allow less of a deterioration, of W's condition than would be the case if he were not transferred but were released immediately into the community from prison. This is an expansive concept of 'treatability', although it does not look out of place amongst the other case law on this question (see Chapter 7).

The decision whether to transfer a prisoner lies with the Secretary of State who 'may, if he is of the opinion having regard to the public interest and all the circumstances that it is expedient to do so by warrant direct that that person be removed to and detained in such hospital as may be specified in the direction': s. 47(1). This provision is very widely worded. It is clear for example that 'all the circumstances' includes such things as the availability of a hospital bed. When he or she does act under this section, it must first be decided in good faith that a proposed transfer is expedient (*Birch* per Mustill LJ at 210; see earlier), but that apart, the courts have traditionally been reluctant to interfere. In *R* v *SSHD, ex p K* [1990] 1 All ER 703 (DC), McCullough J, in a wide-ranging discussion of the powers given to the Secretary of State by Part III of the Act, said, *obiter*, that 'the Secretary of State is never obliged to act under s. 47, even if he thinks that the necessary preconditions are fulfilled' (716).

This view may now have to be modified in the light of the decision of the European Court in *Aerts*, where it was held to be a breach of Art. 5(1)(e) to hold a person judged suitable for hospital treatment on remand in a prison, in which suitable treatment was not available, for seven months. The case of a prisoner awaiting transfer is essentially similar to that of a person held in a prison until a hospital bed is found. If this view is correct, then given the numbers of mentally disordered persons held in prisons, its implications for the Home Office may be considerable. The opposing view is that Art. 5 is not engaged by transfer decisions because it deals only with the initial detention and not with the conditions in which detention is served (*R* v *Deputy Governor or Parkhurst Prison, ex p Hague* [1992] 1 AC 58 (HL). In *R* v *Mersey Care NHS Trust, ex p Munjaz, R* v *Airedale NHS Trust (Appeal) ex p S* [2005] UKHL 58, [2005] 3 WLR 793, [2005] HRLR 42, at para. 30, Lord Bingham held that, although Art. 5 'cannot found a complaint directed to the category of institution within an appropriate system', it 'may avail a person detained in an institution of an inappropriate type', which seems clearly to support the view that, on a suitable fact situation, Art. 5 might provide relief. The same judge observed, in *R v Drew* [2003] UKHL 25, [2003] 1 WLR 1213, [2003] 4 All ER 557 at para. 18, that the Home Secretary is bound to act in compliance with the Convention, and in *R v SSHD and National Assembly of Wales, ex p D* [2004] EWHC 2857 (Admin), Stanley Burnton J held that s. 47 is more than simply permissive (para. 33):

once the prison service have reasonable grounds to believe that a prisoner requires treatment in a mental hospital in which he may be detained, the Home Secretary is under a duty expeditiously to take reasonable steps to obtain appropriate medical advice, and if that advice confirms the need for transfer to a hospital, to take reasonable steps within a reasonable time to effect that transfer...The steps that are reasonable will depend on the circumstances, including the apparent risk to the health of the prisoner if no transfer is effected.

He then linked a failure properly to utilise s. 47 to a possible breach of Art. 8 of the Convention (para. 33), although there was no breach on the facts of that case, the delay in D's transfer being explained by legitimate reasons, namely difficulty in arriving at a diagnosis and the lack of a suitable hospital placement (para. 48).There is always, in addition, as Stanley Burnton J noted, Art. 3, but as seen earlier, the attitude of the European Court, in cases such as *Kudla v Poland* (2002) 35 EHRR 11, is that Art. 3 is not easily engaged.

A transfer direction made under s. 47 is deemed to have the same effect as a hospital order: s. 47(3). An order made under s. 47 can be accompanied by an order made under s. 49, (a 'restriction direction') by which the restrictions contained in s. 41 may apply to a transferee: s. 49(1), (2). It is the policy of the Home Secretary to impose restrictions in all cases, except when a patient is transferred within days of his or her release date and is not judged to constitute a threat to the public. This policy was challenged in *R v Secretary of State for the Home Department, ex p T* [2003] EWHC 538. T argued that an order under ss. 47 and 49 is analogous to one made under ss. 37 and 41, and hence should only be made when there is a demonstrable need for public protection. The High Court, although accepting that no one had suggested that T was a danger to the public (para. 12), rejected this submission, because ss. 47 and 49 deal with sentenced prisoners and hence there is no reason why the policy of the Secretary of State under s. 49 should reflect the approach of the courts when deciding the appropriate sentence at trial. Maurice Kay J held that the policy of the Secretary of State properly emphasised the need for public protection and was lawful. If a restriction direction is made, it will automatically cease to apply on that person's prison release date (s. 50(2)), defined in s. 50(3) as 'the day (if any) on which he would be entitled to be released (whether uncon-ditionally or on licence)', ignoring for these purposes any powers the parole board would have if the transferred person were detained in a prison, and any discretionary powers for earlier release available for use by the Secretary of State. After that day the patient, if still in hospital, will be detained as if held under s. 37. There were 346 trans-fers under ss. 47 and 49 in 2004, up from 296 in 2003 and 223 in 2002, having hovered at around an average of 250 annually for the previous decade (Home Office Research, Development and Statistics Directorate, 2005: Table 3).

There is also provision for the transfer of other than sentenced prisoners under s. 48, defined to include remand prisoners, civil prisoners and those held under the Immigration Act 1971 or s. 62 of the Nationality, Immigration and Asylum Act 2002: s. 48(2). Section 48 applies only to prisoners suffering 'from mental illness or severe mental impairment of a nature or degree which makes it appropriate for him to be detained in hospital for medical treatment and . . . is in urgent need of such treatment'. A patient so transferred is treated as though transferred on a hospital order (s. 47(3)) and, again, it is unusual for an order to be made under s. 48 without an accompanying direction being made under s. 49(1). The use of ss. 48 and 49 increased markedly from 1987, when 77 untried or unsentenced prisoners were transferred to hospital, to 1994, when there were 536 such transfers. It is clear that the rise in numbers through the 1990s was linked to the increase in the number of regional and medium-secure unit beds. Two out of three transfers were in respect of persons charged with violent or sexual offences in Mackay and Machin's research (1998; 2000). Thereafter, the rate fell back unevenly but steadily, against the backdrop of an ever-increasing prison population. There were 481 transfers in 1996, 464 in 1991 and 392 transfers in 2000, after which numbers began to rise again, reaching 421 transfers in 2002 and 485 in 2004 (Home Office Research, Development and Statistics Directorate, 2005: Table 3).

For all transfers, the receiving hospital must be specified in the direction (ss. 47(1), 48(1)) and although it does not follow from this that the agreement of that hospital must be obtained before a direction is made, this has been the normal practice of the Secretary of State: see *R* v *Secretary of State for the Home Department, ex p T* [1994] 1 All ER 794 (DC). The Butler Committee (Committee on Mentally Abnormal Offenders, 1975: para. 2.29) noted the practice without comment. This is understandable, particu-larly because, under the terms of s. 47(2), a transfer direction under either ss. 47 or 48 will cease to have effect if the person named in the direction has not been transferred within 14 days of its making. Under the 1959 Act regime, the delay in the time from when a prisoner was first referred for transfer to the actual transfer increased steadily. Grounds (1990) found that, in the decade 1974–83, the mean wait was 7.5 months, with a quarter of patients waiting a year or more. This increase took place against the back-drop of a fall in the number of prisoners recommended for transfer by prison service doctors, despite, at that time also, an ever-increasing prison population. The reasons for this fall include: the introduction of waiting lists at Broadmoor for transfer patients; a disinclination on the part of psychiatrists to accept chronic patients (Dolan and Shetty, 1995; Cheadle and Ditchfield, 1982; Tidmarsh, 1978, cited in Grounds, 1990) and those diagnosed as having personality disorders (Hargreaves, 1997; National Institute for Mental Health in England, 2003a); the difficulties experienced by special hospitals when trying to secure a bed for patients able to move into less secure accommodation (see Chapter 3).

In the 1990s, when the numbers transferred rose significantly, the average waiting period also seemed to have decreased. Huws *et al.* (1997) found that the average wait from the initial request from a prison doctor for a second opinion to the actual transfer had fallen throughout this period and was by then less than two months. In Mackay and Machin's research (1998; 2000), involving remand prisoners transferred under s. 48, the mean wait was 14 days. Mean waits can be misleading, however. As Larkin and Close (1996) have pointed out, the mean waiting times obscure the fact that referrals are classified as either urgent or routine, with the former being processed in around a third of the time of the routine referrals. In their audit of the referral system as it operates at Rampton hospital, a mean waiting time of 41.4 days disguised the fact that urgent cases were admitted within 20.6 days, compared with a mean of 61.5 days for routine cases. By any measure, though, the situation seems to have worsened again more recently. In November 2005, Louis Appleby, the National Director of Mental Health, and John Boyington, the Director of Health and Offender Partnerships wrote (Appleby and Boyington, 2005) to all strategic health authority prison leads and mental health leads, PCT commissioners, and care service improvement partnerhips prison mental health regional leads, in bald terms, stating that 'there are currently some unacceptable delays in the transfer of acutely mentally ill prisoners to and from hospital under ss. 47 and 48 of the Mental Health Act 1983'. They were referring to the 'prison traffic light' reporting system, which, in September 2005, stated that there were 51 prisoners waiting, after acceptance by an inpatient mental health service provider, for more than 12 weeks for transfer to hospital under the Mental Health Act (HM Prison Service, 2006: 2). In *R* v *SSHD and National Assembly of Wales, ex p D* [2004] EWHC 2857 (Admin), Stanley Burnton J, although holding that there was no breach of Art. 8 in the delayed transfer of D in that case (see above) did also say, by way of observation, that the lack of a national database of available hospital beds hindered the process of transferring D, commenting that 'the Claimant has not suggested that the lack of such a database caused an infringement of his Convention rights, and the practicalities of establishing and maintaining such a database have not been investigated. The position might be otherwise in future' (para. 60).

A transfer direction need not be signed until a bed has been found and the purpose of s. 47(2) is, therefore, not clear. Worse, as Grounds pointed out, under the 1959 regime, it was, and still is under the 1983 Act, possible for transfers to take place 'on the basis of out of date medical reports, long after the initial recommendation' (1990: 548). In *R* v *Secretary of State for the Home Office, ex p Gilkes* [1999] 1 MHLR 6 (HC), it was held that, if there is fluctuation in the medical condition of the person in respect of whom transfer is being contemplated, it is unreasonable of the Home Secretary to rely on dated medical reports. In addition, it was held in *Varbanov* v *Bulgaria* Application No. 31365/96 (2000) that reliance on outdated reports could amount to a breach of Art. 5(1)(e) of the Convention, whilst as already suggested, not to act within a reasonable time in that situation may also constitute a breach, if suitable treatment is not forthcoming in prison (*Aerts*). In summary, the 1983 Act here, as in many other places, provides a 'safeguard' provision that, in practice, is of no relevance whatever. It is instructive to compare s. 47(2) with s. 11(5), which provides that no application is to be made under ss. 2, 3 or 7 unless the applicant has personally seen the patient within the previous 14 days.

There are other concerns with the operation of the transfer provisions. The most significant is the effect that a transfer to hospital has on the length of time that the individual spends in custody. It is established that a determinate prison sentence, and the tariff for those given a discretionary life sentence, continues to run whilst the prisoner is in hospital following transfer for prison: *R v Secretary of State for the Home Department, ex p H & Ors* [1994] 3 WLR 1110 per Rose LJ at 1120C. But things are not necessarily so straightforward. Grounds found that one consequence of the reduction of the availability of hospital beds for transferees was that transfers took place at a later stage in the prisoner's sentence. One consultant at Broadmoor gave evidence to the Butler Committee that, because of the difficulties, some prison doctors had given up trying to get patients onto the Broadmoor waiting list for transfer and that '[b]ecause of the waiting list we have had to admit patients very near the end of their sentences' (para. 3.41, cited in Grounds, 1990: 57). In consequence, there was a risk that patients would be detained in hospital beyond the date at which they would otherwise have been released from prison. This will usually be the earliest release date (ERD), although it may be the latest date of release (LDR), that is, the last date of a determinate sentence served in full, with no remission or parole. The Butler Committee dismissed these concerns as 'almost entirely theoretical' (Committee on Mentally Abnormal Offenders, 1975: para. 3.42). Others argued that a transfer direction should not survive the patient's ERD, and that further detention past that date should be permissible only if that patient was first sectioned under s. 3 (Gostin, 1977). The 1983 Act took a middle course. Now, under s. 50(2),(3), where a restriction direction is made, it must not survive the ERD for persons sentenced to less than four years' imprisonment, or the date of release on licence (when two thirds of the sentence has been served, rather than the ERD, which is the date on which such a person would be eligible for parole, usually at the halfway point of the sentence) for persons serving sentences of longer than four years, rather than subsisting until the LDR, as was the case under the 1959 Act. The practical effect of this is that a transferee remaining in hospital when the restriction order ceases to have effect may apply to a mental health review tribunal for discharge from that date.

Nothing was done in 1983, or since, however, to prevent the transfer of a person from prison shortly before that person's ERD, or even, as in *R v SSHD and National Assembly of Wales, ex p D* [2004] EWHC 2857 (Admin), on the actual day of release (see also the case discussed at Mental Health Act Commission, 2005: para. 5.74–5). Despite the confidence of Butler, it seems clear that late transfer was, and continues to be, a problematic issue. Grounds found that, in the 1960s, transfers were typically 23 months before ERD; in the 1970s, this had fallen to ten months, a change 'not due to any significant reduction in the mean length of their sentences' (1991: 59). In addition, length of stay in hospital after transfer (four years mean, with 7.4 years mean for sex offenders) meant that '[m]ost [62 per cent] of the patients transferred to Broadmoor ... continued to be detained in the hospital well beyond their LDRs – in some cases for many years' (1991: 62); and this 'extra' period of detention bore a 'strong relationship' to the gravity of the offence. There is evidence to suggest that the situation has changed in the last decade. In Huckle's study of transferees to hospitals in South Wales over the three-year period 1992–5, 66 per cent of transfers took place within three months of the offender's arrival in prison (1996: 39). Huws et al.'s research into the operation of the 1983 Act in special hospitals in the period 1984–91 found no correlation between time in hospital and the gravity of the offence (1997: 81), although 44 per cent of transferees were detained beyond their LDR, with 59 per cent held beyond their ERD. Compared with the earlier figures, this seems to be an improvement, yet the numbers detained in hospital longer than they would otherwise have been, had they not been transferred, remains disquietingly high.

In addition, Huws et al.'s results are not strictly comparable with those of Grounds, because a high percentage – 81 per cent of the latter's sample – had left hospital by the end of the study period, whilst in Huws et al.'s research, only 56 per cent had left the hospital (1997: 81). The arguments made three decades ago by Gostin, that there should be a requirement that detention post-ERD should have to be justified on medical grounds, such as in the form of a s. 3 admission at that point, seem to be as strong as ever, particularly because the making available of a right to apply to a tribunal for discharge post-ERD seems to have had little impact (only 17 out of 351 transferees to special hospitals in the period 1984–91 were discharged by a tribunal: Huws et al., 1997: 81). Of particular concern is Huws et al.'s finding that 6 per cent of transferees (21 individuals) were transferred late into their sentences – within six weeks of ERD – on grounds of 'worry about their release' (1997: 77); 4 per cent (15) of transfers took place within one week of ERD. Of these patients, 66 per cent (14) were suffering from a personality disorder. Their mean sentence length was 3.7 years, and mean time in hospital, 2.8 years (1997: 78). The period in hospital does not differ significantly from the mean time in hospital of those transferred earlier in their sentence, but, of course, for the late transferees, virtually all of this period was in excess of the sentence given by the court at the time of conviction. It may well be, as Huws et al. suggest, that prisoners suffering from a personality disorder, unlike mentally ill prisoners, do not come to the attention of prison medical services until they are assessed prior to their proposed release from prison (1997: 82), because those suffering from such disorders do not necessarily appear to be 'mad'.

But this does not detract from the crucial point here, which is that transfers should, under the terms of s. 47, only take place on medical grounds. 'Concerns about release' that are not concerned directly with the need for treatment to improve or prevent a deterioration in the patient's state of mental health, are not per se a good enough reason for transfer. It seems odd that psychopaths feature so largely in this group, when elsewhere their treatability is, at best, suspect. It is difficult not to feel a lurking sense of unease that, as in *R v Rampton Hospital Authority, ex p W* [2001] EWHC Admin 134 and

South West London and St George's Mental Health NHS Trust v *W* [2002] EWHC 1770, when release is imminent, psychopaths are suddenly deemed (deploying a problematic definition) 'treatable', albeit not in large numbers. Of course, such suspicions can be hard to prove, but it is noteworthy that in *R* v *Nottingham Healthcare NHS Trust, ex p M* [2002] EWCA Civ 1728, at para. 37, Pill LJ held that: 'The treatability test must of course be applied in good faith and not used as a cover for decisions taken on other grounds.'

If, as is usual, a transfer to hospital has restrictions attached under s. 49, that person can be transferred back to prison if, before the expiry of that prison sentence (measured by reference to the patient's ERD on licence, ignoring for these purposes any powers of the parole board: s. 50(3)), the patient's doctor (RMO) notifies the Secretary of State that the person concerned no longer requires hospital treatment or has proven to be untreatable: s. 50(1)(a). In *R* v *Shetty, ex p IR* [2003] EWHC 3022, the High Court held, on a judicial review application, that its role in respect of claims by IR that the decision of the Secretary of State to recall him to prison breached his rights under Arts. 3 and 5 ECHR, was to conduct a 'heightened' review of that decision, but did not extend to the court deciding for itself that there had been a breach. The court concluded that the Secretary of State's decision, itself based on a 'most anxious scrutiny' of the situation, was in breach of neither Article. The Secretary of State may alternatively release that person on licence (which allows conditions that cannot be attached to a order for discharge from hospital) or discharge him or her if that would have been possible had he or she been in prison: s. 50(1)(b), and see *R* v *SSHD, ex p Abdul Miah* [2004] EWHC 2569 (Admin). In either case, the restriction direction automatically lapses. Alternatively, the Secretary of State has powers under s. 42(2) to discharge any person held under restrictions (see further Chapter 8). The nature of what is entailed by the requirement that the RMO notify the Secretary of State was litigated in the *Nottingham* case (above). M had been transferred to Rampton hospital from prison for treatment early in 2000. In March 2002, his RMO, following a case conference at the hospital at which the preponderance of opinion was the M should be returned to prison, made an urgent request under s. 50(1), on the grounds that M was no longer treatable, and was actively resisting and/or trying to dictate his treatment and undermine his RMO and named nurse. M sought judicial review of this decision, on the basis that some of those involved in his treatment did not share the view of his RMO. The Court of Appeal held that the RMO did not have to provide an inventory of the various views of his or her colleagues to the Secretary of State (para. 39). Nevertheless, 'there is a duty upon an RMO before giving a notification to make proper enquiries within the hospital as to whether the treatability test is satisfied and to consider views expressed, as well as his own first hand knowledge and experience, before making a recommendation. The extent of enquiry and of disclosure of information will depend on the circumstances of the particular case and will normally be judged as at the moment of decision' (para. 41).

M had also argued that he should have been allowed to make formal representations to the Secretary of State in order to dispute the view as to his treatability expressed by the RMO. On this point, the court held that 'There will be cases in which circumstances, including information available to the Secretary of State, either in the documents by which the notification is given, or from other sources, create a duty in the Secretary of State to make further enquiries or take further action or both' (para. 47), but this was not such a case. Nor was there any right for the patient to make representations to the Secretary of State, or to be consulted about a proposed transfer. Finally, the court dealt cursorily with the relevance of Art. 8 of the Convention, holding that 'Transfer from prison to hospital and hospital back to prison, as a part of a high-security custodial regime, cannot in present circumstances be said to breach the Article notwithstanding the differences in medical treatment which may occur. I do not of course exclude the possibility that some aspects of a custodial regime might attract a case for a breach' (at para. 49).

If the patient was on remand before transfer to hospital, the transfer direction, and any accompanying restriction direction, is automatically brought to an end if, and when, that individual is returned to court and his or her case disposed of. Disposal may be by means of a hospital order, in addition to the other options open to a sentencing court: s. 51(2). A hospital order can be made if, on a reapplication of the criteria for s. 37, this is warranted and the court, after 'considering any depositions or other documents' thinks it 'proper' to make a hospital order: s. 51(6). In *R v Snaresbrook Crown Court, ex p K* 2001 WL 1422891, Pill LJ held that, even with the aid of depositions, it is difficult to know what is 'proper' because it cannot be known if the information in the depositions would have been accepted as evidence, and to sentence a person without convicting him or her is 'a drastic step, one that should only be taken in exceptional circumstances' (at para. 35). If, before that time, the RMO notifies the Secretary of State that the patient no longer requires treatment or is untreatable, the Secretary of State has a discretion to order by warrant the return of the individual to prison (s. 51(3)), which can also be ordered by the court having jurisdiction to try the case if the Secretary of State declines to act: s. 51(4). If there has been no action under either ss. 51(3) or (4), the court having jurisdiction over the case may make a hospital order (with or without a restriction order) without convicting the defendant, and this may be done in his or her absence if the conditions in s. 51(6) apply (s. 51(5)(b)) and it is 'impracticable or inappropriate to bring the detainee before the court': s. 51(5)(a). In *ex p K*, the Divisional Court (Pill LJ at para. 32) held that:

the word 'inappropriate' in section 51(5) must be construed restrictively. The section must not be used as a routine and easy way of avoiding a potentially troublesome trial... I would not necessarily restrict the word 'inappropriate' so as to mean 'physically impossible' but a high degree of disablement or relevant disorder must be present. The section does not apply in a situation in which all that is involved is possible inconvenience for the Crown and inevitable distress for the defendant and others likely to be concerned in a trial.

If this is only done in 'exceptional' circumstances, it will also be no breach of the right to a fair hearing that is protected by Art. 6 of the Convention (at para. 37). But, in any case, the Court of Appeal decided, in the later case of *R v Griffiths* [2002] WL 1311144, the s. 51(5) powers are only applicable before a trial has begun. If doubts about whether it is appropriate for the defendant to attend the trial surface after it has begun ('beginning, broadly with the swearing in of the jury' per Tomlinson LJ, in *Snaresbrook*, at para. 48.) the appropriate mechanism is that of unfitness to plead (per Keene LJ, in *Griffiths*, at para. 21).

6.7 Concluding comments

The stated aim of this chapter was to evaluate the policy of diversion on its own terms, to ask: 'Does diversion work?' It can now be seen that there can be no easy or unqualified answer to that question. The policy of diversion *does* work, but only imperfectly. The system, as a whole, is shot through with some common problems. Foremost amongst these are: a shortfall in funding; lack of coherent central guidance; lack of effective training of criminal justice personnel and others, such as persons to act as AAs. Diversion practice has been left, to a large extent, to those working at local level, and the result is service provision that is patchy, both in terms of geographical spread and of quality. There is also uncertainty, amongst police officers, lawyers and courts, as to the appropriate scope and target population of the policy of diversion.

Added to these considerations, the MHA 1983 at various points – notably the powers to remand to hospital – places legal limitations on the potential of early diversion, although for reasons that are not readily apparent. The removal of these legal–structural limitations on diversion should be of pressing concern to those involved in the reform of mental health law. The heavy-handed mechanisms that currently exist to deal with pleas of unfitness and insanity also require further reform. Even so, the limited time, resources and information available to sentencing, particularly magistrates', courts makes it likely that the remand prison population will continue to feature large numbers of persons who are mentally disordered. Ultimately, the extent to which this is an acceptable feature of our criminal justice system is a political, rather than a legal, medical, or even philosophical, question. And that we seem, as a society, to be equivocal in our response is possibly the most fundamental limitation on the potential for diversion.

One way in which this ambivalence manifests itself is as reluctance on the part of sentencers to make full use of the range of options available under the MHA 1983. In part, this seems to be because of a perception that defendants sentenced to hospital will be released inappropriately early. Such fears are largely unwarranted; for some, mainly personality disordered, defendants 'diversion' can mean a much longer period of incarceration than would otherwise have been the case, with hospitalisation late in a prison sentence being used as an extension of, rather than an alternative to, imprisonment. Such factors speak in turn of the more deeply seated tension between treatment and control, and it is clear that diversion policy has always been circumscribed, not so much by moral or philosophical questions of criminal responsibility and desert, but by more pragmatic considerations of public safety and risk management.

As mentioned at the start of this chapter, current government policy is to diminish the need for diversion at the custodial end of the system, by improving the quality of healthcare in prisons. As far as hospitals are concerned, the government's plans are that detention will depend on a broad concept of treatability; the House of Lords and European Court have ruled that detention in such circumstances will not breach any Convention right (see the discussion in Chapter 8). The courts have thus licensed the government's plans to use hospitals for purely custodial reasons. Prisons become more like hospitals, as hospitals become more like prisons. That the policy of public protection is, in principle, a legitimate one is beyond debate, nor can there be any doubt that the imperfect dovetailing of the mental health and criminal justice systems means that some individuals fall between the two. An example is provided by *R v Swindon Borough Council, ex p Stoddard* (1998) 2 July, unreported (DC). S was at the end of a prison sentence, passed for an offence of violence. S was suffering from an untreatable personality disorder, which by common opinion, including his own, rendered him at significant risk of violent reoffending. The case arose because S was unable to obtain secure community care accommodation from his local authority, even though it had assessed him as being in need of such provision and it was accepted that the duty of the authority was to supply the accommodation under the relevant community care legislation (see Chapter 9). This was because the authority had been unable to find a provider of secure accommodation that would agree to take a patient who was not 'sectionable'. Moses J held that there could be no breach of duty by the local authority or providers of accommodation in such circumstances. The judgment means that local authorities and health authorities, and the providers of services to those authorities, can avoid responsibility for persons such as S. Moreover, the court also accepted the view of the Home Office that the powers of the Secretary of State to recall prisoners released on license, contained in s. 39, Criminal Justice Act 1991, can only be used to recall a prisoner on the basis of behaviour *after* release, and cannot be used to *prevent* release, however great the perceived risk.

Individuals like S fall between the mental health and criminal justice regimes. To reform the law to deal with such situations is legitimate. Our objection to the way in which the reform process has been approached by the government is that it is putting the cart before the horse. In our view, it is wrong, in principle, for hospitals, and the mental health system, to be *predicated on* public protection: that is the role of the criminal justice system. Initially, the plan was for discrete powers for the control and detention of those diagnosed as suffering from an untreatable 'dangerous and severe personality disorder' (Department of Health, 1998a: para. 4.33; see also Home Office and Department of Health, 1999), but by the time of the draft bill 2002, the government had decided to legislate one regime for all patients. The irony of the current, and much less ambitious, set of proposals for reform is that policy towards those that the mental health services do want to treat is still being propelled by policy towards those that they do not: the 'dangerous psychopath' is the axis around which mental health policy more broadly is being reconstituted. If this is social control, then it also looks a lot like 'social control' of medical professionals, and conspiracy theorists perhaps need to look elsewhere for the prime instigator of these measures. Perhaps we should all look, ultimately, at our own views (Health Education Authority, 1997) and their implications.

7

Treatment in Hospital

7.1 Introduction

The medical treatment of many mentally disordered persons in hospital now corresponds closely, in numerous ways, to the medical treatment of other patients. They are likely to be admitted to the same district general hospital as are patients with physical complaints. In either case, the emphasis is on throughput, and hospitalisation is likely to be for as short a period as possible. For the vast majority of psychiatric patients, admitted 'informally' under s. 131 MHA 1983, the law applicable to their medical treatment is that relevant to all other hospital patients. An informal patient in a psychiatric facility may (in theory, at least) refuse treatment, leave hospital at any time, access the same complaints procedures, and so on, in exactly the same way as may any other hospital patient.

For detained patients, the position is different. Part IV of the MHA 1983 lays out a legal regime that allows for treatment without consent. The policy behind the MHA 1983 is that it is justifiable to override the autonomy of detained patients and impose treatment, for the good either of the patient or of others. But Part IV of the 1983 Act is double-edged: the libertarian critique of 'psychiatric treatment as social control' in its less radical form (Gostin, 1975) was a potent influence on the construction of the 1983 Act; hence, Part IV also provides that even detained patients have an absolute right to refuse the most invasive treatments, i.e. those of psychosurgery, which may change the personality of the patient through the destruction of brain tissue or through the surgical implantation of hormones to reduce male sexual drive. Such treatments are used relatively rarely. The main 'physical treatments' are drug therapies and electroconvulsive therapy (ECT), and these too are subject to a system of safeguards, requiring either the consent of the patient or a second opinion. For ECT, the safeguards system applies from the first administration of the treatment to a patient, but it does not come into operation in respect of drug treatments until three months after such treatment has first been administered. Once three months have passed, drug treatments may only be given without consent if a second opinion that it is desirable to do so is provided, by one of the doctors appointed by the state for this purpose, known as a 'second opinion appointed doctor' (SOAD). In turn, the whole system is overseen by the Mental Health Act Commission (MHAC), which visits and inspects facilities, runs the SOAD system, and produces biennial reports. These safeguards are designed to compensate for the removal of the patient's right to refuse treatment.

Part IV of the MHA 1983 can be read as a truce between two competing models of psychiatric treatment: between 'medicine' and as 'control'. Its detail weaves notions of treatment and control, of autonomy and beneficence, and of rights and their overriding together in complex, and sometimes perplexing, patterns. The *Bournewood* litigation (discussed in detail in Chapter 4) illustrated some of the difficult questions about the reach of Part IV. For example, it is not clear why the equation between detained patients and restrictions on medical treatment is made. Do the same concerns about inappropriate treatment not apply to informal patients? Perhaps not, if informal patients are able, in fact, to exercise their legal rights – but as seen in Chapter 4, 'informal' does not necessarily mean 'voluntary', and capacity is often an issue. There is a risk that, if law sees only its own inventions (here, 'the autonomous individual') rather than real people, some of whom will be far from autonomous, there may be no real protection of their interests, whatever the law may say. This was, essentially, the view taken late in 2004, when the *Bournewood* litigation reached the European Court of Human Rights, although the government had, by then, already accepted the force of these points and proffered suggested reforms as Part 5 of the Mental Health Bill 2002. Following the abandonment of that bill, the subsequent bill of 2004, and further consultation (Department of Health, 2005d), the intention now is to introduce what has already become known as the 'Bournewood procedure' for those who lack capacity and who do not positively object to hospitalisation, through amendment to the Mental Capacity Act 2005. If the patient does object to hospitalisation, he or she must be detained under the Mental Health Act (Department of Health, 2006j: 4, and see preface). In either case, there will be new restrictions on the clinical freedom of those providing treatment to such patients.

The expansion of the class of detained patients to include such persons raises the question whether 'detained patients' are properly seen as a homogenous class, given the range of accommodation in which patients may be held, from open wards in district hospitals to high-security intensive wards in the special hospitals. Although the primary concern of this chapter is to detail and analyse the legal rules that are relevant to the medical treatment of both informal and detained patients, considerations such as this underline the importance of studying those rules in their context, asking not only 'what are the rules?' but also 'do they work, and if so, how?' It also means that an informed legal debate must rest on at least a basic understanding of the medical practices that law seeks to regulate.

Consequently, this chapter opens with a consideration of the range of interventions that come under the heading of medical treatment for mental disorder. The extent to which treatment can be seen as beneficial or benevolent, and indeed as 'medical' at all, is unavoidably put into question by such a discussion. In addition, the law and practice of treatment in hospital will be examined. Here the main subtheme is the relation between 'medicalism' and 'legalism'. The history of mental health law in this country is often seen in terms of a tension between 'medicalism' and 'legalism', the former understood in terms of clinical freedom and the latter as fetters on that freedom. But a close analysis of the 1983 Act reveals that the provisions of the common law and the mechanisms in the 1983 Act that were designed to protect the rights of patients have very often failed to do so. Indeed, 'legalism' has tended not to oppose, but to support 'medicalism', with the law mandating the exercise of broad medical discretion. The passage of the Human Rights Act 1998 has changed the landscape to some extent, generating case law that has placed new procedural requirements on treatment providers and SOADs. There has also been substantive change as the courts have inched cautiously in the direction of accepting a human rights-based right to refuse treatment for some (in fact, very few) detained patients.

The final section of the chapter considers the relevance of the emergency measures used when a patient's behaviour is risking harm to self or others. These measures occupy a sort of conceptual hinterland between the poles of treatment and control, and an analysis of them helps to facilitate the development of a fairly sophisticated understanding of that relationship. The chapter concludes with a consideration of the implications, for the broader questions, of how the mental health system should be conceptualised, and the relevance of legal discourses – particularly that of 'rights' – to its operation.

7.2 Medical treatment for mental disorder

The history of treatment for mental disorder – particularly its recent history – is marked by change and innovation. Yet for all this, there is a remarkable degree of continuity in the way in which mental distress has been approached across time and space. So called 'non-psychiatrised' societies, for example, utilise practices of constraint and control, in response to individuals deemed to be 'insane', which are familiar in design and intent to those practised elsewhere as psychiatric interventions (Mason, 1993). At the Sanctuary of Asklepios, at Epidauros in the Argolid, which was a sizeable healing centre by the end of the fourth century BC, the practices of the healer Asklepios were applied. It is said that Asklepios, when confronted by patients suffering from distress, hallucinations or delusions, would use one of two tactics: either he would talk to the afflicted individual, trying to transmit to that person the sense of calm that the Sanctuary insisted upon, or he would throw snakes into patients' beds while they slept, the idea being that the patient, on waking to find him or herself surrounded by snakes, would be shocked out of his or her condition. Sedgwick (1982) notes a similar bifurcation in ancient Rome. In India, there are textual references dating back even further, to 1500 BC, that recommend the root of the plant *Rauwolfa serpentina* as a remedy for what would now be called psychiatric disturbance, which, as Silverstone and Turner (1995: 4) note, 'was found in the 1950s to be soundly based, and resperine was among the first of the newer "antipsychotic" drugs'.

It is altogether too neat to suggest that these three approaches continue in an unbroken line to the present. Asklepios' 'talking cure' is not the forerunner of modern psychoanalysis or of psychotherapy, although these two interventions are known today as the 'talking cures'. Similarly, it would be inaccurate to suggest that modern ECT techniques are the descendants of Asklepios' 'snake treatment', because although ECT involves the administration of an electric shock, it does not attempt to 'shock' the patient out of his or her disorder. It is, however, only fairly recently that such 'shock treatments' passed out of common usage. Even in the 1930s, paraldehyde, laxatives and cold baths were being prescribed for psychotic patients. ECT today is often bracketed together with the use of drugs, under the heading of 'physical treatments'. Talking cures and physical treatments are the two main typologies of treatment for mental disorder. Although all treatments are used in hospitals, drug treatments are the main plank of treatment provision within mental health (Rogers and Pilgrim, 2005: 143). One survey found that 98 per cent of patients in hospital were given drug treatments, with 60 per cent given psychotherapeutic treatments (Rogers, 1993).

7.2.1 Physical treatments

7.2.1.1 Drug treatments

Psychiatric drugs constitute around a quarter of all prescriptions dispensed by the National Health Service. In 2002, NICE estimated that the treatment of schizophrenia alone, involving some 185,000 patients annually, costs £1bn per annum (or 3 per cent of the total health budget) in hospital and drug costs (National Institute for Health and Clinical Excellence, 2002), a figure that, in both absolute and real terms, has risen markedly over the last few years (Howlett, 1998: 97). Silverstone and Turner (1995) provide a useful typology of psychiatric drug treatments.

  1 **Antipsychotics**: drugs with therapeutic effects on psychoses and other types of psychiatric disorder. In addition, they frequently produce extrapyramidal effects, such as tremor and rigidity.

  2 **Antidepressants**: drugs effective in the treatment of pathological depressive states.

  3 **Anti-anxiety drugs**: substances that reduce pathological anxiety, tension and agitation, without therapeutic effect on disturbed cognitive or perceptual processes. These drugs usually raise the convulsive threshold and do not produce extrapyramidal or autonomic effects. They may produce drug dependence.

  4 **Psychostimulants**: drugs that increase the level of alertness and/or motivation.

  5 **Psychodysleptics**: drugs producing abnormal mental phenomena, particularly in the cognitive and perceptual spheres . . .

  6 **Nooceptive drugs**: drugs that improve cognitive function and memory.

(Silverstone and Turner, 1995: 7–8)

Antipsychotic drugs are also known as 'neuroleptics' or 'major tranquillisers'; anti-anxiety drugs are known as 'minor tranquillisers', although this term is a misnomer because these drugs can have effects that are far from minor. Antipsychotic drugs are further divided, between those that are 'typical', which means tried and tested, with known benefits and side effects (for example, chlorpromazine), and 'atypical antipsychotics', a newer strain of neuroleptics said to bestow equal, or more, benefit on patients to that of the 'typical' neuroleptics (Lewis *et al.*, 2006; Sanger, 2006), but with fewer side effects. (There is, however, a risk of fatal side effects with one of the better known of the new-comers, clozapine, necessitating the entry onto the national blood monitoring programme of those prescribed the drug.) Recent research has demonstrated that, in fact, 'atypicals' do not always score better than more established drugs when it comes to side effect (Bagnall *et al.*, 2003). The other main difference between the two is cost: a year's supply of typical antipsychotics for one patient costs around £70; the newer atypical drugs cost around £1,220 per patient per year (National Institute for Health and Clinical Excellence, 2002). Hogman (1996, cited in Howlett, 1998) conducted a survey of the prescribing practices of 761 members of the Royal College of Psychiatrists in the treatment of schizophrenia. It was found that a majority of respondents continued to prescribe chlor-promazine rather than the newer drugs, despite its well-known and significant side effects, essentially on grounds of cost. To counter this, NICE has recommended that, where typical neuroleptics are not working well in the treatment of schizophrenia, psychiatrists should be free to prescribe atypical drugs, citing as well as therapeutic benefits, the hidden savings in terms of hospitalisation and other consequences of poor treatment of schizophrenia. The availability of atypical drugs at the discretion of the professional involved was said, by NICE, to be likely to add £70m to the direct cost of the treatment of schizophrenia. This move was welcomed by the Royal College of Psychiatrists (2002) and the mental health charity MIND (MIND, 2002), although the latter expressed concern that the money required to give effect to this policy might be taken from elsewhere in the mental health budget. This is an understandable concern, given recent reports that up to £25m of the £75m that was earmarked as additional expenditure on mental health at the end of 2001 had, in fact, been spent elsewhere in the NHS to reduce waiting lists (Goodchild, 2002).

The 'official' typology of psychiatric drugs is found in the British National Formulary (BNF). The BNF, which is published twice annually by the BMA and the Royal Pharmaceutical Society of Great Britain, lists drugs by category (for example, antipsychotic drugs are Category 4.2.1, while antipsychotic depot compounds are Category 4.2.2) and provides information on side effects. It also gives advisory maximum doses for most drugs. Within each BNF category, there is a surprisingly wide range of drugs avail-able. Albers *et al.* (2001), for example, list 16 different antipsychotics, and 20 different antidepressants, amongst many other drugs used in comtemporary treatment. The number of drugs is ever increasing, and this, in itself, indicates that existing drug treat-ments are problematic: the search continues for better acting drugs with fewer side effects (Barondes, 2005). Nevertheless, there is support from randomised clinical trials (RCTs) for each of these drug treatments (Bagnall *et al.*, 2003), albeit that there is some controversy over the extent to which RCTs are always truly independent from drug company influence (Charlton, 2005); there is something approaching a consensus that the new drug treatments that appeared in the latter half of the twentieth century 'have improved the quality of life for many hundreds of thousands of seriously distressed people' (Lacey, 1996: 80). It is not a matter of controversy, then, that psychiatric drug use can produce beneficial effects. But such drugs invariably also carry the risk of detrimental effects that may outweigh any benefits gained. In a purely clinical sense, the skill consists in getting the balance between benefits and risks to the optimum level, although this does nothing to address the moral–political questions surrounding drug treatments, particularly when given without full and informed consent.

The benefits to be derived from drug treatments are by no means universal: the treatment of schizophrenia is a case in point. Antipsychotic medicines have become established as the main treatment of this condition since the introduction, in the 1950s, of chlorpromazine (known in the UK as 'Largactyl'). As Lacey comments, 'with the honourable exception of the work of a few multidisciplinary teams, the treatment of schizophrenia in Britain is limited to the use of drugs to control its symptoms' (1996: 89). Antipsychotic drugs cannot 'cure' schizophrenia, although it is unusual that symptoms will remain acute. When a person suffers the acute onset of a bout of schizophrenia of short duration, Silverstone and Turner recommend the gradual reduction of medication, beginning one year after the illness goes into remission (1995: 119), on the basis that around 50 per cent of such patients 'do well' without long-term drug treatment; this must be done with care, because inappropriately rapid reduction is associated with adverse consequences for the patient (Matthews and Weston, 2003). It has also been suggested that early intervention increases the likelihood of a satisfactory outcome (Birchwood et al., 1997). For some, however, it will be necessary to take medication, if intermittently, over a number of years, possibly for life. Much seems to depend on the 'type' of schizophrenia. Positive (extrovert) symptoms generally respond better to drugs than negative (introvert) symptoms. In cases of chronic schizophrenia, drugs are often administered in depot form. Depot preparations are slow release and long lasting, and so reduce the frequency of injections needed. Administration by depot allows a lower total dose and appears to be a more successful approach for patients who require drug treatments over long periods (Johnson, 1990). Despite these advantages, however, there are concerns about the heightened risk of some side effects, particularly impotence and other sexual dysfunction, estimated by Stone (1992), in a review of the literature, to stand at 50 per cent.

Some patients report total satisfaction with drug treatments. Jameson (1996: 54), for example, an individual receiving ongoing drug treatment for schizophrenia, has written that he is 'profoundly thankful because now I can get on with my life ... the state I am in at present is, I am convinced, as good as cure'. For others, though, symptoms are not relieved by antipsychotic medicine, or are only kept at bay for relatively short periods. One survey (Crow et al., 1986) found that 58 per cent of patients had relapsed within two years. Nor does the prescription of higher doses produce a more favourable outcome (Royal College of Psychiatrists, 1993). Indeed, higher doses are, not surprisingly, associated with increased risks of side effects, as is polypharmacy – the prescription of two or more drugs simultaneously – and research has shown that both are widely practised (Fennell, 1996), particularly in forensic and high-security settings (Parker et al., 2002; Tavernor et al., 2000; see further below), whilst 'megadosing' is not unusual for patients unresponsive to lower dosages (Royal College of Psychiatrists, 1993; Parker et al., 2002; Tavernor et al., 2000). The side effects of antipsychotic medicine are potentially manifold, and include, amongst many others, lethargy, blurred vision, impotence, nausea, constipation, reduced sexual arousal, sterility, skin disorders, and an increased propensity for violence. Very rarely, patients die as a result of the drugs they are prescribed (see Appleby *et al.*, 2000). Recent research has indicated the particular danger of the antispychotic drug, thioridazine (Reilly *et al.*, 2002). Other serious iatrogenic effects are 'pseudoparkinsonism', known colloquially as the 'Largactyl shuffle', with symptoms including shaking hands, difficulty in maintaining balance, a shuffling walk, lack of facial expression, that in its worst manifestations 'may progress to a complete seizing up with a virtual absence of movement' (Silverstone and Turner, 1995: 122). The condition affects 20–40 per cent of patients prescribed antipsychotic medicine (*ibid.*), and patients often require antiparkinsonian medication. This feature of medication for schizophrenia – that medications aimed at primary symptoms will often require further medication to suppress the side effects of the initial medication – is by no means an issue that is limited to medical treatment for mental disorder, but it is arguably an issue of particular importance here, given that the client population will contain many who are either vulnerable by reason of their mental disorder, or detained under the MHA 1983, or both.

The condition known as 'tardive dyskinesia' may develop after prolonged use of antipsychotics and, very rarely, after a small number of doses – or even just one. The symptoms of tardive dyskinesia are, ironically, those perhaps most closely associated in the popular mind with the symptoms of madness (Silverstone and Turner, 1995: 124): 'hyperkinetic involuntary movements which are most frequently limited to the face, lips, tongue, jaw and neck, but which can involve the trunk, arms and hands.' The 'mad person', rocking ceaselessly, puckering cheeks, and engaging in other compulsive, repetitive movements is often not exhibiting symptoms of his or her illness, but of its treatment. Tardive dyskinesia, which affects between 10 and 30 per cent of those treated (1995: 125), can be a permanent consequence of antipsychotic drug treatment, and may not be apparent until medication is stopped. Even then, it may not be clear that the condition is a side effect; it has recently been suggested (although very much against the grain of conventional wisdom) that tardive dyskinesia may even be a symptom of schizophrenia (Fenton *et al.*, 1997). In any case, the problem of separating symptoms from side effects, particularly when patients are receiving more than one antipsychotic compound, as they often are, is another issue common to many psychiatric drug treatments.

It is a feature of medicine generally that, for a number of reasons, many patients are unwilling to take their drugs. The issue has a particular resonance in the context of psychiatric treatment, however, because discontinuance by patients in the community is a major factor in the debate over community care (see Chapter 9). Patients in hospital are often similarly reluctant to take their medication, but in hospital situations, there is a temptation for staff to administer medication covertly. The sixth Biennial Report of the Mental Health Act Commission (MHAC) gives an example of medication being covertly given to patients in tea (1995: para. 5.8) and expresses 'fears that such practices may be widespread in many nursing homes'. Covert administration is most probably lawful in the case of a detained patient if the requirements of Part IV of the 1983 Act are complied with, but will only be so in the case of an informal patient if that patient lacks the capacity to give his or her consent and the treatment is in the best interests of the patient. The MHAC (1995: para. 5.9) advises that 'professional judgment must be relied upon in making decisions on this important ethical issue'. This statement is not only potentially misleading as to the legal situation, but it also risks reinforcing the view, amongst medical professionals, that law is only of advisory status and need not be adhered to if it is contraindicated by 'professional judgment'. In 2001, the UKCC, the nursing professional body, issued a position statement on covert administration (UKCC, 2001). This requires that the refusal of a competent patient should be respected, but that the covert administration of medicine to a patient lacking capacity to take treatment decisions might be justified if in the best interests of the patient. This, as we suggest, may accurately state the legal situation – but it is an open question whether such deceptive practices can ever be morally justified (Welsh and Deahl, 2002).

7.2.1.2 Electroconvulsive therapy

Apart from drug treatments, the main physical treatment given in hospital is electro-convulsive therapy (ECT). The administration of electric shocks has a long history in psychiatry, but ECT in its present form was first used in the treatment of mental illness in 1938, and continued in fairly common usage, as a treatment for schizophrenia, into the 1950s (Fennell, 1996: 140). It is still sometimes used for such patients if they are unresponsive to drug treatments, and is now an established treatment for depressive disorders and affective psychoses. Farrell (1997: 130) explains the procedure: 'ECT is carried out under anaesthetic, with the use of muscle relaxant, by placing electrodes on either temple and forehead and passing a small electric shock across the brain for approximately four seconds. This electric "shock" induces a short epileptic fit'. Quite how this affects the patient's disorder is not understood (ECT Anonymous, n.d.), but it is claimed that ECT can have a beneficial effect on mood and functioning that can be extremely rapid (Gregory *et al.*, 1985), and ECT is sometimes used as an emergency treatment when a patient's depression is particularly acute and the patient is refusing food (Fennell, 1996: 200). A typical treatment plan consists of around 12 'doses' of the treatment. It has been estimated that 'around 20,000 people have ECT every year' (Farrell, 1997: 130). In the Department of Health's two-month survey of the use of ECT (January–March 1999), there were 2,835 patients (1,900 or two thirds of whom were female) in receipt of 16,482 doses of ECT, and 75 per cent of patients were not formally detained under the Act (Department of Health, 1999c: Figure 1 and para. 4.15) and so were afforded no special protection over and above that of the common law (see below). When the survey was repeated, with data collected from January to March 2002 (Department of Health, 2003e), the numbers in receipt of ECT had fallen to 2,300, col-lectively receiving 12,800 doses in the survey period, but it remained the case that three quarters – 73 per cent – of recipients were informal patients, and, again, around two thirds were female. The Mental Health Act Commission now collects data on the use of ECT, but this only reveals ECT use involving a SOAD, so the position of informal patients is not covered. There were 3,810 requests for a second opinion in the period

2003–5, more than two thirds (2,640) involving female patients (Mental Health Act Commission, 2005: Figure 64).

Despite its longevity, ECT remains intensely controversial. The beneficial effects of ECT often seem to be short-lived (Farrell, 1997: 130; McCall *et al.*, 2004). Personal testimony from patients both for and against ECT can be found. Perkins (1996), for example, details how her depression prevented her from functioning, because she was 'unable to think properly' (1996: 66) and how, after receiving a course of six doses of ECT, she was back at work within a week. Perkins experienced little in the way of side effects, although she did suffer from memory problems whilst having the course of treatment. In a recent survey involving 54 patients, 85 per cent thought themselves slightly, or much, better for having received a course of ECT treatment (Benbow and Crentsil, 2004). In contrast, Taylor (1996) describes the course of 12 ECT treatments given to him as 'barbaric or inhuman'. Taylor experienced a number of side effects, including severe headaches, neck ache, memory loss, disorientation, and 'total confusion and a confused sense of time and space', which left him in a 'vegetative, numb or stupified condition' (1996: 64). Taylor reports that, although the intensity of these effects lessened over time, memory problems, low self-esteem and a state of confusion were semi-permanent effects of the treatment. Such stories are fairly common. Other potential side effects include heart problems, strokes and falls, of which the risks are greater for older patients; this is a live issue given that, in one survey in Sheffield, the findings of which are typical, the mean age of patients in receipt of ECT was 68.5 years (Openmind, 1995). In the same Sheffield study, women were twice as likely to be given ECT as were men, which is to be expected because women are much more likely to be diagnosed as suffering from depressive or affective disorders than are men, and this is even more the case amongst the elderly population. The Department of Health's survey of the use of ECT found that 44 per cent of female and 36 per cent of male recipients were over the age of 65 (Department of Health, 1999c: 1). O'Leary and Lee (1996) found that 32 per cent of patients given ECT in one study were dead seven years later – double the expected rate – and for those under 65 years, the death rate was five times the normal rate.

The conditions in which ECT treatment is administered were inspected by the Mental Health Act Commission in 2000–1. Of the 230 sites visited, 68 had a dedicated ECT suite of three rooms including a separate waiting room and recovery room; 64 had a nurse trained in basic life support and resuscitation; 73 had a named consultant who visited regularly (MHAC, 2001: Figure 3). This means that the majority of sites had none of these things. Only 95 sites were able to provide evidence of a written ECT policy or a copy of the Royal College of Psychiatrists' *ECT Handbook to Commissioners* (*ibid.*). There was substantial compliance with all of the above factors in 48 of the 230 sites: this is simply unacceptable practice. A private member's bill, intended to tighten the legal restrictions on the use of ECT, was introduced into Parliament in December 1997, but was dropped early in 1998. The 2002 draft bill proposed some tightening of the current safeguards that apply under the 1983 Act, requiring, when the patient does not consent, an RMO to apply to a tribunal for permission to treat (cl. 118), and extending legal protection against unwarranted treatment, and the need to seek prior approval for, inter alia, administering ECT to informal patients lacking capacity (Part V). The explanatory notes to the bill state the government's view that ECT, along with other invasive treatment, breaches Art. 8(1) but can be justified under Art. 8(2) of the Convention (Department of Health, 2002: para. 173). The 2004 Bill contained similar provision to prevent the administration of ECT to a refusing, competent patient (cl. 178–9). This is welcome in principle, but why is ECT singled out for special consideration? In any case, there are well-documented problems with the application of tests of capacity and with providing patients with sufficient information upon which to provide an informed consent (MHAC, 2005: para. 474–5), which threaten to undermine any such scheme. The 2006 Bill is silent on this issue.

Irrespective of this, legal challenge to the use of ECT can be expected under Arts. 3 (on the application of which the government is silent) and 8 of the Convention, whether the Mental Health Act is eventually reformed or not. Such challenge has, to date, been narrowly avoided, in *R v Dr H, South West London and St George's Mental Health NHS Trust and Dr B, ex p K* [2003] EWHC 357 (Admin), 2003 WL 933333. In this case, a stay of proceedings was ordered as the patient in question was no longer in need of the treatment when, following the initial granting of an injunction to prevent ECT being administered, the substantive application came before the High Court. The long-term trend in the use of ECT is down. There were an estimated 65,930 administrations in 1997–8, compared to 105,466 in 1990–1 and 137,940 in 1985 (Department of Health, 1999c: para. 44.18). The Department of Health (2003) found a significant reduction in the use of ECT between 1999 and 2002, and the number of requests to the MHAC for a second opinion in respect of the proposed administration of ECT (which relates only to the treatment of detained patients, see later) has fallen year on year since 2001–2, at which time there were 2,179 requests, to 2004–5, when there were 1,653. The drop from 2003–4 to 2004–5, of 13.6 per cent (Mental Health Act Commission, 2005: Figure 60), is particularly noticeable, and may well be due to the publication by NICE, in 2003, of guidelines on the use of ECT (National Institute for Health and Clinical Excellence, 2003). The essence of the guidance is that ECT should only be used as an intervention of last resort; guidance which, although unpopular with the Royal College of Psychiatrists, was welcomed by MIND and by service users' groups (MIND, 2003).

7.2.1.3 Psychosurgery

The third type of physical treatment requiring a mention is 'psychosurgery' or neurosurgery. The way in which psychosurgical operations work is only imperfectly understood, but it seems that the creation of lesions separating the frontal lobe cortex from the limbic lobe may reduce unwanted emotions (Dally and Connolly, 1981: 68). Thanks to the 'horror' films produced by Hammer studios and others, psychosurgery evokes images of surgeons far madder than any patient, gleefully sawing through patients' craniums. Modern techniques, still controversial in that brain tissue is destroyed with the intention of inducing permanent personality changes in the patient, use radioactive rods attached to a metal frame placed on the patient's head, from which they can be inserted into the brain to effect the lesion. A new technique, deep brain stimulation

(DBS), is being developed at various centres in North America and Europe, and is similar to neurosurgery. Unlike neurosurgery, DBS apparently does not entail the destruction of brain tissue and, therefore, does not, in the opinion of the MHAC, fall under the special protection afforded, by s. 57, MHA 1983, to patients receiving psycho-surgery; as such, it can be given to informal patients under common law powers: Mental Health Act Commission, 2005: para. 485. Having been used for all manner of conditions in the past, psychosurgery is now used only as a last-resort intervention in a small number of (mainly female) patients suffering from depression or obsessional disorders (Mental Health Act Commission, 1995: Appendix 4.1). MHAC data, although involving small numbers, reveals that both doctors and patients often perceive psychosurgery to have a beneficial effect and only rarely a detrimental effect (1995: para. 5.1), although Matthews and Eljamel (2001) found that 50 per cent of patients derive a lasting benefit from the operation. There is evidence to show that it is only in very rare cases that a patient will be symptom-free two years after the treatment has been given and, for rather more patients than doctors, the treatment is felt to achieve no change in their condition (Dally and Connolly, 1981: 74).

Psychosurgery was a common treatment before the advent of the 1950s drug revolu-tion in psychiatry – 10,365 prefontal leucotomies were performed in the decade 1942–52, as were several hundred operations utilising other psychosurgical techniques (Dally and Connolly, 1981: 68) – but is now practiced only a handful of times annually. There were only seven requests (involving four female and three male patients) for a second opinion (without which treatment cannot be given) in the period 2003–5, down from 13 in 2001–3 and a high of 65 in 1989–91 (Mental Health Act Commission, 2005: Figure 65). The MHAC refused three of the 13 requests for a second opinion authoris-ing treatment in 2001–3 (Mental Health Act Commission, 2003: para. 10.60). The view of the law is that psychosurgery is the most serious of all medical treatments for mental disorder, and its practice is made subject to a special legal regime (in s. 57 of the MHA 1983) that, unusually, applies to both detained and informal patients. In Scotland, it was initially provided, by s. 47(2) of the Incapacity (Scotland) Act 2000 and The Adults with Incapacity (Specified Medical Treatments) (Scotland) Regulations 2002, SSI 2002/275, that psychosurgery could be practised on patients lacking capacity to con-sent. Amidst widespread objections, however, and a statement from doctors at the only Scottish site where the operation is performed, in Dundee, that they would not perform the treatment on patients lacking capacity, the Regulations were modified before they came into force (by The Adults with Incapacity (Specified Medical Treatments) (Scotland) Amendment Regulations. 2002, SSI 2002/302). The amendment removed psychosurgery from the list of treatments that could be provided to non-consenting patients, on the basis that this step, unprecedented in Europe, required further deliberation.

The English and Welsh Mental Health Bill of 2002 proposed that psychosurgery would be available in the treatment of patients lacking capacity, if three members of the expert panel were to decide it was warranted in the best interests of a patient with no reasonable prospect of becoming competent, and who was unlikely to resist the treat-ment (cl. 115). The 2004 Bill replaced this, providing that a patient lacking capacity could only be treated if authorised by the High Court (cl. 194). It remains to be seen what becomes of this policy proposal. The agenda produced in 2006 was silent on this question. Will it prove to be that one consequence of the topical focus on the rights to bodily autonomy, and freedom from degrading and inhuman treatment, is that the rights of those lacking capacity to claim them for themselves be will lessened? It is, perhaps, in these apparently marginal areas, involving no more than a few tens of people each year, that the first signs of that lessening may be seen.

7.2.2 Non-physical treatments

It is rare to find hospital inpatients subject to a treatment regime that comprises only psychotherapy. Most often, psychotherapy or therapy involving psychoanalytical techniques will be given alongside drug treatments. Psychotherapy comes in various forms, from one-to-one sessions to various species of group therapy, as does psychoanalysis. The basic difference between them is that psychotherapy is led by the therapist, whereas psychoanalysis tends to be led by the patient and the analyst's role is more that of facilitator. Both are part of the larger group of 'non-physical treatments', which also includes such things as counselling and occupational therapy. There is, in fact, a somewhat bewildering array of types and subtypes of therapies, many of which are practised outside the hospital setting. Although, as seen above, talking cures have a long history, it is Sigmund Freud who is usually credited with the development of modern psychoanalysis. Freud viewed mental distress, in particular neuroses, as the manifestation of unconscious conflict between the 'id', the 'ego' and 'superego', representing innate sexual and aggressive drives, and social rules, respectively. The aim of therapy, therefore, is to draw out and verbalise the particular instance of this conflict that is distressing the patient or 'client', and this entails the exploration of the client's life, very often childhood, experiences. Freud's emphasis on the importance of the libido, as well as the normative assumptions, particularly relating to the gender relationship, which underpinned his work, have been subject to much criticism from feminists (e.g. Firestone, 1971: ch.3; Russell, 1995: 22–4) and later psychoanalysts, and the result is that psychoanalysis is theoretically controversial; there are now a number of neo-Freudian and post-Freudian schools. Other, less commonly practised, psychoanalytical techniques include Jungian therapy, which draws on Durkheimian ideas about the 'collective conscience' as a context in which to situate individual episodes of mental distress, and Gestalt therapy, which rejects the emphasis on past experiences in preference of an approach that allows clients to articulate present needs rather than past traumas.

Group therapies attempt to address problems that people experience in their relations with others, or to provide a supportive environment in which it is possible to divulge information about oneself; as such, they are broadly comparable with individualised talking cures. Again, there are various species of group therapy, ranging from self-help groups to closely supervised sessions, with groups typically comprising 12 or so patients and one or two therapists (Roberts and Pines, 1991). Groups can be semi-permanent institutions with a core of semi-permanent members. If group therapy implicitly moves away from the medical model, the concept of 'medical treatment' is expanded further still by occupational therapy, which uses all sorts of everyday activities to accentuate positive, and identify negative, attitudes, to engender feelings of self-worth through creative activity, and to encourage patients to develop lasting interests and mechanisms for coping with stressful situations or relationships. At the extreme point of this way of thinking is the 'therapeutic community': small wards or units in hospitals in which the whole regime is conceived of as therapeutic. Such units are uncommon, but not unknown. The best-known example is probably the regime that operates at Grendon Underwood, which, although in the prison system, specialises in the treatment of personality-disordered offenders.

A more controversial psychotherapeutic intervention is behaviour modification (BM), which comprises a range of interventions designed to modify behaviour, essentially through a programme of rewards and deprivations. The use of techniques such as high-decibel noise, drugs such as anectine, which cause loss of muscle control, as well as a host of other punitive techniques – cold baths, unpleasant tasting food (such as the self-explanatory 'Rampton cocktail'), physical violence and electric shocks – is well documented as occurring in prisons, juvenile correctional programmes and elsewhere, as well as in mental hospitals (Adams, 1998; Butler and Rosenthal, 1985: ch.14), although it must be said that at least some of these practices were 'punishment', as distinct from 'deprivation', and therefore not strictly within the realms of BM. Nevertheless, BM is so potentially controversial that it merits its own chapter in the Code of Practice, in which it is provided that '[n]o treatment should deprive a patient of food, shelter, water, warmth, a comfortable environment, confidentiality or reasonable privacy' (Department of Health & Welsh Office, 1999: para. 18.1). The Code of Practice picks out for particular comment the BM technique known as 'time out' – which excludes the patient in question from participation in some activity for a period of between seconds and 15 minutes (the maximum period allowed under the Code: Department of Health & Welsh Office, 1999: para. 18.10) in immediate response to inappropriate behaviour. Hospitals should have clear written policies on the use of time out (1999: para. 18.10), which should be monitored, and the technique should form part of a programme and should not be a spontaneous reaction to unwanted behaviour (1999: para. 18.9). The aim of this advice is to attempt to delineate an area of lawful practice of this control technique, as distinct from its use as an act of abuse or punishment. It remains contentious, though, that such techniques are ever used as part of a treatment plan (Adams, 1998: 74).

The efficacy of psychotherapeutic intervention depends, to a large extent, on the attitude of the patient. Without the consent of the patient, 'talking cures' cannot easily proceed. This is obviously less true of BM, although, even here, a recalcitrant patient may often be able to resist the attempted modification of his or her behaviour. On the other hand, as with physical treatments, patients may often consent with less-than-total willingness, for a variety of reasons. There is no doubt that the talking cures can have substantial beneficial effects, but side effects are also an ever-present part of the package. These include the 'deterioration effect', when a patient's condition worsens whilst on a course of therapy; and therapy and therapeutic relationships are inherently double-edged. For example, negative stereotypes and power imbalances may be rein-forced, rather than challenged, by therapy. Another potential 'effect' of the combination of a power imbalance between therapist and client, and the vulnerability of the latter, is sexual abuse (Garrett, 1994). In group therapy, individuals who stand out from the rest of the group in some way – presenting different symptoms from the rest, or being in a minority in terms of race, age, gender or IQ – may find therapy isolating or dispiriting, rather than therapeutic (Manor, 1994). As *One Flew Over the Cuckoo's Nest* (Kesey, 1977) graphically illustrates, group therapy can inflict profound damage on the psyche of individual members.

The various talking cures are often delivered as outpatient services, but they do have a significant role to play in hospital, in the treatment of neuroses, as already mentioned; psychotherapies grounded in learning theory, and BM techniques, are used in the treatment of mental impairment. A key contemporary issue here is the treatment of psychopathy. Although of problematic scope and treatability, in Tennent *et al.*'s research (1993), 61 per cent of psychiatrists questioned (267 of 435) took the view that psychopathy was sometimes treatable, while less than 1 per cent thought it was never treatable. It cannot be said that drug treatments are never effective in the treatment of psychopathy (Stein, 1993), although there is general agreement amongst psychiatrists that drug treatments are the least effective of the options on offer (Tennent *et al.*, 1993). Prins (1995), in a review of the literature, reports that '[c]alm confrontation' of the unacceptable elements in the behaviour of psychopaths, either in peer group contexts or one-to-one encounters, may have some lasting beneficial effect, with some 'symptoms' (such as chronic antisocial behaviour, abnormal aggression and lacking control over impulses) being more amenable to talking cures than others (such as lack of shame, inability to experience guilt and 'pathological eccentricity' – Tennent *et al.*, 1993: 65). Prins emphasises the three therapeutic virtues of 'consistence, persistence and insistence' (1995: 313). There is, as yet, little more than anecdotal evidence of the success of this approach, and more recently, the government has been keen to emphasise the role of drug treatments – principally antipsychotic drugs, including atypical neuroleptics, as well as antidepressants and mood stabilisers such as lithium – in tandem with psycho-logical therapies in the treatment of personality disorders (Bateman and Tyrer, 2002; Craissati *et al.*, 2002; National Institute for Mental Health in England, 2003a: 23–5).

7.3 Medical treatment in hospital: law and practice

7.3.1 The position at common law

7.3.1.1 The right to refuse treatment

For all patients, treatment providers should act in accordance with the guidance issued by the General Medical Council (1998), the Royal College of Psychiatrists (2000), the UKCC (1998) as well as the various documents published by the Department of Health (listed at Department of Health, 2001c). As far as the law is concerned, for detained patients, Part IV of the 1983 Act lays down a statutory regime to govern and regulate their medical treatment for mental disorder in hospital. Part IV of the Act, however, applies only to treatment for mental disorder (s. 63, see below), and a detained patient's common law right to consent to or refuse other treatments is unaffected (for detailed discussion of the common law, see Montgomery, 2002: ch. 10). The vast majority of inpatients are informal. There are, with the exception of psychosurgery and certain types of hormone therapy (see below), no special provisions in the 1983 Act in respect of their medical treatment, and the common law applies to treatment for mental disorder as it does to other forms of medical treatment. The basic rule is that no treatment may be given without consent (Lord Donaldson in *Re T (Adult: Refusal of Treatment)* [1992] 3 WLR 782 (CA) at 799):

Every adult has the right and capacity to decide whether or not he will accept medical treatment, even if a refusal may risk permanent injury to his health or even lead to premature death . . . it matters not whether the reasons for the refusal were rational or irrational, unknown or even non-existent.

A well-known illustration of the operation of the rule is provided by *Re C (Adult: Refusal of Treatment)* [1994] 1 ALL ER 819, [1994] 1 WLR 290 (HC). The case involved C, who had been a patient in Broadmoor from the early 1960s, diagnosed on admission as suffering from chronic paranoid schizophrenia. In 1993, it was discovered that C was suffering from a gangrenous infection in his right leg, which, in the opinion of a consultant vascular surgeon, would lead to imminent death if the lower leg were not amputated. C refused to consent to this treatment for a variety of reasons. The main issue in the case was the test of capacity to be applied in the context of medical treatment (see Chapter 11), but the relevant point here is that the court, having decided that C did have the capacity to make his own treatment decisions, simply applied the general rule expressed by Lord Donaldson MR in *Re T*. In this case, the treatment in question was not related to C's mental disorder, but according to the strict letter of the law for informal patients, the outcome of the case would have been the same had it been. A more recent example is provided by the decision Dame Butler-Sloss, the president of the Family Division, in *Re W (Adult: Refusal of Treatment)* [2002] C8002041. The president held, in the case of an untreatable psychopathically disordered prisoner, who had self-harmed and then refused treatment with the real risk that that would lead to his death, that, as he had capacity, his right to refuse treatment had to be respected.

7.3.1.2 Problems with the right to refuse: information, coercion and capacity

It is not so clear, however, that patient autonomy and the right to refuse treatment is always so well respected in practice. Three issues are of particular concern: information provision, coercion, and capacity or the mental ability to give or refuse consent. Questions of capacity are discussed in detail in Chapters 10 and 11. The focus here is on the first two factors, which are applicable to both informal and detained patients.

7.3.1.2.1 Information

The common law requirements for the provision of information to patients about their proposed treatment and its attendant risks are governed by the *Bolam* standard, laid down in the case of *Bolam* v *Friern Hospital Management Committee* [1957] 2 ALL ER 118 (HC), which essentially leaves the decision to the psychiatric profession. *Bolam* involved a patient who suffered physical injury as a result of being insecurely restrained whilst being given ECT. He sued for negligence and was unsuccessful, the court deciding that, because the restraint that had been applied, in this case, was in line with common practice, no negligence had been committed. This approach was transposed to the provision of information by the House of Lords in *Sidaway* v *Board of Governors of the Bethlem Royal Hospital and the Maudsley Hospital* [1985] 1 AC 870. The general rule is that liability will not attach to a failure to divulge information to a patient concerning inherent risks or side effects, if the person withholding that information (Lord Diplock at 893):

acted in accordance with a practice accepted as proper by a body of responsible and skilled medical opinion

Notice that it is 'a' body of medical opinion. Lord Diplock said that 'there may be a number of different practices which will satisfy [the *Bolam* test] at any particular time', and as long as a respondent can produce evidence to show that nondisclosure of a particular risk is the practice of one body of responsible medical opinion, it is immaterial that another body of opinion does not share that view or practice. This obviously gives a considerable degree of latitude to the professional judgment of those charged with a patient's treatment. This is, however, subject to the caveat that Lord Bridge reserved to the courts a power of veto over the prevailing standards and norms of medical practice. He said (at 900):

the judge might in certain circumstances come to the conclusion that disclosure of a particular risk was so obviously necessary to an informed choice on the part of the patient that no reasonably prudent medical man would fail to make it . . .

   The kind of case I have in mind would be an operation involving a substantial risk of grave adverse consequences, as for example, [a] 10 per cent risk of stroke from the operation . . . In such a case, in the absence of some cogent clinical reason why the patient should not be informed, a doctor . . . could hardly fail to appreciate the necessity for an appropriate warning.

It is a moot point as to when a risk becomes 'substantial'; likewise what counts as 'grave adverse consequences'. Nevertheless, given the serious unwanted effects of much medical treatment for mental disorder, it might well be argued that the 'safety net' constructed by the House of Lords is of more relevance to mental patients than many others. The risk of tardive dyskinesia in long-term antipsychotic medicine use, for example, is somewhere between 10 and 30 per cent, as seen above. On the other hand, it may be that there will often be cogent clinical reasons to justify non-disclosure of even substantial risks. The *Bolam* approach is dictated by the standards of the professions involved, which can, in turn, be affected by the provisions of the Code of Practice, by pushing practice in the direction of full disclosure of information. In this respect, the Code is disappointing. It does repeat the more empowering aspects of *Sidaway* in requiring that patients' questions be answered 'fully, frankly and truthfully' (Department of Health and Welsh Office, 1999: para. 15.16). But it also echoes the language of the *Bolam* approach, stating that consent will be valid if given on the basis of an understanding, in broad terms, of the nature, likely effects and risks of the treatment, and '[a]dditional information is a matter of professional judgment for the doctor proposing the treatment' (1999: para. 15.15). If this is 'legalism', then it is also an example of the tendency of 'legalism' to sanction 'medicalism'.

The courts may offer more hope than the Code in this respect. In *Bolitho v City and Hackney HA* [1997] 4 ALL ER 771, [1998] AC 252, the House of Lords signalled that expert evidence must still satisfy minimum legal standards. Lord Browne-Wilkinson, [1997] 3 WLR 1151 at 1159, explained that:

The court has to be satisfied that the exponents of the body of opinion relied upon can demonstrate that such opinion has a logical basis. In particular, in cases involving, as they so often do, the weighing of risks against benefits, the judge before accepting a body of opinion as being responsible, reasonable or respectable, will need to be satisfied that, in forming their views, the experts have directed their minds to the question of comparative risks and benefits and have reached a defensible conclusion on the matter.

In the specific context of information provision, the Court of Appeal in *Pearce v United Bristol Healthcare NHS Trust* [1999] PIQR 53 (CA) seemed to move the test away from *Bolam*'s emphasis on the reasonable medical professional, and towards the 'reasonable patient': a legal construction often seen as implying an 'informed consent' requirement into information provision (per Lord Woolf, MR, at 59):

if there is a significant risk which would affect the judgment of a reasonable patient, then in the normal course it is the responsibility of a doctor to inform the patient of that significant risk, if the information is needed so that the patient can determine for him or herself as to what course she should adopt.

For some, this statement is evidence that 'information disclosure and the supremacy of the "reasonable doctor test" may be the first *Bolitho* casualty' (Brazier and Miola, 2000). The relationship between doctrinal change and on-the-ground practice is, however, a problematic one in general (Jones, 1999), and in the specific context of mental disorder, there will often be capacity-related problems with the application of a test based even notionally on a concept of the 'reasonable patient'.

As far as the ethics of disclosure are concerned, Bean (1986: 134) points out that it is inevitable, given the current state of knowledge, that full information cannot be given, but he goes on to argue that 'full information' is provided when the patient is told that there is a lacuna in the professional knowledge concerning the workings of the treatment. The argument that some knowledge is 'too technical' to allow it to be effectively imparted to patients is rejected by Bean, on the grounds that the important factor, given that 'consent is a moral commitment on behalf of the informer to provide information upon which the decision can be made' (1986: 136), is the way in which information is given and the environment created by that person – is it conducive to the patient feeling able to ask questions? – rather than a question of the accurate communication of technical and abstract details.

By whatever criteria, however, there seems to be a good deal of patient dissatisfaction with the information that is provided about the purpose and potential effects of treatments, particularly drug treatments (Rogers *et al.*, 1993). In general terms, there is a body of evidence that shows that patients are often unsure about their legal status and rights (Bean, 1980; Hoyer, 1986; Goldbeck *et al.*, 1997). Goldbeck *et al.* found that, in a study of 111 detained patients, only 32 per cent 'recalled having received verbal information about their detention and legal rights from medical staff' (1997: 577); the same number acquired the information from other patients. Overall, only 46 per cent believed that they had been given enough information (*ibid.*), although a sizeable proportion of patients had not correctly understood the legal relevance of the information they had been given. Monahan *et al.* (1995) found that between 40 and 50 per cent of involuntary patients did not appreciate their informal status. Campbell *et al.* (1998) found that 80 per cent of patients in MIND's survey for reporting adverse drug incidents felt that they had not been given enough information about their treatment and 75 per cent reported that they had not been warned about side effects. Brown *et al.* (2001) surveyed 68 long-stay psychiatric inpatients, finding that two out of three did not know the purpose of their medication and 90 per cent had no knowledge of possible side effects. Nevertheless, consent was routinely given, although, significantly, only a minority of patients appreciated that the giving of consent was their own choice. Similarly, the Mental Health Act Commission has reported that some patients, deemed by hospital staff to have consented to treatment, 'have little awareness of the nature of the treatment' (1997: para. 5.2.1). Although the remit of the MHAC is limited to the treatment of detained patients, and the studies of patients' awareness of relevant information tend similarly to focus on detained patients, it seems reasonable to suppose that informal patients are no better off, and may even be worse off, because the law relevant to them, as case law, is, if anything, more opaque than the provisions of Part IV of the 1983 Act. The Healthcare Commission (2004) carried out a large survey, involving 11,350 patients who had received medication in the previous year. The majority – at least 80 per cent – had only ever been in hospital on an informal basis. Thirty-five per cent reported that they had been told nothing about potential side effects, and 11 per cent had not been told the purpose of their medication. The MHAC's eighth report (Mental Health Act Commission, 1999: para. 6.11) records examples of the use of the compulsory powers in Part IV in relation to non-consenting informal patients. This practice, which often depends on the patient's ignorance of the legal position, is strictly unlawful, and an informal patient treated without consent on this basis will have the possibility of an action in battery, as well as possible claims under Arts. 3 and 8 of the Convention.

7.3.1.2.2 Coercion

The law does not recognise that a prison environment may, of itself, undermine an individual's freedom to give or refuse consent (*Freeman v Home Office* [1984] QB 524 (HC).

It follows that the same is true of psychiatric hospital inpatients, particularly when 'informal' and, in theory at least, free to leave at any time. Yet there are various ways in which an informal patient may, in reality, feel coerced into consenting to treatment (Poulsen, 2002). It would follow from some of the arguments and research considered in Chapters 2 and 3 that the mere fact of being in hospital, assigned to the role of 'mental patient', is inherently coercive. Bean (1986: 139) defines coercion, not as pressure, but as the exploitation of vulnerability, and it takes little thought to appreciate that the status of informality means that a patient is always potentially vulnerable to pressure to conform to the wishes of his or her treatment providers. Indeed, this pressure may well be self-imposed: a patient does not need a naked threat to realise that lack of cooperation may lead to the use of the holding powers in s. 5 followed by 'sectioning' (see Chapter 4). Alternatively, informal patients who refuse to cooperate with the regime may be discharged, which may be an equally coercive prospect for some. Richardson (1993: 243) suggests that a patient may consent to treatment in order to appease the doctor, or through a concern that refusal to cooperate will lengthen the time spent in hospital, and Hart's (1996) personal testimony bears this view out.

Although there is a relative dearth of information on coercion and informal patients, Kjellin and Westrin (1998) found that 28 per cent of 99 voluntary patients reported coercive measures used against them, whilst in Finland, Kaltiala-Heino *et al.* (1997) reported a figure of 23 per cent, using a rather tight definition of coercion that excluded support, persuasion and other milder interventions (1997: 318). In both case, not unexpectedly, the figure was much higher for detained patients. Kaltiala-Heino *et al.* (1997) also found that the use of coercion in treatment negatively affects the therapeutic relationship and 'is related to poorer treatment outcome' (1997: 318). Winick (1994) argues that this is because a failure to include the patient in drawing up a plan of treatment denies the patient the opportunity to set a goal for the treatment, yet 'the conscious setting of a goal is virtually indispensable to its achievement' (1994: 102). Conversely, there is no evidence to suggest that the coercive administration of treatments as diverse as psychotherapy and antipsychotic medicine achieves beneficial results (1994: 107), and there is evidence to suggest that coercion in treatment has its own set of unwanted effects, including severe somatic problems, 'learned helplessness' or institutionalisation, and even death in some rare cases (1994: 109).

Notwithstanding *Freeman*, it is generally true that consent to treatment obtained by coercion is invalid. Consent is nullified, inter alia, on grounds of duress. In the field of medical law, the leading case is *Re T (Adult: Refusal of Treatment)* [1992] 3 WLR 782 (CA), in which Lord Donaldson said (at 797) that to test for the presence of duress:

[t]he real question in each such case is 'Does the patient really mean what he says or is he merely saying it for a quiet life, to satisfy someone else or because the advice and persuasion to which he has been subjected is such that he can no longer think and decide for himself?'

It is only possible to speculate how many informal patients who complain of coercion in the administration of treatment would satisfy this test. We suspect that the numbers may be not inconsiderable. For detained patients, coercion may be even more difficult to spot. A detained patient may be treated for mental disorder with drugs for three months without consent, after which time treatment requires either consent or a second opinion. A patient may well consent to such treatment out of a view that the second opinion will inevitably authorise the treatment (as is, indeed, almost always the case), and so there is no point in refusing, which may only anger their doctor who will, as a consequence, then have to go through the whole second opinion procedure. If this is so, patients may consent, feeling under duress to do so, although the coercion in such a situation is virtually invisible (Richardson, 1993: 243, and see later in this chapter).

7.3.1.2.3 Capacity

Concerns about information provision and coercion presume that the recipient is able to digest and act on information, and has a conscious will that is capable of being over-ridden by coercive tactics. For some patients, these presumptions will not hold, because the mental capacity to make treatment and other decisions will be lacking. In the course of the *Bournewood* litigation, it was estimated by the MHAC that, had the judgment of the Court of Appeal been allowed to stand, the increase in admissions under Part II would have been increased by 48,000 per annum, on the grounds that such persons lacked capacity to consent to informal admission. While capacity to consent to treatment is not the same as consent to admission (see Chapter 10), the groups will have considerable overlap: clearly, capacity is an issue in the treatment of many patients. The way in which capacity should be evaluated, and its application in the context of medical treatment, are discussed in Chapters 10 and 11 respectively. Here, it is sufficient to note that, whether under common law, or under the Mental Capacity Act 2005, which will replace the common law when it comes into force (see preface), it is lawful to treat a person lacking capacity in what the treatment provider judges to be the patients' best interests.

Historically, the question of best interests has been determined by an application of the *Bolam* standard, but, emboldened perhaps by the approach to medical evidence taken in *Bolitho*, recent judgments indicate that, when a court is asked to make a declaration, it must make a substantive judgment as to best interests (see, for example, *Re S (Adult Patient: Sterilisation: Patients' Best Interests)* [2000] 3 WLR 1288 (CA)). Not only is this approach immensely preferable to the application of *Bolam* in this context, in terms of policy, because *Bolam* only ever enforced a minimum rather than an optimum standard, it also conforms better to the requirement of the European Court. In *Herczegfalfy* v *Austria* (1992) 15 EHRR 437, the Court held that, in order to avoid a breach of Art. 3, and most probably also of Art. 8, of the Convention, it must be 'convincingly shown' that treatment that is, prima facie, degrading – which arguably applies to all of the physical treatments in one way or another – is a 'medical necessity' (para. 82).

7.3.2 Treatment under compulsion: detained patients

The MHA 1959 was silent on the question of patients' rights to refuse treatment and doctors' and nurses' rights to impose it. It was a commonly held view that the powers in that Act, to detain patients for treatment or for 'observation (with or without medical treatment)' (s. 25(2)(a), necessarily implied a right to treat detained patients with or without consent. This may have been because it was assumed that mental patients lack capacity to consent to treatment by virtue of their condition (Hoggett, 1996: 133), although it seems that this view was assumed rather than debated. As Fennell (1996: 168) notes, '[q]uestions of consent to treatment did not loom large in the Percy Commission's thinking', working as it was on the underlying assumption that the function of the 1959 Act was to give statutory recognition to the 'transformation of the mental health services from an essentially custodial to a more dynamically therapeutic function' (Unsworth, 1987: 232) that had been made possible as a consequence of the development of the new treatments from the 1930s and, in particular, the 'drugs revolution' of the 1950s. As far as mental health professionals were concerned, their practices were by now fully 'medicalised' and '[t]herapeutics were not conceived as a potential source of antagonism between doctors and patients' (1987: 322). This view was reflected in the composition of the Percy Commission, which, as Unsworth notes, had 'no aggressive advocate of greater formal legal safeguards ... as a counterweight to the professional preoccupation with therapeutic goals' (1987: 267) that dominated the Commission's thinking.

A decade later, however, the dominance of therapeutic perspectives was increasingly under challenge for a number of reasons. The public outlook on madness was not, in fact, changed radically by the advent of the drug revolution, and media coverage of cases such as those of Brady and Hindley, and Graham Young (Holden, 1974, later to be the subject of the film *The Young Poisoner's Handbook*) bolstered the view of the mentally ill as 'other' and as dangerous. At the same time, the 'new legalism' began to develop out of concerns that hospital patients were being used as guinea pigs in trials of new, potentially life-threatening drugs of unproven efficacy, but with seriously problematic side effects; concerns that 'treatment' was being used as 'punishment' in some instances (Fennell, 1996: 170–2); and concerns that the implied right to treat that some detected in the fabric of the 1959 Act was at odds with the common law right to refuse treatment (Jacob, 1976). In consequence, although the Butler Commission rejected the need for general provisions relating to consent to treatment (Committee on Mentally Abnormal Offenders, 1975: para. 3.54), by the time of the debates leading eventually to the 1983 Act, the arguments in favour of legislation on this question were in the ascendancy.

The chief architect of the 'new legalism' was Larry Gostin, then legal officer at MIND. Gostin (1975; 1983) promoted 'the ideology of entitlement', which comprised three strands:

(a) that good health care is a right that service users should be able to enforce through the courts;

(b) that legal constraints should be placed on the power and discretion of service providers; and

(c) that hospitalisation should not affect the ability of patients to exercise general legal rights such as the right to vote or to go to court.

The second of these strands led to the requirement that those wishing to treat non-consenting detained patients must seek a second opinion before so doing finding its way into the 1983 Act. The Act was, in general terms, seen as a return to 'legalism', with its provisions relating to the medical treatment of detained patients being seen as a key expression of this shift. The 1983 Act was never a simple shift from medical to legal control of inpatient treatment, however. For most of its lifetime, there has been no legal regulation, other than that provided by the common law, as far as the treatment of informal patients is concerned; the common law inclination has traditionally been to give control to the medical professionals. In addition, to the extent that the 1983 Act did inaugurate a new era of legal controls over medical discretion, the substance of the procedures required by that Act nevertheless left considerable power in medical hands. The second opinion scheme is the prime example of this. Gostin had argued that the second opinion should be provided by a multidisciplinary team or even by a court (1975: 120), and this was the government's preferred option, but in the event, as Fennell (1990: 34) notes. '[t]he political influence of the Royal College of Psychiatrists on the shape of the second opinion procedures was to ensure that the decision was taken by doctors on the basis of medical criteria'. Moreover, the type of 'rights' that the legislation, and Part IV in particular, gave to patients 'are public law, due process, rights; not rights to deal, but entitlements that certain procedural and substantive limits will be adhered to in the way that they are *dealt with*' (Fennell, 1986: 58–9, emphasis in original). And with judicial review proceedings dominated by the conservative *Wednesbury* approach, it can be said that the legal rights given to patients under Part IV of the 1983 Act have been something of a chimera, ultimately tokenistic.

One of the main innovations in the draft Mental Health Bills of 2002 and 2004 was the proposed introduction of a system closer to that advocated by Gostin, with an *a priori* multidisciplinary scrutiny of treatment plans by a tribunal with a power of veto. This proposal, which, in effect, constitutes an admission that the second opinion scheme has failed sufficiently to protect the rights of patients, has subsequently been dropped, for reasons perhaps to do with the costs of running such a system, and partly perhaps because of pressure from the medical profession. In any case, medical dominance of this area looks set to continue, albeit that the courts, in cases brought under the Human Rights Act, have made it clear that they require a greater degree of rigour to accompany the operation of the system, which has traditionally been seen by doctors as little more than a bureaucratic matter, of compliance with the letter, but not necessarily the spirit, of the law. In addition, this case law provides an example of the fact that, following the Human Rights Act, when judicial review or other proceedings raise issues of human rights, the courts must now concern themselves with matters of substance that previously would not have been reviewable. Indeed, it might be said that, whilst the government has procrastinated over the reform of mental health law, it has, in any case, been reformed to a significant extent by the passage of the 1998 Act – and not in the ways in which the government might necessarily have wished to see. We shall look now at the jurisprudence on Part IV, before turning to consider the human rights-generated case law, although it is increasingly difficult to distinguish the one from the other.

7.3.2.1 The application of Part IV of the 1983 Act

The powers of compulsory treatment, currently contained in Part IV of the 1983 Act, apply to all patients who are 'liable to be detained' except patients detained under s. 4 (s. 56(1)(a)), and other short-term detentions under ss. 5(2), 5(4), 35, 135, 136, and 37(4): s. 56(1)(b). Part IV does apply, however, to patients on leave of absence under s. 17, because they remain 'liable to be detained' unless the section expires; excluded from the ambit of Part IV are restricted patients discharged by the Secretary of State or a tribunal (see Chapter 8), who have not been recalled to hospital: s. 56(1)(c). With one exception, Part IV of the Act does not apply to informal patients, the position of whom is governed by the common law.

For every patient detained under the Act there will be a 'responsible medical officer' (RMO), who must be a registered medical practitioner: s. 64(1). The main function of the RMO will be to supervise the administration of treatment to the patient: s. 34(1). An RMO has other specific duties and responsibilities concerning, for example, leave of absence and discharge. It is expected that RMOs will be consultants (Department of Health and Welsh Office, 1998: para. 61). If the RMO is not available when swift action is required, as, for example, when an application for discharge has been made by the nearest relative of a patient under s. 23 (see Chapter 8) then 'the doctor who is for the time being in charge of the patient's treatment (who should normally be another consultant) should exercise the functions of the RMO' (1998: para. 61). The government intends to rename RMOs. The new title will be 'appproved clinician' (AC). It is also intended that a greater pool of professionals will be able to act as AC, which 'may include psychiatrists, psychologists, nurses, social workers and occupational therapists' (Department of Health, 2006d: 2). Appropriate training will be required. In principle, this change is to be welcomed. The current Memorandum gives the impression that ordinarily patients will have regular consultations with their RMOs, but in practice, RMOs, who are allocated around 70 patients each (Peay, 1989: 64), will see them only infrequently, and patients will have much greater contact with nursing staff, their named nurse in particular. In some situations, other professionals will have much greater contact with the patient on a regular basis. It makes sense, therefore, for the professional best acquainted with the particular patient to be AC. Whether consultant psychiatrists will be willing to relinquish control – it is intended that the AC will take over the responsibility for authorising the patient's treatment (Department of Health, 2006d: 2) – remains to be seen. Any change will take a while to percolate through, as all current RMOs will automatically gain AC status.

7.3.2.2 The meaning and scope of 'medical treatment for mental disorder'

Section 145(1) currently defines 'medical treatment' for the purposes of the Act as that which 'includes nursing, and also includes care, habilitation and rehabilitation under medical supervision' (s. 145(1), to be amended by any new bill to make it clear that it includes treatment given or authorised by other professionals who might act as AC, Department of Health, 2006j: 2, and see preface). It is also clear that steps or actions that are a necessary prerequisite to the substantive treatment are covered by the statutory definition. In *B* v *Croydon Health Authority* [1995] 1 ALL ER 683 (CA), it was established that forced feeding could, and did on the facts of that case, amount to medical treatment. In this case, a 24-year-old woman, B, had been detained under s. 3, having been diagnosed as suffering from 'psychopathic disorder' in the form of a borderline personality disorder, coupled with post-traumatic stress disorder arising from acts of sexual abuse that she had suffered over a prolonged period of time. B's condition manifested as depression and a compulsion to self-harm. As discussed earlier, the treatability of personality disorders is problematic, but in B's case, it was thought that she might benefit from psychoanalytic psychotherapy.

Once detained, B was prevented from self-harm and, in response, she started to refuse food. Her condition became so serious that it was not possible to provide her with psychotherapy sessions until she regained weight, and she continued to deteriorate until her life expectancy was estimated at two to three months. Threatened with being fed by nasogastric tube without her consent, B sought an injunction against the defendant health authority, which was granted, but at a full hearing in the High Court, it was held lawful to administer the treatment, because feeding by force came within the s. 145(1) definition. In the Court of Appeal, Hoffman LJ (at p.687) noted that 'a range of acts ancillary to the core treatment fall within the definition' in s. 145(1). He continued, with the concurrence of the other members of the court:

It does not, however, follow that every act which forms part of that treatment within the wide definition in s. 145(1) must in itself be likely to alleviate or prevent deterioration of that disorder. Nursing and care concurrent with the core treatment or as a necessary prerequisite to such treatment or to prevent the patient from causing harm to himself or to alleviate the consequences of the disorder are, in my view, all capable of being ancillary to a treatment calculated to alleviate or prevent a deterioration of the psychopathic disorder.

Hoffman and Neill LJJ both made reference to s. 62 (discussed further below), which permits controversial treatments, otherwise made subject to special restrictions by ss. 57 and 58 (also see below), to be given without compliance with prior formalities in emergency situations. If the patient's life is at risk, or there is a need to prevent serious suffering to the patient, or to prevent the patient acting dangerously to the self or others, treatment that is 'immediately necessary', subject to some limitations, may be given. As Hoffman LJ pointed out, the wording of s. 62 seems to contemplate the treatment of symptoms of the patient's condition – such as acting in a dangerous manner, or here, refusing food – as well as its causes, and therefore it can be presumed that the intention behind the Act was that the treatment of such would be covered by the concept of treatment for the mental disorder from which the patient is suffering.

A similar definition was offered in *Reid* v *Secretary of State for Scotland* [1999] 2 AC 512 [1999] 2 WLR 28, by Lord Hope of Craighead, who said (at [1999] 2 AC 531) that:

Medication or other psychiatric treatment which is designed to alleviate or prevent a deterioration of the mental disorder plainly falls within the scope of the expression. But I think that its scope is wide enough to include other things which are done for either of those two purposes under medical supervision... It is also wide enough to include treatment which alleviates or prevents a deterioration of the symptoms of the mental disorder, not the disorder itself which gives rise to them.

In *Pountney* v *Griffiths* [1976] AC 314, a case heard under the 1959 Act but which is still relevant today, the House of Lords took the view that, when a patient is detained under the MHA for medical treatment, the exercise of powers of control and discipline are necessarily implied. Suitable arrangements for visits to patients by family and friends are, according to the court, an obvious part of a patient's 'treatment' and this, in turn, licensed, as 'treatment', the restraint of the patient in the course of 'ushering him back to his quarters when permitted visiting time is ended' (per Lord Edmund-Davies at 335). It is therefore clear that, if force is necessary in order to administer treatment under Part IV to a detained patient, then that force is seen as part of the patient's 'medical treatment'. This has been underlined in subsequent case law. In *R* v *Broadmoor Special Hospital Authority, ex p S and Ors* (1998) *The Times*, 17 February (see Chapter 3), the Court of Appeal held that these unspoken powers are ancillary not to Part IV of the Act, but to the section authorising detention (usually s. 3 or s. 37). Auld LJ went on to explain that the Mental Health Act:

leaves unspoken many of the necessary incidents of control flowing from a power of detention for treatment, including: the power to restrain patients, to keep them in seclusion, to deprive them of their personal possessions for their own safety and to regulate the frequency and manner of visits to them, a power of control and discipline.

The Court of Appeal approved the view expressed in *R* v *Home Secretary, ex p Leach* [1994] QB 198 (CA) that there could be no definitive list of such powers, but that those for which it could be demonstrated that there existed 'a self-evident and pressing need' would be implied by the courts. Elsewhere is his judgement in *Reid*, Lord Hope said that '[t]he definition [in s. 145(1)] is a wide one, which is sufficient to include all manner of treatment the purpose of which may extend from cure to containment' (529, and the same phrase was used by Lord Hope in *R* v *Ashworth Hospital* [now Mersey Care NHS Trust], *ex p Munjaz* [2005] UKHL 58 at para. 66).

Clearly, this is a very broad approach, which has licensed as medical treatment, for example, the care plan that was upheld in *South West London and St George's Mental Health NHS Trust* v *W* [2002] EWHC 1770 (see Chapter 6). Similarly, in *R* v *Oxfordshire Mental Healthcare NHS Trust, ex p F* [2001] EWHC Admin 535, Sullivan J held that the transfer of a patient from one hospital to another could come within the s. 145(1) definition, if the purpose of that transfer was to enable better treatment to be provided. In *Munjaz*, the House of Lords held that 'seclusion' (solitary confinement: see below) comes within the s. 145(1) definition. In sum, 'medical treatment' for these purposes is anything designed to treat, control or manage the patient, in the broadest sense of those words, and clearly moves beyond the 'medical' as the term is commonly understood.

7.3.2.3 Treatment 'for the mental disorder from which he is suffering': s. 63

It is not enough, to justify treatment under Part IV, that it is medical treatment within the definition in s. 145(1); s. 63 requires such treatment to be 'medical treatment given to [him or her] for the mental disorder from which [he or she] is suffering'. If this is the case, then the consent of the patient shall not be required if the treatment 'is given by or under the direction of the responsible medical officer'. This is a wide and controversial power. In *R v Ashworth Hospital, ex p B* [2003] EWCA Civ 547, the Court of Appeal held that the section licenses only treatments given for the mental disorder that the patient is classified as suffering from, and no other. In the view of the court, a patient, like B in that case, with a dual diagnosis, but who is detained only on the basis of one of those disorders because the other is not of a nature or degree making hospital treatment appropriate, could not be treated under s. 63, or any of the other powers in Part IV of the Act for that second, minor, disorder. Dyson LJ (at para. 42) emphasised that 'Part IV must be interpreted in its context'. That is, Dyson LJ held that Part IV should be conceptualised as a further set of safeguards, to be applied to the treatment of patients, once detained and once classified in accordance with those procedures. Therefore its reach, in terms of enabling treatment without consent, could be no greater than the perimeters set at that earlier stage of detention and classification: at this stage, those matters are set and may not be undermined by treating disorders that have not been shown to justify detention.

This decision was, however, subsequently reversed by the House of Lords ([2005] UKHL 20, [2005] 2 AC 278, [2005] 2 All ER 289, [2005] 2 WLR 695). The leading opinion was that of Baroness Hale of Richmond, who gave five reasons for her conclusion. Firstly, she held that (para. 22):

The Act's definition of 'mental disorder' encompasses, not only each of the four specific forms of disorder that may be relevant under the Act, but the broader concepts of 'arrested development' and 'any other disorder or disability of mind'. Thus, the natural and ordinary meaning of the words is that the patient may be treated without consent for any mental disorder from which he is suffering, and any treatment ancillary to that.

Baroness Hale held, secondly, that, when in the 1983 Act the intention is to be specific about the mental disorder in question – for instance, when the issue is whether a person should be admitted to hospital under s. 3, or whether the patient's diagnosis should be reclassified under ss. 16(1) or 72(5) – the Act uses the phrase 'form of disorder'. Therefore (at para. 23, emphasis in original):

If it had been intended to limit section 63 to treatment for the specific form of mental disorder under which the patient was detained, then the section would have read 'for the *form of* mental disorder from which he is suffering'.

Thirdly, her Ladyship pointed out that s. 63 applies to the treatment of patients detained under ss. 2 and 46 of the 1983 Act, and those detained under the Criminal Procedure Act 1964, in respect of whom there is no requirement to specify the type of disorder that justifies detention. Persons held under these provisions can clearly be treated for all, or any, mental disorder(s) from which they suffer, and 'It would be surprising if the same words had a different meaning when the patient is detained under these provisions from the meaning it has when he is detained under the others' (para. 24).

Fourthly, in her view, the historical context of the 1983 Act showed that the powers to classify and reclassify a patient's condition relate back to the justification for admission and detention, and not forward to the subsequent treatment given to the patient (para. 25). The powers to classify and reclassify were in operation under the 1959 Act because, under that Act, there were greater restrictions on the powers to *detain* a 'psychopathic' or 'subnormal' person than one judged 'mentally ill' or 'severely subnormal'; that Act was silent on the question of *treatment*. Finally, Baroness Hale held that, because the only powers available to reclassify a restricted patient, such as the applicant in this case, are in the hands of a MHRT, and can only be used after a tribunal has determined an application to it, there is no link intended in the scheme of the Act between classification and liability to receive treatment. Tribunal applications are only available at prescribed times and 'It is unlikely that Parliament intended that the patient could not be treated without his consent in the meantime, particularly as the patient may find ways of delaying the tribunal hearing' (para. 28). By the same token, an RMO has no power to reclassify a restricted patient, and 'The obvious reason for this was that the classification was irrelevant to the continued authority to detain' (para. 28).

In the view of Baroness Hale, her analysis of the law was in accord with the policy considerations behind s. 63: the important issue is that patients receive treatment of appropriate quality and are protected from inappropriate treatment. Limiting treatment to that for the disorder for which the patient is detained does not address that point. Her Ladyship also recognised that diagnosis of mental disorder is often problematic, and that this is often because of co-morbidity between mental illness and psychopathic disorder. To restrict treatment options, as argued for by the applicant, would limit the ability of treatment providers to provide optimum treatment. The present case provided an illustration of the negative consequences of this for the patient. Having had his mental illness successfully contained by the treatment given, such that he did not require further hospitalisation for that reason, the ground was now cleared to allow B's underlying personality disorder to be addressed. On the interpretation of the law contended for by the applicant, however, this would not be possible, and so although his possible discharge would (needlessly, in the view of Baroness Hale) be frustrated because he remained dangerous by reason of his personality disorder, it would not be possible to provide treatment for this, unless and until a MHRT could be persuaded to reclassify him.

This decision, from one point of view, refuses to allow legalism and bureaucratic requirements to constrain the discretion of the RMO to offer the best package of treatment to fit the particular, and changing, profile of the patient (Bartlett, 2006). It can, however, be criticised on a number of grounds. First, to deduce that, because a patient admitted under a short-term section can be treated for 'mental disorder' in the generic sense, so too can a patient admitted under a long-term section, does not countenance the fact that the purpose of the short-term sections is different from that of the long-term sections. The short-term sections are designed to facilitate the determination of whether a person who appears to be mentally disordered is, in fact, so disordered; if so, the identification of the mental disorder from which the patient is suffering might occur with greater precision; it might also be discovered whether that disorder is of a nature or degree warranting longer term hospitalisation for treatment. In other words, s. 2 uses the vague criteria of 'mental disorder' because that section should only be used when no firmer diagnosis, prognosis or treatment plan can, at that point, be made. If there is no doubt about such questions, the patient should be admitted under s. 3. Accordingly, it is possible to admit a person under s. 2 with a disorder that would not permit admission under s. 3. On the reading of the law provided by Baroness Hale, it is now, however, lawful to treat a person held under s. 3 for some mental disorder that would not have been sufficient to justify his or her initial admission for treatment, which effectively obliterates the distinction between ss. 2 and 3, and the underlying policy, of differentiating between the short-term detention (with lesser safeguards, justified on that basis) and longer term detention, that the two sections, read together, articulate. The only way to avoid this is to understand 'the mental disorder' in s. 63 as referring back to the grounds for admission, whether that is 'mental disorder' under s. 2 or 'the mental disorder' diagnosed as the basis for admission under s. 3.

Second, it is for the same reason that s. 63 has to be couched in such general terms. If the wording of the section were limited to the 'form of mental disorder', it would not be possible to treat, and, given that treatment is defined so broadly, to assess a person admitted under s. 2. Third, the historical analysis really adds little to the interpretation of the current law on this point. As Baroness Hale pointed out, the 1959 Act linked the question of classification and reclassification to the questions of admission and continued detention, and was silent as to the legality of treatment. But the very fact that what is now Part IV of the 1983 Act was subsequently added to the statutory scheme renders the situation so different as to defy comparison with its predecessor. To say, in other words, that the question of classification was linked only to admission and continued detention, in a scheme where that was all there was to be linked to, tells us nothing about the linkages in a scheme that has other substantive components, in the form of the restrictions added in 1983 to the treatments that can be given to a patient. In any case, it is not clear that it is appropriate to rest present-day policy decisions on historical arguments: it is better to accept that law is 'language which is "always speaking" and can change its meaning in the light of changing social conditions' (Hale LJ in the Court of Appeal in *R* v *Tower Hamlets LBC, ex p Abdul W* [2002] EWCA Civ 287 at para. 31).

In the final analysis, this case decides a question of policy. The House of Lords, in the form of Baroness Hale – who has, of course, been one of the very best mental health lawyers in this country for many years – has opted to establish a default position that maximises the scope for professional discretion and freedom, and plays down the idea that Part IV should be seen as a 'safeguard'. Whether, in any case, this will change things very much for patients is debatable. As discussed in the previous edition of this book (pp. 353–4), the decision of the Court of Appeal, that s. 63 is limited to treatment for the mental disorder from which the patient is classified as suffering, was so hedged around with exceptions that it provided no real impediment to the discretion of the RMO to treat other disorders.

So, as far as the scope of treatment for mental disorder is concerned, then, there is little in the jurisprudence of the courts that limits it. Both the Court of Appeal in this case (see Simon Brown LJ at para. 78) and the House of Lords (see Baroness Hale at para. 22) held that s. 63 does not apply to treatment for any physical disorder. This, in theory at least, is clearly correct. Section 63 cannot be used to force any other sort of treatment on a detained patient for any reason. A detained patient does not lose his or her common law and human rights to refuse treatment for a condition, illness, or injury that it not connected to his or her mental disorder. Yet whether that general statement of principle is reflective of the reality of the situation is very much, in our view, an open question, and an examination of the case law reveals considerable ambiguity in how the line between mental disorder and physical disorder has been drawn.

The modern case law starts with *B v Croydon Health Authority* [1995] 1 ALL ER 683 (CA). In this case, Hoffman LJ held that it was not appropriate to take an 'atomistic' view of the treatment of a patient's condition. By this, as seen above, he meant that it was not important for legal purposes to distinguish between causes and symptoms, or effects. But in the later case of *Tameside and Glossop Acute Services Trust v CH* [1996] 1 FLR 762 (FD) – in which *Croydon* was 'applied' – the concept of a 'symptom', and the nexus between the mental disorder in question and the proposed treatment, was arguably stretched beyond even the generous limits set by the Act. In this case, CH had been detained under s. 3 as suffering from schizophrenia, one manifestation of which was said to be psychotic paranoia manifesting, inter alia, as distrust of medical staff. She was in the 38th week of pregnancy and there were concerns that the foetus was not growing properly because it was not being provided with nourishment by the placenta. The likelihood was that, without intervention, the foetus would die *in utero*. Dr G, the consultant obstetrician and gynaecologist responsible for this aspect of CH's care, was concerned that CH, who had refused to cooperate with antenatal care in the earlier stages of her pregnancy, might continue to do so, even though she had given her consent to a proposed induction of the birth. The trust applied to the High Court for an order that it would be lawful to treat CH as necessary to save the life of the foetus, including the performance of a caesarean section operation without her consent should that prove necessary.

The latest edition of the Code of Practice, citing *Croydon*, advises that treatment for physical disorder cannot be given under Part IV 'unless it can reasonably be said that the physical disorder is a symptom or underlying cause of the mental disorder' (Department of Health and Welsh Office, 1999: para. 16.5). From one point of view, the situation in *Tameside* falls clearly outside of this situation: in no way might it be said that CH's pregnancy was a 'symptom or underlying cause' of her schizophrenia. On the other hand, there was evidence before the court from CH's doctor, Dr M, that the birth of a stillborn child 'will have a profound deleterious effect both in the short and the longer term' (at 767), confirming CH's paranoid delusions about those responsible for her treatment. An alarming picture of CH's future was painted (767): 'If she does not trust the services, she is likely constantly to relapse and not make a recovery with treatment. If she fails to recover she would be unable to care for the child. She would require constant readmissions.' If, on the other hand, the court authorised the proposed treatment, '[t]he prognosis if she delivers a healthy infant is that she can recover from her psychosis and be able to provide care and support for her child. She will then be in a stable mental condition and rational and free from psychotic symptoms' (767). Essentially, CH's doctor presented the court with a choice between, on one hand, a psychotic patient and a child either dead *in utero* or born but uncared for, and a mentally healthy mother and child on the other. Small wonder, then, that the judge, Wall J, chose the latter option. To do this, he adopted the 'holistic' approach taken in *Croydon*, and held that the prognosis, if the treatment was not administered to save the foetus, was such that it would clearly be of benefit to CH's mental health for the treatment to proceed (773): 'It is not... stretching language unduly to say that achievement of a successful outcome of her pregnancy is a necessary part of the overall treatment of her mental disorder.' Accordingly, the treatment fell within s. 63.

In their discussion of this case, and other forced caesarean cases decided at common law, Widdett and Thomson (1997) take issue with the assumptions behind the assertion presented as incontrovertible fact that CH's disorder would vanish from view on the birth of a healthy child. As they say, '[h]aving a child is clearly constructed as curative and normalising' (1997: 86). By the same token, the decision to intervene against CH's wishes 'may be located within broader stories regarding female instability during pregnancy' (1997: 85). Widdett and Thomson point to the orthodoxies of nineteenth-century medical science, which posited female health and ill health – both physical and mental – to be in a direct relation to the proper functioning of an individual's reproductive organs. The logic employed in *Tameside* is no different (1997: 87): '... the prognosis for her mental health was polarised by the possible outcomes of her pregnancy.' This is not merely some 'theoretical' point. It structures the judgment and outcome of the case precisely by overriding a different view of CH that emerged from a report produced by the official solicitor's agent, at the request of CH's lawyers, which Wall J tells us, found her to be 'well oriented and clearly aware of the problems suffered by the foetus' (768). According to this report, CH claimed that it was she who had suggested the possible need for a caesarean-section operation, and had resisted the planned induction of the foetus only because it was her view that, with antibiotics, its health would improve, which it, in fact, did. In sum, this report portrays CH as rational and intent on saving her baby, yet its contents were rejected in favour of the evidence of Drs G and M. This, Widdett and Thomson suggest, demonstrates the pull of a particular, normative, ideology of femininity. (CH's capacity to consent, also at issue in the trial, is discussed in Chapter 10.)

One might ask at this point whether, on the basis of the holistic logic employed in these cases, it will ever be the case that any treatment of a physical disorder, injury or illness, of a detained patient will not be treatment for that patient's mental disorder, because any treatment is designed to make the recipient 'feel better' and therefore can be said to be of benefit to his or her mental health. In both the *Croydon* and *Tameside* cases, the earlier decision of *Re C (Adult: Refusal of Treatment)* [1994] 1 ALL ER 819, [1994] 1 WLR 290 (HC) was distinguished. As discussed above, this case stands for the proposition that, at common law, a competent adult patient has an absolute right to refuse treatment, notwithstanding that the patient is suffering from a mental illness.

Although C suffered from schizophrenia and was a detained patient in a special hospital, the court in that case made no mention of s. 63 of the 1983 Act. According to the courts in *Croydon* and *Tameside*, this was because, in *Re C*, 'the gangrene was entirely unconnected with the mental disorder' (per Hoffman LJ, in *Croydon*, at 688), so that 'Treatment of C's gangrene was not likely to affect his mental condition: the manner in which the delivery of the defendant's child is likely to have a direct effect on her mental state' (per Wall J, in *Tameside*, at 773). This might – assuming it is factually correct – convey the distinction between cases caught by, and those outside, s. 63 as a matter of principle, with the latter being physical disorders 'entirely unconnected with the mental disorder'. Nevertheless, the distinction between those treatments that are, and those that are not, in some way 'connected' seems problematic, particularly in light of the 'holistic' attitude adopted by the courts in these cases. In *Re C*, the relevance of s. 63 was not even argued, and so its positing as being on the 'other side of the line' can only be *ex post facto*. More than this, though, had it been argued in *Re C*, it may well have been, on the logic employed in *Croydon* and, particularly, *Tameside*, that the treatment might have been carried out under s. 63. The court in that case was concerned only to examine C's capacity to take his own decisions, and not the connection between his mental disorder and his refusal to consent. Even so, the court was presented with evidence relevant to this latter issue. Dr E accepted instructions from C's solicitor to see, and report upon, C's ability to refuse consent. He gave evidence to the court that schizophrenia is an all-pervasive illness and manifested in C's case in the form of 'grandiose and persecutory delusions as well as ... [a] mismatch between words spoken and the accompanying emotional display' (821–2). Dr E considered that C was not competent to consent because, although he understood the information that was given to him about the state of his leg, as a result of his mental disorder, he did not believe it (822). In addition, we are told that C's schizophrenia manifested at this time in the delusions that he was a doctor, and that his carers were intent on destroying his body with their interventions (823). Although Thorpe J recorded that Dr E 'did not find any direct link between C's refusal and his persecutory delusions' (823), the crucial point is that a direct link is not required by the decisions in *Croydon* and *Tameside*. In the holistic universe, all things are linked to all others.

Thus, it might be argued that there is here a causal connection between the physical and mental disorders, such that treatment under s. 63, as this section has been interpreted in *Croydon* and *Tameside*, would have been lawful. C's attitude towards the proposed treatment on his leg was a 'symptom' of his disorder in this broad sense. It may be possible to go further still, and argue that the treatment licensed in the leading House of Lords decision on the treatment of incapacitated patients at common law, *F v West Berkshire DHA* [1990] 2 AC 1 might, on the logic of *Croydon* and *Tameside*, have been lawfully performed under s. 63. The House of Lords held that the performance of a sterilisation operation on F was lawful by operation of the common law principle of necessity. In the opinion of Lord Brandon of Oakbrook in that case (at 55), with which Lord

Griffiths (at 70) agreed (no other member of the House mentioning the MHA at all), it was not necessary to detail Part IV of the 1983 Act, because it clearly did not apply. But the fact is that the evidence in F that was used to demonstrate that treatment at common law without F's consent would be lawful because it was in her 'best interests' also shows, clearly, that the decision whether to treat or not had a direct bearing on F's mental condition. In the words of Lord Brandon, 'it would, from a psychiatric point of view, be disastrous for her to conceive a child' (at 53). How is this different from *Croydon* or, especially, *Tameside*? Part of the answer is that F was not a detained patient, but this was not the point of distinction upon which Lord Brandon relied, holding that Part IV of the 1983 Act was not relevant because 'it does not contain any provisions relating to the giving of treatment to patients for any conditions other than their mental disorder' (at 55).

One is left, consequently, wondering where, for the purposes of s. 63, the line is to be drawn. The above analysis of the jurisprudence on this question seems to suggest that the 'limit' of s. 63 has a decidedly 'postmodern' quality to it: that is, it is a limit that continually recedes as one approaches it (Cornell, 1992), rather like the end of a rainbow. On a less esoteric level, the conclusion must be that the Court of Appeal in *Croydon* was *per incuriam* in adopting the 'holistic' approach, or at least that the High Court in *Tameside* was in error for applying that approach in such a way as to elide the clear distinction, on the face of s. 63, between 'mental' and 'physical' disorders. This is not only because to do so is to institutionalise a system whereby persons detained in hospital for treatment for mental disorder are placed in an inferior position is respect of their rights to refuse treatments for physical disorders, purely on the fact of their detention, nor because of the more technical point that this implicitly goes against the decision of the House of Lords in *F*, which is binding on the lower courts, but because this effaces the distinction between treatment of physical and mental conditions. Even if this distinction is philosophically problematic (because it is not clear that a mind/body distinction can rigidly be drawn), it functions, in practice, as a protective barrier for the rights to autonomy of persons detained in hospitals. The approach of the Court of Appeal in *Croydon*, and the application of that approach in *Tameside*, effectively removed that protective barrier.

It is difficult not to notice that the gender of the plaintiff in *Re C* was male, and in the other cases, female. The courts in both *Croydon* and *Tameside* might also have referred to *Secretary of State for the Home Department* v *Robb* [1995] 1 ALL ER 677(HC), a case decided shortly before *Croydon*, in which it was held that a male prisoner, Robb, who was on hunger strike, had the right to refuse food even if that were to lead to his death. Despite the fact that Robb had been diagnosed as suffering from a personality disorder, his capacity to consent to, or refuse, treatment was agreed by four psychiatrists and a psychologist. The court did not even consider the possibility that Robb's refusal to accept food might be seen as a manifestation of his mental condition. If they had done so, it is possible that arrangements could have been put in train for his transfer to hospital for treatment (as was suggested by a psychiatrist employed by the official solicitor, acting as *amicus curiae*: see 680). Instead, in order to uphold Robb's right to refuse treatment, Thorpe J, in the High Court, was obliged to disapprove the earlier case of *Leigh v Gladstone* (1909) 26 TLR 139 – then the only legal authority directly on the question of forced feeding – in which it had been held lawful to force-feed hunger-striking suffragettes, imprisoned for criminal acts carried out in pursuance of female suffrage, on the grounds that this was 'of little relevance or weight in modern times' (at 681). It is easy to see how, from a feminist viewpoint, this aspect of the case merely enhances the thoroughly patriarchal context of this body of law.

The treatment of mental disorder is shot through with gendered assumptions. Clearly, the arguments of Widdett and Thomson are well made, but the present authors do not subscribe to the thesis of gendered judicial conspiracy as being the determining factor in analysing the jurisprudence on the scope of s. 63. Looking more closely at the two cases involving male patients – *Re C* and *Robb* – it is clear that the court was not, in fact, dealing with life-and-death situations. C, although refusing to consent to the amputation of his leg, did consent to conservative treatment. By the time of the High Court hearing, C's gangrenous infection had cleared up and the wound was healing (822) and there had been 'a dramatic aversion of the risk' (at 823). In Robb's case, the hunger strike that was the subject of the legal proceedings was only the latest in a history of such behaviour. On previous occasions, Robb had 'achieved nothing' (per Thorpe J at 679), and on the instant occasion, 'his determination to continue on his hunger strike to the end has wavered. On one occasion he began to accept nutrition and was transferred to a local hospital so that the return to nutrition could be overseen medically' (at 680). One cannot help but suspect that the view that Robb did not intend to refuse food to the point of death informed Thorpe J's ruling that he could lawfully do so. By contrast, in the cases involving female patients – *Croydon* and *Tameside* – the prospect of a death consequent upon the judicial decision was much more real. This analysis might seem to be upset by the ruling in *Re JT (Adult: Refusal of Medical Treatment)* [1998] 1 FLR 48, in which the court, following *Re C*, upheld the right of a young woman detained under s. 3 on grounds of mental impairment to refuse life-saving dialysis for kidney problems caused by renal failure, having judged her competent to make her own decision. But in that case, the situation was that, without cooperation from the patient, the treatment could not be successful, and so a court order that she comply would not have substantively altered the reality of the situation that JT was going to die. Here, s. 63 was barely mentioned, and then only to confirm its inapplicability (per Wall J at 51). Thus, and without denying the importance of the normative constructions of appropriate gendered behaviour that can be found in this body of case law, we would argue that the best predictor of outcome is whether judicial intervention can authorise procedures that, in the view of the court, are necessary to save the life of the patient. Of course, the flipside of this point is that, when the life of the patient really is at stake, her or his autonomy to refuse treatment is more apparent than real.

This analysis is reinforced by the decision in *R v Collins and Ashworth Hospital, ex p Brady* (2001) 58 BMLR 173 (QB), in which s. 63 was again directly at issue. B had been detained in Ashworth special hospital from 1985 with a diagnosis of personality disorder, following his transfer from prison. He had determined to refuse food. This was in response to a decision from the hospital management to move him from one part of the hospital complex to another, for security reasons. This had involved B being subject to an unannounced 'snatch' by a six-strong control and restraint team in full riot gear, including visored helmets (see Hines, 1999). At this point, his RMO was also changed, with Dr C taking over the role. B was not told the reason for these events and feared (although, it seems, needlessly) that his move within the hospital was a preliminary step with a view to his eventual transfer back to prison, to which he strongly objected. Initially, his decision to refuse food was admittedly a tactic, which he had used on several previous occasions, in his ongoing battle of wills with the hospital authorities. After some time, however, B stated that he had now formed the view, rationally, that he wished to starve to death. In response to B's refusal to accept food, Dr C authorised his feeding by force. As we have seen, *Croydon* had established that feeding by force could be 'medical treatment for mental disorder from which [the patient] is suffering' under the MHA. Maurice Kay J held that (i) the feeding by force of B was covered by s. 63, and (ii) B lacked capacity to make this treatment decision, and could therefore have, in the alternative, been given the treatment under the common law 'best interests' principle. Here, unlike the cases of *C* and *Robb*, it seems that the court, in common with those responsible for the care and treatment of B, were not prepared to call his bluff, and so the course of action that would ensure that his life would not be lost was ordered.

It is perhaps not surprising to find that s. 63 has been read expansively, nor that this is explicable in terms of a judicial wish to act so as to preserve life wherever possible. But the above discussion shows that the problems with this are manifold. Surely the better approach – and arguably the better reading of the provision – is to limit the reach of s. 63 to cover treatment of the 'core condition', and only those physical conditions that are either manifestations of an underlying mental disorder or which give rise directly to a mental disorder? One relevant authority, not referred to on this point in any of the case law here under analysis, is *R v MHAC, ex p X* (1988) 9 BMLR 77 (DC). In this case, it was held that if a 'sexually deviant' patient's sexual deviance is 'inextricably linked' with his or her mental disorder, so that treatment for one is treatment for the other, then it will be lawful to treat the sexual deviancy under the compulsory powers in Part IV. This case, as a matter of law, seems to demonstrate the right balance. Applied to the present situation, it does not unduly stretch the causal link, or the idea of a 'symptom' as a sign or an indication of an underlying condition.

This would mean that *Croydon* was correctly decided, but that *Tameside* was not. Even those who are apprehensive about the conceptualisation of eating disorders as mental illness agree that such disorders are the manifestation of some underlying aetiology, which is psychological in character (Bordo, 1988; 1993; Orbach, 1993; Eckerman, 1997; Bridgeman and Millns, 1998: 545–74) and can thus be said to be 'symptoms' of mental disorder in the sense meant by the 1983 Act. There is, on the other hand, no such relation between pregnancy and mental disorder: neither is per se causative of the other. The approach of the Court of Appeal in *St George's Healthcare NHS Trust* (for facts, see Chapter 5) possibly comes closest to this view, although because the point was not argued – it could not be claimed by those using the MHA that the basis for its use was a link (actual or perceived) between S's alleged mental disorder and her pregnancy – in reality, the support to be gleaned from that decision is slight. Nor is there any mention in the *St George's* case of the line of authorities starting with *Croydon*. In the recent past, however, another line of argument has been opened up for patients who wish to resist the imposition of treatment under s. 63. This is concerned not with the question of how to conceptualise medical treatment, nor with the question of how to draw the line between 'mental' and 'physical' disorder, but with the question of whether the Human Rights Act has superimposed limits on the clinical freedom of RMOs, over and above those imposed by the common law (in the form, for example, of an action for negligence) or by the 1983 Act, to impose treatment under this section.

7.3.2.4 Section 63 and Convention rights

On its face, s. 63 is clear: 'the consent of a patient shall not be required' if treatment under this section 'is given by or under the direction' of the RMO. The common law right to refuse treatment simply does not apply to s. 63. Indeed, at the time that the Human Rights Act 1998 came into force, in October 2000, even the common law right to refuse was under attack on various fronts. It had been constantly challenged by a string of cases concerned with forced caesarean sections. At a more general level, it had been drawn very narrowly by the Court of Appeal in *Re T*; it was further challenged by the High Court in *Brady*. Maurice Kay J, in passing, cast doubt on the decision in *Robb*, holding (at para. 72) that, because it has been established (in *Reeves v Commissioner of Police* [1999] 3 WLR 363) that a duty of care is owed by prison and hospital authorities to those under their charge who are deemed to be at risk of suicide:

It would be somewhat odd if there is a duty to prevent suicide by an act (for example, the use of a knife left in a cell) but not even a power to intervene to prevent self-destruction by star- vation. I can see no moral justification for the law indulging its fascination with the difference between acts and omissions in a context such as this and no logical need for it to do so.

This was a somewhat alarming statement for those who wished to see law remain true to its claim to uphold the autonomy of the individual. Subsequently it has been held, in cases like *Re B (Consent to Treatment: Capacity)*, sub nom *B (Adult: Refusal of Medical Treatment)* [2002] EWHC 429, [2002] 2 All ER 449 and *Re W (Adult: Refusal of Treatment)* [2002] C8002041, that the duty of care owed to a person is subservient to that person's right to self-determination when the two are in potential conflict. But the common law gave no mechanism by which to import this thinking into s. 63. Things began to change, however, with the incorporation of the Convention rights into English and Welsh law by the 1998 Act.

R v RMO, Broadmoor Hospital and Ors, ex p Wilkinson [2001] EWCA CIV 1545 involved a patient, W, detained in Broadmoor for a number of decades by virtue of a hospital order and restriction order, with a diagnosis of psychopathic disorder. His RMO, who felt that W was also suffering from an underlying mental illness, namely a psychotic disorder, which might respond positively to appropriate treatment, deter- mined to treat him with antipsychotic medication, but W refused to give his consent, although, in the view of the RMO, he did not have capacity to give or refuse consent. The treatment was administered, and it was necessary to use force to secure administration. W then sought legal advice in order to seek to challenge the administration of further doses of the medication. He obtained a report from an independent consultant psychiatrist, Dr G. Dr G's report was at variance with the views of the RMO and another doctor, Dr H, who supported the RMO, in a number of respects. In particular, he: (i) disagreed with the diagnosis of W as suffering from a psychotic mental illness and hence with the likelihood that antipsychotic medication would benefit him; (ii) disagreed that W lacked capacity; (iii) disagreed with the decision to administer the treatment by force. On this latter point, his particular reason was that W had coronary heart disease, was at risk of heart attack, and had, in fact, had an angina attack after the first dose of antipsychotic medication had been administered by force.

This case was one of an interlocutory appeal, on the question of whether, on an application for judicial review, witnesses could be compelled to attend and submit to cross-examination. It was not necessary for the Court of Appeal to decide on issues of substance, but the court did consider the implications of the Convention rights of patients for the operation of s. 63. As far as Art. 3 is concerned, Simon Brown and Hale LJJ cited at length from the decision of the European Court of Human Rights in *Herczegfalfy* v *Austria* (1992) 15 EHRR 437, at para. 82:

The Court considers that the position of inferiority and powerlessness which is typical of patients confined in psychiatric hospitals calls for increased vigilance in reviewing whether the Convention has been complied with... The established principles of medicine are admittedly in principle decisive in such cases; as a general rule, a measure which is therapeutic necessity cannot be regarded as inhuman or degrading. The Court must nevertheless satisfy itself that the medical necessity has been convincingly shown to exist.

Effectively, this is to change the important question from one of procedure to one of substance; and attach a seemingly very high burden of proof to the requirement to show that the treatment in question is of 'therapeutic' or 'medical' necessity. The Court of Appeal in *Wilkinson* was clear that the implication for the law of England and Wales is that, where such a necessity cannot be convincingly shown, and provided that the treatment in question can be said, in the particular circumstances, to reach a (in fact, fairly highly pitched) minimum level of severity (see *T and V* v *UK* (1999) 7 BHRC 659), a right to refuse treatment must be superimposed onto s. 63 by operation of Art. 3. Even when treatment does not reach the prescribed level of severity, so that Art. 3 is inapplicable, there might still be a breach of Art. 8(1), unless the treatment can be justified by reference to the factors listed in Art. 8(2). In the words of Simon Brown LJ (at para. 30):

If in truth this appellant has the capacity to refuse consent to the treatment proposed here, it is difficult to suppose that he should nevertheless be forcibly subjected to it... its impact on the appellants rights above all to autonomy and bodily inviolability is immense and its prospective benefits (not least given his extreme opposition) appear decidedly speculative.

Of course, this factual question, strictly speaking, was not one for the Court of Appeal. But Simon Brown LJ was clearly of the view that, on these facts, it did not seem to be the case that the treatment in question was a therapeutic necessity such as to justify its imposition in the face of W's refusal, and there are hints, in the judgment of Hale LJ, that she shared his view (see for example, para. 82).

The obligation to act in a way compatible with Convention rights is imposed on public authorities, including the courts, by ss. 6(1) and (3)(a) of the Human Rights Act 1998, and it was the unanimous view of the Court of Appeal in *Wilkinson* that this entailed changes in the way in which judicial review of decisions to impose treatment without consent should be conducted. In *Brady*, decided under the old law, the essence of B's dispute concerned an issue of 'precedent fact' – that his refusal of food was a symptom of his personality disorder. B's contention was that this was a rational decision entirely unconnected with his mental disorder. Maurice Kay J held that the context of the Act, and the wording of s. 63 in particular, made it plain that the decision as to whether s. 63 applied in a particular case was one for the clinical decision of the RMO, and not for the court. Hence, this was a case, in his view, that called for a so-called Super-*Wednesbury* approach (see Chapter 5), under which the task of the court is to review the decision taken, not to reopen the determinations of fact upon which the RMO based his or her decision. Because B could not 'get behind' what appeared to be compliance with s. 63, the merit of his point was not assessed and, as seen above, he lost his case.

In *Wilkinson*, the Court of Appeal held that, in cases that raise questions of human rights, the *Brady* route – that is of applying the so-called 'Super-*Wednesbury*' approach – is, following the coming into force of the Human Rights Act, 'no longer appropriate in the case of the forcible treatment of detained patients' (Simon Brown LJ at para. 27). Instead, the approach outlined by the House of Lords in *Daly* (see Chapter 5) should now be taken. This means a review of 'somewhat greater' intensity (per Lord Steyn in *Daly* at 547). The court proceeded to elaborate on the precise implications of this in the context of detained patients. Simon Brown LJ held that following the Human Rights Act (at para. 26):

It seems to me that the court must inevitably now reach its own view both as to whether this appellant is indeed incapable of consenting (or refusing consent) to the treatment programme planned for him [by the RMO] and depending upon the court's conclusion on that issue, as to whether the proposed forcible administration of such treatment [breaches any of the patient's substantive human rights].'

Hale LJ (at para. 83) said much the same thing:

Whatever the position before the Human Rights Act, the decision to impose treatment without consent is a potential invasion of [the patient's] rights under Article 3 or Article 8. Super-*Wednesbury* is not enough. The appellant is entitled to a proper hearing, on the merits, of whether the statutory grounds for imposing this treatment upon him against his will are made out: i.e. whether it is treatment for the mental disorder from which he is suffering and whether it should be give to him without his consent having regard to the likelihood of its alleviating of preventing a deterioration of his condition . . .

As such, it is no longer open to a court to side-step questions of the suitability, and proportionality, of non-consensual treatment by recourse to some version of the *Wednesbury* approach. Instead, a substantive judgment will be required.

Simon Brown LJ gave some consideration to the approach that should be taken in making a substantive decision. In somewhat guarded language, he rejected the application of the *Bolam* test in this context (para. 31), as did Hale LJ (para. 64). In the later case of *R v Dr M and Ors, ex p N* [2003] 1 WLR 562 [2002] EWCA Civ 1789 (CA), a case factually very similar to *Wilkinson*, the Court of Appeal adopted a different approach, holding that, although the *Bolam* test must be satisfied, 'That is a necessary, but not a sufficient, condition of treatment' (Dyson LJ at para. 29). If the treatment in question is not in accordance with any responsible medical opinion, it cannot satisfy the test of medical necessity laid down in *Herczegfalfy*; that it is in accordance with a body of medical opinion does not mean that it does 'convincingly' satisfy that test. Rather, 'the court has to decide in the light of all the evidence in the case whether the treatment should be permitted' (*ibid.*). In this regard, the court suggested what amounts to a 'checklist' of seven factors that a court should consider (para. 19):

- the degree of certainty that the patient does suffer from a treatable mental disorder;
- the seriousness of that disorder;
- the seriousness of any risk posed to others;
- the likelihood that treatment will alleviate the patient's condition;
- the probable extent of any alleviation;
- the likelihood that treatment will have adverse consequences for the patient;
- the probable severity of those consequences.

The courts rather gave with one hand and took away with the other, as far as patients are concerned, however. In *ex p N* (para. 27), and again in *R v RMO and SOAD, ex p JB* [2006] EWCA Civ 961 (para. 56), the Court of Appeal rejected the argument that, if a responsible body of medical opinion did not agree that the treatment in question should be given, it was not open to a court to conclude that a case for treatment could be convincingly made. It is, then, not enough for a patient to produce medical evidence that he or she should not be given the treatment. That evidence must be such as to persuade the court that it cannot convincingly be shown that treatment is a necessity, which, as Simon Brown LJ anticipated in *Wilkinson* (at para. 31), has rarely proven to be the case. In cases such as *ex p N* and *ex p JB*, the patient, despite providing evidence that the treatment in question was not warranted, was unable to prevent his or her treatment without consent. In these cases, the courts have departed from the traditional view of the operation of *Bolam* – that the courts may not choose between competing responsible medical opinions, which is based on the fact that, as medical laypersons, judges are ill-equipped to make such a choice – in pronouncing themselves convinced that the treatment in question has been convincingly shown to be necessary. There is something odd, then, that to date, High Court judges have felt themselves able to reject *all* medical opinion proffered in support of the patient in *all* cases subsequent to *Wilkinson*, in each case being 'convinced' that the treatment should be given.

Thus, although *Wilkinson* does represent some sort of a breakthrough, its impact should not be overestimated. Moreover, in practice, the *Herczegfalfy* test offers less than it might, and the need for 'medical necessity' to be 'convincingly shown' has been severely watered down by later decisions of the Court of Appeal, each involving patients refusing to consent to treatment ordered by their RMO. In *ex p N*, the court 'disagreed' that 'convincingly shown' amounted to the same as the criminal law burden of proof. In the court's view, 'The standard is a high one. But it does not need elaboration or further explanation' (para. 18). In *ex p JB*, Auld LJ doubted that it is possible to express the test of medical necessity (para. 42):

in terms of evidential proof. It is rather a value judgment as to the future – a forecast – to be made by a court in reliance on medical evidence . . . If it is to be expressed in forensic terms at all, it is doubtful whether it amounts to more than satisfaction of medical necessity on a balance of probabilities, or as a 'likelihood' of therapeutic benefit.

The Court of Appeal in *ex p JB* further held, endorsing *obiter* remarks of Dyson LJ in *ex p N*, that the test of medical necessity involved only one question: subissues, such as (in *ex p JB*) whether the RMO's diagnosis was correct, and if so, whether the treatment was appropriate for it in the circumstances, should not be examined, nor need be proven, separately (para. 34). The 'medical necessity' test should be applied to the over-all situation. This view was based on 'the need for realism and practicality' (para. 39), and applied the reasoning of the House of Lords in *ex p B* (above) that, given the diffi-culties in diagnosis and prognosis, any higher standard, or more exacting procedure, would not be easily attainable. As such, a successful appeal to the House of Lords is unlikely. On the other hand, it may be that the Strasbourg Court would take the view that this telescoped approach to analysis of the fact situation, coupled with a 'balance of probabilities' test, is too far removed from the *Herczegfalfy* requirement of 'convin-cingly shown to exist' to be able satisfactorily to perform its task of complying with the positive obligations under Arts. 3 and 8.

It may be, however, that it would find no such thing. The court in *Herczegfalfy* decided that 'therapeutic' or 'medical necessity' is defined 'according to the psychi-atric principles generally accepted at the time' (para. 83), which, in its deference to the state of psychiatric knowledge, is on all fours with the approach taken in *ex p JB*. The facts of *Herczegfalfy* demonstrate the point. H, on hunger strike in an Austrian psychiatric facility, was fed by force, had drugs administered to him by force, which he resisted, leading to loss of teeth, bruising and broken ribs, and was restrained with handcuffs and a belt strapped around his ankles for two weeks. The court found the prolonged use of physical restraints 'worrying' (para. 83) but accepted that, as it was in accordance with accepted psychiatric principles, it was medically necessary.

Although the court in *Wilkinson* was clear that treatment without consent might be prevented if in breach of Arts. 8 and/or 3, it was not, however, clear in terms of who benefited from this protection. For Simon Brown LJ, the distinction between those having, and those lacking, capacity was of increasing importance. He referred to the

Report (2000) of the European Committee for the Prevention of Torture and Inhuman or Degrading Treatment or Punishment, at para. 41:

Patients should, as a matter of principle, be placed in a position to give their free and informed consent to treatment. The admission of a person to a psychiatric establishment on an involuntary basis should not be construed as authorising treatment without his consent. It follows that every competent patient, whether voluntary or involuntary, should be given the opportunity to refuse treatment or any other medical intervention. Any derogation from this fundamental principle should be based on law and only relate to strictly defined exceptional circumstances.

This, said Simon Brown LJ, 'gives some indication of modern thinking on this sensitive subject' (para. 29). This seems to indicate a sharp distinction between those with capacity and those lacking it, but our view is that this is not how Simon Brown LJ should be understood. He did accept that the 'therapeutic necessity' test applied equally to patients lacking capacity (para. 31). It has been held that Art. 3 has no application in the case of a person in a persistent vegetative state (PVS), because 'Article 3 requires the victim to be aware of the inhuman or degrading treatment which he or she is experiencing or at least be in a state of physical or mental suffering' (Dame Butler Sloss in *NHS Trust A v M, NHS Trust B v H* [2001] Fam 348 at 363), but awareness here should be pitched at as low a level as possible. A person's human rights are not lessened by his or her inability to understand them fully, and as Hale LJ pointed out in *Wilkinson*, 'most people are able to appreciate that they are being forced do something against their will even if they are not able to make the decision that it should or should not be done' (para. 79), so that (para. 64):

The wishes and feelings of an incapacitated person will be an important element in determining what is, or is not, in his best interests. Where he is actively opposed to a course of action, the benefits which it holds for him will have to be carefully weighed against the disadvantages of going against his wishes, especially if force is required to do this.

The approach of Hale LJ chimes with the dicta of the European Court in *Keenan v UK* [1998] 26 EHRR CD64 at para. 112, where the Court stated that there may be a breach of Art. 3 even where the applicant is not able to understand any ill effects of his or her treatment. And this seems to be right in terms of underlying principle, which, as Wicks (2001: 22) points out, 'appears to be the concept of human dignity rather than individual self-determination or autonomy'. This is not to dispute, however, that capacity is a significant factor that impacts on the question of justification for treatment without consent.

At the other end of the spectrum, Hale LJ was at pains to point out that 'I do not take the view that detained patients who have the capacity to decide for themselves can never be treated against their will' (at para. 810). In her Ladyship's view, it remains lawful, in general terms, to treat a patient with capacity under compulsion with the sole aim of benefiting the health of the person subject to the treatment, particularly in view of the fact that the test for capacity is pitched at a relatively low level (para. 80). This view was applied by Silber J in the High Court in *R v RMO, ex p PS* [2003] EWHC 2335 and

R v Dr SS and Dr AC, ex p PB [2005] EWHC 86, both of which concerned patients found to have capacity who were refusing to consent to drug treatments. In both cases, it was held that treatment did not breach either Arts. 3 or 8 simply by reason of the patient having capacity, nor need the criteria for treatment be limited to the need to prevent harm to others. It was lawful to treat on the basis of the health of the patient. In *R v RMO and SOAD, ex p T* [2005] EWHC 1688, Collins J held that whether a refusing patient who objected 'irrationally' to medication had capacity or not was 'an academic argument' (para. 39), because, in either case, it was in the patient's best interests for the treatment to be given.

In *ex p PB*, Silber J also held that there was no breach of Art. 14 by reason of treating a patient with capacity against his or her will under Part IV (the actual section at issue in that case was s. 58(3)(b): see below), when compared to the absolute right to refuse of the common law, because there is an objective reason for the difference, namely that a person treated under Part IV has a condition requiring detention and meets the criterion of treatability (para. 215).

The importance of capacity was further discussed in a case similar to *Wilkinson* on the material facts, *R v S and Otrs, ex p B* [2006] EWCA Civ 28. Lord Philips CJ, giving the judgment of the court, endorsed the approach taken in the earlier cases, holding that 'capacity is not the critical factor in determining whether treatment can be administered without consent' (para. 42). This statement was based on a particular reading of the philosophical relation between autonomy and beneficence as it is played out in the text of the 1983 Act. For Lord Philips, the situation whereby a patient with capacity might refuse treatment that 'objectively' is in his or her best interests, particularly if such treatment is designed to maintain that person's mental health and capacity to give consent, when that patient might be given the treatment if lacking capacity, 'borders on the absurd' (para. 42). Rather, the 1983 Act should be read as (paras. 47–8):

an integrated package of detention and treatment ... The overall objective of detention of a dangerous patient ought to be that the patient should be rehabilitated and able to return to society. This of itself militates against an approach that ignores the overall object of the MHA package, looks at the patient in detention, and imposes a threshold requirement that treatment without consent can only be justified if the treatment is necessary to stop the patient causing harm to others or to protect the patient from serious harm.

In other words, the court deconstructs the distinction between autonomy and beneficence by suggesting that the ultimate function of beneficent intervention is the restoration of autonomy: 'best interests' is philosophically grounded on the idea of autonomy. From this perspective, questions of capacity are of lesser importance. For the purposes of Convention rights – under Arts. 8 and 14, as well as Art. 3 – 'when considering the severity of treatment the fact that it is imposed by compulsion is more significant than the question of whether the patient has or has not capacity to consent to the treatment' (para. 50). The court referred to the *Report* of the European Committee on Torture, discussed by Simon Brown LJ in *Wilkinson*, as well as to a number of other international documents. One of these, the Council of Europe's *White Paper on the Protection of the*

Human Rights and Dignity of People Suffering from Mental Disorder (Council of Europe, 2000), suggests that there should be an absolute right for a patient with capacity to refuse psychiatric treatment. Other documents provide for a right to refuse, except if necessary to protect the safety of the patient or others, but not on the basis of the health of the patient (Council of Europe, 1997; Art. 7, and UN General Assembly Resolution 46/119, principles 9 and 11). In *Wilkinson*, Hale LJ had stated that 'we have not yet reached the point where it is an accepted norm that detained patients who fulfil the ... criteria for capacity can only be treated against their will for the protection of others or their own safety' (para. 80). The court in *ex p B* cited this passage, pointed out that the Richardson Committee reported a lack of consensus on this question, and referred to the fact that *Herczegfalfy* had recently been followed in the case of a person with capacity who had been fed by force whilst in criminal detention (*Nevmerzhitsky* v *Ukraine* Application No. 54825/00 (unreported) 5 April 2005). In addition, the Council of Europe followed up its 2000 White Paper with Recommendations in 2004, which concur with the position articulated in the UK courts (see Council of Europe, 2004, recommendation 18). So, five years on, that point still has not been reached. If anything, the power of the state to override a competent patient's refusal is more entrenched now than it was when *Wilkinson* was decided.

Nonetheless, the philosophy of Lord Philips is, with respect, problematic, because it elides the differences between health and protection as justifications for intervention, and in particular, claims that 'If detention of a patient for treatment pursuant to section 3 is justified on the ground that treatment is necessary for the protection of others, it is illogical to contend that a higher standard has to be applied to justify the administration of the treatment itself' (para. 47), when there is, in fact, a very logical argument that, whilst detention on grounds of public safety can be justified, this does not, of itself, license the qualitatively greater invasion of liberty, of imposing treatment without consent, nor does it necessarily imply that treatment can be justified in the absence of third-party interests in need of protection. This represents that law, for example, of Ontario. Ultimately, this is not a question of logic, but of morality or politics (on the philosophical argument generally, see Price, 1994). The running together of detention and treatment, and the criteria for the two, is very much in line with the approach taken by the House of Lords in *ex p B* (above). In either case, the purpose is to facilitate the maximum clinical freedom possible. This does not mean that there will never be a breach of Art. 3, but it does seem to mean that questions of capacity will not loom large in determining whether a breach has occurred.

Treatment without consent may also be in breach of Art. 8, and it is generally easier to show a breach of Art. 8 than of Art. 3 (*Raninen* v *Finland* [1997] 26 EHRR 563 at para. 63): an action can infringe a person's right to respect for private life, without it amounting to inhuman or degrading treatment. To date, the courts have tended, however, to conflate the two Articles, taking the view that, in either case, 'the only question was whether the treatment had been convincingly shown to be medically necessary. If so, there would be no breach of Article 3, even if the high threshold were otherwise crossed, nor of Article 8, since the interference with the right to respect for private life would be proportionate and would be justified within the terms of Article 8.2' (per Collins J in *R v Haddock* [2005] EWHC 921 (Admin) at para. 12). In *Herczegfalfy*, which involved a detained patient lacking capacity, his claim under Art. 8 was dismissed by the court because the patient was unable to demonstrate that he was not by reason of his mental disorder '*entirely* incapable of taking decisions for himself' (para. 86, emphasis added) over the period that the treatment was administered to him. The implication is that the situation may have been different if the patient had (greater) capacity, but as mentioned above, the European Court recently applied the same approach to a prisoner with capacity in *Nevmerzhitsky*. As with Art. 3, it seems that here, too, it is the necessity and extent of compulsion, not capacity, that is the central issue. In either case, it will be far from easy for a dissenting patient to make a substantive case.

The precise question on appeal in *Wilkinson* was concerned with the ruling in the High Court of Jowitt J, that the three doctors who had provided written reports to the court (the RMO and the SOAD in favour of the treatment; Dr G opposing the treatment) should not be required to attend the substantive judicial review hearing in order to be cross-examined on their witness statements. This application was denied by the High Court, on the grounds that to entertain cross-examination would, in effect, turn the review process into a fact-finding tribunal, this being beyond the ambit of the powers of judicial review in cases that raise no issue of precedent fact. It was against this preliminary finding that W appealed to the Court of Appeal. His appeal was grounded in Art. 6 of the Convention, on the basis that the refusal of the court to allow cross-examination deprived him of his right to a fair trial, and in turn, denied him the protection that a substantive merits hearing would afford to his rights under Articles 2, 3, 8 and 14.

The court allowed the appeal and ordered that the three doctors attend the substantive hearing for cross-examination. But this does not mean that oral evidence will be required in every case. In *ex p N*, the court pointed out that, in *Wilkinson*, Hale LJ had said that cross-examination should be ordered 'if necessary', and where, as in *N*, the judge had formed the view, on the basis of reading the various reports, that the necessity of treatment was convincingly shown, oral evidence or cross-examination was not necessary (at para. 37), nor should it often be necessary. In *ex p JB*, in which Art. 6 was the central issue, Auld LJ (para. 65) held that 'the court, in *Wilkinson*, could not have intended or contemplated that every case would require the hearing and testing of oral medical evidence'. The court here was responding to the concerns raised by Simon Brown LJ in *Wilkinson* (para. 31), that the attendance of medical professionals at court and their cross-examination would add to cost of, and delay, the resolution of the dispute between patients and their RMOs. This is an understandable concern, but how confident are we that the judge, a lawyer, will be able sufficiently to analyse conflicting expert medical opinion without the benefit of seeing that opinion put to challenge? Finally, it should be noted here that the Court of Appeal in *Wilkinson* gave conflicting opinions about the viability of mechanisms, other than that of judicial review, by which a patient could secure a full merits hearing of grievances grounded in both common law and Convention rights (this question is considered further in Chapter 12).

7.3.2.5 Restrictions on the general power

Section 63 does not apply in all situations. Certain procedures – the physical treatments – are taken out of the ambit of the general authority to treat in s. 63 and made subject to specific safeguards in ss. 57 and 58. The backbone of the safeguards system is the regime of second opinions that must be obtained for the provision of the treatments in question, which is administered by the Mental Health Act Commission (MHAC). This section looks at the legal requirements that apply to this system. The following section considers how the scheme actually works in practice.

Section 57, because of the serious and controversial nature of the treatments in question, applies both to patients who are liable to be detained and to informal patients, whether or not resident in hospital: s. 56(2). It does not, however, apply to detained patients excluded from the ambit of Part IV by virtue of s. 56(1) (see above). Jones (2006: 309) argues that there is no good reason for this omission, which appears to be an oversight. Section 57 covers surgical treatment that destroys brain tissue or the functioning of brain tissue (psychosurgery)(s. 57(1)(a)), and 'such other forms of treatment as may be specified for the purposes of this section by regulations made by the Secretary of State': s. 57(1)(b). To date, only one treatment has been so specified: 'the surgical implantation of hormones for the purposes of reducing male sex drive' ('chemical castration'), added by reg. 16, Mental Health (Hospital, Guardianship and Consent to Treatment) Regulations. 1983, SI 1983/893. There are powers to extend the ambit of s. 57 via the Code of Practice (s. 118(2)), but they have not been used.

Before either of these treatments can be given, it is necessary that the patient consent: s. 57(2). This means that treatment under s. 57 can neither be given to patients who lack capacity to consent to the treatment, nor those who actively refuse to consent. Section 57(2)(a) further provides that, before the treatment can be given, an independent doctor (known as a 'second opinion appointed doctor' or SOAD), and two other persons appointed by the Secretary of State for the purpose, certify that the patient has consented and understands the nature, purpose and likely effects of the treatment. The Secretary of State's powers have been delegated to the Mental Health Act Commission: s. 121(2)(a). The appointed persons need not be members of the Commission, but the Commission has stated that, in cases of requests for second opinions under s. 57 they will be (Department of Health and Social Security, 1984: para. 8(i)). It is also required, by s. 57(2)(b), that the SOAD certify that the treatment should be given because it is likely to alleviate the patient's condition or prevent its deterioration. Before so doing, the SOAD 'shall consult with' two other persons who have been professionally involved with the patient's treatment, one of whom must be a nurse and the other of whom neither a nurse nor a doctor: s. 57(3).

Section 58 is concerned with two types of treatment: ECT (inserted by reg. 16 of the 1983 Regulations into s. 58(1)(a)), and the administration of medicine to a patient by any means, at any time after three months has elapsed since the first time in that period of detention when the patient was given medicine for his mental disorder: s. 58(1)(b). Section 58(1)(b) is known as the 'three-month rule'. Its purpose is to protect patients from the continual administration of drugs under the general power in s. 63, if there is no obvious benefit to the patient in so doing. There can be only one three-month period in any one period of detention, and a period of detention is not interrupted by a change in the section under which the patient is detained (Department of Health, 1998i: para. 195) nor by the transfer or renewal of the authority to detain the patient (Department of Health and Social Security, 1984: para. 15), although such changes in the detail of a patient's continuing detention have been used (unlawfully) to justify the commencement of a new three-month period (Mental Health Act Commission, 1995: para. 3.8). The Secretary of State has powers to extend the three-month period by s. 58(2), although these have not been used. The MHAC has recommended that forced feeding should be brought under s. 58 (1997: para. 5.2.8), and is it difficult not to support this proposal.

Before either of these treatments is given, it must be certified either that the patient has consented and the RMO or SOAD has certified in writing both that the patient has consented and that the patient is capable of understanding the nature, purpose and likely effects of the treatment (s. 58(3)(a)), or that a SOAD (and not the RMO) has certified that the patient is not competent to consent, or has refused to consent, but that the treatment should be given because it is likely to alleviate the patient's condition or prevent its deterioration: s. 58(3)(b). Section 58 sits alongside the common law requirement, that the treatment must be in the best interests of its recipient, which must also be satisfied for the treatment to be lawful (*R v S and Ors, ex p B* [2006] EWCA Civ 28, per Lord Philips at para. 62). In *Wilkinson*, Hale, LJ held that the *Re C/Re MB* test of capacity applies to the determination of capacity under s. 58(3)(b) (para. 66), and it can be assumed that the replacement test now found in s. 2 of the Mental Capacity Act 2005 does too, although in *R v Dr SS and Dr AC, ex p PB* [2005] EWHC 86, Silber J held, *obiter*, that, because s. 58 requires a patient only to be 'capable' of understanding, the test 'is not whether the person *actually* understands' (para. 87, emphasis added); although this view was subsequently rejected by the Mental Health Act Commission (2005: para. 1.58), this is what the section says. In the case of treatment under s. 58(3)(b), the SOAD must also consult with a nurse and one other person, being neither a nurse nor a doctor concerned with the patient's treatment before issuing the certificate: s. 58(4). It was the existence of these safeguards, such that treatment under s. 58(3)(b) can only be given in 'very limited circumstances' (para. 128), that underpinned the decision of Silber J in *ex p PB*, that s. 58(3)(b) can be said to satisfy the requirement of Art. 8(2) of the Convention and that any breach of Art. 8(1) must be 'necessary in a democratic society . . . for the protection of health'.

By s. 59, a patient who consents to treatment under ss. 57 or 58 may consent to more than one treatment under the respective section, and to a 'treatment plan' that does not need to have a specified end point. MHAC policy is to limit all certificates given to between one and two years (Mental Health Act Commission, 2005: para. 4.60), and to one year for patients in high-security accommodation or in receipt of 'high dose or complex treatment plans' (Mental Health Act Commission, 1997: para. 5.2.3). A certificate signed by a SOAD following a request for a second opinion may be similarly open-ended, although the MHAC view is that a certificate authorising psychosurgery should be time-limited to eight weeks, and it has been said that time limitation is also likely in the context of drug treatments (Jones, 2003: 326). There is no definition of 'medicine' in the 1983 Act, but the MHAC view is that it 'will broadly encompass any substance intended to influence the mental disorder' (Department of Health and Social Security, 1984: para. 15). In *Croydon*, Hoffman LJ held that 'ordinary food in liquid form, such as would be used in tube feeding, is not a medicine within the meaning of s. 58' (at 687), although it is 'medical treatment' under s. 63. The MHAC has expressed the view that a placebo is not medicine and is therefore not caught by s. 58 (1999: para. 6.17). But this 'fails to address the reality of the situation which is that a placebo is offered to a patient as "medicine" which, hopefully will lead to an improvement in his or her condition' (Jones, 2006: 325) and, in light of the broad approach taken in *Croydon*, the better view is most probably that the treatment is 'medicine' for these purposes.

Consent to treatment may be retracted at any time: s. 60; treatment under s. 57 must then cease. Treatment under s. 58 may continue only if the safeguards in s. 58(3)(b) are first complied with, although there is a period of grace given by s. 62(2), during which treatment given under ss. 57 or 58 can continue, even though consent has been withdrawn, if the RMO 'considers that discontinuance of the treatment or of the treatment plan would cause serious suffering to the patient'. Section 61 provides that, in respect of treatment given in accordance with ss. 57 or 58(3)(b) (that is, treatment under that section in respect of which the patient has refused or is unable to consent), the RMO must report on the treatment and the patient's condition to the Secretary of State as part of the requirement of reports renewing the authority to detain under ss. 20, 41(6) or 49(3), as the case may be.

It has been a notable feature of the operation of the MHA 1983 that these statutory provisions have generated very little litigation. The reason for this is fairly clear, and it is that, under traditional judicial review principles, there has been no way effectively to challenge decisions taken under the authority of Part IV: the so-called '*Brady* approach'. This has, in turn, given rise to a culture in which often, for professionals and patients alike, adherence to the bureaucratic process – the completion of the relevant form (and sometimes not even that) – means that the treatment may be given. But the SOAD procedure was challenged in *Wilkinson*. W had been a detained patient for a number of decades and the 'three-month rule' had long since ceased to be relevant. Accordingly, the treatment fell under s. 58(1)(b). In the view of the RMO, W did not have capacity to make this treatment decision, and so it was necessary to go through the second opinion procedure provided for by s. 58(3)(b). Because the RMO was concerned that W's objections to the treatment would be of greater veracity if he were forewarned, it was arranged for the SOAD visit to be unannounced and for the first dose of treatment to be given immediately thereafter. Dr H was the SOAD in this case and he certified a treatment plan for a number of treatments of antipsychotic medicine to be given to W.

W challenged the substantive decisions of the RMO and the SOAD, as discussed above, and the discussion in the context of s. 63 is equally applicable to treatment under ss. 57 and 58. W also challenged the legality of the SOAD procedure more generally. This was done first by reference to Art. 6, on the basis that the decision to subject him to treatment by force constituted a determination of his civil rights, and the SOAD procedure did not afford the 'fair and public hearing' by an 'independent and impartial tribunal' required by Art. 6(1). Simon Brown LJ held that, if the SOAD procedure were the only mode of review of the decision of an RMO that was open to a patient, there would be a 'plain' breach of Art. 6(1), because the 'certification process ... could hardly be said to involve a fair and public hearing' (para. 35). As it is, and always has been, open to a patient to bring a tortious claim for assault in respect of past treatment, however, and as it had been held in *Wilkinson* that it is now also open to a patient to seek a full merits review of the legality of past or proposed future treatment, the requirements of Art. 6(1) were, in fact, satisfied (para. 34).

His lordship further held that anything less than a full merits review would constitute a breach of Art. 6 (para. 35), but also made clear that it 'does not ... entitle a mental patient in every case to challenge a treatment plan before being subjected to it'. Hale LJ, expressing the same view, explained that the 'RMO and SOAD are not determining his civil rights and liabilities. They are merely deciding to impose or authorise treatment in the belief that the statutory grounds for doing so exist' (para. 84). In the Scottish case of *M, Petitioner* 2003 SLT 219 (Outer House), M, a detained patient, argued that the administration of antipsychotic medication against his will was in breach of Art. 6, because it was a 'determination of his civil rights and obligations' (i.e. the common law right to refuse treatment), and because his RMO, who made that determination, was not 'an independent and impartial tribunal' as the Article requires. The court held (at 224) that Art. 6 is relevant to gate-keeping provisions, which regulate entry to, and continued membership of, a class of persons, because it is these decisions that 'determine' the rights that members of that class shall have. But it is not relevant to the substantive rights that domestic law provides for members of that class, because the entitlement or access to civil rights has already been determined at the point of initial, or continued, detention. This is how one should understand Simon Brown LJ's holding that the 'ambush' tactics, as used in *Wilkinson*, were not in breach of Art. 6 (para. 34). The main impact of this approach will be to focus the minds of litigants and their legal advisers instead on Arts. 3 and 8 and the 'medical necessity' test when framing objections to forced treatment.

The court in *Wilkinson* did take the opportunity to require a more rigorous approach to the SOAD procedure than had previously been followed. Simon Brown LJ referred to the advice given to SOADs by the Mental Health Act Commission. At the time, this told SOADs that, before certifying the treatment plan of the RMO, they should determine that although 'the treatment authorised may not be in accordance with the SOADs personal practice [it] should be reasonable in the opinion of the SOAD'. Similar advice is given in the Code of Practice (see para. 16.21). Simon Brown LJ, calling for 'a less deferential approach than appears to be the norm' (para. 33) from SOADs, made clear that, although a SOAD must, of course, 'pay regard' to the opinions of the RMO, 'that does not relieve him of the responsibility of forming his own independent judgment as to whether or not the treatment should be given' (para. 33, see also Brooke LJ at para. 49 and Hale LJ at para. 71), which is 'not merely approval of the RMO's decision on the basis that it is not manifestly unsound' (*R v S and Ors, ex p B* [2006] EWCA Civ 28 per Lord Philips at para. 68).

The role of the SOAD was again at issue in the later case of *R v Feggetter and MHAC, ex p JW* [2002] WL 498885, CA. In this case, the patient, JW, was in dispute with his RMO about the continuation of drug treatment in the form of antipsychotic medicine. JW had consented to such treatment in the past, but had withdrawn his consent, partly because of the unpleasant side effects of the medication and partly because he wanted a 'drug-free' period because he thought this might be beneficial for the investigation of various physical complaints from which he suffered. The RMO, nevertheless, determined to continue with the treatment despite JW's refusal, and so a SOAD visit was arranged at which the SOAD, Dr F, certified the RMO's treatment plan under s. 58(3)(b). The SOAD's reasons were not disclosed to JW, who sought permission for leave to bring an application for judicial review of the refusal of the SOAD to provide his reasons. That application was refused on the basis that there was no provision either on the face of the MHA or in the accompanying Code of Practice that required a SOAD to provide his or her reasons to the patient. On appeal, the Court of Appeal decided the point by reference to common law principles. Specifically, Brooke LJ held that earlier case law on the question of what fairness requires of an administrative decision had established that there is a class of administrative decision 'where the subject-matter is an interest so highly regarded by the law (for example, personal liberty) that fairness requires that reasons, at least for particular decisions, be given as of right' (per Brooke, LJ at para. 24). Following the decision in *Wilkinson*, his lordship had 'no hesitation in holding that a decision to administer medical treatment to a competent non-consenting adult patient falls into this category' (at para. 25). Hence, Brooke, LJ concluded that (para. 34):

fairness demands that a SOAD should give written and adequate reasons for his opinion when certifying under section 58 of the Mental Health Act 1983 that a detained patient should be given medication against his will, and that these reasons should be disclosed to the patient unless the SOAD or the RMO considers that such disclosure would be likely to cause serious harm to the physical or mental health of the patient or any other person.

This is because it is SOAD decisions that sanction 'the violation of the autonomy of a competent adult patient' (para. 25). Of course, it must be right that reasons need not be given if the patient does not have the capacity to understand them, but this will rarely be the case, even where the capacity to consent or refuse is lacking. The reference to the likelihood of 'serious harm' of the types described, justifying the non-disclosure to the patient, mirrors the wording of s. 7(1) of the Access to Medical Reports Act 1988 and art. 5(1) of the Data Protection (Subject Access Modifications) (Health) Order 2000. Following the general tenor of the judgment in this case, however, it may well be that the reasons for non-disclosure may themselves be subject to review.

This, though, is not to open the floodgates to applications for leave for judicial review by patients aggrieved by the operation of s. 58. Brooke LJ (at para. 29) also made clear that:

The law will not require a SOAD to dot every 'i' and cross every 't' when giving reasons for his opinion. So long as he gives his reasons clearly on what he reasonably regards as the substantive points on which he formed his clinical judgment, this will suffice ... Unless a patient can show a real prospect of establishing that a SOAD has not addressed any substantive point which he should have addressed, or that there is some material error underlying the reasons that he gave, the court will not grant permission [for legal challenge].

The court further determined that the SOAD's reasons should be conveyed to the patient by the RMO. Brooke LJ pointed out that the RMO was in the best position to determine if disclosure was likely to cause significant harm to the patient. He then went on to lay out the appropriate procedure (paras. 32 and 33):

In future, therefore, the SOAD should send a statement of his reasons to the RMO or to the hospital ... together with any opinion he may have on the desirability of withholding them from the patient on "serious harm" grounds. The RMO should then make them available to the patient to read, unless it is a case in which reliance can properly be placed on the "serious harm" exemption from disclosure ... The reasons should be prepared and passed to the RMO for disclosure as soon as practicable.

These need not, however, be given to the patient before the administration of the treatment.

Potter LJ expressly stated that it was not necessary to consider Convention rights, specifically Art. 8, to decide this case (para. 50). Brooke LJ, as mentioned above, held that the case was decidable on ordinary public law principles. He did, however, following a reference to *Wilkinson*, hold that 'With the coming into force of the Human Rights Act 1998 the time has come, in my judgment, for this court to declare that fairness requires that a decision by a SOAD which sanctions the violation of the autonomy of a competent adult patient should be accompanied by reasons' (para. 25). Brooke LJ thus rather ran together the common law principles and the patient's Convention rights. Sedley LJ, by contrast, was more careful to keep the two sources of law separate. For him, the common law's requirement that powers given by legislation must be used fairly was 'the engine of modern public law, and there is no reason to believe that its force is spent' (at para. 44); the present case is an example of its continued use and development. Moreover, on this particular question, in some ways, the common law offers better protection than the Convention: for example, although it is debatable whether Art. 6 – which does not apply in a non-judicial setting – applies to the operation of the SOAD system, the common law rules about fairness and due process do, which means that 'the difficult argument about the point at which Article 6 bites on the s. 58 process is of only secondary relevance' (para. 46).

In general terms, Sedley LJ was of the view that 'Given the present divergences between the common law and the Convention ... care is required ... in mapping the route by which their respective standards and controls are to be imported into public law functions' (para. 49). He also pointed out, however, that the Human Rights Act provides both for the protection of Convention rights *qua* Convention rights (in s. 6 of the 1998 Act) and for the fusion of Convention rights with common law (in s. 3 of the 1998 Act), in which latter case 's. 3 ceases to be a supplanting mechanism and instead settles in as a strong canon of construction' (para. 48). As far as the present case was concerned, the effect of this is that s. 132 of the MHA, which places a duty on hospital managers to inform detained patients about their legal status, its implications, and how it can be challenged, should be interpreted as requiring that a patient be informed of the reasons for the imposition of treatment without consent under s. 58. Moreover, 'Even if s. 132 were not there, exactly the same result would in my opinion be arrived at through s. 58 itself, because what matters for s. 3 purposes is not the particular configuration of the statute but whether (a) its subject matter attracts Convention rights and, if it does, (b) its terms nevertheless block their application' (*ibid.*). Hence, in the view of His Lordship, the case was proven to the benefit of JW both under common law principles and as a breach of Art. 8 of the Convention. Subsequent to the decision in *Feggetter*, the MHAC issued new Guidance to RMOs (Mental Health Act Commission, 2002; see MHAC, 2006a) and SOADs (MHAC, 2002a; see MHAC, 2006b). It is to the operation of the SOAD system that we now turn.

7.3.3 The operation of the scheme of second opinions and reports

The second opinion scheme is operated by the Mental Health Act Commission. It organises the provision of the SOADs required to authorise treatment, who will visit the hospital in question with two other colleagues. The MHAC also reports biennially on the operation of the scheme. The second opinion scheme was one of the major innovations brought in by the MHA 1983. It came as part of a compromise deal with the medical profession, which gave psychiatrists an express legal right to treat without consent for the first time, at the expense of being 'encumbered' in the exercise of that right 'by the erection of a complex and intricate system of formal safeguards for the protection of patients which represents the high water mark of legalism in the Act' (Unsworth, 1987: 324). Section 57 in particular, which requires the RMO to seek a second opinion even when the patient consents to the treatment is seen as 'a significant intrusion into the doctor-patient relationship' (1987: 325). There is no doubt that the regime is bureaucratic, and on the face of it at least, restrictive of the autonomy of the psychiatric profession.

Information for RMOs, SOADs and others with responsibilities for running the regime of second opinions and reports is to be found in the revised Code of Practice (Department of Health and Welsh Office, 1999), the Memorandum (Department of Health, 1998i) on various parts of the Act, and MHAC guidance (Department of Health and Social Security, 1984), and guidance notes on specific issues, which were revised in April 2006 (see Mental Health Act Commission, 2006). The Code of Practice provides that, although overall responsibility for compliance with the requirements of the Act rests with hospital managers (Department of Health and Welsh Office, 1999: para. 16.23), '[t]he patient's RMO is personally responsible for ensuring that Part IV procedures are followed in relation to that patient' (para. 16.24), including ensuring that requests for a SOAD visit are made to the MHAC, and making the arrangements for such visits. When a RMO is considering the use of any of the treatments to which ss. 57 or 58 apply, the first step is to consult the patient and seek his or her consent

(1999: paras. 16.7, 16.9, 16.11). The patient will only be able to give a valid consent if competent to do so. As discussed above, the phraseology used in the Act is that, to be competent, the patient must be 'capable of understanding the nature, purpose and likely effects' of the proposed treatment (ss. 57(2)(a), 58(3)(a)), to which the Code of Practice adds (1999: para. 15.10) that the requirement is that the patient be capable of understanding the principal risks and benefits of the treatment and of not having it, and refers to the test for capacity laid down in *Re C* (now in s. 2 of the Mental Capacity Act 2005), which, as seen above, was held to apply in this context by Hale LJ in *Wilkinson*. NICE guidance (2003: para. 1.4) states that a 'valid consent... enabled by the provision of full and appropriate information' is required for ECT, and the Code of Practice (Department of Health and Welsh Office, 1999: para. 16.10) advises that patients should be provided with information leaflets in addition to the RMO personally seeking consent. The MHAC produces a series of such leaflets for patients. It is not clear whether the Code's requirement of informed consent would be enough, as a matter of law, to raise a greater entitlement to information in respect of ECT compared to other treatments: ECT is a serious intervention, but not necessarily more serious than the other treatments covered by these sections. Consent, of course, depends on having capacity to give it (see also *R v Mental Health Act Commission, ex p X* (1988) 9 BMLR 77 discussed in Chapter 10).

When a valid consent is forthcoming for treatments under s. 58, the RMO need not seek a second opinion. He or she must complete the appropriate form as required by reg. 16, 1983 Regulations, which is Form 38. This form requires the RMO to state that the requirements of s. 58(3)(a) have been met, namely that the patient has the capacity to consent and has, in fact, consented to the treatment, and to give a description of the treatment or treatment plan comprising either the proposed maximum number of doses of ECT (Department of Health and Welsh Office, 1999: para. 16.9a) or drugs, proposed by BNF class rather than name, the method of administration (whether oral or depot antipsychotics, for example) and the dose range, including whether the proposed dosages are above BNF recommended maxima (1999: para. 16.14). The MHAC reports (1997: para. 5.2.2) that its advice to SOADs, when a second opinion is required, is to specify, on the appropriate form (Form 39, see below), the number of preparations authorised from a BNF category, along with the upper dose limit, because this 'allows SOADs to set a clear ceiling on what is authorised' whilst still allowing scope for 'slight changes' to be made by the RMO (*ibid.*). When particularly problematic drugs are to be given – the MHAC refers to Clozaril (the trade name in the UK of the antipsychotic drug clozapine, which carries a substantial risk of serious, even fatal, blood disorders, and cannot be given unless the patient's blood is tested on a weekly basis, so is only used when other antipsychotic medicine has been tried and failed – Lacey, 1996: 95), and newly available antipsychotic medicines not yet in the BNF – 'the individual name of the drug and a specific dose range must be recorded' (MHAC, 1997: para. 5.2.2). The clear implication of this undoubtedly good practice in relation to Form 39 is that patients who consent and so are given treatment under Form 38 do not have these protections. Although the MHAC has powers under s. 61 of the 1983 Act to time-limit any treatment given under Form 39 (Mental Health Act Commission, 2005: para. 4.58), this depends on the RMO informing the MHAC that treatment has been given, or a period or treatment renewed, using Form 39, which does not happen in a quarter of cases (MHAC, 2003: 10.28), so it is clear that, even under Form 39, patients are not protected from the administration of inappropriate treatment. In any case, because each BNF category includes a number of different drugs (see earlier), under the current requirements, the discretion of the RMO to switch drugs within a category, exceed recommended doses, practice polypharmacy or any combination of the three, is largely unfettered. There is force in Richardson's point that the Code of Practice, at this point, lets patients down by giving RMOs scope to adhere to the letter, but not the spirit, of the legislative scheme to the extent that it may be questionable whether a patient's consent can really be regarded as genuine (1993: 243). Such concerns are sharpened by the 'prevalence of bad practice' in respect of recording consent or conclusions about capacity in patients' notes (Mental Health Act Commission, 2001: para. 2.20; 2005: Figure 54), because, without accurate notes, it is very difficult to verify that any given individual's treatment is within the law.

Concerns about Form 38 and treatment under s. 58(3)(a) are compounded by the fact that there is no statutory procedure for reviewing the use of Form 38, and although the Code of Practice urges that its use be reviewed regularly at local level, with a new form being completed at each review, providing that it continues to be appropriate to do so (Department of Health and Welsh Office, 1999, para. 16.35), and although these forms are regularly examined on general MHAC visits, there is an obvious temptation for an RMO to deem a consenting patient competent to do so, to avoid needing to instigate the SOAD procedure. In the case of s. 57 patients, as already mentioned, consent is a prerequisite to any treatment, but even when a patient does consent, there will still be the need for a second opinion. This is not the case under s. 58. The efficacy of judgments of capacity is, therefore, crucial. As Fennel puts it, '[i]t scarcely upholds the principle of self-determination if a RMO accepts the consent of a patient who does not understand the decision being made, or who has not been given information about the treatment's nature, purpose and effects' (1996: 194). Although there has been no systematic research into the reality of these concerns, the most recent MHAC Report, in common with its predecessors, recounts that failure to comply with the Code of Practice in respect of Form 38 is common, with forms not completed by the current RMO, and patients being given treatments not mentioned on the form (Mental Health Act Commission, 2005: Figure 54). PRN ('as required') medication is a particular concern because this can, in practice, mean regular high doses or 'cocktails' being given. The MHAC has suggested that the 1983 Act provides 'insufficient protection' for patients from the use of high doses and cocktails in the first three months of a period of detention (2005: 4.53). Over the year 2004–5, 11 per cent (899) of SOAD visits were concerned with patients in receipt of medicine dosages in excess of the BNF, as a result of which, 82.1 per cent (738 cases) of treatment plans proceeded unchanged, although there was partial change in 15.4 per cent (139) of cases and significant change in 2.5 per cent (22) (2005: 4.54). In addition, there is often a lack of written evidence that patients have given consent based on discussions with the doctor, and 'Commissioners frequently see patients who are deemed to be consenting but whose medical and nursing notes throw doubt on their capacity to do so' (Mental Health Act Commission, 2001: para. 2.20). It seems that often 'compliance has been taken as consent or that patients deemed consenting have little awareness of the nature of the treatment' (MHAC, 1997: para. 5.2.1.). A graphic example of the way in which institutional practices can conflate compliance and consent is provided by the relative dearth of requests for a SOAD emanating from Broadmoor hospital in two years after the implementation of the MHA 1983 (Richardson, 1993: 244). During this period, 89 requests came from Broadmoor, with an average patient population of 494 individuals, compared with 413 requests from Rampton and 262 from Ashworth, with average populations of 590 and 562 respectively. It transpired that, at Broadmoor, a patient would only be considered for transfer or discharge if accepting treatment.

For treatment under s. 57 or under s. 58 without the consent of the patient, a SOAD team visit will be necessary. It is the RMO's responsibility to make, or ensure the making of, the arrangements for these visits, which entails contacting the MHAC, and making sure that the relevant information is available to the team on arrival. When the team arrives, the SOAD must first check that the patient's detention documents are in order (if the patient is not lawfully detained, treatment under Part IV cannot be given), and review the patient's clinical notes and the treatment plan at issue. There should also be consultation with the patient and RMO, and others who have relevant information, before the treatment is authorised. Before a RMO can give treatment under s. 57, the SOAD and other MHAC appointees must fill in Form 37: s. 64(2) and Sch. 1, 1983 Regulations. Information required by this form includes the type of treatment that is to be given, the fact that the patient has given consent and has the legal capacity to do so, and that it is expected that the treatment will have a beneficial effect on the patient's condition. If treatment under s. 58 is given without the consent of the patient, the SOAD team must complete Form 39. Similar information is required as with Form 37, tailored though to the specific requirements of the relevant subsections of s. 58.

The completion of these forms provides the legal authority for treatment to be given. They require the signatories to certify that the requirements of ss. 57 and 58 have been complied with. Completed forms must be returned to the MHAC, irrespective of whether or not the SOAD authorises the treatment in question. A further level of paperwork has been instigated by the MHAC. Form MHAC 2 applies to treatment given under s. 58(3)(b). It must be completed and returned to the MHAC by the SOAD, along with Form 39. This form requires the provision of a greater detail than the forms applicable under the 1983 Regulations, covering: the case history of the patient; the opinions formed about the patient and the treatment by the SOAD; whether the patient consented to the treatment; whether the SOAD required the RMO to amend the proposed treatment or treatment plan in any way; approved dosages of drugs, particularly if above normal levels (as set by the BNF); whether emergency treatment has been given under s. 62 before the SOAD visit.

Finally, Form MHAC 1 must be completed by the RMO, following treatment given under s. 58(3)(b) pursuant to the requirements of s. 61, which requires the RMO to report on treatment given under ss. 57(2) or 58(3)(b) and the patient's condition to the MHAC, in the case of restricted patients, six months after the commencement of the restriction direction or order and thereafter annually (s. 61(2)), and, in the case of other patients, on the occasion of the renewal of the authority to detain: s. 61(1). The MHAC reviews the information provided and will organise a new SOAD visit when appropriate (Department of Health and Welsh Office, 1999: para. 16.36). The information required by Form MHAC 1 largely duplicates that obtained from Form 39, although, in addition, the RMO is required to detail treatments that have been given under s. 58(3)(b), progress made by the patient and the RMO's future intentions regarding further treatment under that section. Despite all of this paperwork, however, the argument made out above, in the context of Form 38, is equally applicable to Forms 37 and 39, and the MHAC forms. That is, it can be argued that the restriction that the requirements of these forms actually places on medical discretion to use potentially dangerous treatments is minimal. In any case, many MHAC1s are either not returned to the MHAC, or are returned with incomplete data (Mental Health Act Commision, 1997: para. 5.17; 2005: para. 4.49), just as many Forms 38 and 39 are also often deficient or confusing in a variety of ways (2001: paras. 2.64, 2.65; 2005: para. 4.59).

Treatment is infrequently given under s. 57. There have only been four applications for a second opinion in respect of proposed hormone treatments under s. 57(1)(b) in the lifetime of the Act: only one of these has resulted in treatment, and there have been no applications since 1988 (Jones, 2006: 311). There is no mystery about why this is the case, however: the most commonly used sexual suppressant is given orally, not surgically (Fennell, 1996: 188), and in *ex p X* it was decided that the section did not extend to hormone analogues, but only to hormones and synthetic hormones, on the grounds that the former are not composed of naturally occurring substances. This left the hormone analogue goserelin outside the scope of the section, even though it is one hundred times more powerful than the hormones and synthetic hormones that are covered by it. Memorably, putting the letter of the statute before its spirit, Stuart Smith LJ held that '[i]f Parliament passes legislation on the control of leopards, it is not to be presumed that leopards include tigers on the basis that they are larger and fiercer'. The court also decided that there must be some sort of incision before it can be said that there has been a 'surgical implant' (Fennell, 1988). The practical result of this is that goserelin and other powerful sexual suppressants can be given under s. 63 for three months, after which time they are most probably covered by s. 58 as 'medicine' (*Croydon*). Psychosurgery has continued to fill a residual, although diminishing, place in treatment for mental disorder. There were only seven applications under s. 57(1)(a) in 2003–5 (Mental Health Act Commision, 2005: para. 4.78), down from 30 in 1995–7, and 64 in 1989–1 (MHAC, 1997: para. 5.3). Interestingly, s. 57 was first used in this way in respect of a detained patient only in the mid-1990s.

Section 58 is much more frequently used, as might be expected. In 2004–5, there were 10,500 referrals for a second opinion for treatments under this section, of which 8,558 were for drug treatments and 1,653 for ECT, with 89 referrals requesting permission to give both treatments (Mental Health Act Commission, 2005: Figures 59 and 60).

The number of requests for a second opinion has increased year on year since the 1983 Act came into force: there were 2,146 requests for a second opinion for drug treatments in 1983–5, rising to 6,195 in 1993–5, 10,848 in 1977–99 and 16,931 in 2003–5 (*ibid.*). The trend for ECT is more complex, rising from 1,886 in 1983–5 to 4,426 in 1997–9, but falling back to 3,811 in 2003–5 (*ibid.*). This may be the effect of the NICE guidelines, published in 2003, extolling a more limited use of ECT (see earlier). The overwhelming majority of referrals (89 per cent in 1997–9) are made in respect of the treatment of mental illness. The numbers for mental impairment, severe mental impairment and psychopathic disorder are of the order of 1–2 per cent, with 5 per cent having a dual diagnosis (MHAC, 1999: para. 6.27). There are clear distinctions along the lines of gender. Women tend to be referred for ECT or drug treatments in equal numbers, whereas men are much more likely to be referred for drug treatments than ECT, and this goes some way, given the rising use of drug treatments and the falling use of ECT, to explaining why the number of second opinions sought in respect of male patients rose from 55 to 59 per cent in 2003–5 (MHAC, 2005: para. 4.64). Men comprise 55 per cent of the total hospital population (Commission for Healthcare Audit and Inspection, MHAC, CSIP and NIMHE, 2005: 15) There are also significant variations by the race of the patients. Black patients are 92 per cent likely to be referred for drug treatments whereas white patients were only around 67 per cent likely, and Asian and others, 75 per cent likely (MHAC, 1999: Table 9). It is probable though, that racial variations under s. 58 are a function of gender differences (MHAC, 1997: para. 5.2): 'over 70 per cent of Black patients referred to for a Second Opinion were male.' This, of course, raises another set of issues about why it is that there are a high number of black men in mental hospitals (see Chapter 4, and see Commission for Healthcare Audit and Inspection, MHAC, CSIP and NIMHE, 2005).

Mental Health Act commission biennial reports have continually referred to a number of practical problems with the operation of the second opinion scheme. The requirement to consult a non-medical person 'professionally concerned' (ss. 57(3), 58(4)) with patient's treatment, for example, is not always easy to satisfy. Social workers and occupational therapists are most frequently consulted, although, on occasion, inappropriate persons are consulted such as the 'ward domestic' (MHAC, 1995: para. 5.13) or a hospital secretary (MHAC, 1997: para. 5.2.2); there may even be no consultation at all (Fennell, 1996: 206). The idea behind the consultation requirement was that it would bring a genuine multidisciplinary dimension to the second opinion process. The reality is that the requirement is little more than 'legalism', in the negative sense of a procedure without a purpose, 'seen as a tiresome formality' (Fennell, 1996: 208) by RMOs. It is not only these 'peripheral' consultations that are a cause for concern. The Code of Practice (Department of Health and Welsh Office, 1999: para. 16.33) provides that consultations should 'only in exceptional cases' be by telephone, and yet Fennell, in an extensive piece of research, found that, as between RMOs and SOADs, 'telephone consultation appeared to be more the norm than the exception' (1996: 204). This does not necessarily render the consultation process deficient, although it does help to raise the suspicion that those operating the scheme are prepared to cut corners on grounds of convenience.

Fennell's research helps provide a more complete picture of the patterns of the SOAD system than that found in the MHAC Reports. Fennell analysed all MHAC2s returned during the period December 1991–August 1992, and MHAC1s returned to the Commission between January and March 1992, with totals of 1,009 and 232 respectively. This gave data about the practices of a large number (276) of hospitals of all types. The majority of applications for a SOAD visit were made in respect of patients held under Part II (839, or 83 per cent, with 164, or 17 per cent, of applications made in respect of patients held under Part III). The overwhelming majority of Part II patients were detained under s.3 on grounds of mental illness (963 applications), of whom around half (445) had a diagnosis of schizophrenic psychosis, the other most common diagnoses being affective psychosis (277) and depressive disorders (216).

In terms of gender, race and age, Fennell found much the same patterns within the treatment of detained patients during this period as those we have discussed above. Women comprised 55 per cent of the sample (566) and men 45 per cent (443). Applications for drug treatment and ECT were about even, but ECT was overwhelmingly a 'woman's treatment': 73 per cent of all requests for a second opinion for ECT were for female patients (197) diagnosed as suffering from affective psychosis or depressive disorder; 77 per cent (167 out of 216) of those diagnosed as suffering from depressive disorder were women, of whom almost all (197, or 93.4 per cent) were given ECT. The gender differential was not just a function of diagnosis, however: of men diagnosed as depressive, 85.7 per cent were given ECT. A similar pattern emerged in respect of affective disorders and schizophrenia (198). The differences became even more marked for elderly patients, because, although ECT was the most likely treatment for both sexes, many more elderly women than elderly men were detained. Young males diagnosed as schizophrenic were, however, markedly more likely than older men to be given ECT: 63 per cent (22 out of 35) of men receiving this treatment were in the 21–35 age group (198), and of the 17 men aged 21–30, five were Afro-Caribbean (*ibid.*), which tallies with the findings of earlier research that black people are more likely to be diagnosed as schizophrenic than white people (Lewis *et al.*, 1990; Berthoud and Nazroo, 1997; Cope, 1989). The overwhelming majority of males diagnosed as schizophrenic, though, were likely to be the subject of a second opinion for drug treatments (86.4 per cent, or 241 out of 279: 198). This reflects the general pattern that men are more likely than women to be given drug treatments: 61 per cent of all such requests for a SOAD were for male patients; although younger patients of both sexes were more likely to be given such treatments, the 'vast majority' (200) for antipsychotic medicines.

A worrying feature revealed by Fennell's research was the willingness of SOADs to certify drug treatment plans that exceeded BNF recommended doses or utilised polypharmacy. Both MHAC1s and MHAC2s showed that 'by far the most common prescribing combination was antipsychotics from both categories 4.2.1 and 4.2.2 together with anticholinergic drugs for side effects' (202), and 56 per cent of all MHAC2 cases followed the above pattern, although more than one antipsychotic medicine was authorised by the SOAD in a higher percentage – 73 per cent – of cases (202). In short, polypharmacy was the norm. No doubt, there are variations in the prescribing practices of different hospitals and different doctors, although the evidence shows that such differences are relatively slight. Fraser and Hepple (1992), for example, found that psychiatric drugs are administered at similar levels at Broadmoor and at a hospital in Newcastle that provides non-secure accommodation: two thirds of patients in both institutions were receiving two or more psychotropic drugs, although administration by depot was more common in Broadmoor. This research did show, however, that women diagnosed as psychopathic were more likely to be given drug treatments than their male counterparts, and patients in the special care unit at Broadmoor were pre-scribed higher dosages than patients housed elsewhere. More recent research (Tavernor *et al.*, 2000) confirms that the use of high dosages of neuroleptics remains common, although it also casts doubt on the therapeutic efficacy of high doses. Parker *et al.* (2002) found that 25 per cent of patients in one forensic secure unit were being treated by polypharmacy, rendering 16 per cent on high dosage levels, but as no single individ-ual drug was administered at levels above the BNF recommended maximum dose, the clinical teams did not view their practices as problematic. Campbell *et al.* (1998) found that 13 per cent (81 out of 622) patients were being given two or more antipsychotics. The charity Age Concern (BBC *News*, 23 July 2001) has expressed concern at practices at the opposite end of the system to the high-security hospitals. The use of sedatives and antipsychotics has increased markedly in recent years in nursing and residential homes, with significant increase, in particular, in the use of atypical antipsychotics, from 252,700 prescriptions for people over the age of 60 in 1999, to 428,000 in 2000. The 'chemical cosh', it seems, whereby drugs are used to control and manage rather than treat patients, is alive and well. Certainly, recent research has shown that much of this drug treatment is 'suboptimal' (Oborne *et al.*, 2003).

In Fennell's research, it was unusual (eight cases) for a SOAD to express concern about polypharmacy, and in only two cases was approval time-limited (1996: 203). Apparently, it was not until a treatment plan involved the use of drugs from four or five BNF categories that SOADs would raise a query. In only 36 cases (3.6 per cent) was Form 39 withheld by the SOAD, either because the technical requirements of the Act had in some way not been complied with, or because of diagnostic concerns or, infre-quently, because the SOAD took the view that the situation was not so serious as to war-rant overruling the refusal to consent of the patient in question. In 13 cases, the SOAD suggested a more interventionist plan than that proposed by the RMO. Overall, the RMO and SOAD were in agreement in around 96 per cent of cases (211), a statistic that has been repeatedly given by the MHAC (1985: para. 11.4; 1987: 22; 1989: 5; 1991: 31; 1999: para. 6.26). In the two most recent reports, the SOAD required significant change to the treatment plan in 3 per cent (Mental Health Act Commission, 2003: Figure 27) and 2.3 per cent (MHAC, 2005: Figure 63) of cases respectively. The Code of Practice accurately captures what has traditionally been seen as the role of the SOAD, which is not to provide a 'second opinion' as such, but rather to decide 'whether the proposed treatment is reasonable in the light of the general consensus of appropriate treatment for such a condition' (Department of Health and Welsh Office, 1999: para. 16.21). The responsibility of the SOAD, therefore, has not been to 'agree' with the specific treatment plan in question, but to be satisfied that it comes within the bounds of treatment that would be given in the circumstances in question by a responsible body of medical opinion. It is not clear how this scheme – which amounts to a statutory version of the *Bolam* approach – can be said 'to protect the patient's rights' as the Code of Practice claims (1999, para. 16.20). Although patients may make a complaint about their treatment (see Chapter 12), there is no appeal against the decision of a SOAD on the face of the 1983 Act. Small wonder, then, that the 'deferential attitude' criticised by Simon Brown LJ in *Wilkinson*, and which the Court of Appeal sought in that case and subsequently to shake up (see above), had developed around the SOAD process.

As far as the SOAD regime is concerned, then, it can be argued that 'the new legalism', as it operated after the coming into force of the 1983 Act, was something of a chimera. In terms of the frame of reference set by the medicalism–legalism debate, it can be said that medicalism remained dominant. A decade ago, Fennell concluded that, '[a]lthough the 1983 Act is often described as representing a return to legalism, it builds on the basic framework of discretionary powers in the 1959 Act' (1996: 181), and there is no convincing evidence that the situation has changed markedly in the intervening years. Moreover, because the system depends on psychiatrists to police psychiatrists, the issue is not only 'discretion', but *medical* discretion. How this was ever seen as 'legalism' is open to question (Rose, 1985) and, in practice, the SOAD system has done little to protect patients from overenthusiastic treatment regimes or abuses of their legal rights.

In 1983, the new legalism, as explained above, found a legislative voice against the backdrop of jaundice about the curative potential of medicalised psychiatry and the failure of the benevolent aspirations behind the 1959 Act. Nowhere is this view to be found better expressed than in Jefferys and Blom-Cooper's oft-quoted foreword to Gostin's *A Human Condition* (1975: 6):

Optimism has given way to scepticism if not pessimism. We are more aware of the complexities of human behaviour, of the unintended and unwelcome side-effects of well-intentioned statutory provision, of the differences in interest and outlook that lie behind an apparent consensus of approach to the treatment of the mentally ill.

By the end of the millennium, there was as good a reason to be sceptical about the solution as there had been about the original problem. The response of the Mental Health Bills of 2002 and 2004 had been to reintroduce, for consultation, the original solution, with second opinions to be given not by SOADs, who would not longer feature in the revised scheme, but by multidisciplinary tribunals to be called mental health tribunals. The reform proposals published in 2006, however, dropped this proposal: it seems that the SOAD system is to continue in more or less its present form. In this case, the issue is to make this system work the best it can. The decisions in *Wilkinson*, *Feggetter*, and the subsequent case law change have made some moves in this direction, but law is not really the key here. The MHAC guidance to RMOs and SOADs (2006a; 2006b) must, if it is to be successful, effect significant cultural change in professional attitudes. In the short term, however, legalism and medicalism share a common enemy, namely a government policy that prioritises issues of control. Of those elements of the reform proposals that have survived into 2006, the proposed adoption of a broad definition of 'mental disorder', together with the dropping of the treatability requirement that currently applies to mental impairment and psychopathic disorder, between them widen the constituency for the administration of treatment without consent, in ways that are controversial (see preface). There is little doubt that the current definition of 'medical treatment' is sufficiently broad to enable measures to control and manage patients who, by medical criteria, are untreatable. This makes it difficult to understand the statutory language of 'medical treatment' other than as a metaphor for the social control of the putatively dangerous. How easily can 'medicalism' or 'legalism' prosper in this political climate?

7.4 Emergency measures: treatment or control?

As noted at Chapter 3, there are relatively high levels of violence in psychiatric facilities. To the extent that patient violence is predictable, attempts by nursing staff to administer medication is a key indicator, although lack of respect for patients and poor communication skills on the part of staff (National Task Force on Violence Against Social Care Staff, 2001: para. 1.4), environmental factors, such as overcrowding, disruption, poor patient mix and poor relations between patients (Mental Health Act Commission, 2001: para. 4.33), also contribute. This, in turn, affects staff retention, which increases the likelihood of further disruption. Violence, however, is not the only way in which an emergency situation may manifest. A depressive patient may refuse treatment to the point of putting his or her life in danger, for example. In addition to the administration of treatment, the range of emergency responses also comprises the practices of 'restraint' and 'seclusion'.

7.4.1 Emergency treatment

The MHA 1983 provides for emergency treatment in s. 62(1):

Sections 57 and 58 above shall not apply to any treatment—

(a) which is immediately necessary to save the patient's life, or

(b) which (not being irreversible) is immediately necessary to prevent a serious deterioration of his condition, or

(c) which (not being irreversible or hazardous) is immediately necessary to alleviate serious suffering by the patient, or

(d) which (not being irreversible or hazardous) is immediately necessary and represents the minimum interference necessary to prevent the patient from behaving violently or being a danger to himself or others.

The disapplication of ss. 57 and 58 means that the treatment of detained patients can be given as though under s. 63, that is, without the consent of the patient. Because s. 57

covers both detained and informal patients, as a matter of law, this seems to entail that the latter may be given emergency treatment, which would otherwise have been covered by that section, under s. 62. In practice, however, the treatments covered by s. 57 are not emergency treatments. The practical effect of this is that s. 62 only applies in reality to detained patients. The scope of s. 62 is limited to treatment that is immediately and minimally necessary, which has been defined tightly at common law in *Devi v West Midlands AHA* [1980] 7 CL 44 (HC). There is no other limitation on life-saving treatment, but for lesser emergencies, the treatment must not be 'irreversible', or 'irreversible and hazardous', as the case may be. These terms are defined in s. 62(3). Treatment is classified as 'irreversible' if it has unfavourable irreversible physical or psychological consequences, and 'hazardous' if it entails significant physical hazard. Although all physical treatments potentially carry the risk of unfavourable irreversible consequences, it is unlikely that the emergency administration of clinically indicated drugs, or ECT, would be so classified by a court, or else s. 62 would be otiose. These treatments are hazardous, in the sense that they may have unwanted detrimental effects, but the definition of this term is limited to significant, physical hazards. Treatments under s. 57 are more problematic, in theory, but in practice, it is most unlikely that the treatments covered by that section would be given in an emergency: as we have seen, its application to hormone therapy is, in reality, non-existent, and psychosurgery is relatively rarely practised, and never in an emergency situation. In its third biennial report, the MHAC stated that it was unusual for drugs to be given in an emergency situation, but more common for ECT to be given, usually pending a SOAD visit (1989: para. 7.6(j)). That this continues to be the case is borne out by subsequent research, which found that the use of s. 62 to provide treatment prior to the giving of a second opinion is recorded on 11 per cent of MHAC2s; of 116 such cases, 112 involved ECT (usually one dose), overwhelmingly for women patients suffering from depressive disorders (Fennell, 1996: 199). The reason for the treatment was to save the life of the patient or prevent a serious deterioration in his or her condition (1996: 200). Around 60 per cent of patients were given ECT within a week of detention under the Act, which seems to indicate that s. 62 is often used for informal, competent, refusing patients who are sectioned for this purpose – but this is not always the case. The MHAC has long reported concern that s. 62 has been used to justify the emergency treatment of informal patients or those excluded from the ambit of Part IV by s. 56 (1993: para. 7.12; 1997: para. 5.2.7), but such treatment is unlawful unless covered by the common law. It has also voiced concerns that s. 62 is being used by psychiatrists purportedly to authorise a course of drug or ECT treatment (Mental Health Act Commission, 1999: para. 6.22). The preferred view is that the use of s. 62 indicates the need to have a treatment plan authorised under s. 58(3)(b). It is not appropriate to use s. 62 repeatedly to treat a non-consenting patient.

The patterns of emergency treatment under the authority of common law are unknown, although it seems that antipsychotic medicine may be used relatively more frequently than under s. 62 (MHAC, 1995: para. 5.14). The general common law principles – that no treatment may be given to an adult without consent, unless the patient lacks capacity, in which case, he or she may be treated without consent to protect life, health or well-being – have been discussed above. If the patient is temporarily incom-petent, the principle of necessity is of more circumscribed application than it is in the treatment of permanently incapacitated patients, and will authorise only such treat-ment as is immediately necessary: *Devi, Re T*. These same principles apply in emergency situations: indeed, cases such as *Re T* did involve emergency situations. Moreover, it is clear that a refusal of treatment made by an adult when competent should continue to bind if the patient loses competence: in *Re T*, the Court of Appeal accepted the validity of an anticipatory refusal, and in the House of Lords' decision in *Airedale NHS Trust* v *Bland* [1993] 2 WLR 316, Lords Mustill, Goff and Keith (at 393, 367, and 360–1 respect-ively) all accepted that a healthcare provider would be guilty of battery if he or she were to treat a patient who had given a valid anticipatory refusal. If a competent patient refuses emergency treatment, the treatment cannot proceed, and the proper course is to 'section' the patient and treat under Part IV. Of course, the procedure may take some time, and the holding powers in s. 5 are of no use here, because they are excluded from the application of Part IV by s. 56. Nevertheless, the law is that any treatment not autho-rised by s. 62 will be unlawful. The law is not always observed, however. The sixth MHAC report refers to 'anecdotal evidence that patients treated in emergency situ-ations, often under Common Law and by inexperienced staff, are particularly subject to harm including collapse and death' (1995: para. 5.14). This concern materialised in the case of David Bennett, to whom medication was administered on the authority of a nurse under s. 62, that is, unlawfully. He was also, at the time, being restrained by nurs-ing staff. He died shortly afterwards (Mental Health Act Commission, 2003: para. 10.31, and see below). ECT carries a risk of death of 0.45 per cent (Fennell, 1996: 198) at the best of times, and the death rate from antipsychotic medicine is slightly lower. It is a real concern that these treatments do seem to be administered by underqualified staff as a heat-of-the-moment response to difficult situations. Each detained patient will have a RMO and informal patients will be under the authority of a named doctor. The Code of Practice provides that emergency treatment of detained patients is the responsibility of the patient's RMO (Department of Health and Welsh Office, 1999: para. 16.40), which must be right, as a matter of law, because treatment under s. 62 is analogous to treatment under s. 63, which specifically provides that this is the case. The situation is, perhaps, not so clear at common law or under the Mental Capacity Act 2005, because, as long as there is consent or the patient lacks capacity to consent, treatment in accordance with the above principles will be lawful, whoever takes the decision to administer it.

7.4.2 Restraint and seclusion

The Code of Practice advises that, ideally, the causes of inappropriate behaviour should be investigated and preventative measures taken (Department of Health and Welsh Office, 1999: paras. 19.4,5), for example, by giving patients adequate explanation of their treatment and the reason for it; the provision of personal space and access to open space; and the structuring of activity and allocation of patients to particular nurses. There is reason to believe that such measures can prove effective. Adshead (1998) has argued that attachment theory – which holds, broadly, that mental health is improved by the formation of relationships of attachment between individuals – can be used to modulate anxiety or arousal in patients, and so minimise or prevent the occurrence of violent or disruptive behaviour. A moving first-hand account of such an attachment having a positive therapeutic value for the patient can be found in Lindsay (1996). On the other hand, however, as Adshead also points out, insecure or unhealthy patient–staff attachments can be a cause of such behaviour. Preventative measures, in other words, may, on occasion, be the cause of violence or disruptive behaviour, or they may fail to prevent its occurrence. Sometimes, there is no apparent cause or warning of an act of violence (Duff *et al.*, 1996). When this is the case, restraint and seclusion are the measures of last resort.

These practices are often described as 'management' in the literature (for example, Department of Health and Welsh Office, 1999: ch. 19). It has been reported that, in some hospitals, the terms 'care and reassurance' or 'care and responsibility' are used (Mental Health Act Commission, 1999: para. 10.10). In either case, such terminology is 'misleading' (MHAC, 2001: para. 4.46) and disingenuous. There is force in Cohen's point (1985: 2) that 'social control', if defined too broadly, becomes a 'Mickey Mouse' concept; but the practices of restraint and seclusion, as is also the case in most, if not all, of the medical practices of the mental health sector, fall comfortably within Cohen's truncated criteria of 'organised responses to crime, delinquency and allied forms of deviant and/or socially problematic behaviour which are actually conceived of as such, whether in the reactive sense … or in the proactive sense' (1985: 3). In this view, 'control' more accurately captures the reality of the situation. As far as the law is concerned, however, these interventions are to be seen as 'treatment'.

7.4.2.1 Restraint

The aim of restraint, that is, the use of physical force against a patient, should be to minimise unacceptable behaviour, and, if used regularly as part of a treatment programme, its use should be reviewed regularly (Department of Health and Welsh Office, 1999: para. 19.14). Physical restraint should be used 'only as a last resort and never as a matter of course' (1999: para. 19.11), and 'the use of tying or hooking a patient to a part of a building or a fixture should never be used' (1999: para. 19.10). The National Institute for Health and Clinical Evidence (NICE, 2005: 53), having reviewed the evidence, found that the core issues in restraint training courses currently in operation include 'taking the patient to the floor', 'sitting and standing the patient', 'restraining hold', 'breakaways', as well as blocking punches and kicks, and separating fighting patients, which gives a flavour of what restraint comprises. If restraint is used on an informal patient, consideration should be given to the invocation of formal powers of detention (1999: para. 19.8). Staff should be trained in the use of restraint techniques (1999: para. 19.9), and courses should be given by persons with a suitable qualification. The MHAC, however, has warned consistently about 'the proliferation of unregulated training courses' (Mental Health Act Commission, 2001: 4.49). Moreover, it is very difficult to measure the effectiveness of training. Although there is anecdotal and impressionistic evidence that better training reduces the incidence of violence on wards, there has been, until very recently, little in the way of detailed and comparative evidence about the efficacy of particular techniques, which means that the substantive content of training is not yet evidence-based (National Audit Office, 2003a; Wright, 2003).

In 2003, the report of the inquiry into the death of a patient, David Bennett, who had died following an incident of the use of restraint, reported that methods used including a hand being held to his throat and nursing staff lying across him whilst he was lying face down on the floor (Norfolk, Suffolk and Cambridgeshire Health Authority, 2003: 19–22). When, in consequence, at the request of the Department of Health and Welsh Assembly, NICE produced guidance on the use of restraint, it noted that 'there was a dearth of evidence in all areas covered by this guideline and all recommendations and good practice points were arrived at by the [Guidelines Development Group, a multi-disciplinary committee comprising senior healthcare professionals, academics and system user representatives] using formal consensus methods' (National Institute for Health and Clinical Excellence, 2005: 11). In other words, in the absence of hard research, the guidelines are based on personal experience and anecdote, and are really more 'best guess' than 'best practice'. The first substantial research on these issues was published in 2006 (Health and Safety Executive, 2006). This showed that restraint training can have beneficial effects, but often only in the short term. It also found that 'What is clear from the research is that where training does not reflect a sound understanding of need, the impact of training is at best negligible and at worst negative' (2006: viii).

The NICE guidelines do now require that all service providers should provide restraint training, and should have policies that link need for training to risk assessment, and which detail frequency and substance of training courses. NICE is fairly prescriptive in this regard. All staff involved in the administration of restraint, either through physical force or tranquillising drugs, should have training in basic life support. In addition (2005: 13):

All staff whose need is determined by risk assessment should receive ongoing competency training to recognise anger, potential aggression, antecedents and risk factors of disturbed/violent behaviour, and to monitor their own verbal and non-verbal behaviour. Training should include methods of anticipating, deescalating or coping with disturbed/violent behaviour.

This is all well and good, but without evidence as to what works and when, it is not apparent that simply formulating guidelines will improve the situation. The knowledge base may be growing (see Health and Safety Executive, 2006: Part 2), but not quickly enough. As the HSE report asks (2006: 30): 'For how long can we continue to operate in this "ad-hoc" manner?'

Although our knowledge of the efficacy of restraint techniques and training remains sketchy, we have a much clearer idea these days of the extent to which restraint is used. In the national survey of inpatients carried out in 2005, it was found that 8 per cent had experienced at least one act of restraint during the previous three months, 1.5 per cent had been subject to five or more acts of restraint, and 0.7 per cent, ten or more such acts. It was also found that the rate of control and restraint among Afro-Caribbean men was

29 per cent higher than the average rate for all inpatients (Commission for Healthcare Audit and Inspection, MHAC, CSIP and NIMHE, 2005: 23). Smith and Humphreys (1997) found that, of patients requiring transfer to intensive psychiatric care wards, 37 per cent were subject to physical restraint in the four hours prior to transfer, and that restraint was used most frequently on patients admitted under s.4 who resisted admission and acted violently on detention. In practice, the formulation of a 'policy' on restraint means the appointment of three persons from amongst nursing staff to act as ward 'restraint teams'.

The use of restraint has a chequered history, particularly, but by no means exclusively, in the special hospitals, and concerns continue to be expressed about practices, including the use of techniques such as the 'wristlock', which can be effective if applied correctly, but often staff fail to retain skills and techniques in which they have been trained (National Institute for Health and Clinical Excellence, 2005). The use of straitjackets remains common on the intensive care wards in the special hospitals (Mental Health Act Commission, 1997: para. 4.5.3), as does the use of mechanical restraint (MHAC, 2003: paras.11.35–11.41; 2005: para. 4.129). The MHAC has reported that there are a worrying number of complaints from patients that restraint is painful and causes injury (1997: para. 10.2.3). Most worrying of all, there have been a number of deaths following the application of restraint, the risk of which is greatly increased if the patient has recently been given more than a small dose of antipsychotic medicine. In combination, restraint and medication can cause acute stress and cardiac arrest (see *Buckley* v *UK* [1997] EHRLR 435). The MHAC found (2001a) that, in 22 of 208 deaths of mental hospital inpatients reported to the coroner as involving unnatural causes, the patient was under restraint at the time of death or had been at some time during the week before death. There is, of course, no necessary connection between recent use of restraint and a subsequent death, and the 22 cases represented only slightly more than 10 per cent of the total. Even so, these statistics are cause for significant concern.

Sometimes, 'restraint' does not capture the nature of the problem nor that of the official response to it. The ninth MHAC report revealed that, 'In this reporting period we have noted a number of uses of the police in full riot gear in response to situations on wards where patients are detained' (Mental Health Act Commission, 2001: para. 4.48). On occasion, nursing staff will also don full riot gear, if deemed necessary in the management of particular patients (see *Brady*, discussed earlier, and Hines, 1999). Those dedicated persons who perform to the best of their abilities in providing treatment to aggressive or disturbed patients deserve a vote of thanks for the difficult and sometimes dangerous responsibility that they shoulder for the general social good. But this does not detract from an argument that it is at this point that the credibility of the medical model of mental disorder begins to look decidedly problematic.

The law does not see it this way. The leading case on the use of restraint remains *Pountney* v *Griffiths* [1976] AC 314 (HL). In that case, a nurse physically restrained a patient when the patient did not respond to a request to return to his ward at the end of a visit from relatives. The patient alleged that the nurse had punched him, and the nurse was convicted of assault by a magistrates' court. The Divisional Court quashed this decision, and the patient appealed to the House of Lords. Before the House, it was accepted that 'a hospital's staff has powers of control over all mentally disordered patients, whether admitted voluntarily or compulsorily, though the nature and duration of the control varies with the category to which the patient belongs' (Lord Edmund-Davies at 334). For detained patients, such powers are inherent in the fact of detention, and hence, in the MHA 1983. In *Tameside*, Wall J, having decided that the performance of a caesarean section operation was lawful under s. 63, held that 'it follows that since the defendant's consent is not required, Dr G is entitled, should he deem it clinically necessary, to use restraint in order to achieve the delivery by the defendant of a health baby' (at 774; see also the cases discussed in Chapter 3). The 1983 Act also contains the latest version of the immunity from suit introduced by the Lunacy Act 1890 in s. 139. In *Pountney*, it was established that that s. 139 protects staff who use reasonable restraint in the course of a patient's treatment (see further Chapter 12). These days, any use of restraint will also have to satisfy the test of 'medical necessity' required by *Herczegfalfy* (see earlier) if a breach of Arts. 3 or 8 of the Convention is to be avoided. Even so, a breach may be found, if the particular act of restraint is disproportionate or arbitrary, even if, in general terms, the treatment in question is necessary (Gostin, 2000: 149). But in truth, *Herczegfalfy*, in which a detained patient was fed by force and sedated, as well as, at times, restrained both physically and mechanically (he was variously handcuffed, strapped to his bed, and had a belt strapped around his ankles), offers little protection over and above that of the 1983 Act. The court held that these actions were necessary in order to treat the patient, who was on hunger strike and resisting treatment.

For informal patients, the legal situation is murkier. There is Crown Court authority that dealings with informal patients are not covered by s. 139 by reason that such are not conducted 'in pursuance of this Act' as that section requires (*R v Runighian* [1977] Crim LR 361), but this may be questionable, because s. 131 does provide for the admission (although only for treatment and not for assessment) of informal patients. There is, in any case, a number of overlapping legal justifications for the use of restraint against an informal patient. There is a common law power exercisable by all citizens to prevent a breach of the peace, which is exercisable in hospitals and residential accommodation. There is a common law right to use force in self-defence, which includes the defence of others. There is also a common law right to confine a person who is insane, as demonstrated by the well-known case of *Fletcher v Fletcher* (1859) 1 El.& El. 420. Finally, there is a generally available power in s. 3(1) of the Criminal Law Act 1967 to use force to prevent a crime or to arrest a person unlawfully at large. The precise nature of each of these powers is debatable (see Hoggett, 1996: 140–2), but the general thrust of the law is clear, which is that, subject to requirements of reasonableness and proportionality, as well as the test of 'medical necessity' required by *Herczegfalfy*, there will be little difficulty for a staff member in finding a legal basis for the restraint of an informal patient.

7.4.2.2 Seclusion

Although the 1983 Act is silent as to the practice known as 'seclusion', the Code of Practice offers the following definition (Department of Health and Welsh Office, 1999: para. 19.16):

Seclusion is the supervised confinement of a patient in a room, which may be locked for the protection of others from significant harm.

Another definition was offered by a patient in 2005 (cited in Mental Health Act Commission, 2005: 306):

Seclusion is the most awful experience: the hopelessness and despair one feels locked in a cell with no knowledge of when one can get out, the powerlessness one feels, the sense of being punished, is overwhelming.

In plain English, seclusion is solitary confinement. It should not be considered as part of a treatment plan (Department of Health and Welsh Office, 1999: para. 19.16) – as is implied by its emergency use status – but it nevertheless falls within the definition of treatment in s. 145(1): Lord Bingham in *R v Ashworth Hospital* (now Mersey Care NHS Trust), *ex p Munjaz* [2005] UKHL 58 at para. 19. As Mason (1992; 1993) discusses, however, at a theoretical level, there are at least three possible explanations for the practice of seclusion: therapeutic, containing and punitive. Ultimately, this is the question of how guidelines, in whatever form, are framed; it will always be an open and empirical question as to which explanation best fits the facts. There is also a lack of consensus as to how seclusion should be defined (Mason, 1992; Exworthy *et al.*, 2001), but there is indisputably a sense in which seclusion that is experienced as punitive *is* punitive. This can be exacerbated by practices such as the use of 'special' clothing whilst a patient is in seclusion, which occurred at least ten times in medium or high-security facilities during the period covered by the MHAC survey (Mental Health Act Commission, 2005: para. 4.276). This is done on the grounds of removing possible means of self-harm, but there is no escaping the fact that this is also ritualistic degradation that any human being is likely to experience as punitive. This is especially true when patients are stripped by staff of the opposite gender (Mason and Whitehead, 2001).

Hospitals are enjoined by the Code to draw up guidelines concerning the use of seclusion, and for the monitoring and review of practice, which should be carried out regularly by hospital managers (Department of Health and Welsh Office, 1999: para. 19.23). The Code itself, however, is fairly prescriptive of the Department of Health view of best practice. Seclusion should only be used as a last resort for the shortest time necessary. It should not be used as punishment, threat, as a consequence of staff shortages or if there is a risk of suicide or self-harm (1999: para. 19.16). The protection of other persons is the 'sole aim' of seclusion. It is the view expressed in the Code that seclusion can be ordered by the nurse in charge of the ward, a senior nursing officer, and even a nursing officer, as well as by a doctor, although, if the initial decision is taken by someone other than a doctor, one should attend immediately (1999: para. 19.18). Seclusion should only take place in a safe, secure and properly identified room, adequately heated, lit, ventilated, with seating, which provides a safe, private environment for the detainee, whilst also allowing complete observation. There should be a nurse within sight and sound of the room at all times (1999: para. 19.19), and present if the patient has also been sedated (para. 19.20): 'The aim of observation is to monitor the condition and behaviour of the patient and to identify at what time seclusion can be terminated.' There should be a documented report every 15 minutes, with a review by two nurses, at least one of whom was not involved with the initial decision to seclude, in the seclusion room, and by a doctor every two and four hours respectively, and if seclusion is to continue for more than eight hours consecutively, or for 12 hours within a 48-hour period, there should be an independent review by a multidisciplinary team not involved in the patient's care at the time that the period of seclusion began (1999: para. 19.21). If seclusion is used in the case of an informal patient, it should be deemed to be an indication that the use of formal powers of detention should be considered (1999: para. 19.16).

The extent to which it is permissible for an institution to implement a policy on seclusion at variance from the terms of the Code was argued before the House of Lords in *R v Ashworth Hospital* (now Mersey Care NHS Trust), *ex p Munjaz* [2005] UKHL 58. Following an earlier, partially successful, legal challenge in 2000 (*R v Ashworth Special Hospital, ex p M* (2000) 2000 WL 1480059, (QB)), Ashworth had revised some elements of its seclusion policy. The revised policy departed from para. 19.21 of the Code, and its requirement of four-hourly medical reviews, in that it required that, from the second day of seclusion, there would be two medical reviews daily, and from the eighth day, three medical reviews each week, only one of which need involve the RMO. There would also, from the second week, be two-hourly review by nursing staff, a weekly multidisciplinary review, a daily review by the ward or site manager, and a monthly report to the hospital's seclusion monitoring group. In addition, the hospital would inform the MHAC of any patient secluded for more than seven days. Under that policy, M was secluded on several occasions for periods of seven and 15 days. M's complaint was that the policy departed too far from the requirements of the Code, so that the infrequency with which his periods of seclusion had been reviewed was unlawful.

By a 3:2 majority, made up of Lords Bingham, Hope and Scott, the House, reversing the decision of a unanimous Court of Appeal, held that the revised policy was in compliance both with domestic law and with the Convention. As far as the domestic law is concerned, the issue was the status of s. 118 MHA 1983 and the Code of Practice published under it. If the Code has the force of law, it would follow that a departure from it is unlawful. Here, the House split 4:1. Lord Bingham examined the terms of the Code, noted that in its Introduction it is stated that 'The Act does not impose a legal duty to comply with the Code', and found it 'plain that the Code does not have the binding effect which a statutory provision or a statutory instrument would have. It is what it purports to be, guidance not instruction' (para. 21, see also Lord Hope at para. 68, Lord Brown at para. 107, and Lord Scott at para. 101, agreeing with Lords Bingham, Hope and Brown). As such, the Code is not a binding document. However (Lord Bingham at para. 21):

It is much more than mere advice which an addressee is free to follow or not as it chooses. It is guidance which any hospital should consider with great care, and from which it should depart only if it has cogent reasons for doing so.

Moreover, 'these reasons must be spelled out clearly, logically and consistently' (Lord Hope at para. 69).

Applying that dicta to Ashworth's policy, all bar Lord Steyn accepted that such reasons had been satisfactorily demonstrated by the hospital. Lord Bingham pointed out (at para. 23) that the Code is silent as to the particular difficulties that attend special hospital patients, and as to the need to seclude a patient for a period of more than a few hours. Lord Hope (para. 70) similarly held that 'special considerations need to be applied to the use of seclusion in a high security hospital, bearing in mind that the very reason why patients are there is because they cannot be dealt with by mental health services elsewhere in a way that will protect others from harm'. In this light, Ashworth's policy, to conduct less reviews of a patient in seclusion than stated in the Code, was reasonable, particularly in view of the other mechanisms in place by which a period of seclusion was reviewed and monitored. Indeed, the policy was able to withstand 'a particularly careful and intense scrutiny' (Lord Hope at para. 74, see also Lord Bingham at para. 24) of the type required when the human rights of an applicant are potentially at issue, whether on an application for judicial review or by way of a claim under the Human Rights Act (see Chapter 5).

By a complicated majority, the House also held 4:1 that there was no breach of Arts. 3 or 5 of the Convention and, 3:2, that there was no breach of Art. 8. Dealing first with Art. 3, Lord Bingham (at para. 29, see also Lord Hope at para. 81) held that Ashworth's policy 'must be considered as a whole' and 'the policy, properly operated, will be sufficient to prevent any possible breach of the Art. 3 rights of a patient secluded for more than seven days'. Lord Hope accepted that Art. 3 imposes a positive obligation on contracting Member States to act reasonably to safeguard Art. 3 rights, which increases in proportion to the likelihood of the risk in question materialising, but found that 'the risk of ill-treatment is very low if full effect is given to the policy' and that it would therefore be disproportionate to require Ashworth to abandon its policy to eliminate that small risk (para. 82). Hence, there was no breach of Art. 3.

Applying *Ashingdane* v *UK* (1985) 7 EHRR 528, Lord Bingham (para. 30, and see Lord Hope at para.s. 83–86) also found Art. 5 to be inapplicable, because the seclusion policy related not to the fact of detention, nor to the type of institution, but only to the particular conditions of detention. Finally Lord Bingham noted 'some difficulty' in appreciating how Art. 8(1) might be said to be engaged by a policy that aimed only to protect third parties and to seclude only for the minimum time necessary to do that (para. 32), but, in any case, went on to hold that, even if Art. 8(1) were engaged, the breach might be justified by reference to several of the grounds listed in Art. 8(2), and 'Properly used, the seclusion will not be disproportionate because it will match the necessity giving rise to it' (para. 33). Lord Hope made substantially the same points, in addition, holding that Ashworth's policy was 'in accordance with the law' as required by Art. 8(2), because, although not made under statutory authority, it did comply with the common law and, as a written and published policy, was sufficiently precise and accessible (paras. 90–2).

For a trenchant critique of this decision, it is necessary to look no further than the dissenting opinion of Lord Steyn, who called it 'a set-back for a modern and just mental health law' (para. 48), which licensed 'a free-for-all in which hospitals are at liberty to depart from the published Code as they consider right' (para. 44). That the majority had upheld a policy, which replaced the 42 reviews called for by the Code in relation to days eight to 14 (and subsequent weeks) of a period of seclusion with the three required by Ashworth's policy, was 'disturbing' (para. 47). Lord Steyn endorsed the decision of the Court of Appeal ([2003] EWCA Civ 1036) that a policy that departs from the Code is unlawful, because, on his analysis, and that of the Court of Appeal, the Code was intended by Parliament to establish 'minimum safeguards and a modicum of centralised protection for vulnerable patients' (para. 44). Departures from the Code should *only* be permitted where a hospital has 'good reason for departing from it in relation to an individual patient' or in relation to a particular class of patients 'who share well-defined characteristics' (para. 46, citing the Court of Appeal at para. 76). Absent good reasons, domestic law is infringed, and there will also a breach of the positive obligation under Arts. 3 and 8 (Court of Appeal, para. 74).

Indeed, Lord Steyn went further than the Court of Appeal, finding that there was also a breach of Art. 5, on the basis that a lawfully detained person has a 'residual liberty'. He cited the well-known Canadian case *Miller* v *The Queen* (1985) 24 DLR (4th) 9, in which the Canadian Supreme Court had held that a prisoner unlawfully subject to solitary confinement had suffered a breach of his residual liberty. He also found support for the concept in the European Court in *Bollan* v *UK* Application No. 42117/98 (see para. 43). This analysis was specifically rejected by Lord Bingham (para. 30), but it maybe that the concept of residual liberty will prove capable of further development. Lord Steyn was joined in the minority by Lord Brown, but only by reason of the latter's view of Art. 8(2)'s requirement that any breach of Art. 8(1) must be 'in accordance with law'. For Lord Brown (para. 127):

Unless it is to the Code that one can look for regulation carrying the force of law it is not in my opinion to be found elsewhere. Hospital policies themselves provide too insubstantial a foundation for a practice so potentially harmful and open to abuse as the seclusion of vulnerable mental patients.

As seen above, this analysis was also specifically rejected, on this occasion by Lord Hope (para. 98) and Lord Scott (paras. 101–3).

Maybe Lord Steyn's view, that the decision of the majority licenses a 'free-for-all', overstates the situation; there must, after all, be 'cogent reasons' to depart from the Code. On the other hand, although Ashworth clearly developed its policy by reference to the Code, as Lord Brown mentioned (para. 126), 75 per cent of patients in long-term seclusion are not *in fact* in 24-hour seclusion, but are nursed on wards and 'interacting with staff and patients', and so it is clear that 'seclusion' is being used at the hospital in a way very different from that envisaged in the Code. One patient mentioned by Lord Brown had been in 'seclusion' at Ashworth for nine years, before his transfer to Rampton, where he was never in seclusion for more than eight hours at a time (for more information, see Mental Health Act Commission, 2005: para. 4.239). This would seem to suggest that perhaps Lord Steyn is not too far wide of the mark after all. At present, neither domestic law nor the Convention offers any real protection to those subject to long-term seclusion, if that seclusion is in accordance with the policy of the hospital in question.

Having said that, it is to be hoped that the substance of the decision of the Court of Appeal in the case of *S v Airedale NHS Trust*, which it heard together with *Munjaz*, but which was not further appealed to the House of Lords, survives. In *Airedale*, S, a patient who had been violent and repeatedly absconded after detention, had been secluded for 12 days in a non-secure hospital because of the unavailability of a bed in a secure unit. His conditions of seclusion were poor: a bare room with no toilet facilities. It was held that the seclusion of S for 12 days in unsuitable conditions, which occurred solely because the facility in question 'could think of no alternative' response to the significant management problems S posed, was unjustified and disproportionate ([2003] EWCA Civ 1036 at para. 81). In our view, the decision of the House of Lords does not affect this; there was, on the evidence, no 'cogent reason' for the seclusion in this case. In this respect, it is to be noted that in *R v MHRT London South and West Region, ex p C* [2001] MHLR 110 (see Chapter 8), Lord Phillips, MR, in determining whether an eight-week wait for a tribunal hearing after an application had been made was in breach of Art. 5.4, cited the decision of the European Court in *Bezicheri v Italy* (1989) 12 EHRR 210, to the effect that resource shortages may not be pleaded in mitigation of a breach of that Article. If it is accepted, following *Munjaz*, that Art. 5 has no application in this situation, nevertheless it is not apparent why the same approach should not apply to Arts. 3 and 8 when, as here, shortage of resources is clearly the real issue.

The 2005 census of hospital inpatients (Commission for Healthcare Audit and Inspection, MHAC, CSIP and NIMHE, 2005: 22) found that, in the three months to 31 March 2005, 3 per cent of patients (1,104 individuals) had experienced at least one period of seclusion, 0.3 per cent (112) five or more periods, and 0.1 per cent (42), ten or more. The MHAC (2005: para. 4.251) found that there were 74 instances of 'isolation' of a patient lasting more than two days in the acute sector and 156 instances in the medium and high-secure sector over a six-month period from 2004–5. There are, in any given year, an unrecorded number of other incidents of solitary confinement not amounting in the opinion of staff (although the MHAC does not always agree – 1997: para. 10.1.2; 2005: para. 4.234) to what the Commission terms 'de facto seclusion' (Mental Health Act Commission, 1999: para. 10.22). It has recommended that the term 'solitary confinement' should be reintroduced to avoid the technical distinctions between what is and what is not seclusion that are made in some hospitals (1999: para. 1024; see the discussion in the Court of Appeal in *Munjaz* at para. 75).

Black and Indian male patients are more likely to be secluded than their white counterparts (Commission for Healthcare Audit and Inspection *et al.*, 2005: 22), and there are particular concerns about the seclusion of female patients (Mason and Whitehead, 2001). The MHAC routinely reports poorly designed seclusion rooms (for example, with blind spots and dangerous fittings); the absence of the basic amenities or furnishings required by the Code; a lack of regard for the dignity and privacy of those secluded; and poor record-keeping (see, e.g., Mental Health Act Commission, 2001: para. 4.40; 2005: paras. 4.247–4.248), with more than half, and sometimes more than three quarters, of facilities failing to comply with the requirements of the Code of Practice regarding the physical environment in which seclusion is carried out and its safety (see MHAC, 2003: para. 11.18) The Commission has long called for a statutory regime for seclusion and restraint (MHAC, 1999: para. 10.25) and although welcome, the more important point is that it is the substance and effect, not the form, of legal regulation, as well as of professional practice (Taxis, 2002; Kaltiala et al., 2003), that requires change. It seems innocuous and inequitable not to acknowledge that detention has different levels of intensity and that seclusion constitutes its most intensive form, and is qualitatively different from detention per se. The concept of residual liberty captures this reality, and so should the law. Following the abolition of the statutory powers to seclude by the Mental Health Act 1959, the courts have evaded the lack of a statutory basis for seclusion by implying it into the 1983 Act (see the Court of Appeal in *Munjaz*, para. 40). That is unacceptable. If seclusion is to be practiced, then there should be a statutory regime, complete with safeguards and rights of appeal, in place.

7.5 Concluding comments: back to the critique of the medical model of treatment for mental disorder

That practices of restraint and seclusion come within the definition of medical treatment in s. 145(1) of the 1983 Act raises difficult enough questions about the 'medicalisation' of our response to mentally distressed or disturbed people. The critique of the 'medicalisation of madness', which now has a long history within the sociology of medicine, aims its criticism more broadly, to encompass not just these 'ancillary' aspects of treatment, but also those at the core of the medical model – the physical and talking treatments. Although treatment for mental disorder is now, seemingly inescapably, eclectic, the medical model of madness continues to dominate, and has been able to expand to accommodate psychological and environmental perspectives on questions of aetiology and treatment. As Pilgrim and Rogers (1999: 121) put it, even though these other aetiological factors are more often taken into account than previously, 'they still legitimize the disease model and the authoritative power of medicine in the diagnosis and treatment of people with personal and social problems'; despite the current eclecticism, physical treatments continue to dominate. It may seem that drug treatments, in particular, are 'properly' medical, but the fact is that the medical model is a social construction. Medicine trades in what Berger and Luckman (1967) call our 'secondary reality', which comprises those elements of experience that are not explicable by recourse to common sense – concepts such as justice, deity, death and madness, for example – for which there is a need to develop specialised knowledges and institutions to provide explanations. How these specialisms have developed and have annexed the social problems that constitute their particular domain is a question in need of explanation. The appropriateness of the medical model may seem to be a matter of common sense, but the key question is really how it has come to be so seen.

Given the dominance of physical treatments, the current state of psychotherapy has a particular relevance here. An umbrella organisation, the UK Council for Psychotherapy (UKCP) was established in 1993, replacing the UK Standing Conference for Psychotherapy, which had been set up in 1989 and had itself replaced earlier prototypes of self-regulation following a private members bill – initially, if indirectly, prompted by the practices of Scientologists – intended to regulate the practice of psychotherapy, which failed to get through Parliament in 1982 (Pokorny, 1994: 515). Also in 1993, a voluntary register of psychotherapists was established. According to Clarkson (1994), the purpose of the UKCP is 'to create a profession and a register so that the public can identify appropriately trained practitioners who are subject to an enforceable Code of Ethics', whilst the voluntary register 'will form the foundation of a Statutory Register of psychotherapists' (1994: 12). National vocational qualifications have been developed, and in 1994, it was 'agreed by all the organisations of the UKCP that entry to psychotherapy training must be at postgraduate level and have an academic content roughly equivalent to a masters degree' (1994: 23). Later in the 1990s, although with some opposition from practitioners dubious of the benefits of further regulation (Mowbray, 1995; Postle, 1999), the UKCP worked with Lord Alderdice on a private members bill, and a Psychotherapy Bill was subsequently introduced in the Lords in May 2000, designed to put the regulation of profession and training requirements on a statutory basis and give statutory authority to a 'General Psychotherapy Council' that the bill would have created. The bill failed to get government support, the government preferring to regulate psychotherapy through the more expeditious method (from a management perspective) of Orders in Council.

For the UKCP, however, the bill was about more than regulation and protection of the public. The proposal for a General Psychotherapy Council, according to the chair of the UKCP (Jung, 2000), was also intended to confirm the professional status of practitioners. That is, for practitioners, the bill was a key stage on the path towards full professionalisation of this branch of medical treatment for mental disorder. The definitions generated from within the ranks of psychotherapists invariably emphasise training and professional status (see Freedman et al., 1975: 2601; Wolberg, 1954: 118, cited in Clarkson, 1994: 12). According to Clarkson, this project is for the benefit of the public, but it is difficult to believe that there are no other intended beneficiaries. The UKCP polices its boundaries (Pokorny, 1994: 515), and it would be naive not to realise that this is because the achievement of professional status is just that: a status, a source of empowerment, which is necessary if psychotherapy is to make any significant inroads into the professional dominance of the psychiatric profession and the Royal College of

Psychiatrists – which has been influential on the shape of the Mental Health Acts of 1959 and 1983 – over the provision of inpatient treatment.

The relevance of this consideration of contemporary developments in the structure of psychotherapy is that, first, it reminds us that 'the medical' comprises that which is so called, nothing more or less. There is no inherent defining quality to interventions that are, or should be, covered by the term; rather, and this is the second point, it is a question of professional and political power plays. As far as psychiatry and physical treatment are concerned, it was the drug revolution of the 1950s that finally made the claims to medical status of the psychiatric profession plausible (see Chapter 3). From a present-day perspective, however, the claims that sounded so plausible forty or fifty years ago have been shown to be problematic. Drug treatments do have beneficial effects, but the degree and longevity of those effects remains a matter of intense controversy, whilst concerns about side effects remains high, at least outside of professional circles. Pilgrim and Rogers see reliance on drug treatments and lack of concern about side effects as a function of psychiatry's relation with the other branches of medicine (1999: 125): 'An over reliance on drug treatment is inextricably linked to a professional strategy on the part of psychiatrists.' And just as psychiatry is parasitic on 'the medical profession', so the process is now being repeated, at one stage removed, in the relation between psychotherapy and psychiatry as it is currently being played out.

It is tempting to conclude, on this basis, that the treatment of mental disorder is more about power and control than about beneficence, and that mental patients are objects in a power play rather than subjects, autonomous individuals with rights. On this view, patients are better understood as 'victims', or more neutrally as 'targets', as simply the stock-in-trade of medical intervention. Hence, what is required is a disempowerment of psychiatry – a demedicalisation of madness – rather than a broadening of the psychiatric power complex through the establishment of new treatments and new professions to administer them, not to mention the development of ever-greater powers of compulsion available for use in the community. This caricature is, in fact, not too far removed from the position of the antipsychiatry movement and its champions, as Atkinson (1995: 33) has argued.

Moreover, it was something like this line of thinking that underpinned the pressures to introduce the legal safeguards for the protection of patients' rights now found in the 1983 Act. And yet, far from being an effective watchdog over the use of medical discretion, the 'return to legalism' turned out, in practice, to be the medical model's 'alibi'. Part IV of the Act has masked the reality of medical freedom with the appearance of legal control. It is at least arguable that Part IV should be understood as a colonisation of legal language and concepts by medicalism. As Fennell (1986: 36) put it, in an early critique of the 1983 Act, the '[l]egal rules provide the medium through which disciplinary power in general is both constituted and exercised, and in this context psychiatric interventions represent a specialised aspect of disciplinary power'. The theoretical flaw in Gostin's 'ideology of entitlement' (see earlier in this chapter), from a critical legal point of view, is that it posits medicalism and legalism as a simple opposition, without appreciating this potential for colonisation.

Rose (1985) has argued, more sociologically, that the ideology of entitlement and the opposition of legal rights to medical discretion wrongly assumes that control and liberty are distinct concepts, when, in fact, '[t]he contemporary psychiatric system operates predominantly not by coercion but by contractuality' (203), and when 'many modern psychiatric practices seek to promote autonomy' (204), using control to help patients gain greater control over their own lives. In consequence, Rose argues, the ideology of entitlement is ill equipped to assess the form that the control–liberty relation should take, and the practical effect is that legalism abdicates power to medical discretion.

This analysis of the reasons for the failure of legalism to deliver its underpinning policy of empowerment also informs the reasoning of those who reject what Lupton (1997) calls the 'orthodox' medicalisation critiques, on the grounds that it utilises an overly simplistic understanding of control. Lupton (1997: 98) argues that:

In their efforts to denounce medicine and to represent doctors as oppressive forces, orthodox critics tend to display little recognition of the ways that it may contribute to good health, the relief of pain and the recovery from illness, or the value that many people understandable place on these outcomes . . . or the ways that patients willingly participate in medical domin-ance and may indeed seek 'medicalisation'.

Most hospital inpatients are not detained, and most consent to treatment, even if that consent is often ambivalent. By the same token, it is arguable that at least some of the case law discussed in this chapter – *Tameside, Croydon,* and *ex p X,* for example – reveals not so much medical attempts to control patients, as the absolute inseverability of control and beneficence, the ultimate aim of which is to restore autonomy. It is import-ant not to overstate this point: on occasion, treatment is more about control than beneficence – *Brady* perhaps comes closest to this – and treatment without consent under Part IV may, of course, be given to patients detained solely for the benefit of other persons. The proposal is to remove the current treatability requirement from detention (see preface), thus allowing 'treatment', which, as the discussion in this chapter has shown, is couched broadly, in the language of benefit to others. But to suggest that this is always, or even usually, the case, or that control can be seen as some sort of 'bottom line' with beneficence a veneer, seems to us to impute, to those providing inpatients treatments, motives both more conspiratorial and sinister than are likely. Indeed, the proposal to remove the treatability requirement has been opposed vigorously by the professional bodies (Kmietowicz, 2002).

There is a need, therefore, to develop a theoretical understanding of the relationships of coercion–consent and control–beneficence that does not structure them opposition-ally, as alternatives, and this, in turn, requires one to think more carefully about what we mean by the phrase 'the medical model'. The present authors' suggestion, derived from Foucault, is that the power of this model should be seen in more 'fundamental' terms, as the medical construction of social reality. The power of psychiatry lies in its ability to produce a reality in which medical treatment for mental disorder is actively sought out.

In other words, although coercion may be, and not infrequently is, present at the actual point of treatment, it is necessary to understand that its absence at this point and its substitution by an apparently consenting patient does not mean that coercion is radically absent. On the contrary, it may well be functioning at the 'deeper' level of constructing a reality, a coercive environment or backdrop against which consent 'seems natural'.

This criticism of the ideology of entitlement and antipsychiatry, then, requires attention to be given not only to the inadequate theorisation of control, but also to the inadequate theorisation of power. It is at this point that the various strands of this discussion so far – the medicalisation critique; the medicalism–legalism relation; the socially constructed nature of the 'medical model' – converge. Again, that convergence is precipitated by the work of Foucault. There are two key innovations in Foucault's thought that are particularly pertinent for us. First, Foucault argued that power should be seen as a positive, productive force as well as a negative, prohibitory one; second, he argued that the power of psychiatry, psychotherapy and so on should be seen more in terms of discourses than of actors. What this amounts to is a view of medical power as that which operates through medical professionals – as the discourses they expound and the discursive techniques or micro-practices (treatments) they apply – rather than as the power being 'held' by them, with 'mental patients' as the 'products' of these discourses and as one measure of their power relations.

There are three key points to be taken from this. First, these power relations are of a particular order: the order of the medical discourses that produced them; legal discourses are of a different order. Richardson (1993: 238) argues that legal discourse is structured around the organising principle of autonomy; medical discourse around beneficence. It may be that the distinction is not as neat as Richardson suggests. As already noted, Rose has pointed out that medical beneficence aims to realise patient autonomy, and, by the same token, the legal positing of autonomous individuals is a beneficent act on the part of law and its framers. In other words, the beneficence– autonomy relation is deconstructable. But at the level of the production of discourse – i.e. in terms of what law and medicine say that they are doing – Richardson's point does hold good. It follows from this that the two cannot operate in tandem (because they do not speak the same language), which is why it is necessary to speak of 'colonisation' rather than of 'fusion'. But there is no a priori reason why the colonisation must be of the legal by the medical. There is no reason, in other words, why the mechanism of legal rights should not operate more effectively than it has during the bulk of the lifetime of the 1983 Act, to shut down areas of medical discretion as constituted by medical discourse (for example, that beneficent motivations justify the treatment of refusing patients without consent) by colonising that situation with autonomy. The post-Human Rights Act decisions of the Court of Appeal seem very much a case in point, particularly if seen as a mechanism by which to develop further the right to refuse consent to treatment, even when treatment is mandated by statute. But as argued earlier in this chapter, neither the law as it currently stands nor existing proposals for reform really posit a fundamental challenge to the operation of medical power, but only a differently shaped conduit through which it is to flow.

Second, Foucault's theory helps explain why the impact on medical powers of rights discourse, or indeed, of the law, however framed, is of limited effect. This is because medical professionals experience legal regulation as a set of negative prohibitions, which is to say that it relies on the weak model of power (as repressive) and, as such, it does not challenge the production of medical knowledge. Rose is sceptical of the ability of 'rights' to effect substantive change, for this reason and for two others, the first of which is that '[t]he doctrines of right and entitlements cannot resolve the issue of whose 'rights' shall prevail; it merely dissimulates the grounds upon which choices are made' (1985 213), and the force of these points must be accepted. The 'question of rights' has been a dominant intellectual problem for all types of jurisprudence and philosophy since at least the time of Plato, and the advent of postmodern thinking has given these debates a new vitality (Morrison, 1997). Rose does, however, concede that 'there might be an argument for the tactical use of rights' (1985: 214) and for us, given the absence of other legal options, this is sufficient. Moreover, the impact of rights discourse is variable: it may be a set of negative impositions, as far as those wishing to provide treatments are concerned, but to the patient, it can be a source of empowerment. Law, like medicine, is in the business of reality construction – and rights discourse at least constructs a reality in which the intended recipients of medical treatment for mental disorder are *a priori* autonomous agents.

The final strand of Rose's criticism of rights discourse is that it has a poor record 'when it comes to the positive changes upon which the strategy bases its claims for progressive mental health policy reform – improving buildings, staffing levels and proficiency, conditions, standards of conduct or treatment regimes, or providing alternatives to institutionalisation' (1985: 210). Again, we accept this point – but for us, it is not *the* point. Rights discourse cannot be the total sum of any strategy of empowerment, and to identify its limitations in affecting policy and resources does not mean that it cannot be effective within these limitations. From a Foucauldian perspective, the list of 'real policy issues' given by Rose itself poses a set of limitations, in the form of the acceptance of the medical discourse on madness that is implied by arguments in favour of increasing the resources put into mental health services, or increased 'proficiency' in the delivery of treatments, when it is not at all clear that it is lack of proficiency that is the problem. By the same token, if the ultimate aim of policy in this area is the empowerment of patients in the face of the constructive power of medical treatment, it is not clear that to shift towards alternatives to institutionalisation will necessarily achieve this, and to run the two concepts of demedicalisation and deinstitutionalisation together is problematic. For Lupton, 'the move towards 'demedicalisation' may be interpreted paradoxically as a growing penetration of the clinical gaze into the everyday life of citizens' (1997: 107). This question has already been discussed in this text (see Chapter 3) and will be discussed further in a later chapter (see Chapter 9), but its relevance here is as a further reminder that 'demedicalisation' can only really be challenged at the level of the production of discourse on madness.

This brings us to the third, and final, point to be taken from Foucault's theory of the operation of power – here emphasising the point that, for Foucault, power is seen as operating through individuals – and the idea of colonisation. It is, of course, not only the discourse of rights that is seeking to colonise contemporary medical knowledge and practices; there is also the government-sponsored discourse of danger and control. Here, too, there is no theoretical reason why medical discourse cannot be colonised by the language of risk: indeed, risk has long been a part of the vocabulary of psychiatry. The problem with the government's proposals, from the point of view of psychiatry, is that, in replacing treatability with 'appropriate treatment', risk is shifted from a component in an essentially medicalised decision to being the dominant factor, thus ousting medical criteria and turning medical professionals, with a mission to provide treatment to those in need, into little more than de facto turnkeys. It can be said that the question of the appropriate policy towards, and regime for, the provision of medical treatment for mental disorder, in or out of hospital, presents in the form of a tension between the politics of control and the politics of rights. The consequence is that psychiatry and the medical model is currently living in times of heightened politicisation.

It is significant, in this climate, that the Royal College of Psychiatrists and the Law Society (2002) issued a joint statement attacking the 2002 Bill. The battle between rights discourse and medical discretion is ongoing, but, for the time, the more pressing battle for both protagonists is to resist the attempt to impose a control paradigm on the provision of medical treatment for mental disorder, and despite all its faults and failings, it can argued that rights discourse has an indispensable role to play in this. In particular, it is submitted that there should be a right to no detention without treatment. As discussed in more detail in Chapter 8, the House of Lords in *A, D and R v Scottish Ministers* [2001] UKPC D5, [2002] UKHRR 1, and more recently, the European Court in *Hutchinson Reid v UK* (2003) 37 EHRR 21. have held that detention without treatment does not per se breach Art. 5(1)(e) ECHR. These cases are based on the jurisprudence developed from the dicta of the European Court in *Winterwerp v The Netherlands* (1979) 2 EHRR 387, that 'a mental patient's right to treatment appropriate to his condition cannot as such be derived from Article 5(1)(e)'. The European Court has made it clear on numerous occasions that the Convention is a document, the interpretation of which requires 'a dynamic and evolutive approach': *Christine Goodwin v UK* (2002) 35 EHRR 18, [2002] 2 FLR 487 at para. 74. The intention behind the Convention was that it would be human rights protection that evolved through the case law, but in this area, it has been the imperatives of control that seem to have been both the domestic and the European Courts' main concern.

This, in our view, is inappropriately conservative. *Winterwerp* is now over two decades old, and it does not reflect much contemporary human rights thinking. Of particular relevance is the view of the Steering Committee on Bioethics' *White Paper on Mental Disorder* (2000), which is that there should be no detention without treatment. The White Paper is posited on the view that it is 'a fundamental principle that treatment must in all cases be administered for the benefit of the patient' defined as 'a real clinical benefit and not only an effect on the administrative, criminal, family or other situation of the patient'. Adherence to this principle would not render medical treatment for mental disorder unproblematic: far from it. But it would, at least, mean that such a system, hemmed in, inter alia, by a right to refuse treatment if competent, would bear some semblance of the medical model, which, for all its faults, is infinitely preferable to the current obsession with risk and danger.

8

Leaving Hospital

8.1 Introduction

The context in which the issue of discharge from hospital must be situated has changed significantly over the last few decades. The shift from chronic to acute patients as the main 'clients' of inpatient services, together with the programme of closure of Victorian asylums and the relocation of psychiatric services into units within general hospitals and into 'the community', means that many patients who would previously have been hospitalised for periods of years, if not decades, now enter hospital, if at all, only for relatively short periods of time. Despite the change of policy, however, our hospitals continue to be overcrowded (see Chapter 3). One consequence of this is that patients are discharged from hospital, or given long-term leave of absence, earlier than would otherwise have been the case (Mental Health Act Commission, 2001: para. 3.5). This is a real cause for concern, because 20 per cent of suicides amongst detained patients occur when the patient is on leave (2001: para. 4.23). Yet mental health patients, as we have been at pains to emphasise, are not a homogeneous group, and some patients, for example, the elderly and institutionalised, continue to spend long periods in hospital. The plight of this group of patients only rarely attracts the attentions of the general media and public; the discharge of restricted patients and others considered, or proven by subsequent events, to be dangerous, by contrast, is rarely out of the news.

In 1995, statutory powers for 'supervised discharge', which allow for the continuing, and to an extent compulsory, treatment and supervision of patients in the community following discharge were introduced. These powers, which may soon be abolished, are considered in Chapter 9. They do not apply to restricted patients (s. 41(3)(aa) MHA 1983), in respect of whom there have long been powers to impose conditions on discharge, and these powers are considered in this chapter. Although the mechanisms for discharging patients from hospital did not feature greatly in the now-abandoned wide-ranging reform of mental health law, and the various mechanisms described in this chapter are likely to continue to exist into the foreseeable future, the system will experience some changes, although not all will be statutory. The government intends to speed up the working of the system under which continued detention can be challenged before a mental health review tribunal (hereafter 'MHRT'), to increase the frequency of entitlement to apply for some patients, and to extend the jurisdiction of tribunals to cover patients subject to the new powers of supervised community treatment (Department of

Health, 2006k). Other changes will be felt in consequence of the amendments that are proposed to the definition of mental disorder, and the legal significance of whether a patient is 'treatable' or not, which widen the criteria for (continued) detention in ways that may not be statistically very significant, but which do constitute a shift in emphasis from treatment to risk (see preface). We shall discuss some of the detailed proposals below, in the context of our consideration of the existing law, policy, and practice.

There are various persons who may initiate or order the discharge of a sectioned patient: the patient's RMO; the managers of the hospital in which the patient is detained; a MHRT; in some circumstances, the patient's nearest relative (NR). The Secretary of State has powers both to discharge and to veto proposals for discharges of restricted patients that come from the RMO or hospital managers. These various possibilities will be considered in turn. For many, if not most, patients, however, discharge is not an event but a process, and before final discharge is agreed to, there will be often be a trial period, during which the patient is given leave of absence – this chapter consequently opens with a consideration of this issue.

8.2 Leave and recall

Leave is seen to have a therapeutic and rehabilitative effect and often features as part of a patient's treatment plan, in a variety of forms, including unaccompanied 'home leave' of various durations, or in the form of short trips alone or under the supervision of nursing staff. As far as patients detained under Part II are concerned, s. 17 gives the non-delegable (Department of Health and Welsh Office, 1999: para. 20.3a) responsibility and power for granting and withholding leave to the patient's RMO, but it is likely that, in practice, RMOs give permission in general terms rather than for each trip outside the hospital (Mental Health Act Commission, 1991: para. 9.7). When a longer period of leave is contemplated, as a trial for discharge, the Code of Practice provides that an RMO should undertake 'any appropriate consultation' (1991: para 20.3.a) before granting leave to an unrestricted patient, although, in any case, there should be 'detailed consultation' with community service providers, carers and appropriate friends and relatives, and patients themselves.

According to the Code, leave should not be granted if the patient refuses to consent to these consultations taking place (para. 20.5). This may cause problems when the patient refuses to agree to the RMO consulting with a specific individual for good reason, as in *JT v UK* [2000] 1 FLR 909. The European Commission held that the inability of a patient to object to a nearest relative was in breach of Art. 8 of the Convention, and the government promised to change the law as part of a 'friendly settlement' of that case (see Department of Health, 2006m). The Department of Health also stated that s. 11 MHA should be interpreted by ASWs with due consideration to the human rights of the patient in the context of admission, and accepted that it is 'also arguable that the issue might arise in other circumstances' (Department of Health, n.d., in Mental Health

Act Commission, 2005: para. 130). Although, in the present context, the decision is for an RMO rather than an ASW, here too a patient has no right to make a legitimate objection to consultations that may entail a breach of her Art. 8 rights, and given that the consequence may be continued detention when leave would otherwise be granted, a claim under Art. 5(1)(e) or 5(4) might also, on some fact situations, be feasible. The key to avoiding any breach is to interpret para. 20.3.a of the Code's requirement for the RMO to undertake 'appropriate' consultations with due consideration to the human rights of the patient.

Leave may be granted for a limited or unlimited period, and may be renewed in the absence of the patient (s. 17(2)), but a period of leave of absence will end on the expiry without renewal of the authority to detain: s. 17(5). This means that the maximum period of leave possible under s. 17 is one year (the period of detention for treatment of a renewed s. 3 admission). It was accepted, following the decision in *R v Hallstrom, ex p W*; *R v Gardner, ex p L* [1986] 2 All ER 306 (DC) that it is unlawful to section a patient, or to renew the authority to detain under the procedure found in s. 20, merely to extend a period of leave. The decision in *Hallstrom* put paid to the practice of using a 'section' as a 'long leash', which had developed after the passage of the 1983 Act as a way around the embargo on ongoing compulsory treatment in the community. Although not over-ruled, the import of this decision has, however, been severely limited by later decisions.

In *Barker v Barking Havering and Brentwood Community Healthcare NHS Trust* [1999] 1 FLR 106, the care plan of B, a patient detained under s. 3, was for graduated, supervised return to the community. She had been granted leave that, at the time that her detention was renewed, allowed her to be absent from the hospital for a number of days each week. B complied with her treatment plan and, on her days in hospital, was assessed rather than treated. She sought judicial review of the decision to renew her detention, on the grounds that the requirements of the relevant section, s. 20(4), were not met. These are, essentially, a repetition of the grounds for initial admission under s. 3. A period of detention cannot be renewed unless the patient is suffering from one of the four types of mental disorder specified in s. 1(2) (see Chapter 2) to a nature or degree that makes it appropriate that the patient receive medical treatment in a hospital (s. 20(4)(a)), and that it is necessary for the health or safety of the patient or others that the patient 'should receive medical treatment and that it cannot be provided unless he continues to be detained': s. 20(4)(c). There is also, in s. 20(4)(b), a treatability require-ment that applies to *all* detained patients, unlike its equivalent in s. 3(2)(b), but this may be satisfied, for mentally ill and severely mentally impaired patients, if the patient, if discharged, would be unlikely to be able to care for him or herself, or obtain the care needed, or would be at risk of serious exploitation: s. 20(4).

In *Hallstrom*, McCullough J had held that these criteria are not satisfied if, at the time of the renewal, it was not, in the opinion of the RMO, necessary that the patient be hos-pitalised. The Court of Appeal in *Barker* agreed with this, but added the gloss that, although it had to be necessary for the purposes of the renewal of a section under s. 20(4)(c) that a patient 'continue to be detained', this did not mean that it was actually necessary that a patient in B's position needed to be confined to a hospital. It was sufficient that detention would be used as a backstop if the care plan for graduated discharge ran into problems. A similar decision was reached by the Administrative Court in *R v Mersey Health Care NHS Trust, ex p DR* [2002] EWHC 1810, 2002 WL 1654941. DR, a patient detained under s. 3, lived at home on leave as part of her care plan. DR's detention was renewed under s. 20 on the grounds that she had a history of failing voluntarily to take her medication, and so hospitalisation for compulsory treatment was a possibility. She challenged that decision, both on the grounds that there was not, in fact, justification for the decision to renew her detention and as a breach of Art. 5(1)(e) of the Convention. The court, following *Barker*, dismissed the first argument on the grounds that the facts showed that treatment in hospital was a significant part of DR's treatment plan. It was further held, although controversially (see Mental Health Act Commission, 2003: para. 9.52 and Figure 20) that the treatment need not be inpatient.

The Art. 5 argument was held to be inapplicable, because DR, if detained, would be so under the provisions of the Act, that is lawfully, and Art. 5 was held not to apply to a patient who is not, in fact, detained. In *R v MHRT and Managers of Homerton Hospital (East London & City Mental Health NHS Trust), ex p CS* [2004] EWHC 2958 (Admin), CS, held under s. 3, had been on leave of absence for three months, and was required to attend the hospital once every four weeks, at which time her progress on leave was monitored by her RMO; CS was given encouragement to engage fully with community-based services. CS applied to a MHRT for an order for discharge, which was denied. On appeal against that decision, CS argued that the facts disclosed that the grounds for detention were no longer made out. Pitchford J found that 'the element of treatment at hospital remained a significant part of the whole' (para. 44), and that, although 'It may be that in the closing stages of the treatment in hospital [the RMO's] grasp on the claimant was gossamer thin, but to view that grasp as insignificant is, in my view, to misunderstand the evidence' (para. 46). CS was consenting to her treatment whilst on leave. The court rejected an argument that an order for guardianship or supervised discharge would be more appropriate than s. 17 leave in such circumstances, in part because 'CS's knowledge of the RMO's powers was a significant element in her willingness to accept the treatment plan' (para. 48). This seems to be very close to saying that CS's apparent consent to treatment was, in fact, underwritten by her fear of the legal powers of her RMO, and we would add our voices to those who 'are disappointed at this judicial attitude and understanding of the nature of consent to treatment' (Mental Health Act Commission, 2005: para. 4.42).

Although the way that s. 20 has been interpreted in these cases is debatable, as a matter of statutory interpretation (Eldergill, 1999), the law as it now stands is reasonably clear. It is *only* when there is *no* intention of hospitalising a patient on leave, and the *only* reason for the extension of a period of detention is to permit continued treatment in the community, that the renewal of authority to detain will be unlawful (for an example of a fact situation in which this was held to be the case, see *R v MHRT and W, ex p Epsom and St Helier NHS Trust* [2001] EWHC Admin 101, discussed later). This situation may also continue indefinitely, because the court in *CS* (at para. 49) held, understandably, given the uncertain nature of mental disorder, that there was no obligation to state in advance a date at which the detaining section of a person on leave of absence must be ended.

Perhaps all of this is what the MHA 1983 has always provided for, and the decision in *Hallstrom* was routinely overestimated in its effect on clinical freedom. *Barker* and subsequent case law is clearly in step with the realities of the care programme approach (see Chapter 9), and the government's policy of providing for the use of compulsion in outpatient care (see Department of Health, 2006l, discussed in Chapter 9). But this area remains a cause for concern, because it offers an alternative to more cumbersome mechanisms from the point of view of the RMO, at the expense of, in practice, removing safeguards against inappropriate compulsion or extending statutory powers beyond their current reach. Section 17 is now defined so broadly that it is not apparent what new powers will, in reality, be added if and when the planned supervised community treatment order (Department of Health. 2006l) comes into force. The MHAC is 'aware anecdotally of patients whose detentions have been renewed several times without recall to hospital'; its attempts to collect more systematic data are frustrated by the non-cooperation of hospitals, although 'a more rigorous exercise' has been promised (2005: para. 4.42).

Leave may be granted subject to conditions that the RMO 'considers necessary in the interests of the patients or for the protection of other persons': s. 17(1). One specific condition that is mentioned in the 1983 Act is that the RMO may direct 'escorted leave', under which the patient remains in the custody of a nominated 'officer' on the staff of the hospital or any other person authorised in writing by the hospital managers, if it appears to him or her 'necessary so to do in the interests of the patient or for the protection of other persons': s. 17(3). 'Interests' is not defined further and is probably open to a broad definition, whilst 'necessary' is defined by the position as it appears to the RMO and not by some objective standard, giving wide scope to the exercise of an RMO's discretion. An 'officer', not defined by the Act, nevertheless features often within it. In *R v Midlands and North West MHRT, ex p PD* [2004] EWCA Civ 311, 2004 WL 412965, the Court of Appeal, in essence, held that an 'officer' means a person employed at the facility in question, and not any other employee of that trust. The Memorandum explains that s. 17(3) is intended, inter alia, to 'allow detained patients to have escorted leave on outings, to attend other hospitals for treatment, or to have home visits on compassionate grounds' (para. 63), but might also include home leave under the custody of a relative, for example. The MHAC reports (2001: para. 4.25) that this does occur, but doubts whether such relatives or friends are aware that they have specific legal powers and duties in respect of the patient.

As far as other conditions are concerned, requirements relating to residence and treatment are most common. The patient and other appropriate persons should be given a copy of any conditions (para. 20.6). A patient given leave remains 'liable to be detained' and therefore subject to the consent to treatment provisions contained in Part IV (s. 56(1)), as well as the aftercare provisions in s. 117 (see Chapter 9). Although this does mean that it is possible, in theory, to administer treatment without consent in the community, the Code of Practice (Department of Health and Welsh Office, 1999: para. 20.7) advises that 'consideration should be given to recalling the patient to hospital' if treatment is refused.

The powers of recall are contained in s. 17(4). The patient's RMO must, by notice in writing to the patient or to the person 'in charge of the patient' (who will be a person appointed under s. 17(3)), revoke the leave of absence and recall the patient to hospital if 'it appears' to the RMO 'that it is necessary so to do in the interests of the patient's health or safety or for the protection of other persons'. Again, this form of words gives a good deal of discretion to RMOs. The Code of Practice directs RMOs to 'consider very seriously the reasons for recalling a patient' including the effects of revocation on the patient, and 'refusal to take medication should not on its own, for example, be a reason for revocation' (1999: para 20.11). These powers must be exercised in compliance with the Convention, and following the decision in *K v UK* (1998) 40 BMLR 20 (see later). This means that a patient should not be recalled in the absence of 'objective medical evidence' that he or she remains mentally disordered, even where recall is deemed necessary on protectionist grounds: in so far as s. 17(4) does allow recall solely on grounds of public protection, it is arguably incompatible with Art. 5(1)(e), as interpreted by the European Court in *Winterwerp v The Netherlands* (1979) 2 EHRR 387. Unlike the powers to recall a conditionally discharged restricted patient, the use of which triggers the right to apply to a tribunal within one month (see later in this chapter), there is no mechanism in the 1983 Act specifically to review a decision taken to recall under s. 17(4).

The MHAC has expressed concerns over the operation of s. 17, including: withholding of authorised leave by nursing staff as punishment or coercion; failure to appreciate the need for compliance with s. 17 for escorted or short trips out of hospital (Mental Health Act Commission, 1995: para. 9.4); no record of leave having been granted; failure to specify conditions or to consult, or to give the patient and other appropriate persons, such as relatives or professional carers, a copy of the conditions of leave, as envisaged in the Memorandum; failure to obtain written permission from the hospital managers before the patient is placed in the custody of someone other than an officer of the hospital (MHAC, 1997: para. 3.4); leave being granted by someone other than the RMO (MHAC, 2001: para. 4.59); and leave not being granted solely because of staff or other resource shortages (MHAC, 2003: para. 9.37). A new concern has emerged with the expansion of private sector-provided beds for detained patients. The MHAC has reported (2005: para. 4.38) 'that the use of s. 17 leave may be constrained within some Independent Hospitals because of an understandable reluctance by the relevant commissioning authorities to fund a bed that is not being occupied'. This, as the Commission notes (*ibid.*), may give rise to successful legal challenge under Art. 5(1)(e).

A predominant concern in the MHAC's sixth report (1995) was the use of s. 17 as an alternative to transferring the patient under s. 19. A formal transfer under that section involves the transference of the authority to detain and all ancillary powers between the respective hospitals, but if a patient is transferred under s. 17, the various powers and duties remain with the first hospital. This means that those responsible for the patient's treatment in the hospital to which he or she has been transferred have no original authority over the patient, but the situation had arisen because transfers under s. 17 are typically used to remove acute patients from a district hospital to an RSU, and RSUs had insisted that such transfers occur under s. 17 rather than s. 19, because there were concerns that otherwise district hospitals would refuse to accept the return of patients from RSUs. Nevertheless, some patients had remained 'on leave' for many years in such cases (Mental Health Act Commission, 1995: para. 9.4). Subsequently, Department of Health guidance was issued on the use of s. 17 (Department of Health, 1996b), but this did not allay the concerns of the MHAC (1997: para. 3.4.1). Formal leave is required whenever a detained patient leaves a hospital site, even if that is to travel to another site managed by the same NHS trust. The MHAC has suggested (1999: para. 4.58) that leave is not required to move to the premises of another trust on the same site, but this has been disputed (Eldergill, 1997: 144, Jones, 2006: 113) on the basis that the staff of the non-detaining trust lack legal authority over such a patient, which the MHAC has subsequently, and correctly in our view, accepted (2003: 9.40–9.44, and see also Recommendation 32).

The provisions of s. 17 apply to patients detained under s. 37 without modification (Sch. 1, Part I, para. 1, MHA 1983), and to restricted patients with the modifications in s. 41(3) and Sch. 1, Part II, para. 3. A restricted patient may not be given leave of absence without the consent of the Secretary of State: s. 41(3)(c)(i) and Sch. 1, para. 3(a). In *R v SSHD, ex p OS* [2006] EWHC 1903 (Admin), the Secretary of State refused to give permission for OS, detained under ss. 37 and 41 following a conviction for manslaughter, to have leave under s. 17. This was so notwithstanding that OS had been conditionally discharged by a tribunal, which had found that there was insufficient threat to public safety to justify his continued detention. A period of leave under s. 17 was a necessary precursor to the implementation of that decision. The Secretary of State based his decision, in part, on the fact that OS, a foreign citizen, who had been denied asylum and was to be deported, might be tempted to abscond if given leave of absence, and that this, in turn, might lead to OS failing to take necessary medication, thus increasing the risk of harm to the public. The High Court upheld that decision as fair and reasonable on the facts. The Secretary of State may attach conditions to his or her consent: *R v Secretary of State for the Home Department, ex p A* [2002] EWHC Admin 1618, [2003] 1 WLR 330. The MHAC (2005: para. 4.42) has reported its 'grave concerns' about reports that the Home Office has agreed to the 'shadowing' of some restricted patients given leave of absence, which involves 'surreptitious surveillance' of the patient when outside the hospital, although in evidence given on behalf of the Secretary of State on 24 July 2006 to the High Court in *ex p OS*, (para. 77) it was said that the practice had been discontinued for over a year.

In *R v Page and SSHD, ex p Hurlock* [2001] EWHC Admin 380, Ouseley J held that, although ss. 17 and 41(3) do not imply an obligation to grant leave when conditional discharge has been ordered by a tribunal but the conditions are not yet met, in such circumstances, an RMO may grant even unescorted leave without first seeking the permission of the Secretary of State. This does not mean that the RMO has an entirely free hand, however. In *R v West London Mental Health NHS Trust, ex p K* [2005] EWHC 1454 (Admin) the RMO of K, a patient detained in Broadmoor, part of the West London Mental Health NHS Trust ('W') under s. 41 MHA 1983, had formed the view that K could be transferred into conditions of lesser security and had arranged for K to have a period of trial leave at an MSU. The MSU was run by an independent sector provider. W declined to fund K's placement in the MSU, partly on the grounds that it was cheaper to provide K with accommodation within the trust's stock than to use an independent provider, and partly on clinical grounds, W having commissioned a medical report from Dr B that disagreed with the RMO's view that K could be appropriately housed in conditions of lesser security. Lightman J (at para. 30) held that the trust:

must give due weight to the views of the RMO, but they are not bound to agree with him. If the managers are to disagree with his clinical judgment, they should have good and substantial reasons for doing so, but it must be recognised that differences of expert medical opinion are not infrequent. If the managers disagree without sufficient reason, their decision may be open to challenge on *Wednesbury* grounds. If the managers do accept that clinical ground to favour a stay at another hospital, the managers must then determine whether the benefit is such that, notwithstanding the impact on the limited resources available for its functions generally, the expenditure should be authorised.

Given that there were both financial and clinical factors to justify a decision not to transfer K, the decision of the trust was upheld. On appeal ([2006] EWCA Civ 118, [2006] 1 WLR 1865), the focus was more on the obligation of the Secretary of State to meet his or her duty under ss. 1(1), 3(1) NHS Act 1977 to promote a comprehensive health service. But the outcome was essentially the same. The desire of the RMO, that a patient be given leave of absence, does not oblige the Secretary of State to use his or her best endeavours to meet it (paras. 54, 61, 65). In holding that resources may properly be taken into account, the court, in this case, followed the approach that has previously been taken in a number of other contexts (see, for example, the *Barry* decision, discussed at length in Chapter 9).

The Secretary of State has powers coexistent with the RMO to recall a patient under s. 17(4): s. 41(3)(c) and Sch. 1, para. 3(b). Section 41(3)(d) and Sch. 1, para. 3(c) provide that s. 17(5) is modified so that a patient given conditional leave of absence either by the RMO or the Secretary of State cannot be recalled to hospital by the RMO after the expiration of 12 months from the day on which that leave of absence began, but can be recalled by the Secretary of State without limit of time. This does not mean, however, that at the expiry of the 12-month period an RMO can do nothing. There is always the option of admission of the patient under the *civil* law of compulsory admission, as happened in *R v North West London Mental Health NHS Trust and Ors, ex p S* [1998] 2 WLR 189 (CA) (see Chapter 6) if the criteria for such admission can be made out.

The substantial discretionary powers of the Secretary of State were challenged in *R v Secretary of State for the Home Department, ex p A* [2002] EWHC 1618; [2003] 1 WLR 330. A, a restricted patient, had been conditionally discharged by a MHRT, but discharge was deferred until suitable accommodation could be found. The Secretary of

State had consented to A being given first escorted, and later unescorted and overnight, leave, with A staying at a hostel into which, as part of his care plan, he would eventually move to permanently under his conditional discharge. But the Secretary of State refused to consent to A being given leave for a period of six weeks, as a trial of his ability to live long-term in the hostel accommodation. This was because, in the opinion of the Secretary of State, it would, in effect, pass control for A, with a violent history of offending, from the Secretary of State to the RMO, and at that time, the Secretary of State was not prepared to do this. Moreover, leave would, in any case, only be consented to under s. 17, as the court found, in exceptional circumstances (para. 49). The Secretary of State preferred to use the powers to discharge a restricted patient subject to such conditions as he thinks fit, and liable to recall at any time, given to him by s. 42 (discussed in detail below): powers that, in the view of the Home Office, were absent from s. 17 leave (because that section only empowers the RMO to impose conditions on leave). After some prevarication on the part of the Home Office, A did eventually commence his trial period in the hostel. A nevertheless sought judicial review both of the substantive decision to refuse consent, and of the policy of only using s. 17 for restriction-order patients in such narrow circumstances, arguing breaches of Art. s 5(1) and (4).

The court held, first, that the Secretary of State's reading of s. 17 was incorrect. Because the RMO can grant leave with conditions under the section, and the Secretary of State can withhold consent to such leave, it follows that the Secretary of State can determine which conditions, including possibly a condition that he be kept informed of the situation when the patient is on leave, should be attached to leave under s. 17 (para. 41). The court further held that it is inappropriate for the Secretary of State to discharge conditionally a patient under s. 42 when he or she has already been discharged conditionally by a tribunal; s. 17 should be used instead (paras. 47, 50). As far as issues of human rights are concerned, the actions of the Secretary of State regarding the implementation of A's leave had, in the view of the court (para. 65), delayed its start by six weeks. In *Johnson* v *UK* (1997) 29 EHRR 296, the European Court held that an unreasonable delay in discharging a person whose mental disorder no longer warranted detention breaches Art. 5(1). Crane J held that this was the case here, the delay being unreasonable because there was no good reason for it (para. 71).

The court declined to issue a certificate of incompatibility between the 1983 Act and the Human Rights Act, however, because no specific 'in principle' breach had been argued before it. Crane J did say that 'possibly section 43(1)(c)(i) might be a candidate' (at para. 56). There must, in our view, be a very strong possibility that this is correct. In *X* v *UK* (1981) 4 EHRR 181, the European Court held the UK in breach of Art. 5(4) because the final decision regarding the discharge of restricted patients was vested solely in the Secretary of State, with no provision for his or her decisions to be reviewed by a court. The 1983 Act amended the domestic law accordingly, by giving MHRTs coextensive powers to order discharge (see later). This does not aid a patient such as A, however, who had already been discharged, albeit conditionally and albeit deferred, by a tribunal. There was, as such, no point in A seeking to challenge the refusal to grant leave by applying to a tribunal for discharge. Because there was no other remedy open to him, he was in a situation exactly analogous to the patient in the *X* case, with release from hospital entirely dependent on the discretion of the Secretary of State, from whose decision there is no right of appeal.

Street (1998: 56) found that 93 per cent of restricted patients had unescorted leave of absence before final discharge, that in the great majority of cases, leave passed without incident, and that around a third of restricted patients discharged from hospital were on leave of absence and living away from hospital at the time. This does not mean that restricted patients are given leave freely – unescorted leave, in particular, will only be granted very close to the end of a period of hospitalisation, during which the patient will have moved into increasingly less secure accommodation – but it does illustrate the widespread use of s. 17 leave.

8.3 Discharge from hospital: the law

8.3.1 Informal patients

There are no special provisions governing the discharge from hospital of informally admitted patients. In theory, informal patients are free to leave at any time, subject to the holding powers contained in s. 5 (see Chapter 4), and subject to having the mental capacity to reach a decision to leave the hospital, which a significant proportion of informal patients will lack. Some, not all, trusts, following the decision of the European Court in *HL* v *UK* (2005) 40 EHRR 32, now use compulsory powers in respect of compliant patients who lack capacity. Those patients who remain on an informal basis rely solely on friends and relatives, and the professional ethics and good practice of hospital staff and managers, to protect them from unwarranted hospitalisation. Informal patients fall outside the remit of the MHAC.

8.3.2 Patients detained under civil law

As far as patients detained under Part II and s. 136 are concerned, the issue is discharge of the authority to detain rather than discharge from hospital. Many patients will be on leave of absence rather than in hospital when discharged from the 'section' on which they are held, and it is from 'liability to detention' that patients are discharged. This means that discharge is not linked directly to the need for hospital treatment and so, for a patient to be discharged, the test is whether he or she should remain liable to detention, rather than whether or not he or she should remain in hospital. By the same token, whether or not a person discharged from a section subsequently leaves hospital is not a legal concern, and it is certainly possible that a patient should remain in hospital but does not need to remain liable to be detained. For example, a threat to the safety of others may have subsided but the need for treatment may not, or a previously refusing patient may have now agreed to consent to treatment. On the discharge of a section, the patient acquires informal status and the above considerations apply. The Memorandum (Department of Health and Welsh Office, 1998: para. 301) does require that, on discharge of a section, it should be made clear to the patient that the authority to detain him or her no longer exists. As discussed in Chapter 3, most patients are discharged within 90 days of admission.

Authority to detain a patient held under Part II will cease automatically if the period of detention expires without it being renewed: ss. 2(4), 4(4), 20(1). It is unlikely that a detention will simply be allowed to lapse (Sackett, 1996: 65). A 'section' may be ended at any time by the making in writing of an 'order for discharge' (s. 23(1)) by the RMO, hospital managers or nearest relative (s. 23(2)(a)), and if the patient is detained in a mental nursing home, by the Secretary of State; if in a NHS trust, it may be by the health authority (HA), special health authority (SHA), or primary care trust (PCT) facilities, or if in a mental nursing home by virtue of a contract between that home and a NHS trust, HA, SHA, or PCT, by those parties also: s. 23(3). Any body or trust given powers to make an order for discharge may delegate them to a committee or subcommittee of at least three members (s. 23(4)), in which case, the decision to discharge must be unanimous: *R v Hospital Managers of Royal Park Hospital, ex p TT* [2003] EWCA Civ 330. This is a controversial decision because an RMO seeking to prevent discharge need (as happened in this case) only convince one member of the committee that discharge is not warranted, whereas the patient must convince all three. The Court of Appeal justified this approach on the basis that the starting point is that the RMO's views are justified, and so should only be overruled by a unanimous committee (Pill LJ at para. 30). It may be that this decision would not survive appeal to the House of Lords. If a preponderance of opinion is in favour of discharge, surely discharge should follow? In reality, it is by far most common to find that a section will be ended by the patient's RMO – 81 per cent in 1991, 76 per cent in 1994 in Sackett's survey – and that, of those left, most will lapse. Most of the remaining orders are made by hospital managers. It is rare that an order for discharge is initiated by a nearest relative.

There are no criteria governing discharge to be found on the face of the MHA 1983. In consequence, the Act seems to allow a patient to be held for the full duration of a period of detention, even if the grounds for admission could no longer be made out at some earlier point, and similarly to allow the discharge of a patient when those grounds remain. The MHAC's first report (Mental Health Act Commission, 1985: para. 8.13) stated that hospital managers 'have the right and the duty' to end a section as soon as the conditions for admission are no longer met, and in *R v MHRT London South and West Region, ex p C* [2000] MHLR 220, Scott Baker J (at para. 20) held that an RMO has a continuing duty to ensure that the conditions for detention are still met. The fundamental authority is the decision of the European Court in *Winterwerp v The Netherlands* (1979) 2 EHRR 387, that continued detention is warranted only so long as the detainee remains of unsound mind such as to warrant hospitalisation. In its later decision in *Johnson v UK* (1997) 27 EHRR 296, however, the Court held that discharge need not be immediate if time is required, for example, to organise aftercare, clearly accepting that factors other than the patient's soundness of mind are relevant to a discharge decision.

Jones (1999: 115) suggested that the criteria should be those that apply to the renewal of a detention for treatment in s. 20(4) (see earlier). The latest edition of the Code of Practice endorsed Jones's suggestion (para. 23.11), advising that hospital managers should appoint review panels to consider the case for discharge, and that this should be done more frequently than required under s. 20; and that, in cases where continued detention is contested, the decision should be made by a multidisciplinary team (para. 23.13).

In *R* v *Riverside Mental Health Trust, ex p Huzzey* (1998) 43 BMLR 167 (HC), Latham J held that, when carrying out a review of a patient's detention, hospital managers should consider the factors in s. 3 (the relevant section in that case), but are not limited to those factors, and might also consider the contents of a report recently made by the RMO (under s. 25, dealt with below) stating that the patient is dangerous. On this authority, the criteria for discharge under s. 23 seem to comprise, at the least, both those relevant to admission in the first place and that mentioned in s. 25. As mentioned earlier, the difference between the criteria in s. 3 and those in s. 20 is that, in the latter, there is a treatability requirement in respect of mental illness and severe mental impairment, but the tone of the judgment in *Huzzey* is very much that the managers can consider any factors felt to be relevant, subject only to the limitations imposed by judicial review. This is also logical because the decision to discharge is the flip side of the decision to renew detention, rather than to admit to hospital in the first place, and so it is the s. 20 criteria that are, prima facie, most relevant. These are the same criteria that apply in a MHRT application (see below). The same logic applies to decisions made by RMOs. This was certainly the view of the law taken by Crane J in *South West London and St George's Mental Health NHS Trust* v *W* [2002] EWHC Admin 1770; Scott Baker J seemed to take a different view in *R* v *Dr F and DE, ex p Wirral Health Authority and Wirral Borough Council* [2001] MHLR 66, holding, at para. 68, that an RMO's power of discharge 'is wholly within the RMO's discretion', subject only to the principles of judicial review. On the other hand, given that any failure to consider the related criteria elsewhere in the statute is prima facie irrational, it may be that this is, in reality, a distinction without a difference.

Each person or body empowered to make an order for discharge can act independently of the others (Department of Health and Welsh Office, 1999: para. 102). The only exception to this is that an order for discharge is not to be made by a nearest relative unless 72 hours' notice has been given to the hospital managers: s. 25(1). In *Re Kinsey* (1999) 21 June, unreported (HC), it was held that the notice had not been given to the hospital managers by a NR who handed a letter requesting the discharge of her son to the hospital receptionist, because to be effective, notice must be given to an officer of the hospital appointed for this task. The reason for the 72-hour delay is to give the RMO time to object to the making of the order in the form of a report to the managers 'certifying that in the opinion of that officer the patient, if discharged, would be likely to act in a manner dangerous to other persons or to himself': s. 25(1). If this is done, the NR may not apply again for the discharge of the patient for six months from the date of the report: s. 25(1)(b).

Section 25 provides one of the rare examples of where the word 'dangerous' actually appears on the face of the Act. This, in itself, is interesting, given the problems in accurately identifying future dangerous behaviour (see Chapter 4), but the more pertinent point here is that the effect of s. 25(1) is, apparently, that a patient can be discharged by an NR, in the face of opposition from the RMO or others involved in the treatment and detention of the patient, if the patient is *not* 'dangerous', *even if* he or she is mentally disordered to a degree that makes hospitalisation appropriate, and even if discharge poses a risk to that patient's health or safety. This was the situation in *Riverside*. In a judgment that also makes it clear that the hospital managers must not simply accept a s. 25 report as accurate, but rather have an active, quasi-judicial role, of accepting or rejecting the RMO's view (see also Department of Health and Welsh Office, 1999: para. 22.2(d)), Latham J held that, under s. 25, dangerouness is the sole issue. There may well be contradictory views in front of the hospital managers because s. 24 gives a medical practitioner, acting on behalf of an NR considering making an order under s. 23, a right of access in private to the patient, and to records relating to the detention and treatment of the patient.

The odds are, however, stacked in favour of the RMO, because the hospital managers are, presumably, only required to ensure that the RMO's opinion is reasonable, and not necessarily one with which they agree. Nevertheless, there are examples of cases in which hospital managers have not followed the advice of an RM, such as *R v Huntercombe Maidenhead Hospital, ex p SR* [2005] EWHC 2361, [2006] ACD 17, 2005 WL 2273357. R, aged 15, was detained under s. 3. Her father wrote to the hospital challenging her detention and this was treated by the hospital managers as an order for discharge under s. 23. R's RMO provided a report affirming that s. 25(1) was met, but the hospital did not accept that R would be 'dangerous' if released and decided that she should be released in accordance with s. 23. The official solicitor challenged that decision on behalf of R, arguing that it was not in R's best interests to be discharged. Because there was much evidence that R was likely to be violent if discharged, Jackson J held that the decision to discharge was, on the facts, perverse and irrational, and would be quashed on that basis (para. 29). Of more general relevance, following the approach in *Huzzey* and *Wirral*, he also held that s. 23 bestows a wide discretion that the hospital managers, in this case, had inappropriately fettered. The managers were not under a legal obligation, having decided that the patient did not meet the dangerousness criteria, to order discharge (para. 20). Other factors could, and should, properly be taken into account. In summary, then, it seems that those in a position to order discharge each have a wide discretion, subject only to judicial review and human rights requirements, to act as they see fit. It also seems that, in cases of dispute, the last word rests with the hospital managers.

8.3.3 Discharge of patients detained under civil law: the practice

All patients should be subject to the 'care programme approach' (see Chapter 9), and there is specific guidance relevant to the discharge plan of a patient who is to be made subject in discharge to the available powers of continued supervision in the community. In its general guidance, the Department of Health (1989) advises that 'planning [for discharge] should start at an early stage', and, if it is known in advance that support will be required on the discharge of non-emergency patients, planning should start 'before admission' (para. 2). The aim of the planning process is to restore the patient to independence in the community to the fullest extent possible (para. 3), and should involve both the primary care team and social services departments, and others who may have a role to play in the continued care and support of the patient (para. 2), such as relatives and GPs. Paragraph 5 provides that '[p]atients should not be discharged until the doctors concerned have agreed and management is satisfied that everything reasonably practicable has been done to organise the care that patient will need in the community', and the patient, or his or her relatives, should be given written guidance on medication, lifestyle, early indicators of relapse and sources of help. Responsibility for overseeing the making of these arrangements should be allocated to a named member of staff (para. 6). As will be discussed further below, and again in Chapter 9, one significant issue affecting the viability of discharge is the availability of suitable provision for the patient in the community, whether in the form of treatment, or of professionals willing to administer them and to take responsibility for the patient, or of accommodation.

There is more to discharge, though, than logistics. It seems that, in practice, a rehearsal of the criteria for admission will structure the consideration of discharge, of both detained and informal patients. This will entail the diagnostic considerations (see Chapter 2), the vulnerability question (in particular, the risk of suicide – see Chapter 3) and the dangerousness question (see Chapter 4). All of this must be considered in the context of the circumstances of the particular patient and so, as with admission, factors such as the patient's willingness to continue to be treated as an outpatient and his or her home circumstances, and the availability of suitable accommodation more generally, will impact significantly on each of these questions (Dell and Robertson, 1988). The various issues to be considered have been structured in the form of 'readiness for release' scales such as that devised by Eisner (1989) and Hogarty and Ulrich (1972). Further guidance was issued by the NHS Management Executive (1994) as part of the initiative to standardise and formalise care in the community. This provides that patients should be discharged 'only when and if they are ready to leave hospital', bearing in mind the availability of outpatient services and the attitude of the patient towards them; it spells out the 'fundamental duty' that those considering discharge have to protect the health, safety and welfare of both the patient and other persons (1994: para. 2).

There is no legal duty on the face of the Act. It has been suggested that there is a common law duty of care placed on those taking discharge decisions (*Holgate* v *Lancashire Mental Hospitals Board* [1937] 4 All ER 294), but more recent decisions do not share this view. The Court of Appeal held in *Clunis* v *Camden and Islington HA* [1998] 2 WLR 902, that a person who had killed a third party shortly after being discharged from hospital and after failing to keep outpatient appointments with his doctor, had no cause of action for negligence against his health authority, both on the grounds that he should not be allowed to profit from his own wrong, and that to find the existence of a duty of care in such circumstances would be counter to public policy. Clunis later went to Strasbourg (*Clunis* v *UK*, 11 September 2001) arguing that the failure of the hospital to maintain control of him in the community amounted to a breach of Art. 8 ECHR, in that the subsequent events would not have occurred but for that failure, and that this put the UK government in breach of its positive obligations under that Article. The court held his complaint inadmissible.

Following *Clunis*, it was similarly held, in *Palmer* v *Tees HA* (2000) 2 LGLR 69 (CA), in which a psychiatric outpatient had abducted, sexually abused and murdered a four-year-old girl, that there was no cause for an action for negligence brought by the child's mother. Relying on the policy arguments, that to find the health authority liable would not prevent further incidents of this nature and would detract from their primary functions, that to issue warnings concerning risk to the public would breach confidentiality, and on the decision of the House of Lords, in *Hill* v *Chief Constable of West Yorkshire* [1989] AC 53, that, in order to be liable for negligence based on the actions of a third party, it must be shown that the victim belonged to a special class of persons at risk (which was judged not to be the case here), it was held that there was no duty of care in such a situation. This is a difficult issue: if there is to be liability in a situation such as that in *Clunis* or *Palmer*, one inevitable consequence would be an increased reluctance to discharge at least some patients who are, in fact, fit for discharge. Yet it is perhaps hard to justify why normal principles of negligence should not apply here. After all, under such principles, healthcare and social service professionals are judged by no harsher a standard than that set by their peers (see further Chapter 12). The courts may be able to pick and chose with the common law, but they do not have jurisdiction to disapply the Human Rights Act 1998 in this situation. In a case such as *Clunis* or *Palmer*, Arts. 2 and 8 might be engaged. In *Osman* v *UK* (2000) 29 EHRR 245, however, the court made it clear that, although the state has a positive duty to protect life, this only applies when the life of an 'identifiable individual or individuals' (at para. 116) is at risk from another. The Convention offers no protection under Art. 2 from a 'random' killing. *Osman* was applied, *mutatis mutandis*, to Art. 8 in *Glaser* v *UK* (2001) 33 EHRR 1. As such, the existing common law decisions do not conflict with the requirements of the Convention.

8.3.4 The discharge of Part III patients

The powers of discharge in s. 23 apply to patients detained in hospital under s. 37, although subject to the modifications in Sch. 1, Part I, para. 8, MHA 1983, which disapplies the power of the nearest relative to order discharge. For patients subject to s. 41 restrictions, Sch. 1, Part II, para. 7 provides similarly, and also adds the requirement to s. 23(1) that any order for discharge can only be made with the consent of the Secretary of State. The powers given to the Secretary of State provide an example of the limitation of medical power and clinical discretion concerning restricted patients, with the implicit message that the clinical gaze fails to consider appropriately all factors relevant to the discharge of presumptively dangerous patients.

The Secretary of State usually prefers, rather than ordering the discharge of a restricted patient under s. 23, to use the more sophisticated powers available in s. 42 to discharge the patient absolutely or, as is usual in the first instance, conditionally. But here, as under s. 23, there are no detailed criteria on the face of the Act by which to make that decision. A restriction order may be ended 'if the Secretary of State is satisfied that ... a restriction order is no longer necessary for the protection of the public from serious harm' (s. 42(1)), in which case the patient is treated as though on a s. 37 order from the date of the discharge of the restrictions by virtue of s. 41(5)). This wording is not more closely defined anywhere else, and, according to Stuart Smith LJ in *R v Parole Board, ex p Bradley* [1990] 3 All ER 828 at 836, it cannot be elaborated with any degree of precision. There is even less guidance on discharge, which the Secretary of State may do by warrant 'if he thinks fit': s. 42(2). All that there has been until recently was an *obiter* comment of Lawton LJ, in *Kynaston v Secretary of State for Home Affairs* (1981) 73 Cr App R 281 (CA), that a patient who is no longer disordered should be discharged. Now, the requirements of Art. 5(1) of the Convention and the dicta of the European Court in *Winterwerp* make it clear that the continued detention of a patient depends on evidence of continuing mental disorder; since the Secretary of State is given significant powers by the 1983 Act, he or she should not leave matters to be decided at the patient's next MHRT hearing. If he or she has information to suggest that a patient is entitled to discharge, he or she should act on it.

In practice, these decisions are taken by the Home Secretary in consultation with various bodies. Section 41(6) of the 1983 Act requires the RMO of a restricted patient to make yearly reports to the Home Secretary, which must contain 'such particulars as the Secretary of State may require'. The purpose of these reports is to prevent the unwarranted detention of restricted patients. The Home Office has issued guidance (Home Office, n.d.), which requires that reports contain information relating to patients' attitudes and motivations, the effects of treatment, and the chances of reoffending, and give reasoned advice on the need for continued detention, and whether detention need be in a special hospital.

The Home Secretary may also call upon the Advisory Board on Restricted Patients (ABRP), set up in 1973, following the recommendation of the Aarvold Committee (Home Office, 1973), in the wake of the release and reoffending of the poisoner, Graham Young. The ABRP draws its membership from the great and the good of legal, forensic psychiatric, probation, social service and criminal justice circles. Its role is to advise the Home Secretary about restricted patients in respect of whom the risks to the public are particularly difficult to predict, or where the case is otherwise potentially controversial. Around fifty cases are referred to the ABRP by the Home Secretary annually, which constitute around 15 to 20 per cent of all discharge and transfer recommendations (Eldergill, 1997: 166). The main concerns of the Home Secretary and the ABRP are essentially the same as those that feature in the discharge of patients not subject to restrictions, although, as might be expected, with the emphasis on the degrees of risk to other persons that the patient, if released, might pose (Green and Baglioni Jr, 1997).

The ABRP reports to the Home Secretary, and to an RMO if his or her recommendation is not agreed with, but not, until fairly recently, to the patient. In *R v Secretary of State for the Home Department, ex p Powell* (1978, unreported), it was held that a patient has no right of access to the recommendations of the ABRP, because the decisions of that body are not open to judicial review. But in *R v Secretary of State for the Home Department, ex p Harry* [1998] 3 All ER 360 (HC), in which a proposal for a patient's transfer had been made by a MHRT (see later) to the Secretary of State, who, in turn, had consulted the ABRP, it was held to be a breach of natural justice if the patient is not allowed an opportunity to make representations both to the ABRP and, following its recommendation, to the Home Secretary. Accordingly, the Home Office changed its practice, and now patients are entitled to make representations, and to be given a copy of the ABRP's report to the Home Secretary and of the Home Secretary's reasons for his or her decision. As Horne (1999) suggests, however, it is important not to overestimate the importance of this victory for patients. *Harry* was also the latest in a long line of cases to confirm the width of the discretion available to the Home Secretary, both to consult whomsoever he or she thinks fit before consenting to a discharge, and to give full weight to considerations of public safety when arriving at a decision.

The ABRP meets several times a year to consider the cases assigned to it by the Home Secretary, which will, in turn, have been recommended for discharge by the patient's RMO. If the patient is in a special hospital, it is unlikely that he or she will be discharged into the community. It is more common that the RMO will recommend that he or she be transferred into increasingly less secure accommodation – RSUs and then general NHS hospitals or, perhaps more likely, hostel accommodation – before final discharge. The Secretary of State may direct the transfer of any patient subject to a hospital order or a transfer direction, either between special hospitals (in respect of which the patient has no right to be consulted (*R v SSHD, ex p Pickering* (1990, unreported) (CA)), or from a special hospital into less secure accommodation: s. 123, reg. 7, 1983 Regulations, SI 1983/893. In either case, a positive RMO recommendation will entail a member of the ABRP visiting the patient. In addition, the NHS trust that processes the RMO's recommendation may also add its opinion to the documentation forwarded to the Home Secretary, even though those providing an opinion may have never seen the patient. Clearly, much of the decision-making process in respect of the discharge of restricted patients from special hospitals into less secure forms of compulsory detention is still carried out 'in private and with few procedural safeguards' (Richardson, 1993: 287).

There are also practical problems facing patients seeking transfer out of a special hospital. Historically, a substantial number of patients have been detained inappropriately in high-security accommodation (Gostin, 1986a; Home Office and Department of Health, 1992; Department of Health, 2000), yet despite the increase in RSU provision, RSUs are often unwilling to accept patients who require more than two years' care, whether dangerous or not (Dolan and Shetty, 1995), giving priority to admissions from the prison system or from local hospitals (Gostin and Fennell, 1992: 211), so that, even when transfer has been approved, alternative hospital accommodation has long been hard to find (Dell, 1980; Smith *et al.*, 1991). The mean wait in one study carried out at Rampton in the early 1990s was 425 days, with individual cases ranging from 149 to 824 days, which also found that delay was, in part, attributable to lags in the process of initiating transfer (Dolan and Shetty, 1995). In consequence, on occasion, what started out as a recommendation by the RMO for transfer becomes a recommendation for discharge by passage of time. According to Gostin and Fennell (1992: 211) '[i]t is not uncommon for a patient on a transfer list to have improved to the point that discharge is appropriate rather than transfer'. Clearly, this situation is less than satisfactory.

This problem does not apply to transfers to prison or between wards within each hospital (Mental Health Act Commission, 1997: para. 4.5.4), but as far as transfer to other NHS accommodation is concerned, the situation has been slow to improve. There were 349 patients from all three special hospitals awaiting transfer in April 2001, not including those suitable but not officially listed for transfer because there is 'no realistic hope of finding them alternative accommodation' (MHAC, 2001: 5.6). By 2003, 'some acceleration in arranging transfers' had been noted (MHAC, 2003: 12.10), which is to be expected, because the accelerated discharge programme (ADP) was then in full effect (see Chapter 3), and personality disorder centres, which provide services for patients transferred out of special hospitals, were being pump-primed by the Department of Health (National Institute for Mental Health in England, 2003: 39). Nonetheless, 'there continue to be a substantial minority of patients who are ready for transfer or discharge, but are waiting Home Office approval, the identification of placements outside the hospital, or an available bed in such a placement' (Mental Health Act Commission, 2003: 12.9), and, again as noted in Chapter 3, the experience of those running special hospitals is that, by 2005, it is 'now more difficult than ever' (Mersey Care NHS Trust, 2005: 5) to find medium-secure accommodation able to accept a patient on transfer, the ADP having filled available space, albeit that the numbers now in need of transfer seem to be significantly lower than in 2001.

There is little that the patient or his or her RMO can do to force the situation. In *R v MHRT and Secretary of State for Health, ex p LH* [2001] 1 MHLR 130 (HC), it was held to be no breach of any Convention right for the Secretary of State to fail to transfer a patient judged as suitable. It is, however, clear, from *Aerts v Belgium* (2000) 29 EHRR 50, that there is a point when conditions of detention are so unsuitable for the patient in question that a breach of Art. 5(1)(e) will be found. In such a case, a mentally ill person held in unsuitable conditions in prison for seven months until a hospital bed could be located for him successfully brought an action under Art. 5. The PCT of a patient's home area may seek suitable transfer accommodation further afield in an effort to circumvent bed shortages locally, but, as the MHAC notes, and the case of *R v Oxfordshire Mental Healthcare NHS Trust and Oxfordshire Health Authority* [2001] 1 MHLR 140 (HC) demonstrates, 'health authorities [now trusts] appear unwilling to fund expensive placements elsewhere' (Mental Health Act Commission, 1999: para. 5.112).

If a patient is able to get to a position in which a decision to discharge can be made, the question arises of whether conditions should be attached. This, like the decision to discharge, is a matter of discretion (unlike in the case of discharge by a tribunal: see later in this chapter), but this does not mean that there are no limitations to its exercise. In *Kynaston*, Lawton LJ held that the Home Secretary should direct the *absolute* discharge of a patient if satisfied that he or she is no longer suffering from mental disorder. In the later Court of Appeal decision in *R v Merseyside Mental Health Review Tribunal, ex p K*

[1990] 1 All ER 694 (discussed further below), it was held that a tribunal can give a conditional discharge to a patient not then suffering from mental disorder, and it would be strange if this power were not also available to the Home Secretary, given that his or her margin of discretion is wider than that of a tribunal (see below). As seen above, although it was held in *Winterwerp* that detention may continue only so long as the patient's mental disorder persists to such a degree as to require hospitalisation, the Court held in *Johnson* v *UK* (1997) 29 EHRR 296 that discharge need not be immediate if it is necessary to make arrangements to smooth the release of the patient into the community.

A conditional discharge will usually require the patient to reside at a particular location, to attend for treatment (although there are no powers to treat without consent: s. 56(1)(c)), and to consent to the supervision of a social worker or probation officer, for a period of five years in a typical case, after which time, if progress has been satisfactory, the supervisor will recommend to the Home Secretary that the discharge be made absolute (Baxter, 1991). Conditional discharge, in the first instance, is the norm: the Home Secretary understandably takes a cautious approach. Only 43 discharges were ordered by the Home Secretary in 2004, all of them conditional, compared with 259 ordered by an MHRT (see later) (Home Office Research and Statistics Directorate, 2005: Table 16).

Section 42(3) further empowers the Secretary of State to recall the patient to hospital at any time unless and until absolutely discharged, at which point the patient will 'cease to be liable to be detained': s. 42(2). Patients recalled are entitled to be provided with reasons as soon as possible and, in any case, within 72 hours (Department of Health, 1993). There are no criteria for the application of s. 42(3), and the fact that these powers are exercisable 'at any time' perhaps indicates that recall is not linked to any breach of the conditions of discharge. Here, as elsewhere, the courts have traditionally been reluctant to fetter the discretion of the Home Secretary to act on the basis of considerations of public safety. In *R* v *Secretary of State for the Home Department, ex p K* [1990] 3 All ER 562, the Court of Appeal held that a conditionally discharged patient can be recalled to hospital even if there is not available to the Home Secretary evidence that the patient is mentally disordered at that time. The court emphasised that the responsibility of the Home Secretary was to balance the rights of the patient against the need to protect the public. K challenged that view in the European Court in *K* v *UK* (1998) 40 BMLR 20. The European Court did not dispute the Court of Appeal's explanation of the considerations properly to be taken into account by the Home Secretary, but held that there will be, as in that case, a breach of Art. 5(1) when recall is not, except in an emergency situation, based on the 'objective medical evidence' required by *Winterwerp*.

The implication of this is, in so far as the Court of Appeal in *K* suggested that a conditionally discharged patient can be recalled on grounds of public safety even if no longer mentally ill, that this view should not be taken in future; and in so far as s. 42(3) does allow recall in such circumstances, there is a strong argument waiting to be made that it is in this respect incompatible with Art. 5(1). In *R* v *SSHD, ex p L* [2005] EWCA Civ 2, [2006] 1 WLR 88, the Court of Appeal held that it is lawful for a patient, initially detained after being found not guilty but insane and sentenced to a hospital order with a restriction order under s. 5(1)(a) of the Criminal Procedure Insanity Act 1964, to be recalled on the basis of a disorder other than the one for which he received treatment in hospital before discharge. In reaching this decision, the court was obliged to distinguish its own decision in *R v Ashworth Hospital, ex p B* [2003] EWCA Civ 547, in which it had held that a patient could not be treated for any disorder other than the one in respect of which he or she had been detained in hospital, the point of distinction being that patients are held under the 1964 Act without there being a need to specify a particular form of mental disorder. But as that decision was later overturned by the House of Lords (([2005] UKHL 20, [2005] 2 AC 278, [2005] 2 All ER 289, [2005] 2 WLR 695; see Chapter 7), the decision in *ex p L* should be reconsidered accordingly. In short, this means that, on the law as it now stands, it is lawful for a patient to be recalled on the basis of a disorder other than the one for which he or she had, before discharge, received treatment in hospital.

There are dicta to be found in the first instance decision in the *K* case, to the effect that it would be unlawful for a patient to be recalled by the Home Secretary under s. 42(3) shortly after discharge by a tribunal, if there had been no change in circumstances in the intervening period ([1990] 1 All ER 703 (HC)). This view was put in doubt by the decision in *R v South Western Hospital Managers and Anor, ex p M* [1994] 1 All ER 161 (HC), but its tenor was affirmed by the decision of the House of Lords in *Von Brandenburg*, discussed later in this chapter. It has also been held that a restriction order is not discharged by implication if the Home Secretary allows the conditions of discharge to lapse: *R v Secretary of State for the Home Department, ex p Didlick* [1993] COD 412 (DC).

Although an RMO has no powers of recall, the decision in *ex p S* (see pp. 221–2) means that, if the grounds can be made out, there is always the option of sectioning a patient under s. 3 as an alternative to formal recall under s. 42(3); and such a patient remains liable to recall under s. 42(3) during and after discharge from detention under s. 3 (*Dlodlo*, see Chapter 6). As such discharge may be ordered by a tribunal, the decisions in these cases effectively allow the Home Secretary to overrule a tribunal decision, which he may want to do given the narrower criteria that are applied by a tribunal and his greater concern for public protection. This seems to raise the possibility that a recall in such circumstances would breach Art. 5(4) if there were to have been no change in the patient's condition or circumstances between discharge and recall, which is the basic thrust of *Von Brandenburg*. On the other hand, if there were to be objective medical evidence to justify the recall, there could be no breach. It might also be open to a court to hold that there are differences between the considerations relevant to those detained under Part II and s. 37 of the 1983 Act, and those in respect of whom a restriction order is in force – in essence a difference between managing treatment and managing risk (Hudson, 2002) – such as to justify a different weighting of the balance of evidence and different conclusions as to the need to detain in hospital. Something like this line of thinking was adopted by the High Court in *R v SSHD, ex p T* [2003] EWHC 538, Maurice Kay J holding, at para. 34, that the consideration relevant to the Home Secretary when deciding whether to impose restrictions on a sentenced prisoner transferred to hospital are not analogous to those relevant to a court contemplating making a hospital order at trial (see Chapter 6).

The number of patients recalled after conditional discharge stood at 55 in 1994, rising to around 80 per year around the turn of the century (Mental Health Act Commission, 2005: para. 5.136), with another hike, to 121 in 2003, and 149 in 2005 (Home Office Research, Development and Statistics Directorate, 2005: Table 3). An audit of all recalls to Ashworth hospital over the period 1981–91 (Dolan *et al.*, 1993) found that the most common reasons for recall were problems with the provision of suitable community services, especially for persons with alcohol and sexual problems, reoffending by patients, and concerns about public safety. Offending rates by discharged restricted patients are relatively low. Of those 127 discharged in 1993, only ten had been convicted of a standard list offence two years later, and only one of those of a grave offence. Eight were convicted of such an offence within five years. Of the 142 discharged in 1999, again, only one had been convicted of a grave offence within two years and two within five years, with a further seven convicted of a standard list offence within two years and 19 within five years (Home Office Research, Development and Statistics Directorate, 2005: Table 17). Street (1998: ch. 8) found that the grave offences covered a wide spectrum of mainly violent crimes, although the numbers were very low (one for manslaughter, three for rape) of all patients discharged in the four years up to 1994. There is evidence to suggest that psychopathically disordered offenders are markedly more likely to reoffend, and for a longer period after discharge, than persons diagnosed as mentally ill, and that conditionally discharged patients are less likely to reoffend than those who are absolutely discharged (Bailey and MacCulloch, 1992), which helps to explain why so few absolute discharges are made.

8.4 Mental health review tribunals: preliminaries and process

Mental health review tribunals (MHRTs) were introduced by the MHA 1959 to provide a mechanism to review the legality of the detention of detained but not informal patients, as well as those subject to guardianship, and now also compulsory aftercare (see Chapter 9). They were devised by the Percy Commission as a replacement for judicial commitment, which was abolished by the 1959 Act. As the admission process was handed over to ASWs and doctors, MHRTs constituted the structural downgrading of legalism, from main player in the admission process to *ex post facto* watchdog. The Mental Health Bills of 2002 and 2004 would have moved back in the direction of the pre-1959 system, with no long-term compulsion possible without the prior approval of a tribunal, but the slimmed-down proposals published in 2006 have abandoned this plan. Despite this, MHRTs continue to have significant legal powers with respect to the continued detention and discharge of patients.

In the context of the 1959 Act, MHRTs might be seen as an island of legalism in a sea of medical power. The 1983 Act extended the legal powers of MHRTs further, largely as a result of the decision of the European Court of Human Rights in *X* v *UK* (1981) 4 EHRR 181, in which it was held that the situation under the 1959 Act regarding the discharge of restricted patients, who could not apply to a tribunal for discharge and whose release was at the discretion of the Home Secretary, violated Art. 5(4) ECHR. Under the 1983 Act, *all* detained patients have a right to have their continued detention in hospital reviewed at periodic intervals by an MHRT with the power, indeed, the duty, if the prescribed criteria are met, to discharge the patient.

8.4.1 Constitution and appointment

The basis of the powers of MHRTs is currently s. 65, together with Sch. 2, MHA 1983, augmented by the Mental Health Review Tribunal Rules 1983 ('the 1983 Rules'), SI 1983/942 (amended by SI 1996/314 and SI 1998/1189), made by the Lord Chancellor under s. 78. Early in 2006, the Department of Health established a Tribunal Rules Advisory Group, with a brief to advise the Department of Health on whether, and if so, how, the current Rules should be updated. There must be an MHRT for every region of England, and one for Wales (s. 65(1A)), and it is the duty of the Secretary of State to determine the regions and to ensure that they cover the whole of England: s. 65(1B). A pool of MHRT members must be appointed by the Lord Chancellor, and, in each region, must include a number of 'legal members', 'medical members' and 'lay members' (as they have come to be known), defined as persons with 'experience in administration... knowledge of social services or such other suitable qualifications and experience as the Lord Chancellor considers suitable': Sch. 2, para. 1. Historically, the system has suffered from a shortage of persons willing and able to act as tribunal members. But concerted efforts have successfully been made over the last few years to improve recruitment. According to Mental Health Review Tribunal Secretariat (2005: 18), the total number of tribunal members has increased from six hundred or so in 2001 to more than a thousand by 2005, with over 250 legal, 100 medical, and 77 lay members recruited over that period. Vacancy rates are down from 22 per cent, 68 per cent and 31 per cent for legal, medical and lay members respectively, in 2001, to a situation where there are now no vacancies for legal or medical members and only 4 per cent for lay members. This is a highly significant achievement: in the past, the non-availability of, in particular, medical members was a major cause of delay in the hearing of applications.

In each region, a legal member will be the 'chairman of the tribunals' (Sch. 2, para. 3), and it is the responsibility of that person to appoint the members for each proceedings or set of proceedings for which an MHRT must be constituted: r. 8(1), 1983 Rules. Each MHRT must consist of at least three members (s. 65(4)), with at least one legal, one medical and one lay member, and the legal member is to be the president of the tribunal so constituted: Sch. 2, paras. 4, 6. In practice, it is rare for more than three members to be present at an MHRT hearing. If the application is by a restricted patient, the president of the tribunal must be selected by the chairman from a list approved by the Lord

Chancellor, and such persons will be those with experience in the criminal courts: r. 8(3), 1983 Rules. Some legal members deal solely with restricted patients. The vast majority are circuit judges, although there are also some recorders and QCs (Department of Health, 1997: Appendix 1).

To prevent a possible conflict of interests, members or officers of the management of the hospital or mental nursing home at which the patient resides, members of the health authority or trust with powers to discharge the patient under s. 23, and anyone with 'a personal connection with the patient or [who] has recently treated the patient in a professional medical capacity' are ineligible from tribunal membership: r. 8(2), 1983 Rules. In *R v Midlands and North West MHRT, ex p PD* [2004] EWCA Civ 311, 2004 WL 412965 the Court of Appeal held that r. 8(2) did not prohibit a consultant psychiatrist, C, employed by the defendant trust from sitting as medical member of the tribunal hearing PD's application. C had not worked at the hospital at which PD was detained and was therefore not an 'officer' of the trust for these purposes (Lord Phillips MR at para. 24), although this will always be a question of fact and context.

There are also questions of natural justice and Convention rights to consider. The test for bias, under both domestic principles of natural justice and the right to a fair trial guaranteed by Art. 6 of the Convention, was authoritatively stated by Lord Bingham in *Porter v Magill* [2001] UKHL 67, [2002] 2 AC 357, [2002] 2 WLR 37, [2002] 1 All ER 465, at para. 103: 'The question is whether the fair-minded and informed observer, having considered the facts, would conclude that there was a real possibility that the tribunal was biased'. This dicta was applied by the Divisional Court in *R v MHRT, ex p M* [2005] EWHC 2791, finding that the test was not satisfied by the fact that the legal member of the tribunal had been the judge who sentenced M. It was also applied by the Court of Appeal in *PD*, upholding the first instance decision, that, on the facts (the main considerations being that C had no contact with the patient or those responsible for his care, and stood neither to gain or lose as a result of his position as medical member), there was neither bias nor the appearance of it in this case. The Court of Appeal refused to consider practical or logistic issues in deciding the case (para. 11). In the new era of trusts operating on a regional basis (the trust in this case is an amalgamation of a number of smaller trusts and now runs 33 sites across a considerable area of the north-west of England), had the decision been otherwise, it would have given rise to a new set of logistic problems for the MHRT Secretariat, which would have been obliged to look further afield to locate medical members deemed sufficiently independent to be acceptable.

8.4.2 Applications and referrals

The process of making a tribunal application can be complicated, confusing, and intimidating for patients. Hospital managers are under a duty to 'take such steps as are practicable' to inform detained patients about their right to apply to an MHRT 'as soon as possible after the commencement of the patient's detention' (s. 132(1)(b), MHA 1983), and a similar duty applies in respect of the patient's nearest relative and his or her rights to apply to a tribunal: s. 132(2). All information must be given both orally and in writing: s. 132(3). The Code of Practice additionally requires that patients wishing to apply to MHRTs be 'given all the necessary assistance to progress with such an application' (Department of Health and Welsh Office, 1999: para. 22.17), including being told about the right to legal representation (see further below) and how to obtain it. A member of staff, trained for the purpose, usually known as the mental health act administrator, should be designated by the managers as responsible for ensuring that patients are given this advice and assistance (1999: para. 14.13.c).

MH v *SSDH* [2005] UKHL 60 concerned a patient, MH, detained under s. 2 MHA 1983, who suffered from severe mental disability, such that she lacked the capacity to make a tribunal application. The House of Lords held that these provisions, coupled with the obligation of hospital managers to refer a case to a tribunal when a patient does not take advantage of his or her right to make an application (see below) means that there is no breach of the requirements of Art. 5(4) of the Convention's requirement that there must be a review of the lawfulness of a patient's detention 'at reasonable intervals': *Winterwerp* (1979) 2 EHRR 387 at para. 39. Baroness Hale pointed out that the right given by Art. 5(4) is to 'take proceedings', as opposed to the right of a person detained on a criminal matter, which is to 'be brought promptly before a judge': Art. 5(3). Hence, so it was held, there is no absolute obligation to hold a hearing in Art. 5(4). Instead, it is a matter for the patient to decide (1999: para. 22). If the patient lacks capacity to make that decision, this does not mean that the detaining section, here s. 2, breaches Art. 5(4): 'Rather, it leads to the conclusion that every sensible effort should be made to enable the patient to exercise that right if there is reason to think that she would wish to do so' (1999: para. 23).

Baroness Hale further pointed out that the patient's nearest relative and 'other concerned members of the family, friends or professionals, can help put the patient's case before a judicial authority' (1999: para. 27). That was so here, but will not always be so: not all patients have concerned family or friends to safeguard their interests, in which case, the patient will be dependent solely on professionals to provide the assistance to make an application. The judgment of the House of Lords in this case leaves open the possibility that there will be a breach of Art. 5(4) *in fact* when suitable assistance for a patient lacking capacity to decide whether or not to make a tribunal application is not forthcoming; we might be inclined to go further, and suggest that the European Court may be more sympathetic to the plight of patients lacking capacity and hold, as did the Court of Appeal in *MH* , before being overturned by the House of Lords, that, to comply with Art. 5(4), there must be steps taken to 'devise a system in which hospital managers were under a duty to refer incompetent patients admitted under section 2 to an MHRT' (Wall LJ, [2005] 1 WLR 1209, [2004] EWCA Civ 1609 at para. 54). At present, despite these mechanisms for information provision, 70 per cent of patients detained under s. 2 do not make a tribunal application (Mental Health Act Commission, 2005: para. 4.112).

8.4.2.1 Applications

When a patient is liable to be detained (except under the short-term civil provisions in ss. 5, 135 and 136, or under a remand order or interim hospital order made by a court: ss. 35, 36, 38), the patient and/or the patient's nearest relative have a right to test the grounds for the continued (liability to) detention by applying to an MHRT under ss. 66, 69 or 70. Basically, the patient may make a fresh application whenever a significant decision relating to the detention is made. An application must be made within the 'relevant period' (s. 66(1)), which varies according to the event triggering the right to apply. On occasion, both the patient and his or her nearest relative have a right to apply, but each can only make one application within each relevant period (s. 77(2)), and there can be no application, except in accordance with the following provisions: s. 77(1). The detail of entitlement to make an application is as follows.

8.4.2.1.1 Patients detained under Part II

The patient alone may make an application:

   (a) within 14 days of admission for assessment: s. 66(1)(a), (2)(a);

   (b) within six months of admission for treatment: s. 66(1)(b), (2)(b);

   (c) within six months of transfer from guardianship to hospital: s.66(1)(e), (2)(e);

   (d) within the period of renewal (which will be six months in the first instance, 12 months thereafter (s. 20(2)(a), (b)) of the authority to detain): s. 66(1)(f), (2)(f).

The patient *or* (but not 'and': s. 66(1)(i)) the nearest relative (provided that the NR was, or was entitled to be, informed of the report) may make an application:

   (a) within 28 days of a report reclassifying the patient's disorder being furnished under s. 16: s. 66(1)(d), (2)(d);

   (b) within six months of the making of an order for supervised discharge under s. 25A: s. 66(1).

The NR alone (s. 66(1)(ii)) may make an application:

   (a) within 28 days of a report being furnished by the patient's RMO under s. 25 blocking discharge by the NR of a patient admitted for treatment: s. 66(1)(g), (2)(d);

   (b) within 12 months (and again in any subsequent period of 12 months during which the order continues in force) of an order made under s. 29 replacing the NR with an acting NR, whether made before or after the patient's admission: s. 66(1)(h), (2)(g).

If an application has been made by a patient detained under s. 2, following which a hearing must take place within seven days (see later), that hearing must take place within that time period even if the patient is subsequently transferred to s. 3: *R v SW Thames MHRT, ex p M* [1998] COD 38 (HC). But an application made by a patient whilst detained under s. 3, but who is made subject to supervised discharge pursuant to ss. 25A, B and C before the hearing has taken place, will lapse and a new application must be made: *R v MHRT, ex p SR* [2005] EWHC 2923 (Admin). Stanley Burnton J distinguished the decision in the *Thames* case, on the basis that, although s. 72(1) (see below) treats applications under ss.2 and 3 of being of the same class, separate provision is made (in s. 72(4A)) for applications from patients subject to supervised discharge. In such cases, a new application must be made.

8.4.2.1.2 Patients detained under a hospital order

Section 66 applies to patients placed under a hospital order by a court in much the same way (s. 40(4)), although with two modifications. First, there can be no application in the first six months of hospitalisation, but such a patient may apply within the second six-month period of the order and thereafter annually. Secondly, a nearest relative may make an application where there has been a report made under s. 16 reclassifying the patient, but not otherwise in the first six months: s. 66(1)(f), (d), Sch. 1, Part I, paras. 2, 9, MHA 1983. An NR may apply in the second six months, and thereafter annually, if the hospital order is renewed: s. 69(1)(a). Although this is very similar to the power that the NR has to apply in respect of a Part II patient when a report has been furnished under s. 25 barring an application for discharge by the NR under s. 23 (see above), the key difference is that, as the power of the NR to order discharge is disapplied by Sch. 1, Pt. 1, para. 8 of the 1983 Act if a hospital order has been made, there is never a need for a report under s. 25 and so dangerousness is never an issue. Hence, a tribunal hearing on application by a NR is not obliged to discharge a patient who can be shown to the satisfaction of the tribunal not to be dangerous, as *is* the case for Part II patients, even where there is a need for hospitalisation on either or both of therapeutic and protectionist grounds (see s. 72(1)(b)(iii) and *R v MHRT, ex p Central and North West London Mental Health NHS Trust* [2005] EWHC 337).

If a person is treated by operation of s. 41(5) as being subject to a hospital order because a restriction order ceases to have effect, he or she may, however, apply within the first six months from the date on which the restriction order ceases to have effect: s. 69(2)(a). This is understandable because, in the vast majority of cases, s. 41(5) is triggered by the Home Secretary using his or her powers under s. 42(1) to end a restriction order, which is a good indication that the patient is no longer considered to constitute a serious risk to other persons. Also, as such patients will, by definition, have been in hospital for a considerable period of time, there is no reason why they should have to wait six months before making an application.

8.4.2.1.3 Patients subject to restrictions

There is a different regime for restricted patients, defined by s. 79(1) as including those subject to a restriction order, limitation direction or a restriction direction. Section 70, MHA 1983 provides that a restricted patient as defined in s. 79 may apply to an MHRT, first, between six and 12 months into their detention (s. 70(a)), and thereafter in any subsequent 12-month period: s. 70(b). Section 70 must be read together with s. 69(2), however, which provides that a person held by virtue of a transfer direction, with or without restrictions, or by a hospital direction, with or without an accompanying limitation direction, may apply within the first six months beginning on the date that the order under that Act was made. The reason for this is that the Home Secretary has the option, in the case of a person transferred from prison to hospital or subject to a hospital direction, to transfer that person (back) to prison if hospital treatment is no longer required: s. 50. Not all restricted patients will be in hospital, because a percentage will have been conditionally discharged. Patients in this category remain liable to recall until absolutely discharged, and consequently may apply to a tribunal once in the second 12 months following discharge, and thereafter, biennially: s. 75(2). If recalled to hospital following conditional discharge, the situation is as if a new order has been made and so s. 70 applies (s. 75(1)(b)), although the Home Secretary must refer such cases to a tribunal within one month (see later).

8.4.2.2 Referrals

The procedure for making an application to an MHRT is patient-led, and not all patients, whether because of cynicism, fear, apathy, or disorder, will activate it. To ensure that all detained patients are subject to an independent review of the grounds for detention, the 1983 Act requires hospital managers, or the Home Secretary, according to the circumstances, to refer cases to an MHRT. It also gives the Secretary of State a wide discretionary power to make referrals.

Hospital managers must refer the case of a patient admitted under s. 3 or transferred to hospital from guardianship if the patient does not make an application, or makes, but subsequently withdraws, an application (s. 68(5)), and the patient's case will not otherwise come before an MHRT, whether by reason of an application made by the patient's nearest relative or a referral by the Secretary of State under s. 67 (see below). This must be done, first, at the expiry of the first period in which an application could be made (that is, six months: s. 68(1)), and thereafter every three years, unless the patient is under 16 years of age, when the period is one year: s. 68(2). In addition to the powers of hospital managers, which do not extend to hospital-order patients, the Secretary of State has discretionary powers 'if he thinks fit, at any time' to refer the case of any patient detained under Part II, or under a hospital order without restrictions made by a court, to an MHRT: s. 67(1), Sch. 1, Part I, para. 1.

The Secretary of State also has discretionary powers to refer 'at any time' the case of patients subject to restrictions (s. 71(1)), whether actually 'detained' or not: s. 71(4). The extent of these powers was considered by the Court of Appeal in *R v SSHD, ex p C* [2002] EWCA Civ 647. C, detained under ss. 37 and 41, had been conditionally discharged by a MHRT. The tribunal had heard reports from medical professionals and a social worker that were in favour of discharge, subject to C residing in hostel accommodation and the availability of a psychiatrist to oversee C's progress, and discharge was deferred to allow these arrangements to be made. The tribunal did hear some conflicting medical evidence to the effect that a condition of psychiatric supervision was required, but it did not follow it, nor did it consider the report of second social worker that was opposed to discharge. When this was discovered by the Home Secretary, he used his powers to refer C's case back to the tribunal, principally on the grounds (1) that it is the preferred policy of the Mental Health Unit of the Home Office that patients be discharged with a condition of psychiatric supervision, (2) that this should have been ordered in this case, and (3) that, as the House of Lords had held in *R v Oxford Regional MHRT, ex p Secretary of State for the Home Department* [1988] 1 AC 120, a tribunal, after ordering discharge, has no power to reconsider the situation of its own motion and, if further evidence comes to light, the use of s. 71 is necessary. The making of the referral had the effect of voiding the tribunal's decision, which is the effect of any referral made under s. 71 by virtue of s. 73(7). Thus, in the view of the Home Secretary, the tribunal was bound to consider the matter afresh. C claimed a breach of Art. 5(4) of the Convention, because the effect of the use of s. 71 here was to deprive him of the effect of the tribunal's decision and hence delay his discharge.

The Court of Appeal, first, used this occasion to hold *Oxford* incompatible with Art. 5(4) (para. 28). (In fact, the court gave its detailed reasons for rejecting *Oxford* in its judgment in *R v SSHD and SSH, ex p IH* [2002] EWCA Civ 646, see below, which it had delivered earlier the same day). Second, the court made it clear that, therefore, in a case in which the conditions of discharge cannot be fulfilled within a reasonable time, the tribunal can reconsider its decision (para. 28). Third, accordingly, there was 'no justification' for the Home Secretary's referral, which undermined the jurisdiction of the tribunal in question (para. 29). Instead, the tribunal should have been 'invited to reconsider' its original decision. There was thus no need for the court to examine the Art. 5(4) issue in connection with this mode of use of s. 71, because it had already been held to be unlawful. Here, as with the requirement that leave is given under s. 17 rather than via s. 42, the courts are prescribing in some detail the limits of the powers open to the Secretary of State. At first instance ([2001] 1 MHLR 100 at 109), Collins J, having held that s. 71 *could* be used in this situation, and where the Secretary of State has information that was not before the tribunal, went on to say that in using it:

the Secretary of State must form the view that it is probable that the material in question would have effected the result in that it would have decided either that a more onerous condition be imposed or that a conditional discharge would not have been ordered.

Although overruled on the availability of s. 71, these comments nevertheless seem relevant to the question of when the Secretary of State should 'invite' a tribunal to reconsider its initial decision.

There is a duty placed on the Home Secretary to make a referral in respect of a detained restricted patient (rather than those 'liable to be detained', which would include conditionally discharged patients and those on leave of absence or absent without leave) whose case has not been considered by a tribunal for three years: s. 71(2). If a conditionally discharged restricted patient is recalled to hospital by the Secretary of State, he or she must also refer that patient's case to a tribunal within one month (s. 75(1)(a)) so that the recall decision can be scrutinised by a tribunal in accordance with specific criteria, as a safeguard against the possible abuse of power by the Secretary of State, who, as seen above, is given powers by the 1983 Act to recall a patient on the basis of other than medical evidence. This, as Hoggett (1996: 180) notes 'is the answer to the precise problem raised by the case of *X v UK*'. As a 'public authority' under s. 6(3) Human Rights Act 1998, the Secretary of State may now not act in a way incompatible with a Convention right (s. 6(1)), to the extent that that is possible whilst also complying with domestic legislation. Hence, the *ex post facto* review of a recall decision by a tribunal may satisfy the Convention but may not satisfy the requirements of the 1998 Act.

Although the general scheme of this process, as evidenced by s. 77(2), is that there should only be one application per patient per relevant period, the situation can arise when an application and a referral, or two applications, both fall due to be heard at the same time or in close succession. For example, hospital managers must refer the case of a s. 3 patient at the end of the first six-month period of detention, if the patient has not made an application during that period, even if the patient does decide to apply on the occasion of the authority for detention being renewed. Because of delays between application and hearing (see later), or because both the patient and his or her nearest relative have exercised a right to make an application, a situation may arise whereby two applications are pending. It is possible for an MHRT to conjoin two applications and hear them together (r. 18(1), 1983 Rules), although both applicants (if there are more than one) have full rights to be provided with documentation, representation, and so on: r. 18(2). Another option, if there are two applications, or an application and a mandatory reference, pending, is to withdraw one application. An application may be withdrawn at any time by the patient, in writing, with the agreement of the tribunal (or the regional chairman), and will be deemed withdrawn if the patient is discharged before the hearing: r. 19(1), (2), 1983 Rules. If an application is effectively withdrawn, another application may be made within the relevant period: s. 77(2). This allows the patient to 'bank' one application for use later in the same relevant period. In other circumstances, it may be that the withdrawal of an application triggers the duty of the hospital managers or the Home Secretary to make a referral, which cannot be withdrawn. The permutations and possibilities open means that there is a tactical aspect to the timing of an application from a purely technical view, in order to ensure that maximum use is made of the tribunal system (Gostin and Fennell, 1992: 77).

8.4.3 Before the hearing

Rule 3(1), 1983 Rules requires that applications to tribunals must be in writing, and 'wherever possible' include the patient's name, address (home and hospital), section under which he or she is currently liable to be detained, whether on leave of absence or not, and any other relevant information. If the application is to be made by the patient's nearest relative, his or her details must also be included: r. 3(2). The application must be signed by the applicant or 'any person authorised by him to do so on his behalf', who may be the member of staff designated to provide assistance, for example. The application must also include information about the applicant's intentions regarding representation. An applicant may represent him or herself (r. 3(2)(e)), or may authorise 'any person' to provide representation, except another patient who is liable to be detained (which includes patients on leave or conditionally discharged, but not informal inpatients) or who is subject to guardianship or aftercare under supervision: s. 78(2)(f); r. 10(1). If a patient does intend to be represented and the name and address of the authorised representative (AR) is known at the time of making the application, that information should be included (r. 3(2)(e)), and in any case, an AR should, on appointment, notify the tribunal of his or her name and address: r. 10(2). If the patient makes no appointment, the tribunal has discretionary default powers to do so on his or her behalf: r. 10(3). The tribunal's powers under r. 10, and other rules dealing with preliminary and incidental matters (rr. 6–8, 12, 13, 14(1), 15, 17, 19, 20, 26 and 28) may be exercised by the chairman of the tribunal alone (r. 5), or by his or her deputy: s. 78(6) and Sch. 2, para. 4, MHA 1983.

Most applicants appoint a lawyer as AR (Eldergill, 1997: 875); only three of 61 patients whose hearings were observed by Perkins (2000) were unrepresented. The Law Society has established the Mental Health Review Tribunal Panel, which admits solicitors, solicitors' clerks and members of the Institute of Legal Executives (ILEX) on satisfactory completion of (it must be said, fairly minimal) training and practice in, and observation of, MHRT work. Both patients and NRs are entitled to advice and assistance under the 'Green Form' scheme, which is means-tested, but, since 1982, legal representation at an MHRT, as well as advice and assistance, has qualified for non-means-tested assistance by way of representation (ABWOR), with the agreement of the Legal Services Commission (Community Legal Services (Financial) Regulations 2000, SI 2000/516). The Tribunals Service has made the applications forms available online. Agreement usually takes about a week, but can be arranged by telephone in emergency situations. Agreement may be refused if it is unreasonable, in all the circumstances, to grant legal aid. As only a relatively small percentage of all patients, and very few restricted patients, are discharged by a tribunal, a strict interpretation of the Regulations might see legal aid frequently being refused, and there are reports that this has happened in the past (Peay, 1989: 47), although it seems that legal aid is now only routinely denied on financial grounds. Once appointed, an AR has the same entitlements as the patient to be supplied by the tribunal with 'all notices and documents' relevant to the application: r. 10(4), 1983 Rules.

The notification of an intention to make an application triggers the duty of the tribunal to contact the managers of the hospital at which the patient is liable to be detained (rr. 2(1)(a), 4(1)(a)), the Secretary of State, if the patient is subject to restrictions (r. 4(1)), and 'other persons interested': r. 7 (although this latter is subject to Art. 8 of the Convention). This, in turn, triggers the duty of hospital managers to provide detailed and wide-ranging information about the patient (r. 6(1)(a), Sch., Part A), and to commission new medical and social work reports on the patient: r. (6)(1)(a), (b), Sch. Part B, para. 1. This must be done 'as soon as practicable', but, in any case, no more than three weeks after receipt by the hospital managers of the notification of the patient's application. If the patient is subject to restrictions, the Secretary of State, subject to the same time limits as hospital managers, must send a 'statement of further information relevant to the application as may be available to him' (r. 6(2)), unless the patient has already been conditionally discharged (and will thus be seeking an absolute discharge under s. 75: see earlier), in which case, the Secretary of State must, within six weeks, provide the information listed in Sch., Part C, which is similar to that in Part A, although tailored to the fact that the patient is not in hospital, and so requests information, for example, about treatment provision or supervision by a probation officer or social worker rather than by an RMO: r. 6(3)(a). Medical and social work reports should be provided by the Secretary of State (Sch., Part D), but, again, only if it is 'reasonably practicable' to do so: r. 6(3)(b). Such reports are, in fact, routinely provided, particularly if the Secretary of State is opposed to discharge. It is unusual for the Secretary of State to be represented at a tribunal hearing. In addition, Part III, Ch. 2 of the Domestic Violence, Crime and Victims Act 2004 provides that the victims of those convicted of a sexual or violent crime, or not convicted but made subject to a hospital order and restriction order under the operation of the Criminal Procedure (Insanity) Act 1964 and related legislation, may make representations to a tribunal which is considering discharging the offender from detention.

A copy of all of this documentation must be forwarded to the patient or his or her authorised representative (rr. 6(5), 10(4)), unless r. 6(4) applies. This allows a tribunal to withhold documents from the applicant, but only if 'disclosure would adversely effect the health or welfare of the patient or others'. The Tribunals Service has made it clear that 'Victims should be made aware that no guarantees can be given that any representations they make will not be disclosed to the patient' (2005: para. 8). The supplier to the tribunal of the documentation in question must state the grounds on which they rely, and it is then the duty of the tribunal to consider, applying the same 'adverse effect' test, whether the grounds are valid, and if it decides that they are, it must withhold the document in question and record the reasons for that decision: r. 12(2). The scope of the test in rr. 6(4) and 12(2) is nowhere closely defined. There is agreement amongst academic writers that it does not extend to protect damage to the therapeutic relationship (see Jones, 2006: 652; Hoggett, 1996: 189). But other boundaries are less clear: how great must the *risk* of adverse effects be? The word used is 'would' not 'might', which seems to indicate that there must be adjudged to be a fairly high degree of risk. A second issue is: how adverse must any effect of disclosure be? There is no modifier, so presumably *any* adverse consequence will suffice to satisfy the Rules. If so, this is questionable in policy terms. Gostin and Fennell (1992: 122) suggest that all information should be disclosed to the patient unless there are 'clear and specific' reasons for non-disclosure.

For some, the present authors included, it is arguable that even this does not go far enough. The right to know information relevant to a judicial decision concerning oneself is a requirement of natural justice, and it is hard to see how there can ever be a justification for non-disclosure, particularly to protect the welfare of others. Rules 6(4) and 12(2) were made in accordance with s. 78(2)(h), which provides that rules may be made allowing non-disclosure if considered to be 'undesirable in the interests of the patient or for other special reasons'. Although the words of the statute still, of course, have the force of law, the fact is that Rules do *not* allow non-disclosure for 'special reasons' (the phrase in s. 78(2)(h) was initially repeated in the Rules until the 1996 amendments) and, as things stand at present, therefore, such should not form part of the reasoning of any decision whether or not to disclose. Whether or not this is the case in practice is difficult to discern. Of course, all of this is now overlain with the requirements of the Convention. The denial of information relevant to a judicial decision about oneself raises issues under Arts. 5, 8 and, especially, 6. The precise contours of the justification for non-disclosure remain to be examined by a court. Part of the problem with policing this power, however, is that these decisions may be taken in private, possibly by one individual (r. 5), which seems to raise its own set of Convention-related problems.

Some, but not all, of these problems are answered by r. 12(3). When there has been a decision not to disclose information to the patient, the status of the authorised representative may prove crucial. By r. 12(3), if the patient has appointed as AR a barrister, solicitor, doctor or other 'suitable person by virtue of his experience or professional qualification', the information in question 'shall' be disclosed to the AR, as long as he or she undertakes not to disclose the information to the patient. This allows an AR access to the full information to ensure that the patient's case is heard and decided fairly and lawfully, and to argue an informed case for disclosure to the patient where a tribunal is 'minded not to disclose any document' to the patient. This is a pragmatic solution to a moral problem, which would most probably satisfy Arts. 5 and 6, but it can place an AR in an impossible position vis-à-vis the patient (see further Chapter 12). In practice, an AR will only rarely face this type of ethical dilemma as, after initial resistance to disclosure of medical reports, particularly from special hospital RMOs (Peay, 1989: 66), it is now rarely the case that all documents are not disclosed to patients, which provides further reason why the Rules should be amended.

An MHRT will not receive information solely from those exercising the authority to detain the patient. The patient is entitled under s. 76 to seek his or her own independent medical report. The purpose of such a report is to provide the patient with advice on whether to make an application to an MHRT, but, of course, if the report advises the making of an application, the patient will want to present it to the tribunal. A doctor 'authorised by or on behalf of a patient' must be given access to the patient in private and may examine records relating to detention and treatment. Although a patient may be denied access to information under rr. 6(4) and 12(2), he or she cannot prevent the disclosure of an unfavourable report that he or she has commissioned, if there is sufficient public interest to justify its disclosure (*W v Edgell and Ors* [1990] 1 All ER 835 (CA)), which means that a report that shows, for example, that a patient is more dangerous than thought to be by the RMO or hospital managers can, as in *Edgell*, be disclosed by the person making it.

Finally, information is also generated by the medical member of the MHRT. Rule 11, 1983 Rules requires the medical member, before the tribunal hearing takes place, to 'examine the patient and take such other steps as he considers necessary to form an opinion of the patient's mental condition'. For this purpose, the medical member has rights of access to the patient and his or her records, similar to those of doctors authorised by the patient under s. 76. If the patient refuses to be examined, a hearing can be postponed (r. 16(1)) or be deemed withdrawn: r. 19(2). The issue of due process is also to the fore here, because r. 11 casts the medical member as both 'witness' and 'decision-maker'. According to the Department of Health (1997: Appendix 13), the medical member should not give his or her opinion to the other members of the tribunal before the hearing, but the risk with this approach is that it is not then heard by the other tribunal members until *after* the hearing, with the applicant neither knowing about it nor having an opportunity to see it. In *R v Mental Health Review Tribunal, ex p Clatworthy* [1985] 3 All ER 699 (HC), Mann J held (at 704) that it would be a breach of natural justice for a tribunal to reach a decision based on the opinion of the applicant's condition that the medical member had formed, without that reasoning being made available to the applicant (see also *R v Avon and Wiltshire Mental Health Partnership NHS Trust, ex p KW* [2003] EWHC 919, 2003 WL 1823101).

This does not necessarily mean that the medical member's findings should be made available as evidence and therefore subject to cross-examination. As Gunn (1986c: 251) has pointed out, Mann J referred to a tribunal resting its decision on the *opinion* of the medical member. Gunn suggests that this is to blur the opinion–evidence distinction, and it may be that it is only *facts* known to the medical member, rather than his or her opinions, that must be disclosed to the applicant. In *R v Ashworth Hospital Authority, ex p H* [2002] EWCA Civ 923, at para. 84, Dyson LJ said, *obiter*, that it is 'the substance of the views' of the medical member that must be, other than under exceptional circumstances, disclosed to the patient or his or her AR.

The position of the medical member survived challenge under Art. 5(4) in *R v MHRT, North and East London Region, ex p H* [2000] CO 2120/2000. The European Court in *DN v Switzerland* Application No. 27154/95 [2001] ECHR subsequently held that there was a breach of Art. 5(4) in the Swiss tribunal system, under which a psychiatrist is both tribunal member and expert witness, because it did not guarantee a patient the independent and impartial hearing required by Art. 5(4). This case was distinguished in *R v MHRT, ex p S* [2002] EWHC 2522 (QBD), on the basis that, in the English and Welsh system, the medical member is not an expert witness, and, provided the medical member keeps (or is seen to keep?) an open mind, the requirement for impartiality is not breached. Research carried out by Richardson and Machin (2000a), however, suggests that it is not so easy in practice for the medical member to juggle the twin roles of witness and decision-maker. Their research suggests (2000a: 111–2) that the advice in *Clatworthy* is not often heeded and the medical member will usually give an account of his or her examination of the patient to the other members of the tribunal prior to the hearing, and, in 50 per cent of cases, will also volunteer an opinion: it also suggests that the distinction between fact and opinion may be easy to draw in the abstract, but in reality, there are no facts that are untainted by opinion in the area of mental health. Two thirds of the tribunal presidents interviewed by the researchers were themselves concerned about a potential lack of fairness arising from the dual role of the medical member, and Richardson and Machin provide examples of the fact that the opinions of medical members can determine the outcome of applications (in all cases in the survey, the tribunal's decision reflected the view of the medical member) when those opinions have not been aired during the proceedings. Perkins similarly found that 'Evidence was often revealed and considered in a haphazard way' (2000: 2). Richardson and Machin conclude with a call for the role of the medical member to be 'radically reconsidered' (2000: 115).

In the two, now abandoned, draft bills of 2002 and 2004, the intention of the govern-ment was to expand the role of tribunals, to cover initial decisions to use compulsion in treatment, and also to separate out the role of medical member and medical witness, at least to an extent. The latest governmental thinking is focused on narrower logistic questions concerned with making the current system function better, and is silent on the role of the medical member (Department of Health, 2006k). The Department of Health has, however, established an advisory group to consider amendments to the MHRT Rules. It would be possible either to abolish the pre-hearing examination or to recognise that examination for what it is, which is a part of the tribunal's deliberations – as Perkins (2000: 1), found to be the case – and so allow the patient to be legally represented at it. The really radical possibility – the abolition of the medical member altogether – is not, at first glance, unattractive. The evidence at the moment is that 'Opinions often [do] not appear to be held very strongly, particularly among lay and legal members' (Perkins, 2000: 3). Moreover, discussions amongst tribunal members only rarely entail consideration of the legal criteria that the tribunal is meant to apply (Richardson and Machin, 2000: 499). This means that, despite the legal status and powers of a tribunal, its decision-making remains largely within a medical paradigm. The abolition of the medical member would entail that the others would be unable merely to make up the numbers, and perhaps tribunals might begin to work as origi-nally intended – as a legal check on medical power. This is, however, a proposal unlikely to find much support in government or professional psychiatric circles.

Rule 13 gives to a tribunal wide powers to make directions designed to expedite hear-ings. In *R v MHRT, ex p B* [2002] EWHC Admin 1553, Scott Baker J urged tribunals to use these powers proactively to ensure that hearings occur in good time. Rule 16 provides that a tribunal may adjourn at any time in order to obtain further information or for any other purpose it deems appropriate, and on adjourning, a tribunal may give directions to expedite prompt hearing of the adjourned application, which is import-ant because one consequence of an adjournment may be that a patient stays in hospital longer than would otherwise have been the case. A tribunal should normally adjourn if there is any doubt whether conditions that it is considering attaching to an order for discharge can be implemented, and a decision to order discharge before while such doubts still exist will be quashed if unreasonable: *R v Secretary of State for the Home Department and Secretary of State for Health, ex p IH* [2002] EWCA Civ 646 at para. 98; *R v MHRT, ex p East London and the City Mental Health NHS Trust* (QBD (Admin)) [2005] EWHC 2329, 2005 WL 2996870.

In *ex p B*, B claimed that an adjournment, at which he had not been represented, had been improperly authorised. Scott Baker J held that the adjournment demonstrated bad practice, because it did not comply with either rr. 13 (no case management directions had been given) or 16 (there was no adjournment by a sitting tribunal) of the MHRT Rules (para. 21). He also stated that an adjournment should specify a specific return date, which had not been the case here (*ibid.*), and that the reasons for an adjournment must be given to the patient or his or her legal representative (para. 23). He did find that an adjournment was warranted on the facts (for which, see below).

In *R v MHRT, ex p Secretary of State for the Home Department* (1987) *The Times*, 25 March (HC) it was held that r. 16 does not permit adjournment in order to see if, with time, the condition of (in that case, a restricted) patient improves (see also *R v Nottingham MHRT, ex p Secretary of State for the Home Department* (1988) *The Times*, 12 October (HC)), and in *R v MHRT, ex p Secretary of State for the Home Department* [2001] ACD 62, it was held that a tribunal may not adjourn in order to consider whether to make a recommendation that it does not have statutory authority to make. A tribunal should 'give serious consideration' to the possibility of adjournment if the unavailability of medical witnesses for cross-examination 'is likely to be critical to [the tribunal's] ultimate decision': *R v Ashworth Hospital Authority, ex p H* [2002] EWCA Civ 923, [2003] 1 WLR 127, per Dyson LJ at para. 85.

8.4.4 Haste and delay in the application process

A truncated procedure applies in the case of applications or references by, or in respect of, patients detained under s. 2. As with other applications, there must be a written, signed application containing the information discussed above (r. 30), but on receipt of an application, the tribunal must fix the date of the hearing to occur within seven days from that date, and give notice of the date, time and location of the hearing to all those involved and who, in the opinion of the tribunal, should have an opportunity to be heard: r. 31. The responsible authority, as soon as it learns that there is to be an application, must supply copies of the admission papers and such information, detailed in Sch. Parts A and B (see earlier), as can reasonably be provided in the time available: r. 32. Documents can be withheld from the patient, as in non-s. 2 applications: r. 32(2). According to the annual report for 1991 (Department of Health, 1992: para. 6), adherence to this timetable can mean hurriedly prepared reports being made available to tribunal members in insufficient time to allow their contents to be digested. Indeed, in Milne and Milne's research into the operation of the MHRT system as it affected one northern hospital in 1988–92, all medical and social work reports bar one were submitted to the tribunal on the day of the hearing (1995: 95).

All of the evidence is that the situation improved little, if at all, in the subsequent years. By the late 1990s, the Department of Health's annual reports (see, for example, Department of Health, 1997) detailed a service in crisis. One main reason for this was the exponential increase in the rate of applications to tribunals. For all categories of patient, 1986 saw 5,046 applications or referrals. By 1996, this had increased to 14,913, reaching 20,157 by the year 2000 (Department of Health, 2001d: 25). Applications by patients detained under s. 2 tripled between 1986 and 1996, from 1,503 to 4,145 (Department of Health, 1997: Appendix 3), and have continued to rise since. Across the various regions, applications under ss. 2 and 3 rose between 1 per cent and 9 per cent in 2000 (Department of Health, 2001d: 25), to a total of around 20,000 applications, which had increased to around 22,000, with hearings up around 1,000 to 12,000, by 2005 (Mental Health Review Tribunal Secretariat, 2005: 22). The ever-increasing numbers of applications, in part, reflects an increasing number of formal admissions, from

17,999 in 1990–1 to 26,707 in 2000–1 (Department of Health, 2002b: Table 1), although thereafter admissions stabilised – there were 26, 752 in 2003–4 (Government Statistical Service, 2006).

As can be seen, there is a considerable falling off of applications – only half of applications by those held under ss. 3 and 37 reach the stage of a hearing, with around 60–70 per cent of s. 2 applications being heard (Mental Health Review Tribunal Secretariat, 2005: 23), either because the patient is discharged before the hearing by the RMO or because the application is withdrawn for some other reason, such as a setback in mental condition, so that the patient feels there is little point in applying at that time (Peay, 1989: 53; Mental Health Act Commission, 2005: para. 4.118). But the main reason is, no doubt, that patients are discharged by RMOs before an MHRT hearing can be scheduled. Eldergill (1997: 206) estimates that this explains 'almost all' of the fall-off of s. 2 cases and 'about half' of it in other non-restricted cases. In restricted cases, for obvious reasons, a majority of applications do result in a hearing.

The higher rate of applications being heard in s. 2 cases is, no doubt, a function of the seven-day timescale that must be adhered to, because there is less time for the situation to change once an application has been made. Despite the legal requirement, not all s. 2 applications were heard within seven days, and in 2000 'The continuing increase of Section 2 applications and a shortage of members to hear them has exacerbated the problem' (Department of Health, 2001d: 26). In the years since 2001, however, things have changed markedly: the average wait between application and hearing fell from 7.5 days in 2001 to less than six days in 2005 (Mental Health Review Tribunal Secretariat, 2005: 23).

This reflects renewed attempts to make this historically poorly funded and poorly run service operate more efficiently. The problems keeping to the seven-day time limit for s. 2 applications had a knock-on effect for other applicants (Wood, 1997: iii), with the consequence that, for non-s. 2 patients, delay, until recently, was the norm. For example, in December 2000, the average wait for non-s. 2, non-restricted patients varied regionally from 7.5 to 9.4 weeks, and for restricted patients from 13.14 to 24.1 weeks. And even this was an improvement on what had gone before: in the Nottingham region, in which Rampton hospital is located, for example, the average wait for restricted patients had fallen from 37.1 weeks in 1998 to 20.5 weeks in December 2000 (Department of Health, 2001d: 26). Despite these improvements, the MHRT Secretariat, which operated out of offices in London, Nottingham, Liverpool and Cardiff, was under-resourced for the job with which it was tasked. Throughout the 1990s, the annual reports of the MHRT regime were replete with attempts of the 15 or so staff in each of the five MHRT regions in England and Wales to cope with the massive workload that the increased number of applications has imposed on them.

The Rules do provide (r. 29(cc)) an eight-week upper time limit between a reference by the Secretary of State and subsequent tribunal hearing in the case of a restricted patient recalled to hospital, which was added following the friendly settlement in *Roux* v *UK* [1997] EHRLR 102. But there are no limits for other patients, except those detained under s. 2, nor is there any mechanism in the Act or Rules whereby a patient can challenge the legality of such delays. In the 1990s, applications for judicial review were headed off by the rather disingenuous and ethically suspect method of allowing the patient in question to jump the queue (see Eldergill, 1997: 787), or they fell away because the patient was discharged (as in *Roux* v *UK* [1997] EHRLR 102). As far as Art. 5(4)'s requirement for the legality of detention to be 'decided speedily by a court' is concerned, in a friendly settlement agreed before the European Commission of Human Rights in *Barclay-Maguire* v *UK* Application No. 91/7/80 (December 1981) (discussed in Gostin, 1982), the UK government suggested 13 weeks as a reasonable maximum waiting time for MHRT applicants. In *Pauline Lines* v *UK* [1997] EHRLR 297, in a friendly settlement, the UK government undertook to amend the 1983 Rules to ensure that no recalled patient waited more than two months after recall for a tribunal hearing. The Commission declared admissible the factually complicated case of L, a conditionally discharged restricted patient, who, after discharge, had been admitted under s. 3 six months before being recalled by the Home Secretary under s. 42(3) and referred to an MHRT, which heard the application seven months after L's admission under s. 3.

As seen above, however, even the 13-week limit has been routinely exceeded, particularly in the case of special hospital patients. The two months' limit seems to have been based on the decision in *E* v *Norway* (1990) 17 EHRR 30, in which an eight-week delay between application and hearing was held to breach Art. 5(4) as 'prima facie, difficult to reconcile with the notion of "speedily" ', although the court did go on to say that 'the special circumstances of the case have to be taken into account' (at para. 64), including, in that case, the fact that the judge was on holiday (accounting for 12 days' delay) and that three weeks passed between hearing and pronouncement of the decision. An example of the importance of the factual situation is provided by *Cotterham* v *UK* [1999] 1 MHLR 97. Although the court had held that a five-month delay was 'excessive' in *Van der Leer* v *The Netherlands* (1990) 12 EHRR 567, and in 1996, the Commission declared admissible *Roux*, on the basis, inter alia, of a six-month delay, it was held in *Cotterham* that, because a ten-month delay from application to hearing was largely the result of the time it took for the patient to obtain an independent medical report and for her solicitors to be able to attend court, the case was inadmissible.

The Human Rights Act 1998 gave a mechanism by which the legality of delay could be litigated in the domestic courts. A test case soon presented itself in the form of *R* v *MHRT London South and West Region, ex p C* [2001] MHLR 110. C had applied to a tribunal for discharge immediately after being detained under s. 3 and his application was listed to be heard, as was the practice in that region, eight weeks later. C sought judicial review claiming that the listing practice breached Art. 5(4), and the Court of Appeal found in his favour. The court noted that r. 6(1)(a), (b), Sch. Part B, para. 1 of the 1983 Rules requires the detaining hospital to provide medical reports to the tribunal within three weeks of receiving notice of an application. The court accepted that, in some complicated cases, a further five weeks' delay may be required, but held that a blanket policy of listing cases for hearing eight weeks after application was unreasonable. In this, it followed the European Court in *E* v *Norway*, emphasising that it was a judgment on the facts (para. 43). The fact of particular relevance was that the listing practice was found to be one of administrative convenience rather than of necessity (para. 64).

Lord Phillips, the Master of the Rolls, also cited the decision of the European Court in *Bezicheri v Italy* (1989) 12 EHRR 210, in support of the proposition that, although an eight-week delay is unlawful without particular reason in the individual case to justify such a delay, 'the Strasbourg Court would not have regard to any alleged constraint of resources' (para. 45), because it is the responsibility of the Contracting State to resource its tribunal system sufficiently so as to enable Convention compliance. Moreover, he said that, where a patient is represented by solicitors experienced in mental health work who request an early hearing date, 'I can see no reason why that request should not be capable of accommodation' (para. 58). This makes it clear to the government that human rights law requires funding, and throws out the invitation to advocates to pressurise continually for the speediest hearing date properly compatible with the needs for a fair trial based on suitable evidence. The court could not be expected to give its view as to what constitutes a reasonable delay, given that so much depends on the facts, but it did suggest that the preferable practice is for the date to be fixed after the medical report required by r. 6 has been obtained, at which point it should be clear whether the case in question is straightforward or complex (para. 60). It was also pointed out that, in most s. 2 cases, a date is fixed within seven days of an application (para. 61). As a rule of thumb, the implication of this is that four to five weeks is the appropriate period between application and hearing in most cases.

Ex p C was followed by *R v MHRT, ex p KB and Seven Ors* [2002] EWHC Admin 639, a conjoined applicant involving eight patients, and *R v MHRT, ex p B* [2002] EWHC Admin 1553. *KB* involved one patient, detained under s. 2, who had waited over four weeks for a hearing, four patients detained under s. 3, who had waited between nine weeks, five days and 22 weeks, one person held under a hospital order, who had waited over nine weeks, and one restricted patient, who had waited 27 weeks. All claimed a breach of Art. 5(4), and the patient detained under s. 2 also claimed a breach of r. 31 of the MHRT Rules. In all cases, the reasons for the delay included the preparation of reports and the timetabling of tribunal hearings, and hearings had been cancelled in all cases. The argument of the applicants was that the delays that each had experienced were 'systemic', caused by under-resourcing and poor administration of the tribunal system (para. 40). Stanley Burton J, following *ex p C*, held that it was open to the court, albeit cautiously (para. 46), to examine the resourcing of the tribunal system. He noted the significant increase in the number of tribunal applications in the decade up to 2000 (para. 52). He noted too that the pressure that this placed on tribunals had been recognised by the Council on Tribunals' *Special Report on MHRTs* (Council on Tribunals, 2000: paras. 2.5–2.9) and had been reported in numerous annuals reports on MHRTs (as discussed above). He quoted from statistics that had been made available to the court, which showed that, of 470 cancelled tribunal hearings in England involving applications by s. 3 patients between September 2000 and August 2001, the reason for cancellation in 75 per cent of cases was the unavailability of a medical member (para. 66). Satisfied that general under-resourcing was the reason for the delay in each case, a breach of Art. 5(4) was accordingly found in each case, and in the case of the patient detained under s. 2, a breach of r. 31 was also found.

The court concluded by underlining that it was neither the fault nor responsibility of the staff of the tribunal system, but of the government, to ensure that Art. 5(4) is complied with (para. 114):

The Chairmen are doing what they can with inadequate resources. Their staff are often working under very great pressure. The Chairmen are not responsible for the lack of tribunal members or the inadequacy of staffing. The evidence before me indicates that the basic responsibility for the delays experienced by patients is that of central government rather than of the regional Chairman or their staff.

In *R v MHRT, ex p B* [2002] EWHC Admin 1553, B was a restricted patient recalled to hospital after conditional discharge, who had to wait from February to October 2001 for a tribunal hearing. The delay was initially caused by a medical report from the detaining hospital, which had been made promptly, which raised doubts about B's treatability. This caused the Home Secretary to seek an adjournment of the tribunal hearing (scheduled for March) in order to seek advice on the implications of the report. Thereafter, the case dragged for one reason or another. Scott Baker J found, as fact, that 'with effective case management the substantive hearing would have taken place a great deal earlier' (para. 53), and in the absence of any explanation from the tribunal that would justify the delay, he found a breach of Art. 5(4).

These cases illustrate the potential of human rights law to require the government to resource the mental health sector adequately, and to impose direct resource costs on the failure to do so. In *R v MHRT and Secretary of State, ex p KB and Eight Ors* [2003] EWHC Admin 193, all nine of the applicants involved in the above two cases sought damages under s. 9 HRA 1998 for their deprivation of liberty, as well as for frustration, distress, damage to mental health, and the loss of the chance of liberty, had the various tribunal hearings taken place earlier than they did. The court dismissed any claim for loss of a chance, but held that the other claims, if proven and, apart from the deprivation of liberty, if proven to be serious, were compensable, measurable by reference to tortious standards. Damages of between £750 and £4,000 were awarded to seven of the claimants. There are other consequences of an ill-functioning tribunal system, as Stanley Burton J noted (para. 8) in *ex p KB and Seven Ors*:

delay prolongs the period of uncertainty for the patient. Cancellations of hearings, particularly if repeated, have other consequences: distress and disappointment for the mentally vulnerable patient, the risk of damage to his or her relationship with the psychiatrists and staff of his or her hospital, loss of trust in the tribunal system, and the waste of scarce resources, as where a RMO or an independent psychiatrist witness cancels a clinic to accommodate a Tribunal hearing which in the event is cancelled shortly before it is due to take place.

Although these decisions provided an important incentive for change, measures to improve the system pre-date them, with the publication in 2001 of the report commissioned by the Lord Chancellor, *Tribunals for Users, One System, One Service* (Lord Chancellor's Department, 2001), which recommended that there be one national system of tribunals, not, as previously, separate administrative systems for each tribunal structure (as well as the MHRT system, there are many other tribunal structures, such as employment tribunals). This suggestion was accepted by the government, which published the White Paper *Transforming Public Services: Complaints, Redress and Tribunals* in 2004 (Department of Constitutional Affairs, 2004). Meanwhile, in 2002, His Honour, Judge Sycamore was appointed as liaison judge, responsible for coordinating arrangements between the Lord Chancellor's Department (now the Department of Constitutional Affairs), the Home Office and the Department of Health. Two full-time regional chairs were appointed to oversee the two remaining regions, the number of MHRT regional offices having been reduced from four to two, and eventually to one, which itself closed when, in April 2006, the National Tribunals Service came into being, the MHRT Secretariat as a separate body came to an end, and MHRTs became one of the tribunals, along with the social security and child support appeals tribunals, employment tribunals and others, to come under the control of the Tribunal Service, run out of the DCA (taking over control from the Department of Health), providing a common administrative structure for all types of tribunal (Kirkham, 2005).

It cannot be doubted that the MHRT system now runs much more efficiently than it did five years ago. But it is too early yet to be sure that it now runs in a wholly acceptable manner. Although improvements in administration, the better use of information technology, the securing of an appropriate number of tribunal members, the retention of full-time administrative staff, and increased resourcing are all necessary and welcome developments, some features of the reinvigorated system give cause for concern. In particular, the number of adjournments on the day of the hearing increased from 1 per cent in 2001 to 10 per cent in 2005 (Mental Health Review Tribunal Secretariat, 2005: 23), and the Mental Health Act Commission's most recently available biennial report continues to report 'communication problems, late cancellations, difficulties in listing cases, lack of Tribunal clerks; and breaches of patient confidentiality through administrative error' (2005: para. 4.108). As the Mental Health Review Tribunal Secretariat accepted (2005: 26), despite the improvements to date, 'there remains a lot still to do'.

8.4.5 At the hearing

Neither the Act nor the Rules prescribe any formal procedural requirements for the conduct of tribunal hearings, except that the last word must be given to the applicant (or the patient, if not the applicant) if he or she wishes it: r. 22(5). This apart, each MHRT may conduct its own hearings as it sees fit, bearing in mind the health and interests of the patient and the desirability of minimal formality: r. 22(1). There is authority for the view that tribunals are properly seen as more inquisitorial and less adversarial: *R v MHRT for the West Midlands and North West Regions, ex p Ashworth Hospital* [2001] EWHC Admin 901, at para. 16 per Stanley Burnton J. In any case, a tribunal must comply with the rules of natural justice (*R v Oxford Regional MHRT, ex p SSHD* [1988] 1 AC 120, [1987] 3 All ER 8, HL), and, as a court and a 'public authority' under s. 6(3)(a)

Human Rights Act 1998, a tribunal must, if possible whilst also acting in accordance with other primary legislation, act in a way compatible with the Convention rights of applicants: ss. 6(1), 6(2) HRA 1998.

In *R v MHRT (Northern Region), ex p N; R v MHRT, ex p DJ* [2006] QB 468, [2006] 2 WLR 850, [2005] EWCA Civ 1605, the Court of Appeal held that it is the civil law burden of proof – on the balance of probabilities – that applies to all issues upon which a tribunal must make a judgment, and this complies with the requirement found in *Winterwerp* (2 EHRR 387 at para. 39) that the presence of mental disorder must be 'reliably shown' (para. 78). Richards LJ did, however, point out that 'The more serious the consequences, the stronger the evidence required in practice to prove the matter on the balance of probabilities' (para. 64). This is an important point, not least because tribunals may hear evidence that would not be disclosable in court proceedings, such as hearsay evidence (r. 14(2)), and should therefore guard against the danger of what Munby J at first instance ([2005] EWHC 587 at para. 129) referred to as 'the well-known problem that constant repetition in "official" reports or statements may, in the "official" mind, turn into established fact something which rigorous forensic investigation shows is in truth nothing more than "institutional folk-lore" with no secure foundation in either recorded or provable fact'.

A MHRT hearing has other features that indicate its inquisitorial rather than adversarial nature. For example, there is a presumption that hearings shall take place in private (r. 21(1)), and nearly all do: only 'one at most' out of six hundred hearings that took place at Ashworth hospital between January 2000 and January 2003 was held in public (*R v MHRT; Ian Stuart Brady and Secretary of State for the Home Department, ex p Mersey Care NHS Trust* [2004] EWHC 1749 per Beatson J at para. 1). Tribunal hearings have to be held wherever there is space within the hospital, and the Council of Tribunals has recently reported 'many of the same issues that we have raised in the past, e.g. the inadequate standard of the tribunal hearing room, delays in the tribunal receiving the papers for the hearing, continuing problems with booking hearing dates in advance, communication difficulties with the secretariat in London'. (2006: para. 41), the worst example being given is of a tribunal hearing taking place in a hospital lobby; other hearings take place in small and cramped rooms where there may or may not be a table for the tribunal to use (Council on Tribunals, 2000: para. 2.26). This can undermine both the dignity and the credibility of proceedings. Clearly, the continuing need for improved resourcing for tribunals comes in many and varied forms.

Although the patient may be accompanied by his or her AR and 'such other person or persons as he wishes' (r. 10(6)), a tribunal sitting in private has discretion as to who may be given access (r. 21(3)), and may exclude a person from any part of the hearing if information disclosable under r. 12(3) is to be discussed: r. 21(4). A tribunal must record its reasons for each of these decisions. 'Information about proceedings before the tribunal and the names of any persons concerned in the proceedings shall not be made public', however, except as the tribunal explicitly directs: r. 21(5). Tribunal hearings trade in confidential medical and other information about patients, but also sometimes in matters that attract a public interest. In *Pickering v Liverpool Daily Post and Echo Newspapers plc* [1991] 1 ALL ER 622, the House of Lords held that information that a named patient has made a tribunal application, that the application has been or will be heard, and whether the patient was discharged by that hearing, can be made public. Information that discloses the evidential base on which a tribunal reached its decision, or information about any conditions imposed on discharge must remain private. This is understandable, but has the unfortunate consequence that media reports cannot include the reason for a discharge decision, which risks adding to public misunderstanding of the work of the tribunal system. In *R v MHRT, ex p T* [2002] EWHC Admin 247, at para. 37, Scott Baker J held that *Pickering* proved only a general framework and that the tribunal's discretion under r. 21(5) to direct that information be made public is not limited by that decision if disclosure of specified information to specified individuals – in that case, information as to the conditions attached to discharge being provided to T, a patient's former partner and mother of his child, who had a justified fear of the patient – is warranted on the facts. He further held that T had no claim under Art. 2 of the Convention, because her life was found not be at risk, nor under Art. 8(1), because there was insufficient evidence to show that the claimed inter- ference with T's private life had reached the necessary level of severity to engage Art. 8 (para. 47). It is clear, however, that in a suitable case, a third party would be able to rely on Art. 8(1) to found a claim to be entitled to the information in question. On the other hand, any such disclosure is also prima facie a breach of the patient's rights under the same Article (para. 48). The crucial factor, accordingly, is the weighting of the public interest, which can justify the breach in either case.

Rule 21(1) provides that a tribunal may be held in public at the request of the patient, if the tribunal is satisfied that to do so will not infringe the interests of the patient: rr. 21(1), 22(1). In *R v MHRT, Brady and SSHD, ex p Mersey Care NHS Trust* [2004] EWHC 1749, a tribunal had acceded to the request of B, that his application be heard in public, on the basis that B had capacity to request a public hearing, which would not be contrary to his interests. The detaining trust objected to this, essentially because of concerns about publicity and security, fearing that B, with a high public profile, would exploit the tribunal as an arena to air grievances that he had about his treatment in hospital, but the tribunal was of the view that it could meet any concerns that the trust might have through the use of r. 21(5), 1983 rules, coupled with the general law on contempt of court.

The trust successfully challenged the tribunal's decision in the High Court. Beatson J gave three reasons for his decision. First, the tribunal had, wrongly in his view, thought that the ruling in *Pickering* was applicable, whereas that case was concerned only with hearings in private (para. 45), and, although r. 21(5) does apply to public as well as private tribunal hearings, there being no indication on its face that it does not (para. 50), it offers no greater protection than the underpinning law on contempt. The relevant law is found in s. 2 of the Contempt of Court Act 1981, which prohibits the dissemination of information aired at the hearing on the narrow grounds that publicity will create a substantial risk that the administration of justice will be seriously impeded or preju- dice. Moreover, s. 2 of the 1981 Act only applies where the proceedings in question are 'active'. In point of fact, then, the tribunal could exercise little control over the dissemination of information made public at the hearing.

This took the judge onto his second point. The tribunal, he held, was wrong to consider only 'short-term' interests of the patient when deciding whether to sit in public or private, and, given its incorrect reading of the powers available to it under r. 21(5), there was no indication that it had given consideration to the 'real difficulties' that the trust might face if the tribunal hearing were to take place in public, because it would be certain to be heavily attended by members of the media, and to be widely reported. Beatson J noted that, under the version of the 1983 Rules that operated under the MHA 1959 regime (the 1960 MHRT Rules), the tribunal was charged to consider, as well as the best interests of the patient, whether the holding of a tribunal in public would 'for any other reason be undesirable' (r. 24(1) 1960 Rules), going on to hold that 'It does not, however, follow from the omission of an express requirement that the tribunal be satisfied that a public hearing would not "for any other reason" be "undesirable", that it is not required to take account of wider considerations' (para. 63). He gave the example of a tribunal applicant held under terrorism legislation, which might properly raise questions of national security if the tribunal were to be held in public (*ibid.*), and noted that the European Court has approved derogations from the principle of a public trial on these grounds (para. 64). Thus, in Beatson J's view, the test under r. 21(1) was to consider all 'relevant considerations', in this case, including 'the concerns about B's safety at such a hearing, and, although indirectly and through the clinical concerns, the impact on B's condition of the considerable security that it was stated would be required' (para. 72).

Third, the tribunal made 'no reference to the nature and extent of B's understanding about the likely impact and ramifications of the hearing being in public or the Claimant's concerns. It appears only to have considered B's understanding in the context of its determination as to his capacity to make the request for a public hearing' (para. 67). In summary, its failure to consider these relevant matters meant that it was appropriate to quash its decision and remit the question to be reheard by the tribunal in the light of the judgment of the court. This is a controversial decision (Hewitt, 2005; Mental Health Act Commission, 2005: paras.1.123–1.130). The judge rewrites the test in r. 21(1) in such a way as to reinstate the words deleted in 1983, arguably an unwarranted exercise in judicial creativity; that test is made subject to a requirement that the patient demonstrate capacity – yet capacity is not mentioned as a gate-keeping factor in r. 21(1), and why should it be, because the tribunal is charged to look at the broader question of the patient's interests? Moreover, the test is hiked up, from capacity to make an application (as the tribunal, erroneously in our view, held) to capacity to foresee the likely consequences of a public hearing. As Hewitt (2005: 95) notes of B's continuing lack of success in litigation: 'The courts have always been able to find sufficient – and sufficiently *legal* – reasons to deny him what he wants, and to do so, moreover, for his own good'.

Whether held in public or in private, other parties to the hearing will include the hospital managers and, in the case of a restricted patient, the Home Secretary. A failure to notify the Home Secretary is a breach of natural justice that will vitiate the hearing: *R v Oxford Regional MHRT, ex p SSHD* [1988] 1 AC 120, [1987] 3 All ER 8, per Lord Bridge at 10, see also *R v MHRT, ex p SS* [2004] EWHC 650, 2004 WL 960902. The Home Secretary will not usually be represented by counsel, except in complicated or controversial cases, for example, where the Home Secretary and the patient's RMO disagree about whether the patient should be discharged (Eldergill, 1997: 164). Richardson (1993: 288) has pointed out that, in cases where the Home Secretary supplies only affidavit evidence, it will not be possible for that evidence to be cross-examined by the applicant. The evidence for discharge will, of course, always be cross-examined, if only by the MHRT members: r. 22(2). Part III, Ch. 2 of the Domestic Violence, Crime and Victims Act 2004 introduced new rights for the victims of those who have been convicted of a serious violent or sexual offence and sent to prison or made subject to hospital and restriction orders to make representations to either the parole board or a MHRT, as the case may be, when the release of the offender is being contemplated. Whilst not strictly a 'party' to the proceedings, victims are given some sort of *locus standi* in relation to MHRT hearings by the 2004 Act.

The lack of a prescribed procedure results in 'stark differences … in the format of hearings' (Peay, 1989: 95). Peay found that some tribunals would hear evidence from the patient, then there would be cross-examination of that evidence by tribunal members and RMOs (if the RMO was opposed to discharge), followed by a hearing of the case against discharge. Others did not provide RMOs with the same opportunities to cross-examine; others heard the RMOs' evidence at a much earlier stage. More recently, Perkins (2000: 1) confirmed that 'great variation' continues to be the norm. The point here is not that 'justice by geography' per se is a bad thing; it is also that the order of proceedings can influence the weight given to the various elements of evidence that are presented, and so the chances of discharge. At the risk of undermining the policy that tribunals should be relatively informal affairs, there is a good argument to be made that tribunals should be required to follow what Peay calls 'standard criminal-court procedure' (1989: 95). It is easy for 'informality' to descend into a denial of the due process rights that have been devised as the best way in which to protect the interests of defendants in criminal trials; MHRT applicants should be in at least as good a position as criminal defendants. An example of the dangers of informality is provided by *R v MHRT, ex p Kelly* (1997) 22 April, unreported (HC). In this case, a conditionally discharged restricted patient had been recalled to hospital by the Home Secretary under s. 42(3), following his arrest on allegations of criminal damage and assault. His case was referred to a tribunal under s. 75(1), but the tribunal declined to order discharge, pointing to the alleged criminal behaviour. On an application for judicial review, the tribunal's decision was quashed as being in breach of the rules of natural justice, because it was found that the tribunal had proceeded on the basis that the patient had committed the criminal offences alleged against him, and had not cross-examined that evidence. But there are examples to be found, in the literature, of similar cases that were not subject to judicial review (see Richardson and Machin, 2000: 505).

It is also worth noting that Ferencz and Maguire (2000) found, in a small survey, that patients were often dissatisfied with tribunals, irrespective of whether they were formal or informal in procedural terms. The main problems identified were that tribunal hearings were alienating experiences, and tribunal members were often (at least seemingly) uninterested in the patients' side of the story, with patients given little opportunity to speak. Ferencz and Maguire argue that tribunal hearings have therapeutic implications in and of themselves, and that tribunals need to be more sensitive to these implications, and, specifically, to improve channels of communication with, and levels of respect for, the patients who appear before them. Due process is a necessary, but not a sufficient, requirement in this regard. A fundamental problem with greater patient participation, however, is that patients' knowledge of the tribunal process is poor. Dolan *et al.* (1999: 267), for example, found that less than 10 per cent of 80 special-hospital patients surveyed understood the powers of tribunals in respect of their own circumstances. Without sufficient information to understand tribunal proceedings fully, it is unlikely that levels of patient satisfaction – which research shows are more linked to the way in which the proceedings were conducted than with substantive outcome (Tyler, 1996) – are unlikely to increase.

8.5 Substantive powers of discharge

The substantive powers of MHRTs are found in ss. 72–5, MHA 1983. Section 72 applies to all patients, other than those subject to restrictions, which are dealt with by ss. 73–5. On hearing an application for discharge from a non-restricted patient, an MHRT has various options open to it. For most patients, an order for discharge is naturally the hoped-for outcome. Discharge can be immediate or deferred to a future specified date: s. 72(3) and s. 73(7) (which applies only to the conditional discharge of restricted patients). A discharge will be deferred if there is a need to make arrangements for some form of care in the community or suitable accommodation. A discharge may be properly deferred, even if the order for discharge has been made following an application by the patients' nearest relative (see earlier in the chapter), seeking to challenge the use by the RMO of his or her powers under s. 25 to veto an application for discharge by the NR under s. 23, notwithstanding that the sole issue for the tribunal in such circumstances is the question of the 'dangerousness' of the patient: *R* v *MHRT, ex p B* [2003] EWHC 815 Admin. The Act places no limit on the length of time for which a discharge may be deferred. Gostin (1986b and supplements: para. 18.09), surely correctly, argues that it is not open to a tribunal to specify a date after the expiry of the authority to detain. It is not lawful to defer discharge in order to give time to consider whether there is any other lawful basis for the patient's continued detention: *Perkins* v *Bath District Health Authority* (1989) 4 BMLR 145 (CA).

If a tribunal decides not to discharge an unrestricted patient, it may recommend that he or she be transferred or given leave of absence (s. 72(3)), or that the patient's RMO consider making a supervision application (for the supervised discharge of the patient into the community: see Chapter 9) in respect of the patient: s. 72(3A). If a recommendation is not taken up within a period specified by the tribunal, the case will go back for further consideration, at which point the tribunal may discharge the patient: r. 24(4), 1983 Rules and *MHRT* v *Hempstock* [1997] COD 443 (HC). The power to make recommendations can, therefore, be a powerful lever over the care of undischarged patients.

There is no power to make recommendations in respect of restricted patients. Richardson (1993) argues that this means that tribunals are of much less relevance to such patients, who are ordinarily held in special hospitals, and for whom the route back into the community is usually via RSUs/MSUs and general NHS hospitals, because the amount of time spent in custody, as Goffman suggested (see Chapter 3), means that it can be hard to assess how the patient might behave outside the institution. As a consequence, special-hospital patients are often not looking to the tribunal to make a direction for discharge but rather are hoping to speed up the process of transfer into conditions of lesser security; the tribunal cannot do this. Tribunals can, and do, make extrastatutory recommendations for transfer or leave of absence to be given to special-hospital patients, but such recommendations have 'very little impact unless supported by the RMO' (Richardson, 1993: 294). In any case, a restricted patient cannot be transferred or given leave of absence without the consent of the Secretary of State: s. 41(3)(c). As with discharge under s. 42(2) (see above), the matter will be considered by the Home Secretary on the advice of the RMO, the ABRP, the hospital managers, and possibly others besides, and the decisions in *Harry* and *ex p LH* (see earlier) have done nothing to limit the discretion of the Home Secretary to decline to act on any recommendations made by a tribunal concerning a restricted patient.

A MHRT may also direct that a patient's disorder be reclassified: s. 72(5). There are (at least) two possible views of the purpose of s. 72(5). The first is that it is a mechanism by which a tribunal, although not wishing to order discharge, can nevertheless exercise some control over the treatment of a patient in hospital. This view, in turn, rests on the assumption that a patient can only be treated using the compulsory powers in Part IV of the 1983 Act for a disorder for which he or she has been classified as suffering from to such an extent as to justify detention in hospital. This view can be seen in cases such as *R* v *Pathfinder NHS Trust, ex p W* [1999] 1 MHLR 142, HC, in which the High Court held that a MHRT's decision as to the appropriate classification of a patient's disorder(s) may not be altered by an RMO unless circumstances change. It is also the view adopted by the Court of Appeal in *R* v *Ashworth Hospital, ex p B* [2003] EWCA Civ 547, Dyson LJ holding that, were it otherwise, 'it is difficult to see what purpose is served by reclassification in sections 16, 20 or 72(5)' (para. 49).

The second view, however, is that the process of reclassification, whether under s. 72(5) or ss. 16 and 20 (through the operation of which a patient's disorder can be reclassified by the RMO when a period of detention is renewed) is merely a matter of housekeeping and accurate record-keeping, with no effect on the treatments that may be given to the patient in question. This was the view taken by the Court of Appeal in

R v *Anglia and Oxfordshire MHRT, ex p Hagan* [2000] Lloyd's Rep Med 119, and by the House of Lords, overturning the decision of the Court of Appeal in *ex p B* ([2005] UKHL 20, [2005] 2 AC 278, [2005] 2 All ER 289, [2005] 2 WLR 695, discussed in Chapter 7). The House held that an RMO may treat under s. 63 for any disorder that is present, irrespective of the patient's formal classification. As such, s. 72(5) has been rendered otiose, and there is little that a tribunal, in a case where it is not prepared to order discharge, can do to limit the discretion of the RMO to treat a patient as he or she sees fit. The fact that s. 72(5) now has no apparent purpose might be taken by some as evidence that the decisions in *Hagan* and, perhaps more significantly, in *ex p B*, constitute an unjustifiable departure from the underlying civil libertarian thinking behind the 1983 Act. It can also be argued that the approach in these cases effectively implements the government's plans to abolish the subcategories of mental disorder, because it is now the case that, as long as the patient is mentally disordered, the powers of compulsion can apply, and the precise diagnosis has already been made a minor and fairly inconsequential issue.

8.5.1 Patients not subject to restrictions

Section 72(1) lays out two avenues of discharge: the first of these is mandatory discharge; the second is discretionary discharge. In either case, discharge may be deferred: *R* v *Mental Health Review Tribunal, ex p Pierce* (1997, unreported) (HC). As discussed earlier, it is discharge from the liability to detain that all Part II and s. 37 patients will seek, which means that, to satisfy the criteria, it is liability to detention that must be found to be unnecessary, rather than actual detention.

8.5.1.1 Mandatory discharge

Section 72(1)(a), which applies only to patients detained under s. 2, provides that 'the tribunal *shall* direct the discharge of a patient', which means that there is no choice about it:

If they are not satisfied (i) that he is then suffering from mental disorder or from mental disorder of a nature or degree which warrants his detention in a hospital for assessment (or for assessment followed by a medical treatment) for at least a limited period; or (ii) that his detention as aforesaid is justified in the interests of his own health or safety or with a view to the protection of other persons.

There does not have to be a quantifiable risk before a tribunal can be satisfied that a patient's continued detention is justifiable on grounds of public protection, as long as it is satisfied that there would be 'a substantial and unacceptable' risk to others if the patient were to be released: *R* v *MHRT, ex p N* [2001] EWHC Admin 1133 per Gibbs J at para. 54.

The wording of s. 72(1)(a), along with that of ss. 72(1)(b) and 73(1)(a), which are the corresponding provisions for patients detained other under s. 2, was amended by the Mental Health Act 1983 (Remedial) Order 2001, SI 2001/3712. Previously, it had been for the patient to satisfy the tribunal that he or she was 'not then' suffering from mental disorder. This was held to breach Art. 5(1) and (4) by the Court of Appeal in *R v MHRT, North and East London, ex p H* [2001] EWCA Civ 415, in a case in which a restricted patient, although judged suitable for discharge by his RMO and an independent psychiatrist, failed to persuade a tribunal that he was not suffering from mental disorder to a degree warranting detention. The court held that the wording of ss. 72(1) and 73(1) could not be read in a way compatible with Art. 5 because the sections allowed the possibility of continued detention, albeit that it had not been 'reliably shown', as required by *Winterwerp*, that the patient was of 'unsound mind'. The remedial order makes it clear that it is for those opposing discharge to prove, or the tribunal to be satisfied, that the patient is suffering from mental disorder, rather than the patient having to prove that he or she is not, which, in any case, as the proving of a negative, is not actually possible. This is a significant change of policy. In cases such as *ex p H*, and *R v SSHD and SSH, ex p IH* [2003] UKHL 59 (see below), in which a tribunal was again not satisfied that a patient was not then suffering from mental disorder, but was also not satisfied that he was then so suffering, this change in policy means the difference between detention and release.

Substantively, the criteria for discharge mirror those for admission in the first place, with the substitution of 'justified' in s. 72(1)(a)(ii) for 'ought to be detained' in s. 2(2)(b), although nothing seems to turn on this, and the addition of the word 'then' to the first, medical, limb of the test. This additional 'then' is what explains the conventional view that an MHRT is not concerned to judge the legality of an admission (see Chapter 5), but what other implications its use may have are debatable. Eldergill (1997: 466) suggests that '[t]he word ['then'] should not, however, be interpreted so literally as to mean that a tribunal must therefore disregard the history of the patient's condition or recent fluctuations in his mental state'. Eldergill gives the example of a patient who appears to be 'well' at the time of the hearing, but who had been 'floridly ill' a short time before. This was also the view of the Court of Appeal in *ex p H*. Lord Phillips, giving the judgment of the court, discussed the case of a schizophrenic patient whose condition is in remission whilst in hospital and in receipt of medication, but about whom there were concerns that, if discharged, the patient would be likely to stop taking the necessary medication and hence become a danger to self or others (*R v London South and West Region MHRT, ex p M* [2000] Lloyds Rep Med 143, QB). He said that Art. 5 does not entail that such a patient must always be discharged; instead, each case must be assessed by weighing the interests of the patient against the public interest (para. 33). And although a patient who is not mentally disordered must be discharged in order to comply with Art. 5(1)(e):

we do not consider that the Convention restricts the right to detain a patient in hospital ... to circumstances where medical treatment is likely to alleviate or prevent a deterioration of the condition. Nor is it necessary under the Convention to demonstrate that such treatment cannot be provided unless the patient is detained in hospital.

It is enough that the patient is mentally disordered and detention is 'a proportionate response' to the presence of mental disorder (para. 33). This signals that the Court of

Appeal will take a restrictive approach to the interpretation of Convention rights when the development of those rights would interrupt the government's plans for the preventative detention of the suspected dangerous on grounds of public protection.

In this, the Court of Appeal was following the lead of the House of Lords, in its guise as the Privy Council, in the Scottish case of *A, D and R v Scottish Ministers* [2001] UKPC D5, [2002] UKHRR 1. The Privy Council held that provisions of the Mental Health (Scotland) Act 1984, added by the Mental Health (Public Safety and Appeals) (Scotland) Act 1999, do not breach Art. 5 of the Convention. These provisions (ss. 64, 66, 68 and 74) provide that a restricted patient may not be discharged from hospital if the Sheriff (who performs the functions carried out by mental health review tribunals in England and Wales) or the Scottish Ministers (with powers analogous to the Secretary of State under the 1983 Act), are satisfied 'that the patient is suffering from a mental disorder the effect of which is such that it is necessary, in order to protect the public from serious harm, that the patient continue to be detained in a hospital, whether for medical treatment or not'. Lord Hope held that the relevant test of compliance with Art. 5(1)(e) is whether the disputed provision is (1) in accordance with domestic law, (2) in accordance with the Convention, in terms of proportionality, procedural fairness and allowing the possibility of legal challenge (*Winterwerp*, para. 43), and (3) arbitrary (*Engel v The Netherlands (No. 1)* (1976) 1 EHRR 647, para. 58).

On the third question, the court in *Winterwerp* had held that 'no one may be confined as a person of unsound mind in the absence of medical evidence establishing that his mental state is such as to justify compulsory hospitalisation' (at para. 39). This was further elaborated in *X v UK* (1981) 4 EHRR 188 at para. 40, shortly after *Winterwerp*. The court explained that what is required is that 'the individual concerned must be reliably shown to be of unsound mind, that is to say, a true mental disorder must be established before a competent authority on the basis of objective medical expertise; the mental disorder must be of a kind or degree warranting compulsory confinement; and the validity of continued confinement depends upon the persistence of such a disorder'. More recently, in *Litwa v Poland* (2001) 22 EHRR 53, at para. 60, the court said that Art. 5(1)(e) allowed the deprivation of liberty 'either in order to be given medical treatment or because of considerations dictated by social policy, or on both medical and social grounds' (see also *Koniarska v UK* Application No. 33670/96 (2000) 12 October (unreported). In *Winterwerp*, however, the court had also made clear (at para. 51) that 'a mental patient's right to treatment appropriate to his condition cannot as such be derived from Article 5(1)(e)'. This led Lord Hope to the conclusion (at paras. 28, 29) that, as far as the claim that detention is only justified if treatment can be provided:

the jurisprudence of the Strasbourg Court does not support this proposition...that the question whether a person who is deprived of his liberty on the ground that he is a person of unsound mind in circumstances which meet the *Winterwerp* criteria should also receive treatment for his mental disorder as a condition of his detention is a matter for domestic law. So too is the place of his detention, so long as it is a place which is suitable for the detention of persons of unsound mind. It follows that the fact that his mental disorder is not susceptible to treatment does not mean that, in Convention terms, his continued detention in a hospital is arbitrary or disproportionate.

The approach of the UK courts was confirmed by the European Court in *Hutchinson Reid* v *UK* (2003) 37 EHRR 211. The Court, citing *Koniarska*, above, held that Art. 5(1) does not require that a patient be treatable in order to be detained (para. 51). Rather, citing *Litwa*, it explained that:

Confinement may be necessary not only where a person needs therapy, medication or other clinical treatment to cure or alleviate his condition, but also where the person needs control and supervision to prevent him, for example, causing harm to himself or other persons.

This is, of course, one necessary break that has to be made with the therapeutic tradition in mental health law, policy, and practice, if the logic of the shift to a risk-management-based perspective is to be followed through. And here, decisively, the European Court makes it. The government has been given an unambiguous green light on this point, and plans to remove the current 'treatability' requirement in England and Wales in the near future, on the basis that it is 'too narrowly focused only on the likely outcome of treatment' (Department of Health, 2006j: 3, and see preface).

For patients detained other than under s. 2, and not subject to restrictions, the criteria for mandatory discharge largely echo those that apply to admission for treatment. The tribunal must discharge the patient if not satisfied that he or she is then suffering from one of the four specified forms of mental disorder, or that he or she is suffering from one of those forms of mental disorder to 'a nature or degree which makes it appropriate for him to be liable to be detained in a hospital for medical treatment' (s. 72(1)(b)(i)), *or* that detention is necessary on grounds of the health or safety of the patient or the protection of other persons (s. 72(1)(b)(ii)), *or*, if the application is made by a nearest relative following the veto by an RMO under s. 25 of an order for discharge made by the NR under s. 23, that the patient would be likely to act in a manner dangerous to others or himself or herself if released: s. 72(1)(b)(iii). Again, the word 'then' has been added to the criteria, compared with those in s. 3. The criteria in s. 72(1)(b)(iii) are relevant *only* on an application by a NR in respect of a patient detained under s. 3: *R (MH)* v *Secretary of State For Health, ex p W* [2004] All ER Digest 188; *R* v *MHRT, ex p W* [2004] EWHC 3266 (Admin).

The courts have interpreted these provisions, particularly s. 72(1)(b)(i), in the manner that is least favourable to the patient. In *R* v *Mental Health Review Tribunal for the South Thames Region, ex p Smith* (1998) *The Times*, 9 December (HC), it was held that the phrase 'nature or degree' in s. 72(1)(b)(i) should be read disjunctively, so that a patient who suffers from a mental disorder of a 'nature' that makes it appropriate that he or she be hospitalised need not be discharged, even if not then suffering from that disorder to a 'degree' that makes hospitalisation appropriate. This decision is in line with, and indeed relied heavily on, academic opinion (Eldergill, 1997: 213), and on medical evidence that a patient exhibiting no symptoms of disorder at the time of a tribunal hearing may soon experience acute symptoms if released from hospital prematurely. The court emphasised that there should be some evidence – prior psychiatric history, for example – upon which to base such a view, and it is, indeed, part of the paradox of hospitalisation that the need for it may only be apparent when the individual concerned is not in hospital. But how does a patient demonstrate his or her sanity when evidence of past disorder is admissible? The obvious risk of the decision in *Smith* is that patients who, in fact, are no longer disordered and in need of hospitalisation will be unable to demonstrate this to the satisfaction of the tribunal. As such, the case is another example of protectionism overriding patients' rights and interests.

Does *Smith* survive the Human Rights Act? The patient certainly is, or should be, in a stronger position following the making of the Remedial Order in 2001, because the burden of proof is on those seeking to ensure continued detention. But on the substantive point of law, it is to be noted that, in *Winterwerp* (at para. 39), the European Court does use the phrase 'kind or degree'. On the other hand, the requirement in *Winterwerp* is for unsound mind sufficient to 'justify' detention, and we would want to argue, as has not been done to date before the European Court, that a test that allows nature 'or' degree permits detention when a person's disorder is of a nature but *not* of a degree to justify compulsory hospitalisation, which is outside of the spirit of the Convention. In our, perhaps optimistic, view, the preferable and Convention-compliant wording must be that the mental disorder in question is of both a nature *and* a degree to warrant detention.

The issue in *R v Canons Park Mental Health Review Tribunal, ex p A* [1994] 2 All ER 659 (CA) was whether the requirement in s. 72(1)(b)(i) that the patient must be discharged if it were not 'appropriate for him to be liable to be detained in a hospital for medical treatment' imported into s. 72 the 'treatability test' that can be found in ss. 3(2)(b), 16(2) or 20(4)(c); a majority of the court decided that it did not. The case involved an application for judicial review made by A, a psychopathically disordered patient who had been refused discharge by an MHRT on the grounds, inter alia, that it did not have to consider whether A was treatable. Kennedy LJ pointed out that the function and position of tribunals differs from that of those concerned with a patient's admission and treatment, because tribunals only have to be satisfied of negatives, i.e., that the patient is not mentally disordered, and so on, whereas, on admission, the burden of proof is on those wishing to admit. Section 72, in other words, does not deal with a situation analogous to that covered by s. 3, and Kennedy LJ, consequently, could 'see no reason why the words of s. 72(1)(b)(i) should be read as a form of legal shorthand' referring to the tests in s. 3 (para. 683). Instead, s. 72 should be read for what it says, and for what it does not say, and it makes no reference to treatability. Moreover, the criteria relevant to discretionary discharge, contained in s. 72(2) (see later) *do* refer to treatability, so there is no purchase to an argument that the absence of treatability as a separate factor in s. 72(1) was an oversight. In the context of s. 72(2), the power to discharge, as discretionary, need not be exercised even if a patient is not treatable, and so to hold that treatability is a factor relevant to mandatory discharge is, in effect, to turn that discretion into a duty.

Of course, the point that a tribunal only has to be satisfied of negatives did not survive *ex p H*, but even without this string to his bow, Roch LJ produced a powerful dissenting opinion in *Canons Park*. Roch LJ referred to the Percy Commission Report (Royal Commission on the Law Relating to Mental Illness and Mental Deficiency 1954–1957), which demonstrated that '[t]he policy of the 1983 Act in relation to patients with psychopathic disorders is treatment not containment' (para. 675), and to the general principle of statutory interpretation that any ambiguity in a statutory provision should be 'resolved in favour of personal liberty'. He further found that the policy behind the Act was driven by the ECHR decision in *X* v *UK*, in which the ECHR had held it unlawful to detain a person on grounds of mental disorder if the reasons for initial admission no longer pertained (per Roch LJ at 676); and moreover that the policy was reflected in the substance of the Act. Roch LJ's interpretation was that, as s. 72(1)(b)(i) used the phrase 'makes it appropriate for him to be liable to be detained' whereas s. 3(2)(a), the comparable subsection, uses the phrase 'makes it appropriate for him to receive medical treatment in hospital', this 'shows that Parliament did not intend to refer simply to the appropriateness test in s. 3(2)(a)' (at 675). Rather, the addition of the words 'liable to be detained' to the criteria that a tribunal must apply 'clearly refer... to the treatability test' (*ibid.*), therefore incorporating that test into the general test of appropriateness.

The decision of the majority in *Canons Park* drew criticism for the reasons given by Roch LJ (Baker and Crichton, 1995; Glover, 1996; Parkin, 1994). In any case, it soon became clear, as a result of the decision of the Privy Council in the Scottish case *Reid* v *Secretary of State for Scotland* [1999] 1 All ER 481 (PC), that the decision of the majority in *Canons Park* can no longer be regarded as good law. *Reid* concerned the equivalent provision in Scottish law to s. 72(1)(b)(i), MHA 1983. Although, technically, only of persuasive influence on the law of England and Wales, the appeal in *Reid* was, in the words of Lord Lloyd (at 484), 'also in reality an appeal against the decision of the Court of Appeal in the *Canons Park* case'. The House resurrected the policy-driven arguments regarding the function of detention and the relevance of the ECHR offered by Roch LJ, holding that a sheriff (who performs the functions of an MHRT for these purposes in Scotland) was bound to order the discharge of an untreatable psychopathic patient. As for the broader policy issue, of whether it is appropriate that dangerously disordered psychopathic persons should be discharged from hospital, this, held Lord Hutton 'is an issue for Parliament to decide and not for judges' (at 516). The patient in that case was, nevertheless, found to be treatable, even though it had not proven possible to alleviate his condition, because life on the hospital ward, with strategies in place to control his anger, did reduce his propensity for aggression, and hence was caught as treatment that alleviated the symptoms of his disorder, as permitted, in England and Wales, by ss. 145(1) and 63 of the MHA 1983. In the later case of *Ruddle* v *Secretary of State for Scotland* (1999) GWD 29–1395, however, the patient was held untreatable even on this broad definition of treatment and so had to be released. This led, in Scotland, to the Mental Health (Public Safety and Appeals) (Scotland) Act 1999, the legality of which was later upheld in the *Scottish Ministers* case involving, inter alia, the same patients as in *Reid* and *Ruddle*. In England and Wales, the resurrected dissent in *Canon's Park* remains the law, but clearly, as far as the superior courts are concerned, the reading of the Convention offered by Roch LJ in that case, in so far as it posits treatability as a requirement of Art. 5(1)(e), does not.

The question of when continued detention becomes inappropriate, and thus in breach of s. 72(1)(b)(i), was considered in *R v MHRT and W, ex p Epsom and St Helier NHS Trust* [2001] EWHC Admin 101. The detaining hospital sought judicial review of the decision of a tribunal to order the discharge of W, a mentally ill patient detained under s. 3. W's illness manifested, inter alia, as a belief that she was unable to swallow, causing severe weight loss and requiring her to be fed by PEG tube whilst in hospital. After regaining weight, she was granted leave of absence, only to lose weight again necessitating her recall to hospital, a pattern that had reoccurred on several occasions. It was likely to occur again at some point in the future; the tribunal's decision was based primarily on the fact that, since the last renewal of her detention by a tribunal, six months previously, W had lived in residential accommodation in the community, at which she could, if necessary, be fed by PEG tube, and had not in that period been recalled to hospital for treatment. The High Court held, first, that there is no automatic right to discharge under s. 72 purely because a patient on leave is not actually receiving medical treatment (para. 46); second, it held that, although a different tribunal may have come to the contrary conclusion, and that a tribunal must so far as possible look to the future as well as to the past in making its decision, the tribunal's decision in this case was reasonable. Sullivan J said that 'there will come a time when, even though it is certain that treatment will be required at some stage in the future, the timing of the treatment is so uncertain that it is no longer "appropriate" for the patient to continue to be liable to be detained' (para. 52), and that this fact situation might reasonably be said to fall into that category.

8.5.1.2 Discretionary discharge

An MHRT should not turn its mind to the possibility of discretionary discharge until it has considered the case for mandatory discharge and rejected it: *R v Mental Health Tribunal for the North Wales Region, ex p P* (20 May 1990) unreported (DC). There are no powers of discretionary discharge in respect of restricted patients: s. 72(7); *Grant v MHRT* (1986) 26 April 1986 (DC). As far as unrestricted patients are concerned, s. 72(1) gives MHRTs a discretionary power to direct the discharge of the patient 'in any case', and s. 72(2) provides that, in the exercise of that discretion, the tribunal 'shall have regard' to the likelihood of medical treatment alleviating or preventing a deterioration in the patient's condition and, if the patient is suffering from mental illness or severe mental impairment, whether he or she would be able to care for himself or herself, to obtain any care needed, and to be able to guard against serious exploitation. This is not, however, an exclusive list of factors, and an MHRT has the discretion to consider any factor that may be relevant to the exercise of its discretion (per Lord Clyde in *Reid* at 504). The discretionary powers are used very rarely, however, and the reason is clear, given that a patient unable to make out his or her case on the basis of the criteria for mandatory discharge is, prima facie, suitable for continued detention.

8.5.2 **Discharge of restricted patients**

8.5.2.1 Absolute discharge

Section 72(7) disapplies s. 72(1) to restricted patients, except as provided by ss. 73 and 74. Section 73(1) provides that a tribunal *must*, on the application or referral of a patient subject to a restriction, direct the absolute discharge of that patient, if satisfied both that at least one of the criteria in s. 72(1)(b) is met *and* 'that it is not appropriate for the patient to remain liable to be recalled to hospital for further treatment': s. 73(1)(b). This is problematic, first because the Remedial Order of 2001 did not change the wording of s. 73(1)(b) as it did that of ss. 72(1)(a), 72(1)(b) and 73(1)(a). It remains for the patient to satisfy the tribunal that liability to recall is not appropriate rather than for those opposing discharge to satisfy the tribunal that it is appropriate. This, in our view, is enough to place s. 73(1)(b) in breach of Art. 5(1) and 5(4). Second, the law as it stands requires that a mentally disordered patient be discharged if no longer dangerous, and a dangerous person be discharged if no longer mentally disordered; s. 72(3) also allows the possibility that a tribunal finds (1) that a patient is not mentally disordered, but (2) it remains appropriate that he or she should remain liable to recall out of a concern for the safety of third parties.

The question of whether a person no longer suffering from mental disorder must be absolutely discharged, or might also be conditionally discharged, and hence subject to recall, was considered by the Court of Appeal in *R v Merseyside MHRT, ex p K* [1990] 1 All ER 694. Some months after K had been conditionally discharged by an MHRT on the grounds that he was not then suffering from a mental disorder, he was convicted of assault and sentenced to six years' imprisonment. In prison, he applied again to an MHRT, for an absolute discharge under s. 75(2), which provides that a conditionally discharged prisoner may apply for absolute discharge when a year has passed since he or she was conditionally discharged, not having been recalled to hospital, and thereafter once every two years. Again, the tribunal found that K was not suffering from a mental disorder, but refused to lift the conditions.

K sought judicial review of both the initial tribunal decision to discharge him conditionally rather than absolutely, and the later decision not to remove the conditions, arguing that, as no longer mentally disordered, he was not a patient within s. 145 (defined as 'a person suffering or appearing to be suffering from mental disorder'), and was therefore entitled to an absolute discharge. The Court of Appeal evaded the difficult question of how mental health legislation can apply to a person who is not mentally disordered. Sir Denys Buckley decided the case on the basis that there had been no decision open to judicial review taken by the second tribunal because that tribunal had not 'discharged' K: he was already discharged. Butler-Sloss LJ, with whom Kerr LJ concurred, merely stated that a patient who has been made subject to restrictions 'remains a patient until he is discharged absolutely', and justified this by reference to the policies behind the 1983 Act, of 'protection of the public' and 'the hoped for progression to discharge of the treatable patient' (at 699), which, so it was implied, would be upset if a patient were to be entitled to absolute discharge as soon after detention as he or she was judged no longer to be mentally disordered. Richardson (1993: 283) argues that this is a 'strained interpretation' and, had the Court of Appeal taken a more autonomy-centred approach, as in treatment cases like *ex p X* (the *Goserelin* case, see Chapter 7), the outcome in *ex p K* might have been different.

The interpretation of s. 73(2) seems uncontroversial on its face. This is why, presumably, counsel for K felt compelled to look elsewhere, to s. 145(1), in order to raise doubts about the legality of the decision not to discharge K absolutely. Arguments based on the ECHR were made before the court in the later case brought by the same patient to challenge his recall to hospital (*R v Home Secretary, ex p K* [1990] 3 All ER 562), but these were neatly side-stepped by holding that the House of Lords' ruling in *R v Secretary of State for the Home Department, ex p Brind* [1990] 1 All ER 649 prevented it from looking to the ECHR, unless the UK statute were to contain ambiguities (although, as a matter of domestic law, how to characterise the relation between ss. 73 and 145 as other than ambiguous is not, in our view, readily apparent). But now, of course, the international law may not be so easily avoided. As discussed earlier in this chapter, the main thrust of the decisions in *Winterwerp* and *Johnson* is that, although a person who is no longer mentally disordered may not be detained, and a conditionally discharged patient who is no longer mentally disordered may not be recalled to hospital (see earlier), this does not mean that a detained patient found not to be suffering from mental disorder at all, or to a nature or degree requiring hospitalisation, is entitled to immediate release; and conditions may be attached to his or her release, as long as there is not an unreasonable delay in release in order for the arrangements in question to be made.

The European Court, then, gives no greater entitlement to absolute discharge than was given by the Court of Appeal in *ex p K*. It is obviously true that s. 73 reflects both protectionist and beneficent concerns, but all the indicators in the 1983 Act are to the effect that these concerns are limited in focus, to persons who *are*, as a point of precedent fact, mentally disordered. Nevertheless, more recent case law, such as *R v MHRT, ex p SSHD* (2005) EWHC 2468 (Admin), takes the same approach as the Court of Appeal in *ex p K*. In that case, it was held that the failure of a tribunal to consider whether a patient should be subject to recall to hospital, and thus be discharged conditionally rather than absolutely as it had ordered, vitiated its decision. A patient in that position is entitled to conditional discharge until the matter is reheard by a tribunal: *R v MHRT, ex p Secretary of State for the Home Department* [2005] EWCA Civ 616.

The companion case to *ex p K* is *R v MHRT, ex p Cooper* [1990] COD 275 (HC), in which it was held that a patient who was no longer dangerous (if he ever had been) was not entitled to absolute discharge solely by virtue of that fact, because the tribunal was not satisfied that the patient should not remain liable to recall on therapeutic grounds. The argument of the patient was to the effect that he had been placed under a restriction order at a time (1963) when such orders were made in respect of fairly minor 'nuisance' offences; had he been convicted more recently, he would have been placed on a hospital order without restrictions, in which case, he would have been entitled to discharge without conditions under s. 72(1) when shown not to be dangerous. It was also contended that s. 73(1)(b) should be understood as limited in scope to the need to protect the public. Both arguments were dismissed by Rose J who, relying on the dicta of Butler-Sloss LJ in *ex p K* that the policy behind the Act is both protectionist and beneficent, saw no reason to limit the scope of the matters to be considered under s. 73(1)(b), and held that a tribunal had no discretion and must order conditional discharge in such a situation. It must be conceded that this is the most straightforward reading of s. 73(1), as a whole, and of s. 73(1)(b) in particular. In *ex p K*, however, it was the interests of the general public that had to be balanced against K's interest in being free from liability to recall. Accordingly, *Cooper* is the more paternalistic, and in a sense more problematic, decision.

If an absolute discharge is granted, the hospital order, and with it, the restriction order, will cease to have effect: ss. 73(3), 75(3). Absolute discharges without prior conditional discharge are rare. There were only 15 in 2004, 22 in each of 2003 and 2002, and 13 in 2001, although this is an increase over the late 1990s (ten in 1996, five in 1997, six in 1998, nine in 1999 and seven in 2000 (Home Office Research, Development and Statistics Directorate, 2005: Table 16)). Most absolute discharges follow a period of conditional discharge: there were 96 such absolute discharges in 2003, 74 per cent of which involved patients conditionally discharged sometime in the previous six years (2005: Table 16, note 4). The main reason for this is undoubtedly that tribunals, in common with the Home Secretary, take a cautious approach to the interpretation of s. 73(1)(b), and do so even in the context of applications under s. 75, from patients already discharged, even though s. 75(3) disapplies ss. 73 and 74, so that, strictly speaking, there are no criteria to be applied when an absolute discharge is sought under that section. In *R v MHRT, ex p C* [2005] EWHC 17, it was said that the lack of criteria for absolute discharge under s. 75 does not render that section incompatible with Arts. 6 and 8 of the Convention, because any tribunal that did not exercise its powers in accordance with the criteria in s. 73, along with ss. 37 and 41, would be liable to judicial review (paras. 56–67).

Even if the evidence is that an applicant is no longer mentally disordered, or not to a nature or degree that warrants hospitalisation, or that he or she is no longer a danger to other persons, a tribunal anxious that the disorder may only be in remission, or that the risk to others is obscured by the constraints placed on a patient's behaviour by the fact of hospitalisation, is unlikely to be easily satisfied that it is not appropriate to leave the door open to the possibility of recall. As seen above, the courts have approved this approach on a number of occasions. In *R v MHRT, ex p Secretary of State* [2001] EWHC Admin 849, the High Court quashed the decision of a tribunal to order the absolute discharge of a patient because the tribunal had failed in its reasons explicitly to explain why it had considered that it was not appropriate for the patient to be liable for recall.

8.5.2.2 Conditional discharge and conditions

If a tribunal is not satisfied that a restricted patient should remain in hospital on an application of the criteria in s. 72(1)(b), but is also not satisfied that it is appropriate for the patient to be discharged absolutely, which it is required to consider by s. 73(1)(b), it must direct the patient's conditional discharge: s. 73(2). A conditionally discharged patient is subject to recall by the Home Secretary using s. 42(3) (s. 73(4)(a)), and must comply with any conditions that are imposed, either by the MHRT on discharge or at a later date by the Secretary of State, who also has powers to vary any condition, however imposed: s. 73(4)(a), (5). The statute does not require that conditions always be imposed (s. 73(4)(b)), but in *R v MHRT, ex p Hall* [2000] 1 WLR 1323 (CA), it was held that a tribunal is under a duty to impose such conditions as it decides are necessary, even if it is apparent that meeting the conditions in question may be difficult. It has been said, by Lord Bridge in *R v Oxford Regional MHRT, ex p SSHD* [1988] 1 AC 120 [1987] 3 All ER 8, at 11–12, that a tribunal hearing an application must first decide whether one or both of the criteria for discharge in s. 72(1)(b) are met, and only then turn its mind to the issue of whether discharge should be absolute or conditional. Lord Bridge went on to say that the first question 'would inevitably be coloured' by the practical possibility of imposing suitable conditions. In practice, the meeting of the criteria for discharge is intimately related to the practical possibility of attaching conditions to the order.

As to the conditions that may be imposed, these are the same as may be imposed on conditional discharge under s. 42 (see earlier). In *SSHD v MHRT for Wales; SSHD v MHRT for Merseyside RHA* [1986] 3 All ER 233 (HC), Mann J held that a condition of discharge that the patient remain in a hospital is 'inconsistent with the duty to discharge' (at 238). Mann J's concern was that to uphold such a condition would undermine the order for discharge, but it also speaks of the lacunae in the powers of tribunals in respect of restricted patients, which is the absence of a power to direct or even, officially, recommend, transfer. In *Merseyside*, the tribunal had concluded that the applicant, who at the time was resident in a special hospital, did not require such a restrictive regime; and the order for discharge was, in fact, an attempt to transfer the patient to conditions of less security with a view to his eventual release. The High Court vetoed this creative use of the legislation. There was a similar attempt to use an order for deferred conditional discharge to transfer a patient out of Rampton special hospital into medium-secure accommodation by a tribunal, which had made repeated recommendations for transfer but to no effect in *MP v Nottinghamshire Healthcare NHS Trust, SSHD, SSH* [2003] EWHC 1782. Again, this met with little success, the court holding that the patient could not lawfully be discharged into such accommodation, and the absence of a power to order transfer of a patient did not breach Art. 5, being a question only of the place, and not of the fact, of detention.

On the other hand, in the *Oxford* case [1987] 3 All ER 8, at 12, Lord Bridge said that residence in a hostel, coupled with compulsory treatment are perfectly proper conditions to be placed on a discharge, and such conditions are often attached to the order for discharge. In *R v MHRT, ex p SSHD, PH* [2002] EWCA Civ 1868, PH, an elderly and physically unwell patient who suffered from chronic paranoid schizophrenia, was conditionally discharged from Broadmoor hospital after 44 years by a tribunal. This was on condition that he live in specialist and secure (although not locked) accommodation with 24-hour supervision, agree to take medication required by his supervising psychiatrist, and that he should not leave his accommodation unless escorted. The

Secretary of State sought judicial review of the conditions, essentially arguing that the tribunal had acted *ultra vires* and in breach of Art. 5(1)(e), because the conditions did not amount to discharge and hence the tribunal's decision was, in effect, a decision for transfer.

The High Court rejected these arguments and the Court of Appeal upheld that decision. The Court of Appeal held that Art. 5(1) did not lay down an absolute standard of deprivation of liberty and that there is only a difference in degree between a restriction, which falls outside Art. 5(1), and a deprivation covered by the Article. It further held, following *HM* v *Switzerland* (2002) 26 February, unreported, that a restriction of liberty designed in the best interests of the patient did not breach Art. 5(1) (para. 17), and that the Secretary of State had failed to demonstrate that this was not the case here, given that the stated intention of the various measures was to monitor and assist PH's discharge out of concern for his own welfare after so long spent in a special hospital. The court did emphasise that every case must be decided on its own facts, but it did specifically overrule the embargo on discharge to hospital accommodation suggested by Mann J in *Merseyside*. In a later case, in which essentially the same conditions were imposed on the discharge of a patient (*R* v *MHRT, ex p Secretary of State* [2004] EWHC 2194) Collins J distinguished *PH*, holding that the conditions were unlawful, on the basis that, in *PH*, 'the crucial matter was that the restrictive conditions were imposed for PH's own benefit and not for the protection of others' (para. 11), whereas in the case in front of him, they were imposed to protect third parties. Moreover, the consent of the patient to be bound by the conditions could not make the deprivation of liberty lawful; the question is simply whether, as a question of fact, the conditions amount to a deprivation of liberty within the meaning of Art. 5(1) of the Convention. If so, there will be a detention for the purposes of domestic law and the tribunal will therefore have acted *ultra vires*: *R* v *MHRT, ex p G* [2004] EWHC 2193.

In *R* v *SSHD and SSH, ex p IH* [2002] EWCA Civ 646, Lord Phillips MR held that, although it is clear from *Winterwerp* that a patient who is no longer mentally disordered is entitled to discharge, albeit that that may be subject to conditions, the Convention does not bestow a right to discharge on persons who are mentally disordered but who are, or may be, eligible for release under the domestic scheme by virtue of ss. 72(1)(a)(ii) or (b)(ii). For such individuals, the decision regarding discharge is properly subject to the availability of appropriate provision in the community and considerations of public safety, nor is there any duty on the state to ensure that appropriate community-based facilities exist (paras 86, 87) – but (at para. 87):

Available resources may make it possible for essential treatment to be provided to a mental patient in the community in circumstances which will not place in jeopardy either his own health or safety or the safety of others. In that event it will be a breach of Art. 5(1) to detain the patient in hospital.

A patient who is mentally disordered, who may be released safely using available resources for aftercare, must be released, but where there are no such resources available, there is no entitlement to discharge in the first place. In such circumstances, there are no conditions under which discharge would be appropriate, and so treatment in hospital remains appropriate: *R v Ashworth Hospital Authority, ex p H* [2001] EWHC Admin 901, per Stanley Burnton J at para. 64.

A conditional discharge may be deferred to allow such arrangements to be made as the tribunal feels are necessary: s. 73(7). This has long between a problematic provision, because the time necessary to make such arrangements can be difficult to predict in advance. The difficulty of the situation was exacerbated by the decision of the House of Lords in *R v Oxford Regional MHRT, ex p SSHD* (also known as *Campbell v SSHD*) [1988] 1 AC 120, [1987] 3 All ER 8. The House held that a tribunal, having decided that conditional discharge should be ordered, and having then decided that discharge should be deferred under s. 73(7), is unable either to undo or to enforce either of those decisions. The upshot of this decision was that, if arrangements have not been made to the satisfaction of the tribunal (perhaps because of reluctance on the part of one or more of the RMO, the hospital managers, the relevant local authority, NHS trust or PCT, or individual consultant psychiatrists to make or accept them), there was no scope for the tribunal to try to force the issue, by replacing its original order with an order for immediate absolute discharge, or to reconsider the nature of the conditions that it initially imposed.

Hence, a patient in that situation cannot be discharged and the matter can only be reconsidered afresh by a tribunal when the patient's case comes before it again by way of application or reference (s. 73(7), MHA 1983), as happened, for example, in *R v MHRT, ex p Booth* [1998] COD 203 (HC). Nor was there any guarantee that the impasse would be resolved by a fresh hearing. The House of Lords thus erected a sharp distinction between the position of patients subject to restriction and of unrestricted patients, in respect of whom, as was held in *Hempstock* (see earlier), a tribunal does have powers to reconsider the question of discharge if there has been a failure to act on recommendations that it has made: this is why the application in the line of case law starting with *Fox* (see Chapter 9) focused instead on the duty placed on NHS bodies and local authorities to provide aftercare under s. 117.

The decision in *Oxford*, was, however, 'set aside' by the House of Lords in *R v SSHD and SSH, ex p IH* [2003] UKHL 59 at para. 27. In that case, a tribunal was not satisfied that IH was then mentally disordered to a nature or degree necessitating his detention in hospital, and so he was entitled to discharge, but nor was it satisfied that he was not mentally disordered. It wished to order that he be discharged, subject to the conditions that he reside in suitable hostel accommodation, under the supervision and direction of a named social worker and a named forensic psychiatrist, and adjourned so that its conditions for discharge could be put in place.

Eight months later, the tribunal reconvened. Evidence was given that it had not been possible to locate a forensic psychiatrist prepared to take responsibility for IH's treatment following discharge, becayse all those forensic psychiatrists who worked in the local authority's area were of the view that discharge of IH was inappropriate at that time. Nevertheless, the tribunal made an order for discharge in the terms laid out above, with discharge to be deferred until the conditions were met. Fifteen months later, no psychiatrist willing to treat IH after discharge had been located, and the Secretary of State referred his case to a new tribunal. This met eight months later, that is, 31 months after the initial adjournment, and 21 months after discharge was ordered. It decided that IH was then, and always had been, suffering from mental illness, albeit that it was then in remission, and that it was appropriate for him to be detained in hospital for treatment.

IH sought a declaration of incompatibility between ss. 73(2) and or (7) of the 1983 Act and Art. 5(1)(e) and 5(4) of the Convention, in relation to the period from the initial decision to conditionally discharge until the later tribunal decided that he should be detained. Lord Bingham, giving the only opinion, held, first, that there was no breach of Art. 5(1)(e) in such circumstances. The case should be contrasted with *Johnson*: 'There is a categorical difference, not a difference of degree' between the two cases. In *Johnson*, the patient was found not to be suffering from mental disorder, in which case, 'the alternative, if those conditions proved impossible to meet, was not continued detention but discharge, either absolutely or subject only to a condition of liability to recall' (para. 28). In *IH*, by contrast, 'there was never a medical consensus, nor did the tribunal find, that the *Winterwerp* criteria were not satisfied . . . the alternative . . . was not discharge . . . but continued detention' (para. 28).

Fennell (2005: 98), discussing this case, argued that, because there is rarely a clear statement that a patient is 'cured' of his or her mental disorder, 'the effect of the ruling is to limit significantly the impact of *Johnson*, and the extent to which Article 5 is capable of imposing positive duties on state authorities to provide after-care to facilitate discharge'. Perhaps the ruling is not as narrow as Fennell suggests, however: although the patient in *Johnson* was found, in fact, not to be suffering from mental disorder, there is reason to think that the crucial distinction is not between those who are not mentally disordered and those who are, or who may be. As can be seen (above), Lord Bingham's point about *Johnson* was that it involved a patient in respect of whom 'the *Winterwerp* criteria were not satisfied'. These criteria do not distinguish the mentally disordered from those who are not, but rather those who do not require hospitalisation for mental disorder from those who do. There must be a mental disorder, which is persisting at the relevant time (these are the first and third criteria respectively), and – the second criterion – 'the mental disorder must be of a kind or degree warranting compulsory confinement': *Winterwerp*, para. 39. In *R v Doncaster MBC, ex p W* [2004] EWCA Civ 378, [2004] 1 MHLR 201, Scott Baker LJ held at para. 39, having referred to the speech of Lord Bingham and that of Lord Phillips in the Court of Appeal, that this is the 'fundamental distinction', in which case the *Johnson* category is broader than Fennell suggests.

On the other hand, this seems to mean that the jurisprudence has constructed a very blurred distinction between the two categories. In the Court of Appeal in *ex p IH*, Buxton and Sedley LJJ held that there was no clear distinction between the two categories. Buxton LJ said, at para. 42, that when the discharge of a patient not then suffering from mental disorder has had conditions attached, 'the justification for the placing of continued restrictions on the subject relates, and can only relate, to the history of mental illness and, as in *Johnson*, to the prospect of recurrence'. This is clearly correct, and the only way to maintain the distinction between a '*Winterwerp* patient' and a '*Johnson* patient' is to narrow the timeframe, looking only at the present, but not the past or the future. Even then, the question 'is this person mentally disordered such as to justify hospitalisation today?' is by no means always easy to answer. Be this as it may, when *ex p IH* reached the House of Lords, Lord Bingham, with the unanimous agreement of the rest of the House, disapproved the approach of Buxton and Sedley LJJ (at para. 28). For him, as seen above, there is a 'categorical' difference between the two types of case. In *Doncaster*, Mance LJ held, at para. 72, that the test is whether or not 'expected treatment . . . [is] an essential pre-requisite of discharge from detention'. But, at the margins, the distinction is between a patient who is not sufficiently disordered as to necessitate hospitalisation and one who is, both of whom require conditions to be attached to discharge and to remain liable to recall, can, and will, be hard to detect, allowing doctors, tribunals and the courts to hold that a person who does not appear to be mentally ill only appears so because his or her illness is in remission, thus satisfying the *Winterwerp* criteria, as was the case in *Doncaster*, for example. This may be correct as a matter of fact in that case, indeed in many, but it will not always be so, and the risk of detention being wrongly warranted by the law is a real one.

The second key element of Lord Bingham's Opinion in *ex p IH* was his finding that there is no 'in principle' incompatibility between the Act and the Convention on the basis that the tribunal did not have the powers essential to being classified as a court, because (para. 26): 'What Article 5(1)(e) and 5(4) require is that the person of unsound mind compulsorily detained in hospital should have access to a court with power to decide whether the detention is lawful and, if not, order his release. This power, the tribunal had.' A breach of Art. 5(4) was found, however, on the basis that, because of the ruling in the *Oxford* case, the tribunal, having made an order for discharge, was precluded from reconsidering it (para. 27). The Court of Appeal had reached the same conclusion (EWCA Civ 646 at para. 71), and Lord Bingham endorsed the substance of the Court of Appeal's judgment. Hence, the situation now, after an order for deferred conditional discharge has been made, is that the tribunal can, and should, monitor the situation, and if there are problems implementing the conditions within a reasonable period of time, the tribunal should consider whether it should:

- further adjourn in order to seek a resolution of the difficulties;

- amend or vary the conditions;

- order a conditional discharge but with no specific conditions, which nevertheless renders the patient liable to recall by the Secretary of State if there are problems following discharge: ss. 73(4)(a), 42(3);

- order that the patient continue to be detained in hospital.

Because it was possible to read the 1983 Act in a manner compatible with these requirements, the court did not make a declaration of incompatibility.

In *Kolanis v UK* (2006) 42 EHRR 12, in a very similar fact situation, the European Court, in turn, endorsed the approach taken by the Court of Appeal and House of Lords in *IH*: first, it endorsed the distinction between the situations of a patient found not to be suffering from mental disorder sufficient to necessitate hospitalisation and one who is was reinforced (para. 69); second, an order for conditional discharge is not necessarily a finding that the patient is no longer mentally disordered, and if the conditions cannot be fulfilled, continued detention does per se not breach Art. 5(1)(e) (para. 70), and in such circumstances there can be 'no question of interpreting Art. 5(1)(e) as requiring the applicant's discharge without the conditions necessary for protecting herself and the public' (para. 71). Third, the absence of a mechanism by which K could exercise her right to challenge her continued detention after conditional discharge had been ordered (a period of a little over a year in this case) did amount to a breach of Art. 5(4) (para. 82), but the Court also seemed to accept that the decision in *IH* had put right any potential future breach of Art. 5(4) (see para. 81). Nonetheless, the law, as it now stands, does not empower tribunals to require compliance with the conditions they impose on discharge, and the practical effect of disagreement between a tribunal and those responsible for making the necessary arrangements will, in most cases, be, as Lord Phillips noted in the Court of Appeal (para 96), that, after *ex p IH* as before it, the patient remains in hospital.

8.5.2.3 Discharge of restricted patients subject to restriction directions

A different procedure applies, by virtue of s. 74, to patients subject to a transfer direction and a restriction direction, even though the effect in hospital is the same as a restriction order (s. 49(2)), because such persons will face the prospect of transfer to prison on discharge from hospital (see Chapter 6). When such a patient applies or is referred to an MHRT, it must hear the case in the ordinary way, but is under a duty to notify the Secretary of State of the outcome of the hearing, and, in particular, whether the patient 'would, if subject to a limitation direction or a restriction order', be entitled to an absolute or conditional discharge (s. 74(1)(a)); 'entitled' means entitled under the criteria relevant to restriction-order patients under s. 73.

If the MHRT decides that the patient should continue to be detained in a hospital, that is what happens. In such circumstances, there is no right for the patient, technically still a prisoner, to apply to the parole board for release, even if he or she would be eligible for release if not in hospital, whether on parole or licence (under the terms of s. 28 Crime (Sentences) Act 1997). In *R v SSHD, ex p P* [2003] EWHC 2953, P, sentenced to life imprisonment but transferred to hospital, and who had served his recommended minimum sentence of ten years, argued that the inability to access the parole board, unless and until a tribunal found that he was suitable for discharge, was in breach of Art. 5(4). The court rejected this: Art. 5(4) requires speedy access to a court, and a tribunal is a suitable court, in the circumstances (paras. 33–7, 72).

If the patient no longer requires hospitalisation, there are various possibilities. If the transfer was initially made under s. 48 (that is, that the transferee was at the time in prison on remand, or as a 'civil prisoner' or held under immigration laws), the Secretary of State, on notification that the patient is entitled to either version of discharge, 'shall', by warrant, direct that the patient be returned to prison (s. 74(4)), usually to face the charges for which the patient had been remanded in custody in the first place, unless the MHRT has used its powers in s. 74(1)(b), which provides that, if the patient satisfies the criteria for conditional discharge, the MHRT has a discretion to recommend that the patient should continue to be detained in hospital. One reason that a tribunal might conclude that it is appropriate for the patient to remain liable to be recalled to hospital for treatment, although not at that time mentally disordered nor a danger to self or others, is that the illness is in remission, and might reoccur if the patient is returned to a prison environment. If such a recommendation has been made, the Secretary of State need not issue the warrant of remittance to prison: s. 74(4). For s. 48 transferees, then, the only outcome of a successful tribunal application or referral will be either return to prison or continued hospitalisation. In 2004, out of 192 unsentenced or untried prisoners in hospital, 93 (48 per cent) returned to prison to await trial or sentence within three months (Home Office Research, Development and Statistics Directorate, 2005: Table 14), although this will be a slight overestimate because this total includes patients remanded in hospital or given a hospital order without conviction by a court. On the other hand, 52 patients remained in hospital six months after first admission. As might be expected, the vast majority of s. 48 transferees, in both directions, are male.

For patients transferred to hospital under s. 47, or psychopathically disordered patients detained in a hospital by virtue of a hospital direction and a limitation direction under s. 45A (which takes effect as a transfer direction and restriction direction made under ss. 47 and 49: s. 45B(2)(a), (b)), there are more possibilities open. According to the wording of the 1983 Act, a MHRT must direct the discharge of the patient (with or without conditions), but only if the Secretary of State agrees, and gives notice to that effect to the tribunal within 90 days of being notified that the grounds for discharge have been made out: s. 74(2). In *Benjamin and Wilson* v *UK* (2003) 36 EHRR 1, s. 74(2) was held by the European Court to breach Art. 5(4) ECHR because the final decision on discharge is not with the tribunal, in consequence of which s. 74(5A) now provides that, if this results in the patient being returned to prison, the parole board has powers to order release, notwithstanding that the restriction direction or limitation direction remains in force; if the parole board makes an order for release, the restriction direction or limitation will cease to have effect. Any discharge will take effect as under s. 73 (s. 74(6)), which means that, on absolute discharge, the patient ceases to be liable to be detained and the orders authorising detention automatically cease: s. 73(3). Hence, there is a possibility that transferred patients may secure early release from custody via a MHRT, if the Secretary of State consents. If conditional discharge is ordered, the powers discussed above, to defer the discharge, to impose and vary conditions, and to recall the patient to hospital, also apply.

At present, if the Secretary of State does not give the notice mentioned in s. 74(2), the hospital managers are under a duty to transfer the patient back to prison at the end of the 90-day period: s. 74(3). For both s. 47 and s. 48 transferees, transfer and restriction directions cease to have effect on the return of the patient to prison: s. 74(5). This duty, like that of the Secretary of State in respect of s. 48 transferees, need not be exercised by hospital managers if the MHRT has recommended, under s. 74(1)(b), that a patient entitled to conditional discharge should nevertheless stay in hospital. An MHRT may feel the need to recommend continued detention in hospital because of the overlap of s. 74 with the powers of the Secretary of State in s. 50, which empowers the Secretary of State, on being notified by the patient's RMO, any other doctor, or an MHRT, that the patient no longer requires treatment in hospital or that there is no effective treatment that can be given, to direct by warrant that the patient be remitted to prison: s. 50(1)(a). A tribunal might wish to counsel against this, for the reasons discussed above. In *R v Nottinghamshire Healthcare NHS Trust, ex p M* [2002] EWHC Admin 1400 HC, however, it was held that, although the Secretary of State must take account of any recent tribunal recommendation, he or she is not bound by it, particularly if there has been a subsequent change in circumstances.

On appeal ([2002] EWCA Civ 1728), the Court of Appeal upheld this decision and further stated that the RMO, acting under s. 50, does not need to provide the Secretary of State with a breakdown of all of the various views of those involved in the treatment of assessment of the patient in hospital (in this case, the RMO had not informed the Secretary of State of the views of two professionals, both of whom were of the opinion, not shared by the RMO, that the patient would benefit from continued hospitalisation). Pill LJ, at para. 41, held that:

there is a duty upon an RMO before giving a section 50(1) notification to make proper enquiries within the hospital as to whether the treatability test is satisfied and to consider views expressed, as well as his own first hand knowledge and experience, before making a recommendation. The extent of enquiry and of disclosure of information will depend on the circumstances of the particular case and will normally be judged as at the moment of decision.

This is a decision for the RMO (paras. 39, 40), because 'It is the judgment of the RMO which is the central feature of the section 50 procedure' (para. 41). As far as the duty of the Secretary of State is concerned, 'There will be cases in which circumstances, including information available to the Secretary of State, either in the documents by which the notification is given, or from other sources, create a duty in the Secretary of State to make further enquiries or take further action or both' (para. 47); this did not support M's argument, that he had a right to make representations to the Secretary of State, particularly when, as in this case, the bone of contention was the issue of treatability. In such a case, the Secretary of State is entitled simply to act on the clinical recommendation of the RMO.

The court dealt briefly with a claimed breach of Art. 8(1) (para. 49):

the Convention does not render unlawful that interference with private life which inevitability follows from a lawfully imposed custodial sentence. Transfer from prison to hospital and hospital back to prison, as a part of a high-security custodial regime, cannot in present circumstances be said to breach the Article notwithstanding the differences in medical treatment which may occur.'

It might be argued, however, that the pertinent Article here is Art. 5(4), and that here is another example of the Minister having power to veto over a tribunal such as was found to violate Art. 5(4) in *X v UK* and *Benjamin and Wilson*. From another point of view,

Art. 5(4) has no application here, either because s. 74(1)(b) provides for a recommendation rather than a decision or because the issue is only where a sentenced prisoner should be detained in his best interests, which does not engage Art. 5 at all because, just as under Art. 8, the issue is not one of freedom or detention but only one of the particular form of detention: *Ashingdane v UK* (1985) 7 EHRR 528 and *R v MHRT and Secretary of State for Health, ex p LH* [2001] 1 MHLR 130, HC.

Benjamin and Wilson was applied by the High Court in *R v SSHD, ex p D* [2002] EWHC 2805, in the case of a 'technical lifer'. This is a person sentenced by a court to life imprisonment, although there was evidence that mental disorder was a significant element of the offence, subsequently treated by the Secretary of State as if a hospital order had been made in his or her case. In this case, D, a transferee, with restrictions, from prison to hospital, had been found by a tribunal to be no longer liable for detention under the 1983 Act. The Secretary of State, in such circumstances, had the discretion to refer the case to the parole board for it to consider whether the individual should also be released from his or her prison sentence. There was no statutory right of access to a parole board hearing. The High Court held that this breached Art. 5(4) and granted a declaration of incompatibility. Once a prisoner had served the 'tariff' (i.e. had reached his or her ERD), there was no room under Art. 5(4) for the exercise of executive discretion over whether he or she should have speedy access to a 'court' (here, the parole board): such access must be as of right.

The result is s. 74(5A) of the 1983 Act, which now gives transferees in such a position a right of access to the parole board, with powers to end any restriction order that remains in force. The government has also abolished the concept of 'technical lifer'. From 2 April 2005, life sentence prisoners transferred to psychiatric hospital for treatment are no longer be considered for technical lifer status. All life-sentence prisoners will have their future release determined by the parole board and be subject to life licence on release (Baroness Scotland, HL Hansard, Col. WS39, 24 Jan 2005). This is, however, a change in form more than substance. As was the situation in *D*, Home Office policy has long been that the Home Secretary will refer the case of a patient sentenced to life imprisonment who is deemed ready to leave hospital by an MHRT, and who has 'passed tariff' for the offence in question, to the parole board, even if he or she does not agree with the MHRT's decision.

The Secretary of State is also empowered, by s. 50(1)(b), to 'exercise any power of releasing [the patient] on licence or discharging him under supervision' that would have been available to the Secretary of State had the patient been remitted to prison. These powers comprise, in brief, release on parole or life licence (in the case of prisoners sentenced to life imprisonment), and are found in the Criminal Justice Act 2003 and Powers of Criminal Courts Act 2000. In addition, the Secretary of State's general power to discharge, by warrant, a restricted patient from hospital absolutely or conditionally under s. 42(2) applies.

Therefore, when notified that the patient satisfies the criteria for discharge, whether absolute or conditional, the Secretary of State has a choice: to consent to the discharge of the patient into the community by the MHRT, with such conditions as the tribunal sees fit (although, of course, he or she has powers to vary those conditions); to use his or her own powers of discharge; to remit the patient to prison; to accept the recommendation of the MHRT that the patient should remain in hospital; or, if there has been no recommendation under s. 74(1)(b), to do nothing and effect the transfer to prison by default under s. 74(3). Each case inevitably turns on its own facts, but it is Home Office policy that, as far as the discharge of life-sentence prisoners is concerned, the powers in s. 50(1)(b) are the preferred option over those in s. 42 (see Gunn, 1993: 331–3), other than in exceptional cases, which means release on life licence rather than conditional discharge. The key difference between the two is that, in the former case, liability to recall subsists for the life of the patient, whereas a conditionally discharged patient may apply from between one and two years after conditional discharge for absolute discharge (s. 75(2)), or be absolutely discharged by operation of law, if the restriction order ceases to have effect and the patient has not been recalled to hospital: s. 42(5).

The policy was challenged in *R v SSHD, ex p Stroud* (1993) COD 75, which elicited from the Home Office the explanation of this preference on grounds of public policy – that persons sentenced to life imprisonment should not be able to circumvent the sentence imposed by resort to the 1983 Act, and that a clear policy allowed consistency of decision-making – decisions being taken by the Home Secretary on the recommendation of the parole board, and in consultation with the Lord Chief Justice and the trial judge, if available. Evidence given on behalf of the Home Office also emphasised that the Home Secretary would consider the use of s. 42 in circumstances under which, for example, the sentencing court had wished to make a hospital order but there was no hospital bed available, or if there had been evidence, not available to the sentencing court, that the patient had been suffering from a mental disorder at the time the offence was committed (Gunn, 1993: 333). In essence, if the Home Secretary is content that the patient could have been given a hospital order at the time of sentence, s. 42 powers will be used. The High Court in *Stroud* found the policy of the Home Secretary to be unimpeachable and that decision was upheld in the Court of Appeal. Gunn (1993: 333) has pointed out that, because it is not possible for a court to make a hospital order following a murder conviction, one would presume that the Home Secretary should consider using s. 42 powers in at least some instances involving persons transferred following such a conviction, given the wide range of situations, of varying moral culpability and of risk to the public, caught by that offence.

As to the choice between s. 74 and s. 50 powers of discharge, although there is no clear data, it seems that s. 74 is more frequently used in tribunal cases. Of *all* of the 417 restricted patients conditionally discharged by either a tribunal or by the Secretary of State in 2004, 259 were discharged by an MHRT, with 43 conditionally discharged by the Home Secretary (Home Office Research, Development and Statistics Directorate, 2005: Table 16). There is a discernible general trend whereby MHRTs are discharging more, and the Home Secretary is discharging fewer, patients than previously. For instance, in 1988, 55 patients were conditionally discharged by the Home Secretary and 70 by tribunals; in 1991, the figures were 48 and 101 respectively. In 1995, the Home

Secretary conditionally discharged only 24 patients, and MHRTs, 140 (Home Office Research, Development and Statistics Directorate, 2002: Table 16; 1997: Table 16). It is not clear what story these figures tell; but it is probably a safe bet to venture that they reveal the increasing reluctance of a series of Home Secretaries to take primary responsibility for the release of potentially dangerous individuals into the community (although reconviction rates remain low), and the increasing numbers of restricted patients detained in hospitals over the past decade or so (see Chapter 6). The number of persons returned to prison to resume a sentence (that is, s. 47 transferees) increased markedly, from 21 in 1986 to 156 in 1996, falling back to 84 in 2001, but up to 135 in 2004 (Home Office Research, Development and Statistics Directorate, 2005: Table 16). It is not clear whether the transfer back to prison of s. 47 patients is achieved by the use of s. 50 or by the use of the default powers of hospital managers in s. 74(3).

8.6 Tribunal and decisions

The president of an MHRT may announce its decision immediately after the hearing, but, in any case, the decision must be communicated in writing within seven days to all parties and, if the patient is subject to restrictions, to the Secretary of State: r. 24(1), 1983 Rules. In fact, the average hearing lasts for 100 minutes (Mental Health Act Commission, 2005: para. 4.117), and most decisions are made and recorded within 15 minutes of its ending (Perkins, 2000: 3). As with disclosure of documents before a hearing, there is a discretion given to MHRTs to decline to disclose full reasons to the patient, and to impose a duty of confidence on other recipients, such as the authorised representative, if there is thought to be a risk to the health or welfare of the patient or others: r. 24(2). There is an obvious risk that r. 24(2) may be used, in effect, to deprive the patient of his or her right, not only to know the reasons for the decision, but to challenge that decision. Clearly, this is another reason why the appointment of a lawyer or doctor as AR is advisable.

An MHRT need only reach a majority decision: r. 23(1). Decisions must be recorded in writing, signed by the president of the tribunal, and must give the reasons for the decision, and, if the decision is based on any of the matters specified in ss. 72(1) or 73(1) or (2), the tribunal must state its reasons for being satisfied regarding those matters: r. 23(2). In general terms, it can be said that 'The Tribunal's reasons must be read as a whole, in a common sense way, not as a legal treatise' (per Sullivan J in *Epsom and St Helier*, at para. 49), and that brevity is acceptable, if the reasons given are clear and reasonable: *R v MHRT, ex p Mersey Care NHS Trust* [2003] EWHC 1182. A decision that fails to address a relevant statutory factor will be quashed by the High Court, using its powers of judicial review: *R v MHRT, ex p Secretary of State* [2001] EWHC Admin 849 (see above).

A trilogy of cases in the mid-1980s established that a MHRT must do more than simply state that the statutory grounds are met or not met, as was the case in *Bone* v

MHRT [1985] 3 All ER 330 (DC). Nolan J referred to a line of case law that showed that 'proper, adequate, reasons must be given' (per Megaw J in *Re Poyser and Mills Arbitration* [1963] 1 All ER 612 (HC) at 616), which are sufficient to 'enable [the parties to the hearing] to know that the tribunal has made no error of law' (per Donaldson P in *Alexander Machinery (Dudley Ltd) v Crabtree* [1974] ICR 120 at 122), holding that merely to rehearse the words of the statute is insufficient. In *R v MHRT, ex p Clatworthy* [1985] 3 All ER 699 (HC), a tribunal decided not to discharge a patient detained under a hospital order on the grounds that the applicant suffered from 'post-schizophrenic personality disorder'. Although this was contrary to the opinions given to the tribunal by the patient's RMO and another doctor, the reasons given did not explain why the tribunal had come to a different clinical view. Mann J quashed the MHRT decision because the reasons given were 'a bare traverse' of the statutory criteria that 'do not enable one to see why the contentions of [the two doctors] were not accepted' (at 703). In the third of these cases, *R v MHRT, ex p Pickering* [1986] 1 All ER 99, a restriction-order patient was not discharged by a tribunal which, by way of giving reasons for that decision, stated that its members were unanimously of the view that the conditions in s. 72(1) were not met; it had noted the 'unhappy history' of the applicant, which included a number of convictions for sexual offences and one for manslaughter, associated with the use of alcohol and considered that the patient might experience stress if released into the community. Forbes J was 'wholly unable to detect' (at 104), from this, which element of which ground in s. 72(1)(b) the tribunal had in mind when refusing the application. Forbes J held that it was 'essential' that the tribunal bear in mind the distinction between the two elements in s. 72(1)(b), that is, the 'diagnostic question' and the 'policy question', and although the decision of a tribunal does not have to be read 'in the air', but need only be comprehensible to those who know what the issues before the tribunal are (at 102), it was not so in this case. The tribunal must also show that it has grappled with the important issues (at 102; see also *R v North East London Regional MHRT, ex p T* [2000] CLY 4173 (HC), and *R v MHRT, ex p SSHD* [2003] EWHC 2864).

In *R v Ashworth Hospital Authority, ex p H* [2002] EWCA Civ 923, [2003] 1 WLR 127, H, a patient detained under s. 3, was absolutely discharged by a tribunal with effect from five minutes after the decision was given. The tribunal seems to have chosen this option, based on its experience that, if the conditional discharge of a special-hospital patient is ordered, 'nothing ever happened' (para. 19). The decision to discharge was made in the face of medical reports from five out of six doctors that discharge was not appropriate at that time. Only one of the five doctors opposed to discharge gave oral evidence to the tribunal, along with the one doctor, Dr W, who favoured discharge. The tribunal recorded that it preferred the evidence of Dr W, which was to the effect that, although H had a long history of violence, there had been no episodes in the previous three years. In addition, Dr W's view was that H had insight into his condition, was compliant with his care plan, and that, despite continuing to be mentally ill, his continued detention was no longer appropriate, provided that H was supervised after discharge (para. 14). The High Court held that the tribunal's decision was '*Wednesbury* unreasonable', because no reasonable tribunal could have come to the conclusion that immediate discharge was appropriate, on the evidence before it, which was unanimously of the view that discharge should only be ordered subject to conditions, if at all. The Court of Appeal upheld this view. As to the tribunal's reasons, these too were found wanting: the Court of Appeal emphasised that it is not enough, where there are disputes of fact, simply to record that one witness was preferred over another; the tribunal's reasons must also demonstrate why the tribunal accepted the evidence in question over conflicting evidence. They must do so in such a way as is comprehensible to the patient and to non-medical or legal professionals, such as social workers, for whom its decision may have various implications (paras. 77–9). Here, the tribunal had not even considered the availability of aftercare and so could not be said to have grappled with the pertinent issues. The more surprising the decision adopted by the tribunal, the greater the necessity to explain that decision (*R v MHRT, ex p East London and City Mental Health NHS Trust* [2005] EWHC 2329 and *R v MHRT, ex p Li* [2004] EWHC 51 (Admin)).

Despite the case law, however, it is questionable how legalistic tribunals actually are. Under the 1959 Act regime, it became clear that many MHRT members did not know the law that they were supposed to be applying. In Peay's (1981) research, less than half of the legal members of tribunals questioned knew that they had a power of discretionary discharge. Fennell (1977) found that tribunal members were informed more by their own views of what 'common sense' required of them than by the statutory criteria. Both of these studies took place before the passage of the 1983 Act – but when Peay (1989) was commissioned, by the then Department of Health and Social Security, to report on the workings of the tribunal system after the 1983 Act had been implemented, she found that little had changed. According to Peay (1989: 212), 'it was not unusual for the decision-making process to be, in essence, back to front; [the members of the tribunal] first determined what outcome they preferred and then selected the evidence to accord with that view'. On occasion, the reason for this was to ensure that patients would continue to be supervised on discharge, but more frequently, the reasoning was grounded in concerns about public safety. Tribunal members were concerned that applicants posed a risk to other persons, but there would be no evidence to support that view. In such situations, continued detention was authorised 'on the legally acceptable grounds that [the tribunal was] satisfied that the patient remained disordered and in need of medical treatment' (1989: 213).

Such creative use of the tests to be applied in ss. 72 and 73 by tribunals will not necessarily lay decisions open to legal challenge, provided that the reasons given for declining to grant the application sought look reasonable on their face, given the discretion allowed to tribunals. An example is *Smith*, (see earlier) in which the court virtually rewrote the tribunal's reasons: for example, being prepared to accept that a tribunal's statement, that 'We considered that [the patient] should not be discharged', implied a rejection of the other alternatives open to it. To the extent that Peay's findings continue to hold good – and Richardson and Machin (2000: 499) more recently found that the requirements of the MHA were discussed by the tribunal members before the hearing in only one of 50 cases, and that there is widespread non-compliance by tribunals with the law, even when it is known and understood by the tribunal members – Peay's research gives weight to the thesis of this book that legal criteria mask medical discretion.

Peay's findings on the role of RMOs in tribunal hearings are a further case in point. In theory, the patient's RMO is a witness before the tribunal; in practice, however, 'without some impetus from the RMO neither [the Home Office nor an MHRT is] likely to initiate change' (1989: 59). In the case of restricted patients, even where a tribunal recommends the patient's transfer or that leave of absence be given, this is unlikely to be implemented by the Home Secretary without the consent of the RMO; and RMOs, like tribunal members, viewed their role vis-à-vis their patients as being determined by clinical rather than legal considerations (1989: 61). The most antilegalistic of the RMOs that Peay interviewed in one special hospital simply ignored the law; others were less antagonistic, but 'adopted the pragmatic view that it was not possible to make the fine distinctions in human behaviour which the law required' (1989: 60). In either case, legal criteria played, at best, a marginal role in dictating RMO's practices, whilst the evidence of RMOs frequently dictated the decisions of MHRTs. Of course, this will not always be the case: sometimes, a tribunal will decide against the evidence of an RMO. RMOs have, however, developed strategies to minimise the likelihood of this happening. For instance, one RMO interviewed by Peay explained that, if he suspected that an MHRT would make a decision of which he disapproved, he would reduce the patient's medication in the period before the hearing so that the patient would appear before the MHRT in as ill and agitated a state as possible, in order to demonstrate to the tribunal that continued detention was appropriate (1989: 70). In summary, although it would be an exaggeration to say that the statutory criteria are irrelevant in practice, it is clear that the criteria in ss. 72 and 73 do not necessarily constitute the only, or even the most important, factors acting on the decision-making processes of MHRTs. Rather, they provide the tools with which decision-makers can justify the outcomes that are reached; and as an attempt to rein in medical discretion with legal criteria, it is far from clear that the tribunal procedure has been successful.

Perhaps not surprisingly, tribunals order discharge relatively infrequently: five out of the 61 hearings, all involving civilly detained patients, observed by Perkins (2000) resulted in discharge. In Richardson and Machin's (2000) study of 50 cases, 18 of which involved restricted patients, 11 orders for discharge were made, only two being for immediate discharge. Failed tribunal applications, which confirm the powerlessness of a detained patient over his or her position, contribute to what Ferencz and Maguire (2000: 50) term the 'cycle of distress' that many patients experience, with hopes for discharge repeatedly dashed. In 2004, there were a total of 11,897 hearings, leading to 1,351 orders for discharge, which is a rate of 11 per cent (Mental Health Act Commission, 2005: Figure 73). Research has shown considerable regional variation, the highest reported figure being 50.3 per cent in Birmingham (Saad and Sashidharan, 1994), compared with 17.1 per cent in Oxford (Wilkinson and Sharpe, 1993), 18.9 per cent in Bradford (McKenzie and Waddington, 1994) and 9.4 per cent in Middlesborough (Milne and Milne, 1995).

The most recent MHRT reports do not provide this level of detail. The tribunals' annual report for 1997 (Department of Health, 1997: Appendix 7) confirms these findings. For example, in 1996, there were 804 hearings in the Anglia and Oxford RHA area, leading to 65 orders for discharge, whereas in South Thames, there were 138 discharges out of 826 hearings. In Wales, 349 hearings realised 94 discharges; in the South and West RHA area, there were 97 discharges from 634 hearings. There are also variations by category of detention and accommodation. One noticeable aspect of the statistics is that non-restricted patients detained in special hospitals have only a slim chance of discharge – in 1996, of 230 applications leading to 164 hearings, there were *no* discharges (1997: Appendix 8) – which reflects the facts that special-hospital accommodation is unusual for patients held under Part II, that such patients in special hospitals are, by definition, thought to be the most dangerous of civilly detained patients, and possibly also that the special hospitals house a group of formerly restricted patients who, although no longer in need of high-security accommodation, cannot be found alternative placements and who tend to be heavily institutionalised (see Chapter 3).

This group apart, restricted special-hospital patients are much less likely to be discharged than others: only 19 patients were discharged from a special hospital by an MHRT in 1996, out of 562 hearings (Department of Health, 1997: Appendix 8). This is to be expected, because, as discussed above, discharge is often not a realistic prospect for these patients. Frequently, the main purpose of an application is to garner information – through access to medical reports – about their situation that is not forthcoming from RMOs, and to vocalise concerns they may have, rather than to seek discharge. Restricted patients held other than in the special hospitals have a better chance of release. There were 138 orders for discharge from 658 hearings in 1996 (1997: Appendix 7), at a 'success rate' (of 1 in 4.8) greater than that of non-restricted patients detained under s. 2 (of around 1 in 6.75) and other than under s. 2 (of around one in eight). More recent data, from 2003, confirms this, with around 22 per cent of hearings involving restricted patients leading to absolute or (much more frequently) conditional discharge (Mental Health Act Commission, 2005: 4.119). Again, this is perhaps to be expected, because restricted patients detained other than in special hospitals have, most likely, been transferred out of a special hospital into less secure accommodation as part of a graduated plan of release. Of course, a tribunal may impose conditions on the discharge of restricted, but not other, patients, and undoubtedly this also helps to explain these, at first sight, counterintuitive figures.

Finally, we must note in passing that, since 2001, data that was put into the public domain by means of annual and then biennial reports by the MHRT Secretariat, for example, regarding the number of tribunal applications resulting in an order for discharge, any regional variations, and the relative 'success rate' of various categories of applicant, is no longer so readily available. The MHAC, which has historically, and in agreement with the Secretary of State, considered that the operation of the tribunal system was beyond its remit, being properly the responsibility of the MHRT Secretariat and the Council on Tribunals, has taken to reporting in more detail on tribunal activity. Moreover, it has had to scour the case law and seek the information mentioned above on request from the MHRT Secretariat in order to do so (see Mental Health Act Commission, 2005: para. 4.119 and note 183). The MHAC noted, with, in our view, considerable understatement, that 'It would be helpful for the MHRT to report its activity with more specificity in its annual report' (2005: para. 4.110). We do not have to be so candid, and wish to state here our dissatisfaction that, in the age of freedom of information and information technology, some data on the working of the mental health system is now harder to come by than was the case some years ago; we hope very much to see a return to previous practice now that responsibility for the MHRT system has been transferred from the Department of Health to the Department for Constitutional Affairs. If official bodies such as the MHAC have to take active steps to access data that should be freely available, what hope does the average patient, professional or indeed interested citizen have?

8.7 Challenging MHRT decisions

8.7.1 Challenges by patients

In 1986, Gunn predicted that the decision of the Court of Appeal in *Hallstrom (No. 1)*, that the embargo on the bringing of proceedings for things 'done in pursuance of' the 1983 Act in s. 139(2) does not apply to applications for judicial review, 'will permit the resolution of some complex problems of interpretation of the Act' (1986a: 292); this has, indeed, proved to be the case. Most of the case law that has been discussed in this chapter and elsewhere has arisen from the High Court's powers of judicial review. Challenges to MHRT decisions have most often been based on claims of illegality relating to a tribunal's alleged misreading of the powers given to it by the 1983 Act, although there are also examples, such as the decision in *Kelly* (see earlier), of arguments based on procedural impropriety, in the form of a breach of the rules of natural justice rather than of the terms of the legislation. Following the decision of the House of Lords in *Daly* (see Chapter 5), as developed inter alia by the decision of the Court of Appeal in *Wilkinson* (see Chapter 7), when issues of human rights are at stake, judicial review hearings will now also contemplate the proportionality of the decision, and proportionality can come very close to on-the-merits review, as discussed in Chapter 5.

If a judicial review application is successful and the tribunal's order is quashed, the situation is as if it had never been made, and so the patient's legal situation will be as it was before the order was made: *R v Finnegan and DE, ex p Wirral Health Authority* [2001] EWCA Civ 1901. A mistake of law (in a case in which a tribunal declined to order the discharge of a patient wrongly thought to be subject to a restriction order) will not invalidate a tribunal decision, however, if the substantive decision would not have been different had the mistake not occurred: *R v MHRT London North and East Region, ex p PW* [2001] 1 MHLR 146, HC.

In *R v Ashworth Hospital Authority, ex p H* [2002] EWCA Civ 923, [2003] 1 WLR 127, the Court of Appeal held that the High Court has jurisdiction to grant a stay of a tribunal decision, pending the outcome of an application for judicial review of that decision. It further held that this power could be utilised after the tribunal's decision had been implemented, provided that there was strong 'and not merely arguable' case that the decision was unlawful, that there was cogent evidence that the patient was dangerous, and that the decision was to be reviewed as speedily as possible (para. 47). The Court of Appeal approved the decision of Sullivan J in the High Court in *R v MHRT, ex p Epsom and St Helier NHS Trust* [2001] EWHC Admin 101. In that case, too, a decision to discharge a patient detained under s. 3 with immediate effect was challenged by the detaining hospital by way of an application for judicial review, and the order of the tribunal was stayed by the High Court until the substantive application could be heard. This was on the basis of, what Sullivan J described as, 'wholly exceptional circumstances', namely that a stay of the order for discharge was necessary to preserve the life of a patient who was refusing food (para. 30).

8.7.1.1 Judicial review or appeal by way of case stated under s. 78(8)?

There is an alternative to judicial review, which is an appeal against the decision of an MHRT, which is by way of case stated, under s. 78(8), MHA 1983. An appeal against the decision of an MHRT on a point of law may be made to the High Court by way of case stated (s. 78(8), RSC Ord. 56, rr. 7–12, as reproduced in Civil Procedure Rules (CPR) 1998, Sch. 1), although any such reference should be based on a specific finding of fact, and not as a mechanism through which to rehearse 'theoretical and academic' questions: Silber J in *MP v Nottinghamshire Healthcare NHS Trust, SSHD, SSH* [2003] EWHC 1782 at para. 39. The question arises whether a patient seeking redress is better served by such an appeal or by an application for judicial review. In *Bone v MHRT* [1985] 3 All ER 330 (HC), the patient, on a s. 78(8) application, was successful in his argument that the tribunal had erred in law in not giving sufficiently clear reasons for its decision not to direct his discharge (see earlier). Nolan J was invited by counsel for the appellant to say that, if the case had come before him by way of an application for judicial review, he would have quashed the tribunal's decision. But Nolan J refused to say this, pointing out that, if there had been an application for judicial review, 'there would have been an opportunity for evidence to be filed as to the facts and issues before the tribunal by all concerned' (at 334). He did, however, advise that 'if any further such case is sought to be brought before the court an application for judicial review should be considered as an alternative to a case stated under s. 78(8) . . . not only because judicial review procedure allows a broader consideration of the issues, but also because it offers a much more comprehensive range of reliefs'. In His Lordship's view, all that the High Court could do on upholding an appeal under s. 78(8) was to give any direction that the tribunal could have given (RSC Ord. 94, r. 11(6), now reproduced in CPR 1998, Sch. 1), and '[n]o such direction could appropriately be made in the circumstances of this case', presumably because the court did not have before it sufficient information upon which any such direction might be based.

Gunn (1986b) took issue with this view of the powers of the court under s. 78(8), on the basis that the High Court can return a case to the tribunal for amendment (r. 11), which arguably includes the power to ask for further facts as found by the tribunal. This might, on occasion, serve to provide the High Court with sufficient information to enable it to use its powers under r. 11(6) of Ord. 94 (CPR 1998, Sch. 1) to make a decision that the tribunal, had it not erred in law, would have been capable of making, in particular, to direct the discharge of the patient, which, as Gunn points out (1986b: 179), 'seems to provide the court with much greater power than the remedies for judicial review'. Even if, in a technical sense, there is a greater 'range' of remedies on judicial review, discharge by the High Court is the outcome that the most patients wish to see.

In the years after *Bone*, the s. 78(8) route has been the one that is most commonly used (Department of Health, 1993c: Appendix 13). There may not always be a choice, however: s. 78(8) is limited to questions of law, and so challenges based on want of jurisdiction that may not be apparent on the face of information available under s. 78(8) may have to proceed by way of judicial review. In this sense, judicial review does allow a broader consideration of the issues, because the High Court may go beyond the facts as found by the tribunal, and admit affidavit evidence from one or more of the parties to the tribunal hearing. Tactics may also be based on the technicalities of application. Gunn (1986b: 179) suggests that, because a case stated has to be requested of the tribunal within 21 days, and leave for judicial review can be sought up to three months after the events complained of, it may be advisable, when both options are open, to request that the tribunal state a case in the first instance, and, if this is not successful, then move for leave to apply for judicial review. This advice must now be reconsidered in the light of the Human Rights Act 1998, but that Act adds nothing to one side or the other in the sense that, in either case, the court must not act in a way that contravenes a Convention right. On the other hand, because judicial review does not technically provide an arena for an on-the-merits review, in some instances at least, s. 78(8) might allow a human rights-based challenge to a MHRT decision where judicial review would not.

8.7.2 Challenges by RMOs

An RMO, or the detaining hospital, might not agree with a tribunal decision to discharge a patient. Judicial review and s. 78(8) are available options, but RMOs have fashioned – and, in *R v South Western Hospital Managers, ex p M* [1994] 1 All ER 161 (HC), the court accepted – an alternative strategy for undermining a tribunal decision, which is, simply to readmit the patient: in this case, the patient, discharged from detention under s. 2 by a tribunal, had not left hospital before she was detained under s. 3 at the instigation of her RMO. In the High Court, Laws J held that M's readmission and continued detention were lawful. The decision to readmit her immediately after her discharge by the tribunal had not been made in bad faith, and the duties bestowed on ASWs to make applications for compulsory detention were not in any way fettered by the existence of a recent tribunal decision. Hence, 'there is no sense in which those concerned with a s. 3 admission are at any stage bound by an earlier tribunal decision' (at 173), even if there has been no change in the patient's condition.

It should be noted that, after such a readmission, it is again open to a patient to apply for discharge and for a MHRT to order it. In this sense, *ex p M* built the 'revolving door' into the scheme of the 1983 Act. In the first edition of this book, we argued that there is a good case for the view that a 'new fact' rule, which functions in many other common law jurisdictions and holds that a prior decision may not be departed from unless justified by the existence of some new fact, should be introduced in the UK. As discussed above, something very like a 'new fact' rule was applied by the High Court, in *R v Pathfinder NHS Trust, ex p W* [1999] 1 MHLR 142, to the powers of an RMO to reclassify a patient's mental disorder in a way that departed from a recent tribunal classification. In addition, it can be argued that, in a situation such as that in *ex p M*, the requirement of Art. 5(4), that the legality of detention should be 'decided speedily by a court' with, as was held in *X v UK* (1981) 4 EHRR 181, the power to order discharge, is also undermined by the approach taken that case.

The Court of Appeal ([2001] EWCA Civ 239; [2002] QB 235; [2001] 3 WLR 588, [2001] 1 MHLR 36) and then the House of Lords ([2004] 2 AC 280, [2003] UKHL 58, [2004] 1 All ER 400, [2003] 3 WLR 1265) confronted these arguments in *R v East London and the City Mental Health NHS Trust, ex p Von Brandenburg*. A MHRT ordered that a mentally ill patient, B, held under s. 2, be discharged. This was on the grounds that B did not suffer from mental illness to a nature or degree that warranted detention, nor was it necessary for his own health or the health and safety of other persons that he be detained. Discharge was deferred for seven days to allow suitable accommodation for B to be located. On the sixth day, B's RMO arranged for his admission under s. 3. As in *ex p M*, B was readmitted before he had left the hospital. He sought judicial review of the decision to readmit, and, when that application was dismissed, B appealed.

The House of Lords, in the form of Lord Bingham, held that B's readmission was lawful on the facts: B had assured the tribunal that he would continue to take his medication following discharge, but had, in fact, declined to do so, with the consequence that 'his condition significantly deteriorated' (para. 13). This part of the judgment is not controversial and, following the appeal to the Court of Appeal, was applied in a similar situation by the High Court in *R v Oxfordshire Mental Healthcare NHS Trust, ex p H* [2002] EWHC 465. But both the Court of Appeal and House of Lords moved significantly in the direction of a new fact rule. In the Court of Appeal, Sedley LJ disapproved the view of Laws J in *ex p M* that an ASW is not fettered in any way by an earlier tribunal decision (para. 38). In the House of Lords, Lord Bingham held (para. 8) that:

The regime prescribed by Part V of the 1983 Act would plainly be stultified if proper effect were not given to tribunal decisions for what they decide, so long as they remain in force, by those making application for the admission of a patient under the Act. It is not therefore open to the nearest relative of a patient or an ASW to apply for the admission of the patient, even with the support of the required medical recommendations, simply because he or she or they disagree with a tribunal's decision to discharge. That would make a mockery of the decision.

He then laid out (at para. 10) something that looks very much like a new fact rule:

An ASW may not lawfully apply for the admission of a patient whose discharge has been ordered by the decision of a mental health review tribunal of which the ASW is aware unless the ASW has formed the reasonable and bona fide opinion that he has information not known to the tribunal which puts a significantly different complexion on the case as compared with that which was before the tribunal.

Lord Bingham provided 'by way of illustration only' three examples: an ASW learns of an earlier suicide attempt, unknown at the time of the tribunal, which invalidates an assessment that the patient does not present a serious risk of self-harm; a patient gives assurances that he or she will continue to take medication and then does not, creating a risk to self or others not apparent at the time of the tribunal hearing; or there is a significant deterioration in the patient's condition after a tribunal has ordered discharge (para. 10). In the absence of information not known to the tribunal, then, any application for readmission will be unlawful.

As for the particular duties of the various actors involved, Lord Bingham emphasised that doctors are required only to express a professional opinion, and so any such rule would not, in any case, be relevant. As for ASWs, ordinarily, in the exercise of his or her duties under s. 13, which requires that the ASW to be 'satisfied that such an application [for admission to hospital] ought to be made', the ASW will be or become aware of any relevant tribunal decision. In the Court of Appeal, Sedley LJ perhaps went furthest in the direction of a new fact rule, holding that 'A recent – and often not so recent – order of a tribunal for discharge will always be a relevant fact . . . it is the duty of the subsequent decision-maker to take it into account; a failure to do so, albeit through ignorance, will vitiate a subsequent decision to seek admission' (para. 41). Lord Bingham 'could not accept' this, however (para. 11): for him, 'if, despite performing these statutory duties in a reasonable way, [the ASW] does not learn of a tribunal decision, I can see no ground for implying a more far-reaching duty of inquiry not expressed in the statute' (para. 11). He did accept that, where there is a decision to make an application for admission following a tribunal decision to discharge, an ASW is under a duty to explain to the patient why the tribunal decision will not protect him or her from readmission, but that duty 'must however be limited' and may require an explanation 'in very general terms'. An ASW cannot be required to make a 'potentially harmful disclosure' to the patient, as, for example, when the ASW's decision to seek readmission is based on information supplied by relatives of the patient or the patient's doctor, in circumstances under which disclosure would risk undermining a 'continuing and trusting relationship' (para. 12).

Be that as it may, the import of this case is, to some extent, opaque. Both the Court of Appeal (Lord Phillips at para. 30) and House of Lords (Lord Bingham at para. 12) did not accept that the effect of their decisions is that a new fact rule now operates in England and Wales. Both courts attempted to ensure both that ASWs and RMOs are free to act according to their own judgment about the need for admission, and that that freedom does not entail a breach of Art. 5(4) of the Convention, by emphasising that, in cases of disagreement, the tribunal prevails (Lord Phillips in the Court of Appeal at para. 31, cited in the opinion of Lord Bingham in the House of Lords at para. 5). In consequence, the courts end up attempting to articulate a very fine distinction. Sedley, LJ, having explained that, 'while not legally bound in the absence of a change of circumstances by a recent MHRT decision in favour of discharge, those concerned in a s. 3

application cannot lawfully ignore it' (para. 42), noted that 'there may be little practical difference between what [B] has sought [namely to show that a 'new fact' rule exists] and what he has achieved' (para. 39). Certainly, it is debatable whether the average ASW or mental health professional would feel totally comfortable with this distinction between 'not legally bound' and 'cannot lawfully ignore'.

The Court of Appeal followed its own ruling in *Von Brandenburg* in the later case of *R* v *Ashworth Hospital Authority, ex p H* [2002] EWCA Civ 923, [2003] 1 WLR 127 (see also *R* v *Finnegan and DE, ex p Wirral Health Authority* [2001] EWCA Civ 1901). As seen above, in *ex p H*, a tribunal had made what was later held to be an irrational, and hence unlawful, decision to order the immediate discharge of H. In response, the hospital had begun judicial review proceedings against the tribunal and had resectioned H. The High Court held that, if a hospital has substantial grounds for thinking that a tribunal has erred in law, *Von Brandenburg* is distinguishable. This view was rejected by the Court of Appeal (per Dyson LJ at para. 56):

To countenance such a course as lawful would be to permit the professionals and their legal advisers to determine whether a decision by a court to discharge a detained person should have effect. I cannot think that this is consonant with Article 5.4.

Dyson LJ, in reaching this decision, based his view on a reading of *Von Brandenburg* in which he seems to view that case as though it has introduced a 'new fact' rule. He summed up the *ratio* of that case as follows (at para. 56):

In the absence of material circumstances of which the tribunal is not aware when it orders discharge, in my judgment it is not open to the professionals, at any rate until and unless the tribunal's decision has been quashed by a court, to resection a patient.

In the light of this, our view is that, matters of legal semantics aside, a new fact rule does now operate in England and Wales. This is surely the most desirable reading of these judgments. And in so far as the ruling in *Von Brandenburg* seems, in theory at least, to leave open the possibility that a discharged patient may be readmitted when there are no new facts justifying that decision (this *must* be the implication of the refusal to recognise the existence of the rule), Dyson LJ's approach is also be to preferred. It is more clearly in line with the requirements of Art. 5(4).

8.8 Absence without leave

Some patients may simply bypass the legal mechanisms by which to challenge detention, and abscond. The MHA 1983 defines 'absent without leave' widely, if blandly, as 'absent from any hospital or other place and liable to be taken into custody': s. 18(6). A detained patient is deemed to be absent without leave if he or she leaves the hospital at which he or she is detained without having been granted leave, fails to return to hospital on the expiry of a period of leave or if recalled, or goes absent from a place at which he or she is required to reside as a condition of leave: s. 18(1)(a), (b), (c). These provisions tie in with the widest definition of absconding in the literature, that of Huws and Shubsachs (1993: 46–7), namely 'the unauthorised absence of the patient from the hospital, an outside working party, or rehabilitation or compassionate leave from the hospital [including d]eliberate evasion of nursing staff in crowded areas whilst outside the hospital'. In *R v SSHD, ex p S* [2003] EWCA Civ 426, S, detained under s. 3 following his release on licence from prison, absconded from hospital in breach of s. 18(6), unaware that his licence had been revoked by the Secretary of State. It was held that he was also, even whilst detained in hospital, unlawfully at large for the purposes of his recall to prison, under (as it then was) s. 39(2) of the Criminal Justice Act 1991. It is an offence both to assist or induce a patient who is liable to be detained to abscond and to harbour a patient who is absent without leave, or to prevent, hinder or interfere with his or her recapture (s. 128(1), (3)), although a patient commits no criminal offence by absconding: *R v Criminal Injuries Compensation Board, ex p Lawton* [1972] 3 All ER 582.

The spectre of the 'escaped madman' is a staple of much modern fiction and attracts media attention. Yet the fact is that absconding from the 'deep end' of the hospital system is rare. Huws and Shubsachs (1993) found that, in the period 1976–88, during which a total of 4,909 persons were detained in a special hospital, there were only 36 escapes. Only seven of these were from hospital, the majority occurring on outings from the hospital. Even so, Huws and Shubsachs (1993: 51, 52) compute that there is only a one in four thousand chance that a patient will abscond when on an outing from hospital. A further 30 special-hospital patients absconded from RSUs, local hospitals or hostels whilst on leave of absence, at a rate of 1 in 2,800. The majority of absconders – around 75 per cent – are, in fact, informal patients (Andoh, 1994: 135). There is a sense in which the idea of an 'informal absconder' is paradoxical, but, in hospital, the same recording practices and reactive procedures apply to the unauthorised absences of both detained and informal patients, and the main issue is not legal status but whether the absconding is a matter of 'grave concern' or not (Andoh, 1994). It is perhaps to be expected that most absconders would be informal patients, who comprise at least 90 per cent of annual admissions; and the fact that around 25 per cent of absconders are detained patients means that, as a proportion of the whole, they are markedly more likely to abscond. The research invariably shows that young males, unemployed, admitted under compulsory powers with admission requiring police involvement, with a prior history of hospitalisation, are most likely to abscond (Tomison, 1989; Farid, 1991; Huws and Shubsachs, 1993; Short, 1995), and there is evidence to suggest that Afro-Caribbean patients are more likely to abscond than others (Falkowski *et al.*, 1990).

Even if the absconder is from the deep end of the hospital system, there is good reason to argue that there will very rarely be cause for 'grave concern' for public safety. Offending by patients absent without leave is minimal. Huws and Shubsachs found that, between 1976 and 1988, absconders from special hospitals committed a handful of petty theft offences. Two serious offences were committed: a rape, and the shooting of a police officer resulting in a manslaughter conviction. Two serious offences is, of course, two too many, but it comes nowhere near the public perception of the risk. These offences were committed by patients who had absconded from hospital; patients who absconded whilst on leave committed no serious offences (Huws and Shubsachs, 1993: 55). Violence is almost never reported to have been a feature of an escape. In the overwhelming majority of instances, absconders pose no significant danger to the public (Brook *et al.*, 1999). There have long been concerns, on the other hand, about the correlation between absconding and risk of suicide (Milner, 1966; Falkowski *et al.*, 1990; Morgan and Priest, 1991; Bannerjee *et al.*, 1995, Mental Health Act Commission, 2001; 2005: para. 4.44 and Figure 51)), so that best practice is to respond immediately on discovering an escape.

Most absconders are not hard to find. Homesickness is a common reason for absconding – the patient's view that they do not need to be in hospital is another (Short, 1995: 281) – and many patients are to be found at home (Bowers, 2003). Most are soon back in the custody of the hospital: a good proportion within hours, and more within 24 hours (89 per cent in Short, 1995: 281; 69 per cent in Huws and Shubsachs, 1993: 51). A sizeable minority of patients return voluntarily (Bowers, 2003). It is extremely rare that a detained patient absent without leave is not apprehended, although on apprehension, a small minority are discharged rather than returned to hospital.

Most patients are returned by the police, or by nursing staff, relatives or friends. Very few absconders remain at large for any length of time. Until the passage of the Mental Health (Patients in the Community) Act 1995, a patient, other than one subject to restrictions, who was not taken into custody within 28 days of the date of absconding, ceased automatically to be liable to be detained. Apparently, around 10 per cent of patients detained under a hospital order achieved discharge in this manner (Walker and McCabe, 1973, in Hoggett, 1996: 166). Section 2(1) of the 1995 Act substituted a new s. 18(4) of the 1983 Act, which now provides that persons detained for treatment, including patients on a s. 37 order, who abscond, may be taken into custody at any time before six months from the first day that he or she was absent without leave, or before the expiry of the period of detention, whichever is the later: s. 18(4)(a), (b). Thus, the maximum period for which a patient may be absent without leave is 12 months, if the authority to detain has been renewed (for at least the second time) shortly before the date of the absconding. A patient who absconds near the end of a period of detention will automatically cause the extension of the period for which he or she is liable to be detained by up to six months. The period of detention (but not the six-month period: s. 18(4)) may be extended by one week if the patient is absent without leave on the day, or within a week, of expiry, and is recaptured or returns voluntarily before the expiry date: s. 21. This is to allow time for arrangements to be made for the renewal of the patient's detention.

None of the above applies to restricted patients, who remain liable to detention regardless of time absent without leave (Sch. 1, Part II, paras. 2, 4), nor to patients held under the short-term Part II powers of detention in ss. 2, 4, 5(2) and 5(4), who may not be retaken once the period of detention has expired (s. 18(5)), nor to patients remanded to hospital for medical reports or for treatment, or on conviction made the subject of an interim hospital order, who may be arrested without warrant by a constable, and returned to the court that made the order, which may (although need not) terminate the order and deal with the offender in some other way: ss. 35(10), 36(8), 38(7). There is no time limit on the liability to arrest of absconders in this category.

The 1983 Act provides, in s. 18(1), that a detained patient absent without leave may be taken into custody by an ASW, any member of staff of the hospital in question, a police officer, and any person authorised in writing by the hospital managers. If the patient is on leave, but with a requirement to reside in another hospital, the staff of that hospital and persons authorised by the managers of that hospital may also retake the patient: s. 18(2). The procedure on absconding depends upon the level of concern raised. Andoh (1994) found that, when there is cause for grave concern – usually when a patient is thought to pose a suicide risk or a risk to the safety of other persons, or to be particularly frail, confused or vulnerable – nursing staff will first search the hospital and grounds, and then, if failing to locate the patient, contact the duty doctor; a decision is then taken about whether to book the patient as absent and call the police. Nursing staff will also telephone the home address of the patient and, if the patient is there, steps will normally be taken either to compel (if detained) or attempt to persuade (if informal) the patient to return. The patient's home address will also be telephoned in cases causing less-than-grave concern. It is possible to use the s. 4 powers to compel the return of an informal patient, although the only powers of entry available in the Act are those in s. 135 (see Chapter 4), requiring the issue of a warrant. Another option for a police officer is to use s. 17(1)(d), PACE 1984, which gives powers to enter and search premises for a person 'unlawfully at large and whom he is pursuing'. The House of Lords in *D'Souza v DPP* [1992] 4 All ER 545 held that a person absent without leave under s. 18 of the 1983 Act is 'unlawfully at large'. As to the reference to pursuit, Lord Lowry held that this limited the availability of this power to situations where there was a chase, and it did not provide a general licence to enter premises. If the requirements of s. 17(1)(d) of the 1984 Act can be made out, reasonable force may be used in their exercise: s. 117, PACE 1984.

Andoh (1994), looking at practices in three hospitals, found that all three always contacted the police when a detained patient had absconded, although if the case was not one of grave concern this would not be done until the patient had broken the hospital's unofficial curfew (typically 11p.m. or midnight). The police were contacted regarding absconding by informal patients less often, but still perhaps surprisingly frequently, on around 15 per cent of such occasions, although at one hospital, at which there was a relatively small number of absconders, the level was higher, at 55 per cent (Andoh, 1994: 135). Police procedure on receipt of a report of absconding shows a high degree of consistency across regions. Cases are categorised as either urgent, requiring full inquiry, or non-urgent, requiring limited inquiry. Cases in the first category involve detained and especially restricted patients, and vulnerable patients. In such cases, 'the police would leave no stone unturned in their efforts to find the missing person' (1994: 132). For example, forces other than the one initially contacted, are brought in if necessary. Otherwise, the practice is to go to the home address of the patient, and merely report back to the hospital whether or not the patient was there.

The reason why, until the passage of the Mental Health (Patients in the Community) Act 1995, a patient who remained at large for 28 days ceased to be liable to be detained was that it was assumed that a patient who coped for that period of time outside of hospital did not need to be detained. Although that period has now been extended, the 28-day period retains its significance. Section 21A (which, with s. 21B, was also introduced by the 1995 Act) provides that, if a patient is returned or returns voluntarily to hospital within 28 days of absconding, the renewal of authority to detain under s. 20 may be made as if the patient had not absconded, and if the period of liability to detention has been extended by a week through the operation of s. 21, the necessary reports may be made during that period, although the renewal of detention is backdated to the date at which the earlier detention ended. Section 21B, by contrast, lays out a procedure similar to that required for initial admission to be followed in the case of patients being returned or returning to hospital more than 28 days after the date of absconding, and thus maintains something of the philosophy behind the pre-1995, 28-day limit, on liability to recapture. In such a case, the patient's liability to detention will automatically terminate one week after his or her return to hospital, unless the requirements of the section are complied with: s. 21B(4). These requirements are that the 'appropriate medical officer', which means the RMO for hospital inpatients (ss. 21B(10), 16(5)(b)), must examine the patient within one week of his or her return, to see if the 'relevant conditions' are satisfied: s. 21B(2). These are those in s. 20(4) (s. 21B(10)), which are essentially the same as for admission for treatment under s. 3. If they are satisfied, the RMO must report to the managers in writing, but before doing so must 'consult' – the decision, however, is solely for the RMO – with one person professionally involved in the patient's treatment and an ASW (who need not be so involved): s. 21B(3). A report, 'duly furnished' to the hospital managers (ss. 21B(2)(b), 10(a)), provides authority for the renewal of the patient's detention in accordance with s. 20(2), that is, for six months if it is the first renewal or 12 months for subsequent renewals. As with s. 21A, any renewal made by virtue of s. 21 is backdated: s. 21B(6). A retaken patient is entitled to a MHRT review of that decision within the period of renewal: ss. 66(1)(f), (2)(f). Of course, prevention is better than cure, and there is a growing literature concerned with strategies to prevent absconding in the first place (Bowers *et al.*, 2003).

8.9 Concluding comments

This has been a long chapter, and so our concluding comments will be brief. In terms of the ongoing theme of this book that questions the nature of the relationship between 'medicalism' and 'legalism', it is evident that the material that has been discussed in this chapter has, again, revealed the limitations of law, in the form of the safeguards built into the 1983 Act, to act as an independent constraint on the exercise of medical discretion. Instead, particularly, but not exclusively, in the case of restricted patients, medicine and law have seemingly worked effectively 'together' to deliver a policy that subordinates the good of the individual to the safety of the many. But, as suggested in Chapter 7, this should more properly be seen as a colonisation of the legal by the medical, with the consequence that law has often been procedure, and sometimes not even that, rather than protection. By and large, although less so in the case of unrestricted patients (Richardson and Machin, 1999), the courts have accepted the need to diminish both the importance of substantive rights and due process for the greater public good, and have been particularly reluctant to interfere with the discretion of the Secretary of State.

As this chapter also shows, however, there are decisions that buck this trend. Pre-Human Rights Act cases like *Clatworthy*, *Kelly*, *Harry* and *Reid* are examples of courts placing, or affirming, real legal constraints on the operation of the discharge system. Following the coming into force of the Human Rights Act, the courts have increased the protection offered to patients in a number of ways, including the introduction of a (de facto) new fact rule, the insistence that lack of resources will not exclude breaches of Art. 5(4) of the Convention caused by unreasonable delays in access to the tribunal system, and the finding that the Kafkaesque situation, under which a patient was required to prove that he or she was not mentally disordered before a tribunal, breached Art. 5(1). Other decisions, particularly the rulings in *Scottish Ministers*, *ex p H*, and *Reid* v *UK*, that the Convention does not require a detained patient to be treatable, demonstrate a rather less proactive approach to the protection of human rights, and too great a readiness to prioritise control and risk management, than some might wish to see.

We have seen in this chapter that the discharge system suffers from a shortage of funding, so that, at one end of the scale, patients may be discharged inappropriately, and at the other, discharge may be denied or delayed because of inefficiencies in the system. It is important not to forget that the hospital system provides care and treatment for vulnerable people, and, when discharge is governed by factors other than therapeutic ones, we should be concerned, even if it is ultimately concluded that consideration of other factors is justified. It is also appropriate to remember that, for most patients, prevention of discharge is not an issue. But, important as these considerations are, we should not lose sight of the larger questions raised, about the social function of our mental health system – and we are yet far from a satisfactory answer.

9

Control, Care and Community

9.1 Introduction

The historical development of the current regime for the care and control of mentally disordered persons in the community has been discussed earlier in this book (see Chapter 3). The focus in this chapter, therefore, will be the system as it currently operates. If conceptualised as a unified and singular system, community care presents as a paradox, in that it simultaneously constructs mentally disordered persons as being both 'of' the community, needing and deserving of its care; and as 'outsiders', from whom the community is in need of protection. This paradox traverses all policy and practice in this area to an extent, but it can be resolved partially by recognition of the fact that 'community care' comprises two – relatively discrete, albeit overlapping – systems. The first that we discuss is the system of *service provision*, in which the key questions concern the ease with which those in need can access services and the quality of those services; the second to be considered is a system of *control* and *supervision*.

It is true that, in the main, the latter system builds on the former, in that it takes the form of *requiring* compliance with services that are otherwise optional or client-led. But the aims of the 'control'-based system are significantly different in orientation to those of the 'service' system, and require separate discussion. In particular, the two systems mobilise very different concepts of 'community'. The former, in theory at least, practises social inclusionism, and sees no difference between the interests of mentally disordered persons and those of the broader community: we all have an interest in the pursuit of optimum levels of public health and welfare. The latter practices social exclusionism and sees the interests of the broader community as being in opposition to those of (potentially dangerous) mentally disordered persons, with the consequence that the rights of the mentally disordered are permitted to be overridden in the public interest.

In practice, the boundaries between optional and mandatory service provision, in terms of constituency, are blurred. For instance, a patient who may be able to leave hospital, if he or she complies with a plan for treatment in the community, may agree to be subject to compulsion. It is an open question whether acceptance of treatment, or other requirements such as place of abode, is really the voluntary acceptance of an optional service in such circumstances, but this is how the law sees it, provided that the services in question do not amount to 'detention', in which case, even consent cannot make them lawful (see *R v MHRT, ex p SSHD, PH* [2002] EWCA Civ 1868, discussed in

Chapter 8). Moreover, risk to others (or to self) is not the only relevant factor in determining who gets subjected to the various powers of compulsion, nor are all the shots called by central government and its policies. Medical criteria and localised decisions are also pertinent, and as we shall see below, psychiatrists and others can prevent, or at least considerably delay, the release into the community of persons ordered to be discharged by a tribunal by refusing to provide the services in question, if that refusal can be medically justified. In addition, the intricacies and subtleties of government policy and professional practice may not translate into public opinion. As Prins (2002: 397) has recently argued, 'we live in "over-reactive" times', in which fear of the 'other', as evidenced, for example, by the moral panic that surrounded and continues to surround paedophilia, leading to vigilantism across the country, seems to be the main concern. In reality, then, the line between inclusionism and exclusionism is dynamic, politically loaded, multifaceted, and problematic.

Both systems have seen, and will see further, reform under the current Labour administration, reacting to its own conclusion, widely shared, that 'community care has failed' (Department of Health, 1998a). Riding on the back of political and media concern about dangerous mentally disordered persons at large in the community, control is at the top of the policy agenda: '[m]aintaining the highest possible levels of public protection will remain our top priority' (1998a: para. 4.24). Significant steps were taken in the 1990s, although the government stopped short, in England and Wales, of introducing treatment under compulsion 'in the community'; supervised community treatment (SCT) is a central plank of the government's truncated plans for reform. Those who adopt a Cohenesque reading of care in the community (see Chapter 3) will find much of interest in these developments, which are discussed further below.

As discussed in Chapter 3, the 'failure of community care' that predicated the latest round of reforms has been understood not only as a failure of control: it has also been seen as a failure of coordination and of cooperation between local authority social service departments (SSDs), health authorities (HAs: now largely replaced by primary care trusts, or PCTs), and local authority housing authorities, caused by inadequate systems, poor management and inadequate resourcing (Department of Health, 1998a: para. 3.2). The Department of Health has been busy over the last few years, developing policies and practices to improve inter-agency cooperation and the use of resources (see later in this chapter). There are difficult political issues at play here. There can be no doubt that the community care system has a potential demand for resources that is of a magnitude beyond the ability of any government to satisfy completely. Indeed, although the welfare state was introduced on the assumption that better access to services would, in the long run, decrease overall demand, the opposite has been shown to be true. The consequences of a healthier, longer living population is one of the key social policy questions of our time, as the ongoing debate about pensions and other benefits demonstrates. Hence, some of the central controversies in the construction and operation of the current system are unlikely to be resolved quickly or easily, by legislation or by any other means. Nevertheless, better legal systems and frameworks can improve the efficacy of service delivery by a number of measures, including, as well as financial considerations, qualitative outcomes (especially consumer satisfaction). And as we shall argue further below, the unintelligibility, to the layperson, of the current legal framework for the provision of community care services and for assessing entitlement to services, in respect of which there are no current proposals for reform, impedes both consumer satisfaction and efficacy, however measured. Clearly, there are many and varied issues and interests jostling for a place in the politics of community care. This chapter offers a discussion of current debates through a critical reading of the current law, policy and practice of community care.

9.2 Services for mentally disordered persons in the community

9.2.1 Community care planning

Part III of the National Health Service and Community Care Act (NHSCCA) 1990 is the locus of a network of duties and entitlements – but although attempting to give coherence to the legal framework for the provision of community care services, this is not a consolidating Act. It has not placed all of the law relevant to community care under one roof, and can really be seen as no more than a starting point for those who wish to study this area in any detail. The Act did nothing to clarify, and in fact, complicated, the philosophical or political basis of community care provision. Its consumerist and managerialist principles are very different from the ideology of welfare that underpinned prototypical community care legislation in the post-war period, of which significant elements remain in force. Little attempt has been made, as of yet, to reconcile these differences (Clements, 1997), or to codify and rationalise what, as will be seen, is a confusing patchwork of statutory provision and supporting secondary legislation and guidance. Nor does it seem that any such attempt is in prospect, despite the ongoing process to reform, in particular, the powers of control over mentally disordered people in the community.

The NHSCCA 1990 places primary responsibility for the effective delivery of community care services on SSDs. Section 46(1) requires every SSD to prepare, publish and keep under review a plan for the provision of community care in its area. This must be done in consultation with housing authorities, the voluntary sector (including organisations representing the interests of private carers such as family members, and voluntary housing and community care organisations), and any other persons as the Secretary of State may direct: s. 46(2). Despite such local autonomy, there is a significant degree of central government control over service provision at local level. The Secretary of State has powers to inspect premises and evaluate management practices, to make regulations, including regulations regarding the transfer of staff between

SSDs and HAs, which must be complied with by SSDs, and to hear complaints and carry out investigations: ss. 48–50, NHSCCA 1990. The Secretary of State also uses 'approvals' (which are permissive) and, in particular, 'directions' (compliance with which is mandatory and which are to be found in LAC (93)10, published by the Department of Health in March 1993), under powers to be found in ss. 7, 7A Local Authority Social Services Act 1970. Central government also has control of gross local government funding, and can target funds through the use of grant funding for services for the mentally ill under s. 7E of the 1970 Act, and by the Mental Health Grant, through which £133.5m was made available in 2003–4 to pump-prime multi-agency initiatives (HSC 2003/002: LAC (2003)1, Department of Health, 2003). In 2006, £90,539m was granted for spending over the years 2006–7 and 2007–8 on mental health services for adolescents and children with mental health problems (Department of Health, 2006n).

There is also a significant degree of discretion to be exercised at local level, in terms of which services to provide, to what extent, and to which individuals, and HSC 2003/002 provides that greater discretion is afforded to SSDs with a track record as 'high performing'. This means that service provision is not standard across the country and so raises issues of equity of entitlement (Bindman *et al.*, 2000), as well as of inter-agency cooperation. There is a statutory duty on SSDs and HAs to cooperate with each other in the delivery of health and welfare services: s. 22, National Health Service Act (NHSA) 1977. Amongst the most important aims of the NHSCCA 1990 were, first, to bring into being a system of care in the community that was 'much more user driven rather than fitting clients into existing services' (Lord Henley, Under-Secretary of State for the Department of Social Security, *Hansard*, HL, Vol. 520, Col. 645); and, second, to 'ensure that a seamless community care service is available which covers both health and social needs' (Baroness Blatch, *Hansard*, HL, Vol. 518, Cols. 1537–38). The extent to which these aspirations have been realised will be discussed later; first, it is necessary to consider what is meant in law by 'community care'.

9.2.2 Community care services

The NHSCCA 1990 does not define 'community care', but 'community care services' are defined by s. 46(3) to comprise those that may be provided under:

- Part III of the National Assistance Act 1948;
- s. 45 of the Health Services and Public Health Act 1968;
- s. 21 and Sch. 8 of the National Health Service Act 1977;
- s. 117 of the Mental Health Act 1983.

These statutes are concerned with the provision of accommodation services, welfare services, and health services, including aftercare, to overlapping groups of clients, the main point of overlap being between services for persons with mental illness and those for elderly persons. Each of the statutory provisions is supplemented by rules,

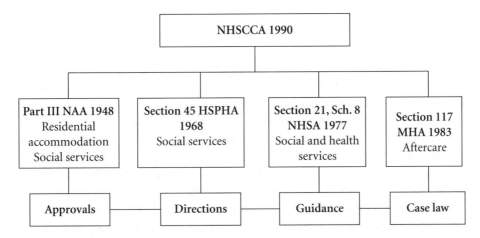

Fig. 9.1 The community care legislation

• Patients transferring between facilities maintain their status (s. 19)

• Upon lapse of authority to detain, patients in hospital revert to informal status (s.131)

regulations, and guidance, as well as by directions and approvals from the Secretary of State (see Figure 9.1).

9.2.2.1 Part III, National Assistance Act 1948

Part III of the National Assistance Act 1948 (NAA) is concerned with the provision of services by SSDs. Sections 21–8 deal with the provision of residential accommodation; s. 29 is concerned with welfare services. Section 21(1)(a) of the 1948 Act gives a discretion to SSDs to provide residential accommodation for adults (the needs of children are covered by the Children Act 1989) who are 'in need of care and attention which is not otherwise available to them'. In *R v Slough BC, ex p M* [2004] EWHC 1109, Collins J (at paras. 43–4) held that:

It is not necessary ... for the need for care and attention to be for care and attention provided by the local authority. It is a general need for care and attention and, as it seems to me, a person who is chronically ill and who, therefore, needs continual medical care and continual provision is, by that very fact, properly said to be in need of care and attention ... Whether that need ... will in a particular case mean that he is required to have accommodation is a wholly different question and it may well be that ... where there are other means whereby these matters can be provided for, section 21 will not come into play at all.

The Court of Appeal upheld this, very wide, definition of 'in need of care and attention' ([2006] EWCA Civ 655 at para. 21), but this does not mean that it is easy to access accommodation via s. 21. There must be no other way of satisfying the need in question, and often there will be at least the possibility of securing accommodation via an application to the local housing authority The presence of informal mechanisms for meeting needs, in the form, for example, of relatives and friends of the client, are also relevant. For example, in *R v Camden LBC, ex p P* [2004] EWHC 55, it was held that P, who suffered from depression, anxiety disorder and obsessive–compulsive behavioural problems for which he had been hospitalised, was not entitled to be provided with accommodation under s. 21 on discharge from hospital, inter alia, because he could be provided with support in his own home by his wife, W. This was despite the fact that the reason that P had applied for accommodation to be provided under s. 21 was that W, who had health problems of her own, was unable to cope with his difficult behaviour, and he was, for that reason, living in bed-and-breakfast accommodation at the time of his application. The couple had, in fact, not lived together for over a year because P, an American citizen, had returned to live with his family in America for a year before returning and being admitted to hospital in London. When P was homeless for six days, W had moved out of her flat so that he could stay there, but she would not stay there with him. The SSD decided that (1) '[P and W] can live together and if they continue to have relationship problems, these should be capable of resolution with advice and guidance', and (2) 'If for some reason [P] is not able to live with his wife, [P] has support available from his family in the USA' (cited at para. 23 of the judgment). The High Court held that this was a reasonable assessment on the facts and therefore P did have care and attention 'otherwise available' to him (para. 29). Whether or not the SSD assessment was correct, this case does underline the extent to which 'informal' care is seen by SSDs and the courts as an integral element of the community care 'system'. In *R v Stockton on Tees BC, ex p Stephenson* [2005] EWCA Civ 960, it was held that an SSD's policy, that it would not reimburse the cost of care provided by a family member, was lawful in principle, on the basis that family members could be expected to provide services on a voluntary basis. A policy is not a rule, however, and where it can be shown, as in *Stephenson*, that a family member has given up paid employment to care for a relative on the understanding and expectation that payment will be made, such a policy cannot simply be applied without consideration of whether it is fair to apply it in the particular circumstances.

The scope of the obligations of an SSD are subject to approvals and directions of the Secretary of State. Directions can be found in Appendix 1 to LAC 93(10), the effect of which is that SSDs have four duties to make arrangements under s. 21(1)(a). The first is in respect of persons who, by reason of 'age, illness, disability or any other circumstance', are in need of such services and are ordinarily resident in the SSD's area. The second is in respect the same classes of persons, who are not ordinarily resident in the SSD's area but who are in urgent need: LAC(93)10, Appendix 1 para. 2(1)(b). The third duty, imposed 'without prejudice to the generality' of the first two, is owed to persons in urgent need of temporary accommodation 'in circumstances where the need for that accommodation could not reasonably have been foreseen', and makes no reference to the ordinary residence of the applicant: Appendix 1, para. 2(2). The fourth, also imposed without prejudice to the generality of the first two, and which applies in respect both of those ordinarily resident in the SSD's area and those with no settled residence in the SSD's area, requires SSDs to make arrangements under s. 21(1)(a) for persons who are, or have been, suffering from mental disorder, and to prevent mental disorder: Appendix 1, para. 3(a), (b).

In *R v Redbridge LB, Camden LB, ex p N* [2003] EWHC 3419 (Admin), Stanley Burnton J rejected an argument that the duty owed to mentally disordered persons by virtue of para. 3(a) and (b) meant that a SSD, in effect, owed a duty to the whole world to provide those services, as long as that person was, in fact, present in its catchment area. Rather, s. 21 and Appendix 1 must be read subject to s. 24(1), which provides that it is for the SSD in whose area the applicant is ordinarily resident to provide any necessary residential accommodation. Any other interpretation of the scope of the duty imposed by para. 3 of Appendix 1 would render s. 24 devoid of effect (para. 39) and would 'enable an applicant in arguable need for residential accommodation...to choose which local authority he is make liable, and possibly in whose area he will live' (para. 40). He further held, with significant implications for applicants who, as in this case, are seeking asylum in the UK, that 'ordinarily resident' or 'settled residence' (the two terms being interchangeable in his view: para. 40) may not cover 'a person of unsettled immigration status', who, therefore, 'may well not be ordinarily resident anywhere' when, following arrival in the UK, he or she is waiting to be 'dispersed' to some location in the UK by the National Asylum Support Service (para. 40).

The linkage between the provision of accommodation and the need for care and attention indicates that this provision is not concerned with the provision of accommodation *per se*: s. 21 provides an entitlement to care rather than to housing. A string of cases, culminating in the decision of the Court of Appeal in *R v Tower Hamlets LBC, ex p Abdul W* [2002] EWCA Civ 287, have held that, in limited circumstances, a need identified under s. 21 may properly be met through the provision of 'ordinary' housing (see further below). An SSD may provide its own accommodation or avail itself of the provision of another SSD, for which it must pay (s 21(4)), although the SSD in whose area the recipient is ordinarily resident retains the responsibility to provide the accommodation: s. 21(6). As discussed in Chapter 3, these days, the vast majority of residential accommodation – 85 per cent of all places – of all is purchased from private providers.

Means-tested charges are payable by recipients of accommodation: s. 22. The amount of a capital that may be taken into account is regulated by the Community Care (Residential Accommodation) Act 1998 and supporting secondary legislation. A resident is required to pay in full for his or her accommodation if he or she has capital above a specified limit (set at £ 21,000 from 10 April 2006): The National Assistance (Sums for Personal Requirements and Assessment of Resources) (Amendment) (England) Regulations 2006, SI 2006/674. Capital of less than £12,750 is disregarded, and those with capital of between £12,750 and £21,000 pay a contribution to the cost of their care. It is also provided, in s. 21(2A), that regulations may specify that certain resources must be ignored for the purposes of assessing whether a person is in need of care and attention not otherwise available under s. 21(1)(a), and The National Assistance (Residential Accommodation) (Disregarding of Resources) (England) Regulations SI 2001/3067 provide that the disregard level for the purposes of assessing need is pegged to the capital disregard level under s. 22. The Secretary of State, acting under powers given to him or her inter alia by s. 22(5) of the 1948 Act, has also made the National Assistance (Residential Accommodation) (Additional Payments and Assessment of Resources)

(Amendment) (England) Regulations 2001, SI 2001/3441, which allow a person assessed as needing residential accommodation under s. 21 to pay a 'top up' in order to live in accommodation that is more expensive than the SSD would usually pay for someone with that person's assessed needs. Policy guidance on charging was issued as part of the Fair Access to Care Services (FACS) initiative in 2002 (Department of Health, 2002g; for the most recent version of the *Guide on Charging for Residential Accommodation*, known as CRAG, see Department of Health, 2006o). Nevertheless, there remains a considerable discretion, subject to judicial review, to develop policies at local level.

There is also a considerable incentive for those likely to be in need of residential accommodation to divest themselves of their assets, in particular their home, in order to avoid having to pay charges for residential accommodation, and, accordingly, reg. 25 of the National Assistance (Assessment of Resources) Regulations 1992, SI 1991/2977 provides that, when capital has been transferred to avoid charges, it may be treated as part of the client's 'nominal' capital for the purposes of assessing liability to charges. In *R v Dorset County Council, ex p Beeson* [2002] EWCA Civ 1812, B had transferred his house by deed of gift to his son. The SSD saw this as an instance for the application of reg. 25. B's son appealed against this finding and the appeal was heard by a three-person complaints panel (two county councillors and an independent chair), which rejected his complaint. B then sought judicial review. At first instance ([2001] EWHC Admin 986), the High Court held that the regulation did not apply in this case. This was because its application is limited to situations in which there had been a transfer specifically and deliberately to avoid liability, and in this case, the evidence of B and his son, that the house had been transferred to provide B's son with accommodation following the breakdown of his marriage, had not been shown to be inaccurate. The Court of Appeal upheld the High Court on this point.

In a Scottish case, *Robertson v Fife Council* [2002] SLT 951, a decision of the House of Lords, the issue was at what point a consideration of 'notional capital' became relevant. In that case, R, an elderly woman in need of residential accommodation, had transferred her property to her sons, their consideration being 'love, favour and affection', and the relevant SSD had decided that reg. 25 applied to that transfer. It therefore determined not to provide care to R until such time as her notional capital was reduced to the statutory limit. Lord Hope of Craighead, with whom the other law lords agreed, held at para. 53 that 'Notional capital can be taken into account at the stage when charges are being made for the services. But it must be left out of account at the earlier stage when decisions are being taken to provide these services. This avoids the prospect of very real hardship which this case has demonstrated'. Thus, disagreements about the amount of notional capital available must not impact on the duty of the SSD to provide services that, by virtue of (in the law of England and Wales) s. 21 of the 1948 Act, they must provide.

Bisset-Johnson and Main (2002) have suggested that, although the practical effect of *Robertson* is sound in policy terms from one point of view – because clients denied access to SSD-run or commissioned accommodation will often, as in that case, be

accommodated in NHS accommodation, which causes 'bed-blocking' in NHS facilities –
it is not clear how an SSD, obliged to accommodate a person that it deems to have
notional capital available, will actually be able to extract that capital from third persons
lawfully in possession of it, in this case, the client's children. They conclude that
'Without legislative action to afford the local authorities a remedy in this situation, the
authorities face serious financial implications' (2002: 282). In *Derbyshire CC v Akril*
[2005] EWCA Civ 308, another case in which property had been transferred by an
elderly person, A, to his children whilst he was in hospital awaiting a nursing home
place, the SSD sought to use s. 423 Insolvency Act 1986 as a mechanism to address this
problem. Section 423 empowers the court to order that property transferred in order to
defraud creditors be restored to the original owner. The High Court made an order
under s. 423 and it was upheld by the Court of Appeal; this seems to go some way to
answering Bisset-Johnson and Main's point.

One final point on this issue is whether the complaints panel procedure (outlined
above) is Convention compliant. In *Beeson*, the High Court held that it is not, being in
breach of Art. 6 ECHR, because it involves a determination of the applicant's civil rights
by a panel that is not sufficiently independent or impartial, which deficits are not
answered by the availability of judicial review. The Secretary of State for Health, as an
interested party, appealed against this part of the judgment, arguing that Art. 6 is not
engaged in such circumstances. The Court of Appeal held that Art. 6 was engaged, given
that the panel is charged to decide a matter relevant to the complainant's civil rights,
namely the question of where he should live and on what terms, and that the panel procedure per se does not satisfy the requirement of that Article for impartiality, but then,
at para. 30, Laws LJ continued:

That is of course right; but it seems to us to miss the real point in issue here, namely whether,
given the quality of the first-instance process such as it is, the addition of judicial review
satisfies Art. 6. If there is no reason of substance to question the objective integrity of the first-
instance process (whatever may be said about its *appearance*), it seems to us that the added
safeguard of judicial review will very likely satisfy the Art. 6 standard unless there is some special feature of the case to show the contrary. Here there is not.

Although it difficult to dispute that the availability of judicial review renders the system, as a whole, compliant with Art. 6, it is perhaps unfortunate that the court did not
take a more robust attitude to the constitution of the complaints panel. Any court or
quasi-court that is two-thirds constituted by officers of one of the parties before it is
clearly unacceptable and should be reformed. The Convention does, it is true, focus on
substantive questions, but the common law has long demanded as a requirement of
natural justice that justice must not only be done, but must be seen to be done, and that
is not the case here.

Section 26(1) of the NAA 1948, as amended, authorises SSDs to make arrangements
for the provision of accommodation with voluntary organisations or 'any other person' –
which means privately run care homes – in order to provide care-home accommodation with personal or nursing care (s. 26(1A)), as long as such homes are registered in

accordance with the Care Standards Act 2000, Part I or Part II, as the case may be. In practice, much residential accommodation is provided by the independent sector (see Chapter 3). The 2000 Act and supporting secondary legislation lays down a detailed regime of registration for care homes, which are defined negatively, as homes that are not 'hospitals' under the terms of the NHSA 1977, but which offer accommodation inter alia for people who are or have been mentally disordered, or who are disabled or infirm, (see s. 3(2), (3) Care Standards Act 2000). Section 6 of the 2000 Act also establishes the National Care Standards Commission (NCSC), now known as the Commission for Social Care Inspection (CSCI), which, by s. 5, is given powers to regulate the provision of care-home accommodation through a licensing system. It is an offence to operate such a home unless it has been registered with the CSCI: s. 11, 2000 Act. The CSCI may refuse to register a care home or may cancel a registration, and the burden of proof is on those alleging that the home and its staff are suitable: *Jones* v *Commission for Social Care Inspection* [2004] EWCA Civ 1713. Cancellation may be done summarily on the order of a magistrate, on the application of the CSCI, to prevent serious risk to a person's life, health or well-being: s. 20(1)(B). There is a tribunal system (the Care Standards Tribunal) to which appeals against decisions of the CSCI or a Magistrate lie: s. 21, 2000 Act. The CSCI must act in accordance with directions and guidance given by the Secretary of State (s. 6(2)), and the Care Homes Regulations 2001 SI 2001/6539, as amended, prescribe detailed requirements as to who is suitable to run such homes, and the manner in which they must be run.

Detailed consideration of the care homes regime is beyond the scope of this text, but there are two important points that should be made about the regime. First, the courts have decided that there is nothing wrong, in principle, with SSDs using the mechanism of contracts with independent providers to impose requirements over and above those specified in the statute, provided that such requirements are reasonable: *R* v *Newcastle-upon-Tyne City Council, ex p Dixon* (1993) 158 Local Government Reports 441 (HC). A contractual term will be found to be unreasonable if compliance with it would threaten the continuing viability of the private homes in question, because that constrains the choice of service users and so frustrates the purpose of the policy behind the Act of 1990: *R* v *Cleveland County Council, ex p Cleveland Care Homes Association and Ors* (1993) 158 Local Government Reports 641 (HC). It is perhaps doubtful that the policy of the Act, however, should be seen to be that care homes should be kept open at any cost. Nevertheless, the judgment in *Cleveland* seems to mean that it is not open to an SSD, motivated by a preference for public-sector provision, to write terms into contracts with independent providers in order to ensure the continued viability of that provision.

Second, although s. 3(2) of the 2000 Act differentiates, as a matter of law, between care homes that provide nursing on the one hand, and hospitals on the other, other provisions of the 2000 Act operate in the direction of collapsing that distinction. In particular, s. 2(3)(b) provides that an establishment that accepts patients detained under the Mental Health Act 1983 is to be deemed an 'independent hospital' rather than a care home. Thus, the definition turns on the type of resident, rather than the type of establishment. The number of detained patients held in private mental nursing homes has risen considerably over the last two decades, from 269 admissions in 1986 to 1,005 in 1996–7 (Department of Health, 2003c: Tables 10, 11), and stood at 1,629 by 2004–5 (Government Statistical Service, 2006: Table 9), although it has been higher. In addition, of course, most hospital inpatients are not detained, and in this much larger group, the crossover between 'hospitals' and 'homes' is significantly more substantial. In short, although the 1983 Act draws a rigid distinction between patients who are in hospital and those who are not (although subject to its provisions on leave of absence – see Chapter 8 – and s. 2(6) of the 2000 Act specifically provides that a patient in a care home on leave of absence from a hospital does not convert that care home into a hospital), in practice, the line between inpatient services and community care can be difficult to draw. This has major implications for the way in which the 'shift' to community care should be understood.

At the other end of the spectrum, a care home is distinguished from 'ordinary' housing: the former being a place in which accommodation is coupled with personal or nursing care. In *Moore v Care Standards Tribunal* [2005] EWCA Civ 627, [2005] 1 WLR 2979, a charity, F, provided care-home accommodation. F then devolved the provision of accommodation to H, a second charity but one that functioned together with F as part of the same organisation, with F continuing to provide the care. F sought to have a number of its homes deregistered on the basis that it had issued the occupants with assured tenancies, such that they were now tenants of their own 'ordinary' accommodation and so the accommodation in question no longer amounted to a care home, because no care was provided by the lessor, H. If the homes in question were now to be regarded as 'ordinary' accommodation, the residents were no longer in residential accommodation and therefore could claim state benefits including welfare benefits and housing benefits. This would save the accommodation provider a considerable sum, because rent was now being paid by the tenants for the accommodation. The Court of Appeal (Sir William Aldous at para. 21) held that:

the intention of the legislature was to include within the Act a range of models of care facilities, but I can see no reason why an establishment cannot provide accommodation within the meaning of that word in section 3 of the Act whether or not the accommodation provided is by lease or licence. The crucial consideration is whether the establishment provides the accommodation together with nursing or personal care... The establishment of a lessor and lessee relationship can be an indicator of a situation where an establishment does not provide both the accommodation and the care, but cannot be determinative.

This is an important decision that both challenges care home providers to maximise the possibility for residents to be supported in independent living, and has considerable financial implications for providers, residents and the Treasury.

As far as welfare services are concerned, s. 29(1) of the NAA 1948 provides a wide discretion for SSDs, subject to approvals and directions made by the Secretary of State, to make arrangements for promoting the welfare of a wide constituency of 'disabled' clients, which includes, inter alia, those 'who suffer from mental disorder of any description'. Section 29 is used for a wide variety of purposes, including the provision of home help and meals, recreational facilities such as televisions, organised outings and holidays, and services ancillary to these, such as the provision of transport to and from recreational facilities, holidays, and so on. Such services may also be charged for, to the extent that it is reasonable to do so, under s. 29(5) and s. 17 Health and Social Services and Social Security Adjudications Act 1983.

Charging policy has largely been left, until recently, to the discretion of individuals SDDs. The Care Standards Act 2000 amended s. 7 of the Local Authority Social Services Act 1970, which gives the Secretary of State powers to issue guidance on the exercise of statutory powers by SSDs, so that the Secretary of State now has power to issue guidance on charging policy, which was done in 2001 (Department of Health, 2001f), followed by practice guidance in 2002 (Department of Health and Department for Work and Pensions, 2002). The basis thrust of this guidance is that persons on Income Support or Jobseeker's Allowance may not be charged for services, and those on one or more of a variety of disability benefits are entitled to an individualised assessment to ensure that charges, if imposed, are reasonably pegged to a client's income. Nevertheless, the statutory requirement is to impose, if charging is imposed, reasonable charges, and this means that SSDs retain a degree of discretion over their policies at local level. In *R v Powys County Council, ex p Hambridge (No. 2)* (2000) BMLR 133 (CA), the SSD had divided service users into three groups: Group A comprised clients whose only income was in the form of Income Support; Group B, which included H, comprised clients in receipt of Income Support and some form of additional disability benefit; Group C comprised clients not in receipt of any state benefit. The SSD's policy was to charge those in Groups B and C at a higher rate than those in Group A. H challenged this policy on the basis that it was in breach of the Disability Discrimination Act 1985, in that it discriminated against disabled persons by reason of requiring them to pay higher charges than clients in Group A. The Court of Appeal rejected this argument, on the basis that, although there was 'discrimination', it was based not on disability but simply on ability to pay, as evidenced by the higher charges also imposed on clients in Group C.

9.2.2.2 Section 45, Health Services and Public Health Act 1968

Section 45, Health Services and Public Health Act 1968 empowers SSDs to make arrangements, subject to approvals and directions of the Secretary of State, for promoting the welfare of 'old people', with the limitation, imposed by s. 45(4)(b), that this provision may not be used as a mechanism 'for making available any accommodation or services required to be provided under the National Health Service Act 1977'. Of course, as has been discussed at various points in this text, there are a considerable number of elderly people with mental health problems and so services for the elderly and services for the mentally disordered will inevitably overlap. Department of Health and Social Security Circular 19/71 (Department of Health and Social Security, 1971) makes it clear, however, that s. 45 of the 1968 Act is designed to catch those elderly people who, because not 'disabled' as defined by s. 29 of the 1948 Act, do not qualify for the provision of services under the Chronically Sick and Disabled Persons Act 1970; this means that this is the least relevant provision for present purposes, because the definition of 'disabled' in s. 29 of the 1948 Act will catch most, if not all, of those who are mentally disordered within the meaning of the MHA 1983. The range of services available under s. 45 of the 1948 Act is very similar to that available under s. 29 of the 1948 Act. Again, such services may be charged for under s. 17, Health and Social Services and Social Security Adjudications Act 1983.

9.2.2.3 Section 21 and Sch. 8, National Health Service Act 1977

Section 21 and Sch. 8, National Health Service Act 1977 are the main sources of non-residential community care services for adults suffering from mental disorder. Paragraph 4AA of Sch. 8 specifically provides that residential accommodation may not be provided to 'any person' under these powers. Section 21(1)(b) and para. 2(1) of Sch. 8 require SSDs to provide care and aftercare for ill persons. LAC(93)10 require SSDs to make arrangements for the provision of day centres offering facilities for training or occupation, for the provision of an adequate number of approved social workers, and for providing social work support for persons living in their own homes, including the identification, diagnosis, assessment and treatment and aftercare of mental disorder, and for ensuring that guardianship orders (see later) can be made. Schedule 8 also permits the provision of ancillary services, such as domiciliary assistance, to persons living in their own homes.

9.2.2.4 Section 117, Mental Health Act 1983

Section 117(2) of the MHA 1983 places a duty on PCTs or HAs and SSDs to provide, in cooperation with voluntary agencies, aftercare services to those patients entitled to receive them 'until such time as the [PCT or HA and SSD] are satisfied that the person concerned is no longer in need of such services'. The duty is placed by the statute on the PCT, HA and SSD in the area in which the patient 'is resident or to which he is sent on discharge'. In *R v MHRT, Torfaen County Borough Council and Gwent AHA, ex p Hall* [1999] 3 ALL ER 132 (HC), a patient, H, who, before hospitalisation, had resided in one area, was to be discharged in another area. There was some buck-passing between HAs as to who was responsible for arranging (and funding) H's care. In the High Court, Scott Baker J held that it is for the service providers in the area in which the patient resided before entering hospital, and no other, to make the necessary arrangements. The only exception to this, when the duty falls on the authorities in the area to which the patient will be discharged, is when a patient was of no fixed abode at the time of initial detention.

Only those released from compulsory detention under the Act are eligible. Section 117(2A) contains a further duty to provide s. 12-approved doctors and 'supervisors' for the care of persons subject to aftercare under supervision (ACUS: see later). The term 'aftercare' is not itself defined nor its components specified in the 1983 Act, and the Code of Practice (Department of Health and Welsh Office, 1999: ch. 27) merely refers to the care programme approach (CPA: see later), which should apply to all persons in contact with service providers, whether formally in receipt of aftercare or not.

In *R v Camden and Islington Health Authority, ex p K* [2001] 3 WLR 553, [2001] MHLR 24 at para. 29 Lord Phillips MR held that 'the nature and extent of [s. 117] facilities must, to a degree, fall within the discretion of the health authority, which must have regard to other demands on its budget'. The content of aftercare has been made clearer by the introduction of 'aftercare under supervision' (discussed further later in this chapter). The most frequent features of an aftercare programme will be some combination of accommodation, medical, educational and training services. These last services may be provided by way of day centres, outpatient provision, or direct to clients in their own homes or in hostel or care home accommodation. Usually such services can be provided without the need for explicit compulsion, because the possibility of return to hospital arises if a patient does not comply with the terms of his or her discharge, but there are powers to force clients to accept services under s. 117. After many years of uncertainty about whether s. 117 services may be charged for, with around two thirds of areas charging for at least some services provided under s. 117 and the other third providing them free (*R v Manchester City Council, ex p Stennett* [2002] UKHL 34 per Lord Steyn at para. 4), it has now been established by the House of Lords in *Stennett*, a test case that conjoined several appeals, that s. 117 imposes a freestanding duty, and is not a gateway into other services, and that, because there is no charging provision in the section, it is not permissible to charge for s. 117 services.

Jones pointed out (2003: 450–1) that the approach taken in *Stennett* can produce anomalies. He gave the example of a patient leaving hospital who will require long-term residential accommodation to be provided after discharge. If that patient was initially sectioned because he or she would not agree to be hospitalised, then, on discharge, the provision of that accommodation, under s. 117, will be free of charge. But if, at the point of initial admission to hospital, that patient was compliant and so the use of a 'section' was not necessary, he or she will have to pay towards the cost of the provision of resi-dential accommodation, because in that case the accommodation will be provided under s. 22 of the 1948 Act. Lord Steyn in *Stennett* held (at para. 13) that 'this view is too simplistic', that the legislation has to deal with the 'generality of cases', and that the dis-tinction between the two cases may reflect the policy view that patients who have been sectioned 'pose greater risks upon discharge to themselves and others than compliant patients'. He also approved the dicta of Buxton LJ in the Court of Appeal ([2001] QB 370 at 386) that s. 117 applies to an 'exceptionally vulnerable class' of patient.

Our response is: (i) simplistic or not, the anomaly identified by Jones exists; (ii) the distinction between informal and sectioned patients is arbitrary to a large degree – the same patient may be 'compliant' one day but not the next, and the significant use of s. 5 of the 1983 Act demonstrates this (see Chapter 4); (iii) as *Bournewood* and its aftermath has made clear, exceptionally vulnerable people are often held 'informally' in hospital. The decision in *Stennett* is welcome, however, and Jones' point is not really directed at s. 117, but rather at the regime under ss. 21 and 22 of the 1948 Act, and raises the ques-tion of whether continued charging under that regime is a defensible policy, at least when services are provided in the form of aftercare, given that the duty under the 1948 Act is only triggered in cases of 'need', defined restrictively. On the other hand, this would be to set up an equally anomalous and problematic distinction between 'aftercare' and 'care', and would impose unmanageable budgetary pressures on SSDs. We can only have the care – and the control – that we are prepared to pay for.

9.2.2.5 Other sources of care and assistance in the community

These then, are 'community care services' as defined by s. 46(3) of the NHSCCA 1990. There is clearly a considerable degree of overlap between the various provisions. Yet these services by no means fill the field, and there are a number of other statutory provisions that, in practice, are as central to the delivery of community care as those singled out by s. 46(3). These various statutory provisions are linked together and weave in and out of the definition of community care services in s. 46(3). A key example is the provision of welfare services under the Chronically Sick and Disabled Persons Act 1970 (CSDPA), access to which is limited to 'disabled' persons. Section 2(1) of that Act places a duty on SSDs to identify local needs for services, which is broadly similar to the duty in s. 46(1) of the 1990 Act, and lists a range of welfare services that must be supplied to those in need of them. From one point of view, the role of the 1970 Act after the enactment of the 1990 Act is to function as a parallel regime, providing services for 'disabled persons', whilst that set up by the 1990 Act is concerned with providing services to others in need of community care services. Yet things are not that simple, for two reasons.

First, s. 2(1) of the 1970 Act, although listing the welfare services in question, refers to s. 29 of the National Assistance Act 1948, which gives SSDs a *power* to supply welfare services. The effect of the 1970 Act was to augment that power with a *duty*. Those to whom the duty under s. 2(1) of the 1970 Act is owed are persons defined as 'disabled' in s. 29 of the 1948 Act, and s. 2(1) of the 1970 Act provides that, if it has been assessed as necessary that the SSD make arrangements in order to meet the needs of the person in question, 'it shall be the duty of [the SSD] to make those arrangements in exercise of their functions under . . . s. 29 [of the 1948 Act]'.

The point is that s. 29 is to be found in Part III of the NAA 1948, which *is* on the list of community care services in s. 46(3) of the 1990 Act. Therefore, it is arguable that services under the 1970 Act are within the s. 46(3), 1990 Act definition, through being linked to Part III of the 1948 Act in this way. This view has been rejected by the High Court on a number of occasions. In *R v Gloucestershire County Council, ex p Mahfood and Ors* (1996) 8 Admin LR 180, at 193, McCowan LJ, sitting in the Divisional Court, held that '[w]hat is authorising the local authority to make arrangements under s. 2 is s. 2'; the same view was reached in the High Court decision in *R v Gloucestershire County Council and Anor, ex p Barry* (1995) 30 BMLR 20. *Barry* went to the House of Lords on a different point (see later) and there is no particularly strong support to be gleaned from their Lordships' opinions for either of these possible interpretations. The view that services which must be provided by virtue of the operation of s. 2(1) of the 1970 Act *are* provided under s. 29 of the 1948 Act was expressed in *R v North Yorkshire County Council, ex p Hargreaves (No. 2)* (1997) *The Times*, 12 June (HC), and in *R v Powys County Council, ex p Hambridge* [1998] 1 FLR 643 (HC). In the latter case, Popplewell J held bluntly (at 650) that '[w]hen providing welfare services under s. 2 [of the 1970 Act] the local authority are exercising their functions under s. 29 [of the 1948 Act]. They are not providing services under s. 2; they are making arrangements under the 1948 Act for the provision of their services'. On appeal ([1998] 96 LGR 627), the Court of Appeal upheld Popplewell J's decision. The practical importance of this question is that, as mentioned above, services under the 1948 Act can be charged for under s. 17, Health and Social Services and Social Security Adjudications Act 1983, whereas there are no provisions to permit charges to be levied under the 1970 Act.

Second, to confuse matters further still, 'disabled' is defined by s. 29 of the 1948 Act to include, inter alia, people aged 18 or over 'who suffer from mental disorder of any description'. Hence, even if welfare services provided under the 1970 Act are not 'community care services', they may be accessed by persons with mental disorder who would also be prima facie entitled to access the same services under the 1990 Act. As might be expected, the complexity of the relationship between the various statutes in this area tends to store up a further set of problems regarding access and entitlement.

9.3 Assessing entitlement, and the nature and scope of the duties owed

9.3.1 Entitlement under the NHSCCA 1990

In the scheme of the 1990 Act, access to the services listed in s. 46(3) is dealt with in s. 47. This prescribes a two-stage procedure to be used in the assessment of the needs of individuals. When it appears to an SSD that a person may be in need of community care services, the SSD *must*, first, carry out an assessment of the person's needs (s. 47(1)(a)). It was said by Stanley Burnton J, in *R v Camden LBC, ex p B* [2005] EWHC 1366, that this refers to 'a person who may be in need at the time, or who may be about to be in need', and there is no duty to consider future needs. This was said in the context of patients who are detained in hospital with little prospect of release in the near future, and should not, in our view, be taken to mean that future needs are not, in general terms, to be considered by a s. 47 assessment. Second, the SSD, 'having regard to the results of that assessment, shall then decide whether his needs call for the provision by them of any such services': s. 47(1)(b). The legal obligation to meet needs does not amount to a duty to promote the best interests of the client (Owen J in *Crookdale v Drury* [2003] EWHC 1938 at para. 52). There is no obligation for an SSD (SSD1) to carry out an assessment of the needs of persons for whom another SSD has responsibility (*R v Southend BC, ex p J* [2005] EWHC 3457), even when, as in that case, those persons have been clients of a service (a day centre) that SSD1 proposes to close. The obligation imposed by s. 47 is to carry out a full community-care assessment of the applicant's various needs. It is not acceptable to assess only the narrower question, of whether an applicant is eligible for the care plan approach (CPA: see further below), which asks only if the applicant has a persistent and enduring mental disorder: *R v Islington LBC, ex p HP* [2004] EWHC 7.

An assessment must comply with the requirements of natural justice. In *R v Wandsworth LBC, ex p G* [2004] EWCA Civ 1170, the issue was whether G, who lived in residential care accommodation, should return to live there following a hospital stay, as she wished to do, or whether she should be moved into a nursing home, as the SSD wished to see happen. The SSD allegedly based its view on a medical report that said that G needed nursing following her stay in hospital, which could only be provided by a nursing home. The Court of Appeal held that this was a view that the SSD is entitled, in principle, to take, but it struck down the SSD's decision because: it had failed to consider all the relevant factors; no written records were kept of the discussions and conclusions supporting its decision; it did not allow G's representative and next friend, her daughter L, to attend relevant meetings; the doctor that had provided an opinion had been asked to confirm the already-made decision of the SSD rather than to make an independent and impartial assessment of the extent of G's needs, and whether they might reasonably be met by providing her with nursing care in her residential care accommodation rather than moving her.

It is not open to an SSD to decline to carry out an assessment, or to hold that a potential service user does not 'appear to be' a person in need, on the grounds that it does not offer the services required to meet any needs that may be identified (*R v Berkshire CC, ex p P* [1997] 95 LGR 449 (HC)), or that it does not have the resources to meet any need that might thereby be identified: *R v Bristol City Council, ex p Penfold* [1998] COD 210 (QB). But it has been said that an SSD may refuse to provide a service if it is *impossible*, for legal reasons, for the SSD to supply it: *R v Swindon BC, ex p Stoddard* (1998) 2 July, unreported (DC), in which an SSD was unable to provide 'community care' accommodation in a regional secure unit, because such facilities only accept 'sectioned' patients.

In addition, an existent and continuing duty may be terminated if the intended recipient of the services in question refuses to accept them (*R v Kensington and Chelsea London Borough Council, ex p Kujtim* [1999] 4 ALL ER 161), but only if that the refusal is unreasonable: *R v Islington LBC, ex p Batantu* (2001) 33 HLR 76 (QB). In *R v Newham LBC, ex p P* 2000 WL 1741487, Henriques J held that a refusal of accommodation is less likely to be categorised as unreasonable if it were made in the absence of legal advice as to the potential implications of refusal, and that the SSD should explain the offer to the client and make sure that its terms are properly understood. The court further held that, if the refusal is reasonable, an SSD that treats that refusal as discharging its duty to assess the client's needs is in breach of s. 47. It is likely that a refusal to accept a reasonable offer of accommodation or other services based on a properly carried-out assessment under s. 47 will be unreasonable: *R v Southwark LB, ex p K* [2001] EWCA Civ 999, [2001] HLR 31 (CA) per Mance LJ at para. 57. But a refusal to accept offered accommodation has been held reasonable when based on the unsuitability of the location of the accommodation (*ex p K*), or because the property was only available on a short-term basis and was expensive for the applicant (*ex p Batantu*). In the first instance decision in *ex p K* (2000 WL 1791525), Hallett J held that the question of whether a refusal to accept an offer of services was reasonable, in that case, by an elderly Kurdish woman with little ability to speak English who suffered from paranoid schizophrenia and whose capacity was in doubt, 'must involve an objective assessment of the whole of the circumstances, whatever the mental capacity of the claimant or the support they derive from others'. This point was not taken on appeal. It would be unfortunate if Hallett J is understood to have prescribed an 'objective' test of reasonableness, to be applied to, by definition, vulnerable people whose lack of 'objectivity' may well be a symptom of the problem that the community care legislation attempts to address. The better view is that an objective assessment of a refusal must take account of the particular, subjective, circumstances of the client refusing the services offered.

At both stages of the assessment process, the way that 'need' is defined is the crucial factor. It is worth pointing out that a 'need' is not a 'right'. As such, although the 1990 Act was purported to herald a new era of user-driven services, the statute retains the paternalistic language of the past. An SSD may involve other agencies in the assessment process, yet there is no provision in the statute for input from the client. Client and carer involvement is a key element of the 'care plan approach' (see later), and so discussion of needs with the client is the norm – but, although the client may express preferences, the final decision is with the SSD: *ex p K* (above).

On the other hand, the distinction between a 'preference' and a 'need' will not always be clear, and an SSD which draws the distinction inappropriately may be liable to successful challenge by way of judicial review. According to the National Assistance Act 1948 (Choice of Accommodation) Directions 1992, para. 2, when it has been decided to provide accommodation under s. 21, the SSD in question must 'make arrangements for accommodation ... for that person at the place of his choice', although this is subject to the SSD deciding that the placement is reasonable and suitable for the client's needs, and is cost-neutral compared to what would have been the SSD's preferred placement: 1992 Directions, para. 3. In *R v Avon County Council, ex p M* [1994] 2 FCR 259 (HC) M, a learning-disabled client, expressed an emphatic preference for a particular care home, but the SSD placed him in another home on grounds of cost. After seeking unsuccess-fully to challenge the decision through the SSD's complaints procedure, M sought judi-cial review, and was successful, on the grounds that his strong preference constituted a psychological need on his part, that required accommodation in the home of his choice in order for it to be satisfied.

In *R v Leicester CC, ex p S* [2004] EWHC 533 (Admin), the respondent SSD decided to provide residential accommodation for S in Leicester, her home city, notwithstand-ing that she had, for several years, lived in Newcastle, and wished to be provided with accommodation there. The High Court quashed the SSD's decision on the basis that it had considered the suitability of the competing placements in Leicester and Newcastle only in terms of the facilities offered, and had not sufficiently, nor sufficiently recently, considered S's particular needs, its last assessment having taken place five years ago. These cases seem to hold out a beacon of hope for client involvement, and while this is accurate in a sense, from another perspective, it merely emphasises that it is what a client needs, rather than what a client wants, that is the decisive factor. Hence, if a want is to be satisfied, it must first be redefined as a need.

An example is provided by *R v Southwark LB, ex p K* [2001] EWCA Civ 999, [2001] HLR 31 (CA). K, a Kurdish woman who had been born and lived in Iraq for most of her 91 years, suffered from paranoid schizophrenia, with failing sight and hearing, and various other physical infirmities, rendering her immobile to a large extent. She had been assessed as being in need of accommodation and care, and had been offered, together with her elderly husband, a placement in residential accommodation. This placement was deemed necessary to meet K's needs by the SSD. It was refused by K and her husband, who wished to be provided with a ground-floor flat, where Mr K, aided by his daughter and other family members, felt they would be able to care for K, who did not speak English (the SSD had been unable to locate Kurdish speakers to participate in the provision of residential care to K). It was also said in evidence that the use of residential accommodation was antithetical to Kurdish culture, in which family members care for the elderly in their own homes. The High Court held that K's needs had been properly assessed and reasonably responded to by the SSD, and the Court of Appeal upheld that decision, notwithstanding the views of a social worker and psychiatrist, which supported those of K and her husband. *Ex p M* was distinguished (at para. 54) on the basis that K's preference did not amount to a need. This is antithetical to the concept of empowerment. Indeed, it may be possible to go further and argue that the assessment procedure under the NHSCCA 1990, as constructed by law, comes close to systematic disempowerment, and *Avon* expresses the exception that proves the rule: that unless clients present as supplicants, which involves clients recasting themselves in the discursive terms of social work as an essentially paternalist discourse, they will be turned away.

Nevertheless, needs are not abstract entities, and a client's needs must be assessed sensitively. For example, services to be provided to clients in their own homes must take account of the particular circumstances of that home life. Obviously, attitudes towards, for example, the use of residential accommodation will vary from client to client and from family to family. A decision to offer a client a care package incorporating residential accommodation, rather than providing services to a client in his or her own home, when that client has a strong preference for staying at home may breach Art. 8 of the Convention, notwithstanding that there may be a strong financial incentive for the SSD to prefer residential care: *R v SW Staffs Primary Care Trust* [2005] EWHC 1894. As in *ex p K*, cultural factors, and issues surrounding language skills, may also often be pertinent. There is some evidence to suggest that mental health services are experienced by actual and potential users from within a particular cultural perspective (Littlewood and Lipsedge, 1997), and the potential of any state system to function as a conduit of racism has been underscored by the events that have unfolded in the wake of the death of Stephen Lawrence. Gender is also a relevant consideration (Thorogood, 1989), and both factors impact on the question of need and how an SSD makes itself aware of needs in its area (Ahmad and Atkin, 1996). There is also a reported lack of knowledge of available mental health services, particularly amongst Asian women (Hatfield *et al.*, 1996), which calls for more assertive, but also sensitive, outreach, if needs are to be identified as readily as in other sections of the community. This assumes that (more) intervention is necessarily a good thing, which is, in reality, an open question. But the point here is that 'need' cannot be assessed accurately outside its broader social context; in this lies both the potential for empowerment and disempowerment in the assessment process under s. 47.

In the 1990s, a dominant and recurring theme was the relationship between needs and resources: is an individual's 'need' to be assessed without reference to external factors, or is it permissible to take such factors, most importantly available resources, into account? The leading decision is that of the House of Lords in *R v Gloucestershire County Council and Anor, ex p Barry* [1997] 2 All ER 1, which was not concerned directly with the 1990 Act but rather with the Chronically Sick and Disabled Persons Act 1970. As discussed earlier, the 1970 Act is not listed as a source of community care services in s. 46(3) of the 1990 Act, and, even if it does come under that section by virtue of its relation to s. 29 of the 1948 Act, it also and simultaneously functions as a parallel regime, concerned with the provision of services to 'disabled' persons. The wording of the provisions of the 1970 Act that deal with access to services is similar, but not identical, to the wording in s. 47(1) of the 1990 Act, but it is possible nonetheless to apply the implications of the opinions handed down in *Barry* to the question of the interpretation of the 1990 Act.

In *Barry*, the situation was that an SSD, pleading lack of resources, intended to withdraw cleaning and laundry services, which it had been supplying to B, a pensioner, under the terms of s. 2(1) of the 1970 Act. This duty is to provide, where 'necessary', a variety of social services to disabled persons who 'need' them. The central thrust of the opinions of a majority of the House of Lords was that, once a need has been assessed to exist, and it had been decided that it was necessary to meet it (because it was not being met in some other way, for example, through the efforts of informal carers), there is a duty to meet it. Lord Clyde said that 'a shortage of resources will not excuse a failure in the performance of the duty' (at 16). But that does not mean 'that a consideration of resources may not be relevant to the earlier stage' of deciding whether or not a need recognised by law could be said to exist and whether it was necessary to meet it. In short, in determining whether or not a *legally* recognised need existed, the issue of available resources was a factor that could properly be taken into account. This was because, in Lord Clyde's view, '[t]he words "necessary" and "needs" are both relative expressions' and their meaning could only be assessed by reference to other factors, such as other, competing needs, types and extent of disabilities, and so on. Once 'external' factors were acknowledged as relevant, the twin issues of cost and resources inevitably became part of the equation. Lord Nicholls of Birkenhead explained (at 12) that:

Once it is accepted...that cost is a relevant factor in assessing a person's needs...then, in deciding how much weight is to be attached to cost, some evaluation or assumption has to be made about the impact which the cost will have upon the authority. Cost is of more or less significance depending upon whether the authority currently has more or less money. Thus, depending upon the authority's financial position, so the eligibility criteria...may properly be more or less stringent.

Barry has recently been applied to the provision of services, in that case, expensive alterations to a family home, provided to a family with two disabled sons under Part III Children Act 1989, on the basis that such services are also triggered by the duty in s. 2(1) of the 1970 Act, in *R v Wandsworth LBC, ex p Spink* [2005] EWCA Civ 302, [2005] 1 WLR 2884, [2005] 2 ALL ER 954 at para. 35. The means of the two boys' parents was a relevant consideration when deciding whether to charge for the provision of the service in question.

As far as its implications for the interpretation of s. 47(1) of the 1990 Act are concerned, the decision of the majority in *Barry* makes clear *both* that the assessment of 'needs' under s. 47(1)(a), *and* the question of whether needs, once identified, must be met under s. 47(1)(b), can properly be answered by the SSD with reference to the availability of resources. Unlike s. 2(1) of the 1970 Act, which provides that, once needs have been identified that must necessarily be met but which will not otherwise be so, 'it shall be the duty of that authority to make those arrangements', s. 47(1)(b) only requires that the SSD make a decision *whether or not* to meet any needs that the assessment has identified, *even if it is 'necessary' that such needs be met* and so an SSD may, subject to the principles of judicial review, and human rights, if pertinent, plead inadequate resources as sufficient reason for deciding against providing the service in question. In essence, the second and third elements of the assessment procedure in the 1970 Act have been telescoped in the 1990 Act. Under the 1970 Act, having, firstly, decided that there is an unmet need, the SSD must, secondly, decide whether it is necessary to meet that need, and, finally, if it is necessary, meet it. Under the 1990 Act, by contrast, the issues of whether it is necessary to meet the need and the fact of meeting it have been conflated, with the consequence that the 'third' stage of the process has been 'colonised' by the language of discretion with its subtext of resource awareness.

This means that the 1990 Act allows the possibility that needs will be identified but not met. Lord Clyde explained that, under the 1970 Act, 'in the strict sense of the word no unmet need will exist' (at 17), because the recognition of needs in the first place is tailored by resource considerations. It may be that there is little difference, from the consumer's point of view, between a need that is legally recognised as such but not met (under the 1990 Act) and a need that is not met because it is not recognised as such through an adjustment of the criteria for assessment to keep needs in line with resources (under the 1970 Act). Nevertheless, Schwehr (1997: 664–5) sees this as, in part at least, a positive development, because 'the notion of unmet need, as widely understood in the field, has finally received attention and recognition by the Lords. Its existence is no longer a matter for shame, concealed by means of mealy-mouthed assessments'. Schwehr suggests that, to avoid successful claims for judicial review on grounds of *Wednesbury* unreasonableness, 'authorities will have to set their criteria in their community care plans very much more carefully, and on the basis of much fuller research, consultation and legal advice than is presently the case' (1997: 666).

It is arguable that in this situation, *R v Secretary of State for the Home Department, ex p Daly* [2001] 2 AC 532 (HL) (see Chapter 5) would now require something more than the application of the traditional *Wednesbury* approach, if Convention rights are pertinent; in many of the cases, the right to respect for family life, protected by Art. 8, is at issue. For example, in *ex p Batantu*, a family of six were living in overcrowded accommodation, and in *ex p Adbul W*, a family of ten were living in a two-bedroom flat at the time of the assessment. Art. 8 was not mentioned in the first case or by the Court of Appeal in the second, and was dealt with summarily by the High Court in that case (at para. 36). In *R v North and East Devon HA, ex p Coughlan* [2001] QB 213, [2000] WLR 622 [2000] ALL ER 850 (discussed further below), Lord Woolf MR, giving the judgment of the Court of Appeal, held (at para. 93) that the closure of a care home, in breach of a promise to keep it open and with savings that were 'not dramatic', was in breach of Art. 8(1) and was not justified under Art. 8(2). The issue has not yet been argued fully in the context of decisions taken under s. 47, although in *ex p Adbul W*, Pill LJ held (at para. 23) that the court should not usurp the duty of the SSD to make a s. 47 assessment, and 'It is for the authority to make that decision, subject to the possibility of challenge by way of judicial review *on any of the ordinary grounds*' (emphasis added).

Whatever the approach to be applied on a judicial review application, Schwehr's argument really seeks to make a virtue from apparent necessity, and to take this approach is to concede that the interpretation of 'need', as it functions in the Acts of 1990 and 1970, adopted by the majority in *Barry*, is necessarily the correct one. Ordinarily, there is little practical point in disputing a recent and fully reasoned decision of the House of Lords, but in the present state of flux that is community care policy, no point can be assumed to be beyond discussion. And there is a powerful counterargument to the position adopted by the majority of the House, which is to be found in the judgments of the majority in the Court of Appeal and, in particular, the dissenting opinion of Lord Lloyd of Berwick in the House of Lords, with which Lord Steyn agreed.

Lord Lloyd accepted that 'need' is a relative concept, but decided that it might nevertheless be defined as 'the lack of what is essential for the ordinary business of living' (at 5), which should be 'assessed against the standards of civilised society' (at 6). In practice, this decision is left to the individual social worker, acting in accordance with standards set at local level by his or her SSD, and although these standards could not be defined precisely, that was no reason to guillotine that judgment through the invocation of questions of resources. His general approach was summed up in his observation that '[e]very child needs a new pair of shoes from time to time. The need is not the less because his parents cannot afford them' (at 6). As far as the words of s. 2(1) of the 1970 Act were concerned, 'there is nothing in the language of the section which permits, let alone suggests, that external resources are to be taken into account when assessing the individual's needs' (at 7). Arguably, the same is true of the 1990 Act. If this approach were to be taken – for example, if any future statute were positively to exclude any consideration of the availability of resources from the process of assessment of need – it is submitted that both logic and justice would be served. To the extent that Schwehr's argument has force, a true picture of the extent of unmet need is better arrived at by a legal framework that highlights the unavailability of services, rather than by denying the existence of needs as a matter of law.

Such an approach also brings into sharp relief the distinction at the stage of meeting identified need that exists between the Acts of 1970 and 1990. Lord Lloyd's opinion rested, in part, on the relevance of s. 47(2) of the 1990 Act. This provides that if, during the process of carrying out the assessment of needs under s. 47(1)(a), 'it appears to the local authority that [the subject of the assessment] is a disabled person', the SSD 'shall proceed to make such a decision as to the services he requires as is mentioned in section 4 of the Disabled Persons (Services, Consultation and Representation) Act, 1986' (s. 47(2)(a)); s. 4 of the 1986 Act places a duty on SSDs to assess disabled persons for services under s. 2 of the 1970 Act. Under the terms of s. 4 of the 1986 Act, this must be done at the request of the disabled person or their carer, but s. 47(2)(a) of the 1990 Act provides that the SSD must act on its own initiative if the need is identified in the course of an assessment carried out under s. 47(1)(a). In other words, in Lord Lloyd's view, disabled persons are, by virtue of s. 47(2) taken out of the discretionary regime of the 1990 Act and relocated into the mandatory regime operating under s. 2 of the 1970 Act. For Lord Lloyd, this was a key plank in his reasoning that the duties under the 1970 Act were to be carried out without reference to resources considerations, because disabled persons were seen by Parliament 'as a special case' (at 8). But, if this is correct, the more pertinent points for present purposes are, first, why, in principle, disabled persons deserve this privileged status over other community care service users, and second, how, in logic, this can be the situation if some service users, in particular, in the context of the present discussion, persons in need of care or assistance by reason of mental disorder, are covered by both Acts.

The response of Lord Clyde, for the majority in *Barry*, was to close down on the relevance of s. 47(2) – and so also avoid these particular difficulties raised at the policy level – by holding that s. 2(1) of the 1970 Act had to be defined not by reference to later legislation, but in 'its own terms in the context in which it was enacted' (at 17), and that the rerouting of disabled persons into the 1970 Act regime by s. 47(2) did not imply substantive differences between the regimes, but rather speaks merely of 'the desire to recognise the distinct procedural situation relative to the disabled' (at 18). One might be suspicious that this is enough to answer Lord Lloyd's point, particularly, as Schiemann LJ noted in *R v Powys County Council, ex p Hambridge* [1998] 96 LGR 627 (CA), it is clearly policy that services for the mentally ill are provided free of charge, whilst the policy in regard of services for the disabled is to charge. Nevertheless, the labyrinthine nature of this area of community care law makes it impossible to argue authoritatively that Lord Clyde's explanation of the function of s. 47(2) is clearly wrong.

Even so, this does not diminish the point that a service user can demand that his or her identified needs must be met under the 1970 Act, but cannot do so under the 1990 Act. Clements (1997: 189) has argued, in the context of a discussion of wholesale reform and simplification of community care legislation, that all assessments of entitlement to services should be governed by what is at present s. 47(1) of the 1990 Act, with s. 47(2) of that Act, s. 4 of the 1986 Act and s. 2 of the 1970 Act repealed. This is a proposal of considerable virtue in that it harmonises the assessment process irrespective of the class of user, but its practical effect would be to bring disabled persons 'down' to the level of entitlement currently afforded to other would-be community care service users. This may, ultimately, be the most realistic proposal, but it is at least arguable that the better option would be to bring other service users 'up' to the level of entitlement currently available under s. 2 of the 1970 Act. One thing is, however, clear: the above analysis of *Barry* reveals that the wording of key statutory provisions is sufficiently loose to bear competing interpretations grounded in competing policy assumptions – that which holds that services must, ultimately, be limited by available resources (as here), and, on the other hand, that which holds that resources must be made available to meet such needs as are determined to exist. It is unfortunate that this vital issue is left to the lottery of the court system (in both the Court of Appeal and House of Lords, a majority decision was handed down, with four judges deciding the case one way, four the other) and the predilections of unelected judges. Any future statute, whichever policy is decided upon, should make that decision abundantly clear on its face; and if the policy is that services should be needs-led rather than resources-led, the means to achieve this must also be provided.

Returning to the present situation, however, the above discussion demonstrates that the 1990 Act was always more concerned with the *management* of services, and with the putting in place of a coherent framework of responsibility and accountability for service provision, than with questions of *entitlement*. As if the legal situation were not already complex enough, the 1990 Act did nothing to alter the fact that each of the statutes defined as providing 'community care services' in s. 46(3) of that Act have their own provisions regarding access and entitlement. And, increasingly over recent years, those seeking access to services have bypassed the 1990 Act, using s. 47 only as a mechanism by which to insist that an assessment be carried out, or as a gateway into the legislation to which s. 46(3) refers, under which, it has been argued, stricter duties are to be found than those imposed by s. 47 of the 1990 Act.

9.3.2 Bypassing the 1990 Act to access services

The nature of the duty imposed under s. 21 of the National Assistance Act 1948 was considered by the Court of Appeal in *R v Sefton Metropolitan Borough Council, ex p Help the Aged and Ors* [1997] 4 All ER 532. As discussed above, an SSD has a duty to provide residential accommodation under this section for those who 'by reason of age, illness, disability or any other circumstance are in need of care and attention which is not otherwise available to them'. In *Sefton*, the defendant SSD had provided an elderly woman, B, with residential accommodation on her leaving hospital. Initially, her available capital was above the £16,000 limit then set by s. 22 of the 1948 Act and para. 20 of the National Assistance (Amendment of Resources) Regulations 1992, made by the Secretary of State, which meant that B funded her own placement by way of charges levied by the SSD under s. 22. When B's capital fell to £16,000, the SSD carried out an assessment of her needs and determined that she was in need of residential accommodation. Because the SSD did not have sufficient funds to provide accommodation for all the elderly people in need in its area, however, it had developed a policy whereby it would not fund residential accommodation until the resident's capital fell to £1,500. Paragraph 20 of the 1992 Regulations, however, required that charges be reduced for persons with capital below £16,000, and that capital of less than £10,000 be discounted by an SSD when deciding whether to charge a recipient of residential care for some, or all, of the cost of that care.

The charity, Help the Aged, brought an application for judicial review to test the legality of the SSD's policy, and this entailed consideration by the Court of Appeal, inter alia, of the nature of the duty owed by an SSD under s. 21 of the 1948 Act. Lord Woolf MR, in the light of *Barry*, felt 'compelled to conclude that there is a limited subjective element in making an assessment of whether the ailments of the person concerned do or do not collectively establish a need for care and attention' (at 543). In his view, however, it is 'very much more difficult' for an SSD to plead lack of resources under s. 21 of the 1948 Act than in the context of s. 29 of that Act or s. 2(1) of the 1970 Act. Part of the reason for this was that the nature of the need – for accommodation – is qualitatively different, by definition of greater severity, from a need for other services. In part also, Lord Woolf emphasised that the requirement of s. 2(1) of the 1970 Act – that it must be 'necessary' to provide the services in question – was absent from s. 21 of the 1948 Act, so that, under the latter provision, there is a duty to meet needs even though it is not 'necessary' that they are met.

The qualitative distinction between a need for accommodation and a need for other services is, however, problematic. It tends to break down in practice, because a failure to provide services in the community increases the likelihood that service users will need residential accommodation. Furthermore, if there is not always a duty, because of limited resources, to meet 'needs' when it has been decided that it is 'necessary' to do so, under the 1970 Act, the implication is, surely, that there should be *greater* scope for the exercise of discretion in the case of needs that are *not* defined as 'necessary' under s. 21 of the 1948 Act and not, as Lord Woolf suggested, *less* scope. Yet this merely points to the problematic nature of the 'policy' on community care provision, because Lord Woolf was surely correct to the extent that there is no reason, in principle, why it should be have to be 'necessary' that services are provided under s. 2(1) of the 1970 Act, but not under s. 21 of the 1948 Act.

This view clearly informed Lord Woolf's ruling that it was not lawful for an SSD to adopt a system of prioritisation that contradicted the clear policy in s. 22 and the attendant Regulations. Hence, when a resident's capital fell to £16,000 (the specified limit), and following an assessment that revealed a need that, even when resources were taken into account, the SSD concluded it was under a duty to meet, then it must do so. It was unlawful to delay meeting a need in such circumstances and 'lack of resources is no excuse' (at 543). Nor did the court have much time for the argument that, because an SSD must, under the terms of s. 21 of the 1948 Act, only provide services 'which are not otherwise available', there was no duty to provide services that were 'otherwise available' by reason of the ability of applicants to fund their own care. This 'totally defeats the intention of s. 22' (*ibid.*), that, under the specified capital limits, an SSD must fund care for those under the financial threshold of entitlement regardless of ability to pay (this part of the judgment is now reflected in the National Assistance (Residential Accommodation) (Disregarding of Resources) (England) Regulations 2001: see above). As such, *Sefton* must be counted as, at least a partial, victory for Help the Aged. The Court of Appeal closed down various 'escape routes' that the SSD had sought to use in avoidance of its statutory duty. And although Lord Woolf's reasoning may be somewhat problematic for the reasons discussed above, the decision in this case seems to suggest that there is a greater possibility of ensuring access to residential provision by going directly to s. 21 of the 1948 Act, rather than via s. 47 of the NHSCCA 1990, which is effectively to render s. 47(1) of the 1990 Act otiose for these purposes.

This view was confirmed when the Court of Appeal, in the later case of *R v Kensington and Chelsea London Borough Council, ex p Kujtim* [1999] 4 ALL ER 161, held that an SSD is not entitled to rely on the discretionary wording of s. 47(1)(b) of the 1990 Act to justify a decision not to provide accommodation to a client assessed as being in need of services under s. 21(1) of the 1948 Act. This also explains, in part, why there has been a 'recent expansion of litigation in this field' (Hale LJ in *ex p Abdul W* at para. 30). It is legitimate to wonder, from the point of view of service users, what the function of the passage of the 1990 Act has been other than to complicate the legal situation and to confront would-be applicants with a virtually unintelligible legal maze masquerading as a 'gateway' into securing entitlement.

Nevertheless, the scheme under s. 21 of the 1948 Act is now reasonably clear as far as the relevance of resources is concerned. It was summarised as a four-stage process by Henriques J in *ex p Batantu*. First, s. 47(1)(a) of the 1990 Act triggers the general duty to carry out an assessment, which must be undertaken irrespective of resources (*R v Bristol City Council, ex p Penfold* [1998] COD 210, QB, above); second, the assessment must take place by reference to the criteria in s. 21, at which point there is the 'limited' ability to consider resource availability in determining whether the criteria are met (*Sefton*). Third, if the criteria are met, there is a duty to meet the needs in question, and here, resources are not at all relevant (*ex p Kujtim*, approved by Lord Hope in *R v Barnet LBC, ex p G* [2003] UKHL 57 at para. 190). Finally, however, resources are relevant to the question of how that duty will be satisfied: an SSD may chose between accommodation A and accommodation B, if both are suitable to meet the client's identified needs, *inter alia* on grounds of cost. This approach was followed by Hale LJ in *R v Tower Hamlets LBC, ex p Abdul W* [2002] EWCA Civ 287 (see paras. 30–3), whose approach was, in turn, endorsed by the House of Lords in *R v National Asylum and Support Service, ex p Westminster City Council* [2002] UKHL 38 per Lord Hoffmann at para. 26.

The duty under s. 21 is a potentially onerous one. In *ex p Kujtim*, Potter LJ (at para. 30) explained that the duty to provide accommodation subsists:

on a continuing basis so long as the need of the applicant remains as originally assessed and if, for whatever reason, the accommodation, once provided, is withdrawn or otherwise becomes unavailable to the applicant, then ... the local authority has a continuing duty to provide further accommodation.

This enables residents of care homes to challenge decisions to close their particular accommodation, on the basis that the closure puts the SSD in breach of its continuing duty, if the resident is of the view that his or her needs are no longer being met (Darton, 2004). This was the situation in *R v Barking and Dagenham LBC, ex p L* [2002] 1 FLR 763 (CA). L had lived in the same residential accommodation, which offered communal dining facilities, for 24 years. The responsible SSD decided that the property needed to be refurbished, and it was proposed that discrete units of accommodation would be provided, with no communal dining facilities offered. L argued that this would be to fail to meet her needs, which included routine and contact with other people, and which were facilitated by communal eating. She further argued that the care plan that the SSD had drawn up to meet her needs was vague or incomplete in various ways, and hence the SSD had failed to carry out a proper assessment of her needs. The Court of Appeal held that L's concerns were not 'intrinsically unreasonable' (at para. 26), but it declined to adjudicate on the acceptability of the care plan that had been devised, because, per Schiemann LJ at para. 27, 'the court is not the appropriate organ to be prescriptive as to the degree of detail which should go into a care plan'; that complaint should be made to the Secretary of State (see below) before seeking redress in the courts.

In this case, the SSD had given various undertakings, to the effect that the new accommodation would be suitable for L. The Court of Appeal released the SSD from those undertakings on the basis that they added nothing to their statutory duties. This is typical, and understandable, because the attitude of the courts generally on this issue is non-interventionist. In *R v Plymouth City Council, ex p Cowl* [2001] EWCA Civ 1935 [2002] 1 WLR 803, C sought judicial review of a decision to close his care home, despite the SSD being willing to settle the matter through its complaints procedure. The Court of Appeal held that, until the complaints procedure had been exhausted, there was no cause of action. In general, the courts have underlined the desirability of resolving such disputes by means other than litigation (*Cowl* led to the issuance of a *Practice Direction* to this effect: [2002] 1 ALL ER 633 [2002] 1 WLR 810).

When decisions have been litigated, it has been held that there is a right to be consulted, as a requirement of procedural fairness. In particular, in *R v North and East Devon Health Authority ex p Coughlan* [2001] QB 213 [2000] 2 WLR 622, Lord Woolf MR held (at para. 108) that:

consultation must be undertaken at a time when proposals are still at a formative stage; it must include sufficient reasons for particular proposals to allow those consulted to give intelligent consideration and an intelligent response; adequate time must be given for this purpose; and the product of consultation must be conscientiously taken into account.

If this is done, and provided that the decision to close a particular facility is not 'Wednesbury unreasonable', it will be lawful and will not, without more, breach any of the human rights of the residents (*R v East Sussex CC, ex p Dudley* [2003] EWHC 1093). Frequently these days, when a SSD-run care home is to be closed, it is proposed, as in this case, that the residents be transferred to accommodation run by the private sector. In *R v Havering LBC, ex p Johnson* [2006] EWHC 1714, the SSD had formulated a plan to close two care homes and transfer two others to a private sector provider. The Secretary of State intervened in the case, arguing that, following such a transfer of responsibility to a private sector operator, that body fell within the scope of s. 6(3)(b) Human Rights Act 1998, being therefore bound to act in a manner compatible with the provisions of that Act (s. 6(1)), that is, compatibly with the substantive Convention rights, because it was now operating 'functions of a public nature'. The High Court rejected this contention, as it did in respect of the residents' contention that their human rights would be significantly less well protected after transfer. The SSD, after transfer, remains bound by the duty in s. 6(1) of the 1998 Act, and must therefore continue to protect the human rights of residents (see also *R* v *Leonard Cheshire Foundation, ex p Heather* [2002] EWCA Civ 366).

This is done both through the terms of contracts under which private providers are engaged and through monitoring the quality of ongoing provision. In *R* v *St Helens BC, ex p Haggerty* [2003] EWHC 803, [2003] HLR 69, the SSD had decided not to renew a contract with S, an independent provider of residential accommodation, with the result that a particular home would have to close. The High Court held that such a decision was amenable to judicial review, and that the SSD must give due consideration to the human rights of the residents when making its decision, but that there was no breach of any of Arts. 2, 3 or 8 of the Convention, the SSD having acted reasonably within available resources.

If, however, there has been a promise that 'has induced a legitimate expectation of a benefit which is substantive, not simply procedural', a court may also insist that it be kept, if to break it 'is so unfair that to take a new and different course will amount to an abuse of power' (per Lord Woolf MR in *R* v *North and East Devon Health Authority, ex p Coughlan* [2001] QB 213 [2000] 2 WLR 622). In that case, C and other residents in her care home had been promised that it would be 'their home for life', but later, the SSD planned to close the home, essentially on grounds of cost. The Court of Appeal held that the closure was not permissible in the face of the promise made to C and the other residents, and that, because few individuals were involved, and because the SSD had failed to show an overriding public interest, it could not now resile from that promise. In the later case of *R* v *Newham LBCC, ex p Bibi* 2000 WL 1544686, the High Court held that a promise was binding even though the SSD making it thought, wrongly, that it had a statutory obligation to provide accommodation. It is clear that any promise must be 'clear and unequivocal' if it is to bind the SSD: Lightman J in *R* v *Walsall MBC, ex p P and R* (2001) 26 April, unreported, at para. 8; see also *R* v *Lincolnshire HA, ex p Collins* [2001] EWHC Admin 665.

As mentioned earlier, the Court of Appeal in *ex p Coughlan* also found a breach of Art. 8 ECHR, but this was for the particular reason that there had been the promise in question, and when that is absent, *Coughlan* may be distinguished, as it was by Maurice Kay LJ in the *Dudley* case at para. 52. In *CH and MH* v *Merton Primary Care Trust* [2004] EWHC 2984, the residents of an NHS care home (technically, hospital provision, but nothing turns on this) had been given a 'home for life' promise of the sort made in *Coughlan*. The trust sought to close the facility and relocate the residents, all with severe learning difficulties, into the community, on the grounds that that was in the best interests of the residents. The High Court held that (1) there was an entitlement that the applicants have their best interests investigated in family proceedings, such proceedings to run side-by-side with their application for judicial review, at which (2) best interests would also be a live issue, as would the Art. 8 rights of the applicants, and (3) following the decision in *Wilkinson* (see Chapter 7), the court was therefore bound by s. 6(1) of the Human Rights Act 1998 to make a substantive judgment on best interests. An SSD (or in this case, PCT) may be able to escape from the terms of a 'home for life' promise by demonstrating that Art. 8(2) applies, and that the best interests of the residents are served by the closure of their home, but, as this case also makes clear, such a claim cannot be blandly asserted by the SSD: it must prove its case to the satisfaction of the courts. A 'home for life' promise may be departed from where the medical interests of the client require it: *R v Wandsworth LBC, ex p G* [2003] EWHC 2941 (the case was appealed but not on this point).

The effect of all of this litigation is that access to residential accommodation under Part III of the 1948 Act is to be assessed differently from access to other welfare services under Part III, because the latter, unless provided in conjunction with s. 2(1) of the 1970 Act, may largely be provided, subject to judicial review, at the discretion of the SSD. Access to services under s. 45 of the Health Services and Public Health Act 1968 is, if anything, more discretionary in nature than access to any other services under any other provisions, because s. 45 provides a power to, but does not impose a duty on, SSDs to provide services for 'the promotion of the welfare of old people'. The main relevance of s. 45 of the 1968 Act for present purposes is that it illustrates yet another permutation of the confused relationship between community care services, as defined by s. 46(3) of the 1990 Act, and other services, because here, the services that are so defined function, in effect, as a safety net for those falling through the 1970 Act rather than the 1990 Act.

Access to the services to be provided under s. 21 and Sch. 8 NHSA 1977 is equally problematic. The services to be provided (see earlier) are defined in s. 21 as 'functions exercisable by local social service authorities', whilst para. 2(1) of Sch. 8 provides that SSDs 'may, with the Secretary of State's approval, and to such extent as he may direct, make arrangements for the purpose of the prevention of illness and for the care of persons suffering from illness and for the after-care of persons who have been so suffering'. Appendix 3 of LAC(93)10 provides that the Secretary of State has approved the making of arrangements under s. 21 in connection with all three of these purposes (Department of Health, 1993b: Appendix 3, para. 3(1), (3)), with the exception of such services for the purpose of prevention of mental disorder, which are the subject of a direction, in para. 3(2). Yet this does not mean that *individual* applicants have a right to access the services in question. The services in question – the provision of training and day centres, a sufficient number of social workers and social work services – are, by their nature, 'general' provisions; the reference to 'persons' rather than 'any person' supports the view that this is a 'general duty' not enforceable by individuals and similar, for example, to the general duty that the police have for the detection and investigation of crime (see *R v Commissioner of Police of the Metropolis, ex p Blackburn* [1968] 1 All

ER 763; *(No. 2)* [1968] 2 All ER 319; *(No. 3)* [1973] 1 All ER 324 (CA)). This view is further supported by the observation of Lord Clyde in *Barry* (at 16) that, apart from s. 2(1) of the Chronically Sick and Disabled Persons Act 1970, there was only one other directly enforceable duty to be found in the statutory regime, and that is contained in s. 117, MHA 1983.

Section 117 MHA 1983 imposes a duty on both PCTs or HAs and SSDs to provide services for mentally disordered persons, but is limited in two ways. First, the financial and other resources of the potential recipient are relevant to whether services under s. 117 are, in the language of the provision, 'called for' (*Tinsley* v *Sarkar* [2005] EWHC 192), as are the resources available to the provider (*R* v *Camden and Islington Health Authority, ex p K* [2001] 3 WLR 553, [2001] MHLR 24 per Lord Phillips MR at para. 29; see also *Brand* v *The Netherlands* Application No. 49902/99, paras. 64 and 65), the Court holding that resources are relevant to the question of whether there has been a breach of Art. 5.

Second, s. 117 only authorises the provision of aftercare to patients leaving hospital following detention under ss. 3, 37, 45A (with or without restrictions), or transfer to hospital under ss. 47 or 48 of the MHA 1983. Section 117 has no application to informal patients or those detained under ss. 2, 4, 5, or 136, if not subsequently transferred to s. 3. Such patients must, therefore, rely on the general powers to provide aftercare in the NHSA 1977, and their attendant problems of enforceability. But, for those who do come under the terms of s. 117, it may be that this provision offers a more fruitful avenue for seeking access to services. The case law on s. 117 has concerned patients discharged by a tribunal, but the same principles should apply when discharge is ordered or initiated by the patient's RMO, the hospital managers, or the nearest relative, and, if the patient is restricted, by the Secretary of State.

That the duties imposed by s. 117 are owed to, and enforceable by, individuals was established in *R* v *Ealing District Health Authority, ex p Fox* [1993] 1 WLR 373; 3 All ER 170 (HC). Otton J pointed out that s. 117(2) provides that 'it shall be the duty' of HAs (these days, PCTs) and SSDs, in consultation with voluntary agencies, to provide aftercare 'for *any person* to whom this section applies' (emphasis added), holding that the duty is not only general, but also entails a specific duty owed to individual patients (1 WLR 373 at 385). What is less certain is the point at which the duty to a specific individual is triggered. Starting with what is clear, the duty is certainly in play from the moment a patient leaves hospital, when there will be a formal passing of responsibility from the hospital to the PCT and SSD for subsequent service provision. Second, it is also clear that there is a duty to make arrangements to enable a conditional or deferred discharge to occur once that has been ordered by a tribunal. Otton J, in *Fox* ([1993] 1 WLR 373 at 387), held that a HA 'acts unlawfully in failing to seek to make practical arrangements for after-care prior to [a] patient's discharge from hospital where such arrangements are required by a mental health review tribunal in order to enable the patient to be conditionally discharged from hospital'. In *R* v *Mental Health Review Tribunal and Ors, ex p Hall* [1999] 1 WLR 1323, at 1335, Scott Baker J reiterated the same view, as did Lord Phillips MR in *R* v *Secretary of State for the Home Department and Secretary of State for Health, ex p IH* [2002] EWCA Civ 646 [2002] 3 WLR 967, at para. 96. The same applies if a tribunal adjourns a hearing in order for the availability of aftercare to be investigated: *ex p IH* at para. 98.

Third, what is not clear is whether there is any enforceable duty *before* a tribunal orders discharge, or indicates that it is considering discharge and adjourns for investigations to be made. There are some *obiter dicta* to be found in the judgment of Kennedy LJ, in the Court of Appeal in *ex p Hall* at 1353, that there is, or may be, a duty to have in place at least an 'embryonic' care plan before a tribunal hearing, but in the later Court of Appeal decision in *R v Camden and Islington Health Authority, ex p K* [2001] 3 WLR 553, [2001] MHLR 24, Lord Phillips MR had accepted the concession made by counsel for the HA that 'a health authority has a *power* to take preparatory steps before discharge of a patient' (paras. 20, 29, emphasis added). This view was endorsed by Scott Baker LJ in *R v Doncaster MBC, ex p W* [2004] EWCA Civ 378, [2004] 1 MHLR 201, at para. 49. Scott Baker LJ went on to hold, however, that a HA's failure to endeavour to use its s. 117 powers 'in the absence of strong reasons, would be likely to be an unlawful exercise of discretion', which is to effectively turn the power into a duty.

In the later case of *R v Camden LBC, ex p B* [2005] EWHC 1366, Stanley Burnton J referred to these authorities, holding that 'Practicality requires s. 117 authorities to be under a duty before discharge, at least in cases where a tribunal has provisionally decided that a conditional discharge is appropriate' (at para. 58), although the s. 117 authority is not fixed with the specific duty to make arrangement until it has been informed that a MHRT has ordered discharge (at para. 72). In the *Doncaster* case in the High Court ([2003] EWHC 192), he had held (at para. 43) that 'if discharge is not contentious, an authority should if practicable plan after-care before a tribunal hearing in order for it to comply with its section 117 duty on the patient's discharge'. The difficulty with this, of course, lies in drawing the lines appropriately between cases (i) where discharge is not contentious, (ii) where it is contentious but there is at least some opinion in favour of it, (iii) where there is some lesser prospect of discharge, and (iv) where there is none. In the *Camden* case, the same judge went on to consider whether the reach of the duty was such that those responsible under s. 117 should proactively monitor the progress of patients in hospital, without waiting for a tribunal hearing, in order to ascertain whether there may be a duty to provide services. On this, in the absence of authority, he concluded, *obiter*, that it would be 'inconsistent with the lack of any express duty imposed by s. 117' (para. 62).

It is true that, under the care programme approach (CPA: see below), providers of care are required to review the needs of patients continually, even when in hospital (or, indeed, prison), but to demand the investigation of aftercare possibilities, when there is very little chance that aftercare will soon be required, would be to impose further burdens on the finite resources of PCTs and SSDs, and other providers of community care, such as CMHTs, for no apparent purpose. Moreover, as Stanley Burnton J noted in *Camden*, services provided under s. 117 are community care services under s. 47 of the NHACCA 1990, which, as seen above, places a duty on SSDs to meet the identified needs of persons not only under s. 117 of the 1983 Act, but also the other legislation listed in s. 46(3), and 'Parliament could not have intended local authorities to have to devote their resources to making assessments of the possible future needs of persons for such services' (para. 65). This must, in general terms, be correct, but in our view, at the very least, there *should* be a duty before a tribunal hearing to consider into which of the categories mentioned above any given case seems likely to fall, and, where the case in question falls into any but the last category, there should be an absolute duty under s. 117. The reason for this is that the nature of the duty before a tribunal hearing is not to *provide* aftercare, but to investigate and report, provisionally, on its suitability and availability for the patient in question. This does not seem to us to be unduly onerous.

Once the duty under s. 117 has been triggered, aftercare must be provided. The section uses mandatory language: 'It shall be the duty' to provide aftercare. This, however, is not how s. 117 has been interpreted by the courts in a number of cases, in which a tribunal has ordered discharge subject to conditions but it has not been possible for those conditions to be met, either because suitable accommodation or professionals willing to take responsibility for the patient cannot be located. In the first of these cases, *Fox*, Otton J refused to make an order of mandamus to compel the HA to act, on the grounds that this would be to compel a psychiatrist to treat against his or her clinical judgment (at 387), but he did make it clear that a HA (a PCT), faced initially with staff who refuse to treat or otherwise supervise a patient following discharge, 'is under a continuing obligation to make further endeavours to provide arrangements', and it is only when such steps have been taken without success that the HA should admit defeat. This approach was confirmed in the later Court of Appeal decisions in *ex p K* and *ex p IH*, and, in the latter case, by the decision of the House of Lords ([2003] UKHL 59). In *ex p K*, Lord Phillips MR held (at paras. 20, 29) that the duty under s. 117 is to use '*reasonable* endeavours' to make arrangements for discharge, but in *ex p IH*, the same judge, giving the unanimous judgment of the Court of Appeal, held that the duty under s. 117 is to use '*best* endeavours to put in place the necessary aftercare' (at para. 96); the same term was used in the House of Lords ([2003] UKHL 59 at para. 29 per Lord Bingham). In *Doncaster*, Scott Baker LJ said (at para. 50) that, in his view, there is no material distinction between the two terms. Our view is that (i) 'best' entails a more onerous duty than 'reasonable', and (ii) given the importance of the issue, is to be preferred.

Whether a PCT/SSD has endeavoured sufficiently to meet its statutory obligation will be a question of fact. Has there been sufficient attempt to identify a suitable placement for the patient, or to make necessary arrangements? In some cases, it is the inability to locate professionals willing to take responsibility for the treatment and supervision of the patient in the community that is the problem. On this, in *ex p K*, Sedley LJ (at para. 55) explained that:

No judge can realistically sit as a court of appeal from a psychiatrist on a question of professional judgment. What a judge must do is ensure that such judgment, to that extent that its exercise is a public law function, is made honestly, rationally and with due regard only to what is relevant.

If, however, the view that the conditions in question cannot be satisfied 'were shown to have been adopted less as an exercise of professional judgment than as a closing of the ranks against an unwelcome decision of the Mental Health Review Tribunal, the courts would not be powerless to intervene' (at para. 53). These dicta were said to apply equally to professional judgments made by social work professionals by Stanley Burnton J in *R v Doncaster MBC, ex p W* [2003] EWHC Admin 192 at para. 45. There are a couple of points to be made here. First, the dichotomy that Sedley LJ constructs between an exercise of professional judgment (which is permissible) and a closing of ranks in the face of an unwelcome tribunal decision (which is not) is problematic. This is because the first collapses into the second in practice: in all of these cases, a 'closing of ranks' followed, and was intimately related to, an act of professional judgment that a tribunal had made an 'unwelcome' decision. Hence, it will be very difficult, if not impossible, to draw the line where Sedley LJ claims that it can be drawn.

Second, the reference to the court 'not being powerless' is opaque. The High Court can, of course, issue a writ of mandamus, requiring the recipient of the writ to comply with the order of the court. It is clear from that later case of *ex p IH* (see Chapter 8) that, in the view of the House of Lords, the onus is on the tribunal to reconsider the terms of discharge when they prove difficult to implement. In practice, an order of mandamus will be made only in the very rarest of situations – when it is clear that an 'unprofessional' closing of ranks has taken place. The court may not be powerless, but to date, those powers have never been used.

Patients have scored no greater success by invoking their Convention rights under Art. 5. In *Doncaster*, Scott Baker LJ held that 'the ECHR places no greater obligations upon section 117 after-care authority than domestic legislation. Provided the authority uses its best endeavours to fulfil the conditions imposed by the tribunal it will meet its obligations both under section 117 and the Convention' (para. 67). Indeed, even when there is a breach of Art. 5(1)(e) and or (4), it is not clear that a patient will have a remedy against those with duties under s. 117. In *ex p K*, Buxton LJ at para. 49 held that the case law of the European Court demonstrated the possibility of an action, in Strasbourg, against 'the State', but in domestic law, 'the State' in this abstract sense was not a possible defendant. Rather, the nature of the patient's complaint, 'being a complaint about *detention*' (emphasis in original), meant that it had to be targeted against those responsible for that detention – in law, the managers of the detaining hospital. And it seems that there can be no action against the hospital, because s. 6(2) of the Human Rights Act 1998 precludes liability of a state organ (and 'public body' for the purposes of s. 6(2)) if, by reason of primary legislation, that body could not have acted differently, in which case, there is no remedy against a hospital under Art. 5(4) in domestic law.

In *Doncaster*, the patient argued that, if those with s. 117 duties were responsible for the continued detention of a patient whose discharge had been ordered, it was irrelevant that they were not the detaining authority. This argument chimes with reality. In such a situation, it is those with s. 117 duties who are holding the hospital doors shut, as it were, from the outside to prevent the patient leaving; it is not the hospital that it holding them shut from the inside. But this view was roundly rejected by Scott Baker LJ, holding that 'the respondent did nothing to cause the unlawful detention of W. It neither knowingly tried to nullify the decision of the tribunal nor failed to use its best endeavours to implement the conditions it had directed' (para. 69). Some may feel that the point is worth taking to Strasbourg. As the European Court has said many times, for example, in *Christine Goodwin* v *UK* (2002) 35 EHRR 18, [2002] 2 FLR 487, the spirit of the Convention requires rights that are 'practical and effective, not theoretical and illusory' (para. 74); in this situation, a patient who has been granted discharge by a tribunal may feel, with some justification, that his or her Convention rights are far from being practical or effective. Moreover, in Strasbourg, issues of how the state constitutes itself and divides responsibility, as Buxton LJ noted, are much less relevant than they are to the domestic courts. But on recent authority (see, for example, *Kolanis*, discussed in Chapter 8), it is perhaps unlikely that patients would score any greater success in Strasbourg than in the domestic courts. The tribunal system has been fixed with the responsibility for monitoring the implementation of conditions and, by extension, the activities of those charged to allow their implementation.

There is one final argument waiting to be made, which is that those responsible for aftercare are 'public authorities' for the purposes of s. 6(1) Human Rights Act 1998. Section 6(1) provides that a public authority must act in a way compatible with Convention rights, and it can be argued that, if a patient's discharge is being blocked by the refusal of psychiatrists, CPNs or social workers to accept responsibility, then those persons are failing to act in accordance with the patient's Convention rights. This, in turn, however, depends on such professionals being recognised as a public authority, which s. 6(3) defines to include 'any person certain of whose functions are functions of a public nature'. In *ex p IH*, both the Court of Appeal and the House of Lords declined to rule on this argument, because it was not necessary to do so for the resolution of that case, and so the point must be counted as still open.

The upshot of the jurisprudence to date is that those with s. 117 duties remain free to make a judgment, on professional grounds, that a patient whose discharge has been ordered should not be discharged. Here, in a battle between the patient's RMO, or those with s. 117 duties, and a tribunal, the RMO and colleagues win. This should be contrasted with the decision in *R* v *East London and the City Mental Health NHS Trust, ex p Von Brandenburg* of the Court of Appeal ([2001] EWCA Civ 239, [2002] QB 235, [2001] 3 WLR 588, [2001] 1 MHLR 36; House of Lords [2004] 2 AC 280, [2003] UKHL 58, [2004] 1 All ER 400, [2003] 3 WLR 1265). As discussed in Chapter 8, it was held in that case that a patient may not be readmitted at the initiation of his or her RMO after discharge by a tribunal in the absence of new circumstances. In that situation, the tribunal wins the battle. The factors relevant to (re)admission and discharge are not analogous, and it might be argued that the RMO's powers in one situation should not necessarily be the flipside of those in the other situation. Nevertheless, there is a sense in which these decisions are anomalous, or perhaps demonstrate that, for RMOs, possession remains nine tenths of the law.

Finally, it is worth pointing out that the Court of Appeal in *Clunis* v *Camden and Islington HA* [1998] 2 WLR 902 held that complainants should not look to the courts to enforce any duty owed under s. 117, unless they have first made a complaint to the Secretary of State to exercise the default powers available in s. 124. These default powers were repealed by s. 66(2) and Sch. 10, NHSCCA 1990, although equivalent powers were inserted as s. 7D, Local Authority Social Services Act 1970 by s. 50, NHSCCA 1990. But it is unlikely that a complaint would elicit the outcome that the applicant wants, because the Secretary of State is concerned more with the general provision of services than with access to them by individuals. On the other hand, it may be arguable on appropriate facts that, if the Secretary of State, who clearly is 'the state' for these purposes and who is not precluded in the exercise of his or her discretion to order the discharge of any patient, fails to take steps to enable discharge to occur when it is being blocked by those with s. 117 duties, there is the possibility of a successful challenge, under Art. 5(4), that avoids the difficulties of linking remedy to defendant that vexed Buxton LJ and subsequent courts.

9.3.3 Other avenues of complaint

It is in itself noteworthy that those seeking access to services have used the mechanism of judicial review with such frequency, because this tells the tale of the paucity of other remedies. The House of Lords effectively closed down the possibility of an action for breach of statutory duty in this area, taking the view that such an action will only be a possibility where there are no avenues of complaint built into the relevant statutory scheme: *Cocks* v *Thanet District Council* [1983] AC 286 and *X* v *Bedfordshire County Council* [1995] 3 All ER 353. Thus, because there are, for example, mechanisms that empower the Secretary of State to issue directions to specific SSDs, it is doubtful that a private law action for breach of statutory duty would lie, and any suggestion that it may do so, in the context of services under s. 117, MHA 1983, to be found in the judgment in *Fox* was firmly scotched by the Court of Appeal in *Clunis*. As mentioned above, the Court of Appeal in that case emphasised that recourse to judicial review should be the last resort for aggrieved individuals. In *R* v *Barking and Dagenham LBC, ex p L* [2002] 1 FLR 763, a case concerning a challenge to a decision to close a care home, the Court of Appeal again took this stance, as it did in a housing case, *Anufrijeva* v *Southwark LBC* [2003] EWCA Civ 1406, [2004] 2 WLR 603.

Advice about complaints procedures is given by HSC 2001/015, LAC(2001)18. This provides that all complaints about SSDs or NHS bodies must be investigated, and there must be ground-level procedures for the informal resolution of complaints, which, in the case of PCTs or NHS trusts, should include face-to-face meetings and the use of conciliation and action by the trust's chief executive. If these measures fail, there is recourse, for complaints about social services, under the Care Standards Act 2000, to be made to the Commission for Social Care Inspection, with a further right of complaint to the Parliamentary or local government ombudsman. For complaints against NHS bodies, HSC 2001/015 requires that trusts provide for an independent review of complaints that cannot be resolved in-house, and for review panels, comprising a lay chair (selected by the Secretary of State), one other lay member and a non-executive member of the trust in question, to provide a report on the complaint in question. Again, there is the prospect of further complaint that, since 2004, has been to the Healthcare

Commission, which also deals with complaints against private providers. For clients seeking access to services, however, it highly unlikely that the complaints systems will give them what they want, geared as they are more towards policing errors and inappropriate treatment and policies rather than clinical decisions to refuse to offer treatment. As such, the complaints system can be more of an obstacle course to be surmounted rather than a source of the satisfaction of grievances.

9.4 A 'seamless' service?

9.4.1 Working together with NHS bodies

In addition to the requirement of collegiate community care planning currently imposed by s. 46, NHSCCA 1990, and the general duty to work together under s. 22, NHSA 1977, s. 47(3) of the 1990 Act provides that if, during the assessment of needs carried out under s. 47(1), it appears to the SSD that there may be a need for health or housing services, the SSD must notify the relevant PCT, HA or local housing authority and 'invite them to assist, to such extent as is reasonable in the circumstances, in the making of the assessment'. The SSD 'shall take into account any services that are likely to be made available by a HA or local housing authority'. Policy guidance issued contemporaneously with the NHSCCA 1990 stressed that 'local collaboration is the key to making a reality of community care' (Department of Health, 1990a; Dowling *et al.*, 2004). The Department of Health (1990b) also introduced the care programme approach (CPA) from 1991. According to the NHS Executive, which, in 1994, endorsed the CPA in the form of guidance (Department of Health, 1994), the main aim of the CPA 'is to ensure the support of mentally ill persons in the community, thereby minimising the possibility of their losing contact with services and maximising the effect of any therapeutic intervention' (1994: para. 9). Paragraph 10 of the guidance detailed the main elements of the CPA as:

- *systematic assessment* of health, social care and housing needs, both in the short and long term;
- a written *care plan* agreed by the patient, relevant professionals, and the patient's carers;
- the allocation of a *key worker* to provide a focal point for contact with the recipient of services, to monitor service delivery and to respond to problems if and when they arise;
- *regular (six-monthly) review* of the patient's progress and ongoing needs.

The various limitations in the statutory scheme do not apply to the CPA, which, for example, applies to all patients discharged from hospital and not only to those covered by s. 117 MHA 1983 (Department of Health, 1994: para. 8).

Throughout the 1990s, however, the CPA suffered from the limitations of inter-agency cooperation. Research carried out by the NHS Executive, in conjunction with NHS regional offices and the Social Services Inspectorate, in 1997 confirmed that a 'seamless' service was far from being realised in many parts of the country. Only slightly more than half of all SSDs had completed a comprehensive assessment of needs in their areas as required by s. 46 of the 1990 Act, and HAs had contributed to only two thirds of the assessments of needs that had been carried out under s. 47. The research also found that 'few community teams are integrated': one reason for this was that SSDs and HAs 'used different systems for recording information about the processes of treatment and care', and, more often than not, the data accumulated by each was not shared (see Department of Health, 1998a: paras. 3.6–3.13). This research also found that, in many SSD areas, a commitment to client empowerment was noticeably lacking. Only half of all SSDs reported having involved service users in the assessment of local needs required by s. 46 (1998a: para. 3.7).

This lack of inter-agency cooperation can be explained, in part at least, on the basis that each agency, and the professions that dominate the various agencies, functions within different paradigms of care. (Questions of interprofessional relationships were considered in Chapter 5.) Equally, in the context of community care, a clash of perspective may be a feature of cooperation at ground level between health professionals and social workers. It was argued, just as it was becoming apparent that the CPA and, especially, joint working was failing to take off, that this is the result of differences in professional ideology, overlain with factors relating to organisational identity, which function as a sort of 'double separation' between SSDs and HAs (now PCTs) and their respective staff (Dalley, 1993; Onyett et al., 1994). Divisions are continually recreated by a separation of the levels of basic professional education and training. The result is an inevitable politicisation of interprofessional relationships, and, although there are initiatives to provide a common training base for those who will staff community care programmes (Barnes, 2006), the professional status of social workers, both in the public mind and in their dealings with psychiatric professionals, especially consultant psychiatrists, remains ambivalent. It is not just a case of a simple binary split between the professional and organisational cultures of health and social service workers respectively: on the medical 'side' of the divide, psychiatric nurses and psychotherapists are jostling for professional position with psychiatrists (see Chapter 7). Evidence was also published that suggested that the introduction of managerialist principles by the 1990 Act (see Chapter 3) impacted negatively on the quality of services, because it encouraged a tendency amongst SSDs and HAs to budget defensively (Wistow, 1994; 1995), a tendency that accelerated as pressure on resources increased.

There were two main practical consequences of this. First, it led to, or at least exacerbated the existence of, a 'grey area' falling between that which is clearly health care and that which is clearly social care, over which responsibility is ill-defined or agreed (Lewis and Glennerster, 1996). Second, the assessment process, and the implementation of the CPA, was not always the consensual experience that the government's guidance might suggest. In this respect, the seemingly innocuous and straightforward advice from the

Department of Health (1995a: para. 3.2.10), that a client's key worker will not always act as care manager, and that for clients with complex needs, the functions of care manager may be shared amongst several professionals, often meant that service delivery was experienced by clients as fractured, possibly even as contradictory or incoherent.

The courts have been called upon on a number of occasions in recent years to adjudicate in disputes between various public authorities over responsibility for the provision of a particular service or in the meeting of a particular need. An example is the dispute that spawned *Avon County Council* v *Hooper and Anor* [1997] 1 All ER 532 (CA). An SSD had provided services for a severely disabled client, H, from his birth in 1978 until his death in 1991. The services in question were those for which an SSD is entitled to charge under s. 17 Health and Social Services and Social Security Adjudications Act 1983, which now allows charges to be levied by an SSD for the provision of non-residential services: LAC(94)1. At the time, however, SSDs could also charge for residential services under this provision, and it was residential accommodation that had been provided in this case, although no charge had been made by the time of H's death. In 1989, the local HA had paid almost £300,000 to H in settlement of a negligence claim arising out of the circumstances of his birth, and had agreed to indemnify H against claims for care provided prior to the date of that settlement. The SSD, who had funded H's care, sued H's estate and the HA in order to recover a proportion of its cost, amounting to £232,000. The court held that it was reasonable for the SSD to levy such a charge, that charges could be levied retrospectively, and that, if a lesser sum is to be payable, the onus is on the chargee to persuade the SSD why that should be the case. But the particular pertinence of this case in the present context is that it shows how far from effective cooperation the actual relationship between an SSD and a HA can be at local level. The Court of Appeal has held, for policy reasons (the court not being able to predict the implications had it found the existence of duties), that neither owes a duty of care to the other: *Islington LBC* v *University College London Hospital NHS Trust* [2005] EWCA Civ 596.

In *R* v *North and East Devon HA, ex p Coughlan* [2001] QB 213, [2000] WLR 622 [2000] ALL ER 850, the Court of Appeal attempted to specify the border between those the responsibilities of HAs or PCTs and SSDs with greater clarity. The case concerned the care of C, who had been severely disabled and left with a serious neurological condition following a road traffic accident in 1971. Since that time, she had been resident in accommodation provided by her HA. The HA now wished to close the facility and transfer C to residential accommodation provided by the SSD. The case involved several issues, but the pertinent one for the present purposes concerned the question of the financing of C's nursing care in the SSD-provided facility. If it was to be provided by the HA as 'nursing care', it had to be provided free of charge (under s. 1(2) National Health Service Act 1977), but if it was to be provided by the SSD, then C was liable to charges (under the terms of the legislation discussed above). The Court of Appeal held that the duty of SSDs to provide accommodation under s. 21, NAA 1948, because it contemplated that those in need of accommodation by reason of age, illness or disability necessarily implied that some nursing care could properly be provided as part of the 'package of care' for which SSDs are responsible. Such nursing care must be that which is 'provided in connection with the accommodation', as required by s. 21(5) NAA 1948. In C's case, her need for nursing was such that it could not be deemed to be part of any 'social care' package, because her disabilities were such that it would not be reasonable for an SSD to be expected to provide for them. The key point here, however, is that the case shows that inter-agency working has been hindered not only by apathy, or a fear of losing control of local budgets, but also by legal uncertainties.

The Conservative administration of the mid-1990s took the first steps towards improving the situation with the publication in 1995 of *Building Bridges: A Guide to Arrangements for Inter-Agency Working for the Care and Protection of Severely Mentally Ill People* (Department of Health, 1995a). This document stated (1995a: para. 1.3.6) that 'multidisciplinary [community care provision] can only function where all those in the team work effectively together for the good of the patient', not only in formulating and delivering service packages, but also in other ways, for example, in sharing information and deciding local priorities. The main principles of inter-agency working were listed in *Building Bridges* (1995a: para. 1.1.1) as including:

- a commitment to joint working at all levels of the agencies involved, including senior management;

- a focus on service users, including sensitivity to the particular needs of individuals (specifically including people from ethnic minorities);

- an agreed and jointly 'owned' strategy for the care of severely mentally ill people;

- agreed and well-understood procedures for accessing services.

It further stated that, while the lead agency for community care services is the SSD, and primary responsibility for the CPA lies with PCTs and HAs, 'if properly implemented, multi-disciplinary assessment will ensure that the duty to make a community care assessment is fully discharged as part of the CPA, and there should not be a need for separate assessments' (1995a: para. 1.3.8). Four years on, when the Department of Health published *Still Building Bridges* (1999e), based on inspections carried out in 1998, it reported that the situation was beginning to improve. The inspections revealed, 'In contrast to the previous inspections . . . a good understanding of the use of care programme approach for assessment and care planning; joint health authority and social services departments strategies in place or in development; services developing in a more flexible way; extensive involvement of users and carers in care planning' (1999e: para. 1.7). Yet it was still the case that 'In most authorities we found assessment systems varied significantly between different professional groups, different agencies and within agencies. There were few examples of holistic inter-disciplinary assessments as expected in Care Management' (1999e: para. 1.21).

Under the Labour administrations since 1997, further steps have been taken to encourage greater cooperation. Two White Papers, published at the end of 1998 (Department of Health, 1998a; 1998b), promised a raft of changes, including more stock, more resources, better integration of management structures, better quality care, more outreach, and a greater emphasis placed on prevention. They were followed by a welter of new guidance to services (Department of Health, 1998e; 1998f; 1998g). For working-age adults, the *National Service Framework for Mental Health* (NFSMH) was introduced in 1999 (Department of Health, 1999; its seven standards are laid out in Chapter 3), both to standardise service quality nationally and to engender improvement in the quality of services. The document applies to both health and social services, and to the whole range of service provision, from outreach to high-security confinement (Department of Health, 1998a: para. 4.3). Standards 4 and 5 deal specifically with inter-agency working, and the NSFMH notes the importance of multidisciplinary initial assessment (Department of Health, 1999: 43). The *National Service Framework for Older People* (Department of Health, 2001e), with supporting guidance (HSC 2002/001; LAC (2002)1), requires that the needs of all older people , including those with mental health problems (2001e: para. 7.6) be subject to the single assessment procedure (SAP), which is multidisciplinary.

Section 26 of the Health Act of 1999 places a duty on health and social service providers to cooperate when performing their functions, s. 30 allows SSDs to channel funds to HAs for joint ventures, and s. 31 establishes 'partnership arrangements', under which social service and health bodies may pool resources, staff, and facilities in order to improve the quality of service provision: s. 31(1). Pursuant to s. 31, the NHS Bodies and Local Authorities Partnership Arrangements Regulations 2000 (SI 2000/617) were made by the Secretary of State, specifying in detail the functions that may be subject to partnerships. Guidance has also been issued on the implementation of partnerships (Department of Health, 2000c; 2002f; Dickinson, 2006), and the scheme certainly incentivised some service providers: by January 2003, there were almost two hundred partnership schemes in operation. A further step towards integrated service delivery was taken by the establishment of care trusts (CTs) by s. 45 Health and Social Care Act 2001, together with the Care Trusts (Applications and Consultation) Regulations 2001 (SI 2001/3788), which allow a PCT or NHS trust, already working in tandem with an SSD, to take over formally the health-related functions of the SSD. This can only be done where designation as a CT is likely to promote the effective delivery of those functions by the trust.

By 2006, there were approximately ten CTs in existence. CTs are, from one point of view, a pragmatic and logical continuation of the process of formalising partnerships that was enabled by s. 31 of the 1999 Act. From another point of view, this is a controversial development, because it enables an NHS body to charge for services (if they would be provided by an SSD were it not for the existence of the CT), thus moving away, some argue, from the NHS principle that services should be provided free at the point of need (Campbell, 2001). CTs are voluntary partnerships and any partner may withdraw from the CT, but it is clear that the carrot of more freedom over budgetary control at local level is underpinned by the stick, to be found in s. 46 of the Health and Social Care Act 2001, of 'directed partnerships', whereby a 'failing' local providers of community care provision can be directed to form a 'partnership' that is, in practice, a CT.

Other recent reforms help to clarify with greater precision the allocation of responsibilities between agencies. Section 49 of the 2001 Act removed the obligation of SSDs to provide nursing care by a registered nurse: all such nursing is now provided by the NHS free of charge. Section 49 was phased in over a period of time, but came fully into effect from 1 April 2003. This partly put into effect the recommendation of the Royal Commission on Long-term Care (1999) to this effect. This lessens the import of the decision of the Court of Appeal in *ex p Coughlan* to a significant extent, although, as the court noted in that case, where the line is to be drawn between 'social care' and 'nursing care' will sometimes be problematic, depending on 'a careful appraisal of the facts of the individual case' (per Lord Woolf MR at para. 30). And it is only nursing care provided by a registered nurse that is to be provided free to SSD-run care home residents; other nursing remains the responsibility of the SSD and may still be charged for by a SSD that provides it. The government has issued a number of circulars giving guidance as to how PCTs should meet the need for continuing NHS care (Department of Health, 2001g) and how they should assess the needs for nursing care of residents in SSD accommodation: Department of Health, 2001f; 2003a. In February 2003, the Health Service Ombudsman published a critical report (Health Service Ombudsman, 2003), which detailed that, in a number of instances, local responses to the *Coughlan* judgment had been unsatisfactory, and that this was partially the fault of the Department of Health, which had not issued detailed guidance on the implications of the judgment for two years (see Department of Health, 2001g); more significantly, it had not picked up, through inspections, on the fact that unlawful criteria were still being used.

There is still the potential, and the incentive, for local service providers to construct (and, although criteria must be agreed at strategic health authority level, it is left to PCTs to apply) eligibility criteria that might attract legal challenge, as happened in *R v Bexley NHS Care Trust, ex p Grogan* [2006] EWHC 44. In this case, the High Court found that B's eligibility criteria, which assessed clients as being on one or the other side of the line demarcated in *Coughlan* by reference to the nature, complexity, intensity or unpredictability of their health needs, to be unlawful. This was because the criteria made no mention of the 'primary health need' approach and did not explain the test that was applied to those criteria. The court went on to note that local problems are, at least partly, the consequence of lack of clarity in the guidance issued by the Department of Health following *Coughlan*, in which there seems to be overlap between the factors that point to NHS-provided care and those that point to SSD-provided care (paras. 63–82).

The Scottish Parliament implemented the full recommendation of the Royal Commission, which was that both nursing and personal care should be free (The Community Care and Health (Scotland) Act 2002). The reason for this recommendation was that, in the view of the Scottish Parliament, it seems equally anomalous that personal care (help with dressing, washing and so on), as opposed to nursing care, should be freely provided in NHS accommodation but be chargeable in SSD accommodation, as it does that nursing care should be provided freely in NHS accommodation but be charged for in SSD accommodation. The government in England and Wales rejected this, on the basis that it would benefit the well-off (Bissett-Johnson and Main, 2002: 279). But this situation also provides a disincentive for patients and their families, once a patient has been admitted to a hospital or other NHS facility, to agree to a transfer to SSD accommodation, and can therefore cause the blocking of beds that would otherwise be available within the NHS. In England and Wales, the government responded to this problem by including in the Queen's Speech for 2002 (which states the government's legislative intentions for the coming year) what subsequently became the Community Care (Delayed Discharge) Act 2003, under which an SSD that fails to make arrangements for (certain classes of) NHS patients who require social service provision of one sort or another will be fined if the consequence of delay is that NHS beds remain blocked. Needless to say, this is a controversial measure (Bielanska, 2003), and the bill was amended in its passage through the House of Lords, so that mentally ill patients are excluded from its ambit (see s. 11(3) Community Care (Delayed Discharge) Act 2003). The problem it addresses is, however, real enough. The National Audit Office (2003) found that, in September 2002, four thousand beds in the NHS were blocked by elderly persons fit to leave hospital if residential accommodation had been available.

As far as the CPA itself is concerned, *Building Bridges* made it clear that 'the CPA can and should be applied to all patients who are accepted by the specialist psychiatric services' (1995a: para. 1.3.6). The CPA must be written into contracts with independent and voluntary providers of services. The earlier advice has now been superseded by *Modernising the CPA*, issued in 1999 (Department of Health, 1999a). The four main elements of the CPA (listed above) are unchanged, as is its coverage (working age adults). As before, 'the key principles of the CPA are applicable to all service users' (1999a: para. 18). There are some superficial changes: key workers have been renamed as care coordinators (usually a community psychiatric nurse or psychiatric social worker: see the discussion at Department of Health, 1995a: paras 3.1.18–3.1.25); the requirement for six-monthly reviews in all cases has been lifted, although regular reviews must continue in all cases. *Building Bridges* made clear that a full multidisciplinary assessment should be reserved for complex cases, but the new approach attempts to systematise this. There are now two levels of the CPA: 'standard' and 'enhanced', depending on the needs of the service user, although in either case a multidisciplinary assessment is required, and there should be 'A single assessment [which] should facilitate access to both health and social services' (1995a: para. 38).

The standard CPA is appropriate when the need is predominantly for support from one agency, when clients are able to self-manage their mental health problems, when there is an active informal support network, or when patients are more likely to maintain contact with service providers, and when clients 'pose little danger to themselves or others' (Department of Health, 1999d: para. 57). The enhanced CPA, which means a more interventionist approach, is indicated when clients have multiple needs, when continued contact with all agencies is not assured, when agencies such as those that function as part of the criminal justice system may be involved with the client, when more frequent and interventionist management may be required, and when clients are more likely to be at risk of harming themselves or others (1999d: para. 58). Generally, 'Elements of risk and how the care plan manages the identified risk must always be recorded' (1999d: para. 63). Also emphasised is the need for joint planning and training of staff, the development of systems for the sharing of information, and a common approach to risk assessment, which, it is made clear, is 'an essential and on-going part of the CPA process' (1999d: para. 31). Under the old system, the broader Department of Health policy of 'care management', which also entails an individualised approach to the treatment of persons within the NHS generally, ran parallel with the CPA, with the latter seen as 'a specialist variant of care management for people with mental health problems' (Department of Health, 1995a: para. 3.2.8). Care management may include the appointment of a nominated care manager, or, if the client has complex needs, managers. The NSFMH (Department of Health, 1999: 45) moved policy in the direction of merging the CPA with care management. *Modernising the CPA* emphasised that 'The CPA *is* Care Management' (Department of Health, 1999d: para. 35, emphasis in original), and requires the integration of the two concepts into a unified approach. A lead officer in each area must work across agencies to ensure the delivery of an integrated service (1999d: para. 40), and service delivery must be audited in accordance with guidance issued by the NHS Executive (1996).

The lasting effects of these developments remain to be seen. In 2002, the Social Services Inspectorate (2002: ch. 5) reported that, whilst there have been real strides made in some areas, in others, there is still much to be done. In 2004, the Commission for Health Improvement published its sector report *What CHI has Found: Mental Health Trusts*, summarising findings made during a number of visits of trusts in 2001–3. This report found a number of problems familiar from a decade or so earlier. For example, 'The picture of IT management for most trusts . . . is poor and information systems to support the delivery of care and the use of information to monitor the quality of care are underdeveloped. Most [local systems] are incompatible with the systems used in other local health organisations and social services, hindering access to up to date clinical information (2004: 14). Generally (2004: 15):

There are good examples of structural approaches to partnership working with primary care trusts, such as jointly funded posts with responsibilities across primary and secondary mental health care . . . There is a range of partnership development between trusts and local authorities . . . However, there is evidence from one of CHI's investigations to suggest that in some cases, local partnerships have not been sufficiently developed to put these arrangements successfully in place.

The CHI also found 'that sometimes differences in cultures, values and approaches of health and social care organisations were creating tensions at team level with some staff unsure about their lines of managerial accountability and professional leadership' (2004: 16), although there are examples of well-established and well-run, formalised partnerships to be found (Rees *et al.*, 2004). There is also continuing evidence that 25 per cent of service users are not consulted at all about the terms of their care plan and only 42 per cent are fully involved; around half of all users are not given a copy of their care plan (Healthcare Commission, 2005: 13). Not all service users have a care plan, and there is evidence that younger clients do better than their older counterparts in this regard, and that the needs of those of Afro-Caribbean or Asian origin are less well met than those of their white counterparts (Sainsbury Centre and Mental Health Act Commission, 2005).

9.4.2 Working with housing authorities

The importance of the integration of SSDs with local housing authorities was a recurrent theme of the 1999 White Paper (see, for example, Department of Health, 1999a: paras. 2.6, 4.55). The interface between these two agencies has often been, at best, haphazard in the past, and whereas PCTs, HAs and SSDs have improved joint working, less progress has been made to improve cooperation between SSDs and local housing authorities (Social Services Inspectorate and Audit Commission, 2001: 27). Partly, this is because of the generic problems facing inter-agency cooperation, discussed above – but there is no doubt that part of this is down to the discretionary language of s. 47(3) of the NHSCCA 1990, under which it is always open to a housing authority to decline the invitation to assess or meet the needs of an individual who must be assessed by an SSD under s. 47(1). That a local housing authority is not required even to assist at the stage of assessment of needs, let alone at the stage of actual provision of services, again casts some doubt on the claims that, under the 1990 Act, service users are to experience a 'seamless service' across local government departments. If a housing authority declines an invitation to assist, it is perfectly possible that an SSD will nevertheless go on to decide that there is a need for independent housing that it, under the terms of the 1948 Act, cannot supply. Even if a local housing authority does assist at the stage of need assessment, there is no provision under the 1990 Act to require it to meet any housing needs that are identified. In sum, this meant that, through most of the 1990s – and in many areas, it continues to be the case – the only way for those in need of housing, other than residential accommodation, to access provision is through private rental or the general housing legislation.

   This is certainly the policy expressed in LAC 93(10) (Department of Health, 1993b): 'no new category of entitlement to housing is created by 1990 Act'. The need to consider independent housing had been a feature of the debates about the future direction of community care in the 1980s. But by the time of the Griffiths Report (1988), upon which the subsequent White Paper and the 1990 Act were largely based, the assumption was that the need was for the provision of services to clients already living in their own homes. Although the much-trumpeted intention of the 1990 Act had been to provide 'the right level of intervention and support to enable people to achieve maximum independence and control over their own lives' (Department of Health, 1990a), LAC(93)10 effectively meant that the role of local housing authorities in the realisation of community care practice would be, at best, marginal. As Cowan (1995a: 216) put it, '[t]his message was crystal clear: either own or occupy your own home or be provided with residential care but do not expect us to provide you with your own independent accommodation'.

Contrary to the view expressed in social work theory (see Chapter 3), the housing elements of the 1990 Act do not reveal a policy of client empowerment; the point is that this is above and beyond local policies, practices, or failure of communication. It is true that there were some moves in the direction of greater user choice, the clearest example being the Community Care (Direct Payments) Act 1996, which gives SSDs a power to provide funds directly to certain classes of service user, including mentally ill persons, who may then purchase their own care (Spandler and Vick, 2005; 2006). The service user had first, however, to persuade the SSD that he or she was in need of community care services, and there are limitations on the use of direct payments for residential accommodation under s. 21 of the 1948 Act, because an SSD is required, under that section, to 'make arrangements' and it has been held that the making of direct payments to service users does not comprise such: *R v Secretary of State for Health, ex p LB Hammersmith and Fulham (and Ors)* (1997) *The Independent*, 15 July (HC).

Attempts by service users in the 1990s to enlarge the scope of community care in this regard, by recourse to litigation against housing authorities, met with little success, notwithstanding that 'a person who is vulnerable as a result of mental illness or handi-cap' is defined as being in 'priority need' of local authority or social housing (s. 189(1)(c), Housing Act 1996), in which case, the authority 'shall secure that accommodation is available for occupation by the applicant' under s. 193(2) of the same Act. The courts have decided that a mentally ill or learning disabled person is vulnerable for that reason, when homeless, if he or she is 'less able to fend for himself than an ordinary homeless person so that injury or detriment to him will result when a less vulnerable man would be able to cope without harmful effects' (*R v Camden London Borough Council, ex p Pereira* [1998] 31 HLR 317 per Hobhouse LJ at 330). This test is capable of being applied narrowly, to exclude persons, who are within the spirit of the legislation, from its protection (see the cases successfully appealed in *Hall and Carter v Wandsworth LBC* [2004] EWCA Civ 1740). But the main blow came in the form of restrictions on access to housing, placed on persons in priority need under what is now s. 189(1)(c), by the decision of the House of Lords in *R v Oldham MBC, ex p Garlick; R v Tower Hamlets LBC, ex p Ferdous Begum* [1993] 2 All ER 65 (HL). The latter case on this conjoined appeal, which was heard before the passage of the Act of 1996, although the statutory definition of 'priority need' has not changed, involved an application for council hous-ing made by F, a learning-disabled woman. This had been rejected by the local housing authority on the basis, inter alia, that F lacked the mental capacity to agree to the appli-cation that had been made in her name (the application was for housing for F and her family), or to accept an offer of housing if one were made.

In the leading opinion on this point, Lord Griffiths confirmed that no duty arose to provide accommodation unless the applicant, even if both vulnerable and in priority need, had sufficient mental capacity to agree to the terms of the tenancy, on the basis that the housing legislation was concerned with housing provision rather than the provision for the severely disabled, which was instead provided under s. 21, NAA 1948. As Edmunds aptly summarises, 'this significant and regrettable decision denies people with a mental illness or mental handicap who are homeless, access in their own right to the complicated network of provisions on local authority assistance' (1994: 358). This does not mean that all persons who are mentally disordered will be unable to access entitlement to housing, but it does mean that those who fail the capacity test (with obscure content) that local housing authorities are licensed to apply after *Garlick* will be excluded. And it is hard to believe that the issue of the resources (in terms of services provided in the home, that would be required to accommodate many such persons in 'conventional' housing) was not within the contemplation of Lord Griffiths in reaching his conclusion on the law (McCabe, 1996), particularly as Lord Slynn dissented, on the basis that there is no reference to a test of capacity on the face of the legislation.

There are further examples of a failure on the part of the courts to embrace and enforce a notion of joined-up service provision. For example, in *R v Brent LBC, ex p Mawcan* (1994) 26 HLR 528 (HC), the court refused to find that it was unreasonable of a local housing authority to place community care clients in 'bed and breakfast' accommodation, even though concerns have been expressed that such accommodation is unsuitable for mentally disordered persons, risking 'ghettoisation' of mentally disordered persons, because many people are reluctant to share such accommodation with the mentally ill (Jodelet, 1991). More alarmingly still, in *R v Wirral MBC, ex p B* (1994) *The Times*, 3 May (HC), it was held that a local housing authority was under no duty to contact the local SSD when contemplating evicting a person known to be in need of community care services. In *Wirral*, B had been evicted from her council property as a result of her awkward and difficult behaviour. She was then held to be intentionally homeless (under what is now s. 191, Housing Act 1996), even though she was acknowledged, by reason of mental illness, to be in priority need. Cowan (1995b) has argued that *Wirral* may be wrongly decided because, in other cases, courts have looked at the background reasons for homelessness when deciding if, in a given case, it can said to be 'intentional'. In *Wirral*, Johnson J held that it is for the client rather than the local housing authority to contact the local SSD. In *North Devon Homes Ltd v B* 2003 WL 1202659, Steel J accepted a different argument: that the eviction of a mentally ill council tenant on the grounds that her behaviour towards her neighbours, which was indeed offensive, was nevertheless in breach both of s. 22 Disability Discrimination Act 1995, which prohibits unjustified discrimination against a disabled person (defined to include mental disorder as understood in the MHA 1983) and B's Art. 8 ECHR right to respect for her family life, which would be the result of her eviction. The decision to evict was held to be unreasonable because B 'cannot help conduct that happens... most if not all of the conduct that is perpetrated is due to her mental problems' (at para. 17), and thus eviction was a response to her disability and hence unlawful. It is to be hoped that this recent High Court decision foretells of a more widespread change of judicial attitude to come.

The *Wirral* case underlines the point that patient advocacy (see Chapter 12) is vitally important if client empowerment is to develop as fully in practice as it has in various strands of social work theory, just as it underlines the degree to which the law must accept its share of culpability for the 'failure' of care in the community. Decisions such as this buttressed a view amongst housing authorities that the onus is primarily on

SSDs acting under the 1948 Act, rather than on local housing authorities acting under the housing legislation, to deal with mentally disordered persons in need of housing. Conversely, 'SSDs might also seek to restrict their definitions of the basis that [the Housing Act 1996] should mop up most cases' (Cowan, 1995a: 223). Cowan (1995a) argued that the problem is exacerbated by the failure to integrate the relevant legislation properly. One element of this is that, under the 1990 Act regime, entitlement is triggered by being 'ordinarily resident' in the SSD area in question. And this remains the case, despite the ruling in *R v Berkshire CC, ex p P* [1997] 95 LGR 449 (HC) that there is no such limitation of the right to be assessed under s. 47(1), because in the key 'community care service' of residential accommodation under s. 21 of the 1948 Act, the phrase *is* applicable. By contrast, the concept used in the housing legislation is 'local connection', currently contained in s. 199 Housing Act 1996. The two concepts are not coterminous, and the decision about whether an applicant has satisfied the requirement is for the SSD or local housing authority respectively. Moreover, s. 198 of the 1996 Act provides that, even if an applicant is in priority need and is not intentionally homeless, a local housing authority may decline to provide accommodation of any sort, if of the view that the applicant does not have a local connection with its area, but does have a local connection with the area of another local housing authority.

In such circumstances, the duty of the first local housing authority in question is only to notify the second one, and the first one need not even offer advice and assistance to the applicant: ss. 197, 198(1), Housing Act 1996. In sum, this means that the potential for 'passing the parcel', both as between SSDs and local housing authorities, and between different local housing authorities, is built into the statutory scheme (for an example involving two housing authorities 'engaged in a struggle to avoid being fixed with responsibility' for the care of a particularly learning-disabled client with complex needs, described as a 'lamentable state of affairs' by Gibbs J at para. 27, see *RW v Sheffield CC* [2005] EWHC 720 (Admin)). The possibility is exacerbated further by directions made by the Secretary of State in relation to the operation by SSDs of s. 21 of the 1948 Act (Department of Health, 1993b: Appendix 1), which, as detailed above, require SSDs to provide residential accommodation for persons in urgent need.

The problems with this situation are twofold: first, there is the potential for a person trying to access residential accommodation to fall between the cracks, with each agency holding the other responsible; second, if the policy behind decarceration and community care is to deinstitutionalise mental health services, the current regime systematically fails, at the level of statutory provision, to permit the realisation of that aim in practice. This is because the legal framework exerts a gravitational pull towards the provision of the community care in care homes. It seems clear that an entitlement to 'ordinary' housing is a prerequisite for a community care policy that has as one of its intentions to reduce the all-too-frequent triadic equation between mental illness, homelessness, and avoidable institutionalisation (Abdul-Hamid and Cooney, 1997).

In the last few years, however, the courts have begun to respond more positively in this regard. The first relevant decision is that of Moses J in *R v Westminster City Council, ex p M, P, A and X* (1997) 1 CCLR 85, who held that 'ordinary' (as opposed to residential) accommodation, rented from a landlord, fell within s. 21 of the 1948 Act. In *R v Bristol City Council, ex p Penfold* [1998] COD 210 (QB), before Scott Baker J, a SSD argued inter alia that it could not provide 'ordinary' housing under s. 21 of the 1948 Act. This has certainly been the view that had routinely been taken of the powers in s. 21. The judge rejected this contention, however, holding (at 218) that 'while s. 21(1)(a) is not a basic safety net for everybody, it can in appropriate circumstances extend to the provision of "normal" accommodation', if that is required to meet a need that might otherwise have been met by other community care circumstances. There were similar outcomes in *R v Wigan MBC, ex p Tammadge* [1998] 1 CCLR 581 and *R v Islington LBC, ex p Batantu* (2001) 33 HLR 76 (QB). In all three cases, an SSD was required by the court to provide suitable 'ordinary' accommodation for a claimant judged to be in need of such.

A dissenting voice was raised by Stanley Burnton J in *R v Tower Hamlets LBC, ex p Abdul W* [2002] EWHC Admin 641, a case concerning a family of ten, living in a two-bedroom flat. The family was on the housing authority's waiting list for more suitable accommodation, specifically a house with five bedrooms. They faced a long wait: the authority gave evidence that 661 applicants were on the list for such properties, but only 27 had become available in the preceding year. W, the father, suffered from schizophrenia and had recently been hospitalised. On release, his care plan stated that W, whose mental health had improved significantly (he was symptom-free for the first time in two decades), required support and his state of mental health monitoring. He also required 'assistance with liasing with the housing department'. W requested an assessment under s. 47(1) of the National Health Service and Community Care Act 1990. This was carried out and a decision was made by the SSD not to offer him any services at that time. W sought judicial review, arguing that his mental health required him to be rehoused, through the use of the powers of the SSD in s. 21 of the National Assistance Act 1948.

Stanley Burnton J, not surprisingly, rejected W's arguments on the facts: the evidence of his care plan and the s. 47(1) assessment was that he did not require services at that time. He also gave consideration to the broader question of the scope of s. 21 in this regard. He drew attention to s. 21(8), which provides that:

Nothing in this section shall authorise or require a local authority to make any provision authorised or required to be made . . . by or under any enactment not contained in this Part of this Act.

This, he suggested (at para. 27) meant that the provision of 'ordinary' housing, which, as seen above, is subject to the regime in the housing legislation, cannot lawfully be provided under s. 21 of the 1948 Act, and this 'is consistent with the view that section 21 is a safety net provision . . . to be relied on when all else fails' (para. 28). He went on to point out that s. 167(2) of the Housing Act 1996 requires a housing authority to give priority when allocating accommodation to persons in overcrowded or insanitary conditions, or who have a medical need for settled housing, from which he deduced that neither 'overcrowding of itself' nor a risk to health give rise to a duty under s. 21. Finally, he pointed out that, if s. 21 could be used in this way, it would undermine the housing authority's system for allocating housing based on need for housing. Evidence was given to the court by the local mental health team leader that '[W]'s housing situation is no different from a number of other families in the borough. There are many families in the borough whose unsatisfactory housing impacts adversely on their physical or mental health' (at para. 15).

Despite the reality and legitimacy of these concerns, Stanley Burnton J was overruled by the Court of Appeal ([2002] EWCA Civ 287). Pill LJ pointed out that it has been established, in *R v Southwark LB, ex p K* [2001] EWCA Civ 999, [2001] MHLR 31 (CA), that the need for care and attention is an absolute requirement of eligibility under s. 21 (at para. 20). He also upheld the first instance view that the SSD had appropriately decided that there was no duty on the facts of this case (para. 26). Third, he confirmed that, once a duty has been shown to exist because of a need for care and attention, the SSD might meet that duty as it saw fit, including the provision of 'ordinary' housing (para. 34). Finally, however, he declined to face head-on the argument made on behalf of the SSD, that, because housing was available (at least in theory) via the housing legislation, W could not be said to be a person in need of accommodation 'which is not otherwise available', as s. 21(1)(a) requires (para. 34).

Hale LJ, giving the other judgment in the Court of Appeal, held that Stanley Burnton's J's analysis of the scope of s. 21 may well have been correct as a matter of historical record. There was substantial reason to think that the original intention behind s. 21(1) was that it should be limited to residential home accommodation, but she went on to say that 'Whatever the words "residential accommodation" may have meant in 1948 . . . they are a good example of language which is "always speaking" and can change its meaning in the light of changing social conditions' (at para. 31). As such, it was proper to conclude that, in principle, if the provision of 'ordinary' housing was required as part of a package to meet a client's need for care and attention, it could lawfully be provided under s. 21(1), and s. 21(8) must be read to be compatible with that. But this did not mean that there was a duty to provide such housing under s. 21 in a case such as the present one, in which the need was for housing rather than care (at para. 32). Hale LJ did not analyse the import of the words 'not otherwise available' in s. 21(1)(a), but the necessary implication of her judgment, and that of Pill LJ, is that these words should not be read to mean that housing cannot be provided under the 1948 Act because it is dealt with, and hence, in some sense, 'otherwise available' through the housing legislation.

On the other hand, it cannot be assumed that, because there is a need for 'ordinary' housing or rehousing, the duty under s. 21 is triggered (Hale LJ at para. 32). That is dependent upon the presence of an unmet need for care and attention, and 'Ordinary housing is not "care and attention". It is simply the means whereby the necessary care and attention can be made available if otherwise it will not' (para. 32). Hale LJ went on to emphasise that s. 21(8) will ordinarily prohibit the provision of 'ordinary' housing under s. 21, by reason of the fact that there is already a power to meet housing needs through the housing legislation (para. 34); s. 21 reaches only so far as the needs of the applicant, and not other members of his or her family (para. 34). The needs of children, as already mentioned, are to be met through the powers available in the Children Act 1989 and should not enter the equation under s. 21 (para. 34), and, if there is a power (not a duty) to provide accommodation for the children of an applicant under s. 21, 'it is not an entitlement or enforceable expectation' (Carnwath LJ in *R v Haringey LBC, ex p O* [2004] EWCA Civ 535 at para. 42). These dicta were applied in *R v Southwark LBC, ex p Mooney* [2006] EWHC 1912, Jackson J holding that no duty under s. 21 had come into existence in the case of an applicant, M, living in accommodation unsuitable for her because of physical disability, along with her three minor children, two of whom had learning difficulties and emotional and developmental problems. The SSD had accepted, following an assessment of M's needs, that her current accommodation was unsuitable, and the HA had accepted her as being in priority need under the terms of the housing legislation. M nevertheless sought judicial review on the basis that the SSD was in breach of its duty under s. 21 to provide her with suitable accommodation. Jackson J held that no such duty had come into existence, there being 'a substantial gap between establishing a need for housing and triggering a duty under s. 21(1) of the 1948 Act' (para. 51).

Although both *Tammadge* and *Batantu* were distinguished by Jackson J (para. 59), in truth, the difference between this case and those is slight, and we suspect that *ex p Abdul W* may prove, in retrospect, to be the high-water mark for the development of s. 21 of the 1948 Act as a mechanism to circumvent the housing legislation and the waiting lists that characterise its functioning. The key distinction is whether a need for accommodation is severable from a need for care and attention, but that is a question capable of being answered differently by different SSDs. Nevertheless, the case law has now established that it is not permissible to adopt a broad interpretation of 'otherwise available'. It is no longer legitimate for an SSD to take the view that, as well as housing provided by local authorities, there is always property available to rent through the private sector and so property in the form of 'ordinary housing' will always be 'available'. Such a reading would, of course, totally defeat the intention of s. 21, and it is much better to interpret that phrase narrowly and pragmatically, as being satisfied if the particular client has no other means of securing required accommodation. This reading does not endorse queue jumping; rather, it gives SSDs to discretion to respond creatively to the identified needs of service users, and is very much in line with the current policy of lessening the reliance on residential accommodation. To be given full effect, however, the decision in *ex p Ferdous Begum* also needs to be reviewed. Articles 8 and 14 of the ECHR may provide the tools to do this, because it is certainly arguable that the decision in that case discriminates against persons lacking capacity in terms or respect for their family life. The Court of Appeal in *ex p Abdul W* emphasised that it should be the SSD rather than a court that decides what needs are present and how they should be met (see Pill LJ at para. 23; Hale LJ at para. 33). And it is perfectly possible that an SSD might conclude that the needs of a particular client, who lacks capacity, are best met by the provision of ordinary housing and the delivery of various services to the client in that housing. Unfortunately, the decision in *ex p Ferdous Begum* seems to prevent an SSD from doing just that.

9.5 **Control in the community**

Community care, and the CPA, are not concerned solely with the provision of 'optional' services, nor are they solely concerned with providing only those services required by the health or welfare of the client. Risk to others, as both *Building Bridges* and *Modernising the Care Programme Approach* make clear, is also a relevant factor. Accordingly, community care law also embraces a degree of compulsion and control over service recipients, through a variety of statutory mechanisms. This raises the question of whether community care should be seen ultimately in terms of care or of control. Indeed, the question runs through the law that has been discussed above. *Building Bridges* made it clear that, of the target group as a whole, it was the severely mentally ill who were to be the prime focus of service provision, and one would perhaps be forgiven for thinking that this is because there is a perception that clients falling into this category are, by definition, in greater need, not of care, but of control and supervision. Similarly, the 'enhanced' CPA introduced in 1999 is designed for those liable to lose touch with services and likely to be a danger to self or others. Such a view is given support by the fact that services for the mentally ill tend to be provided free of charge regardless of ability to pay, unlike services for disabled persons. There has been a quantitative increase in the number of control-based measures available for use in recent years, but it is more difficult to gauge the extent to which there has been a qualitative shift. Certainly, the public and political will for 'more control' seems to exist, and the main reason for this is the perception that, collectively, the mentally ill (particularly schizophrenics) and those with personality disorders, constitute a significant risk to public safety. At the heart of this view is an equation between (the failure of) community care and apparently motiveless homicides by mentally disordered persons. Before discussing the available legal powers of control in the community, it is therefore first necessary to consider the extent to which recent developments are based on accurate perceptions of the risk to public safety.

9.5.1 **Homicide and community care**

The relationship between community care and homicide is one of extreme controversy. Although not the first such incident, it was the killing of Jonathon Zito by Christopher Clunis, on Finsbury Park Tube station in December 1992, which propelled the issue into the public and political domain. Following this incident, the Department of Health (1994), in the form of the NHS Executive, published guidance on discharge and aftercare. As well as attempting to lay down standards of best practice, it also required HAs to initiate independent inquiries following homicides by mentally disordered persons in their areas and to publish the reports generated by the inquiries (para. 34); numerous such reports have since been published. The issue of homicide, particularly committed against strangers in public places, by persons known to the mental health system (although often not in receipt of any care or supervision at the time of the killing) was the most highly profiled aspect of mental health policy and practice in the media in the 1990s. Attempting to unravel any precise relationship between homicide and community care is, however, a complex operation.

Homicide rates in England and Wales are relatively low. There were 765 deaths initially classified by the police as homicide in 2004–5, a 12 per cent decrease from the 869 recorded the previous year (Home Office, 2006a: 5). This compares to 627 in 1996 and 563 in 1986 (Home Office Research and Statistics Directorate, 1996). One school of thought, represented, for example, by Tidmarsh (1995) and Muijen (1996), takes the view that there is no appreciable relationship between community care, mental disorder, and homicide rates. Following a review of the evidence, which shows that '[t]he rate of mentally abnormal homicide appears to be constant world-wide' (1995: 2), Tidmarsh argues that '[t]he criminal statistics show no trend over the years which would give ammunition to those who are alarmed about community care' (*ibid.*). Muijen (1996: 151) calculates that somewhere between 3 and 7 per cent of homicides are related to mental disorder. Home Office statistics seem to corroborate this view. They routinely record only a small percentage of homicides as attributable to mental disorder: the figure was 4 per cent in 2001–2 (Home Office Research and Statistics Directorate, 2003: 4). The majority, over 40 per cent in 2001–2 (*ibid.*), of homicides are recorded as being carried out for reasons of quarrel, revenge or loss of temper, and a much more useful indicator of the use of violence is whether the offender is, at the time, under the influence of alcohol (44 per cent of all violent offenders in 2005–6) or drugs (23 per cent) (Home Office, 2006a: Table 5.06).

Such conclusions are, however, vigorously disputed by Howlett (1998), who argues that the Home Office statistics 'are insufficiently detailed to ascertain the numbers of mentally ill people who commit homicide' (1998: 82), for example, by not showing how many homicides following quarrels or loss of temper, or carried out in revenge, were committed by mentally disordered persons. He points instead to data produced by the National Confidential Inquiry into Suicide and Homicide by People with Mental Illness (Appleby, 1997). A total of 408 homicide convictions were notified to the inquiry in the year from April 1996. Of these, in 327 instances, court files were made available, which showed that, in 238 cases, the court requested a psychiatric report. Of these 238 cases: 17 per cent (39) had 'symptoms of mental illness' at the time of the killing; 43 per cent had a mental disorder of some sort; 25 per cent had previous contact with adult mental health services; 12 per cent had had contact with those services in the year before the homicide was committed. This gave the inquiry a figure of 50 homicides (and 1,000 suicides) committed by persons who had had contact with mental health services no more than a year before the homicide was committed. If the numbers of such homicides has increased in line with the general increase, the expected figure in 2006 would be around 65. The report of the National Confidential Inquiry (Department of Health, 2001j), *Safety First: Five-Year Report of the National Confidential Inquiry into Suicide and Homicide by People with Mental Illness*, found that (2001j: findings 32–40):

- around a third of all perpetrators of homicide had a diagnosis of mental disorder based on life history: the most common diagnoses were alcohol dependence, drug dependence and personality disorder;

- 7 per cent of people convicted of homicide in England and Wales, and 6 per cent in Scotland, were committed to psychiatric hospital;

- 5 per cent of all perpetrators of homicide in England and Wales (7 per cent of those with a psychiatric report), and 2 per cent in Scotland, had a diagnosis of schizophrenia;

- 9 per cent of people convicted of homicide had a diagnosis of personality disorder;

- 15 per cent of people convicted of homicide in England and Wales (for whom reports were available), and 5 per cent in Scotland, had symptoms of mental illness at the time of the offence;

- these mentally ill perpetrators had a lower rate of previous convictions for violence than those who were not mentally ill at the time of the offence;

- alcohol and drugs were more likely to contribute to the offence in people convicted of homicide who were not mentally ill;

- mentally ill perpetrators were less likely to kill a stranger than those without mental illness;

- 9 per cent of all perpetrators in England and Wales had been in contact with mental health services in the year before the offence. At least 18 per cent had been in contact with services at some time.

Unravelling these findings is problematic. As can be seen, some of the definitions on which they are based, such as the broad definition of mental disorder that is used, are much wider than those deployed, for instance, by the 1983 Act, which means that the relationship between homicide and mental disorder is, to some extent, an artefact of the definitions deployed (Shaw *et al.*, 2006). But they do demonstrate that the idea that the mentally ill are a risk to the general population, rather than to those known to them, is false, although they do also demonstrate that rather more homicides are committed by mentally disordered persons than some would accept. What is not clear is whether the incidence of homicide by mentally disordered persons is increasing. In an authoritative review, Taylor and Gunn (1999) found that, over the previous four decades, there has been an annual 3 per cent *decline* in the contribution of mentally ill persons to criminal homicide statistics, but more recent research reached conclusions closer to those of Howlett and the National Confidential Inquiry, with 10 per cent of homicides carried out whilst the perpetrator was actively mentally ill (the illness most commonly being schizophrenia), and 34 per cent of perpetrators suffering from a diagnosed mental disorder, usually a personality disorder or dependence on alcohol or drugs (Shaw *et al.*, 2006).

Whatever the truth of this, it is clear that, in relative terms, the numbers of mentally disordered persons involved in homicides, unlike suicides, remain low, at least by comparison to public perception of the risk. But perhaps that is not the point. The findings of the National Inquiry do tend to support research suggesting that there is an, albeit complex, link between mental disorder and violence (Bowden, 1996). Included in that hundred or so individuals a year are many of the most highly publicised homicides and other acts of violence by mentally disordered persons in recent years, including those carried out by Michael Stone, Christopher Clunis, Horrett Campbell, Andrew Robinson, and others. It might be thought that the appropriate policy response to such events would be to improve access to community care services and the framework for the delivery of such services, and, as seen above, there are some moves in that direction. But the government has also revived the concept of a 'community treatment order', which had been discarded in 1995 in favour of more limited powers. This development shall be discussed further below. First, we shall look at the existing statutory powers: guardianship and aftercare under supervision (ACUS).

9.5.2 Guardianship

Guardianship is seen as an alternative to compulsory admission to hospital and continuing hospitalisation (Department of Health and Welsh Office, 1999: para. 13.2). It can therefore function as both preventative care and aftercare. Guardianship is a concept that has long been known to mental health law. The basic idea is that a nominated person or body assumes responsibility for the supervision of a patient's care in the community, and, so the Code of Practice suggests (1999: para. 13.6), acts as 'advocate' in securing necessary services for the person subject to the guardianship order. As with admission to hospital under Part II, MHA 1983, however, the making of an order does not require the consent of the patient.

Under the Mental Deficiency Act 1913, 'idiots' and 'imbeciles' could be taken into guardianship, the effect of which was to give to the guardian the powers of a father over the person subject to the order. The MHA 1959 extended the scope of guardianship to cover mentally ill persons, but s. 34 of that Act maintained the formula whereby a person appointed as a guardian of a mentally disordered person enjoyed 'all such powers as would be exercisable by him in relation to the patient ... if he were the father of the patient and the patient were under the age of 14 years'. This would seem to mean, in so far as this issue was given any thought at the time, that a guardian might, amongst other things, consent to medical treatment on behalf of the mentally disordered person.

When the MHA was overhauled in 1983, the opportunity was taken to reword this infantising (and sexist) provision and specify the powers of a guardian with greater clarity and limitation. The White Paper that preceded the reforms of the early 1980s (Department of Health and Social Security, 1981: paras. 43, 44) rejected arguments that guardianship should permit treatment in 'the community' without consent (although these arguments have continued unabated to the present) and opted instead for a more restrictive 'essential powers' approach. Accordingly, the 1983 Act now provides that a guardian has three powers: to require the patient to reside at a specified place; to require that the patient attend at places and times for the purposes of medical treatment, education, occupation or training; to require that access to the patient is given to a doctor, ASW, or other person specified by the guardian (s. 8(1), MHA 1983). Whether these 'essential powers' do, in fact, contain the essentials of guardianship, which according to the Code of Practice 'is to enable patients to receive community care where it cannot be provided without the use of compulsory powers' (1999: para. 13.1) is at least debatable. It is accepted law that there is 'no power under the 1983 Act to give treatment to a mentally disordered person who withholds consent [or, presumably, who cannot consent] unless he is detained in hospital': *R v Hallstrom, ex p W (No. 2)* [1986] 2 All ER 306 (HC) per McCullough J at 313; see also *T v T* [1988] 1 All ER 613 (HC) at 617, per Wood J. In addition, the power to require attendance for treatment, and so on, is not supported with any power to take and convey the patient to the place in question, and although a patient may be absent from the place where he or she has been required to reside, is deemed by the guardian to be absent without leave and so can be returned by a social worker or police officer if apprehended before the expiry of the guardianship order or six months from the date first absent, whichever is the later (s. 18(3), (4), MHA 1983), there is no power to detain the patient at the place of residence in question.

If the purpose of guardianship is to give the guardian sufficient powers to ensure and require that patients accept treatment in order to obviate what would otherwise be a need for compulsory detention, then clearly the powers given by s. 8 of the 1983 Act are not sufficient for that purpose. Thus, in practice, the paradoxical situation is that, to be effective, these 'compulsory' powers rely on the cooperation, or at least absence of positive resistance, of patients. This is the first reason why guardianship under the 1983 Act failed to live up to expectations. The second reason is concerned with the criteria for the making of a guardianship order. It is open to a criminal court to make a guardianship order rather than a hospital order (s 37(1), MHA 1983), but this is infrequently done (12 times in 2004–5, although up from three in 2001–2: NHS Health and Social Care Information Centre, 2005: Table 1). Rather, guardianship orders are usually made under the civil powers contained in Part II of the 1983 Act. These largely mirror the requirements of admission for treatment under s. 3. Applications may be made by either an ASW or the patient's NR (s 11(1)), and must be founded on the written recommendations of two doctors. The requirements and limitations in ss. 11 and 13, discussed in Chapter 5 in relation to admission to hospital for treatment, also apply here, as does the initial time limitation of six months, and the pattern of renewal, with attendant medical reports (but no consultations) under s. 20(6). Differences are that it must be necessary for the patient's *welfare* (rather than, in s. 3(2)(b), his or her health or safety) that an application is made (s 7(2)(b)), which is a much broader concept, and there is no treatability test in s. 7. But, as with admission under s. 3, the patient must be suffering from one of the four specific forms of mental disorder (s 7(2)(a)), which incorporates into the criteria for admission into guardianship the requirements of s. 1 of the Act, namely that mentally impaired, severely mentally impaired, and psychopathically disordered persons are only eligible for guardianship if abnormally aggressive or seriously irresponsible conduct results from, or is associated with, the disorder in question.

This is not too much of a problem in practice, as far as psychopathy is concerned, because guardianship is rarely used for such patients (there were four new cases in England in 2004–5 – NHS Health and Social Care Information Centre, 2005: Table 1), but it means that the majority of persons with learning disabilities, for whom guardianship was designed, who are not normally aggressive nor irresponsible, are not eligible for guardianship. This, as Gunn (1986: 147) bluntly notes, is 'a mistake', which was poignantly underlined by the case of Beverley Lewis (Fennell, 1989). Nevertheless, in *Re F (Mental Health Act: Guardianship)* [2000] 1 FLR 192, the Court of Appeal confirmed that the criteria for the making of a guardianship order should be construed narrowly, and overruled the High Court, which had found that 'seriously irresponsible' behaviour was exhibited by a person who wished to leave her voluntary residential accommodation and return home against the advice of her carers (see further Sandland, 2000).

The third reason why guardianship has been used less than was expected before the passage of the 1983 Act is that it usually falls to local authority social services authorities to act as guardian (958 from a total of 966 cases in 2004–5, NHS Health and Social Care Information Centre, 2005: Table 1). Section 7(5) of the MHA 1983 provides that an application for guardianship must name the proposed guardian, who can be either a local social services authority or any other person (including the applicant, so that an ASW or NR can both make an application and act as guardian), but SSDs have a power of veto over an application naming any other person as guardian. It is also to the relevant SSD that an application for guardianship must be forwarded, within 14 days of the second medical recommendation: s. 8(2). Once an application for guardianship has been accepted by an SSD, whether or not it will actually act as the patient's guardian, it is required, under Part III, reg 13 of the Mental Health (Hospital, Guardianship and Consent to Treatment) Regulations. 1983, SI 893/1983 (as amended by SI 807/ 1997), made by the Secretary of State acting under the powers given in s. 9, to arrange for the patient to be visited by a doctor at least every three months, and by a s. 12-approved doctor at least once every year, in addition to carrying out the functions mentioned in s. 8.

If, as rarely happens, a private guardian is appointed, he or she will be under the supervision of the SSD, and must act in accordance with any directions that the SSD gives him or her, as well as appointing a doctor to oversee the patient's medical treatment, and keeping the SSD informed of any changes of address of the patient and doctor. An SSD or private guardian will also owe a common law duty of care to the patient. Persons subject to guardianship have much the same rights to apply to an MHRT as do other patients subject to Part II of the 1983 Act (s 66(1)(c)), which will entail a further layer of paperwork for all concerned (the Secretary of State's powers of referral in s. 67 are also applicable here). From the point of view of an SSD, it is easy to see how guardianship can be seen to carry all the burdens of compulsory admission to hospital but few of the benefits. Guardianship should not be used in isolation, but only as part of the broader, comprehensive CPA (Department of Health and Welsh Office, 1999: paras. 13.1, 13.4); in the majority of cases, it will be hard to demonstrate what the invocation of guardianship will add to the effective operation of a care plan.

There has been a noticeable increase in the use of guardianship in recent years: from 41 new cases in 1982–3 to 226 in 1992–3, to 372 in 1995 (Mental Health Act Commission, 1997: para. 8.8), rising to 540 in 2001–2, and peaking with 1,024 individuals subject to a guardianship order on 31 March 2002 (Department of Health, 2002b: Table 1).

Although falling slightly subsequently, there were still 966 persons subject to an order on 31 March 2005 (NHS Health and Social Care Information Centre, 2005: Table 1). For reasons that are not absolutely clear, the increase in the use of guardianship seems to have continued despite the introduction of the seemingly more attractive alternative of ACUS in 1996 (Mental Health Act Commission, 1999: para. 4.122). Most probably, this is because the two orders aim at different target populations: ACUS is aimed, in the main, at young, potentially dangerous, mentally ill (mainly schizophrenic) men; guardianship, by contrast, seems to be used as part of the care plan for, mainly, female patients of pensionable age having dementia or learning difficulties (Gordon, 1998). There are examples of its successful use with younger mentally ill persons, notably Andrew Robinson, who later went on to kill a member of staff whilst he was detained under s. 3. As in that case, however, an order is often allowed to lapse, or is not renewed, and is often a precursor to the provision of residential accommodation (Gordon, 1998); by comparison with the other powers in Part II, its use is still minimal. Not surprisingly, thought has long been given to recasting guardianship (Law Commission, 1995), but the Department of Health (1994) decided to wait until the impact of the introduction of aftercare under supervision (ACUS: see below) could be assessed. As mentioned above, ACUS proved to have little effect on guardianship, which now seems set to continue to play a part in any reformed mental health system. The same cannot be said, however, for ACUS itself.

9.5.3 From aftercare under supervision to supervised community treatment

There was a flurry of activity by the Conservative administration in the mid-1990s, concerned to be seen to be doing something about the (perceived) problem of inadequate legal powers to control the actions of dangerous mentally disordered persons in the community. Supervision registers were introduced in 1994 via Department of Health guidelines (NHS Management Executive, 1994), which required all HAs to ensure that providers of mental health services were contractually obliged to draw up, maintain and use supervision registers of patients most at risk of harm to self or others, as part of a broader mental health information system. Lowe-Ponsford *et al.* (1998) reported that, for a mixture of pragmatic and principled reasons, around half of the consultant psychiatrists in one health region felt that the registers should be abolished; and only one quarter of those surveyed felt that they should not. The picture nationally was uneven (Cohen *et al.*, 1996). The main reasons were that the additional paperwork outweighed any benefits of maintaining a register, and the point of the registers was somewhat oblique. In 1999, the Department of Health (1999a: para. 59) announced the abolition of supervision registers from April 2001, on the basis that, with the revamping of the CPA, they were now superfluous. From one point of view, supervision registers were tried and failed and there is little more to be said. From another point of view, the failure of supervision registers reveals the danger of building policy and practice on the basis of knee-jerk reactions to a small number of incidents and an overblown view of the risk to the public.

Swiftly following supervision registers, new powers to subject an individual, on leaving hospital, to continued supervision in the community in the form of ACUS were introduced by the Mental Health (Patients in the Community) Act 1995. These were designed to add teeth to the duty placed on HAs (and now PCTs), and SSDs, to provide aftercare under s. 117, MHA 1983. As discussed above, SSDs, in tandem with other agencies, are required to make and review care programmes and to appoint a 'care coordinator' who is primarily responsible for seeing that the requisite services are provided to patients in the community. Until the 1995 Act, however, the use of these services had been optional. The Royal College of Psychiatrists had been campaigning for a number of years for greater powers of control to be available for patients following discharge, arguing that patients who would be able to cope outside hospital if they could be forced to take necessary medication were being failed by a system that allowed total freedom from coercion until sectionable. It is this group of patients – often seen as being caught in the 'revolving door' by the original policy of the 1983 Act – that the 1995 reforms were primarily aimed at. As such, ACUS also had evident attractions for hospital managers who have to manage beds within a system that, as discussed in Chapter 3, is at breaking point.

On the other hand, there was resistance to greater powers of coercion outside of hospital from other quarters (Harrison, 1995), and the ECHR was thought by some to circumscribe measures that introduce compulsion without detention (Crichton, 1994). As a consequence, the 1995 Act is essentially a compromise that attempts to mollify both of these views (Parkin, 1996), and, like guardianship, stopped short of compulsory treatment in the community. The main feature of the 1995 Act is to add a degree of compulsion to the use of aftercare services provided under s. 117 for all those detained or liable to be detained in hospital (s. 25A(1)(a)) – except restricted patients, who have their own regime of conditional discharge (see Chapter 8) – by adding a number of sections to the MHA 1983 (ss. 25A–25J). Section 25D gives health and local authorities powers similar to those available under a guardianship order (see earlier), but with the significant additional power of conveyance to a place of residence, or a place for treatment (s. 25D(4)), using force, if necessary. The power to take and convey must be used only when it is appropriate to do so. Under the ECHR, as interpreted in *X* v *UK* (1981) 4 EHRR 188, it is lawful to arrest ('take') a person without a medical examination only where it would be impracticable to conduct one in an emergency situation. A period of ACUS lasts for six months in the first instance (s. 25G(1)), is renewable once for a further six months and thereafter annually, and, as with renewal of detention in hospital under s. 20, there is an elaborate procedure of examinations, consultations and reports required for the renewal of an order.

After a slow start (Knight *et al.*, 1998), the number of patients placed on ACUS has increased gradually (Davies, 2002). In 1997–8, only 318 applications were made in England (Mental Health Act Commission, 1999: para. 4.120). By 1999–2000, this had increased to 562; by 2004–5, to 643 (Government Statistical Service, 2006: Table 7). Nevertheless, given that the government estimated that there would be 3,000 patients suitable for ACUS (Department of Health, 1993d), these numbers are disappointing.

This is partly explained by the fact that s. 25B of the 1995 Act makes an application for ACUS – a bureaucratic process necessitating the coordination of various professionals – the responsibility of the RMO, constituting a substantial increase in the paperwork of RMOs in general psychiatric hospitals (Mohan *et al.*, 1998). Criteria similar to those used in s. 3 must be applied (see s.25A), although, compared with the terms of that section, the 'dangerousness' and 'vulnerability' criteria are here couched more narrowly: risks must be 'substantial' and harm must be 'serious', which means that the test for ACUS is harder to satisfy than the test for admission into hospital.

The RMO must also decide that ACUS 'is likely to help to secure' that the patient receives the services in question: s. 25A(4)(a), (b), (c). But, because there is no sanction for breach of the terms of ACUS, other than to 'consider' whether to detain the patient again (s. 25E, but this can only be done if the criteria for detention can be made out), it is not clear how ACUS can help, given that there should already be a care plan in place for each patient. It is little wonder that RMOs seem to have preferred to use s. 17 leave of absence, which not only allows them to bypass a significant amount of bureaucracy but also allows them to retain greater control over a patient in the community – because of ongoing liability to detention and the ease of using the procedure for recall to hospital (see Chapter 8) – than does ACUS. Section 3 of the 1995 Act extended the maximum period of leave under s. 17 from six months to a year, and, when the Court of Appeal in 1999 in *Barker* reinterpreted, and largely did away with, the limits on the use of s. 17 laid down in *Hallstrom* (see Chapter 8), the needs of psychiatrists for greater control of patients in the community had been substantially met.

The government, however, never gave up on the freestanding order for control in the community. The intention now is to abolish ACUS and replace it with what is to be called supervised community treatment (SCT) (Department of Health, 2006n). SCT will only be available for patients detained under s. 3 or by virtue of a hospital order without restrictions, but it will not be used routinely. Rather, it 'will address the specific problem where patients – who leave hospital – do not continue with their treatment, their health deteriorates and they require detention again – the so-called 'revolving door' (2006n: 1); 'Only people who would be a risk to their own health or safety or that of others if they did not continue to receive their treatment when discharged from hospital can be considered for SCT' (2006n: 2). Persons subject to SCT will have to comply with 'requirements . . . to ensure that they stay in contact with mental health services and practitioners can monitor them for signs of deteriorating health', although there are to be no powers to treat without consent outside hospital (*ibid.*). A refusing patient may, however, be recalled to hospital where 'clinically necessary' (*ibid.*). Requirements are likely to be concerned with contact with mental health professionals, compliance with treatment programmes, sometimes coupled with residence, although requirements must not amount to detention, if compliance with Art. 5(1) of the Convention is to be complied with (see *R* v *MHRT, ex p Secretary of State for the Home Department, PH* [2002] EWCA Civ 1868, discussed in Chapter 8).

It is not clear whether the use of the word 'recall' indicates that the section under which the patient was detained before being made subject to SCT continues to subsist after the patient leaves hospital (elsewhere, the document uses the word 'redetain'). If so, this would be a point of distinction between the SCT and ACUS, but would blur the distinction between SCT and s. 17 leave. There is an important point of principle at stake here: despite its relative lack of use, the 1995 Act was important because it marked the appearance of powers of compulsion over patients who were neither detained in hospital nor 'liable to be detained', such that it cannot be disputed that, at some level, ACUS marked a 'dispersal' of coercive powers. It was this that distinguished ACUS from s. 17 leave, and makes it fallacious to argue that ACUS did not mark any extension of the mental health system because powers of control, and to require treatment to be undertaken, outside of hospital already exist under that section. And it is not necessary to deny any benevolent intent behind the introduction of ACUS in order to argue that it is also an extension of the state's disciplinary powers: from a Foucauldian perspective, for example, benevolence is a key conduit for the spread of control. This is perhaps how one should interpret the findings of Knight *et al.* (1998) that, in one third of cases in which ACUS is used, an illegal requirement to accept medication *was* stipulated as part of the patient's care plan. If SCT is to be more akin to the situation of a detained patient on leave than it is to that of a discharged patient subject to extra controls after discharge, then, at some theoretical level, it marks a retreat in the march of the disciplinary state; if not, the same objections that were levelled at the introduction of ACUS, and at the two earlier versions of SCT, to be found in the now abandoned draft bills of 2002 and 2004, continue to apply.

In practical terms, however, there is little to distinguish SCT from ACUS. With SCT, as with ACUS, it will be for the patient's RMO (to be renamed clinical supervisor) to decide that SCT should be used, based on criteria similar to those that govern admission to hospital under s. 3 of the 1983 Act (2); any requirements to be placed on the patient must be agreed with the relevant approved mental health professional (AMHP) (the proposed replacement for the ASW), who must also provide a second opinion before any decision to recall a patient to hospital can be taken. The three-month rule, and the need for the CS to consult a SOAD, will apply to any drug treatment given as part of the package (which speaks of the reality that, although not legally obliged to accept treatment outside of hospital, patients must nevertheless agree to treatment as a condition of discharge); patients subject to SCT will have the same rights to apply to a tribunal as detained patients, with a specific right to apply if recalled to hospital for more than 72 hours and a SCT order will last for six months in the first instance, renewable annually thereafter.

It seems, to us, likely that SCT will be no more popular than ACUS, not least because, from the point of view of the RMO, it suffers with the same defects by comparison with leave under s. 17. Indeed, SCT imposes further limitations on the RMO because, unlike under s. 17, there will be 'clear criteria as to the circumstances in which people may be recalled to hospital for compulsory treatment' and 'The clinical supervisor must obtain a second opinion from an AMHP in order to redetain a patient'. It remains to be seen whether SCT, if and when introduced, does manage to tempt RMOs away from their preference for s. 17, but our best guess is that this is unlikely.

Finally, much of the criticism of the plans to extend control over patients in the community that attended both the introduction of ACUS and the publication of the draft bills of 2002 and 2004 was based on pragmatics rather than principle. For example, Tessa Jowell MP, speaking in the Parliamentary debates that preceded the 1995 Act, expressed concerns that the use of these powers of compulsion 'will damage community care – driving people from services rather than encouraging them to use them, especially if, as will be likely, supervisors try to get the police involved' (Hansard, HC, Vol. 264, Col. 1163, cited in Jones, 1999: 137). Similar concerns were voiced in 2002. The Royal College of Psychiatrists and the Law Society (2002: para. 8) described the plans for the medical treatment order (as it was then to be called) and treatment under compulsion in the community as 'ethically dubious and practically unworkable'. Liberty (2002: para. 24) argued that the proposal 'is likely to discourage cooperation; and to undermine if not destroy the therapeutic relationship in the community', thereby increasing rather than diminishing the risk to the public. In 2002, the objections of many, as Liberty (2002: para. 25) noted, are not to SCT in principle – the problem of the revolving-door patient is well recognised – but to the way in which the 2002 Bill abandoned the principle of reciprocity that featured so strongly in the Richardson Report, and posited a scheme that overemphasises control and has little to say about how the SCT would integrate with intensive community support services, or how such would be funded. We suggested in the last edition of this text that, if the government could address this point, opposition to the extension of powers of compulsion in the community would significantly lessen. The 2006 plans promise and require that 'An appropriate package of treatment and free support services will be put into place by the NHS and local authority social services before a patient leaves hospital on SCT' (Department of Health, 2006n: 2). If this is done, then, in truth, whether or not SCT comes into existence or ACUS is abolished is, perhaps, not such an important question as is commonly thought. The 'need' for such an order, after all, is perhaps more to do with (party) politics than risk management or clinical need (Eastman, 1997).

9.6 Concluding comments

The government's focus on increased powers of control in the community is unfortunate, firstly because it is unwarranted – as seen in Chapter 8, there are already significant powers to require treatment in the community through the use of s. 17 leave and conditional discharge. Equally important is appropriate and assertive outreach: help, not control. In this respect, there have been significant strides in recent years under the aegis of the National Service Framework, although this seems to have been at the cost of improvements waiting to be made elsewhere in the system. Secondly, although the White Paper of 1998 promised 'legislative powers which work with the grain of comprehensive local services' (Department of Health, 1998a: para. 2.24), and subsequently various measures to improve inter-agency cooperation have been introduced, the focus on control obscures the lack of proposals to reform the tangled legislative system for service delivery that, as documented earlier in this chapter, is at best, confused, and at worst, counterproductive.

This, in our view, is unfortunate. Community care, as far as entitlement to services is concerned, has become a lawyer's playground, and we will not be surprised if others cannot find their way through the 'maze of interacting statutory provisions', as the law was recently described by Lord Phillips MR in *R v Wandsworth LBC, ex p Spink* [2005] EWCA Civ 302, [2005] 1 WLR 2884, [2005] 2 ALL ER 954 at para. 1. Clements (1997) suggests that the focus of reform should be on philosophical consistency – the current swathe of legislation has substantial elements that reflect the post-war ideals of the Welfare State, which tend to disempower by responding to 'need' and giving over the definition of that concept to professionals, cut across with a number of more empowering provisions (for example, the Disabled Persons (Services, Consultation and Representation) Act 1986). The result is that the community care user is incoherently conceptualised by the current regime. The consequences of that incoherence, as this chapter has shown, are plain to see. It is hard not to suspect that the subtext of policy under the Conservative government was to shift primary responsibility for care in the community from the state to the families and other informal carers of mentally disordered persons (Lewis, 1989). The saving grace of the Labour administration's 1998 White Paper was that it claimed to reverse that trend, and to accept, on behalf of the community, that community care is the responsibility of us all, and of the state, and is not just a problem of individuals and their families. Yet its subsequent proposals do minimise the role of the family; for some, this evinces a preoccupation with the politics of risk, not the acceptance that risk is best minimised through effective, and sufficiently resourced, service delivery.

High-profile politics aside, it must be remembered that, although the system is a long way from perfect, it does work much of the time, particularly for learning-disabled clients. And there is little doubt that inter-agency working is better now than it was a decade, or even half a decade, ago. There have also been some welcome developments in the courts, enabling community care service users to access local authority housing stock via the community care legislation in some, albeit limited, circumstances. But, more often, the courts have proven to have greater concern for the economic and risk management concerns of central government and those who operate the system than they have for the rights of service users, as in the decision in *Barry* and the case law on the extent of the duties owed under s. 117 of the 1983 Act. Ultimately, community care law, policy and practice are about the way in which a community sees itself and its aspirations. It is, perhaps, understandable that this translates easily into a focus on control and public safety – but, *a priori*, this is to fracture 'community', positing the mentally ill as 'other'. It is worth reflecting on this: is this the system we want? Or is there another way?

10

Mental Capacity: Broad Issues and Basic Concepts

10.1 Introduction

Mental capacity, as distinct from mental illness, has so far been in the background of this book. There have been references to it, in the discussion of the *Bournewood* litigation in Chapter 4 and in the discussion of the treatment provisions, ss. 57 and 58 of the 1983 Act, in Chapter 7, for example, but the question of how capacity is to be determined, and the effects of a finding of incapacity, have been left largely unexplored.

Capacity determines both the authority of an individual to make a decision, and the legal responsibility for that decision. A patient lacking the capacity to consent to treatment for a specific physical ailment, for example, may sometimes be treated for that ailment notwithstanding his or her express objection to the treatment: he or she no longer has control over whether or not treatment will be given, and responsibility for the treatment will lie elsewhere. Precisely what happens when an individual is found incapable of making a decision will be discussed in some detail in Chapter 11, but the person lacking capacity, the individual most affected, will no longer normally control the decision. Absent a valid and applicable advance refusal of medical treatment, medical decisions will instead pass to a substitute decision-maker, who will be under a corresponding responsibility to decide in the patient's 'best interests'.

Capacity is a problematic topic for a book such as this. It cannot be omitted, because it so heavily overlaps, or is perceived so heavily to overlap, with the lives of the people with mental health problems; at the same time, it also concerns people who are not mentally ill in the conventional sense. Thus, a person affected by a severe stroke may lack mental capacity for a variety of decisions (see, for example, *Re S (Hospital Patient: Court's Jurisdiction)* [1995] 3 All ER 290 (CA)). While we would not expect such a person to be within the purview of mental health law as understood in the rest of this book, he or she is subject to many of the same legal provisions regarding incapacity. In addition, mental disability alone is insufficient to render an individual incapable of making decisions. People with mental disabilities, like all other adults, are presumed competent until shown to be otherwise: MCA 2005, s. 1(2); *Re C (Adult: Refusal of Medical Treatment)* [1994] 1 All ER 819 at 824; *Masterman-Lister v Brutton and Co, Jewell and Home Counties Dairies* [2002] EWCA Civ 1889. At issue, instead, is the ability to make the specific decision at issue. While characteristics of specific psychiatric conditions may enlighten that investigation, they in no way determine its outcome.

Investigation of the concept of capacity therefore overlays mental disability with a new set of criteria. The issues are substantively broader than much of the discussion in preceding chapters. Up to now, primary concerns have been confinement, medical treatment, and the mechanics of community care. Incapacity, by comparison, can be raised in a multitude of legal contexts. While particular attention will be given later to matters of current interest to mental health lawyers, this is an essentially arbitrary restriction. If the concern is capacity, why focus on these subjects rather than capacity to contract, to write a will, to marry, to consent to sexual activity, or to commit a tort or crime, particularly when these issues may also be of relevance to people with mental health problems? In deference to that wider relevance of capacity, this chapter includes an overview of some of the contexts and tests of incapacity – but this can only provide a flavour. For the relevance of capacity to specific legal contexts, students should have reference to texts and litigation in the specific area of law concerned.

The discussion of capacity covers the next two chapters. This chapter will provide an introduction to the sorts of test that might be used to determine capacity and the advantages and problems each entails, and it will discuss the possible ways in which decisions could be made for a person lacking capacity. Chapter 11 provides an introduction to the MCA 2005.

Before this discussion, a linguistic caveat is appropriate. There is a legal presumption of capacity: it is, in general, those claiming incapacity who have the onus of proving it (*Snook* v *Watts* (1848) 11 Beav 105). There are exceptions to this rule at common law. Those propounding a will may be required to demonstrate the capacity of the testator, if those challenging the will have put it at issue (*Battan Singh* v *Amirchand* [1948] AC 162 (JCPC)). Further, once incapacity of a certain type (such as contractual) is found, the onus will be on the individual alleging a return of capacity so to demonstrate (*Birkin* v *Wing* (1890) 63 LT 80). These are exceptions, however. The presumption of capacity needs to be stressed at this time, in part, because articulation of tests of capacity, including those below, tend to be phrased in terms of what is required for capacity to be found. As a matter of writing style, this does away with a considerable number of negatives and greatly simplifies sentence structures; it is misleading in so far as it suggests that capacity needs to be demonstrated. With the caveats above, it is instead for those who challenge capacity to prove its absence.

10.2 Legal structures of capacity

10.2.1 Property and affairs

Until 1959, the legal control of the property and affairs, as well as personal decision-making, of people lacking capacity was based on the role of the monarch as *parens patriae*, the father of the people. This ancient jurisdiction, codified at the beginning of the fourteenth century, gave the Crown the power and responsibility to manage the estates and persons of 'lunatics' and 'idiots'. Historically, the exercise of this authority was delegated by the Crown, usually to the Lord Chancellor, and then following the major court reforms of the late nineteenth century, to all High Court judges, assisted by a variety of administrative officers, including the Masters in Lunacy and the Lord Chancellor's Visitors. (For a summary of the history of this jurisdiction, see Bartlett, 2001a: 117–21.) A series of statutes commencing in the nineteenth century refined the power until 1959, at which time the MHA abolished it and placed both personal and financial guardianship on a purely statutory basis.

The jurisdiction in financial matters (or, more properly matters of 'property and affairs') was, for present purposes, preserved largely unchanged. It was brought forward into Part VII of the MHA 1983, and will remain in effect until the MCA 2005 comes into force. The same cannot be said of personal guardianship, to which the 1959 Act made fundamental changes: see below.

The result is that the financial aspects of incapacity have a long history, a history that has evolved rather than one that has been subject to sudden diversion. While the prerogative authority of the Lord Chancellor gave way to the statutory authority of Part VII of the MHA 1983, the statutory language of the test for intervention has remained largely unchanged. In 1853, the inquiry was whether the individual was 'of unsound mind, and incapable of managing himself or his affairs, at the time of the inquiry' (s. 47, Regulation of Commissions in Lunacy Act 1853; see also definition of 'lunatic' in s. 2). In the 1983 Act, the court is to intervene where 'after considering medical evidence, [it] is satisfied that a person is incapable, by reason of mental disorder, of managing and administering his property and affairs' (s. 94(2)). If the test is met, the Court of Protection takes control of the estate. While, a hundred years ago, the Lord Chancellor could appoint a person to be committee (pronounced with the emphasis on the first and third syllables) to handle the day-to-day management of the estate, Part VII of the MHA 1983 allows a receiver to be appointed to perform an analogous function (s. 99). Under the MCA 2005, a broadly analogous function will be performed by a 'deputy'.

Incremental development does not, of course, mean no development. At one time, the tradition was that those dependent on the incapacitated person would be made guardians of the person, because they had an interest in ensuring the continued good health of the incapacitated person; presumed heirs were instead given the role of committee, because they had an interest in appropriate frugality in the care of the incapacitated individual. That approach disappeared in the nineteenth century, and today, family members are frequently appointed as receivers irrespective of their presumed interests in the estate of the individual.

The effect of a finding of incapacity over property and affairs has also developed over time. At the beginning of the nineteenth century, a finding of lunacy did not necessarily preclude the individual from dealing with their estates, as, for example, by signing a relevant contract (*M'Adam* v *Walker* (1813) 1 Dow 148 at 177–8). A so-called lucid interval was always acknowledged to be a possibility, and contracts signed in such conditions were binding. That ceased to be the case with *Re Walker* [1905] 1 Ch 160: contracts signed by persons found incapable under the statute were void (see also *Re Beaney (Deceased)* [1978] 2 All ER 595 at 600). The result is that, throughout the twentieth century, the statutory process was, in general, an extremely blunt instrument: the individual either retained complete control over his or her estate, or forfeited all control. Unusually, for incapacity law, the finding was global, in so far as it affects all matters of property and affairs relating to the estate. This situation will change with the introduction of the MCA 2005. Under the new statute, an individual with capacity to make a specific decision regarding his or her property or affairs can do so; the statute expressly precludes a court-appointed deputy from making any decision that the individual has capacity to make: s. 20(1).

Clearly, not all those who may have difficulties caring for their estates have been under the control of Part VII of the Mental Health Act. For those that are not – and in any event, once the MCA 2005 comes into effect – issues may still arise as to the validity of contracts signed, gifts made, or other property dealings by those alleged to be lacking capacity. The rules here are notably different from those applying to those under Part VII of the MHA 1983. Incapacity in this context is decision-specific: inability to make one decision does not imply inability to make another decision. Further, the consequences of incapacity are different. Incapacity per se does not affect the validity of a contract. The contract can still be enforced by the second party unless that party knew, or ought reasonably to have known, at the time the contract was signed that the first party lacked capacity: *Imperial Loan Company* v *Stone* [1892] 1 QB 599. In that event, the contract will be voidable rather than void. In the event of a retrospective finding that the individual lacked capacity, the contract can be confirmed by the court: *Baldwyn* v *Smith* [1900] 1 Ch 588.

This provides a good example of how different aspects of 'capacity law' interact, and how they do not entirely meet in a coherent whole. Under the twentieth-century law, the legal status of the contract depended on whether an order had been made under what is now Part VII of the MHA 1983. There was no obligation on anyone to apply for such an order, and in that sense, the legal status of the contract seems to risk arbitrariness. There is, further, no obvious way that the other party to the contract would be aware of such an order, pivotal though it might turn out to be. The new statutory scheme will have some of the same tensions: determining the legal status of an action taken in the past is not necessarily the same as determining whether a substitute decision-making process will apply in the future.

Decisions regarding capacity therefore arise in specific litigation, on specific facts, throughout the legal system. Courts have often been coy in their definition of what needs to be shown as a matter of substance to find incapacity in contractual and similar matters. Up to the late nineteenth century, delusion was pivotal to the finding of incapacity (see Bartlett, 1996). Leonard Shelford (1847), in the leading mid-century legal treatise on lunacy, stated (at 42):

The absence or presence of delusion so understood, forms the true and only test, or criterion, of absent or present insanity. In short, delusion in that sense of it, and insanity, seem to be almost, if not altogether, convertible terms; so that a patient under a delusion, so understood, on any subject or subjects, in any degree, is, for that reason, essentially mad or insane on such subject or subjects in that degree.

If the individual was deluded on a matter relevant to the decision at hand, incapacity followed; otherwise, the courts might be hesitant to intervene, lest the merely eccentric lose their rights.

By the last few decades of the nineteenth century, this point of definition was being lost. *Jenkins* v *Morris* (1880) 14 Ch 674 provides a particularly startling indication of that move. The dispute revolved around the land of Thomas Price, who had believed his land to be impregnated with sulphur, and thus of limited value. He sold it to the defendant, Morris, at a price that would have been favourable had the land been polluted with sulphur, but which was, in fact, well under its real value. The statement of Jessel MR (at 683) shows a startling departure from the delusion standard:

[I]t is suggested that [the trial judge] should have told [the jury] that [Price] was not competent to manage this business unless he was free from delusions as connected with the farm in question, and that he was not free from those delusions because he thought the farm was impregnated with sulphur. I am not prepared to say that he was bound to tell the jury all that under the particular circumstances of this case; for it must be recollected that, although a man may believe a farm to be impregnated with sulphur and not fit for himself to live in, he may still be a shrewd man of business, and may even believe that the other side may not know of the impregnation of the farm with the sulphur, and that in consequence he may get a higher price for it than if it was known that it was so impregnated. He may have been perfectly right in his conclusion upon that subject, and the jury may have thought that it was so. The judge, in fact, says that he was a shrewd man of business.

The delusion went to the heart of the contract concerned, yet the court confirmed capacity. Indeed, the court allowed the possibility of the truth of the delusion, without inquiring into the facts surrounding either the land or the mental state of the vendor – a marked departure from the previous judicial approach. By the close of the twentieth century, language of delusion, which is at the basis of the case law upon which the modern edifice of capacity is built, is rarely used, although there can be little doubt that delusional beliefs will be relevant to a determination of capacity.

While there has been considerable retreat from the hard-line position of *Jenkins*, the courts have been more circumspect regarding how capacity is now to be assessed. The movement is from a test based on delusion to a test based on intellectual ability more broadly, away from simply the correct perception of facts at the basis of a decision, toward a standard of reasoning and analysis requisite to reach judgments. At the same time, there is no obvious acknowledgement in the courts of the changing use of the nineteenth-century language.

Indeed, there has been a marked hesitation about attempting overly to define the range of factors relevant to contractual capacity. In *Manches* v *Trimborn* (1946) 174 LT 344, Scott LJ held (at 345):

Therefore, if I were directing a jury, I should tell them that the degree of mental incapacity which the defence would have to establish to their satisfaction, was such a degree of incapacity as would interfere with the capacity of the defendant to understand substantially the nature and effect of the transaction into which she was entering. In some cases, criminal and testamentary, judges have felt able to give juries a good deal more assistance as to what faculties ought to be in question in determining responsibility for the commission of a crime, on the one hand, or for the making of a will, on the other hand; but I doubt if in a case of this kind, I could give the jury any further help than what I have already said.

That said, a few principles may be drawn.

Certainly, the individual must be able to understand the nature of the document and the parties. Some decisions also require the individual to understand the nature of the overall transaction, or the effect of the transaction on their estate more broadly. *Re Beaney (Deceased)*, for example, involved a gift by an old lady, near the end of her lifetime, of her house, her sole significant asset, to one of her children, with the effect that, at her death, there was little available for her other children. In the circumstances of the case, the court held that it was necessary that Mrs. Beaney understand more than that she was making a gift, that the subject matter of the gift was her house, and that the recipient of the gift was her daughter. It held that she also needed to understand that she was disposing of the bulk of her estate, and the effect that this would have upon the claims of the other potential beneficiaries under her will. Similarly, in *Manches*, it was held that the individual needed to understand not only that she was signing a cheque, and that this would involve the transfer of funds in the stated amount from herself to the payee, but also the essentials of the transaction of which the cheque was a part.

Incapacity to contract does not preclude an individual from making a will. Instead, capacity for this purpose will depend on ability to understand the document in question. Here there is a classic threshold test, defined in *Banks* v *Goodfellow* (1870) 5 QB 549 at 565:

It is essential to the exercise of such a power that a testator shall understand the nature of the act and its effects; shall understand the extent of the property of which he is disposing; shall be able to comprehend and appreciate the claims to which he ought to give effect.

The right to marry, interestingly, tends to be available for individuals with a lower level of capacity than the right to make a will. The courts seem content to emphasise that the contract of marriage is an easy one to understand, although it is necessary that the parties understand 'the responsibilities normally attaching to marriage': *In the Estate of Park* [1954] P 89 at 127; see also *Durham* v *Durham* (1885) 10 P 80; *Bennett* v *Bennett* [1969] 1 WLR 431 at 433; *Sheffield City Council* v *E* [2004] EWHC 2808)

The differential level of capacity between testamentary and matrimonial matters is surprising, because marriage revokes previous wills of the parties: s. 18, Wills Act 1837. The different capacities can, in turn, lead to ominous results. As with other contracts, marriages of those lacking capacity are voidable, not void, and are not open to challenge following the death of one of the parties. A clandestine marriage of an individual lacking capacity will thus be unchallengeable following the death of the incapacitated party. His or her previous will would be revoked by the supposed marriage, and the new spouse would acquire rights on intestacy (*Re Roberts (Deceased)* [1978] 1 WLR 653; *In re Davey* [1981] 1 WLR 165). This result seems an invitation for the unscrupulous to prey on wealthy persons of low capacity and poor health.

10.2.2 Personal decision-making

This history of personal guardianship is more complex, as the MHA 1959 made fundamental changes to the previous system. The *parens patriae* system was previously available to control the personal decision-making of people found lacking capacity, in much the same way that it had been used for decisions regarding property and affairs (Bartlett, 2001a). The indications are that it was only very seldom used, however. Much more significantly, the Mental Deficiency Acts of 1913, 1926 and 1939 allowed for statutory supervision and guardianship of persons under its purview. In 1955, there were 79,300 people under these systems of care (Royal Commission on the Law Relating to Mental Illness and Mental Deficiency 1954–1957, 1957: Table 15).

The 1959 Act changed the structure for these decisions. For decisions related to personal care, guardianship ceased to be based on capacity at all: *parens patriae* was abolished for people lacking capacity. Instead, guardianship could be imposed whenever the welfare of the patient required it: see Chapter 9. Guardianship also became available only for people with one of the four specific forms of mental disorder – mental illness, subnormality, severe subnormality or psychopathy. For those for whom guardianship was available, however, the 1959 Act left the authority of the guardian unchanged: the guardian had the authority over the incapacitated person possessed by a father over his 14-year-old child.

Court processes were no longer required for the commencement of guardianship, but only the relatively informal certification by two doctors and a social worker: see further Chapter 9. This removal of a role for the court can be understood as a part of the trend away from formal proceedings evident throughout the Percy Commission and the subsequent Act.

The 1983 Act restricted guardianship in two ways. First, the definitions of the mental subnormalities, now relabelled mental impairments, were narrowed for the Act as a whole. Not only is the person now required to be suffering from a state of arrested or incomplete development of mind, which includes impairment of intelligence, but that must, in turn, now result in 'abnormally aggressive or seriously irresponsible conduct.' (s. 1(2)) No matter the severity of their disorder, persons with developmental disorders are not eligible for guardianship unless this final condition is met, and recent litigation has held that this must be read restrictively: s. 1(2); see *Re F (Mental Health Act: Guardianship)* [2000] 1 FLR 192, discussed further in Chapter 2. The powers of the guardian were also limited. Under the MHA 1983, the guardian has only specifically enumerated powers: the power to require an individual to reside at a given place (but not to detain them there), to require that the individual attend at specific times and places for medical treatment (but not to consent to the treatment), and the power to require access to the individual to be given to a medical practitioner, approved social worker, or other person specified in the guardianship order (s. 8).

The result was perceived to create a lacuna in the law: no personal decisions could be made for people incapacitated for reasons outside the mental disability criteria in s. 1 of the 1983 Act, and outside the powers specifically enumerated in s. 8, no personal decisions regarding an incapacitated person could be made at all.

It is sometimes suggested that the *parens patriae* powers disappeared by inadvertence: see, e.g., *In Re TF (An Adult: Residence)* [2000] 1 MHLR 120 at 127, per Thorpe LJ. This is not a justifiable reading. Whether or not the legislative intentions were wise, there is no doubt that the legislature understood that the law of *parens patriae* was being abolished in 1959 in so far as it related to incapacitated adults, and it is similarly clear that the legislators were aware that the restriction of powers in 1983 would create a marked reduction in the decisions that could be made under guardianship. The view, at the time, was that guardianship restricted civil rights, rather than enhancing them. The White Paper that served as the basis for the 1983 Act commented that the 1959 powers were 'very wide, as well as somewhat ill-defined, and out of keeping, in their paternalistic approach, with modern attitudes to the care of the mentally disordered' (Department of Health and Social Security, 1981).

The development of the court's jurisdiction in this area has been largely reactive, and therefore lacks the overall coherence of a planned programme. The initial court decisions to deal with the guardianship gap involved consent to medical treatment. *F v West Berkshire Health Authority* [1989] 2 All ER 545 (HL) involved the sterilisation of an adult incapacitated by reason of developmental handicap. Surgical intervention without consent is, generally, a battery, and the question before the court was who could consent on F's behalf. A declaration of the courts was sought in advance of the surgery, to clarify the legal position. By extending the common law doctrine of necessity, the court held that the doctor was permitted to treat an incapacitated adult without consent, as long as the treatment was in the best interest of the patient.

F has since been applied in other contexts related to personal guardianship. Its closest parallel is *R v Bournewood, ex p L* (see Chapter 4), where the House of Lords again invoked the doctrine of necessity, per Lords Goff and Steyn. Because the question in *F* had been whether a battery would be committed by the doctors performing surgery on an individual unable to consent, so the question in *Bournewood* was whether the tort of false imprisonment would be committed by the facility by restricting the movements of a mentally incapacitated but compliant patient.

The subsequent case of *Re S (Hospital Patient: Court's Jurisdiction)* [1995] 3 All ER 290 concerned a Norwegian artist incapacitated by a stroke. Here, the dispute was whether his estranged wife or his current common law partner would make decisions about his personal care. The case concerned whether the common law partner had a sufficient interest in the case to have standing to commence an application before the court. The court held that she did, and in that sense, the case is significant. Unlike *F*, there was no suggestion that she herself would be directly liable for errors in decision-making about S. The case thus expanded the range of applicants to those personally concerned about the care of an individual, whether potential tortfeasors or not.

Prior to *S*, the courts had only provided advice as to whether a course of conduct would be tortious or otherwise illegal. *S* is sometimes read as establishing a new authority of the court to make apparently binding declarations in the best interests of a person lacking capacity. Whether the case bears that interpretation is a moot point – it actually restricts itself to the question of standing – but that step is clearly taken in *In Re TF (An Adult: Residence)* [2000] 1 MHLR 120. In that case, the court held that it was in the best interests of TF to live in local authority accommodation, and the local authority was given authority to exert such force on her as to keep her from harm's way. In *Re S (Adult Patient) (Inherent Jurisdiction: Family Life)* [2002] EWHC 2278, the court went to far as to hold that it could appoint a substitute decision-maker for a person lacking capacity.

The result was a much more expansive role for the court than merely determining whether a certain course of action would render a carer subject to civil or criminal penalty under existing law. In essence, it seems to have been a shift back to *parens patriae* in all but name. It is difficult to fault the sentiments behind the courts' actions: personal decisions do need to be made on behalf of people lacking capacity, after all. At the same time, the jurisprudential developments were open to criticism both doctrinally and practically (see Bartlett, 2005, ch. 1; Kennedy, 1997). The doctrinal basis for the development of what was, in essence, a new development was shaky at best. In its implementation, the new power was subjected to few safeguards. In the exercise of this new 'declaratory' jurisdiction, medical evidence was not necessarily introduced to substantiate incapacity (e.g., *A v A Health Authority and Anor, In Re J (A Child), R (S) v Secretary of State for the Home Department* [2002] EWHC 18). The sole criterion for decision-making was the best interests of the person lacking capacity, defined only by a 'balance sheet approach', comparing benefits and detriments of different courses of action: *Re A (Male Sterilisation)* [2000] 1 FLR 549. No express threshold of harm needed to be shown prior to the an order being made to remove a person lacking capacity from family care into institutional care: *Newham London Borough Council v S (Adult: Court's Jurisdiction)* [2003] EWHC 2278; *Re S (Adult Patient) (Inherent Jurisdiction: Family Life)* [2002] EWHC 2278.

For these reasons, the passage of the MCA 2005 is a welcome event. It provides a considered and coherent structure to the law surrounding personal decision-making on behalf of people lacking capacity and will be discussed in detail in Chapter 11. Whether it entirely ousts the jurisdiction of the court as it has been developed in the recent past is an open question (see Bartlett, 2005: 92–6), but it may certainly be hoped that it will be used for most personal decisions taken on behalf of those lacking capacity.

10.3 Tests of capacity

It is notable that the most developed analytic discussions of capacity come not from the legal literature, but from medics. Lawyers must approach this literature with some care. It is generally written in the context of consent to medical treatment, and may be difficult to apply to other areas of competency assessment. Nonetheless, it does provide a useful framework for what sorts of option are available to determine capacity.

10.3.1 Status approaches

It might be possible to say that all persons of a certain status are to be deemed incompetent. Laws relying on status tend to be unclear as to whether they are based on a presumption of incapacity in the status group, or a different social policy objective. Thus, it was until 2003 a crime for a man to have sexual intercourse with a woman who is mentally 'defective', or to engage in homosexual activity with men with severe mental handicaps: see s. 8, Sexual Offences Act 1956; s. 1(3), Sexual Offences Act 1967, now superseded by s. 30, Sexual Offences Act 2003. It might be asked whether the basis for these prohibitions is that the individuals concerned would be lacking the capacity to consent, or whether it is, instead, a different social policy against the sexual behaviour in question (see Carson, 1989a: 361). Similarly, as discussed in Chapter 7, involuntary patients in psychiatric facilities have no right to refuse most treatment in the first three months following their detention (MHA 1983, ss. 58(1)(b) and 63). Is this based on a belief that such patients would be unable to consent in any event, or are there other overriding policy considerations that would justify treatment over the objection of a competent patient in these circumstances? The justification of the Percy Commission for the use of compulsion suggests a considerable element of the former. The Commission takes as a starting point that people with mental difficulties ought to be able to receive treatment on the same basis as physical patients (Royal Commission on the Law Relating to Mental Illness and Mental Deficiency 1954–1957, 1957: para. 136):

But mental disorder has special features which sometimes require special measures. Mental disorder makes many patients incapable of protecting themselves or their interests, so that they if are neglected or exploited it may be necessary to have authority to insist on providing them with proper care. In many cases it affects the patient's judgment so that he does not realise that he is ill, and the illness can only be treated against his wishes at the time.

The Commission goes on to note, in addition, the potential risks that a patient's behaviour may create for society more generally, but the references to the patients' inability to protect the self and the patient's affected judgment may suggest that issues of capacity are, indeed, a part of its thinking. On that interpretation, confinement becomes not dissimilar to a status-based test of capacity.

The apparent advantage of a status-based test is its ease of administration, and the certainty of class membership that might go along with it. That, of course, depends on the status chosen. If the status were being involuntarily confined in a psychiatric facility, or indeed being a patient in a psychiatric facility, the line might be relatively clear. This would, however, throw the net too widely, because many people in these groups may be competent in all matters of legal concern. In addition, those lacking capacity to make a decision but not in the status group, would remain legally capable, and thus able to make decisions they *ex hypothesi* lack the capacity to make.

Selecting a more sensitive status such as 'severe mental handicap' would have similar problems that some people who might be expected to retain authority over decisions might lose that authority, and some who ought, perhaps, to be relieved of responsibility would keep it. In addition, that sort of standard would lack precise definition, making the apparent ease of administration largely illusory.

A status-based approach would be unlikely to prove acceptable as a test of capacity on any scale, in any event. As noted above, English law has long compartmentalised capacity. Where European jurisdictions may use a concept of judicial personhood to which many legal rights attach together, that has never been the English way. Capacity to contract has always been distinct from capacity to make a will, or to consent to medical treatment, for example. While this may make for some uncertainty vis-à-vis third parties, because a given individual may be competent for some decisions and not for others, it does have the advantage of ensuring that the individual retains as much freedom and control over his or her life as he or she is capable of exercising. For this reason, the Law Commission rejected any form of a status-based test of capacity (see Law Commission, 1995: 32). The rejection of such a test similarly corresponds to the experience of those who work with people with mental health or learning difficulties, that they may well be quite perceptive on some matters, but without capacity on others.

If status is not the appropriate way to go, mechanisms must be articulated to assess the individual choices that persons of marginal capacity make, to determine whether the decisions are to be respected. The following discussion presents a variety of alternatives. The overall categorisation relies to a considerable degree upon the classic paper of Roth *et al.* (1977).

10.3.2 Evidencing a choice

The ability to evidence a choice is considered a *sine qua non* for capacity. It is unusual as a criterion for incapacity, because the inability to evidence a choice may flow from physical rather than mental factors. Nonetheless, it is difficult to see how the intellectually competent intentions of an individual unable to communicate those intentions can be respected. The concern here, as relating to intellectual capacity, is that all reasonable efforts be made to ascertain any competent wishes. In particular, the distinction must be made between a person who is unable to evidence a choice, and one who acquiesces, who may be able to choose, but, for whatever reason, does not do so. It is not obvious, for example, whether the case presented by Roth *et al.* (1977: 280) to illustrate the evidencing of a choice standard is, under that standard, capable or not:

Case 1 A 41-year-old depressed woman was interviewed in the admission unit. She rarely answered yes or no to direct questions. Admission was proposed; she said and did nothing but looked apprehensive. When asked about admission, she did not sign herself into the hospital, protest, or walk away. She was guided to the inpatient ward by her husband and her doctor after being given the opportunity to walk the other way.

The individual was clearly compliant, but notwithstanding Roth's implication, it is not clear that she actually evidenced a choice. Note further that the individual apparently did, rarely, answer 'yes' or 'no' to direct questions. We are left to wonder about whether more sensitive interrogation of the patient's wishes would have demonstrated a clearer choice, and the degree to which the 'choice' was not a real choice, but flowed instead from the influence of those wishing to admit the patient.

Certainly, the ability to manifest a choice must be a *sine qua non* to capacity, but should any manifestation suffice? The English courts have occasionally nullified apparent choices by patients on the ground that they did not reflect such a 'real' choice. In *Re MB (Medical Treatment)* [1997] 2 FLR 426, the Court of Appeal held that a refusal based on a phobia regarding hypodermic needles did not evidence a real choice on the part of the patient. Similarly, in *Re T (Adult: Refusal of Treatment)* [1992] 3 WLR 782, for example, T refused a blood transfusion following a conversation with her mother, a Jehovah's Witness who opposed blood transfusions on religious grounds. T's own religious beliefs were not entirely clear, and she had shown no antipathy to the transfusion prior to the conversation. The refusal occurred in the context of an emergency: T's life was at risk following an unsuccessful caesarean section operation. In this context, the refusal was held not to constitute a real choice on the part of T, but instead smacked of the undue influence of the mother. Significantly, doctors 'encouraging' patients to consent to treatment does not come under similar scrutiny. The difficulty here is that to divide it from 'true' choice, 'untrue' choice requires a set of criteria, and thus a more ornate test of capacity such as those discussed below.

While it is difficult to criticise the evidencing of a choice as a necessary condition for capacity, ought it to be a sufficient condition? Such a position is not without its advantages: it would, after all, be inexpensive and easy to administer. Ought any decision that can be articulated by an individual be respected? Buchanan and Brock (1986: 32–3) provide a rather pointed criticism of the standard:

This standard respects every expressed choice of a patient, and so is not, in fact, a criterion of *competent* choice at all. It entirely disregards whether defects or mistakes are present in the reasoning process leading to the choice, whether the choice is in accord with the patient's conception of his or her good, and whether the choice would be harmful to the patient. It thus fails to provide any protection for patient well-being, and is insensitive to the way the value of self-determination itself varies with differences in people's capacities to choose in accordance with their conceptions of their own good.

Typical of many modern commentators, Buchanan and Brock equate capacity with the reasoning process to reach a decision, a view that will be reflected in the remainder of the criteria discussed below. Yet why should this be the case? Law and society respect the manifestly irrational decisions of people whose capacity is not called into question. Thus people with cancer may refuse treatment on the manifestly unfounded basis that they do not believe the doctor's diagnosis, and people are permitted to engage in spending sprees or expensive and frivolous hobbies entirely beyond their means. The rationality of some of these decisions is highly dubious, yet they are respected; on what basis should some irrational decisions be respected, and not others? This question will circulate through all of the discussions of capacity below. There is often, in the case law, an implied expectation that those of marginal capacity should justify their eccentricities more than those whose capacity is not in doubt; it is not clear why this should be so (see Carson, 1993: 314–6).

Buchanan and Brock argue that the decision might be at variance with the individual's conception of his or her good. Their point here does not represent paternalism according to the values of an outside source such as a doctor; it is instead that the use of the standard is somehow inconsistent with the individual's *own* view of his or her own good. This is a complex statement that warrants unpacking: to begin with, it presupposes a specific vision of self-determination. Margaret Somerville posits various definitions of self-determination and autonomy (1994: 185–8). In one, simple, version, self-determination means no more than the ability to register a choice, again rendering a concern about self-determination in the current context circular. Other definitions centre on a more developed notion of the individual as a person, a 'self' in the philosophic sense. Such a higher standard is required in the analysis of Buchanan and Brock, who require as a basis for capacity that the individual have 'a set of values or conception of the good' (1986: 25). Various questions flow from this.

To begin with, is it necessarily obvious that the simple version of self-determination is to be avoided in all cases? The removal of decision-making authority from the individual may have its own costs, both to third parties in the form of assumption of responsibility, and to the individual, in terms of loss of self-respect and the respect of others. Can these costs not sometimes outweigh the benefits? To pick an extreme example, would the simple ability to manifest a choice not be a perfectly acceptable system to decide what sort of sandwich a person will eat for lunch? If it is acknowledged that loss of the decision-making authority per se has its costs, should some decisions not merely be left where they are? This would suggest that the nature or seriousness of the decision might have a role to play in the standard of capacity applied to it.

A more complex meaning of autonomy raises theoretical difficulties, since it implicitly or explicitly imports a notion of a 'self', with a variety of characteristics. These characteristics will almost certainly be value-laden – in much the same way as was discussed regarding the 'rational' subject above – and much of the discussion of the remaining conceptualisations of capacity will involve defining some of those characteristics. Here, the point is instead to question the appropriateness of relying on that sort of concept. The question becomes not only whether a concept of the self should be required, but also which self. One view would allow paternalistic intervention as a justified displacement of personal autonomy when the latter would 'frustrate the exercise of choices, which are part of the individual's attempts to pursue his own conception of how to live.' (quoted in Fennell, 1990: 29). The difficulty here is to ascertain when the 'conception of how to live' is crystallised. As people progress through their lives, including those parts of their lives in which they are to some degree disabled, expectations of what constitutes a good or acceptable level of life may change. Adoption of a more complex standard of self may imply a tendency to privilege the views of the patient when he or she had been of robust capacity, and to marginalise the views of the patient when capacity becomes marginal.

In a testamentary context, there is some support in the case law for this approach, particularly when the will is executed shortly before the death of the testator. Thus *Harwood* v *Baker* (1840) 3 Moore 282 involved a will that left the testator's entire estate to his second wife, disinheriting the remainder of his family. The testator was held to be incompetent to execute the will, on the basis that he had not shown an antipathy to these relatives when his capacity had not been in doubt. (at 313–4). Similarly, in *Battan Singh* v *Amirchand* (above), a will, leaving the testator's estate to two friends who had apparently cared for the testator, was disallowed, preferring a will leaving the estate to nephews living on another continent and seen only infrequently, who had been the beneficiaries of an earlier will. While the testator did know the scope of his estate, his prior views as to who should receive the benefit of it held sway.

Certainly, the views of the individual when competent may affect the appropriate decision to be taken when he or she has lost capacity, but it is much less obvious that the fact that a person's views change over the course of time somehow indicates incapacity. If capacity is to be determined with reference to a 'self', it is fair to ask what self that is, the self of robust earlier days, or the self that is progressing through infirmity. It is not obvious that the answer to that question needs to be the same for all decisions. Should wills be subject to a different test than, for example, treatment to which the patient would have consented in earlier times, but now refuses? The use as the criterion of capacity of mere ability to evidence a choice privileges the existing self to the exclusion of all previous personal characteristics. That is one unambiguous solution to the problem; the versions that follow provide others.

10.3.3 'Reasonable' outcome of choice

Where the previous standard of capacity was based on the mere ability to make a choice, this version assesses capacity on the basis of the outcome of the choice. In theory, it is an objective test: could the reasonable person have reached the decision of the individual in question, in the circumstances in question? This is no more a test of 'capacity' or 'competency' than the previous test, however: reasoning ability does not enter into the equation, nor, at least not expressly, do the reasons for which the choice was made. Here, again, the problem of the right to irrational or wrong decisions enters the picture. It is nonsensical to claim that people may do irrational things with their money, or refuse life-saving treatment for whatever reason they choose, if, when their capacity is called into question, the irrationality of the decision is precisely what will render the individual incapable of making the decision.

Nonetheless, there is a persistent set of claims that this standard is used frequently in practice. Physicians, for example, are alleged often to be content to treat a patient as competent as long as they are accepting treatment, but that the patient will be treated as incompetent if treatment is refused (see, e.g., Law Commission, 1995: para. 3.4; Gunn, 1994: 16; Roth *et al.*, 1977: 281).

Doctors are by no means the only culprits here, however. While courts do not, at least officially, judge capacity simply on the objective reasonableness of the individual's choice, there is precedent for the application of different standards of capacity, depending on the decision reached by the allegedly incompetent person. This was the approach in *Evans* v *Knight and Moore* (1822) 1 Add 229 (at 237–8):

[W]here a mental aberration is proved to have shown itself in the alleged testator, the degree of evidence necessary to substantiate any testamentary act depends greatly on the character of the act itself. If it purports to give effect only to probable intentions, its validity may be established by comparatively slight evidence. But evidence, very different in kind and much weightier in degree, is required to the support of an act which purports to contain dispositions contrary to the testator's probable intentions, or savouring, in any degree, of folly or frenzy.

Here, the will was 'precisely such a disposition as natural affection would dictate' (at 238), apparently an objective test, and the will was unsurprisingly upheld. More recently, Bernard Dickens has claimed that the common law similarly varies the standard of consent in a medical context, depending on whether treatment is consented to or refused (1994: 287). In practice, courts are extremely hesitant to allow a finding of capacity when the result will be that recommended medical treatment will not be provided: see further below. Certainly, notwithstanding their protestations to the contrary, the judicial decisions do often seem at pains to explain that such 'irrational' decisions may not be so irrational after all, if they are to be upheld: see, for example, *Re B (consent to treatment: capacity), sub.nom B (Adult: Refusal of Medical Treatment), Re B V NHS Hospital Trust* [2002] EWHC 429, [2002] 2 ALL ER 449, [2002] 1 FLR 1090.

Certainly, one can see the logic of the standard of capacity varying in proportion to the complexity of the decision; this will indeed be implied in the standards that follow. In so far as 'irrational' decisions have more complex ramifications than socially approved decisions, an assumption that may or may not be true, a higher level of capacity would often be expected of the former decisions. The approach of the courts in cases such as *Evans* would appear to be quite different: the issue is not the complexity of the decision, but the agreeableness of its outcome.

At issue here, then, appears to be a range of social factors, quite independent of the abilities of the individual. The testamentary cases appear to support Victorian ideologies of the family and inheritance of wealth; the medical cases appear to support the desirability of medical treatment. This begs the question of whether capacity is an appropriate mechanism to enforce what are effectively social policy goals. If the objective is to re-enforce specific doctrines of the family, it is not obvious why only those of marginal capacity should be subject to the policy, while those clearly possessing capacity enjoy greater freedom to leave their estate to whom they choose. If the objective is to ensure that specific forms of treatment are carried out, it is not obvious why only those of marginal capacity should lose the right to refuse them. In essence, if a specific outcome is worth enforcing, why is it worth enforcing only for those of marginal capacity, rather than through intervention that would affect all in society?

That is not, of course, the same question as the severity of impact of the decision. Ought different standards of capacity apply for decisions that will affect the individual differently? It was posited above, for example, that the social costs of an incapacity finding may outweigh the benefit of such a finding, so that, in some situations, the mere ability to evidence a choice may be an appropriate standard of capacity. That is, in its way, a result-oriented test, because the ramifications of a decision either way by an individual of low capacity are viewed as sufficiently small to be outweighed by other social factors. How far should the law go, down this road?

Roth *et al.* (1977: 283) propose a system under which the test of capacity would vary with the risk–benefit ratio of proposed treatment. Thus treatments of high risk and low benefit would require minimum capacity to refuse, just as treatments of high benefit and low risk would require minimum capacity to consent. Consenting to the former, or refusing the latter, would require a higher standard of capacity. The difficulty here is that the risks and benefits are likely to be assessed by the doctor, and may or may not reflect the patient's priorities.

10.3.4 **Rational reasons approach**

This version of capacity assesses aspects of the reasoning process itself, insisting that the individual reach a decision based on rational reasons. It is thus, to begin with, expected that rational processing of information to reach a rational conclusion will occur: those with, for example, severe affective disorders may be found to lack capacity on that ground alone. The decision may also be found to be irrational if the reasoning process is founded in mental disorder. This approach thus begins to look at the quality of the decision-making process, rather than simply at the outcome of the process.

The case law does occasionally expressly reflect the rational reasons test. Certainly, there is a tendency to insist on the ability to manipulate information in a rational way for a finding of capacity to be made. *Jenkins v Morris* (see above) presents a particularly clear example of a rather pure form of the test: the concern of the court in that case involved the ability of the vendor of the land to reason, based on the apparently incorrect belief that his land was impregnated with sulphur; the focus on the vendor's abilities, the court's view that he might be a 'shrewd man of business', suggests a focus on his abilities. He would fairly clearly not have sold his land in this fashion, however, but for the mistaken belief in the pollution of the land. If this belief were the function of a mental disability, the wrong result would seem to have been achieved by the test.

For this reason, the tendency in recent years has been to attempt to consider irrational reasoning processes based in the mental disorder. The approach has been to examine the reasoning process with reference to the ethical framework of the individual during their life, prior to their capacity being called into question. This is, of course, only a partial answer to the problem, because it still looks to the process, rather than the information upon which the process is based. The veracity of the information is discussed in other approaches to incapacity, below.

Other problems of this approach will now be obvious. It may well be the case that the individual in question was never of unquestioned capacity, in which case, the approach cannot apply. Alternatively, once again, this would expressly privilege a version of the individual's 'self' frozen at a specific point in the past to the prejudice of any legitimate personal progress or change since that time. Consider a decision of an ageing individual, apparently based on religious grounds, when previously the individual had not been a believer: the development might well be the product of a mental abnormality; at the same time, many people apparently develop religious beliefs later in life, and it would be inappropriate to deprive those of marginal capacity of that rather common experience. The problem is how it will be determined which of these is the case. Here, again, there would appear to be the risk of an objective, result-based test: if the behaviour were that of a reasonable believer, it might be allowed – but then, what constitutes 'reasonableness' of religious belief?

A more fundamental complication going to the heart of the test is that a number of factors used by most people to make decisions are simply not rational in any real sense. Few 'rational' individuals would not be frightened of invasive medical treatment, for example. If this were to weigh into the decision made by the marginally capable person, would it be a point against the decision in this model, notwithstanding that it would equally be a factor in the decision of a person of unquestioned capacity?

10.3.5 Ability to understand

This articulation focuses on the capacity to understand and reason. As such, it bears some similarity to the rational reasons test, but where that test was interested primarily in distinguishing 'true' views from those affected by a mental disorder, this test does not centre on that distinction, but rather directly on the cognitive performance of the individual. Because this test focuses on cognitive ability in preference to outcome, it thus acknowledges that the person with capacity may choose to make irrational or unwise decisions. The test is based on the view that an individual who has the relevant reasoning ability should have authority to choose as they see fit.

At least in theory, this may be divorced from the actual information upon which the decision in question is to be made, as long as the level of understanding is such that the individual would have sufficient understanding to make the decision. In practice, because the test is likely to involve a determination of capacity regarding a specific decision, some reference to that context may occur – but not necessarily. The medical profession, in particular, has developed a variety of apparently objective tests to judge reasoning and understanding ability.

There are a wide variety of these tests, of which the 'mini mental state examination' and the Wechsler scales – particularly the Wechsler adult intelligence scale (WAIS) – are the best known. The tests employ a variety of methods. The mini-mental state examination, developed in 1975, is a short test, taking roughly five to ten minutes to administer. It purports to test the individual's spatial and temporal orientation, their attention and calculation abilities, their recall, and their linguistic capacity. In practice, it involves the individual in: answering a variety of questions relating to date, time, and place; repeating three objects named by the assessor, counting forward by sevens (or spelling 'world' backwards); following simple oral or written commands, writing a sentence and copying a design of interlocking pentagons (Folstein *et al.*, 1975). The Hopkins competency assessment test, designed specifically for medical capacity, takes a slightly different approach, where questions are answered that relate to essays read aloud to the individual. The essays relate to informed consent to medical treatment, and are written to varying degrees of difficulty (Janofsky *et al.*, 1992). Other tests use vignettes about specific treatment situations, about which the individual is quizzed regarding recall and assessment of relevant information (see, e.g., Marson *et al.*, 1995).

The argument in favour of this sort of test is that it moves away from the judgment of an individual assessor as to the value of the decision in question. The risk of standards based on assessment of relevance of information in the specific situation in which the decision is to be made is that the person assessing capacity may lack objectivity. Thus doctors recommending treatment presumably want, in good faith, to give the treatment, believing it to be to the benefit of the patient, and reasons for refusing treatment risk being perceived as lacking capacity. Tests based on ability allow assessment divorced from these professional values. These tests at least purport to be objective.

This very objectivity is equally the difficulty of the tests. The mini-mental state examination, perhaps the most frequently used of this sort of test and strong on objectivity, provides an illustration. The difficulty is that, while it may measure cognitive function, it is at best difficult to see how the cognitive function correlates with capacity. As discussed above, capacity is determined with reference to specific decisions, and incapacity in one context does not necessarily imply incapacity in another. The questions on the mini-mental state exam are divorced from all of these contexts: is it really possible that the ability of an individual to make a will, or to consent to medical treatment, or both, is appropriately judged on the basis of their ability to count upwards by sevens, or to copy a design of intersecting pentagons? Such tests may be relevant to identify particular cognitive difficulties that may, in turn, be relevant for some capacity determinations, but it is difficult to see that they can be central to the analysis.

Further, care must be taken in this form of testing to ensure an absence of hidden bias. The mini-mental state exam, for example, requires the individual both to read and to write a sentence. A person who is illiterate will thus be prejudiced on the test, for reasons entirely divorced from their capacity. Similarly, persons confined for an extended period of time may lose track of the day or month, or indeed even of seasons, if they are unable to go outside the institution, where these matters become significant. In this context, the test appears particularly problematic, because it would be measuring not cognitive ability, but instead the adverse effects of institutionalisation.

The approach of reading a paragraph and questioning the individual on the information seems more satisfactory – but it, too, can be seen as problematic. Do people actually respond to or understand hypothetical situations in the same way as they do their own lives? In addition, the vignettes or essays tend to focus on specific factual contexts: generally capacity to consent to treatment. How much assistance will they be outside the area for which they are designed?

The introduction of fact situations also begins to introduce some of the subjective issues that the tests were otherwise to exclude. Consider a patient with a religious objection to blood transfusions discussing a hypothetical vignette about a patient to undergo heart surgery. The importance of avoiding a blood transfusion would not be an answer suggested by the vignette in response to a question about the desirability of treatment, but the individual may well mention it in this case. The vignette approach appears to assume a closed universe of information, and it is not obvious how it accounts for information imported by the person being tested.

Even these tests present difficulties in application to specific decisions made by specific individuals. It is not merely that the test will be of limited application outside of its subject area; it is also unclear how well or badly one must do on a test for a resultant finding of incapacity. Here, the test developed by Marson *et al.* (1995) deserves special note, because that test does attempt to include a variety of thresholds into one instrument. While an interesting approach that may lead the way to testing that is more sensitive to varying standards, it is nonetheless problematic. Different decisions require different degrees of capacity, even within a single subject area: incapacity for one contract or one treatment does not mean incapacity for all. It is difficult to see how statistical scores that are validated according to one set of objective vignettes can take account of capacity when the decision in question may vary considerably from that portrayed in the vignette.

All of this would seem to indicate a pressure to assess capacity in the context of the actual decision that occasions the determination of capacity. This does not, at least in theory, mean a departure from a standard of *ability* to understand. This distinction is drawn particularly in the gloss of Stuart-Smith LJ on s. 57(2)(a) of the MHA 1983, where the language reads 'capable of understanding' and not 'understands'. Thus the question is capacity and not actual understanding: *R* v *Mental Health Act Commission, ex p X* (1988) 9 BMLR 77 at 85. In cases where, for example, capacity to make a will is contested after the death of the testator, ability to understand may well be determined according to whether the deceased must have been able to understand the required material for the testamentary disposition in question, based largely on circumstantial evidence, because there may be no evidence of his or her *actual* understanding of the material. Nonetheless, the move to a focus on the specific situation will often mean that the ability to understand collapses into the actual understanding of the individual.

10.3.6 Actual understanding

This test focuses on the actual understanding of the individual at the time the decision was made, about the actual decision itself. It has a concreteness that ability to understand lacks. Roth *et al.* (1977: 282) make this point as follows:

Unlike the ability-to-understand test, in which the patient's comprehension of material of a certain complexity is used as the basis for an assumption of comprehension of other material of equivalent complexity (even if this other material is not actually tested), the actual understanding test makes no such assumption. It tests the very issues central to patient decision-making about treatment.

The move away from the ability to understand in the abstract does, of course, have its difficulties. By placing the assessment back in the context of the specific decision, it reintroduces the pressures related to that decision into the capacity assessment. As was the case with the rational reasons approach, the risk is that a failure to decide in a specific way may be thought to indicate incapacity: if the decision is unexpected or perceived as inappropriate, the individual *must* have misunderstood the situation.

It further places an onus on the person doing the assessment to ensure that appropriate information has been given to the individual prior to the assessment of capacity being made. This may be relatively unproblematic in some contexts: doctors are already required to explain treatments to patients prior to performance of the treatment, for example. If the patient understands, they are competent and such an explanation would have been necessary in any event; if not, all that is lost is some of the doctor's time. If the individual is dead, however, as will be the case for a contested will, it may well be difficult to determine whether a lack of knowledge flowed from a lack of understanding, the test for capacity here, or a failure by those surrounding the individual to make information about the estate available to the testator.

Under this standard, the individual clearly needs to understand the information relevant to making the actual decision in question. But do they need to believe it? The nineteenth-century tradition was very much in the affirmative: decisions based on delusions were at the core of incapacity (Bartlett, 1996). Particularly if the temptation to use the fact of an 'inappropriate' decision to indicate a lack of understanding is resisted, the standard of actual understanding may still be met if the decision were to have been made under a delusion. The way in which understanding has been defined in the previous sections, after all, is based largely on abstract information, and the ability to manipulate it. Even in the test of actual understanding, the question is whether an individual is actually aware of relevant material and able to manipulate it. There is no obvious requirement that the individual *believe* the information in question; this is the problem addressed by the next test, appreciation.

10.3.7 Appreciation of information

Appreciation of information is the test proposed by the Law Commission in its 1995 proposals on mental capacity, and incorporated into the MCA 2005. Under this test, individuals will lack capacity if they are 'unable to make a decision based on the information relevant to the decision, including information about the reasonably foreseeable consequences of deciding one way or another or failing to make the decision' (Law Commission, 1995: 39; see also MCA 2005, s. 3(4)). This suggests not only a minimum level of ability to understand information, but also that the individual must be able to use that information, including information about the probable consequences of a decision one way or the other, as the basis of his or her decision. It is nonetheless clear that the individual need not exercise his or her judgment prudently: an unwise decision will not mean that an individual lacks capacity (1995: 39–40; MCA 2005, s. 1(4)).

The influence of this standard can be seen in many areas of English capacity law. It is, perhaps most clearly, present in the context of consent to medical treatment, where it is implied in the requirement that a patient be able to weigh information in the balance to arrive at a choice: see *Re C (Adult: Refusal of Medical Treatment)* at 295; *Re MB (Medical Treatment)* at 437. It is also present by implication in much of the remainder of English incapacity law. Thus for testamentary capacity, *Banks v Goodfellow* required that the testator understand 'the nature of the act *and its effects*', and also 'to comprehend and appreciate the claims to which he ought to give effect': (1870) 5 QB 565, emphasis added. The failure to realise that signing a will would, for example, disinherit a child, and perhaps to understand the relative needs of children for a share in the estate, would thus render the will invalid. This was certainly the result in *Re Beaney (Deceased)* (see earlier), in which it was held that capacity to make a gift of the sole major asset of the donor, as the donor approached the end of her life, required not only that she was making a gift and that the recipient of that gift was one daughter, but also that the gift would effectively deny the donor's other children a share in her estate. In *In the Estate of Spier (Deceased)* [1947] WN 46, a man was held not to have the capacity to marry, because while he certainly knew that he was going through a ceremony of marriage, he 'was lacking in a proper capacity to take care of his own person and property, and that the very nature of the disease was such as to act towards incapacitating him from deciding whether his own health justified him in taking this very important step'. In this formulation, although not in some of the others regarding capacity to marry discussed above, the expectation that capacity to marry will involve understanding of the property ramifications and consideration of one's health suggests a much more sophisticated standard of capacity than merely understanding information; it suggests a standard more analogous to appreciation.

The standard raises various sets of problems. One will now be familiar: the expectation that a decision will be based on specific criteria, requiring acknowledgement of specific future results of the decision, risks privileging one set of criteria over others. For example, the individual might be thought incompetent, because they are failing to give adequate concern to the fact that they might die without the treatment, or, more controversially, that a foetus might cease to be viable unless the potential mother is treated. Such cases will be considered below, in the context of consent to medical treatment, but the problem is not necessarily confined to medical issues. The application of a standard based on appreciation to testamentary matters, for example, would seem to make it relatively difficult for a person of marginal capacity to disinherit someone. It is, perhaps, possible to minimise this risk by interpreting the test to allow the individual to weight criteria as they wish, as long as he or she acknowledges the possible result. Nonetheless, there is a real potential that the criteria be used for ends not relevant to capacity itself. Another familiar problem concerns how one is to determine how much of the lack of appreciation is the result of an inability to appreciate, a skill that the medical tests discussed above do not measure, and how much a problem of information not being provided, or not provided in an accessible form.

An additional problem is simply whether this approach sets the standard of capacity too high: what level of specificity is expected for the understanding of future ramifications of deciding in various ways? The reality is that people of robust capacity may make decisions quickly, or for reasons that ignore longer term effects. Does a standard that requires appreciation of these factors require decisions of marginally capable people that are of higher standard than those of unquestioned capacity? The higher the standard, the more people will fall outside it. The standard of appreciation is sufficiently high that it does not tend to occur in the medical literature; is it therefore a standard that is too high for at least some legal contexts?

10.4 Capacity in context

As noted at the beginning of this chapter, the law presumes that all adults, including those with mental disabilities, have capacity to make decisions: incapacity must be demonstrated. The presumption of capacity for those with mental health difficulties is not a legal fiction: it reflects the actual abilities of a majority of psychiatric patients. The MacArthur treatment competence study set out to measure capacity of newly admitted inpatients in psychiatric facilities in three American cities (Applebaum and Grisso, 1995; Grisso et al., 1995a; Grisso and Applebaum, 1995b). Patients with schizophrenia were tested, along with those with major depression. There were two control groups. The first was drawn from the population living in the communities served by the facilities, but without psychiatric histories. This allowed control based on socio-economic factors. A second control was drawn from a population hospitalised for a purely medical problem, ischemic heart disease (angina), to allow a control based on the possible effect of hospitalisation upon capacity. A variety of measures were used to assess whether the patients could understand treatment disclosures, whether patients could perceive, acknowledge and understand their disorder, and whether they were able to think rationally about proposed treatments. These are recognisable as pivotal concepts in the assessment of capacity, discussed earlier in this chapter.

The findings of the MacArthur study (Grisso and Applebaum, 1995b) make very interesting reading. The study did find that patients with mental illness scored less favourably, as a group, on the tests of understanding, appreciation and reasoning than did the physically ill and community controls. This was due largely to relatively poor performance by some schizophrenic patients, a group tending to manifest more severe symptoms. They were at pains to point out (1995b: 169) that this result could not, however, be applied indiscriminately to individual people with schizophrenia:

Even so, on any given measure of decisional abilities, the majority of patients with schizophrenia did not perform more poorly than other patients and non-patients. The poorer mean performance of the schizophrenia group for any particular measure was due to a minority within that group.

In concrete terms, roughly a quarter of the schizophrenic group showed impaired performance on each of the particular tests assessing understanding information, appreciation and reasoning. Roughly half of the group of schizophrenic patients showed impairment on at least one of these tests. For the depressed patients, impairment on the individual tests ranged from about 5 to 12 per cent, and just under a quarter showed impairment in at least one of the three areas. About 12 per cent of those hospitalised for angina showed such impairment in at least one area, and 4 per cent of the community control.

While the MacArthur study is refreshing in its statistical rigour, it is not without its problems, as its authors acknowledge. Of those approached to participate in the study, 15 to 20 per cent, depending on the site, declined. Between 1 and 20 per cent of psychiatric admissions, again depending on the site, were not approached to participate due to the intervention of their doctors (Grisso and Applebaum, 1995b: 151). The authors cite the latter group as, perhaps, resulting in underestimation of impairment, because clinicians' requests were 'often' based on judgments that the patient was too acutely disturbed to participate, suggesting they would be likely to fall in the impaired range on the tests (1995b: 152 and 169–70). Sadly, there is no indication of the reasons that the former, larger, group did not participate, and so no indication of how they would have altered the statistical profile.

Notwithstanding their best attempts, the patient samples are not entirely evenly matched. This shows up most significantly in the angina control group. Roughly 20 per cent of the angina group were from a relatively high socio-economic class, compared with 1 per cent of the schizophrenics and 4 per cent of the patients with major depression. Fully 80 per cent of the schizophrenics, and 64 per cent of the depressives, were from the lowest socio-economic classes, compared with 51 per cent of the angina patients. These criteria were based on education and level of employment (1995b: 151). While the study was administered orally, therefore removing literacy as a factor, it is difficult to see that ability to articulate could have been removed, and the authors acknowledged that results for the understanding of treatment information tests were correlated positively with socio-economic status (1995b: 161). On that basis, it is unsurprising that the psychiatric patients scored lower on these tests than did the angina patients. This argument, it must be said, is not persuasive when comparing the psychiatric sample with the community groups, where considerably better pairing was achieved.

Perhaps more problematic, it is not obvious that the study escaped the medical internalism that can so easily monopolise capacity determination. This is perhaps clearest on the tests of appreciation (perceptions of disorder), a section that evaluated both whether the patient acknowledged their disorder, and whether they acknowledged the potential of treatment. This test was not administered to the community groups, sensibly enough because they had been screened to ensure that they had no disorder. It is the second of these tests that is interesting for current purposes: about 13 per cent of the schizophrenic patients, and 14 per cent of the depressive individuals, failed to acknowledge the potential value of treatment; for angina patients, this number was zero. The authors elaborate (1995b: 164) on the reasons for denial among the psychiatric patients:

The most frequent reasons given by schizophrenia patients for devaluing treatment, especially medication, involved beliefs that it was intended to harm them in some way. In contrast, the most frequent reason given by depression patients for devaluing treatment was the belief that they were 'too sick' for anything to help them.

The account fails to acknowledge a distinctive quality of the psychiatric sample groups: they were much more likely to have been veterans of the psychiatric system. The breakdown of statistics does not indicate how many of the angina patients were on their first admission, and thus their first major encounter with treatment, but almost three quarters had been admitted no more than twice before. By comparison, 84 per cent of the schizophrenic patients and 45 per cent of the depressives had been admitted to a psychiatric facility at least three times previously. The statistics offer no insight into the experiences of the patients in these prior admissions. To what degree can the comments of the schizophrenics be read as, at least partly, coloured by adverse effects of medication in past admissions? If the confinement was not a happy one, and an appropriate sense of trust was not established between patient and doctor, might this, in part, explain the belief that the medication was not only harmful, but intended to harm? Admittedly, three quarters of the individuals in this class were diagnosed with schizophrenia of a paranoid type, but that cannot be understood as a full explanation, because about half of those giving full acknowledgement to the treatment shared that diagnosis.

As for the people with severe depression, is it not possible that they are right? If previous treatments had failed to provide a lasting solution for them, is a belief that they are 'too sick' to be helped necessarily an indicator of incapacity? Is it possible that, instead of the depressives lacking capacity for not acknowledging the potential of treatment, the angina patients were unduly optimistic about treatment? It has been speculated that mild depression might, indeed, improve rationality to make treatment decisions (Taylor, 1989), because persons in full health tend to undervalue risks of treatment and overvalue benefits, relative to a hypothetical 'rational' person. There is some empirical study to support this view (Costello, 1983). In the MacArthur study, the patients were instead diagnosed with major depression; nonetheless, it is fair to ask whether a pattern of repeat confinements and no lasting medical solution might lead a competent patient to believe that more medication was not the answer.

The design of the MacArthur study must also be remembered. The patients were tested promptly upon admission, generally before any psychiatric medication would have time to take effect (Grisso and Applebaum, 1995b: 152). Assuming that the beneficial effects of these drugs would outweigh increased impairment caused by adverse effects, it would be reasonable to expect these people to score better on the three tests as time passed, suggesting that the levels of impairment in entire patient psychiatric populations may be lower than the study would suggest. Equally, the fact of admission would generally suggest a particularly acute point in the patient's psychiatric symptoms. Because the study finds a correlation between severe symptoms and impairment, it may well be the case that impairment of those with psychiatric problems in the community is also less frequent than the rate contained in the study.

Finally, as the authors make clear (1995b: 170), the study measured impairment, not incapacity (emphasis in original):

[D]eterminations of incompetence require a judgment that the *degree* of deficits in the abilities relevant in a particular case is sufficiently great to warrant a declaration of incompetence, with consequent invalidation of the person's choice. There is no numerical criterion that can represent this judgment across cases, because the degree of deficits in ability that logically will be required may be expected to vary in relation to the specific disorder, proposed treatments, probable consequences, and other contextual factors that vary from one case to another.

Some patients may have been impaired relative to the control groups in ways that one might expect to be relevant to capacity to make treatment decisions; the study does not purport to claim that they were impaired enough that they would lack capacity to make a specific treatment decision. That determination would depend on the specific information needed to be understood in the context of the specific treatment in question.

This last reservation is addressed by a recent English study by Cairns *et al.* (2005). The study applied the MacArthur capacity assessment tool, along with a clinical assessment, to 112 patients admitted to the psychiatric ward of a London hospital, to determine whether those people had capacity to make treatment decisions about the treatment proposed for them by their attending psychiatrist. Just over 40 per cent lacked capacity, with mania and psychosis statistically correlated to the lack of capacity.

The MacArthur study does demonstrate that the discussion of the variety of tests of incapacity with which this chapter began is not only an academic exercise. If ability to understand proposed treatment were to be the only test of capacity, 72 per cent of the schizophrenic sample and 95 per cent of the severely depressed sample would presumably be of unquestioned capacity, because they showed no impairment in this area. If the test of capacity were, instead, one of understanding, reasoning and appreciation jointly, a different picture results. Roughly half of the schizophrenic sample and 24 per cent of the severely depressed sample showed impairment on at least one of these tests, making their capacity appropriately the subject of particular scrutiny.

For this reason, inconsistencies in the determination of capacity are unfortunate, and notwithstanding the fairly uniform adoption of the standard in *C*, the case law shows considerable variation in application. This may, in part, be because capacity determination has tended to be litigated in unusual and specific fact situations. The capacity of pregnant women refusing treatment has been particularly prominent in recent case law: see *St. George's Healthcare NHS Trust* v *S* [1998] 2 FLR 728; *Norfolk and Norwich Healthcare (NHS) Trust* v *W* [1996] 2 FLR 613; *Re MB* (above); *T* (above); *Tameside and Glossop Acute Services Trust* v *CH*, [1996] 1 FLR 762; *A Metropolitan Borough Council* v *DB* [1997] 1 FLR 767; *Re S (Adult: Refusal of Medical Treatment)* [1992] 4 All ER 671. The refusal to consent to a blood transfusion owing to religious beliefs is another common theme: *Re S (Adult: Refusal of Medical Treatment)*; *Re L* (see Chapter 11); *Re S (A Minor) (Consent to Medical Treatment)* [1994] 2 FLR 1065; *Re T*. None of these cases purport to distinguish their facts from the more general common law. In a few of the pregnancy cases, the pregnant woman had been admitted to a psychiatric facility, so the capacity and treatment provisions of the MHA 1983 were discussed expressly. These cases are nonetheless very specific fact situations, with particular pressures. Treatment was eventually authorised in every one except *St. George's NHS Trust*, which was an appeal of a treatment authorisation by the court after the treatment had been performed. It remains to be argued and considered how far they may be extended to cases involving impairment of understanding rather than religious belief, and when the viability of a foetus is not at issue.

The cases involving the capacity of minors must also be approached with some care. Often, the litigation will be in the context of particularly controversial fact situations. The leading case, *Gillick* v *West Norfolk and Wisbech AHA* [1985] 3 All ER 402, for example, concerns whether children with capacity but under the age of 16 years may receive birth control treatment. *L*, *T*, and *S* all involved religious objections to blood transfusions, and *DB* was a pregnancy case. Perhaps more significantly, minors are subject to a different legal regime. While consent by a minor with capacity will render medical treatment legal, a treatment refusal by a competent minor can still be overridden by the minor's parent or the courts. This reflects a policy decision in society that minors are to be particularly protected by the state, and decisions made about them to be subject to special scrutiny, to ensure that the decisions are in the minor's best interests. It is not a policy that has general legal foundation for adults.

The test in *C* has the advantage of avoiding these difficulties: this was a case about an adult psychiatric patient, whose situation was uncomplicated by pregnancy or religious views. As discussed above, the case requires all three of the comprehension measures of the MacArthur survey or, to place it in the language of this chapter, establishes a test where information must be appreciated.

While this test tends to be adopted on its face in the more recent cases above, its application tends to vary markedly from that of Thorpe J. In *Re C* itself, there was no doubt that C had impaired decision-making ability, but this did not result in a finding of incapacity. C's evidence in court was described by the court as follows (at 822–3):

He expressed the grandiose delusions of an international career in medicine during the course of which he had never lost a patient. He affirmed his complete faith in God and, subject to one reservation, in the Bible. He expressed complete confidence in his ability to survive his present trials aided by God, the good doctors and the good nurses. Although he recognised that he would die, death would not be caused by his foot. As he made clear in re-examination, that was his belief, although he could not say that that would not happen. Throughout he expressed his rooted objection to amputation. He did not ascribe the condition of his foot to persecution by authority. As in his interview with Dr. Gall, he accepted the possibility of death as a consequence of his retaining his limb.

While this was his evidence in court, his doctor at Broadmoor testified that C did also have a 'persecutory delusion that whatever treatment is offered is calculated to destroy his body.' (at 823). Thorpe J also summarised his view of C's behaviour in court (at 823):

C himself throughout the hours that he spent in the proceedings seemed ordinarily engaged and concerned. His answers to questions seemed measured and generally sensible. He was not always easy to understand and the grandiose delusions were manifest, but there was no sign of inappropriate emotional expression. His rejection of amputation seemed to result from sincerely held conviction. He had a dignity of manner that I respect.

Pivotal to the court's finding that C had requisite capacity to consent was the legal finding that causation between delusion and decision must be demonstrated for a finding of incapacity, another theme discussed above. His Lordship must be right on the law here, but it is applied in a spirit that is very generous to C. The persecutory delusion cited by his Broadmoor doctor does not seem to figure in his analysis, reliance instead being placed on C's testimony in court. Similarly, C's grandiose delusion that he had previously had an international medical career, his belief notwithstanding medical advice that he would survive his injury, and his belief, again in direct contradiction to the medical evidence, that he would not die from his injured foot were held insufficient to warrant a finding that he lacked capacity. The court drew the following conclusion (at 824):

Although his general capacity is impaired by schizophrenia, it has not been established that he does not sufficiently understand the nature, purpose and effects of the treatment he refuses. Indeed, I am satisfied that he has understood and retained the relevant treatment information, that in his own way he believes it, and that in the same fashion he has arrived at a clear choice.

How are we to understand this finding and, in particular, the phrase 'in his own way, he believes it'? While he sets the most stringent of criteria for the test of capacity, Thorpe J appears to require a considerable weight of evidence to displace the presumption of capacity. To use the MacArthur language, while he holds that inadequate ability in any one of the tests of understanding of information, appreciation and reasoning will be sufficient to render an individual incapable, he equally seems to find that a very significant impairment is necessary to deprive the individual of capacity – a much more significant impairment than that used by the MacArthur authors for their statistics. To use an academic image, it is the difference between setting difficult examination questions and being charitable to the student in setting the marking scheme.

C can be juxtaposed in this context with *Tameside and Glossop Acute Services Trust v CH*. CH was already pregnant when she was detained in a psychiatric ward, and throughout the litigation, it was clear that she wanted her child to be born alive and healthy. She also had a history of schizophrenia, dating back some fifteen years. It was discovered in her 31st week of pregnancy that her foetus was suffering from intra-uterine growth retardation. By her 37th week of pregnancy, the medical evidence was that the situation was becoming serious: either the baby would need to be born through induction or caesarean section, or it would not be born alive. CH had agreed to induction to occur several days hence, but her doctor was concerned that she would change her mind. He therefore approached the court for a declaration that a caesarean section could be performed, should it be necessary.

The issues in the case are various. The question of whether the caesarean section could constitute treatment for mental disorder within the meaning of s. 63 of the MHA 1983 were noted in Chapter 7: it could. Here, the issue is whether CH had capacity to consent. Strictly speaking of course, it did not matter, because the treatment could be imposed upon her over her competent objection anyway, due to the court's view of the first issue. Nonetheless, the findings of the court on the capacity point are striking.

While represented by a guardian *ad litem*, CH was not called in the case, notwithstanding that the matter was not yet an emergency, and as a result, all evidence is seen through the filter of the trust's submission and an affidavit from the official solicitor's agent. While it is dangerous to speculate what evidence CH might have provided if called, the case report does cry out that there is another side to the story.

The court purports to follow the test in *C*, but adopts a markedly different approach to the evidence. First, it is difficult to characterise CH's fundamental position as incorrect, irrelevant, or irrational. This basic position was summed up by her doctor as follows (at 765):

In her deluded way she is doing the best to protect the baby. Her understanding is that the baby is premature and that if it is delivered small it will not survive. I cannot get through to her that if we leave it where it is it will die.

She was correct in her belief that the child, if induced, would be born prematurely. The second statement must be viewed with some scepticism. On the facts, it was not obvious that CH rejected the medical advice she was given: she had, after all, consented to the induction of the delivery; the application was occasioned by a concern of the doctor that she would change her mind. The possibility of a caesarean section had been raised with her, but she had declined on the basis that 'it was unnecessary at the moment – she wanted to hang on because she wanted a week of antibiotics' (at 766). The statement from the official solicitor's agent, who interviewed her, indicated that the antibiotics had, indeed, assisted the development of the foetus. In that interview, she reiterated that she would consent to a caesarean section or induction of labour should it become necessary. One is left to wonder where the evidence of incapacity in this position was.

The second part of the statement might suggest that there had been a failure of trust between CH and her medical advisers, a failure the doctors appear to acknowledge in the case. Again, it is not difficult to see why this might be the case: CH had a history of pathological reactions to the major tranquillisers that would have been the drug of choice during her current psychiatric treatment. The reactions had been sufficiently severe that the foetus would be put at risk if she experienced them while pregnant, and, as a result, she was on less intrusive medication. Such problematic treatment in the past might be unlikely to engender a relationship of trust between CH and the treatment staff on a subsequent admission. It would seem that she believed some of the drugs she was receiving for her psychiatric disorder were harming her foetus (at 766). Whether or not she was right, would not any expectant mother be sceptical? There was evidence from her doctor that CH 'is unable to accept [the medical staff's] advice and perceives it as malicious and harmful to her child.' (at 766): once again, must this be evidence of incapacity? CH was in a controlled situation where, effectively, she could not select her own doctors. Is it really a mark of incapacity for the patient to be sceptical of doctors that she did not select and could not change?

The court's finding regarding her capacity is nothing if not pithy, perhaps, in part, because CH's guardian *ad litem* conceded her incapacity (at 771):

As to the first of the questions posed by Mr. Francis, the evidence is overwhelming that the defendant lacks the capacity to consent to, or to refuse medical treatment in relation to the management of her pregnancy. Mr. Francis accepts this on her behalf. I agree with Dr. M's evidence that she fails all three of the tests laid down in *Re C*. In particular, she is suffering from the delusion that the doctors wish to harm her baby and is incapable of understanding the advice which she is given.

Yet is the standard in *Re C* really applied here? Thorpe J seemed to insist merely on a minimal level of capacity: can it really be said that CH did not meet that standard? The court in *Tameside* makes no reference to the degree of impairment necessary to found an incapacity finding, but its approach seems to set a much higher threshold than that envisaged by Thorpe J.

How are these differing approaches to be understood? The temptation is to view *Tameside* as the anomaly, because it involves the complicating factor of the viability of the foetus. *C*, too, involved an unusual situation in its way: because Broadmoor did not have a resident surgeon who would perform the amputation, C was admitted, on a temporary basis, to a general hospital. The doctor at that hospital took the view that C was competent, and that his refusal of the amputation should be respected; it was the view of Broadmoor that the operation should go ahead, either now or in the event that it was medically necessary at a future time when C lacked capacity, which created the need for the court decision. The *C* case can therefore be understood not so much as a conflict between C and the doctor wishing to treat him, but as between C and Broadmoor, with the surgeon in charge of the amputation supporting C's position.

Viewed in this light, the *C* case can be seen as part of a line of cases about whether the courts ought to encourage treatments about which the treating doctors have reservations. The courts have traditionally been extremely hesitant to do this: see, e.g., *Re J* [1992] 4 All ER 614 at 623, 625–6. Usually, there will be no such medical dispute between the patient's treatment team, and the medical view of best interests will be clear. Where that is the case, it is rare, if ever, that the courts have not found a way for the treatment to occur. On this view, *Tameside* is the more typical case.

Indeed, one can occasionally see the courts adopting a lower threshold of capacity, when necessary to allow treatment. *R v Mental Health Act Commission, ex p X* (1988) 9 BMLR 77 was a case involving a treatment arguably under s. 57 of the MHA 1983. Section 57 treatments cannot be given to patients lacking capacity, so, for the treatment to proceed, a finding that X was capable was of more than academic interest. In that case, where both X and his medical advisers favoured the treatment, the court was content that competency would be shown on the basis of adequate capacity to understand, whether or not there was actual understanding or actual appreciation. This is certainly a correct literal reading of s. 57(2)(a) of the statute, which refers expressly to a patient '*capable* of understanding the nature, purpose and likely effects of the treatment in question' (emphasis added), but it nonetheless stands in rather stark contrast to the approach in the later cases of *C* and *Tameside*.

It would be harsh to view the law of capacity as simply a mechanism by which courts allow treatment to occur, but it would be equally unwise to accept uncritically the claim of Jones and Keywood that 'the courts have been emphatic in rejecting the rationality or reasonableness of the outcome as a measure of incompetence' (1996: 112) That is certainly the courts' claim; but it is less obviously a description of the courts' practice.

10.5 How should decisions be made for those lacking capacity?

Once it has been determined that an individual lacks capacity to make a specific decision or set of decisions by the appropriate process, the issue arises as to how, if at all, those decisions should be able to be made regarding the individual. That implies the selection of both a decision-maker and a set of criteria or principles upon which to base the decision. These are, at least in theory, quite separate processes. A doctor might be selected as the decision-maker, for example, but be required to make the decision on non-medical criteria, such as what the patient would have chosen prior to losing capacity.

It would be possible, of course, to devise a system where no one made the decision. As discussed earlier, this was the situation introduced for personal decisions by the 1983 MHA, but it is currently in retreat: see Chapter 11. While it is fashionable to disparage such a system, it may well be that, in some cases, no action is the best action. If an individual is, on the evidence, reasonably likely to regain capacity with reasonable promptness, it may well be that the best course of action is to leave things unchanged, so that the individual can make their own decisions when capacity is regained. Often, however, this will not be an appropriate response. Failure to act might result in an individual remaining incapacitated, when their condition might be improved. It might result in a pointless diminution of their assets, or a life of poverty because assets are not realised. It may also leave the individual unprotected, and subject to exploitation by those who would wish to take advantage.

If intervention is appropriate, there are a variety of approaches to the substantive criteria for decision-making.

10.5.1 The place of the incapacitated person

Conceptually, capacity is a gatekeeper concept, a mechanism by which individuals either retain or lose authority over, and responsibility for, decisions that affect their lives. If the individual loses that authority and responsibility through incapacity, the question arises as to what status, if any, they continue to hold in the criteria of decision-making. As Buchanan and Brock point out (1986: 50–1), the tradition in legal, ethical and biomedical literature has tended to place the interest of the individual at the centre of the decision-making process:

The dominant tendency, both in recent legal doctrine and in the bioethics literature, has been to view the rights of incompetent individuals as an extension of the rights of competent individuals, through arrangements by which these rights are exercised for the incompetent by others. Although many bioethicists are sharply critical of attempts to apply this approach to those incompetent individuals who were never competent, it is generally agreed that the appropriate starting point for a theory of decision-making for incompetents is in the rights of competent individuals.

This appears initially counterintuitive. If the finding of incapacity is a process by which the individual is taken out of the decision-making process, why should the criteria of decision-making be perceived in terms of the rights that individual would have possessed if competent? Obviously, these individuals remain people whose views, even if lacking capacity ought to be considered; and clearly that is particularly important when the decision in the area of incapacity will affect options in areas where the individual continues capable. Yet is this sufficient to exclude all other criteria? The reality is that the individual has lost personal autonomy, and no surrogate decision-making structure will reintroduce that personal control over their life. If the individual control that is the value at the heart of autonomy is irretrievable, why should the rights of a competent individual serve as the model for decision-making? What is wrong with allowing factors unrelated to the individual, such as social interests or the interests of carers, into the decision-making equation?

Traditionally, the degree to which the interests or views of such third parties could be taken into account in English law was context specific. Historically, relations between trustee and beneficiary, and between guardian and ward, the relations created under the old *parens patriae* system, were fiduciary in nature. The relationships between principal and agent, including those created in enduring powers of attorney for the management of the property and affairs of those lacking capacity, are similarly fiduciary. Students familiar with the law of equity will recognise the maxims and principles that will apply to these relationships. It is expected that those in fiduciary positions will act to safeguard the interests of those under their care, and they must avoid even potential conflicts of interest. This will, of course, be problematic if carers, whether family or professionals, are the decision-makers, because it is difficult to see that they will not be personally affected by decisions made regarding the incapacitated person. While the fiduciary relationship requires the trustee or guardian to act solely for the benefit of the vulnerable person, that is, of course, quite a different matter from making the decisions that the vulnerable person would have made. The law of equity never required this; indeed, the trustee or guardian was, and is, expected to exercise independent judgment.

If the principle is that the interests of the incapacitated person hold sway, to the exclusion of the interests of professionals, family, carers, the state and society at large, the question still remains as to how the incapacitated person is to be embodied in the decision-making. There have traditionally been three ways, which will be examined in turn: advance directives, substituted judgment and best interests.

10.5.2 Advance directives

Advance directives allow an individual to make decisions while competent, which will be binding in any subsequent period of incapacity. Historically, they had no formal recognition in England. A move towards this form of advance planning was made by the Enduring Powers of Attorney Act 1985, which allowed donors of powers of attorney in a specific form to determine who would manage their estate in the event of subsequent incapacity. They did not, however, allow advance determination of how decisions would be made in the personal realm, where property or affairs were not at issue. The first step in that direction was taken by Thorpe J, in *Re C* [1994] 1 All ER 819 (HC), regarding medical treatment (discussed earlier). It would seem from that case that advance refusals of treatment are without formality requirements: they do not need to be in writing, signed or witnessed. All that appears to be required is clear evidence of a decision by a patient that the treatment in question should not be performed in the event that the patient lacks capacity to consent at the time.

The advance directive in the *C* case was hypothetical: the patient had recovered, and the issue was what would occur in the event that he suffered from a similar condition in the future. In *Re AK (Medical Treatment: Consent)* [2001] 1 FLR 129, the problem was more immediate, but the result was the same. The advance refusal of treatment of a patient with motor neurone disease was upheld, and treatment in violation of that directive following subsequent incapacity was held to be tortious (at 134). The case reaffirms the law, that an advanced refusal of treatment is binding upon subsequent incapacity, and once again, there is no suggestion of formalities requirements.

In *AK*, as in *C*, the court had the luxury of being able to receive evidence from the patient directly, because incapacity had not been lost. The limited case law on advance refusals when the individual has already lost capacity suggests a considerable reluctance of the courts to rely on the advance decision, particularly in life-threatening situations. Issues of onus and standard of proof are considered in *HE v A Hospital NHS Trust* [2003] EWHC 1017, [2003] 2 FLR 408. That case holds that the presumption of capacity applies to advance decisions, and that it is for the person challenging capacity to make out his or her case. Beyond that, the applicability of the advance decision is to be demonstrated by the person propounding it. While the standard of proof remains within the civil burden, it is at the high end of that sphere: clear and convincing evidence must be presented, and any ambiguity is to be resolved in favour of the preservation of life (paras. 23–4). While it is for an individual alleging revocation of an advance directive to raise a serious question on the point, once a doubt has been raised, the burden is on the person propounding the decision to demonstrate the continued validity and applicability of the decision (para. 43).

Refusal of medical treatment remains the only context in which advanced decisions have been formally recognised in English law. Other jurisdictions have more generous provisions in place: see, for example, the Ontario Substitute Decisions Act 1992, SO 1992, c. 30, which effectively allows an individual to create binding preferences for virtually all decisions related to personal care, consent to treatment, or estate management.

If the model of decision-making for those lacking capacity is deemed to be an extension of the rights of the individual when competent, the advance directive has a considerable theoretical attraction. How better to introduce the wishes of the incapacitated individual into the process, than by his or her own proclaimed wishes prior to incapacity?

While certainly appealing in this regard, the matter is not as straightforward as it might first appear. The individual may have made a variety of directives at different times: is only the most recent to be taken into account for purposes of the decision? How well informed was the individual about the consequences of their statement? Did they realise, for example, that the refusal of a certain treatment might cause death, or that the failure to sell certain shares might result in insufficient funds to pay nursing home costs? Did they realise the legal effect of the statement, that it would indeed bind a subsequent decision? How are changes of circumstance to be accounted for? Thus, an individual refusing treatment for a physical condition in advance might, or might not, have refused a new treatment for the condition, discovered after the directive had been made. Should the directive still preclude such treatment? The appeal of the advance directive is that the individual would decide now, if competent, in the manner they proscribed earlier. But this is not necessarily true. As people's capacities change, their expectations of life may change with them; what was unthinkable previously may become acceptable, or even desirable.

Some of these matters may be appropriately addressed through the provision of formal safeguards. It is difficult to see, for example, that an individual with capacity, attending at a lawyer's office to sign an official-looking document purporting to restrict future choices in the event of incapacity, will have any doubt as to what they are doing. That does not address all the problems, however; and it must be remembered that increasing formality restricts the use of the process, through both social and economic rationing. The risk of a formal system is that it will be available only to those with money and in the know about the process.

10.5.3 Substitute judgment

The substitute judgment model of decision-making requires that decisions be made as they would have been by the incapacitated person, but for the incapacity. In *In re D (J)* *(Court of Protection)* [1982] 1 Ch 237 at 243–4, Sir Robert Megarry V-C establishes five principles for making decisions in this way, in the context of the authority of the court to make a will for a person lacking capacity.

(1) It is to be assumed that the patient is having a brief lucid interval at the time when the will is made.

(2) During the lucid interval, the patient has a full knowledge of the past, and a full realisation that as soon as the will is executed he or she will relapse into the actual mental state that previously existed, with the prognosis as it actually is.

(3) It is the actual patient who has to be considered and not a hypothetical patient. One is not concerned with the patient on the Clapham omnibus.

(4) During the hypothetical lucid interval, the patient is to be envisaged as being advised by competent solicitors.

(5) In all normal cases, the patient is to be envisaged as taking a broad brush to the claims on his bounty, rather than an accountant's pen.

While some of these apply most directly to the specific context of a testamentary disposition, a slightly more detailed account will provide insight into the precise nature, and the strengths and weaknesses of the substitute judgment approach.

The essence of the substitute judgment approach is in the first three principles. The objective is for the decision-maker to stand in the shoes of an incompetent person experiencing a hypothetical, temporary return to capacity, albeit a capacity tempered by the knowledge that, immediately the decision is made, they will return to their incapacitated state. The decision is thus to be grounded in the character the incapacitated individual would have if competent, but in the specific situation in which the individual actually finds him or herself. While conceptually clear, this may involve complications in practice. People are not consistent, and here, as with the advance directive model, inconsistencies are difficult to absorb into the system.

According to the third principle, the decision-maker is to take into account the idiosyncrasies of the incapacitated individual: the approach is one of substituting judgment. Thus the decision-maker should take into account the religious or political views, and antipathies or affection for specific persons or causes of the individual affected by the decision. To this end, reference is to be made to the individual as they were prior to losing capacity (at 244). A formal advance directive, or a clearly stated view when competent, therefore, will normally be of considerable evidential value in determining the decision to be taken. Nonetheless, the court in *D(J)* does leave itself with some leeway (at 244):

No doubt allowance may be made for the passage of years since the patient was last of full capacity, for sometimes strong feelings mellow into indifference, and even family feuds evaporate.

This may perhaps be merely an acknowledgement that people change over time, and that people lacking capacity may do so as well as anyone else. Earlier in this chapter, the danger was noted of assessing capacity on the basis of an earlier time when the subject was of undisputed capacity. Similarly, it was noted that advance directives are problematic when circumstances change, as, for example, when new treatments become available for a condition where the directive would refuse all treatment. In so far as the court here is addressing this sort of problem, the statement seems unobjectionable, and, indeed, conceptually necessary to distinguish the substitute decision model from the less flexible advance directive.

It is questionable, however, whether the statement is instead a mechanism to allow other non-subjective factors to enter into the determination of the decision-maker. It continues as follows (at 244):

Furthermore, I do not think that the court should give effect to antipathies or affections of the patients which are beyond reason. But subject to all due allowances, I think that the court must seek to make the will which the actual patient, acting reasonably, would have made if notionally restored to full mental capacity, memory and foresight.

The reference to antipathies that are 'beyond reason', and to the individual 'acting reasonably' suggest a move away from the pure subjective standard. In so far as the antipathies are the result of mental disorder, the reservation is uncontroversial; indeed, the purpose of substitute decision-making rules is to ensure that such delusional notions are not part of the decision-making process. If, instead, it refers to antipathies of the individual when competent, as seems likely given the context, it is a notable departure from the subjective standard. On a subjective basis, the incapacitated person should, after all, be allowed to continue their irrational dislike of some of their family. The comment seems to be opening the way for factors, such as a respect for family values, to be introduced to paper over the cracks of old family disputes.

Perhaps, in this context, it is appropriate to remember that substitute decision-making involves the law awarding authority to another. Arguably, there are some things in which the law ought not to allow itself to be involved, and there are assumptions law ought to make, whether true or not. This can be seen in the fourth principle, the assumption that the individual would have the benefit of competent professional advice. The reality is that many people do not get such advice, if indeed they receive advice at all, and do not discover the deficiency until it is too late. Assume that as an individual's previous will had been badly drafted: if one looks to the individual and their specific situation to the exclusion of all else, there is no reason to assume that they would have had better luck with the lawyer, when they sought to draft a new will. Yet the courts, reasonably, have rejected this approach, because it would not meet social expectations of the court's function. The court cannot be seen to make decisions on the basis of bad advice, even if that is the advice that the client would probably have received. Similarly, it would be difficult to defend the Court of Protection taking investment decisions for a client by selecting random stocks from the daily newspaper, even if this was how the client invested. At some point, fetishising a substitute decision model in its purest form becomes counterproductive and unhelpful to the client.

The final principle identified in *D(J)*, that the incapacitated person is deemed to take 'a broad brush to the claims on his bounty, rather than an accountant's pen' (at 244), applies most directly to the specific situation of that case: the writing of a will by the court. The point is that a legacy is not to be decided on the basis of a minute arithmetical calculation of previous gifts and specific kindnesses to the testator. It would seem to have little application outside the specific context of that case.

A problem with the substitute decision model becomes immediately obvious: what if the individual never had capacity for the decision in question? How is the decision-maker to infer what the views of the incapacitated person would be, if he or she has never had capacity? The tendency would appear to be to lapse into other social values to justify a decision. In the testamentary context, some of these are contained in the test of capacity itself. Recall that capacity to draft a will required, among other things, an ability to 'comprehend and appreciate the claims to which he ought to give effect' (*Banks* v *Goodfellow* (1870) 5 QB 549 at 565). *Smee* v *Smee* (1879) 5 P 84 elaborated upon this, indicating that the testator ought to be able 'rationally to consider the claims of all those who are related to him, and who, according to the ordinary feelings of mankind, are supposed to have some claim to his consideration when dealing with his property as it is to be disposed of after his death.' (at 92). At issue was 'not merely the amount and nature of his [the testator's] property but, the interest of those who by personal relationship or otherwise had claims upon him' (at 92).

There seems to be something of an expectation that the person who had never been competent would behave in a way something akin to the social norms identified above. In *Re C* [1991] 3 All ER 866, for example, the individual in question was aged 75 and had been institutionalised for 65 years, owing to a severe developmental disability. At the time of the application to draft a statutory will, Hoffman J held that she had 'little memory, understanding or capacity to communicate,' (at 867) and that she had always been incapable of making a testamentary disposition (at 868). At issue was whether the statutory will might include a considerable bequest to the institution in which C lived, and where she appeared to have been happy for a considerable time.

Hoffman J acknowledged that there was no way of knowing what C's preferences would have been, because she had never been competent (at 870): 'In all relevant respects, the record of her individual preferences and personality are a blank on which nothing has been written. Accordingly, there is no material on which to construct a subjective assessment of what the patient would have wanted to do.' In these circumstances, 'the court must assume that she would have been a normal decent person, acting in accordance with contemporary standards of morality' (p. 870). Here, C's decision would be swayed by two factors: that she had been in the care of the community, through the National Health Service and voluntary organisations, for much of her life; that she had inherited her wealth. The court therefore held that she would have bequeathed her estate to the mental health charity associated with her institution and to her family on this basis. At the time of the hearing, the estate was valued at £1.5m. The court ordered an immediate gift of £400,000 to the family and £100,000 to the charity. A will was then to be drawn giving a special legacy of £10,000 to B, a volunteer with the charity who had been particularly kind to C, taking her on outings and visiting her regularly, which 'will I hope be accepted as symbolic of the debt which people like Miss C and their families owe to voluntary workers who ameliorate their lives' (at 872). A special bequest of £15,000 was to be made to a first cousin twice removed who had Down's syndrome, because 'Miss C would wish to recognise her community of misfortune with this child by a special provision' (at 872). The residue of the estate would be divided equally between the family and the charity.

It is as difficult to fault this result as it is disarmingly easy to do so. It is fair to ask why the facility should benefit, albeit indirectly, through its charitable arm. The point of the National Health Service is that a reasonable quality of service ought to be available to people such as C as a matter of right. We do not expect individuals to leave bequests to their general practitioners, even if they have received long and good service from them; indeed, the law presumes against the validity of such gifts, and bequests in such situations are void for undue influence: see *Rhodes* v *Bate* (1866) 1 Ch App 252; *Mitchell* v *Homfray* (1881) 8 QBD 587; *Dent* v *Bennett* (1839) 4 My & Cr 268. Why would we expect C to leave a bequest to the facility, which is, in some ways, in an analogous position? At the same time, the family's moral claim is doubtful. C's mother died in 1918, and it was not clear whether her father had maintained any contact prior to his death in 1953. Hoffman J held that 'few if any other members of her fairly extensive family appear to have been aware of her existence' (at 867). It is not entirely obvious why C would wish to leave funds to such people. The court found that it was because she had inherited her money; it is not obvious that this is sufficient to justify a share to the relatives. The recognition of 'community of misfortune' with the child with Down's syndrome seems, at best, speculative, and while it is certainly easy to sympathise with the gift to B, the reasons appear to flow directly from Hoffman J's view of social obligation, rather than C's substituted judgment.

On the other hand, without the will, the family would inherit the entire estate on intestacy. This seems an equally inappropriate result, given the limited relationship between the parties.

If competent, C would presumably have made a will, thus, on a substituted judgment approach, the court was right to do so in her stead – but in order to do so, the decision-maker must create a fictional construction of the character of the incapacitated person, a construction that is entirely fictional in the case of a person who has never had capacity, and at least partly fictional in any event, if supposed circumstances following incapacity are to be taken into account, as in *Re D(J)*. The values of autonomy implied in the model, the respect provided to the individuality of the person and the right for decisions to be made in a fashion consistent with their views when competent, are laudable; but, in the end, the reality cannot be expected to match the ideal.

10.5.4 Best interests

The best interests approach is, perhaps, the most frequently applied of the mechanisms to determine decision outcome in English incapacity law. It is certainly the test of general application in matters of consent to medical treatment unless an advance refusal of treatment applies, and more recently has been used as a framework in making personal decisions about people lacking capacity more broadly: see *Newham London Borough Council* v *S (Adult: Court's Jurisdiction)* [2003] EWHC 1909, and *Re S (Adult Patient) (Inherent Jurisdiction: Family Life)* [2002] EWHC 2278, [2003] 1 FLR 292. Further, in so far as the 'best interests' of the individual may be equated with 'benefit' to the individual, it is one part of the approach contained in Part VII of the MHA 1983 that has been applied to decisions related to the property and affairs of incapacitated persons (s. 95(1)).

For such a significant portion of incapacity law, remarkably little guidance was provided as to what the approach actually entails. Consistent with the prevailing view of tort liability in medical matters in the late 1980s, *F* took the view that the physician's view of best interest need only be consistent with that of a responsible body of his or her professional colleagues: *F* at 78. This view was limited by *Re A (Male Sterilisation)* [2000] FLR 549 (at 555):

Doctors charged with the decisions about the future treatment of patients and whether such treatment would, in the cases of those lacking capacity to make their own decisions, be in their best interests, have to act at all times in accordance with a responsible and competent body of relevant professional opinion. That is the professional standard set for those who make such decisions. The doctor, acting to that required standard, has, in my view, a second duty, that is to say, he must act in the best interests of a mentally incapacitated patient. I do not consider that the two duties have been conflated into one requirement.

This would appear to require something more akin to correctness, rather than mere consistency with professional opinion. Quite how a professional is to obtain any certainty as to the correctness of their assessment was not clear. Prior to the introduction of the MCA 2005, therefore, the best advice must be to apply to court in the event of any doubt.

At common law, the determination of best interests was decided according to a 'balance sheet' approach, explained as follows (at 560) by Thorpe LJ in *A (Male Sterilisation)*:

There can be no doubt in my mind that the evaluation of best interests is akin to a welfare appraisal ... [T]he first instance judge with the responsibility to make an evaluation of the best interests of a claimant lacking capacity should draw up a balance sheet. The first entry should be of any factor or factors of actual benefit ... Then on the other sheet the judge should write any counterbalancing dis-benefits to the applicant ... Then the judge should enter on each sheet the potential gains and losses in each instance making some estimate of the extent of the possibility that the gain or loss might accrue. At the end of that exercise the judge should be better placed to strike a balance between the sum of the certain and possible gains against the sum of the certain and possible losses. Obviously, only if the account is in relatively significant credit will the judge conclude that the application is likely to advance the best interests of the claimant.

Little guidance was provided as to what should be included on the balance sheet, although a certain amount may perhaps be surmised. If the substituted judgment approach can be characterised in legal terms as a set of subjective criteria, the best interests approach, reasonably, should be objective. At issue ought to be how the reasonable individual would decide in the position of the incapacitated person in question, rather than how the actual incapacitated person would have decided.

There is judicial support for this view, in the words of Ungoed-Thomas J, that the decision-maker should act 'as a properly advised decent sane person in the patient's position would act': *In re TB* [1967] Ch 247 at 253. This does not restrict the best interests test to a specific set of professional criteria. If the 'sane person' in the position of the patient would consider a wide variety of factors, that same variety would fall to be considered under the best interests test. This is confirmed in *Re MB (Medical Treatment)* [1997] 2 FLR 426, a case involving surgical intervention, where Butler-Sloss LJ held that 'Best interests are not limited to best medical interests' (at 439). A similar view can be seen in *In re W (EEM)* [1971] 1 Ch 123 at 125, where the court was charged with deciding whether commencement of divorce proceedings would be to the 'benefit' of the incapacitated person:

The first question which arose on these sections was the scope of the word 'benefit'. It seems clear to me that it is not restricted to material benefit, but that it is of wide significance comprehending whatever would be beneficial in any respect, material or otherwise.

In that case, the court considered the following relevant to determining whether the divorce proceedings would be to the benefit of W: the sanctity of marriage, in so far as that would be relevant to the reasonable person in W's position; the religious views of W; public policy in so far as it would have affected W's views; the effects on W's children; pending legal changes to divorce legislation; financial considerations for W.

The focus on how W would approach matters suggests a blurring of the distinction between the substitute judgment and best interest approaches. Indeed, the court in *W* goes so far as to cite *In re CL* [1969] 1 Ch 587, for the proposition that 'it is for the benefit of the patient that the court should do what it is satisfied that he would have done even though it be not for his financial or material benefit' (*W* at 135–6, citing *CL* at 597). This may, in part, be a reflection of the specifics of the statutory provisions further defining the court's role, although not specifically relevant to the issue in question, which allowed the court to act 'for making provision for other persons or purposes for whom or which the patient might be expected to provide if he were not mentally disordered': perhaps, but not necessarily, a substitute judgment test. It may also reflect a view that the individual would be the best judge of their best interests, given the breadth of factors that may be taken into account in assessing best interests.

If that is the case, it suggests that the distinction between substitute judgment and best interests approaches is not merely that of subjective versus objective view. Where characteristics of the subject are known, the test would become a substitute judgment; as less reliable or recent information were available, the application of an objective stand-ard, the reasonable individual in the position of the one in question, would become increasingly significant. This reflects the approach in medical cases, where the decision-maker is bound by the prior competent wishes of the patient if they are known, and where best interests are resorted to only in the absence of such wishes. As noted above, a similar process must, of necessity, happen in the substitute judgment approach: if the individual has never had capacity, a decision must be made according to a mythical per-sonality constructed for the incapacitated person. The two tests start to look remarkably similar.

The best interests approach is, however, open to other interpretations. In some formulations, external factors might be used to override the competent wishes previously expressed of the incapacitated person. Section 4 of the MCA 2005, for example, requires that determination of the best interests of an individual lacking capacity would include consideration, among other factors, of his or her present (and therefore incompetent) wishes, and the need to permit and encourage the individual to be involved as fully as possible in any decision made for them. This seems laudable. Other formulations of the best interests test might include a wide array of considerations. Counsel in *W (EEM)*, for example, argued that both the sanctity of marriage and social policy supporting marriage militated against allowing the divorce to proceed (at 132). In the actual case, the court rejected that contention, except in so far as it might have affected W's views, but it does raise the issue of what policy factors ought to be insisted upon, if any, in the determination of best interests.

The result of these outside factors might be decisions being made about the individual, or treatment performed on the individual, to which they may be known to have objected when capable. This seems, intuitively, to be a violation of the individual's autonomy. There is, rationally (or not), a sense that the incapacitated individual is somehow a vestige of the capable one, and the failure to acknowledge the continuity of the person by respecting prior wishes or relying on the decision that he or she would have made, appears at best to marginalise, if not violate, that person.

The degree to which interests other than those of the patient may be considered in the determination of best interests is startlingly unclear. Certainly, family and carers are to be consulted as a matter of good practice by the doctor, but it is equally clear, in *F*, that the decision as to best interests rests with the doctor (at 567). While Lord Goff in *Bland* reiterates that view (at 871), he also refers (at 869) to the effects of the treatment on family members:

It is reasonable also that account should be taken of the invasiveness of the treatment and of the indignity to which, as the present case shows, a person has to be subjected if his life is pro-longed by artificial means, which must cause considerable distress to his family – a distress which reflects not only on their own feelings but their perception of the situation of their relative who is being kept alive.

A similar view is taken by the court in *Re S (Medical Treatment: Adult Sterilisation)* [1998] 1 FLR 944 (at 946–7):

The question is what is best for S? As to the wishes of her parents, their opinions as to the nature and extent of the risk of pregnancy and their reaction to an adverse decision by the court – these are matters to be taken into account. However, the opinion of the parents as to the outcome of the central balancing exercise is certainly not determinative of the matter; that is one for the court alone.

Countervailing authority is found in the argument of Lord Mustill, in *Airedale NHS Trust* v *Bland* [1993] AC 789 at 896, where both the pain caused to the family, and the expense or other unpleasantness caused to the state as a whole, are held to be matters inappropriate for the court's consideration:

Threaded through the technical arguments addressed to the House were the strands of a much wider position, that it is in the best interests of the community at large that Anthony Bland's life should now end. The doctors have done all they can. Nothing will be gained by going on and much will be lost. The distress of the family will get steadily worse. The strain on the devotion of a medical staff charged with the care of a patient whose condition will never improve, who may live for years and who does not even recognise that he is being cared for, will continue to mount. The large resources of skill, labour and money now being devoted to Anthony Bland might in the opinion of many be more fruitfully employed in improving the condition of other patients, who if treated may have useful, healthy and enjoyable lives for years to come.
   This argument was never squarely put, although hinted at from time to time. In social terms it has great force, and it will have to be faced in the end. But this is not a task which the courts can possibly undertake. A social cost-benefit analysis of this kind, which would have to embrace 'mercy-killing' to which exactly the same considerations apply, must be for Parliament alone, and the outcome of it is at present quite impossible to foresee. Until the nettle is grasped, we must struggle on with the existing law, imperfect as it is.

Lord Mustill's view is certainly the more consistent with the themes of self-determination that Lord Goff espouses elsewhere in *Bland*, and he is right to point to the difficulty of moving beyond the individual patient to allow other social factors to enter the equation. The difficulties are, at least, twofold: first is the difficulty of ascertaining what would constitute best interests, when the interests of a wide variety of people and of the state as a whole might be theoretically relevant; second is the risk of creeping extension of this approach – when do matters of convenience to carers (professional or family) and the state become matters of legitimate interest and concern in the determination of overall best interests?
   The most recent relevant case does little to clarify. In *Re A (Male Sterilisation)* [2000] 1 FLR 549 (CA), Butler-Sloss P held that neither a mother's moral views regarding sterilisation of her son, nor social questions such as the protection of vulnerable women whom the son might meet, for example, at his group home, were relevant in a determination of whether the sterilisation operation ought to be performed (at 556).

By comparison, Thorpe LJ specifically left the questions relating to the interests of third parties open (at 558). The third judge, Schiemann LJ, did not take a specific view.

This issue is, of course, of considerable importance in a mental health framework. In a climate of increased concern by the state about controlling patients living in the community, and at a time when both community care and institutional budgets are increasingly stretched, resulting in overstretched staff, the use of drugs risks blurring the line as to best interests of the patient, or best interests of others. While an increasingly important area of concern, it is not obvious that the courts will have an occasion to address it, because there is, at this time, no requirement except in unusual circumstances that courts oversee treatment provided in the best interests of incompetent patients.

This raises a question of process as to how best interests decisions are made, and the degree of deference owed to medical decision-makers in the event that they are potentially incorrect in their assessment of the patient's best interests. In practice, a given medical condition may be amenable to a variety of treatments, and it is long-established law that doctors practising any of these treatments that are used by a respectable body of their colleagues will not be held to be negligent: *Bolam v Friern Hospital Management Committee* [1957] 2 All ER 118. The question in the current context is whether whichever of these treatments selected by the doctor will meet the best interests threshold for treatment of the patient, or whether some more structured assessment of best interests needs to be made, and whether, upon application to the court, it is appropriate for the court, after determining best interests, broadly to leave to the individual practitioner the question of which of these treatments ought to be pursued.

It is these tensions that render problematic the failure of the courts to articulate the best interests test in greater detail. If it were simply an extension of the substitute judgment approach to take account of individuals whose personal characteristics when competent cannot be known, a detailed set of criteria would be difficult to create, because each decision would be so heavily reliant on its facts – but if this is the approach, the courts should say so. If, on the other hand, other factors are to be taken into consideration, the courts should be clear as to what those factors are.

10.6 Who should make decisions for those lacking capacity?

If the authority to make decisions on behalf of another is to be granted, there are various possible bodies that might exercise it. The selection of such a decision-maker involves a variety of concerns. The authority to make decisions on another's behalf may involve the delegation of considerable power. The decision-maker must be trusted to make decisions of appropriate standard, according to the appropriate criteria. The incapacitated person may be in a vulnerable position vis-à-vis the decision-maker, physically, emotionally, or financially. The decision-maker must be an individual who will not abuse that position of vulnerability. At the same time, there is a social and practical interest that decisions are made expeditiously and efficiently.

Traditionally, this decision-making has been the role of the court, or has at least been overseen by the court. Thus, prior to the MHA 1959, authority over personal decisions rested with High Court judges, through their *parens patriae* jurisdiction. The MHA 1959 abolished this power as it applied to adults, collapsing it into the guardianship provisions of that Act, but, following restrictions to guardianship in the MHA 1983, the courts have been reinventing a role for themselves in these matters: see earlier. The difficulty with courts assuming this role more broadly is similar to the difficulty of courts in making incapacity determinations. The courts tend to be expensive, impersonal, often slow, and bureaucratic, and these difficulties compound themselves when moving from the temporally specific determination of incapacity, to the long-term supervision of the care of persons lacking capacity. The courts are also likely to have no direct knowledge of the individual: whatever approach of decision-making is adopted, the court will need to be guided by evidence. This will be problematic if a quick decision is required, and is likely to be expensive in any event. Courts do, however, tend to be strong on due process safeguards, which, at their best, provide some protection to the person lacking capacity against abuse.

Alternatively, the decisions might be allocated to an administrative body. This has been the situation, for example, for estate management under Part VII of the MHA by the old Court of Protection, which was less a real court than an administrative office. Such professionalisation of the caring functions has the advantage that those in charge of decisions are themselves sufficiently talented to make good decisions, or at least decisions meeting a professional standard. Administrative bodies also risk the perception that decision-making is too far removed from the individual, performed by bureaucrats, and if professionals do all of the work, it can also be expensive. For both of these reasons, courts and administrative bodies have tended to find individuals who are closer to the individual to make the day-to-day decisions. These have variously been called committees, guardians, tutors, receivers and managers, depending on the system in question, but the court or administrative body generally keeps some sort of overarching control to ensure appropriate exercise of the decision-making power by the individual.

Other systems appoint individuals to make the decisions without the intervention of a court or administrative body. Frequently, a family member will be designated by statute to make decisions on behalf of an incapacitated individual (see, for example, Ontario's Consent to Treatment Act, SO 1992, c. 31, s. 17(1)). *F* offered a different approach, where the doctor proposing treatment would make the decision. While often bringing the decision much closer to the individual, and rendering decisions considerably less bureaucratic, less expensive and more flexible, both approaches have their problems.

The professional is likely to be recommending a certain course of conduct because of a belief that it is the right course of conduct. There are professional values at stake, and quite possibly a bona fide desire that a specific decision be made in a specific way. For doctors and lawyers alike, involvement of a competent client in the decision-making allows those values to be tested by the individual most affected, according to values outside those of the professional. At issue is a reality check on the professional vision, an acknowledgement that the decision of the client or patient is not merely based on a professional standard of quality of outcome. Whether the decision-making criterion is substitute judgment or best interests, it is nonetheless to be based on how the outcome would best suit the life of the incapacitated individual as a whole, not only according to a specific professional code. Professionals are generally not trained to take account of this wider array of factors. The advantage of involving the family or other layperson in the decisions involving an incapacitated individual is that this reference to the individual circumstances of the incapacitated person, outside the professional gaze, is maintained.

At the same time, there is no guarantee that the family member will be intellectually or emotionally able to interrogate the decision of the professional, or otherwise to manage the affairs of the incapacitated person. The family member may mean well, but may not be qualitatively good at decision-making, on whatever standard of quality is selected. Equally problematic is that they, like the professionals, may well be affected by the outcome of the decision, and it is doubtful that either family or professional can keep their own interests separate from those of the incapacitated person. Sending his or her mother to a private nursing home may mean that the decision-maker's inheritance will be spent on nursing home fees, and the decision-maker may feel, wrongly in law but perhaps consistent with some social views, that they have some sort of quasi-proprietorial claim over the inheritance. Can the decision-maker really be relied upon to keep this factor outside consideration when determining accommodation for a parent?

Equally problematic is the availability of information upon which to base decisions, and how it is to be safeguarded. It seems indisputable that the individual with authority to make a decision on behalf of another must have access to the information upon which to base the decision. In most, if not all, cases, this will mean that a considerable amount of personal information must be made available. The current law is generally silent about the availability of such information. Doctors will have the relevant medical information in their files already, removing that access problem in the event that they make the decision; they will not, or at least not necessarily, have the non-medical information that seems to be relevant for decision-making under any of the models above. Other professionals are likely to be in a similar situation for decisions in their fields. On the other hand, there is nothing in the current law that gives family members or other decision-makers access to doctors' or other professionals' files in the event of the client's incapacity. It must be the case that access can be given to those with decision-making authority; but release of the information has its problems too.

The first difficulty concerns the privacy of the incapacitated person. This is, in part, a matter of personal dignity: it is not obvious that the individual concerned would have wished family members, for example, to know aspects of their private life. Consider *Re S (Hospital Patient: Court's Jurisdiction)* [1995] 3 All ER 290, where the dispute was between the estranged wife and the current cohabiting partner of the incompetent person, as to who would have decision-making authority over his care. The wife eventually received custody of S's person and estate (*Re S (Hospital Patient: Foreign Curator)* [1996] Fam 23), a set of duties which might well have included support for the cohabiting partner. The personal and financial relations between S and the cohabiting partner might well be something he would have wished to keep private from his wife; yet she may well have needed to be given access to the information to fulfil her duties over the estate. This situation is particularly problematic, because it also affects the privacy rights of the cohabiting partner, who might also have wished the details of her relationship with S to be kept private from the wife. The result, disclosure to the wife, may therefore be a less-than-ideal solution.

Involvement of laypeople as decision-makers also carries with it the complication that it may be difficult to control the information after it is disclosed to them. The relations between decision-maker and incapacitated person are almost certainly fiduciary in nature. A duty of confidentiality is a classic fiduciary duty, and such a duty would presumably attach to the information. As a matter of practice, however, can the family member be relied upon not to disclose the information to others? Enforcement would have to be by way of court application – an expensive process, and one often requiring an additional guardian figure to take the action on behalf of the person lacking capacity. Even if successful, the result would be fine or imprisonment, and it is doubtful that these would be appropriate for what may well have been an indiscretion by the family member. At the same time, lack of confidentiality can be problematic, because it may alert the less scrupulous in society to a vulnerable individual.

All of this suggests that decisions might be better made by professionals such as doctors, lawyers, court staff or professional trustees. These people tend to be overseen by their relevant professional bodies, and are likely to understand better their duty of confidentiality. The first difficulty here, of course, is that these people also generally expect payment, and this must come either from the public purse or from the incapacitated person. They are also unlikely to have personal knowledge of the incapacitated person, meaning that high-calibre decisions will involve considerable investigation, and the corresponding time commitment. The professionals concerned are not necessarily trained in such investigation, and such investigations are unlikely to be seen by them as an efficient use of time. An additional difficulty is social. Families often view the care of vulnerable loved ones as at the core of what it is to be a family. The family members may find the removal of that role frustrating and alienating, at a time when they may already be distressed at witnessing the situation of their incapacitated member.

10.7 Concluding comments

A proper understanding of how the concepts of capacity and substituted decision-making are applied cannot be limited to an assessment of the case law. Not only are there the usual legal problems that the decisions of the court may, or may not, be appropriately or correctly applied by those in charge of administering the law, it is also the case that the reported cases themselves are problematic. While modern cases refer to the nineteenth-century precedents, they appear to be applying other standards – but they are not always forthcoming on what those standards are. The cases themselves further contain tensions as to how they are to be interpreted.

A proper assessment would require a systematic analysis of how the decisions are, in fact, being made. This is not possible. There is no general mechanism to report those found to be lacking capacity, nor, in general, to monitor the decisions being made about these people. This makes socio-legal analysis of incapacity difficult. It is not known, for example, what gender or racial mixes in this category are, although a comfortable majority of those under the control of Part VII of the MHA 1983 are women, owing, perhaps in part, to women's longer average lifespans; Cairns *et al.* did find that being black was correlated to a finding of incapacity for treatment decisions in their study (2005: 381).

A number of the same questions arise in assessing the meaning of incapacity as arose in the discussion of the meaning of mental illness in Chapter 2. Certainly, the test of incapacity, like the test of mental illness, is culturally defined. A particularly clear example of this may be seen in the test of capacity to marry, enunciated in *Durham* v *Durham* (1885) 10 P 80 (at 82):

I may say this much in the outset, that it appears to me that the contract of marriage is a very simple one, which does not require a high degree of intelligence to comprehend. It is an engagement between a man and a woman to live together, and love one another as husband and wife, to the exclusion of all others. This is expanded in the promises of the marriage ceremony by words having reference to the natural relations which spring from that engagement, such as protection on the part of the man, and submission on the part of the woman.

Clearly, the references to 'protection on the part of the man' and 'submission on the part of the woman' are not understood as part of the bargain by all modern bridal couples. Yet if that attitude is based in a particularly Victorian image of marriage, it is difficult to see what would be substituted at the start of the twenty-first century that might be less culturally based. While a modern test might reflect modern culture, the individual would still be judged on whether they had the culturally appropriate understanding.

Further, it is at least open to question how submissive Victorian wives, in fact, were (and how protective their husbands). Even in the Victorian age, did this represent a realistic view of marriage, a view of marriage that would have reflected the expectation of real nineteenth-century couples? Or was it a moral ideal that many married couples would have realised they might not attain? And, if the latter, ought people to have been judged according to a standard reflecting a moral ideal rather than a practical reality? A similar difficulty is likely to arise in a modern context. The ideals of marriage remain firm among moralists, but are increasingly challenged in practice. Ought capacity to be judged according to the culture of the moralists?

Some of these difficulties were acknowledged in the most recent case on capacity to marry, *Sheffield City Council* v *E* [2004] EWHC 2808. The court defined the duties attaching to marriage in the following terms (para. 132):

Marriage, whether civil or religious, is a contract, formally entered into. It confers on the parties the status of husband and wife, the essence of the contract being an agreement between a man and a woman to live together, and to love one another as husband and wife, to the exclusion of all others. It creates a relationship of mutual and reciprocal obligations, typically involving the sharing of a common home and a common domestic life and the right to enjoy each other's society, comfort and assistance.

It is not obvious that this definition escapes the problems outlined above. For example, the court carefully removes gender imbalance from the criteria, a change that may reflect a broad cultural shift in some parts of English and Welsh society, but does it follow that all cultures in our multicultural Britain have redefined marriage in these egalitarian terms?

While particularly clear in the marriage context, these cultural issues extend into all areas of capacity. Thus, the testamentary test in *Banks* v *Goodfellow* required that the testator understand, among other things, 'claims to which he ought to give effect'. This tends to refer to close family members, yet it is clearly a mere cultural value that these people are entitled to inherit upon the demise of the testator. Even as regards capacity to commit a crime, the knowledge that the act was 'wrong' is to be understood in a moral way, 'according to the ordinary standard adopted by reasonable men': *R* v *Codere* (1916) 12 Cr App R 21 at 27. It seems inappropriate to find individuals incapable owing to the wrong set of cultural values, yet how is a test of capacity to be formulated that is free of cultural bias?

The law of incapacity creates roles of authority and dependence, discipline and control, power and subordination, themes running through the remainder of this book. In so far as the existing laws relating to incapacity are specific to the decision in question, allowing for capacity in some areas but not others, it is not obvious that the law of incapacity will be analogous to one of Goffman's total institutions (1961): more like care in the community, it will have some of those characteristics but not others. Thus, there will still be issues of learned dependency, particularly significant here because they may affect later capacity. There is also the risk of conflicts in those in charge of decision-making, between the best interests of the person lacking capacity as perceived by that person or by the law, and the personal convenience or view of best interests of the decision-maker.

Similarly, there will be Foucauldian resonances, because the modern view of capacity is linked closely with the concept of rationality. Indeed, it is difficult to find a concept closer to the heart of Foucault's opus than the allocation of rights, of legal personhood, on the basis of a test of rationality. The study of incapacity thus involves the knowledge of the margin of personhood itself. Given the emphasis that Foucault places on the relationship between knowledge and power, the way in which incapacity is to be understood should be of no small importance to those who take his work seriously.

11

The Mental Capacity Act 2005

11.1 Context and overview of the Act

The MCA 2005 is expected to come into effect in April 2007, following an 18-year gestation period. It has grown from a project that the Law Commission commenced in 1989. The Commission proposed a comprehensive statute on decision-making for people lacking capacity, including formalising the appointment of substitute decision-makers, codifying a test of incapacity and of best interests, providing a set of standards and processes regarding medical research when subjects lack capacity, codifying advance treatment refusals, and providing an enhanced Court of Protection to oversee the new law. The Commission's work and proposals received broadly, although not universally, favourable responses (Carson, 1993; Gunn, 1994; Fennell, 1994; Freeman, 1994; Parkin, 1995; Fennell, 1995; Bartlett, 1997). Nonetheless, the proposals were put out for further consultation with the publication of a Green Paper by the Lord Chancellor's Department in 1997 (Lord Chancellor's Department, 1997), and a White Paper in 1999 (Lord Chancellor's Department, 1999).

The White Paper stated that the Law Commission's work would be largely enacted, but without the proposals on research (Law Commission, 1995: Part VI) and advance statements on health care (Part V), although the latter would still be governed by common law, discussed above. These issues, which for some time risked scuppering the entire reform project, seem odd objections. The concerns with the research aspects of the proposals seem to have been based in a squeamishness regarding research on people lacking capacity. While this concern is certainly legitimate, there was, at the time of the Law Commission report, no developed or coherent law concerning this research, leaving much to local practice. If research into disabling conditions is to be pursued, much of it will need to be done on individuals lacking capacity. The Law Commission was proposing the introduction of formalised safeguards for such research – surely, in principle, a good thing.

The concern about advance directives flowed from concerns about whether advanced refusals of medical treatment sanctioned euthanasia. Whatever the merits of those concerns, it is difficult to see them as relevant to the bill, because common law already allowed an individual to refuse treatment prospectively, even if such a refusal would result in his or her death. The bill proposed only to give that arrangement a statutory framework.

A bill was considered by a joint scrutiny committee of the House of Commons and House of Lords in 2003 (House of Commons and House of Lords, 2003), and the bill was finally passed into law two years later. The concern about advance directives was sufficient that only a last-minute intervention by the Prime Minister ensured passage through the Lords, and, as a result, the Act specifically provides that it does not alter the law related to murder, manslaughter, or assisted suicide (s. 62).

As a result, the Act passed bears considerable similarity to that proposed by the Law Commission. The exception is that the Commission's proposals regarding public law protections for people lacking capacity have not been included. These would have established objective thresholds that would have had to be met prior to intervention by state actors in the lives of people lacking capacity. Instead, the Act provides a system of advocates that may need to be consulted at key events, such as admission to hospitals or care homes for significant periods, or the provision of serious medical treatment.

The MCA essentially provides a set of mechanisms for substitute decision-making for people lacking capacity. It is designed to sit alongside much of the common law, but not necessarily to supersede it. A probate court concerned about whether the will of a deceased person was validly executed, for example, will not necessarily turn for guidance to the MCA. It will instead continue to rely on the existing body of jurisprudence regarding capacity to make a will; the MCA will be relevant if a living person were found, under the MCA criteria, not to have capacity to make a will. In that event, the Act provides a system by which a substitute decision-maker, the Court of Protection in the case of a will, can act on the person's behalf.

As noted in Chapter 10, such systems have long been in place for decisions regarding the property and affairs of people lacking capacity. Most recently, these have been governed by Part VII of the MHA 1983 and, to a lesser degree, by the Enduring Powers of Attorney Act 1985. Both of these statutory regimes are superseded by the MCA. For personal decisions, the MCA is entering new legislative space. As discussed in Chapter 10, the *parens patriae* power of the Crown created a system to make personal decisions on behalf of an individual lacking capacity that was in place until 1959, although the indications are that it was seldom used for this purpose. The provisions of the Mental Deficiency Acts, used much more frequently, were similarly superseded by the MHA 1959. The guardianship provisions of the 1959 Act were not based on capacity, but rather on welfare, and, by the end of the 1980s, were used only rarely. Certainly, personal decisions for those lacking capacity must have been made prior to the MCA 2005, but they were made outside a codified legal framework. In this sense, the MCA 2005 opens new legislative space.

This chapter outlines the contours of that space. While the various aspects of the MCA will be discussed in some detail below, an overview may assist at this stage. The MCA refers to a person lacking capacity (or, in some contexts, reasonably believed to be lacking capacity) as 'P', and a person empowered to make decisions on behalf of that person as 'D'. This convention is similarly followed in this chapter.

The Act opens with a statement of principles (s. 1), designed to guide interpretation of the remainder of the Act. These are drawn from the common law and from good practice. While they are uncontroversial, they are important guides to how the Act is meant to be understood.

The Act then defines what it means to lack capacity to make a decision (ss. 2–3). Although it has some idiosyncrasies of its own, the definition broadly reflects the common law as it has developed in the context of capacity to consent to medical treatment. Thus, to lack capacity, P must either fail to understand the information relevant to a decision, fail to retain it, or fail to be able to use the information to arrive at a decision. Significantly, the assessment refers to the specific decision to be made: there is nothing inconsistent with an individual having capacity to make some decisions, but not others. This is consistent with the common law, but represents a change from decision-making under Part VII of the MHA 1983 and the Enduring Powers of Attorney Act 1985. Under the former, a finding that an individual lacked capacity deprived that individual of authority to make any decisions relating to his or her property or affairs; under the latter, the attorney similarly had authority to make all decisions consistent with the power. The attorney thus had authority to make decisions whether or not the donor retained or reacquired capacity to make some of those decisions, unless the power provided to the contrary. Under the MCA, all substitute decision-makers are precluded from making decisions that the individual has the power to make.

The MCA places advance refusals of medical treatment on a statutory footing (ss. 24–6). Much of this reflects the common law regarding such advance decisions, although particular requirements are introduced for such refusals if reliance on them would result in the death of the individual: these must be in writing, signed and witnessed; and they must expressly envisage that they will apply if the patient's life is in danger. Advance refusals of medical treatment are the only decision to which the new statutory best interests tests will not apply. If an individual, while competent, makes a valid and applicable advance refusal of treatment and the need for such treatment arises, it is in law as if the individual were competent and refusing the treatment. For somatic treatments, that ends the matter. For treatments for mental disorder, however, P's refusal can be overridden by ss. 63 and 58 of the MHA 1983, if he or she is detained under that Act: see Chapter 7.

For all other decisions, the statutory test of best interests applies (s. 4). This contains a variety of substantive conditions, not entirely consistent with each other in theoretical approach. Some aspects of the test focus on the subjectivity of P, such as the requirement to take into account P's current wishes, and any wishes expressed while competent. Others are more objective, but focus on the particular situation of P: D is required to take into account the likelihood that P will regain capacity, for example. Yet others are entirely objective: D is required to consider 'all the relevant circumstances' in reaching a decision as to best interests. No guidance is provided as to how the various aspects of the test are to be balanced in a given case. The test also includes procedural elements, providing a list of people with whom D must consult in ascertaining best interests. For particularly serious decisions, such as those involving medium or long-term admission to psychiatric facilities or care homes, independent advocates are to be provided for people lacking capacity where others are unavailable to advise on best interests.

The Act specifically holds that D must always act in the best interests of P (s. 1(5)). For substitute decision-makers other than the Court of Protection, a further express limitation is created if the decision would result in the 'restraint' of P, where restraint is taken to mean either doing an act requiring force consequent on P's resistance, or restricting P's liberty of movement. Such actions will only be permitted to prevent harm to P, and where the restraint is proportional to the seriousness and likelihood of the harm prevented. Significantly, any violation of rights under Art. 5 of the ECHR is greater than 'restraint' under the MCA 2005: such decisions can only be made by the Court of Protection. As passed in 2005, therefore, the MCA cannot be taken to be a solution to the *Bournewood* problem. The government's proposed amendments to the MCA to take account of these problems are discussed elsewhere in this volume (see Chapter 4).

The Act envisages several types of substitute decision-maker. Individuals with capacity to do so will be able to sign powers of attorney that will take effect in the event of capacity being lost – a so-called 'lasting power of attorney' (LPOA). The system is broadly similar to the enduring powers of attorney (EPOA) system under the 1985 Act, but unlike EPOAs, LPOAs will be allowed to be created for personal decisions as well as for decisions concerning property and affairs. Once the LPOA is registered with the Public Guardian, the donee will be entitled to make decisions covered by the LPOA that the donee lacks capacity to make. These decisions must, however, be made in the donee's best interest.

Alternatively, the Court of Protection will be able to appoint one or more 'deputies' to make decisions for a person lacking capacity. These individuals will be responsible to the Court, normally via the Public Guardian, and will again be required to make decisions for P according to the best interests criteria. They will not be able to be given authority over decisions within the scope of an LPOA, and they, like the donee of an LPOA, will have jurisdiction only if the individual lacks the capacity to make the specific decision in question.

If neither of these substitute decision-makers exist, the Act provides a broad mechanism where anyone who reasonably believes that P lacks capacity can make decisions regarding P's 'care or treatment' in P's best interests. This is the most radical departure in the Act, because it provides a near unbounded authority for altruism. Such flexibility comes at a cost, however: here, as elsewhere in the Act, there are few procedural safeguards to oversee D's exercise of his or her decision-making authority.

A new offence of ill-treating or neglecting a person lacking capacity is created by the Act (s. 44).

The entire process is to be overseen by a reconstituted Court of Protection. Unlike the body of the same name formulated under Part VII of the Mental Health Act 1983, the new version will more closely resemble a court in its operational style: it will be a superior court of record, staffed by judges. It will have broad jurisdiction over matters under the MCA, including disputes regarding whether a person lacks capacity and what the best interests of P are. It can determine the validity and applicability of advance refusals of medical treatment, and can intervene in the event that the donee of an LPOA is not acting in the best interests of P. It can make decisions on behalf of P, including making a will, and, as noted above, it can appoint a deputy to make decisions on behalf of P.

The research provisions of the Act require that any research done on people lacking capacity concerns the impairing condition or its treatment. Such research will be allowed only if the benefit to P will not be disproportionate to the burdens of the research, or, where the research is to provide knowledge rather than to benefit P personally, where inconvenience to P will be minimal. A variety of procedural safeguards are introduced to ensure that these standards are met, and if P appears to object to the research, he or she must be withdrawn from it. Further discussion of the research proposals is outside the scope of this book, and readers are referred to discussions elsewhere (e.g. Bartlett, 2005: 2.123–2.134).

Although passed in 2005, the Act is currently expected to come into force in April 2007 and remains, to a considerable degree, a work in progress (for revised implementation timetable, see preface). The statutory instruments that will contain much of the procedural detail are now beginning to appear, but there is much left to come. Further, we await guidance envisaged by the Act directed to donors and donees of LPOAs, and persons to be consulted when research is contemplated. Perhaps most significantly, we await a final Code of Practice. A draft Code was published prior to the passage of the Act (Department of Constitutional Affairs, 2004a), available, as of October 2006, online at http://www.dca.gov.uk/menincap/mcbdraftcode.pdf. A major consultation exercise followed the publication of this draft Code, however. A final Code is expected shortly, and it is not clear how significant the changes will be from the draft version. Finally, as noted elsewhere in this text, the government has indicated plans to amend the MCA 2005, to take account of the human rights issues in *HL* v *UK* (the *Bournewood* litigation). While a briefing document has been published by the government (Department of Health, 2006b), at the time of writing, a bill has not yet been introduced.

For all these reasons, it is recommended that readers check the relevant sources for new developments.

As noted in Chapter 10.1, the law relating to incapacity has a considerable overlap with mental health law, but they are not the same field. This chapter is only an introduction to the MCA 2005 and, for a more detailed analysis, readers are referred to the relevant guides to the Act (Bartlett, 2005; Greaney *et al.*, 2005; Jones, 2005).

11.2 The principles of the Act and the meaning of incapacity

The MCA commences with the following statement of principles:

1(1) The following principles apply for purposes of this Act—

(2) A person must be assumed to have capacity unless it is established that he lacks capacity.

(3) A person is not to be treated as unable to make a decision unless all practicable steps to help him to do so have been taken without success.

(4) A person is not to be treated as unable to make a decision merely because he makes an unwise decision.

(5) An act done, or decision made, under this Act for or on behalf of a person who lacks capacity must be done, or made, in his best interests.

(6) Before the act is done, or the decision is made, regard must be had to whether the purpose for which it is needed can be as effectively achieved in a way that is less restrictive of the person's rights and freedom of action.

These principles are not new. Those contained in subss. (2), (4), and (5) flow from the common law, albeit with subs. (5) now referring to the statutory definition of best interests, rather than to the common law one. Those contained in subss. (3) and (6) are largely statements of existing good practice. Nonetheless, some comments may be made about the principles.

Subsection (2) reiterates the common law presumption of capacity. The relevance of the presumption will be slightly different under the Act, however, particularly regarding persons of marginal capacity ostensibly agreeing to their care. Prior to the introduction of the Act, it mattered little in practice whether these people had capacity: if they did, they were giving valid consent; if they did not, the care would be nonetheless be legal if in their best interests, based on the principle of necessity established in *F v West Berkshire*. Under the MCA, the situation will have changed, in some cases. In the event that a valid and applicable LPOA has been signed or a deputy appointed by the court, decisions made on behalf of persons lacking capacity must be made by these substitutes. Whether or not such a substitute has been appointed, best interests will now be determined under the Act, using a procedure considerably more robust than that of common law.

The principles in subss. (3) and (4), in effect, serve to buttress the general presumption of capacity in subs. (2). Subsection (4) makes it clear that lack of capacity is not to be determined by the outcome of the decision made: capacity is to be determined by functional ability to make decisions, not according to the desirability of the outcome of a choice. Subsection (3) requires that all practicable steps be taken to assist the person to make a decision before he or she is found to lack capacity. This re-enforces that the presumption of capacity is not rebutted if obtaining a competent decision would be merely inconvenient. Reasonable steps must be taken to get a competent decision, including, for example, use of alternate methods of communication such as sign language or, in the event that capacity is perceived to vary over the course of the day, asking for a decision at a time when the individual is most likely to have capacity.

Subsection (6) is the principle of least restrictive alternative, and, as such, has long been at the core of much good practice relating to people with disabilities. Different articulations of the principle of least restrictive alternative have slightly different emphases. This particular version focuses on minimal restriction of the person's 'rights and freedom of action'.

What it means for a person to lack capacity is defined in ss. 2 and 3 of the Act. The Act imposes a diagnostic threshold: for the purposes of the Act, any incapacity must flow from 'an impairment of, or a disturbance in the functioning of, the mind or brain' (s. 2(1)), whether permanent or temporary (s. 2(2)). Except for a few property provisions, the Act will only apply if P is over the age of 16. Children will, therefore, be dealt with under other legislation or the common law. Much of this other law continues to apply until the individual reaches the age of 18 years, however: *Re R (A Minor) (Wardship: Medical Treatment)* [1991] 4 All ER 177; *Re W (A Minor) (Medical Treatment: Court's Jurisdiction)* [1992] 3 WLR 758. Persons between the ages of 16 and 18 years may be dealt with either under the MCA or these other legal powers.

The pivotal definition of incapacity is contained in s. 3(1):

3(1) For the purposes of section 2, a person is unable to make a decision for himself if he is unable—

(a) to understand the information relevant to the decision,

(b) to retain that information,

(c) to use or weigh that information as part of the process of making the decision, or

(d) to communicate his decision (whether by talking, using sign language or any other means).

The individual must be able to understand information relevant to the reasonably foreseeable consequences of deciding one way or another, or of failing to make a decision (s. 3(4)). The Act therefore imposes the same standards of capacity for whichever way an individual is to decide: there is no different standard of capacity dependent on whether the individual agrees with professional advice, for example. The information is to be put to the individual in a way that is appropriate to his or her circumstances (s. 3(2)). It may be necessary to use visual aids or simple language, for example. Similarly, it would be necessary to provide the information in a language understood by the individual. The individual need only retain the information for a short time (s. 3(3)).

The similarity of the test in s. 3 to the common law test of capacity to consent to medical treatment discussed above (Chapter 10) will be obvious, with the conspicuous difference that the MCA contains no reference to believing the information. This seems appropriate, beccause individuals may fail to believe information for a wide variety of reasons, some of which will bespeak incapacity, and others not. If an individual fails to believe his or her doctor on the basis that the doctor is inexperienced, for example, it does not follow that the individual lacks capacity. If, on the other hand, the individual's lack of belief is the result of psychosis, the individual will almost certainly lack capacity, presumably on the basis that it affects the individual's ability to use or weigh information under subs. (c).

Section 2(3) provides that lack of capacity cannot be established 'merely' by reference to a person's age, appearance, or any condition or aspect of behaviour that might lead to unjustified assumptions about that person's capacity. The intent of the provision is laudable: decisions regarding capacity should not be made according to stereotypes.

The meaning of the word 'merely' is problematic, however, because it suggests that the stereotypical category may be a factor in determining capacity, as long as it is accompanied by others. It is difficult to see that this is appropriate: stereotypical assumptions should not be permitted to influence decisions regarding capacity at all.

The incapacity of an individual is to be determined according to the specific decision to be made. As is the case at common law, there is nothing legally inconsistent with an individual having capacity for some decisions and not others. He or she may have the ability to contract, but not to consent to medical treatment, or may indeed have the ability to conclude some contracts (or consent to some medical treatments), and not others. This represents no change to the common law position, but constitutes a marked change from the situation under Part VII of the Mental Health Act. An individual found incapable under Part VII lost all his or her rights to contract and contracts purportedly signed by these individuals were void: *Re Walker* [1905] 1 Ch 160; *Re Beaney (Deceased)* [1978] 2 All ER 595 at 600. Under the MCA, this is no longer the case, and, indeed, donees of LPOAs and court-appointed deputies are specifically precluded from making decisions that an individual has capacity to make at the relevant time: ss. 11(2); 20(1). The result in the law of contract, presumably, is drawn from the current common law for contracts signed by people not under Part VII. Such people are presumed to have capacity, and contracts signed by them will be enforceable unless both the contrary is shown and the other party to the contract was aware, or ought reasonably to have been aware, of P's incapacity at the time the contract was concluded: *Imperial Loan Company* v *Stone* [1892] 1 QB 599.

11.3 Best interests

The definition of best interests in the Act is contained in s. 4. The section combines a variety of the approaches discussed in Chapter 10. Section 4(6) requires D to consider, in so far as reasonably ascertainable, P's past and present wishes and feelings, in particular written statements made by P when he or she had capacity, the beliefs and values that would be likely to influence P's decision if he or she had capacity, and any other factors P would consider if able to do so. These elements, relating to the subjective views of P, suggest the influence of a substitute judgment model of decision-making: what P would want, however irrational or improbable, matters to the determination of his or her best interests.

The inclusion of P's current (and therefore, by definition, incompetent) wishes warrants note. This is, undoubtedly in part, a matter of common humanity: if P is clearly averse to a decision, and particularly a decision concerning his or her care or bodily integrity, enforcement of that decision may be traumatic for that person. Absent cogent reason to the contrary, such results are to be avoided. More subtly, the provision acknowledges that, while law must draw a hard line between 'capable' and 'incapable' decision-making to determine who is legally authorised to make decisions, the realities of life are far more complex. The requirement that current views are to be taken into account acknowledges that P has views that may matter considerably in decision-making, even if legal responsibility for the decision lies elsewhere.

Other factors further emphasise the importance of P's autonomy. Subsection 4(3) requires D to consider whether P is likely to regain capacity to make the decision in question, and if so, when that will be. The implication is that D ought to avoid deciding in a fashion that will bind P, once he or she has regained capacity. D's decisions should control P's affairs only for the period of the incapacity, if it is reasonably possible so to limit those decisions. As a further acknowledgement of P's autonomy, subs. 4(4) requires D to involve P as far as practicable in the decision-making process.

At the same time, the list of factors for determination of best interests is not closed: s. 4(2) requires D to take into account 'all the relevant circumstances' (emphasis added). Objective best interests are also therefore relevant to the overall determination.

The Act provides no guidance as to how the objective criteria are to be balanced against the criteria more directed to the individual's autonomy. Presumably, the balance will depend both on the decision to be taken, and on P's individual circumstances. The views that the individual had when competent would be particularly important when the Court of Protection exercises its power to make a will on behalf of P, for example. Decisions necessitated by practical necessity may have a stronger objective component. While the prior competent views of P may be relevant in delaying as long as possible a decision to enter a nursing home, the realities of the situation may make it necessary at some point to override those wishes. Subjective factors might be of particular importance for a decision relating to medical treatment to which P, while competent, had expressed a firm religious objection. Objective factors would be of higher relevance when P had never had capacity, and therefore where values he or she would take into account are a matter of speculation.

This flexibility is potentially one of the considerable strengths of the Act. It also has the potential to undermine the Act. Section 4 is an attempt to strike a careful balance between autonomy and objective best interests. The best interests test is at the core of the legislative scheme, and if it is not is appropriately applied in individual decisions, much of the appeal of the Act will be lost.

Subsection 4(1) provides that best interests cannot be determined 'merely' on the basis of P's age, appearance, condition or behaviour that would lead to 'unjustified' assumptions about his or her best interests. The criticism here is similar to that noted regarding determination of capacity, above: 'merely' suggests that these criteria may be factors in decision-making, as long as they are not the only factors. If they lead to 'unjustified' assumptions, however, it is not obvious why they should be factors at all.

Subsection 4(5) provides that, where the best interests determination relates to life-sustaining treatment, D must not be motivated by a desire to bring about P's death.

These all, together, constitute the substantive requirements of s. 4. The section also includes procedural requirements. D must take account of the views of the following people, and must consult them, if 'practical and appropriate' to do so:

(a) anyone named by P as someone to be consulted on the matter in question or on matters of that kind;

(b) anyone engaged in caring for P, or interested in his or her welfare;

(c) any donee of a lasting power of attorney granted by P; and

(d) any deputy appointed for P by the court (s. 4(7)).

The individuals listed in (b) through (d) are to be consulted whether or not they have direct responsibility for the decision in question. Thus, the donee of an LPOA that concerns consent to medical treatment only should normally be consulted regarding other care-related matters, unless it is not 'appropriate' to do so. This is significant not only because the views of these people may be enlightening, but also to ensure consistency between decisions regarding P.

The purpose of consulting these people is to determine P's best interests, and, in particular, to ascertain P's past and present wishes and feelings, the beliefs and values P would have brought to the decision, and what P would have considered if he or she had been able to do so. The focus is the best interests of P, not of the person consulted. The concerns of the person consulted may be relevant to P's best interests, either because they would be taken into account by P or because they may alter the options for the decision – P's best interests may best be served by returning to live with the consultee, but that is of little assistance if the consultee is not prepared to take on that responsibility – but it is P's best interests that are at the heart of the consultation. Decisions taken on behalf of P will often impact, sometimes significantly, on the lives of the consultees. How practical it will be for consultees to make this distinction between P's best interests and their own best interests is, at best, an open question.

The Act provides no guidance on whether this consultation affects any right to confidentiality of P. By necessary implication, it must be possible to disclose relevant information regarding a decision to the individual whose advice is being sought; otherwise, it is not obvious how the consultee is meant to be meaningfully involved. At the same time, it does not follow that P would wish all people on the list to know his or her affairs. If there is cogent reason to believe that P would not wish information divulged to a consultee, it would presumably not be 'appropriate', to use the language of s. 4(7), to consult that individual. A consultee who, for example, was believed to have been abusing P would not be appropriately consulted (see, *mutatis mutandum, JT v UK* [2000] 1 FLR 909; *R (On the application of M) v Secretary of State for Health* [2003] EWHC 1094. Most questions of confidentiality will not be so stark, however.

The Act is similarly silent on whether any information provided to the consultee in the best interests determination is impressed with a duty of confidentiality: is the consultee liable for telling others the information? A coherent argument can be made that such a duty is created, at least in some cases, on the basis that confidential information provided to another with the express or implied expectation that it will be kept confidential, is impressed with a duty on the recipient not to disclose it to others (see, e.g., *Attorney-General v Guardian Newspapers (No. 2)* [1990] 1 AC 109, per Lord Goff). This begs the question, however, of whether the information provided to the consultee is provided in circumstances under which it would be expected to remain confidential. How far does the duty extend to information that is not legally confidential, but may not widely be known? There may be cogent reasons that P would not wish such information to be widely known; but it is not obvious how far the law will go to preclude this. The traditional relationship between guardian and ward was fiduciary in nature; a coherent argument can be made to the effect that the relationship between D and P is of a similar character. In that event, it may well be the case that a duty of confidentiality impresses onto information learned in the course of that relationship, and a duty not to disclose is imposed on any information that P would wish not generally known. That is certainly the position contained in the draft Code of Practice under the MCA (Department of Constitutional Affairs, 2004a: paras. 6.26, 7.48). When D is a professional, such as a doctor or lawyer, such duties may also be imposed by (and enforced through) professional obligations and organisations. When D is a family member, different social dynamics apply: D may well think it appropriate to share information within the family. Again, it is not clear that a duty of confidentiality would impress onto these additional family members. In so far as D's disclosure is in breach of a duty of confidentiality, it is further not obvious how it is to be enforced. The traditional mechanism is litigation; but it is not obvious that this is an appropriate response to loose tongues within the family.

For decision-makers other than the Court of Protection, some latitude is provided in the determination of best interests. The compliance with s. 4 will be sufficient 'if (having complied with the requirements of subsections (1) to (7) [D] believes that what he does or decides is in the best interests of the person concerned.' (s. 4(9)).

Several questions arise regarding this subsection. First, it would seem that, if there is no compliance with subss. (1) to (7), the best interests test is not met. To be realistic, however, decisions will be made by carers who may have no knowledge of the Act: families do not necessarily seek advice from a lawyer when decisions must be taken for a frail loved one. This raises the question of the legal status of decisions taken in good faith, but not in compliance with subss. (1) to (7), leaving the carers at risk of legal liability for these decisions. There are several possible responses. It may be that the courts would hold the carers liable in such circumstances. 'Ignorance of the law,' the adage goes, 'is no excuse'. Depending on the circumstances of the case, this would seem an inappropriate result: the carers may well themselves be emotionally fragile as they witness the frailty of their family member; the addition of legal liability seems extraordinarily harsh. Alternatively, the courts might read down the provisions of s. 4, declining to insist that the substantial and procedural safeguards in the section are observed in their entirety. This would also be an unfortunate result. The best interests test is at the core of the MCA; to weaken this core provision would fundamentally alter its ethos. This might well be disastrous for the overall implementation of the Act. As a final alternative, the court could conceivably hold that the Act does not destroy the common law jurisdiction that grew from cases following *F* v *West Berkshire*. In this analysis, the actions might be justified not by the Act, but might still be legal at common law. This would also be a poor result, because it would still allow the safeguards and subtleties of the Act to be circumvented. The Act was the result of considerable thought and consultation; it would be most unfortunate for it to be gutted in such a fashion. The difficulty is that the courts must presumably choose one of these three choices – and none of them are attractive.

Second, a particular question regarding determination of best interests arises regarding care teams. Various members of these teams may be relying on the determination of best interests at various times, sometimes for a variety of disparate care and treatment-related decisions. How far are team members entitled to rely on the pursuit of aspects of s. 4 by other team members, in their determination of best interests? Subsection (9) seems to presuppose that D, as an individual, will have followed all aspects of the best interests test personally, but it is likely to prove impractical and inefficient for each and every member of a care team to consult with all of the people listed in s. 4(7). It will surely result in better decision-making for a small number of the team to make these enquiries, in greater depth. The answer in this case may lie in the specific wording of s. 4(7). This requires each D on the team to take account of the views of the people listed in the section, but it requires consultation only if 'practical and appropriate'. At least arguably, once the views have been obtained, it is no longer appropriate for other care members to return to re-receive the information.

11.3.1 'Serious medical treatment' and admission to NHS or local authority accommodation

Sections 35–41 of the MCA make additional provisions for the determination of best interests when 'serious medical treatment' or admission to NHS or local authority facilities will be for longer than prescribed times. These sections establish an independent advocacy service. When a decision of these types is contemplated, an independent advocate must be called in to advise on best interests, when no one other than a professional is suitable to be consulted regarding P's best interests. The advocates are intended to provide support to P, so that he or she can participate as fully as possible in the decision and this process includes: obtaining relevant information, and, in particular, ascertaining what P's wishes and feelings would be likely to be if P had capacity; ascertaining alternative courses of action; obtaining a further medical opinion regarding treatment, if appropriate (s. 36). To this end, the advocate has a right to examine and copy health records, social service records, and records made pursuant to the Care Standards Act 2000.

The decisions that trigger these additional provisions are:

- admission to an NHS hospital (not just a psychiatric hospital or ward) for a period expected to exceed 28 days, or transfer to a different hospital where admission is expected to extend to such a period;

- admission to an NHS care home (or transfer to a different care home) for a period expected to exceed eight weeks;

- admission to local authority residential accommodation (or transfer to different local authority accommodation) provided pursuant to s. 117 of the MHA, or ss. 21 or 29 of the National Assistance Act 1948, where such accommodation is expected to continue for at least eight weeks; or

- where 'serious medical treatment' is proposed for P.

The first three of these, involving admission to hospital or care homes, do not include situations where the admission is 'imposed' pursuant to the MHA (ss. 38(2), 39(3)). 'Imposed' is not defined in the MCA. It would certainly include involuntary admission under s. 3, or under Part III of the MHA. It would also include admission under s. 2, when it was expected that a s. 3 admission would follow. It is less obvious whether it would include admission on the authority of a guardian, under s. 8 of the MHA. Certainly, such admissions cannot be viewed as voluntary in any meaningful sense: see Chapter 4. It would, however, be anomalous for these not to be included in the advocacy protections. The protections are designed to ensure a second and disinterested assessment of the need for these admissions, when the only carers are professionals. As noted in Chapter 9, the vast bulk of guardians are now local authorities – i.e. professionals. In the event that there is no non-professional to advise on the best interests of P, it is not obvious why the decisions of these professional guardians should escape scrutiny.

'Serious medical treatment' is defined by the Mental Capacity Act 2005 (Independent Mental Capacity Advocates) (General) Regulations 2006:

> 4(2) Serious medical treatment is treatment which involves providing, withdrawing or withholding treatment in circumstances where—
>
> (a) in a case where a single treatment is being proposed, there is a fine balance between its benefits to the patient and the burdens and risks it is likely to entail for him,
>
> (b) in a case where there is a choice of treatments, a decision as to which one to use is finely balanced, or
>
> (c) what is proposed would be likely to involve serious consequences for the patient. (SI 2006/ 1832).

This definition is interesting, in that it would seem to include relatively minor treatments when there is a choice of treatment, or where the risks and benefits of the proposed treatments are finely balanced. In this context, 'serious' does not necessarily mean serious in the colloquial sense. Sadly, s. 4(2)(c) adds little to guide in the scope of decisions for which advocacy is to be required: seriousness of consequences is likely to be in the eye of the beholder. The spirit of the Act would suggest that this should be determined, at least in part, according to what the views of P would be if competent, but the fact that an independent advocate may be required indicates that there is no family member or similar person to ask about such views.

11.4 Decisions by substitutes

The selection of substitutes mandated by the MCA can be arranged in hierarchical form. Donees of LPOAs will have been appointed by P when he or she was competent to do so; deputies are appointed by the Court of Protection. While the Court of Protection may revoke the LPOA under some circumstances, or may itself make decisions on behalf of P even if an LPOA is in effect, it cannot appoint a deputy to make decisions inconsistent with those of a donee of the LPOA who is acting within his or her authority (s. 20(2)). In the absence of a valid and applicable LPOA and of a court-appointed deputy with the relevant authority, carers may make decisions regarding care and treatment as the need arises.

The decision-making authority of substitutes extends only to decisions for which P lacks capacity, or for which D reasonably believes P to lack capacity. This applies even if an LPOA has been registered or where a court has appointed a deputy to make decisions for P (ss. 11(7)(a), 20(1)). All substitutes are also bound by valid and applicable advance decisions to refuse medical treatment.

Some decisions remain outside the scope of the Act entirely. Nothing in the Act allows an individual to vote on behalf of P (s. 29). Significantly for this volume, decisions regarding treatment under Part IV of the Mental Health Act are outside the scope of the MCA (s. 28). The breadth of this section is discussed below. Finally, a number of decisions related to family law and personal relationships are outside the scope of the MCA (s 27), including:

- consent to marriage or civil partnership;
- consent to sexual relations;
- giving consents relating to new reproductive technologies required by the Human Fertilisation and Embryology Act 1990;
- consent to divorce or dissolution of civil partnership based on two years of separation;
- consent to placement of a child for adoption, or the making of an adoption order.

In these matters, if the individual lacks capacity to decide him or herself, law provides no mechanism for substitute decision-making. For the first three items, the matter in question cannot therefore occur; for the final two, the specificity of the statutory provision should be noted. The MCA does not say that divorce is impossible when one of the parties lacks capacity, nor that the children of such a person can never be adopted. What is precluded is instead the route to these outcomes that is based on the consent of P.

In general, decisions under the Act are to be made based solely on the best interests criteria in s. 4. The main exception is where the restraint of P would result from a decision taken by the donee of an LPOA, by a court-appointed deputy, or under the general defence available to carers. D restrains P if force is used, or its use is threatened, to secure the doing of an act that P resists, or where P's liberty of movement is restricted, whether or not P resists (ss. 6(4), 11(5), 20(12)). Restraint is not prohibited under the MCA. Instead, substitute decision-makers may use it only if it is necessary to prevent harm to P, and where the restraint is a proportionate response to the seriousness and likelihood of that harm occurring.

The Act holds that any action that would deprive P of his or her liberty under the European Convention on Human Rights constitutes more than restraint: ss. 6(5), 11(6), 20(13). Such decisions are therefore outside the authority of the above-named decision-makers, and under the MCA, as currently drafted, available only to the Court of Protection. The Act, as it now stands, cannot practically cope with the decision in *HL v UK* (the *Bournewood* case), discussed in Chapter 4. The government has issued a briefing sheet (Department of Health, 2006b) signalling proposed amendments to the MCA to meet the problems in *Bournewood*. These proposed amendments are also discussed in Chapter 4.

11.4.1 The new Court of Protection

The Act is overseen by a new Court of Protection. The nomenclature here is perhaps confusing, because 'Court of Protection' was also the label used for the body charged with administering Part VII of the MHA 1983. That body was headed by a Master appointed under the Supreme Court Act 1981, and while it certainly held hearings, its jurisdiction was strictly limited by Part VII of the 1983 Act. Essentially, it made determinations as to whether individuals lacked capacity to administer their property and affairs, and if they did not, took over that administration from them. In addition, it was permitted to draft wills on behalf of people lacking the capacity to do so.

The new Court of Protection, by comparison, will instead be staffed by judges. It will have a broad jurisdiction on matters related to incapacity. It may make declarations as to whether an individual has capacity to make a decision, and as to whether an act done in relation to such a person is lawful (s. 15). It may make decisions related to an individual's personal welfare or property and affairs, when that person lacks the capacity to do so. Both these categories are defined, but in broad terms (ss. 17 and 18). It will have the power to draft a will on behalf of P, a power broadly analogous to that contained in ss. 96 and 97 of the MHA 1983. Apart from the decisions noted above in s. 27, the court has an exceptionally wide latitude of authority to make decisions and determinations on behalf of people lacking capacity.

The court is given specific powers relating to LPOAs and advance decisions to refuse treatment. For the former, these deal with the creation of powers (such as whether the individual had capacity to create the power, or whether the power was created by undue influence or fraud), or meaning or effect of the power, including giving directions to the donee of the power. The court is also given a role in supervision of powers, being able to order that the power not be registered if the potential donee is behaving outside his authority or not in P's best interests (s. 22 (3)), or by requiring reports, accounts or other documentation during the authority of the donee (s. 23). For advance decisions to refuse treatment, the court has specific powers to determine the validity and applicability of these decisions. In neither of these instances, does the court have the authority to alter the terms of the instrument itself.

The common law had established a number of situations where a court application was considered to be mandatory prior to a doctor proceeding with medical treatment. These included sterilisations for non-therapeutic purposes (*F v West Berkshire*) and termination of life-sustaining treatment for people in a permanent vegetative state (*Airedale NHS Trust v Bland* [1993] AC 789). While the court no doubt has jurisdiction to provide directions and determinations relating to best interests in such cases, there is no requirement under the Act that it be consulted prior to these procedures. The draft bill of the Law Commission, upon which the MCA is so closely based, did include such a requirement for termination of life-sustaining treatment, unless it was expressly within the authority of the donee of an LPOA (Law Commission, 1995: cl. 10), so its exclusion from the 2005 Act must not be considered accidental.

While the court is given a broad jurisdiction, the limitations of the Act must nonetheless be acknowledged. The MCA itself creates mechanisms to make decisions that P himself or herself could have made; there is no authority under the act to require others to provide services for P. In some cases, other legislation or common law may create such duties. If an individual has a right to social services provision, for example, the court might no doubt invoke that law to reach a specific result regarding P. These authorities are few and limited, however. In the end, the court will often have its options limited by the services that others are prepared to provide. As an obvious example, the courts have held that there is no jurisdiction to require the provision of medical services that the attending physician views not to be desirable for his or her patient: see *Re J* [1992] 4 All ER 614, and, in a psychiatric context, *R v Ealing District Health Authority, ex p Fox* [1993] 3 All ER 170 at 183.

The court is aided in its administration of the Act by the Office of the Public Guardian, and by the Court of Protection Visitors. The latter are the former Lord Chancellor's Visitors, and include both lay and medical members who may visit people lacking capacity and provide reports to the Public Guardian or to the court.

The court is given the authority to appoint one or more deputies to make decisions on behalf of P. Again, and unlike the receivers appointed under Part VII of the MHA 1983, the deputy may be given authority to make personal or property-related decisions, or both. The deputy must be at least 18 years of age, or, for decisions related to property and affairs, a trust corporation. The deputy has a right to payment for expenses, and can be remunerated if the court so specifies in the order of appointment. Deputies may be required to post security with the Public Guardian, and to provide such reports to the Public Guardian as are required by the court: s. 19.

The MCA provides that the powers given to a deputy are to be as limited in scope and duration as reasonably practicable under the circumstances (s. 16(4)(b)), and may make the deputy subject to such duties or directions as the court thinks appropriate: s. 16(5). Nonetheless, the Act provides some specific restrictions on the powers of deputies. A deputy cannot prohibit contact between P and an individual named by the court. For example, in the case of a family feud, the deputy could not preclude contact between P and members of P's family named by the court. A deputy further cannot require a change of medical practitioners in charge of P's health care. The deputy may not sell P's property, or execute a will for P.

The deputy may also not be given powers that conflict with those given to a donee of an LPOA: s. 20(4). The policy of the Act would seem to be that the choices made by a substitute decision-maker appointed by the individual when competent take precedence over choices made by the court.

11.4.2 Lasting powers of attorney

Lasting powers of attorney (LPOAs) provide the most effective mechanism for people with capacity to make provision for any subsequent loss of capacity. Like regular powers of attorney, they are mandates signed by a donor, allowing the person named in the power, the attorney, to act on the donor's behalf in those matters listed in the power. At common law, however, regular powers of attorney ceased to have effect upon the incapacity of the donor: *Drew* v *Nunn* (1879) 4 QB 661. This remained the case until the Enduring Powers of Attorney Act 1985, which allowed powers executed in a specific form to remain valid, notwithstanding incapacity. The traditional power of attorney could extend only to the 'property and affairs' of an individual. The courts were content to give this phrase a broad meaning: see, e.g., *Re W* [1970] 2 All ER 502, where the phrase was taken to include representing P's interest in a divorce proceeding. Nonetheless, it did not extend to making decisions about personal decisions about P, including those related to P's care and treatment. With the introduction of the MCA, this restriction is removed: LPOAs can cover personal decisions, as well as those related to property and affairs.

With the introduction of the MCA, no new powers may be signed under the 1985 Act. Powers created under that Act prior to the introduction of the MCA will still be valid. People who are competent to do so may nonetheless wish to consider creating a new power under the MCA, particularly if they wish the power to extend to personal decision-making.

It is likely that LPOAs will prove popular. Around 15,000 enduring powers of attorney were registered annually under the old regime (*Masterman-Lister* v *Brutton & Co, Jewell & Home Counties Dairies* [2002] EWCA Civ 1889 at para. 15). Because the information required to be submitted upon registration with the court is minimal, little is known about the people, estates, or exercise of authority under this scheme. Suto *et al.* (2002) were able to determine the mean age at the time of registration to be 83 years, roughly 13 years higher than those under Part VII of the MHA 1983. Further, the standard deviation for the EPOA group was nine years, less than half of that for the Part VII group, and a higher percentage were women: 71 compared to 66 per cent. It does seem that the EPOA process, therefore, was about the estates of old women. It seems unlikely that the numbers of people executing the new LPOA will decrease. Less obvious is whether the frequency will increase, and if so, whether this will change the demographic profile of the donors.

The LPOA is potentially a very flexible instrument for individuals to plan for future incapacity. Different LPOAs may be signed for different decisions, so different donees might be appointed to make decisions regarding investments and those regarding personal care, or, indeed, those decisions relating to housing and medical treatment. An LPOA may appoint more than one donee to make a type of decision, and if so, may specify whether the donees will act jointly or separately. For decisions relating to property and affairs, a trust corporation may be a donee. The donee of the power may make decisions regarding life-sustaining treatment, although only if the power expressly confers that authority: s. 11(8).

The donee is permitted to define the scope of the LPOA as he or she would like. To use an example from the draft Code of Practice, the donee may require that the donee invest only in ethical investments – those operating in a socially and environmentally responsible manner (Department of Constitutional Affairs, 2004a: para. 6.14). It is not entirely clear what happens if the restriction on the power would require a decision not in the best interests of P, as defined in s. 4. Consider a restriction, for example, allowing a donee to make personal care decisions for P, but requiring decisions not be taken that would result in P's admission to a care home. While P's views would be clear, and those are to be taken into account in the best interests determination, P's views are not determinative of best interests: at some point, the restriction in the power might conflict with P's best interests.

The power will not allow the donee to make the decision to admit P to a home. On one reading, such a decision would be entirely outside the scope of the power. Others are not technically bound by the power, however, and if the decision in question is outside the scope of the power, it is not obvious that they would be precluded from making it. In some contexts, this is an attractive result. If violation of the donor's wishes were the only way forward, it would provide a way through a practical impasse. This is a problematic result, however: P presumably chose the specific donee in the belief that P's wishes would be respected; it seems counterintuitive that a substitute – either one that *ex hypothesi* P did not choose to make the decision, or indeed, the donee purporting to act under a different legal authority such as the general defence – should be able to circumvent P's wishes based on a technical legal argument. This is particularly problematic when the test of best interests does not provide guidance as to how the views of the individual are to be balanced against other factors in the best interests assessment. If another legal authority, such as the general defence, were to be relied upon, there is no legal requirement in the Act that anyone be notified of the decision, let alone a requirement that the decision inconsistent with P's wishes be given court scrutiny. The restriction in the power might be left meaning remarkably little.

The other reading would be that the authority is taken to occupy a field of decision-making, with a direction as to how decisions within that field are to be taken. As such, as a personal decision, the admission to a home would be within the authority of the power, but a decision that the donee would be precluded from making. An advantage of this approach is that the wishes of P could not simply be circumvented by, for example, an individual purporting to rely on the general defence: the restriction in the LPOA is meaningful. If this approach is adopted, however, a collision is possible between the restriction and P's best interests as defined under s. 4. The Act is not entirely clear how such a conflict is to be resolved. Certainly, the principles state that decisions are to be taken in the individual's best interests: s. 1(5). That general principle is not followed in specific contexts, however, with advance refusal of medical treatment being the most obvious. The MCA itself specifically requires that decisions under the MCA be made *both* in accordance with P's best interests *and* subject to any conditions or restrictions specified in the instrument: s. 9(4).

It is not clear how the Court of Protection would approach the situation. The court has a variety of powers relating to LPOAs, but altering their terms is not one of them.

Much may depend on the individual case setting the precedent. The courts may, perhaps, be more content to allow a restriction to hold sway when investment decisions are at issue, and more concerned about best interests when health or personal care decisions are at issue. It is difficult to see that such a distinction can be justified, however, because the point of principle and the statutory construction would be the same in each case.

The formalities requirements regarding an LPOA are contained in ss. 10 and 13 and in Sch. 1 to the Act. Both donor and donee must be over the age of 18. The LPOA must be made in writing, on the prescribed form, signed, and witnessed.

The LPOA may be relied upon only after it has been registered. The provisions regarding registration are contained in Sch. 1 of the MCA. Registration occurs initially with the Public Guardian. Registration is intended to be a largely administrative affair in most cases. The LPOA itself requires the donor to list the persons he or she wishes to be notified prior to registration. There is no formal requirement that evidence of incapacity be provided, although the donor will, of course, be able to object to the registration. In that event, the LPOA cannot be registered without an order of the court.

The Court of Protection is currently expected to come into being in April 2007 (now October 2007, see preface), and the role it will establish for itself in relation to donees of LPOAs remains to be seen. Certainly, as noted above, it has considerable authority to supervise donees, but it is not clear how resolutely it will choose to exercise its powers. Similar powers existed under the Enduring Powers of Attorney Act. These were considered in the case of *In re R (Enduring Power of Attorney)* [1990] 1 Ch 647. That case involved the alleged promise of a life interest in property and continuing support for a paid companion, formerly housekeeper, employed by R for some twenty years. It was alleged that, in detrimental reliance upon these promises, the companion remained with R, accepting wages well below the market value of her labour. R executed a power of attorney containing an express prohibition of gifts to friends or relatives. When R was admitted to a nursing home, the attorney terminated the employment of the companion, and commenced proceedings to evict her from the flat where she and R had lived. The companion applied to the court to enforce the promise of continued support, relying on the general authority of the court to give directions with respect to the management or disposal by the attorney of the property and affairs of the donor: s. 8(2)(b)(i), EPAA 1985 (similar in content to MCA s. 23(1)).

The court declined to order the attorney to honour the promises. The court held that the powers of the court in s. 8(2)(b) concerned merely administrative matters; they could certainly not be used to override the clause of the power, expressly permitted by the Act, precluding gifts to friends or relatives. The court's approach should instead be one of non-intervention (at 652):

The purpose and effect of the Enduring Powers of Attorney Act 1985 is to enable somebody to give a power of attorney, which will endure despite a supervening incapacity, to a person of his choice, and to empower that person to deal with his property in the way that he thinks fit.

In part, this is irreproachable. It is difficult to see that it would be an appropriate exercise of the court's powers to circumvent a clause in the power, expressly authorised by the

Act. In this context, the case stands as a warning of the need to ensure proper advice prior to execution, because mistakes (if indeed this was a mistake) cannot necessarily be rectified later.

The broader principle, that the court ought to adopt a non-interventionist approach generally, may be more controversial. It is certainly an arguable view, but it does not flow inevitably from the statutory provisions. The powers contained in the relevant sections may be used to assist or to control the donee. Thus the rendering of accounts is one way in which donees are shown to be doing their job appropriately, and the clause concerning remuneration of donees specifically allows for the repayment of excessive fees. The power of the court to determine the meaning or effect of the instrument is similarly ambiguous: it may be seen to assist or to confine the donee's discretion, depending on the circumstance. Further, the power to require the donee to furnish information or documents may be an important tool in controlling a donee. To label these powers as concerning 'administrative matters' (at 651) solves nothing.

Whether the court has the power to intervene, of course, is a different question from whether the court ought to exercise such a power. The issue here is how one is to view the enduring power of attorney. The court in *R* emphasised its private law roots, and certainly it may well be the case that donors execute such powers in the expectation that it will leave the management of their affairs in the private sphere of the family. It is similarly arguable that those who wish their affairs administered by a particular person following incapacity should have that wish respected, and the court should not usurp that role. Further, an expansive reading of the court's power to intervene does reduce the distinctions between the enduring or lasting power of attorney process and a court-appointed deputy: if the attorney is not to have independent power, how are they, in practice, to be different from such a deputy? If a non-interventionist approach is adopted, as it is in *R*, it does emphasise the importance of the donor's selecting an attorney who can be trusted to administer the estate as the donor would wish, because that donor will have a broad discretion, broadly free of court intervention.

Arguments may also be advanced for a more expansive view of the court's intervention. The protection of those lacking capacity has been understood as an appropriate role of the state for close to a millennium. It can be difficult to know how successful or appropriate an attorney will be in the role, until he or she has actually taken it up. Are we really to leave an unfortunate and incapacitated donor in the largely unmonitored control of the donee? Are the other safeguards on enduring powers really so strong that we can rest assured that such powers cannot be used by the unscrupulous for self-advantage? If a deputy is sufficiently inept at his or her role, the court has the authority to revoke the LPOA (s. 22(4)), but this is an extreme outcome. Is there not space for some role of the court in supporting a donee of mixed abilities in the exercise of their functions rather than removing them entirely, thereby more closely approximating the relationship envisaged by the donor? And how, if not through the use of the court's directory powers, is this to be accomplished? The *R* case leaves a stark choice in the case of this sort of difficulty: remove the attorney and appoint a receiver, or live with the less-than-ideal administration. Is it at least arguable that a less severe use of the court's powers allows for a kinder middle ground, more in keeping with what the donor must presumably have wanted?

11.4.2.1 Capacity to make an LPOA

An individual may make or revoke an LPOA only if he or she has capacity to do so. The Act makes no requirement of medical evidence to this effect, although it is, of course, prudent for such evidence to be collected at the time the power is signed, in cases of doubt. The meaning of incapacity in this context has been litigated in the context of enduring powers of attorney in the case of *Re K, Re F* [1988] 1 All ER 358. The question in these cases was whether capacity to execute the power was different from capacity to make the decisions covered by the power. In these cases, it was agreed that the donors were incapable of managing their property and affairs at the time the power was signed, but understood the nature and effect of the power. The court upheld the powers, establishing the following test of capacity (at 363):

What degree of understanding is involved? Plainly one cannot expect that the donor should have been able to pass an examination on the provisions of the 1985 Act. At the other extreme, I do not think that it would be sufficient if he realised only that it gave cousin William power to look after his property. Counsel as *amicus curiae* [for the Official Solicitor] helpfully summarised the matters which the donor should have understood in order that he can be said to have understood the nature and effect of the power: first, if such be the terms of the power, that the attorney will be able to assume complete control over the donor's affairs; second, if such be the terms of the power, that the attorney will in general be able to do anything with the donor's property which the donor could have done; third, that the authority will continue if the donor should be or become mentally incapable; fourth, that if he should be or become mentally incapable, the power will be irrevocable without the confirmation of the court.

There is certainly an appeal to this approach. Intuitively, there does seem to be a difference between understanding what an enduring power of attorney does, and understanding the full range of one's property and affairs and what needs to be done to maintain them. A donor may not understand the full range of their property, but may still be perfectly aware that they want their child, for example, to manage the property in the event of their own incapacity.

While the result of the court may be desirable, reaching the result is not nearly so easy, because, as noted above, incapacity revoked a power of attorney at common law: *Drew v Nunn*. The reason for this would seem to be that the essence of the power is to allow the attorney to act for the donor. When the donor ceases to have a contracting mind, he or she cannot perform the acts the power purports to grant to the attorney. Therefore, the attorney can no longer perform them either, and the power is revoked (*Drew v Nunn* at 666). The argument in *K* was that the donor could not create a power that the law would have revoked. The court circumvents this argument by suggesting that the revocation in this context is metaphorical, because the donor performed no actual act to revoke it, and that a more accurate phrasing was that 'at least for some purposes the power ceased to have effect *as if* he had revoked it' (at 361, 364):

> The rule is therefore concerned with whether the power can be validly exercised rather than with its essential validity. Of course, for most purposes it will make no difference whether one says that the power has ceased to be exercisable or has become invalid. But the fact that the power cannot be validly exercised does not commit one to the proposition that it is for all purposes invalid.

This approach raises the issue of what the status of the power is in such circumstances at common law: is it a valid power, but held in abeyance? Would the restoration of the donor to full capacity resurrect the authority of the attorney, if the power itself was valid but not exercisable? There is no suggestion of this in *Drew* v *Nunn*, where the donor did recover capacity. In that case, the court seemed to think that revoked meant revoked.

Even if this theoretical distinction is accepted, it is still not entirely adequate to reach the result in *K*, because, at the time that the powers in that case were signed, the donors did not have the legal ability to deal with their own property. On the theory of *Drew* v *Nunn*, how could they purport to pass on to the agent powers that they did not have at the time the powers were signed? The court addressed this problem in the following terms (at 362):

> In one sense Miss K did possess the powers to manage her property because she owned it. She could not exercise those powers on a regular basis because she lacked the mental capacity. But there is no logical reason why, though unable to exercise her powers, she could not confer them on someone else by an appropriate juristic act.

Surely this is sophistry. The force of the *Drew* judgment is that an attorney cannot do things that the donor cannot do. If that is the case, the distinction drawn by the court is specious: it would be contrary to *Drew* that the agent be able to exercise powers that the donor could not. It might, theoretically, be possible for the donor to grant to the agent the powers of an incapacitated person over property, but it is difficult to see that such powers would be of much use. The old rule was instead that a person lacking capacity to manage their own affairs could not appoint an agent to do so. This rule is contained in cases such as *Stead* v *Thornton* 3 B & Ad 357 and *Tarbuck* v *Bispham* 2 M & W 2 at 8, cases cited in argument to the court in *Drew* (at 664), but apparently not to the court in *K*. Whatever the merits of the result in K, the reasoning is problematic.

The result may be doctrinally problematic, but it seems that the law in *Re K, Re F* is now part of the legal landscape. It seems likely that it will be applied to capacity to make and revoke LPOAs.

11.4.3 The general defence

In the absence of a valid, applicable and registered LPOA, a valid and applicable refusal of treatment, a court-appointed deputy with authority for a decision, or an applicable decision of the Court of Protection, the MCA provides a general defence for those providing 'care or treatment' to P: s. 5. 'Care' is not defined in the Act, and 'treatment' is defined only as 'including a diagnostic or other procedure' (s. 64(1)), but it is reasonable to suspect that the phrase will be given a wide reading by the court, at least as regards personal decision-making. The draft Code of Practice provides an illustrative list of circumstances, including routine physical care, routine shopping or purchase of services, and healthcare procedures (Department of Constitutional Affairs, 2004a: para. 5.5).

The defence takes effect if D has taken 'reasonable steps' to determine whether P lacks capacity, and where D reasonably believes both that P lacks capacity and that the decision proposed is in P's best interests. In that event, it is as if P had consented to the act in question, or consented to D's doing the act. Once again, this is a mechanism merely to provide a decision: D has no new defence for civil or criminal liability in doing the act in question negligently.

It is with the general defence that the MCA is at its boldest and most innovative. Effectively, s. 5 expands the decision-making structure in F, under which doctors make necessary decisions on behalf of patients following appropriate consultation and consideration of best interests, to most personal decisions regarding incapacitated individuals. As envisaged in F, a doctor will be able to treat in the best interests (now as defined in the statute) of P. The Law Commission, which initially recommended a general power broadly similar to that contained in s. 5, also envisaged it to be used for third-party relationships, such as carers arranging for milk to be delivered to P, or arranging that P's roof be repaired (Law Commission, 1995: para. 4.7). Such decision-making structures – effectively, agency arrangements – seem to be within the scope of s. 5, as long as they would be able to be established by a competent consenting person.

The mechanism has considerable strengths. It is nearly infinitely flexible, allowing the individual to retain control over those decisions for which they remain competent but allowing other decisions to be made with the minimum of administrative hassle. It reflects what is actually happening, in the sense that the move to increased community living is inevitably resulting in more decisions being taken by carers ranging from live-in family to well-meaning neighbours and friends on a relatively ad hoc basis. The legal status of these decisions is now at best complicated; the proposed bill would place them on a firm legal footing.

While these advantages are significant, a general mechanism of this type has not been without its critics. Bartlett (1997), discussing the Law Commission proposal, notes that there is no expectation that all decisions under this authority will be taken by the same individual, leading to a potential lack of coordination between decision-makers, who may not even know of each other's existence. Similarly, it is not clear how a potential decision-maker under this power would know of the court orders or continuing power of attorney that would deprive them of authority. The MCA creates a right to payment for 'necessary' goods and services out of P's funds (s. 7; see further below). Particularly if D is not closely related to P, it is not clear how D would know enough about P's financial situation to know whether some of the more significant interventions anticipated, such as replacing a roof, would be within the budget of the individual. There is no restriction on D him or herself receiving payment for goods or services rendered to P, suggesting the risk of conflicts of interest. And here, as with many of the Law Commission's proposals, Bartlett argues that there are insufficient mechanisms of policing proposed, to ensure that the powers granted are being exercised effectively and appropriately.

Is Bartlett unduly alarmist? He is also the primary author of this chapter, and thus obviously does not think so. To put the other side, however, the problems will be minimised if the procedural aspects of the best interests test, requiring communication between carers, work effectively and if those carers feel it appropriate to share necessary information. Yet it is appropriate to remember here that law operates as part of a broader social structure. Will persons with knowledge of the finances or life expectancy of an individual necessarily feel it appropriate to share that information with someone else, perhaps outside the family, who thinks (perhaps quite rightly) that a new roof is necessary? The mechanism does not handle disagreement or lack of trust between carers particularly effectively. D must have a reasonable belief that the act is in P's best interests, but while the views of other carers are to be sought, they do not bind D as to his or her view of P's best interests. For doctors and similar professionals, there are professional disciplinary structures and employment hierarchies that can be brought into play to challenge decisions in a relatively informal and inexpensive way. Such mechanisms do not exist outside professional bodies. The only obvious control on these decisions is a court application, a potentially expensive process for which legal aid may not be available.

The general defence is at its most convincing in cases where reasonable people make good decisions in good faith. The problems arise outside of this protected realm. How frequently will people make bad decisions, albeit in good faith? How frequently will bad people take advantage? Will the stereotyped double-glazing salesman, for example, really use the provision to sell new windows to vulnerable old ladies of marginal capacity? We will not know the answer to these questions, because the general defence operates entirely in the private realm: decisions taken in reliance upon the mechanism need be reported to no one, and therefore we will have no way to judge the relative merits and demerits of the provision's impact. The problem is deeper than such a statistical survey, in any event: even if, as will almost certainly be the case, the considerable bulk of decisions are good ones, is this sufficient? If the state is to grant powers to third parties over its most vulnerable citizens, is there not a corresponding political duty to ensure that these powers are exercised appropriately? Or, to put the reverse philosophical view, do we really trust the state to second-guess personal decisions made about vulnerable people by their friends, neighbours, and family – the people who know the vulnerable person best?

11.4.4 Payment for goods and services

Section 7 of the MCA provides a right for a supplier to be paid a reasonable price for 'necessary' goods or services provided to P. Section 8 further provides that, for acts requiring expenditure performed in reliance on the general defence (s. 5), it is lawful for D to pledge P's credit to pay those expenses, and to apply money in P's possession to defray the expenditures. Section 8(2) expressly contemplates that D may pay himself or herself out of P's funds for expenditures borne by D on P's behalf. While this has the advantage of allowing considerable flexibility – carers may be able to be reimbursed with minimal fuss – there is no formal need to account for these payments, leaving some risk of abuse. That said, the draft Code of Practice states that the intent is not that D would, by virtue of this provision, have signing authority over P's bank accounts or investments (Department of Constitutional Affairs, 2004a: para. 5.38), providing some potential limit to the funds available to D.

The right to payment under s. 7 applies to 'necessary' goods and services. 'Necessary' is, in turn, defined as 'suitable to a person's condition in life and to his actual requirements at the time when the goods or services are supplied': s. 7(2). This is, in essence, a consolidation of the common law and the statutory provisions in the Sale of Goods Act 1979, and the jurisprudence flowing therefrom will apply to the MCA provisions. It can be quite an expansive definition. Thus in *In re Bevan* [1912] 1 Ch 196, the incompetent person had made a living letting property. Necessaries in that case included all expenses related to rent audit of the properties, and even renovation expenses for one of the rental properties (see, generally, Matthews, 1982).

The MCA therefore creates rights of suppliers to be paid for goods or services. Beyond the right to apply money actually in P's possession to these expenses, however, ss. 7 and 8 provide no additional mechanism to be paid. Certainly, if an EPOA or LPOA covering financial decisions is in effect, or a deputy with the relevant authority appointed, the donee or deputy will have authority to reimburse the expenses in question. Alternatively, and outside the scope of the MCA, social services regulations allow a carer to act as an 'appointee' of a person lacking capacity, and so to claim benefits on their behalf. That may be of practical importance, because it provides a steady (albeit modest) income that a carer may use for the benefit of P.

Outside these cases, it may be that the only way to effect actual payment of the debt owed pursuant to ss. 7 or 8 may be an application to the Court of Protection. While this may seem unfortunate for those acting in good faith under the MCA, the nuisance must be balanced against the risk that the unscrupulous may take financial advantage of the vulnerable.

11.5 Advance decisions regarding treatment

The Act places advance decisions to refuse treatment on a statutory footing. These may be made by a person over 18 years of age who has capacity to do so, to take effect in the event of subsequent incapacity. While the definition of capacity is that contained in ss. 2 and 3 of the MCA, this form of decision-making is unusual in that the best interests provisions of the Act have no application. If a valid advance decision to refuse treatment applies, it is as if the individual makes a competent refusal of that treatment: s. 26(1).

The decision must refer to 'treatment'. This is defined in the MCA, rather unhelpfully, as 'includ[ing] a diagnostic or other procedure': s. 64(1). Certainly, the term is likely to be taken to include all medical procedures, but nothing express in the Act restricts it to medical treatment. How far it may be read as extending beyond medical care into other forms of personal care remains to be seen.

As noted above, the effect of a valid and applicable advance decision is the same as if the treatment were refused by a competent person. Two caveats flow from this. First, if the treatment may be provided notwithstanding the competent refusal of consent, it may be provided notwithstanding the advance decision. The obvious example here is treatment provided to detained patients under ss. 63 and 58 of the MHA 1983. Because consent of the patient is not necessary for these treatments, so they would not be precluded by a valid and applicable advance decision, although, of course, the advance decision would still constitute a factor that a doctor might wish to take into account in deciding whether such enforcement of treatment was appropriate under these sections. The advance decision can, of course, preclude treatment of informal patients, or detained patients for treatments other than for mental disorder, because these treatments require the consent of the patient. Second, the effect of the decision can be no more than a refusal of treatment. Nothing in the Act creates a power to insist on the provision of a specific treatment – only to refuse it. In this, the Act reflects the common law position: see *R (Burke)* v *General Medical Council* [2005] EWCA 1003. Preferences regarding treatment that the individual would want are, of course, relevant to the best interests determination (see above), but they are not binding.

The advance decision to refuse treatment applies only if it is valid and applicable. The former of these terms refers to whether there is a legally effective decision: has the individual withdrawn it, or done something clearly inconsistent with it (s. 25(2))? Such inconsistency includes, but is not limited to, giving authority to a donee of an LPOA do make the decision in question. Donors of LPOAs may therefore wish to make it clear on the face of those instruments whether they are intended to supersede any advance decision to refuse treatment. Section 25 does not specifically state that the advance decision will be invalid if the individual lacked capacity to make it. Whether one wishes to characterise this scenario as a nullity or as an invalid decision seems a matter of semantics: clearly, in such a case, the decision has no effect.

By comparison, applicability refers to whether the decision applies to the situation now at issue. The decision will not be applicable if it does not refer to the treatment proposed, or if there are conditions precedent in the decision that have not been met: s. 25(4). The decision will also not be applicable if the individual has capacity to make the decision at the time it needs to be made (s. 25(3)); in that event, the individual consents or not as he or she wishes. The decision will further not be applicable if 'there are reasonable grounds for believing that circumstances exist which P did not anticipate at the time of the advance decision and which would have affected his decision had he anticipated them': s. 25(4)(c). A simple example of such a condition would be where an individual makes an advance decision to refuse medication for a specific disorder because of adverse effects of the medications available at the time the decision was made. If medications developed since that time do not have the adverse effects in question, it might be reasonable to think that the individual would not have refused such newer medication. The advance decision might therefore be inapplicable regarding the newer medications.

Like the position at common law, there is no general requirement that advance refusals be in writing; unlike the position at common law, there is such a formalities requirement for advance refusals regarding life-sustaining treatment. These must be in writing, signed and witnessed, and must state expressly that they are to apply if the life of the individual is at risk: s. 25(5). There may be unfortunate consequences for persons who made advance refusals of life-sustaining treatment at common law. Such decisions that satisfy the formalities requirement will continue to be valid, but for those that do not, there are no provisions in the Act recognising previously valid refusals made prior to the introduction of the Act. Individuals with capacity might make a new decision if they are made aware of the requirements of the Act, but if the individual is now incapable of making an advance decision, there will be no way for him or her to refuse the treatment in question.

The MCA provides that practitioners will be not be liable if they provide treatment unless they are 'satisfied' that a valid and applicable advance refusal applies: s. 26(2). They will further not be liable for withholding treatment if they 'reasonably believe' that a valid and applicable advance refusal applies to the treatment: s. 26(3). The intention here is to provide legal protection for practitioners in the case of honest and reasonable doubt. In case of doubt, of course, the Court of Protection also has jurisdiction to make declarations regarding validity and applicability, and treatment may be performed to sustain life or prevent a serious deterioration of P's condition pending the court's decision: s. 26(5).

11.6 Rough edges

The statutory structures of the MCA unquestionably represent a considerable improvement to the previous law relating to people lacking capacity. Nonetheless, there are some problems and complexities warranting further consideration.

One ongoing problem relates to people who lack capacity to make decisions about their accommodation, and who are placed in environments (usually hospitals or care homes) where they are deprived of their liberty. The European Court of Human Rights has held that the situation under current law constitutes a breach of Art. 5 of the ECHR: see *HL* v *UK* Application No. 45508/99 (2005) 40 EHRR 32 (the *Bournewood* case). The MCA, as passed in 2005, precludes all substitute decision-makers under the MCA except the Court of Protection from making decisions that would result in such deprivations of liberty. The government has published a briefing paper (Department of Health, 2006b), indicating an intention to amend the MCA to take account of the *Bournewood* case, but at the time of writing, no actual bill has been published (see now the 2006 Bill discussed in the preface). While some of the concerns regarding the Act generally discussed below will also apply to the *Bournewood* situation, the case itself and the government response are discussed in detail in Chapter 4.

11.6.1 Safeguards and enforcement

A strength of the MCA is its procedural flexibility and informality. Decisions may be taken and care provided for people lacking capacity with minimal bureaucratic hassle. This strength is also the Act's weakness, however. Decisions within the ambit of the Act may be of profound importance to a person lacking or of marginal capacity, and it may be of considerable importance to ensure that they are made appropriately. The substantive provisions of the MCA in this regard are laudable, but there are relatively few procedural safeguards to ensure that those standards are met. The Court of Protection has ample jurisdiction to make appropriate orders when it is made aware of problems, although it is not yet clear how interventionist the court will be in its use of those powers: see the discussion above regarding LPOAs, for example. The court also has some investigative resources provided through the Public Guardian and the Court of Protection Visitors.

It is less obvious how problems will come to the attention of the court and the Public Guardian. Certainly, in appropriate cases, the Court of Protection may require deputies to report back to the court or to the Public Guardian regarding the exercise of their duties: s. 19(9)(b). No similar power exists over donees of LPOAs to provide routine reports. LPOAs must be registered before being relied upon, but this will generally be a purely administrative process: absent express objection by the donor or a person required by the LPOA to be notified of the registration, the Official Guardian is obliged to register the document (Sch. 1, s. 4(5)). For decisions of donees once the LPOA is registered, and, in any event, for decisions made under the general defence, no official of the court will routinely be made aware of decisions being taken. As such, there is no routine procedural accountability for decisions made under the Act. Certainly, people with concerns might apply to the court on behalf of P, but this is a potentially expensive proposition. Alternatively, they might notify the Public Guardian, who, with the assistance of the Court of Protection Visitors, has authority to investigate. It remains to be seen whether this office will have sufficient resources for the job, however, and how it will respond to such complaints. Finally, if the decision-maker is a professional, it may be possible to complain through professional channels, because a failure to look after an individual's best interests may give rise to professional censure: see *Pembrey* v *General Medical Council* [2003] UKPC 60, for example. These responses rely upon a person other than P and D raising the alarm, however: they will not be discovered as a matter of routine administration of the MCA.

This raises the question of when complaints are lodged. A perusal of the case law arising under the previous common law structure would suggest that cases came to the attention of the court when there was a row over care, generally between family carers and professionals: see, e.g., *Re S (Adult Patient)(Inherent Jurisdiction: Family Life)*

[2002] EWHC 2278 (Fam), [2003] 1 FLR 292; *In Re TF (An Adult: Residence)* [2000] 1 MHLR 120; *HL v UK* (above); *Newham London Borough Council v S and Anor (Adult: Court's Jurisdiction)* [2003] EWHC 1909 (Fam), [2003] All ER (D) 550. Consideration of these cases suggests that the facts quickly become considerably more complex than the best interests of P, with recriminations flying between the carers. While it does seem that such cases should be considered in a more dispassionate forum, it is not obvious that such disagreements ought to be the primary trigger for the institution of safe-guards, as seems now, in practice, to be the usual case. What happens if abuse does not trigger a sufficiently fractious relationship between carers that one of them goes to the courts? It may well be that either substandard decision-making or abuse occurs outside these contentious relationships. This may involve malice or, one hopes more frequently, a decision-maker who means well but is ill-suited to the decision-making role. That might be because such a role does not suit D's character or talents, or it might be through a lack of information and support: it certainly does not follow that bad decision-making flows only from evil people. At the same time, for people who are vulnerable through a lack of capacity, poor decision-making can have unfortunate con-sequences. It is not at all obvious that there are meaningful safeguards in place for such situations. The government's proposed response to the *Bournewood* litigation is intended to provide some safeguards when people without capacity are deprived of their liberty, but even here, the onus to commence the process of safeguards is to rest with the person depriving P of liberty: see Chapter 4. This is a significant limitation to a system of safeguards.

At issue here is, in part, a problem with law. Generally, legal systems assume an individual with the will to challenge an inappropriate decision. That is precisely the assumption that cannot be made regarding people lacking capacity, and when that individual is absent, the problem is how procedures that ensure the provision of civil rights are to be triggered. In the context of civil confinement of people lacking capacity, this problem was considered in *R (MH) v Secretary of State for Health* [2005] UKHL 60, reversing [2004] EWCA Civ 1609. In this case, MH was admitted to a psychiatric facil-ity under s. 2 of the MHA 1983. She had Down's syndrome, and lacked the practical abilities both to apply for a review tribunal hearing and to instruct lawyers on her behalf. Her case was made more compelling by the fact that an application had been made under s. 29 to displace her mother as nearest relative. This had the effect of extending the s. 2 admission until the nearest relative issue had been resolved. This did not occur for almost two years, although the Secretary of State had exercised his discre-tion to order a review tribunal hearing for MH in this period. Counsel acting on her behalf said that MH was effectively deprived of a hearing under these circumstances, in violation of Art. 5(4) of the ECHR. In effect, because MH lacked the capacity to apply for a tribunal hearing herself, the argument was that one ought to be provided for her automatically. This argument was successful in a unanimous Court of Appeal. The court held that MH was effectively deprived of a hearing into her rights in a situation where a capable person would not have been so deprived. That, in the view of Buxton LJ (at para. 18), could not have been the intent of the framers of the ECHR.

An appeal to the House of Lords was successful, however. Baroness Hale, for a unanimous House of Lords, held that the right in Art. 5(4) was to apply for a hearing, and that there was no right to an automatic hearing. In her view, other safeguards in the system, in particular the rights of nearest relatives to apply for hearings, were sufficient to safeguard the Art. 5(4) rights of people lacking capacity in this context. That may be an appropriate reading of regarding Art. 5(4), but in MH's case, the only reason that there was a tribunal determination of her situation was because the Secretary of State exercised his discretion to order a hearing. Discretion, it might be argued, is a slender reed upon which to hang rights. Indeed, the matter was only brought to the attention of the Secretary of State through the actions of MH's mother. Had the mother been compliant, it is difficult to see that MH's rights would ever have been considered in any legal forum.

Attempts are being made to deal with this in the *Bournewood* context by a process of routine reporting, assessments, and authorisations for these people; but there are no such moves outside this limited context. Indeed, while it may arguably be implicit in the ethos of the MCA, nothing in the Act expressly indicates that a person of marginal capacity need to be told that a decision has been reached that they lack capacity, and that decisions are to be made on their behalf. As discussed above, however, decisions taken by D in good faith and without negligence may nonetheless bind the individual, and have financial consequences to the person thought to lack capacity. If a full explanation to that individual is not made at each stage of the process, it is difficult to see that the right of that person to apply to court will be meaningful.

This, in turn, raises questions about the right to a hearing upon the removal of civil rights, provided under Art. 6 of the ECHR. There may be some room for doubt as to whether the informal process meets the required standard. A similarly informal process for the conduct of litigation by a litigation friend under the Civil Procedure Rules was called into question by Kennedy LJ in the case of *Masterman-Lister* v *Brutton & Co, Jewell & Home Counties Dairies* [2002] EWCA Civ 1889. His Lordship noted that the complainant in *Winterwerp* v *Netherlands* [1979] 2 EHRR 387 argued that admission to a psychiatric facility automatically deprived him of his right to manage his property and affairs, in violation of his Art. 6 rights. His Lordship noted (para 17):

That complaint was accepted by the European Court of Human Rights, but neither Order 80 nor CPR 21.1 contain any requirement for a judicial determination of the question of whether or not capacity exists.

This suggests that his Lordship considered that some form of judicial determination ought to be conducted as a matter of routine.

A more formalised system might go considerably further in providing safeguards to ensure appropriate decision-making. It would, however, undercut the flexibility at the core of the MCA, which is one of its real advantages. It would further need to be a much bigger bureaucracy than is envisaged under the MCA and it might involve practical difficulties. Families tend to view the right to make decisions about their loved ones as a private matter from which the state should be excluded; and where more extensive systems of involvement have been tried, they have not always been successful for this reason (see Bartlett, 2001: 41). On the other hand, decisions taken under the MCA are given statutory authority and are to be made on a statutory basis: in that sense, the state is implicated. As a constitutional question, can, or should, the state really turn its back on how those decisions are made?

11.6.2 Interface with the Mental Health Act

The express basis of the relationship between the MCA and the MHA 1983 is contained in s. 28(1) of the MCA:

28(1) Nothing in this Act authorises anyone—

(a) to give a patient medical treatment for mental disorder, or

(b) to consent to a patient's being given medical treatment for mental disorder,

if, at the time when it is proposed to treat the patient, his treatment is regulated by Part 4 of the Mental Health Act.

The provision applies only to 'medical treatment' for 'mental disorder', terms that are given the same meaning as under the MHA 1983: MCA s. 28(2). As discussed elsewhere in this book, these terms are given expansive meanings under the MHA 1983, but they are not infinite in scope. Treatment that is not for mental disorder is outside the scope of s. 28(1), and therefore instead within the scope of the MCA.

As discussed elsewhere in this text, Part IV of the MHA 1983 regulates treatment in a variety of ways. Section 57 prohibits some treatments – currently psychosurgery and surgical implantation of hormones to reduce male sex drive – without the competent consent of the patient. The MCA provision makes it clear that this provision is paramount over the MCA provisions: these treatments may not be performed on a patient lacking capacity.

Part IV also regulates treatment for people confined under the MHA 1983. Sections 63 and 58 of the MHA 1983 allow treatment under certain circumstances for patients who have capacity but refuse treatment, or who lack capacity to consent to the proposed treatment. These provisions are discussed in detail in Chapter 7. For medical treatment for mental disorder to continue for more than three months in these circumstances, or for the provision of ECT at any time, a second opinion must be obtained pursuant to procedures prescribed in the Act, unless the patient offers competent consent. For persons confined under the MHA, the above section of the MCA makes it clear that these provisions continue to apply. An advance refusal of such treatment will be relevant to the exercise of medical discretion under the MHA 1983, but it will not preclude the treatment. The best interests test of the MCA has no formal application in such cases, although, in so far as it represents a codification of best practice, some practitioners under the MHA may nonetheless look to it for assistance. Thus, while it will be appropriate for doctors acting under Part IV of the MHA to take into account the wishes of the patient, there is no statutory requirement that they do so.

Apart from s. 57, Part IV does not regulate the treatment of informal patients. Treatment of these patients thus would appear to be available under the MCA. This is an uncomfortable result, particularly for ECT. The requirement under s. 58 of the MHA 1983 that a second opinion be obtained whenever ECT is performed without the competent consent of a confined patient attests to the fact that it is a particularly controversial treatment, at least in the public's perception. Particularly for patients whose liberty is deprived other than under the MHA 1983 – *Bournewood* patients – it seems counterintuitive that similar safeguards would not be required when treatment occurs under the MCA. The government's proposed response to *Bournewood* may go some distance to meeting these concerns, because it envisages an advocate appointed for these people. It is less clear whether the MCA will be suitably robust in this regard for other people lacking capacity to consent to ECT. As discussed above, somewhat minimal safeguards are provided for 'serious medical treatment'. The definition of that phrase makes no specific reference to ECT, however.

ECT is a particularly controversial example of a broader question: does the MCA adequately protect incapable people who are to be prescribed psychiatric treatment? People lacking capacity are a highly vulnerable group, and psychiatric medications can be very highly intrusive. Are the safeguards sufficient?

Section 28 of the MCA refers only to Part IV of the MHA 1983. It therefore applies neither to involuntary admissions to facilities nor to guardianship, both of which are covered by Part II of the MHA 1983. Certainly, involuntary admissions under the MHA 1983 are not precluded by the MCA.

More complex is whether the MCA can be used to avoid safeguards contained in the MHA 1983. As an obvious example, involuntary admission under s. 3 of the MHA 1983 requires an individual to fall under one of four categories of mental disorder: mental illness, mental impairment, severe mental impairment, or psychopathy. As discussed in Chapter 2, the mental impairments require an impairment of intelligence and social functioning that is 'associated with abnormally aggressive or seriously irresponsible conduct on the part of the person concerned': MHA 1983, s. 1(2). If a person with a mental impairment does not behave in that fashion, he or she cannot be confined under the MHA 1983. While the government is intending to abolish the four categories of mental disorder in the near future, it has stated that it will be retaining this safeguard for people with intellectual disabilities. If a person cannot be detained under the MHA 1983 for this reason, however, is there any bar to their being detained under the MCA? The individual would clearly come under the *Bournewood* decision, so the answer, in the short term, must be 'no'. Once the government's response to *Bournewood* is in place, however, it would seem that there is nothing in the MCA that will preclude such a result. Depending on the phrasing of the legislation implementing the *Bournewood* response, it may well be that the safeguard for people with mental impairments under the MHA 1983 will be able to be circumvented routinely by the MCA.

Guardianship creates a different set of difficulties. When the MCA was passed, it was the government's intention to abolish guardianship under s. 7 of the MHA 1983, and the MCA makes no reference to such guardianship. The government's intention appears to have changed, so it is necessary to assess how guardianship fits with the MCA mechanisms.

As discussed elsewhere (see Chapter 9), the MHA 1983 gives limited powers to a guardian. He or she may require the subject of the guardianship to reside at a specific place (but does not have the power to detain him or here there), require the subject to attend for a place for medical treatment, occupation, education or training (but has no power to consent on the person's behalf), and require access to the subject to be given to specified professionals such as doctors: MHA 1983, s. 8(1). These powers are narrower than, but would be included in, the scope of personal care and treatment decisions contemplated by the MCA. They may therefore overlap with the decision-making authority of a donee of an LPOA, a court-appointed deputy, a person relying on the general defence, or the Court of Protection. There is the consequent possibility of conflicting decisions and conflicting authority.

Because the guardianship powers are narrower than those available to a donee of an LPOA or deputy, it is difficult to see that it would normally be appropriate to apply for guardianship when one of those individuals already has the relevant authority, at least after P has lost capacity. The application for guardianship is to be made only if guardianship is 'necessary' in the interests of the subject's welfare or for the protection of others: MHA 1983, s. 7(2)(b). It is difficult to see that this will be the case, if a donee or deputy already exists who must, by definition, act in the best interests of P. If there is doubt as to whether D is operating in the best interests of P, the appropriate response is an application to the Court of Protection, rather than the creation of a guardian and the consequent creation of conflicting authorities.

The reverse is not necessarily true: if a guardian exists, it may nonetheless be appropriate for the subject to make an LPOA if competent to do so, or for the court to appoint a deputy. These substitutes might be given authority wider than that of the guardian. When such an individual takes over the relevant decision-making, it will normally be appropriate to terminate the guardianship as no longer necessary.

If a guardian exists, however, it will not necessarily be appropriate or helpful to appoint a deputy. First, the guardian will have authority whether or not the subject has capacity; if the subject has not lost capacity, he or she will be able to make the relevant decisions under the MCA. If coercion of a person with capacity is required, guardianship may, perhaps, have a role. Indeed, the result of a combination of guardianship with the general defence may occasionally yield highly favourable results. Under the guardianship, the subject could be required to attend at a doctor's office. There, if the subject were to lack capacity, treatment could be provided under the general defence. If the individual were not to lack capacity, there would still be sufficient coercion to be assured that he or she had been given the appropriate information about treatment, and had made an informed choice.

While the interaction between guardianship and the general defence has some potential benefits, it has potential problems as well. The MCA is clear that a person providing personal care and treatment may rely on the general defence only if there is no deputy or donee of an LPOA with the relevant decision-making authority: s. 6(6).

There is no such restriction on decisions within the authority of a guardian, and it is not obvious which decision would prevail in the event of conflicting decisions as to where an individual is to live, for example.

This problem is amplified because of both substantive and procedural difficulties. D under the MCA is governed by the best interests test under that Act. The guardian is not. Where D's decision as to best interests must be reasonable and can be scrutinised by the Court of Protection, the guardian's is subject merely to the *Wednesbury* test. Any dispute about the guardian's reasonableness will not be settled in the Court of Protection, but elsewhere by judicial review. The litigation would therefore be at the Court of Appeal before both sets of problems would come before the same court.

12

Legal Responses and Advocacy
for Clients

12.1 Introduction

In conclusion, I may say that this seems to me one of the very cases which Parliament had in mind when they said that such an action as this should not be brought without the leave of the court. It is an unfortunate feature of mental illness that those afflicted by it do not realise the need for their being under the care and control of others. They resent it, much as a small child or a dumb animal resents being given medicine for its own good, and they are apt to turn round and claw and scratch the hand that gives it.

Richardson v London County Council [1957] 1 WLR 751 at 760–1, per Denning LJ

The quotation is shocking to readers at the beginning of the twenty-first century. After thirty years of the politics of disability and patients' rights, Lord Denning's words may sound like reflections of a bygone era – but are they?

As we have seen in the preceding chapters, there is no shortage of legal rules and standards contained in the MHA 1983, MCA 2005, community care legislation and common law. These rules are, of course, relevant only if there are mechanisms in place to ensure that they are followed. The questions underlying this chapter are whether the law provides adequate mechanisms for those brought under the mental health system to ensure that they are dealt with in a manner that is consistent with the substantive and procedural rules provided by the law, and whether sufficient recompense is available in the event that the standards are not complied with.

In addition, as we have seen, involvement in the psychiatric system can impact fundamentally on the lives of individuals. The extreme example is institutionalisation, which affects all aspects of the individuals' lives: how they spend their time; what they eat; when and where they sleep; what treatment they receive; who they are permitted to have contact with, etc. Care in the community is less overtly controlling, but may nonetheless structure the lives of clients in particular ways. Much of this lies outside the scope of the legal or statutory standards, but it nonetheless has a considerable impact on the individual's life. Lawyers who work with disadvantaged clients will recognise this sort of situation, where the client is concerned about a complex set of problems, where the legal and extralegal mix together in a tangled mass. This chapter will also ask whether there is a role for law or for lawyers in addressing client dissatisfaction with these less expressly legal issues.

The legal forms of redress are primarily judicial review, civil or criminal actions, and the various complaints processes associated with NHS trusts. These will be examined in turn below. In the event that a lawyer, paralegal or other authorised person is to act on behalf of the client, involvement in any of these systems raises pragmatic issues of advocacy. Some of these will be examined at the end of the chapter.

12.2 Mental health review tribunals and judicial review

These remedies have been discussed at many points in this text (see, primarily, Chapters 5 and 8). The objective here is not to repeat that substantive discussion, but instead to summarise what these remedies can do in a mental health context.

12.2.1 Mental health review tribunals

Although mental health review tribunals (MHRTs) have substantial powers, their jurisdiction is purely statutory. There is no jurisdiction to consider matters beyond those listed in s. 72 of the MHA 1983. The tribunal system's governing legislation is not geared to require a patients' rights approach. Admittedly, the successful challenge to the release criteria under the Human Rights Act now means that the onus on the hospital man-agers to show that the confinement criteria are met, rather than on the patient to show that confinement criteria are not met (*R v MHRT N and E London Region, ex p H* [2001] 3 WLR 512; [2002] QBD 1), presents a much more attractive playing field to the patient – but the culture of review boards has not traditionally been built on patient rights. While MHRTs do have a discretion to release patients, even if the confinement criteria are met, this discretion rarely results in an unqualified release; an MHRT can, however, recommend the grant of a leave of absence to an unrestricted patient, or the transfer of the patient to another hospital or into guardianship, or into aftercare under supervision (ss. 72(3), 72(3A)), and can further consider the case in the event that these recommendations are not complied with. Again, this allows some flexibility of outcome, which may work for or against the patient. Yet, as seen in Chapter 8, the indications are that the tribunals are extraordinarily sympathetic to the doctors' positions. Moreover, many issues important to patients are not within the remit of MHRTs: tribunals have no direct role in determination of appropriateness of treatment, for example, or in addressing inappropriate living conditions in the facility. While, in theory, these are matters that could be considered under a tribunal's general discretion to release an individual from confinement, this would be an extraordinarily tangential way to approach disagreements regarding treatment or conditions.

The Mental Health Review Tribunal Rules do contain some basic due process provisions, such as right to notice (r. 20), the right to representation (r. 10), and the duty on

MHRTs to give reasons for their decisions: r. 23 (see Chapter 8). Several of these rules are, at best, problematic. Rule 11 requires the medical member of the tribunal to be both witness and judge. The exceptions and limitations in r. 12, relating to the disclosure of documents to the patient and/or his authorised representative, may considerably restrict the ability of advocates to determine the truth of factual allegations contained in any document disclosed with the r. 12(3) limitation (that the information must not be disclosed to the client: see Chapter 8), because an advocate may be unable to verify the accuracy of statements without disclosing the information in question to his or her client. Similarly, it would seem very difficult to ask other persons who might be able to confirm or deny the information about its veracity, because it is difficult, in practice, to see how this could be accomplished without disclosing the content of the document.

Rule 12(3) can, therefore, drive a wedge between advocate and client. The difficulty was recognised in the Ontario case of *Re Egglestone and Mousseau and Advisory Review Board* (1983) 42 OR (2d) 268 (at 276):

I would expect that faced with the order made here counsel should obtain the consent of his client to accept the documentary review on this limited basis, otherwise he may not feel at liberty to receive the information at all.

Such instructions in advance cannot be perceived as a solution, however. Either the client refuses the disclosure on this basis, in which case neither advocate nor client will know the information and it is difficult to see how the case can properly be argued, or the client consents, and the advocate will know information that will inform decision-making that the client will not know, furthering the marginalisation and disempowerment of the client. In this scenario, the result may be little short of Kafka: the client will be asked for instructions on the conduct of the case, without being able to be told why the instructions are being asked for.

12.2.2 Judicial review

As has been seen at various points throughout this book, both judicial review and habeas corpus are potentially powerful mechanisms by which to challenge decisions made by those who implement mental health services, both in hospital and in the community. But as has also been seen, both are of limited effect, and if the decision of the Court of Appeal in *Barker* (see Chapter 5) is anything to go by, it seems that the availability of habeas corpus will become increasingly limited in the future. Despite our misgivings about such a development, judicial review is of potentially broad scope, extending to any statutory power of decision. There have been some notable victories using judicial review by those seeking access to community services, although overall it can be said that the courts have, more often than not, failed to take a stance that is likely to empower clients or to give their advocates much scope to challenge decisions (see Chapter 9). As far as inpatients are concerned, both the decisions of MHRTs and of individual doctors, social workers and others made pursuant to MHA 1983 are subject to review. Thus in *Hallstrom* (see Chapter 8), the detention of a patient under s. 3 was successfully challenged on the basis that one of the medical reports did not represent the true view of the doctor: see also Gunn (1986a: 292).

The combination of judicial review with alleged violations of the Human Rights Act similarly has considerable potential. In *R v Feggetter, MHRC, ex p John* [2002] EWCA 554, for example, the applicant successfully challenged a failure by a SOAD to provide adequate reasons for a decision that involuntary treatment should proceed. While the case was really decided on the basis of traditional judicial review principles and the public law duty to give reasons, the framing of the case with reference to the Human Rights Act added an aura to the proceedings that may have assisted the applicant.

The placement of an application for judicial review in a Human Rights Act context may further have practical effects for the applicant. Particularly in cases where the alleged violation is 'fundamental' – concerning the right to life (Art. 2) or freedom from torture or inhuman or degrading treatment (Art. 3) – or of Arts. 8 (right to privacy and family life) or 14 (freedom from discrimination), where proportionality is likely to be of particular importance, it has been held that the court must be put in a position to reach its own view on any conflict of evidence, including medical evidence: *R (Wilkinson) v RMO of Broadmoor Hospital and MHAC SOAD* [2001] EWCA Civ 1545, at paras. 25–6, 53, 62. That may include, for example, cross-examination on affidavits. A subsequent panel of the Court of Appeal has emphasised that such detailed evidence-gathering by the reviewing court will not be required in every case (*R (N) v Dr M and Ors* (2002) WL 31676213, at paras. 32–9), but nonetheless, in cases of dispute where the rights at issue require it, it would seem that the duty for the reviewing court to hear evidence is now unquestioned.

Several limitations of judicial review must be noted. First, remedies are discretionary: a prima facie case by an applicant will not necessarily result in relief (see Chapter 5). Second, the courts are content to accord specialist tribunals such as the MHRTs considerable latitude both in their findings of fact and, to a lesser degree, in their interpretation of their constitutive legislation. Similarly, while it is now clear that decisions regarding treatment under s. 58 are judicially reviewable, at least under the HRA, the courts have thus far been notably deferential to medical opinion. There might still be some room for argument in particular cases – medication beyond recommended maximum dosages, for example – but there is little evidence of enthusiasm in the courts for giving credence to patient rights in any substantial way. Finally, judicial review will only be available when there is a statutory power of decision: decisions occurring outside the statute will not be within its scope.

The review tribunal process, habeas corpus, and judicial review all have their place in assuring that the standards contained in the various legislation are applied. They do little to affect decisions made regarding patients or situations not directly subject to legislation, however: they have virtually no application, for example, to informal hospital inpatients. Further, while they may ensure that decisions are corrected after they are made, they are unlikely to provide recompense in damages for the results of such decisions, nor do they hold individuals directly responsible. That is the function of civil and criminal law, and it is to those areas that this chapter now turns. There are, as we have seen, numerous statutes applicable to the care and treatment of mentally disordered persons. The following discussion will focus on the relevant provision of the MHA 1983, but the points made here also provide a flavour of the issues relevant to statutory provisions regarding civil and criminal liability more generally.

12.3 Controlling the starting gate: s. 139

Section 139, MHA 1983 provides:

> 139(1) No person shall be liable, whether on the ground of want of jurisdiction or on any other ground, to any civil or criminal proceedings to which he would have been liable apart from this section in respect of any act purporting to be done in pursuance of this Act or any regulations or rules made under this Act, or in, or in pursuance of anything done in, the discharge of functions conferred by any other enactment on the authority having jurisdiction under Part VII of this Act, unless the act was done in bad faith or without reasonable care.

> (2) No civil proceedings shall be brought against any person in any court in respect of any such act without the leave of the High Court; and no criminal proceedings shall be brought against any person in any court in respect of any such act except by or with the consent of the Director of Public Prosecutions.

These subsections do not apply to actions against the Secretary of State, health authorities or NHS trusts (s. 139(4), as amended by the National Health Service and Community Care Act 1990, s. 66(1), Sch. 9, para. 24(7)), nor to offences for which leave of the Director of Public Prosecutions is already required as condition precedent to prosecution: s. 139(3). Nonetheless, s. 139 does limit recourse by patients against those who control them, and cases commenced without compliance with that section are a nullity: *Seal v Chief Constable of South Wales Police* [2005] EWCA Civ 586, [2005] 1 MHLR 137. For this reason, the scope and effects of the section should be analysed with some care.

12.3.1 Scope

Section 139 expressly applies to both criminal and civil matters, and to actions taken relating to the management of the property and affairs of the patient under Part VII of the statute. Regarding the Part VII protection, the section would seem broad enough to cover both persons involved in applications to invoke the jurisdiction of the Court of Protection, and receivers and others putting the orders of that body into effect. It does not apply to judicial review: *Hallstrom*, see Chapter 8. The logic here is that, notwithstanding that judicial review applications are heard in the civil court structure, they do not determine 'liability' for decisions, but rather correctness of decisions ([1985] 3 All ER 775 at 783–4).

The provisions extend not only to acts actually done pursuant to the statute, but also to acts purporting to be done pursuant to the statute. The leading case here is *Poutney* v *Griffiths* [1976] AC 314 (HL). As will be recalled from Chapter 7, the case concerned the use of restraint by a nurse in ushering a patient back to his ward at the end of a visit from his family. The patient alleged that he had been assaulted by the nurse, and the nurse, although claiming that he had only lightly brushed against the patient, was duly convicted. The House of Lords held that the conviction could not stand because the events occurred in pursuance of the statute, and therefore there could be no proceedings without leave having first been obtained. The court noted that the detention of an individual in hospital necessarily involved the exercise of control and discipline, as a necessary corollary to the administration of treatment (see Chapter 7). This would perhaps be uncontroversial if the nurse's version of the facts were to be accepted, but it is, at best, doubtful that they were so accepted by the triers of fact at first instance. It is far less obvious that an unprovoked punch, as was the case in the patient's version of events, is appropriately considered part of the exercise of control and discipline. That said, might it be seen to be an act '*purporting* to be done' in pursuance of the legislation? The view of the House of Lords is extraordinarily expansive on the scope of s. 139(1), particularly when combined with the expansive readings of 'medical treatment' that have flowed from s. 145.

The current view is that s. 139 refers only to detained patients, not to those admitted informally: *R* v *Runighian* [1977] Crim LR 361. This authority is merely at Crown Court level, suggesting that some hesitation is appropriate before uncritical reliance is placed upon it. The summary of the case in the *Criminal Law Review* is brief, but it suggests that the decision was reached on the basis that s. 5 of the 1959 Act, now s. 131 of the 1983 Act, did not mandate the admission of informal patients: it merely indicated that the statute did not preclude such admissions. Informal admissions were, instead, by private arrangement. Such a reading would, of course, not apply to situations where the statute specifically governs informal patients, such as the treatment safeguards contained in s. 57. More generally, the reading is not obviously consistent with *R* v *Kirklees MBC, ex p C* [1992] FLR 117, discussed in Chapter 4, where the court appears to see s. 131 and private arrangements as creating separate admission routes, with the bulk of informal patients admitted pursuant to s. 131. Nevertheless, as the possibility of admission pursuant to s. 131 was not disputed in that case, the argument may still be open.

Also problematic will be the issue of when an individual living in the community falls outside the scope of the Act, so as to render s. 139 inoperative. Clearly, the creation of a plan for aftercare pursuant to s. 117 of a person formerly detained under the Act and about to be released will be within the scope of the section. Will the performance of the aftercare, as distinct from the formation of the plan for aftercare, also fall within the scope of the section? The preferable view would be that it will not, in so far as the individual has been released from the facility and is a regular individual in the community, separate from the facility. In reality, such a clean split is unlikely to occur. If the individual is not simply released, but subjected to aftercare under supervision under s. 25A, then the implementation of the care plan under s. 25D would appear to be caught by

s. 139. If the discharged individual is not subjected to a s. 25A order, he or she is still likely to remain an outpatient. Should outpatients be covered by the section? It would seem not. They have no status under the Act, and it is therefore difficult to see that they can be treated pursuant to it. If an outpatient is actually a detained patient on leave of absence pursuant to s. 17, however, a much closer nexus to the Act is present, and the applicability of s. 139 is considerably more likely.

Prosecutions of offences under the MHA 1983, which already may be only instituted by, or with the consent of, the Director of Public Prosecutions are not subject to the section: s. 139(3). This currently applies only to offences under s. 127, concerning ill treatment or wilful neglect of patients.

The section covers not only events in purported compliance with the legislation, but also with 'any regulations or rules' made under the statute. This extension will be particularly important for matters flowing from review tribunal proceedings and applications before the Court of Protection, both of which are regulated to a considerable degree by statutory instruments. It is a nice question whether purported reliance on the Code of Practice brings a defendant within the protection of the section: often, the question will be only academic, because acts performed within the guidance of the Code will be sufficiently related to some authority in the statute that a plea of *purported* pursuance of the statute will be successful. In the event that informal patients are deemed to be admitted and treated outside the statute, however, there may still be an issue as to whether their admission, treatment and management, as advised in the Code of Practice, renders the section applicable. Alternatively, it is perhaps arguable that the applicability of many of the provisions of the Code to informal patients suggests that these patients are treated pursuant to the statute, rather than as a result of the private arrangements by which they were admitted.

Section 139 refers specifically to 'acts' performed in purported pursuance of the statute. It is another nice question as to whether acts include omissions in this context. Jaconelli and Jaconelli (1998:153) argue that it does not. If they are correct, it would be the case that failure to treat would be outside the scope of the section, but maltreatment would be within it, for example. While this seems counterintuitive, the section is quite clear in its reference to 'any act purporting to be done'; it is not obvious that this wording can conveniently include omissions.

The section will, of course, be relevant to patients and former patients who wish to pursue remedies against those administering the legislation. The wording does not limit the category of plaintiff to whom it applies, however. Thus the section will also apply to a plaintiff suing, for example, on the basis that an individual acted negligently in allowing a detained patient to escape, when that escape results in an assault on the plaintiff: see *In re Shoesmith* [1938] 2 KB 637.

12.3.2 Leave to commence an action

The immediate effect for a plaintiff or complainant whose action falls within s. 139 is that leave must be sought to commence the action. In the case of a criminal matter, consent must be sought from (or the prosecution instituted by) the Director of Public Prosecutions. For a civil action, it is the leave of the High Court that is required. The requirement for leave to be granted is that the plaintiff demonstrate that the act complained of was done in bad faith, or without reasonable care: s. 139(1).

The section might loosely be understood as creating standards relating both to the defendant's conduct and to the appropriateness of the plaintiff's case. On the one hand, there is a sense that people charged with the administration of the MHA 1983 should not be held liable because they genuinely and in good faith make a mistake in their duties. This approach is manifest, for example, in *Richardson* v *London County Council* [1957] 1 WLR 751 (at 760):

Parliament has wisely provided that he [the plaintiff] is not to be allowed to bring an action of this kind unless there is substantial ground for believing them [the officers who confined the plaintiff] to have been guilty of want of good faith or want of reasonable care.... [A]lthough these public authorities may have misconstrued the Act and although they may have done things which there was no jurisdiction to do, nevertheless, so long as they acted in good faith and in a reasonable manner, they are to be protected from having actions brought against them.

While the need for 'substantial' grounds must be read in the context of subsequent statutory reform and case law, the remainder of the comment continues to reflect one judicial approach to the section. In general, wrongful confinement is a tort of strict liability; an action will succeed whenever a detention is unlawful. Section 139 may therefore be understood as precluding otherwise winnable cases. As Jaconelli and Jaconelli point out, this alteration will be particularly significant in torts of strict liability, such as breach of statutory duty, false imprisonment, and battery (1998: 154). It will be less likely to be significant when the action is in negligence, because a want of due care forms a part of the action in these cases in any event. Even in these cases, as Hale (Hoggett, 1996: 250) points out, there are residual disadvantages. The plaintiff must receive leave from a High Court judge, even if the claim is in the jurisdiction of the county courts; at that hearing, the plaintiff has the burden of showing that the case should continue.

The section also looks to the plaintiff, on a long-standing assumption that those with histories of mental health difficulties will be more likely than the general public to sue unreasonably and with unwinnable cases. It was to these claims that Lord Denning referred in the quotation with which this chapter commenced. In this context, the section can be seen to overlap considerably with the restrictions already available to the courts relating to claims having no real prospect of success: see Civil Procedure Rules, r. 24.2. Indeed, as Hale suggests, given the existence of these rules, it is not obvious that this aspect of the section is necessary or desirable (Hoggett, 1996: 250):

Only a minority of patients, even of those compulsorily detained, are suffering from disorders which make it at all likely that they will harass other people with groundless accusations. Rather more of them are suffering from disorders which make it likely that they will not complain at all, even if they have every reason to do so.... There is no evidence that the floodgates would open if section 139 were entirely repealed. There is more evidence, from a series of reports and investigations, that mental patients are in a particularly powerless position which merits, if anything, extra safeguards rather than the removal of those available to everyone else.

The recent trend seems, at least at first blush, to be to restrict the application of s. 139, and thus to provide the plaintiff with increased access to the courts. This is, in part, the result of changes to the wording of s. 139(2) in the 1983 legislation. Where the 1959 Act had required a potential plaintiff to demonstrate a 'substantial ground' for the contention that the potential defendant had acted in bad faith or without reasonable care, that requirement was removed from the 1983 legislation. The leading case is *Winch* v *Jones* [1985] 3 All ER 97 (CA). Lord Donaldson MR identified the problems that the section is intended to address in the following fashion (at 100–1):

To be more specific, there are two fundamental difficulties. First, mental patients are liable, through no fault of their own, to have a distorted recollection of facts which can, on occasion, become pure fantasy. Second, the diagnosis and treatment of mental illness is not an exact science and severely divergent views are sometimes possible without any lack of reasonable care on the part of the doctor. The intention of Parliament, as it seems to me, was quite clearly that no one should be prevented from making a valid claim that they have suffered by reason of negligence in the exercise of powers conferred by the Mental Health Acts and that no one should be harassed by an invalid claim.

Thus both the aspects of the section discussed above were noted. His Lordship then addressed the standard by which the court should decide whether leave ought to be granted (at 102):

As I see it, the section is intended to strike a balance between the legitimate interests of the applicant to be allowed, at his own risk as to costs, to seek the adjudication of the courts on any claim which is not frivolous, vexatious or an abuse of the process and the equally legitimate interests of the respondent to such an application not to be subjected to the undoubted exceptional risk of being harassed by baseless claims by those who have been treated under the Mental Health Acts. In striking such a balance, the issue is not whether the applicant has established a prima facie case or even whether there is a serious issue to be tried, although that comes close to it. The issue is whether, on the materials immediately available to the court, which, of course, can include material furnished by the proposed defendant, the applicant's complaint appears to be such that it deserves the fuller investigation which will be possible if the intended applicant is allowed to proceed.

While the onus therefore remains on the plaintiff, it is necessary to meet only a relatively low threshold in order for leave to be granted. This is consistent with the procedures for the hearing of the application. Affidavit evidence from both parties may be considered (*Carter* v *Metropolitan Police Commissioner* [1975] 1 WLR 507), but it is not to be turned into a trial on the affidavit evidence, and Parker LJ, in *Winch* v *Jones*, holds that cross-examination on that evidence ought never to be permitted (at 103). Affidavits might show that 'some allegation made by an intending plaintiff is totally refuted by incontrovertible evidence', but he was unwilling to go much further in interrogating the merits of the case. For Parker LJ, the appropriate standard was whether there was a 'reasonable suspicion that the authority had done something wrong' (at 103).

The approach in *Winch* is intended to keep the leave application from turning into a full-scale trial. While that end is laudable, it does raise possible difficulties: for example, if the relatively low threshold and summary investigation process required by *Winch* is relied upon, can the standards contained in s. 139(1) be relied upon as the case progresses and more facts become available? For the vexatious plaintiff, this is likely to be an academic problem, because the granting of leave under s. 139(2) does not preclude an application to strike the proceedings as frivolous or vexatious at a later point in the process: *X v A, B and C and the MHAC* (1991) 9 BMLR 91. If, instead, the facts show that there was no want of reasonable care, a negligence action can be dismissed either at trial or on summary judgment.

If instead the action is for wrongful confinement, for example, the question arises as to whether s. 139(1) actually alters the nature of the tort, or merely provides a procedural safeguard at the beginning of the process. In the event that leave is granted, does the eventual trial include the bad faith or want of due care provisions as a part of the substance of the tort that the plaintiff must demonstrate? Or, once leave is granted, does the tort revert back to its usual rules, where any illegal confinement can yield damages? The cases relating to s. 139 have tended to be about leave, rather than about final result, so the question may still technically be open. The Court of Appeal in *Wilkinson* clearly understood subs. (1) as creating a bar to a finding of liability on the part of the individual, but the question as to whether this is a procedural or a substantive bar remains significant, because of the potential effect on hospital and health authority liability, discussed below.

12.3.3 Section 139 and vicarious liability

In general, employers are liable for the torts of employees acting within the scope of their employment, through the doctrine of vicarious liability. This is, of course, a separate matter from direct liability of employer in situations where a tort performed by an employee is not involved, such as a failure by an NHS trust to maintain a building adequately, or to provide adequate staffing for a facility. In such situations of direct liability, only the employer will be liable. In situations of vicarious liability, liability will be joint: both employer and employee will be liable, as would be the case when leave is given pursuant to s. 139 and a plaintiff is successful in their suit against the individual doctor or social worker. In most cases, the employer of the doctors and other staff charged with the administration of the MHA 1983 will be a health authority or NHS trust, parties specifically excluded from the protection of s. 139. The question, therefore, arises as to whether the employers can remain vicariously liable, notwithstanding that leave is not granted under s. 139 to sue the doctor or nurse individually.

The arguments turn on whether vicarious liability is a 'master tort' or a 'servant tort'. If the former, vicarious liability of the employer is based on a theory that the employee acts on express or implied instructions of the employer, and therefore the tort of the employee is equally the tort of the employer. If the latter, the liability is based solely on the tort of the employee, and the liability of the employer is some form of indemnity flowing from the employment relationship.

The standard view in English tort law texts is that vicarious liability is a servant tort (Stanton, 1994: 128; Rogers, 2006: 879–83; Heuston and Buckley, 1996: 431–2). These accounts tend to rely to a considerable degree on *Imperial Chemical Industries Ltd* v *Shatwell* [1965] AC 656 (HL). In that case, the view was stated by all five law lords that, unless the servant could be held liable in damages, the employer could not be. That said, the facts in that case were rather unusual, and there are occasional judicial pronouncements to the contrary: see, e.g., *Twine* v *Bean's Express Ltd* [1946] 1 All ER 202; *Norton* v *Canadian Pacific Steamships* [1961] 1 WLR 1057 at 1063. The possibility that vicarious liability remains a master tort was specifically left open by Henry J in *Furber* v *Kratter* (1988) unreported (HC), a case involving inappropriate solitary seclusion in a psychiatric facility, allegedly without nursing care and without clothing, reading or writing material, where leave was sought pursuant to s. 139. If, following the opening left in *Furber*, vicarious liability is perceived as a master tort, the employer might well remain liable, notwithstanding the unavailability of an action against the employee because of s. 139.

This line of argument is complicated by the fact that, in some parts of the MHA 1983, duties are vested directly in employees such as approved social workers or medical officers. Specific statutory duties are not generally delegable. It becomes problematic to adopt a theory of implied instructions from employer to employee, when the employee and not the employer is charged with the duties alleged to be violated.

Even if vicarious liability is a servant tort, that does not necessarily end the matter. If, as was argued to be a possibility above, s. 139 does not alter the substantive law but instead merely removes an action for damages against some people, the tort arguably continues to exist. Just because (in the absence of bad faith or a want of reasonable care) an individual doctor cannot be sued for wrongful confinement, the argument would go, it does not necessarily follow that the tort has ceased to exist, but merely that one of the parties cannot be sued for it: see Jaconelli and Jaconelli (1998: 159). The issues here would seem to be: first, the degree to which s. 139 does in fact affect substantive law; second, whether the employer can be called upon to indemnify damages for which the employee has not been found liable.

Can this arrangement of split liability reflect the legislative intent of the section? While such an intent may seem improbable, Jaconelli and Jaconelli point to the fact that the subsection removing health authorities and the Secretary of State from the scope of the provision was drafted as the case of *Ashingdane* v *UK* (1984) 6 EHRR 69; (1985) 7 EHRR 528 neared the European Court of Human Rights, challenging the authority of the predecessor of s. 139. While both the Commission recommendation, reported at (1984) 6 EHRR 69, and the eventual court decision, (1985) 7 EHRR 528, upheld the predecessor of s. 139, it was more reluctant to do so for the health authority and government than it was for individual members of staff. Jaconelli and Jaconelli argue that the exclusion of health authorities and the Secretary of State from the scope of the section is to be read in that context.

This view was adopted by the majority in *Wilkinson*: see paras. 24, 58; para. 42 contra. The argument here does not appear to engage with the principles of tort noted above. The question was further not argued before that court, and was arguably a collateral issue in a case primarily concerned with alleged Human Rights Act violations. It nonetheless provides rather weak authority for the view that hospitals, health authorities and the Secretary of State are not protected by the terms of s. 139(1), even if this subsection does protect the individuals for whom these bodies are vicariously liable.

12.4 Criminal prosecutions

Subject to the provisions of s. 139, the regular criminal law continues to apply to those contained in the mental health system. In addition, however, the MHA 1983 provides its own, additional offences in Part IX of the Act.

Section 126 provides penalties of up to two years' imprisonment and an unlimited fine for persons who, without lawful authority or excuse, possess documents relating to the administration of the Act that they know, or believe, to be false. While the documents to which the section applies are specified in s. 126(3), the class is quite broad, including applications under Part II, medical or other recommendations, or reports under the Act, and 'any other document required or authorised to be made for any of the purposes of this Act'. The actual deception by the person creating the document remains under the broader criminal law; this section makes it an offence knowingly to possess such documents.

Section 128 makes it an offence to induce, or knowingly to assist, detained persons to absent themselves without leave. The provision extends not merely to those detained under Part II of the Act, but also to persons detained in a place of safety under s. 137, and also to those subject to guardianship under s. 7. Similarly, the harbouring of individuals absent without leave, or assisting them to prevent their recapture, is made an offence. Section 129 essentially makes it an offence to interfere with inquiries and inspections authorised by the Act. The interferences prohibited are listed specifically in the section: refusing to allow the inspection of premises; refusing to allow access to, or visiting, interviewing, or examination of, persons; refusing to produce records and documents; refusing to withdraw when an interview is permitted under the Act to be held in private.

Section 127 creates a number of offences related to the ill treatment or wilful neglect of patients. Managers, officers and staff of hospitals and mental nursing homes can be held liable for ill-treating or wilfully neglecting persons receiving treatment as inpatients of those facilities. These individuals can similarly be held liable regarding ill treatment or wilful neglect on the premises of outpatients receiving treatment at the hospital or mental nursing home: s. 127(1).

The offences in s. 127(1) are restricted to the staff of the facilities in question; not so the remaining offences provided in the section. Section 127(2) is broader still:

> It shall be an offence for any individual to ill-treat or wilfully to neglect a mentally disordered patient who is for the time being subject to his guardianship under this Act or otherwise in his custody or care (whether by virtue of any legal or moral obligation or otherwise).

This applies to any individual who cares for another who is mentally disordered, whether through guardianship or otherwise. Thus, in *R v Newington* (1990) Cr App R 247 (CA), the statute was applied to the owner of a residential home for the elderly. There was no doubt that the section could apply to her, although the mental disorder of the individuals allegedly ill treated had to be demonstrated (at 254).

While s. 127(2) will be of particular relevance for those living in the community and in facilities other than those identified in s. 127(1), it is also presumably broad enough to encompass many of the situations contained in s. 127(1). The elements of the offences are nonetheless somewhat different. Section 127(2) requires proof of the mental disorder of the individual, and of a specific relation between the accused and the individual – guardian, custodian or carer. Section 127(1) requires a patient–staff relationship in a hospital or mental nursing home, and, it would seem from the wording of the subsection, that the individual will be 'receiving treatment for mental disorder'. The current trends in case law would seem to be according a markedly broad interpretation to the phrase 'treatment for mental disorder', suggesting that it may not be a high hurdle for a prosecutor to leap; nonetheless, in the event of ill treatment of an individual not actually receiving such treatment, s. 127(2) might be considered, in the event that the complainant is mentally disordered and in the care of the potential accused.

Section 127(2A) inserted by the Mental Health (Patients in the Community) Act 1995, s. 2(1), Sch. 1, para. 18, is broader still:

> It shall be an offence for any individual to ill-treat or wilfully to neglect a mentally disordered patient who is for the time being subject to after care under supervision.

Here, no express relationship is implied between the potential defendant and the patient. Indeed, it is not even expressly required that the defendant know that the individual is mentally disordered and subject to aftercare under supervision, although proof of those facts would undoubtedly be required to make out the offence. Curiously, this provides people subject to aftercare under supervision with wider protection than that available to those subject to guardianship under s. 7. While ill treatment or wilful neglect of either by a carer will found a remedy, additional protection to those subject to guardianship is within the remit of s. 127(2), which prohibits ill treatment or wilful neglect only by their guardians. The lives of those subject to each form of control in the community may be quite similar; it is not obvious why the punitive sanctions against those abusing them ought to be different.

Common to all of the s. 127 offences is the phrase 'ill-treat or wilfully to neglect'. The leading case on the meaning of this phrase is *Newington*. In that case, the Court of

Appeal held that ill treatment should be pleaded separately from wilful neglect, because the latter would require consideration of a particular state of mind, where the former would not (at 252). The nature of the state of mind was not particularly articulated, because *Newington* was a case of ill treatment. The court summed up the elements of this aspect of the offence in the following terms (at 254):

In our judgment the judge should have told the jury that for there to be a conviction of ill-treatment contrary to the Act of 1983 the Crown would have to prove (1) deliberate conduct by the appellant which could properly be described as ill-treatment irrespective of whether this ill-treatment damaged or threatened to damage the health of the victim and (2) a guilty mind involving either an appreciation by the appellant at the time that she was inexcusably ill-treating a patient or that she was reckless as to whether she was inexcusably acting in that way.

The court held that a case may be made out, notwithstanding that no actual injury or unnecessary suffering or injury to health was caused (at 253). This suggests a relatively wide scope to 'ill-treatment'. Michael Gunn (1990: 361) has suggested that it may well be wide enough to include inadequate feeding or heating, the use of harsh words or bullying. Violence does not necessarily constitute ill treatment if it was used, for example 'for the reasonable control of a patient' (*Newington*, at 253). From the earlier case of *R* v *Holmes* [1979] Crim LR 52, it is clear that the offence can be made out from a single assault; a course of conduct is not necessary.

Proceedings under s. 127 must be instituted by, or with leave of, the Director of Public Prosecutions (DPP): s. 127(4). The effect of this provision is to take s. 127 offences outside the scope of s. 139. Thus, s. 127 prosecutions may be commenced without proof of bad faith or want of due care.

Local social service authorities are given specific authority to 'institute proceedings' for all the offences in Part IX by s. 130, although this is 'without prejudice to any provision of this Part of this Act requiring the consent of the Director of Public Prosecutions for the institution of such proceedings'. The effect of this caveat is ambiguous. To begin with, what is clear is that local social service authorities have standing to prosecute the offences under the Act. They must also seek consent of the DPP to institute a prosecution under s. 127, the only section in Part IX where such consent is expressly required. The ambiguity arises in the interface between ss. 130 and 139: does the authority to 'institute proceedings' mean an authority to institute such proceedings without the leave of the DPP otherwise required by s. 139(2)? The specific maintenance of the role of the DPP 'under this Part' might be taken to imply a modification of that officer's role under s. 139, which is contained in a different part of the Act. On this reading, s. 139 would not apply. At the same time, s. 139(3) specifically exempts from its remit Part IX offences, which the DPP must already institute or consent to the institution of. This implicitly brings the remaining Part IX offences under the scope of s. 139(2), and there is nothing that would remove the local social services authority from that subsection. It is not clear which of these readings the courts would adopt.

In some cases, the issue will be academic. It is difficult to see how leave would be required under s. 139 for an action against an individual who assists another to escape, for example, even given the broadest interpretation of acts 'purporting to be done in pursuance of this Act'. In other cases, the matter will be effectively a procedural nicety. It is difficult to see how an individual who knowingly makes false statements on an admission application can be said to be acting other than in bad faith, suggesting that the grant of leave under s. 139 would be a formality. Cases may well be more compli- cated, however: the obstruction offences contained in s. 129 provide an example. Arguably, these may involve imperfect compliance with the Act, and a misguided view of the law by the potential defendant. Prima facie, s. 139 might provide a defence, if prosecutions by the local social services authority are, in fact, covered by that section. The relationship between ss. 130 and 139 is thus not entirely of academic interest.

A variety of offences outside of the current MHA refer specifically to people with mental disabilities. For example, ss. 30–45 of the Sexual Offences Act 2003 prohibit a wide variety of sexual activity with or in the presence of a person lacking capacity or with a mental disorder impeding choice. This precluded conduct includes sexual touching of such a person, inciting or inducing that person to engage in sexual activity, or engaging in sexual activity in the presence of that person. For care workers, these matters are more strict: the prohibitions apply to any person with a mental disorder, not merely the incapacitated or where that disorder impedes choice.

It is appropriate to close this section by returning to its first point: the broader crim- inal law also applies to people contained in the mental health system. Thus, an assault on a patient by a member of staff is not merely an offence under s. 127; it may also give rise to a charge of common assault: see, e.g., *Newington*. A manifest lack of care such as results in the death of a person with mental disorder, unable to care for himself or herself, may result in a conviction for manslaughter in the event that an individual undertakes to provide care to that individual and fails adequately to do so: *R v Stone, R v Dobinson* [1977] 1 All ER 341. Advocates should be aware of such wider possibilities of the criminal law.

12.5 Civil actions for damages

Subject again to the provisions of s. 139, the general laws of contract and tort apply to people in the mental health system as much as anywhere else. Contract will be of lim- ited assistance when dealing with NHS trusts and health authorities, because no con- tract exists between these bodies and their patients: *Pfizer* v *Ministry of Health* [1965] 1 All ER 152. The same logic would apply to community care facilities, unless the client pays directly for the care received.

Tort provides a more encouraging line of authorities. Any exhaustive analysis of the torts that might assist people in the mental health system is, of course, beyond the scope of this book: it could easily comprise a separate volume. That said, advocates should think creatively, and not leap instantly to an action in negligence. Assault or battery may be an effective mechanism to seek redress for inappropriately aggressive behaviour directed at the client by hospital or community care staff. Occupier's liability applies as much in psychiatric facilities as it does elsewhere, providing redress for injury flowing from a person's entry into premises, whether on a short-term or long-term basis. Wrongful confinement may be used to challenge detentions, and has the advantage that, once the confinement is shown, it is for the defendant to justify their actions. Rather than discuss the variety of torts in a summary fashion, the discussion that follows will instead examine a few more specific difficulties raised in recent mental health litigation. These issues have tended to arise in the context of negligence law.

To begin with a basic principle, it is uncontroversial that there is a duty of care between healthcare professionals, such as doctors and nurses, and their patients. The duty arises when the doctor–patient relationship is crystallised, or when the patient is accepted as a patient in a hospital (McHale *et al.*, 1997: 149). This duty is therefore broad enough to include care both inside and outside psychiatric facilities. This gives the patient the right to expect the standard of care that the 'reasonable doctor' occupying the position of the potential defendant would have provided: general practitioners are subject to the standard of the reasonable general practitioner; psychiatric specialists are subject to the standard of the reasonable psychiatric specialist etc.

In theory, this ought to provide many people in the mental health system with civil redress for medical misadventure or other errors by these professionals. For example, patients given megadoses of cocktails of psychiatric medication (see Chapter 7) might think they can sue in the event that they suffer adverse effects. Until recently, it would be difficult to see that such an action would succeed. The test of whether the standard of care was breached was whether a responsible body of medical opinion would have behaved as the defendant did: *Bolam* v *Friern HMC* [1957] 2 All ER 118. Because megadosing is not uncommon in psychiatric facilities, this test would be difficult to surmount. Recently, however, a caveat has been introduced on the *Bolam* test, by *Bolitho* v *City and Hackney HA* [1997] 3 WLR 1151, where the House of Lords acknowledged, per Lord Browne-Wilkinson at 1159, that the professional views must stand up to objective scrutiny:

The court has to be satisfied that the exponents of the body of opinion relied upon can demonstrate that such opinion has a logical basis. In particular, in cases involving, as they so often do, the weighing of risks against benefits, the judge before accepting a body of opinion as being responsible, reasonable or respectable, will need to be satisfied that, in forming their views, the experts have directed their minds to the question of comparative risks and benefits and have reached a defensible conclusion on the matter.

The intrusiveness of this revised standard on medical authority is limited. The views of doctors will clearly continue to have considerable sway in court. In megadosing, however, doctors are failing to be governed by the maximum dosages of drugs recommended by the manufacturers of those drugs, maxima presumably based on scientific testing and experimentation. In such extreme situations, *Bolitho* might be invoked to challenge the appropriateness of the doctor's decision. Except in such rather unusual situations, however, a fairly uniform medical view that the doctor's actions were inappropriate would be necessary to found a negligence action; such uniform views opposing a course of action by a doctor are uncommon.

Megadosing might also be addressed through a negligence action based on insufficient information provision. Informal patients, of course, have the same treatment rights as any other member of the community. This means that they must consent to any treatment they are given, assuming they have the capacity to do so (see Chapters 10 and 11). Similarly, some confined patients are treated on their consent pursuant to s. 58. Treatment on the patient's consent in these contexts must meet the usual common law standard, as established by *Sidaway* v *Governors of Bethlem Royal Hospital* [1985] AC 871, *Pearce* v *United Bristol Healthcare NHS Trust* [1999] PIQR 53 (CA), *Chester* v *Afshar* [2004] UKHL 41, 2004 WL 2289136 (HL), [2005] 1 AC 134, [2004] 4 All ER 587, [2004] 3 WLR 927.

This means that they must be informed of the major risks and benefits of treatment. The precise scope of this in a megadosing context has yet to be litigated, but it seems, at the very least, arguable that it would be necessary to disclose that the dosage is in excess of the manufacturer's recommended maximum. Information provision can be a double-edged sword, however, because, if the information is provided, including possible adverse effects from the megadose, a court might find that the patient had voluntarily assumed the risk of resulting adverse effects, and no action would therefore lie: *volenti non fit injuria*. It is questionable whether this is an appropriate result. If consenting to the medication is understood by the patient as the only hope for release from the facility, is the consent to the risk 'voluntary' in the sense that ought to invoke the defence?

The legal relationship between doctor and patient becomes more complex when the doctor is exercising a statutory function under the 1983 Act. Liability for signing a medical certificate as part of a process for involuntary admission will serve as an example. More recently, it has been expressly held that the duty of care of doctors signing such certificates is still an open question: *X (Minors)* v *Bedfordshire County Council* [1995] 3 All ER 353 at 384; *Clunis* v *Camden and Islington Health Authority* [1998] 2 WLR 902 at 914. This was somewhat surprising, because the broadly held belief up until that time had been that a duty of care did exist, as evidenced by a considerable trail of litigation: e.g. *Winch* v *Jones* (see earlier; leave granted to sue doctor for negligence in confinement); *O'Neill* v *Morrison* (1994) unreported (CA) (similar situation: leave refused but no implied doubt as to duty of care); *Buxton* v *Jayne* [1960] 1 WLR 783 (leave granted to bring action against duly authorised officer of local authority – analogous in the 1959 Act to the social worker in the 1983 Act – for lack of care in confining plaintiff).

Both *X* and *Clunis* rely for this proposition on the case of *Everett* v *Griffiths* [1921] 1 AC 631 (HL), in which, notwithstanding the tentative views of Viscounts Haldane and Cave that such a duty did exist, the fact that no negligence was found in the completion of the medical certificate in question allowed the matter to be left open. A majority of the House of Lords continued to leave the matter open in *Harnett* v *Fisher* [1927] AC 573, although Lord Atkinson offers the opinion that the doctor signing such a certificate 'is simply engaged as a medical man by a patient to give an opinion as to the patient's state of health, as he would be to diagnose the state of health of any patient who in his daily practice called upon him to prescribe for him' (at 596). This suggests that, in his Lordship's view, the standard duty of care applied to the duties of a doctor in signing such certificates. The content of these cases may be inconclusive, but reliance upon these cases is not convincing in any event. The statutory regime under consideration was that contained in the Lunacy Act 1890 where the medical certificate was but one piece of evidence necessary to apply for an order for confinement. The order itself was signed by, and was subject to the discretion of, a Justice of the Peace. The removal of this extra layer of bureaucracy is significant. Now, the requisite medical certificates and the application pursuant to ss. 2 or 3 are sufficient for confinement. The certificates, therefore, have a legal effect that they did not have previously, suggesting that a new analysis is necessary.

The obvious starting place for such an analysis is *X* v *Bedfordshire*. In that case, one of the issues was whether the social workers and psychiatrists interviewing children as part of the determination as to whether the children ought to be placed in care gave rise to an action in damages, in the event that it was performed negligently. Lord Browne-Wilkinson, speaking for a unanimous House of Lords, held that it did not, on the basis that such a duty would not be 'just and reasonable' within the meaning of *Caparo Industries plc* v *Dickman* [1990] 2 AC 605. His Lordship reasoned that a complex and interdisciplinary statutory system had been established, in which liability of individuals could not easily be disentangled. Second, child protection proceedings were inherently delicate, involving a complex balancing exercise, and the court should hesitate before criticising the balancing of conflicting priorities by the authorities. Third, liability in damages might induce local authorities to be more cautious and defensive in their approach. Fourth, he held that the fraught relations that often existed between parents of the children concerned and social workers would breed hopeless, vexatious and costly litigation. He further held that the statutory remedies, although not providing for compensation, did allow for scrutiny of decisions. Finally, he held that the doctors were retained to advise the local authorities, not the plaintiffs, and hence that no patient–doctor relationship was, in fact, established (at 380–4).

A number of these arguments simply do not apply to the doctor or social worker involved in a confinement under the MHA 1983. Certainly, the statutory regime is complex, but the roles of the various professionals are kept distinct. Any negligence or impropriety of these individuals would be clearly definable by reference to the statute. Issues of the delicacy of the proceedings and the risk of vexatious litigation are already dealt with through s. 139, discussed earlier. Two others can be dismissed relatively briefly. Certainly, the availability of a civil remedy might induce those in charge to 'adopt a more cautious and defensive approach to their duties' (at 381); but is caution necessarily a bad thing, particularly when considerable violations of civil rights will result from the actions? It should further be recalled that the existence of a duty of care is but one element required for success in a negligence action. A breach of the duty is also necessary, and success on this head will require proof of a want of reasonable care, a criterion already allowing room for error in the event of difficult circumstances.

The negligence action is to provide a mechanism to call decision-makers to account, to explain themselves. This is further relevant to the issue of statutory remedies, because, as discussed above, the review tribunals provided by the statute do not determine the validity of the initial detention, but only the appropriateness of continued detention. The statute does not provide a mechanism for the initial detention to be considered; unlike that in the child welfare situation, this is left to the broader law of judicial review.

This leaves the most interesting of the grounds for decision in X: the question of who is the client of the doctor or social worker. In X, Lord Browne-Wilkinson addressed the matter as follows (at 383):

The social workers and the psychiatrists were retained by the local authority to advise the local authority, not the plaintiffs. The subject matter of the advice and activities of the professionals is the child. Moreover, the tendering of any advice will in many cases involve interviewing and, in the case of doctors, examining the child. But the fact that the carrying out of the retainer involves contact with and a relationship with the child cannot alter the extent of the duty owed by the professionals under the retainer from the local authority. The Court of Appeal drew a correct analogy with the doctor instructed by an insurance company to examine an applicant for life insurance. The doctor does not, by examining the applicant, come under any general duty of medical care to the applicant. He is under a duty not to damage the applicant in the course of the examination: but beyond that his duties are owed to the insurance company and not to the applicant.

The role of the certifying doctors and social worker is by no means as clear-cut. Certainly, some doctors or social workers will be brought in only for purposes of the certification, and will have no other professional relationship with the individual. This suggests a relatively close parallel to the doctors and social workers in X. Frequently, however, at least one of the certifying doctors will be the patient's general practitioner. In the event that the certificate will involve a readmission, the other doctor may well be the individual's psychiatrist, who may continue to serve in that role following the individual's admission to hospital. In both of these cases, the medical professionals signing the certificates are in an ongoing professional relationship with a patient. Can it really be said that the signing of the certificates is severable from the remainder of that relationship, so that it, unlike the programme of treatment of which the admission must form an integral part, is not contained within the doctor–patient relationship?

A finding that the actions of doctors related to medical certification was not within the patient–doctor duty of care would lead to anomaly. Consider a case where a doctor informed a patient that, if he or she did not consent to informal admission, the doctor would institute civil confinement. If the patient were to rely on the doctor and go into hospital as an informal patient, the situation would be analogous to a patient entering hospital for a physical ailment on doctor's advice, and the duty of care would be beyond question. If, instead, the patient were to call the bluff of the doctor and the doctor were to sign the certificate, the duty of care would not exist. The duty would be a function of whether the patient agreed to follow the doctor's advice voluntarily – a most unusual result.

An appeal of *X* v *Bedfordshire* to the ECHR was successful, of reasons of mixed relevance in the current context: *Z* v *UK* [2001] 2 FLR 612; (2002) 34 EHRR 3. It was held that the level of abuse to which the children had been subjected constituted a breach of Art. 3, and the consequent failure to provide a domestic remedy in damages constituted a breach of Art. 13. Because the case did not involve psychiatric care or treatment, the Art. 3 violation is of no direct relevance for current purposes, and because Art. 5 contains in it an express right to damages, recourse to Art. 13 is unlikely to be necessary for psychiatric cases involving wrongful confinement, although there may be relevance for other forms of psychiatric malpractice. The court does not expressly overrule tort law, but instead awards damages for a convention breach. The case does not expressly affirm a duty of care in domestic law, therefore, but does provide a salient reminder of the overlapping jurisdiction of the Convention: see below.

The move towards increasing care in the community similarly raises difficulties relating to the scope of the duty of care and the doctor–patient relationship. The leading case is *Clunis*. In that case, the plaintiff was released from Guy's Hospital in south London. Because he wished to live in north London, aftercare was arranged by Guy's with a north London hospital, and Dr Sargeant, a psychiatrist at that hospital, agreed to serve as responsible medical officer under the aftercare plan. Notwithstanding appointments established for him on 9 October and 13 November 1992, the plaintiff, Clunis failed to attend at the hospital. Dr Sargeant contacted Clunis's last general practitioner, who indicated that Clunis had been removed from his list due to aggressive and threatening behaviour. Dr Sargeant then contacted Guy's Hospital and social services, to arrange a mental health assessment visit. This was to take place on 30 November, but Clunis was not at home at the relevant time, and the assessment, therefore, did not take place. Dr Sargeant made an appointment to see Clunis on 10 December, which he again did not attend. On 17 December, social services notified Dr Sargeant of a telephone call from the police, indicating that Clunis was 'waving screwdrivers and knives and talking about devils'. Later that day, Clunis killed a bystander in an unprovoked attack, by stabbing him with a knife. At trial, a plea of diminished responsibility was accepted, based on a diagnosis of schizo-affective disorder.

Clunis commenced a suit against Dr Sargeant, alleging negligence in her follow-up of his care plan. The case is, therefore, interesting, because it lies at the intersection of several issues. First, there is the issue of the duty of care owed by doctors to persons in care in the community in general, and on aftercare under s. 117 in particular. Second, there is the issue that the negligence alleged was one of omission: the doctor should have intervened more to ensure that appropriate care was given, notwithstanding the inevitable conclusion that Clunis did not, at the time, want the treatment. Finally, there was the issue of whether the action was barred on policy grounds, because it stemmed from Clunis's own criminal act in killing the bystander: *ex turpi causa non oritur actio*. The defendants applied to have the claim struck out as disclosing no cause of action. This was unsuccessful, but their appeal succeeded and the case was dismissed on the basis of the first and third of these issues. In neither case is the reasoning of the court entirely satisfactory.

On the issue of *ex turpi causa*, the court held (at 911) that the claim arose out of the commission of a criminal offence:

In the present case we consider the defendant has made out its plea that the plaintiff's claim is essentially based on his illegal act of manslaughter; he must be taken to have known what he was doing and that it was wrong, notwithstanding that the degree of his culpability was reduced by reason of mental disorder. The court ought not to allow itself to be made an instrument to enforce obligations alleged to arise out of the plaintiff's own criminal act and we would therefore allow the appeal on this ground.

The difficulty with the court's reasoning is that the court conflated the entire action for damages to an action for damages flowing from the death of the bystander. No doubt, in monetary terms, this was where most of the damages lay, but the failure to provide appropriate medical care would appear to have had adverse effects not directly related to the homicide. Certainly, it would appear that, by the morning in question, Clunis was psychotic. The unpleasant experience of having those psychotic delusions before the attack would presumably constitute actionable damage, if the duty of care and breach were successfully shown. There is no reason for those damages to be lost as a result of the *ex turpi* ruling.

Of greater relevance for current discussion is the fact that the Court of Appeal failed to find a duty of care between Dr Sargeant and Clunis. Perhaps unsurprisingly, given the lack of express statutory language, the court held that s. 117, the duty to provide aftercare services to a formerly detained patient, created a public law duty, rather than a private law action in damages. More problematically, it held (at 913–14) that the provision of aftercare services under the statute was inconsistent with a coexisting common law duty of care:

Bearing in mind the ambit of the obligations under s. 117 of the Act and that they affect a wide spectrum of health and social services, including voluntary services, we do not think that Parliament intended so widespread a liability as that asserted by Mr Irwin [counsel for Clunis]. The question of whether a common law duty exists in parallel with the authority's statutory obligations is profoundly influenced by the surrounding statutory framework.... So, too, in this case, the statutory framework must be a major consideration in deciding whether it is fair and reasonable for the local health authority to be held responsible for errors and omissions of the kind alleged. The duties of care are, it seems to us, different in nature from those owed by a doctor to a patient whom he is treating and for whose lack of care in the course of such treatment the local health authority may be liable.

Certainly, a variety of professional individuals and voluntary agencies may be involved in the patient's aftercare. It is not obvious that this should negate a duty of care, however, because the aftercare received by a formerly detained patient under s. 117 may well, in all outward appearances, be similar to the care in the community received by any other patient, only for the latter, the care will be outside the terms of the statute. Precisely analogous arguments to those rehearsed by the court above will apply. Therefore, either the court is saying that there is no duty of care between psychiatrists or health authorities and their patients living in the community – a truly startling statement – or it must be asked why the provision of essentially similar services by statutory obligation under s. 117 rather than merely by good practice should *remove* the duty of care.

Perhaps the escape route for the court might have been that Clunis terminated one therapeutic relationship with Guy's upon his release from that facility, and, because he never attended an appointment with Dr Sargeant, never commenced a new one. As a result, at the time of the homicide, there was no duty of care in effect: Clunis had slipped through the cracks between therapeutic relationships. But even this is problematic. In general, the duty of care between hospital and patient arises when there is an express or implied undertaking that the patient will be treated: *Cassidy* v *Ministry of Health* [1951] 1 All ER 574. Such an express undertaking would appear to have existed in this case, and was manifest by Dr Sargeant's continuing, albeit unsuccessful, attempts to establish a therapeutic relationship with Clunis. It is, perhaps, arguable that the relationship, and hence the duty, did not exist in this case, because it had been repudiated by Clunis's refusal to attend the treatments. In any event, this is not how the court approached the issue.

A broader question arises as to the strategic benefits from a patient's rights perspective of litigation complaining of a doctor's failure to intervene in the life of a patient, either by failing to confine the individual under ss. 2 or 3, or to launch guardianship proceedings under s. 7. Certainly, there is a legal coherence to such actions. If a duty of care exists between doctor and patient, then the patient has a right to expect the doctor to exercise a certain standard of care. Because the doctor's role appropriately includes diagnosis of mental illness and consequent responsibilities under the Act, it seems tautological that the patient ought to be able to insist that these roles are fulfilled to the appropriate standard of care. The failure to do so, as was alleged in the *Clunis* case, can be tragic; more often it is more mundane, but nonetheless may detract from the longer term quality of life of the patient, and may therefore be actionable. All that is asked, the argument runs, is the exercise of a reasonable professional standard of care. At the same time, such litigation must encourage doctors to err on the side of intervention. As we saw in Chapter 4, the dangerousness of the mentally ill is significantly over-predicted, and institutionalisation has its disadvantages as well as its benefits. Is it really the case that doctors should be encouraged to intervene more?

12.6 Applications under the Human Rights Act

It will be clear from the remainder of this book that the Human Rights Act offers a panoply of new issues for litigation. The objective in this section is not to catalogue these potential issues, but rather to consider how far the Human Rights Act offers a distinct set of processes for redress, which, in turn, may avoid some of the hurdles contained elsewhere. If the Human Rights Act overlays previously existing mental health law with a new set of procedures for redress, it is equally appropriate to emphasise that it contains its own sets of hurdles. Some of these are procedural: thus, the Human

Rights Act requires, for example, that proceedings must be brought by a 'victim' – a narrower class than can launch judicial review proceedings. Others are substantive: alleged abuses of rights have to attain a sufficient *gravitas* to constitute violations of the Act. Sometimes this is implied in the relevant Article, and defined jurisprudentially. Thus, not all inappropriate treatment will be considered inhuman or degrading under Art. 3. Issues relating to the circumstances of the treatment and its severity will also be relevant. Other Articles more expressly include restrictions to the rights in the phrasing of the Article itself. Particularly regarding these Articles, a doctrine of 'proportionality' has developed, allowing reasonable limitations to be set on the right, if consistent with a legitimate state objective to be obtained. While the Human Rights Act offers some important new directions for litigation, therefore, it is in no way a patient rights free-for-all.

The way in which Human Rights Act processes overlay pre-existing mental health law does, however, provide some potential for patient advocacy. Key among these is the fact that an entire process or section of the statute may be challenged as constituting a breach of human rights, rather than only the application of facts to the legislation in question. The possibilities for systemic advocacy are thus markedly increased. There may also be advantages for individual claimants as well. As we have seen elsewhere in this book, actions that may be legal under domestic law may nonetheless constitute breaches of the Act, providing a new set of substantive rights.

The procedural niceties of Human Rights Act applications are still very much under development. As noted above, there may be distinct advantages to including human rights issues in judicial review proceedings, because, in appropriate cases, the court may be prepared to hear oral evidence. Section 8(1) of the HRA further provides near-infinite flexibility in the redress awarded by the court, making these applications potentially attractive.

Of particular relevance in the current context is the question of whether s. 139 applies to these proceedings. In *Wilkinson*, a majority of the court took the view that it did: paras. 54 and 61. Once again, however, the question had not been argued before the court, and Hale LJ expressly indicated that her view in this regard was provisional. An alternative view is found in *R (W) v Doncaster Metropolitan Borough Council* [2003] EWHC 192 (Admin). In that case, Stanley Burton J held that s. 139 did apply to judicial review cases in which damages were claimed, but distinguished these cases from applications under the Human Rights Act (para. 56):

I doubt whether liability for the unlawful infringement of the rights of a patient under Article 5.1 is precluded by section 139(1) of the MHA. In such a case, the patient has a Convention right to compensation under Article 5.5. Section 3 of the HRA requires the Court to construe legislation in a way that is compatible with that right. Moreover, Parliament did not have breach of the Convention in mind when it enacted section 139(1) of the MHA. Despite the general words of that section, I should have been disposed to read it down so as not to apply to the breaches of Convention rights. The interpretation of general words so as to exclude specific cases that Parliament could not have intended to be included in them is a standard mode of statutory interpretation.

It is submitted that this is the stronger view. As noted above, Convention rights have procedural and substantive hurdles of their own. While the views in *Wilkinson* extended only to cases that would be tortious absent s. 139, it is the case that some human rights violations may occur without bad faith or a want of reasonable care on the part of the perpetrator. Particularly if the view were to prevail that NHS trusts and government cannot be vicariously liable for the behaviour of those protected by s. 139(1), the financial ramifications for such human rights violations would fall entirely on the patient. For the patient to receive the compensation that is his or her right under Art. 5.5, he or she would be required to appeal to the European Court of Human Rights in Strasbourg. The purpose of the Human Rights Act was to make that journey unnecessary. It is difficult to see that it can have been the legislative intent to make it unnecessary for all but psychiatric patients.

Such a result would further raise difficulties under Art. 14 of the ECHR, the non-discrimination provision. Disability is not contained expressly within that provision, but the wording of that Art. makes it clear that the classes upon which discrimination is prohibited is not closed. In *Pretty* v *UK* (2002) 35 EHRR 1, the ECtHR held (para. 88):

For the purpose of Article 14, a difference in treatment between persons in analogous or relatively similar positions is discriminatory if it has no objective and reasonable justification, that is if it does not pursue a legitimate aim or if there is not a reasonable relationship of proportionality between the means employed and the aim sought to be realised.

It is difficult to see what legitimate aim is pursued by forcing psychiatric patients, unlike the rest of the British public, to appeal to Strasbourg for their Art. 5.5 rights.

It is to be acknowledged that this may significantly restrict the effect of s. 139(1). Consistent with ECHR jurisprudence, the Privy Council has held that incompatability with domestic law relating to psychiatric confinement will constitute a breach of Art. 5: *A (A Mental Patient) v Scottish Ministers and Advocate-General (Scotland)* [2002] SC (PC) 63, [2002] HRLR 6. In this area, the overlap between domestic illegality and human rights violation is complete. In that event, even entirely innocent and technical violations of admissions procedures may give rise to actions in damages, gutting, to a considerable degree, the effect of s. 139. That is nonetheless what the ECHR would appear to provide; there is no obvious reason to deny that Convention right to those in psychiatric facilities.

12.7 Complaint processes

For much of what clients will want, litigation is not the appropriate model: not only is it expensive, it frequently will not provide a remedy to the client's actual problem. There may not be a lot of point in suing because a client is unhappy with the medication they are receiving, or unable, for religious or cultural reasons, to eat the food served in a hospital, although these may be significant problems for the client. It is not obvious that civil actions would succeed for such problems; even if they did, they would provide a remedy in damages, not preferable medication or different food. For many such day-to-day difficulties, a direct approach to the doctor or hospital manager may provide the best chance of a resolution to the problem. The presence of an advocate may give the client's concerns increased credence by such authority figures, which may trigger a solution. In other instances, the advocate's negotiation skills may allow otherwise unforeseen solutions to be reached.

Even if the matter is one for which other legal avenues appear appropriate, informal dispute resolution mechanisms should be considered. Thus tribunals tend to be sympathetic to the RMO's views of the appropriateness of detention, for example. It may well be the case that some sort of negotiated plan with the RMO directed towards release of the client may bring results more effectively than a review tribunal hearing.

Particularly for issues of day-to-day living outside the scope of tribunals, internal complaint processes within the hospital or community care facility might be considered. A variety of such mechanisms exist. NHS trusts are now required to operate complaints processes, headed by a complaints manager. This is a separate structure from the trust's disciplinary system, although the structure of most complaint systems seems to assume that the complaint will be about an individual, rather than an inappropriate policy. Increasingly, these processes will have advocacy programmes running in parallel in the trust, to assist complainants. At their best, these advocacy services will be staffed by people whose knowledge of the workings of the trust will be considerably better than an external advocate, and who may therefore be particularly effective at having the complainant's matter resolved.

In the event that the client is not content with the result of a complaint through one of these internal processes, the complaint may then be forwarded to the Mental Health Act Commission. The Commission has a fairly broad authority under the Act to visit people detained pursuant to the Act in hospitals and mental nursing homes; and to investigate complaints of detainees under the Act if the complaint has not been adequately dealt with through an internal process: s. 120(1), MHA 1983. The Commission has powers of investigation – a distinct advantage in ensuring that the substance of a complaint is considered – but its jurisdiction extends only to confined patients, not to those informally admitted, nor to outpatients or persons on aftercare with supervision, although the Commission does have jurisdiction to investigate complaints relating to events that occurred during a period of detention even if that detention has now ceased.

Complaints may also be lodged with the Health Services Commissioner for England, a position established through the Health Service Commissioner Act 1993. The Commissioner's jurisdiction extends to individuals providing health services, and also health authorities and NHS trusts. Until 1996, complaints relating to clinical judgment were outside the Commissioner's remit; that was changed by s. 6 of the Health Service Commissioner (Amendment) Act 1996. The Commissioner has powers of investigation, suggesting that this may be an inexpensive way for a client's concern to be investigated.

There can thus be seen to be a potential overlap between the jurisdictions of the Mental Health Act Commission and the Health Services Commissioner. The bodies have informally agreed that matters relating to the circumstances or consequences of detention of psychiatric patients will be dealt with by the former body; otherwise, they will fall to the latter.

Finally, many professionals working in the mental health sector are subject to internal professional disciplinary processes: for example, doctors, nurses and health visitors are all subject to such professional regulation. In the event that the concern is with the professionalism of such an individual, a complaint to the relevant professional body – i.e. the General Medical Council or the UK Central Council for Nursing, Midwifery and Health Visiting – might be considered.

12.8 Advocacy

The right of people with mental health difficulties to representation is established in a variety of sources. The Mental Health Review Tribunal Rules 1983 establish the right of a party to representation before those tribunals. The representative may be virtually anyone authorised by the party. Legal aid is available for these proceedings (see Chapter 8).

For litigation before the courts, the usual rules regarding representation apply. The apparent openness of the courts is, however, subject to the individual's right to participate in litigation. The rule is that a 'patient' may sue or be sued only through a 'litigation friend': CPR r. 21.2. These rules take effect if the individual is 'a person who, by reason of mental disorder within the meaning of the Mental Health Act 1983, is incapable of managing and administering his own affairs': CPR r. 21.1. The rules adopt the term 'patient', a usage that will be reflected in the discussion that follows. While the 'patient' must be suffering from a 'mental disorder' as contained in the broad definition of s. 1(2) of the MHA, there is no requirement that the individual in question be contained in a psychiatric facility or even under active medical care for their disorder at the time of the litigation. In that sense, 'patient' may be a very misleading term.

The leading case concerning capacity to litigate is *Masterman-Lister v Brutton & Co, Jewell & Home Counties Dairies*. Consistent with a functional approach to capacity, based on the specific decisions to be made, the court focused particular concern on issues relating to the litigation in question: paras. 18, 75. Kennedy LJ adopted the following articulation of the standards involved (at 26):

So the mental abilities required include the ability to recognise a problem, obtain and receive, understand and retain relevant information, including advice; the ability to weigh the information (including that derived from advice) in the balance in reaching a decision, and the ability to communicate that decision . . . [T]he court should have regard to the complexity of decisions under consideration but not to the court's own valuation of the gravity of those decisions because it is not for the court to decide in a non-medical treatment case what is or is not serious in the life of the person before it.

While r. 21.2 requires that persons within this class must have a litigation friend, there is no routine mechanism for the prompt and effective enforcement of this provision.

Rule 21.3 requires claimants against patients to apply for a litigation guardian in cases where none exists; it is not necessarily obvious how such claimants will know that the person subject to the proceedings is a patient. This may lead to awkward results, because steps in proceedings taken against patients in contravention of r. 21.3 are of no effect unless subsequently ratified by the court under r. 21.3(4).

Further, the rules for the appointment of such friends are remarkably lax. For persons wishing to act on behalf of a patient, a court order is often unnecessary: r. 21.4. Instead, it is sufficient that a 'certificate of suitability' be filed with the court after service on all parties under r. 6.6, to the effect that the individual (r. 21.4(3)):

(a) can fairly and competently conduct proceedings on behalf of the patient; and

(b) has no interest adverse to that of the patient; and

(c) where the patient is a claimant, undertakes to pay any costs in relation to the proceedings to which the patient may become liable, subject to a right to be reimbursed from the assets of the patient.

No evidence of incapacity need be filed with this form. Rule 6.6 further does not require the patient to be served with the form unless the court orders otherwise, although the carer with whom the patient lives must be served. It may well be, therefore, that the patient knows nothing of the litigation. If the patient, in fact, lacks capacity, this may, in some cases, have minimal adverse consequences, but this begs the question of whether the patient does, in fact, lack capacity, and raises questions about the dignity afforded to clients of marginal capacity. Challenges to the appointment of litigation friends under r. 21.7, and appointments by the court under r. 21.6 must be accompanied by evidence, but the nature of that evidence is unspecified, and need not be specifically medical. This absence of judicial process has led to the consistency of the current appointment process with Art. 6 of the ECHR being called into question: see *Masterman-Lister*, para. 17.

Advocates should be aware that the authority of the client to conduct proceedings is not only an issue upon the commencement of proceedings. Indeed, the issue regarding client authority may change over the course of litigation. Thus, a client may be capable of providing instructions up to the time of settlement or judgment in a case, but, due to specific incapacities, be unable to provide instructions as to how a large sum of damages is to be dealt with. In that event, the appointment of a litigation guardian may become appropriate at that time: *Masterman-Lister*, paras. 27, 83. The authority of a solicitor to act ceases upon a client subsequently becoming a person under disability, and proceedings occurring after that time would seem to be a nullity. In civil actions, the solicitor may become personally liable for costs thrown away by other parties, in the event that the case proceeds after the client becomes a person under disability and without the appointment of a next friend: *Yonge v Toynbee* [1910] 1 KB 215.

The effect of the appointment of a litigation friend, or the conduct of the litigation by the Court of Protection, is that the patient, while remaining technically the party in the matter, ceases to be involved in the conduct of the litigation: the next friend takes on the role. Next friends can be anyone the court sees fit to appoint, although the official solicitor often assumes this role. The litigation is, of course, to be conducted for the benefit of the patient; there is an inevitable loss of control of the litigation by the patient him or herself. In the event that the loss of capacity is likely to be temporary, it may be worth considering delay of the proceedings until it is regained. In this context, it should be noted that limitation periods do not run against people in their incapacity: s. 28, Limitations Act 1980.

As to the mechanics of representing individuals within the mental health system, Eldergill (1997: ch. 16) provides a valuable 'how to' guide, complete with not only discussion of general principles, but also checklists, a pro forma case summary, and advice on the minutiae of conducting interviews. Quite appropriately, he emphasises the essential similarity between representation in this context and any other form of client advocacy (1997: 884):

> In terms of professional conduct, the principles are the same as for any client attending the office: to serve the client without compromising the solicitor's integrity or his overriding duty to the court and the judicial process. . . . To summarise, the usual principles governing the solicitor–client relationship apply and few problems will arise provided the solicitor is courteous and avoids being patronising.

While this is, and must be, the overarching principle, as Eldergill acknowledges, representation of this sort of client has its own quirks. Additional patience and empathy may be required to gain the client's trust, to help the client to formulate their wishes and instructions. Particular care may be necessary to explain the situation the client is in. While information about detention and treatment rights is required to be given to clients by s. 132, MHA 1983, the client may or may not remember the information. In a study of detentions under the Scottish Mental Health Act, for example, Goldbeck *et al.* (1997: 577) found that less than a third of detained patients recalled receiving this information. While 87 per cent understood that they were detained, only 30 per cent could correctly identify the legal order that was the basis of the detention. This is not necessarily an indictment of those providing the information. Section 132 requires that the information be given 'as soon as practicable after the commencement of the patient's detention', and thus at a time when the client may well be facing new and frightening surroundings, and a barrage of other information. It is perhaps unsurprising that they do not remember it. Nonetheless, the advocate may have to explain the legal situation, starting at the basics.

As in all relationships with clients, the solicitor should not jump to conclusions about what the client wants. The client may well want to be released from the facility; but alternatively or additionally, the client may want a different treatment regime that, if provided, might make continuation in the facility considerably more palatable or even agreeable. Assuming the client has the capacity to instruct, it is inappropriate that advocates 'second-guess' the client's wishes or instructions due to concerns about whether the instructions are in the client's clinical or social best interests. Virtually all other professionals in the mental health system are professionally obliged to act in the client's best interests: that role is already taken, many times over. In the same way that a solicitor would not second-guess the instructions of other clients, the instructions of these clients should be respected, consistent, of course, with the solicitor's duty to the court and judicial process. The fact that the client's views should not be second-guessed does not, of course, mean that the advocate should encourage the client to have a closed mind about other results. An advocate may be able to negotiate a partial solution to a problem, and here, as in any other solicitor–client relationship, a partial victory may be preferable to the client than the risk of an all-or-nothing hearing.

All of this is based on the assumption that the client is able to give competent instructions. What is the role of the advocate if the client does not have this ability? Romano (1997: 750–9) identifies four logically possible responses of the advocate in this situation: follow the client's wishes as if the client is competent; have a guardian appointed; have the advocate act as de facto guardian; withdraw. None of these is ideal, but some are perhaps more problematic than others. In court proceedings, the directions are fairly clear: withdraw until a litigation friend is appointed. The hard line of the court rules does not directly apply to tribunal applications, however, and it seems counter-intuitive to remove to a third party the rather specific right to challenge a confinement, for example, which is provided to the patient under the Act. For this reason, it is also dubious whether the advocate should act as guardian: it is still not the client making the decisions. In addition, as Romano points out (1997: 755), the role of advocate is different and conflicting from that of guardian:

While the advocate has an obligation to consult with the client regarding what the advocate should do on his behalf, the guardian's role is to determine the best interests of the client and act accordingly. This shift in responsibility from taking instructions to giving them can result in the advocate disregarding many important ethical rules which should ordinarily govern the advocate–client dynamic.

Arguably, the advocate is in a particularly poor position to fulfil the role of guardian in any event. He or she is unlikely to have known the client prior to the commencement of the professional relationship, and therefore unlikely to be aware of the values of the client when capable. There is real danger here that the advocate will move in directions of which the client may not approve, if the client regains capacity.

Continuing based on the client's wishes is also a profoundly problematic option, even in a review tribunal setting where the rules of court do not apply. The difficulty is that continuation with a hearing may have an adverse result. The client has a right to only one hearing per certificate, and if the client is detained under s. 3, it will be six months or a year before the right to another tribunal hearing arises. It is conceivable that a negligence action might lie against a solicitor for the loss of the right to a hearing in this period, in the event that the solicitor proceeded on instructions of an incapable client to a hearing early in the certificate.

That leaves withdrawal, which would seem to be the only appropriate course of action. It, too, is problematic, particularly if the advocate sees what appears to be a winning argument. It also does not preclude the client from proceeding to the tribunal and representing him or herself. It seems counterintuitive to deny representation, to which the client has a prima facie right under the rules of the tribunal, for a hearing that is going to go forward in any event. Withdrawal finally suggests that the client must pass two hurdles to obtain relief from the tribunal: he or she must not merely convince the tribunal of the justice of their case; he or she must also convince their advocate of their ability to instruct. Care must therefore be taken not to set the standard of capacity to instruct so high as to preclude meritorious cases from reaching the appropriate forum. Yet, if the advocate really cannot get proper instructions, it is not obvious what else can be done.

Above all, clients should be treated professionally, with respect, dignity, and emotional commitment. We are now at the end of this book – the time for the reader to look back and to consider where we have been. The legal issues described in this book involve fundamental rights and liberties, and the needs of some of society's most vulnerable people. Conceptually, mental health law contains implied premises as to what it is to be a citizen, what the role of the state is with reference to the vulnerable and the bizarre in society, and what the relative roles of law and medicine are in the regulation and control of deviance. It is a field where what is usually assumed becomes problematic. It has been suggested that the law may have unforeseen effects – some beneficial, some not. Above all, it has been argued that this is an area of considerable legal and social complexity. It is not a realm of simple answers; it is a field of considerable difficulty – but a field offering corresponding intellectual rewards. Mediocre advocacy will not suffice: clients deserve – and need – better. And that is the final challenge of this book, to the advocates and potential advocates who read it.

Bibliography

ABDUL-HAMID, W. and COONEY, C. (1997) 'Homelessness, mental illness and the law', *Medicine, Science and Law* 37(4): 341–4.

ADAMS, R. (1998) *The Abuses of Punishment*, London: Macmillan.

ADSHEAD, G. (1998) 'Psychiatric staff as attachment figures: understanding management problems in psychiatric services in the light of attachment theory', *British Journal of Psychiatry* 172: 64.

AHMAD, W.I.U. and ATKIN, K. (1996) *Race and Community Care*, Buckingham: Open University Press.

AKINKUNMI, A. and MURRAY, K. (1997) 'Inadequacies in the Mental Health Act 1983 in relation to mentally disordered remand prisoners', *Medicine, Science and Law* 37(1): 53.

ALBERS, L.J., HAHN, R.K. and REIST, C. (2001) *Handbook of Psychiatric Drugs 2001–2*, Laguna Hills, CA: Current Clinical Strategies Publishing.

ALLDERIDGE, P. (1985) 'Bedlam: fact or fantasy?', in W.F. Bynum, R. Porter and M. Shepherd (eds) *The Anatomy of Madness*, Vol. 2, London: Tavistock.

ANDOH, B. (1994) 'Hospital and police procedures when a patient absconds from a mental hospital', *Medicine, Science and Law* 34(2): 130.

ANDOH, B. (1995) 'Jurisprudential aspects of the "right" to retake absconders from mental hospitals in England and Wales', *Medicine, Science and Law* 35(3): 225.

ANON. (1996) 'Why we run for cover', in J. Read and J. Reynolds (eds) *Speaking Our Minds: An Anthology*, Basingstoke: Macmillan.

APPELBAUM, P. and GRISSO, T. (1995) 'The MacArthur treatment competence study I: mental illness and competence to consent to treatment', *Law and Human Behavior* 19(2):105.

APPELBAUM, P.S. (1985) 'Standards for civil commitment: a critical review of the literature', *International Journal of Law and Psychiatry* 7: 133.

APPLEBY, L. (1997) *The National Confidential Inquiry into Suicide and Homicide by People with Mental Illness: Progress Report*, London: Department of Health.

APPLEBY, L. and BOYINGTON, J. (2005) *Letter regarding prison transfer* (later published together with HM Prison Service, 2006).

APPLEBY, L., THOMAS, S., FERRIER, N., LEWIS, G., SHAW, J. and AMOS, T. (2000) 'Sudden unexplained death in psychiatric inpatients', *British Journal of Psychiatry* 176: 405–6.

ARBER, S., GILBERTY, G.N. and EVANDROU, M. (1988) 'Gender, household composition and receipt of domiciliary services by elderly disabled people' *Journal of Social Policy* 17: 153.

ARMSTRONG, W. (1999) ' "Nature or degree" in the Mental Health Act 1983', *Journal of Mental Health Law* 2: 154–8.

ATKINSON, P. (1995) *Medical Talk and Medical Work*, London: Sage.

AUDINI, B. and LELLIOTT, P. (2002) 'Age, gender and ethnicity of those detained under Part II of the Mental Health Act 1983', *British Journal of Psychiatry* 180: 222.

Audit Commission (1986) *Making a Reality of Community Care*, London: HMSO.

AUSTIN, C., LE FEUVRE, M., O'GRADY, J., SWYER, B. and VAUGHAN, P. (2003) 'Improving psychiatric information for magistrates' courts', *Justice of the Peace and Local Government Law* 167(1/1): 6–7.

BAGNALL, A-M., JONES, L., GINNELLY, L., LEWIS, R., GLANVILLE, J., GILBODY, S., DAVIES, L., TORGERSON, D. and KLEIJNEN, J. (2003) 'A systematic review of atypical antipsychotic drugs in schizophrenia',

Health Technology Assessment 7(13), York: York Publishing Services.

BAILEY J. and MacCULLOCH, M. (1992) 'Patterns of reconviction in patients discharged directly to the community from a special hospital: implications for aftercare', *Journal of Forensic Psychiatry* 3(3): 445.

BAKER, E. (1992) 'Dangerousness: the neglected gaoler – disorder and risk under the Mental Health Act 1983', *Journal of Forensic Psychiatry* 3(1): 31.

BAKER, E. (1994) 'Human Rights, *M'Naghten* and the 1991 Act', *Criminal Law Review* 84: 553.

BAKER, E. and CRICHTON, J. (1995) '*Ex parte* A: psychopathy, treatability and the law', *Journal of Forensic Psychiatry* 6(1): 101.

BANNERJEE, S. *et al.* (1995) *Deaths of Detained Patients: A Review of Reports to the Mental Health Act Commission*, London: Mental Health Foundation.

BARHAM, P. (1992) *Closing the Asylum: The Mental Patient in Modern Society*, London: Penguin.

BARNES, D. (2006) 'The outcomes of partnerships with mental health service users in interprofessional education: a case study', *Health and Social Care in the Community* 14(5): 426–35.

BARNES, M. and MAPLE, N. (1992) *Women and Mental Health: Challenging the Stereotypes*, Birmingham: British Academy of Social Workers and Ventura Press.

BARNES, M., BOWL, R. and FISHER, M. (1990) *Sectioned: Social Services and the Mental Health Act 1983*, London: Routledge.

BARONDES, S.H. (2005) *Better than Prozac: Creating the Next Generation of Psychiatric Drugs*, Oxford: Oxford University Press.

BARTLETT, P. (1996) 'Sense and nonsense: sensation, delusion and the limitation of sanity in nineteenth-century law', in L. Bently and L. Flynn (eds), *Law and the Senses*, London: Pluto.

BARTLETT, P. (1997) 'The consequences of incapacity', *Web Journal of Current Legal Issues* 4.

BARTLETT, P. (1999) *The Poor Law of Lunacy: The Administration of Pauper Lunatics in Mid-Nineteenth-Century England*, London: University of Leicester Press/ Cassell.

BARTLETT, P. (1999a) 'The asylum, the workhouse and the voice of the insane poor in nineteenth-century England', *International Journal of Law and Psychiatry* 21(3): 1.

BARTLETT, P. (2001) 'English mental health reform: lessons from Ontario?' *Journal of Mental Health Law*: 27–43.

BARTLETT, P. (2001a) 'Legal madness in the nineteenth century', *Social History of Medicine* 14(1): 107–31.

BARTLETT, P. (2003) 'Capacity and confinement: when is detention not detention?', in K. Diesfeld and I. Freckelton (eds) *Involuntary Detention and Therapeutic Jurisprudence: International Perspectives on Civil Commitment*, Aldershot: Ashgate, Dartmouth.

BARTLETT, P. (2003a) 'The test of compulsion in mental health law: capacity, therapeutic benefit and dangerousness as possible criteria', *Medical Law Review* 11: 326.

BARTLETT, P. (2005) *Blackstone's Guide to the Mental Capacity Act 2005*, Oxford: Oxford University Press.

BARTLETT, P. (2006) 'Psychiatric treatment: in the absence of law?', *Medical Law Review* 14: 124–31.

BARTLETT, P. and WRIGHT, D. (1999a) 'Community care and its antecedents', in P. Bartlett and D. Wright (eds) *Outside the Walls of the Asylum*, London: Athlone.

BARTLETT, P. and WRIGHT, D. (eds) (1999) *Outside the Walls of the Asylum: The History of Care in the Community 1750–2000*, London: Athlone.

BARTLETT, P., LEWIS, O. and THOROLD, O. (2006) *Mental Disability and the European*

Convention on Human Rights, Leiden: Martinus Nijhof.

BATEMAN, A.. and TYRER, P. (2002) *Effective Management of Personality Disorder*, London: Department of Health.

BAXTER, R. (1991) 'The mentally disordered offender in hospital: the role of the Home Office', in K. Herbst and J. Gunn (eds) *The Mentally Disordered Offender*, London: Butterworth-Heinemann.

BBC News (23 July 2001) 'Concern over sedative use'.

BEAN, P. (1980) *Compulsory Admissions to Mental Hospitals*, Chichester: John Wiley.

BEAN, P. (1986) *Mental Disorder and Legal Control*, Cambridge: Cambridge University Press.

BEAN, P. (2001) *Mental Disorder and Community Safety*, Basingstoke: Palgrave.

BEAN, P. and MOUNSER, P (1993) *Discharged from Mental Hospitals*, London: Macmillan.

BEAN, P. and NEMETZ, T. (1994) *Out of Depth and Out of Sight*, London: Mencap.

BEAN, P. and NEMETZ, T. (1997) *Final Report to the Mental Health Foundation on the Evaluation of the Southampton MIND Appropriate Adult Scheme*, London: Mental Health Foundation.

BEAN, P. and NEMETZ, T. (1995) *Out of Depth and Out of Sight*, London: Mencap.

BEAN, P., BINGLEY, W., BYNOE, I., FAULKNER, A., RASSABY, E. and ROGERS, A. (1991) *Out of Harm's Way*, London: MIND.

BEBBINGTON, P.E., FEENEY, S.T., FLANNIGAN, C.B., GLOVER, G.R., LEWIS, S.W. and WING, J.K. (1994) 'Inner London collaborative audit of admissions in two health districts: II. ethnicity and the use of the Mental Health Act', *British Journal of Psychiatry* 165: 734.

BEEBE, M., ELLIS, D. and EVANS, R. (1973) 'Research report on statutory work under the Mental Health Act 1959: experience in the London Borough of Camden', *The Human Context* 5: 377.

BENBOW, S.M. and CRENTSIL, J. (2004) 'Subjective experience of electroconvulsive therapy', *Psychiatric Bulletin* 28: 289–91.

BENTALL, R.P., JACKSON, H.F. and PILGRIM, D. (1988) 'Abandoning the concept of "schizophrenia": some implications of validity arguments for psychological research into psychotic phenomena', *British Journal of Clinical Psychology* 27: 303.

BENTALL, R.P., JACKSON, H.F. and PILGRIM, D. (1988a) 'The concept of schizophrenia is dead: long live the concept of schizophrenia', *British Journal of Clinical Psychology* 27: 329.

BERGER, P. and LUCKMANN, T. (1967) *The Social Construction of Reality*, London: Penguin.

BERTHOUD, R. and NAZROO J. (1997) 'The mental health of ethnic minorities', *New Community* 23(3): 309.

BHUI, K. and BHUGRA, D. (2002) 'Mental illness in Black and Asian ethnic minorities: pathways to care and outcomes', *Advances in Psychiatric Treatment* 8: 26.

BHUI, K., STANSFELD, S., HULL, S., PRIEBE, S., MOLE, F. and FEDER, G. (2003) 'Ethnic variations to and use of specialist mental health services in the UK: systematic review', *British Journal of Psychiatry* 182: 105.

BIELANSKA, C. (2003) 'The Community Care (Delayed Discharge) Bill: Is it a cure for bed-blocking?' *Elderly Client Adviser* 8(2).

BINDMAN, J., GLOVER, G., GOLDBERG, D. and CHISHOLM, D. (2000) 'Expenditure on mental health care by English health authorities: a potential cause of inequity', *British Journal of Psychiatry* 177: 267–74.

BIRCHWOOD, M., McGORRY, P. and JACKSON, H. (1997) 'Early intervention in schizophrenia', *British Journal of Psychiatry* 170: 2.

BIRD, A. (1998) *Philosophy of Science*, London: UCL Press.

BIRMINGHAM, L., MASON, D. and GRUBIN, D. (1996) 'Prevalence of mental disorder in remand prisoners: consecutive case study', *British Medical Journal* 313: 1521.

BIRMINGHAM, L., MASON, D. and GRUBIN, D. (2000) 'Mental illness at reception into prison', *Criminal Behaviour and Mental Health* 10: 77–87.

BISSETT-JOHNSON, A. and MAIN, S. (2002) 'The Community Care and Health (Scotland) Act 2002 and *Robertson v Fife Council*', *Scottish Law Times* 34: 279–84.

Black Health Workers and Patients Group (1983) 'Psychiatry and the corporate state', *Race and Class* 25: 49.

BLUGLASS, R. (1987) 'The Mental Health Act 1983 in practice', *Medico-Legal Journal* 55(3): 151.

BLUMENTHAL, S. and WESSELY, S. (1992) 'National survey of current arrangements for diversion from custody in England and Wales', *British Medical Journal* 305: 1322.

BLUMENTHAL, S. and WESSELY, S. (1994) *The Patterns of Delay in Mental Health Review Tribunals*, London: HMSO.

BOAST, N. and CHESTERMAN, P. (1995) 'Black people and secure psychiatric facilities', *British Journal of Criminology* 31(2): 218.

BORDO, S. (1988) 'Anorexia nervosa: psychopathology as the crystallisation of culture', in I. Diamond and L. Quinby (eds) *Feminism and Foucault: Reflections on Resistance*, Boston: Northeastern University Press.

BORDO, S. (1993) *Unbearable Weight: Feminism, Western Culture and the Body*, Berkeley: University of California Press.

BOTT, E. (1976) 'Hospital and society', *British Journal of Medical Psychology* 49: 97.

BOWDEN, P. (1996) Violence and mental disorder', in N. Walker (ed) *Dangerous People*, London: Blackstone Press.

BOWERS, L. (2003) 'Runaway patients', *Mental Health Practice* 7(1): 10–12.

BOWERS, L., ALEXANDER, J. and GASKELL, C. (2003) 'A trial of an anti-absconding intervention in acute psychiatric wards', *Journal of Psychiatric and Mental Health Nursing* 10: 410–16.

BOYLE, M. (1990) *Schizophrenia: A Scientific Delusion?*, London: Routledge.

BOYLE, M. (1994) 'Schizophrenia and the art of the soluble', *The Psychologist* 7: 399.

BRABBINS, C.J., and TRAVERS, R.F. (1994) 'Mental disorder among defendants in Liverpool magistrates' court', *Medicine, Science and Law* 31(4): 279.

BRADFORD, B., McCANN, S. and MERSKY, H. (1986) 'A survey of involuntary patients' attitudes toward their commitment', *Psychiatric Journal of the University of Ottawa* 11: 162.

BRAHAMS, D. (2004) 'Suicides in UK prisons', *Medico-Legal Journal* 72(1): 1–2

BRAZIER, M. and MIOLA, J. (2000) 'Bye-bye *Bolam*: a medical litigation revolution?', *Medical Law Review* 8: 85.

BRIDGEMAN J. and MILLNS, S. (eds) (1998) *Feminist Perspectives on Law: Law's Engagement with the Female Body*, London: Sweet and Maxwell.

British Medical Association and Association of Police Surgeons (1994) *Health Care of Detainees in Police Stations*, London: BMA.

British Medical Association and the Law Society (1995) *Assessment of Mental Capacity: Guidance for Doctors and Lawyers*, London: BMA.

BROOK, R. (1573) *La Grande Abridgement*, 2 vols., n.p.

BROOK, R., DOLAN, M., and COOREY, P. (1999) 'Absconding of patients detained in an English Special Hospital', *Journal of Forensic Psychiatry* 10(1): 46–58.

BROOKE, D., TAYLOR, C., GUNN J. and MADDEN, D. (1996) 'Point prevalence of mental disorder in unconvicted male prisoners in England and Wales', *British Medical Journal* 313: 1524.

BROWN, D., ELLIS, T. and LARCOMBE, K. (1993) *Changing the Code: Police Detention Under the Revised PACE Codes of Practice*, London: HMSO.

BROWN, H. and SMITH, H. (eds) (1992) *Normalisation: A Reader for the Nineties*, London: Routledge.

BROWN, K.W., BILLCLIFF, N. and McCABE, E. (2001) 'Informed consent to medication in long-term psychiatric patients', *Psychological Bulletin* 25:132–4.

BROWN, N. (1991) 'Section 5(2) audit', *Psychiatric Bulletin* 15: 706.

BUCHANAN, A. (2002) 'Psychiatric detention and treatment: a suggested criterion', *Journal of Mental Health Law* 6: 35–41.

BUCHANAN, A. and BROCK, D. (1986) 'Deciding for others', *The Milbank Quarterly* 64 (Supp. 2): 17.

BUSFIELD J. (1986) *Managing Madness: Changing Ideas and Practice*, London: Unwin Hyman.

BUSFIELD J. (1996) 'Professionals, the state and the development of mental health policy' in T. Heller *et al.* (eds) *Mental Health Matters: A Reader*, London: Macmillan.

BUTLER, P. and KOUSOULOU, D. (2006) *Women at Risk: The Mental Health of Women in Contact with the Judicial System*, London: The London Development Centre and the Care Service Improvement Partnership.

BUTLER, R. and ROSENTHAL, G. (1985) *Behaviour and Rehabilitation*, Bristol: Wright.

BUTLER, T. (1993) *Changing Mental Health Services: The Politics and the Policy*, London: Chapman and Hall.

BYNUM, W. (1981) 'Rationales for therapy in British psychiatry 1780–1835' in A. Scull (ed) *Madhouses, Mad-Doctors and Madmen*, London: The Athlone Press.

CAIRNS, R., MADDOCK, C., BUCHANAN, A., DAVID, A., HAYWARD, P., RICHARDSON, G., SZMUKLER, G. and HOTOPF, M. (2005) 'Prevalence and predictors of mental incapacity in psychiatric inpatients', *British Journal of Psychiatry* 187: 379.

CALLANAN, M., DUNNE, T., MORRIS, D. and STERN, R. (1997) *Primary Care, Serious Mental Illness and the Local Community: Developing a Commissioning Framework*, Tunbridge: Salamons Centre.

CAMPBELL, D. (1996) 'Cash-hit courts "are not using" mental tests', *The Guardian*, 11 July.

CAMPBELL, F. (2001) 'Care trusts could mark the beginning of the end for the NHS', *The Guardian*, 28 February.

CAMPBELL, P., COBB, A. and DARTON, K. (1998) *Psychiatric Drugs: Users' Experiences and Curent Policy and Practice*, London: MIND.

CAPLAN, P. (1995) *They Say You're Crazy: How the World's Most Powerful Psychiatrists Decide Who's Normal*, Reading, MA: Addison-Wesley.

CARDINAL, M. (1996) 'The words to say it', in S. Dunn, B. Morrison and M. Roberts (eds) *Mind Readings: Writers' Journeys through Mental States*, London: Minerva.

Care Service Improvement Partnership and National Institute for Mental Health (2006) *National Suicide Prevention Strategy for England Annual Report on Progress 2005*, London: Care Service Improvement Partnership.

Care Service Improvement Partnership and the National Institute for Mental Health in England (2006a) *10 High Impact Changes for Mental Health Services*, London: Care Service Improvement Partnership.

CARSON, D. (1989a) 'The sexuality of people with learning difficulties', *Journal of Social Welfare and Family Law*: 355.

CARSON, D. (1989b) 'Prosecuting people with mental handicap', *Criminal Law Review*: 87.

CARSON, D. (1993) 'Disabling progress: the Law Commission's proposals on mentally incapacitated adults' decision-making', *Journal of Social Welfare and Family Law*: 304.

CASTEL, R. (1985) 'Moral treatment: mental therapy and social control in the nineteenth century', in S. Cohen and A. Scull (eds)

Social Control and the State, Oxford: Basil Blackwell.

CAVADINO, M. (1989) *Mental Health Law in Context: Doctor's Orders?*, Aldershot: Dartmouth.

CAVADINO, M. (1991) 'Mental illness and neo-Polonianism', *Journal of Forensic Psychiatry* 2: 295.

CAVADINO, M. and DIGNAN, J. (1997) *The Penal System: An Introduction*, 2nd edn, London: Sage.

Central Council for Education and Training in Social Work (1993) *Requirements and Guidance for the Training of Social Workers to be Considered for Approval in England and Wales under the Mental Health Act 1983*, CCETSW Paper No.19.27, London: CCETSW.

Centre for Public Innovation (2005) *Review into the Current Practices of Court Liason and Diversion Schemes*, London: CPI.

CHADWICK, P.D. (1997) *Schizophrenia: The Positive Perspective*. London: Routledge.

CHARLTON, B.G. (2005) 'If "atypical" neuroleptics did not exist, it wouldn't be necessary to invent them: perverse incentives in drug development, research, marketing and clinical practice', *Medical Hypotheses* 6: 1005–9.

CHEADLE, J. and DITCHFIELD, J. (1982) *Sentenced Mentally Ill Offenders*, London: Home Office Research and Planning Unit.

CHEUNG, P., SCHWEITZER, I., TUCKWELL, V. and CROWLEY, K. (1997) 'A prospective study of assaults on staff by psychiatric inpatients', *Medicine, Science and Law* 37(1): 46.

CHO, N. (2002) 'Nearest relatives of gay and lesbian patients', *Journal of Mental Health Law* 8: 323–7.

CLARKSON, P. (1994) 'The nature and range of psychotherapy', in Clarkson, P. and Pokorny, M. (eds) *The Handbook of Psychotherapy*, London: Routledge.

CLARKSON, P. and POKORNY, M. (eds) (1994) *The Handbook of Psychotherapy*, London: Routledge.

CLEMENTS, L. (1997) 'Community care: towards a workable statute', *Liverpool Law Review* 19(2): 181.

COCOZZA J. and STEADMAN, H. (1978) 'Predictions in psychiatry: an example of misplaced confidence in experts', *Social Problems* 25(3): 265.

COHEN, A., DOLAN, B. and EASTMAN, N. (1996) 'Research on the supervision registers: inconsistencies in local research ethics committees responses', *Journal of Forensic Psychiatry* 7(2): 413.

COHEN, R. and HART, J. (1995) *Student Psychiatry Today: A Comprehensive Textbook*, 2nd edn, Oxford: Butterworth-Heinmann.

COHEN, S. (1985) *Visions of Social Control*, Cambridge: Polity.

COID, J. (1988) 'Mentally abnormal offenders on remand I: rejected or accepted by the NHS?', *British Medical Journal* 296: 1779.

COID, J., BEBBINGTON, P., JENKINS, R., BRUGHA, T., LEWIS, G., FARRELL, M. and SINGLETON, N. (2002) 'The national survey of psychiatric morbidity among prisoners and the future of prison medical care', *Medicine, Science and the Law* 42(3): 245–50.

COID, J., KAHTAN, N., GAULT, S. and JARMAN, B. (2000) 'Ethnic differences in admissions to secure forensic psychiatry services', *British Journal of Psychiatry* 177: 241.

Commission for Health Improvement (2004) *What CHI has Found: Mental Health Trusts*, London: Commission for Health Improvement.

Commission for Healthcare Audit and Inspection, MHAC, CSIP and NIMHE (2005) *Count Me In: Results of a National Census of Inpatients in Mental Health Hospitals and Facilities in England and Wales*, London: Commission for Healthcare Audit and Inspection.

Commission for Social Care Inspection (2005) *The State of Social Care in England 2004–5*, London: Commission for Social Care Inspection.

Commission for Social Care Inspection (2006) *Annual Report 2005–6*, London: HMSO.

Committee on Mentally Abnormal Offenders (the 'Butler Committee') (1975) *Report of the Committee on Mentally Abnormal Offenders*, Cmnd 6244, London: HMSO.

COMYN, J. (1822) *Digest of the Laws of England*, 5th edn, 8 vols., A. Hammond (ed), London: Strahan.

COOKE, D. (1991) 'Treatment as an alternative to prosecution: offenders diverted for treatment', *British Journal of Psychiatry* 158: 785.

COPE, R. (1989) 'The compulsory detention of Afro-Caribbeans under the Mental Health Act', *New Community* 15(3): 343.

COPE, R. (1993) 'A survey of forensic psychiatrists' views on psychopathic disorder' *Journal of Forensic Psychiatry* 4: 215.

CORNELL, D. (1992) *The Philosophy of the Limit*, London: Routledge.

COSTELLO, E. (1983) 'Information processing for decision-making in depressed women: a study of subjective expected utilities', *Journal of Affective Disorders* 5: 239.

Council of Europe (2000) *White Paper on the Protection of the Human Rights and Dignity of People Suffering from Mental Disorder* Info?

Council of Europe (2004) *Recommendations* (adopted by the Committee of Ministers 22 Sept)

Council on Tribunals (2000) *Mental Health Review Tribunals: Special Report*, Cm 4740, London: HMSO.

Council on Tribunals (2001) *Annual Report 2000–1*, London: HMSO.

Council on Tribunals (2002) *Annual Report 2001–2*, London: HMSO.

Council on Tribunals (2006) *Annual Report 2005–6*, HC1210, London: HMSO.

COWAN, D. (1995a) 'Accommodating community care' *Journal of Law and Society* 22(2): 212.

COWAN, D. (1995b) 'Community care and homelessness', *Modern Law Review* 58(2): 256.

COWEN, H. (1999) *Community Care, Ideology and Social Policy*, Hemel Hempstead: Prentice Hall.

CRAISSATI, J., HORNE, L. and TAYLOR, R. (2002) *Effective Treatment Models for Personality Disordered Offenders*, London: Department of Health.

CRAWFORD, D. (1984) 'Problems with assessment of dangerousness in England and Wales', *Medicine and Law* 3: 141.

CREPAZ-KEAY, D. (1996) 'A sense of perspective: the media and the Boyd Inquiry', in G. Philo (ed) *Media and Mental Distress*, London: Longman.

CRICHTON, J. (1994) 'Supervised discharge', *Medicine, Science and Law* 34(4): 319.

CRICHTON, J. (1995) 'Psychiatric inpatient violence: issues of English law and discipline within hospitals, *Medicine, Science and the Law* 35(1): 53.

CRICHTON, J.H.M. and CALGIE, J. (2002) 'Responding to inpatient violence at a psychiatric hospital of special security: a pilot project', *Medicine, Science and Law* 42(1): 30–3.

CROW, T., MACMILLAN, J., JOHNSON, A. and JOHNSTONE, E. (1986) 'The Northwick Park study of first episodes of schizophrenia II: a controlled trial of prophylactic neuroleptic treatment', *British Journal of Psychiatry* 148: 120.

CUMMING, E. and CUMMING, J. (1957) *Closed Ranks: An Experiment in Mental Health Education*, Cambridge, MA: Harvard University Press.

DALLEY, G. (1993) 'Professional ideology or organisational tribalism?', in J. Walmsley, J. Reynolds, P., Shakespeare and R. Wollfe (eds) *Health, Welfare and Practice: Reflecting on Roles and Relationships*, London: Sage.

DALLY, P. and CONNOLLY, J. (1981) *Physical Methods of Treatment in Psychiatry*, Edinburgh: Churchill Livingstone.

DARTON, R. (2004) 'What types of home are closing? The characteristics of homes which closed between 1996 and 2001', *Health and Social Care in the Community* 12(3): 254–64.

DAVIES, S. (2002) 'Compulsory treatment in the community: current legal powers' *Advances in Psychiatric Treatment* 8: 180–8.

DAVIS, S. (1991) 'Violence by psychiatric inpatients: a review', *Hospital and Community Psychiatry* 42: 585.

DEAHL, M. and TURNER, T. (1997) 'General psychiatry in no-man's land', *British Journal of Psychiatry* 171: 6.

DEAN, C. and WEBSTER, L. (1991) 'The Mental Health Act 1983: characteristics of detained patients', *Journal of Forensic Psychiatry* 2(2): 185.

DELL, S. (1980) 'Transfer of special hospital patients into National Health Service hospitals', in J. Gunn and D. Farrington (eds) *Abnormal Offenders, Delinquency and the Criminal Justice System*, Chichester: John Wiley.

DELL, S. (1982) 'Diminished responsibility reconsidered', *Criminal Law Review*: 809.

DELL, S. and ROBERTSON, G. (1988) *Sentenced to Hospital*, Oxford: Oxford University Press.

DELL, S., GROUNDS, A., JAMES, K. and ROBERTSON, G. (1991) *Mentally Disordered Remand Prisoners: Report to the Home Office*, unpublished.

Department of Constitutional Affairs (2004) *Transforming Public Services: Complaints, Redress and Tribunals*, Cm 6243, London: HMSO.

Department of Constitutional Affairs (2004a) *Draft Code of Practice to the Mental Capacity Bill*, London: DCA.

Department of Health (1986) *Mental Health Act: Approved Social Workers*, LAC(86)15, London: Department of Health.

Department of Health (1989) *Discharge of Patients from Hospital*, HC(89)5, London: Department of Health.

Department of Health (1989a) *Caring for People*, London: Department of Health.

Department of Health (1989b) *Working for Patients*, London: Department of Health.

Department of Health (1990a) *Community Care in the Next Decade and Beyond*, London: HMSO.

Department of Health (1990b) *The Care Programme Approach for People with a Mental Illness Referred to Specialist Psychiatric Services*, HC(90)23, London: Department of Health.

Department of Health (1992) *Mental Health Review Tribunals for England and Wales Annual Report 1991*, London: Department of Health.

Department of Health (1993a) *Community Care Plans (Consultation) Directions 1993*, LAC(93)4, London: Department of Health.

Department of Health (1993b) *Approvals and Directions for Arrangements from 1 April 1993 Made Under Schedule 8 to the National Health Service Act 1977 and sections 21 and 29 of the National Assistance Act 1948*, LAC(93)10, London: NHS Executive, Department of Health.

Department of Health (1993c) *Mental Health Review Tribunals for England and Wales Annual Report 1992*, London: Department of Health.

Department of Health (1993d) *Legal Powers on the Care of Mentally Ill People in the Community: Report of the Internal Review*, London: Department of Health.

Department of Health (1994) *Guidance on the Discharge of Mentally Disordered People and their Continuing Care in the Community*, HSG(94)27, London: Department of Health.

Department of Health (1995a) *Building Bridges: A Guide to Arrangements for Inter-Agency Working for the Care and Protection of Severely Mentally Ill People*, London: Department of Health.

Department of Health (1995b) *Mental Health Act 1983: Memorandum on Parts I to VI, VIII and X*, London: HMSO.

Department of Health (1995c) *Mentally Disordered Offenders*, produced for LAG and Doughty Street Chambers Conference.

Department of Health (1995d) *Inpatients Formally Detained under the Mental Health Act 1983 and other Legislation, England: 1987–8 to 1992–3*, Statistical Bulletin 1994/9, London: Department of Health.

Department of Health (1996a) *The Spectrum of Care*, London: Department of Health.

Department of Health (1996b) *The Use of 'Trial Leave' under Section 17 of the Mental Health Act 1983 to Transfer Patients between Hospitals*, HSG (96)28, London: Department of Health.

Department of Health (1997) *Mental Health Review Tribunals for England and Wales Annual Report 1996*, London: Department of Health.

Department of Health (1997a) *The New NHS: Modern, Dependable*, Cm 3807, London: HMSO.

Department of Health (1998a) *Modernising Mental Health Services: Safe, Sound and Supportive*, London: HMSO.

Department of Health (1998b) *Modernising Social Services: Promoting Independence, Improving Projection, Raising Standards*, Cm 4169, London: HMSO.

Department of Health (1998c) *Community Care Statistics 1998*, London: Department of Health.

Department of Health (1998d) *Inpatients Formally Detained in Hospitals under the Mental Health Act 1983 and other Legislation, England: 1987–8 to 1997–8*, London: Department of Health.

Department of Health (1998e) *A First Class Service: Quality in the New NHS*, London: HMSO.

Department of Health (1998f) *National Service Frameworks*, HSG(98)074, LASSL(98)6, London: Department of Health.

Department of Health (1998g) *Partnership in Action: New Opportunities for Joint Working between Health and Social Services*, London: Department of Health.

Department of Health (1998h) *Press Release 98/391*, London: Department of Health.

Department of Health (1998i) *Mental Health Act 1983: Memorandum on Parts I to VI, VIII and X*, London: Department of Health

Department of Health (1999) *A National Service Framework for Mental Health*, London: Department of Health.

Department of Health (1999a) *Reform of the Mental Health Act 1983: Proposals for Reform*, Cm 4480, London: Department of Health.

Department of Health (1999b) *Report of the Committee of Inquiry into the Personality Disorder Unit, Ashworth Special Hospital* (the 'Fallon Report'), Cm 4194-II, London: HMSO.

Department of Health (1999c) *Electro Convulsive Therapy: Survey Covering the Period from January 1999 to March 1999, England*, Statistical Bulletin 1999/22, London: Department of Health.

Department of Health (1999d) *Effective Care Co-ordination in Mental Health Services: Modernising the Care Programme Approach*, London: Department of Health.

Department of Health (1999e) *Still Building Bridges: The Report of a National Inspection of Arrangements for the Inspection of Care Programme Approach with Care Management*, CI 99/3, London: Department of Health.

Department of Health (2000) *Report of the Review of Security at the High Security Hospitals*, London: Department of Health.

Department of Health (2000a) *The NHS Plan*, Cm 4818-I, London: Department of Health.

Department of Health (2000b) *An Organisation with a Memory*, London: HMSO.

Department of Health (2000c) *Implementation of Health Act Partnership Arrangements*,

HSC 2000/10, LAC(2000)9, London: Department of Health.

Department of Health (2001) *Community Care Statistics 2001: Residential Personal Social Services for Adults, England*, Bulletin 2001/29, London: Department of Health.

Department of Health (2001a) *England's New Mental Health Institute: A World First*, Press Release 2001/0310, London: Department of Health.

Department of Health (2001b) *Building a Safer NHS for Patients*, London: Department of Health.

Department of Health (2001c) *Good Practice in Consent: Achieving the NHS Plan Committment to Patient-Centred Practice*, NHS Executive HSC 2001/023, London: Department of Health.

Department of Health (2001d) *Mental Health Review Tribunal Report April 1999 to March 2001*, London: Department of Health.

Department of Health (2001e) *The National Service Framework for Older People*, HSC 2001/007, LAC(2001)12, London: Department of Health.

Department of Health (2001f) *Guidance on free nursing care in nursing homes*, HSC 2001/17, LAC (2001)26, London: Department of Health.

Department of Health (2001g) *Continuing Care: NHS and Local Council's Responsibilities*, HSC 2001/15, LAC (2001)18, London: Department of Health.

Department of Health (2001h) *Fairer Charging Policies for Home Care and other Non-residential Social Services: Guidance for Councils with Social Service Responsibilities*, LAC(2001)32, London: Department of Health.

Department of Health (2001j) *Safety First: Five-Year Report of the National Confidential Inquiry into Suicide and Homicide by People with Mental Illness*, London: Department of Health

Department of Health (2002) *Community Care Statistics 2002 Supported Residents (Adults), England*, Bulletin 2002/19, London: Department of Health

Department of Health (2002a) *Patient Care in the Community: Community Psychiatric Nursing Summary Information for 2001–2, England*, London: Department of Health.

Department of Health (2002b) *Mental Health Taskforce: An Introduction*, London: Department of Health.

Department of Health (2002c) *2000–1 Survey of Reported Violent or Abusive Incidents, Accidents Involving Staff and Sickness Absence in NHS Trusts and Health Authorities, in England*, London: Department of Health.

Department of Health (2002d) *Draft Mental Health Bill*, Cm 5538, London: HMSO.

Department of Health (2002e) *Draft Mental Health Bill Explanatory Notes*, Cm 5538-II, London: Department of Health.

Department of Health (2002f) *Guidance on Section 31 Partnership Arrangements*, London: Department of Health, Health and Social Care Joint Unit.

Department of Health (2002g) *Fair Access to Care Services: Guidance on Eligibility Criteria for Adult Social Care*, LAC (2002)13, London: Department of Health.

Department of Health (2002h) *Guardianship under the Mental Health Act 1983 England 2002*, London: Department of Health.

Department of Health (2003) *Mental Health Grant Guidance*, HSC 2003/002, LAC (2003)1, London: Department of Health.

Department of Health (2003a) *Guidance on NHS-Funded Nursing Care*, HSC 2003/006, LAC (2003)007, London: Department of Health.

Department of Health (2003b) *Charging for Residential Accommodation Guide (CRAG)*, London: Department of Health.

Department of Health (2003c) *Inpatients Formally Detained in Hospitals Under the Mental Health Act 1983 and Other Legislation, NHS Trusts, High Security Psychiatric Hospitals and Private Facilities: 2001–2*, London: Department of Health.

Department of Health (2003d) *Reforming NHS Financial Flows: Introducing Payment by Results*, London: Department of Health.

Department of Health (2003e) *Electro Convulsive Therapy: Survey Covering the Period from January 2002 to March 2002, England*, Statistical Bulletin 2003/08, London: Department of Health.

Department of Health (2004a) *Draft Mental Health Bill*, Cm 6305 London: HMSO.

Department of Health (2004b) *Inpatients Formally Detained in Hospitals under the Mental Health Act 1983 and other Legislation, England: 1993–4 to 2003–4*, Bulletin 2004/22, London: Department of Health.

Department of Health (2004c) *The NHS Improvement Plan: Putting People at the Heart of Public Services*, Cm 6268, London: Department of Health

Department of Health (2004d) *Choose and Book: Patient's Choice of Hospital and Booked Appointment: Policy Framework for Choice and Booking at the Point of Referral*, London: Department of Health.

Department of Health (2004e) *The National Service Framework for Mental Health: Five Years On*, London: Department of Health.

Department of Health (2005) *Commissioning a Patient-Led NHS*, Gateway ref.: 5312, London: Department of Health.

Department of Health (2005a) *Creating a Patient-Led NHS: Delivering the NHS Improvement Plan*, Gateway ref: 4699 London: Department of Health.

Department of Health (2005b) *Health Reform in England: Update and Next Steps*, London: Department of Health.

Department of Health (2005c) *Community Care Statistics 2005 Supported Residents (Adults), England*, Bulletin 2005/10, HSCIC, London: Department of Health.

Department of Health (2005d) Bournewood *Consultation: The Approach Taken in the European Court of Human Rights in the Bournewood Case*, London: Department of Health.

Department of Health (2005d) *Delivering Race Equality in Mental Health Care: An Action Plan for Reform Inside and Outside Services and the Government's Reponse to the Independent Inquiry into the Death of David Bennett*, London: HMSO.

Department of Health (2006a) *The Mental Health Bill: Plans to Amend the Mental Health Act 1983*, Briefing sheets A1 to A8, April, Gateway ref. 6420 (available online at http://www.dh.gov.uk/PolicyAndGuidance/ HealthAndSocialCareTopics/MentalHealth /fs/en), London: Department of Health.

Department of Health (2006b) *Bournewood Briefing Sheet*, June, Gateway ref. 6794, London: Department of Health.

Department of Health (2006c) *Inpatients Formally Detained in Hospitals under the Mental Health Act 1983 and other Legislation, England: 1994–2005 to 2004–5*, London: Department of Health.

Department of Health (2006d) *The Mental Health Bill: Plans to Amend the Mental Health Act*, Briefing sheet – Professional Roles – A4, April, Gateway ref. 6420, London: Department of Health.

Department of Health (2006e) *Health Reform in England: Update and Commissioning Framework*, Gateway ref. 6865, London: Department of Health.

Department of Health (2006f) *Our Health, Our Care, Our Say: A New Direction for Community Services*, Cm 6737, London: Department of Health.

Department of Health (2006g) *The NHS in England: The Operating Framework for 2006/7*, London: Department of Health.

Department of Health (2006h) *Practice-based Commissioning: Achieving Universal Coverage*, Gateway ref. 6503, London: Department of Health.

Department of Health (2006i) *Form KHO3 Returns* (available online at http://www. performance.doh.gov.uk/hospitalactiv- ity/data_requests/download/beds_ open_overnight/bed_05_summary.xls)

last accessed 7/9/06, London: Department of Health.

Department of Health (2006j) *The Mental Health Bill: Plans to Amend the Mental Health Act 1983*, Briefing Sheet – Criteria – A2, April, Gateway ref. 6420, London: Department of Health.

Department of Health (2006k) *The Mental Health Bill: Plans to Amend the Mental Health Act 1983*, Briefing sheet – MHRT – A6, May, Gateway ref. 6420, London: Department of Health.

Department of Health (2006l) *The Mental Health Bill: Plans to Amend the Mental Health Act 1983*, Briefing sheet – Supervised Community Treatment – A3, April, Gateway ref. 6420, London: Department of Health.

Department of Health (2006m) *The Mental Health Bill: Plans to Amend the Mental Health Act 1983*, Briefing sheet – Nearest Relative – A5, April, Gateway ref. 6420, London: Department of Health.

Department of Health (2006n) *Child and Adolescent Mental Health Service (CAMHS) Grant Guidance 2006–7 and 2007–8*, HSC 2006/001, London: Department of Health.

Department of Health (2006o) *Charging for Residential Accommodation Guide (CRAG) in Support of The National Assistance (Assessment of Resources) Regulations 1992 (SI 1992/2977*, London: Department of Health.)

Department of Health (2006p) *Mental Health Bill*, HL Bill 1 2006–7, 5412, London: Department of Health.

Department of Health and Department for Work and Pensions (2002) *Fairer Charging Policies for Home Care and other Non-residential Social Services: Practice Guidance*, London: Department of Health.

Department of Health and Home Office (1992) *Review of Health and Social Services for Mentally Disordered Offenders and Others Requiring Similar Services: Final Summary Report*, Cm 2088, London: HMSO.

Department of Health and Home Office (1996) *Mentally Disordered Offenders: Sentencing and Discharge Arrangements*, Discussion paper, London: Department of Health and Home Office.

Department of Health and Home Office (2000) *Reforming the Mental Health Act* (White Paper), Cm 5016, London: HMSO.

Department of Health and Home Office (2000a) *Reforming the Mental Health Act: Part II High Risk Patients*, Cm 5016-II, London: HMSO.

Department of Health and Home Office (2002b) *Consultation on the Draft Mental Health Bill*, London: Department of Health.

Department of Health and National Institute for Mental Health in England (2005) *Offender Mental Health Care Pathway*, London: Department of Health.

Department of Health and Social Security (1971) *Better Services for the Mentally Handicapped*, London: HMSO.

Department of Health and Social Security (1971) *Welfare of the Elderly: Implementation of Section 45 of the Health Services and Public Health Act 1968*, Circular 19/71, London: Department of Health and Social Security.

Department of Health and Social Security (1975) *Better Services for the Mentally Ill*, London: HMSO.

Department of Health and Social Security (1980) *Report of the Review of Rampton Hospital*, Cmnd 8073, London: HMSO.

Department of Health and Social Security (1981) *Reform of Mental Health Legislation*, Cmnd 8405, London: HMSO.

Department of Health and Social Security (1984) *Mental Health Act Commission: Guidance For Responsible Medical Officers – Consent to Treatment*, Circular DDL (84) 4, London: Department of Health and Social Security.

Department of Health and Welsh Office (1993) *Mental Health Act 1983 Code of Practice*, London: HMSO.

Department of Health and Welsh Office (1998) *Mental Health Act 1983: Memorandum on Parts I to VI, VIII and X*, London: HMSO.

Department of Health and Welsh Office (1999) *Mental Health Act 1983 Code of Practice*, 3rd edn, London: HMSO.

Department of Health and Welsh Office (1999a) *Review of the Mental Health Act 1983* (the 'Richardson Report'), London: Department of Health.

DERSHOWITZ, A. (1970) 'The law of dangerousness: some fictions about predictions', *Journal of Legal Education* 23: 24.

DEUTSCH, A. (1973) *The Shame of the States*, New York, NY: Arno.

DICKENS, B. (1994) 'Medical consent legislation in Ontario', *Medical Law Review* 2: 283.

DICKINSON, H. (2006) 'The evaluation of health and social care partnerships: an analysis of approaches and synthesis for the future', *Health and Social Care in the Community* 14(5): 375–83.

DIGBY, A. (1985) 'Moral treatment at the retreat, 1796–1846', in W. Bynum, R. Porter, and M. Shepherd (eds) *The Anatomy of Madness: Volume II – Institutions and Society*, London: Tavistock.

DIGBY, A. (1985a) *Madness, Morality and Medicine: A Study of the York Retreat, 1796–1914*, Cambridge: Cambridge University Press.

DILLON, J. (2003) 'Women in Broadmoor "should not be there" ', *The Independent on Sunday*, 9 March.

DIXON, L., ADAMS, C. and LUCKSTED, A. (2000) 'Update on family psychoeducation for schizophrenia', *Schizophrenia Bulletin* 26: 5–20.

DIXON, L.B. and LEHMAN, A.F. (1995) 'Family interventions for schizophrenia', *Schizophrenia Bulletin* 21: 631–43.

DOLAN, M. and SHETTY, G. (1995) 'Transfer delays in a special hospital population', *Medicine, Science and Law* 35(3): 237.

DOLAN, M., COOREY, P. and KULUPANA, S. (1993) 'An audit of recalls to a special

hospital' *Journal of Forensic Psychiatry* 4(2): 249–60.

DOLAN, M., GIBB, R. and COOREY, P. (1999) 'Mental health review tribunals: a survey of special hospital patients' opinions', *Journal of Forensic Psychiatry* 10(2): 264–75.

DOWLING, B., POWELL, M. and GLENDENNING, C. (2004) 'Conceptualising successful partnerships', *Health and Social Care in the Community* 12(4): 309–17.

DUFF, L., GRAY, R. and BRISTOW, F. (1996) 'The use of control and restraint techniques in acute psychiatric units', *Psychiatric Care* 3: 230–4.

DUFF, R. (1986) *Trials and Punishment*, Cambridge: Cambridge University Press.

DUNN, S., MORRISON, B. and ROBERTS, M. (eds) (1996) *Mind Readings: Writers' Journeys Through Mental States*, London: Minerva.

EAGLES, J. (1991) 'The relationship between schizophrenia and immigration: are there alternatives to psychosocial hypotheses?', *British Journal of Psychiatry* 159: 783.

EASTMAN, N. (1996) 'Hybrid orders: an analysis of their likely effects on sentencing practice and on forensic psychiatric practice and services', *Journal of Forensic Psychiatry* 7(3): 481.

EASTMAN, N. (1997) 'The Mental Health (Patients in the Community) Act 1995: a clinical analysis', *British Journal of Psychiatry* 170: 492.

EASTMAN, N. and PEAY, J. (1998) 'Sentencing psychopaths: is the "hospital and limitation direction" an ill-considered hybrid?', *Criminal Law Review*: 93.

ECKERMANN, L. (1997) 'Foucault, embodiment and gendered subjectives: the case of voluntary self-starvation', in A. Peterson and R. Bunton (eds) *Foucault Health and Medicine*, London: Routledge.

ECT Anonymous (n.d.) *On what is known with scientific confidence about the effects of ECT*, London: ECT Anonymous.

EDELSOHN, G. and HIDAY, V. (1990) 'Civil commitment: a range of patient attitudes', *Bulletin of the American Academy of Psychiatry and Law* 18: 65.

EDMUNDS, R. (1994) 'Locking the mentally ill out of the homelessness legislation', *Journal of Forensic Psychiatry* 5(2): 355–69.

EGGLESTONE, F. (1990) 'The Home Office: the advisory board on restricted patients', in R. Bluglass and P. Bowden (eds) *Principles and Practice of Forensic Psychiatry*, Edinburgh: Churchill Livingstone.

EISNER, H. (1989) 'Returning the not-guilty by reason of insanity to the community: a new scale to determine readiness', *Bulletin of the American Academy of Psychiatry and the Law* 17(4): 401.

ELDERGILL, A. (1997) *Mental Health Review Tribunals Law and Practice*, London: Sweet and Maxwell.

ELDERGILL, A. (1999) 'Case note on *Barker* v *Barking and Brentwood Community NHS Trust and Others*', *Journal of Mental Health Law* 1(1): 68.

ELDERGILL, A. (2002) 'Is anyone safe? Civil compulsion under the Draft Mental Health Bill', *Journal of Mental Health Law* 8: 331–59.

EMMINS, C. (1986) 'Unfitness to plead: some thoughts prompted by Glenn Pearson's case', *Criminal Law Review*: 604.

European Committee for the Prevention of Torture and Inhuman or Degrading Treatment or Punishment (2000) *Report*, Strasbourg: Council of Europe.

EVANS, J. and TOMISON, A. (1997) 'Assessment of the perceived need for a psychiatric service to a magistrates' court', *Medicine, Science and Law* 37(2): 161.

EVANS, S., HUXLEY, P., WEBBER, M. *et al.* (2005) 'The impact of "statutory duties" on mental health social workers in the UK', *Health and Social Care in the Community* 13(2): 145.

EXWORTHY, T. and PARROTT, J. (1997) 'Comparative evaluation of a diversion from custody scheme', *Journal of Forensic Psychiatry* 8(2): 406.

EXWORTHY, T., MOHAN, D., HINDLEY, N. and BASSON, J. (2001) 'Seclusion: punitive or protective?', *Journal of Forensic Psychiatry* 12(2): 423–33.

FAHY, T. (1989) 'The police as a referral agency for psychiatric emergencies', *Medicine Science and the Law* 29(4): 315.

FALKOWSKI J., WATTS, V., FALKOWSKI, W. and DEAN, T. (1990) 'Patients leaving hospital without knowledge or permission of staff: absconding', *British Journal of Psychiatry* 156: 488.

FANTHORPE, U.A. (1996) 'Walking in darkness', in S. DUNN, B. MORRISON and M. ROBERTS (eds) *Mind Readings: Writers' Journeys through Mental States*, London: Minerva.

FARID, B. (1991) 'Absconders from a district general hospital', *Psychiatric Bulletin* 15: 736.

FARRELL, E. (1997) *The Complete Guide to Mental Health*, London: Vermilion.

FENNELL, P. (1977) 'The mental health review tribunal: a question of imbalance', *British Journal of Law and Society* 2: 186.

FENNELL, P. (1986) 'Law and psychiatry: the legal constitution of the psychiatric system', *Journal of Law and Society* 13(1): 35.

FENNELL, P. (1988) 'Sexual suppressants and the Mental Health Act', *Criminal Law Review*: 660.

FENNELL, P. (1989) 'The Beverley Lewis case: was the law to blame?', *New Law Journal* 139: 559.

FENNELL, P. (1990) 'Inscribing paternalism in the law: consent to treatment and mental disorder' *Journal of Law and Society* 17(1): 29.

FENNELL, P. (1991a) 'Diversion of mentally disordered offenders from custody', *Criminal Law Review*: 333.

FENNELL, P. (1991b) 'Double detention under the Mental Health Act 1983: a case of extra-Parliamentary legislation' *Journal of Social Welfare and Family Law*: 194.

FENNELL, P. (1992) 'The Criminal Procedure (Insanity and Unfitness to Plead) Act 1991', *Modern Law Review* 55(4): 547.

FENNELL, P. (1994) 'Statutory authority to treat, relatives and treatment proxies', *Medical Law Review* 2: 30.

FENNELL, P. (1994a) 'Mentally disordered suspects in the criminal justice system', *Journal of Law and Society*: 57.

FENNELL, P. (1995) 'The Law Commission proposals on mental incapacity', *Family Law*: 420.

FENNELL, P. (1996) *Treatment Without Consent: Law, Psychiatry and the Treatment of Mentally Disordered People since 1845*, London: Routledge.

FENNELL, P. (2005) 'Convention compliance, public safety, and the social inclusion of mentally disordered people', *Journal of Law and Society* 32(1): 90–110.

FENTON, W., BLYLER, C., WYATT, R. and McGLASHAN, T. (1997) 'Prevalence of spontaneous dyskinesia in schizophrenic and non-schizophrenic patients', *British Journal of Psychiatry* 171: 265.

FERENCZ, N. and MAGUIRE, J. (2000) 'Mental health review tribunals in the UK: applying a therapeutic jurisprudence perspective', *Court Review* Spring: 48–52.

FINCH, J. (1984) 'Community care: developing non-sexist alternatives', *Critical Social Policy* 9: 6.

FIRESTONE, S. (1971, republished 1979) 'Freudianism: the misguided feminism', in *The Dialectic of Sex: The Case for a Feminist Revolution*, London: Jonathan Cape/The Women's Press.

FLANNIGAN, C., GLOVER, G., FEENEY, S., WING, J., BEBBINGTON, P. and LEWIS, S. (1994) 'Inner London collaborative audit of admissions in two health districts: I. Introduction, methods and preliminary findings', *British Journal of Psychiatry* 165: 734.

FLANNIGAN, C., GLOVER, G., WING, J., LEWIS, S., BEBBINGTON, P. and FEENEY, S. (1994a)

'Inner London collaborative audit of admissions in two health districts: III. Reasons for acute admission to psychiatric wards', *British Journal of Psychiatry* 165: 750.

FOLSTEIN, M., FOLSTEIN, S. and McHUGH, P. (1975) ' "Mini-mental state": a practical method for grading the cognitive state of patients for the clinician' *Journal of Psychiatric Research* 12: 189.

FORSYTHE, B., MELLING, J. and ADAIR, R. (1999) 'Politics on lunacy: central state regulation and the Devon Pauper lunatic asylum, 1845–1914' in J. Melling and B. Forsythe (eds) *Insanity, Institutions and Society, 1800–1914: A Social History of Madness in Comparative Perspective*, London: Routledge.

FOUCAULT, M. (1965) *Madness and Civilization: A History of Insanity in the Age of Reason*, trans. R. Howard (1973), New York: Random House.

FOUCAULT, M. (1977) *Discipline and Punish: The Birth of the Prison*, London: Allen Lane.

FOUCAULT, M. (1980) 'Lecture Two, 14 January 1976' in C. Gordon (ed) *Power/ Knowledge*, Brighton: Harrvester Press.

FOUCAULT, M. (1986) *The Foucault Reader*, P. Rabinow (ed), London: Penguin.

FOUCAULT, M. (1988) 'The dangerous individual', in L. Kritzman (ed) *Michel Foucault: Politics, Philosophy, Culture: Interviews and Other Writings*, London: Routledge.

FRASER, K. and HEPPLE, J. (1992) 'Prescribing in a special hospital', *Journal of Forensic Psychiatry* 3(2): 311.

FREEDMAN, A., KAPLAN, H. and SADOCK, B. (1975) *Comprehensive Textbook of Psychiatry*, 2 vols., Baltimore: Williams and Wilkins.

FREEMAN, M. (1994) 'Deciding for the intellectually impaired', *Medical Law Review* 2: 77.

FRITH, C. (1994) 'Letter to . . .', *The Psychologist* 7: 490.

GANESVARAN, T. and SHAH, A. (1997) 'Psychiatric inpatient suicide rates: a 21-year study', *Medicine, Science and Law* 37(3): 202–9.

GARCIA, I., KENNETT, C., QURAISHI, M. and DURCAN, G. (2005) *Acute Care 2004: A National Survey of Adult Psychiatric Wards in England*, London: Sainsbury Centre for Mental Health.

GARFINKEL, H. and BITTNER, E. (1967, republished 1984) ' "Good" organizational reasons for "bad" clinical records', in H. Garfinkel, *Studies in Ethnomethodology*, Cambridge: Polity.

GARRETT, T. (1994) 'Sexual contact between psychotherapists and their patients', in General Medical Council (1999) *Seeking Patient's Consent: The Ethical Considerations*, London: GMC.

GELDER, M., GATH, D., MAYOU, R. and COWEN, P. (1996) *Oxford Textbook on Psychiatry*, 3rd edn, Oxford: Oxford University Press.

General Medical Council (1998) *Seeking Patients' Consent: The Ethical Considerations*, London: GMC.

GILBOY, J. and SCHMIDT, J. (1971) ' "Voluntary" hospitalization of the mentally ill', *Northwestern Law Review* 66: 429.

Glasgow Media Group (1996) *Media and Mental Distress*, G. Philo (ed), London: Longman.

GLOVER, N. (1996) ' "Treatability": its scope and application', *Journal of Forensic Psychiatry* 7(2): 353.

GLOVER-THOMAS, N. (2002) *Reconstructing Mental Health Law and Policy*, London: Butterworths.

GOFFMAN, E. (1961, republished 1991) *Asylums: Essays on the Social Situation of Mental Patients and Other Inmates*, London: Penguin.

GOLDBECK, R., MACKENZIE, D. and BENNIE, P. (1997) 'Detained patients' knowledge of their legal status and rights', *Journal of Forensic Psychiatry* 8: 573.

GOLDBERG, D., BENJAMIN, S. and CREED, F. (1994) *Psychiatry in Medical Practice*, 2nd edn, London: Routledge.

GONDOLF, E., MULVEY, E. and LIDZ, C. (1991) 'Psychiatric admission of family violent versus non-family violent patients', *International Journal of Law and Psychiatry* 14(2): 245–54.

GOODCHILD, S. (2002) 'Scandal of the missing millions', *The Independent*, 1 September.

GORDON, C. (1998) 'Guardianship in Oxfordshire: hits and misses', *Psychiatric Bulletin* 22: 233.

GOSTIN, L. (1975) *A Human Condition*, vol. 1, London: MIND.

GOSTIN, L. (1977) *A Human Condition*, vol. 2, London: MIND.

GOSTIN, L. (1982) 'Human rights, judicial review and the mentally disordered offender', *Criminal Law Review*: 792.

GOSTIN, L. (1983) 'The ideology of entitlement: the application of contemporary legal approaches to psychiatry', in P. Bean (ed) *Mental Illness: Changes and Trends*, Chichester: John Wiley.

GOSTIN, L. (1986a) *Institutions Observed*, London: King's Fund.

GOSTIN, L. (1986b) *Mental Health Services, Law and Practice*, London: MIND.

GOSTIN, L. (2000) 'Human rights of persons with mental disabilities: The European Convention on Human Rights', *International Journal of Law and Psychiatry* 23(2): 125.

GOSTIN, L. and FENNELL, P. (1992) *Mental Health: Tribunal Procedure*, London: Longman.

Government Statistical Service (1998) *Health and Personal Social Service Statistics England 1998*, London: HMSO.

Government Statistical Service (2002) *Health and Personal Social Service Statistics England 2002*, London: HMSO.

Government Statistical Service (2006) *Inpatients Formally Detained in Hospitals under the Mental Health Act 1983 and Other Legislation, England: 1994–5 to 2004–5,*

Bulletin: 2006/09/HSCIC, London: The Information Centre.

GRAY, N., LAING, J. and NOAKS, L. (eds) (2002) *Criminal Justice, Mental Health and the Politics of Risk*, London: Cavendish.

GRAY, N.S., O'CONNOR, C., WILLIAMS, T., SHORT, J. and MACCULLOCH, M. (2001) 'Fitness to plead: implications from case law arising from the Criminal Justice and Public Order Act 1994', *Journal of Forensic Psychiatry* 12(1): 52–62.

GREANEY, N., MORRIS, F. and TAYLOR, B. (2005) *Mental Capacity Act 2005: A Guide to the New Law*, London: Law Society.

GREEN, B. and BAGLIONI JR, A. (1997) 'Judging suitability for release of patients from a maximum security hospital by hospital and community staff', *International Journal of Law and Psychiatry* 20(3): 323.

GREENBERG, N., LLOYD, K., O'BRIEN, C., MCIVER, S., HESSFORD, A. and DONOVAN, M. (2002) 'A prospective survey of section 136 in rural England (Devon and Cornwall)', *Medicine, Science and Law* 42(2): 129–32.

GREENHALGH, N., WYLIE, K., RIX, K. and TAMLYN, D. (1996) 'Pilot mental health assessment and diversion scheme for an English metropolitan petty sessional division', *Medicine, Science and Law* 36(1): 52.

GREGORY, S., SHAWCROSS, C.R. and GILL, D. (1985) 'The Nottingham ECT study: a double-blind comparison of bilateral, unilateral and simulated ECT in depressive illness', *British Journal of Psychiatry* 146: 520–4.

GRIFFITHS, R. (1988) *Community Care: Agenda for Action*, London: HMSO.

GRISSO, T. and APPELBAUM, P. (1995b) 'The MacArthur treatment competence study: III. Abilities of patients to consent to psychiatric and medical treatments', *Law and Human Behavior* 19(2): 149.

GRISSO, T., APPELBAUM, P., MULVEY, E. and FLETCHER, K. (1995a) 'The MacArthur treatment competence study. II. Measures of abilities related to competence to consent to treatment', *Law and Human Behavior* 19(2): 127.

GROUNDS, A. (1990) 'Transfers of sentenced prisoners to hospital', *Criminal Law Review*: 544.

GROUNDS, A. (1991) 'The transfer of sentenced prisoners to hospital 1960–83: a study of one special hospital', *British Journal of Criminology* 31(1): 54.

GRUBIN, D. (1991) 'Unfit to plead in England and Wales 1976–88: a survey', *British Journal of Psychiatry* 158: 540.

GRUBIN, D. (1993) 'What constitutes unfitness to plead?', *Criminal Law Review*: 748.

GUDJONSSON, G. (1992) *The Psychology of Interrogations, Confessions and Testimony*, Chichester: Wiley.

GUDJONSSON, G. (1995) ' "Fitness for interview" during police detention: a conceptual framework for forensic assessment', *Journal of Forensic Psychiatry* 6(1): 185.

GUDJONSSON, G., CLARE, I., RUTTER, S. and PEARSE, J. (1993) *Persons at Risk During Interviews in Police Custody: The Identification of Vulnerabilities*, Royal Commission on Criminal Justice Research Study No.12, London: HMSO.

GUDJONSSON, G., HAYES, G. and ROWLANDS: (2000) 'Fitness to be interviewed and psychological vulnerability: the views of doctors, lawyers and police officers', *Journal of Forensic Psychiatry* 11(1): 74–92.

GUNN, J. and JOSEPH, P. (1993) 'Remands to hospital for psychiatrists' reports: a study of psychiatrists' attitudes to section 35 of the Mental Health Act 1983', *Psychiatric Bulletin* 17: 197.

GUNN, J., MADEN, A. and SWINTON, M. (1991) 'Treatment needs of prisoners with psychiatric disorders', *British Medical Journal* 313: 338.

GUNN, M. (1986) 'Mental Health Act guardianship: where now?', *Journal of Social Welfare Law*: 144–52.

GUNN, M. (1986a) 'Judicial review of hospital admissions and treatment in the community under the Mental Health Act 1983', *Journal of Social Welfare Law*: 290.

GUNN, M. (1986b) 'Case note on *Bone v Mental Health Review Tribunal*', *Journal of Social Welfare Law*: 177.

GUNN, M. (1986c) 'Case note on *R v Mental Health Review Tribunal, ex parte Clatworthy*', *Journal of Social Welfare Law*: 249.

GUNN, M. (1990) 'Case note on *R v Newington*', *Journal of Forensic Psychiatry* 1: 360.

GUNN, M. (1993) 'Patients subject to restriction direction and release', *Journal of Forensic Psychiatry* 4(2): 330.

GUNN, M. (1994) 'The meaning of incapacity', *Medical Law Review* 2: 8.

GUNN, M.J. and HOLLAND, T. (2002) 'Some thoughts on the proposed Mental Health Act', *Journal of Mental Health Law* 8: 360–72.

HALL, A., PURI, B., STEWART, T. and GRAHAME, P. (1995) 'Doctors' holding powers in practice: section 5(2) of the Mental Health Act 1983', *Medicine, Science and Law* 35(3): 231–6.

HALLECK, S. (1979) 'The future of psychiatric criminology', in C. Jeffrey (ed) *Biology and Crime*, Beverley Hills, CA: Sage.

HAMILTON, J. (1990) 'Special hospitals and the state hospital', in R. Blugrass and P. Bowden (eds) *Principles and Practice of Forensic Psychiatry*, London: Churchill Livingstone.

HARDIE, T., BHUI, K., BROWN, P., WATSON, J. and PARROTT, J. (1998) 'Unmet needs of remand prisoners', *Medicine, Science and Law* 38(3): 233.

HARGREAVES, D. (1997) 'The transfer of severely mentally ill prisoners from HMP Wakefield: a descriptive study', *Journal of Forensic Psychiatry* 8(1): 62.

HARRISON, G., INEICHEN, B., SMITH, J. and MORGAN, H. (1984) 'Psychiatric hospital admissions in Bristol: II. Social and clinical aspects of compulsory admission', *British Journal of Psychiatry* 145: 605.

HARRISON, K. (1995) 'Growing opposition to "uncontroversial" bill', *Openmind*, April/May: 5.

HART, H. (1961, republished 1994) *The Concept of Law*, Oxford: Clarendon Press.

HART, L. (1995) *Phone At Nine Just To Say You're Alive*, London: Pan.

HART, L. (1996) 'Stay calm and charm them', in J. Read and J. Reynolds (eds) *Speaking Our Minds: An Anthology*, London: Macmillan.

HATFIELD, B., HUXLEY, P. and MOHAMAD, H. (1997) 'Social factors and compulsory detention of psychiatric patients in the UK: the role of the approved social worker in the 1983 Mental Health Act', *International Journal of Law and Psychiatry* 20(3): 389–97.

HATFIELD, B., MOHAMAD, H., RAHIM, Z. and TANWEER, H. (1996) 'Mental health and the Asian communities: a local survey', *British Journal of Social Work* 26: 315.

HAYCOCK, J. (1993) 'Comparative suicide rates in different types of involuntary confinement', *Medicine, Science and Law* 33(2): 128.

Health and Safety Executive (2006) *Violence and Aggression Management Training for Trainers and Managers: A National Evaluation of the Training Provision in Healthcare Settings*, Research Report 440, London: HMSO.

Health Education Authority (1997) *Making Headlines: Mental Health and the National Press*, London: Health Education Authority.

Health Service Ombudsman (2003) *NHS Funding for Long-term Care*, HC 399, London: Health Service Ombudsman.

Healthcare Commission (2004) *Patient Survey Report: Mental Health*, London: Healthcare Commission.

Healthcare Commission (2005) *Survey of Users 2005 Mental Health Services*, London: Commission for Healthcare Audit and Inspection.

Healthcare Commission (2005) *The National Audit of Violence (2003–5) Final Report*, London: The Royal College of Psychiatrists.

Healthcare Commission (2006) *National Survey of NHS staff 2005: Summary of Key Findings*, London: Commission for Healthcare Audit and Inspection.

Healthcare Commission and the Commission for Social Care Inspection (2006) *Improvement Review Of Adult Community Mental Health Services*, London: Commission for Healthcare Audit and Inspection.

HEUSTON, R.F.V. and BUCKLEY, R.A. (1996) *Salmond and Heuston on the Law of Torts*, 21st edn, London: Sweet and Maxwell.

HEWITT, D (2005) 'A private function', *Journal of Mental Health Law*: 83–95.

HEWITT, D. (2000) 'Widening the "Bournewood gap"', *Journal of Mental Health Law* 4: 196–204.

HEYWOOD and MASSEY. *See* WHITEHORN.

HIDAY, V. (1992) 'Coercion in civil commitment: process, preferences and outcomes', *International Journal of Law and Psychiatry* 15: 359.

HILSON, C. (2003) 'The Europeanization of English administrative law: judicial review and convergence', *European Public Law* 9(1): 125–45.

HINES, D. (1999) *Independent Investigation into Complaints Raised by Ian Stewart Brady Relating to His Transfer to Lawrence Ward and Re-feeding at Ashworth Hospital*, London: Department of Health.

HIRST, D. and MICHAEL, P. (1999) 'Family, community and the lunatic in mid-nineteenth-century North Wales' in P. Bartlett and D. Wright (eds) *Outside the Walls of the Asylum*, London: Athlone.

HM Prison Service (2003) *Clinical Governance: Quality in Prison Healthcare*, Prison Service Order 3100, 16 January.

HM Prison Service and Department of Health (2002) *Mental Health Inreach Collaborative Launch Document*, London: Department of Health.

HM Prison Service and Department of Health (2003) 'Ministerial foreword', in *Prison Health*, London: Department of Health.

HM Prison Service and NHS Executive (1999) *The Future Organisation of Prison Health Care*, London: Department of Health.

HM Prison Service Prison (2006) *Transfer of Prisoners to and from Hospital under Sections 47 and 48 of the Mental Health Act 1983*, Service Instruction 03/2006, London: HM Prison Service.

HM Prison Service, Department of Health and The National Assembly for Wales (2001) *Changing the Outlook: A Strategy for Developing and Modernising Mental Health Services in Prisons*, London: Department of Health.

HM Stationery Office (2004) *Domestic Violence, Crime and Victims Act 2004 Explanatory Notes*, London: HMSO.

HODGSON, J. (1997) 'Vulnerable suspects and the appropriate adult', *Criminal Law Review*:785.

HOGARTY, G. and ULRICH, R. (1972) 'The discharge readiness inventory', *Archives of General Psychiatry* 23: 419.

HOGE, S., APPELBAUM, P. and GREER, A. (1989) 'An empirical comparison of the Stone and dangerousness criteria for civil commitment', *American Journal of Psychiatry* 146: 170.

HOGGETT, B. (1996) *Mental Health Law*, 4th edn, London: Sweet and Maxwell.

HOGMAN, G. (1996) *Is Cost a Factor? A Survey by the National Schizophrenia Fellowship of the Experiences and Views of Psychiatrists on New Drugs for the Treatment of Schizophrenia*, London: National Schizophrenia Fellowship.

HOLDAWAY, S. (1983) *Inside the British Police*, Oxford: Basil Blackwell.

HOLDEN, A. (1974) *The St Albans Poisoner*, London: Hodder and Stoughton.

Home Office (1973) *Report on the Review of Procedures for the Discharge and Supervision of Psychiatric Patients subject to Special Restrictions* (the 'Aarvold Committee'), Cmnd 5191, London: HMSO.

Home Office (1990) *Provision for Mentally Disordered Offenders*, Circular 66/1990, London: HMSO.

Home Office (1991) *Guidance on the Criminal Procedure (Insanity and Unfitness to Plead) Act 1991*, Circular 93/91, London: HMSO.

Home Office (1992) *Report of the Committee of Inquiry into Complaints about Ashworth Hospital*, 2 vols., Cmnd 2028, London: HMSO.

Home Office (1996) *Protecting the Public*, Cm 3190, London: HMSO.

Home Office (1997) *Restricted Patients: Reconvictions and Recalls by the End of 1995*, London: Home Office.

Home Office (2003) *Prison Population Brief*, London: Home Office.

Home Office (2003a) *Guidance For Appropriate Adults*, London: Home Office.

Home Office (2006) *Population in Custody Monthly Tables: July 2006, England and Wales*, London: Home Office.

Home Office (2006a) *Crime in England and Wales 2005–6*, Bulletin 12/06, London: Home Office Research, Development and Statistics Directorate.

Home Office (n.d.) *Restricted Patients Detained in Special Hospitals: Information for the Special Hospitals Service Authority*, London: Home Office.

Home Office and Department of Health (1992) *Review of Health and Social Services for Mentally Disordered Offenders and Others Requiring Similar Services*, Cmnd 2088, London: HMSO.

Home Office and Department of Health (1999) *Managing Dangerous People with Severe Personality Disorders: Proposals for Policy Development*, London: Home Office and Department of Health.

Home Office and Department of Health (2002) *Consultation on Draft Mental Health Bill*, London: Department of Health.

Home Office Research and Statistics Directorate (1996) *Criminal Statistics: England and Wales 1996 Statistics Relating to Crime and Criminal Proceedings for the Year 1995*, London: HMSO.

Home Office Research and Statistics Directorate (1997) *Statistics of Mentally Disordered Offenders in England and Wales 1996*, London: Home Office Research and Statistics Directorate.

Home Office Research and Statistics Directorate (1998a) *Statistics of Mentally Disordered Offenders in England and Wales 1997*, London: Home Office Research and Statistics Directorate.

Home Office Research and Statistics Directorate (1998b) *The Prison Population in 1997: A Statistical Review*, London: Home Office Research and Statistics Directorate.

Home Office Research and Statistics Directorate (2003) *Crime in England and Wales 2001–2: Supplementary Volume*, London: Home Office.

Home Office Research, Development and Statistics Directorate (2002) *Statistics of Mentally Disordered Offenders 2001*, Bulletin 13/02, London: Home Office Research, Development and Statistics Directorate.

Home Office Research, Development and Statistics Directorate (2005) *Statistics of Mentally Disordered Offenders 2004*, Bulletin 22/05, London: Home Office Research, Development and Statistics Directorate.

Home Office, Mental Health Unit (1997) *Crime Sentences Act*, HO Circular 52/1997, London: Home Office.

HORNE, J. (1999) 'The advisory board on restricted patients and tribunal recommendations', *Journal of Mental Health Law* 1(1): 62–7.

House of Commons and House of Lords (2003) *Report of the Joint Committee on the Draft Mental Incapacity Bill*, PP (2002–3) HL 189 and HC 1083.

House of Commons and House of Lords (2005a) *Report of the Joint Scrutiny Committee on the Mental Health Bill*, PP HL (2004–5) 79/HC (2004–5) 95.

HOUSTON, R. (1999) ' "Not simple boarding": care of the mentally incapacitated in Scotland during the long eighteenth century', in P. Bartlett and D. Wright (eds) *Outside the Walls of the Asylum*, London: Athlone.

HOWARD, H. (2003) 'Reform of the insanity defence: theoretical issues', *Journal of Criminal Law* 67(1): 51–67.

HOWLETT, M. (1998) *Medication, Non-Compliance and Mentally Disordered Offenders*, London: The Zito Trust.

HOYER, G. (1986) 'Compulsorily admitted patients' ability to make use of their legal rights', *International Journal of Law and Psychiatry* 8: 413.

HUCKLE, P. (1996) 'A survey of sentenced prisoners transferred to hospital for urgent psychiatric treatment over a three-year period for one region', *Medicine, Science and Law* 36(4): 37.

HUDSON, B. (2002) 'Balancing rights and risks: dilemmas of justice and difference' in N. Gary, J. Laing and L. Noaks (eds) *Criminal Justice, Mental Health and the Politics of Risk*, London: Cavendish.

HUGHES, D. (1991) 'The reorganisation of the National Health Service: the rhetoric and reality of the internal market', *Modern Law Review* 54: 88.

HUME, C. and PULLEN, I. (1994) *Rehabilitation for Mental Health Problems: An Introductory Handbook*, 2nd edn, Edinburgh: Churchill Livingstone.

HUWS, R. and SHUBSACHS, A. (1993) 'A study of absconding by special hospital patients: 1976 to 1988', *Journal of Forensic Psychiatry* 4(1): 45.

HUWS, R., LONGSON, D., REISS, D. and LARKIN, E. (1997) 'Prison transfers to special hospitals since the introduction of the Mental Health Act 1983', *Journal of Forensic Psychiatry* 8(1): 74.

HUXLEY, P. (1985) *Social Work Practice in Mental Health*, Aldershot: Gower.

HUXLEY, P., EVANS, S., WEBBER, M. and GATELY, C. (2005) 'Staff shortages in the mental health workforce: the case of the disappearing approved social worker', *Health and Social Care in the Community* 13(6): 504

INEICHEN, B., HARRISON, G. and MORGAN, H. (1984) 'Psychiatric hospital admissions in Bristol: I. Geographic and ethnic factors', *British Journal of Psychiatry* 145: 600.

IRELAND, J.L. (2004) 'Nature, extent and causes of bullying among personality-disordered patients in a high-secure hospital', *Aggressive Behavior* 30(3): 229–42.

IRELAND, J.L. (2004a) *Patient-to-Patient Bullying in a High Secure Forensic Setting: A Study of Mental Health and Women's Services*, Research funded by National Forensic Mental Health Research and Development Programme, MRD 12/44, London: MRD.

IRELAND, J. L. (2006) 'Exploring definitions of bullying among personality disordered patients in a high-secure hospital', *Aggressive Behavior* 32(5): 451–63.

IRELAND, J. L. and BESCOBY, N. (2004) 'A behavioural assessment of bullying behaviour among personality disordered patients in a high-secure hospital', *Aggressive Behavior* 31(1): 67–83.

IRELAND, J.L. and SNOWDEN, P. (2002) 'Bullying in secure hospitals' *Journal of Forensic Psychiatry* 13(3): 538–54.

JACOB, J. (1976) 'The mental patient's right to his psychosis', *Modern Law Review* 17: 17.

JACONELLI, J. and JACONELLI, A. (1998) 'Tort liability under the Mental Health Act 1983', *Journal of Social Welfare and Family Law* 20: 151.

JAMES, A. (2001) *Raising Our Voices: An Account of the Hearing Voices Movement*, London: Handsell Publications.

JAMES, D. (2000) 'Police station diversion schemes: role and efficacy in central London', *Journal of Forensic Psychiatry* 11(3): 532–55.

JAMES, D. and HAMILTON, L. (1991) 'The Clerkenwell scheme: assessing efficacy and cost of a psychiatric liaison service to a magistrates' court', *British Medical Journal* 303: 282.

JAMES, D., CRIPPS J. and GRAY, N. (1998) 'What demands do those admitted from the criminal justice system make on psychiatric beds?', *Journal of Forensic Psychiatry* 9(1): 74.

JAMES, D., CRIPPS J., GILLULEY P. and HARLOW, P. (1997) 'A court-focused model of forensic psychiatry provision to central London: abolishing remands to prison?', *Journal of Forensic Psychiatry* 8(2): 309.

JAMESON, R. (1996) 'Schizophrenia from the inside', in J. Read and J. Reynolds (eds) *Speaking Our Minds: An Anthology*, London: Macmillan.

JAMISON, K. (1993) *Touched with Fire: Manic-Depressive Illness and the Artistic Temperament*, New York: Simon and Schuster.

JAMISON, K. (1996) *An Unquiet Mind: A Memoir of Moods and Madness*, London: Picador.

JANOFSKY, J., McCARTHY, R. and FOLSTEIN, M. (1992) 'The Hopkins competency assessment test: a brief method for evaluating patients' capacity to give informed consent', *Hospital and Community Psychiatry* 43:2: 132.

JEFFERSON, T. (1988) 'Race, crime and policing: empirical, theoretical and methodological issues', *International Journal of the Sociology of Law* 16: 521.

JEFFERYS, M. and BLOM-COOPER, L. (1975) 'Foreword' in Gostin, L. (1975) *A Human Condition*, vol. 1, London: MIND.

JODELET, D. (1991) *Madness and Social Representations*, Hemel Hempstead: Harvester Wheatsheaf.

JOHNSON, C., SMITH, J., CROWE, C. and DONOVAN, M. (1993) 'Suicide amongst forensic psychiatric patients', *Medicine, Science and Law* 33(2): 137.

JOHNSON, D. (1990) 'Organising a depot clinic', *Practical Reviews in Psychiatry* 2(10): 1.

JOHNSTONE, G. (1996) *Medical Concepts and Penal Policy*, London: Cavendish.

JONES, K. (1972) *A History of the Mental Health Services*, London: Routledge & Kegan Paul.

JONES, M. (1998) *Textbook on Torts*, 6th edn, London: Blackstone.

Jones, M. (1999) 'Informed consent and other fairy stories', *Medical Law Review* 7: 103.

JONES, M. and Keywood, K. (1996) 'Assessing the patient's competence to consent to medical treatment', *Medical Law International* 2: 107.

JONES, R. (1999) *Mental Health Act Manual*, 6th edn, London: Sweet and Maxwell.

JONES, R. (2003) *Mental Health Act Manual*, 8th edn, London: Sweet and Maxwell.

JONES, R. (2005) *Mental Capacity Act Manual*, London: Sweet and Maxwell.

JONES, R. (2006) *Mental Health Act Manual*, 10th edn, London: Sweet and Maxwell.

JOYCE, J., MORRIS, M. and PALIA, S. (1991) 'Section 5(2) audit', *Psychiatric Bulletin* 15: 224.

JUNG, C.G. (2000) 'The CG Jung page', UKCP website (online at www.cgjungpage.org).

JUSTICE (1994) *Unreliable Evidence? Confessions and the Safety of Convictions*, London: Justice.

KALTIALA, R., HEINO, C., TUOHIMAKI, J., KORKEILA, V. and LEHTINEN, R. (2003) 'Reasons for using seclusion and restraint in psychiatric inpatient care', *International Journal of Law and Psychiatry* 26(2) 139–49.

KALTIALA-HEINO R., LAIPPALA, P. and SALOKANGAS, R. (1997) 'Impact of coercion on treatment outcome', *International Journal of Law and Psychiatry* 20(3): 311.

KANE, J., QUITKIN, F., RIFKIN, A., WEGNER, J., ROSENBERG, G. and BORENSTEIN, M. (1983) 'Attudinal changes of involuntary committed patients following treatment', *Archives of General Psychiatry* 40: 374–7.

KARP, D. (2001) *The Burden of Sympathy: How Families Cope with Mental Illness*, New York: Oxford University Press

KENDELL, R. (1991) 'Relationship between the DSM-IV and the ICD-10', *Journal of Abnormal Psychology* 100: 297.

KENNEDY, I. (1997) 'Case note on R (Adult: Refusal of Treatment) [1996] 2 FLR 99', *Medical Law Review* 5:104.

KERRIGAN, K. (2002) 'Psychiatric evidence and mandatory disposal: Article 5 compliance?', *Journal of Mental Health Law*: 130–8.

KERRIGAN. K. (2000) 'Mentally disordered suspects: the lessons of R v Aspinall', *Journal of Criminal Law* 64(1): 80–8.

KESEY, K. (1977) *One Flew Over the Cuckoo's Nest*, Harmondsworth: Penguin.

KEYWOOD, K. (1996) 'Rectification of incorrect documentation under the Mental Health Act 1983', *Journal of Forensic Psychiatry* 7: 79–91.

KING, M. (1991) 'Child welfare within law: the emergence of a hybrid discourse', *Journal of Law and Society* 18(3): 303.

KIRKHAM, R. (2005) 'Reforming the tribunal sector', *Journal of Social Welfare and Family Law* 27(2): 185–97.

KJELLIN, L. and WESTRIN, C-G. (1998) 'Involuntary admissions and coercive measures in psychiatric care', *International Journal of Law and Psychiatry* 21(1): 31–42.

KMIETOWICZ, Z. (2002) 'New mental health bill may conflict with advice from the GMC', *British Medical Journal* 325: 678.

KNIGHT, A., MUMFORD, D. and NICHOL, B. (1998) 'Supervised discharge order: the first years in the South and West Region', *Psychiatric Bulletin* 22: 418.

LACEY, R. (1996) *The Complete Guide to Psychiatric Drugs*, 2nd edn, London: Vermilion.

LAING, J. (1995) 'The mentally disordered suspect at the police station', *Criminal Law Review*: 371.

LAING, J. (1996) 'The proposed hybrid order for mentally disordered offenders: a step in the right direction?', *Liverpool Law Review* 18(2): 127.

LAING, J. (1997) 'The likely impact of mandatory and minimum sentences on the disposal of mentally disordered offenders', *Journal of Forensic Psychiatry* 8(3): 504.

LARKIN, E. and CLOSE, A. (1996) 'Performing well? Referrals to Rampton Hospital in 1993', *Journal of Forensic Psychiatry* 7(1): 177.

Law Commission (1995) *Mental Incapacity*, LC No. 231, London: HMSO.

Law Society (2002) 'Response to the Draft Mental Health Bill', London: Law Society (reprinted in *Journal of Mental Health Law* 8: 373–5).

LAWSON, W., HEPLER, N., HOLLIDAY, J. and CUFFEL, B. (1994) 'Race as a factor in inpatient and outpatient admissions and diagnosis', *Hospital and Community Psychiatry* 45: 72.

LEFF, J. (1993) 'Comment on crazy talk: thought disorder or psychiatric arrogance by Thomas Szasz', *British Journal of Medical Psychology* 66: 77.

LEIGH, I. (2002) 'Taking rights proportionately: judicial review, the Human Rights Act and Strasbourg', *Public Law*: 265–87.

LELLIOTT, P. and AUDINI, B. (2003) 'Trends in the use of Part II of the Mental Health Act 1983 in seven English local authority areas', *British Journal of Psychiatry* 182: 68–70.

LEWIS, B. (1996) 'Therapy room', in J. Read, and J. Reynolds (eds) *Speaking Our Minds: An Anthology*, London: Macmillan.

LEWIS, G. (2002) *Sunbathing in the Rain: A Cheerful Book about Depression*, London: Flamingo.

LEWIS, G., CROFT-JEFFREYS, C. and DAVID, A. (1990) 'Are British psychiatrists racist?', *British Journal of Psychiatry* 157: 410.

LEWIS, J. (1989) ' "It all really starts in the family": community care in the 1990s', *Journal of Law and Society* 16: 83.

LEWIS, J. and GLENNERSTER, H. (1996) *Implementing the New Community Care*, Buckingham: Open University Press.

LEWIS, S.W., BARNES, T.R., DAVIES, L., MURRAY, R.M., DUNN, G., HAYHURST, K.P., MARKWICK, A., LLOYD, H. and JONES, P.B. (2006) 'Randomized controlled trial of effect of prescription of clozapine versus other second-generation antipsychotic drugs in resistant schizophrenia', *Schizophrenia Bulletin* 32(4): 715–23.

LIBERTY (2002) *Liberty's Response to the Department of Health Consultation on the Draft Mental Health Bill*, London: Liberty.

LINDSAY, W. (1996) 'By definition', in J. Read and J. Reynolds (eds) *Speaking Our Minds: An Anthology*, London: Macmillan.

LITTLECHILD, B. (1995) 'Reassessing the role of the "appropriate adult" ', *Criminal Law Review*: 540.

LITTLEWOOD, R. (1992) 'Psychiatric diagnosis and racial bias: empirical and interactive approaches', *Social Science and Medicine* 34: 141.

LITTLEWOOD, R. and LIPSEDGE, M. (1997) *Aliens and Alienists*, 3rd edn, London: Routledge.

LONG, C. and MIDGELY, M. (1992) 'On the closeness of the concepts of the criminal and the mentally ill in the nineteenth century: yesterday's opinion reflected today', *Journal of Forensic Psychiatry* 3(1): 63.

Lord Chancellor's Department (1997) *Who Decides? Making Decisions on Behalf of Mentally Incapacitated Adults*, (Green Paper), Cm 3803, London: HMSO.

Lord Chancellor's Department (1999) *Making Decisions: The Government's Proposals for Making Decisions on Behalf of Mentally Incapacitated Adult*, (White Paper) Cm 4465, London: HMSO.

Lord Chancellor's Department (2001) *Tribunals for Users, One System, One Service*, London: HMSO.

LORING, M. and POWELL, B. (1988) 'Gender, race and DSM-III', *Journal of Health and Social Behaviour* 29: 1.

LOWE-PONSFORD, F., WOLFSON, P. and LINDESAY, J. (1998) 'Consultant psychiatrists' views on the supervision register', *Psychiatric Bulletin* 22: 409.

LUPTON, D. (1997) 'Foucault and the medicalisation critique', in A. Peterson and R. Bunton (eds) *Foucault, Health and Medicine*, London: Routledge.

MACKAY, R.D. (1990) 'Fact and fiction about the insanity defence', *Criminal Law Review*: 247.

MACKAY, R.D. (1995) *Mental Condition Defences in the Criminal Law*, Oxford: Clarendon.

MACKAY, R.D. (2002) 'On being insane in Jersey, Part 2: the appeal in *Jason Prior v Attorney General*', *Criminal Law Review*: 728–34.

MACKAY, R.D. (2004) 'On being insane in Jersey, Part 3: the case of the *Attorney General v O'Driscoll*' *Criminal Law Review*: 291–6.

MACKAY, R.D. and GEARTY, C.A. (2001) 'On being insane in Jersey: the case of *Attorney General v Jason Prior*', *Criminal Law Review*: 560–3.

MACKAY, R.D. and KEARNS, G. (1994) 'The continued underuse of unfitness to plead and the insanity defence', *Criminal Law Review*: 576.

MACKAY, R.D. and KEARNS, G. (1997) 'The trial of the facts and unfitness to plead', *Criminal Law Review*: 644.

MACKAY, R.D. and KEARNS, G. (2000) 'An upturn in unfitness to plead? Disability in relation to the trial of the facts under the 1991 Act', *Criminal Law Review*: 532–46.

MACKAY, R.D. and MACHIN, D. (1998) *Transfers from Prison to Hospital: The Operation of Section 48 of the Mental Health Act 1983*, London: Home Office.

MACKAY, R.D. and MACHIN, D. (2000) 'The operation of section 48 of the Mental Health Act 1983', *British Journal of Criminology* 40: 727–45.

MACKAY, R.D., MITCHELL, B.J. and HOWE, L. (2006) 'Yet more facts about the insanity defence', *Criminal Law Review*: 399–411.

MACLEOD, S. (1996) 'The art of starvation', in S. Dunn, B. Morrison and M. Roberts (eds) *Mind Readings: Writers' Journeys through Mental States*, London: Minerva.

MANNION, R. and STREET, A. (2006) *Payment by Results and Demand Management: Learning from the South Yorkshire Laboratory*, Centre for Health Economics Research Paper, 14 January 2006, York: University of York.

MANOR, O. (1994) 'Group psychotherapy', in P. Clarkson and M. Pokorny (eds) *The Handbook of Psychotherapy*, London: Routledge.

MARKUS, K. (2003) 'Leonard Cheshire Foundation: what is a public function?', *European Human Rights Law Review* 1: 92–100.

MARSON, D., INGRAM, K., CODY, H. and HARRELL, L. (1995) 'Assessing the competency of patients With Alzheimer's disease under different legal standards', *Archives of Neurology* 52: 949.

MASON, T. (1992) 'Seclusion: definitional interpretations', *Journal of Forensic Psychiatry* 3(2): 261–9.

MASON, T. (1993) 'Seclusion: an international comparison', *Medicine, Science and Law* 34(1): 54.

MASON, T. and WHITEHEAD, E. (2001) 'Some specific problems of secluding female patients', *Medicine, Science and Law* 41(4): 315–24.

MATHIESEN, T. (1983) 'The future of control systems: the case of Norway' in D. Garland and P. Young (eds) *The Power to Punish: Contemporary Penality and Social Analysis*, London: Heinemann.

MATTHEWS, K. and ELJAMEL, M.S. (2001) *The Neurosurgery for Mental Disorder in Dundee Report* Dundee: Dundee Neurosurgery for Mental Disorder Service.

MATTHEWS, P. (1982) 'Contracts for necessaries and mental incapacity', *Northern Ireland Legal Quarterly* 33(2): 149.

MATTHEWS, T. and WESTON, S.N. (2003) 'Experience of thioridazine use before and after the Committee on Safety of Medicines' warning', *Psychiatric Bulletin* 27: 87–9.

MAYS, J. (1995) *In the Jaws of the Black Dogs: A Memoir of Depression*, Toronto: Penguin.

McCABE, D. (1996) 'No place like home', *Community Care*, 22 August: 27.

McCALL, W.V., DUNN, A. and ROSENQUIST, P.B. (2004) 'Quality of life and function after electroconvulsive therapy', *British Journal of Psychiatry* 185: 405–9.

McCONVILLE, M. and HODGSON, J. (1993) *Custodial Legal Advice and the Right to Silence*, Royal Commission on Criminal Justice Research Report No.16, London: HMSO.

McGUE, M., GOTTESMAN, I. and RAO, D. (1985) 'Resolving genetic models for the transmission of schizophrenia', *Genetic Epidemiology* 2: 99.

McHALE J. and FOX, M., with MURPHY, J. (1997) *Health Care Law: Text and Materials*, London: Sweet and Maxwell.

McKENZIE, I. and WADDINGTON, D. (1994) 'Mental health review tribunals in Bradford', *Psychiatric Bulletin* 18: 55.

McKENZIE, I., MORGAN, R. and REINER, R. (1990) 'Helping the police with their enquiries', *Criminal Law Review*: 22.

Mental Health Act Commission (1985) *First Biennial Report 1983–5*, London: HMSO.

Mental Health Act Commission (1987) *Second Biennial Report 1985–7*, London: HMSO.

Mental Health Act Commission (1989) *Third Biennial Report 1987–9*, London: HMSO.

Mental Health Act Commission (1991) *Fourth Biennial Report 1989–91*, London: HMSO.

Mental Health Act Commission (1993) *Fifth Biennial Report 1991–3*, London: HMSO.

Mental Health Act Commission (1995) *Sixth Biennial Report 1993–5*, London: HMSO.

Mental Health Act Commission (1997) *Seventh Biennial Report 1995–7*, London: HMSO.

Mental Health Act Commission (1999) *Eight Biennial Report 1997–9*, London: HMSO.

Mental Health Act Commission (2001) *Ninth Biennial Report 1999–2001*, London: HMSO.

Mental Health Act Commission (2001a) *Deaths of Detained Patients in England and Wales: A Report by the Mental Health Act Commission on Information Collected from 1 February 1997 to 31 January 2001*, London: Department of Health.

Mental Health Act Commission (2002) *Guidance for RMOs: R (on the application of Wooder) v Dr Feggetter and the Mental Health Act Commission*, GN 1B/02, Nottingham: Mental Health Act Commission.

Mental Health Act Commission (2002a) *Guidance for SOADs: R (on the application of Wooder) v Dr Feggetter and the Mental Health Act Commission*, GN 1A/02, Nottingham: Mental Health Act Commission.

Mental Health Act Commission (2002b) *Annual Report 2001–2*, Nottingham: Mental Health Act Commission.

Mental Health Act Commission (2003) *Placed Amongst Strangers: Tenth Biennial Report 2001–3*, London: HMSO.

Mental Health Act Commission (2005) *11th Biennial Report 2003–5*, London: HMSO.

Mental Health Act Commission (2006) *Guidance* (available online at http://www.mhac.org.uk/Pages/guidancenotes.html).

Mental Health Act Commission (2006a) *Guidance for RMOs: R (on the application of Wooder) v Dr Feggetter and the Mental Health Act Commission*, Nottingham: MHAC.

Mental Health Act Commission (2006b) *Guidance for SOADs: R (on the application of Wooder) v Dr Feggetter and the Mental Health Act Commission*, Nottingham, MHAC.

Mental Health Review Tribunal Secretariat (2005) *Activity Report April 2001–March 2005*, London: Mental Health Review Tribunal Secretariat.

Mersey Care NHS Trust (2005) *Strategic Business Plan 2004–7 Progress Report*, Paper MC 017/05, Liverpool: Mersey Care Trust

MIDELFORT, E. (1980) 'Madness and civilisation in early modern Europe: a reappraisal of Michel Foucault', in Malament, B. (ed) *After the Reformation: Essays in Honor of J.H. Hexter*, Manchester: Manchester University Press.

MILNE, E. and MILNE, S. (1995) 'Mental health review tribunals: why the delay?', *Journal of Forensic Psychiatry* 6(1): 93.

MILNE, S., BARRON, P., FRASER, K. and WHITFIELD, E. (1995) 'Sex differences in patients admitted to a regional secure unit', *Medicine, Science and Law* 35(1): 57.

MILNER, G. (1966) 'The absconder', *Comprehensive Psychiatry* 7: 147.

MIND (1997) *Without Prejudice*, London: MIND.

MIND (2002) 'Sexual harassment on mixed wards still a major problem', MIND press release, 24 April, London: MIND.

MIND (2003) 'Psychiatrists appeal to NICE to drop new restrictions on ECT fails as users' views win respect', MIND press release, 26 March, London: MIND.

MIND (2004) *The National Service Framework for Mental Health: What Progress Five Years On?* London: MIND

Ministry of Health (1963) *Health and Welfare: The Development of Community Care*, London: HMSO.

MOHAN, D., THOMPSON, C. and MULLEE, M. (1998) 'Preliminary evaluation of supervised discharge in the South and West Region', *Psychiatric Bulletin* 22: 421.

MOKHTAR, A. and HOGBIN, P. (1993) 'Police may underuse section 136', *Medicine, Science and Law* 33(3): 188.

MONAHAN, J. (1981) *Predicting Violent Behavior*, Beverly Hills, CA: Sage.

MONAHAN, J. (1984) 'The prediction of violent behavior: toward a second generation of theory and policy', *American Journal of Psychiatry* 141(1): 10.

MONAHAN, J. (1988) 'Risk assessment of violence among the mentally disordered: generating useful knowledge', *International Journal of Law and Psychiatry* 11: 249.

MONAHAN, J. (2006) 'A jurisprudence of risk assessment: forecasting harm among prisoners, predators, and patients', *Virginia Law Review* 92: 390.

MONAHAN, J. and STEADMAN, H. (eds) (1994) *Violence and Mental Disorder: Developments in Risk Assessment*, Chicago, IL: University of Chicago Press.

MONAHAN, J., HOGE, S., LIDZ, C., ROTH, L., BENNETT, N., GARDNER, W. and MULVEY, E. (1995) 'Coercion and commitment: understanding involuntary mental hospital admission', *International Journal of Law and Psychiatry* 18(3): 249.

MONAHAN, J., RUGGIERO, M. and FRIEDLANDER, H. (1982) 'Stone-Roth model of civil commitment and the California dangerousness standard', *Archives of General Psychiatry* 39: 1267.

MONAHAN, J., STEADMAN, H., APPELBAUM, P., GRISSO, T., MULVEY, E., ROTH, L., CLARK ROBBINS, P., BANKS, S., and SILVER, E. (forthcoming) 'The classification of violent risk', *Behavioral Sciences and the Law*.

MONAHAN, J., STEADMAN, H.J., SILVER, E., APPELBAUM, P., CLARK ROBBINS, P., MULVEY, E.P., ROTH, L.H., GRISSON, T. and BANKS, S. (2001) *Rethinking Risk Assessment: The MacArthur Study of Mental Disorder and Violence*, Oxford: Oxford University Press.

MONTANDON, C. and HARDING, T. (1984) 'The reliability of dangerousness assessments: a decision making exercise', *British Journal of Psychiatry* 144: 149.

MONTGOMERY, J. (2002) *Health Care Law*, 2nd edn, Oxford: Oxford University Press.

MOODLEY, P. and THORNICROFT, G. (1988) 'Ethnic group and compulsory detention', *Medicine, Science and Law* 28(4): 324–8.

MORGAN, H. and PRIEST, P. (1991) 'Suicide and other unexpected deaths among psychiatric inpatients: the Bristol confidential inquiry', *British Journal of Psychiatry* 158: 368.

MORRIS, J. (1993) *Independent Lives: Community Care and Disabled People*, London: Macmillan.

MORRISON, W. (1997) *Jurisprudence: From the Greeks to Postmodernism*, London: Cavendish.

MOWBRAY, R. (1995) *The Case Against Psychotherapy Registration: A Conservation Issue for the Human Potential Movement*, London: The Trans Marginal Press.

MUIJEN, M. (1996) 'Scare in the community: Britain in moral panic', in T. Heller, J. Reynolds, R. Gomm, R. Muston and S. Pattison (eds) *Mental Health Matters: A Reader*, Basingstoke and London: Macmillan.

MURPHY, E. (1991) *After the Asylums: Community Care for People with Mental Illness*, London: Faber.

National Appropriate Adult Network (2005) *National Standard 1 Recruitment and Selection of Appropriate Adults; National Standard 2 Support, Supervision, Development and Retention of Appropriate Adults*, London: NAAN.

National Appropriate Adult Network (2005a) *National Standard 3 Training*, London: NAAN.

National Appropriate Adult Network (2005b) *National Standard 4 Service Delivery*, London: NAAN.

National Association for the Care and Rehabilitation of Offenders (2005) *Findings of the 2004 Survey of Court Diversion/ Criminal Justice Mental Health Liaison Schemes for Mentally Disordered Offenders in England and Wales*, London: NACRO.

National Audit Office (2003) *Ensuring the Effective Discharge of Older Patients from NHS Acute Hospitals*, HC 392, London: National Audit Office.

National Audit Office (2003a) *A Safer Place to Work: Protecting NHS Hospital and Ambulance Staff from Violence and Aggression: Report prepared by the Comptroller and Auditor General*, HC 527, London: National Audit Office.

National Institute for Health and Clinical Excellence (2002) '*NICE recommends new antipsychotic drugs as one of the first line options for schizophrenia*', Press release 2002/030, London: NICE.

National Institute for Health and Clinical Excellence (2003) *Guidance on the Use of Electroconvulsive Therapy*, London: NICE.

National Institute for Health and Clinical Excellence (2005) *Violence: The Short-term Management Of Disturbed/Violent Behaviour in Inpatient Psychiatric Settings and Emergency Departments*, London: NICE.

National Institute for Mental Health for England (2003) '*User/survivor and carer experiences*', London: National Institute for Health for England.

National Institute for Mental Health in England (2003) *Inside Outside: Improving Mental Health Services for Black and Minority Ethnic Communities in England*, London: Department of Health.

National Institute for Mental Health in England (2003a) *Personality Disorder: No Longer a Diagnosis of Exclusion – Policy Implementation Guidance for the Development of Services for People with Personality Disorder*, London: Department of Health.

National Task Force on Violence Against Social Care Staff (2000) *Report of the National Task Force on Violence Against Social Care Staff*, London: Department of Health.

National Task Force on Violence Against Social Care Staff (2001) *National Action Plan*, London: Department of Health.

NEMETZ, T. and BEAN, P. (2001) 'Protecting the rights of the mentally disordered in police stations: the use of the appropriate adult in England and Wales', *International Journal of Law and Psychiatry* 24: 595–605.

NHS Executive (1994) *Introduction of Supervision Registers for Mentally Ill People from 1 April 1994*, HSG(94)5, London: Department of Health.

NHS Executive (1996) *An Audit pack for Monitoring the CPA*, HSG(96)6, London: Department of Health.

NHS Executive (1998) *A First Class Service: Quality in the New NHS*, London: Department of Health.

NHS Executive (1999) *Clinical Governance: Quality in the New NHS*, HSC 1999/065, London: Department of Health.

NHS Health Advisory Service/Department of Health and Social Security Social Services Inspectorate (1988) *Report on the Services Provided by Broadmoor Hospital*, HAS/SSI(88) SH 1, London: Department of Health and Social Security.

NHS Health and Social Care Information Centre (2005) *Guardianship under the Mental Health Act 1983, England 2005*, London: Department of Health.

NICHOLSON, R., EKENSTAM, C. and NORWOOD, S. (1996) 'Coercion and the outcome of psychiatric hospitalisation', *International Journal of Law and Psychiatry* 19:2: 201.

NORFOLK, G. (1997) 'Fitness to be interviewed: a proposed definition and scheme of examination', *Medicine, Science and Law* 37(3): 228.

NORFOLK, SUFFOLK and Cambridgeshire Health Authority (2003) *Independent Inquiry into the Death of David Bennett*, Cambridge: Norfolk, Suffolk and Cambridgeshire Health Authority.

NORRIS, C., FIELDING, N., KEMP, C. and FIELDING J. (1992) 'Black and blue: an analysis of the influence of race on being stopped by the police', *British Journal of Sociology* 43(2): 207.

O'DOHERTY, S. (2003) 'Judicial review: the death of *Wednesbury*', *Justice of the Peace* 167: 24–6.

O'LEARY, D. and LEE, M. (1996) 'Seven-year prognosis in depression: mortality and readmission risk in the Nottingham ECT cohort', *British Journal of Psychiatry* 169: 423–9.

OBORNE, A.C., HOOPER, R., SWIFT, C.G. and JACKSON, S.H.D. (2003) 'Explicit, evidence-based criteria to assess the quality of prescribing to elderly nursing home residents', *Age and Aging* 32: 102–8.

Office for National Statistics (2006) *Suicides* (available online at http://www.statistics.gov.uk/cci/nugget.asp?id = 1092) last accessed 16 February 2007.

ONYETT, S., HEPPLESTON, T. and BUSHNELL, D. (1994) 'A national survey of community mental health team structure and process', *Journal of Mental Health* 3: 175.

OPENMIND (1995) 'Older women and ECT', *Openmind* 74: 10.

ORBACH, S. (1993) *Hunger Strike: The Anorectic's Struggle as a Metaphor for our Age*, Harmondsworth: Penguin.

OWEN, A.L., SASHIDHARAN, S.P. and EDWARDS, L.I. (2000) 'Availability and acceptability of home treatment for acute psychiatric disorders: a national survey of mental health trusts and health authority purchasers', *Psychiatric Bulletin* 24: 169–71.

OWEN, S., AVIS, M. and KHALIL, E. (2004) *A Scoping Exercise for a Health Strategy for Women in Custody in England and Wales: Final Academic Report Submitted to the HM Prison Service*, London: Department of Health.

PALMER, C. (1996) 'Still vulnerable after all these years', *Criminal Law Review*: 633.

PARKER, J., De VILLIERS, J. and CHURCHWARD, S. (2002) 'High-dose antipsychotic drug use in a forensic setting', *Journal of Forensic Psychiatry* 13: 407–15.

PARKIN, A. (1994) 'Case note on *R v Canons Park Mental Health Review Tribunal, ex parte A*', *Journal of Social Welfare and Family Law*: 331.

PARKIN, A. (1995) 'Where now on mental incapacity?', *Web Journal of Current Legal Issues* 2.

PARKIN, A. (1996) 'Caring for patients in the community', *Modern Law Review* 59(3): 414.

PARKMAN, S., DAVIES, S., LEESE, M., PHELAN, M. and THORNICROFE, G. (1997) 'Ethnic differences in satisfaction with mental health services among representative people with psychosis in south London: PriSM study 4', *British Journal of Psychiatry* 171: 260.

PARSONS, S., WALKER, L. and GRUBIN, D. (2001) 'Prevalence of mental disorder in female remand prisons', *Journal of Forensic Psychiatry* 12(1): 104–202.

PEAY, J. (1981) 'Mental health review tribunals: just or efficacious safeguards?', *Law and Human Behaviour* 5: 161.

Peay, J. (1988) 'Offenders suffering from psychopathic disorder: the rise and demise of a consultation document', *British Journal of Criminology* 28: 67.

Peay, J. (1989) *Tribunals on Trial: A Study of Decision-Making under the Mental Health Act 1983*, Oxford: Clarendon.

Peay, J. (1997) 'Mentally disordered offenders', in M. Maguire, R. Morgan and R. Reiner (eds) *The Oxford Handbook of Criminology*, Oxford: Oxford University Press.

Peay, J. (2002) 'Mentally disordered offenders', in M. Maguire, R. Morgan and R. Reiner (eds) *The Oxford Handbook of Criminology*, 3rd edn, Oxford: Oxford University Press.

Peay, J. (2003) *Decisions and Dilemmas: Working with Mental Health Law*, Oxford: Hart.

Peay, J. Roberts, C. and Eastman, N. (2001) 'Legal knowledge of mental health professionals: report of a national survey', *Journal of Mental Health Law* 5: 44–55.

Pegler, J. (2002) *A Can of Madness*, London: Chipmunka.

Perkins, E. (2000) *Decision-making in Mental Health Review Tribunals*, London: Department of Health.

Perkins, R. (1996) 'Choosing ECT', in J. Read and J. Reynolds (eds) *Speaking Our Minds: An Anthology*, London: Macmillan.

Perring, C. (1992) 'The experience and perspectives of patients and care staff of the transition from hospital to community-based care', in S. Ramon (ed) *Psychiatric Hospital Closure: Myths and Realities*, London: Chapman and Hall.

Perrucci, R. (1974) *Circle of Madness: On Being Insane and Institutionalized in America*, New Jersey: Prentice-Hall.

Pierpoint, H. (2001) 'The performance of volunteer appropriate adults: a survey of call outs', *Howard Journal of Criminal Justice* 40(3): 255–71.

Pierpoint, H. (2006) 'Reconstructing the role of appropriate adult in England and Wales', *Criminology and Criminal Justice* 6(2): 219–37.

Pilgrim, D. (1995) 'Letter to…', *The Psychologist* 8: 9.

Pilgrim, D. and Rogers, A. (1999) *A Sociology of Mental Health and Illness*, 2nd edn, Buckingham: Open University Press.

Pokorny, M. (1994) 'Structure of the United Kingdom Council for Psychotherapy and list of its member organisations', in P. Clarkson and M. Pokorny (eds) *The Handbook of Psychotherapy*, London: Routledge.

Polythress, N.G., Bonnie, R.J., Monahan, J., Otto, R. and Hodge, S.K. (2002) *Adjudicative Competence: The MacArthur Studies*, New York: Plenum.

Porter, R. (1987a) *Mind-Forg'd Manacles: A History of Madness in England from the Restoration to the Regency*, London: Athlone Press.

Porter, R. (1987b) *A Social History of Madness: Stories of the Insane*, London: Nicholson and Weidenfeld.

Postle, D. (1999) '*Psychotherapy professionalisation and statutory regulation*', available on G.O.R.I.L.L.A. (online at http://www.mind-gymnasium.com/confront UKPP/bathbcp.htm).

Poulsen, H.D. (2002) 'The prevalence of extralegal deprivation of liberty in a psychiatric hospital population', *International Journal of Law and Psychiatry* 15: 29–36.

Pourgourides, C., Prasher, V. and Oyebode, F. (1992) 'Use of section 5(2) in clinical practice', *Psychiatric Bulletin* 16: 14.

Price, D. (1994) 'Civil commitment of the mentally ill: compelling arguments for reform', *Medical Law Review* 2: 321.

Priebe, S. and Turner, T. (2003) 'Reinstitutionalisation in mental health care', *British Medical Journal* 326: 175–6.

Prins, H. (1995) 'What price the concept of psychopathic disorder?', *Medicine, Science and Law* 35: 307.

Prins, H. (2002) '*Cui bono*? Withholding treatment from violent and abusive patients in NHS trusts: "we don't have to take this"', *Journal of Forensic Psychiatry* 13(2): 291–406.

PRIOR, L. (1993) *The Social Organisation of Mental Illness*, London: Sage.

PRIOR, L. (1996) 'The appeal to madness in Ireland', in D.Tomlinson and J. Carrier (eds) *Asylum in the Community*, London: Routledge.

PRIOR, P. (1992) 'The approved social worker: reflections on origins', *British Journal of Social Work* 22: 105.

PRITCHARD, E. (2006) *Appropriate Adult Provision in England and Wales*, London: NAAN.

PROCHASKA, F. (1988) *The Voluntary Impulse: Philanthropy in Modern Britain*, London: Faber and Faber.

RABIN, C. and ZELNER, D. (1992) 'The role of assertiveness in clarifying roles and strengthening job satisfaction of social workers in multidisciplinary mental health settings', *British Journal of Social Work* 22: 17.

RAMON, S. (1992) 'The context of hospital closure in the Western world, or why now?', in S. RAMON (ed) *Psychiatric Hospital Closure: Myths and Realities*, London: Chapman and Hall.

RASSABY, E. and ROGERS, A. (1987) 'Psychiatric referrals from the police', *Bulletin of the Royal College of Psychiatrists* 11: 78.

READ, J. and REYNOLDS, J. (eds) (1996) *Speaking Our Minds: An Anthology*, London: Macmillan.

REED, J. (1994) *Report of the Department of Health and Home Office Working Group on Psychopathic Disorder*, London: Department of Health and Home Office.

REED, J. (1996) 'Psychopathology: a clinical and legal dilemma', *British Journal of Psychiatry* 168: 4.

REED, J. (2002) 'Delivering psychiatric care to prisoners: problems and solutions', *Advanced Psychiatric Treatment* 8(2): 117–25.

REED, J. and LYNE, M. (2000) 'Inpatient care of mentally ill people in prison: results of a year's programme of semistructured inspections', *British Medical Journal* 320: 1031–4.

REES, G., HUBY, G., McDADE, L. and McKECHNIE, L. (2004) 'Joint working in community mental health teams: implementation of an integrated care pathway', *Health and Social Care in the Community* 12(6): 527–36.

REILLY, J.G., AYIS, S.A., FERRIER, I.N. and JONES, S.J. (2002) 'Thioridazine and sudden unexplained death in psychiatric inpatients', *British Journal of Psychiatry* 180: 515–22.

RETHINK (2006) *A Cut Too Far: A Rethink Report into Budget Cuts Affecting Mental Health Services*, London: Rethink

RICHARDSON, G. (1993) *Law, Process and Custody: Prisoners and Patients*, London: Weidenfeld and Nicolson.

RICHARDSON, G. and MACHIN, D. (1999) 'A clash of values? Mental health review tribunals and judicial review', *Journal of Mental Health Law* 1(1): 3.

RICHARDSON, G. and MACHIN, D. (2000) 'Judicial review and tribunal decision making: a study of the mental health review tribunal', *Public Law* Autumn: 494–514.

RICHARDSON, G. and MACHIN, D. (2000a) 'Doctors on tribunals: a confusion of roles', *British Journal of Psychiatry* 176: 110–15.

RICKFORD, D. (2003) *Troubled Inside: Responding to the Mental Health Needs of Women in Prison*, London: Prison Reform Trust.

RICKFORD, D. and EDGAR, K. (2005) *Troubled Inside: Responding to the Mental Health Needs of Men in Prison*, London: Prison Reform Trust.

RIORDAN, S., WIX, S., KENNEY-HERBERT, J. and HUMPHREYS, M. (2000) 'Diversion at the point of arrest: mentally disordered people and contact with the police', *Journal of Forensic Psychiatry* 3(1): 683–90.

ROBERTS, J. and PINES, M. (eds) (1991) *The Practice of Group Analysis*, London: Routledge.

ROBERTSON, G. (1989) 'The restricted hospital order', *Psychiatric Bulletin* 13: 4.

ROBERTSON, G., PEARSON, R. and GIBB, R. (1996) 'Police interviewing and the use of appropriate adults', *Journal of Forensic Psychiatry* 7(2): 297.

ROGERS, A. (1990) 'Policing mental disorder: controversies, myths and realities', *Social Policy and Administration* 24: 226.

ROGERS, A. (1993) 'Coercion and "voluntary" admission: an examination of psychiatric patient views', *Behavioral Sciences and the Law* 11: 259.

ROGERS, A. and FAULKNER, A. (1987) *A Place of Safety: MIND's Research into Police Referrals to the Pscyhiatric Services*, London: MIND.

ROGERS, A. and PILGRIM, D. (2001) *Mental Health Policy in Britain: A Critical Introduction*, 2nd edn, Basingstoke: Palgrave.

ROGERS, A. and PILGRIM, D. (2005) *A Sociology of Mental Health and Illness*, Maidenhead: Open University Press.

ROGERS, A., PILGRIM, D. and LACEY, R. (1993) *Experiencing Psychiatry: Users' Views of Services*, London: Macmillan.

ROGERS, W. (2006) *Winfield and Jolowicz on Tort*, 17th edn, London: Sweet and Maxwell.

ROMANO, D. (1997) 'The legal advocate and the questionably competent client in the context of a poverty law clinic', *Osgoode Hall Law Journal* 35: 737.

ROMILLY, C., PARROTT, J. and CARNEY, P. (1997) 'Limited duration restriction orders: what are they for?', *Journal of Forensic Psychiatry* 8(3): 562.

ROSE, N. (1985) 'Unreasonable rights: mental illness and the limits of the law', *Journal of Law and Society* 12(2): 199.

ROSE, N. (1986) 'Law, psychiatry and rights', in P. Miller and N. Rose (eds) *The Power of Psychiatry*, Cambridge: Polity Press.

ROSENHAN, D.L. (1973) 'On being sane in insane places', *Science* 179: 250.

ROSSAU, C. and MORTENSEN, P. (1997) 'Risk factors or suicide in patients with schizophrenia: nested case-study analysis', *British Journal of Psychiatry* 171: 355–69.

ROTH, L. (1979). 'A commitment law for patients, doctors and lawyers', *American Journal of Psychiatry* 136: 1121.

ROTH, L., MEISEL, A. and LIDZ, C. (1977) 'Tests of competency to consent to treatment', *American Journal of Psychiatry* 134(3): 279.

ROTH, M. (1990) 'Psychopathic (sociopathic) personality', in R. Blugrass and P. Bowden (eds) *Principles and Practice in Forensic Psychiatry*, London: Churchill Livingstone.

ROWLANDS, R., INCH, H., RODGER, W. and SOLIMAN, A. (1996) 'Diverted to where? What happens to the diverted mentally disordered offender', *Journal of Forensic Psychiatry* 7(2): 284.

Royal College of Psychiatrists (1993) *Consensus Report on the Use of High Dosage Antipsychotic Medicine*, CR26, London: Royal College of Psychiatrists.

Royal College of Psychiatrists (1998) *Management of Imminent Violence*, London: Royal College of Psychiatrists.

Royal College of Psychiatrists (1998a) *Psychiatric Beds and Resources: Factors Influencing Bed Use and Service Planning*, London: Royal College of Psychiatrists.

Royal College of Psychiatrists (2000) *Good Psychiatric Practice 2000*, CR83, London: Royal College of Psychiatrists.

Royal College of Psychiatrists (2002) 'Response to the Draft Mental Health Bill', reprinted in *Journal of Mental Health Law* 8: 376–9.

Royal College of Psychiatrists and the Law Society (2002) *Joint Statement on the*

Reform of the Mental Health Act 1983, London: Royal College of Psychiatrists and Law Society.

Royal Commission on Criminal Justice (1993) *Report of the Royal Commission on Criminal Justice*, Cm 2263, London: HMSO.

Royal Commission on Criminal Procedure (1981) *Report of the Royal Commission on Criminal Procedure*, Cmnd 8092, London: HMSO.

Royal Commission on Long-term Care (1999) *With Respect to Old Age: Long-term Care – Rights and Responsibilities* (the 'Sutherland Report'), Cm 4192-I, London: HMSO.

Royal Commission on the Law Relating to Mental Illness and Mental Deficiency 1954–1957 (the 'Percy Commission') (1957) *Report*, Cmnd 169, London: HMSO.

RUSCHENA, D., MULLEN, P., BURGESS, P., CORDNER, S., BARRY-WALSH J., DRUMMER, O., PALMER, S., BROWNE, C. and WALLACE, C. (1998) 'Sudden death in psychiatric patients', *British Journal of Psychiatry* 172: 331.

RUSSELL, D. (1995) *Women, Madness and Medicine*, Cambridge: Polity.

SAAD, K. and SASHIDHARAN, S. (1994) 'Mental health review tribunals', *Psychiatric Bulletin* 16: 470.

SACKETT, K. (1996) 'Discharges from section 3 of the Mental Health Act 1983: changes in practice', *Health Trends* 28: 66.

Sainsbury Centre and Mental Health Act Commission (2005) *Back on Track? CPA Care Planning for Service Users who are Repeatedly Detained under the Mental Health Act*, London: Sainsbury Centre for Mental Health

Sainsbury Centre for Mental Health (2005) *Acute Care 2004: A National Survey of Adult Psychiatric Wards in England*, London: The Sainsbury Centre for Mental Health.

Sainsbury Centre for Mental Health (2006) *Under Pressure: The Finances of Mental Health Trusts in 2006*, London: The Sainsbury Centre for Mental Health.

SANDLAND, R. (1994) 'The common law and the "informal" minor patient', *Journal of Forensic Psychiatry* 5(3): 569.

SANDLAND, R. (2000) 'Mental Health Act guardianship and the protection of children', *Journal of Mental Health Law*: 186–95.

SANGER, D. (2006) 'The pharmacology and mechanisms of action of atypical antipsychotic drugs: dopamine and beyond', *Annals of General Psychiatry* 5(Suppl 1):S34

SASHIDHARAN, S. (2001) 'Institutional racism in British Psychiatry', *Psychiatric Bulletin* 25: 244.

SCHWEHR, B. (1997) 'The relevance of resources to the assessment of need and the provision of services for the disabled', *Journal of Forensic Psychiatry* 8(3): 662.

Scottish Executive Central Research Unit (2001) *Mentally Disordered Offenders and the Use of Hospital Directions and Interim Hospital Orders*, Crime and Criminal Justice Research Findings No 56, Edinburgh: Scottish Executive.

SCULL, A. (1977) *Decarceration: Community Treatment and the Deviant – A Radical View*, Englewood Cliffs, NY: Prentice Hall.

SCULL, A. (1979) *Museums of Madness*, Harmondsworth: Penguin.

SCULL, A. (1993) *The Most Solitary of Afflictions: Madness and Society in Britain, 1700–1900*, New Haven: Yale University Press.

SCULL, A. (1996) 'Mental patients and the community: a critical note', *International Journal of Law and Psychiatry* 9: 383.

SEDGWICK, P. (1982) *Psychopolitics*, London: Pluto Press.

SHAH, A. (1993) 'An increase in violent behaviour among psychiatric inpatients: real or apparent?', *Medicine, Science and Law* 33: 227.

SHAW, J., HUNT, I.M., FLYNN, S., MEEHAN, J., ROBINSON, J., BICKLEY, H., PARSONS, R., McCANN, K., BURNS, J., AMOS, T., KAPUR, N. and APPLEBY, L. (2006) 'Rates of mental disorder in people convicted of homicide: National Clinical Survey', *British Journal of Psychiatry* 188: 143–7.

SHELFORD, L. (1847) *Practical Treatise of the Law Concerning Lunatics, Idiots, and Persons of Unsound Mind*, 2nd edn, London: Sweet.

SHORT, J. (1995) 'Characteristics of absconders from acute admission wards', *Journal of Forensic Psychiatry* 6(2): 277.

SHUBSACHS, A., HUWS, R., CLOSE, A., LARKIN, E. and FALVEY, J. (1995) 'Male Afro-Caribbean patients admitted to Rampton hospital between 1977 and 1986', *Medicine, Science and Law* 35(4): 336.

SILVERSTONE, T. and TURNER, P. (1995) *Drug Treatment in Psychiatry*, 5th edn, London: Routledge.

SINGLETON, N., MELTZER, H. and GATWARD, R. (1998) *Psychiatric Morbidity among Prisoners in England and Wales*, Office of National Statistics, London: HMSO.

SMITH, A. and HUMPHREYS, M. (1997) 'Physical restraint of patients in a psychiatric hospital', *Medicine, Science and Law* 37(2): 145.

SMITH, D. (1990) 'K is mentally ill: the anatomy of a factual account', in *Texts, Facts, and Femininity: Exploring the Relations of Ruling*, London: Routledge.

SMITH, J., DONOVAN, M. and GORDON, H. (1991) 'Patients in Broadmoor hospital from the south-western region: an audit of transfer procedures', *Psychiatric Bulletin* 15: 81.

SMITH, J.C. (2000) 'Comment on *R v Antoine*', *Criminal Law Review*: 621–6.

SMITH, R. (1981) *Trial by Medicine: Insanity and Responsibility in Victorian Trials*, Edinburgh: Edinburgh University Press.

SMYTH, M.G. and HOULT, J. (2000) 'The home treatment enigma', *British Medical Journal* 320: 305–9.

Social Services Inspectorate (2002) *Modernising Mental Health Services: Inspection of Mental Health Services*, London: Department of Health.

Social Services Inspectorate and Audit Commission (2001) *Delivering Results*, London: Audit Commission.

SOLOMKA, B. (1996) 'The role of psychiatric evidence in passing "longer than normal" sentences', *Journal of Forensic Psychiatry* 7(2): 239.

SOMERVILLE, M. (1994) 'Labels versus contents: variance between philosophy, psychiatry and law in concepts governing decision-making', *McGill Law Journal* 39: 179.

SOOTHILL K. *et al.* (1981) 'Compulsory admissions to mental hospitals in six countries', *International Journal of Law and Psychiatry* 4: 327.

SOOTHILL, K., KUPITKSA, P. and MACMILLAN, F. (1990b) 'Compulsory hospital admissions: dangerous decisions?', *Medicine, Science and Law* 30(1): 17.

SOOTHILL, K., KUPITKSA, P., BADIANI, D. and MACMILLAN, F. (1990a) 'Compulsory admission to mental hospitals: a replication study', *International Journal of Law and Psychiatry* 13: 179.

SPANDLER, H. and VICK, N. (2005) 'Enabling access to direct payments: an exploration of care co-ordinators decision making practices', *Journal of Mental Health Law* 14(2): 145–55.

SPANDLER, H. and VICK, N. (2006) 'Opportunities for independent living using direct payments in mental health', *Health and Social Care in the Community* 14(2): 107–15.

SPENCE, S. and McPHILLIPS, M. (1995) 'Personality disorder and police section 136 in Westminster: a retrospective analysis of 65 cases over six months', *Medicine, Science and Law* 35(1): 48.

SPITZER, R. (1976) 'More on pseudoscience in science and the case for psychiatric diagnosis', *Archives of General Psychiatry* 33: 459.

STANTON, K. (1994) *The Modern Law of Tort*, London: Sweet and Maxwell.

STARMER, K. (2003) 'Two Years of the Human Rights Act', *European Human Rights Law Review* 1: 14–23.

Steering Committee on Bioethics (2000) *White Paper on the Protection of the Human Rights and Dignity of People Suffering from Mental Disorder, Especially as Involuntary Patients in a Psychiatric Establishment*, Council of Ministers's documents, 23 (Addendum), Strasbourg: Council of Europe.

STEIN, G. (1993) 'Drug treatment of personality disorders', in P. Tyre and G. Stein (eds) *Personality Disorder Reviewed*, London: Gaskell Books.

STONE, H. (1992) 'Depot neuroleptics: involuntary castration?', *Journal of Forensic Psychiatry* 3(1): 7.

STREET, R. (1998) *The Restricted Hospital Order: From Court to the Community*, Home Office Research Study 186, London: Home Office Research and Statistics Directorate.

STURDY, H. and PARRY-JONES, W. (1999) 'Boarding-out insane patients: the significance of the Scottish system 1857–1913', in P. Bartlett and D. Wright (eds) *Outside the Walls of the Asylum*, London: Athlone.

STYRON, W. (1990) *Darkness Visible*, London: Cape.

STYRON, W. (1996) 'Darkness visible', in S. Dunn, B. Morrison and M. Roberts (eds) *Mind Readings: Writers' Journeys through Mental States*, London: Minerva.

SUTO, W., CLARE, C. and HOLLAND, A. (2002) 'Substitute financial decision-making in England and Wales: a study of the Court of Protection', *Journal of Social Welfare and Family Law* 21(4): 37.

SUZUKI, A. (1991) 'Lunacy in seventeenth- and eighteenth-century England: analysis of Quarter Sessions records Part I', *History of Psychiatry* 2: 437.

SUZUKI, A. (1992) 'Lunacy in seventeenth- and eighteenth-century England: analysis of Quarter Sessions records Part II', *History of Psychiatry* 3: 29.

SUZUKI, A. (1995) 'The politics and ideology of non-restraint: the case of the Hanwell Asylum', *Medical History* 39: 1.

SZASZ, T. (1970) *Ideology and Insanity: Essays on the Psychiatric Dehumanisation of Man*, Garden City: Doubleday.

SZMUKLER, G. and HOLLOWAY, F. (2000) 'Reform of the Mental Health Act: health or safety?', *British Journal of Psychiatry* 177: 196–200.

TAVERNOR, R., SWINTON, M. and TAVERNOR, S. (2000) 'High-dose antipsychotic medication in maximum security', *Journal of Forensic Psychiatry* 11: 36–48.

TAXIS, J.C. (2002) 'Ethics and praxis: alternative strategies to physical restraint and seclusion in a psychiatric setting', *Issues in Mental Health Nursing* 23(2): 157–70.

TAYLOR, J. and GUNN, J. (1984) 'Violence and psychosis: 1 – Risk of riolence among psychotic men', *British Medical Journal* 288: 1945.

TAYLOR, L. (1996) 'ECT is barbaric', in J. Read and J. Reynolds (eds) *Speaking Our Minds: An Anthology*, London: Macmillan.

TAYLOR, P. and GUNN, J. (1999) 'Homicides by people with mental illness: myth and reality', *British Journal of Psychiatry* 174: 9.

TAYLOR, S. (1989) *Positive Illusions: Creative Self-deception and the Healthy Mind*, New York, Basic Books.

TENNENT, G., TENNENT, D., PRINS, H. and BEDFORD, A. (1993) 'Is psychopathic disorder a treatable condition?', *Medicine, Science and Law* 33: 63.

THACKREY, M. and BOBBITT, R. (1990) 'Patient aggression against clinical and non-clinical staff in a VA medical center', *Hospital and Community Psychiatry* 41: 195.

THOMAS, C., STONE, K., OSBORN, M., THOMAS, P. and FISHER, M. (1993) 'Psychiatric morbidity and compulsory admission among UK-born Europeans, Afro-Caribbeans and Asians in Central Manchester', *British Journal of Psychiatry* 163: 91.

THOMAS, D.A. (2004) 'The Criminal Justice Act 2003: custodial sentences', *Criminal Law Review*: 702–11.

THOMAS, P. (1997) *The Dialectics of Schizophrenia*, London: Free Association Books.

THOMAS, T. (1986) *The Police and Social Workers Community Care Practice Handbooks*, London: Gower.

THOMPSON, A., SHAW, M., HARRISON, G., DAVIDON, H., GUNNELL, D. and VEUE, J. (2004) 'Patterns of hospital admission for adult psychiatric illness in England: analysis of hospital episode statistics data', *British Journal of Psychiatry* 185: 334–41.

THOMPSON, R. (2005) 'Community law and the limits of deference', *European Human Rights Law Review* 3: 243–58.

THOMSON, M. (1996) 'Family, community and state: the micro politics of mental deficiency', in A. Digby and D. Wright (eds) *From Idiocy to Mental Deficiency*, London: Routledge.

THOMSON, M. (1998) 'Community care and the control of mental defectives in inter-war Britain', in P. Horden and D. Smith (eds) *The Locus of Care*, London: Routledge.

THORNICROFT, G. (2004) 'Specifying needs appropriate to placement outside special hospitals over time', *The Research Findings Register*, Summary No. 1296 (available online at http://www.refer.nhs.uk/ViewRecord.asp?ID=1296) last accessed on 7 August 2006.

THORNICROFT, G. (2006) *Shunned: Discrimination Against People with Mental Illness*, Oxford: Oxford University Press.

THOROGOOD, N. (1989) 'Afro-Caribbean women's experience of the health service', *New Community* 15(3): 319.

TIDMARSH, D. (1978) *Broadmoor Ins and Outs*, unpublished paper presented to the Forensic Section of Royal College of Psychiatrists, Broadmoor Hospital, 23 May.

TIDMARSH, D. (1995) 'Homicide and community care', *Journal of Forensic Psychiatry* 6(1): 1.

TOEWS J., EL-GUEBALY, N. and LECKIE, A. (1984) 'Patients' attitudes at the time of their commitment', *Canadian Journal of Psychiatry* 26: 251.

TOMISON, A. (1989) 'Characteristics of psychiatric hospital absconders', *British Journal of Psychiatry* 154: 368.

Tribunals Service (2005) *New Procedures Concerning the Rights of Access to MHRT Hearings of Victims of Certain Criminal Offences Committed by Patients*, London: Tribunals Service.

TYLER, T.R. (1996) 'The psychological consequences of judicial procedures: implications for civil commitment hearings', in D.B. Wexler and B.J. Winick (eds) *Law in a Therapeutic Key: Developments in Therapeutic Jurisprudence*, Durham, NC: Carolina Academic Press.

UK Central Council for Nursing, Midwifery and Health Visiting (1998) *Guidelines for Mental Health and Learning Disabilities Nursing: A Guide to Working with Vulnerable Clients*, London: UKCC.

UK Central Council for Nursing, Midwifery and Health Visiting (2001) *UKCC Position Statement on the Covert Administration of Medicines: Disguising Medicine in Food and Drink*, London: UKCC.

United Nations (1991) *General Assembly Resolution 46/119*, 17 December 1991.

UNSWORTH, C. (1987) *The Politics of Mental Health Legislation*, Oxford: Oxford University Press.

VAUGHAN, P., KELLY, M. and PULLEN, M. (2001) 'The working practices of the police in relation to mentally disordered offenders and diversion services', *Medicine, Science and Law* 41: 13–20.

WALKER, N. (1996) 'Hybrid orders', *Journal of Forensic Psychiatry* 7(3): 469.

WALKER, N. and McCabe, S. (1973) *Crime and Insanity in England Vol. 1: The Historical Perspective*, Edinburgh: Edinburgh University Press.

WALLCRAFT, J. (1996) 'Some models of asylum and help in times of crisis', in D. Tomlinson and J. Carrier (eds) *Asylum in the Community*, London: Routledge.

WALMSLEY, J., ATKINSON, D. and ROLPH, S. (1999) 'Community care and mental deficiency 1913 to 1945', in P. Bartlett and D. Wright (eds) *Outside the Walls of the Asylum*, London: Athlone.

WEBB, A. and HOBDELL, M. (1980) 'Co-ordination and team work in the health and personal social services', in S. Lonsdale, A. Webb and T. Briggs (eds) *Teamwork in the Personal Social Services*, London: Croom Helm.

WELSH, S. and DEAHL, M. (2002) 'Covert medication: ever ethically justifiable?', *Psychiatric Bulletin* 26: 123–6.

West London Mental Health NHS Trust (2004) *Annual Report and Accounts 2003/04*, London: West London Mental Health NHS Trust.

West London Mental Health NHS Trust (n.d.) *Broadmoor Hospital General Information Booklet*, London: West London Mental Health NHS Trust.

WEST, D. (1996) 'Sexual molesters', in N. Walker (ed) *Dangerous People*, London: Blackstone.

WHELAN, R. (1999) *Involuntary Action: How Voluntary is the 'Voluntary' Sector?*, London: Institute of Economic Affairs.

WHITE, C. (2002) 'Re-assessing the social worker's role as an appropriate adult', *Journal of Social Welfare and Family Law* 24(1): 55–65.

WHITE, S. (1992) 'The Criminal Procedure (Insanity and Unfitness to Plead) Act', *Criminal Law Review*: 4.

WHITEHORN, N. (1991) *Heywood and Massey, Court of Protection Practice*, London, Sweet and Maxwell.

WICKS, E. (2001) 'The right to refuse medical treatment under the European Convention on Human Rights', *Medical Law Review* 9: 17–40.

WIDDETT, C. and THOMSON, M. (1997) 'Justifying treatment and other stories', *Feminist Legal Studies* 5: 84.

WILKINSON, P. and SHARPE, M. (1993) 'What happens to patients discharged by mental health review tribunals?', *Psychiatric Bulletin* 17: 337.

WILLIAMS, J. (2000) 'The inappropriate adult', *Journal of Social Welfare and Family Law* 22(1): 43–57.

WILLIAMS, M., LLOYD. K. and HAYRE, C. (2005) 'Mental disordered offenders and prison health care in remand settings', *Prison Service Journal* 162: 24–8.

WILSON, P. (1996) 'The Law Commission's report on mental incapacity: medically vulnerable adults or politically vulnerable law?', *Medical Law Review* 4: 227.

WING, J. (1988) 'Abandoning what?', *British Journal of Clinical Psychology* 27: 325.

WINICK, B. (1994) 'The right to refuse mental health treatment: a therapeutic jurisprudence analysis', *International Journal of Law and Psychiatry* 17(1): 99.

WISTOW, G. (1994) 'Community care futures: inter-agency relationships: stability or continuing change', in M. Titterton (ed) *Caring for People in the Community*, London: Jessica Kingsley.

WISTOW, G. (1995) 'Coming apart at the seams', *Health Service Journal* 2: 24.

WOLBERG, L. (1954) *The Technique of Psychotherapy*, New York: Grune and Stratton.

WOOD, J. (1997) 'Foreword', in Department of Health, (1997) *Mental Health Review Tribunals for England and Wales Annual Report 1996*, London: Department of Health.

WRIGHT, D. (1997) 'Getting out of the asylum: understanding confinement of the insane in the nineteenth century', *Social History of Medicine* 10: 137.

WRIGHT, S. (2003) 'Control and restraint techniques in the management of violence in inpatient psychiatry: a critical review', *Medicine, Science and Law* 43(1): 31–8.

ZEDNER, L. (1991) *Women, Crime and Custody in Victorian England*, Oxford: Oxford University Press.

Index

Aarvold Committee 368
ability to understand 513–15
abnormally aggressive or
    seriously irresponsible
    conduct
    guardianship 490, 503
    Mental Health Act 2005 576
    mental illness, definition of 48
    mental impairment, definition
        of 36–9
    psychopathic disorders 40–1
ABRP (Advisory Board on
    Restricted Patients) 368–9
absconding see absence without
    leave
absence without leave 429–33
    arrest 431–2
    assisting persons in being
        absent, offence of 590
    discharge by absconding,
        achieving 431, 433
    duration of absence 431
    entry and search, police
        powers of 432
    extension of detention 431,
        433
    gender 430
    harbouring, offence of 590
    hospitals, absence from
        429–30
    informal patients 430
    meaning 429–30
    Mental Health Act 1983
        429–32
    Mental Health Review
        Tribunals 397–8
    police 431–2
    public protection 430–1
    race 430
    reports 433
    restricted patients 254–5, 398
    suicide, risk of 431, 432
    warrants, issue of 431–2
absolute discharge
    conditionally discharged
        persons 406–8
    dangerousness 406–8
    fitness to stand trial 232–3
    liberty and security, right
        to 406

Mental Health Act 1983 406–8
Mental Health Review
    Tribunals 406–8, 423
mental health system 379
recall, liability to 406–8
restricted patients 406–8,
    415, 417
Accelerated Discharge
    Programme (ADP) 98
accommodation see also housing;
    housing authorities; National
    Assistance Act 1948, Pt III,
    accommodation services
    under; residential
    accommodation
acquiescence to admission
    115–20, 153
actus reus 233–8
ACUS see aftercare under
    supervision (ACUs)
adjournments 386–7, 392
admission see admission for
    assessment; admission for
    treatment;
    admission to hospital; emergency
    admissions; informal
    admission
admission for assessment 111,
    126–8
    approved social workers
        (ASWs) 128, 164–5
    best interests of the patient 557
    certificates, requirement for
        128
    civil confinement 122–4,
        126–7, 180
    code of practice 128
    criteria 126–8
    dangerousness requirement
        128
    mental disorder
        nature and degree to require
            hospitalization, meaning
            of 127–8
        patient suffering from a
            126–7
    Mental Health Act 1983
        section 2 126–8, 138
    Mental Health Review
        Tribunals 377, 387

nearest relatives 173
taking patient to hospital 180
admission for treatment 128–33
    approved social workers 164–5
    certificates, requirement for
        129
    civil confinement 122–5,
        128–33, 164–5
    criteria 128–30
    informal admission 112–14,
        116
    Mental Health Act 1983
        section 3 128–33
    Mental Health Review
        Tribunals 377
    mental impairment 129
    nearest relatives 173
    Percy Commission 131
    psychopathic disorders 129,
        130–1
    severe mental impairment 131
    social control 131
    treatability test 129–32
admission of person already in
    hospital
    holding power for doctors and
        nurses 133–4, 138–9
    immediate restraint, necessity
        for 134
    informal admissions 133
    leave, attempts to 133–4, 153
    Mental Health Act 1983
        section 5 133–4, 138–9
admission to hospital 111–54 see
    also admission for assessment;
    admission for treatment
    already in hospital, admission
        of patients 133–4, 138–9
    capacity 149–51
    civil confinement 111, 120–6,
        153
    dangerousness 145–9, 151
    emergency admissions 134–5,
        138
    holding power for doctors and
        nurses 133–4, 138–9
    immediate restraint, necessity
        for 134
    informal admissions 111–20,
        133, 153

admission to hospital (*cont.*)
Justices of the Peace, powers
of, 135–6
leave, attempts to 133–4, 153
Mental Health Act 1983
section 5 133–4, 138–9
outpatient admissions 138
police 111, 136–8
policy 145
standards 154
Stone system 151–3
admissions *see* admission for
assessment; admission for
treatment;
admission to hospital; emergency
admissions; informal
admission
ADP (Accelerated Discharge
Programme) 98
advance decisions regarding
treatment 569–71
best interests test 547, 570
change of circumstances
570–1
civil confinement 570
common law 545, 571
Court of Protection 548–9,
559, 571
drug therapy 570–1
euthanasia 545
formalities 571
informal patients 570
lasting powers of attorney 57,
562
Mental Health Act 2005
545–7, 569–71
refusal of treatment, as 545,
547, 570
personal care 569
substitute decision-making
558
treatment, definition of
569–70
advance directives 545, 547 *see*
also advance decisions
regarding treatment
capacity 528–31
change of circumstances
570–1
enduring powers of attorney
528
medical treatment, refusal of
528–9
standard of proof 528–9
substitute judgment 530–1
adversarial approach 392–3

Advisory Board on Restricted
Patients (ABRP) 368–9
advocacy 604–8 *see also*
representation
best interests of the patient
556–7
complaints 603
guardianship 488, 607
housing authorities 480–1
Human Rights Act 1998 601
independent advocates 556–7
informal admission 119
local authority
accommodation 556
medical treatment, consent to
556
Mental Health Act 2005 546
NHS accommodation 556
professional advocates,
appointment of 119
residential accommodation
556
role 556
affairs and property *see* property
and affairs, capacity and
Afro-Caribbean origins, persons
of 55, 140–3 *see also* race
aftercare in the community 21,
491–5 *see also* aftercare under
supervision (ACUs)
codes of practice 447–8
conditional discharge 410–12,
464–5
criminal proceedings 591
damages 598–600
discharge from hospital
availability of suitable care
following 366
blocking 464–9
duty to provide aftercare
464–9
Human Rights Act 1998 29–30
mandatory orders 466–7
Mental Health Act 1983 584–5
public authorities, Convention
rights and 468
refusal to provide 436
supervision 491–5
aftercare under supervision
(ACUs) 491–5
abolition of 493, 495
care programmes 492
coercion 492–5
dangerousness 491, 493
guardianship 491
health authorities 492

introduction of 492, 495
Primary Care Trusts 492
recalls 493–4
residence, power to convey to a
place of 492
responsible medical officers
(RMOs) 493
reviews 492
social services departments
492
supervised community
treatment (SCT),
replacement with 493–5
supervision registers 491–2
treatment, power to convey to
a place of 492
use of 492–3
aggressive conduct *see*
abnormally aggressive or
seriously irresponsible
conduct; violence
alcohol and drug dependency
35, 42–6, 202, 215
alcohol testing 99
anorexia 5–6
anti-anxiety drugs (minor
tranquillisers) 278
anti-depressants 8–9, 279
antipsychotics (neuroleptics or
major tranquillisers) 14, 78,
278–81, 290, 330–1
antisocial or dissocial personality
disorders 40–2
appeals
case stated 425–6
fitness to stand trial 223
appointment of receivers 499,
560, 564
appreciation of information
516–19, 526
appropriate adult scheme,
operation of 205–14
absence of appropriate adult,
interviews in 206, 208–9
cautions 206
confessions 207, 208–9, 212
detecting the need for
appropriate adult 209–10
diversion from prosecution
205–14, 272
evidence, exclusion of 212–14
facilitating communication, as
206–7
fitness for interview 211–12
forensic medical examiners,
role of 211–12

guardians, 207–8
guidance 206
interpreters 208
legal advice, right to 207
Mental Health Act 1983 205–6
miscarriages of justice 213
National Appropriate Adult
   Network (NAAN) 209,
   213–14
PACE and codes 205–14
parents 207–9, 214
persons who should act as
   appropriate adults 207–9
police detecting the need for
   appropriate adult 209–10
privilege 207
relatives 207–9, 214
retained, whether system of
   appropriate adults should
   be 212–14
role of 205–7, 212
samples, taking 206
silence, right to 207
social workers 209
solicitors
   acting as 208, 213
   role of attending 206–7
training 207–8, 209, 210, 213,
   272
vulnerable suspects 205–7
victim support volunteers 209
voluntary sector 209, 214
young offenders 205–6, 207,
   209
approved social workers (ASWs)
   21, 87 see also approved social
   workers (ASWs), civil
   confinement and
assessment, admission for 128
emergency admissions 135
habeas corpus 187–8
leave and recall 354–5
Mental Health Review
   Tribunals 427–9
police 140
approved social workers (ASWs),
   civil confinement and 123,
   155–65, 174
admission for treatment
   164–5
approved mental health
   professionals 163
assessments, admissions for
   164–5
British Association of Social
   Workers (BASW) 161

doctors, interaction with
   181–3
emergency admissions 134–5
entry and inspection, powers
   of 178–9
family and relatives,
   consultation of 163–4
interviews 177–9
local authorities 161–2
Mental Health Act 1983 160,
   162–4
mental welfare officers 160,
   161–2
multidisciplinary teamwork
   181–3
nearest relatives 160, 163–73
   appearing to be nearest
     relative, consulting
     persons 168–9
   consultation with 163–4,
     166–9
   reasonable enquiry, duty of
     168–9
   views of 163
number of 162
police 179
professionalisation 160–2
qualifications 161
psychiatrists, interaction with
   181–3, 197–8
recruitment problems 162
Richardson Committee 163
   training 160–3
violence or hostility towards
   178
welfarism 160–1
armed forces 195, 263
arrest 136–7, 140–4, 179, 431–2
arrested or incomplete
   development of mind 34–9,
   129, 300, 503
artistic genius, image of the 3
Ashworth Hospital 24, 66, 97–9,
   102–3, 327, 341–3, 373, 393
assault 593–4
assessments see also admission
   for assessment
accommodation services
   458–69
approved social workers,
   interviews with 177–9
bail 203, 218–19
civil confinement 174–9
declining to carry out 451
general practitioners 175–7,
   180–1

housing authorities 478–82
medical recommendations
   174–7
outpatient 203
police 137, 139
remand 218, 219
residential accommodation
   451, 458–63
services in the community
   450–72
social services departments
   450–70, 472–6
systematic assessments 470
termination 451–2
transfer from prison to
   hospital 264
without hospitalization 174
ASWs see approved social
   workers (ASWs)
asylum-based provision
administration 75, 77
beds, number of 80–1
boarding out-patients, system
   of 82
care in the community 71, 79,
   85
closure of asylums 85
Commissioners in Lunacy 75
compulsory admissions,
   statistics on 81
county asylums 18, 19, 72,
   75–8, 112
criminal lunatics 18
decarceration policies 79–82
decline in, reasons for 78–82
doctors 77–8
drug therapies, growth in
   78–80
duration of stay 81–2
growth in, reasons for 78
hospitals, opening of 77
informal admissions 112
Justices of the Peace 75, 77–8
medical certificates needed for
   admission 78
moral treatment 73–4
normality, concept of 74
open door policies 80
opiates, use of 73
paupers 18, 75–6, 82
poor law 75–6, 82
prisons 76
private sector 78
professionals, involvement of
   75–9
reform 72–3

asylum-based provision (*cont.*)
  rise and fall of 71–82, 109
  social reform movements
      72, 75
  specialists 78
  standards 72–4
  surveillance 73–4
  transquillisers 78
  Vagrancy Acts 74–5
  work, inability to 76–7
  workhouses 76, 82
  York Retreat 73, 74
asylum-seekers 150, 441
attachment theory 336
attorney, powers of *see* lasting
    powers of attorney; powers of
    attorney
autonomy
  best interests of the patient
      536–7, 553
  capacity 509–10, 527
  compulsion, treatment of
      detained patients under
      309, 313
  hospital, treatment in 348–9
  second opinions and report
      system 322–4

bail
  assessment 218–19
  bail information schemes
      217–18
  conditions 215
  diversion 203, 219–30
  further offending, risk of
      217–18
  Mental Health Act 1983 218–19
  outpatient assessments 203
  previous convictions for
      violent or sexual offences
      218–19
  refusal of 217–19
  remand 215–19
battery 292, 335, 503, 593–4
behaviour modification 287
best interests of the patient,
    capacity and 504–5,
    534–8, 558
  advance decisions regarding
      treatment 547, 570
  advocates 556
  assessment, admission for 557
  autonomy 536–7, 553
  balance sheet approach 534–5
  care teams 556
  civil confinement 557

code of practice 555
common law 555
confidentiality 554–5
consultation 554, 556
Court of Protection 548, 553,
    559–60
definition 552
deputies 548
external factors 536
factors, list of 553
families 555, 557
fiduciaries 555
general defence 567–8
guardians 557, 577
ignorance of the law 555
independent advocates 556–7
involuntary admissions 557
lasting powers of attorney
    554, 562
legal status of decisions 555
local authority
    accommodation, admission
    to 556–7
medical treatment, consent to
    534–8, 553–4, 556–7
Mental Capacity Act 2005
    536, 547–8, 550, 552–7, 573,
    575, 577–8
NHS accommodation,
    admission to 556–7
objectivity 535–6, 547, 553
opinion, responsible body of
    534
personal decisions 504–5
procedural requirements
    553–4
representation 606–7
residential accommodation,
    admission to 556–7
restraints 548
safeguards 555
second opinions and report
    system 319
self-determination 536–7
serious medical treatment
    556–7
sterilisation 537–8
subjectivity 535–6, 547, 552,
    553
substitute decision-makers
    548, 558
substitute judgment 535–6,
    538, 552
wills 553
wishes and feelings of patient
    552–4, 556

bias 275, 385, 514
blood transfusions, refusal of
    508, 515, 521–2
Bolam test 290–1, 294, 312, 594
British National Formulary
    (BNF) 279, 330–1
Broadmoor 18, 66, 97–103, 266,
    268–9, 327, 331, 525
bullying 103

caesareans 303–4, 523–5
capacity 27, 29, 497–544 *see also*
    best interests of the patient,
    capacity and; Mental Capacity
    Act 2005; substitute
    decision-making, capacity and
  ability to understand 513–15
  actual understanding 515–16,
      518–19
  administrative bodies 539
  admission to hospital 149–51
  advance directives 528–31
  appreciation of 516–19, 526
  asylum seekers 150
  autonomy 509–10, 527
  battery 503
  best interests of the patient
      534–8, 504–5
  bias in tests 514
  blood transfusions, refusal of
      508, 515, 521–2
  Bournewood patients 26, 151
  caesareans 523–5
  change of circumstances
      570–1
  children 522
  choice
      evidencing a 507–10
      reasonable outcome of
          510–12
  civil confinement 116,
      149–51, 506
  common law partners,
      decision-making by 504
  compartmentalised capacity
      507
  compliance 507–8
  compulsion, treatment of
      detained patients under
      295, 314–17
  confidentiality 541
  consent 115–20, 149–51
  context, capacity in 518–26
  contracts 500–2
  Court of Protection 499, 539
  court, role of the 504–5, 539

Crown 498–9
culture 542–3
dangerousness 151
decision-making for persons lacking capacity 503–5, 526–41
declarations 505
depression 519, 520–1
discharge from hospital 362
doctors as decision-makers 539
drug therapy 282, 520–1
due process 539
emergency medical treatment 335
enduring powers of attorney 528, 546
evidencing a choice 507–10
false imprisonment 504
family members 499, 539–41
fiduciaries 527, 541
fitness to stand trial 225
gender 542
gifts 502
guardians 503–4, 527, 539
Hopkins competency test 514
hospital
    admission to 149–51
    discharge from 362
    treatment in 276, 294
housing authorities 479–80
idiosyncrasies of person, taking into account 530–1
informal admissions 26, 115–20, 294
information
    appreciation of 516–19, 526
    availability of 540–1
    privacy 541
    provision of 516
inhuman or degrading treatment 29
instructions, ability to give 607
irrationality 508–13, 524, 543–4
Law Commission 507, 516
lay persons as decision-makers 541
legal presumption of capacity 498, 506
legal structures of capacity 498–505
litigation 500–1, 604–7
Lord Chancellor 499

lucid intervals 500–1, 530
MacArthur treatment competence study 518–23
marginal capacity, persons with 507, 509, 511, 513, 518
marriage 502–3, 517, 542–3
medical treatment
    blood transfusions, refusal of 508, 515, 521–2
    caesareans 523–5
    consent to 6–7, 9, 150, 497, 505–11, 513–17, 521–6
    information, appreciation of 517
    pregnant women refusing 521–5
    refusal of 289, 294, 508, 511, 515, 521–5, 528–9
Mental Deficiency Acts 503, 546
Mental Health Act 1959 503–4, 539
Mental Health Act 1983 499, 500, 506, 515, 522, 524, 526, 539, 542, 546
Mental Health Review Tribunals 376, 395
mini mental state examination 513–15
moral ideals 543
necessity 504
objectivity 514
Ontario 149
parens patriae 498–9, 503–5, 539, 546
paternalism 509–10
perceptions of disorder, tests of 519–20
Percy Commission 506
personal decision-making 503–5, 546, 548, 559, 560–2, 567, 569–70, 577
persons who should make decisions 538–41
pregnant women refusing medical treatment 521–5
presumption of capacity 498, 506
privacy 541
professionals
    advice from, presumption of 531
    decision-making by 539–41
    investigations 541
    payment of 541

property and affairs 498–503, 517, 546, 548, 559, 560–1, 565, 583
psychosurgery 285–6
race 542
rational reasons test 512–13, 516
rationality 508–13, 524, 543–4
reasonable outcome of choice 510–12
reform 23
religious belief 508, 513, 515, 521–2, 553
representation 604–7
Richardson Committee 24, 149
risk-benefit ratio 512
schizophrenia 518–21
second opinions and report system 319, 320, 322, 325–7
self-determination 509–10
severe mental handicap 507
severity of impact of decision 512
sexual behaviour 506
social norms 532
social policy 506, 511
socio-economic classes, 518, 519
standard of proof 528–9
status approaches 506–7, 526–8
sterilisation 504
substitute judgments 529–33, 542
tests of capacity 225, 499, 501, 505–21, 551, 561, 565
third parties 527
total institutions 543
trustees 527
understand
    ability to 513–15, 518–19
    actual understanding 515–15, 518–19
vulnerability, standard of 150–1
Wechsler adult intelligence scale (WAIS) 513–14
wills 498, 502–3, 510, 511, 515, 517, 530–3, 543
care and attention, persons in need of 439–41, 458–9, 484–4
care in the community 82–95 see also carers; services in the community
asylums 71, 79, 85

care in the community (*cont.*)
  Audit Commission. *Making a Reality of Community Care* 83
  Better Services for the Mentally Handicapped White Paper 83
  Better Services for the Mentally Ill. White Paper 83
  care plan approach 92, 93–4
  Caring for People. White Paper 88
  civil liberties 92–5
  colonisation 86–95
  community mental health centres (CMHCs) 85, 94
  community mental health teams (CMHTs) 85, 94–5
  community psychiatric nurses (CPNs) 85
  community treatment orders 23, 356–7
  compulsory admission, discharge of people subject to 91
  concept of community 84
  control 92–3
  convergence 86–95
  decarceration 91
  development of 82–5
  divergence 86–95
  domiciliary services 67, 68, 92, 453–4
  European Convention on Human Rights 92–3
  failure of community care 84–5
  family, care by the 13–14, 64, 68, 84, 440, 572–5
  femininity, care and 84
  funding 89–90
  grant aid 90
  Griffiths Report 83
  group homes 91, 92
  guardianship 82
  health authorities 86–8
  homicides 93–4
  hospital services
    beds, number of 85
    closure of hospitals 83
    definition of hospitals 91
    impact on 82–91
    nursing homes 91
    providers or acquirers of care 88
  Independent Living Movement 84
  inter-agency living 93
  learning disabilities 84
  local authorities 66–7, 86–90
  managerialism 88, 89–90
  market principles and practices 88–90
  Mental Health Act 1959 60
  Mental Health Act 1983 584–5
  mental health system 63–8, 82, 109
  monitoring of persons in own homes 92
  National Assistance Act 1948 86
  National Confidential Inquiry into Suicide and Homicide by People with a Mental Illness 93–4
  National Health System 86–9
  National Service Framework for Mental Health (NSFMH) 85, 495
  normalisation theory 84
  nursing care 85, 88, 91
  Payment by Results (PbR) 89
  Percy Commission 82
  Primary Care Trusts 88–90
  private sector 88
  providers or acquirers of care, characterized as 88
  psychiatric profession, domination of 87–8, 89
  psychiatrisation of social problems 90
  rehabilitation model 84
  residential care 85, 88, 90, 94–5, 109
  severe and dangerous personality disorders (SDPDs) 94
  social control 92–5
  social reintegration, concept of 84
  social workers 87–8
  suicides 93–4
  supervised community treatment (SCT) 92
  supervision registers 92
  supplementary benefit 88
  welfare state, development of the 86
  welfarism 88
care plans 92–4, 450–2, 455, 461, 465, 470, 478
Care Programme Approach (CPA)
  discharge from hospital 365–6
  enhanced 476–7
Care Service Improvement Partnership 60
Care Standards Tribunal 444
care trusts (CTs), establishment of 474
carers
  coercion 113
  families 13–14, 64, 68, 84, 440, 572–5
  informal admission 113
  local authorities 68
  Mental Capacity Act 2005 572–5
  police 136
  respite care 13, 166
case stated, appeals by way of 425–6
cautions 206
certificates *see* medical certificates
challenging behaviour, race and 143
challenging civil confinement
  habeas corpus 187–90, 197
  Human Rights Act 1998 196–7
  judicial review, 190–6
  legality, challenging 185–97
  Mental Health Act 1983 Part II 185–97
  Mental Health Review Tribunals, applications to 185–7
  nearest relatives 169–73
charges
  accommodation services 441–3, 448, 458–60
  control in the community 485
  divestiture of assets 442–3
  means-testing 441–3, 458–60
  services in the community welfare services 446
charities
  funding 15
  government, relationship with 15
  hospitals 17–19
  lobbying by 15
  Madhouse Acts 17–18
  private facilities 12
Charter of Fundamental Rights of the EU 27
chemical castration 318, 328, 575

children and young persons
  accommodation services 439
  appropriate adult 205–6, 207,
    209
  capacity 522
  damages 596–8
  housing authorities 483–4
  informal admission 115–16
  Mental Capacity Act 2005 551
  nearest relatives 167–8, 172–4
  parental responsibility, persons
    with 172–4
  services in the community 438
civil action by patients *see also*
  damages, actions for
  affidavit evidence 587–8
  capacity 500–1, 604–7
  course of proceedings, capacity
    during 605
  leave to commence actions 586
  litigation friend 574, 605–5,
    607
  Mental Health Act 1983 583
  property and affairs, capacity
    and 500–1
  representation 604–7
  striking out 588
civil confinement 120–6 *see also*
  approved social workers
  (ASW), civil confinement and;
  challenging civil confinement;
  nearest relatives, civil
  confinement and
  access to patient, denial of
    179–80
  accommodation services
    444–5
  admission 111, 120–6, 153
    assessments 122–4, 126–7,
      173, 377, 387
    mechanics and dynamics of
      173–85
    Stone system of admission
      criteria 151–3
    treatment for, 122–5,
      128–33, 173
  advance decisions regarding
    treatment 570
  applications 155
    documents, rectification
      and scrutiny of 183–5
    execution of applications
      179–80
    forms 173–4
    nearest relatives 174, 177
    prerequisites for 173–80

arrest 179
assessments
  admissions for 122–3, 124,
    126–7
  medical recommendations
    174–7
  social work 174
  without hospitalisation
    174
attention of mental health
  system, methods of coming
  to 156–7
authorisation, duration of 179
benefit to individual criterion
  120–5
best interests of the patient
  557
capacity 116, 149–51, 506, 557
certificates from medical
  practitioners, two 123, 155,
    595–7
civil rights 160, 175
code of practice 174–7
  documents, rectification
    and scrutiny of 183–4
  emergency admissions 176,
    177
  execution of application
    179
  interviews with approved
    social workers 177
  medical recommendations
    174–6
  multidisciplinary teamwork
    180
consent 116, 153, 197–8
contagious diseases,
  quarantine for 146
criminal justice system 200,
    584
criteria 120–1, 124, 126, 155
damages 595–7
dangerousness 120–1, 151–3,
    158
diagnosis 177
discharge from hospital 362–7
doctors, role of 159, 181–3
documents
  rectification of 183–5
  scrutiny of 183–5
drug therapy 281–2
due process 155
duration of detention, 125
economics 121–2
emergency admissions 125,
    176–7

emergency medical treatment
    334
entry, powers of 178–80
execution of applications
    179–80
family and relatives 157, 159
forms 173–4
general practitioners 157, 158,
    175–7, 180–1
guardianship 489, 490
history of 120–1
home, referrals from patient's
    156–7
hospital
  admissions to 120–6, 153
  discharge from 362–7
  taking the patient to 180
  treatment in 275–6
informal admission 114, 116
inspection, powers of
    178–9
justifications 120–2,
    159–60
Justices of the Peace 19–20,
    123–4, 159–60, 179
legal knowledge of
  professionals 176
mechanics and dynamics of
  admission 173–85
medical recommendations
    174–7
  code of practice 174–5
  emergency admissions
    176–7
  general practitioners
    175–6, 180–1
  previous acquaintance with
    patient, doctor must have
      175–6
  psychiatrists 175–6
  two, requirement for
    174–6, 180–1
Mental Capacity Act 2005
    573, 576
Mental Health Act 1959
    19–20
Mental Health Act 1983
    122–3, 138, 155–98
Mental Health Review
  Tribunals 185–97, 423
mental impairment, definition
  of 36
multidisciplinary teamwork
    180–3
National Health Service 159
paperwork 155

civil confinement (*cont.*)
Percy Commission 159–60,
181
persons who are admitted 158
police 124, 126, 179–80
previous acquaintance with
patient, doctor must have
175–6
previous admissions 158
procedure 123, 124–5
process of 155–98
professionals 155–6
protective custody 122
psychiatrists 175–6
public place, referral from 157
race 143
rectification of documents
183–5
referrals 156–8
sedation 179
self-referrals 157
social class 158
social control 157
social workers 159, 174
Stone system of admission
criteria 151–3
taking the patient to hospital
180
therapeutic considerations 158
treatability 122
treatment
admissions for 122–3,
124–5, 128–33
advance decisions 570
trial periods 139
US Constitution, standards in
120
use of force 179
violent resistance 180
warrants of entry 179–80
civil partners 167
civil rights *see also* European
Convention on Human Rights;
Human Rights Act 1998
care in the community 92–5
Charter of Fundamental
Rights of the EU 27
civil confinement 160, 175
guardianship 504
Mental Capacity Act 2005
573, 574
mental impairment, definition
of 37–9
nearest relatives 166
severe mental impairment
37–8

UN Declaration on the Rights
of Mentally Retarded
Persons 34
clinical trials 279–80
clothing, use of special 340
CMHCs (community mental
health centres) 67–8, 85, 94
CMHTs (community mental
health teams) 67, 85, 94–5,
204
codes of practice
admission for assessment 128
aftercare 447–8
behaviour modification 287
best interests of the patient
555
civil confinement 166, 174–7,
179–80, 183–4
compulsion, treatment of
detained patients under
303–4
confidentiality 555
discharge from hospital 364
documents, rectification and
scrutiny of 183–4
emergency admissions 135,
176, 177
emergency medical treatment
335–6
execution of application 179
experts 38
general defence 567
goods and services, payment
for 569
guardianship 115, 488–9
information, right to 290–1
interviews with approved
social workers 177
lasting powers of attorney 562
leave and recall 354–5, 358
medical recommendations
174–6
Mental Capacity Act 2005 549
Mental Health Act 1983 22,
585
Mental Health Review
Tribunals 376
multidisciplinary teamwork
180
nearest relatives 166
Richardson Committee 25
seclusion 340–3
second opinions and report
system 318, 321, 324–6, 332
services in the community
447–8

coercion *see also* use of force
aftercare under supervision
(ACUs) 492–5
carers 113
consent 292–4
guardianship 577
hospital, treatment in 292–4,
349
informal admission 113,
293–4
refusal of medical treatment
292–4
supervised community
treatment (SCT) 494–5
cohabitees as nearest relatives
167–8
College of Physicians 15, 17
Commissioners in Lunacy 18, 75
Committee for the Prevention of
Torture and Inhuman or
Degrading Treatment 29
community care *see* care in the
community
community mental health
centres (CMHCs) 67–8, 85, 94
community mental health teams
(CMHTs) 67, 85, 94–5, 204
community psychiatric nurses
(CPNs) 67–8, 85, 203–4
community treatment orders 23,
356–7, 488
complaints procedures 602–4
advice on 469–70
advocacy 603
Care Standards Act 2000
469–70
damages 603
directions 469
drug therapy 602–3
Healthcare Commission
469–70
Health Services Commissioner
603–4
informal dispute resolution
603
Mental Capacity Act 2005
572–3
Mental Health Act
Commission 603–4
Primary Care Trusts 469–70,
603
private sector 470
responsible medical officers
(RMOs) 603
services in the community
469–70

compulsion, treatment of
detained patients under
294–324
admission 122–4, 128–33,
164–5
antipsychotic medication
309–10
approved clinicians (ACs) 297
autonomy 309, 313
beneficence 313
Bolam test 312
burden of proof 313
Butler Commission 295
caesareans 303–4
capacity 295, 314–17
care in the community 91
checklist 312
classified as suffering from,
treatment for disorder
patient is 300–2
code of practice 303–4
coercion 293–4
common law 296, 303, 315
consent 295–6, 300, 305–6,
309–10, 313, 316–17
drug therapy 295, 309–10, 315
entitlement, ideology of 295
fair trials 317
force feeding 298, 306–9, 311
gender 306–7
Human Rights Act 1998 296,
309–17
inhuman or degrading
treatment 310, 313–17
judicial review 296, 317
legalism 295–6, 301
meaning and scope of medical
treatment for mental
disorder 297–9
medical evidence 312, 317
mental disorder from which he
is suffering, meaning of
299–309
Mental Health Act 1983
296–317
Mental Health Review
Tribunals 301
multidisciplinary approach
296
necessity 310, 313–14, 317
nursing staff, contact with 297
opinion, responsible body of
312
Percy Commission 295
personality disorders,
treatability of 298

physical disorders, treatment
for 303–8
pregnancy 303–4, 309
prisons 62–3
private life, right to respect for
311, 313–14, 316–17
psychopathic disorders 301
reclassification of disorder
300–1
refusal of medical treatment
289, 293–4
remand 220, 221
responsible medical officers
(RMOS) 297, 309–10, 313,
317
restrictions on general power
318–24
Richardson Committee 316
safeguards 302
second opinions, system of
318–33
self-determination 309
sterilisation 305–6
treatability 26
use of force 299, 310
Wednesbury unreasonableness
296, 311
compulsory powers *see* civil
confinement; compulsion,
treatment of detained patients
under
conceptualising mental health
law 1–32
conditional discharge
absolute discharge 406–8
aftercare, availability of
410–12, 464–5
conditions 408–14
deferred discharge 411–12
liberty and security, right to
409–10, 412–14
Mental Health Act 1983
408–14
Mental Health Review
Tribunals 379–80, 386,
408–14, 420–1, 423
restricted patients 249, 408–19
transfer from special hospitals
409–10
condoms, supply of 102
confessions 205, 207, 208–9, 212
confidentiality
best interests of the patient
554–5
capacity 541
code of practice 555

families 541, 555
fiduciaries 555
Mental Health Review
Tribunals 419
consent *see also* medical
treatment, consent to
capacity 115–20
civil confinement 116, 153,
197–8
coercion 292–4
compulsion, treatment of
detained patients under
295–6, 300, 305–6, 309–10,
313, 316–17
disclosure 290–2
drug therapy 275
emergency medical treatment
334–5
informal admission 112,
115–20, 153
informed consent 324
mental impairment, definition
of 37–8
psychosurgery 285
psychotherapy 287
remand to hospital 221
retracing consent 320
second opinions and report
system 318–20, 324–7
sexual offences 37–8
treatment, without 358
construction of self, disorder as
5–9
contagious diseases, quarantine
for 146
contracts
damages 593
Mental Capacity Act 2005 552
necessaries 569
private sector 444
property and affairs, capacity
and 500–2
control in the community 92–3,
485–96
aftercare 436, 491–5
charges 485
civil confinement 157
compulsory powers 435–6
dangerousness 436
drug therapy 15
emergency medical treatment
336
failure of community
care 436
guardianship 488–91
homicide 485–8

control in the community (*cont.*)
　hospital, treatment in 276–7,
　　347–9
　Mental Health Act 1983 584
　mental health system 379
　Primary Care Trusts 436
　psychopathic disorders 40
　public protection 485
　restraint 336
　restriction orders 254–5
　seclusion 336
　social exclusion 435–6
　social inclusion 435–6
　social services departments 436
　supervised community
　　treatment (SCT) 493–5
　supervision 435, 485, 491–5
　treatment
　　admission for 131
　　balance between control
　　　and 109
　violence 487–8
conveyance to hospital 180
Court of Protection *see also*
　deputies (Court of Protection)
　administration 560
　advance decisions 548–9, 559
　best interests test 549, 553,
　　560
　capacity 539
　common law 559–60
　declarations 559
　goods and services, payment
　　for 569
　judges 559
　jurisdiction 548–9, 559–60,
　　572
　lasting powers of attorney
　　559–60, 562–3, 572
　Law Commission 560
　lay and medical members 560
　medical treatment
　　consent to 559–60
　　withdrawal of 559–60
　Mental Capacity Act 2005
　　545–6, 548–9, 559–60, 572,
　　577–8
　Mental Health Act 1983 16,
　　548, 559, 585
　personal decisions 559
　property and affairs 499, 559
　Public Guardian 560, 572
　restraint 548
　sterilisation 559–60
　supervision 559
　Visitors 560, 572

wills 546, 553, 559
court-based pre-sentencing
　diversion 214–39 *see also*
　sentencing as diversion
　bail, remand or 215–19
　Crown Court 214
　custodial sentences 214
　either way offences 214
　fitness to plead 238–9
　fitness to stand trial 223–38,
　　272
　hospital, remand to 219–39
　indictable offences 214
　local initiatives 219
　magistrates' courts 214, 238–9
　remand
　　bail or 215–19
　　hospital, to 219–39
　resources, lack of 219
　schemes aimed at mentally
　　disordered offenders,
　　operation of 218
　special verdict 239–41, 272
　unfitness to plead 238–9
CPA *see* Care Programme
　Approach (CPA)
CPNs (community psychiatric
　nurses) 67–8, 85, 203–4
criminal confinement *see also*
　court-based pre-sentencing
　diversion; sentencing as
　diversion
　19th century legislation 18
　appropriate adult 205–14
　asylum-based provision 18
　bail 203, 215–19
　diversion 219–39, 272
　fitness to stand trial 223–38
　remand to hospital 219–39,
　　272
　special verdicts 239–41, 272
criminal justice, mental
　disorder and 199–274 *see
　also* court-based
　pre-sentencing diversion;
　criminal confinement;
　criminal proceedings;
　diversion from
　prosecution; remand to
　hospital, diversion from
　criminal justice system and
　alcohol and drug dependency
　　202
　civil confinement 200
　dangerous and severe
　　personality disorders,

persons suffering from
　273–4
　dangerousness 200–1, 273–4
　falling between mental health
　　and criminal justice system,
　　persons 273–4
　folk devils 201
　homicides 200
　lunatics, mythology of
　　criminal 201
　medical model 199
　Mental Health Act 1983 202
　popular understanding of links
　　between mental disorder
　　and crime 201
　prison 202
　　transfer to hospital from
　　　262–72
　public protection, policy of
　　273–4
　punishment 202
　risk management and control
　　199–202
　special verdict 239–42
　transfer from prison to
　　hospital 263–72
　treatment 202
criminal proceedings
　absence without leave,
　　assisting detained persons
　　in being 590
　aftercare 591
　assault 593
　civil confinement 584
　Director of Public
　　Prosecutions, leave of
　　592–3
　false documents 590
　false statements 593
　harbouring 590
　ill-treatment or neglect 548,
　　590–2
　informal patients 584
　inquiries and inspections,
　　interfering with 590
　manslaughter 593
　Mental Heath Act 1983 583–4,
　　590–3
　police 140
　prosecutions 585, 590–3
　restraint 584
　sexual relations with persons
　　receiving treatment 593
　social services departments
　　592–3
Crown Prosecution Service 204

custodial sentences *see* imprisonment, prisons

damages, actions for 593–600
  aftercare 598–600
  assault and battery 593–4
  Bolam test 594
  child protection proceedings 596–8
  civil confinement 596–7
  complaints 603
  contract 593
  drug therapy
    information, provision of 595
    megadosing 595
    negligence and 594–5
  duty of care of health care professionals 594–600
  ex turpi causa rule 598–9
  habeas corpus 189
  homicide 598–9
  Human Rights Act 1998 196, 601
  information, provision of 595
  inhuman or degrading treatment 598
  involuntary admissions, signing medical certificates for 595–7
  judicial review 190–1
  liberty and security, right to 598
  local authorities 596
  medical treatment, consent to 595
  Mental Health Act 183 593–600
  negligence 593–600
  occupiers' liability 594
  standard of care 594–6, 600
  tort 593–4
  vicarious liability 589
  volenti non fit injuria 595
dangerous and severe personality disorders (DSPDs) 24, 273–4
dangerousness
  absolute discharge 406–8
  admission to hospital 128, 145–9, 151–3
  aftercare under supervision (ACUs) 491, 493
  assessment, admission for 128
  capacity 151

civil confinement 120–1, 151–3, 158
contagious diseases, quarantine for 146
control in the community 436
criminal justice system 200–1, 273–4
criteria 146–8
dangerous and severe personality disorders 24, 273–4
discharge from hospital 364–6
discrimination 147–8
European Convention on Human Rights 147–8
hospital
  admission to 145–9, 151
  discharge from 364–6
  orders 245–6
  transfer from prison to 265
media 2–3
Mental Health Act 1983 24, 145–6
nearest relatives 169
perceptions of 2–3
predictions 147–8
special control 146
MacArthur Project in the US 146–8
Mental Health Review Tribunal 378
race 149
release 22, 364–5
restriction orders 249–54
Richardson Committee 25
services in the community 436
severe and dangerous personality disorders (SDPDs) 94, 254
standards 25, 146–9
Stone system of admission criteria 151–3
transfer from prison to hospital 265
violence 146–7
day centres 13, 447
decisional competence test 224–5
decision-making *see* capacity; personal decision-making, capacity and; property and affairs, capacity and; substitute decision-making, capacity and; substitute

judgment, capacity and deep brain stimulation 284–5
defective, meaning of 37
deferred discharge 397, 411–12
definitions 2–3
  mental disorder 26, 34–6
  Mental Health Act 1983 34–50, 57–8
  mental illness 46–50
  mental impairment 34, 36–9
  psychopathic disorders 35, 39–52
  severe mental impairment 34
delay
  discharge from hospital 387–93, 434
  hospital orders 246–7
  housing authorities, waiting lists of 484
  Mental Health Review Tribunals 26, 29, 387–93, 434
  special hospitals, waiting lists at 266
  transfer from prison to hospital 266–7
  waiting lists 266, 484
delusions 501, 516, 522–3, 531
Department of Health 24–6
  draft bills 25–6
  hospital, treatment in 16
  policies, guidance and directives from 21
  prisons 62
depression 3, 4, 8–9, 279, 282–3, 285, 519, 520–1
deputies (Court of Protection)
  appointment 557–8
  best interests test 548
  contact with individual, prohibiting 560
  expenses, payment of 560
  goods and services, payment for 569
  guardianship 577
  lasting powers of attorney 548, 558, 560
  Mental Capacity Act 2005 548, 552, 559–60, 577
  personal decisions 560
  powers 560
  property and affairs 560
  Public Guardian 548, 560
  remuneration 560
  restrictions 560

deputies (*cont.*)
  substitute decision-making
    548, 557–8
developmental disorders 4, 19,
  20, 503
deviance, understanding of 54
diagnosis
  civil confinement 177
  Diagnostic and Statistical
    Manual of Disorders
    (DSM-IV-TR) 48–9
  diagnostic threshold 551
  discharge from hospital 366
  Mental Capacity Act 2005 551
  mental disorder, definition
    of 35
  mental illness, definition of
    48–50
  police 137
  psychopathic disorders 42
  race 142
  schizophrenia 50–1
  signs of mental illness 49–50
  WHO International
    Classification of Diseases
    48–9
diminished responsibility
  235–6, 241
directions *see* hospital and
  limitation directions;
  restriction directions,
  discharge of patients subject
  to Director of Public
  Prosecutions (DPP) 585–6,
  592–4
disability discrimination
  Charter of Fundamental
    Rights of the EU 27
  definition 450
  employment 27
  housing 27, 480
  reasonable adjustments 27
  services in the community
    446, 450
  Treaty of Amsterdam 27
  welfare services 446
discharge *see* absolute discharge;
  conditional discharge;
  discharge from hospital;
  Mental Health Review
  Tribunals (MHRTS),
  discharge from hospital and;
  restriction directions,
  discharge of patients subject
  to discharge from hospital
  353–434 *see also* conditional

discharge; Mental Health
Review Tribunals (MHRTS),
discharge from hospital and
  absconding 431, 433
  absolute discharge 232–3, 379,
    406–8, 423
  absence without leave 429–33
  accommodation 366
  Advisory Board on Restricted
    Patients 368–9
  availability of suitable
    provision in community
    366
  capacity 362
  care programme approach
    365–6
  civil confinement 362–7
  code of practice 364
  colonisation 434
  conditions 370–1, 373
  consultation 368
  criteria 363–4, 368
  dangerousness 364–6
  diagnostic considerations 366
  expiry of period of detention
    363
  funding 434
  hospital and limitation
    directions 257, 258–9
  hospital orders 367–73
  Human Rights Act 1998 367,
    434
  informal patients 362–3
  judicial review 364, 369
  leave and recall 354–62
  liability to detention 362, 371
  liberty and security, right to
    368, 370
  medicalism and legalism,
    tension between 433–4
  Mental Health Act 1983
    362–73
  Mental Health Act
    Commission 363
  nearest relatives 364–5, 367
  negligence 366–7
  number of patients recalled
    373
  orders for discharge 363
  persons who may initiate or
    order discharge 354
  planning for discharge 366
  practice 365–7
  private life, right to respect for
    367
  public protection 371, 373

  recall 354–62
  reoffending rates 373
  reports 364
  representations, patient's right
    to make 369
  responsible medical officers
    (RMOs) 363–5, 368–72
  restriction orders 367–8,
    372–3
  review panels 364
  sectioning, ending 362–7
  Secretary of State, consent of
    367–72
  special hospitals 369–70
  supervision 353, 365–6
  transfer directions 369–70
  treatability requirement 364
  vulnerability 366
disclosure of documents 383–5,
  387, 581
discretionary discharge 403–4,
  405
discretionary life sentences 24
discrimination
  dangerousness 147–8
  disability discrimination 27,
    446, 450, 480
  housing authorities 480
  services in the community
    446, 450
  welfare services 446
diseases, quarantine for
  contagious 146
dissocial personality disorders
  40–2
diversion from prosecution 199,
  202–14 *see also* court-based
  pre-sentencing diversion;
  remand to hospital, diversion
  from criminal justice
  system and; sentencing as
  diversion
  appropriate adult scheme,
    operation of 205–14,
    272
  bail, outpatient assessments
    for 203
  community mental health
    teams (CMHTs) 204
  community psychiatric nurses
    (CPN) 203–4
  confessions 205
  criminal process, within the
    204–19
  Crown Prosecution Service
    204

early diversion from criminal process 203–4, 272

forensic medical examiners, referrals from 204

hospitals used for custodial reasons 273

informal diversion 203–4

Mental Health Act 1983 203, 272

miscarriages of justice 204–5

outpatient assessments, for 203

PACE and codes 204–5

place of safety, removal by police to 203

police 203, 205, 272

public interest 204

public protection, policy of 273

success of 272

transfer from prison to hospital 263–72

tranquillisers 8–9, 14, 78, 278–81, 290, 330–1, 337

divestiture of assets 442–3

doctors *see also* general practitioners; medical personnel; psychiatrists

approved social workers (ASWs) 181–3

asylum-based provision 77–8

capacity 539

civil confinement 159, 181–3

decision-making by 539

role of 159, 181–3

second opinion appointed doctors (SOADs) 275, 277, 318–33

domiciliary care 67, 68, 92, 453–4

dopamine 52

DPP (Director of Public Prosecutions) 585–6, 592–4

dress 101–2, 340

drug and alcohol testing 99

drug dependency 32, 42–6, 202, 215

drug therapy

advance decisions regarding treatment 570–1

advertising 14–15

anti-anxiety drugs (minor tranquillisers) 278

anti-depressants 8–9, 279

antipsychotics (neuroleptics or major tranquillisers) 14,

278–81, 290, 309–10, 330–1

asylum-based provision 78–80

British National Formulary (BNF) 279, 330–1

capacity 282, 520–1

changing drugs 326

chlorpromazine 280

complaints 602–3

compulsion, treatment of detained patients under 295, 309–10, 315

consent 275

control, used for 15

costs of drugs 279

covert administration of medicine 281–2

damages 594–5

depot preparations 280

detained persons 281–2

discontinuance by patients in the community 281

emergency medical treatment 333–5

high doses 280

hospital, treatment in 275, 278–82, 288, 347

informal admissions 282

information, provision of 595

manufacturers 14–15

medical certificates 320

megadosing 595

Mental Health Review Tribunals 400

National Institute for Clinical Excellence (NICE) 279

negligence 594–5

nooceptive drugs 278

number of drugs available 279

opiates 73

polypharmacy 280–1, 326, 330–2

prescriptions 14

pseudoparkinsonism 281

psychodysleptics 278

psychopathy 288

psychostimulants 278

randomised clinical trials (RCTs) 279–80

reduction in medication 280

refusal of treatment 8–9, 281–2

restraint 338

safeguard systems 275

schizophrenia 52, 279–81

second opinions and report system 318–22, 325–6, 339, 330–2

sedation 179, 331

side effects 14–15, 278–81, 290, 347

supervised community treatment (SCT) 494

tardive dyskinesia 281, 290

thioridazine 281

three-month rule 318–19, 320

typology of 278, 279

use of force 310

violence 333

DSPDs (dangerous and severe personality disorders) 24, 273–4

dual detention 222

eccentricity 501, 509

ECT *see* electroconvulsive therapy (ECT)

either way offences 214, 238

elderly people

informal admission 113

services in the community 446–7

electroconvulsive therapy (ECT) 275, 277–8

conditions of use 283–4

depression 282–3

emergency medical treatment 334

guidance 284

history of ECT 282

informal patients lacking capacity 284

inhuman or degrading treatment 284

Mental Capacity Act 2005 575–6

private life, right to respect for 284

procedure 282, 283–4

safeguards 275, 283–4

second opinions and report system 318–19, 325, 329, 330

side effects 283

success of 283

emergencies *see also* emergency admissions; emergency medical treatment

housing authorities 481

emergencies (*cont.*)
  National Assistance Act 1948
    440
  temporary accommodation,
    persons in need of 440
emergency admissions 134–5,
  138
  approved social workers
    (ASWs) 134–5
  civil confinement 125, 176–7
  code of practice 135, 176, 177
  criteria 136–7, 140
  justices of the peace 135–6
  medical certificates 135
  medical recommendations
    176–7
  Mental Health Act 1959 138
  Mental Health Act 1983
    section 4 134–6
  nearest relatives 134–5
  police 135–7, 140
  private places, persons in 135–6
  procedure 134–5
  reasonable cause standard 135
  social workers 134–6
  transfer from prison to
    hospital 267
emergency medical treatment
  277, 333–45
  attachment theory 336
  battery 335
  capacity 335
  care and responsibility or care
    and reassurance 336
  code of practice 335–6
  common law 334–5
  consent 334–5
  detained patients 334
  drug therapy 333–5
  electroconvulsive therapy 334
  informal patients 334, 335
  irreversible and hazardous,
    treatment must not be 334
  medical recommendations
    176–7
  Mental Capacity Act 2005 335
  Mental Health Act 1983 333–4
  Mental Health Act
    Commission (MHAC)
    334–5
  necessity 335
  responsible medical officers
    (RMOs) 335–6
  restraint 336–9
  seclusion 340–5
  social control 336

  violence 333, 336
employment laws 27
enduring powers of attorney
  advance directives 528
  goods and services, payment
    for 569
  lasting powers of attorney
    548, 561, 564
  Mental Capacity Act 2005 547
  popularity of 561
  powers of attorney 561, 563–5
  property and affairs, capacity
    and 546
  registration 561
entitlement, ideology of 295,
  347–8
entry, powers of 178–80, 432
escorted leave 357
European Convention on Human
  Rights *see also* fair trials;
  inhuman or degrading
  treatment; liberty and
  security, right to; private life,
  right to respect for
  care in the community 92–3
  dangerousness 147–8
  European Court of Human
    Rights, jurisprudence of 30
  family life, right to respect for
    456, 480, 484, 582
  home, right to respect for
    462–3
  Human Rights Act 1998 27–8
  life, right to 216–17, 394
euthanasia 545
eviction 480
ex turpi causa rule 598–9
experts 30, 38, 384–6

facts, trial of the 227–8
  acquittals 234–6
  actus reus, commission of the
    233–7
  criminal procedure, as 228–9
  fair trials 228–9
  fitness to stand trial 227–9,
    233–7
  mens rea 234–6
  murder 234–7
fair trials
  accommodation services 443
  compulsion, treatment of
    detained patients under 317
  facts, trial of 228–9
  fitness to stand trial 223,
    227–30

  independent and impartial
    tribunal 321, 385
  Mental Health Review
    Tribunal 375, 384
  public hearings 320–1, 323
  representation 605
  second opinions and report
    system 320–1, 323
  transfer from prison to
    hospital 271–2
false documents, offence of
  providing 590
false imprisonment 188, 504
false statements, offence of
  providing 593
Fallon Committee report 24–5,
  98–100
families *see also* nearest
  relatives
  appropriate adult 207–9, 214
  approved social workers
    163–4
  best interests of the patient
    555, 557
  capacity 499, 539–41
  carers 13–14, 64, 68, 84, 440,
    572–5
  civil confinement 157, 159,
    163–4
  common law partners 504
  confidentiality 541, 555
  consultation of 163–4
  costs of care 440
  Court of Protection,
    applications to 120
  family life, right to respect for
    456, 480, 484, 582
  homes, persons whose liberty
    is curtailed in 120
  housing 13, 480, 484
  informal admission 120
  judicial review 582
  leave and recall 357
  local authorities 64, 68
  Mental Capacity Act 2005
    572–5
  privacy 541
  public support for 13
  referrals by 157
  respite care 13
  stereotyping 13
  Victorian values about family
    involvement 165–6, 168
feeble-mindedness 43
fiduciaries 527, 541, 555
fitness for interview 211–12

fitness to plead *see* unfitness to plead

fitness to stand trial 223–38
 absolute discharge 232–3
 abuse of process 230–1
 acquittals 234–6
 actus reus, commission of the 233–7
 appeals 223
 burden of proof 224
 capacity test 225
 cognitive test 224
 Crown Court 223–4
 decisional competence test 224–5
 defence, issue raised by the 223–4
 defences 235–6
 disability, defendants under a 223–4
 diminished responsibility 235–6
 diversion 223–38, 272
 facts, trial of the 227–9, 233–7
 fair trials 223, 227–30
 fluctuates, where mental state of defendant 227
 hospital orders 226, 230–3, 235–6, 238
 innocence, presumption of 228
 juries 224, 225–7, 231
 jury directions 224
 liberty and security, right to 231
 magistrates' courts 224
 medical evidence 223–4, 226, 230–2
 mens rea 234–6
 Mental Capacity Act 2005 225
 murder 232, 234–7
 provocation 236
 remand to hospital 223–38
 restriction orders 232, 235–6, 238
 Scotland 237
 special verdict 235, 239
 standard of proof 224, 227
 stay of proceedings 230
 supervision orders 228–9, 232–3
 tests 224–5, 227–8, 231
 time for consideration of issue 225–6
folk devils 201

force feeding 6–7, 298, 306–9, 311, 319, 320
forensic medical examiners 204, 211–12
freedom of information 424
Freudian therapy 286
funding
 care in the community 89–90, 438, 474
 charities 15
 direct funding of service users 479
 discharge from hospital 434
 government 16
 hospital-based provision 109
 housing authorities 479
 local authorities 90, 438
 National Health Service 70–1, 89
 Payment by Results (PbR) 89
 prisons 62
 Responsible Medical Officers (RMOs) 297

gender
 absence without leave 430
 Afro-Caribbean men, over-representation over 140–1
 capacity 542
 care in the community 84
 compulsion, treatment of detained patients under 306–7
 medical model 35
 restriction orders 253
 second opinions and report systems 329, 330
 services in the community 453–4
 women, over-representation in system of 35
general defence
 best interests test 567–8
 care or treatment, persons providing 566–7
 code of practice 567
 good faith 568
 goods and services, payment for 567–9
 guardianship 577–8
 lasting powers of attorney 562, 572
 Law Commission 567–8
 Mental Capacity Act 2005 566–8

 personal decisions 567
 reasonable steps to determine capacity 567
general practitioners
 assessments 157, 158, 175–7, 180–1
 civil confinement 157, 158, 175–7
 forensic medical examiners 211
 medical recommendations 175–6, 180–1
 mental health system 63–4, 67–8
genetics 51–2
Gestalt therapy 286
gifts 502
goods and services, payment for
 code of practice 569
 Court of Protection 569
 deputies 569
 enduring powers of attorney 569
 expenses 569
 general defence 567–9
 lasting powers of attorney 569
 Mental Capacity Act 2005 569–70
 necessaries 569
 suppliers, rights of 569
government *see also* health authorities; local authorities; National Health Service; social services departments
 central and local government, relationship between 16
 funding 16
 policy 16
 sectors, competition between 15–16
GPs *see* general practitioners
grant aid 90
group homes 12, 85, 91–2
group therapy 130, 286–7, 288
guardianship
 abnormally aggressive or seriously irresponsible conduct 490, 503
 advocate, as 488, 607
 aftercare under supervision (ACUs) 491
 aims of 82, 488–9
 appropriate adult 207–8
 best interests of patient 557, 577
 capacity 503–4, 527, 539
 care in the community 82

guardianship (*cont.*)
 certification 503
 civil rights 504
 code of practice 115, 488–9
 coercion 577
 compulsory detention 489, 490
 control in the community
  488–91
 court, role of the 503, 504, 539
 deputies 577
 developmental disorders 503
 general defence 577–8
 guardianship orders 489
 hospital orders 244
 informal admission 114–15
 lasting powers of attorney 577
 learning disabilities, persons
  with 489–90
 medical treatment, consent to
  488–9
 Mental Capacity Act 2005 27,
  576–8
 Mental Deficiency Acts 19, 82,
  488
 mental disorder 503
 Mental Health Act 1959 503,
  539
 Mental Health Act 1983 20–1,
  489–90, 503, 577
 mental illness 503
 necessity 577
 Percy Commission 503
 personal decisions 503–4, 577
 powers 82, 114–15
 private guardians 490
 psychopathy 489–90, 503
 representation 607
 residence 114–15, 503
 restrictions 503, 578
 severe subnormality 503
 social services departments
  490
 sterilisation 504
 subnormality 503
 supervision 490
 treatment requirement 503
 UN Declaration on the Rights
  of Mentally Retarded
  Persons 34
 unfitness to plead 238–9
 use of 490–1
 Wednesbury unreasonableness
  578

habeas corpus, writ of 188–90,
 581

approved social workers
 (ASWs) 187–8
civil confinement, challenging
 187–90, 197
damages 189
false imprisonment 188
Human Rights Act 1998
 189–90
judicial review, 189
liberty and security, right to
 189–90
Mental Health Review
 Tribunals 187
nearest relatives 187–8
release, orders for immediate
 188–9
vicarious liability 588–90
habitual drunkards, detention
 of 43
harbouring persons absent
 without leave 590
health authorities
 aftercare under supervision
  (ACUs) 492
 care in the community 86–8
 nursing care 88
 services in the community
  436, 447, 464, 472–4
health professionals *see*
 Approved Social Workers
 (ASWs); doctors; general
 practitioners; medical
 personnel; nurses;
 psychiatrists; Responsible
 Medical Officers (RMOs);
 social workers
Health Services Commissioner
 603–4
Healthcare Commission 469–70
Hearing Voices Network 9
hearings *see also* fair trials
 deprivation of 573–4
 duration of 419
 exclusions from 393–4
 hospital managers 395–6
 liberty and security, right to
  573–4
 Mental Capacity Act 2005
  573–4
 Mental Health Review
  Tribunal 377–8, 381–7,
  392–7, 419
 notice 387
 parties 395–6
 public hearings 320–1, 323,
  394–5

Secretary of State 383, 395–5
history of mental health law and
 provision *see also*
 asylum-based provision;
 Mental Health Act 1959
 19th century legislation 18
 charitable hospitals 17–19
 Commissioners in Lunacy 17,
  75
 electroconvulsive therapy 282
 hospital, treatment in 277–8
 justices of the peace,
  inspection and licensing by
  17
 Lunacy Act 1890 18–19, 159,
  339, 596
 Madhouse Acts 17–18, 112
 Mental Deficiency Acts 43,
  546
 Mental Treatment Act 1930 19
 Metropolitan Commissioners
  in Lunacy 17
 private madhouses 17–18
 property and affairs, capacity
  and 498–500
 release 21–2
 Trial of Lunatics Act 1883 239
 Victorian and Edwardian
  social policy 43
holding powers 133–4, 138–9
home leave *see* leave and recall
home, right to respect for 462–3
homelessness 3, 479–80
homes for life promises 462–3
homicide
 care in the community 93–4
 community treatment orders
  488
 control in the community
  485–8
 criminal justice system 200
 damages 598–9
 facts, trial of the 234–7
 hospital orders 232, 245
 inquiries 485–6
 manslaughter 593
 murder 219, 232, 234–7, 239,
  241, 245
 National Confidential Inquiry
  into Suicide and Homicide
  by People with a Mental
  Illness 93–4
 rates 486–7
 special verdict 239, 241
homosexuality 55–7
 armed forces 195

judicial review 195
illness model 56–7
pathological conceptions of 56–7
private life, right to respect for 195
sexual deviance, as 43–4
social attitudes, changes in 56–7
statistical abnormality of 56
Hopkins Competency Assessment Test 514
hormone implantation 318, 328, 575
hospital *see* admission to hospital; discharge from hospital; hospital and limitation directions; hospital-based provision; hospital orders; hospital, treatment in; remand to hospital, diversion from criminal justice system and; special hospitals; transfer from prison to hospital
hospital and limitation directions 256–63
armed forces 263
criteria 257–62
Crown Court, committal to 263
culpability 259–62
definition 257
hospital orders 256–63
interim hospital orders 256–7, 262–3
medical evidence 258
Mental Health Act 1983 256–8, 262
prison
transfer from 257, 262
transfer to 256–7, 258–62
psychiatrists 260
psychopathic disorders 246, 257–62
punitive element 259, 261–2
release 257, 258–9
restriction directions, discharge of patients subject to 415
Scotland 260, 261
sentencing as diversion 256–63
treatability 258, 262–3
hospital-based provision 63–6, 109 *see also* admission to hospital; discharge from

hospital; transfer from prison to hospital
accommodation services 444–5
already in hospital, admission of persons already in 133–4, 138–9, 153
Approved Mental Health Professional 87
asylum-based provision 77
beds
closure of 107–8
number of 85
care in the community 82–91
charities 19
closure of hospitals 83
custodial reasons, used for 273
definition of hospitals 91
fire-fighting approach 107–8
funding 109
holding power for doctors and nurses 133–4, 138–9
immediate restraint, necessity for 134
informal admissions 133
leave, attempts to 133–4, 153
Madhouse Acts 17–18
Mental Health Act 1983 section 5 133–4, 138–9
nursing homes 91
treatment and control, balance between 109
hospital directions *see* hospital and limitation directions
hospital, discharge from *see* discharge from hospital
hospital managers
hearings 395–6
information on patients, provision of 382–3
Mental Health Review Tribunals 379, 381–3, 395–6
referrals by 379, 381
hospital orders
admissions 246
Advisory Board on Restricted Patients 368–9
availability of places 246–7
conditions 368
criteria 245, 247–9
custody threshold 247–9
dangerousness 245–6
delay 246–7

discharge 245, 248–9, 257, 258, 367–73
fitness to stand trial 226, 230–3, 235–6, 238
guardianship orders 244
homicide 245
hospital and limitation directions 256–63
imprisonment, as alternative to 244
interim hospital orders 256–7, 262–3
inhuman or degrading treatment 247
life sentences 248
magistrates' courts 245
medical evidence 246
Mental Health Act 1983 section 37 244–9
Mental Health Review Tribunals 248–9, 378, 383, 420
murder 232, 245
police involvement, increase in 107
psychopathic disorders 246, 257, 259–60
recalls 372–3
release 245, 248–9, 257, 258, 272–3
remand to hospital 221
representations, patient's right to make 369
restriction orders 232, 235–6, 245, 249–55, 260, 367–8, 372–3, 414–18
return to prison 248–9
Richardson Committee 24
sentencing as diversion 243–9
sexual offences 245
special verdict 239–41
suitability of offender 247–8
summary offences 245
total institutions 104–7
transfers 265, 266, 271, 369–70
treatability requirement 246
unfitness to plead 238
violence 104–6, 245
unrestricted 245
hospital, treatment in 275–352
see also compulsion, treatment of detained patients under; emergency medical treatment in hospital; medical treatment, consent to; refusal of medical treatment
autonomy 348–9

hospital, treatment in (*cont.*)
    behaviour modification 287
    beneficence 346–9, 351–2
    Bournewood procedure 276
    capacity 276, 294
    civil confinement 275–6
    coercion 292–4, 349
    colonisation 347, 349, 351
    common law 276–7, 288–94
    consent 348–50
    constraint and control 277,
        348–9
    control model 276–7, 347–9
    demedicalisation 350
    Department of Health 16
    detained patients 275–6
    drug therapies 275, 278–82,
        288, 347
    electroconvulsive therapy
        (ECT) 275, 277–8, 282–4
    entitlement, idea of 347–8
    force-feeding 6–7
    group therapy 130, 286–7,
        288
    history of medical treatment
        277–8
    Human Rights Act 1998 277
    informal admissions 275–6
    information, right to 290–2
    legalism 276–7, 347
    liberty and security, right
        to 351
    medical model 276, 345–52
    medicalism and legalism,
        tension between 276–7
    Mental Capacity Act 2005 276
    Mental Health Act 1983
        275–7
    Mental Health Act
        Commission 275
    non-physical treatments
        286–8
    occupational therapy 286, 287
    physical treatments 275,
        277–86
    politicisation 351
    power relations 349–51
    psychoanalysis 286
    psychopathy, treatability of
        288
    psychosurgery 284–6, 318,
        328
    psychotherapy 286, 287–8,
        346–7
    remand 219, 220, 221–3, 273
    rights discourse 350

risk 351
safeguards system 275, 347
Sanctuary of Asklepios 277–8
second opinions and reports,
    operation of schemes of
    275, 277, 318–33
shock treatments 277–8
talking cures 277–8, 287–9
therapeutic communities 287
treatability requirement,
    removal of 348
hospitals *see* admission to hospital;
    discharge from hospital;
    hospital and limitation
    directions; hospital-based
    provision; hospital orders;
    hospital, treatment in; remand
    to hospital, diversion from
    criminal justice system and;
    special hospitals; transfer
    from prison to hospital
housing *see also* housing
    authorities; National
    Assistance Act 1948, Pt III,
    accommodation services under
    families 13, 120
    homelessness 3, 479–80
    homes, persons whose liberty
        is curtailed in 120
    mental health system 65
housing authorities
    assessment of needs 478–82
    capacity 479–80
    care and attention 483–4
    children 483–4
    direct funding of service users
        479
    disability discrimination 27,
        480
    eviction, notification to social
        services departments of
        480
    family life, right to respect for
        480, 484
    homelessness 479–80
    inter-agency cooperation
        478–82
    local connection 481
    National Health Service and
        Community Care Act 1990
        478–9
    ordinary housing 481–4
    overcrowding 482–3
    patient advocacy, importance
        of 480–1
    priority need 479, 484

residential accommodation
    483
services in the community
    436, 438, 478–84
social services departments,
    integration with 478–84
urgent need, persons in 481
vulnerable persons 479–80
waiting lists 484
human rights *see* civil rights;
    European Convention on
    Human Rights; Human Rights
    Act 1998
Human Rights Act 1998 26–30,
    59, 600–2 *see also* fair trials;
    inhuman or degrading
    treatment; liberty and
    security, right to; private life,
    right to respect for
    advocacy 601
    aftercare 29–30
    civil confinement, challenging
        196–7
    common law 197
    compulsion, treatment of
        detained patients under
        296, 309–17
    damages 196, 601
    discharge from hospital 367,
        434
    effective remedy, right to an
        194
    European Convention on
        Human Rights 27–8
    European Court of Human
        Rights, jurisprudence
        of 30
    experts 30
    family life, right to respect for
        456, 480, 484, 582
    habeas corpus 189–90
    home, right to respect for
        462–3
    hospital, treatment in 277
    judicial review 191–2, 194,
        196–7, 582, 601
    judiciary, resulting in cultural
        changes to 30
    leave and recall 361
    life, right to 216–17, 394
    list of Convention
        rights 28
    Mental Capacity Act 2005
        549, 574
    Mental Health Act 1983 23,
        309–17

Mental Health Review
  Tribunals 380–1, 389–90,
  393, 403, 426, 434, 580
merits reviews 197
nearest relatives 165–6, 167,
  171–3
proportionality 197, 601
public authorities 191–2, 196
public functions, private
  bodies performing 191–2
remedies 196
seclusion 342
second opinions and report
  systems 323–4
services in the community
  461–3, 467
special hospitals 101
total institutions 99–101
treatability 29
vicarious liability 602
victims 196, 601
Wednesbury unreasonableness
  194
hyperglycaemia 240

identifying the insane 4–9,
  13–14
idiosyncrasies of person, taking
  into account 530–1
idiots 17–19
illegality 193, 424
ill-treatment and neglect, offence
  of 548, 590–2
images of the mentally ill *see*
  perceptions of the mentally ill
immoral conduct *see*
  promiscuity, immoral
  conduct, sexual deviancy and
  drug or alcohol dependency
implantation of hormones 318,
  328, 575
imprisonment *see also* prison
  diversion 214, 243
  hospital orders as alternative to
    244
  imprisonment for public
    protection (IPP) 243
  life sentences 24, 248, 417–18
  Parole Board 414–15, 417
  remand 215–19
  restriction directions,
    discharge of patients subject
    to 417–18
  technical lifer, concept of 417
incapacity *see* capacity; Mental
  Capacity Act 2005

incomplete development of mind
  34–9, 129, 503
independent and impartial
  tribunal 321, 385
Independent Living Movement
  84
indictable offences 214, 222–3,
  238
informal admission 111–20, 153
  absence without leave 430
  acquiescing incapacitated
    people 115–20, 153
  advance decisions regarding
    treatment 570
  already in hospital, admission
    of persons already in 133
  authorisation 118–19
  Bournewood patients 26,
    115–16, 118–20
  capacity 26, 115–20, 294
  carers, coercion by 113
  children 115–16
  civil confinement
    capacity to consent, patients
      without 116
    disadvantages compared to
      114
  coercion 113, 293–4
  common law 27, 112
  consent 112, 115–20, 153
  county asylums 112
  criminal proceedings 584
  disadvantages 113–14
  discharge from hospital 362–3
  drug therapy 282
  emergency medical treatment
    334, 335
  family homes, persons whose
    liberty is curtailed in 120
  gender 114
  guardians, powers of 114–15
  hospital, treatment in 275–6
  Justices of the Peace 112
  lasting powers of attorney
    118–19
  liberty and security, right to
    113, 116–18
  medical treatment, refusal of
    293–4
  Mental Capacity Act 2005
    118–20, 576
  Mental Health Act 1983 20,
    112–20 584–5
  Mental Treatment Act 1930 19
  necessity 117
  Percy Commission 116

procedural safeguards 114
professional advocates,
  appointment of 119
psychogeriatric patients 113
race 141, 143–4
release 116–17
representatives, appointment
  of 119
restraint 336, 339
services in the community
  448–9
staff, training of 119
supervising authorities 118
treatment 112–14, 116, 570
women 114
wrongful confinement 116
information
  appreciation of 516–19, 526
  availability of 540–1
  belief in 551
  capacity 516–19, 526, 540–1
  code of practice 290–1
  damages 595
  drug therapy 595
  freedom of information 424
  hospital managers 382–3
  hospital, treatment in 290–2
  medical treatment
    consent to 517
    refusal of 290–1
  Mental Capacity Act 2005
    516–17, 547, 551
  Mental Health Review
    Tribunal 382–5, 387, 393–4
  privacy 541
  provision of 516
  public, disclosure to the
    393–4
  Secretary of State 382–3
  understand, failure to 547, 551
  use information, failure to be
    able to 547, 551
  wills 517
informed consent 291, 324
inhuman or degrading
  treatment
  Committee for the Prevention
    of Torture and Inhuman or
    Degrading Treatment 29
  compulsion, treatment of
    detained patients under
    310, 313–17
  damages 598
  hospital orders 247
  Human Rights Act 1998 601
  judicial review 195–6, 582

inhuman or degrading (*cont.*)
  refusal of medical treatment
    292, 294
  remand 216
  restraint 339
  seclusion 342
  sentencing as diversion 243
  transfer from prison to
    hospital 270
innocence, presumption of 228
inquiries 98, 485–6, 590
inquisitorial approach 392–3
in-reach programmes 62
insane, identification of 2–10
inspection 5, 17, 95, 178–9, 473,
  590
institutionalisation 109, 579
  discultarisation 96–7
  reinstutionalisation 109
  total institutions 96–7
instructions, ability to give 607
intellect of mentally ill people
  3–4
interagency cooperation *see*
  multidisciplinary teamwork
interdisciplinary nature of
  mental health law 31
interpreters 208
irrationality 193, 429, 508–13,
  524, 543–4

joint ventures 474
judgment *see* substitute
  judgment, capacity and
judicial review
  accommodation services 443
  civil confinement, challenging
    190–6
  compulsion, treatment of
    detained patients under
    296, 317
  damages 190–1
  discharge from hospital 364,
    369
  effective remedy, right to an 194
  Europeanization of 197
  family life, right to respect for
    582
  habeas corpus 189
  homosexuals, exclusion from
    armed forces of 195
  Human Rights Act 1998
    191–2, 194, 196–7, 582, 601
  illegality 193
  inhuman or degrading
    treatment 195–6, 582

irrationality 193
leave 192–3, 426
limitations 582
mandatory orders 23–4, 190
medical evidence 582
Mental Health Act 1983 27,
  191, 192–3 581–3
Mental Health Review
  Tribunals 187, 424–6,
  581–2
merits, review on the 195–6,
  197
nearest relatives 193
private life, right to respect for
  195, 582
private sector 191–2
procedural impropriety 193
prohibitory orders 190
proportionality 194–6
public functions, private
  bodies performing 191–2
quashing orders 190
reasons 191, 582
remedies 190–3, 426, 582
residential care homes 191–2
second opinions and report
  system 320, 322–3
services in the community
  469
substantive powers of review
  193–6
Super-*Wednesbury* test 193–4
Wednesbury unreasonableness
  193–5
Jungian therapy 286
juries
  directions 224
  fitness to stand trial 224,
    225–7, 231
justices of the peace
  admission to hospital 135–8
  approved social workers
    (ASWs) 135
  asylum-based provision 75,
    77–8
  civil confinement 123–4,
    159–60, 179
  emergency admissions 135–6
  informal admission 112
  inspection and licensing 17
  Madhouse Acts 17
  medical certificates 135
  Mental Health Act 1983
    section 135 135–6
  police, issue of warrants to
    135–6

powers of 135–6
private places, persons in
  135–6
reasonable cause standard 135
social workers 135–6

key workers 470, 472, 476

Largactyl shuffle 281
lasting powers of attorney
  (LPOA)
  advance decisions on medical
    treatment 57, 562
  appointment 557
  best interests test 554, 562
  code of practice 562
  common law 565–6
  Court of Protection 548,
    559–60, 562–3, 572
  deputies (Court of Protection)
    548, 558, 560
  enduring powers of attorney
    548, 561, 564
  ethical investments 562
  flexibility 561
  formalities 563
  general defence 562, 572
  goods and services, payment
    for 569
  guardianship 577
  informal admission 118–19
  medical evidence 565
  medical treatment, consent to
    554
  Mental Capacity Act 2005
    550, 552, 561–6, 572, 577–8
  notification 563
  personal decision-making
    548, 561–2
  property and affairs 548, 561,
    565
  Public Guardian 548, 563
  registration 548, 563, 572
  removal of attorney 564–5
  remuneration 564
  residential care home,
    admission to 562
  revocation 557, 564, 565–6
  substitute decision-making
    548, 557–8
  supervision 563
  tests for capacity 565
  terms, alteration of 562–3
  trust corporations 561
Law Commission 22–3
  capacity 507, 516

Court of Protection 560
general defence 567–8
Mental Capacity Act 2005
545–6
Law Society Mental Health
Review Tribunal Panel 382
learning disabilities 39, 84,
489–90
least restrictive alternative,
principle of 550
leave and recall
approved social workers
(ASWs) 354–5
code of practice 354–5, 358
community treatment orders
356–7
conditions 357–61
consent, treatment without
358
consultation 354–5, 358
duration of leave 355
escorted leave 357
grounds for renewal of
detention 355–6
hospitals 354–62
Human Rights Act 1998 361
liberty and security, right to
355–6, 361
maximum period 355
Mental Health Act 1983
354–62
Mental Health Act
Commission 358–9
Mental Health Review
Tribunals 361–2
nearest relatives, consultation
with 354
private life, right to respect
for 354
private sector 358, 360
public protection 358–9
relatives, custody of 357
responsible medical officers
(RMOs) 354–61
restricted patients 359–62
Secretary of State,
discretionary powers of
360–1
surveillance 359
transfers 358–9
treatability requirement 355
leave of absence see absence
without leave
leave to commence actions
affidavit evidence 587–8
civil proceedings 586

Director of Public
Prosecutions 586
Mental Health Act 1983
585–8
strict liability 586
striking out 588
substantial grounds, meaning
of 586, 587
leaving hospital see discharge
from hospital; Mental Health
Review Tribunals, discharge
from hospital and
legal aid 16, 382, 604
legal presumption of capacity
550
legal profession 16 see also
representation
legal responses see civil actions;
criminal proceedings; judicial
review; Mental Health Review
Tribunals
legalism
compulsion, treatment of
detained patients under
295–6, 301
discharge from hospital
433–4
hospital, treatment in 276–7,
347
medicalism 276–7, 433–4
Mental Health Review
Tribunals 373–4, 421–2,
434
second opinions and report
system 324, 329, 332–3
liberty and security, right to
absolute discharge 406
compulsory treatment 63
conditional discharge 409–10,
412–14
damages 598
discharge from hospital 368,
370
fitness to stand trial 231
habeas corpus 189–90
hearings, deprivation of
573–4
hospital, treatment in 351
Human Rights Act 1998 28–9,
602
informal admission 113,
116–18
leave and recall 355–6, 361
medical evidence 29
Mental Capacity Act 2005
571–4

Mental Health Review
Tribunals 376, 385, 389–91,
400–5, 428–9
prisons 63
restraint 548, 558–9
restriction directions,
discharge of patients subject
to 415–17
seclusion 342–4
services in the community
467
special verdict 241
transfer from prison to
hospital 264–5, 267–8,
270
unsound mind, persons of
28–9
licence, recall on 273
life, right to 216–17, 394
life sentences 24, 243, 248,
417–18
limitation directions see hospital
and limitation directions
litigation friend 574, 604–5, 607
living wills see advance decisions
regarding treatment; advance
directives
lobbyists 15
local authorities
approved social workers
161–2
care homes 66–7
care in the community 66–7,
86–8, 90
Care Standards Act 2000 66–7
carers 68
central and local government,
relationship between 16
civil confinement 161–2
damages 596
discretion 438
domiciliary services 68
families and friends, care
by 68
funding 90, 438
grant aid 90
independent advocates 556
local authority
accommodation 88, 90,
556–7
long-term mentally ill 85
nursing homes 66–7
private sector, competition
with 88
providers of services, as 88
residential care 66–8, 90

local authorities (*cont.*)
  services in the community
    438
  social workers 67, 161–2
Lord Chancellor 18, 499
LPOA *see* lasting powers of
    attorney (LPOA)
lucid intervals 500–1, 530
lunatics
  Lunacy Act 1890 18–19, 159,
    339, 596
  Royal prerogative 18
  mythology of criminal lunatics
    201

MacArthur treatment
  competence study 146–8,
    518–23
Madhouse Acts 17–18
  admission 17
  charitable hospitals 17–18
  Commissioners in Lunacy 17
  inspection 17
  justices of the peace,
    inspection and licensing
    by 17
  licensing 17
  Metropolitan Commissioners
    in Lunacy 17
  private madhouses 17–18
magistrates' courts
  diversion 214, 238–9
  fitness to stand trial 224
  hospital orders 245
  remand 215, 219, 220–3,
    238–9
  restriction orders 250
  special verdict 239
  unfitness to plead 238–9
mail, withholding 102–3
managerialism 88, 89–90,
  109–10, 437
managers of hospital *see* hospital
  managers
mandatory discharge 399–405
mandatory orders 23–4, 190,
  466–7
manslaughter 593
marginal capacity, persons with
  decision-making 507, 509,
    511, 513, 518
  Mental Capacity Act 2005
    550, 572, 574
  representation 605
marriage
  capacity 502–3, 517, 542–3

culture 542–3
moral ideals 543
property and affairs, capacity
  and 502–3, 517
means-testing charges 441–3,
  458–60
medical certificates
  assessment, admissions for
    128
  asylum-based provision 78
  civil confinement 123, 155,
    595–7
  damages 595–7
  drug therapy 320
  emergency admissions 135
  Mental Health Act 1959 19–20
  reasons 322–3
  second opinions and report
    system 318–23
  treatment, admission for 129
  two doctors 19–20, 174–6,
    180–1
medical model 7–9, 276–7
  Afro-Caribbeans,
    over-representation in
    system of 55
  criminal justice system 199
  hospital, treatment in 276,
    345–52
  mental illness, definition of 49
  neutrality of 55
  over-representation in system
    55
  promiscuity, immoral
    conduct, sexual deviancy
    and drug or alcohol
    dependency 43
  race 142
  schizophrenia 50–1
  second opinions and report
    system 332–3
  women, over-representation
    of 35
medical personnel 11–12, 15, 64
  see also Approved Social
    Workers (ASWs); doctors;
    general practitioners; nurses;
    psychiatrists; Responsible
    Medical Officers (RMOs);
    social workers
  approved mental health
    professionals 87, 163
  care in the community 87–8,
    89
  College of Physicians 15, 17
  efficiency 12

duty of care 594–600
good faith 17
managerialism 89
Mental Capacity Act 2005
  572–3
morale 12
National Task Force on
  Violence against Social Care
  Staff 105
nearest relatives, tensions with
  165–7
power 11–12
psychiatric profession,
  domination of 87–8, 89
status enhancement 11
tensions between 11
training 163
violence against 104–6
medical recommendations
  assessments 174–7
  civil confinement 174–7
  code of practice 174–6
  emergency admissions 176–7
  general practitioners 175–6,
    180–1
  Mental Health Act 1083
    122–3, 138
  Mental Health Review
    Tribunals 398
  previous acquaintance with
    patient, doctor must have
    175–6
  psychiatrists 175–6
  restricted patients 251–2, 256,
    398
  two, requirement for 174–6,
    180–1
medical records, access to 384–5
medical treatment *see also* drug
  therapy; emergency medical
  treatment; hospital, treatment
  in; medical treatment, consent
  to; refusal of medical
  treatment
  Court of Protection 559–60
  electroconvulsive therapy 275,
    277–8, 282–4, 318–19, 325,
    329, 330, 334, 575–6
  hormones, surgical
    implantation of 318, 328,
    575
  psychosurgery 285–6, 318,
    328, 575
  sterilisation 305–6, 504,
    537–8, 559–60
  withdrawal of 559–60

medical treatment, consent to
  advance decisions regarding
    treatment 569–71
  advance directives 6–7, 9, 16
  best interests of the patient
    534–8, 553–4, 556–7
  blood transfusions, refusal of
    508, 515, 521–2
  caesareans 303–4, 523–5
  capacity 6–7, 9, 150, 497,
    505–11, 513–17, 521–6
  Court of Protection 559–60
  damages 595
  Department of Health 16
  force-feeding 6–7
  guardianship 488–9
  independent advocates 556
  information, appreciation of
    517
  informed consent 291
  lasting powers of attorney 554
  Mental Capacity Act 2005
    547, 552, 575–6
  pregnant women refusing
    303–4, 521–5
  religious objections 553
  serious medical treatment
    556–7
  subjectivity 553
medical treatment, refusal of *see*
  refusal of medical treatment
medication *see* **drug therapy**
medium secure units (MSUs) 66
mens rea 234–6
mental age 4
mental capacity *see* **capacity**
Mental Capacity Act 2005 21,
  545–79
  abnormally aggressive or
    seriously irresponsible
    conduct 576
  advance decisions 545–7,
    569–71
  advocates system 546
  appreciation of information
    516–19, 526
  best interests test 536, 547–8,
    550, 552–7, 573, 575, 577–8
  Bournewood litigation 571–4,
    576
  children 551
  civil confinement 573
  civil rights 573, 574
  code of practice 549
  common law 545–7, 550,
    551–2, 572–3

complaints 572–3
complexities 571–8
compulsory admissions for
  treatment 576
context and overview 545–9
contract 552
Court of Protection 545–6,
  548–9, 559–60, 572, 577–8
  deputies 548, 552, 559–60,
    577
  wills 546
decision-making 23, 27, 545,
  571–2
definition of incapacity
  549–52
deputies 548, 552, 559–60, 577
diagnostic threshold 551
electroconvulsive therapy
  575–6
emergency medical treatment
  335
enduring powers of attorney
  547
enforcement 572–5
entry into force 549
euthanasia 545
family carers 572–5
fitness to stand trial 225
flexibility 574–5
general defence 566–8
goods and services, payment
  for 569–70
guardianship 27, 576–8
guidance 549
hearings, deprivation of
  573–4
hormones, surgical
  implantation of 575
hospital, treatment in 276
Human Rights Act 1998 549,
  574
ill-treating or neglecting
  person lacking capacity,
  criminal offence of 548
incapacity, meaning of 549–52
informal patients 118–20, 576
informality 572
information
  appreciation of 516–17
  belief in 551
  understand, failure to 547,
    551
  use information, failure to
    be able to 547, 551
lack of capacity, definition of
  547, 551

lasting powers of attorney
  550, 552, 561–6, 572, 577–8
Law Commission 545–6
least restrictive alternative,
  principle of 550
liberty and security, right to
  571–4
liberty, deprivations of 571,
  576
litigation friend 574
marginal capacity, persons
  with 550, 572, 574
medical treatment, consent to
  547, 552, 575–6
medical treatment, refusal of
  294, 545, 547
Mental Health Act 1983 552,
  575–8
mental illness 576
mental impairment 39, 576
nearest relatives 573–4
necessity 550
personal decision-making
  505, 546
presumption of capacity 550
principles 546–7, 549–52
problems and complexities
  571–8
procedural flexibility 572
professionals 572–3
property and affairs 499, 500,
  546
psychopathy 576
psychosurgery, consent to 575
Public Guardian 572
research 545, 549
restraints 548
safeguards 572–5
second opinions and report
  system 319, 325
severe mental impairment 576
standards 545, 551
statement of principles 546–7
statutory instruments 549
stereotyping 551–2
substitute decision-making
  546, 548, 557–69, 571–2
tests 551
treatment, compulsory
  admissions for 576
Wednesbury unreasonableness
  578
White Paper 545
wills 546
Mental Deficiency Acts
  guardianship 19, 82, 488

Mental Deficiency Acts (*cont.*)
    personal decisions 503–4
    promiscuity, immoral
        conduct, sexual deviancy
        and drug or alcohol
        dependency 43
    property and affairs, capacity
        and 546
mental disorder *see also* hospital,
    treatment in
    assessment, admission for
        126–8
    definition of 26, 34, 35–6
    diagnosis 35
    gateway definition, as 35
    guardianship 503
    medical evidence 35
    mental disorder from which he
        is suffering, meaning of
        299–309
    nature and degree to require
        hospitalisation, meaning of
        127–8
    specific types 35–6
mental disorder, medical
    treatment for *see* hospital,
    treatment in
Mental Health Act 1959
    capacity 539
    care in the community 60
    certification by two doctors
        19–20
    compulsory admissions
        19–20
    developmental disorder 20
    emergency admissions 138
    guardianship 503, 539
    justices of the peace,
        compulsory admissions and
        19–20
    mental health review tribunals,
        introduction of 20
    National Health Service 19
    parens patriae power 20
    promiscuity, immoral
        conduct, sexual deviancy
        and drug or alcohol
        dependency 43, 44
Mental Health Act 1983
    19th century clauses, relevance
        or applicability of 21–2
    absence without leave 429–42
    absolute discharge 406–8
    aftercare 584–5
    alcohol or drugs, dependence
        on 35, 42–6

already in hospital, admission
    of persons already in
    133–4, 138–9
appropriate adult 205–6
approved social workers 160,
    162–4
assessment, admission for
    126–8, 138
bail 218–19
capacity 499, 500, 506, 515,
    522, 524, 526, 539, 542, 546,
    558
care in the community 584–5
civil confinement 122–3, 138,
    155–98
civil proceedings 583
code of practice 22, 585
Community Treatment
    Orders, proposal for 23
compulsion, treatment of
    detained patients under
    296–317
conditional discharge 408–14
control 584
Court of Protection 548, 559,
    585
criminal justice system 202,
    583–4, 590–3
dangerous persons with
    personality disorders,
    confinement of 24
dangerousness 24, 145–6
definitions 34–50, 57–8
discretionary life sentences 24
diversion 203, 243–4, 272–3
emergency admissions 134–6
emergency medical treatment
    333–4
Fallon Committee 24
guardians 489–90, 503, 577
    reduction in role of 20–1
hospitals
    hospital and limitation
        directions 256–8, 262
    hospital orders 244–9
    hospital, treatment in
        275–7
    transfer from prison to
        hospital 263–72
Human Rights Act 1998 23,
    309–17
informal admissions 20,
    112–20, 584–5
judicial review 27, 191–3,
    581–3
leave and recall 354–62

leave to commence actions
    585–8
legal responses 579
Lunacy Act 1980 18–19
medical recommendations
    122–3, 138
Mental Capacity Act 2005
    552, 575–8
mental disorder, definition of
    34, 35–6
Mental Health Review
    Tribunals 186–7, 375–9,
    424, 580
mental illness, definitions of
    46–50
mental impairment, definition
    of 34, 36–9
nearest relatives 169, 172
omissions 585
outpatients 585
police 136–8, 139
powers of attorney 561
promiscuity or other immoral
    conduct 35, 42–6
property and affairs 499, 500,
    546, 583
prosecutions, consent of DPP
    to 585
psychopathic disorder,
    definition of 35, 39–42
psychosurgery 285
reform 22–4
remand to hospital 219–22,
    272
restraint 339
restriction directions,
    discharge of patients subject
    to 414–19
restriction orders 249–50
Richardson Committee 23–4
scope 27, 33
seclusion 340–1
second opinions and report
    system 318–33
sentencing as diversion 243–4,
    272–3
services in the community
    438, 447–9, 464
severe mental impairment,
    definition of 34
sexual deviancy 35, 42–6
sources of mental health law
    17–22
standards 22
statutory interpretation 22
structure 34–46

substitute decision-making
558
transfer from prison to
hospital 263–72
treatment, admission for
128–33
vicarious liability 588–90
Mental Health Act Commission
(MHAC)
complaints 603–4
discharge from hospital 363
emergency medical treatment
334–5
Health Services Commissioner
603–4
hospital, treatment in 275
investigations 603
leave and recall 358–9
Mental Health Review
Tribunals 423–4
restraint 336–8
seclusion 340–1, 344
second opinions and report
system 318–19, 321, 324–7,
330–3
visits 603
mental health care, other
interests involved in 11–17
Mental Health Review Tribunals
185–6, 419–29 *see also* **Mental**
Health Review Tribunals
(MHRTS), discharge from
hospital and
absolute discharge 423
admissions 185–7
amendment, return a case for
425–6
annual reports 422–4
approved social workers
427–9
burden of proof 29
case stated, appeal by way of
425–6
challenging 419–22, 414–9
civil confinement 185–7
patients, by 424–6
responsible medical officers
(RMOs) 428–9
civil confinement 185–97, 423
compulsion, treatment of
detained patients under
301
conditional discharge 420–1,
423
confidentiality 419
delay 26, 29

discharge 185–6, 419–29
discretion 185–6
evidence, conflicting 420–1
freedom of information 424
grounds for continued
detention 185–6
habeas corpus 187
hospital orders 248–9, 420
Human Rights Act 1998 426,
434, 580
illegality 424
introduction of 20, 373
irrationality 429
judicial review 187, 424–6,
581–2
jurisdiction 185–6, 580
leave and recall 361–2
legalism 421–2
liberty and security, right to
428–9
Mental Health Act 1959 20
Mental Health Act 1983
186–7, 424, 580
Mental Health Act
Commission 423–4
merits review 424
mistake of law 424, 429
natural justice 424
new fact rule 427–9, 434
procedural impropriety 424
proportionality 424
public protection 421
reasons 393, 419–22, 425
release 580
representation 604, 607
responsible medical officers
(RMOs)
challenging decisions
426–9
role of 422
restricted patients 422–3
Rules 580–1, 604
special hospitals 423
stay of proceedings 424–5
time limits 419
Wednesbury unreasonableness
420–1
writing 419
Mental Health Review Tribunals
(MHRTS), discharge from
hospital and 353–4, 373–429
absolute discharge 406–8
access to medical records
384–5
accompanied, patient's right to
be 393–4

adjournments 386–7, 392
adversarial approach 392–3
applications 375–9
assistance with 376
capacity to make 376
contents 381–2
delay 387–92, 434
forms 382
fresh 377
haste in process 387–92
increase in 387–8, 390
more than one application
381
notice 382
time for 377, 378, 388–9
withdrawal of 381, 388
writing 381
appointment 374–5
assessment, admissions for
377, 387
authorised representatives
(AR) 381–2, 384
before hearing, discharge
388–9
bias 375, 385
burden of proof 393, 400, 403
capacity 376, 395
chairman of the tribunals 374
code of practice 376
composition 374–5
conditional discharge 379–80,
386, 408–14
conflicts of interest 375
constitution 374–5
continued detention 399–405
cross-examination 396
dangerousness 378
deferred discharge 397
delay 387–93, 434
directions 386
disclosure of documents
383–5, 387, 581
discretionary discharge
403–4, 405
evidence 393
expert witnesses 384–6
fair trials 375, 384
forms 382
hearings 377–8, 392–7
before 381–7
discharge before 388–9
duration of 419
exclusions from 393–4
notice 387
parties 395–6
public hearings 394–5

Mental Health Review (*cont.*)
  Secretary of State,
    representation at hearing
    of 383
  timetable 387
hearsay 393
hospital managers
  hearings 395–6
  information on patient,
    provision of 382–3
  referrals by 379, 381
hospital orders 378, 383
Human Rights Act 1998
  380–1, 389–90, 393, 403
improvements in system 392
independent and impartial
  tribunal 385
informality 396
information
  patient, provision of
    information on 382–5,
    387
  public, disclosure to the
    393–4
inquisitorial approach 392–3
introduction of MHRTs 373
Law Society Mental Health
  Review Tribunal Panel 382
leave of absence 397–8
legal aid 382
legal representation 382, 386
legalism 373–4, 434
liberty and security, right to
  376, 385, 389–91, 400–5
life, right to 394
listing practice 389–90
mandatory discharge 399–405
medical evidence 402–3
medical members
  abolition 386
  bias 385, 581
  expert witnesses 384–6, 581
  information generated by
    384–5
  liberty and security, right to
    385
  opinions of 384–5
  role of 385
medication, risk that patient
  will not take 400
Mental Health Act 1983 375–9
Mental Health Act
  administrators 376
National Tribunals Service,
  creation of 392
natural justice 375, 383, 385,
  392, 396

nearest relatives 375–8, 381,
  397, 402
opinions 384–5
patient participation,
  problems with 397
Percy Commission 373
powers 374–5
private life, right to respect
  for 394
private, sitting in 393–5
proportionality 401
psychopathic disorders,
  persons with 403–4
public protection 399–401
reasons 393, 419
recall decisions 380–1
reclassification of disorders
  398–9
recommendations 398
referrals 379–81
refusal of discharge 397–8
regions 374
reports 382–4, 387, 391, 393
representation 381–2, 383–4,
  386, 390
re-sectioning following
  release 30
responsible medical officers
  (RMOs) 377, 396,
  397–400
restricted patients 374–5,
  378–80, 388, 406–19
  absolute discharge 406–8
  conditional discharge
    408–14
  leave of absence 398
  recommendations 398
  restriction directions,
    discharge of restricted
    patients subject to
    414–19
  special hospitals 398
  transfers 398
restriction orders 378–9,
  383
Rules 374–5, 383–9, 392,
  394–5
Secretary of State
  hearings 383, 395–6
  information on patient,
    provision of 382–3
  referrals by 379–81
  restricted patients, transfer
    of 398
substantive powers of
  discharge 397–419, 434
supervision applications 398

time limits 377, 378, 380–2,
  387, 388–9, 419
transfers 397–8
  hospital, to 377, 378–9
  restricted patients 398
treatability requirement
  402–5
treatment
  admission for 377
  control over 398–9
  future, requirement for
    404–5
victims, representations by
  396
mental health system
  absolute discharges 379
  accommodation, provision
    of 65
  asylum-based provision, rise
    and fall of 71–82, 109
  beds, number of 65–7
  care homes, number of beds
    in 67
  care in the community 63–7,
    82, 109
  Care Standards Act 2000 66–7
  community mental health
    centres (CMHCs) 67–8
  community mental health
    teams (CMHTs) 67
  community psychiatric nurses
    (CPNs) 67–8
  conditional discharges 379
  contemporary system,
    overview of 60–71
  definition 61
  domiciliary services 67, 68
  duration of CPN episodes 68
  duty to provide services
    64–5
  experiences of 63–4
  family and friends, care by 64,
    68
  first contacts 68
  funding 70–1
  general practitioners 63–4,
    67–8
  history of 60
  hospital provision 63–6, 109
  Human Rights Act 1998 59
  independent sector 67
  local authorities 66–8
    Care Standards Act 2000
      66–7
    care homes 66–7
    carers 68
    domiciliary services 68

nursing homes 66–7
residential accommodation
66–8
social workers 67
managerialism 109–10
medium secure units (MSUs)
66
Mental Health Task Force 69
National Director of Mental
Health 69
National Health Service,
funding of 70–1
National Institute for Clinical
Excellence (NICE) 69
National Institute for Mental
Health for England
(NIMHE) 69–70
*National Service Framework for
Mental Health* (NSFMH)
68–70
nursing homes 66–7
occupancy rates 65–6
overview 59–110
physical definition of
system 64
primary care sector 63
Primary Care Trusts 63, 64–5,
70, 108
prisons 61–3
private care provision 64
professionals 64
regional secure units (RSUs)
66
reinstitutionalisation 109
residential accommodation
66–8, 109
social services departments,
spending of 68
social workers 67, 68
special high security hospitals,
provision of 65–6, 108
surveillance 68
Mental Health Task Force 69
mental illness
abnormally aggressive or
seriously irresponsible
conduct 48
definition 46–50
diagnosis 48–50
Diagnostic and Statistical
Manual of Disorders
(DSM-IV-TR) 48–9
guardianship 503
lay interpretation 47–8
medical model 49
Mental Capacity Act 2005 576

Mental Health Act 1983 46–50
pseudo-patients 50
psychopathic disorders 47–8
signs of mental illness 49–50
WHO International
Classification of Diseases
48–9
mental impairment
abnormally aggressive or
seriously irresponsible
conduct 36–9
civil confinement 36
civil rights 37–9
definition of 34, 36–9
learning disabilities 39
medical evidence 37
medical experts 38
Mental Capacity Act 2005 39,
576
Mental Health Act 1983 34,
36–9
remand to hospital 220
restriction orders 252–3
second opinions and report
system 329, 333
severe mental impairment and,
difference between 36 -8
sexual offences, consent and
37–8
transfer from prison to
hospital 264
treatment, admission for 129
Mental Treatment Act 1930 19
**Metropolitan Commissioners in
Lunacy** 17
MHAC *see* **Mental Health Act
Commission (MHAC)**
MHRT *see* **Mental Health Review
Tribunals**
MIND 12, 15
mini mental state examination
513–15
miscarriages of justice 21, 204–5
M'Naghten **rules** 239–41
MSUs (medium secure units) 66
multidisciplinary teamwork
approved social workers
(ASWs) 181–3
civil confinement 180–3
code of practice 180
compulsion, treatment of
detained patients
under 296
housing authorities
478–82
police 140

second opinions and report
system 329, 332
services in the community
436–7, 470–8, 495–6
murder
facts, trial of the 234–7
fitness to stand trial 232,
234–7
hospital orders 245
remand to hospital 219
restriction orders 232
special verdict 239, 241

**National Assistance Act 1948,
Pt III, accommodation
services under** 438, 439–45
assessment of needs 458–69
asylum seekers 441
care and attention, persons in
need of 439–41, 458–9
Care Standards Tribunal 444
charges
divestiture of assets 442–3
means-testing 441–3,
458–60
children 439
compulsory admissions 444–5
divestiture of assets 442–3
fair trials 443
family care, costs of 440
hospitals 444–5
informal care 440
judicial review 443
licensing 444
means-tested charges 441–3,
458–60
National Care Standards
Commission (NCSC) 444
nursing homes 444–5
ordinary residence 440–1
private sector 443–4
registration 444
restoration of property to
original owners 443
social services departments
438, 439–46, 458–60
temporary accommodation,
persons in urgent need of
440
urgent need, persons in 440
voluntary organizations
443–4
**National Assistance Act 1948,
welfare services under** 439,
445–6, 449
care in the community 86

National Assistance (*cont.*)
  Care Standards Act 2000 446
  charges 446
  disability discrimination 446
  disabled persons 445–6
  social security 446
  social services departments
    445–6
National Care Standards
  Commission (NCSC) 444
National Health Service 11–12
  see also Primary Care Trusts
  (PCTs)
  accommodation, admission
    to 556
  best interests test 556–7
  care in the community 86–9
  civil confinement 159
  creation of 87–8
  funding 70–1
  independent advocates 556
  Mental Health Act 1959 19
  National Health Service Act
    1977 438, 447
  National Health Service and
    Community Care Act 1990
    437, 438–9, 449–70
  National Health Service
    bodies, working together
    with 470–8
  prisons, partnership with 61–2
  private sector, regulation of 12
  services in the community
    437–9, 447, 449–70
  structure of, changing the
    88–9
  Working for Patients White
    Paper 88
National Institute for Clinical
  Excellence (NICE) 69, 279,
  336–7
National Institute for Mental
  Health in England (NIMHE)
  60, 69–70
National Service Framework for
  Mental Health (NSFMH)
  68–70
  care in the community 85, 495
  list of standards 68–9
  prisons 61
  services in the community
    452–3, 456
National Task Force on Violence
  against Social Care Staff 105
natural justice 375, 383, 385,
  392, 396, 424

NCSC (National Care Standards
  Commission) 444
nearest relatives *see also* nearest
  relatives, civil confinement
  and
  appointment 26
  civil confinement 123, 155–6,
    158, 165–74, 177
  consultation with 354
  discharge from hospital
    364–5, 367
  habeas corpus 187–8
  judicial review 193
  leave and recall 354
  Mental Capacity Act 2005
    573–4
  Mental Health Review
    Tribunals 375–8, 381, 397,
    402
  police 136
  poor relief 22
  release 21–2
  replacement 26
nearest relatives, civil
  confinement and 123, 155–6,
  158
  abolition of role of nearest
    relative, proposal for 166–7
  admission for assessment 173
  admission for treatment 173
  appearing to be nearest
    relative, persons 168–9
  applications 174, 177
  approved social workers
    (ASWs) 160, 163–73
    appearing to be nearest
      relative, consulting
      persons 168–9
    consultation with 163–4
    reasonable enquiry, duty of
      168–9
    views of 163
  carers, respite for 166
  children
    Children Act 1989,
      responsibility under the
      167–8
    parental responsibility
      172–4
  civil partners 167
  civil rights 166
  code of practice 166
  cohabitees 167–8
  dangerous patients 169
  definition 167–8
  delegation 168, 169

  discharge, power of 173
  emergency admissions 134–5
  family support and care 165
  Human Rights Act 1998 165–6,
    167, 171–3
  interim orders 173
  justification for involvement of
    the family 165–6
  lay and professions, tension
    between 165–7
  list of relatives 167
  Mental Health Act 1983 169,
    172
  objections to confinement by
    nearest relatives 169–73
  ordinarily resides with, relative
    that patient 168–9
  parental responsibility, persons
    with 167–8
  private life, right to respect for
    172–4
  reasonable enquiry, duty of
    168–9
  removal and replacement of
    nearest relative, 168,
    169–72
  substitution 168, 169–72
  treatment, admission for 173
  Victorian values about family
    involvement 165–6, 168
necessaries 569
necessity
  compulsion, treatment of
    detained patients under
    310, 313–14, 317
  emergency medical treatment
    335
  guardianship 577
  informal admission 117
  Mental Capacity Act 2005
    550
  personal decisions 504
  restraint 134, 339
negligence
  damages 593–600
  discharge from hospital
    366–7
  drug therapy 594–5
  duty of care 594–600
  health professionals 594–600
  neglect and ill-treatment,
    offence of 548, 590–2
neuroleptics 8–9, 14, 78, 278–81,
  290, 330–1
neurosurgery *see* psychosurgery
next friends 605–6

NFSMH *see* National Service Framework for Mental Health (NSFMH)

NHS *see* National Health Service

NICE (National Institute for Clinical Excellence) 69, 279, 336–7

NIMHE (National Institute for Mental Health in England) 60, 69–70

non-physical treatments 286–8

nooceptive drugs 278

normality, concept of 74

normalisation theory 84

Northern Ireland, psychopathy as category of disorder in 41

nurses 11, 12
  care in the community 85, 88, 91
  community psychiatric nurses (CPNs) 67–8, 85, 203–4
  compulsion, treatment of detained patients under 297
  compulsory detention into, discharge of people from 91
  contact with 297
  health authorities 88
  personal care 475–6
  services in the community 451, 472–3, 475–6

nursing homes
  accommodation services under National Assistance Act 1948 444–5
  beds, number of 85
  care in the community 91
  local authorities 66–7

obedience test 96

obsessional disorders 285

occupational therapy 286, 287

occupiers' liability 594

old people *see* elderly people

opiates 73

opinions *see* second opinions and report system

PACE and codes 180, 204–14

paedophilia 43, 44–5

parens patriae 20, 498–9, 503–5, 539, 546

Parole Board 414–15, 417

paupers 18, 75–6, 82

Payment by Results (PbR) 89

PCTs *see* Primary Care Trusts (PCTs)

perceptions of the mentally ill
  crime and mental disorder, links between 201
  dangerousness 2–3
  factors influencing mental disorder 9–10
  folk devils 201
  homelessness 3
  media 2–3
  poverty 3

Percy Commission
  capacity 506
  care in the community 82
  civil confinement 159–60, 181
  compulsion, treatment of detained patients under 295
  guardianship 503
  informal admission 116
  Mental Health Review Tribunals 373
  treatment, admission for 131

personal decision-making, capacity and 503–5
  advance decisions regarding treatment 569–70
  battery 503
  best interests of the patient 504–5
  common law partners 504
  Court of Protection 559, 560
  court, role of the 504–5, 559
  declarations 505
  deputies (Court of Protection) 560
  false imprisonment 504
  general defence 567
  guardianship 503–4, 577
  lasting powers of attorney 548, 561–2
  Mental Capacity Act 2005 505, 546
  Mental Deficiency Acts 503
  Mental Health Act 1959 503–4
  necessity 504
  parens patriae 503–5
  powers of attorney 561
  sterilisation 504
  substitute decision-making 558

personality disorders 24–5, 253, 298

pharmaceutical manufacturers 14–15

physical treatment in hospital 275, 277–86, 303–8

place of safety, removal to 126, 135–6, 138, 179, 203, 219, 242, 262, 590

pleas *see* unfitness to plead

police
  72 hour detention period 137–8
  absence without leave 431–2
  admission to hospital 111, 136–8
  agencies, relationship with other 140
  appropriate adult 205–14
  approved social workers (ASWs) 140, 179
  arrest 136–7, 140–4
  assessments 137, 139
  bed closures 107
  carers 136
  civil confinement 124, 126, 179–80
  criminal offences 140
  diagnosis of mental disorder 137
  diversion from prosecution 203, 205, 272
  emergency admissions 136–8, 140
  entry and search powers 179–80, 432
  hospital, admission to 107, 111, 136–8
  increased involvement of 107
  interviews 205
  Mental Health Act 1983 section 136 136–8, 139
  nearest relatives 136
  PACE and codes 180, 204–14
  place of safety, removal to 138, 203
  powers 136–8
  psychiatrists, contacting 140
  public places, persons in 136–8, 140
  race 141–4
  regional variations 139–40
  standards 136–8
  taking patient to hospital 180
  warrants for emergency admissions, issue of 135–6

polypharmacy 280–1, 326, 330–2

poor law 75–6, 82

poverty 18, 22
  asylum-based provision 75–6,
    82
  perceptions 3
  poor law 75–6, 82
  poor relief, nearest relatives
    and 22
powers of attorney *see also* lasting
  powers of attorney (LPOA)
  advance directives 528
  common law 561
  court's power of intervention
    564
  enduring powers of attorney
    528, 547–8, 561, 563–5, 569
  goods and services, payment
    for 569
  Mental Health Act 1983 561
  personal decisions 561
  promises, honouring 563–4
  property and affairs 561
  tests for capacity 565
predictions
  dangerousness 147–8
  future events, intervention
    and 55
preferences 452–3
prefrontal leucotomies 285
pregnant women 303–4, 309,
  521–5
pre-sentencing diversion *see*
  court-based pre-sentencing
  diversion
presumption of innocence 228
pressure groups 15
previous convictions for violent
  or sexual offences 218–19
Primary Care Trusts (PCTs)
  aftercare under supervision
    (ACUs) 492
  care in the community 88–90
  complaints 469–70, 603
  control in the community 436
  funding 70, 89
  mental health system 63–5,
    70, 108
  prisons 62
  services in the community
    436, 447, 464, 466–7, 472–5
  special hospitals 108
  tariffs 89
prisons *see also* transfer from
  prison to hospital
  asylum-based provision 76
  Changing the Outlook 61
  compulsory treatment 62–3

criminal justice system 202,
  262–72
  Department of Health 62
  diversion 214
  funding 62
  hospital orders 248–9
  in-reach programmes, funding
    of staff for 62
  liberty and security, right
    to 63
  Mental Health Bill 2002 62
  NHS, partnership with 61–2
  National Service Framework
    for Mental Health 61
  Primary Care Trusts 62
  recall on licence 273
  release 273
  remand 215–19
  restriction directions,
    discharge of patients subject
    to 414–19
  return to 248–9
  task forces 62
  transfer to 414–19
  treatment available in prison
    273
Pritchard test 231
private life, right to respect for
  capacity 541
  compulsion, treatment of
    detained patients under
    311, 313–14, 316–17
  discharge from hospital 367
  families 541
  information 541
  judicial review 195, 582
  leave and recall 354
  Mental Health Review
    Tribunals 394
  nearest relatives 172–4
  refusal of medical treatment
    292, 294
  restraint 339
  seclusion 342–3
  second opinions and report
    system 323–4
  special hospitals 100, 101–2
  surveillance 100
  transfer from prison to
    hospital 267, 271
private sector providers 12, 64
  accommodation services
    443–4
  asylum-based provision 78
  care in the community 88
  charities 12

complaints 470
contracts 444
group homes 85
Human Rights Act 1998 191–2
judicial review 191–2
leave and recall 358, 360
local authorities, competition
  with 86
Madhouse Acts 17–18
National Health Service 12
public functions, private
  bodies performing 191–2,
  461–2
registration 444
regulation 12
residential care 85
services in the community
  461–2
social security 85
transfer to 461–2
privilege 207
procedural impropriety 193,
  424, 461
professionals *see* Approved Social
  Workers (ASWs); doctors;
  general practitioners; medical
  personnel; nurses;
  psychiatrists; Responsible
  Medical Officers (RMOs);
  social workers
prohibitory orders 190
promiscuity, immoral conduct,
  sexual deviancy and drug or
  alcohol dependency
  control of tendencies 45–6
  decision-making 44
  dependency, meaning of 45–6
  drunkards, detention of
    habitual 43
  feeble-mindedness 43
  homosexuality 43–4
  medicalised model 43
  Mental Deficiency Act 1913 43
  Mental Health Act 1959 43, 44
  Mental Health Act 1983 35,
    42–6
  paedophilia 43, 44–5
  psychopathic disorders 43–4
  remand 215
  Victorian and Edwardian
    social policy 43
property and affairs, capacity
  and 498–503
  contracts 500–2
  Court of Protection 499, 559,
    560

Crown 498–9
deputies (Court of Protection)
    560
enduring powers of attorney
    546
family members 499
gifts 502
history 498–500
lasting powers of attorney
    548, 561, 565
litigation 500–1
Lord Chancellor 499
lucid intervals 500–1
marriage 502–3, 517
Mental Capacity Act 2005
    499, 500, 546
Mental Deficiency Acts 546
Mental Health Act 1983 499,
    500, 546, 583
parens patriae 498–9, 546
powers of attorney 561
test for intervention 499
trust corporations 561
wills 502–3
proportionality
Human Rights Act 1998 197,
    601
judicial review 194–6
Mental Health Review
    Tribunals 401, 424
research 549
restraint 548, 558
sentencing as diversion 242
prosecutions 585, 590–3 *see also*
    diversion from prosecution
protection of the public *see*
    public, protection of the
protective custody 122
provocation 236
pseudoparkinsonism 281
pseudopatients 50
psychiatric drugs
psychiatrists
approved social workers
    (ASWs) 181–3, 197–8
civil confinement 181–3,
    197–8
hospital and limitation
    directions 260
medical recommendations
    175–6
police contacting 140
race 142
restriction orders 250–1
role of 11
stereotyping 142

psychiatry 2, 9
psychoanalysis 286
psychodysleptics 278
psychogeriatric patients 113
psychopathic disorder
abnormally aggressive or
    seriously irresponsible
    conduct 40–1
antisocial or dissocial
    personality disorders 40–2
compulsion, treatment of
    detained patients under
    301
compulsory admission 41
definition of 35, 39–42
diagnosis 42
drug therapy 288
Fallon Committee 24
guardianship 489–90, 503
hospitals
hospital and limitation
    directions 246, 257–62
hospital orders 246, 257,
    259–60
remand 220
transfer from prison to
    hospital 264, 269–70
treatment in 129, 130–1,
    288
Mental Capacity Act 2005 576
Mental Health Act 1983 35,
    39–42
Mental Health Review
    Tribunals 403–4
mental illness, definition of
    47–8
Northern Ireland 41
promiscuity, immoral
    conduct, sexual deviancy
    and drug or alcohol
    dependency 43–4
remand to hospital 220
restriction orders 252–3, 255
Scotland 41
second opinions and report
    system 329, 333
sentencing as diversion 243
social control 40
transfer from prison to
    hospital 264, 269–70
treatability 24, 41–2
treatment, admission for 129,
    130–1
psychostimulants 278
psychosurgery
capacity 285–6

consent 285
deep brain stimulation
    284–5
depression 285
Mental Health Act 1983 285
Mental Capacity Act 2005 575
obsessional disorders 285
prefrontal leucotomies 285
Scotland 285
second opinions and report
    system 318, 328
psychotherapy
consent 287
power imbalances 287–8
professionalisation of 346–7
qualifications 346
register of psychotherapists
    346
UK Council for Psychotherapy
    346–7
public authorities *see also* health
    authorities; local authorities;
    National Health Service;
    Primary Care Trusts; social
    services departments
aftercare 468
Human Rights Act 1998
    191–2, 196
public functions, private
    bodies performing 191–2,
    461–2
services in the community
    461–2
Public Guardian 548, 560, 563,
    572
public perception *see* perceptions
public, protection of the *see also*
    dangerousness
absence without leave
    430–1
control in the community
    485
criminal justice system 273–4
discharge from hospital 371,
    373
diversion from prosecution
    273
imprisonment for public
    protection (IPP) 243
leave and recall 358–9
Mental Health Review
    Tribunals 399–401, 421

quarantine for contagious
    diseases 146
quashing orders 190

race
  absence without leave 430
  action plans 144
  Afro-Caribbeans 140–3
    men, over-representation of
      140–1
    over-representation 55,
      140–1
  capacity 542
  challenging behaviour 143
  civil confinements 143
  dangerousness 149
  detention 140–5
  diagnosis 142
  geographic variations 141
  informal admissions 141,
    143–4
  medical model 55, 142
  over-representation 55, 140–1
  police, section 136 arrests by
    141–4
  policy documents 144
  psychiatrists, stereotyping by
    142
  referrals 143
  restriction orders 253
  schizophrenia 142–3
  seclusion 344–5
  second opinions and report
    system 329, 330
  services in the community
    453–4, 478
  special high security hospitals
    108
Rampton 66, 97, 99–100, 267,
  369–70, 388, 409
randomised clinical trials (RCTs)
  279–80
rational reasons test 512–13, 516
rationality 193, 429, 508–13,
  524, 543–4
real life, suspension of 96
reasonable outcome of choice
  510–12
reasons
  judicial review 191, 582
  medical certificates 322–3
  Mental Health Review
    Tribunals 393, 419–22, 425
  second opinions and report
    system 322–4
recall
  absolute discharge 406–8
  aftercare under supervision
    (ACUs) 493–4
  licence, recall on 273

Mental Health Review
  Tribunals 380–1
prison 248–9, 273
restriction directions,
  discharge of patients subject
  to 415
supervised community
  treatment (SCT) 493–4
receivers, appointment of 499,
  560, 564
recommendations see medical
  recommendations
referral process
  civil confinement 156–8
  community psychiatric nurses
    (CPNs) 204
  diversion from prosecution
    204
  families 157
  forensic medical examiners
    (FMEs) 204
  home, referrals from the
    156–7
  hospital managers 379, 381
  Mental Health Review
    Tribunals 379–81
  public places, referrals from
    157
  race 143
  Secretary of State 379–81
  transfer from prison to
    hospital 267
reform
  capacity 23
  Department of Health White
    Paper 24–5
  Fallon Committee 24–5
  Law Commission 22–3
  Richardson Committee 23–4
  services in the community
    457–8
  social workers 22–30
refusal of medical treatment
  275, 288–94
  advance decisions regarding
    treatment 545, 547, 570
  advance directives 528–9
  battery 292
  Bolam test 290–1, 294
  capacity 289, 294, 508, 511,
    515, 521–5
  coercion 292–4
  common law 288–9
  consent 290–4
  detained patients 289, 293–4
  disclosure of risks 290–2

drug therapy 8–9, 279–81
guidance 288–9
informal admissions 289,
  292–4
information, right to 290–2
informed consent 291
inhuman or degrading
  treatment 292, 294
Mental Capacity Act 2005 294
opinion, responsible body of
  medical 290–1
private life, right to respect for
  292, 294
warnings of substantial risk
  290–1
regional secure units (RSUs) 66
rehabilitation model 84
relatives see families; nearest
  relatives
release see also discharge from
  hospital
  19th century 21–2
  dangerousness 22
  earliest release date (ERD)
    268–70
  graduated release 264
  habeas corpus 188–9
  hospital orders 245, 248–9,
    257, 258, 272–3
  informal admission 116–17
  latest date of release (LDR)
    268–9
  Mental Health Review
    Tribunals 30, 580
  nearest relatives 21–2
  prisons 273
  re-sectioning 30
  restriction orders 254
  services in the community
    447–9
  transfer from prison to
    hospital 264–6, 268–70
religion
  blood transfusions, refusal of
    508, 515, 521–2
  capacity 508, 513, 515, 521–2,
    553
  medical treatment, consent to
    508, 515, 521–2, 553
remand see remand in custody;
  remand to hospital, diversion
  from criminal justice
  system
remand in custody
  assessments 218
  bail or 215–19

drug or alcohol abuse, persons
with 215
inhuman or degrading
treatment 216
life, right to 216–17
magistrates 215
prison population 215–17
screening 216–17
suicide 216–17
violent offenders 216–17
remand to hospital, diversion
from criminal justice system
and 219–39, 272
accused persons, definition of
220–1
assessment 219
bail 219–30
compulsory treatment 220,
221
consent 221
Crown Court, 219, 220, 222
diversion 219—39
dual detention 222
duration 219
fitness to plead 238–9
fitness to stand trial 223–38
hospital orders 221
indictable offences 222–3
lack of hospital places 219
magistrates' court 219, 220–3,
238–9
medical criteria 221
Mental Health Act 1983
219–22, 272
mental impairment 220
murder, persons convicted of
219
psychopathic disorder 220
reports, for 219, 220–3
responsible medical officers,
powers of 222
severe mental impairment 221
summary offences 222
transfer from prison to
hospital 271
treatability test 223
treatment, for 219, 220,
221–3, 273
remedies see also damages,
actions for
effective remedy, right to an
194
Human Rights Act 1998 194,
196
judicial review 23–4, 190–4,
426, 466–7, 582

reoffending rates 373
reports see also second opinions
and report system
absence without leave 433
discharge from hospital 364
Mental Health Review
Tribunals 381–2, 383–4,
386, 390
out-of-date 267–8
remand to hospital 219, 220–3
sentencing as diversion 242
transfer from prison to
hospital 267–8
representation
advice, right to legal 207
appropriate adult 206–7, 213
authorised representatives
(AR) 381–2, 384
best interests test 606–7
capacity to litigate 604–7
course of proceedings, capacity
during 605
fair trials 605
guardians, advocates as 607
informal admission 119
instructions, ability to give
607
legal aid 16, 382, 604
litigation friend 604–5
appointment 605, 607
certificates of suitability
605
challenging appointments
605
marginal capacity, patients
with 605
Mental Health Review
Tribunals 382, 386, 604,
607
next friends 605–6
time limits 606
understanding of clients 606
withdrawal 607–8
research 545, 549
residence
aftercare under supervision
(ACUs) 492
discharge from hospital 366
guardianship 114–15, 503
power to convey to a 492
requirement to reside in
specific place 114–15
residential accommodation
abuse 95
assessments 451, 458–63
beds, number of 67, 85

best interests test 556
care in the community 88, 90,
94–5, 109
charges 448
closure 461–3, 472–3
group homes 12, 85, 91–2
home for life promises
462–3
housing authorities 483
independent advocates 556
inspection 95
judicial review 191–2
lasting powers of attorney 562
local authorities 66–8, 88, 90,
556–7
mental health system 66–8,
109
preferences 452–3
private care 85
refusal of 451–2
registration 95
scandals 108
services in the community
447–8, 451–3, 458–63,
472–3
social security 85, 88
respite care 13, 166
Responsible Medical Officers
(RMOs)
aftercare under supervision
(ACUs) 493
complaints 603
compulsion, treatment of
detained patients under
297
discharge from hospital
363–5, 368–72
emergency medical treatment
335–6
funding 297
independent and impartial
tribunal 321
leave and recall 354–61
Mental Health Review
Tribunals 377, 396–400,
422, 426–9
remand to hospital 222
restriction directions,
discharge of patients subject
to 416
second opinions and report
system 319, 320–33
supervised community
treatment (SCT) 494
team visits 327–8
training 297

restraint
  aims 336
  already in hospital, admission
    of persons already in 134
  best interests test 548
  common law 339
  Court of Protection 548
  criminal proceedings 584
  death, causing 337, 338
  drugs 338
  emergency medical treatment
    336–9
  extent of use 337–8
  guidance 337
  immediate restraint, necessity
    for 134
  immunity 339
  informal admissions 336, 339
  inhuman or degrading
    treatment 339
  liberty and security, right to
    548, 558–9
  necessity 134, 339
  Mental Capacity Act 2005 548
  Mental Health Act 1983 339
  Mental Health Act
    Commission 336–8
  National Institute for Clinical
    Excellence (NICE) 336–7
  physical restraint 336–8
  private life, right to respect for
    339
  proportionality 548, 558
  restraint teams 338
  risk assessment 337
  self-defence, right to 339
  social control 336
  special hospitals 338
  straitjackets 338
  substitute decision-making
    558–9
  training 336–7
  tranquillisers 337
restricted patients see also
  restriction directions,
  discharge of patients subject
  to; restriction orders
  absolute discharge 406–8
  Advisory Board on Restricted
    Patients (ABRP) 368–9
  conditional discharge 408–14
  leave and recall 359–62
  leave of absence 398
  Mental Health Review
    Tribunals 374–5, 378–80,
    388, 398, 406–19, 422–3

  recommendations 398
  Secretary of State 398
  special hospitals 398
  transfers 398
restriction directions, discharge
  of patients subject to 414–19
  absolute discharge 415, 417
  conditional discharge 415–19
  hospital and limitation
    directions 415
  hospital
    continued detention in
      414–18
    transfer to 265, 270–1, 414
  hospital orders 417–18
  liberty and security, right to
    415–17
  life imprisonment 417–18
  Mental Health Act 1983
    414–19
  Parole Board 414–15, 417
  prison, transfer to 414–19
  recall, liable to 415
  responsible medical officers
    (RMOs) 416
  Secretary of State 414–19
  technical lifer, concept of 417
  transfer directions 265, 270–1,
    414–16
restriction orders
  conditional discharges 249
  control 254–5
  Crown Court, committal to
    the 250
  criteria 250
  dangerousness 249–54
  discharge from hospital
    367–8, 372–3
  duration of 255, 256
  fitness to stand trial 232,
    235–6, 238
  gender 253
  hospital orders 232, 235–6,
    245, 249–55, 260
  leave of absence 254–5
  limited duration, restriction
    orders of 256
  magistrates' courts 250
  medical evidence 250–2, 256
  medical recommendations
    251–2, 256
  Mental Health Act 1983
    section 41 249–56
  Mental Health Review
    Tribunals 378–9, 383
  mental impairment 252–3

  monitoring by mental health
    unit (MHU) of Home
    Office 255
  murder 232
  nature of restrictions 254–6
  psychiatrists 250–1
  psychopathic disorders 252–3,
    255
  race 253
  release 254
  restricted patient regime
    254–6
  risk assessment 250–1
  sentencing as diversion
    249–56
  serious harm, risk of 250–2
  severe and dangerous
    personality disorders
    (SDPD) 254
  sexual offences 253
  socially disadvantaged persons
    253
  special verdict 241
  therapeutic concerns 254
  treatability requirement 254
  violent offences 250–1, 253
Richardson Committee
  approved social workers 163
  capacity 24, 149
  code of practice 25
  dangerousness standards 25
  decision-making 25
    open and fair 25
    patient's involvement in 25
  general principles, set of 23,
    25
  hospital, confinement in 24
  involuntary treatment 24
  mandatory orders, flexibility in
    23–4
  Mental Health Act 1983 23–4
  proposals 23–4
  reviews 24, 25
  securing 25
RMOs see Responsible Medical
  Officers (RMOs)
romanticisation of mental
  illness 4
Rosenhan study 54
Royal Prerogative powers 17, 18
RSUs (regional secure units) 66

safety, removal to place of 126,
  135–6, 138, 179, 203, 219, 242,
  262, 590
Sanctuary of Asklepios 277–8

scaremongering 2–3
schizophrenia 4, 6
  abandonment of concept
    of 53
  biochemical factors 52
  capacity 518–21
  case study 50–5
  causal theories 51–2
  chlorpromazine 280
  deviance, understanding of 54
  diagnosis 50–1
  Diagnostic and Statistical
    Manual of Disorders
    (DSM-IV-TR) 48–9
  dopamine levels 52
  drug efficacy 52
  drug therapy 52, 279–81
  genetics 51–2
  medical model 50–1
  medical theories 52
  multiple causes, as having 53
  neurodevelopment models 52
  race 142–3
  second opinions and report
    system 330
  social causes 53–4
  socio-economic status 53–4
  split personality 51
  symptoms 50, 51
  WHO International
    Classification of Diseases
    48–9
Scotland
  compulsory admission 41
  fitness to stand trial 237
  hospital and limitation
    directions 260 261
  psychopathic disorders 41
  psychosurgery 285
  services in the community
    475–6
  treatability 404
SCT see supervised community
  treatment (SCT)
SDPDs (severe and dangerous
  personality disorders) 94, 254
search, powers of 99–101, 432
seclusion
  authorisation 340
  clothing, use of special 340
  code of practice 340–3
  conditions 344–5
  emergency medical treatment
    340–5
  guidelines 340
  Human Rights Act 1998 342

inhuman or degrading
    treatment 342
  liberty and security, right to
    342–4
  Mental Health Act 1983 340–1
  Mental Health Act
    Commission 340–1, 344
  monitoring 341–2
  private life, right to respect
    for 342–3
  punishment, as 340
  purpose of 340, 342–3
  race 344–5
  reports 341
  reviews 341–2
  social control 336
  special hospitals 342
second opinions and report
  system 318–33
  age 330
  autonomy 322–4
  best interests of patient 319
  Brady approach 320, 348
  capacity 319, 320, 322, 325–7
  certification 318–23
    duration of 320
    reasons 322–3
  code of practice 318, 321,
    324–6, 332
  compulsion, treatment of
    detained patients under
    318–33
  consent 318–20, 324–7
    informed 324
    retracting 320
  discontinuance of treatment
    320
  drug therapy 318–22, 325,
    329, 330–1
    certificates, duration of
      320
    changing drugs 326
    polypharmacy 326, 330–2
    sedatives 331
    three-month rule 318–19,
      320
  electroconvulsive therapy
    318–19, 325, 329, 330
  fair and public hearings
    320–1, 323
  force feeding 319, 320
  forms 326–8
  gender 329, 330
  hormones, surgical implants of
    (chemical castration) 318,
    328

Human Rights Act 1998 323–4
  independent and impartial
    tribunals 321
  judicial review 320, 322–3
  legalism 324, 329, 332–3
  medicalism 332–3
  Mental Capacity Act 2005
    319, 325
  Mental Health Act 1983
    318–33
  Mental Health Act
    Commission (MHAC)
    318–19, 321, 324–7, 330–3
  mental impairment 329, 333
  more than one treatment,
    consent to 319–20
  multidisciplinary approach
    329, 332
  non-medical professionally
    concerned persons,
    consultation with 329
  operation of schemes of
    324–33
  physical treatments 318
  private life, right to respect for
    323–4
  psychopathic disorder 329,
    333
  psychosurgery 318, 328
  race 329, 330
  reasons 322–4
  responsible medical officers
    (RMOs) 319, 320–33
  safeguards 318, 319–20
  schizophrenia 330
  second opinion appointed
    doctors (SOADs) 275, 277,
    318–33
  severe mental impairment 329
  special control 333
  supervised community
    treatment (SCT) 494
  time limits 319–20, 325–6
Secretary of State
  discharge from hospital
    367–72
  hearings 383, 395–6
  hospital orders 367–72
  leave and recall 360–1
  Mental Health Review
    Tribunals 379–83, 395–6,
    398
  referrals 379–81
  restricted patients
    discharge of 414–19
    transfer of 264, 398

Secretary of State (*cont.*)
    services in the community
        437–8
    transfer from prison to
        hospital 264
sectioning *see* civil confinement
sedation 179, 331
self-defence, right to 339
self-determination 309, 509–10,
    536–7
self-harm 105–6, 115, 298, 340,
    428
self-referrals 157
sentencing *see* court-based
    pre-sentencing diversion;
    sentencing as diversion
sentencing as diversion 242–63
    extension period 242
    hospital and limitation orders
        256–63
    hospital orders 243–9
    hospital, transfer to 243
    imprisonment for public
        protection (IPP) 243
    inhuman or degrading
        treatment 243
    life sentences 243
    medical reports 242
    Mental Health Act 1983
        243–4, 272–3
    minimum term 242
    mitigation 242
    proportionality 242
    psychopathic disorders 243
    restriction orders 249–56
    seriousness of offence 242
    sexual offences 242–4
    specified offences 242–3
    violent offences 242–3
seriously irresponsible conduct
    see abnormally aggressive or
    seriously irresponsible
    conduct
services *see* goods and services,
    payment for
services in the community
    435–84 *see also* National
    Assistance Act 1948 Part III,
    accommodation services
    under
    aftercare 447–8
        code of practice 447–8
        discharge, blocking 464–9
        duty to provide 464–9
        features of 448
        mandatory orders 466–7

public authorities,
    Convention rights and
        468
    refusal to provide 436
allocation of responsibility
    between agencies 475
alternative sources of care and
    assistance 449–50
approvals 438
assessment of entitlement
    450–72
    declining to carry out 451
    systematic 470
    termination of 451–2
beds, blocking of 476
breach of statutory duty 469
care coordinators 476
care management 477
care plans 450–2, 455, 461,
    465, 470, 478
care programme approach
    465–6, 470–3, 476–7
Care Standards Act 2000 446
care trusts (CTs),
    establishment of 474
charges 446, 448–9, 472,
    474–6
children and adolescents 438
closure of facilities 461–3,
    472–3
code of practice 447–8
community care planning
    437–8
complaints 469–70
compulsory detention, release
    from 447–9
conditional discharges,
    aftercare and 464–5
consultation with other
    agencies 437
consumerism 437
dangerousness 436
definition 438
directions 438
disabled persons 445–6,
    449–50, 454, 457–8
discretion 438
domiciliary services 453–4
elderly people 446–7
eligibility criteria 475
failure of community care 436
family life, right to respect for
    456
funding 438, 474
gender 453–4
grey areas 471

guidance 470, 475, 477
health authorities 436, 447,
    464, 472–4
Health Services and Public
    Health Act 1968 438, 446–7
home for life promises 462–3
home, right to respect for
    462–3
housing authorities 436, 438,
    478–84
Human Rights Act 1998
    461–3, 467
informal patients 448–9
inspections 473
inter-agency cooperation 436,
    470–8, 495–6
integrated care 436, 470–8,
    495–6
joint ventures 474
judicial review 469
key workers 470, 472, 476
knowledge, lack of 453–4
legitimate expectations 462
liberty and security, right
    to 467
local authorities 438
managerialism 437
mandatory orders 466–7
Mental Health Act 1983
    section 117 438, 447–9, 464
National Assistance Act 1948,
    welfare services under
    445–6
National Health Service Act
    1977 438, 447
National Health Service and
    Community Care Act 1990
    437, 438–9, 449–60, 470
    bypassing 458–69
National Health Service
    bodies, working together
    with 470–8
National Service Framework
    for Mental Health
    (NFSMH) 474, 495
natural justice 451
need 452–8
    definition of 452–3, 456
    preferences and 452–3
    resources and 454–6,
        458–60
nursing care 451, 472–3,
    475–6
packages of care 473
partnership arrangements
    474, 477–8

personal care 475–6
preferences 452–3
Primary Care Trusts 436, 447,
    464, 466–7, 472–5
private sector facilities
    public function, private
        bodies with 461–2
    transfer to 461–2
procedural fairness 461
professional education and
    training 471
race 453–4, 478
reform and simplification
    457–8
refusal to accept services
    451–2
residential accommodation
    447, 472
    assessment 451, 458–63
    charges 448
    closure of 461–3, 472–3
    home for life promises
        462–3
    preferences 452–3
    refusal of 451–2
resources 454–6, 458–60
reviews 470
Scotland 475–6
Secretary of State, powers of
    437–8
service provision 435–6
    mandatory 435–6
    optional 435–6
social exclusion 435–6
    social inclusion 435–6
social security 446
social services departments
    436, 437–8, 447
    assessment of entitlement
        450–70, 472–6
    discretion 438
    elderly people 446–7
    high performing 438
    National Health Service Act
        1977 447
    welfare services 445–6
standards 474
supervision 435
Wednesbury unreasonableness
    455–6, 461–2
welfare services 445–6, 449
**severe and dangerous personality
    disorders (SDPDs)** 94, 254
severe mental impairment
    capacity 507, 576
    civil rights 37–8

definition 24
Mental Capacity Act 2005 576
Mental Health Act 1983 24
mental impairment and,
    difference between 36
remand to hospital 221
second opinions and report
    system 329
treatment, admission for 131
severe subnormality 503
sex *see* gender
sexual activity, consent to 506
sexual deviancy *see* promiscuity,
    immoral conduct, sexual
    deviancy and drug or alcohol
    dependency
sexual harassment 103
sexual offences
    bail 218–19
    consent 37–8
    hormones, surgical
        implantation of 575
    hospital orders 245
    mental impairment, definition
        of 37–8
    previous convictions 218–19
    restriction orders 253
    sentencing as diversion 242–4
    sexual relations with persons
        receiving treatment 593
shock treatments 277–8
silence, right to 207
social and environmental factors
    10
social exclusion 435–6
social inclusion 435–6
**social norms, substitute
    judgment and** 532
social reintegration, concept of
    84
social policy
    capacity 506, 11
    promiscuity, immoral
        conduct, sexual deviancy
        and drug or alcohol
        dependency 43
    Victorian and Edwardian
        social policy 43
social reform movements 72, 75
social security 16, 85, 88, 446
**social services departments
    (SSDS)** 27
    accommodation services 438,
        439–46, 458–60
    aftercare under supervision
        (ACUs) 492

control in the community 436
criminal proceedings 592–3
eviction, notification of 480
guardianship 490
housing authorities,
    integration with 478–84
services in the community
    436–8, 446–7, 450–70,
    472–6
spending of 68
welfare services 445–6
social workers 11, 68 *see also*
    **approved social workers
    (ASWs)**
    appropriate adult 209
    assessments 174
    British Association of Social
        Workers (BASW) 87
    care in the community 87–8
    civil confinement 159, 174
    development of profession 87
    discharge from hospital 87
    judicial review 135–6
    local authorities 67
    role 87
    training 87–8
socio-economic class
    capacity 518, 519
    civil confinement 158
    schizophrenia 53–4
solicitors *see* representation
solitary confinement *see*
    seclusion
sources of mental health law
    17–30
special high security hospitals
    65–6, 108
    Ashworth 24, 66, 97–9, 102–3,
        327, 341–3, 373, 393
    black persons 108
    Broadmoor 18, 66, 97–103,
        266, 268–9, 327, 331, 525
    closure of, proposal for 108
    Fallon Report 108
    lesser security, transfer to
        conditions of 108
    Rampton 66, 97, 99–100, 267,
        369–70, 388, 409
    Tilt Report 108
    total institutions, as 108
special hospitals *see also* **special
    high security hospitals**
    Accelerated Discharge
        Programme (ADP) 98
    bullying 103
    conditional discharge 409–10

special hospitals (*cont.*)
  condoms, supply of 102
  directions 99–101
    challenging 100–1
  discharge from hospital
    369–70
  dress 101–2
  Fallon Report 98–100
  Human Rights Act 1998 101
  inquiries into 98
  mail, withholding 102–3
  Mental Health Review
    Tribunals 423
  Primary Care Trusts 108
  private life, right to respect for
    100, 101–2
  random drug and alcohol
    testing 99
  restraint 338
  searches 99–101
  seclusion 342
  security and management,
    lapses in 98–9
  sexual harassment 103
  squat searches 101
  staff and inmates, barriers
    between 103–4
  surveillance 100
  Tilt Report 99–100
  total institutions, as 98–104
  transfer
    conditional discharge
      409–10
    prison, from 266
    problems with 97–8
  transsexuals, dress and 102
  transvestites, dress and 101–2
  trial transfers 97
  visits 100
  waiting lists 266
  Wednesbury unreasonableness
    102–3
special verdict 239–42
  Crown Court 239
  diminished responsibility 241
  diversion 239–41, 272
  fitness to stand trial 235
  hospital orders 239–41
  hyperglycaemia 240
  internal/external causes model
    240
  liberty and security, right
    to 241
  magistrates' orders 239
  M'Naghten Rules 239–41
  murder 239, 241

restriction orders 241
standard of proof 239
Trial of Lunatics Act 1883 239
unfitness to stand trial 239
split personality 51
squat searches 101
staff, abuse of 104–6
state of arrested or incomplete
  development of mind
status
  approaches 506–7, 526–8
  capacity 506–7, 526–8
  medical personnel, status
    enhancement of 11
  socio-economic status 53–4
stay of proceedings 230, 424–5
stereotyping 4, 10, 13, 142, 551–2
sterilisation
  best interests test 537–8
  capacity 504
  compulsion, treatment of
    detained patients under
    305–6
  Court of Protection 559–60
  guardianship 504
Stone system of admission
  criteria 151–3
straitjackets 338
subnormality 503
substitute decision-making,
  capacity and
  advance decisions 558
  best interests test 548, 558
  briefing sheet 559
  Court of Protection deputies
    548, 557–8
  deputies 548
  hierarchy 557–8
  lasting powers of attorney
    (LPOA) 548, 557–8
  liberty, deprivation of 571–2
  Mental Capacity Act 2005
    546, 548, 557–69, 571–2
  Mental Health Act 1983 558
  personal decisions 558
  restraints 558–9
  voting 558
substitute judgment, capacity
  and 529–33, 542
  advance directives 530–1
  best interests test 535–6, 538,
    552
  idiosyncrasies of person,
    taking into account 530–1
  lucid intervals 530
  principles 530

professional advice,
  assumption that patient
  would have had 531
safeguards 548
social norms 532
wills 530–3
suicide
  absence without leave 431,
    432
  care in the community 93–4
  National Confidential Inquiry
    into Suicide and Homicide
    by People with a Mental
    Illness 93–4
  remand 216–17
  secondary adjustment, as 106
  standards on prevention 106
  total institutions 106
summary offences 222, 238, 245
supervised community
  treatment (SCT)
  aftercare under supervision
    (ACUs) 493–5
  coercion 494–5
  compulsory treatment 92
  control in the community
    493–5
  drug therapy 494
  recall 493–4
  responsible medical officers
    (RMOs) 494
  second opinions 494
supervision *see also* supervision
  orders
  aftercare under supervision
    (ACUs) 491–5
  control in the community 92,
    365–6, 435, 485, 490–5
  Court of Protection 559
  discharge from hospital 353,
    365–6
  guardianship 490
  informal admission 118
  lasting powers of attorney 563
  Mental Health Review
    Tribunals 398
  registers 92
  services in the community
    435
  supervised community
    treatment (SCT) 92, 491–5
supervision orders
  fitness to stand trial 228–9,
    232–3
  revocation or amendment 238
  treatment component 233

supervision and treatment
  orders 238
surgery *see* psychosurgery
surgical implantation of
  hormones 318, 328, 575
surveillance 30, 68
  asylum-based provision 73–4
  leave and recall 359
  private life, right to respect
    for 100
  special hospitals 100
  total institutions 100

taking the patient to hospital
  180
talking cures 277–8, 287–9
tardive dyskinesia 281, 290
technical life, concept of 417
temporary accommodation,
  persons in urgent need
  of 440
testamentary capacity 498,
  502–3, 510, 511, 515, 517, 543
  see also wills
tests of incapacity 225, 499, 501,
  505–21, 551, 561, 565
therapeutic benevolence
therapeutic communities 287
thioridazine 281
Thorazine 78
three month rule, drug therapy
  and 318–19, 320
Tilt Report 99–100, 108
torts
  damages 593–4
  master tort or servant tort
    588–9
  vicarious liability 588–9
total institutions
  bed occupancy rates 107
  capacity 543
  disculturalisation or
    institutionalisation 96–7
  duration of stays 107
  experience of 95–108
  Fallon Report 98–9
  hospital sector 104–7
    bed closures, 107
    violence in 104–6
  Human Rights Act 1998
    99–101
  obedience test 96
  public/private split 95–6
  secondary adjustments 96,
    106
  self-harm 106

special high security hospitals
  108
special hospitals 98–104, 108
  staff, abuse of 104–6
  suicide 106
  surveillance 100
  suspension of real life 96
  violence 104–6
  Weberian model of modernist
    institutions 95
transfer directions, persons
  subject to 265, 270–1, 369–70,
  414–16
transfer from prison to hospital
  62, 263–72
  assessments 264
  availability of beds 266–8
  back to prison, transfer 270
  criminal justice system
    263–72
  criteria 264–5
  dangerousness 265
  delay 266–7
  diversion from prosecution
    263–72
  fair trials 271–2
  graduated release 264
  hospital and limitation
    directions 257, 262
  hospital orders 265, 266,
    271
  inhuman or degrading
    treatment 270
  liberty and security, right to
    264–5, 267–8, 270
  medical reports, out-of-date
    267–8
  Mental Health Act 1983
    sections 47–49 263–72
  Mental Health Review
    Tribunals 377, 378–9
  mental impairment 264
  private life, right to respect for
    267, 271
  psychopathic disorder 264,
    269–70
  public interest 264
  receiving hospitals,
    specification of 266
  referrals 267
  release 264–6, 268–70
    earliest release date (ERD)
      268–70
    latest date of release (LDR)
      268–9
  remand 271

restriction directions 265,
  270–1, 414
routine cases 267
screening 263
Secretary of State, decisions by
  the 264
sentencing as diversion 243
special hospitals, waiting lists
  at 266
treatability test 264, 269–71
urgent cases 267
waiting lists 266
transfers *see also* **transfer from**
  prison to hospital
  conditional discharge 409–19
  directions, persons subject to
    transfer 265, 270–1,
    369–70, 414–16
  discharge from hospital
    369–70
  hospital and limitation
    directions 256–7, 258–62
  leave and recall 358–9
  Mental Health Review
    Tribunals 377–9, 397–8
  prison, to 414–19
  private sector, to 461–2
  restricted patients 398,
    414–19
  special high security hospitals
    108
  special hospitals 97–8, 108,
    409–10
  trial transfers 97
tranquillisers 8–9, 14, 78,
  278–81, 290, 330–1, 337
transsexuals, dress and 102
transvestites, dress and 101–2
treatability
  civil confinement 122
  compulsory admission 26
  discharge from hospital 364
  Fallon Committee 24
  guardianship 503
  hospital and limitation
    directions 258, 262–3
  hospital orders 246
  hospital, treatment in 348
  Human Rights Act 1998 29
  leave and recall 355
  Mental Health Review
    Tribunals 402–5
  personality disorders 29
  psychopathy 24, 41–2
  remand to hospital 223
  restriction orders 254

treatability (*cont.*)
  Scotland 404
  standards of 26
  transfer from prison to
    hospital 264, 269–71
  treatment, admission for
    129–32
treatment *see also* compulsion,
  treatment of detained patients
  under; medical treatment;
  treatability
  admission for treatment
    122–5, 128–33, 164–5, 377
  aftercare under supervision
    (ACUs) 492
  community treatment orders
    23, 356–7, 488
  consent 357
  control and, balance between
    109
  criminal justice system 202
  discontinuance of 320
  future treatment, requirement
    for 404–5
  general defence 566–7
  Mental Health Review
    Tribunals 377, 398–9, 404–5
  power to convey to a place of
    492
  prisons 273
  supervised community
    treatment (SCT) 92, 493–5
  supervision orders 233, 238
  treatment, definition of
    569–70
Trial of Lunatics Act 1883 239
trial periods 139
tribunals *see* Mental Health
  Review Tribunals

UN Declaration on the Rights of
  Mentally Retarded Persons 34
understanding
  ability to understand 513–15,
    518–19
  actual understanding 515–15,
    518–19
  capacity 513–15, 518–19
  failure to understand
    information 547, 551
  Mental Capacity Act 2005
    547, 551
  representation 606
unfitness to plead
  actus reus 238
  diversion 238–9

either way offences 238
guardianship orders 238–9
hospital orders 238
indictable offences 238
magistrates' courts 238–9
remand to hospital 238–9
summary offences 238
supervision and treatment
  orders, revocation or
  amendment of 238
unfitness to stand trial *see* fitness
  to stand trial
urgency *see* emergencies;
  emergency admissions;
  emergency medical
  treatment
use of force *see also* coercion
  civil confinement 179
  compulsion, treatment of
    detained patients under
    299, 310
  drug therapy 310
  force feeding 6–7, 298, 306–9,
    311, 319, 320

Vagrancy Acts 74–5
verdicts *see* special verdict
vicarious liability
  damages 589
  delegation 589
  health authorities 588–90
  Human Rights Act 1998 602
  master tort or servant tort
    588–9
  Mental Health Act 1983
    588–90
victim support volunteers
  209
victims, representation by 396
violence *see also* homicide;
  murder
  approved social workers
    (ASWs) 181–3, 197–8
  assault 593–4
  attachment theory 336
  bail 218–19
  battery 292, 335, 503, 593–4
  civil confinement, resistance to
    180
  control in the community
    487–8
  dangerousness 146–7
  drug therapy 333
  emergency medical treatment
    333, 336
  hospital orders 104–6, 245

National Task Force on
  Violence against Social Care
  Staff 105
previous convictions 218–19
remand 216–17
restriction orders 250–1, 253
sentencing as diversion
  242–3
staff, against 104–6
total institutions 104–6
zero tolerance campaign
  105–6
Visitors 560, 572
volenti non fit injuria 595
voluntary admission *see* informal
  admission
voting 558

waiting lists 266, 484
Wechsler Adult Intelligence Scale
  513–14
Wednesbury unreasonableness
  compulsion, treatment of
    detained patients under
    296, 311
  guardianship 578
  Human Rights Act 1998
    191–2
  judicial review 193–5
  Mental Capacity Act 2005 578
  Mental Health Review
    Tribunals 420–1
  services in the community
    455–6, 461–2
  special hospitals 102–3
  super-*Wednesbury* 193–4, 311
welfare services *see* National
  Assistance Act 1948, welfare
  services under
welfare state, development
  of the 86
welfarism 88, 160–1
WHO International Classification
  of Diseases 48–9
wills
  best interests test 553
  capacity 498, 502–3, 510, 511,
    515, 517, 543
  Court of Protection 546, 553,
    559
  culture 543
  information, appreciation of
    517
  lucid intervals 530
  Mental Capacity Act 2005
    546

professional advice,
assumption that patient
would have had 531
property and affairs, capacity
and 502–3
social norms 532
substitute judgment 530–3

work, inability to 76–7
workhouses 76, 82
writ of habeas corpus *see* habeas
corpus, writ of
wrongful confinement 116

York Retreat 73, 74

young people *see* children and
young persons

zero tolerance campaign on
violence against staff 105–6